PROFESSIONAL
BAKING

Photography by    J. GERARD SMITH

Featuring recipes from

Le Cordon Bleu

L'Art Culinaire

Paris—1895

with a foreword by

ANDRÉ J. COINTREAU

*President, Le Cordon Bleu*

WILEY

JOHN WILEY & SONS, INC.

# WAYNE GISSLEN

# PROFESSIONAL
# BAKING

## FIFTH EDITION

Published by John Wiley & Sons, Inc., Hoboken, New Jersey.
Published simultaneously in Canada.

Photographs on pages 40, 120, and 128 were taken at Turtle Bread Company, Minneapolis, Minnesota.
Design and page make up by Mauna Eichner and Lee Fukui.

For general information on our other products and services, or technical support, please contact our Customer Care Department within the United States at 800-762-2974, outside the United States at 317-572-3993 or fax 317-572-4002.

Wiley also publishes its books in a variety of electronic formats. Some content that appears in print may not be available in electronic books.

For more information about Wiley products, visit our Web site at http://www.wiley.com.

*Library of Congress Cataloging-in-Publication Data:*

Gisslen, Wayne, 1946-
  Professional baking / Wayne Gisslen ; photography by J. Gerard Smith. — 5th ed.
      p. cm.
  Includes bibliographical references and index.
  ISBN 978-0-471-78349-7 (Trade) — ISBN 978-0-471-78348-0 (College)
  1. Baking. 2. Food presentation.   I. Title.
  TX763.G47 2009
  641.8'15—dc22
                            2007020433

Printed in the United States of America

10 9 8 7 6 5 4 3 2 1

This book is dedicated to
Anne and Jim Smith and their family.

# Contents

# Recipe Contents

Recipes in blue type were developed and tested by Le Cordon Bleu.

## Chapter 13
## Pies

## Chapter 14
## Pastry Basics

## Chapter 15
## Tarts and Special Pastries

## Chapter 16
## Cake Mixing and Baking

## Chapter 17
## Assembling and Decorating Cakes

## Chapter 18
## Specialty Cakes, Gâteaux, and Torten

*Chapter* 19
# Cookies

*Chapter* 20
# Custards, Puddings, Mousses, and Soufflés

## Chapter 21
# Frozen Desserts

## Chapter 22
# Fruit Desserts

## Chapter 23
## Dessert Presentation

## Chapter 24
## Chocolate

# About Le Cordon Bleu

With more than 30 schools on five continents and a student body made up of over seventy different nationalities, Le Cordon Bleu is well known and highly regarded throughout the gastronomic world. Le Cordon Bleu and its master chefs are renowned for their tradition of excellence in the culinary arts and hospitality management, and are committed to furthering the appreciation of fine food and fine living. Already involved in consulting and the promotion of a variety of culinary products, Le Cordon Bleu has successfully developed partnerships worldwide with major hospitality and culinary institutions, professional organizations and with the cruise industry.

## Le Cordon Bleu Addresses

**Le Cordon Bleu Paris**
8, rue Léon Delhomme
75015 Paris
France
Phone: 33 1 53 68 22 50
Fax: 33 1 48 56 03 96
E-mail: paris@cordonbleu.edu

**Le Cordon Bleu Ottawa**
453 Laurier Avenue East
Ottawa, Ontario
K1N 6R4 Canada
Phone: 1 613 236 CHEF (2433)
Fax: 1 613 236 2460
Toll-free: 1 888 289 6302
E-mail: ottawa@cordonbleu.edu

**Le Cordon Bleu Thailand**
Dusit Thani Building
946 Rama IV Road
Bangkok 10500
Thailand
Tel: 66 2 237 8877
Fax: 66 2 237 8878
E-mail: thailand@cordonbleu.edu

**Le Cordon Bleu, Inc.**
**Corporate Office**
40 Enterprise Ave
Secaucus, New Jersey 07094
USA
Phone: 1 201 617 5221
Fax: 1 201 617 1914
Toll-free: 1 800 457 2433 (CHEF)
E-mail: info@cordonbleu.edu

**Le Cordon Bleu London**
114 Marylebone Lane
London, W1U 2HH
United Kingdom
Phone: 44 20 7935 3503
Fax: 44 20 7935 7621
E-mail: london@cordonbleu.edu

**Le Cordon Bleu Tokyo**
Roob-1, 28-13 Sarugaku-Cho
Daikanyama, Shibuya-Ku
Tokyo 150-0033
Japan
Phone: 81 3 5489 0141
Fax: 81 3 5489 0145
E-mail: tokyo@cordonbleu.edu

**Le Cordon Bleu Kobe**
The 45th 6F, 45 Harima-cho
Chuo-Ku,Kobe-shi
Hyogo 650-0036
Japan
Phone: 81 78 393 8221
Fax: 81 78 393 8222
E-mail: kobe@cordonbleu.edu

**Le Cordon Bleu Australia**
Days Road, Regency Park
South Australia 5010
Australia
Phone: 61 8 8346 3700
Fax: 61 8 8346 3755
E-mail: australia@cordonbleu.edu

**Le Cordon Bleu Peru**
Av.Nunez de Balboa 530
Miraflores, Lima 18
Peru
Phone: 51 1 242 8222
Fax: 51 1 242 9209
E-mail: info@cordonbleu.edu

**Le Cordon Bleu Liban**
Rectorat B.P.446
USEK University—Kaslik
Jounieh
Lebanon
Phone: 961 9640 664/665
Fax: 961 9642 333
E-mail: liban@cordonbleu.edu

**Le Cordon Bleu Mexico**
Universidad Anahuac del Sur
Avenida de las Torres #131, Col.
Olivar de los Padres
C.P.01780
Del Alvaro Obregon, Mexico D.F.
Phone: 52 55 5628 8800
Fax: 52 55 5628 8837
E-mail: mexico@cordonbleu.edu

*http:www.cordonbleu.edu*
*info@cordonbleu.edu*

## U.S. School Locations

### Arizona
Scottsdale Culinary Institute
8100 E. Camelback Road
Scottsdale, Arizona 85251
Tel: (480) 990 3773

### California
California Culinary Academy
625 Polk Street
San Francisco, California 94102
Tel: (415) 771 3500

California School of Culinary Arts
521 East Green Street
Pasadena, California 91101
Tel: (626) 403 8490

### Florida
Le Cordon Bleu College of Culinary
Arts—Miami
3221 Enterprise Way
Miramar, FL 33025
Tel: (954) 438 8882

Orlando Culinary Academy
8511 Commodity Circle
Orlando, Florida 32819
Tel: (407) 888 4000

### Georgia
Le Cordon Bleu College of
Culinary Arts—Atlanta
1957 Lakeside Parkway, Suite 515
Tucker, Georgia 30084
Tel: (770) 938 4711

### Illinois
Culinary & Hospitality Institute of
Chicago
361 West Chestnut
Chicago, Illinois 60610
Tel: (312) 944 0882

### Minnesota
Le Cordon Bleu College of Culinary
Arts—Minneapolis/St. Paul
1440 Northland Drive
Mendota Heights, Minnesota 55120
Tel: (651) 905 3400

### Nevada
Le Cordon Bleu College of Culinary
Arts—Las Vegas
1451 Center Crossing Road
Las Vegas, Nevada 89144
Tel: (702) 365 7690

### New Hampshire
Atlantic Culinary Academy
23 Cataract Avenue
Dover, New Hampshire 03820
Tel: (603) 742 1234

### Oregon
Western Culinary Institute
921 SW Morrison Street, Suite 400
Portland, Oregon 97205
Tel: (800) 848-3202

### Pennsylvania
Pennsylvania Culinary Institute
71 Liberty Avenue
Pittsburgh, Pennsylvania 15222
Tel: (412) 566 2433

### Texas
Le Cordon Bleu College of Culinary
Arts—Dallas
11830 Webb Chapel Road,
Suite 1200
Dallas, Texas 75234
Tel: (214) 647 8500

Texas Culinary Academy
11400 Burnet Road Suite 2100
Austin, Texas 78758
Tel: (512) 837 2665

*www.lecordonbleuschoolsusa.com*

# Foreword

Le Cordon Bleu was delighted to work once again with author Wayne Gisslen on the fifth edition of *Professional Baking*. This continued collaboration underlines the importance of classic pâtisserie and baking techniques at the service of the global gastronomic world. It has always been the philosophy of Le Cordon Bleu that through mastering and understanding the importance of these techniques, processes, and methods, students gain the skills and confidence necessary to become not only excellent professionals but also creators of their own works of art. Le Cordon Bleu sees this fifth edition of *Professional Baking* as an important tool in this endeavor.

Founded in Paris in 1895, Le Cordon Bleu today has become a network of over thirty schools and programs in five continents and has more students worldwide than any other culinary education provider. Le Cordon Bleu maintains close relations with the culinary industry, and benefits from its international recognition, setting the standard of excellence. Known for classical French cuisine, Le Cordon Bleu continues to teach long celebrated culinary traditions while creating a balanced, harmonious, and flavorsome repertoire of contemporary and international cuisines.

Le Cordon Bleu's authority on culinary techniques, training, and development are recognized and supported by noted establishments including the Ministry of Tourism of Shanghai, China, and the government of Australia. Le Cordon Bleu also provides training in the French culinary arts to many organizations, including chefs of the Club Managers Association of America and Regent Seven Seas Cruises.

Each year Le Cordon Bleu master chefs pass on their knowledge and experience to a student body of over seventy nationalities, and share their expertise and craft at a variety of annual festivals and culinary events around the world. Selected for their skill and professional experience, our chefs hail from Michelin starred restaurants and top hotel kitchens, and are winners of numerous international competitions.

Through its expansion worldwide, Le Cordon Bleu has proven that French culinary techniques can be applied to a variety of world cuisines. Each campus reflects the influences of its host country. Students and master chefs alike are encouraged to explore and experiment using the ingredients available to them to adapt and create new flavors and encourage new trends in cuisine and fine dining.

*Professional Baking* has been a mainstay in North American universities, community colleges, and culinary schools. It has been used to train hundreds of thousands of pastry chefs and bakers, many of whom continue to use the book in their kitchens. Created by the talented Wayne Gisslen, the text teaches, through its clear writing style, precise photography, and recipes, first to understand and then to perform—presenting a no-nonsense view of the workings of a professional kitchen.

Wayne Gisslen has balanced his practical knowledge with a clean, pedagogical and consistent approach to make this a reference for a lifetime. *Professional Baking*'s flexible format is the reason why we consider it to be the best textbook for promoting good theory and practice, and it has the adaptability to be used all over the world. For Le Cordon Bleu this is a necessary tool for any kitchen, at work or at home. In the fifth edition of *Professional Baking*, Le Cordon Bleu chefs, and Wayne Gisslen unite once again to combine their knowledge and experience resulting in a definitive text and reference book. Our collaboration with Wayne Gisslen is the result of a strong partnership and friendship that has grown over the years and we thank him for his generosity and support.

ANDRÉ J. COINTREAU
President and CEO
Le Cordon Bleu International

# Preface

Each new edition of **Professional Baking** is released into a world of growing interest in fine baking. The rebirth of artisan baking was well underway when the previous edition was published, but this interest has continued to grow. Professionals as well as enthusiastic amateurs and even some consumers are looking for more detailed information about the technical aspects of baking. At the same time, related concerns, such as concern about food allergies, diet, and health, have had an important impact on the art and science of baking and pastry-making.

**Professional Baking**, which has been a widely used resource and teaching tool for more than twenty years, continues to grow and change with the industry. This fifth edition incorporates a wealth of new material designed to help the beginning baker and the experienced professional meet the demands of a changing environment. Even with these changes, however, the focus of text is, at it has always been, on a solid grounding in the basics, presented in a straightforward and easy-to-grasp style.

## What's New

As with past revisions, **Professional Baking, Fifth Edition** has been planned in close collaboration with instructors representing schools with a variety of baking programs. The revision process began early, soon after the publication of the previous edition, as I collected suggestions and responses from as many sources as possible. Instructors who daily face the challenge of teaching their craft in a changing industry have brought a wealth of insight, and I am grateful for their contributions. The following are some of the significant additions to the fifth edition as a result of this dialog:

- A new chapter on baking for special diets, including low-fat, low-sugar, gluten-free, and dairy-free diets (chapter 27).

- A revised and enlarged chapter on ingredients, including more detailed information on all categories of ingredients and more detail on fruits, including ripening characteristics and trim yield (chapter 4).

- An expanded section on how to work with formulas and recipes, including bakeshop math.

- A new section on bakeshop sanitation.

- More information on baking tools and equipment.

- An expanded chapter on the history of baking.

- New sidebars explaining the history and cultural background of various bakery products, as well as details concerning specialty equipment, ingredients, nutrition, and other topics of interest.

- More detailed information on controlling gluten development and on the baking process.

- More detailed information on basic yeast dough techniques.

- New material on liquid shortening cakes, including formulas.

- A new section on sugar confections.

- A revised discussion of dessert plating concepts and techniques.

- New formulas, plus dozens more revised and improved.

## The Goal of This Text

The goal of **Professional Baking** is to provide students with a solid theoretical and practical foundation in baking practices, including selection of ingredients, proper mixing and baking techniques, careful makeup and assembly, and skilled and imaginative decoration and presentation. It is designed as a primary text for use in colleges and culinary schools, baking courses within broader food service curricula, and on-the-job training programs. It is also valuable as a manual for cooks and bakers, both professional and amateur.

The methods and procedures in this book are primarily those of small bakeshops and food service organizations. The emphasis is on producing high-quality handcrafted items. Development of manual skills is stressed. Such skills are a valuable asset even to students who eventually move on to more industrialized, automated production like that found in large commercial bakeries.

The text focuses on both understanding and performing. The practical material is supported by a systematic presentation of basic theory and ingredient information so students learn not only what techniques work but also why they work. Procedures for basic bread and pastry doughs, cake mixes, creams, and icings form the core of the material. Much of the text is devoted to step-by-step procedures and production techniques. The discussion of techniques is reinforced with straightforward formulas that allow students to develop their skills while working with large or small quantities.

Those students who have developed a good understanding and mastery of basic techniques are usually eager to progress to fine pastries and other advanced work. The basic techniques and formulas that form the core of the book are supplemented with explanations of advanced techniques and formulas, enabling students to learn and practice a broad range of skills for producing fine pastries, cakes, and decorative pieces. Emphasis here is on developing manual skills for careful detailed work rather than on producing large quantities. Those whose careers or interests lead them to restaurants rather than bakeries and pastry shops will find a detailed discussion of the principles of designing and plating appealing dessert presentations.

## The Organization of the Text

Two factors strongly influence the arrangement and organization of **Professional Baking**. The first is the dual emphasis already mentioned—the emphasis on both understanding and performing. It is not enough to present students with a collection of formulas, nor is it enough to give them a freestanding summary of baking theory and principles. They must be presented together, and the connections between them must be clear. Thus, when students practice preparing specific items, their study of theory helps them understand what they are doing, why they are doing it, and how to get the best results. At the same time, each formula they pr.epare helps reinforce their understanding of the basic principles. Knowledge builds upon knowledge.

The second factor is that most of a baker's activities fall naturally into two categories: (1) mixing, baking, and/or cooking doughs, batters, fillings, creams, and icings, and (2) assembling these elements (for example, baked cake layers, fillings, and icings) into finished pieces. The first category of tasks requires careful selection of ingredients, accurate measurement, and close attention to mixing and baking procedures. Naturally, most of the detailed guidelines and procedures in this book are devoted to these kinds of tasks. The second category, the assembly of prepared components, is less a matter of scientific accuracy than of manual skills and artistic abilities.

This division of tasks is so well known to the practicing baker that it is usually taken for granted. Consequently, it is often neglected in written materials. As far as possible, the arrangement of subjects in this text reflects the working practices of bakeshops and kitchens. In a typical facility, operations such as mixing pie doughs, cooking fill-

ings, preparing icings, and mixing and baking cake layers are done separately and in advance. Then, depending on demand, finished products can be assembled quickly, shortly before they are needed. In this book, the procedures for mixing and baking cakes, for example, are discussed separately from the procedures for assembling, icing, and decorating them. These are very different techniques, and students find it helpful to approach them in a realistic context. Similarly, basic creams and icings are fundamental elements required for making a wide range of pastries, cakes, and other desserts; hence, they are treated early in the text.

Although the arrangement of chapters represents a logical grouping of products and procedures, it is not intended to dictate the order in which instructors should teach the units. Every curriculum has different requirements and constraints, so the sequence of instruction varies from school to school and instructor to instructor. The arrangement of material in this text is designed to encourage flexibility. Instructors are encouraged to teach the material in any order that suits their needs. Of course, baking techniques are highly interdependent; frequent cross-references help students understand these connections.

An important element in the text is the participation of the instructor, whose ideas and professional experience are invaluable. There is no substitute for firsthand seeing and doing under the guidance and supervision of experienced teachers. Baking is an art as much as a skill, and on many points bakers and pastry chefs differ in their preferences. The text frequently explains possible variations in theory and procedure, and students are encouraged to consult their instructor for the techniques he or she prefers. Throughout the book, the instructor's input is encouraged. Exposure to a variety of formulas and techniques can only enrich students' education and enhance their skills.

The text is designed for readability and practicality. Discussions of baking theory are presented in easy-to-read, point-by-point explanations. Techniques and makeup methods are detailed in concise yet complete step-by-step procedures. The format emphasizes and highlights key points in bold type, italics, and numbered sequences, so the basic information can be located and reviewed at a glance.

## The Formulas

Nearly 900 formulas and recipes are included for the most popular breads, cakes, pastries, and desserts. These formulas are not selected at random, merely for the sake of having formulas in the book. Rather, they are carefully chosen and developed to teach and reinforce the techniques students are learning and to strengthen their understanding of basic principles. The goal is for students to understand and use not only the formulas in this book but any formula they encounter.

The formulas in this book are instructional—that is, their purpose is not merely to give directions for producing baked goods but also to provide an opportunity to practice, with specific ingredients, the general principles being studied. Directions within formulas are often abbreviated. For example, instead of spelling out the straight dough method for breads in detail for each dough mixed in this way, this book refers the student to the preceding discussion of the procedure. By thinking and reviewing, students derive a stronger learning experience from their lab work.

Many formulas are followed by variations. These are actually whole formulas given in abbreviated terms. This feature encourages students to see the similarities and differences among preparations. For example, there seems little point in giving a formula for cream pie filling in the pie chapter, a formula for custard filling for éclairs and napoleons in a pastry chapter, and separate formulas for each flavor of cream pudding in a pudding chapter without pointing out that these are all basically the same preparation. Skill as a baker depends on understanding and being able to exercise judgment, not just on following recipes. The ability to exercise judgment is essential in all branches of cookery but especially so in baking, where the smallest variation in procedure can produce significant changes in the baked product. The formulas in this text will help students develop judgment by requiring them to think about the relationships between general procedures and specific products.

Students are encouraged to study chapter 2 before actually proceeding with any of the formulas. The second section of the chapter explains the principles of measurement, the various formats used for the formulas and recipes in this book, techniques for converting yield, and U.S. and metric measurements and bakers' percentages.

# Features

## CD-ROM

The CD-ROM, designed to complement the book, accompanies the academic edition of this book and utilizes Wiley CulinarE-Companion™, a professional-level software program. The CD-ROM contains nearly 900 formulas from this book plus a range of useful features that make them easy to adapt and manipulate to suit individual needs. Users can:

- Add, edit, modify, and print formulas, portion sizes, and yield, and create shopping lists.

- Search recipes by main ingredient, meal, and cuisine type.

- Resize formulas using baking formulas in U.S. or metric measurements or baker's percentages.

- Perform metric conversions instantly.

- Calculate nutritional analyses of formulas in U.S. Food and Drug Administration (FDA) format and update nutritional analysis if an ingredient is changed.

## Mixing Method Cards

A group of four laminated Mixing Method Cards accompany the academic version of the book. They detail mixing methods for Quick Breads, Cakes, Cookies, and Yeast Doughs.

## Supplements

To enhance the mastery of the material in **Professional Baking**, the following student and instructor supplements are available:

The **Study Guide** (ISBN 978-0-471-78350-3) contains review materials, practice problems, and exercises. (Answers to questions are included in the **Instructor's Manual**.)

The **Instructor's Manual with Study Guide Solutions** (ISBN 978-0-470-25392-2) includes teaching suggestions and test questions. Test questions are also available in electronic form on a Free Instructor's Resource CD-ROM (ISBN 978-0-470-25860-6) and on our Web site, available to course instructors upon request.

The newly updated and revised Web site contains information for the student and instructor. It is available at www.wiley.com/go/gisslen.

WebCT and Blackboard online courses are available for this book. Visit www.wiley.com/go/gisslen for more information, or contact your Wiley representative.

# Acknowledgments

In the previous edition of this book, I began this section with a heartfelt expression of gratitude to all the chefs and instructors who have offered criticism and suggestions over the years. I can do no better than repeat what I wrote then. A book of this nature and scope must always be more than a one-person job. I would like to thank a large group of people who are in many ways the unsung heroes of **Professional Baking**, namely, the many instructors and other readers of the book who have corresponded with me and my editors over the years or who have responded thoughtfully to our questions and surveys. These instructors face many challenges every day as they work to transmit the knowledge and skills of our craft to their students in an array of learning environments. They have helped me understand from their points of view the difficulties instructors face, and this has helped me develop the text, from edition to edition, into a more inclusive and flexible teaching and learning tool. These reviewers have truly been an integral part of the development of **Professional Baking** from the first edition, and I am grateful to them. Most of the changes and additions to the fifth edition have been in response to their input. To give them due recognition, I have added a list of reviewers following these acknowledgments. No doubt I have inadvertently missed some people, so I would like to thank every instructor who has talked or corresponded with me about this book and given me ideas for its improvement.

Second, I would like to express my gratitude to the staff of Le Cordon Bleu, whose participation made such a great improvement in the previous edition and whose contributions still form an important part of this new edition. Thanks especially to André Cointreau, president of Le Cordon Bleu, for making this collaboration possible. Julie Walsh and Laurent Duchêne are the two remarkable pastry chefs who developed and tested the many formulas that found a place in the text. I thank them very much. In addition, a number of students worked with chefs Walsh and Duchêne during our photography session in London: Saori Matsunuma, Yuka Eguchi, Kaori Tsuboi, Erika Kahn, Michele Perle, Townley Morrison, James Rizzo, Daniel Schumer, and Benjamin Coffin.

Chef Lou Sackett has been a very valuable resource in my effort to improve and fine-tune the content of **Professional Baking** and has spent a great deal of time reviewing the manuscript. I am grateful for her input.

Photographer Jim Smith has worked with me on all my projects for more than twenty-five years, and his work is such an important part of these texts that he is truly a partner in their development. Once again his work has added immeasurably to this new edition. I would like to thank not only Jim but also his great team, including Anne Smith, Jason Torres, Justin Allen, and Judy Lieberman, for the great working relationship and friendship that has developed. In addition, my gratitude goes to a great team who helped with food preparation for our most recent photography session: Chef-Instructors Rick Forpahl and David Eisenreich of Hennepin Technical College, and their students Eric Aho, Vince Jones, Derek Evancevich, Rachel Adams, Melanie Plifka, Keith Soltesz, Megan Flannery, Luz Maria Pereira, John Alrick, and Bradley Buth.

Testing new formulas and recipes and retesting old ones is an important part of the work of a new edition, and I would like to extend my thanks to Jennifer Peck for her skilled and knowledgeable assistance both in recipe testing and in preparation for photography. In addition, I am grateful to J. Marshall of Pastry Chef Central for donating important baker's tools.

I would like to extend recognition and gratitude to a great pastry chef and teacher, Leo "Sonny" Silverman, my first inspiration and mentor in fine pastry and decorative work. Finally, I wish to thank everyone at John Wiley and Sons who worked so hard on this project: Kerstin Nasdeo, Julie Kerr, Christopher Guiang, Jeff Faust, Tom Hyland, Lynne Marsala, Michael Mukhoyan, Alexey Zhukov, Vladimir Karphkhin, Andrey Grigoryev, Maxim Mukhoyan, Oleg Solovyov, Olga Braslavets, and Sergey Semin, and especially my editor and friend, Melissa Oliver.

# Reviewers

**Robert L. Anderson**, Des Moines Area Community College, Ankeny, Iowa

**Anne Baldzikowski**, Cabrillo College, Aptos, California

**Thomas Beckman**, The Cooking and Hospitality Institute of Chicago, Chicago, Illinois

**Karla V. Boetel**, Des Moines Area Community College, Ankeny, Iowa

**Eric Breckoff**, J. Sargeant Reynolds Community College, Richmond, Virginia

**Mark S. Cole**, Del Mar College, Corpus Christi, Texas

**Martha Crawford**, Johnson & Wales University, Providence, Rhode Island

**Chris Crosthwaite**, Lane Community College, Eugene, Oregon

**John R. Farris**, Lansing Community College, Lansing, Michigan

**Joseph D. Ford**, New York Food and Hotel Management, New York, New York

**Carrie Franzen**, Le Cordon Bleu—Minneapolis, Minneapolis, Minnesota

**Robert J. Galloway**, Dunwoody Industrial Institute, Minneapolis, Minnesota

**David Gibson**, Niagara College of Applied Arts and Technology, Niagara Falls, Ontario, Canada

**Kathryn Gordon**, Art Institute of New York City, New York, New York

**Jean Hassell**, Youngstown State University, Youngstown, Ohio

**Iris A. Helveston**, State Department of Education, Tallahassee, Florida

**Nancy A. Higgins**, Art Institute of Atlanta, Atlanta, Georgia

**Roger Holden**, Oakland Community College, Bloomfield Hills, Michigan

**George Jack**, The Cooking and Hospitality Institute of Chicago, Chicago, Illinois

**Mike Jung**, Hennepin Technical College, Brooklyn Park, Minnesota

**Frederick Glen Knight**, The Southeast Institute of Culinary Arts, St. Augustine, Florida

**Paul Krebs**, Schenectady County Community College, Schenectady, New York

**Jeffrey C. LaBarge**, Central Piedmont Community College, Charlotte, North Carolina

**Fred LeMeisz**, St. Petersburg Vocational Technical Institute, St. Petersburg, Florida

**Laurel Leslie**, Kapiolani Community College, Honolulu, Hawaii

**Janet Lightizer**, Newbury College, Brookline, Massachusetts

**Valeria S. Mason**, State Department of Education, Gainesville, Florida

**Elizabeth McGeehan**, Central New Mexico Community College, Albuquerque, New Mexico

**John Oechsner**, Art Institute of Atlanta, Atlanta, Georgia

**Philip Panzarino**, New York City Technical College, Brooklyn, New York

**Jayne Pearson**, Manchester Community College, Manchester, Connecticut

**Kenneth Perry**, Le Cordon Bleu, Minneapolis, Minnesota

**Richard Petrello**, Withlacoochee Vocational-Technical Center, Inverness, Florida

**Willaim H. Pifer**, Bellingham Technical College, Bellingham, Washington

**Gunter Rehm**, Orange Coast College, Costa Mesa, California

**Kent R. Rigby**, Baltimore International College, Baltimore, Maryland

**Lou Sackett**, Yorktowne Business Institute School of Culinary Arts, Lancaster, Pennsylvania

**Kimberly Schenk**, Diablo Valley College, Pleasant Hill, California

**Peter Scholtes**, George Brown College, Toronto, Ontario, Canada

**George L. Southwick**, Ozarks Technical Community College, Springfield, Missouri

**Simon Stevenson**, Connecticut Culinary Institute, Suffield, Connecticut

**Patrick Sweeney**, Johnson County Community College, Overland Park, Kansas

**Chris Thielman**, College of DuPage, Glen Ellyn, Illinois

**Andrea Tutunjian**, Institute of Culinary Education, New York, New York

**F. H. Waskey**, University of Houston, Houston, Texas

**J. William White**, Pinellas County School System, St. Petersburg, Florida

**Ronald Zabkiewicz**, South Technical Education Center, Boynton Beach, Florida

PROFESSIONAL

# BAKING

## Chapter 1

# The Baking Profession

B aking is one of the oldest occupations of the human race. Since early prehistoric human beings made the transition from nomadic hunters to settled gatherers and farmers, grains have been the most important foods to sustain human life, often nearly the only foods. The profession that today includes baking artisan sourdough breads and assembling elegant pastries and desserts began thousands of years ago with the gathering of wild grass seeds and the grinding of those seeds between stones.

Today the professions of baker and pastry chef are growing quickly. Thousands of skilled people are needed every year. Baking offers ambitious workers the chance of finding satisfaction in an industry that is challenging and rapidly changing.

Before you start your practical studies, covered in the remaining chapters of this book, it is good to know a little about the profession you are entering. This chapter gives you a brief overview of the baking professions, including how it got to where it is today.

**After reading this chapter, you should be able to:**

1. Describe the major events in the history of baking from prehistoric times to the present.

2. Name the principal career positions in modern food service and bakery operations.

3. Name and discuss four attitude characteristics possessed by successful bakers and pastry cooks.

# BAKING—HISTORICAL BACKGROUND

**G**rains have been the most important staple food in the human diet since prehistoric times, so it is only a slight exaggeration to say that baking is almost as old as the human race.

## The First Grain Foods

Before human beings learned to plant, they gathered wild foods. The seeds of various wild grasses, the ancestors of modern grains, were rich in nutrients and valued by prehistoric peoples as important foods. These seeds, unlike modern grains, had husks that clung tightly to them. People learned that by toasting the seeds, probably on hot rocks, they could loosen the husks and then remove them by beating the seeds with wooden tools.

The early development of grain foods took place mostly in the eastern Mediterranean regions, because, it seems, this was an area where wild grains were especially abundant.

Because of the lack of cooking utensils, it is probable that the earliest grain preparation was made by toasting dry grains, pounding them to a meal with rocks, and mixing the meal to a paste with water. Because the grains had already been cooked by toasting them to remove the husks, the paste needed no further cooking. Later it was discovered that some of this paste, if laid on a hot stone next to a fire, turned into a flatbread that was a little more appetizing than the plain paste. Unleavened flatbreads, such as tortillas, are still important foods in many cultures.

Unleavened flatbreads made from grain pastes are the first step in the development of breads as we know them.

To understand how breads developed, one must also understand a little about how grains developed. As you learn in a later chapter, modern yeast breads depend on a combination of certain proteins to give them their structure. For all practical purposes, only wheat and its relatives contain enough of these proteins, which form an elastic substance called *gluten*. A few other grains also contain gluten proteins, but they do not form as good a structure as wheat gluten.

Further, the proteins must be raw in order to form gluten. Because the earliest wild grains had to be heated in order to be freed from their husks, they could be used only to make grain pastes or porridges, not true breads. Over time, prehistoric people learned to plant seeds and, eventually, they planted only seeds of plants whose seeds were easiest to process. As a result, hybrid varieties developed whose husks could be removed without heating the grains. Without this step, modern breads could not have come about.

## Ancient Leavened Breads

A grain paste left to stand for a time sooner or later collects wild yeasts (microscopic organisms that produce carbon dioxide gas) from the air and begins to ferment. This was, no doubt, the beginning of leavened (or raised) bread, although for most of human history the presence of yeast was mostly accidental. Eventually, people learned they could save a small part of a dough to leaven the next day's batch.

Small flat or mounded cakes made of a grain paste, whether leavened or unleavened, could be cooked on a hot rock or other hot, flat surface, or they could be covered and set near a fire or in the embers of a fire. The ancient Egyptians developed the art of cooking leavened doughs in molds—the first loaf pans. The molds were heated and then filled with dough, covered, and stacked in a heated chamber. These were perhaps the first mass-produced breads. Breads made from wheat flour were costly and affordable for only the richest people. Most people ate bread from barley and other grains.

By the time of the ancient Greeks, about five or six hundred years BCE, true enclosed ovens were in use. These ovens were preheated by building a fire inside them. They had a door in the front that could be closed, so the oven could be loaded and unloaded without losing much heat.

The breads baked in these ovens were still, for the most part, simply cakes of baked grain pastes mixed with a little of the paste from the day before to supply wild yeasts for leavening. Such flat or slightly mounded breads were called **maza**. Maza, especially maza made of barley, were the staple food of the time. In fact, in ancient Greece, all foods were divided into two categories, maza and **opson**, meaning things eaten with maza. Opson included vegetables, cheese, fish, meat, or anything else except bread. Often the opson was placed on top of the flat bread, forming the ancestors of modern pizzas.

Writings from ancient Greece describe as many as eighty kinds of bread and other baked grain products developed by professional bakers. Some of these could be called true breads rather than flatbreads or maza, because they were made with kneaded doughs containing wheat flour, which provided gluten proteins.

Several centuries later, ancient Rome was slow to develop breads. Not until master bakers arrived from Greece did grain foods develop much beyond porridges and simple flatbreads. By the latter period of the Roman Empire, however, baking was an important industry. Bakeshops were often run by immigrant Greeks.

An important innovation in Roman baking was introduced by the Gauls, a European people who had been conquered by the Romans. The Gauls, the ancestors of the modern French, had developed beer making. They discovered that adding the froth from beer to bread dough made especially light, well-leavened breads. The froth contained yeast from beer fermentation, so this process was the beginning of the use of a controlled yeast source for making bread doughs.

Many of the products made by Roman bakers contained quantities of honey and oil, so these foods might be called pastries rather than breads. That the primary fat available was oil placed a limit on the kinds of pastries that could be made. Only a solid fat such as butter enables the pastry maker to produce the kinds of stiff doughs we are familiar with, such as pie doughs and short pastries.

## Baking in the Middle Ages

After the collapse of the Roman Empire, baking as a profession almost disappeared. Not until the latter part of the Middle Ages did baking and pastry making begin to reappear as important professions in the service of the nobility. Bread baking continued to be performed by professional bakers, not homemakers, because it required ovens that needed almost constant tending. Because of the risk of fire, baking ovens were usually separated from other buildings and were often outside city walls.

In much of Europe, tending ovens and making bread dough were separate operations. The oven tender maintained the oven, heated it properly, and supervised the baking of the loaves that were brought to him. In early years, the oven may not have been near the workshops of the bakers, and one oven served the needs of several bakers. It is interesting to note that in many bakeries today, especially in the larger ones, this division of labor still exists. The chef who tends the ovens bakes the proofed breads and other products that are brought to him or her and may not have any part in the mixing and makeup of these products.

Throughout the Middle Ages, part of the bread maker's job was sifting, or bolting, the whole-grain flour that was brought to him by customers. Sifting with coarse sieves removed only part of the bran, while sifting with finer sieves removed most or all of the bran and made whiter flour. Because more of the grain is removed to make white flour, the yield is lower and, thus, white bread was more expensive. Ordinary people couldn't afford white bread. Not until around 1650 CE did bakers start buying sifted flour from mills.

Because bread was the most important food of the time, many laws regulated such factors as bolting yields, bread ingredients, and loaf sizes.

It was also in the Middle Ages that bakers and pastry chefs in France formed guilds in order to protect and further their art. Regulations prohibited all but certified bakers from baking bread for sale, and the guilds had enough power to limit certification to their own members. The guilds, as well as the apprenticeship system, which was well developed by the sixteenth century, also provided a way to pass the knowledge of the baker's trade from generation to generation.

To become master bakers, workers had to go through a course of apprenticeship and obtain a certificate stating they had gained the necessary skills. Certified master bakers could then set up their own shops. Master bakers were assisted by apprentices, who were not paid and were learning the trade, and by journeymen, who were paid servants and who may have completed an apprenticeship but had not gained a master baker's certificate.

## Sugar and Pastry Making

Bakers also made cakes from doughs or batters containing honey or other sweet ingredients, such as dried fruits. Many of these items had religious significance and were baked only for special occasions, such as the Twelfth Night cakes baked after Christmas. Such products nearly always had a dense texture, unlike the light confections we call cakes today. Nonsweetened pastry doughs were also made for such products as meat pies. In the 1400s, pastry chefs in France formed their own corporations and took pastry making away from bakers. From this point on, the profession of pastry making developed rapidly, and cooks developed many new kinds of pastry products.

Honey was the most important sweetener. Sugarcane, the source of refined sugar, was native to India and grown in southern regions of Asia. To be brought to Europe, sugar had to pass through many countries, and each overland stop added taxes and tolls to the already high price. To Europeans, sugar was a rare and expensive luxury item.

The European arrival in the Americas in 1492 sparked a revolution in pastry making. Caribbean islands proved good for growing sugar, so the supply became more abundant and prices dropped. Cocoa and chocolate, native to the New World, were available in the Old World for the first time. Once the new ingredients became widely available, baking and pastry became more and more sophisticated, and many new recipes were developed. By the seventeenth and eighteenth centuries, many of the basic pastries we know today, including laminated or layered doughs like puff pastry and Danish dough, were being made. Also in the eighteenth century, processors learned how to refine sugar from sugar beets. At last Europeans could grow sugar locally.

# From the First Restaurants to Carême

Modern food service is said to have begun shortly after the middle of the eighteenth century. Just as bakers and pastry cooks had to be licensed and were members of guilds, which controlled production, so too were caterers, roasters, pork butchers, and other food workers licensed members of guilds. An innkeeper, in order to serve meals to guests, had to buy the various menu items from those operations that were licensed to provide them. Guests had little or no choice and simply ate what was available for that meal.

In 1765, a Parisian named **Boulanger** (whose name, incidentally, means "bread baker") began advertising on his shop sign that he served soups, which he called *restaurants* or *restoratives*. (Literally, the word means "restoring.") According to the story, one of the dishes he served was sheep's feet in a cream sauce. The guild of stew makers challenged him in court, but Boulanger won by claiming he didn't stew the feet *in* the sauce but served them *with* the sauce. In challenging the rules of the guilds, Boulanger changed the course of food service history.

For the bread baker, two important events during this period were the publication of the first two major books on bread making: *L'art du meunier, du boulanger et du vermicellier* (*The Art of the Miller, the Bread Baker, and the Pasta Maker*) by Malouin in 1775, and *Le parfait boulanger* (*The Perfect Bread Baker*) by Parmentier in 1778.

The nineteenth century saw not only a revolution in food service but also in the development of modern baking as we know it. After the French Revolution in 1789, many bakers and pastry cooks who had been servants in the houses of the nobility started independent businesses. Artisans competed for customers with the quality of their products. The general public—not just aristocrats and the well-to-do—were able to buy fine pastries. Some of the pastry shops started during that time still serve Parisians today.

A new invention in the eighteenth century changed the organization of the commercial kitchen, which had been centered around an open cooking fire. This invention was the stove, which provided a more controllable heat source. Commercial kitchens became divided into three departments: the stove, run by the cook, or **cuisinier**; the rotisserie, run by the meat chef, or **rôtisseur**; and the oven, run by the pastry chef, or **pâtissier**. The pastry chef and the meat chef reported to the cuisinier, who was also known as **chef de cuisine**, which means "head of the kitchen." Although the stovetop was a new feature of this reorganized kitchen, the baker's oven was still the wood-fired brick oven that had long been in use.

The most famous chef of the early nineteenth century was **Marie-Antoine Carême**, also known as Antonin Carême, who lived from 1784 to 1833. His spectacular constructions of sugar and pastry earned him great fame, and he elevated the jobs of cook and pastry chef to respected professions. Carême's book, *Le pâtissier royal*, was one of the first systematic explanations of the pastry chef's art.

Ironically, most of Carême's career was spent in the service of the nobility and royalty, in an era when the products of the bakers' and pastry chefs' craft were becoming more widely available to average citizens. Carême had little to do with the commercial and retail aspects of baking.

In spite of his achievements and fame as a pastry chef, Carême was primarily not a baker but a chef de cuisine. As a young man, he learned all the branches of cooking quickly, and he dedicated his career to refining and organizing culinary techniques. His many books contain the first systematic account of cooking principles, recipes, and menu making.

Portrait of Marie-Antoine Carême, from M.A. Carême. *L'art de la cuisine française au dix-neuvième siècle. Traité élémentaire et pratique*, 1833. Division of Rare and Manuscript Collections, Cornell University Library.

# Modern Baking and Modern Technology

The nineteenth century was a time of great technical progress. Automated processes enabled bakers to do many tasks with machines that once required a great deal of manual labor. The most important of these technological advances was the development of **roller milling**. Prior to this time, flour was milled by grinding grain between two stones. The resulting flour then had to be sifted, or bolted, often numerous times, to separate the bran. The process was slow. Roller milling, described in chapter 4 (see page 57), is much faster and more efficient. This was a tremendous boost to the baking industry.

Another important development of the period was the new availability of flours from the wheat-growing regions of North America. These wheat varieties were higher in protein than those that could be grown in northern Europe, and the export of this wheat to Europe promoted the large-scale production of white bread.

In the twentieth century, advances in technology, from refrigeration to sophisticated ovens to air transportation that carries fresh ingredients around the world, contributed immeasurably to baking and pastry making.

Preservation techniques have helped make available and affordable some ingredients that were once rare and expensive. Also because of modern food preservation technology, it is now possible to do some or most of the preparation and processing of foods before shipping rather than in the bakeshop or food service operation itself. Thus, convenience foods have come into being. Today it is possible to avoid many labor-intensive processes, such as making puff pastry, by purchasing convenience products.

Modern equipment has helped change production techniques and schedules. For example, dough sheeters speed the production of laminated doughs such as Danish dough while at the same time producing a more uniform product. Retarder-proofers hold yeast doughs overnight and then proof them so they are ready to bake in the morning. It is possible to prepare some foods farther in advance and in larger quantities, holding them in good condition until ready for finishing and serving.

## ❋❳ ESCOFFIER ❲❋

Georges-August Escoffier (1847–1935), the greatest chef of his time, is still revered by chefs and gourmets as the father of twentieth-century cookery. His main contributions were (1) the simplification of the classical menu, (2) the systematizing of cooking methods, and (3) the reorganization of the kitchen.

Escoffier's books and recipes are still important reference works for professional chefs. The basic cooking methods and preparations we study today are based on Escoffier's work. His book *Le guide culinaire*, which is still widely used, arranges recipes in a simple system based on main ingredient and cooking method, greatly simplifying the more complex system handed down from Carême. Learning classical cooking, according to Escoffier, begins with learning a relatively few basic procedures and understanding basic ingredients.

Although Escoffier didn't work as a bread baker, he applied the same systems to the production of desserts that he did to that of savory food. Several of the desserts he invented, such as peach Melba, are still served today.

# Modern Styles

All these developments have helped change cooking styles and eating habits. The evolution in cooking and baking that has been going on for hundreds of years continues. It is helpful to explore a little further the changes in restaurant cooking styles, because the changes in baking and pastry have followed a similar course.

A generation after **Escoffier**, the most influential chef in the middle of the twentieth century was Fernand Point (1897–1955). Working quietly and steadily in his restaurant, La Pyramide, in Vienne, France, Point simplified and lightened classical cuisine. Point's influence extended well beyond his own lifetime.

Many of Point's apprentices, such as Paul Bocuse, Jean and Pierre Troisgros, and Alain Chapel, went on to become some of the greatest stars of modern cooking. They, along with other chefs of their generation, became best known in the 1960s and early 1970s for a style of cooking called **nouvelle cuisine**. They took Point's lighter approach even further and urged simpler, more natural flavors and preparations, with lighter sauces and seasonings and shorter cooking times. In traditional classical cuisine, many dishes were plated in the dining room by waiters. Nouvelle cuisine, however, emphasized artful plating presentations done by the chef in the kitchen. In the pastry chef's department, this practice is the beginning of the modern plated dessert.

A landmark event in the history of modern North American cooking was the opening of Alice Waters' restaurant, Chez Panisse, in Berkeley, California, in 1971. Waters' philosophy is that good food depends on good ingredients, so she set about finding dependable sources of the highest-quality vegetables, fruits, and meats and preparing them in the simplest ways. Over the next decades, many chefs and restaurateurs followed her lead, seeking the best seasonal, locally grown, organically raised food products.

During the latter part of the twentieth century, as travel became easier and as immigrants arrived in Europe and North America from around the world, awareness of and taste for regional dishes grew. Chefs became more knowledgeable not only about the traditional cuisines of other parts of Europe but also of Asia, Latin America, and elsewhere. Many of the most creative chefs are inspired by these cuisines and use some of their techniques and ingredients. Master pastry chefs such as Gaston Lenôtre have revitalized the art of fine pastry and have inspired and taught a generation of professionals.

The use of ingredients and techniques from more than one regional cuisine in a single dish has become known as **fusion cuisine**. Fusion cuisine can produce poor results because it is not true to any one culture and becomes too mixed up. This was especially true in the 1980s, when the idea of fusion cuisine was new. Cooks often used a mixture of ingredients and techniques without a good feeling for how everything worked together. The result was sometimes a jumbled mess. But those chefs who have taken the time to study in depth the cuisines and cultures they borrow from have brought new excitement to cooking and to restaurant menus. In the pastry department, ingredients such as passion fruit, mangoes, and lemongrass, once strange and exotic, are now commonly found.

Bakers, chefs, and consumers have often reacted against technology in food production by rediscovering old-fashioned foods and production methods. Bakers, especially, are looking to reclaim the flavors of old-fashioned breads that were lost as baking became more industrialized and baked goods became more refined, standardized, and—some would say—flavorless. Inspired by the example of Lionel Poilâne (p. 131), bakers are researching methods for producing the handmade sourdough breads of times past, and they are experimenting with specialty flours in their search for flavor. On restaurant dessert menus, this trend can be seen in the old-fashioned, homestyle desserts that sit comfortably side by side with ornate, ultramodern pastry presentations.

# BAKING AND PASTRY CAREERS

At the beginning of the twenty-first century, the popularity of fine breads and pastries is growing even faster than new chefs can be trained. Those entering a career in baking or pastry making today find opportunities in many areas, from small bakeshops and neighborhood restaurants to large hotels and wholesale bakeries.

# Restaurant and Hotel Food Service

As you learned earlier in this chapter, one of Escoffier's important achievements was the reorganization of the kitchen. He divided the kitchen into departments, or stations, based on the kinds of foods they produced. A station chef was placed in charge of each department. This system, with many variations, is still used today, especially in large hotels with traditional kinds of food service. In a small operation, the station chef may be the only worker in the department. But in a large kitchen, each station chef might have several assistants.

Station chefs in large kitchens include the sauce chef (*saucier*), who is responsible for sauces and sautéed items; the fish chef (*poissonier*); the roast chef (*rôtisseur*); and the pantry chef (*chef garde manger*). Desserts and pastries are prepared by the pastry chef (*pâtissier*). Station chefs report to the executive chef, or *chef de cuisine*, who is in charge of food production. In the largest kitchens, the position of executive chef is mostly managerial. The executive chef may do little or no cooking personally. The *sous chef* assists the executive chef and is directly in charge of the cooking during production.

The pastry department is usually separated physically from the hot kitchen, for many reasons. Many desserts and confections must be prepared in a cool environment. In addition, the separation helps prevent creams, icings, and batters from absorbing the aromas of roasted, grilled, and sautéed foods.

In a small to medium-size restaurant, the pastry chef may work alone, preparing all the dessert items. Often the pastry chef starts work early in the morning and finishes before dinner service starts. Another cook or the dining room staff then assembles and plates the desserts during service.

In large restaurants and hotels, the chef in charge of baking and desserts is the executive pastry chef. This is a management position comparable to the executive chef in the hot kitchen. The executive pastry chef supervises workers in the department, including specialists such as the bread baker (*boulanger*), who prepares yeast goods including such breakfast items as brioche, croissants, and Danish pastry; the ice cream maker (*glacier*), who makes frozen desserts; the confectioner or candy maker (*confiseur*); and the decorator (*décorateur*), who prepares showpieces, sugar work, and decorated cakes.

In hotels, the work of the baking and pastry department can be extensive, including preparing not only desserts and breads for all the on-premise restaurants, cafés, and room service but also breakfast breads and pastries and all baked goods, including specialty cakes and decorative work, for the banquet and catering departments. Such large operations provide many opportunities for the baker wishing to get a wide range of experience.

Caterers, institutional volume feeding operations (schools, hospitals, employee lunchrooms), executive dining rooms, and private clubs may require the services of bakers and pastry chefs. The required skills vary from one establishment to another. Some prepare all their baked goods in-house, while others rely on convenience products and finished wholesale bakery foods.

# Bakeries

Retail bakeries include independent bakeshops as well as in-store bakery departments in grocery stores and supermarkets. High-end supermarkets, in particular, have provided many new opportunities for creative bakers and pastry chefs. A few grocery stores have even installed wood-burning hearth ovens for baking handcrafted artisan breads.

The **head baker** is the worker in charge of the production in a retail bakery. The head baker is in charge of a staff that may range from a few bakers who share most tasks to, in a larger bakery, many specialists who work in different departments, such as breads and yeast goods, cakes, and decorated items. Even bread-making tasks can be divided among different workers, with some workers mixing, proofing, and making up the doughs and others baking the items and managing the ovens.

Wholesale bakeries accomplish the same tasks as retail bakeries, except production may be more automated and industrialized. Equipment such as mixers and ovens handle large volumes of doughs and baked goods. In addition to finished items, wholesale bakeries may produce unfinished products such as cake layers, cookie dough, and puff pastry dough for sale to restaurants, hotels, caterers, supermarkets, and other food service operations.

# Professional Requirements

What does it take to be a good baker or pastry chef?

The emphasis of a food service education, whether in baking and pastry or in the hot kitchen, is on learning a set of skills. But in many ways, *attitudes* are more important than skills because a good attitude will help you not only learn skills but also persevere and overcome the difficulties you may face in your career.

Mastery of skills is, of course, essential to success. There are, however, general qualities that are also important for the new pastry chef or baker, just graduated from school, who wants to advance in the industry. The following are a few of the important ones.

## Eagerness to Work

Baking professionally is demanding, both physically and mentally. By the time they graduate, students know their fellow students who have been the hardest working, especially those who seek extra work, extra opportunities to learn, are the most successful. Once they have graduated, bakers and chefs who give the most effort are the ones who advance the fastest.

One of the hardest discoveries for new culinarians is the repetitive nature of the work—doing the same tasks over and over, whether making up hundreds of dinner rolls a day or thousands of cookies for holiday sales. Successful bakers and chefs approach repetition as an opportunity for building skills. Only by doing a cooking task over and over can you really master it, really understand every nuance and variable.

Overcoming the stress created by hard work requires a sense of responsibility and a dedication to your profession, to your coworkers, and to your customers or clients. Dedication also means staying with a job and not hopping from kitchen to kitchen every few months. Sticking with a job for at least a year or two shows prospective employers you are serious about your work and can be relied on.

## Commitment to Learning

Never stop learning. Read. Study. Experiment. Take continuing education courses. Network with other chefs. Share information. Join appropriate professional associations, like the American Culinary Federation or the Retail Bakers of America. Join the alumni association of your school and keep in touch with your fellow graduates. Enter competitions to hone your skills and to learn from your competitors. Learn management and business skills. Keep up with the latest developments in technology, baking techniques, and food trends while you refresh your basic skills. Remember that learning to bake and cook and manage a kitchen is a lifelong process.

In return, help others learn. Share your knowledge. Be a mentor to a student. Teach a class. Help a coworker. Judge a competition. Contribute to professional workshops and seminars. Do what you can to raise the skill level of the profession.

## *Dedication to Service*

Food service, as its name implies, is about serving others. Baking and cooking professionally mean bringing enjoyment and well-being to your guests. Good service requires sourcing high-quality ingredients and handling them with care and respect; guarding the health of guests and coworkers with full attention to food safety and sanitation; treating others with respect; making guests feel welcome and coworkers feel valued; and maintaining a clean, attractive work environment. Look after others, and your own success will follow.

## *Professional Pride*

Professionals take pride in their work and want to make sure it is something to be proud of. A professional cook maintains a positive attitude, works efficiently, neatly, and safely, and always aims for high quality. Although it sounds like a contradiction, professional pride includes a strong dose of humility, for it is humility that leads chefs to dedicate themselves to hard work, perpetual learning, and commitment to service. A professional who takes pride in his or her work recognizes the talent of others in the field and is inspired and stimulated by their achievements. A good baker or pastry chef demonstrates pride by, in turn, setting a good example for others.

# TERMS FOR REVIEW

| | | | |
|---|---|---|---|
| gluten | pâtissier | fusion cuisine | glacier |
| maza | chef de cuisine | saucier | confiseur |
| opson | Carême | poissonier | décorateur |
| Boulanger | roller milling | chef garde manger | head baker |
| cuisinier | Escoffier | sous chef | |
| rôtisseur | nouvelle cuisine | boulanger | |

# QUESTIONS FOR DISCUSSION

1. What characteristic of modern wheat flour makes it possible to make an elastic, yeast-fermented dough? Why was it not possible for prehistoric people to make such doughs from the earliest wild grains?

2. What historical event did the most to make sugar widely available? How so?

3. What contribution did beer production make to the process of bread making?

4. Briefly describe how commercial kitchens were organized after the invention of the stove in the eighteenth century.

5. What is nouvelle cuisine? How did nouvelle cuisine affect the style of desserts served in restaurants?

6. Describe the organization of a large modern hotel kitchen. Name and describe specialty positions that may be found in large bakeries.

# Basic Professional Skills: Bakeshop Math and Sanitation

**R**ecipes and formulas are fundamental tools of the kitchen and bakeshop. They indicate ingredients to be purchased and stored. They give measuring and preparation instructions for the items to be produced. And they are the focus of other management tools and techniques, including modifying quantities and determining costs.

In this chapter, you are introduced to bakeshop production through a discussion of the kinds of measurements and mathematical calculations necessary for baking and of the basic processes common to nearly all baked goods.

In the final portion of this chapter, you will find a brief overview of a critically important subject: bakeshop sanitation.

**After reading this chapter, you should be able to:**

1. Describe the problems and limitations of written formulas.

2. Describe the two basic functions of standardized formulas.

3. Explain the importance of weighing baking ingredients.

4. Use a baker's balance scale.

5. Calculate raw fruit yields based on trimming losses.

6. Use formulas based on baker's percentages.

7. Convert formulas to different yields.

8. Calculate EP unit costs.

9. Calculate formula costs.

10. Describe steps to prevent food-borne diseases in the areas of personal hygiene and food handling techniques.

# FORMULAS AND MEASUREMENT

A *recipe* is a set of instructions for producing a certain dish. In order to duplicate a desired preparation, it is necessary to have a precise record of the ingredients, their amounts, and the way in which they are combined and cooked. This is the purpose of a recipe.

Bakers generally talk about **formulas** rather than recipes. If this sounds to you more like a chemistry lab than a food production facility, it is with good reason. The bakeshop is very much like a chemistry laboratory, both in the scientific accuracy of the procedures and in the complex reactions that take place during mixing and baking.

Note there are no exact rules about the use of the word *formula* (but see sidebar). Some bakers use the term for flour goods only, while referring to *recipes* for items such as pastry cream, fruit fillings, and dessert mousses. Other bakers are in the habit of calling all recipes *formulas*. Still others always use the word *recipe*. In this book, we use the word *formula* for most products, although you will also see the word *recipe* used occasionally.

The primary function of a formula, of course, is to give a set of ingredients and quantities for making a product. But a formula is useful for related purposes also. A written formula provides a means of modifying quantities and yields and determining costs. These functions require the use of math. Procedures for working with formula math are the main focus of this section.

## ⁂ FORMULAS AND MOPs ⁂

Strictly speaking, the term *formula* refers only to the list of ingredients and quantities. The directions for using those ingredients, referred to in this book as the *procedure*, is known by many chefs as the *method of preparation*, or MOP. There are relatively few MOPs, or basic procedures, and these are applied to nearly all the products of the bakeshop. To a trained baker, these MOPs are so well understood that they need not be repeated with every formula, as explained in the text below.

One of the major purposes of this book is to familiarize you with the principal procedures used in the bakeshop so you too can use professional formulas.

## The Uses and Limitations of Formulas and Recipes

In spite of their importance, written formulas and recipes have many limitations. No matter how detailed a formula is, it assumes you already have certain knowledge—that you understand the terminology it uses, for example, and that you know how to measure ingredients.

Before talking specifically about baking formulas, let's briefly consider recipes in general. Many people believe that learning how to cook means simply learning recipes. A professional cook, on the other hand, learns to work by mastering a set of basic procedures. A recipe is a way of applying basic techniques to specific ingredients.

The main purpose of learning basic cooking principles is not to be able to cook without recipes but rather to understand the recipes you use. As we said above, every recipe assumes you have certain knowledge, so you can understand the instructions and follow them correctly.

If you have leafed through this book, you know it is not just a book of formulas and recipes. Although it contains hundreds of formulas, they take up only part of it. Your main concern is learning techniques and procedures that you can apply to any formula.

Bakers use a relatively small number of basic mixing techniques to prepare doughs and batters. For this reason, a baker's formula may consist only of a list of ingredients and quantities and the name of the mixing method. A trained baker can produced a finished product with this information alone. In fact, often the name of the mixing method isn't even necessary because the baker can tell from the ingredients and their proportions which mixing method is needed. To accustom you to this way of working, and to emphasize the importance of learning basic mixing methods well, most of the formulas in this book indicate the name of the required mixing method without repeating the steps for each formula. In each case, you should review the basic procedures as needed before using a formula.

Some recipes supply very little information, and some supply a great deal. But no matter how detailed it is, a written recipe can't tell you everything, and some judgment by the cook is always required. This is especially true in the hot kitchen, where cooks must always make adjustments for ingredient product variation—some carrots are sweeter than others, some oysters are saltier than others, and so on.

In the bakeshop, there is less product variation. For example, flour, yeast, sugar, butter, and other basic ingredients are pretty consistent, especially when purchased from the same source. Nevertheless, many other factors can't be accounted for when writing a recipe. For example:

- Equipment varies from bakeshop to bakeshop. For example, different mixers as well as different sizes of mixer process dough differently, and ovens vary in their baking properties.

- It is impossible to give exact instructions for many processes. For example, a bread formula may indicate a mixing time, but the exact time needed for a particular batch will vary. The baker must be able to judge by the feel and texture of the dough when it has developed properly.

## Standardized Recipes and Formulas

A **standardized recipe or formula** is a set of instructions describing the way a particular establishment prepares a particular item. In other words, it is a customized recipe developed by an operation for the use of its own cooks, pastry chefs, and bakers, using its own equipment, to be sold or served to its own patrons.

Formula formats differ from operation to operation, but nearly all of them try to include as much precise information as possible. The following details may be listed:

- Name of the recipe.

- Yield, including total yield, number of portions, and exact portion size.

- Ingredients and exact amounts, listed in order of use.

- Equipment needed, including measuring equipment, pan sizes, portioning equipment, and so on.

- Directions for preparing the dish. Directions are kept as simple as possible.

- Preparation and cooking times.

- Directions for holding the product between preparation and service.

- Directions for portioning, plating, and garnishing.

- Directions for storing leftovers.

As you can tell, some of these points apply more to the pastry or dessert station in a restaurant than they do to retail bakeries. Bread recipes don't require instructions for plating and garnishing, for example. Nevertheless, the basic principles apply to bakeries as well as to restaurant kitchens.

### The Functions of Standardized Formulas

An operation's own recipes are used to control production. They do this in two ways:

* They control quality. Standardized formulas and recipes are detailed and specific. This is to ensure the product is the same every time it is made and served, no matter who cooks it.

* They control quantity. First, they indicate precise quantities for every ingredient and how to measure that quantity. Second, they indicate exact yields and portion sizes and how to measure and serve those portions.

### The Limitations of Standardized Formulas

Standardized formulas have the same problems as all recipes—the problems we discussed earlier regarding variations in ingredients, equipment, and vagueness of instructions. These problems can be reduced by writing the recipe carefully, but they cannot be eliminated. Even if an operation uses good standardized recipes, a new employee making a dish for the first time usually requires some supervision to make sure he or she interprets the instructions the same way as the rest of the staff. These limitations don't invalidate standardized recipes. If anything, they make exact directions even more important. But they do mean that experience and knowledge are still very important.

## Instructional Recipes and Formulas

The formulas in this book are *not* standardized. Remember that a standardized formula is custom-made for a particular operation. The formulas in this book, obviously, are not.

The purpose of a standardized formula is to direct and control the production of a particular food item. Directions must be as complete and exact as possible.

The purpose of the instructional formulas in this book is to teach basic baking and cooking techniques. They provide an opportunity for you to practice, with specific ingredients, the general procedures you have learned.

If you glance at any of the formulas in this book, you will see they do not contain all the features of standardized formulas, as described in the previous section. In particular, you will see the following differences:

1. **Instructions for preparation.**

   In most cases, formulas in this book follow a discussion of a basic procedure. The formulas are examples of the general procedure, and they give you experience in applying what you have learned. The information you are given in the formula instructions is intended primarily to encourage you to think and to learn a technique, not just to turn out a product. You should consult your instructor when you have a question about a procedure.

2. **Variations and optional ingredients.**

   Many formulas are followed by variations. These are actually whole formulas given in abbreviated terms. It is possible to write them out as separate, full-length formulas. (You are encouraged to do this before preparing a variation, as a learning experience.)

   Giving formulas as variations rather than as separate formulas encourages you to see the patterns behind each. Again, you are learning techniques, not just formulas. You develop more understanding of what you are doing if you see coconut cream pie and chocolate pudding as variations of the same basic techniques rather than as separate, unrelated formulas.

Your instructors may have their own variations, or they may wish to make changes in the basic formulas in order to teach you certain points. Unlike standardized formulas, instructional formulas are not engraved in stone.

## Reading Formulas and Recipes

Before starting production, you must read the entire recipe carefully and completely. The following are some of the tasks you must do as you read the recipe and get ready for production. Chefs call these advance preparations their *mise en place* (meeze on plahss; French for "put in place"). A good mise en place is essential for efficient operation of a bakeshop or kitchen.

### Formula Modifications

- Determine the yield of the printed recipe and decide if it needs modification. If you need to convert the recipe to a different yield (discussed later in this chapter), do all the math beforehand.

- Determine if any other changes are needed, such as ingredient substitutions, to get the desired result. Write them down.

### Ingredients

- Assemble and measure all ingredients. If all ingredients are scaled in advance, production can go quickly and without interruption. Also, it's better to find out in advance if you don't have enough of an ingredient so you can get more before starting production.

- Prepare all ingredients as necessary, such as sifting flour, separating eggs, and bringing butter to room temperature. Many of these steps are indicated in the recipe, but many may not be. Professional formulas often assume the experienced baker knows, for example, that butter should be removed from the refrigerator in advance so it is soft enough to be used in creaming-method cake batters.

### Procedures

- Read the entire procedure or method of preparation carefully and make sure you understand it.

- If a mixing method is indicated only by name, such as Creaming Method, look up and review the procedure if you need to refresh your memory. Make sure you understand each step of the general procedure and how to apply it to your specific formula.

- Look up any terms or key words you don't know.

### Tools and Equipment

- Determine what equipment you need. Required equipment is generally listed in standardized recipes but not in recipes from other sources. Read every step of the procedure and write down which tools and equipment you need in each step.

- Assemble all tools and equipment.

- Prepare equipment as needed. For example, line sheet pans with parchment, grease cake pans, preheat ovens.

## Units of Measure— U.S. System

| Weight | | |
|---|---|---|
| 1 lb | = | 16 oz |

| Volume | | |
|---|---|---|
| 1 gal | = | 4 qt |
| 1 qt | = | 2 pt |
| | | or |
| | | 4 cups |
| | | or |
| | | 32 (fl) oz |
| 1 pt | = | 2 cups |
| | | or |
| | | 16 (fl) oz |
| 1 cup | = | 8 (fl) oz |
| 1 (fl) oz | = | 2 tbsp |
| 1 tbsp | = | 3 tsp |

| Length | | |
|---|---|---|
| 1 ft | = | 12 in. |

*Note:* One fluid ounce (often simply called *ounce*) water weighs 1 ounce. One pint water weighs approximately 1 pound.

## Abbreviations of U.S. Units of Measure Used in This Book

| | |
|---|---|
| Pound | lb |
| Ounce | oz |
| Gallon | gal |
| Quart | qt |
| Pint | pt |
| fluid ounce | fl oz |
| Tablespoon | tbsp |
| Teaspoon | tsp |
| Inch | in. |
| Foot | ft |

# Measurement

One of the primary functions of a formula is to indicate the ingredients and correct quantities or measurements to be used to make a product.

Ingredients are almost always weighed in the bakeshop, rather than measured by volume, because measurement by weight is more accurate. Accuracy of measurement, as we have said, is essential in the bakeshop. Unlike home baking recipes, a professional baker's formula will not call for 6 cups flour, for example.

To demonstrate to yourself the importance of weighing rather than measuring by volume, measure 1 cup flour in two ways: (a) Sift some flour and lightly spoon it into a dry measure. Level the top and weigh the flour. (b) Scoop some unsifted flour into the same measure and pack it lightly. Level the top and weigh the flour. Note the difference. No wonder home recipes, which usually indicate volume measures of dry ingredients, can be so inconsistent!

The baker's term for weighing ingredients is *scaling*.

The following ingredients, and *only* these ingredients, may sometimes be measured by volume, at the ratio of 1 pint per pound or 1 liter per kilogram:

- ◆ Water
- ◆ Milk
- ◆ Eggs

Volume measure is often used when scaling water for small or medium-sized batches of bread. Results are generally good. However, whenever accuracy is critical, it is better to weigh. This is because 1 pint water actually weighs slightly more than 1 pound, or approximately 16.7 ounces. (This figure varies with the temperature of the water.)

For convenience, volume measures of liquids are frequently used when products other than baked flour goods—such as sauces, syrups, puddings, and custards—are being made.

## Units of Measure

The system of measurement used in the United States is complicated. Even people who have used it all their lives sometimes have trouble remembering things like how many fluid ounces are in a quart and how many feet are in a mile.

The first table above lists equivalents among the units of measure used in the bakeshop and kitchen. You should memorize these thoroughly so you don't lose time making simple calculations. The second table above lists the abbreviations used in this book.

## The Metric System

The United States is the only major country that uses the complex system of measurement we have just described. Other countries use a much simpler system called the **metric system**.

### Basic Units

In the metric system, there is one basic unit for each type of measurement:

The **gram** is the basic unit of weight.

The **liter** is the basic unit of volume.

The **meter** is the basic unit of length.

The **degree Celsius** is the basic unit of temperature.

Larger or smaller units are made simply by multiplying or dividing by 10, 100, 1000, and so on. These divisions are expressed by prefixes. The ones you need to know are:

*kilo-* = 1000

*deci-* = ⅒ or 0.1

*centi-* = ¹⁄₁₀₀ or 0.01

*milli-* = ¹⁄₁₀₀₀ or 0.001

Once you know these basic units, you do not need complicated tables such as the first table on page 20. The table below summarizes the metric units you need to know in the bakeshop.

## Converting to Metric

Most Americans think the metric system is much harder to learn than it really is. This is because they think about metric units in terms of U.S. units. They read there are 28.35 grams in 1 ounce and are immediately convinced they will never be able to learn metrics.

Most of the time, you do not need to worry about being able to convert U.S. units into metric units and vice versa. This is a very important point to remember, especially if you think the metric system might be hard to learn.

The reason is simple. You will usually be working in either one system or the other. You will rarely have to convert from one to the other. Many people today own imported cars and repair them with metric tools without worrying about how many millimeters are in 1 inch. Occasionally you might find a metric formula you want to try in a U.S. kitchen. Even then, much modern equipment, such as digital scales, measures in both metric and U.S. units, so conversion isn't needed. When it is necessary to convert, you can refer to a table such as the one in appendix 1 without having to memorize exact conversion factors. For most purposes, all you have to remember is the information in the table on this page.

To become accustomed to working in metric units, it is helpful to have a feel for how large the units are. The following rough equivalents may be used to help you visualize metric units. They are *not* exact conversion factors. (When you need exact conversion factors, see appendix 1.)

| Metric Units | | |
|---|---|---|
| **Basic units** | | |
| **Quantity** | **Unit** | **Abbreviation** |
| Weight | gram | g |
| Volume | liter | L |
| Length | meter | m |
| Temperature | degree Celsius | °C |
| **Divisions and multiples** | | |
| **Prefix/Example** | **Meaning** | **Abbreviation** |
| kilo- | 1000 | k |
| Kilogram | 1000 grams | kg |
| deci- | ⅒ | d |
| Deciliter | 0.1 liter | dL |
| centi- | ¹⁄₁₀₀ | c |
| Centimeter | 0.01 meter | cm |
| milli- | ¹⁄₁₀₀₀ | m |
| Millimeter | 0.001 meter | mm |

A *kilogram* is slightly more than 2 pounds.

A *gram* is about ¹⁄₃₀ ounce. A half-teaspoon of flour weighs a little less than 1 gram.

A *liter* is slightly more than 1 quart.

A *deciliter* is slightly less than ½ cup.

A *centiliter* is about 2 teaspoons.

A *meter* is slightly longer than 3 feet.

A *centimeter* is about ⅜ inch.

0°C is the freezing point of water (32°F).

100°C is the boiling point of water (212°F).

An increase or decrease of 1 degree Celsius is equivalent to about 2 degrees Fahrenheit.

## Metric Formulas and Recipes

American industry will probably adopt the metric system someday. Many recipe writers are already eager to get a head start and are printing metric equivalents.

As a result, you will see recipes calling for 454 g flour, 28.35 g butter, or a baking temperature of 191°C. No wonder people are afraid of the metric system!

Kitchens in countries that use the metric system do not work with such impractical numbers any more than we normally use figures like 1 lb 1¼ oz flour, 2.19 oz butter, or a baking temperature of 348°F. That would defeat the purpose of the metric system, which is to be simple and practical. If you have a chance to look at a French cookbook, you will see nice, round numbers such as 1 kg, 200 g, and 4 dL.

**The metric measures in the formulas in this book are NOT equivalent to the U.S. measures given alongside them.** You should think of the metric portion of the formulas as separate formulas with yields that are close to but not the same as the yields of the U.S. formulas. To give exact equivalents would require using awkward, impractical numbers. If you have metric equipment, use the metric units, and if you have U.S. equipment, use the U.S. units. You should rarely have to worry about converting between the two.

For the most part, the total yield of the metric formulas in this book is close to the yield of the U.S. formulas while keeping the ingredient proportions the same. Unfortunately, it is not always possible to keep the proportions exactly the same because the U.S. system is not decimal-based like the metric system. In some cases, the metric quantities produce slightly different results due to the varying proportions, but these differences are usually extremely small.

Digital professional scale.
Courtesy of Cardinal Detecto

## Measuring by Weight

A good balance scale should be accurate to ¼ oz (0.25 oz) or, if metric, to 5 g. Dry ingredients weighing less than ¼ oz can be scaled by physically dividing larger quantities into equal portions. For example, to scale ¹⁄₁₆ oz (0.06 oz), first weigh out ¼ oz, then divide this into four equal piles using a small knife.

For fine pastry work, a small battery-operated digital scale is often more useful than a large balance scale. A good digital scale is relatively inexpensive. It can instantly measure quantities to the nearest ⅛ oz or the nearest 2 g. Most digital scales have a zero or tare button that sets the indicated weight to zero. For example, you may set a container on the scale, set the weight to zero, add the desired quantity of the first ingredient, again set the weight to zero, add the second ingredient, and so on. This speeds the weighing of dry ingredients to be sifted together, for example.

When very small quantities of items such as spices are required in formulas in this book, an approximate volume equivalent (usually in fractions of a teaspoon) is also included. However, remember that careful weighing on a good scale is more accurate. Approximate volume equivalents of selected ingredients are given in appendix 4.

In order to make formula conversions and calculations easier, fractions of ounces that appear in the ingredient tables of the formulas in this book are written as decimals. Thus, 1½ oz is written as 1.5 oz and ¼ oz is written as 0.25 oz. A list of decimal equivalents is included in appendix 3.

### AP Weight and EP Weight

In the hot kitchen, cooks are regularly concerned with the trimming yield of vegetables, fruits, meats, and other ingredients. For example, 1 lb raw, whole turnips yields much less than 1 lb trimmed, peeled turnips. In the bakeshop, bakers need not be concerned

---

### ❋⟩ SCONE FLOUR ⟨❋

British bakers have a convenient method for measuring baking powder when small quantities are needed. They use a mixture called **scone flour**. To make 1 lb scone flour, combine 15 oz flour and 1 oz baking powder; sift together three times. One oz (¹⁄₁₆ lb) scone flour thus contains ¹⁄₁₆ (0.06 oz) baking powder. For each ¹⁄₁₆ oz baking powder you need in a formula, substitute 1 oz scone flour for 1 oz of the flour called for in the formula.

## Procedure for Using a Baker's Balance Scale

The principle of using a baker's scale is simple: The scale must balance before setting the weights, and it must balance again after scaling. The following procedure applies to the most commonly used type of baker's scale.

1. Set the scale scoop or other container on the left side of the scale.

2. Balance the scale by placing counterweights on the right side and/or by adjusting the ounce weight on the horizontal bar.

3. Set the scale for the desired weight by placing weights on the right side and/or by moving the ounce weight.

   For example, to set the scale for 1 lb 8 oz, place a 1-lb weight on the right side and move the ounce weight to the right 8 oz. If the ounce weight is already over 8 oz, so you cannot move it another 8, add 2 lb to the right side of the scale and subtract 8 ounces by moving the ounce weight 8 places to the left. The result is still 1 lb 8 oz.

4. Add the ingredient being scaled to the left side until the scale balances.

with trimming yield of the ingredients they use most: flour, sugar, fats, and so on. However, it is important to be able to make the proper yield calculations when working with fresh fruits. How many pounds of whole apples must the baker order, for example, if 5 lb peeled, sliced apples are needed?

The percentage yield of a fruit or vegetable indicates, on the average, how much of the **AP weight** (as purchased weight) is left after trimming to produce the ready-to-cook item, or **EP weight** (edible portion weight).

To determine the percentage yield of a fruit, follow these steps:

1. Weigh the item before trimming. This is the AP weight.

2. Trim and peel the item as necessary to get the edible portion.

3. Weigh the trimmed item. This is the EP weight.

4. Divide the EP weight by the AP weight. For example, 5 lb trimmed (EP) divided by 10 lb before trimming (AP) equals 0.5.

5. Multiply this number by 100 to get the percentage. For example, 0.5 × 100 equals 50%.

The most accurate yield percentages are the ones you calculate yourself, because they are based on the items you actually use in your bakeshop. For approximate or average yield percentages of most commonly used fruits, refer to the section on fruits beginning on page 580 in this book.

Once you have a yield percentage for an item, save this number to refer to as necessary. You can use this figure to do two basic calculations.

1. **Calculating yield.**

   Example: You have 10 lb AP apples. Yield after trimming is 75%. What will your EP weight be?

   First, change the percentage to a decimal number by moving the decimal point two places to the left.

$$75\% = 0.75$$

   Multiply the decimal by your AP weight to get EP yield.

$$10 \text{ lb} \times 0.75 = 7\frac{1}{2} \text{ lb or } 7 \text{ lb } 8 \text{ oz}$$

2. **Calculating amount needed.**

   Example: You need 10 lb EP apple slices. What amount of untrimmed fruit do you need?

   Change the percentage to a decimal number.

$$75\% = 0.75$$

   Divide the EP weight needed by this number to get the AP weight.

$$\frac{10 \text{ lb}}{0.75} = 13.33 \text{ lb or } 13 \text{ lb } 5\frac{1}{3} \text{ oz}$$

# Baker's Percentages

The most important information conveyed by a baker's formula is the *ratios* of the ingredients to each other. For example, if you know a particular bread dough requires exactly two-thirds as much water as flour, you can always know the exact amount of water to add to the flour, whether you are making a large or a small quantity. *Ratios are the simplest and most basic way of expressing a formula.*

Bakers use a simple but versatile system of percentages for expressing their formulas. **Baker's percentages** indicate the amount of each ingredient used as a percentage of the amount of flour used.

To put it differently, the percentage of each ingredient is its total weight divided by the weight of the flour, multiplied by 100%, or:

$$\frac{\text{total weight of ingredient}}{\text{total weight of flour}} \times 100\% = \% \text{ of ingredient}$$

Thus, flour is always 100%. If two kinds of flour are used, their total is 100%. Any ingredient that weighs the same as the amount of flour used is also given as 100%. The cake formula ingredients listed on page 26 illustrate how these percentages are used. Check the figures with the above equation to make sure you understand them.

Please remember these numbers do not refer to the percentage of the total yield. They are simply a way of expressing *ingredient proportions.* The total yield of these percentage numbers will always be greater than 100%.

Baker's percentages make it easy to see at a glance the ingredient ratios and, therefore, the basic structure and composition of the dough or batter. In addition, they make it easy to adapt the formula for any yield, as you will see in a later section. A third advantage is that single ingredients may be varied and other ingredients added without changing the whole formulation. For example, you can add raisins to a muffin mix formula while keeping the percentages of all the other ingredients the same.

Baker's percentages are the most basic way of expressing a formula, so they are also a useful tool for developing new formulas. When devising a new formula, a baker thinks about the best ratio of ingredients, as indicated by percentages. Once the proper ratios are established, the baker can then translate them into weights, so that the formula can be tested. Most of the formulas in this book were devised this way.

Clearly, a percentage system based on the weight of flour can be used only when flour is a major ingredient, as in breads, cakes, and cookies. However, the principle can be used in other formulas as well by selecting a major ingredient and establishing it as 100%. Many bakers use the percentage system for flour goods only (doughs and batters), but it is helpful to extend the benefits of this system to other products. In this book, *whenever an ingredient other than flour is used as the base of 100%, this is indicated at the top of the formula above the percentage column.* See, for example, the formulas for almond filling on page 201. These recipes indicate "almond paste at 100%," and the weights of the sugar, eggs, and other ingredients are expressed as percentages of the weight of the almond paste. (In some formulas in this book, especially those without a predominant ingredient, percentages are not included.)

# Formula Yields

Yields for the formulas in this book are indicated in one of two ways. In most cases, the yields are given as a total of the ingredient quantities. For example, in the sample formula on page 26, the yield tells us how much cake batter the formula makes. This is the figure we need to know for the purpose of scaling the batter into pans. The actual weight of the baked cake will vary depending on pan size and shape, oven temperature, and so on.

Other formulas of this type, in which the yield is the total weight of the ingredients, include formulas for bread doughs, coffee cake fillings, pastry doughs, and cookie doughs.

In some formulas, however, the yield is not the same as the total weight of ingredients. For example, see the recipe for French buttercream, page 425. When sugar and water are boiled to make a syrup, about half the water evaporates. Thus, the actual yield is less than the total weight of the ingredients.

In this book, when the yield is not the same as the total weight of the ingredients, the yield is indicated above the ingredients list rather than below it.

Also, please note that all yields, including percentage totals, are rounded off to the next lower whole number. This eliminates insignificant fractions and makes reading easier.

## *Basic Formula and Recipe Conversion*

Unless you are working in an operation that uses only its own standardized formulas, you frequently will be required to convert formulas to different quantities. For example, you may have a formula for 20 lb dough but need only 8 lb.

Converting formulas and recipes is an important technique. It is a skill you will probably need to use many times in this book and in your career. There is no "best" yield to write recipes for, as every operation, every school, and every individual has different needs.

Nearly everyone instinctively can double a formula or cut it in half. It seems more complicated, though, to change a formula from 10 to 18 kg, say, or from 20 to 12 qt. Actually, the principle is exactly the same: You multiply each ingredient by a number called a *conversion factor*, as in the first procedure given here.

The two procedures are general ones. These procedures are also used for recipes in the hot kitchen. The second of the two, for changing portion sizes, is applicable to some of the dessert recipes in this book but is, of course, not used when portion sizes are not given, as in formulas for bread dough. Then, in the next section, we look at procedures for making calculations with baking percentages.

## Conversion Calculations Using Percentages

Using baker's percentages simplifies formula and ingredient calculations. The two procedures below are used regularly in the bakeshop.

### Procedure for Calculating the Weight of an Ingredient When the Weight of Flour Is Known

1. Change the ingredient percentage to decimal form by moving the decimal point two places to the left.

2. Multiply the weight of the flour by this decimal figure to get the weight of the ingredient.

   Example: A formula calls for 20% sugar and you are using 10 lb flour. How much sugar do you need?

   $$20\% = 0.20$$
   $$10\ lb \times 0.20 = 2\ lb\ sugar$$

   *Note:* In the U.S. system, weights normally must be expressed all in one unit, either ounces or pounds, in order for the calculations to work. Unless quantities are very large, it is usually easiest to express weights in ounces.

Example: Determine 50% of 1 lb 8 oz.

$$1\ lb\ 8\ oz = 24\ oz$$
$$0.50 \times 24\ oz = 12\ oz$$

Example (metric): A formula calls for 20% sugar and you are using 5000 g (5 kg) flour. How much sugar do you need?

$$20\% = 0.20$$
$$5000\ g \times 0.20 = 1000\ g\ sugar$$

### Procedure for Converting a Formula to a New Yield

1. Change the total percentage to decimal form by moving the decimal point two places to the left.

2. Divide the desired yield by this decimal figure to get the weight of flour needed.

3. If necessary, round off this number to the next highest figure. This will allow for losses in mixing, makeup, and panning, and it will make calculations easier.

4. Use the weight of flour and remaining ingredient percentages to calculate the weights of the other ingredients, as in the previous procedure.

Example: In the sample cake formula in the table, how much flour is needed if you require 6 lb (or 3000 g) cake batter?

$$377.5\% = 3.775$$
$$6\ lb = 96\ oz$$

96 oz/3.775 = 25.43 oz or, rounded off, 26 oz (1 lb 10 oz)
3000 g/3.775 = 794.7 g or, rounded off, 800 g

| Ingredients | U.S. Weight | Metric Weight | % |
|---|---|---|---|
| Cake flour | 5 lb | 2500 g | 100 |
| Sugar | 5 lb | 2500 g | 100 |
| Baking powder | 14 oz | 125 g | 5 |
| Salt | 12 oz | 63 g | 2.5 |
| Emulsified shortening | 2 lb 18 oz | 1250 g | 50 |
| Skim milk | 3 lb | 1500 g | 60 |
| Egg whites | 3 lb | 1500 g | 60 |
| *Total weight:* | *18 lb 14 oz* | *9438 g* | *377.5%* |

## Problems in Converting Formulas

For the most part, converting baking formulas to different yields works well. As long as ingredient ratios stay the same, you are making the same dough or batter. But when you make very large conversions—say, from 2 lb dough to 100 lb—you may encounter problems. In general, the major pitfalls are in one of the following categories.

### Surface and Volume

If you have studied geometry, you may remember that a cube with a volume of 1 cubic foot has a top surface area of 1 square foot. But if you double the volume of the cube, the top surface area is not doubled but is in fact only about 1½ times as large.

What in the world, you ask, does this have to do with cooking? Consider the following example.

Suppose you have a good recipe for ½ gal dessert sauce, which you normally make in a small saucepan. You want to make 16 gal sauce, so you multiply all ingredients by a conversion factor of 32 and make the sauce in a steam kettle. To your surprise, not only do you end up with more sauce than you expected, but it turns out rather thin and watery. What happened?

Your converted recipe has 32 times as much volume to start, but the amount of surface area has not increased nearly as much. Because the ratio of surface area to volume is less, evaporation is less. This means less reduction and less thickening occur, and the flavors are not as concentrated. To correct this problem, you would have to either simmer the sauce longer or use less liquid.

The surface/volume problem shows up in the difference between making a single loaf of bread at home and making a large quantity of bread in the bakery. The home bread baker uses warm water to make a bread dough and must find a way to keep the dough warm enough so it ferments properly. The ratio of surface area to volume in a small amount of dough is so high the dough cools quickly. The commercial baker, on the contrary, often uses ice water when making bread dough to ensure the dough doesn't become too warm (see p. 123). The ratio of surface to volume is low, and the dough retains the heat generated by mixing.

When making large adjustments in formula yields, you must also determine if adjustments in procedure or ingredient percentages are needed.

### Equipment

When you change the size of a formula, you must often change the equipment, too. This change often means the recipe does not work in the same way. Bakers and cooks must be able to use their judgment to anticipate these problems and to modify their procedures to avoid them. The example just given, of cooking a large batch of dessert sauce in a steam kettle, is among the kinds of problems that can arise when you change cooking utensils.

Other problems can arise because of mixers or other processing equipment. For example, if you break down a dough formula to make only a small quantity, you might find there is so little dough in the mixing machine that the beaters don't blend the ingredients properly.

Or you might have a recipe for a muffin batter you usually make in small quantities, mixing the batter by hand. When you increase the recipe greatly, you find you have too much to do by hand. Therefore, you use a mixer but keep the mixing time the same. Because the mixer does the job so efficiently, you overmix the batter and end up with poor-quality muffins.

Many mixing and stirring jobs can be done only by hand. This is easy with small quantities but difficult with large batches. The result is often an inferior product. On the other hand, some handmade products are better if they are produced in large batches. It is hard, for example, to make a small batch of puff pastry because the dough cannot be rolled and folded properly.

# Selection of Ingredients

In addition to measuring, there is another basic rule of accuracy in the bakeshop: Use the exact ingredients specified.

As you will learn in chapter 4, different flours, shortenings, and other ingredients do not function alike. Baker's formulas are balanced for specific ingredients. For example, do not substitute bread flour for pastry flour or regular shortening for emulsified shortening. They won't work the same way.

Occasionally, a substitution may be made, such as active dry yeast for compressed yeast (see p. 84), but not without adjusting the quantities and rebalancing the formula.

# Cost Calculations

Food service operations are businesses. Chefs and bakers must be aware of the basics of food cost calculations, even if they aren't responsible for the management of budgets, invoices, and expenses. This section discusses the most basic calculations.

## Ingredient Unit Costs

The first simple calculation you need for all further calculations is for *unit cost*. Often the purveyor's invoice indicates unit cost: for example, 10 lb apricots at $2.00 per pound, totaling $20.00 (10 × $2.00 = $20.00). In other cases, you must make this calculation, using the following formula:

Total cost ÷ number of units = unit cost

Example 1. A case of mangoes weighing 15 lb costs $25.00. What is the cost per pound?

$25.00 ÷ 15 lb = $1.67 per lb

Example 2. A 45-kg sack of patent flour costs $20.00. What is the cost per kilogram?

$20.00 ÷ 45 kg = $0.45 per kg (rounded up)

## EP Unit Costs

Calculation of AP and EP quantities, as discussed on pages 22–24, is necessary not only for determining quantities needed for preparing formulas and recipes but also for determining costs. After all, when you buy fresh fruit by weight, for example, you are paying for the entire fruit, even if you discard peels, cores, and pits.

In the first example above, we determined that we are paying $1.67 per AP pound of mangoes. But we discard the peel and pit, so the cost per EP pound is greater than $1.67. We use the following formula to calculate the yield cost, or EP unit cost:

AP unit cost ÷ yield percentage = EP unit cost

Using a yield percentage of 75% (see p. 23), we can calculate the cost of our peeled, pitted mangoes using this formula. First, convert the percentage to a decimal by dividing it by 100:

75% ÷ 100 = 0.75
$1.67 ÷ 0.75 = $2.23 per EP lb

## Formula Costs

To determine the cost of preparing a formula or recipe, we first determine the cost of each ingredient. Then we add the costs of all the ingredients to get the total cost of the formula.

When we have calculated the total cost, we can then determine the unit cost of the finished product. Units may be any measure we require: per ounce, per kilogram, or per serving portion (portion cost).

For the most accurate costing, you should determine the number of units actually sold, rather than the unit yield of the formula. Keep in mind that ingredients or product lost through spillage or other waste must still be accounted for and paid for. Using units sold or served accounts for these costs.

The following general procedure explains the basic steps in calculating formula cost.

## Procedure for Calculating Formula Costs

1. List all ingredients and quantities of the formula as prepared.

2. Determine the EP unit cost of each ingredient (see above).

3. Convert the quantities in the formula to the same units used for the EP costs. (For example, to convert ounces to pounds, divide by 16, as in the example below.)

4. Calculate the total cost of each ingredient by multiplying the EP unit cost by the number of units

needed. Round up fractions of a cent to the next highest cent.

5. Add the ingredient costs to get the total formula cost.

6. To get unit costs, divide the total formula cost by the number of units produced (or, for better accuracy, the number of units actually sold, as explained above). Round up fractions of a cent to the next highest cent.

### Example: Costing a Formula
### Item: Biscuit Dough

| Ingredients | Amount | Amount in Converted Units | EP Unit Cost | Total |
|---|---|---|---|---|
| Bread flour | 1 lb 4 oz | 1.25 lb | $0.40/lb | $0.50 |
| Pastry flour | 1 lb 4 oz | 1.25 lb | $0.38/lb | $0.48 |
| Salt | 0.75 oz | 0.05 lb | $0.48/lb | $0.03 |
| Sugar | 2 oz | 0.125 lb | $0.55/lb | $0.07 |
| Baking powder | 2.5 oz | 2.5 oz | $0.18/oz | $0.45 |
| Butter | 14 oz | 0.875 lb | $2.80/lb | $2.45 |
| Whole milk | 1 lb 10 oz | 1.625 lb | $0.40/lb | $0.65 |
| | | Total cost | | $4.63 |
| | | Quantity produced | | 5.3 lb or 85 oz |
| | | Cost per unit | | $0.88 per lb or $0.06 per oz |

# FOOD SAFETY AND SANITATION

In chapter 1 we discussed some of the requirements for success in the food service industry, including professional pride. One of the most important ways of demonstrating professional pride is in the area of sanitation and safety. Pride in quality is reflected in your appearance and work habits. Poor hygiene, poor grooming and personal care, and sloppy work habits are nothing to be proud of.

In addition, poor sanitation can cost a lot of money. Poor food handling procedures and unclean kitchens cause illness, unhappy customers, and even fines, summonses, and lawsuits. Food spoilage raises food costs. Finally, poor sanitation and safety habits show lack of respect for your customers, for your fellow workers, and for yourself.

This section briefly outlines the guidelines for food safety in the bakeshop, with enough information to build basic awareness. Be aware, however, that entire books and courses of study are devoted to food sanitation. Consult the bibliography at the end of this book to find more detailed information on this subject.

## Food Hazards

Preventing food-borne illness is one of the most important challenges facing every food service worker. To prevent illness, a food worker must understand the sources of food-borne disease.

Most food-borne illness is the result of eating food that has been **contaminated**. To say that a food is contaminated means it contains harmful substances that were not present originally in the food. In other words, contaminated food is food that is not pure. In this section, we first discuss the substances that can contaminate food and cause illness. Afterward, we consider how these substances get into food to contaminate it and how food workers can prevent contamination and avoid serving contaminated food.

Any substance in food that can cause illness or injury is called a **hazard**. Food hazards are of three types:

Biological hazards.

Chemical hazards.

Physical hazards.

### Biological Hazards

The most important kinds of biological hazard to consider are microorganisms. A **microorganism** is a tiny, usually single-celled organism that can be seen only with a microscope. A microorganism that can cause disease is called a **pathogen**. Although these organisms sometimes occur in clusters large enough to be seen with the naked eye, they are not usually visible. This is one reason why they can be so dangerous. Just because food looks good doesn't mean it is safe.

Four kinds of microorganisms can contaminate food and cause illness: bacteria, viruses, fungi, and parasites. Most food-borne diseases are caused by bacteria, and these are the pathogens we focus on here. Many of the measures we take to protect food from bacteria also help prevent the other three kinds of microorganisms.

## Bacterial Growth

Bacteria multiply by splitting in half. Under ideal conditions for growth, they can double in number every 15 to 30 minutes. This means a single bacterium can multiply to one million in less than 6 hours! The following conditions are needed for bacterial growth:

1. **Food.**
   Bacteria require food in order to grow. They like many of the foods we do. Foods with sufficient amounts of protein are best for bacterial growth. These include meats, poultry, fish, dairy products, and eggs, as well as some grains and vegetables.

2. **Moisture.**
   Bacteria require water in order to absorb food. Dry foods do not support bacterial growth. Foods with a very high salt or sugar content are also relatively safe, because these ingredients make the bacteria unable to use the moisture present.

3. **Temperature.**
   Bacteria grow best at warm temperatures. Temperatures between 41°F and 135°F (5°C and 57°C) promote the growth of disease-causing bacteria. This temperature range is called the *Food Danger Zone*.
   *Note:* In the past, 45°F (7°C) and 140°F (60°C) were considered the lower and upper limits of the Food Danger Zone. Health experts now recommend a slightly lower temperature range to provide an extra measure of safety.

4. **Acidity or alkalinity.**
   In general, disease-producing bacteria like a neutral environment, neither too acidic nor too alkaline. The acidity or alkalinity of a substance is indicated by a measurement called *pH*. The scale ranges from 0 (strongly acidic) to 14 (strongly alkaline). A pH of 7 is neutral. Pure water has a pH of 7.

5. **Oxygen.**
   Some bacteria require oxygen to grow. These are called *aerobic*. Some bacteria are *anaerobic*, which means they can grow only if no air is present, such as in metal cans. Botulism, one of the most dangerous forms of food poisoning, is caused by anaerobic bacteria. A third category of bacteria can grow either with oxygen or without it. These bacteria are called *facultative*. Most bacteria in food that cause disease are facultative.

6. **Time.**
   When bacteria are introduced to a new environment, they need time to adjust to their surroundings before they start growing. This time is called the *lag phase*. If other conditions are good, the lag phase may last about 1 hour or somewhat longer.
   If it weren't for the lag phase, food-borne disease would be much more common than it is. This time delay makes it possible to have foods at room temperature *for very short periods* in order to work on them.

## Protection against Bacteria

Because we know how and why bacteria grow, we should be able to keep them from growing. Because we know how bacteria get from place to place, we should know how to keep them from getting into our food.

There are three basic principles of protecting food against bacteria. These principles are the reasons behind nearly all the sanitation techniques we discuss in the rest of this chapter.

1. **Keep bacteria from spreading.**

   Don't let food touch anything that may contain disease-producing bacteria, and protect food from bacteria in the air.

2. **Stop bacteria from growing.**

   Take away the conditions that encourage bacteria to grow. In the kitchen, our best weapon is temperature. *The most effective way to prevent bacterial growth is to keep foods below 41°F (5°C) or above 135°F (57°C).* These temperatures won't necessarily kill bacteria; they'll just slow down their growth greatly.

3. **Kill bacteria.**

   Most disease-causing bacteria are killed if they are subjected to a temperature of 170°F (77°C) for 30 seconds or higher temperatures for shorter times. This enables us to make food safe by cooking and to sanitize dishes and equipment with heat. The term *sanitize* means to kill disease-causing bacteria.

   Certain chemicals also kill bacteria. These may be used for sanitizing equipment.

## Other Biological Hazards

*Viruses* are even smaller than bacteria. They consist of genetic material surrounded by a protein layer. Viruses cause disease when they multiply inside the body. They do not grow or multiply in food, as bacteria do. Therefore, food-borne viral diseases are usually caused by direct contamination from people, food contact surfaces, or contaminated water.

*Parasites* are organisms that can survive only by living on or inside another organism. They take their nourishment from the organism they are living in. Human parasites are usually very small, but they are larger than bacteria. Most foods that can carry parasites are used in the hot kitchen rather than the bakeshop, although raw fruits and milk can possibly be contaminated.

Molds and yeasts are examples of *fungi* (singular form: fungus). These organisms are usually associated with food spoilage rather than food-borne disease. Some fungi, like bread yeasts, are valuable to us. Some molds, however, produce toxins that can cause disease. Peanuts, tree nuts, corn, and milk can carry a serious mold-produced toxin that can be fatal to some people.

Some plants are naturally poisonous because they carry *plant toxins*. The best-known plant toxins are those found in certain wild mushrooms. The only way to avoid plant toxins is to avoid the plants in which they occur, as well as products made with those plants. In some cases, the toxins can be transferred in milk from cows that have eaten the plant (such as jimsonweed and snakeroot) or in honey from bees that have gathered nectar from the plants (such as mountain laurel). Other toxic plants to avoid are rhubarb leaves, water hemlock, apricot kernels, and nightshade.

An *allergen* is a substance that causes an allergic reaction. Allergens affect only some people, and these people are said to be *allergic* to that specific substance. Not all allergens are biological hazards, but the most important ones are, so we discuss them together in this section.

Foods to which some people are allergic include wheat products, soy products, peanuts and tree nuts, eggs, milk and dairy products, fish, and shellfish. Nonbiological allergens include food additives such as nitrites, used in cured meats, and monosodium glutamate (MSG), often used in Asian foods.

Because these products are common and perfectly safe for most people, it is difficult to avoid serving them. For the sake of people who are sensitive to these foods, food service personnel, especially dining room staff, must be well informed of the ingredients in all menu items and be able to inform customers as needed.

## Chemical and Physical Hazards

Some kinds of chemical poisoning are caused by the use of defective or improper equipment or equipment that has been handled improperly. The following toxins (except lead) create symptoms that show themselves quickly, usually within 30 minutes of eating poisoned food. By contrast, symptoms of lead poisoning can take years to appear. To prevent these diseases, do not use the materials that cause them.

1. **Antimony.**
   Caused by storing or cooking acid foods in chipped gray enamelware.

2. **Cadmium.**
   Caused by cadmium-plated ice-cube trays or containers.

3. **Cyanide.**
   Caused by silver polish containing cyanide.

4. **Lead.**
   Caused by lead water pipes, solder containing lead, or utensils containing lead.

5. **Copper.**
   Caused by unclean or corroded copper utensils, acid foods cooked in unlined copper utensils, or carbonated beverages in contact with copper tubing.

6. **Zinc.**
   Caused by cooking foods in zinc-plated (galvanized) utensils.

Other chemical contamination can result from exposure of foods to chemicals used in commercial food service establishments. Examples include cleaning compounds, polishing compounds, and insecticides. Prevent contamination by keeping these items physically separated from foods. Do not use them around food. Label all containers properly. Rinse cleaned equipment thoroughly.

*Physical contamination* is contamination of food with objects that may not be toxic but may cause injury or discomfort. Examples include pieces of glass from a broken container, metal shavings from an improperly opened can, stones from poorly sorted dried beans, soil from poorly washed fruits, insects or insect parts, and hair. Proper food handling is necessary to avoid physical contamination.

# Personal Hygiene and Safe Food Handling

Earlier in this section, we said that most food-borne disease is caused by bacteria. Now we change that statement slightly to say that *most food-borne disease is caused by bacteria spread by food workers*.

## Cross-Contamination

At the beginning of this section, we defined *contamination* as harmful substances not present originally in the food. Some contamination occurs before we receive it, which means that proper purchasing and receiving procedures are important parts of a sanitation program. But most food contamination occurs as a result of **cross-contamination**, which may be defined as the transferring of hazardous substances, mainly microorganisms, to a food from another food or another surface, such as equipment, worktables, or hands.

## Personal Hygiene

For the food worker, the first step in preventing food-borne disease is good personal hygiene. Even when we are healthy, we have bacteria all over our skin and in our nose and mouth. Some of these bacteria, if given the chance to grow in food, will make people ill.

1. Do not work with food if you have any communicable disease or infection.

2. Bathe or shower daily.

3. Wear clean uniforms and aprons.

4. Keep hair neat and clean. Always wear a hat or hairnet.

5. Keep mustaches and beards trimmed and clean. Better yet, be clean-shaven.

6. Wash hands and exposed parts of arms before work and as often as necessary during work, including:

   ◆ After eating, drinking, or smoking.

   ◆ After using the toilet.

   ◆ After touching or handling anything that may be contaminated with bacteria.

7. Cover coughs and sneezes, then wash hands.

8. Keep your hands away from your face, eyes, hair, and arms.

9. Keep fingernails clean and short. Do not wear nail polish.

10. Do not smoke or chew gum while on duty.

11. Cover cuts or sores with clean bandages.

12. Do not sit on worktables.

## Procedure for Washing Hands

1. Wet your hands with hot running water. Have the water as hot as you can comfortably stand, but at least 100°F (38°C).

2. Apply enough soap to make a good lather.

3. Rub hands together thoroughly for 20 seconds or longer, washing not only the hands but the wrists and the lower part of the forearms.

4. Using a nail brush, clean beneath the fingernails and between the fingers.

5. Rinse hands well under hot running water. If possible, use a clean paper towel to turn off the water to avoid contaminating the hands by contact with soiled faucets.

6. Dry hands with clean single-use paper towels or a warm-air hand dryer.

## Use of Gloves

If used correctly, gloves can help protect foods against cross-contamination. If used incorrectly, however, they can spread contamination just as easily as bare hands. Health departments in some localities require the use of some kind of barrier between hands and foods that are ready to eat—that is, foods that will be served without further cooking. Gloves, tongs, and other serving implements, and bakery or deli tissue can serve as barriers. To be sure gloves are used correctly, observe the following guidelines.

## Guidelines for Using Disposable Gloves

1. Wash hands before putting on gloves or when changing to another pair. Gloves are not a substitute for proper handwashing.

2. Remove and discard gloves, wash hands, and change to a clean pair of gloves after handling one food item and before starting work on another. In particular, never to fail to change gloves after han-

dling raw meat, poultry, or seafood. Gloves are for single use only. Remember that the purpose of using gloves is to avoid cross-contamination.

3. Change to a clean pair of gloves whenever gloves become torn, soiled, or contaminated by contact with an unsanitary surface.

## Food Handling and Preparation

We face two major sanitation problems when handling and preparing food. The first is *cross-contamination*, discussed above.

The second problem is that, while we are working on it, food is usually at a temperature between 41°F and 135°F (5°C to 57°C), or in the Food Danger Zone. The lag phase of bacteria growth (p. 31) helps us a little but, to be safe, we must keep foods out of the danger zone whenever possible.

1. Start with clean, wholesome foods from reputable purveyors. Whenever applicable, buy government-inspected dairy and egg products.

2. Handle foods as little as possible. Use tongs, spatulas, or other utensils instead of hands when practicable.

3. Use clean, sanitized equipment and worktables.

4. Clean and sanitize cutting surfaces and equipment after handling raw foods and before working on another food.

5. Clean as you go. Don't wait until the end of the workday.

6. Wash raw fruits thoroughly.

7. When bringing foods out of refrigeration, do not bring out more than you can process in 1 hour.

8. Keep foods covered unless in immediate use.

9. Limit the time foods spend in the Food Danger Zone.

10. Taste foods properly. Using a ladle or other serving implement, transfer a small amount of the food to a small dish. Then taste this sample using a clean spoon. After tasting, do not use the dish and spoon again. Send them to the warewashing station or, if using disposables, discard them.

11. Don't mix leftovers with freshly prepared foods.

12. Cool and chill foods quickly and correctly, as explained in the following guidelines. Chill custards, cream fillings, and other hazardous foods as quickly as possible by pouring them into shallow, sanitized pans, covering them, and refrigerating. Do not stack the pans.

## Guidelines for Cooling Foods

1. Never put hot foods directly into the cooler. Not only will they cool too slowly but also they will raise the temperature of other foods in the cooler.

2. If they are available, use quick-chill units or blast chillers to cool foods quickly before transferring them to cold storage.

3. Use ice-water baths to bring down temperatures of hot foods quickly.

4. Stir foods as they are cooling to redistribute the heat in the food and help it cool more quickly.

5. Divide large batches into smaller batches. This increases the amount of surface area for the volume of food and helps it cool more quickly. Pouring foods into flat, shallow pans also increases surface area and cooling speed.

# The HACCP System

Once you have learned the principles of food safety, you must apply them in the bakeshop or kitchen. Many food service operations have designed food safety systems that enable food workers to keep a close check on food items whenever there is a risk of contamination or of the growth of pathogens. One effective food safety system is called the *Hazard Analysis and Critical Control Point* system, or **HACCP**. Versions of this system have been widely adopted throughout the food service industry.

The following discussion is a brief introduction to the basic concepts of HACCP. For a more detailed explanation, refer to other published material listed in the bibliography (p. 757). The discussion below is based on information presented in those books.

## The Steps of the HACCP System

The purpose of HACCP is to identify, monitor, and control dangers of food contamination. It is a system of seven steps:

1. Assess hazards.

2. Identify critical control points (CCPs).

3. Set up standards or limits for CCPs.

4. Set up procedures for monitoring CCPs.

5. Establish corrective actions.

6. Set up a recordkeeping system.

7. Verify that the system is working.

These steps are the basis of the following discussion.

## The Flow of Food

HACCP begins with a concept called the **flow of food**. This term refers to the movement of food through a food service operation, from receiving through the stages of storage, preparation, and service, until it gets to the consumer.

The flow of food is different for each item prepared. Some menu items involve many steps, including receiving of ingredients, storing ingredients, preparing ingredients (such as trimming fruit), cooking, holding, serving, cooling, storing leftovers, reheating leftovers, and so on. Even the simplest items undergo several steps. For example, a cake that is bought already prepared from a commercial baker and served as dessert goes through at least the following steps on its way to the customer:

> Receiving.
>
> Storing.
>
> Serving.

## Hazards and Critical Control Points

At each of these steps, as foods flow through the operation, risks can lead to dangerous conditions, or *hazards*. These hazards can be divided into three categories:

1. *Contamination*, such as cross-contamination from a soiled cutting surface; torn packaging that permits insect infestation; working on food without washing hands; spilling cleaning chemicals on food.

2. *Growth of bacteria and other pathogens* due to such conditions as inadequate refrigeration or storage and holding hot foods below 135°F (57°C).

3. *Survival of pathogens or the continued presence of toxins*, usually because of inadequate cooking or heating or inadequate sanitizing of equipment and surfaces.

Note that these hazards correspond to the sanitation techniques discussed on pages 31–32 (keep bacteria from spreading, stop bacteria from growing, kill bacteria). The important difference is that the hazards addressed by HACCP include chemical and other hazards in addition to disease-causing organisms.

At each step where there is a risk of one of these hazards, it is possible to take action that eliminates the hazard or reduces it to a minimum. These steps are called **critical control points**, or CCPs. In simple language, setting up an HACCP system starts with reviewing the flow of food to figure out where something might go wrong, then deciding what can be done to decrease or eliminate that possibility. In the language of HACCP, these steps are called assessing the hazards and identifying critical control points.

## Setting Standards and Following Procedures

The next step in designing an HACCP food safety system is setting up procedures for critical control points. At each CCP, food workers need to know the standards that must be met, the procedures to follow to meet the standards, and what to do if they are not met. To reduce the chances of making mistakes, these standards and procedures are written out. Whenever possible, they should be included in the operation's recipes.

Some procedures are general and include the sanitation rules discussed earlier in this chapter. *Examples:* Wash hands before handling food and after handling raw foods; hold foods above 135°F (57°C) or below 41°F (5°C). Others apply to specific items. *Examples:* Cook a beef roast to an internal temperature of at least 145°F (63°C) and ensure it stays at that temperature for at least 3 minutes.

Careful observation is needed to know when standards are met. This often involves measuring. The only way to know, for example, that a roast has reached the required internal temperature is to measure it, using a clean, sanitized thermometer.

Managers must ensure that all employees are trained to follow procedures and have the equipment needed to do so.

Once these procedures are developed, additional steps in setting up the HACCP system are important to ensuring its effectiveness: monitoring CCPs, taking corrective action if procedures are not followed, keeping records of all aspects of the system, and verifying that the system is working.

As this brief introduction to HACCP implies, establishing such a system to control all aspects of food production requires more information than this chapter has space for. Refer to the bibliography for more detailed information.

## Learning More about Food Safety

It is important for you to understand that food safety and sanitation is a large and complex topic. The material in this chapter is only an introduction to the study of food safety. To advance in a food service career, you will be required to demonstrate a detailed knowledge of the subject well beyond what can be presented in such a short space. Entire textbooks are devoted to kitchen sanitation and safety. Many organizations, including local and regional health departments and organizations such as the National Restaurant Association (in the United States), sponsor training programs leading to certificates of competency in food safety. Cooks in supervisory positions in the United States may be required to hold such a certificate by state or local law. In Canada, many provinces have their own safety regulations, and food service operators should be familiar with these as well as with federal regulations. The health and safety of your clientele depends on your diligent study.

# TERMS FOR REVIEW

| | | | |
|---|---|---|---|
| recipe | kilo- | hazard | parasite |
| formula | deci- | microorganism | fungus |
| standardized formula | centi- | pathogen | plant toxin |
| scaling | milli- | Food Danger Zone | allergen |
| metric system | scone flour | aerobic | cross-contamination |
| gram | AP weight | anaerobic | HACCP |
| liter | EP weight | facultative | flow of food |
| meter | baker's percentage | lag phase | critical control point |
| degree Celsius | contaminated | virus | |

# QUESTIONS FOR DISCUSSION

1. Below are ingredients for a white cake. The weight of the flour is given, and the proportions of other ingredients are indicated by percentages. Calculate the weights required for each.

   | | |
   |---|---|
   | Cake flour | 3 lb (100%) |
   | Baking powder | 4% |
   | Shortening | 50% |
   | Sugar | 100% |
   | Salt | 1% |
   | Milk | 75% |
   | Egg whites | 33% |
   | Vanilla | 2% |

2. In the formula in question 1, how much of each ingredient is needed if you want a total yield of 4½ lb batter?

3. Why are baking ingredients usually weighed rather than measured by volume?

4. Make the following conversions in the U.S. system of measurement:

   3½ lb  = ___ oz

   6 cups = ___ pt

   8½ qt  = ___ fl oz

   ¾ cup = ___ tbsp

   46 oz = ___ lb

   2½ gal = ___ fl oz

   5 lb 5 oz divided by 2 = ___

   10 tsp = ___ fl oz

5. Make the following conversions in the metric system:

   1.4 kg = ___ g

   53 dL = ___ L

   15 cm = ___ mm

   2590 g = ___ kg

   4.6 L = ___ dL

   220 cL = ___ dL

6. Which of the following foods can become contaminated by disease-causing organisms?

   chocolate éclairs

   dinner rolls

   baked custard

   biscotti cookies

   crisp baked meringues

   bread sticks

   chocolate bars

7. How often should you wash your hands when working on food?

8. Why is temperature control an effective weapon against bacterial growth? What are some important temperatures to remember?

## Chapter 3

# Baking and Pastry Equipment

**M**uch of a baker's art and craft involves simple tools. Learning to be a skilled baker requires developing a great deal of manual skill using these tools. For example, a pastry bag is nothing more than a cone-shaped piece of fabric or plastic, open at both ends. Although its construction is simple and it requires no operating manual, hours of practice are required to become skilled at using a pastry bag for decorative work.

At the other extreme are large machines such as floor-model mixers, ovens of many types, and dough-handling equipment such as molders, dividers, and sheeters. Of these, perhaps only ovens are essential to a baker's work. The other items are important laborsaving devices that enable the worker to produce goods in large quantities with greater speed. Without them, much of the work of a bakeshop would not be economically feasible.

This chapter is an outline of the most important pieces of equipment used by bakers and pastry chefs, from large equipment to containers and molds to hand tools. In addition to the tools discussed in this chapter, most bakeshops contain an array of equipment also found in most kitchens, including pots and pans, spoons, ladles, spatulas, knives, and so on. Learning to use these tools is the subject of much of this book.

**After reading this chapter, you should be able to:**

1. Identify the principal pieces of equipment used in baking and pastry making and indicate their uses.

# EQUIPMENT SANITATION AND SAFETY

Before we look at specific items, we must first consider points related to the use of equipment in general.

## Safety

Baking equipment can be dangerous. From large mixers to small hand tools such as knives, equipment found in the bakeshop can inflict serious injuries if not used carefully and properly.

Never use a piece of equipment until you are thoroughly familiar with its operation and all its features. You must also learn how to know when a machine is not operating correctly so you can shut it down immediately and report the malfunction to a supervisor.

Remember that not all models are alike. Each manufacturer introduces slight variations on the basic equipment. While all deck ovens or all vertical mixers, for example, operate on the same basic principles, each model is slightly different, if only in the location of the switches. It is important to study the operating manual supplied with each item or to be taught by someone who already knows that item well.

## Sanitation

Thorough, regular cleaning of all equipment is essential. Most large equipment can be partially disassembled for cleaning. Read the operating manual, which should describe these procedures in detail, or get the information from someone who knows the equipment.

When purchasing equipment, look for models that have been tested and certified by recognized agencies that certify products and write standards for food, water, air, and consumer goods. Three prominent agencies are NSF International (www.nsf.org, formerly the National Sanitation Foundation), CSA International (www.csa-international.org), and Underwriters Laboratory (www.ul.com). These three agencies are accredited by ANSI, the American National Standards Institute, as Standards Developing Organizations (SOOs). They are also accredited by ANSI to certify equipment (such as baking and other commercial food equipment) against the American National Standards that have been developed by each of these SOOs. The standards, and the certifications of these three agencies, are recognized internationally. Products meeting their testing requirements are labeled or marked accordingly (see below). Criteria govern such factors as design and construction (for example, sealed joints and seams as well as accessible and component parts), materials used (for example, nontoxic materials, smooth and easily cleanable surfaces), and performance testing.

NSF International certification mark.
Courtesy NSF International

SANITATION
NSF/ANSI STD. NO.

The CSA sanitation mark.
Courtesy of the Canadian Standard Association

The Underwriters Laboratory logo.
Reproduced with permission of Underwriters Laboratory, Inc.

# LARGE EQUIPMENT

Mixers, ovens, and dough-handling equipment take up most of this category.

# Mixers

Mixers of various types are essential tools in the bakeshop. While small quantities of doughs and batters can be mixed by hand, commercial baking in any quantity would be next to impossible without power mixers. Two main types of mixer are used in small and medium-size bakeshops. Other types of specialized equipment are used in large industrial bakeries.

## Vertical Mixer

Also called a *planetary mixer*, the vertical mixer is the most common type used in baking as well as in cooking. The term *planetary* is descriptive of the motion of the beater attachment. Just as a planet spins on its axis while revolving around the sun, so the beater attachment spins on its axis while rotating in an orbit to reach all parts of the stationary bowl. Tabletop mixers range in capacity from 5 to 20 quarts (4.75 to 19 L). Floor models are available as large as 140 quarts (132 L).

Small table-model mixer.
Courtesy of Hobart Corporation

Vertical mixers have three main mixing attachments:

1. The paddle is a flat blade used for general mixing.
2. The wire whip is used for such tasks as beating egg foams and cream.
3. The dough arm or dough hook is used for mixing and kneading yeast doughs. Dough hooks may be standard *J*-hooks or spiral hooks.

Be sure to use the right size attachment for the bowl. Using a 40-quart paddle with a 30-quart bowl could cause serious damage. Also, make sure both the bowl and the mixing attachment are firmly in place before turning on the machine.

Additional special attachments are also available. These include the following:

- The sweet dough arm combines the actions of the dough arm and the flat paddle and is used for mixing sweet doughs.
- The wing whip is used for mixing materials too heavy for the standard wire whip.
- The pastry blender is used to blend fat and flour, as in making pie doughs.

Large floor-model mixer.
Courtesy of Hobart Corporation

Mixer attachments: (left) whip, (center) paddle, (right) dough arm. Courtesy of Hobart Corporation

The availability of such a variety of attachments points up one of the main advantages of the planetary mixer: its versatility. With a single machine, the baker can produce a great variety of doughs, batters, creams, meringues, and other goods. In addition, vertical mixers have an attachment hub that can be used to power many other tools, such as grinders and slicers. This makes vertical mixers useful in the kitchen as well as the bakeshop.

## Spiral Mixer

Spiral mixers are designed for doughs and heavy batters and are used primarily for making large quantities of yeast doughs for breads and bagels. Unlike vertical mixers, spiral mixers do not have interchangeable bowls and agitator arms. The agitator arm is in the shape of a spiral, and both the bowl and the spiral arm rotate to develop the dough quickly and efficiently. In a typical model, the bowl may be set to rotate in either direction. Dough capacities range from 5 to 30 pounds (2.3 to 14 kg) for small machines to more than 500 pounds (230 kg) in large machines.

Spiral mixer.
Courtesy of TMB Baking, Inc.

Because they are used exclusively for mixing doughs, they do not have the versatility of vertical mixers, as described above. However, they have several important features and advantages that make them the preferred mixers of bread bakers and pizza makers:

Because they are used exclusively for mixing doughs, they do not have the versatility of vertical mixers, as described above. However, they have several important features and advantages that make them the preferred mixers of bread bakers and pizza makers:

* Spiral mixers blend and develop dough more efficiently than planetary mixers. Because of their design, they develop dough more intensively and in less time, resulting in lower machine friction and dough warming (see p. 123).
* The design of the bowl and beater allows for a wide range of dough capacity for each machine. For example, a medium-size mixer may handle as little as 10 pounds (4.5 kg) dough or as much as 200 pounds (90 kg). By contrast, a vertical mixer bowl handles only a narrow range of dough weights; too large or too small a quantity will not mix properly.
* Spiral mixers are sturdier and more rugged than vertical mixers. They handle more dough and last longer with less repair and maintenance.

Three main varieties of spiral mixer are available:

1. **Fixed-bowl mixers.** These have a nonremovable bowl. The dough must be lifted out by hand.
2. **Removable-bowl mixers.** These have a bowl that may be removed from the machine, usually on a wheeled trolley. These are useful for high-volume operations, because a new bowl of ingredients may be wheeled into place as soon as the earlier batch is removed.
3. **Tilt mixers.** On these machines, the entire machine tilts up to deposit the finished dough onto a tray or another container.

Most spiral mixers have two operating speeds, although some specialized machines for stiff doughs have only one speed. In a typical mixing procedure, the baker uses the first speed for the first phase of dough mixing, when the ingredients are blended, and switches to the second speed for the later phase of dough development. Machines with automated controls have timers to regulate each phase of mixing.

Similar to spiral mixers are fork mixers. Instead of a single spiral agitator or beater, these machines have a two-pronged fork-shaped beater that enters the bowl at about a 45-degree angle. Like spiral mixers, fork mixers are used specifically for bread doughs.

### Horizontal Mixer

Horizontal mixers are large, industrial-size mixers capable of handling as much as several thousand pounds of dough at a time. Each model is designed to work best with a specific range of products, such as bread doughs, pastry doughs, or soft doughs and batters. Beater or agitator designs differ for each of these specialized models.

Many horizontal mixers are equipped with water jackets that surround the mixing container. Water of the desired temperature is circulated through the jacket, enabling the operator to control the dough temperature with great precision.

## Dough-Handling Equipment

### Dough Fermentation Trough

This item is used to hold mixed yeast doughs during fermentation. Small operations might simply use large mixing bowls on stands instead.

### Divider

Dividers cut scaled pieces of dough into equal portions by means of a die or cutter attached to a hydraulic or mechanical lever assembly. For example, a di-

**Continuous Mixer**

Another type of mixer used in large bakeries is the *continuous mixer*. Here, small amounts of scaled ingredients enter the machine continuously at one end. The ingredients are blended and developed into a dough as they move through the machine. The finished dough emerges at the other end of the machine. These mixers are efficient because instead of having to blend, say, 200 pounds of flour into a dough all at once, they may take in the flour in 5-pound increments, making the blending much easier.

Horizontal mixer.
Courtesy of The Peerless Group

Divider.
Courtesy of American Baking Systems and S.A. Jac NV

vider may cut a 3-pound piece of dough (called a *press*) into 36 pieces, 1⅓ ounces each, for making dinner rolls. After they are divided, the individual pieces must be rounded by hand (see p. 118).

## Divider-Rounder

This machine divides the dough as does a simple divider, and it then automatically rounds the individual portions, greatly speeding makeup of the dough products.

## Dough Sheeter

A sheeter rolls out portions of dough into sheets of uniform thickness. It consists of a canvas conveyor belt that feeds the dough through a pair of rollers. To make thin sheets, the dough usually must be passed through the rollers several times. The operator decreases the space between the rollers after each pass.

## Molder

A molder rolls and forms pieces of bread dough for standard loaves, baguettes, and rolls, eliminating the need to perform these tasks by hand.

## Proofer

A proofer is a special box in which the ideal conditions for fermenting yeast doughs can be created. The box maintains a preset warm temperature and humidity level appropriate to the specific dough.

## Retarder

Chilling or refrigerating yeast dough slows or retards the rate of fermentation so the dough can be stored for later baking. A retarder is a refrigerator that maintains a high level of humidity to prevent the dough from drying out or crusting.

## Retarder-Proofer

This machine is, as the name suggests, a combination retarder and proofer. A dough can be retarded for a preset time, after which the machine switches to proofing mode and warms up to a second preset temperature and humidity level. For example, breakfast breads can be made up the previous day, held, and be fully proofed and ready to bake when the shop opens the next morning.

Divider-rounder.
Courtesy of TMB Baking, Inc.

Sheeter. Courtesy of American Baking Systems and S.A. Jac NV

Molder. Courtesy of American Baking Systems and S.A. Jac NV

Proofer.
Courtesy of Bevles

Retarder-proofer.
Courtesy of TMB Baking, Inc.

# Ovens

Ovens are, of course, the workhorses of the bakery and pastry shop and are essential for producing breads, cakes, cookies, pastries, and other baked items. Ovens are enclosed spaces in which food is heated, usually by hot air (except in the case of microwave ovens, which are not especially useful in a bakeshop). Several kinds of oven are used in baking.

Steam is important in baking many kinds of breads, as discussed in chapter 6. Ovens used in bakeshops, including deck ovens, rack ovens, and mechanical ovens, may have steam injected into them during part of the baking cycle.

Deck oven.

Courtesy of Macadams Baking Systems (Pty) Ltd.

## Deck Oven

Deck ovens are so called because the items to be baked—either on sheet pans or, in the case of some breads, freestanding—are placed directly on the bottom, or deck, of the oven. There are no racks for holding pans in deck ovens. Deck ovens are also called *stack ovens* because several may be stacked on top of one another. Breads baked directly on the floor of the oven rather than in pans are often called *hearth breads*, so another name for these ovens is *hearth ovens*. Deck ovens for baking bread are equipped with steam injectors.

## Rack Oven

A rack oven is a large oven into which entire racks full of sheet pans can be wheeled for baking. Normal baker's racks hold 8 to 24 full-size sheet pans, but racks made specifically to go into rack ovens usually hold 15 to 20 pans. Rack ovens hold one to four of these racks at once. The ovens are also equipped with steam injectors.

Although this usage is not strictly correct, you may hear the term *rack oven* used for conventional ovens such as those found in restaurant ranges because the pans are placed on racks rather than directly on the bottom, as in deck ovens.

## Mechanical Oven

In a mechanical oven, the food is in motion while it bakes. The most common type is a revolving oven, in which the mechanism is like that of a Ferris wheel. This mechanical action eliminates the problem of hot spots, or uneven baking, because the mechanism rotates the foods throughout the oven. Because of their size, they are especially useful in high-volume operations. Revolving ovens can be equipped with steam injectors.

A typical revolving oven is shown in the illustration. Each of the multiple trays in such an oven holds one or more sheet pans. The operator loads one tray at a time through the narrow door in the front.

Rack oven.

Courtesy of Lang Manufacturing Company

## ❊{ WOOD-FIRED }❊ OVENS

Wood-fired brick ovens are similar in function to deck ovens in that items are baked directly on the oven floor. These ovens are used in some operations that produce artisan breads as well as in some restaurants that serve pizzas and similar items. The heat is generated by a wood fire built inside the oven. This fire heats the thick brick floor and walls, which retain enough heat to bake foods. Gas-fired brick ovens are similar, but the heat is more easily controlled.

Revolving oven.

Courtesy of Baxter/ITW Food Equipment Group, LLC

## Convection Oven

Convection ovens contain fans that circulate the air and distribute the heat rapidly throughout the interior. The forced air makes foods cook more quickly at lower temperatures. Because the strong forced air can distort the shape of items made with batters and soft doughs, and because the airflow may be strong enough to blow baking parchment off sheet pans, convection ovens are not as versatile for the baker as are the other kinds of ovens discussed here.

## Steam-Jacketed Kettle

Convection oven.
Courtesy of Vulcan-Hart Company

Steam-jacketed kettles, or steam kettles, have double walls between which steam circulates. Liquids in the kettle itself are heated quickly and efficiently. Although restaurants may use large floor-mounted kettles for making stocks, smaller table models are more useful in the bakeshop for making custards, creams, and fillings. Tilting kettles with a pouring lip are called *trunnion kettles*. Table models range in capacity from a few quarts or liters to 40 quarts (38 L).

Steam-jacketed kettle.
Courtesy of Vulcan-Hart Company

## Fryer

Fryers are needed in the bakeshop for doughnuts and other fried items. Small operations often use standard deep fryers (or even stovetop kettles), but larger doughnut fryers are best if you make doughnuts in quantity. They should be used in conjunction with screens for lowering the doughnuts into the fat and for removing them when fried. In the fryer in the illustration, the proofed doughnuts are arranged on the screen at the right side of the fry kettle. The operator then manually lowers the screen into the hot fat by means of the two raised handles. The illustration also shows, on the left side, a batter depositor for cake doughnuts.

Doughnut fryer.
Courtesy of Belshaw, Bros., Inc.

# PANS, CONTAINERS, AND MOLDS

**M**any of the pots and pans found in the hot kitchen are also used in the bakeshop. For example, saucepans are used to boil syrups and to cook creams and fillings. This section, however, concentrates on specialty containers and molds for the bakery. The following is a representative sample of the more important of these, in alphabetical order. Molds are of two types: those for baking dough or batter items, and those for giving shape to refrigerated items such as mousses and bombes. Other containers, such as mixing bowls, are included in the list.

Baba mold

1. **Baba mold.**
    A small thimble-shaped mold for making babas (p. 191).

Banneton

Barquette

Charlotte mold

Full-size and half-size hotel pans

Loaf pan

Pullman pan

2. **Banneton.**
   A bentwood basket, available in various shapes, for holding and giving shape to certain hearth bread doughs as they proof. Similar canvas-lined baskets are also available.

3. **Barquette.**
   A small boat-shaped mold for petits fours and small tartlets.

4. **Bombe mold.**
   A dome-shaped mold for frozen desserts (p. 566).

5. **Brioche mold.**
   A flared pan with fluted sides for making brioche (p. 193).

6. **Cake pans.**
   While most cake pans are round, other shapes, such as hearts, are available for specialty cakes. Cake pans come in many sizes.

7. **Cake ring.**
   See *Charlotte ring*.

8. **Charlotte mold.**
   The classic charlotte mold is round, tapered, and flat-bottomed, with two handles near the top rim. Except for the Apple Charlotte (p. 592), which is baked in this mold, classic charlottes are made with a Bavarian cream filling and refrigerated until set, not baked.

9. **Charlotte ring.**
   Also called *cake rings*, these are stainless-steel rings in various diameters and heights, most often used for making molded desserts and for shaping and holding desserts made of layers of cake, pastry, and fillings. The rings are removed after the fillings have set and before serving or display. (See chapter 18. A charlotte ring in use is illustrated on page 454.)

10. **Chocolate molds.**
    Used for all sorts of chocolate work, from large display pieces to bite-size truffles. (See chapter 24.)

11. **Cornstick pan.**
    Special baking pan with indentations shaped like small ears of corn. Used for baking cornbread items.

12. **Flexipan.**
    This is the brand name for a line of nonstick baking pans made of a flexible silicone material. Flexipans are available in dozens of shapes and sizes to make a wide range of products, from muffins and quick-bread loaves to petits fours.

13. **Hotel pan.**
    A rectangular pan, usually made of stainless steel. Designed to hold foods in service counters. Also used for baking and steaming, and often used for baked items such as bread pudding. The standard size is 10 × 20 inches (325 × 530 mm). Fractions of this size (½, ⅓, and so on) are also available. Standard depth is 2½ in. (65 mm), but deeper pans are also available.

14. **Loaf pan.**
    A rectangular pan, usually with slightly flared sides, used for baking loaf breads. Loaf pans can also be used for molding refrigerated and frozen desserts. A special type of loaf pan is the Pullman pan, which has straight, not flared sides, and a removable lid, for baking Pullman loaves of bread (p. 180).

**15. Madeleine pan.**

A special baking pan with shell-shaped indentations, used for baking madeleines (p. 417).

**16. Mixing bowls.**

The most useful mixing bowls are made of stainless steel and have round bottoms. They are used for general mixing and whipping. The round construction enables the whip to reach all areas for thorough mixing or whipping.

**17. Muffin pan.**

Metal baking pan with cup-shaped indentations for baking muffins. (See chapter 10.) Pans are available for making muffins in several sizes.

**18. Petit four molds.**

Tiny metal molds in a variety of shapes, used for baking an assortment of little tartlets, financiers (p. 373), and other petits fours.

**19. Pie pan.**

Shallow pan with sloping sides, used for baking pies. Disposable aluminum pie pans are usually used in retail bakeshops.

**20. Savarin mold.**

Small ring-shaped or doughnut-shaped metal mold for baking savarins (p. 191).

**21. Sheet pan.**

A shallow, rectangular pan (1 in./25 mm deep) for baking sheet cakes, cookies, rolls, and other baked goods. A full sheet pan measures 18 × 26 inches (46 × 66 cm). Half-sheet pans are 13 × 18 inches (33 × 46 cm). Perforated sheet pans are the same size, but the bottom is full of tiny holes. These allow even baking and browning of breads and rolls because the holes allow the oven's hot air to circulate freely around the items as they bake.

*Pan extenders* are metal or fiberglass frames that fit inside sheet pans. They give straight sides to sheet cakes and make the pan deeper. Extenders are usually 2 inches (5 cm) high.

**22. Springform pan.**

A cake pan with a removable bottom. Used primarily for baking cheesecakes and other items too delicate to be easily removed from standard cake pans.

**23. Tart pan.**

A shallow (1 in./2.5 cm deep) metal pan, usually with fluted sides, used for baking tarts. Standard pans are round, but square and rectangular pans are also available. They may be made in one piece or with a removable bottom to make removal of the baked tart from the pan easier.

Tart pans make multi-serving pastries, but smaller tartlet pans make single-portion tartlets. Like tart pans, these come in a variety of sizes. The smallest usually are in one piece and lack the removable bottom.

**24. Tube pan.**

A deep cake pan with a tube in the center. The tube promotes even baking of angel food cakes and similar items.

Madeleine pan

Savarin mold

Sheet pan

Springform pan

Tart pan

Tube pan

Blowtorch

Straight spatula

Bench brush

Chinois

China cap

Icing comb

Cookie cutters and pastry cutters

Roller cutter

# HAND TOOLS

1. **Blowtorch.**
   A tool used for caramelizing and controlled browning of various pastry items and for caramelizing the sugar topping of crème brûlée. Butane or propane is used as fuel, depending on the model.

2. **Bowl knife.**
   Also called a *straight spatula* or *palette knife*, this tool has a long, flexible blade with a rounded end. Used mostly for spreading icing on cakes and for mixing and bowl scraping. A variant with an angled blade is called an *offset spatula*. The bent blade allows spreading and smoothing batters and fillings inside pans.

3. **Brushes.**
   Pastry brushes are used to brush items with egg wash, glaze, and so on. Larger bench brushes are used to brush flour from tabletops and from the surface of dough. Oven brushes are used to clean excess flour from deck ovens.

4. **Chinois and china cap.**
   A chinois is a conical strainer with a fine mesh, used mostly for straining sauces. A china cap is also a conical strainer; this one is made of perforated steel, so it doesn't strain as finely. A china cap is usually lined with several layers of cheesecloth if the liquid must be well strained.

5. **Comb, icing.**
   A small plastic tool, usually triangular, with serrated edges in various patterns, for decorating icings and other pastry and decorative items.

6. **Cutters.**
   Many types of cutters are used in the pastry department. Cookie cutters and pastry cutters, available in many shapes, cut decorative shapes by stamping them from rolled-out dough. Roller cutters have a handle on each end, like a rolling pin, and are rolled over rolled-out dough to cut repetitive shapes quickly and efficiently, with minimal loss of dough to trimmings and scraps. Roller cutters are often used for croissants (p. 205).

7. **Pastry bag.**
   A cone-shaped cloth or plastic bag with an open end that can be fitted with metal or plastic tubes or tips of various shapes and sizes. Used for shaping and decorating with items such as icing; for filling certain kinds of pastries and other items, such as éclairs; and for portioning creams, fillings, and doughs. Use of the pastry bag and tubes for decorative work is discussed and illustrated in chapter 17.

8. **Peel.**
   A thin, flat wooden board or steel sheet with a long handle, used for inserting and removing hearth breads from deck ovens. Because they are thinner than traditional wooden peels, steel peels are easier to slide under baked loaves.

Peel

### 9. Roller docker.

A tool that pierces holes in rolled-out dough to prevent bubbling during baking. It consists of a handle attached to a rotating tube fitted with rows of spikes.

Roller docker

### 10. Rolling pins.

Many types of rolling pin are used in the bakeshop for rolling out doughs. Perhaps the most versatile pin, used for most general rolling tasks, is simply a solid hardwood rod, about 2 inches (5 cm) thick and 20 inches (50 cm) long. A French rolling pin is about 2 inches (5 cm) thick at the center and tapered toward the ends. It is useful for rolling pie doughs and other doughs that must be rolled to a circular shape. For large quantities or heavy work, a heavy ball-bearing pin may be used. This pin is 3 to 4 inches (8 to 10 cm) thick and has a swiveling rod inserted through the center, with a handle at each end. Textured rolling pins are used to emboss designs, such as a basketweave pattern, in sheets of marzipan and pastillage.

Ball-bearing rolling pins, straight wooden rolling pins, and textured rolling pin

### 11. Scrapers.

A bench scraper, also called a *dough scraper*, is a small rectangle of stainless steel with a handle along one of the long edges. It is used for cutting and portioning dough and for scraping tabletops. A bowl scraper is a piece of plastic about the same size, but with one curved edge and no handle. It is used for scraping out the contents of mixing bowls.

Bench scraper

Bowl scraper

### 12. Sieve.

A round metal screen supported in a stainless-steel hoop frame. It is used for sifting flour and other dry ingredients. Also called a *drum sieve* or *tamis* (pronounced tah-mee).

### 13. Strainer.

A round-bottomed, cup-shaped tool made of screen mesh or perforated metal, with a handle on one side. Used for separating solids from liquids, such as draining the juice from fruit. Screen-mesh strainers can also be used for sifting dry ingredients, like a sieve.

Sieve

### 14. Turntable.

A round, flat disk that swivels freely on a pedestal base. Used for holding cakes for decorating.

### 15. Wire rack

A wire grate used to hold baked goods as they are cooling, or to hold items such as cakes while liquid icings, such as fondant, are applied.

Turntable

### 16. Whip.

Loops of stainless-steel wire fastened to a handle. Whips with a few stiff wires are used for mixing and blending, and whips with many flexible wires are used for whipping foams, such as whipped cream and egg foams. Also called *whisk*.

Whips

# MISCELLANEOUS TOOLS AND EQUIPMENT

Hydrometer

Ice cream freezer

1. **Acetate.**

   A type of clear plastic. Acetate strips are used for lining charlotte molds (see above) in the production of certain cakes, pastries, and refrigerated desserts. For retail display, the strips can be left on after the charlotte rings are removed to support the dessert while displaying the layers. Acetate sheets are most often used in decorative chocolate work, as illustrated in chapter 24.

2. **Couche.**

   A sheet of heavy linen or canvas, used for supporting certain breads, such as baguettes, as they are proofed. The cloth is placed on a sheet pan and pleated to form troughs to hold the loaves so they can proof without spreading.

3. **Hydrometer.**

   Also called a *sugar densimeter*, *saccharometer*, and *Baumé hydrometer*. Used to test the density of sugar syrups. (Sometimes called a *thermometer*, but this is inaccurate because it doesn't measure temperature.) It is a glass tube that is weighted at one end. It is floated in the solution to be tested, and because it floats higher in denser solutions, the density can be read off the scale marked along the length of the tube at the point where the surface of the liquid meets the tube.

4. **Ice cream freezer.**

   Machine for churning and freezing ice creams and sorbets. It consists of a large refrigerated canister or container with a paddle, called a *dasher*, that rotates inside. The ice cream or sorbet mix freezes against the walls of the canister but is continually scraped off and remixed to prevent the formation of ice crystals. Unlike home models, which depend on a salted ice water mixture to create freezing temperatures, commercial ice cream freezers contain a built-in electrically operated freezing unit.

5. **Marble.**

   A stone material used for tabletop or work surfaces in pastry shops. The hard, cool surface of marble is ideal for working with pastry doughs as well as for tempering chocolate and for some decorative work, such as pastillage. Marble slabs may be installed on top of under-the-counter refrigerated storage boxes. This keeps the marble cool even in warm weather.

6. **Parchment paper.**

   Also called *baking paper* or *silicone paper*, this is a sheet of treated nonstick paper sized to fit standard sheet pans. When used to line pans, parchment eliminates the need for greasing the pans. Also used to make piping cones for decorative work. (See chapter 17.)

7. **Rack, cooling.**

   A wire rack used to hold baked goods while cooling. The rack allows air circulation around the items.

8. **Silicone mat.**

   Flexible fiberglass mat coated with nonstick silicone, used to line baking sheets. Available to fit full and half-size sheet pans. Also used in sugar work (see chapter 26). The mats withstand temperatures up to about 480°F (250°C) and can be reused indefinitely if well cared for and not folded or creased. There are several manufacturers of silicone mats, but they are often known by one brand name, Silpat.

### 9. Thermometers.

Thermometers have many uses in the bakery, and there are many types of specialized thermometers. The sugar thermometer, also called a *candy thermometer*, is one of the most important. It is used for measuring the temperature, and hence the concentration, of boiling sugar syrups (p. 261). The chocolate thermometer is used for tempering chocolate (p. 639). Other thermometers measure the temperature of bread doughs, frying fat, and the interiors of ovens, refrigerators, and freezers (to check the accuracy of the equipment's thermostat).

In addition, tools for special decorative work are illustrated in the appropriate chapters. See the following pages:

Chocolate, p. 639     Sugar, p. 673

Pastillage, p. 662     Marzipan, p. 659

Sugar thermometer

Chocolate thermometer

## Chapter 4

# Ingredients

The following introduction to baking ingredients is necessarily simplified. Hundreds of pages could be written—and have been—on wheat flour alone. Much of the available information, however, is technical and of concern primarily to large industrial bakers. In this chapter, you will find the information you need to produce a full range of baked items in a small bakeshop or a hotel or restaurant kitchen.

**After reading this chapter, you should be able to:**

1. Understand the characteristics and functions of the major baking ingredients.

2. Make appropriate adjustments in formulas when substituting ingredients, such as dry milk for liquid milk and dry yeast for cake yeast.

3. Identify the main types of wheat flours by sight and feel.

# WHEAT FLOUR

Wheat flour is the most important ingredient in the bakeshop. It provides bulk and structure to most of the baker's products, including breads, cakes, cookies, and pastries. While the home cook depends almost entirely on a product called *all-purpose flour*, the professional baker has access to a wide variety of flours with different qualities and characteristics. To select the proper flour for each product and to handle each correctly, you should understand each type of flour and how it is milled.

## Wheat Varieties

The characteristics of a flour depend on the variety of wheat from which it is milled, the location in which it is grown, and its growing conditions. The most important thing for the baker to know is that some wheats are *hard* and some are *soft*. **Hard wheats** contain greater quantities of the proteins called *glutenin* and *gliadin*, which together form gluten when the flour is moistened and mixed. The subject of gluten is discussed in more detail later in this chapter and in chapter 5.

Gluten development, as you will learn, is one of the baker's major concerns when mixing doughs and batters. **Strong flours**—that is, flours from hard wheats with high protein content—are used primarily to make breads and other yeast products. **Weak flours**—that is, flours from **soft wheats** with low protein content—are important in the production of cakes, cookies, and pastries.

Six principal classes of wheat are grown in North America:

1. **Hard red winter.** This wheat is grown in large quantities. It has a moderately high protein content and is used primarily for bread flours. The term *red* in the name refers to the dark color of the bran and husk layers of the wheat berry, not to the interior of the grain, which is white.

2. **Hard red spring.** This wheat has the highest protein content of North American wheats and is an important component of strong bread flours.

3. **Hard white.** This high-protein wheat is grown in small quantities for bread flours. One interesting use for this wheat is for making whole wheat flours that are lighter in color and not as strong in flavor as whole wheat flours made from red wheat.

4. **Soft white.** This is a low-protein wheat useful for pastries, cakes, crackers, and other products in which a softer wheat is required.

5. **Soft red winter.** This is another low-protein wheat used for cake and pastry flours.

6. **Durum.** This is the hardest of the six wheat classes. It is used primarily for spaghetti and other macaroni products.

Different varieties are grown in Europe. For example, four principal wheat strains grown in France—Recital, Scipion, Soissons, and Textel—are softer—that is, lower in protein—than most North American varieties.

## Composition of Wheat

The wheat kernel consists of three main parts:

1. The **bran** is the hard outer covering of the kernel. It is darker in color than the interior of the grain. It is present in whole wheat flour as tiny

brown flakes, but it is removed in the milling of white flour. (In the case of whole wheat flour made from white wheat, the bran flakes are a much lighter, creamy white color.)

Bran is high in dietary fiber and also contains B vitamins, fat, protein, and minerals.

2. The **germ** is the part of the kernel that becomes the new wheat plant if the kernel is sprouted. It has a high fat content that can quickly become rancid. Therefore, whole wheat flour containing the germ has poor keeping qualities.

Wheat germ is high in nutrients, containing protein, vitamins, and minerals as well as fat.

3. The **endosperm** is the white, starchy part of the kernel that remains when the bran and germ are removed. This is the portion of the wheat kernel that is milled into white flour. Depending on its source, the wheat endosperm contains about 68 to 76% starch and 6 to 18% protein. The endosperm also contains small amounts of moisture, fat, sugar, minerals, and other components. These are discussed in more detail when we consider the composition of flour in a later section.

## The Milling of Wheat

The purpose of milling wheat is twofold:

1. To separate the endosperm from the bran and germ.

2. To grind the endosperm to a fine powder.

### Stone Grinding

Until modern roller milling (described below) was invented, wheat was made into flour by grinding it between two large stones. Once the grain was ground, it was sifted to remove some of the bran. This sifting is called **bolting**. Bolted flour is lighter in color and finer in texture than whole wheat flour, but of course some of the flavor and nutrients are removed with the bran and germ. In specialty markets, one can still find stone-ground flour, especially unbolted whole wheat flour, and other stone-ground meals, such as cornmeal.

Stone-grinding is laborious and time-consuming, and it does not produce a product that is easy to separate into the precise grades of flour demanded by modern baking. It wasn't until the break system was invented in the nineteenth century that the full range of flour grades in use today became available.

### Roller Milling and the Break System

Modern milling of wheat into flour is accomplished by a fairly complex and highly refined system that uses grooved steel rollers. In what is called the **break system**, the rollers are set so the space between them is slightly smaller than the width of the kernels, and the rollers rotate at different speeds. When the wheat is fed between them, the rollers flake off the bran layers and germ and crack the endosperm into coarse pieces. By sifting the broken grains, the parts can be separated. Approximately 72% of the wheat kernel can be separated as endosperm and milled into flour. The remaining 28% consists of bran (about 14%), germ (about 3%), and other outer portions called *shorts* (about 11%).

To further understand how milling works, one must understand that the outer parts of the endosperm—that is, the parts closest to the bran—are higher in protein than the inner parts. When the grain is cracked in the mill, the outer parts break into larger pieces and the inner parts into smaller pieces. In addition, the

Kernel of wheat.
Provided by the Wheat Foods Council

parts closest to the bran are darker in color than the creamy white interior of the endosperm.

Sifting separates the flour into **streams**. This means the grain is passed through rollers many times, and each time the rollers are closer together. After each pass through the rollers, part of the endosperm is fine enough to be sifted off as flour. The first streams come from the interior of the kernels. Later streams consist of the outer portions of the endosperm. By repeated sifting and breaking, different grades of flour can be obtained from one type of wheat. These grades are described in the following section.

## Flour Grades

As described above, different grades of flour come from different portions of the endosperm. Modern milling processes were developed to separate these portions.

### Patent Flour

Flour from the interior of the endosperm, extracted during the first streams of milling, is considered the highest grade of flour and is called **patent flour**. It is fine in texture because the granules from the interior of the grain are the smallest. It is whiter in color than other grades and has high-quality protein. It is nearly completely free of any trace of bran or germ.

Different grades of patent flour are available, depending on the amount of endosperm extracted. Fancy patent, also called *extra short*, is made from only the inner 40 to 60% of the endosperm. Short patent may contain up to 80% of the endosperm, while long patent consists of up to 95% of the endosperm.

Most bakers use the term *patent flour* to mean strong patent flour used for breads. However, any flour made from the interior of the endosperm is patent flour, even if made from soft wheat. Cake flour and pastry flour are also patent flours. You should be aware of these two uses of the term to avoid confusion.

### Clear Flour

The portion of the endosperm left after the patent flour is removed is called **clear flour**. This flour comes from the outer parts of the endosperm and thus is darker in color and higher in protein. Clear flour is usually separated into more than one grade. First clear is a dark flour, tan in color, that is often used in rye breads, where its dark color is not noticed and its high protein content contributes much-needed gluten. Even though it is dark, first clear is lighter in color than second clear, which is a low-grade flour not usually used in food production.

It was stated earlier that the outer parts of the endosperm are higher in protein than the interior. Thus, for each type of wheat, clear flour is higher in protein than patent flour. However, the quality of the protein in patent flour is better. This means that the gluten that is formed from these proteins stretches well and makes a strong, elastic film. Clear flour is higher in protein, but the protein is not as high in quality.

### Straight Flour

**Straight flour** is made by combining all the streams of the milling process. In other words, it is made from the entire endosperm. Because it contains the darker parts of the grain as well as the whiter interior, straight flour is darker in color than patent flour. In addition, it contains small amounts of bran and germ that weren't separated during milling.

Straight flour is not often used in North American baking. Some European flours are straight flours.

### Extraction

**Extraction** refers to the amount of flour milled from a given amount of grain. It is expressed as a percentage of the total amount of grain. For example, whole wheat flour is said to be 100% extraction because if you start with 100 pounds of grain, you end up with 100 pounds of whole wheat flour. As a second example, if a grade of flour is described as 60% extraction, this means it would take 100 kg whole grain to produce 60 kg of this grade of flour. The remaining 40% is bran, germ, shorts, and darker, lower grades of flour. Patent flour is a low-extraction flour, while straight flour is a high-extraction flour.

## Composition of Flour

White flour consists mostly of starch. This starch supplies the bulk of baked goods such as breads. Yet the other components of flour, especially protein, are of most concern to the baker because of the way they affect the dough-making and baking processes. This section describes each of the major components of white flour.

### Starch

White flour consists of about 68 to 76% starch. Starches are complex carbohydrates whose molecules consist of long chains of simpler sugars bound together. The starches in flour are contained in granules. Most of these tiny granules remain intact until they come in contact with water during the mixing process, at which time they absorb water and swell in size. Starch can absorb from one-quarter to one-half its weight in water.

A very small amount of the starch is broken down into sugars during milling or storage. This sugar is available as food for yeast.

### Protein

About 6 to 18% of white flour is protein, depending on the variety of wheat. Proteins act as binding agents that hold the starch granules together in the endosperm.

About 80% of the proteins in flour are called *glutenin* and *gliadin*. These two proteins, when combined with water and mixed in a dough, form an elastic substance called **gluten**. Controlling the development of gluten, as you will learn in the next chapter, is one of the primary concerns of the baker. Without gluten, it is impossible to make our familiar yeast-raised breads, because gluten provides their structure.

Gluten proteins can absorb about 1 to 2 times their weight in water.

Other proteins present in white flour are enzymes, most importantly **amylase**, also called **diastase**. This enzyme breaks down starch into simple sugars, which is important for yeast fermentation. Yeast is able to ferment sugars but not starch; amylase makes fermentation possible even in bread doughs with no added sugar.

### Moisture

The moisture content of flour in good condition ranges from 11 to 14%. If it becomes higher than this, spoilage is likely to occur. For this reason, flour should always be stored covered in a dry place.

### Gums

Like starches, *gums* are forms of carbohydrate. Gums make up 2 to 3% of white flour. The most important gums are called **pentosans**. They are significant because they have a much greater ability to absorb water than either starches or proteins. Pentosans absorb 10 to 15 times their weight in water, so even though they are present in small quantities, they have an important effect on dough formation.

Gums also serve as a source of dietary fiber.

### Fats

Fats and fat-like substances (*emulsifiers*) comprise only about 1% of white flour, but it is necessary to be aware of them. First, they are important for gluten development. Second, they spoil easily, giving flour an off flavor. For this reason, flour has a limited shelf life and should be used in a timely manner.

### Ash

**Ash** is another term for the mineral content of flour. When bakers are buying flour, they look at two important numbers in the flour's description: the protein content and the ash content. The ash content is determined by burning a sample of flour in a controlled environment. The starch and protein, when burned completely, turn to carbon dioxide gas, water vapor, and other gases, but the minerals do not burn and are left as ash. In general, the higher the ash content, the darker the flour. This is because the bran and the outer parts of the endosperm contain more minerals than the whiter, inner portions of the endosperm. Similarly, whole-grain flour is higher in ash than white flour. In conventional baking, bakers like a relatively low ash content because it makes whiter breads. Today, many artisan bakers of handmade breads look for darker flour with a higher ash content because it makes breads with a more robust wheat flavor.

Ash content for wheat flours ranges from about 0.3% for white cake flour to about 1.5% for whole wheat flour.

### Pigments

Orange-yellow pigments called **carotenoids** are present in flour in tiny amounts. Because of these pigments, unbleached flour is creamy in color rather than pure white. As flour ages after it is milled, oxygen in the air bleaches some of these pigments, turning the flour somewhat whiter in color.

## Absorption

**Absorption** refers to the amount of water a flour can take up and hold while being made into a simple dough, based on a predetermined standard dough consistency or stiffness. It is expressed as a percentage of the weight of flour. Thus, if the absorption ratio of a certain grade of flour is described as 60%, this means 60 pounds water combined with 100 pounds flour would yield a dough of standard consistency.

What accounts for differences in absorption ratio of different flours? Remember that the starch, protein, and pentosan gums in flour all absorb water (p. 59). Consider these facts:

- Because starch is the largest component of flour, it absorbs most of the water. However, it absorbs only one-quarter to one-half its weight in water, so a small variation in starch content results in a small variation in absorption.

- Pentosan gums absorb 10 to 15 times their weight in water, but because they are present in such tiny quantities, they don't account for much variation in absorption ratios.

- Proteins are present in significant amounts and absorb up to twice their weight in water. Thus, variations in the absorption ratio of different flours are caused primarily by variations in protein content.

For all practical purposes, the absorption ratio of water by flour is a function of the protein content. *The higher the protein content of the flour, the more water it can absorb.* Obviously, this is an important consideration for the baker. She will have to adjust the water in her bread formulas if she starts using flour of a different protein content.

### Flour Treatments and Additives

Millers may add small amounts of various compounds to improve the dough-making and baking qualities of flour. All additives must be indicated on the product label. Bakers also may purchase additives and add them to flour as needed.

## Enzymes

As described above, the enzyme amylase, more commonly called *diastase* by bakers, is naturally present in flour, but usually in too small a quantity to be helpful for yeast. Malt flour (described on p. 70) is high in diastase. It may be added by the miller, or the baker may add it in the bakeshop.

## Aging and Bleaching

Freshly milled flour is not good for bread making. The gluten is somewhat weak and inelastic, and the color may be yellowish. When the flour is aged for several months, the oxygen in the air matures the proteins so they are stronger and more elastic, and it bleaches the color slightly.

Aging flour is costly and haphazard, however, so millers may add small quantities of certain chemicals to accomplish the same results quickly. Bromates, specifically potassium bromate, added to bread flours mature the gluten but do not bleach the flour a great deal. Bromate use is decreasing because of concerns about its safety, and it is not used at all in Canada and Europe. Other additives, such as ascorbic acid (vitamin C), are used instead.

Chlorine is added to cake flour because not only is it a maturing agent but also it bleaches the flour to pure white.

## Nutrients

**Enriched flour** is flour to which vitamins and minerals (primarily iron and B vitamins) were added to compensate for the nutrients lost when the bran and germ were removed. Most white flour used in North America is enriched.

## Dough Conditioners

**Dough conditioners**, also called *dough improvers*, are sometimes added by the baker for the production of yeast products. They contain a variety of ingredients that improve gluten development, aid yeast fermentation, and delay staling. The use of dough conditioners is regulated by law in Canada and the United States, so it is important not to use too much. Also, adding too much to yeast doughs decreases bread quality.

## Vital Wheat Gluten

**Vital wheat gluten** is wheat gluten in a concentrated form, usually about 75% by weight. It is added to flour to improve the quality of yeast-raised doughs. It can increase the volume of yeast breads and aid in the development of gluten during mixing.

# Types of Patent Flour

Bakers generally use the term *patent flour* to mean *patent bread flour*. Technically, all white flour except clear flour and straight flour is patent flour, including cake and pastry flours.

## Bread Flour

Patent flour made from hard wheat has enough good-quality gluten to make it ideal for yeast breads. Patent bread flours typically range from 11 to 13.5% protein and 0.35 to 0.55% ash. They are available bleached or unbleached. Bread flour with added malt flour to provide extra diastase enzymes is also available.

Bread flour

## High-Gluten Flour

Flour with an especially high protein content is sometimes used in hard-crusted breads and in such specialty products as pizza dough and bagels. It is also used to strengthen doughs made from flours that contain little or no gluten. See, for example, the formula for Chestnut Bread on page 168. (The name of this flour is slightly misleading; the flour is high not in gluten but in gluten-forming proteins. There is no gluten in flour until certain proteins absorb water and a dough is mixed.)

A typical high-gluten flour has 14% protein and 0.5% ash.

## Cake Flour

**Cake flour** is a weak or low-gluten flour made from soft wheat. It has a soft, smooth texture and a pure white color. Cake flour is used for cakes and other delicate baked goods that require low gluten content.

Protein content of cake flour is approximately 8%, and ash content is approximately 0.3%.

## Pastry Flour

**Pastry flour** is also a weak or low-gluten flour, but it is slightly stronger than cake flour. It has the creamy white color of patent flour rather than the pure white of cake flour. Pastry flour is used for pie doughs and for some cookies, biscuits, and muffins.

Pastry flour has a protein content of about 9% and an ash content of about 0.4 to 0.45%.

## European Flour Types

In much of Europe, a flour grading system based on ash content is dominant. For example, the grades T45 and T55 are white wheat flours with low ash for breads and pastries. T65 includes high-gluten flours, and T80, T110, and T150 are whole wheat flours of increasing darkness. Other flours are included in this grading system. For example, T170 is dark rye flour.

Bread flours from European wheats are generally lower in protein than North American bread flours. Typically, they have a protein content of around 11.5%. Some North American mills have begun supplying similar flour to artisan bread bakers seeking to imitate classic European breads.

## Hand Test for Flour Strength

A typical small bakery keeps three white wheat flours on hand: cake flour, pastry flour, and a bread flour such as patent. You should be able to identify these three by sight and touch, because sooner or later someone will dump a bag of flour into the wrong bin or label it incorrectly, and you will need to be able to recognize the problem.

Cake flour

Pastry flour

Hand test for flour strength (from left to right): bread flour, pastry flour, cake flour

Bread flour feels slightly coarse when rubbed between the fingers. If squeezed into a lump in the hand, it falls apart as soon as the hand is opened. Its color is creamy white.

Cake flour feels very smooth and fine. It stays in a lump when squeezed in the hand. Its color is pure white.

Pastry flour feels smooth and fine, like cake flour, and can also be squeezed into a lump. However, it has the creamy color of bread flour, not the pure white color of cake flour.

## Types of Flour

| Flour | Protein | Ash |
|---|---|---|
| Straight flour | 13–15% | 0.4–0.45% |
| Patent bread flour | 11–13.5% | 0.35–0.55% |
| Clear flour | 17% | 0.7–0.8% |
| High-gluten flour | 14% | 0.5% |
| Cake flour | 8% | 0.3% |
| Pastry flour | 9% | 0.4–0.45% |
| All-purpose flour | 11–11.5% | 0.39–4.4% |

## Other Wheat Flours

**All-purpose flour**, seen in retail markets, is not often found in bake-shops, although it is often used as a general-purpose flour in restaurants, where it is purchased under the name *restaurant and hotel flour*. This flour is formulated to be slightly weaker than bread flour so it can be used for pastries as well. A professional baker, however, prefers to use flours formulated for specific purposes, because these give the best results. All-purpose flour has a protein content of about 11 to 11.5%.

**Durum flour** is made from durum wheat, a high-gluten wheat of a different species than those used for most flour. It is used primarily to make spaghetti and other dried pasta. In the bakeshop, it is occasionally used in specialty products, such as Italian semolina bread (*semolina* is another name for durum flour or durum meal). Durum flour has a protein content of 12 to 15%.

**Self-rising flour** is a white flour to which baking powder and, sometimes, salt has been added. Its advantage is that the baking powder is blended in uniformly. However, its use is limited by two factors. First, different formulas call for different proportions of baking powder. No single blend is right for all purposes. Second, baking powder loses its aerating or leavening power with time, so the quality of baked goods made from this flour can fluctuate.

**Whole wheat flour** is made by grinding the entire wheat kernel, including the bran and germ. The germ, as you have learned, is high in fat, which can become rancid, so whole wheat flour does not keep as well as white flour.

Because it is made from wheat, whole wheat flour contains gluten-forming proteins, so it can be used alone in bread making. (Protein content is typically 12 to 13%.) However, bread made with 100% whole wheat flour is heavier than white bread because the gluten strands are cut by the sharp edges of the bran flakes. Also, the fat from the wheat germ may contribute to the shortening action. This is one reason why most whole wheat breads are strengthened with white flour. Another reason is that the flavor of 100% whole wheat is stronger than many people care for, and the lighter flavor imparted by a blend of flours is often preferred by customers.

Whole wheat flour

**Bran flour** is flour to which bran flakes have been added. The bran may be coarse or fine, depending on specifications.

**Cracked wheat** is not a flour but a type of meal, in which the grains are broken into coarse pieces. It is used in small quantities to give texture and flavor to some specialty breads.

# OTHER FLOURS, MEALS, AND STARCHES

Wheat flour is the only flour with gluten of sufficient quantity and quality for making regular yeast breads. Some other grains, primarily rye and spelt, also contain gluten proteins, a fact important to people with gluten sensitivity or celiac disease. Nevertheless, the proteins do not form a good, elastic gluten useful for bread making. With the exception of a few specialty baked goods, these other flours and meals are mixed with wheat flour for most baking purposes.

## Rye

Next to white and whole wheat, rye is the most popular flour for bread making. Although **rye flour** contains some proteins, these do not form gluten of good quality. This is because although it contains enough gliadin, rye flour does not contain enough glutenin. Therefore, breads made with 100% rye flour are heavy and dense. To make a lighter rye loaf, it is necessary to use a mixture of rye and hard wheat flours. Typical formulas call for 25 to 40% rye flour and 60 to 75% hard wheat flour.

Rye flour is also high in pentosan gums—about 4 times as much as wheat flour. The gums give some structure to rye breads, but they also interfere with gluten development and make rye doughs stickier than wheat doughs.

Rye flour is milled much like wheat flour. The lightest rye flours, from the inner part of the kernel, have a low extraction rate, corresponding to patent flour. The following grades and types are generally available:

Dark rye flour

**Light rye.**  The lightest is nearly white. It has a very fine texture and a high percentage of starch, with little protein.

**Medium rye.**  This is a straight flour, milled from the whole rye grain after the bran is removed. Thus, it is darker than light rye and has a higher protein content.

**Dark rye.**  Like clear flour milled from wheat, dark rye comes from the part of the rye grain closest to the bran. Thus, it is darker than other rye flours and has a lower percentage of fine starch particles.

**Whole rye flour.**  This product is made from the whole rye kernel, including the bran and germ.

**Rye meal or pumpernickel flour.**  *Rye meal* is a dark, coarse meal made from the entire rye grain, including the bran and germ. Products labeled *pumpernickel* are sometimes cut into flakes rather than ground into coarse meal. Rye meal is used for pumpernickel bread and similar specialty products.

**Rye blend.**  This is a mixture of rye flour (generally 25 to 40%) and a strong wheat flour, such as clear flour.

## Corn

Wheat and rye account for the great majority of the grain flours and meals used in the bakeshop. Other grains are used mainly to add variety to baked goods.

Of these other grains, corn is perhaps the most important. (*Note:* In Great Britain, corn is referred to as *maize*, while the word *corn* simply means "grain.")

Corn contains no gluten-forming proteins, although it does contain significant quantities of other proteins and is therefore important in vegetarian diets.

Corn is most often used by the baker in the form of yellow cornmeal. Blue cornmeal is also available. Most cornmeal is made from only the endosperm, because the oil in the germ becomes rancid quickly. However, whole-grain cornmeal is also available. Cornmeal is available in grinds from fine to coarse. Coarse cornmeal produces a crumbly, somewhat gritty texture in cornbreads, a quality that is desirable in some products.

Other important corn products are discussed below in the section on starches.

Yellow cornmeal

## Spelt

Spelt is considered an ancestor of modern wheat. Like wheat, it contains gluten proteins, but they form a rather weak gluten structure that can't withstand much mixing. Spelt has a lower absorption ratio than wheat.

Spelt was unheard of by most bakers not long ago, but it has enjoyed increased popularity, partly because of increased interest in vegetarian diets and the desire for more variety in dietary sources of protein. It is found increasingly as an ingredient in specialty breads.

## Oats

Long familiar as breakfast porridge, oats in various forms also find uses in the bakeshop. Although rich in protein, including enough gluten proteins to make them off-limits for people allergic to gluten, oats do not form a gluten structure when mixed into a dough. Oats are high in gums, which supply dietary fiber. The gum content accounts for the gummy or gluey texture of oatmeal porridge.

**Rolled oats,** commonly used for porridge, are made by steaming oat grains to soften them and then flattening them between rollers. They are used to give textural interest to multigrain breads, as toppings for specialty loaves, and as an ingredient in some cookies.

**Steel-cut oats** are whole grains that have been cut into small pieces. They are occasionally used in small quantities in specialty breads. They have a long cooking time and a chewy texture.

**Oat flour** is whole-grain oats ground into fine flour, which can be mixed with wheat flour in small quantities for specialty breads.

**Oat bran** is a good source of dietary fiber that is often used as a muffin ingredient.

## Buckwheat

Buckwheat is technically not a grain because it is the seed not of a grass but of a plant with branched stems and broad, arrow-shaped leaves. Whole buckwheat is often ground into a dark, strong-tasting flour, while buckwheat endosperm alone is ground into a lighter-colored flour with a somewhat milder taste. When the grains are crushed into small pieces, they are called *buckwheat groats* and can be cooked like rice.

Buckwheat flour is most commonly used for pancakes and crêpes, but it can also be used in small quantities in specialty breads and multigrain products.

## Soy

Soy is not a grain but rather a bean or legume. Nevertheless, it may be ground into a flour like a grain. Unlike regular grains, however, it is low in starch. It is, however, high in fat and protein, although it contains no gluten proteins. The rich protein content makes it valuable in vegetarian diets.

Soy flour used in baking usually has had part of the fat removed. Raw soy flour contains enzymes that make it useful in baking. These enzymes aid yeast action and bleach the pigments in wheat flour. Raw or untoasted soy flour should be used in small quantities in yeast breads, generally about 0.5%. Higher quantities give an unpleasant beany flavor to breads and produce poor texture.

When soy flour is toasted, the enzymes are destroyed and the flour has a pleasanter flavor. Toasted soy flour can be used to add flavor and nutritional value to baked products.

## Rice

Rice flour is smooth, white flour milled from white rice. It has a small amount of protein but no gluten, so it is often used in gluten-free baked products.

## Other Grains and Flours

Many other grains, such as amaranth, millet, teff, and barley, have limited used in the bakeshop, either as flour or as whole grains. Other starchy non-grain foods, such as potatoes and chestnuts, can be dried and ground into flour for special products. See, for example, the formula for Chestnut Bread on page 168. Cooked potato starch is sometimes added to yeast breads, because the starch is easily broken down by diastase enzymes into forms of sugar that yeast can use.

## Starches

In addition to flours, other starch products are used in the bakeshop. Unlike flour, they are used primarily to thicken puddings, pie fillings, and similar products. The most important starches in dessert production are as follows:

1. *Cornstarch* has a special property that makes it valuable for certain purposes. Products thickened with cornstarch set up almost like gelatin when cooled. For this reason, cornstarch is used to thicken cream pies and other products that must hold their shape.

2. *Waxy maize* is made from a different type of corn. It is almost always manufactured into a form called *modified food starch*. Waxy maize and other modified starches have valuable properties. Because they do not break down when frozen, they are used for products that are to be frozen. Also, they are clear when cooked and give a brilliant, clear appearance to fruit pie fillings.

   Waxy maize does not set up firm like cornstarch but rather makes a soft paste that has the same consistency hot and cold. Thus, it is not suitable for cream pie fillings.

3. *Instant starches* are precooked or pregelatinized so they thicken cold liquids without further cooking. They are useful when heat will damage the flavor of the product, as in fresh fruit glazes, such as strawberry.

---

### ❧ AMYLOSE AND AMYLOPECTIN STARCHES ❧

Starch molecules fall into two principal categories. Amylose molecules are long, straight chains, while amylopectin molecules have many branches. Most grain starches are high in amylose starches, while starches from roots and tubers, such as potatoes and arrowroot, are high in amylopectin starches. The differences between the two types can be summarized as follows:

Amylose starches, after cooking, get thicker and cloudier as they cool. They form a firm gel when cooled. They tend to break down and release liquid after long storage or after freezing.

Amylopectin starches do not get thicker as they cool, and they remain fairly clear. They remain stable when frozen and do not release liquid in storage or after freezing.

# SUGARS

Sugars or sweetening agents have the following purposes in baking:

◆ They add sweetness and flavor.

◆ They create tenderness and fineness of texture, partly by weakening the gluten structure.

◆ They give crust color.

◆ They increase keeping qualities by retaining moisture.

◆ They act as creaming agents with fats and as foaming agents with eggs.

◆ They provide food for yeast.

We customarily use the term *sugar* for regular refined sugars derived from sugarcane or beets. The chemical name for these sugars is **sucrose**. However, other sugars of different chemical structure are also used in the bakeshop.

Sugars belong to a group of substances called **carbohydrates**, a group that also includes starches. There are two basic groups of sugars: **simple sugars** (or *monosaccharides*, which means "single sugars") and **complex sugars** (or *disaccharides*, meaning "double sugars"). Starches, or *polysaccharides*, have more complex chemical structures than sugars. Sucrose is a disaccharide, as are maltose (malt sugar) and lactose (the sugar found in milk). Examples of simple sugars are glucose and fructose.

All these sugars have different degrees of sweetness. For example, lactose is much less sweet than regular table sugar (sucrose), while fructose (or fruit sugar, one of the sugars in honey) is much sweeter than sucrose.

All sugars share one characteristic that is important for bakers and pastry chefs to understand: They are *hygroscopic*. This means they attract and hold water. Some sugars are more hygroscopic than others. Fructose, found in honey, is much more hygroscopic than sucrose, or table sugar.

For some purposes, this characteristic is desirable. For example, baked goods containing sugar stay moist longer than those with little or no sugar. For other purposes, this is undesirable. For example, spun sugar (p. 673) can be held for only a limited time, because it attracts moisture from the air and becomes sticky. Sugar used for dusting can attract moisture and dissolve.

## Invert Sugar

When a sucrose solution is heated with an acid, some of the sucrose breaks down into equal parts of two simple sugars, dextrose and levulose. A mixture of equal parts of dextrose and levulose is called **invert sugar**. It is about 30% sweeter than regular sucrose.

Invert sugar has two properties that make it interesting to the baker. First, it holds moisture especially well—that is, it is very hygroscopic—and, therefore, helps keep cakes fresh and moist. Second, it resists crystallization. Thus, it promotes smoothness in candies, icings, and syrups. This is why an acid such as cream of tartar is often added to sugar syrups. The acid inverts some of the sugar when it is boiled, preventing graininess in the candy or icing.

Invert sugar is produced commercially and is available as a syrup. It is also present in honey.

---

### ❊ DEXTROSE AND LEVULOSE ❊

The names for the two sugars that make up invert sugar mean, literally, "right sugar" and "left sugar." To put it simply, this is because their molecules contain the same numbers of atoms and have the same basic structure, but they are mirror images of each other. If one can be said to coil to the right, the other coils to the left.

Another name for dextrose is *glucose*. This is the name it is usually known by in the bakeshop, except when it is purchased as a dry powder.

# Regular Refined Sugars, or Sucrose

Refined sugars are classified by the size of the grains. However, there is no standard system of labeling, so the names of the granulations vary depending on the manufacturer.

## Granulated Sugar

Solid sugars (clockwise from top left: 10X sugar, brown sugar, regular granulated sugar, superfine granulated sugar)

**Regular granulated sugar,** also called *fine granulated sugar* or *table sugar*, is the most familiar and the most commonly used.

**Very fine** and **ultrafine sugars** (also called *caster sugar*) are finer than regular granulated sugar. They are prized for making cakes and cookies because they make a more uniform batter and can support higher quantities of fat.

**Sanding sugars** are coarse and are used for coating cookies, cakes, and other products.

**Pearl sugar** is a type of sanding sugar. It consists of opaque, white grains and does not easily dissolve in water. This characteristic, as well as its appearance, makes it useful for decorating sweet dough products. Pearl sugar is also called *sugar nibs*.

In general, finer granulations are better for mixing into doughs and batters because they dissolve relatively quickly. Coarse sugars are likely to leave undissolved grains, even after long mixing. These show up after baking as dark spots on crusts, irregular texture, and syrupy spots. Also, fine sugars are better for creaming with fats because they create a finer, more uniform air cell structure and better volume.

Coarse sugar, on the other hand, can be used in syrups, where its mixing properties are not a factor. Even a very coarse sugar dissolves readily when boiled with water. In fact, coarse crystalline sugar is often purer than fine sugar and makes a clearer syrup.

## Confectioners' or Powdered Sugars

*Confectioners' sugars* are ground to a fine powder and mixed with a small amount of starch (about 3%) to prevent caking. They are classified by coarseness or fineness.

10X is the finest sugar. It gives the smoothest texture in icings.

6X is slightly coarser in texture than 10X. For this reason, it is less likely to form lumps or to dissolve in moisture. It is used mostly for dusting the tops of desserts.

Coarser types (XXX and XX) are used for dusting and whenever 6X or 10X are too fine.

Confectioners' sugar is also known as *icing sugar* because of its importance in making many kinds of icing.

## Dehydrated Fondant

Dehydrated fondant, also known as *fondant sugar*, is a dried form of fondant icing. It is different from confectioners' sugar in that it is much finer than even 10X, and it does not contain any starch to prevent caking.

During the manufacture of fondant, part of the sucrose is changed to invert sugar. This helps keep the sugar crystals tiny, which makes for a very smooth, creamy icing with a good shine.

Fondant is discussed with other icings in chapter 17.

## Brown Sugar

**Brown sugar** is mostly sucrose (about 85 to 92%), but it also contains varying amounts of caramel, molasses, and other impurities, which give it its characteristic flavor. The darker grades contain more of these impurities. Basically, brown sugar is regular cane sugar that has not been completely refined. However, it can also be made by adding measured amounts of these impurities to refined white sugar.

Brown sugar was, at one time, available in 15 grades that ranged from very dark to very light. Today, only two to four grades are generally available.

Because it contains a small amount of acid, brown sugar can be used with baking soda to provide some leavening (see p. 84). It is used in place of regular white sugar when its flavor is desired and its color will not be objectionable. Of course, it should not be used in white cakes.

Keep brown sugar in an airtight container to prevent it from drying out and hardening.

Demerara sugar is a crystalline brown sugar. It is dry rather than moist like regular brown sugar. Demerara sugar is sometimes used in baking, but it is more often served as a sweetener with coffee and tea.

## Non-Nutritive Sweeteners

Also known as *sugar substitutes*, these products are discussed together with other dietary issues in chapter 27.

# Syrups

**Syrups** consist of one or more types of sugar dissolved in water, often with small amounts of other compounds or impurities that give the syrup flavor. The most basic syrup in the bakeshop, called **simple syrup**, is made by dissolving sucrose in water. **Dessert syrup** is simple syrup with added flavorings. These sucrose syrups are discussed in more detail in chapter 12.

## Molasses

**Molasses** is concentrated sugarcane juice. Sulfured molasses is a byproduct of sugar refining. It is the product that remains after most of the sugar is extracted from cane juice. Unsulfured molasses is not a byproduct but a specially manufactured sugar product. It has a less bitter taste than sulfured molasses.

Molasses contains large amounts of sucrose and other sugars, including invert sugar. It also contains acids, moisture, and other constituents that give it its flavor and color. Darker grades are stronger in flavor and contain less sugar than lighter grades.

Molasses retains moisture in baked goods and therefore prolongs freshness. Crisp cookies made with molasses can soften quickly because the invert sugars absorb moisture from the air.

Liquid sugars (clockwise from top left: molasses, honey, low-conversion glucose syrup, corn syrup)

## Glucose Corn Syrup

**Glucose** is the most common of the simple sugars (monosaccharides). In syrup form, it is an important bakeshop ingredient. Glucose is usually manufactured from cornstarch. Starch, as explained on page 66, consists of long chains of simple sugars bound together in large molecules. The manufacturing process breaks these starches into glucose molecules.

Not all the starch is broken into simple sugars during the process. In low-conversion syrups, only one-fourth to one-third of the starch is converted to glucose. As a result, these syrups are only slightly sweet. They are also very thick, because there are many larger molecules in the solution. Low-conversion syrups are less likely to burn or caramelize. They are useful for icings, candies, and sugar pieces, such as pulled sugar.

Regular, all-purpose **corn syrups** are medium-conversion glucose syrups in which nearly half the starch is converted to glucose. Corn syrup is useful for imparting moistness and tenderness to baked goods.

Dark corn syrup is regular corn syrup with added flavorings and colorings. In bakeshop usage, it is considered similar to a very mild molasses.

## Honey

Honey is a natural sugar syrup consisting largely of the simple sugars glucose and fructose, plus other compounds that give it its flavor. Honeys vary considerably in flavor and color, depending on their source. Flavor is the major reason for using honey, especially as it can be expensive.

Because honey contains invert sugar, it helps retain moisture in baked goods. Like molasses, it contains acid, which means it can be used with baking soda as a leavening.

## Malt Syrup

**Malt syrup**, also called *malt extract*, is used primarily in yeast breads. It serves as food for the yeast and adds flavor and crust color to the loaves. Malt is extracted from barley that has been sprouted (malted) and then dried and ground.

There are two basic types of malt syrup: *diastatic* and *nondiastatic*. Diastatic malt contains a group of enzymes called *diastase*, which breaks starch into sugars that can be acted on by yeast. Thus, diastatic malt, when added to bread dough, is a powerful food for yeast. It is used when fermentation times are short. It should not be used when fermentation times are long because too much starch will be broken down by the enzyme. This results in bread with a sticky crumb.

Diastatic malt is produced with high, medium, or low diastase content.

Nondiastatic malt is processed at high temperatures that destroy the enzymes and give the syrup a darker color and stronger flavor. It is used because it contains fermentable sugar and contributes flavor, crust color, and keeping qualities to breads.

Whenever malt syrup is called for in formulas in this book, nondiastatic malt is intended. Only one formula requires diastatic malt. If malt syrup is not available, you may substitute regular granulated sugar.

Malt is available in two other forms. *Dried malt extract* is simply malt syrup that has been dried. It must be kept in an airtight container to keep it from absorbing moisture from the air. *Malt flour* is the dried, ground, malted barley that has not had the malt extracted from it. It is obviously a much less concentrated form of malt. When used in bread making, it is blended with the flour.

# FATS

The major functions of fats in baked items are:

- ◆ To add moistness and richness.
- ◆ To increase keeping quality.
- ◆ To add flavor.
- ◆ To assist in leavening when used as a creaming agent or to give flakiness to puff pastry, pie dough, and similar products.

Many fats are available to the baker. Each has distinctive properties that make it suitable for different purposes. Among the properties a baker must consider when selecting a fat for a specific use are its melting point, its softness or hardness at different temperatures, its flavor, and its ability to form emulsions.

## Saturated and Unsaturated Fats

Some fats are solid at room temperature, while others are liquid. The liquid fats we usually refer to as **oils**. Whether the fats are solid or liquid depends on the fatty acids that make up the fat molecules (see sidebar).

Fatty acids consist primarily of long chains of carbon atoms to which hydrogen atoms are attached. If a fatty acid chain contains as many hydrogen atoms as it can possibly hold, it is called **saturated**. If the chain has empty spaces that could hold more hydrogen, it is called **unsaturated**. (One or more places along the carbon chain can lack hydrogen atoms.) Saturated fats are solid at room temperature, while unsaturated fats are liquid.

Natural fats consist of a mixture of many fat compounds. The more saturated fats are in the mixture, the more solid the fat is. The more unsaturated fats are in the mixture, the softer it is.

To produce solid, pliable fats for the bakeshop, manufacturers submit oils to a treatment called **hydrogenation**. This process bonds hydrogen atoms to the empty spaces in fatty acid chains, changing them from unsaturated to saturated. By controlling the process, the manufacturer can give the fat exactly the desired blend of saturated and unsaturated fats to produce a shortening with the exact characteristics desired, such as softness, moldability, and melting point.

## Fat Emulsions

Most bakery ingredients mix easily with water and other liquids and actually undergo a change in form. For example, salt and sugar dissolve in water; flour and starch absorb water and the water becomes bound up with the starch and protein molecules. Fat, on the other hand, does not change form when it is mixed with liquids or other bakery ingredients. Instead, it is merely broken down into smaller and smaller particles during mixing. These small fat particles eventually become more or less evenly distributed in the mix.

A uniform mixture of two unmixable substances, such as a fat and water, is called an **emulsion**. Mayonnaise is a familiar example of an emulsion from outside the bakeshop—in this case, an emulsion of oil and vinegar. There are also emulsions of air and fat, such as that formed when shortening and sugar are creamed together in the production of cakes and other products (see p. 86).

Fats have differing abilities to form emulsions. For example, if the wrong shortening is used in certain cakes, the emulsion may fail because the batter contains more water than the fat can hold. We then say that the batter curdles or breaks.

### Shortenings

Any fat acts as a shortening in baking because it shortens gluten strands and tenderizes the product. However, we generally use the word *shortening* to mean any of a group of solid fats, usually white and tasteless, that are especially formulated for baking. Shortenings generally consist of nearly 100% fat.

Shortenings may be made from vegetable oils, animal fats, or both. During

---

### ⁎{ LIPIDS }⁎

Fats are members of a larger group of compounds called *lipids*. Lipids are organic compounds that are not soluble in water. Other lipids include cholesterol and emulsifiers, such as lecithin.

Technically, fats are *triglycerides*, which are molecules made up of three fatty acid chains attached to the three carbon atoms of a glycerin molecule. The physical characteristics of each fat are determined by what kind of fatty acid chains make up the compound.

---

### ⁎{ HYDROGENATION AND FAT STABILITY }⁎

As explained in the text, one purpose of hydrogenation is to produce fats with desired physical characteristics. A second reason is to reduce the ability of the fat to spoil, or become *rancid*, by reacting with the oxygen in the air. The more unsaturated a fat is, the more likely it is to become rancid. Saturated fats are more stable, because all the places along the carbon chain are filled by hydrogen atoms, which gives oxygen less opportunity to react with the fat.

manufacturing, the fats are hydrogenated. This process turns liquid oils into solid fats. Because shortenings are used for many purposes, manufacturers have formulated different kinds of fats with different properties. There are three main types: regular or all-purpose (AP) shortenings, high-ratio plastic shortenings, and high-ratio liquid shortenings.

## Regular Shortenings

*Regular shortenings*, or all-purpose shortenings, have a fairly tough, waxy texture, and small particles of the fat tend to hold their shape in a dough or batter. They are called *plastic* shortenings, which means they are moldable at room temperature. Regular shortenings can be manufactured to varying degrees of hardness. They have a good creaming ability. This means that a good quantity of air can be mixed into them to give a batter lightness and leavening power (see p. 86). Also, this type of shortening melts only at a high temperature.

Because of their texture, regular shortenings are used for flaky products such as piecrusts and biscuits. They are also used in many other pastries, breads, and products mixed by creaming, such as certain pound cakes, cookies, and quick breads.

Unless another shortening is specified in a formula, regular shortening is generally used.

Fats (from left: lard, butter, margarine, shortening)

## High-Ratio Plastic Shortenings

These are soft shortenings that spread easily throughout a batter and quickly coat the particles of sugar and flour. They are called *high-ratio* because they were devised for use in cake batters that contain a high ratio of sugar and liquid to flour. Because they contain added emulsifying agents, they can hold a larger quantity of liquid and sugar than regular shortenings can. Thus, they give a smoother and finer texture to cakes and make them moister. Because of the added emulsifiers, this shortening is also commonly referred to as **emulsified shortening**.

On the other hand, high-ratio shortening does not cream well. When recipe instructions call for creaming shortening and sugar, regular shortening rather than high-ratio shortening should be used.

When emulsified shortening is used to make high-ratio cakes—cakes with a high ratio of sugar and liquid to flour—a simpler mixing method can be used because this shortening spreads so well (see chapter 16).

In addition, high-ratio shortening is often used in icings because it can hold more sugar and liquid without curdling.

The term *emulsified shortenings* is not, strictly speaking, an accurate one. Pure fat cannot be emulsified, because an emulsion is a mixture of at least two substances. It would, perhaps, be more accurate to call them *emulsifier* or *emulsifying* shortenings. However, the term *emulsified shortenings* is the more widely recognized and commonly used term.

## High-Ratio Liquid Shortenings

High-ratio liquid shortenings, also called *liquid cake shortenings*, are less hydrogenated than plastic shortenings, so they are liquid and pourable, although they are thick and cloudy or opaque in appearance. They contain more emulsifiers than high-ratio plastic shortenings. They are effective shortenings in high-ratio cakes. The emulsifiers make the cakes moist and fine-textured. Also, because they are so good at incorporating air during mixing, they increase the volume and tenderness of cakes.

High-ratio liquid shortenings, because they spread through the batter so well, simplify mixing. Also, the quantity of shortening in a batter can often be reduced because the shortening is so effective. For example, in the formula for yellow cake batter on page 405, the shortening quantity can be reduced to 50% with only a small change in quality; the cake will be only slightly drier and firmer.

# Butter

Fresh butter in North America consists of about 80% fat, about 15% water, and about 5% milk solids. Most North American butter is made from sweet cream. Many European butters have a higher fat content—about 82% or even more— and a lower moisture content. In addition, they are more likely to be made from cultured cream (crème fraîche, p. 76, and sour cream are examples of cultured cream used in the kitchen), which gives them a somewhat fuller flavor.

Butter is graded according to U.S. Department of Agriculture (USDA) standards, although grading is not mandatory. Grades are AA, A, B, and C. Most operations use grades AA and A because flavors of the lower grades may be off. In Canada, grades are Canada 1, Canada 2, and Canada 3.

Butter is available salted and unsalted. Unsalted butter is more perishable, but it has a fresher, sweeter taste and is thus preferred in baking. Also, because salt masks off flavors that might be absorbed during storage, it is harder to tell if salted butter has foreign flavors that might detract from the finished baked goods. If salted butter is used, the salt in the formula may have to be reduced. It is difficult to know for sure, however, how much to reduce the salt content, because salted butters vary in their composition.

Shortenings are manufactured to have certain textures and hardnesses so they will be particularly suited to certain uses. Butter, on the other hand, is a natural product that doesn't have this advantage. It is hard and brittle when cold, very soft at room temperature, and it melts easily. Consequently, doughs made with butter are much harder to handle. Also, butter is more expensive than shortening.

On the other hand, butter has two major advantages:

1. **Flavor.** Shortenings are intentionally flavorless, but butter has a highly desirable flavor.

2. **Melting qualities.** Butter melts in the mouth. Shortenings do not. After eating pastries or icings made with shortening, one can be left with an unpleasant film of shortening coating the mouth.

For these reasons, many bakers and pastry chefs feel the advantages of butter outweigh its disadvantages for many purposes. Shortening is not often used in fine French pastries. Frequently, you may blend 50% butter and 50% shortening to get both the flavor of butter and the handling qualities of shortening.

# Margarine

*Margarine* is manufactured from various hydrogenated animal and vegetable fats, plus flavoring ingredients, emulsifiers, coloring agents, and other ingredients. It contains 80 to 85% fat, 10 to 15% moisture, and about 5% salt, milk solids, and other components. Thus, it may be considered a sort of imitation butter consisting of shortening, water, and flavoring.

Unlike the margarines sold by retail grocers, bakers' margarines are formulated in different ways for different purposes. Following are the two major categories.

## Cake Margarines or Bakers' Margarines
These types of margarine are soft and have good creaming ability. They are used not only in cakes but also in a wide variety of other products.

### Pastry Margarines

These margarines, also called *roll-in compounds*, are tougher and more elastic than cake margarines and have a waxy texture. They are especially formulated for doughs that form layers, such as Danish dough and puff pastry.

*Puff pastry margarine*, the toughest of these fats, is sometimes called *puff pastry shortening*. Puff pastry made with this margarine generally rises higher than pastry made with butter. However, as the fat doesn't melt in the mouth like butter, many people find the pastry unpleasant to eat.

*Roll-in margarine* is somewhat softer in texture than puff pastry margarine and has a lower melting point. It can be used in Danish pastries, croissants, and puff pastry.

## Oils

Oils are liquid fats. They are not often used as shortenings in baking because they spread through a batter or dough too thoroughly and shorten too much. Some breads and a few cakes and quick breads use oil as a shortening. Beyond this, the usefulness of oil in the bakeshop is limited primarily to greasing pans, deep-frying doughnuts, and serving as a wash for some kinds of rolls.

## Lard

Lard is the rendered fat of hogs. Because of its plastic quality, it was once highly valued for making classic American flaky piecrusts and biscuits, and it is still sometimes used for these products. Since the development of modern shortenings, however, it is not often used in the bakeshop.

## Storage of Fats

All fats become rancid if exposed to the air too long. Also, they tend to absorb odors and flavors from other foods. Highly perishable fats, such as butter, should be stored, well wrapped, in the refrigerator. Other fats and oils should be kept in tightly closed containers in a cool, dry, dark place.

# MILK AND MILK PRODUCTS

Next to water, milk is the most important liquid in the bakeshop. As we will discuss in chapter 5, water is essential for the development of gluten. Fresh milk, being 88 to 91% water, fulfills this function. In addition, milk contributes to the texture, flavor, crust color, keeping quality, and nutritional value of baked products.

In this section, we discuss milk products in two parts: first, an explanation and definition of the available products; and second, guidelines for using milk products in baking.

The table on page 75 lists the water, fat, and milk solids content of the most important milk products. Milk solids include protein, lactose (milk sugar), and minerals.

## Categories and Definitions

When we talk about milk and cream used in food service, we are nearly always talking about milk from cows. Milk from other animals, including goats, sheep, and water buffaloes, is used to make some cheeses, but most of the liquid milk we see, except for a small amount of goat milk, is milk from dairy cattle.

Milk is used as a beverage and also in cooking. Similarly, other milk products, including cream, butter, and cheese, are eaten as purchased and also used in cooking.

## Pasteurization

Liquid milk, directly as it comes from the cow and before it has had anything done to it, is called *raw milk*. Because raw milk may contain disease-causing bacteria or other organisms, it is almost always **pasteurized** before being sold or before being processed into other products. Pasteurized milk has been heated to 161°F (72°C), held at this temperature for 15 seconds to kill disease-causing organisms, and then quickly chilled. By law, all Grade A liquid milk and cream must be pasteurized. (Grades B and C are used in food processing and industrial uses and are rarely seen in food service or in the retail market.)

Even after pasteurizing, milk and cream are highly perishable products. Some cream products are **ultrapasteurized** to extend their shelf life. Heating the product to a much higher temperature (275°F/135°C) for 4 seconds kills not only disease-causing bacteria but nearly all organisms that cause spoilage. Ultra-pasteurized products must still be refrigerated both before and after opening.

**Ultra-High-Temperature (UHT) pasteurization** involves even higher temperatures. The resulting product is packed into sterile cartons. If the cartons are unopened, the milk will keep at room temperature for up to 10 months. Once opened, the milk must be refrigerated like regular pasteurized milk. UHT milk has a somewhat cooked taste and is better suited to cooking than for drinking as a beverage.

## Fresh Milk Products

**Whole milk** is fresh milk as it comes from the cow, with nothing removed and nothing (except vitamin D) added. It contains about 3½% fat (known as **milk fat** or **butterfat**), 8½% nonfat milk solids, and 88% water.

**Skim** or **nonfat milk** has had most or all of the fat removed. Its fat content is 0.5% or less.

**Low-fat milk** has a fat content of 0.5 to 2%. Its fat content is usually indicated, usually 1% and 2%.

*Fortified nonfat* or *low-fat milk* contains added substances that increase its nutritional value, usually vitamins A and D and extra nonfat milk solids.

Except, of course, for nonfat milk, natural liquid milk contains fat, which, because it is lighter than water, will gradually separate and float to the top in the form of cream. **Homogenized milk** has been processed so the cream doesn't separate. This is done by forcing the milk through very tiny holes, which breaks the fat into particles so small they stay distributed in the milk. Nearly all liquid milk on the market has been homogenized.

## Composition of Milk Products

| | Water (%) | Fat (%) | Milk Solids (%) |
|---|---|---|---|
| Fresh, whole | 88 | 3.5 | 8.5 |
| Fresh, skim | 91 | trace | 9 |
| Evaporated, whole | 72 | 8 | 20 |
| Evaporated, skim | 72 | trace | 28 |
| Condensed, whole[a] | 31 | 8 | 20 |
| Dried, whole | 1.5 | 27.5 | 71 |
| Dried, skim | 2.5 | trace | 97.5 |

[a]Condensed milk also contains 41% sugar (sucrose).

## Fresh Cream Products

**Whipping cream** has a fat content of 30 to 40%. Within this category, you may find light whipping cream (30 to 35%) and heavy whipping cream (36% or more). Extra-heavy cream, also called *manufacturer's cream*, has a fat content of 38 to 40% or more and is generally available only on the wholesale market. Whipping cream labeled *ultrapasteurized* keeps longer than regular pasteurized cream. Pure ultrapasteurized cream does not whip as well as regular pasteurized cream, so additives such as vegetable gums are added to make it more whippable.

**Light cream**, also called *table cream* or *coffee cream*, contains 18 to 30% fat, usually about 18%.

**Half-and-half** has a fat content of 10 to 18%, too low to be called *cream*.

## Fermented Milk and Cream Products

**Sour cream** has been cultured or fermented by added lactic acid bacteria, which makes it thick and slightly tangy in flavor. It has about 18% fat.

**Crème fraîche** (kremm fresh) is a slightly aged, cultured heavy cream. It is widely used for sauce-making in Europe because of its pleasant, slightly tangy flavor and its ability to blend easily into sauces. Unlike regular heavy cream, it usually doesn't require tempering and can be added directly to hot sauces. It is available commercially but is expensive. A close approximation can be made by warming 1 quart (1 L) heavy cream to about 100°F (38°C), adding 1½ ounces (50 mL) buttermilk, and letting the mixture stand in a warm place until slightly thickened, about 6 to 24 hours.

**Buttermilk** is fresh, liquid milk, usually skim milk, which has been cultured or soured by bacteria. It is usually called *cultured buttermilk* to distinguish it from the original buttermilk, which was the liquid left after butter-making. Buttermilk is used in recipes calling for sour milk.

**Yogurt** is milk (whole or low-fat) cultured by special bacteria. It has a custardlike consistency. Most yogurt has additional milk solids added, and some of it is flavored and sweetened.

## Milk Products with Water Removed

**Evaporated milk** is milk, either whole or skim, with about 60% of the water removed. It is then sterilized and canned. Evaporated milk has a somewhat cooked flavor.

**Condensed milk** is whole milk that has had about 60% of the water removed and is heavily sweetened with sugar. It is available canned and in bulk.

**Dried whole milk** is whole milk that has been dried to a powder. **Nonfat dry milk** is skim milk that has been dried in the same way. Both are available in regular form and in instant form, which dissolves in water more easily.

## Cheese

Two types of cheese are used in the bakeshop, primarily in the production of cheese fillings and cheesecakes.

**Baker's cheese** is a soft, unaged cheese with a very low fat content. It is dry and pliable and can be kneaded somewhat like a dough. Generally available in 30-pound and 50-pound packs, it can be frozen for longer storage.

**Cream cheese** is also a soft, unaged cheese, but it has a higher fat content, about 35%. It is used mainly in rich cheesecakes and in a few specialty products.

Two other cheeses are occasionally used for specialty products. *Mascarpone* is a type of Italian cream cheese with a tangier flavor than American-style

Baker's cheese

Cream cheese

Mascarpone

Ricotta

Ricotta impastato

cream cheese. It is used to make the filling for tiramisú (p. 474). Another Italian cheese, *ricotta*, was originally made from the whey left over from making cheese out of cow's milk or sheep's milk, although now it is more often made from whole milk than from whey. It has many uses in the kitchen and bakeshop. A smooth, relatively dry ricotta called *ricotta impastato* is used to make a filling for cannoli (p. 246). Regular ricotta has too much moisture for this purpose.

## Artificial Dairy Products

A wide variety of imitation cream and dessert topping products are made from various fats and chemicals, which are listed on the label. They are used in some institutions because they keep longer and are generally less expensive than dairy products. Some people feel they are acceptable, but many find their flavors objectionable.

## Guidelines for Using Milk Products in Baking

### Fresh Liquid Milk

Whole milk contains fat, which must be calculated as part of the shortening in a dough. For this reason, whole and skim milk are not interchangeable in a formula unless adjustments are made for the fat. Refer to the table on page 75 for the fat content of milk products.

Acid ingredients, such as lemon juice, cream of tartar, and baking powder, normally should not be added directly to milk, as they will curdle it.

| Substituting Dry Milk for Liquid Milk | |
|---|---|
| **To substitute for** | **Use** |
| 1 lb skim milk | 14.5 oz water + 1.5 oz nonfat dry milk |
| 1 lb whole milk | 14 oz water + 2 oz dried whole milk |
| 1 lb whole milk | 14 oz water + 1.5 oz nonfat dried milk + 0.5 oz shortening or 0.7 oz butter |
| 1 kg skim milk | 910 g water + 90 g nonfat dry milk |
| 1 kg whole milk | 880 g water + 120 g dried whole milk |
| 1 kg whole milk | 880 g water + 90 g nonfat dry milk + 30 g shortening or 40 g butter |

### Buttermilk

When buttermilk is produced, the lactose in the milk is converted to lactic acid. When buttermilk is used in place of regular milk in baked goods such as cakes or muffins, this acidity must, in most cases, be neutralized by adding baking soda to the formula. Then, because the soda and acid together release carbon dioxide, this extra leavening power must be compensated for by reducing the baking powder, as follows:

| For each quart (2 lb) buttermilk: | For each liter (1 kg) buttermilk: |
|---|---|
| 1. Add 0.5 oz baking soda. | 1. Add 15 g baking soda. |
| 2. Subtract 1 oz baking powder. | 2. Subtract 30 g baking powder. |

Substituting plain milk for buttermilk requires a different calculation. If a formula includes buttermilk and baking soda, you must add another acid to react with the soda when you substitute plain milk. Adding cream of tartar is usually the simplest method of supplying acid. For each teaspoon (5 mL) baking soda, add 2 teaspoons (10 mL) cream of tartar to make up for the lost acid of the buttermilk.

## Cream

Cream is not often used as a liquid in doughs and batters, except in a few specialty products. In these instances, because of its fat content, it functions as a shortening as well as a liquid.

Cream is more important in the production of fillings, toppings, dessert sauces, and cold desserts such as mousses and Bavarian creams. For detailed instructions on whipping heavy cream into a foam, see chapter 12, page 264.

## Dried Milk

1. Dried milk is often used because of its convenience and low cost. In many formulas, it is not necessary to reconstitute it. The milk powder is included with the dry ingredients and water is used as the liquid. This practice is common in bread making and in no way reduces quality. Unlike fresh liquid milk, which must be heated to destroy enzymes that can be harmful to bread doughs, dried milk contains no active enzymes and can be used without further preparation.

2. Proportions for reconstituting dry milk can be calculated from the table on page 77. For easy use, the equivalents in the table above can be used.

3. Heat-treated dry milk, not low-heat-processed dry milk, should be purchased by the bakeshop. In the heat-treated product, certain enzymes that can break down gluten have been destroyed.

# Storage of Milk Products

Fresh milk and cream, buttermilk and other fermented milk products, and cheese must be kept refrigerated at all times.

Evaporated milk in unopened cans may be kept in a cool storage area. After opening, store it in the refrigerator.

Condensed milk in large containers keeps for a week or more after opening if kept covered and in a cool place. The sugar acts as a preservative. Stir before using because the sugar tends to settle to the bottom and sides.

Dried milk should be kept in a cool, dark place. It does not need refrigeration, although you should store it well away from ovens and other heat sources. Keep the container tightly closed to prevent the milk from absorbing moisture from the air.

# EGGS

Eggs should be well understood by the baker because they are used in large quantities in the bakeshop and are more expensive than many of the other high-volume ingredients, such as flour and sugar. For example, half or more of the ingredient cost of the average cake batter is for the eggs.

## Composition

A whole egg consists primarily of a yolk, a white, and a shell. In addition, it contains a membrane that lines the shell and forms an air cell at the large end, and two white strands called *chalazae* that hold the yolk centered.

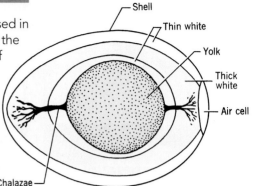

The parts of an egg. The diagram shows, in simplified form, the location of the parts of an unbroken egg, as described in the text.

- ◆ The yolk is high in both fat and protein, and it contains iron and several vitamins. Its color ranges from light to dark yellow, depending on the diet of the chicken.

- ◆ The white is primarily albumin protein, which is clear and soluble when raw but white and firm when coagulated. The white also contains sulfur.

- ◆ The shell is *not* the perfect package, in spite of what you may have heard. It is not only fragile but also porous, allowing odors and flavors to be absorbed by the egg and allowing the egg to lose moisture even if unbroken.

The table below lists the average water, protein, and fat content of whole eggs, whites, and yolks.

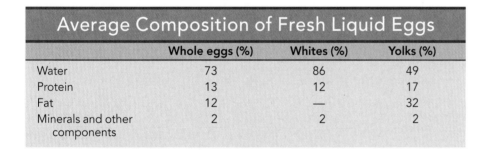

| Average Composition of Fresh Liquid Eggs | | | |
|---|---|---|---|
| | Whole eggs (%) | Whites (%) | Yolks (%) |
| Water | 73 | 86 | 49 |
| Protein | 13 | 12 | 17 |
| Fat | 12 | — | 32 |
| Minerals and other components | 2 | 2 | 2 |

## Grades and Quality

### Grades

In the United States, eggs are graded for quality by the USDA. There are three grades: AA, A, and B. The best grade (AA) has a firm white and yolk that stand up high when broken onto a flat surface and do not spread over a large area. As eggs age, they become thinner and are graded lower. The figure on page 80 shows the differences among grades AA, A, and B.

In Canada, there are four egg grades: A, B, C, and Canada Nest Run.

As a baker, you will not be concerned so much with the firmness of yolks and whites. Rather, you will want eggs that are clean and fresh-tasting, free of bad odors and tastes caused by spoilage or absorption of foreign odors. One bad-smelling egg can ruin an entire batch of cakes.

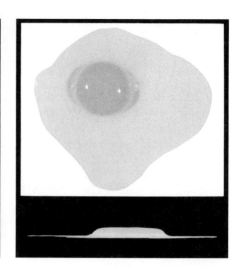

Egg grades: (a) Grade AA, (b) Grade A, and (c) Grade B, as seen from the top and side. Note how the white and yolk lose thickness and spread more in the lower grades.
Courtesy of USDA

## Maintaining Quality

Proper storage is essential for maintaining quality. Eggs keep for weeks if held at 36°F (2°C) but lose quality quickly if held at room temperature. In fact, they can lose a full grade in one day at warm bakeshop temperatures. There's no point in paying for Grade AA eggs if they are Grade B by the time you use them. Store eggs away from other foods that might pass on undesirable flavors or odors.

## Size

Eggs are also graded by size. The table below gives the minimum weight per dozen (including shell) of each size category. Note that each size differs from the next by 3 ounces per dozen. European eggs are also graded by size, with size 1 being the largest (70 g each, or about 2.5 oz) and 7 being the smallest (45 g each, or about 1.6 oz). This weight includes the shell.

Large eggs are the standard size used in baking and in food service. Shelled large whole eggs, yolks, and whites have the following approximate weights.

**Average Large Eggs, Approximate Weights without Shell**

| | |
|---|---|
| One whole egg = 1.67 oz | 47 g |
| One egg white = 1 oz | 28 g |
| One yolk = 0.67 oz | 19 g |
| 9½ whole eggs = 1 lb | 21 whole eggs = 1 kg |
| 16 whites = 1 lb | 36 whites = 1 kg |
| 24 yolks = 1 lb | 53 yolks = 1 kg |

## Egg Size Classifications

| Size | Minimum Weight per Dozen | |
|---|---|---|
| | U.S. | Metric |
| Jumbo | 30 oz | 850 g |
| Extra large | 27 oz | 765 g |
| Large | 24 oz | 680 g |
| Medium | 21 oz | 595 g |
| Small | 18 oz | 510 g |
| Peewee | 15 oz | 425 g |

To measure small quantities or odd quantities of whole egg, such as 0.5 oz or 15 g, beat the whole egg or eggs and then measure by weight.

# Market Forms

1. **Fresh eggs** or **shell eggs.**

2. **Frozen eggs.** Frozen eggs are usually made from high-quality fresh eggs and are excellent for use in baking. They are pasteurized and are usually purchased in 30-pound tins.

   To thaw, place them unopened in the refrigerator and hold for two days, or place in a defrosting tank containing running water at 50° to 60°F (10° to 15°C) for about 6 hours. Do not defrost at room temperature or in warm water. Stir well before using.

   Whole eggs

   Whole eggs with extra yolks

   Whites

   Yolks

   Frozen yolks usually contain a small amount of sugar (usually about 10%; check the label) to keep the components from separating while frozen. When sugared yolks are used in products such as cakes, you should allow for their sugar content by reducing the sugar in the formula by the same amount. For example, if you are using 20 ounces of yolks with 10% sugar, subtract 2 oz (20 oz × .10) from the sugar in the formula.

3. **Dried eggs.**

   Whole

   Yolks

   Whites

   Dried eggs are sometimes used in the bakeshop, though less often than frozen eggs. The whites are frequently used for making meringue powders. Dried egg products are also used by commercial manufacturers of cake mixes.

   Dried eggs are incorporated in baked goods in two ways: by reconstituting them with water to make liquid eggs, or by mixing them with the dry ingredients and adding the extra water to the liquid portion of the formula.

   *It is important to follow manufacturers' instructions for the ratio of egg to water because egg products vary.* After mixing, let the eggs stand to allow time for the water to be absorbed. This takes 1 hour for whole eggs and yolks, and sometimes 3 hours or more for whites. Mix again before using. The following are typical ratios for reconstituting eggs:

   | Product | Ratio of egg to water by weight |
   | --- | --- |
   | Whole eggs | 1:2.5 |
   | Yolks | 1:1 to 1:1.5 |
   | Whites | 1:5.5 to 1:6 |

Unlike most dried products, dried eggs do not keep well. Keep refrigerated or frozen, tightly sealed.

# Pasteurized Eggs and Sanitation

In recent years, cases of salmonella food poisoning have been caused by raw or undercooked eggs. As a result, cooks have been made more aware of sanitation concerns with respect to eggs. Pasteurized egg products are used in more operations. For a more detailed discussion of eggs and food safety, see appendix 6, page 748.

# Functions

Eggs perform the following functions in baking:

1. **Structure.**  Like gluten protein, egg protein coagulates to give structure to baked products. This is especially important in high-ratio cakes, in which the high content of sugar and fat weakens the gluten.

    If used in large quantities, eggs make baked products more tough or chewy unless balanced by fat and sugar, which are tenderizers.

2. **Emulsifying of fats and liquids.**  Egg yolks contain natural emulsifiers that help produce smooth batters. This action contributes to volume and to texture.

3. **Leavening.**  Beaten eggs incorporate air in tiny cells or bubbles. In a batter, this trapped air expands when heated and aids in leavening.

4. **Shortening action.**  The fat in egg yolks acts as a shortening. This is an important function in products that are low in other fats.

5. **Moisture.**  Eggs are mostly water (see the table on p. 79). This moisture must be calculated as part of the total liquid in a formula. If yolks are substituted for whole eggs, for example, or if dried eggs are used, adjust the liquid in the formula to allow for the different moisture content of these products.

6. **Flavor.**

7. **Nutritional value.**

8. **Color.**  Yolks impart a yellow color to doughs and batters. Also, eggs brown easily and contribute to crust color.

# LEAVENING AGENTS

Unlike liquids and solids, gases expand greatly when they are heated. *Leavening* is the production or incorporation of gases in a baked product to increase volume and to produce shape and texture. These gases must be retained in the product until the structure is set enough (by the coagulation of gluten and egg proteins and the gelatinization of starches) to hold its shape.

The three main gases that leaven baked goods are carbon dioxide, steam, and air. Two of these gases, steam and air, are present in all baked goods.

An essential part of the leavening process is the formation of *air cells* during mixing. Even if a properly mixed dough or batter appears dense and compact, it actually contains millions of tiny air cells. Leavening gases are trapped in these air cells, and the air cells expand as they fill with gases and as the gases are heated. The walls of the cells are formed largely from gluten proteins and sometimes egg proteins. They hold the gases and form the structure of the baked item. More details of the leavening process are discussed in chapter 5.

In this section, we discuss the most important ingredients or agents that supply gases for leavening.

Exact measurement of leavening agents is important because small changes can produce major defects in baked products.

# Yeast

Yeast is the leavening agent in breads, dinner rolls, Danish pastries, and similar products. This section discusses the characteristics of yeast. The handling of yeast and its use in yeast doughs are discussed in chapter 6.

## Yeast Fermentation

**Fermentation** is the process by which yeast acts on sugars and changes them into carbon dioxide gas and alcohol. This release of gas produces the leavening action in yeast products. The alcohol evaporates completely during and immediately after baking.

Fermentable sugar in bread dough comes from two sources:

1. It is added to the dough by the baker.

2. It is produced from flour by enzymes that break down the wheat starch into sugar. These enzymes are present in the flour and/or are added by the baker in the form of diastatic malt (see p. 70).

Yeast is a microscopic plant that accomplishes this fermentation process by producing enzymes. Some of these enzymes change complex sugars (sucrose and maltose) into simple sugars. Others change the simple sugars into carbon dioxide gas and alcohol. The following formula describes this reaction in chemical terms:

$$C_6H_{12}O_6 \quad \rightarrow \quad 2CO_2 \quad + \quad 2C_2H_5OH$$

simple sugar       carbon dioxide       alcohol

Because yeast is a living organism, it is sensitive to temperature.

| | |
|---|---|
| 34°F (1°C) | Inactive (storage temperature) |
| 60° to 70°F (15° to 20°C) | Slow action |
| 70° to 90°F (20° to 32°C) | Best growth (fermentation and proofing temperatures for bread doughs) |
| Above 100°F (38°C) | Reaction slows |
| 140°F (60°C) | Yeast is killed |

In addition to leavening gases, yeast also contributes flavor to bread doughs. Flavor molecules are produced by the yeast during fermentation. For this reason, breads produced by long fermentations usually have more flavor than short-fermentation products.

## Types of Yeast

The yeast added to bread dough by the baker may be a commercially produced yeast or a wild yeast culture that is present in *sourdough starter*. The preparation, use, and handling of sourdough starters is discussed in chapter 7.

Commercial yeast is available in three forms:

1. **Fresh yeast**, also called **compressed yeast**, is moist and perishable and is preferred by professional bakers. It is usually purchased in 1-pound (450 g) cakes. Under refrigeration and carefully wrapped to avoid drying, fresh yeast lasts up to 2 weeks. For longer storage (up to 4 months),

Fresh yeast

it may be frozen. Avoid using fresh yeast that has discolored or become moldy.

Some bakers crumble compressed yeast and add it directly to the dough in a straight-dough procedure. However, the yeast is mixed more evenly into the dough if it is first softened in twice its weight of warm (100°F/38°C) water. See chapter 6 for information on mixing procedures.

2. **Active dry yeast** is a dry, granular form of yeast. Active dry yeast must be rehydrated in 4 times its weight of warm water (105°F/41°C) before use. When using active dry yeast in a bread formula, use part of the water in the formula to dissolve the yeast. Do not add additional water.

   About 25% of the yeast cells in active dry yeast are dead due to the harsh conditions of the drying process. The presence of the dead cells can have a negative effect on dough quality. For this reason, active dry yeast has never been popular with professional bakers.

3. **Instant dry yeast** is a fairly new product (it was invented in the 1970s). It is also a dry granular form of yeast, but it does not have to be dissolved in water before use. It can be added in its dry form because it absorbs water much more quickly than regular dry yeast. In fact, the preferred way of incorporating it in a bread formula is to mix it with the dry flour.

   Unlike active dry yeast, instant yeast contains very little dead yeast, so less of it is needed. In general, you need only 25 to 50% as much instant yeast as fresh compressed yeast, or about 35% on average.

   Instant yeast also produces more gas, and produces it more quickly than regular dry yeast. This characteristic makes it appropriate for short fermentations or no-time doughs (explained on p. 121). For long fermentations and pre-ferments (see p. 131), fresh yeast may be a better choice. Fermentation times for instant yeast must be carefully monitored to avoid overfermentation or overproofing. Instant dry yeast is sometimes called *rapid-rise* or *quick-rise* yeast.

   As the illustration shows, instant yeast is nearly identical in appearance to active dry yeast. You must rely on the packaging for proper identification.

In most formulas in this book, when yeast is required, fresh yeast is specified. To substitute dry yeast or instant yeast, use the following guidelines:

◆ To convert fresh yeast to regular active dry yeast, multiply the quantity by 0.5. For example, if the formula calls for 1.5 oz fresh yeast, multiply by 0.5 to get 0.75 oz active dry yeast.

◆ To convert fresh yeast to instant dry yeast, multiply the quantity by 0.35. For example, if the formula calls for 40 g fresh yeast, multiply by 0.35 to get 14 g instant yeast.

Yeast contributes flavor in addition to leavening action.

# Chemical Leaveners

**Chemical leaveners** are those that release gases produced by chemical reactions.

## Baking Soda

Baking soda is the chemical **sodium bicarbonate**. If *moisture* and an *acid* are present, soda releases carbon dioxide gas, which leavens the product.

Heat is not necessary for the reaction (though the gas is released faster at high temperatures). For this reason, products leavened with soda must be baked at once, or gases will escape and leavening power will be lost.

Acids that react with soda in a batter include honey, molasses, brown sugar,

Active dry yeast; instant dry yeast

buttermilk, sour cream, yogurt, fruit juices and purées, chocolate, and natural cocoa (not Dutch processed). Sometimes cream of tartar is used for the acid. The amount of soda used in a formula is generally the amount needed to balance the acid. If more leavening power is needed, baking powder, not more soda, is used.

## Baking Powder

Baking powders are mixtures of baking soda plus one or more acids to react with it. They also contain starch, which prevents lumping and brings the leavening power down to a standard level. Because baking powders do not depend for their leavening power on acid ingredients in a formula, they are more versatile.

*Single-acting baking powders* require only moisture to release gas. Like baking soda, they can be used only if the product is to be baked immediately after mixing. For all practical purposes, no single-acting baking powders are sold today, although you can make it yourself, as explained in the sidebar. Practically, single-acting baking powders release gas too quickly to be useful for most products.

*Double-acting baking powders* release some gas when cold, but they require heat for complete reaction (see sidebar: Acid Salts). Thus, cake batters made with these can incorporate the leavening agent early in the mixing period and then stand for some time before being baked.

Do not include more baking powder than necessary in a formula because undesirable flavors may be created. Also, excess leavening may create an undesirably light, crumbly texture. Cakes may rise too much and then fall before they become set.

## Baking Ammonia

**Baking ammonia** is a mixture of ammonium carbonate, ammonium bicarbonate, and ammonium carbamate. It decomposes rapidly during baking to form carbon dioxide gas, ammonia gas, and water. Only heat and moisture are necessary for it to work. No acids are needed.

Because it decomposes completely, it leaves no residue that could affect flavor when it is properly used. However, it can be used only in small products that are baked until dry, such as cookies. Only in such products can the ammonia gas be completely driven off.

Because ammonia releases gases very quickly, it is sometimes used in products in which rapid leavening is desired, such as cream puffs. Use of ammonia enables the baker to lower the cost of such products by reducing the quantity of eggs. However, the quality of the resulting goods is lowered as well.

## Storage of Chemical Leaveners

Baking soda, powder, and ammonia must always be kept tightly closed when not in use. If left open, they can absorb moisture from the air and lose part of their leavening power. They must be stored in a cool place, because heat also causes them to deteriorate.

---

### ❊⟩ MAKING ⟨❊ SINGLE-ACTING BAKING POWDER

A simple, homemade baking powder may be made by mixing the following ingredients in the proportions indicated (using volume measure rather than weight).

| | | |
|---|---|---|
| Baking soda | 1 tbsp | 15 mL |
| Cornstarch | 1 tbsp | 15 mL |
| Cream of tartar | 2 tbsp | 30 mL |
| Yield: | 4 tbsp | 60 mL |

---

### ❊⟩ ACID SALTS ⟨❊

Technically, the ingredients in baking powder are not acids but acid salts. This means they do not release an acid or act like an acid until they are dissolved in water. For simplicity, however, we refer to these compounds as acids.

Different baking powders contain different combinations of acid salt that react with different speeds. How they react is referred to as their *dough reaction rate*, or DRR. Fast-acting baking powders release about two-thirds of their gases during mixing and one-third during baking. Slow-reacting powders release about one-third of their gases during mixing and two-thirds during baking.

Release of some gases during mixing helps create the air cells needed for leavening, as explained above. However, it is important that some gases are also released during baking for proper leavening to occur.

Fast-acting acids include cream of tartar (potassium acid tartrate) and MCP (monocalcium phosphate).

Slow-acting acids include SAS (sodium aluminum sulfate) and SAPP (sodium acid pyrophosphate).

---

## Air

Air is incorporated into all doughs and batters during mixing. The formation of air cells is important even in products leavened by yeast or baking powder because the air cells collect and hold the leavening gases.

Some products are leavened mostly or entirely by air. In these products, air is incorporated into the batter primarily by two methods: creaming and foaming. This air expands during baking and leavens the products.

1. *Creaming* is the process of beating fat and sugar together to incorporate air. It is an important technique in cake and cookie making. Some pound cakes and cookies are leavened almost entirely by this method.

2. *Foaming* is the process of beating eggs, with or without sugar, to incorporate air. Foams made with whole eggs are used to leaven sponge cakes, while angel food cakes, meringues, and soufflés are leavened with egg white foams.

## Steam

When water turns to steam, it expands to 1,100 times its original volume. Because all baked products contain some moisture, steam is an important leavening agent.

Puff pastry, cream puffs, popovers, and piecrusts use steam as their primary or only leavening agent. If the starting baking temperature for these products is high, steam is produced rapidly and leavening is greatest.

# GELLING AGENTS

The two ingredients discussed in this section are chemically and nutritionally unrelated. Gelatin is a protein and pectin is a soluble fiber, a type of carbohydrate that is not absorbed by the body. However, they both are used to thicken or to solidify (gel) soft or liquid foods.

Other thickening and gelling agents include starches, discussed on page 66.

## Gelatin

*Gelatin* is a water-soluble protein extracted from animal connective tissue. When a sufficient quantity of gelatin is dissolved in hot water or other liquid, the liquid will solidify when cooled or chilled. When used in smaller quantities, the liquid will thicken but not solidify.

Gelatin thickens and gels because of the nature of its proteins, which form long strands. When present in small quantities, the strands get tangled with one another, so the liquid does not flow as freely. When present in large enough quantities, the strands bond with one another to form a network that traps the liquid to keep it from flowing at all.

### Gelatin Forms

Culinary gelatin is available in a powdered form and in sheets. Powdered gelatin is most widely available to North American kitchens, although sheet gelatin, also called *leaf gelatin*, is also available and often preferred by pastry chefs. The sheet form is especially easy to use because it is premeasured (the sheets are of uniform weights). Also, when using sheet gelatin, it is not necessary to measure the liquid for soaking it. This is explained below.

As explained in the sidebar, equal weights of powdered and sheet gelatin do not have the same gelling power. The following equivalents are useful:

◆ Ten teaspoons powdered gelatin equal 1 ounce.

---

### ⁕{ BLOOM }⁕

When used in connection with gelatin, the term *bloom* has two meanings.

1. The process of softening gelatin in water is called *blooming*. To bloom gelatin, combine it with water or other liquid according to the procedures explained in the text.

2. The bloom rating is a measure of the strength of the gel formed by the gelatin. The higher the number, the stronger the gel. Gelatins with higher bloom ratings set faster and have less taste to detract from the main ingredients.

Powdered gelatin usually has a bloom rating of about 230.

Sheet gelatin varies in bloom rating, but sheets with lower bloom rating weigh more, so the gelling power per sheet is the same no matter the bloom rating. Typically, manufacturers label sheet gelatin "gold," "silver," and "bronze," as follows:

| | | | |
|---|---|---|---|
| Gold | 200 bloom | 2 g per sheet | 0.07 oz per sheet |
| Silver | 160 bloom | 2.5 g per sheet | 0.09 oz per sheet |
| Bronze | 130 bloom | 3.3 g per sheet | 0.12 oz per sheet |

---

- One ounce (30 g) powdered gelatin has the same gelling power as 20 sheets of sheet gelatin.

- One teaspoon powdered gelatin weighs about 2.8 g or 1/10 oz.

- One teaspoon powdered gelatin has the same gelling power as 2 sheets of gelatin.

The reference table below lists volume equivalents for a range of weights of gelatin.

Sheet gelatin is available in sizes ranging from 1.7 g to 3.3 g (see sidebar: Bloom).

Powdered gelatin and sheet gelatin can be used interchangeably, but they are handled differently. Guidelines for handling the two products and for substituting one for the other are described below.

Sheet and granulated gelatin

## Weight-Volume Equivalents for Powdered Gelatin

| U.S. | | Metric | |
|---|---|---|---|
| Weight | Approximate volume | Weight | Approximate volume |
| 0.1 oz | 1 tsp | 1 g | 1.75 mL |
| 0.12–0.13 oz | 1¼ tsp | 2 g | 3.5 mL |
| 0.16–0.17 oz | 1⅔ tsp | 3 g | 5 mL |
| 0.2 oz | 2 tsp | 4 g | 7 mL |
| 0.25 oz | 2½ tsp | 6 g | 10 mL |
| 0.33 oz | 3⅓ tsp | 8 g | 14 mL |
| 0.4 oz | 4 tsp | 10 g | 18 mL |
| 0.5 oz | 5 tsp | 12 g | 21 mL |
| 0.75 oz | 7½ tsp | 14 g | 25 mL |
| 1 oz | 10 tsp | 16 g | 28 mL |
| | | 20 g | 36 mL |
| | | 30 g | 54 mL |

## *Using Gelatin in Formulas*

Using gelatin in a formula requires three main steps:

1. The gelatin is softened in water or other liquid. It absorbs 5 times its weight in water.

2. The softened gelatin is added to hot ingredients, or it is heated with other ingredients, until it dissolves.

3. The mixture is chilled until it sets.

Most of the formulas in this book that require gelatin were developed using powdered gelatin (others were developed using sheet gelatin). The following guidelines will help you use recipes requiring gelatin:

- When a formula was developed using sheet gelatin, no soaking liquid is indicated in the ingredient list. In the procedure, the instructions direct you to soften the gelatin in cold water. To use sheet gelatin, add the indicated weight of gelatin to a generous quantity of cold water and soak until soft. Remove the soaked sheets from the water, drain well, and incorporate into the formula. (See p. 272 for an illustration of using sheet gelatin to make chiboust cream.)

- Always use very cold water to soak sheet gelatin. If the water is warm, some gelatin will dissolve and be lost.

- To substitute powdered gelatin when no quantity of soaking liquid is given, measure the gelatin, then add 5 times its weight of cold water. Let stand until the water is absorbed.

- When a formula was developed using powdered gelatin, the quantity of water for soaking is usually indicated. Either powdered gelatin or sheet gelatin can be used in these formulas. Add the measured gelatin to the measured water and soak. Then add the gelatin and the soaking liquid to the mixture in the formula.

- For an example of a formula developed using sheet gelatin but indicating no soaking liquid in the ingredient list, see Fruit Glaçage, page 434. For an example of a formula developed using powdered gelatin and for which the quantity of soaking liquid is indicated, see Vanilla Bavarian Cream, page 534.

Bavarian creams, chiffon pie fillings, and many mousses depend on gelatin for their texture. More information on the use of gelatin in these products is included in chapter 13.

## Pectin

Vegetable gums are carbohydrates that consist of molecules in long chains, somewhat like starches. They can absorb a great deal of water, which makes them useful for thickening or gelling liquids.

*Pectin* is perhaps the most familiar of these gums. It is present in many fruits. In general, unripe fruits have more pectin than ripe fruits. One of the reasons fruits get softer as they ripen is that the pectin breaks down.

Pectin is extracted from fruits and used to thicken or gel fruit preserves, jams, and jellies. It can also be used to make fruit glazes, because the pectin thickens or sets fruit juices and purées. An important advantage of pectin over an ingredient such as cornstarch is that it makes a clear, not cloudy, gel.

---

### ❋❴ VEGETABLE GUMS ❵❋

In addition to pectin, several other gums are used in food production. Most of these are used by manufacturers and are not likely to be found in the bakeshop. The following three gums, however, are sometimes used by pastry chefs and retail bakers:

**Agar-agar,** also known simply as *agar* or *kanten* (its Japanese name) is derived from seaweed and sold in the form of dry strands or powder. It is used much like gelatin, except it does not need to be refrigerated in order to gel. This makes it especially good for use in warm weather and for products that will not be refrigerated. Unlike gelatin, which is an animal product, agar-agar can be used on vegetarian menus.

As a rule of thumb, 1 part agar by weight has as much gelling power as 8 parts gelatin.

**Gum tragacanth,** often called *gum trag,* is extracted from a bush native to the Middle East. It is used by pastry chefs to make gum paste, a decorative product similar to pastillage (p. 662).

**Xanthan gum** (zan than) is often used to provide structure in gluten-free formulas (see p. 705).

Pectin alone, when added to a liquid, thickens but does not solidify or gel. In order for pectin to gel, an acid (such as fruit juice) and a high sugar content are necessary. This is one reason jams and jellies contain so much sugar.

Fruits high in pectin will gel naturally, without needing additional pectin. Such fruits include cranberries, apples, and plums. Citrus peels also contain pectin; this characteristic is useful in the production of marmalade.

For making jellies, the amount of pectin you need to add varies with the fruit. As a rule of thumb, 1.75 ounces (50 g) powdered pectin gels 2 quarts (2 L) fruit juice or fruit pulp.

Several fruit preparations in chapter 22 require the use of pectin.

# FRUITS AND NUTS

## Fruit Products

Nearly any kind of fresh fruit can be used in the production of desserts. In addition, a wide variety of dried, frozen, canned, and processed fruit products are important ingredients in the bakeshop. The following is a list of some of the most important fruit products. Use of these products is covered in appropriate chapters throughout the book. You will find more detailed information on fresh fruits in chapter 22.

**Fresh.**

apples

apricots

bananas

berries

cherries

figs

grapefruit

grapes

kiwi

kumquats

lemons

limes

mangoes

melons

nectarines

oranges

papayas

passion fruit

peaches

pears

pineapples

plums

rhubarb (actually not a fruit but a stem)

**Canned and frozen.**

apples, sliced

apricots, halves

blueberries

cherries, both sour and sweet

peaches, slices and halves

pineapple, rings, chunks, nibs, crushed, juice

strawberries

**Dried.**

apricots

currants (actually very small raisins)

dates

figs

raisins, light and dark

prunes

**Candied and glacé.**

cherries

citron

figs

fruitcake mix

lemon peel

orange peel

pineapple

**Other processed fruits.**

apricot glaze or coating

jams, jellies, and preserves

prepared pie fillings

fruit purées and fruit compounds, usually frozen (widely used for such products as fruit Bavarians, sauces, soufflés, and other desserts)

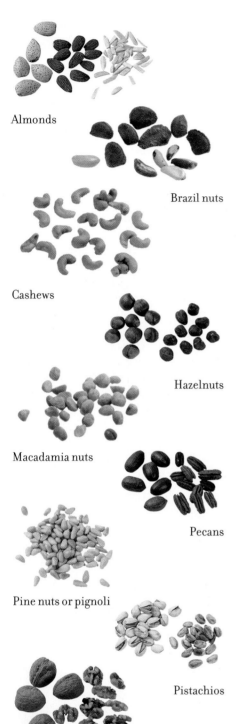

Almonds

Brazil nuts

Cashews

Hazelnuts

Macadamia nuts

Pecans

Pine nuts or pignoli

Pistachios

Walnuts

# Nuts

Most nuts are available whole, halved, or broken or chopped. Because they are high in oil, all nuts can become rancid. Store them, tightly closed, in a cool, dark place.

**Almonds.** The most important nut in the bakeshop. Available natural (skin on) and blanched (skin off) in many forms: whole, split, slivered, chopped, and ground (almond flour).

**Brazil nuts.**

**Cashews.**

**Chestnuts.** Must be cooked. Forms used in bakeshops are purée and glacé (in syrup).

**Coconut.** Sweetened coconut is used primarily for cake decoration.
    Unsweetened coconut is used as an ingredient in a great variety of goods such as cookies, macaroons, cakes, and fillings. Many types are available, based on the size of the individual grains, flakes, or shreds. The smallest types are extra-fine, about the texture of granulated sugar, and macaroon, about the texture of cornmeal. Large sizes include short and long shred, chip, and flake.

**Hazelnuts.** Best if toasted before use. Also available ground (hazelnut flour or meal).

**Macadamia nuts.**

**Pecans.** More expensive than walnuts. Used in premium goods.

**Peanuts.**

**Pine nuts** or **pignoli.** Small kernels that are usually toasted to enhance flavor. Especially important in Italian pastries.

**Pistachios.** Often used in decorations because of the attractive green color of the kernel.

**Walnuts.** One of the most important nuts in the bakeshop, along with almonds and hazelnuts.

# Nut Products

**Almond paste.** An expensive but highly versatile nut paste used in a variety of cakes, pastries, cookies, and fillings. It is made from 2 parts finely ground almonds and 1 part sugar, plus enough moisture to bring it to the proper consistency.

**Kernel paste.** A product similar to almond paste, but less expensive. It is made from apricot kernels, which have a strong almondlike flavor.

**Macaroon paste.** This product stands between almond paste and kernel paste in that it is made from a blend of almonds and apricot kernels.

**Marzipan.** Essentially a sweetened almond paste, used in decorative and confectionery work. This product can be purchased or made in the bakeshop from almond paste.

**Praline paste.** A confectionery paste made from almonds and/or hazelnuts and caramelized sugar, all ground to a paste. It is used as a flavoring for icings, fillings, pastries, and creams.

**Nut flours.** Nuts ground to a powder but not so ground as to turn to a paste. Almond flour is the most widely used. Nut flours are often used in fine pastries.

# CHOCOLATE AND COCOA

Chocolate and cocoa are derived from cocoa or cacao beans. When the beans are fermented, roasted, and ground, the resulting product is called **chocolate liquor**, which contains a white or yellowish fat called **cocoa butter**.

Much more information on the characteristics of chocolate and on handling chocolate can be found in chapter 24, which is completely devoted to this specialty. The brief summary of chocolate products in this chapter is an overview of those used in the bakeshop.

## Cocoa

**Cocoa** is the dry powder that remains after part of the cocoa butter is removed from chocolate liquor. *Dutch process cocoa*, or *dutched cocoa*, is processed with an alkali. It is slightly darker, smoother in flavor, and more easily dissolved in liquids than is natural cocoa.

Natural cocoa is somewhat acidic. When it is used in such products as cakes, it is possible to use baking soda (which reacts with acid) as part of the leavening power.

Dutched cocoa, on the other hand, is generally neutral or even slightly alkaline. Therefore, it does not react with baking soda (see table below). Instead, baking powder is used as the sole leavening agent. If you are substituting dutched for natural cocoa, you must increase the baking powder by 1 ounce (30 g) for each ½ ounce (15 g) soda omitted.

If not enough soda is used in chocolate products, the color of the finished product may range from light tan to dark brown, depending on the quantity used. If too much is used, the color will be reddish brown. This color is desired in devil's food cakes but it may not be wanted in other products. When switching from one kind of cocoa to another, you may have to adjust the soda in your recipes.

### ⁕{ SAVORY }⁕ INGREDIENTS

The ingredients listed in this chapter by no means comprise all the ingredients used by bakers or by any worker preparing a dough product. Pizza is only one example of a yeast dough product that may include nearly any food ingredient in the kitchen. Even simpler yeast breads may contain ingredients such as olives, aged cheeses, or meat products. Herbs, both fresh and dried, are used in many savory bread items, such as the rosemary focaccia on page 167. The baker has a limitless list of ingredients upon which to exercise his or her creativity and is not limited to the ingredients discussed in this chapter.

### Baking Soda Needed to Balance the Acidity of Typical Cocoa Products

| | Amount of baking soda per lb | Amount of baking soda per kg |
|---|---|---|
| Natural cocoa | 1.25 oz | 80 g |
| Dutched cocoa | 0 | 0 |
| Unsweetened chocolate | 0.8 oz | 50 g |
| Sweet chocolate | 0.4 oz | 25 g |

Natural cocoa

Dutched cocoa

## Unsweetened or Bitter Chocolate

Unsweetened chocolate is straight chocolate liquor. It contains no sugar and has a strongly bitter taste. Because it is molded in blocks, it is also referred to as *block cocoa* or *cocoa block*. It is used to flavor items that have other sources of sweetness.

Unsweetened chocolate is also known as *bitter chocolate*. Do not confuse this product with *bittersweet chocolate*, which is a category of sweetened chocolate with a low sugar content.

In some less expensive brands, some of the cocoa butter may be replaced by another fat.

## Sweet Chocolate

Sweet chocolate is bitter chocolate with the addition of sugar and cocoa butter in various proportions. If the percentage of sugar is low, sweetened chocolate may be called *semisweet* or, with even less sugar, *bittersweet*. Both of these products must contain at least 35% chocolate liquor, and their sugar content ranges from 35 to 50%. A product labeled *sweet chocolate* may contain as little as 15% chocolate liquor. Do not confuse sweet chocolate with milk chocolate (described below). In this book, when sweet chocolate is specified in a recipe, any sweetened chocolate may be used, although the results will, of course, vary. Bittersweet chocolate is specified if a good grade of chocolate with a high chocolate liquor content is essential for the best results.

Because sweet chocolate has only half the chocolate content of bitter chocolate, it is usually not economical to add it to products that are already highly sweetened because twice as much will be needed. For example, it is better to use bitter chocolate when making chocolate fondant from plain white fondant.

Good-quality chocolate products—including not only dark chocolate but also milk chocolate and white chocolate (see below)—are often called **couverture**, which means "coating" in French. When couverture is used to coat candies, cookies, and other products, the chocolate must be prepared by a process called **tempering**. This involves carefully melting the chocolate without letting it get too warm, then bringing the temperature back down to a certain level. The process requires a fair amount of skill. See page 641 for procedures.

Less expensive chocolates, which have part of the cocoa butter replaced by other fats, are easier to handle and don't require tempering. However, they do not have the flavor and eating qualities of good chocolate. These products are sold under such names as *cookie coating*, *cake coating*, *baking chocolate*, and *coating chocolate*. Do not confuse coating chocolate with couverture. These two products are entirely different, even though *couverture* means "coating." It would be less confusing if this lower-quality chocolate were referred to only as *baking chocolate*, without using the word *coating*.

## Milk Chocolate

Milk chocolate is sweet chocolate to which milk solids have been added. It is usually used as a coating chocolate and in various confections. It is seldom melted and then incorporated in batters because it contains a relatively low proportion of chocolate liquor.

## Cocoa Butter

Cocoa butter is the fat pressed out of chocolate liquor when cocoa is processed. Its main use in the bakeshop is to thin melted couverture to a proper consistency.

## White Chocolate

White chocolate consists of cocoa butter, sugar, and milk solids. It is used primarily in confectionery. Technically, it should not be called chocolate, because

---

### ❊{ FAT CONTENT }❊
### OF COCOA

When chocolate liquor is pressed to remove cocoa butter from cocoa solids, not all the cocoa butter is pressed out. Therefore, cocoa powder contains some fat in the form of cocoa butter. In Canada and the United States, a product labeled *cocoa* contains a minimum of 10% cocoa butter. Regular cocoa has a fat content of 10 to 12% and is known as *10/12 cocoa*. High-fat cocoa has a fat content of 22 to 24% and is known as *22/24 cocoa*. Both types are used in the bakeshop. For hot cocoa beverage, 22/24 cocoa is more often used.

European cocoa usually has a fat content of 20 to 22 and is called *20/22 cocoa*.

Low-fat cocoa, with a fat content below 10%, must be specially labeled and is more difficult to manufacture. It is expensive and not generally used in the bakeshop.

it contains no cocoa solids. However, the name white chocolate is in common use. Some inexpensive brands, in which another fat is substituted for the cocoa butter, not only contain no cocoa solids but none of the other components of chocolate either. These products don't deserve the name *chocolate* at all.

# Substituting Cocoa and Chocolate

Because cocoa is the same as bitter chocolate, only with less cocoa butter, it is often possible to substitute one product for the other. Shortening is usually used to take the place of the missing fat. However, different fats behave differently in baking. Regular shortening, for example, has about twice the shortening power of cocoa butter, so only half as much is needed in many products, such as cakes. The procedures below take this difference into account.

Because of these varying factors as well as the different baking properties of cakes, cookies, and other products, it is recommended that you test-bake a small batch when making a substitution in a formula. You can then make additional adjustments, if necessary. *No single substitution ratio is adequate for all purposes.*

## Procedure for Substituting Natural Cocoa for Bitter Chocolate

1. Multiply the weight of the chocolate by $5/8$. The result is the amount of cocoa to use.

2. Subtract the weight of the cocoa from the original weight of chocolate. Divide this difference by 2. The result is the amount of shortening to add to the formula.

Example: Replace 1 lb chocolate with natural cocoa.

$$5/8 \times 16\,oz = 10\,oz\ cocoa$$

$$\frac{16\,oz - 10\,oz}{2} = 3\,oz\ shortening$$

## Procedure for Substituting Bitter Chocolate for Natural Cocoa

1. Multiply the weight of the cocoa by $8/5$. The result is the amount of chocolate to use.

2. Subtract the weight of cocoa from the weight of chocolate. Divide by 2. Reduce the weight of shortening in the mix by this amount.

Example: Substitute bitter chocolate for 1 lb natural cocoa.

$$8/5 \times 16\,oz = 26\,oz\ chocolate\ (rounded\ off)$$

$$\frac{26\,oz - 16\,oz}{2} = \frac{10}{2} = 5\,oz\ less\ shortening$$

## Starch Content of Cocoa

Cocoa contains starch, which tends to absorb moisture in a batter. Consequently, when cocoa is added to a mix—for example, to change a yellow cake to a chocolate cake—the quantity of flour is reduced to compensate for this added starch. Exact adjustments will vary depending on the product. However, the following may be used as a rule of thumb:

Reduce the flour by ⅜ (37.5%) of the weight of cocoa added.

Thus, if 1 pound cocoa is added, the flour is reduced by 6 ounces. Or, if 400 g cocoa is added, reduce the flour by 150 g.

Chocolate, of course, also contains starch. When melted chocolate is added to fondant, for example, the fondant gets stiffer because of this starch and usually requires thinning. Often, however, the drying effect of the starch is balanced by the tenderizing effect of the cocoa butter. Methods of incorporating both chocolate and cocoa in various products are discussed in appropriate chapters.

# SALT, SPICES, AND FLAVORINGS

## Salt

Salt plays an important role in baking. It is more than just a seasoning or flavor enhancer. It also has these functions:

- Salt strengthens gluten structure and makes it more stretchable. Thus, it improves the texture and grain of breads. When salt is present, gluten holds more water and carbon dioxide, allowing the dough to expand more while holding its structure.

- Salt inhibits yeast growth. It is therefore important for controlling fermentation in bread doughs and preventing the growth of undesirable wild yeasts.

For these reasons, the quantity of salt in a formula must be carefully controlled. If too much salt is used, fermentation and proofing are slowed. If not enough salt is used, fermentation proceeds too rapidly. The yeast uses too much of the sugar in the dough and, consequently, the crust doesn't brown well. Other results of overfermentation are described in chapter 6.

Because of the effect of salt on yeast, never add salt directly to the water in which yeast is softened.

## Spices

Spices are plant or vegetable substances used to flavor foods. Plant parts used as spices include seeds, flower buds (such as cloves), roots (such as ginger), and bark (such as cinnamon). Spices are generally available whole or ground. Ground spices lose their flavor rapidly, so it is important to have fresh spices always on hand. Keep them tightly sealed in a cool, dark, dry place.

Because a small amount of spice usually has a great deal of flavoring power, it is important to weigh spices carefully and accurately. A quarter-ounce too much of nutmeg, for example, could make a product inedible. In most cases, it is better to use too little than too much.

The following are the most important spices and seeds in the bakeshop:

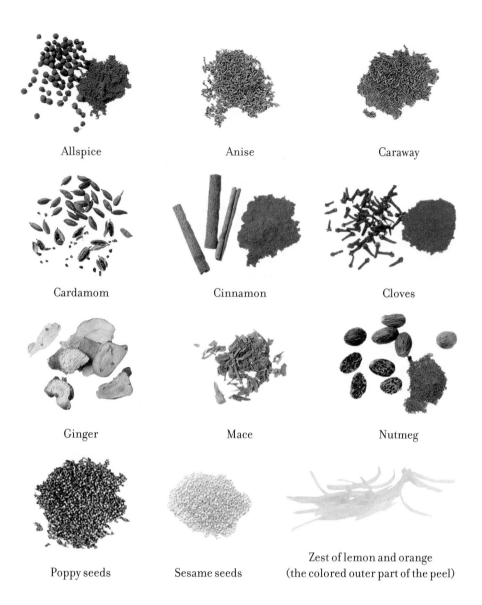

Allspice    Anise    Caraway

Cardamom    Cinnamon    Cloves

Ginger    Mace    Nutmeg

Poppy seeds    Sesame seeds    Zest of lemon and orange
(the colored outer part of the peel)

# Vanilla

Vanilla is the most important flavoring in the pastry shop. The source of the flavor is the ripened, partially dried fruit of a tropical orchid. This fruit, called *vanilla bean* or *vanilla pod*, is readily available, but at a high price. In spite of their cost, vanilla beans are valued by pastry chefs for making the finest-quality pastries and dessert sauces and fillings.

There are several ways to flavor products directly with vanilla beans. The simplest is simply to add one to a liquid when the liquid is heated, allowing the flavors to be extracted. Then remove the bean. For a stronger flavor, split the bean lengthwise before adding it. Then, when the bean is removed, scrape out the tiny black seeds from the inside of the pod (see page 269) and return them to the liquid.

Vanilla beans can also be used to flavor items that are not heated, such as whipped cream. Simply split the bean lengthwise, scrape out the seeds, and add them to the preparation.

A more common and economical way of flavoring with vanilla is to use vanilla extract. Vanilla extract is made by dissolving the flavoring elements of vanilla beans in an alcohol solution. To use, simply add the indicated quantity of the liquid as directed in the recipe.

Vanilla beans

If a formula calls for vanilla beans, there is no exact equivalent if you must substitute vanilla extract. This is because the strength of the flavor extracted from the bean depends on many factors, such as how long it was left in the liquid, whether or not it was split, and so on. However, a rule of thumb is to substitute ½ to 1 teaspoon (2.5 to 5 mL) extract for each vanilla bean.

Pure natural vanilla powder is available in a pure white color, so it can be used to give a good vanilla flavor to white products, such as flat icing or whipped cream, without discoloring them.

## Extracts and Emulsions

**Extracts** are flavorful oils and other substances dissolved in alcohol. These include vanilla, lemon, bitter almond, cinnamon, and coffee. Coffee extract can be approximated if it is not available. Dissolve 5 ounces (150 g) instant coffee powder in 12 ounces (360 g) water.

**Emulsions** are flavorful oils mixed with water with the aid of emulsifiers such as vegetable gums. Lemon and orange are the most frequently used emulsions. Their flavor is strong. For example, it takes less lemon emulsion than lemon extract to give the same flavor.

Flavorings in general may be divided into two categories: natural and artificial. Natural flavorings are usually more expensive but have a superior flavor. Artificial vanilla is a compound called *vanillin*, widely used in industrially made baked goods but lacking the rich, complex flavor profile of natural vanilla. Because flavorings and spices are used in small quantities, it is not much more expensive to use the best quality. Trying to save a few pennies on a cake by using inferior flavorings is false economy.

## Alcohols

Various alcoholic beverages are useful flavoring ingredients in the pastry shop. These include sweet alcohols, often called *liqueurs*, nonsweet alcohols, and wines.

Many liqueurs are fruit-flavored. The most important of these are orange (including Cointreau, Grand Marnier, and Triple Sec) and cassis or blackcurrant. Other important flavors are bitter almond (amaretto), chocolate (crème de cacao), mint (crème de menthe), and coffee (crème de café, Kahlúa, Tía Maria).

Nonsweet alcohols include rum, cognac, Calvados (a brandy made from apples), and kirschwasser (a colorless brandy made from cherries; see p. 585).

The two most important wines are both sweet wines: Marsala (from Sicily) and Madeira (from the Portuguese island of the same name).

# TERMS FOR REVIEW

hard wheat
soft wheat
strong flour
weak flour
bran
germ
endosperm
bolting
break system
stream
patent flour
bread flour
clear flour
straight flour
extraction
gluten
amylase
diastase
pentosan
ash
carotenoid
absorption
enriched flour
dough conditioner
vital wheat gluten
cake flour
pastry flour

all-purpose flour
durum flour
self-rising flour
whole wheat flour
bran flour
cracked wheat
rye blend
rye meal
sucrose
carbohydrate
simple sugar
complex sugar
invert sugar
granulated sugar
confectioners' sugar
brown sugar
syrup
simple syrup
dessert syrup
molasses
glucose
corn syrup
malt syrup
emulsion
oil
saturated
unsaturated

hydrogenation
regular shortening
emulsified shortening
margarine
pasteurized
ultrapasteurized
UHT pasteurization
whole milk
milk fat
butterfat
skim milk
nonfat milk
low-fat milk
homogenized milk
whipping cream
light cream
half-and-half
sour cream
crème fraîche
buttermilk
yogurt
evaporated milk
condensed milk
dried whole milk
nonfat dry milk
baker's cheese
cream cheese

leavening
fermentation
fresh yeast
compressed yeast
active dry yeast
instant dry yeast
chemical leavener
sodium bicarbonate
single-acting baking
    powder
double-acting baking
    powder
baking ammonia
creaming
foaming
gelatin
pectin
almond paste
kernel paste
chocolate liquor
cocoa butter
cocoa
dutched cocoa
couverture
tempering
extract

# QUESTIONS FOR DISCUSSION

1. Why is white wheat flour used in rye breads? in whole wheat breads? Some bakeries in Europe produce a kind of pumpernickel bread with 100% rye flour. What would you expect its texture to be like?

2. Describe how to distinguish bread, pastry, and cake flours by touch and sight.

3. Why does white flour have better keeping qualities than whole wheat flour?

4. What is the importance of aging in the production of flour? How is this accomplished in modern flour milling?

5. What is clear flour? What products is it used for?

6. List four functions of sugars in baked foods.

7. What is invert sugar? What properties make it useful in baking?

8. True or false: 10X sugar is one of the purest forms of sucrose. Explain your answer.

9. What is the difference between regular and emulsified shortening? between cake margarine and pastry margarine?

10. What are some advantages and disadvantages in using butter as the fat in pie dough?

11. List six functions of eggs in baked goods.

12. What is the difference between single-acting and double-acting baking powders? Which is most frequently used, and why?

13. Explain how to use sheet gelatin in a recipe. Explain how to substitute powdered gelatin for sheet gelatin.

## Chapter 5

# Basic Baking Principles

When you consider that most bakery products are made of the same few ingredients—flour, shortening, sugar, eggs, water or milk, and leavenings—you should have no difficulty understanding the importance of accuracy in the bakeshop, as slight variations in proportions or procedures can mean great differences in the final product. To achieve the desired results, it is not only important to weigh all ingredients accurately, as discussed in chapter 2. It is also important to understand all the complex reactions that take place during mixing and baking, so you can control these processes.

In this chapter, you are introduced to bakeshop production through a discussion of the basic processes common to nearly all baked goods.

**After reading this chapter, you should be able to:**

1. Explain the factors that control the development of gluten in baked products.

2. Explain the changes that take place in a dough or batter as it bakes.

3. Prevent or retard the staling of baked items.

# MIXING AND GLUTEN DEVELOPMENT

**M**ixing of doughs and batters is a complex process. It involves more than just blending the ingredients together. In order to help us control the mixing processes or methods that apply to the products in this book, from bread doughs to cake batters, it is helpful to understand the many reactions that take place during mixing.

## Basic Mixing Processes

In general, there are three phases of mixing in the production of doughs and batters:

1. Blending the ingredients.

2. Forming the dough.

3. Developing the dough.

These phases overlap one another. For example, the dough begins to form and to develop even before the ingredients are uniformly blended. Nevertheless, thinking of mixing processes in this way helps understand what is going on.

Different products contain different ingredients in various proportions. Compare, for example, French bread dough and cake batter. The first has no fat or sugar, while the second has large quantities of both. The first has a smaller percentage of liquid in the mix, so it is a stiff dough, which bakes into a chewy product, rather than a semiliquid like the cake batter, which bakes into a tender product. Because of these and other differences, the two products require different mixing methods. A main focus of much of the rest of this book is the correct mixing methods for the many products made in the bakery. For each of the mixing methods, one goal is to control the three stages of mixing listed above.

In this discussion, we focus on two special processes that occur during mixing: air cell formation and hydration of the components.

### Air Cells

Air cells are visible in the cut surface of bread and other baked items. These air cells form the porous texture of the interior of the item. (The interior of baked good is referred to by bakers as the **crumb**. In other words, a loaf of bread, for example, consists of two parts, the crust and the crumb.)

Air cells are a necessary part of the leavening process. They consist of open spaces surrounded by elastic cell walls made primarily of proteins such as gluten or egg albumin. When gases are formed by leavening agents, they collect inside the air cells. As the gases expand during baking, the cell walls stretch and enlarge. Eventually, the heat of baking causes the cell walls to become firm, giving structure and support to the baked item.

It is important to understand that no new air cells form during baking. All the air cells that enable leavening are formed during mixing.

Air cells begin forming as soon as the mixing process starts. Plenty of air is present between the particles of flour and other dry ingredients. In some cases, as with certain cakes, additional air cells are introduced when certain liquid ingredients are added, as when egg foams are folded in.

Air cells are usually rather large at the beginning of mixing, but as mixing continues, these large cells become divided into smaller ones as gluten and other proteins develop and stretch to form more cell walls. This means the length of mixing determines the final texture of the item. In other words, proper mixing is required to get the desired texture.

## Hydration

**Hydration** is the process of absorbing water. The many ingredients in baked goods absorb or react with water in different ways. All these processes are necessary for dough formation.

Starch is, by weight and volume, the largest component of bread doughs and most other doughs and batters. It does not dissolve in water, but it does attract and bind with water molecules and undergoes a change in form. Water molecules become attached to the surface of starch granules, forming a kind of shell around them. During baking, the heat causes the hydrated starch to gelatinize. Gelatinization helps form the structure of baked goods and is discussed later in this chapter (pp. 105–106). Without hydration during mixing, gelatinization could not take place.

Proteins, too, are mostly insoluble in water, but they also attract and bind with water molecules during mixing. Gluten proteins in dry flour form tight coils. Once they come into contact with water, they begin to uncoil. Mixing then causes the straightened proteins to stick together and form long gluten fibers. In other words, water is essential for the formation of gluten.

Yeast requires water in order to become active and begin fermenting sugars and releasing carbon dioxide gas for leavening.

Salt, sugar, and chemical leaveners such as baking powder have no effect on baked items in their dry form. They must be dissolved in water in order to carry out their many functions.

Finally, water has many other functions. For example, controlling water temperature enables the baker to control the temperature of the dough or batter. Adjusting the quantity of water or other liquid enables the baker to adjust the consistency or softness of a dough or batter.

# Controlling Gluten Development

Flour is mostly starch, as you know, but it is the content of gluten-forming proteins, not the starch, that concerns the baker most. Gluten proteins are needed to give structure to baked goods. Bakers must be able to control the gluten, however. For example, we want French bread to be firm and chewy, which requires much gluten. On the other hand, we want cakes to be tender, which means we want very little gluten development.

**Glutenin** and **gliadin** are two proteins found in wheat flour and, in much smaller quantities, in a few other grains, such as rye and spelt. During mixing, these two proteins combine with water (that is, they are hydrated) and form a stretchable substance called **gluten**. As explained above, gluten forms when hydrated glutenin and gliadin proteins uncoil and attach to each other to form long chains. During mixing, these protein chains gradually stretch and become intertwined, forming an elastic network we call the *gluten structure*.

**Coagulation** is the firming or hardening of gluten proteins, usually caused by heat. When gluten proteins coagulate during baking, they solidify into a firm structure. Soft, pliable bread dough is converted into firm bread crumb that holds its shape. A side effect of coagulation is that the proteins release much of the water they absorbed during mixing. Some of this water evaporates, and some is absorbed by the starch.

Ingredient proportions and mixing methods are determined, in part, by how they affect the development of gluten. The baker has several methods for adjusting gluten development.

## Selection of Flours

The proteins in wheat flour, especially in patent flour from hard wheat, form *good-quality gluten*—that is, the gluten is strong and elastic. Proteins in clear flour (see p. 58) are abundant, but the gluten they form is of slightly lower quality.

Wheat flours are classified as strong or weak, depending on their protein content. Strong flours come from hard wheat and have a high protein content. Weak flours come from soft wheat and have a low protein content. Thus, we use strong flours for breads and weak flours for cakes. (The protein content of flours is discussed in greater detail in chapter 4.)

Rye proteins form poor-quality gluten and are not sufficient for normal breads, although a few specialty breads, heavy in texture, are made from all rye. Spelt also contains a small amount of gluten protein but it is of low quality. Most other grains, such as corn, buckwheat, and soy, contain no gluten proteins at all. To make bread from rye or other grains, the formula must be balanced with some high-gluten flour, or the bread will be heavy.

## Fat and Other Tenderizers

Any fat used in baking is called a **shortening** because it shortens gluten strands. It does this by surrounding the particles and lubricating them so they do not stick together. Thus, fats are tenderizers. A cookie or pastry that is very crumbly, which is due to high fat content and little gluten development, is said to be *short*.

You can see why French bread has little or no fat, while cakes contain a great deal.

In the two-stage cake mixing method (p. 384), the flour is mixed so thoroughly with shortening that very little gluten development takes place, even with several minutes of mixing.

Sugar is another tenderizer that inhibits gluten development. Sugar is hygroscopic (p. 67), meaning it attracts and binds to water. Water that is attracted to sugar is not available to hydrate gluten. For this reason, a special mixing method is used for some sweet doughs, in which the gluten is developed in a separate step, before the sugar is added (p. 114).

## Water

Because gluten proteins must absorb water before they can be developed, the amount of water in a formula can affect toughness or tenderness.

In general, glutens absorb about twice their weight in water. Much of the water added to flour is absorbed by starch, so it is not all available to the proteins. Starving proteins of water keeps products tender by preventing gluten development. Piecrusts and crisp cookies, for instance, are made with very little liquid in order to keep them tender. Adding even a little extra water to these formulas activates more gluten and toughens the product.

Once all the gluten proteins are hydrated, additional water is of no use in developing gluten. In fact, if a great deal of water is added, the glutens are diluted and weakened.

The condition of the water used in bread doughs, specifically hardness and pH, also affects gluten. **Water hardness** refers to the mineral content of the water, especially its calcium content. Water with a high mineral content is called *hard*. The minerals in hard water strengthen gluten, often too much, making the dough too elastic and hard to work. Water that is too soft makes dough that is too slack and sticky. Either water treatments or dough conditioners can be used to counteract these effects.

The **pH** of water is a measure of its acidity or alkalinity, on a scale of 0 to 14. A strong acid has a pH of 0, while a strong alkali has a pH of 14. Pure water, being neutral, has a pH of 7. The mineral content of water often raises its pH.

The strongest gluten development takes place with a slightly acid pH of 5 to 6. The tenderness of a baked item can be adjusted by adding either an acid, such as fruit juice, to lower the pH beyond the 5 to 6 range, or adding an alkali, such as baking soda, to raise the pH above this range. Sourdoughs, being acidic, make doughs that are softer and stickier than regular yeast doughs.

## Mixing Methods

When the ingredients of a dough are mixed, three important processes take place:

1. The mixing action blends the water with the flour so the flour proteins can hydrate. This is the first step in the development of gluten.

2. Air is mixed into the dough. The oxygen in the air reacts with the gluten and helps strengthen it and make it more elastic.

3. The mixing action develops the gluten by stretching and aligning the gluten strands into an elastic network.

In the case of bread dough, the dough is soft and sticky at first. As the gluten develops, the dough becomes smooth and less sticky. When the dough reaches the ideal state of development, it is said to be **mature**. If mixing continues, gluten strands break and the dough becomes sticky and stringy. Overmixing results in poor loaf volume, because the broken gluten is no longer able to support the structure.

In products for which tenderness is desired, such as cookies, cakes, and short dough, the mixing time is kept short. Some gluten development is desired for these products, or they will be too crumbly. Pie doughs will not hold together, biscuits will slump rather than rise properly, and cookies will crumble. However, overmixing results in toughness.

**Dough relaxation** is an important technique in the production of most doughs. After mixing or kneading, gluten becomes stretched and tight. At this point, it becomes difficult to work or mold the dough. A period of rest or relaxation allows the gluten strands to become used to their new length and shape, and they become less tight. The dough can then be handled more easily, and it has less of a tendency to shrink.

## Leavening

Yeast fermentation helps gluten development because the expansion of air cells by yeast stretches the gluten just as mixing does. After a period of fermentation, the gluten in yeast dough is stronger and more elastic.

While it strengthens gluten, leavening also tenderizes the product. This is because the cell walls become thinner as they are stretched, making the finished product easier to chew.

Too much fermentation, on the other hand, can hurt the gluten structure, because the gluten becomes overstretched. Gluten strands tear and lose their elasticity. Overfermented doughs have poor texture, similar to overmixed dough.

Adding too much baking powder to a product such as a cake batter has an effect similar to overfermenting a yeast dough. The protein structure of the batter is stretched too far and can't hold, so it is likely to collapse. The result is a dense cake with poor volume.

## Temperature

Gluten develops more at a warm room temperature than at cold temperatures. Thus, the ideal temperature for mixing bread dough is 70° to 80°F (21° to 27°C). By contrast, tender products such as pie dough are best made with ice-cold water and mixed at a cool temperature to limit gluten development.

## Other Ingredients and Additives

**Salt** is an important additive in yeast doughs. Not only does it help regulate yeast fermentation but also it strengthens gluten and makes it more elastic. Yeast doughs without salt are harder to handle, and the gluten is more likely to tear.

**Bran** inhibits gluten development because it prevents some of the gluten strands from sticking together, and the sharp edges cut through gluten strands that have formed. Whole-grain breads are likely to be denser or heavier in texture. The texture of the mixed dough is not smooth and silky, and it tears easily.

Other solid food particles added to bread dough, such as herbs, nuts, olives, grated cheese, and even ground spices have a similar effect on gluten development.

**Dough conditioners** contain a mixture of ingredients, one of whose main functions is to strengthen gluten. Selection of dough conditioners depends on many factors, such as the hardness and pH of the water and the selection of flours.

**Milk**, including pasteurized milk, contains an enzyme that interferes with gluten development. Milk used in yeast doughs should be scalded by heating it to a simmer (180°F or 82°C) and then cooling before incorporating it in the dough.

# THE BAKING PROCESS

The changes to a dough or batter as it bakes are basically the same in all baked products, from breads to cookies and cakes. You should know what these changes are so you can learn how to control them.

The stages in the baking process are as follows. Be aware that many of these steps happen at the same time, not one after the other. For example, escape of water vapor and other gases begins almost at once, but it is more rapid later in the baking process.

## Melting of Fats

Solid fats mixed into a dough or batter trap air, water, and some leavening gases. When the fats melt, these gases are released and the water turns to steam, both of which contribute to leavening.

Different fats have different melting points, but most fats used in baking melt between 90° and 130°F (32° and 55°C). Gases released early in baking are more likely to escape because the structure isn't set enough to trap all of them. This is why puff pastry made with butter, with a low melting point, doesn't rise as high as puff pastry made with puff paste shortening. On the other hand, the high melting point of shortening makes the pastry unpleasant to eat.

## Formation and Expansion of Gases

The gases primarily responsible for leavening baked goods are carbon dioxide, which is released by the action of yeast and by baking powder and baking soda; air, which is incorporated into doughs and batters during mixing; and steam, which is formed during baking.

Some gases—such as carbon dioxide in proofed bread dough and air in sponge cake batters—are already present in the dough. As they are heated, the gases expand and leaven the product.

Some gases are not formed until heat is applied. Yeast and baking powder form gases rapidly when first placed in the oven. Steam is also formed as the moisture of the dough is heated.

As the product rises, the cell walls become thinner as they are stretched by the expanding gases. This tenderizes the product.

Production and expansion of gases starts immediately at the beginning of baking. Yeast dies at 140°F (60°C) and stops producing carbon dioxide. However, production of steam continues throughout the baking process.

As the gases are formed and expand, they are trapped in a stretchable network formed by the proteins in the dough. These proteins are primarily gluten and sometimes egg protein.

## Killing of Yeast and Other Microorganisms

In addition to yeast, doughs may contain other organisms, including bacteria and molds. Most of these, including yeast, die when the interior temperature of the item reaches about 140°F (60°C), although some microorganisms may survive to a slightly higher temperature.

When yeast dies, fermentation stops and no more carbon dioxide gas is released.

## Coagulation of Proteins

Gluten and egg proteins are the proteins primarily responsible for the structure of most baked goods. They provide this structure only when they are heated enough to coagulate, or become firm. Recall that proteins consist of molecules in the form of long chains. This process begins slowly at 140° to 160°F (60° to 70°C). Gradually these chains bond to each other to form a solid structure. To visualize this process, think of eggs, which are liquid when cold but become firmer as they are heated, until they are quite solid.

While this process is going on, gases are continuing to expand and the protein strands continuing to stretch. Finally, when coagulation is complete, the air cells can no longer expand and the product stops rising. Much of the water that bonded with the protein during mixing is released and either evaporates or is absorbed by starch. Once the protein structure has completely coagulated, the baked item is able to hold its shape.

The exact temperatures at which coagulation begins and is completed depends on several factors, including the other ingredients that are present. Sugars and fats, especially, affect the coagulation temperature of protein. Most proteins, however, are completely coagulated by the time they reach 185°F (85°C).

Correct baking temperature is important. If the temperature is too high, coagulation starts too soon, before the expansion of gases reaches its peak. The resulting product has poor volume or a split crust. If the temperature is too low, the proteins do not coagulate soon enough, and the product may collapse.

## Gelatinization of Starches

Starch molecules make up the majority of most baked goods. Thus, starch is an important part of the structure. Although starches by themselves generally can't support the shape of the baked item, they give bulk to the structure.

Starches make a softer structure when baked than proteins do. The softness of the crumb of baked bread is due largely to the starch. The more protein structure there is, the chewier the bread is.

Starch molecules are packed into tiny, hard granules. These granules attract and bond to water during mixing. As they are heated during baking, the water is absorbed into the granules, which swell greatly in size. Some of the starch granules break open and release starch molecules. During this process, starch molecules bond with any available water. This is why the interior of baked doughs are fairly dry, while unbaked doughs are moist. Most (but not all) of the water is still present but has bonded with starch.

This process, called **gelatinization**, begins when the interior reaches about 105°F (40°C) and continues throughout baking, or until about 200°F (95°C).

Depending on how much water is present in the dough or batter, not all the starch gelatinizes, because not enough water may be available. In dry products such as cookies and pie dough, a lot of the starch remains ungelatinized. In products made from a batter with a high water content, such as some cakes, a larger percentage of the starch gelatinizes.

## Escape of Water Vapor and Other Gases

Throughout the baking process, some of the water turns to steam and escapes into the air. If this takes place before the proteins coagulate, it contributes to leavening. In addition to steam, carbon dioxide and other gases escape as well. In yeast products, alcohol produced by the fermentation process is one of these gases.

Another result of the loss of moisture is the beginning of crust formation. As moisture is lost from the surface, the surface becomes harder. The crust begins to form even before browning starts. Baking breads with steam injected into the oven slows crust formation by delaying the drying of the surface. Delaying crust formation allows the bread to continue rising.

Loss of moisture continues even after the product is removed from the oven, as it cools.

A measurable amount of moisture is lost during baking. If a baked product of a specific weight is required, allowance must be made for moisture loss when scaling the dough. For example, to get a 1-pound loaf of baked bread, it is necessary to scale about 18 ounces dough. The percentage of weight loss varies greatly, depending on such factors as proportion of surface area to volume, baking time, and whether the item is baked in a pan or directly on the oven hearth.

## Crust Formation and Browning

A crust is formed as water evaporates from the surface and leaves it dry. Browning cannot occur until the surface temperature rises to about 300°F (150°C), and this can't happen until the surface dries. Browning begins before the interior of the item is completely baked and continues for the rest of the baking period.

Browning occurs when chemical changes occur to starches, sugars, and proteins. Although this is often referred to as **caramelization**, it is only part of the story. Caramelization involves only the browning of sugars. A similar process, called the **Maillard reaction**, causes most of the crust browning of baked goods. This is a process that occurs when proteins and sugars together are subjected to high heat. Maillard browning also occurs on the surface of meats and other high-protein foods.

The chemical changes caused by caramelization and Maillard browning contribute to the flavor and appearance of the baked item.

Milk, sugar, and egg, when included in doughs and batters, increase browning.

# AFTER BAKING

Many of the processes that take place during baking continue after the item is removed from the oven, while some of these processes reverse. We can divide this period into two stages, cooling and staling, although there is no exact dividing line between the two. In a sense, staling begins immediately, and cooling is only the first part of this process.

## Cooling

Moisture continues to escape after the item is removed from the oven. At the same time, cooling begins, which causes the gases still inside the item to contract. If the protein structure is completely set, the product may shrink slightly but hold its shape. If the product is underbaked, however, the contraction of gases may cause it to collapse.

When baked goods are removed from the oven, the surface is drier than the interior crumb. During cooling, the moisture content tries to equalize throughout the item. As a result, crisp crusts gradually become softer.

Proteins continue to solidify and bond to one another during cooling. Many products are fragile when they are still hot, but cooling makes them firm enough to handle. It is best not to handle or cut most baked goods until they have cooled.

Fats that melted during baking resolidify. This process also helps make the texture firmer.

Starches continue to gelatinize while the interior is still hot. Also, starch molecules bond with each other and become more solid as the product cools. This process is called *starch retrogradation* and is responsible for staling.

## Staling

*Staling* is the change in texture and aroma of baked goods due to a change of structure and a loss of moisture by the starch granules. Stale baked goods have lost their fresh-baked aroma and are firmer, drier, and more crumbly than fresh products. Prevention of staling is a major concern of the baker, because most baked goods lose quality rapidly.

As indicated, starch retrogradation begins as soon as the item begins to cool. As starch molecules bond with each other, the starch forces out moisture and becomes harder and drier. Even though this moisture may then be absorbed by other ingredients such as sugar, the result is that the texture of the item feels drier. Because this is a chemical reaction of the starch, breads become drier in texture even when tightly wrapped.

Starch retrogradation is more rapid at refrigerator temperatures than at room temperature, but it nearly stops at freezer temperatures. Thus, bread should not be stored in the refrigerator. It should be left at room temperature for short-term storage or frozen for long-term storage.

Chemical staling, if it is not too great, can be partially reversed by heating. Breads, muffins, and coffee cakes, for example, are frequently refreshed by placing them briefly in an oven. Remember, however, that this also results in more loss of moisture to the air, so the items should be reheated only just before they are to be served.

Loss of crispness is caused by absorption of moisture, so, in a sense, it is the opposite of staling. The crusts of hard-crusted breads absorb moisture from the crumb and become soft and leathery. Reheating these products to refresh them not only reverses chemical staling of the crumb but also recrisps the crusts.

Loss of crispness is also a problem with low-moisture products such as cookies and piecrusts. The problem is usually solved by proper storage in airtight wraps or containers to protect the products from moisture in the air. Pre-baked pie shells should be filled as close to service time as possible.

In addition to refreshing baked goods in the oven, three main techniques are used to slow staling:

1. **Protecting the product from air.** Two examples of protecting baked goods are wrapping bread in plastic and covering cakes with icing, especially icing that is thick and rich in fat.

   Hard-crusted breads, which stale rapidly, should not be wrapped, or the crusts will quickly become soft and leathery. These bread products should always be served very fresh.

2. **Adding moisture retainers to the formula.** Fats and sugars are good moisture retainers, so products high in these ingredients keep best.

   Some of the best French bread has no fat at all, so it must be served within hours of baking or it will begin to stale. For longer keeping, bakers often add a very small amount of fat and/or sugar to the formula.

3. **Freezing.** Baked goods frozen before they become stale maintain quality for longer periods. For best results, freeze soon after baking in a blast freezer at –40°F (–40°C), and maintain at or below 0°F (–18°C) until ready to thaw. Breads should be served quickly after thawing. Frozen breads may be reheated with excellent results if they are to be served immediately.

   Refrigeration, on the other hand, speeds staling. Only baked goods that could become health hazards, such as those with cream fillings, are refrigerated.

# TERMS FOR REVIEW

| | | | |
|---|---|---|---|
| crumb | coagulation | dough relaxation | gelatinization |
| hydration | shortening | salt | caramelization |
| glutenin | water hardness | bran | Maillard reaction |
| gliadin | pH | dough conditioner | starch retrogradation |
| gluten | mature (dough) | milk | staling |

# QUESTIONS FOR DISCUSSION

1. List and describe briefly the three stages of mixing of a dough or batter.

2. What are air cell walls made of? Describe how air cells are formed. Name two functions of air cells.

3. Describe what happens when gluten proteins come in contact with water during mixing.

4. What is the result of overmixing on bread dough? pie dough?

5. Discuss seven factors that affect the development of gluten in batters and doughs.

6. Why do some cakes fall if they are removed from the oven too soon?

7. Which kind of cake would you expect to have better keeping qualities—a sponge cake, which is low in fat, or a high-ratio cake, which is high in both fat and sugar?

## Chapter 6

# Understanding Yeast Doughs

**I**n its simplest form, bread is nothing more than a baked dough made of flour and water and leavened by yeast. In fact, some hard-crusted French breads contain only these ingredients, plus salt. Other kinds of bread contain additional ingredients, including sugar, shortening, milk, eggs, and flavorings. But flour, water, and yeast are still the basic building blocks of all breads.

Yet, for something that seems so simple, bread can be one of the most exacting and complex products to make. Success in bread making depends largely on your understanding of two basic principles: gluten development, which was discussed in chapter 5, and yeast fermentation, which has already been touched on and is described in further detail here.

This chapter focuses on the basic procedures in the production of many kinds of yeast products. Special attention is given to mixing methods and to control of fermentation. In chapter 8, these procedures are applied to specific formulas.

**After reading this chapter, you should be able to:**

1. List and describe the twelve basic steps in the production of yeast goods.

2. Explain the three basic mixing methods used for yeast doughs.

3. Understand and control the factors affecting dough fermentation.

4. Recognize and correct faults in yeast products.

# YEAST PRODUCT TYPES

Although all yeast doughs are made according to the same basic principles, it is useful to divide yeast products into categories such as the following.

## Lean Dough Products

A *lean dough* is one that is low in fat and sugar.

- Hard-crusted breads and rolls, including French and Italian breads, kaiser rolls and other hard rolls, and pizza. These are the leanest of all bread products.

- Other white and whole wheat breads and dinner rolls. These have a higher fat and sugar content and sometimes also contain eggs and milk solids. Because they are slightly richer, they generally have soft crusts.

- Breads made with other grains. Rye breads are the most common. Many varieties of rye bread are produced, with light or dark flours or with pumpernickel flour, and with various flavorings, especially molasses and caraway seeds.

## Rich Dough Products

There is no exact dividing line between rich and lean doughs but, in general, *rich doughs* are those that contain higher proportions of fat, sugar, and sometimes eggs.

- Nonsweet breads and rolls, including rich dinner rolls and brioche. These have a high fat content, but their sugar content is low enough to allow them to be served as dinner breads. Brioche dough, made with a high proportion of butter and eggs, is especially rich.

- Sweet rolls, including coffee cakes and many breakfast and tea rolls. These have high fat and sugar content and usually contain eggs. They generally have a sweet filling or topping.

## Laminated or Rolled-In Yeast Dough Products

*Rolled-in doughs* or laminated doughs are those in which a fat is incorporated into the dough in many layers by using a rolling and folding procedure. The alternating layers of fat and dough give the baked product a flaky texture.

Laminated doughs vary in sugar content from about 4% for some croissant doughs to 15% or more for some Danish doughs. However, most of the sweetness of laminated yeast dough products comes from the fillings and toppings.

Croissant and Danish doughs are the main laminated yeast dough products. In general, Danish dough products contain eggs, while croissants do not, although there are exceptions to this rule.

---

### ❧ LAMINATED DOUGHS ❧

Laminated doughs—doughs that consist of many layers of fat sandwiched between layers of dough—include yeast-leavened doughs, such as Danish and croissant doughs, and doughs that contain no yeast but rather are leavened by steam and air only, namely, the various types of puff pastry.

Because the procedure for enclosing the fat and rolling and folding the dough to increase the number of layers is similar for these two types of products, they are often discussed together in a pastry unit, separate from yeast doughs.

It is important to realize, however, that handling and making up yeast doughs is fundamentally different than handling and making up doughs for other pastries. Remember that fermentation continues in Danish dough while it is being rolled, folded, and made up. As a result, it handles differently from puff pastry, even though the steps in the rolling procedure are similar. Careless handling can easily result in overfermented doughs with decreased quality. Puff pastry, on the other hand, can be rolled and made up over a longer period without loss of quality, as can other pie and pastry doughs that contain no leavening agents. Including croissant and Danish doughs with other yeast-leavened doughs emphasizes the production principles and procedures that all yeast doughs have in common.

# YEAST DOUGH PRODUCTION

There are twelve basic steps in the production of yeast breads. These steps are generally applied to all yeast products, with variations depending on the particular product. In particular, many of the handcrafted artisan breads that have become popular require more complex procedures. These procedures are reserved for chapter 7, where we take the time to describe them fully. This chapter gives you the information you need to produce the conventional yeast formulas in chapters 8 and 9. To prepare the sourdough breads and some of the specialty items in chapter 8, you are advised to prepare by reading chapter 7.

| | |
|---|---|
| 1. Scaling ingredients | 7. Benching |
| 2. Mixing | 8. Makeup and panning |
| 3. Bulk fermentation | 9. Proofing |
| 4. Folding or punching | 10. Baking |
| 5. Scaling or portioning of dough | 11. Cooling |
| 6. Rounding | 12. Storing |

As you can see, mixing ingredients into a dough is only one part of a complex procedure.

This section describes each of these steps, including the basic procedures. In the next sections, dough making and fermentation are discussed in greater detail. Specific makeup procedures are included with the formulas in chapters 8 and 9.

## Scaling Ingredients

All ingredients must be weighed accurately.

Water, milk, and eggs may be measured by volume. They are scaled at 1 pint per pound (1 kg/L). However, it is more accurate to weigh these liquids (p. 20), especially if quantities are large. Procedures for weighing ingredients in the bakeshop are discussed in detail in chapter 2.

Special care must be taken when measuring spices and other ingredients used in very small quantities. This is particularly important with salt, which affects the rate of fermentation (p. 94).

## Mixing

Mixing yeast doughs has three main purposes:

- To combine all ingredients into a uniform, smooth dough.
- To distribute the yeast evenly throughout the dough.
- To develop the gluten.

The first half of chapter 5 is devoted to a detailed explanation of the mixing process for doughs and batters in general. This information is important for all dough products and should be reviewed as necessary. The following section contains additional information and procedures needed for the proper mixing of yeast doughs.

The three phases of mixing in the production of doughs and batters are described on page 100. During the first phase, flour and other dry ingredients are hydrated or combined with liquid ingredients. Bread bakers often refer to this phase as the ***pickup stage*** because the loose dry ingredients are gradually picked up and incorporated by the developing dough.

In the second phase, all the dry ingredients are hydrated and form a rough dough. Bakers call this the ***cleanup stage*** because the dough forms enough to pull away from (or clean up) the bowl into a compact mass.

In the development phase, the dough is further mixed and gluten is developed to the desired degree. Bakers often divide this phase into two stages, the ***initial development phase***, in which the dough still appears rough and undermixed, and the ***final development stage***, in which the gluten becomes smooth and elastic.

Three principal mixing methods are used for yeast doughs: the straight dough method, the modified straight dough method, and the sponge method (also called the *sponge-and-dough method*).

## Straight Dough Method

In its simplest form, the ***straight dough method***, also called the *direct dough method*, consists of only one step: Combine all ingredients in the mixing bowl and mix. With fresh yeast, many bakers make good-quality products using this procedure. However, the yeast may not be evenly distributed in the dough. It is therefore safer to mix the yeast separately with a little of the water. If active dry yeast is used, it is, of course, essential to mix the yeast with water before incorporating it in the dough.

Instant dry yeast, on the other hand, need not be blended with water for use because it is moistened and becomes active in the dough so quickly. The usual method for incorporating instant dry yeast is to mix it in dry form with the flour.

---

### Procedure: Straight Dough Mixing Method for Yeast Products

**1a.** In the mixing bowl that is to be used for mixing the dough, soften fresh yeast or active dry yeast in a little of the water.

Fresh yeast: Mix with about 2 times its weight in water, or more.

- Ideal water temperature: 100°F (38°C).

Active dry yeast: Mix with about 4 times its weight in water.

- Ideal water temperature: 105°F (40°C).

**1b.** If using instant dry yeast, mix it directly with the flour.

**2.** Add the flour to the mixing bowl.

**3.** Add the remaining ingredients to the top of the flour in the mixing bowl.

**4.** Mix to a smooth, developed dough.

---

## Modified Straight Dough Method

For rich sweet doughs, the straight dough method is modified to ensure even distribution of the fat and sugar. In this procedure, the fat, sugar, eggs, and flavorings are first blended until uniform before the dough is developed.

## Procedure: Modified Straight Dough Method

1. If using fresh or active dry yeast, soften the yeast in part of the liquid, using a separate container. If using instant dry yeast, mix it with the flour.

2. Combine the fat, sugar, salt, milk solids, and flavorings and mix until well combined, but do not whip until light.

3. Add the eggs gradually, as fast as they are absorbed.

4. Add the liquid and mix briefly.

5. Add the flour and yeast. Mix to a smooth dough.

## Sponge Method

Sponge doughs are prepared in two stages. For this reason, the procedure is often called the *sponge-and-dough method*. This procedure gives the yeast action a head start.

The first stage is called a **sponge**, a **yeast starter**, or a **yeast pre-ferment**. All of these terms mean the same thing. Pre-ferments are discussed in more detail in chapter 7.

There are many variations of the **sponge method**, so the steps indicated in the procedure here are general. Variations on the sponge method are discussed in more detail in chapter 7 because they play an important part in the production of artisan breads. The procedure given on this page, however, will enable you to prepare the conventional sponge doughs in this book.

A note on the system of bakers' percentages (p. 24) is needed here. There are two possible ways to express percentages when using a sponge:

1. Consider the sponge or pre-ferment as a separate formula. Express the flour in the sponge as 100%. Then, in the main formula, express the total weight of the sponge as a percentage of the flour weight in the main formula.

2. Consider the sponge as part of the main formula. Express the flour in the sponge as a percentage of the total flour in the complete formula.

Each method has advantages, and bakers have their own preferences. In this book, both methods are used, depending on the formula, so you can have experience working with each.

## Procedure: Sponge Method

1. Combine part or all of the liquid, all of the yeast, and part of the flour (and, sometimes, part of the sugar). Mix into a thick batter or soft dough. Let ferment until double in bulk.

2. Fold (punch down) and add the rest of the flour and the remaining ingredients. Mix to a uniform, smooth dough.

## Mixing Times and Speeds

The first two purposes of mixing—combining the ingredients into a dough and distributing the yeast—are accomplished during the first part of this step. The remaining time is necessary to develop the gluten. Overmixed and undermixed doughs have poor volume and texture (review "Mixing and Gluten Development," p. 100).

Mixing times given in formulas in this book are *guidelines only*. You must learn to tell by sight and feel when a dough is thoroughly mixed. This can be done only through experience. A properly developed dough feels smooth and elastic. A lean dough should not be sticky.

The **windowpane test** is a good indication of complete and proper gluten development. To apply the test, take a small ball of the developed dough and

Windowpane test for gluten development.

stretch it as shown in the photo. It should form a thin, translucent membrane. Please note that this test works best for standard white breads. Whole-grain doughs do not form a gluten window because the particles of bran break or interfere with the gluten strands. Also, many sourdoughs do not easily form a gluten window because the acidity of the dough affects the gluten.

Mixing speeds in formulas should be taken as guidelines rather than as firm instructions. Small mixers, whose motors and gears are not as strong as those of larger mixers, can be damaged if they are run at too high a speed with stiff bread doughs. In such cases, a lower speed than the one indicated in the formula should be used. For the same reason, batches of stiff dough should be kept small. Too large a batch puts excessive strain on the machine.

Follow the recommendations of the mixer manufacturer with regard to mixing times and batch sizes; manufacturers' recommendations should take priority over the instructions in this book. If a slower speed is used, extend the mixing time as necessary to obtain a properly mixed dough. Depending on the mixer, developing a dough at first or slow speed requires approximately twice as much time as at second speed.

Rich doughs are generally undermixed slightly because a greater tenderness is desired for these products. Rye breads are also mixed less because of their weaker gluten, which tears easily.

Overmixing is a common error in bread making. Gluten that is developed too long stretches nearly as far as it can and loses its elasticity. Then it tears instead of stretches, and molding is more difficult. The texture and volume of overmixed products are less desirable.

Salt, used in proper quantities, helps alleviate this problem because it makes gluten stronger and more elastic.

## Procedure for Fermenting Yeast Dough

Place the dough in a container large enough to allow for expansion of the dough. Cover the container and let the dough rise at a temperature of about 80°F (27°C) or at the temperature indicated in the specific formula. Ideally, the fermentation temperature is the same as the temperature of the dough when it is taken from the mixer. Fermentation should be in an environment of high humidity, or the fermenting dough should be kept covered to avoid drying or crusting.

If proper containers are not available or if humidity is too low to prevent a crust from forming on the dough, you may oil the surface of the dough lightly.

Fermentation times indicated in formulas are general guidelines only. Fermentation is complete when the dough is doubled in volume. A dent remains or fills very slowly after the fingers are pressed lightly into the top of the dough if fermentation is complete. If the dough springs back, fermentation is not complete.

# Bulk Fermentation

**Fermentation** is the process by which yeast acts on the sugars and starches in the dough to produce carbon dioxide gas ($CO_2$) and alcohol. The action of the yeast is described in chapter 4 (p. 83).

Gluten becomes smoother and more elastic during fermentation, so it stretches farther and holds more gas. An underfermented dough will not develop proper volume, and the texture of the product will be coarse. A dough that ferments too long or at too high a temperature becomes sticky, hard to work, and slightly sour. An underfermented dough is called a **young dough**. An overfermented dough is called an **old dough**.

Doughs with weak gluten, such as rye doughs and rich doughs, are usually underfermented or "taken to the bench young."

Yeast action continues until the yeast cells are killed when the temperature of the dough reaches 140°F (60°C) in the oven. It is important to be aware that fermentation continues during the next steps in yeast dough production—punching, scaling, rounding, benching, and makeup or molding. *Failure to allow for this time may result in overfermented doughs.* Doughs that are to be made into rolls and loaves requiring a great deal of makeup time should be slightly underfermented to prevent the dough from being too old by the time makeup is complete.

More detailed information on dough making and on controlling fermentation is given in the sections beginning on page 122.

# Folding or Punching

After fermentation is completed, the dough is folded over to compress it and to give additional slight development to the gluten. This step accomplishes four objectives:

- It expels carbon dioxide.
- It redistributes the yeast for further growth.
- It relaxes the gluten.
- It equalizes the temperature throughout the dough.

Folding the dough after bulk fermentation is traditionally called **punching**, but some bakers dislike this term because it misleadingly suggests the process involves simply hitting the dough with the fist. This is not the case.

For some products, additional bulk fermentation and folding may be required after this step, although most breads need only one bulk fermentation period.

Large quantities of dough are more easily folded on a workbench, although small batches can easily be folded in the bowl or container in which they are fermented. Both methods are described in the procedure at the right.

# Scaling or Portioning Dough

Using a baker's scale, divide the dough into pieces of the same weight, according to the product being made.

During scaling, allowance is made for weight loss due to evaporation of moisture in the oven. This weight loss is approximately 10 to 13% of the weight of the dough. Allow an extra 1½ to 2 ounces dough for each 1 pound baked bread, or 50 to 65 g per 500 g.

Actual baking loss depends on baking time, size of the unit, and whether it is baked in a pan or freestanding.

Scaling should be done rapidly and efficiently to avoid overfermenting the dough.

If a dough divider is used to make rolls, the dough is scaled into presses, which are then divided into 36 equal pieces (see p. 44). For example, if 1⅓-ounce rolls are desired, the presses should be scaled at 3 pounds (36 × 1⅓ oz), plus 6 ounces to allow for baking loss. Presses are rounded, relaxed, and divided; the divided units may or may not be rounded again, depending on the product.

## Procedure for Folding Dough

### Method 1: On Workbench

1. Dust the workbench with flour and turn out the fermented dough onto the bench so the top side is down.

2. Grasp the dough on one side, pull up (a), and fold over the center so about one-third of the dough mass is folded over.

3. Press down on the folded portion to expel gases (b).

4. Brush dusting flour from the top of the dough (c) so it doesn't become folded into the dough, which would make streaks in the finished bread.

5. Repeat steps 2 through 4 on the remaining three sides (d).

6. Turn the dough over so the seams are on the bottom. Lift the dough and return it to the dough container.

### Method 2: In the Dough Container

1. Pull up the dough on one side, fold it over the center, and press down.

2. Repeat on the remaining sides of the dough.

3. Turn the dough upside down in the container.

# Rounding

After scaling, the pieces of dough are shaped into smooth, round balls. This procedure forms a kind of skin by stretching the gluten on the outside of the dough into a smooth layer. **Rounding** simplifies the later shaping of the dough and also helps retain gases produced by the yeast.

Your instructor will demonstrate rounding techniques. Machines are also available that divide and round portions of dough automatically.

# Benching, Bench Proofing, or Intermediate Proofing

Rounded portions of dough are allowed to rest for 10 to 20 minutes. This relaxes the gluten to make shaping the dough easier. Also, fermentation continues during this time.

In large operations, the rounded dough is placed in special proofers for this rest. Smaller operations place the dough in boxes that are stacked on one another to keep the dough covered. Or the dough may simply be placed on the workbench and covered—hence the term **benching** or bench rest.

# Makeup and Panning

The dough is shaped into loaves or rolls and then placed in pans or on baking sheets. **Hearth breads**—breads baked directly on the bottom of the oven—may be placed in floured baskets or other molds after makeup.

Proper makeup or molding is of critical importance to the finished baked product. All gas bubbles should be expelled during molding. Bubbles left in the dough will result in large air holes in the baked product.

For both pan breads and hearth breads, the seam must be centered on the bottom to avoid splitting during baking. For units baked in pans, the pan size must be matched to the weight of the dough. Too little or too much dough will result in a poorly shaped loaf.

Breads and rolls take a great many forms. Many shapes and techniques are presented in chapters 8 and 9.

# Proofing

**Proofing** is a continuation of the process of yeast fermentation that increases the volume of the shaped dough. Bakers use two terms so they can distinguish between fermentation of the mixed dough and proofing of the made-up product before baking. Proofing temperatures are generally higher than fermentation temperatures.

Underproofing results in poor volume and dense texture. Overproofing results in coarse texture and some loss of flavor.

French bread is generally given a long proof to create its characteristic open texture. Its strong gluten withstands the extra stretching of a long proof.

Rich doughs are slightly underproofed because their weaker gluten structure does not withstand too much stretching.

---

## Procedure for Proofing Yeast Dough Items

1. For lean yeast doughs, place the made-up products in a proof box at 80° to 85°F (27° to 30°C) and 70 to 80% humidity, or as indicated in the formula. Proof until double in bulk.

   Rich doughs, especially rolled-in doughs, are usually proofed at a lower temperature (77°F or 25°C) so the butter does not melt out of the dough.

   Avoid using too much humidity. This weakens the surface of the dough and causes uneven proofing.

   If a proof box is not available, come as close to these conditions as you can by covering the products to retain moisture and setting them in a warm place.

2. Test-proof by sight (the unit doubles in bulk) and by touch. When touched *lightly*, properly proofed dough springs back slowly. If it is still firm and elastic, it needs more proofing. If the dent remains in the dough, the dough is probably overproofed.

# Baking

As you recall from chapter 5, many changes take place in the dough during baking. If necessary, review pages 104–106. The most important changes are:

1. **Oven spring**, which is the rapid rising in the oven due to production and expansion of trapped gases as a result of the oven heat. The yeast is very active at first but is killed when the temperature inside the dough reaches 140°F (60°C).

2. Coagulation of proteins and gelatinization of starches. In other words, the product becomes firm and holds its shape.

3. Formation and browning of the crust.

In order to control the baking process, the following factors should be considered.

## Oven Temperature and Baking Time

Temperatures must be adjusted for the product being baked. At the proper temperature, the inside of the unit becomes completely baked at the same time the crust achieves the desired color. Therefore:

1. Large units are baked at a lower temperature and for a longer time than small rolls spaced apart.

2. Rich doughs and sweet doughs are baked at a lower temperature because their fat, sugar, and milk content makes them brown faster.

3. French breads made with no added sugar and a long fermentation require very high temperatures to achieve the desired crust color.

   ♦ Popular American lean breads are baked at 400° to 425°F (205° to 220°C).

   ♦ Some French breads are baked at 425° to 475°F (220° to 245°C).

   ♦ Rich products are baked at 350° to 400°F (175° to 205°C).

A golden-brown crust color is the normal indication of doneness. Loaves that are done sound hollow when thumped.

## Washes

Many, if not most, yeast products are brushed with a liquid, called a **wash**, just before baking. The most common washes are as follows:

1. *Water* is used primarily for hard-crusted products, such as French bread. Like steam in the oven (see below), the water helps keep the crust from drying too quickly and thus becoming too thick.

2. *Starch paste* is used primarily for rye breads. In addition to keeping the crust from drying too quickly, the starch paste helps give a shine to the crust.

   To make a starch paste, mix 1 ounce light rye flour with 1 quart water (60 g rye per 500 mL water). Bring to a boil while stirring. Cool. If necessary, thin with water to the consistency of cream.

3. *Egg wash* is used to give a shiny brown crust to soft breads and rolls and to rich doughs and Danish. It is made by mixing beaten eggs with water or, sometimes, milk. Proportions vary greatly depending on how strong a wash is desired.

4. *Commercial aerosol washes (sprays)* provide a quick and easy way to give shine and also to help toppings such as seeds adhere.

Photo taken at Turtle Bread Company

Baker's lames

Photo taken at Turtle Bread Company

## Cutting or Scoring

A break on the side of the loaf is caused by continued rising after the crust is formed. To allow for this expansion, the tops of hard-crusted breads are cut before baking. Slashes are made on the top of the loaf with a baker's *lame* (lahm; French for "blade," a curved or straight razor blade attached to a handle) or other sharp knife or razor immediately before it is put into the oven, as shown in the figure. The pattern created by the cuts also contributes to the appearance of the bread.

Small rolls often bake completely without a break, so they are usually cut for the sake of appearance only.

*Note:* The term *docking* is often used for this procedure. However, many bakers feel this term should be reserved for a different process—namely, the piercing or perforating of pastry and pie doughs. To avoid confusion, this book uses the terms *cutting* and *scoring* for the slashing of bread crusts, but you should be aware of the other term because you will hear it used.

## Loading the Ovens

Proofed doughs are fragile until they become set by baking. They should be handled carefully when being loaded into the ovens, and they should not be disturbed during the first part of baking.

Breads and rolls are baked either directly on the bottom of the oven (hearth breads) or in pans.

1. **Hearth breads.** To load the ovens, place the proofed units on a peel that is well dusted with cornmeal. Slide the peel into the oven. Then, with a quick snap, remove the peel, leaving the loaves or rolls in place. To remove baked items, quickly slide the peel under them and pull them out. The illustration shows a peel in use.

2. **Pan breads and rolls.** Freestanding items may be baked on sheet pans instead of on the hearth. Bakers generally refer to such breads and rolls as *hearth breads* even if they are not baked directly on the bottom of the oven. Sprinkle the pans with cornmeal to keep the units from sticking and to simulate the appearance of hearth-baked items. Pans may also be lined with silicone paper. Perforated sheet pans or screens are also available. These allow better air circulation and therefore permit more even browning.

   Sandwich loaves and other pan breads are, of course, baked in loaf pans or other appropriate pans. Details are given in the makeup section of chapter 8.

## Steam

Hard-crusted breads are baked with steam injected into the ovens during the first part of the baking period. Rye breads also benefit from baking with steam for the first 10 minutes.

The steam helps keep the crust soft during the first part of baking so the bread can expand rapidly and evenly without cracking or breaking. If steam were not used, the crust would begin forming earlier and thus would become thick and heavy. Also, crust that forms too early is likely to split as the interior continues to expand. The steam also helps distribute the heat in the oven, further aiding oven spring. When the moisture of the steam reacts with the starches on the surface, some of the starches form dextrins. Then, when the steam is withdrawn, these dextrins, along with sugars in the dough, caramelize and turn brown. The result is a thin, crisp, glazed crust.

Rich doughs, those with higher fat or sugar content, do not form crisp crusts and are usually baked without steam.

## Cooling

After baking, bread must be removed from the pans and cooled on racks to allow the escape of the excess moisture and alcohol created during fermentation.

Small rolls spaced on baking sheets are often cooled on the pans when air circulation is adequate. On the other hand, if condensation is likely to make the bottoms of the rolls soggy, it is better to cool them on racks.

If soft crusts are desired, breads may be brushed with melted shortening before cooling.

Do not cool bread in a draft because the crust may crack.

Like other dough products, breads continue to undergo physical and chemical changes after they are removed from the oven. Review page 107 for a summary of these changes.

## Storing

Breads to be served within 8 hours may be left on racks. For longer storage, wrap cooled breads in moistureproof bags to retard staling. Bread must be thoroughly cool before wrapping, or moisture will collect inside the bags.

Wrapping and freezing maintains quality for longer periods. Refrigeration, on the other hand, increases staling.

Hard-crusted breads should not be wrapped (unless frozen) because the crusts will soften and become leathery. Alternatively, use porous bags or wrapping material that protects the bread from contamination but allows moisture to escape.

# TYPES OF DOUGH-MAKING PROCESSES

## Straight Dough

In the typical small retail shop, most breads are mixed by the straight dough method—that is, all ingredients are mixed in one operation, as described on page 114. The dough is then given a bulk fermentation time (that is, until molding and proofing) of 1 to 2½ hours. This is called a **short-fermentation straight dough**.

A **no-time dough** is made with a large quantity of yeast, preferably instant dry yeast, taken from the mixer at a higher temperature (up to 90°F/32°C) and given only a few minutes' rest before being scaled and made up. It is also given a shorter proof. This process should be used only in emergencies because the final product does not have a good texture and flavor.

**Long-fermentation doughs** are fermented for 5 or 6 hours or longer, sometimes overnight, at a temperature of 75°F (24°C) or lower. During this time, it is usually advisable to fold or punch the dough several times. The advantage of this method is that the long, slow fermentation greatly enhances the flavor of the product. Some of the best European breads are made this way. The major disadvantage—besides being harder on the work schedule—is that the fermentation is harder to control because of fluctuations in temperature and other factors. Doughs often become overfermented. In spite of this disadvantage, long fermentation has been revived with the interest in artisan breads (see chapter 7).

To avoid the problems of a long-fermentation straight dough but achieve the flavor created by a long fermentation, one can use the sponge method.

### Sponge Processes

The sponge process involves a two-stage mixing method, as described on page 115. First, a sponge is made of water, flour, and yeast and allowed to ferment. Then the dough is made by mixing in the remaining ingredients. The finished dough may be given a short fermentation, or, if the sponge has had a long fermentation, it may be scaled immediately, like a no-time dough.

### Advantages of the Sponge Method

- Shorter fermentation time for the finished dough.

- Scheduling flexibility. Sponges can usually be held longer than finished dough.

- Increased flavor, developed by the long fermentation of the sponge.

- Stronger fermentation of rich doughs. High sugar and fat content inhibits yeast growth. When the sponge method is used, most of the fermentation is complete before the fat and sugar are incorporated.

- Less yeast is needed, because it multiplies during the sponge fermentation.

# CONTROLLING FERMENTATION

Proper fermentation—that is, fermentation that produces a dough that is neither underripe (young) nor overripe (old)—requires a balance of time, temperature, and yeast quantity.

## Time

Fermentation times vary, so the time to punch the dough is indicated not by clock but by the appearance and feel of the dough. Fermentation times given in the formulas in this book are guidelines only.

To vary the fermentation time, you must control the dough temperature and the amount of yeast.

## Temperature

Ideally, dough is fermented at the temperature at which it is taken from the mixer. Large bakeries have special fermentation rooms for controlling temperature and humidity, but small bakeshops and restaurant kitchens seldom have this luxury. If a short-fermentation process is used, however, the fermentation is complete before the dough is greatly affected by changes in shop temperature.

### Water Temperature

Dough must be at the proper temperature, usually 78° to 80°F (25.5° to 26.7°C), in order to ferment at the desired rate. The temperature of the dough is affected by several factors:

- ◆ Shop temperature.

- ◆ Flour temperature.

- ◆ Water temperature.

Of these, water temperature is the easiest to control in the small bakeshop. Therefore, when the water is scaled, it should be brought to the required temperature. On cold days, it may have to be warmed, and on hot days, using a mixture of crushed ice and water may be necessary. Also, if a long fermentation is used, the dough temperature must be reduced in order to avoid overfermenting.

## Procedure for Determining Water Temperature

1. Multiply the desired dough temperature by 3.

2. Add together the flour temperature and room temperature, plus 20°F (11°C) to allow for the friction caused by mixing (see *Note*).

3. Subtract the result of step 2 from that of step 1. The difference is the required water temperature.

   Example: Dough temperature needed = 80°F

   Flour temperature = 68°F

   Room temperature = 72°F

   Machine friction = 20°F

   Water temperature = ?

1. $80° \times 3 = 240°$
2. $68° + 72° + 20° = 160°$
3. $240° - 160° = 80°$

Therefore, the water temperature should be 80°F.

*Note:* This procedure is precise enough for most purposes in the small bakeshop. However, there are other complications, such as variations in machine friction, that you may want to consider if you wish to be even more exact. To make these calculations, see appendix 5.

## Yeast Quantity

If other conditions are constant, the fermentation time may be increased or decreased by decreasing or increasing the quantity of yeast (see procedure below). In general, use no more yeast than is needed. Excessive yeast results in inferior flavor.

## Procedure for Modifying Yeast Quantities

1. Determine a factor by dividing the old fermentation time by the fermentation time desired.

2. Multiply this factor by the original quantity of yeast to determine the new quantity.

   $$\frac{\text{Old fermentation time}}{\text{New fermentation time}} \times \frac{\text{old yeast}}{\text{quantity}} = \frac{\text{new yeast}}{\text{quantity}}$$

   Example: A formula requiring 12 oz yeast has a fermentation time of 2 hours at 80°F. How much

yeast is needed to reduce the fermentation time to 1½ hours?

$$\frac{2 \text{ hours}}{1\frac{1}{2} \text{ hours}} \times 12 \text{ oz yeast} = 16 \text{ oz yeast}$$

*Caution:* This procedure should be used within narrow limits only. An excessive increase or decrease in yeast quantities introduces many other problems and results in inferior products.

### Small Batches

When very small quantities of dough—only a few pounds—are made, the dough is more likely to be affected by shop temperature. Thus, it may be necessary to slightly increase the yeast quantity in cool weather and slightly decrease it in hot weather.

## Other Factors

The salt in the formula, the minerals in the water, and the use of dough conditioners or improvers affect the rate of fermentation. See page 94 for a discussion of salt and its effect on fermentation.

Water that is excessively soft lacks the minerals that ensure proper gluten development and dough fermentation. On the other hand, water that is very hard—that is, has high mineral content and, as a result, is alkaline—also inhibits the development of the dough. These conditions are more of a problem for lean doughs than for rich doughs. In most localities, small bakeshops can overcome these problems with the proper use of salt or, in areas with alkaline water, by adding a very small amount of a mild acid to the water. Dough conditioners, buffers, and improvers that can correct these conditions are available from bakers' suppliers. Their use should be determined by local water conditions.

The richness of the dough must also be considered. Doughs high in fat or sugar ferment more slowly than lean doughs. This problem can be avoided by using a sponge instead of a straight dough.

## Retarding

*Retarding* means slowing the fermentation or proof of yeast doughs by refrigeration. This may be done in regular refrigerators or in special retarders that maintain a high humidity. If regular refrigerators are used, the product must be covered to prevent drying and the formation of a skin.

### Retarded Fermentation

Dough to be retarded in bulk is usually given partial fermentation. It is then flattened on sheet pans, covered with plastic wrap, and placed in the retarder. The layer of dough must not be too thick because the inside will take too long to chill and thus will overferment. When needed, the dough is allowed to warm before molding. Some doughs high in fat are made up while chilled so they do not become too soft.

### Retarded Proof

Made-up units to be retarded are made from young dough. After makeup, they are immediately placed in the retarder. When needed, they are allowed to warm and finish their proof, if necessary. They are then baked.

A valuable laborsaving tool for medium to large bakeshops is the **retarder-proofer**. As the name suggests, this equipment is a combination of freezer/retarder and proofer, with thermostats for both functions and with timers to automate the process. For example, the baker can make up a batch of rolls in the afternoon or evening and place them in the retarder-proofer with the controls set for retarding or freezing. The baker sets the timer for the proper hour the following morning. The machine automatically begins to raise the temperature, proofing the rolls so they are ready to bake in time for breakfast.

# BREAD FAULTS AND THEIR CAUSES

Because of the complexity of bread production, many things can go wrong. To remedy common bread faults, check the following troubleshooting guide for possible causes and correct your procedures.

| FAULT | CAUSES |
|---|---|
| **SHAPE** | |
| Poor volume | Too much salt |
| | Too little yeast |
| | Too little liquid |
| | Weak flour |
| | Under- or overmixing |
| | Oven too hot |
| Too much volume | Too little salt |
| | Too much yeast |
| | Too much dough scaled |
| | Overproofed |
| Poor shape | Too much liquid |
| | Flour too weak |
| | Improper molding or makeup |
| | Improper fermentation or proofing |
| | Too much oven steam |
| Split or burst crust | Overmixing |
| | Underfermented dough |
| | Improper molding—seam not on bottom |
| | Uneven heat in oven |
| | Oven too hot |
| | Insufficient steam |
| **FLAVOR** | |
| Flat taste | Too little salt |
| Poor flavor | Inferior, spoiled, or rancid ingredients |
| | Poor bakeshop sanitation |
| | Under- or overfermented |

| FAULT | CAUSES |
|---|---|
| **TEXTURE AND CRUMB** | |
| Too dense or close-grained | Too much salt |
| | Too little liquid |
| | Too little yeast |
| | Underfermented |
| | Underproofed |
| Too coarse or open | Too much yeast |
| | Too much liquid |
| | Incorrect mixing time |
| | Improper fermentation |
| | Overproofed |
| | Pan too large |
| Streaked crumb | Improper mixing procedure |
| | Poor molding or makeup techniques |
| | Too much flour used for dusting |
| Poor texture or crumbly | Flour too weak |
| | Too little salt |
| | Fermentation time too long or too short |
| | Overproofed |
| | Baking temperature too low |
| Gray crumb | Fermentation time or temperature too high |
| **CRUST** | |
| Too dark | Too much sugar or milk |
| | Underfermented dough |
| | Oven temperature too high |
| | Baking time too long |
| | Insufficient steam at beginning of baking |
| Too pale | Too little sugar or milk |
| | Overfermented dough |
| | Overproofed |
| | Oven temperature too low |
| | Baking time too short |
| | Too much steam in oven |
| Too thick | Too little sugar or fat |
| | Improper fermentation |
| | Baked too long or at wrong temperature |
| | Too little steam |
| Blisters on crust | Too much liquid |
| | Improper fermentation |
| | Improper shaping of loaf |

# TERMS FOR REVIEW

| | | | |
|---|---|---|---|
| lean dough | sponge | punching | straight dough |
| rich dough | yeast starter | rounding | no-time dough |
| rolled-in dough | yeast pre-ferment | benching | long-fermentation dough |
| pickup stage | sponge method | hearth breads | retarding |
| cleanup stage | windowpane test | proofing | retarder-proofer |
| initial development phase | fermentation | overn spring | |
| final development phase | young dough | wash | |
| straight dough method | old dough | short-fermentation | |

# QUESTIONS FOR DISCUSSION

1. What are the main differences in ingredients between French bread and white sandwich bread?

2. Why is Danish pastry dough flaky?

3. What are the twelve steps in the production of yeast products? Explain each briefly.

4. What are the three major purposes of mixing yeast doughs?

5. Explain the differences in procedure between the straight dough method and the sponge method. How is the straight dough method sometimes modified for sweet doughs, and why is this necessary?

6. What are the purposes of punching a fermented dough?

7. How much French bread dough will you need if you want to make 16 loaves that weigh 12 ounces each after baking?

8. List four advantages of the sponge method for mixing bread doughs.

9. What is the importance of water temperature in mixing yeast doughs?

# 7

# Understanding Artisan Breads

C onsumer interest in flavorful, handmade breads has grown tremendously in recent years. In North America, this has stimulated bakers to research and experiment with traditional European breads in order to offer their customers distinctive, handcrafted products. More and more restaurants are either making their own breads on the premises or purchasing from local bakers who practice baking more as a craft than as an industry. Many fine European bakeries have preserved and practiced these techniques for generations, but to most practitioners in North America, they are new discoveries.

In chapter 6, you learned the basic procedures for producing conventional yeast products of many types. These principles and techniques hold true for artisan breads as well, but additional complexities must be understood before you can produce fine sourdoughs and other artisan breads.

**After reading this chapter, you should be able to:**

1. Select flour for making artisan breads.

2. Prepare yeast pre-ferments.

3. Prepare and maintain a sourdough starter.

4. Mix bread doughs using the technique called *autolyse*.

5. Bake artisan breads properly.

# WHAT IS ARTISAN BREAD?

*Artisan bread* has many definitions. Most of the possible definitions include expressions like *homemade, handmade, made in small quantities, lacking in preservatives,* and *using traditional techniques.* But for every definition, it is possible to find exceptions. Clearly, those terms don't completely define what we understand to be artisan breads or separate them from conventional breads. After all, every bread formula in this book can be made by hand in small quantities, yet many of them would not be considered artisan. At the same time, commercial bakeries use machines to transform thousands of pounds of flour a day into high-quality breads that nearly anyone would call artisan, or that at least have all the eating qualities of artisan breads. Furthermore, now that supermarket chains are selling mass-produced loaves with *artisan* on the label, the word is harder than ever to define, if not impossible.

The dictionary defines an *artisan* as a "skilled manual worker, a craftsperson." An artisan bread, then, is one made by hand by a skilled baker. This is a good start, but it is not precise. Another definition sometimes given is that artisan breads are made using traditional methods. This is also important, but we still must determine what is meant by *traditional methods.* We may not be able to come up with a definition of artisan bread that satisfies everyone, but we can list the characteristics that, according to many bakers, should be present.

**Handmade.** This is the characteristic most closely related to the dictionary definition of *artisan.* Does this mean that machinery cannot be used at all? A home baker can make bread from start to finish without machinery, but clearly it would be difficult for a bakery to produce enough bread to be commercially viable without using even a mixer. Some form of machinery is used in virtually every baking operation. Nevertheless, hand work plays an important role in artisan production, and the manual skill and judgment of the artisan baker are essential. By necessity, then, artisan bread production is usually small-scale, not high-volume. Making artisan bread is not an automatic or purely mechanical process.

**Use of pre-ferments and sourdough or culture starters.** A *pre-ferment* is a fermented dough or batter used to provide leavening for a larger batch of dough. The discussion of the sponge mixing method in the previous chapter introduced the subject of pre-ferments. As we learned, one advantage of using a sponge is that it creates more flavor by means of a long, slow fermentation. A sourdough starter is similar to a yeast pre-ferment, except it uses wild yeast instead of commercial yeast. Pre-ferments and sourdough starters are discussed in more detail in this chapter.

**No chemical additives or preservatives.** The classic artisan bread is a crisp-crusted bread that contains nothing but flour, water, and salt, and it is leavened either by wild yeast (sourdough) or commercial yeast. Other ingredients may be added for specialty breads, including dough ingredients such as milk, eggs, and butter, and add-ins such as herbs, spices, nuts, dried fruit, and olives. But all ingredients should be recognizable by the consumer as familiar food items.

**Traditional production methods.** Bread has been made for centuries without the use of machinery except, of course, ovens, and until recently those ovens were wood-fired. Today's artisan bakers try to duplicate as much as possible these traditional methods. As already noted, at least part of the production should be by hand, even if mixers are used to make the dough. Bakers also seek out flours similar to those used for old-fashioned European breads, most notably flours with slightly lower protein content and higher ash (see p. 60). Also, because the fermentation process is so important for flavor, doughs are usually fermented for longer times at lower temperatures, often without the use of proof boxes. Hearth ovens or deck ovens are invariably used, and some bakeries have even installed wood-fired hearth ovens for their breads.

## FLOUR

As any chef knows, choosing high-quality ingredients is an important part of cooking the finest dishes. Unlike the cook in the kitchen, however, the bread baker has few ingredients to worry about. Flour, of course, is the baker's main ingredient, so the quality of flour in the bakeshop affects nearly all the baker's products, and especially bread.

One of the great inspirations for bread bakers today is the late Lionel Poilâne, whose famous breads were shipped around the world. Poilâne was particular about his selection of flours, insisting on using only organically grown wheat that conformed to his exacting specifications. Today's artisan bakers, in North America as well as Europe, are following his lead and seeking out the best organic flours, often made from wheat grown in small quantities.

As we have said, artisan bread bakers in North America often try to replicate the traditional breads of France and other European countries, so they look for flour that is similar to European flours. This means, first of all, flour with a protein content around 11.5% rather than the 12.5% common to North American bread flours.

Keep in mind that lower protein content means a lower absorption ratio (p. 60). This means that if you are substituting a lower-protein flour in a formula in which you have always used a higher-protein patent flour, you must use less liquid in order to get the same dough consistency. Whenever you change flours, it is best to test a small batch to see how the new flour performs.

Second, while North American straight flours are about 72% extraction (see p. 58), artisan breads are often made with higher-extraction flour, anywhere from 77 to 90%. This means the flour is darker and has a higher ash content, resulting in fuller flavor. In addition, the higher mineral content is beneficial to the long, slow fermentations favored for artisan breads. If it is not possible to find such flours, they can be approximated in two ways. The easier way is to mix a little whole wheat flour with the white flour. A more laborious way, but one that gives a closer approximation to a high-extraction flour, is to sift whole wheat flour through a fine sieve to remove the coarse flakes of bran. You can save the bran for another use.

## PRE-FERMENTS AND SOURDOUGH STARTERS

Chapter 6 introduced the subject of pre-ferments (also spelled preferments) with its discussion of the sponge method of bread mixing. Pre-ferments give the fermentation a strong head start, and they contribute to flavor by extending the fermentation period. In addition, the use of pre-ferments allows the baker to reduce or eliminate the amount of commercial yeast used. Third, short-fermentation straight doughs may be difficult to handle, requiring the use of dough conditioners and other additives. Pre-ferments, on the other hand, naturally improve the dough texture, making it easier to work without resorting to additives.

There are two basic types of pre-ferments: *yeast pre-ferments*, sometimes called *yeast starters*, and *sourdough pre-ferments*, usually called *sourdough starters* or *natural starters*. (Note that some bakers use the term *pre-ferment* only for yeast starters. In this book, we use the term generically for any fermented dough used to provide leavening.)

Sourdough starters are similar to yeast pre-ferments except they are made with wild yeasts. As a result, they are handled somewhat differently. These starters are "sour" because of the acidity created in the dough during the long fermentation. This acidity affects not only the flavor of the bread but also the texture. The starches and proteins are modified by the acids, resulting in a moister crumb and better keeping qualities.

Note that some sourdough cultures produce only a mild acidity, resulting in a bread that does not taste particularly sour (see the discussion of bacterial fermentation on page 134). The term *sourdough*, however, is commonly used for wild cultures of any degree of acidity. Some bakers prefer the terms *levain* (p. 133) or *culture starter* to describe this category, reserving *sourdough* for those cultures with a strong acidity only.

# Yeast Pre-Ferments

The basics of yeast pre-ferments were introduced in chapter 6 in the discussion of the sponge mixing method (p. 115). The general procedure outlined there is applicable to any pre-ferment. However, additional information is useful to the baker of artisan breads because pre-ferments are subject to many variations.

Many traditional terms are used for types of pre-ferment. Unfortunately, the terminology is not used consistently. Some of the terms are introduced here, but you may find that some bakers use them in different ways. As artisan breads become more common, these terms will probably become more standardized. Even the word *sponge* is used in different ways. As used by this book and by many bakers, a sponge is any yeast pre-ferment. Other bakers use the word *sponge* only for a thin, batterlike pre-ferment.

Unlike sourdoughs, which can last indefinitely, yeast starters have a limited life and are best made fresh for each new batch of dough. Overfermented yeast pre-ferments should be discarded because a dough made from them will not handle well, and the bread will have undesirable flavors.

The most important types of pre-ferments are noted in the following sections.

## *Poolish*

This type of starter is said to have originated in Poland, and the word **poolish** comes from "Polish." A poolish (or *poolisch*) is a thin yeast starter made with equal parts flour and water (by weight), plus commercial yeast. In other words, a formula for poolish is 100% flour, 100% water, and varying percentages of yeast, depending on the desired speed of fermentation.

To contribute maximum flavor, a poolish is made with only a small quantity of yeast and given a long fermentation at room temperature. The poolish bubbles up and increases in volume, and when it is at its peak, it starts to fall back slightly and the top surface appears wrinkled. A poolish given a slow fermentation may hold its peak quality for several hours. After this period, the acidity will increase and the quality will deteriorate.

If a shorter fermentation is needed, use more yeast. In this case, however, the starter will be at its peak of quality for a shorter time before it starts to deteriorate. See the table for yeast quantities and fermentation times.

## Yeast Quantities and Approximate Poolish Fermentation Times

| Quantity of fresh yeast (percent of flour used in poolish) | Quantity of dry yeast (percent of flour used in poolish) | Approximate fermentation time at room temperature (65°–68°F or 18°–20°F) |
|---|---|---|
| 3.5% | 1.4% | 2 hours |
| 2% | 0.8% | 4 hours |
| 1% | 0.4% | 8 hours |
| 0.5% | 0.2% | 12–16 hours |

## Biga

**Biga** is the Italian term for pre-ferment. Although the word can, in theory, refer to a starter of any consistency, it is usually used for stiff pre-ferments. Because stiffer doughs ferment more slowly than wet ones, a biga is generally made with more yeast. Use about 2 times the quantity of yeast as in a poolish to get the same fermentation time.

A typical biga contains 100% flour, 50 to 60% water, and about 1 to 1.5% fresh yeast.

## Levain-Levure

This is the general French term for yeast pre-ferment. It is usually stiff like a biga, but the term is sometimes used for thin pre-ferments like the poolish as well. The word **levure** means "yeast." Do not confuse **levain-levure** with the word *levain* alone. **Levain** means "sourdough" or "culture starter," and *pain au levain* means "sourdough bread."

## Scrap Dough

Scrap dough is simply a piece of fermented bread dough saved from a previous batch. It is sometimes known as **pâte fermentée** (pot fer mawn tay), meaning "fermented dough." Saving a piece of fermented dough, preferably in the retarder so it doesn't overferment, is an easy and common way to get the benefits of using a pre-ferment without having to make one separately. Of course, it is also possible to make a batch of bread dough just to use as a pre-ferment.

Because scrap dough is actually bread dough, it differs from other ferments in that it contains salt as well as flour, water, and yeast. The salt slows the fermentation. To balance the salt, a scrap dough contains more yeast than the other types of pre-ferments we have discussed.

When pure pre-ferments like the poolish and biga are used in bread, they are usually the only source of leavening. On the other hand, scrap dough is usually used in smaller quantities—that is, as a smaller proportion of the finished bread dough—and may not be strong enough to ferment the bread on its own. Yeast may be added in addition to the scrap dough when the final bread dough is mixed. In other words, such a bread dough is a straight dough (p. 121) to which scrap dough is added. This method, in which both a pre-ferment and a fresh addition of yeast are used to provide leavening, is sometimes called **mixed fermentation**.

# Sourdough Starters

For purposes of this discussion, we define a *sourdough* as a dough leavened by a sourdough starter. A *sourdough starter* is a dough or batter that contains wild yeasts and bacteria, has a noticeable acidity as a result of fermentation by these organisms, and is used to leaven other doughs.

Sourdough starter is also called a *natural sour* or *natural starter*. Before commercially prepared yeast was available, bread was started by mixing flour and water and letting this mixture stand until wild yeasts began to ferment it. This starter was then used to leaven bread. A portion of the starter was saved, mixed with more flour and water, and set aside to leaven the next day's bread. This process is still used today.

There are two important points to notice in these definitions: the presence of wild yeasts, not commercial yeasts, and the importance of bacteria.

## Wild Yeasts

The wild yeasts in sourdough starters are not the same organisms as commercial yeasts. Consequently, they act somewhat differently. Also, different wild yeasts are found in different regions and environments. For example, the wild yeast that gives San Francisco sourdough its distinctive flavor is not the same as wild yeasts found in other parts of the world. If a starter is brought from one region to another, the sour may gradually change character because the yeasts in the new location apparently take over.

Wild yeasts can tolerate more acidity than commercial yeasts. If a dough made with commercial yeast becomes too sour or acidic, the yeast is likely to die, and the resulting bread will have an off taste. Wild yeasts used in starters can tolerate and grow in higher levels of acidity.

Although you can approximate sourdough breads using yeast pre-ferments, the complex flavor and moist texture or crumb of a true sourdough can be made only with a true natural starter containing wild yeasts.

## Bacterial Fermentation

The second important point is that sourdough starters contain bacteria as well as yeast. The most important of these bacteria belong to a group called *Lactobacilli* (singular form: *Lactobacillus*). Like the yeast, these bacteria ferment some of the sugars in the dough and create carbon dioxide gas. In addition, they create acids. These acids give sourdough its sourness. As in the case of wild yeasts, the exact strains of bacteria present vary from starter to starter, so each starter has unique characteristics.

Two kinds of acid are created by the bacteria: lactic acid and acetic acid. Lactic acid is a weak or mild acid. Acetic acid, which is the acid in vinegar, is a strong acid. Getting a good balance of these two acids is an important goal of the baker. The balance of these acids gives the bread its characteristic sourdough flavor. Too much acetic acid in the dough makes the bread taste harsh and vinegary. Lactic acid is necessary to balance the flavor, but if the dough contains only lactic acid and little or no acetic acid, the bread has little sourdough flavor.

The ways in which the baker maintains the starter and controls the fermentation process affect the formation of these two acids.

## Starting and Maintaining Natural Starters

As we have said, the microorganisms (yeasts and bacteria) that create sourdough starters differ from place to place. In addition, different bakers look for different results in their sourdough breads. Thus, the procedures for creating, maintaining, and using natural starters vary considerably. We begin this section with a general explanation of the important factors that should be considered.

We then present a general procedure for making a natural starter. Please keep in mind that, until your starter is well established and strong and you have baked breads with consistent quality with this starter, your procedures will be somewhat experimental.

## Source of Microorganisms

As you have read, if a flour-and-water dough or batter is left to stand long enough, sooner or later it is likely to start fermenting, either from yeasts and bacteria in the air and environment or from yeasts and bacteria that were already present in the flour. Unfortunately, however, just letting a dough stand and hoping for the best is not the ideal way to make a batch of bread. To create a starter, the baker usually looks for a more reliable source of fermentation.

Wild yeasts are naturally present on the surface of fruits and on the surface of whole grains, and these are the most common sources used for creating natural sours. Mixing whole-grain rye flour into a batter or dough with water and letting it stand until it ferments is one of the best and most reliable ways of creating a starter. The initial fermentation usually takes at least two or three days. Rye is a good environment for wild yeasts, and starters begun with rye are more likely to be more successful than starters begun with wheat flour only. Whole-grain rye generally contains more of these organisms, but if it is not available, use the darkest rye you can find. Light rye is made from the interior of the grain and contains fewer organisms.

Another popular way to create a sour is to mix a batter or loose dough with regular bread flour (wheat) and bury pieces of fruit (grapes are often used) or vegetable in it until it begins to ferment. Then remove the fruit. Some bakers feel this method is not as good as using rye because grain is the natural environment for the yeasts on rye, whereas the yeasts on fruit are not as adapted for growing in grain or flour.

Formulas for both types of starter are included in the next chapter. Of course, results will vary depending on your location.

## Refreshing the Starter

After the initial fermentation has begun, the starter must be refreshed or fed regularly so the yeasts and bacteria are nourished and will multiply until they are strong enough to ferment a bread dough. Depending on the environment and other factors, this can take several weeks. The yeasts and bacteria must regularly be supplied with fresh food, in the form of wheat flour, so they can grow. The basic procedure is to combine a portion of the fermenting starter with additional flour and water in the correct ratio (see next section) and again letting the mixture ferment.

You can imagine that if you continually add more flour and water to a starter, soon you will have more starter than you can use. For this reason, part of the starter is discarded each time it is refreshed.

Because every starter is different, it is impossible to predict how much time is needed between refreshments. Generally, it may take two days or more at the beginning of the process, but as the yeasts and bacteria multiply, the starter gets stronger and faster-acting. A developed starter is usually refreshed every day or even more often if the temperature is warm.

## Flour-Water Ratio in the Starter

Some sourdough starters are stiff doughs, similar to the type of pre-ferment called a *biga* (p. 133). A stiff starter is sometimes referred to by its French name, *levain*. Others are looser batters, with the same consistency as a poolish (p. 132). Thin starters are sometimes called **barms**. The two types are handled somewhat differently and yield slightly different results.

A thick, doughlike starter is relatively stable and does not need to be refreshed as often. It can be refrigerated without being refreshed for several days or even a week. Stiff starters favor the production of both lactic acid and acetic acid. Furthermore, the starter will produce more acetic acid under refrigeration than at room temperature. Often a baker will retard a stiff starter with the goal of increasing the ratio of acetic to lactic acid.

A thin starter is less stable and must be refreshed more often. It ferments more quickly than a stiff starter and can become strongly acidic in a short time, so it must be monitored carefully. Thin starters favor the production primarily of lactic acid.

The type of starter you choose to make depends on the flavor profile (balance of acids) you would like and on your production schedule. Professional bakeshops can usually manage the demanding feeding schedule of a thin starter. The fact that wet starters ferment more quickly may make them more adaptable to a bakeshop's schedule. Casual or amateur bakers often start with a thin starter because it is easier to mix, but they may find that a stiff starter is easier to maintain in the long run.

## AUTOLYSE

Artisan bakers usually take an extra step during the mixing of the final dough. This step is called *autolyse* (pronounced auto-lees). To mix a bread dough in this fashion, first combine the flour and water and mix at low speed just until all the flour is moistened and a dough is formed. Turn off the mixer and let stand for approximately 30 minutes.

During the autolyse, the flour hydrates fully, meaning the water is completely absorbed by the flour's proteins and starches. Also, the enzymes in the dough begin acting on the proteins before they are too stretched by mixing. This improves the gluten structure in the bread, making the finished dough easier to handle and to mold. It also improves the texture of the baked bread. Because of the improved gluten structure, mixing time is reduced, meaning less air is mixed into the dough, improving the dough's color and flavor. This is because the oxygen in the air has a bleaching effect.

Notice that only the flour and water are included in the autolyse. The yeast or starter, the salt, and other ingredients are not added until after this rest period. If the yeast or starter were added to the dough before the autolyse, the yeast action would increase the acidity of the dough, and this acidity would inhibit the action of the enzymes. If the salt were added, it would interfere with water absorption by the gluten proteins.

After the autolyse period is over, add the remaining ingredients and finish mixing the dough.

## FERMENTATION

After the finished dough is made, the next step in the production of yeast breads is fermentation. The basics of this stage of production are explained in chapter 6. Additional information is useful for the baker making artisan breads.

One of the advantages of using pre-ferments is the improvement in flavor and texture caused by the extended fermentation time. This holds true for the

## General Procedure for Making a Sourdough Starter

The following is only a general procedure and is subject to many variations, as described in the above text.

1. Combine the ingredients for the first stage as directed in the formula. Most starters fall into two groups:

   ◆ Mix together whole rye flour and water (a).

   ◆ Or mix together bread flour and water. Add the selected fresh fruit or vegetable.

2. Cover the starter and let stand at room temperature until it begins to ferment. Continue to let ferment until it bubbles up, increases in volume, and then falls back (b). This will probably take two or three days.

3. Refresh the starter. Mix together bread flour, water, and all or some of the starter from step 1. Use the quantities or ratios in your formula, or use the following guidelines:

   ◆ A typical stiff starter, or *levain*, may use the following ratio:

   | | |
   |---|---|
   | Flour | 100% |
   | Water | 50–60% |
   | Fermented starter | 67% |

   ◆ A typical thin starter, or *barm*, may use the following ratio:

   | | |
   |---|---|
   | Flour | 100% |
   | Water | 100% |
   | Fermented starter | 200% |

4. Cover and let stand at room temperature until well fermented. It should be sticky and full of bubbles, and it should have increased in volume at least 50% (c). This may take about 2 days, depending on the room temperature.

5. Repeat the refreshment as in step 3.

6. Continue to ferment and refresh as in steps 4 and 5. As the starter becomes stronger and more active, the fermentation will eventually take only 1 day or less. Once the starter has reached this level of activity, it is ready to use (d). Total time varies greatly, but will average about 2 weeks.

7. After the starter is fully developed, it can be refrigerated to slow its activity and increase the time between refreshments. Do not refrigerate a starter unless it has been refreshed recently, or the yeast may use up its food. Bring a refrigerated starter to room temperature before using it to make bread.

8. The developed starter may be used as is in formulas, or it may be used as a *storage starter*. This means it is a source of leavening that the baker keeps and maintains in storage. To use this storage starter, the baker removes a quantity of it as needed and refreshes this portion of it with the amounts of flour and water specified in an individual bread formula. This starter is then called an *intermediate starter*. For best results, always use either a refreshed starter or an intermediate starter in a bread formula. A storage starter taken from the refrigerator may not be active enough to provide the best fermentation.

fermentation of the finished bread dough as well. Yeast will ferment at any temperature between 33° and 105°F (1° to 40°C). If the temperature is too low, however, fermentation will be slow and acidity will be produced. On the other hand, a high temperature promotes excessively rapid fermentation and the development of off flavors. As you recall, most production breads are fermented in proof boxes at a temperature of about 80°F (27°C).

A lower temperature is preferable for artisan breads. Before the development of proof boxes, doughs were simply fermented at room temperature. Attempting to duplicate these conditions, artisan bakers may use fermentation temperatures in the range of 72° to 75°F (22° to 24°C). At these slightly cooler temperatures, doughs made with a yeast pre-ferment may take two to three hours to ferment until double in bulk.

Sourdoughs ferment more slowly. A sourdough may take eight hours to ferment at these cooler temperatures. Some bakers make sourdoughs at the end of the workday and allow them to ferment overnight. The following morning, they then make up, proof, and bake the loaves.

It is possible to ferment any of these doughs—yeast pre-ferment doughs and sourdoughs—at a still lower temperature of about 68°F (20°C). Keep in mind, however, that the fermentation period will be longer. More acidity will develop because the acid-forming bacteria will be more active than the yeast. This increased acidity may or may not be desirable, depending on the product. You may want to experiment with the results of various fermentation temperatures and times.

# BAKING

The types of artisan breads described in this chapter are usually baked as hearth breads. That is, they are baked directly on the deck or floor of deck or hearth ovens. If you must bake them in rack ovens, it is best to use perforated pans rather than solid pans, because the perforated pans allow for better heat circulation and more even browning of the crust.

Underbaking is a common fault. Most lean hearth breads are best baked in a hot oven preheated to 425° to 450°F (218° to 232°C) until the crust takes on a rich, deep brown color. Use the lower end of this range for large loaves and the hotter temperatures for small products. Small products need a higher temperature so the crust browns sufficiently in the shorter baking time. A well-browned crust has a richer flavor because of the well-caramelized starches and the browned proteins. Pale golden crusts have a blander flavor. In addition, taking care to bake the bread fully ensures a crisp crust that is less likely to be softened by excessive moisture from the interior of the bread.

Steam should be used for at least the first 15 minutes of baking. Injecting moisture into the oven delays the formation of the crust so the bread can expand fully. Thus the crust will be thin and crisp rather than thick and hard. The moisture also affects the starches on the surface of the bread, aiding in creating a more attractively browned crust.

# ARTISAN BREAD FORMULAS

**N**ow that we have surveyed the concepts, ingredients, and techniques used by artisan bakers, we return to the discussion that opened this chapter: What is artisan bread?

In presenting the basic procedures for making artisan breads, in this chapter we focused on the most fundamental bread formulas—that is, formulas consisting only of flour, water, salt, and leavening in the form of a yeast pre-ferment or sourdough starter. The same concepts are also applied to many specialty breads, such as breads flavored with nuts, olives, dried fruit, and so on. Furthermore, bakers specializing in fine handcrafted breads find they can increase sales by offering not only crisp-crusted sourdough breads but also a variety of rich dough products such as brioche (p. 193) and kugelhopf (p. 190), preparing these products with the same care as their lean breads. Are these products artisan breads as well? As we have said, it is hard to define the term in a way everyone agrees on.

The formulas in the following chapter begin with a variety of simple straight dough breads and rolls. These are intended to illustrate the basic yeast dough procedures discussed in chapter 6. Probably no one would consider these artisan breads, but that doesn't mean they should not be prepared with care, skill, and attention to detail. The latter part of chapter 8 includes many specialty breads, including sourdough breads, multigrain loaves, and specialty products. Which of these are artisan breads? That is for you to determine.

## TERMS FOR REVIEW

| | | | |
|---|---|---|---|
| artisan bread | levure | mixed fermentation | natural starter |
| pre-ferment | levain-levure | sourdough | lactobacilli |
| poolish | levain | sourdough starter | barm |
| biga | pâte fermentée | natural sour | autolyse |

## QUESTIONS FOR DISCUSSION

1. What do bakers mean by the term *artisan bread*? Can you give examples from local bakeries?

2. Describe the types of flour bakers favor for making artisan breads.

3. What is the difference between a natural starter and a yeast starter? Describe the source of yeast for each.

4. Describe the kinds of acids that make a sourdough sour. Where do these acids come from?

5. Describe how to mix a bread dough using the technique called *autolyse*.

6. What is the difference between fermenting artisan bread doughs and fermenting conventional bread doughs?

## Chapter 8

# Lean Yeast Doughs

The basic yeast dough production methods discussed in chapters 6 and 7 apply to the formulas presented in this chapter. Therefore, the methods are not repeated in detail for each formula. The basic procedures are indicated, and you should refer to these chapters if you need to refresh your memory of the details.

The discussion of yeast doughs is divided into two chapters. This chapter presents lean dough products, representing a complete range of formula types, from basic white loaves and dinner rolls to sourdoughs to artisan breads to popular specialty items like bagels, pita, focaccia, and crumpets. Chapter 9 completes the study of yeast products with a range of rich doughs, including Danish, brioche, and sweet roll doughs.

Large bakeries have machinery that automatically forms loaves and rolls of many types. In a small bakeshop, however, the baker still makes up most products by hand. Learning how to shape loaves, rolls, and pastries is an important part of the art and craft of fine baking.

**After reading this chapter, you should be able to:**

1. Prepare lean straight doughs and doughs made with a sponge or pre-ferment.

2. Prepare natural starters and yeast starters, and mix sourdoughs using them.

3. Make up a variety of loaf and roll types using lean doughs.

4. Prepare a variety of specialty bread items with nonstandard makeup and baking techniques, including English muffins, crumpets, and bagels.

# INTRODUCTION TO HANDCRAFTED BREADS

**N**ot many years ago, bread was somewhat of an afterthought in most restaurants, and there was not much variety or even attention to quality. In many cities today, however, fine restaurants vie with one another to serve the most interesting selections of fresh artisanal breads. Customers are often given a choice from among four, five, or even more types of bread. Handcrafted specialty breads are appearing in neighborhood bakeries, and everyone seems to have discovered the delights of sourdough.

Traditional formulas such as hard rolls, soft rolls, Italian bread, white and whole wheat loaf breads, and American-style rye bread form the core of this chapter. It is important to learn the basics of yeast dough production well, and this is easiest to do when you are working on familiar formulas without unusual techniques and exotic ingredients. Not only will you learn how to mix basic yeast doughs but you will also practice making up a variety of loaf and roll types by hand to develop your manual skills. Then you can proceed with confidence to specialty handcrafted items. Working with sourdoughs, in particular, is more challenging than working with straight doughs, so your earlier practice and experience will benefit you.

The conventional yeast dough formulas in this chapter are augmented with specialty items. These include newly popular breads, such as olive bread, prosciutto bread, ciabatta, multigrain breads, and focaccia, and are joined by several sourdough bread formulas, including a traditional French country bread, or *pain de campagne.*

Making and fermenting dough is a craft distinct from making up rolls and loaves using these doughs. Each dough may be made into many types of loaves and rolls, and each makeup method may be applied to many formulas. Therefore, most makeup techniques—except for a few unique procedures for specialty items—are described in a section at the end of the chapter rather than repeated after every formula.

# CRISP-CRUSTED BREAD FORMULAS

**T**he crisp, thin crusts of French, Italian, and Vienna breads and of hard rolls are achieved by using formulas with little or no sugar and fat and by baking with steam. Because the crust is part of the attraction of these items, they are often made in long, thin shapes that increase the proportion of crust.

These breads are usually baked freestanding, either directly on the hearth or on sheet pans. (Perforated sheet pans are especially useful, as they allow better circulation of hot air around the product.) The water content must be low enough that the units hold their shape in the oven.

In practice, French and Italian bread formulas in North America are widely interchangeable. Some of them have little resemblance to breads in France and Italy, but nevertheless they may be popular and of good quality. The best practice is to follow regional preferences and to produce good-quality products that appeal to your customers.

To create the open-cell structure characteristic of French bread, give the loaves a very full proof before baking.

Two unusual breads are included in this section. Fougasse is a traditional shape from the French countryside. It is made with a basic French bread dough but formed into a large, flat, ladder-shaped loaf and coated with olive oil. Ciabatta (its Italian name refers to its resemblance to a beat-up old slipper) is made with a very slack dough. Because it is so sticky, it is handled as little as possible and simply deposited on sheet pans without being shaped into loaves. This gives it a very light, open texture.

## HARD ROLLS

*For large-quantity measurements, see page 718.*

| Ingredients | U.S. | | Metric | % | Procedure |
|---|---|---|---|---|---|
| Water | 13 | oz | 750 g | 59 | **MIXING** |
| Yeast, fresh | 0.75 | oz | 22 g | 3.5 | Straight dough method (p.114) |
| Bread flour | 1 lb 6 | oz | 625 g | 100 | 10 minutes at second speed (see p. 116) |
| Salt | 0.5 | oz | 14 g | 2.25 | **FERMENTATION** |
| Sugar | 0.5 | oz | 14 g | 2.25 | |
| Shortening | 0.5 | oz | 14 g | 2.25 | About 1 hour at 80°F (27°C) |
| Egg whites | 0.5 | oz | 14 g | 2.25 | **MAKEUP** |
| *Total weight:* | *2 lb 5* | *oz* | *1073 g* | *171%* | See pages 172–176. |
| | | | | | **BAKING** |
| | | | | | 425°F (218°C) for loaves; 450°F (230°C) for rolls. Steam for first 10 minutes. |

## VIENNA BREAD

*For large-quantity measurements, see page 718.*

| Ingredients | U.S. | | Metric | % | Procedure |
|---|---|---|---|---|---|
| Water | 13 | oz | 370 g | 59 | **MIXING** |
| Yeast, fresh | 0.75 | oz | 22 g | 3.5 | Straight dough method (p. 114) |
| Bread flour | 1 lb 6 | oz | 625 g | 100 | 10 minutes at second speed (see p. 116) |
| Salt | 0.5 | oz | 14 g | 2.25 | **FERMENTATION** |
| Sugar | 0.6 | oz | 18 g | 3 | |
| Malt syrup | 0.25 | oz | 6 g | 1 | About 1 hour at 80°F (27°C) |
| Oil | 0.6 | oz | 18 g | 3 | **MAKEUP** |
| Eggs | 0.9 | oz | 25 g | 4 | See pages 172–176. |
| *Total weight:* | *2 lb 6* | *oz* | *1098 g* | *175%* | **BAKING** |
| | | | | | 425°F (218°C) for loaves; 450°F (230°C) for rolls. Steam for first 10 minutes. |

# ITALIAN BREAD

*For large-quantity measurements, see page 718.*

| Ingredients | U.S. | | Metric | % | Procedure |
|---|---|---|---|---|---|
| Water | 1 lb 1 | oz | 460 g | 61 | **MIXING** |
| Yeast, fresh | 0.75 | oz | 20 g | 2.75 | Straight dough method (p. 114) |
| Bread flour | 1 lb 12 | oz | 750 g | 100 | 8–10 minutes at second speed (see p. 116) |
| Salt | 0.5 | oz | 15 g | 2 | **FERMENTATION** |
| Malt syrup | 0.13 oz (¾ tsp) | | 4 g | 0.5 | 1½ hours at 80°F (27°C) or 2 hours at 75°F (24°C) |
| *Total weight:* | *2 lb 14* | *oz* | *1249 g* | *166%* | **MAKEUP** |

**MAKEUP**

See pages 172–176.

**BAKING**

425°F (218°C) for loaves; 450°F (230°C) for rolls. Steam for first 10 minutes.

## VARIATIONS

## WHOLE WHEAT ITALIAN BREAD

*For large-quantity measurements, see page 718.*

Use the following proportions of flour in the above formula.

| Ingredients | U.S. | Metric | % |
|---|---|---|---|
| Whole wheat flour | 12 oz | 325 g | 43 |
| Bread flour | 1 lb | 425 g | 57 |

Increase the water to 59–60% to allow for the extra absorption by the bran. Mix 8 minutes.

## PIZZA

Optional addition: Add 2.5% vegetable oil or olive oil (0.63 oz/18 g) to Italian Bread formula. For dough to be retarded, also add 1% sugar (0.25 oz/8 g). Ferment, scale (see the table below), and round. After bench rest, sheet or roll out and apply tomato sauce, cheese, and toppings. Bake without proofing.

Baking temperature: 550°F (290°C).

Pizza Margherita before baking.

Pizza Margherita after baking.

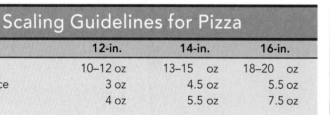

## Scaling Guidelines for Pizza

| | 12-in. | 14-in. | 16-in. |
|---|---|---|---|
| Dough | 10–12 oz | 13–15 oz | 18–20 oz |
| Tomato sauce | 3 oz | 4.5 oz | 5.5 oz |
| Cheese | 4 oz | 5.5 oz | 7.5 oz |

## ⊰ PIZZA ⊱

Naples, Italy, takes pride in being the birthplace of pizza. Today the Associazione Verace Pizza Napoletana sets down the rules by which its members must abide if they wish to claim that they serve authentic Neapolitan pizza. The rules state that the dough must contain only flour, water, salt, and natural yeast and that it must be made by hand or in an approved mixer. The pizza must be shaped by hand and baked on the hearth of a wood-burning oven. Toppings are limited to a list of approved ingredients.

Two pizzas—Margherita, topped with tomatoes, basil, and buffalo mozzarella; and Marinara, topped with tomatoes, garlic, oregano, and olive oil—are considered the original and true Neapolitan pizzas.

Pizza has grown beyond its origins to become an international favorite. In North America, most of the pizzas served make no claim to being authentically Italian and instead sport toppings such as barbecued chicken, beef with peppers and taco seasonings, and smoked salmon with artichokes, in addition to old favorites like sausage and pepperoni.

# FRENCH BREAD (STRAIGHT DOUGH)

*For large-quantity measurements, see page 719.*

| Ingredients | U.S. | | | Metric | % | Procedure |
|---|---|---|---|---|---|---|
| Water | 1 lb | 1 | oz | 460 g | 61 | **MIXING** |
| Yeast, fresh | | 0.75 | oz | 20 g | 2.75 | Straight dough method (p. 114) |
| Bread flour | 1 lb | 12 | oz | 750 g | 100 | 8–10 minutes at second speed (see p. 116) |
| Salt | | 0.5 | oz | 15 g | 2 | **FERMENTATION** |
| Malt syrup | | 0.13 | oz | 4 g | 0.5 | 1½ hours at 80°F (27°C) or 2 hours at 75°F (24°C) |
| Sugar | | 0.5 | oz | 12 g | 1.75 | |
| Shortening | | 0.5 | oz | 12 g | 1.75 | **MAKEUP** |
| **Total weight:** | **2 lb 15** | | **oz** | **1273 g** | **169%** | See pages 172–176. |

**BAKING**

425°F (218°C) for loaves; 450°F (230°C) for rolls. Steam for first 10 minutes.

**VARIATION**

## WHOLE WHEAT FRENCH BREAD

*For large-quantity measurements, see page 719.*

Use the following proportions of flour in the above formula.

| Ingredients | U.S. | Metric | % |
|---|---|---|---|
| Whole wheat flour | 12 oz | 325 g | 43 |
| Bread flour | 1 lb | 425 g | 57 |

Increase the water to 63–64% to allow for the extra absorption by the bran. Mix 8 minutes.

# FRENCH BREAD (SPONGE)

*For large-quantity measurements, see page 719.*

| Ingredients | U.S. | | Metric | % | Procedure |
|---|---|---|---|---|---|
| **Sponge** | | | | | **MIXING** |
| Bread flour | 8 | oz | 250 g | 33 | Sponge method (p. 115) |
| Water | 8 | oz | 250 g | 33 | **FERMENTATION** |
| Yeast, fresh | 0.5 | oz | 15 g | 2 | Sponge: 4 hours at 75°F (24°C) or overnight at 65°F (18°C) |
| Malt syrup | 0.25 | oz | 8 g | 1 | |
| **Dough** | | | | | Dough: 30 minutes at 80°F (27°C) |
| Bread flour | 1 lb | | 500 g | 67 | **MAKEUP** |
| Water | 6.5 | oz | 202 g | 27 | See pages 172–176. |
| Salt | 0.44 oz (2¼ tsp) | | 13 g | 1.75 | **BAKING** |
| **Total weight:** | **2 lb 7** | **oz** | **1238 g** | **164%** | 425°F (218°C) |

**VARIATION**

## COUNTRY-STYLE FRENCH BREAD

*For large-quantity measurements, see page 719.*

Use the following proportions of flour and water in the dough stage of the above formula.

| Ingredients | U.S. | | Metric | % |
|---|---|---|---|---|
| Clear or bread flour | 6 | oz | 200 g | 25 |
| Whole wheat flour | 10 | oz | 300 g | 42 |
| Water | 7.25 oz | | 225 g | 30 |

Make up the dough into round loaves.

 **FRENCH BREAD**

The long, slender loaf called the *baguette* (bah get) is the classic French loaf familiar to most people in North America. However, the terms *French bread* and *baguette* are not interchangeable. Many types of bread are produced in France other than the light, crusty baguette.

Baguettes should be made only with lean doughs that produce a crisp crust. It is not a good practice to make baguette-shaped loaves with ordinary soft-crusted white bread and sell it labeled as French bread.

# BAGUETTE

*For large-quantity measurements, see page 718.*

| Ingredients | U.S. | | Metric | % | Procedure |
|---|---|---|---|---|---|
| Bread flour | 2 lb 2 | oz | 1000 g | 100 | **MIXING** |
| Salt | 0.67 | oz | 20 g | 2 | Straight dough method (p. 114) |
| Yeast, fresh | 0.75 | oz | 25 g | 2.5 | 3–5 minutes at first speed |
| Water | 1 lb 4 | oz | 600 g | 60 | 15 minutes at second speed (see p. 116) |
| *Total weight:* | *3 lb 7* | *oz* | *1645 g* | *164%* | **FERMENTATION** |

**FERMENTATION**

1 hour at 80°F (27°C)

**MAKEUP**

See page 174. Scale at 11 oz (320 g).

**BAKING**

475°F (250°C) for 20 minutes with steam

---

*VARIATION*

## FOUGASSE

Scale dough at 18 oz (540 g). See page 176 for makeup.

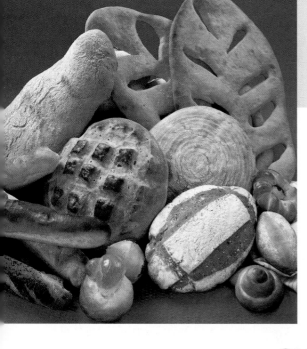

An assortment of hearth breads: in back, ciabatta and fougasses; in center, two differently formed pains de campagne; in front, baguettes, French rye, and assorted dinner rolls.

# CUBAN BREAD

*For large-quantity measurements, see page 719.*

| Ingredients | U.S. | | Metric | % | Procedure |
|---|---|---|---|---|---|
| Water | 15 | oz | 465 g | 62 | **MIXING** |
| Yeast, fresh | 1 | oz | 30 g | 4 | Straight dough method (p. 114) |
| Bread flour | 1 lb 8 | oz | 750 g | 100 | 12 minutes at first speed |
| Salt | 0.5 | oz | 15 g | 2 | **FERMENTATION** |
| Sugar | 1 | oz | 30 g | 4 | 60 minutes at 80°F (27°C) |
| *Total weight:* | *2 lb 9* | *oz* | *1290 g* | *172%* | **MAKEUP** |

**MAKEUP**

Scale at 20 oz (625 g).

Round loaves (p. 175).

Score top with a cross.

**BAKING**

400°F (200°C)

# CIABATTA

*For large-quantity measurements, see page 719.*

| Ingredients | U.S. | | Metric | % |
|---|---|---|---|---|
| **Sponge** | | | | |
| Water | 1 lb 1 | oz | 480 g | 72 |
| Yeast, fresh | 1 | oz | 30 g | 4 |
| Bread flour | 1 lb | | 450 g | 67 |
| Virgin olive oil | 6 | oz | 180 g | 27 |
| **Dough** | | | | |
| Salt | 0.5 oz | | 15 g | 2 |
| Bread flour | 8 | oz | 220 g | 33 |
| *Total weight:* | *3 lb* | | *1375 g* | *205%* |

## Procedure

### MIXING

Sponge method

1. Warm the water to about 100°F (37°C). Dissolve the yeast in the warm water.

2. Add the yeast mixture to the flour for the sponge. Add the oil.

3. Mix to form a soft dough. Beat well for approximately 5 minutes or until the sponge starts to become smooth.

4. Cover and leave at room temperature until doubled in size, approximately 1 hour.

5. Stir down and add the ingredients for the dough. Beat for a few minutes to form a smooth dough, which will be very soft and sticky.

### FERMENTATION

Cover and allow to ferment at room temperature until doubled in size, approximately 1 hour.

### MAKEUP AND BAKING

1. Lightly oil sheet pans. Handling the fermented dough as little as possible, scale it into portions weighing about 18 oz (550 g). This is usually done by approximation to avoid handling the dough. Deposit the dough on a greased and floured sheet pan (a).

2. Shape very lightly into rough ovals or rectangles on the oiled pans (b). The dough will be very sticky; handle as little as possible.

3. Dust the tops with extra flour (c). Proof at room temperature until the dough doubles in volume and the flour on the top starts to crack slightly.

4. Bake at 425°F (220°C) for about 30 minutes or until golden. Cool on a wire rack.

# SOFT-CRUSTED BREAD AND RYE BREAD FORMULAS

This category includes sandwich-type breads baked in loaf pans, soft rolls, braided breads, and straight-dough rye (sour rye breads are in the next section). Many of these formulas incorporate milk, eggs, and higher percentages of sugar and fat.

## WHITE PAN BREAD

*For large-quantity measurements, see page 719.*

| Ingredients | U.S. | | | Metric | % | Procedure |
|---|---|---|---|---|---|---|
| Water | | 12 | oz | 300 g | 60 | **MIXING** |
| Yeast, fresh | | 0.75 | oz | 18 g | 3.75 | Straight dough method (p. 114) |
| Bread flour | 1 lb 4 | | oz | 500 g | 100 | 10 minutes at second speed (see p. 116) |
| Salt | | 0.5 | oz | 12 g | 2.5 | |
| Sugar | | 0.75 | oz | 18 g | 3.75 | **FERMENTATION** |
| Nonfat milk solids | | 1 | oz | 25 g | 5 | 1½ hours at 80°F (27°C) |
| Shortening | | 0.75 | oz | 18 g | 3.75 | **MAKEUP** |
| **Total weight:** | 2 lb 3 | | oz | **891 g** | **178%** | See page 179. |

**BAKING**

400°F (200°C)

### VARIATION

## WHOLE WHEAT BREAD

*For large-quantity measurements, see page 719.*

Use the following proportions of flour in the above formula.

| Ingredients | U.S. | | Metric | % |
|---|---|---|---|---|
| Bread flour | 8 | oz | 200 g | 40 |
| Whole wheat flour | 12 | oz | 300 g | 60 |

## WHITE PAN BREAD (SPONGE)

*For large-quantity measurements, see page 720.*

| Ingredients | U.S. | | | Metric | % | Procedure |
|---|---|---|---|---|---|---|
| **Sponge** | | | | | | **MIXING** |
| Flour | 1 lb | | | 500 g | 67 | Sponge method (p. 115) |
| Water | | 11 | oz | 340 g | 45 | **FERMENTATION** |
| Yeast, fresh | | 0.6 | oz | 18 g | 2.5 | |
| Malt syrup | | 0.13 | oz | 4 g | 0.5 | Sponge: about 4 hours at 75°F (24°C) |
| **Dough** | | | | | | Dough: about 15 minutes at 80°F (27°C) |
| Flour | | 8 | oz | 250 g | 33 | **MAKEUP** |
| Water | | 3.5 | oz | 112 g | 15 | See page 116. Especially suitable for Pullman loaf. |
| Salt | | 0.5 | oz | 15 g | 2 | |
| Nonfat milk solids | | 0.75 | oz | 22 g | 3 | |
| Sugar | | 1.25 | oz | 38 g | 5 | **BAKING** |
| Shortening | | 0.75 | oz | 22 g | 3 | 400°F (200°C) |
| **Total weight:** | 2 lb 10 | | oz | **1319 g** | **176%** | |

# SOFT ROLLS

*For large-quantity measurements, see page 720.*

| Ingredients | U.S. | | | Metric | % | Procedure |
|---|---|---|---|---|---|---|
| Water | | 12.5 | oz | 375 g | 60 | **MIXING** |
| Yeast, fresh | | 0.75 | oz | 22 g | 3.5 | Straight dough method (p. 114) |
| Bread flour | 1 lb 5 | | oz | 625 g | 100 | 10–12 minutes at second speed (see p. 116) |
| Salt | | 0.4 | oz (2 tsp) | 12 g | 2 | |
| Sugar | | 2 | oz | 60 g | 9.5 | **FERMENTATION** |
| Nonfat milk solids | | 1 | oz | 30 g | 4.75 | 1½ hours at 80°F (27°C) |
| Shortening | | 1 | oz | 30 g | 4.75 | **MAKEUP** |
| Butter | | 1 | oz | 30 g | 4.75 | See pages 176–184. |
| **Total weight:** | **2 lb 7** | | **oz** | **1180 g** | **189%** | **BAKING** |
| | | | | | | 400°F (200°C) |

**VARIATIONS**

### CINNAMON BREAD

Make up Soft Roll Dough as for loaves (p. 179) but, after flattening each unit, brush with melted butter and sprinkle with Cinnamon Sugar (p. 199). After baking, while still hot, brush tops of loaves with melted butter or shortening and sprinkle with cinnamon sugar.

### RAISIN BREAD

Scale 75% raisins (1 lb/470 g). Soak in warm water to soften; drain and dry. Add to Soft Roll Dough 1–2 minutes before end of mixing.

# EGG BREAD AND ROLLS

*For large-quantity measurements, see page 720.*

| Ingredients | U.S. | | | Metric | % | Procedure |
|---|---|---|---|---|---|---|
| Water | | 10.5 | oz | 312 g | 50 | **MIXING** |
| Yeast, fresh | | 0.75 | oz | 22 g | 3.5 | Straight dough method (p. 114) |
| Bread flour | 1 lb 5 | | oz | 625 g | 100 | 10–12 minutes at second speed (see p. 116) |
| Salt | | 0.4 | oz (2 tsp) | 12 g | 2 | |
| Sugar | | 2 | oz | 60 g | 9.5 | **FERMENTATION** |
| Nonfat milk solids | | 1 | oz | 30 g | 4.75 | 1½ hours at 80°F (27°C) |
| Shortening | | 1 | oz | 30 g | 4.75 | **MAKEUP** |
| Butter | | 1 | oz | 30 g | 4.75 | See pages 176–184. |
| Eggs | | 2 | oz | 60 g | 9.5 | **BAKING** |
| **Total weight:** | **2 lb 7** | | **oz** | **1181 g** | **188%** | 400°F (200°C) |

# 100% WHOLE WHEAT BREAD

*For large-quantity measurements, see page 720.*

| Ingredients | U.S. | | | Metric | % | Procedure |
|---|---|---|---|---|---|---|
| Water | 1 lb 2 | | oz | 515 g | 69 | **MIXING** |
| Yeast, fresh | | 0.75 | oz | 22 g | 3 | Straight dough method (p. 114) |
| Whole wheat flour | 1 lb 10 | | oz | 750 g | 100 | 8 minutes at second speed (see p. 116) |
| Sugar | | 0.5 | oz | 15 g | 2 | |
| Malt syrup | | 0.5 | oz | 15 g | 2 | **FERMENTATION** |
| Nonfat milk solids | | 0.75 | oz | 22 g | 3 | 1½ hours at 80°F (27°C) |
| Shortening | | 1 | oz | 30 g | 4 | **MAKEUP** |
| Salt | | 0.5 | oz | 15 g | 2 | See page 175. |
| **Total weight:** | **3 lb** | | | **1384 g** | **185%** | **BAKING** |
| | | | | | | 400°F (200°C) |

# CHALLAH

*For large-quantity measurements, see page 720.*

| Ingredients | U.S. | | Metric | % | Procedure |
|---|---|---|---|---|---|
| Water | 8 | oz | 200 g | 40 | **MIXING** |
| Yeast, fresh | 0.75 | oz | 20 g | 3.75 | Straight dough method (p. 114) |
| Bread flour | 1 lb 4 | oz | 500 g | 100 | 10 minutes at second speed (see p. 116) |
| Egg yolks | 4 | oz | 100 g | 20 | **FERMENTATION** |
| Sugar | 1.5 | oz | 38 g | 7.5 | 1½ hours at 80°F (27°C) |
| Malt syrup | 0.13 | oz | 2 g | 0.6 | **MAKEUP** |
| Salt | 0.4 | oz (2 tsp) | 10 g | 1.9 | See pages 180–184. |
| Vegetable oil | 2 | oz | 62 g | 10 | **BAKING** |
| **Total weight:** | **2 lb 4** | **oz** | **482 g** | **183%** | 400°F (200°C) |

# MILK BREAD (PAIN AU LAIT)

*For large-quantity measurements, see page 720.*

| Ingredients | U.S. | | Metric | % | Procedure |
|---|---|---|---|---|---|
| Yeast, fresh | 1 | oz | 30 g | 3 | **MIXING** |
| Milk | 1 lb 2 | oz | 500 g | 50 | Straight dough method (p. 114) |
| Bread flour | 2 lb 4 | oz | 1000 g | 100 | 10–15 minutes at second speed (see p. 116) |
| Sugar | 3.5 | oz | 100 g | 10 | **FERMENTATION** |
| Salt | 0.75 | oz | 20 g | 2 | 60–90 minutes at 77°F (25°C) |
| Eggs | 3.5 | oz | 100 g | 10 | **MAKEUP** |
| Butter or margarine | 5 | oz | 150 g | 15 | Any method for soft rolls, pages 176–184. Glaze with egg wash. |
| Malt syrup | 0.33 | oz | 10 g | 1 | **BAKING** |
| **Total weight:** | **4 lb 4** | **oz** | **1910 g** | **191%** | 425°F (220°C) |

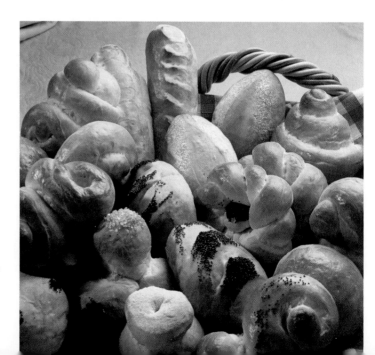

Assorted rolls made with milk bread (pain au lait) dough.

# LIGHT AMERICAN RYE BREAD AND ROLLS

*For large-quantity measurements, see page 721.*

| Ingredients | U.S. | | Metric | % | Procedure |
|---|---|---|---|---|---|
| Water | 12 | oz | 350 g | 60 | **MIXING** |
| Yeast, fresh | 0.75 | oz | 22 g | 3.75 | Straight dough method (p. 114) |
| Light rye flour | 8 | oz | 250 g | 40 | 5–6 minutes at second speed (see p. 116) |
| Bread flour or clear flour | 12 | oz | 350 g | 60 | **FERMENTATION** |
| Salt | 0.4 | oz (2 tsp) | 12 g | 2 | 1½ hours at 80°F (27°C) |
| Shortening | 0.5 | oz | 15 g | 2.5 | **MAKEUP** |
| Molasses or malt syrup | 0.5 | oz | 15 g | 2.5 | See pages 176–180. |
| Caraway seeds (optional) | 0.25 | oz | 8 g | 1.25 | **BAKING** |
| Rye flavor | 0.25 | oz | 8 g | 1.25 | 400°F (200°C). Steam for first 10 minutes. |
| **Total weight:** | **2 lb 2** | **oz** | **1030 g** | **173%** | |

**VARIATION**

Add up to 10% Rye Starter (p. 154) to the formula to contribute flavor.

# ONION RYE

*For large-quantity measurements, see page 721.*

| Ingredients | U.S. | | Metric | % | Procedure |
|---|---|---|---|---|---|
| Water | 12 | oz | 300 g | 60 | **MIXING** |
| Yeast, fresh | 0.75 | oz | 18 g | 3.75 | Straight dough method (p. 114) |
| Light rye flour | 7 | oz | 175 g | 35 | 5 minutes at second speed (see p. 116) |
| Clear flour | 13 | oz | 325 g | 65 | **FERMENTATION** |
| Dried onions, scaled, soaked in water, and well drained | 1 | oz | 25 g | 5 | 1½ hours at 76°F (24°C), punch down, then 1 more hour |
| Salt | 0.4 | oz (2 tsp) | 10 g | 1.9 | **MAKEUP** |
| Caraway seeds | 0.25 | oz | 6 g | 1.25 | See pages 176–180. |
| Rye flavor | 0.25 | oz | 6 g | 1.25 | **BAKING** |
| Malt syrup | 0.5 | oz | 12 g | 2.5 | 400°F (200°C). Steam for first 10 minutes. |
| **Total weight:** | **2 lb 3** | **oz** | **877 g** | **175%** | |

**VARIATION**

## ONION PUMPERNICKEL (NONSOUR)

*For large-quantity measurements, see page 721.*

Use the following proportions of flour in the above formula.

| Ingredients | U.S. | Metric | % |
|---|---|---|---|
| Rye meal (pumpernickel flour) | 4 oz | 100 g | 20 |
| Medium rye flour | 3 oz | 75 g | 15 |
| Clear flour | 13 oz | 325 g | 65 |

Dough may be colored with caramel color or cocoa powder.

# SEVEN-GRAIN BREAD

| Ingredients | U.S. | | Metric | % | Procedure |
|---|---|---|---|---|---|
| Water | 1 lb 10 | oz | 815 g | 62 | **MIXING** |
| Yeast, fresh | 1 | oz | 30 g | 2.4 | Straight dough method (p. 114) |
| Bread flour | 1 lb 8 | oz | 750 g | 57 | Sift together the bread flour, rye flour, barley |
| Rye flour | 6 | oz | 185 g | 14 | flour, and cornmeal; add the oats, flax seeds, |
| Barley flour | 2 | oz | 65 g | 5 | and millet and mix well. This ensures even dis- |
| Cornmeal | 3 | oz | 90 g | 7 | tribution of the flours. |
| Rolled oats | 3 | oz | 90 g | 7 | Mix 10 minutes at first speed. |
| Flax seeds | 2 | oz | 65 g | 5 | **FERMENTATION** |
| Millet | 2 | oz | 65 g | 5 | 1½ hours at 75°F (24°C) |
| Salt | 0.75 | oz | 24 g | 1.8 | **MAKEUP** |
| *Total weight:* | *4 lb 5* | *oz* | *2179 g* | *166%* | See pages 175 and 179. Make up as desired |
| | | | | | for loaf pans or round loaves. |

*Note: For the purposes of calculating with percentages, all seven grains are included as part of the total flour, even though three of them are not ground.*

**BAKING**

425°F (220°C)

See pages 175 and 179.

## VARIATION

### MULTIGRAIN BREAD

Use 80% bread flour and 20% whole wheat flour in the basic recipe and omit the remaining flours and grains. Separately, prepare a cold soaker (see sidebar) using 35% commercial nine-grain mixture and 35% water. Let stand, covered, until the grains are soft and the water is absorbed, 8 hours or more. Drain the soaker. Mix the bread dough 5 minutes, add the soaker, and then continue mixing until the gluten is developed.

## ❧ SOAKERS ❧

Adding large quantities of whole or cracked grains to bread doughs can have two undesirable effects. First, the grains absorb water from the dough, resulting in a dry baked loaf. Second, the grains may not hydrate sufficiently, resulting in hard chunks in the bread that are difficult to eat.

The seven-grain bread formula on this page contains a relatively small quantity of small, fairly tender grains, and there is sufficient water in the formula to hydrate them. Thus, they can be added directly to the other ingredients.

However, if larger quantities of grains are added, especially if those grains include large, hard grains such as wheat berries, it is better to prepare what is known as a *soaker*. This procedure hydrates the grains before they are included in the bread dough.

Two kinds of soakers, hot and cold, are used. For large, hard grains, a hot soaker is preferred. To prepare a hot soaker, bring the required quantity of water to a boil, as indicated in the formula. Pour the water over the grains and stir. Cover tightly and let stand 4 hours or more, or until the grains are softened and cooled. Drain and add to the dough as indicated in the formula.

Use a cold soaker for smaller and softer grains. Pour cold or room-temperature water over the grains, stir, cover, and let stand until softened. If a cold soaker is used for hard grains, it may be necessary to prepare it one day ahead of time. In warm weather, store the soaker in the refrigerator to inhibit fermentation or enzyme activity.

# SOURDOUGH FORMULAS AND SPECIALTY BREADS FOR THE ARTISAN BAKER

This section begins with several formulas for yeast starters, also called *yeast pre-ferments*, and for sourdough starters, also called *natural starters*. These starters are explained in detail in chapter 7. Please review that material if necessary before preparing these formulas.

Pre-ferments provide leavening and improve the flavor and texture of the finished bread. True sourdough breads use only a sour starter for leavening. However, it is also possible to use a starter primarily as an ingredient to improve flavor and texture and to rely on additional yeast for leavening. This type of process is called *mixed fermentation*, as explained on page 133, and can be used with any type of pre-ferment, whether it is a natural starter or yeast starter. When mixed fermentation is used, the formula can be expressed as if it were a straight dough formula, and the separately made starter is one of the ingredients. This section includes examples of mixed fermentation in addition to a number of pure sourdough formulas.

Sourdoughs, especially sour rye doughs, are stickier than regular doughs, so handling the dough and making up loaves requires more skill and practice. Care should be taken not to overmix the dough. Use low speed to avoid damaging the gluten.

Underproof sourdough breads slightly. Proofed units are fragile. Steam should be used in baking to allow the crust to expand without breaking.

The final formulas in the chapter include a number of specialty breads and other yeast dough items. Some of these are produced by methods unlike those of other breads. English muffins and crumpets are made on a griddle rather than baked in an oven. Both of these items are toasted before being eaten. **English muffins** are split in half before toasting, and crumpets are toasted whole. True **bagels**—dense, chewy, and boiled in a malt syrup before baking—are unlike the soft imitation bagels widely sold today (sidebar and formula on p. 165).

Production methods for these items are modified for use in a small bakeshop. Large producers have special equipment for bagels, English muffins, and crumpets.

Additional formulas in this chapter include two popular ones for focaccia, which is closely related to pizza dough; an unusual and flavorful bread made with chestnut flour; a flatbread called *pita*, which puffs up when baked to form a hollow center; and an Amish-style soft pretzel.

## BASIC YEAST STARTER (BIGA)

*For large-quantity measurements, see page 721.*

| Ingredients | U.S. | | Metric | % | Procedure |
|---|---|---|---|---|---|
| Bread flour | 15 | oz | 450 g | 100 | **MIXING** |
| Water | 9 | oz | 270 g | 60 | Straight dough method (p. 114) |
| Yeast, fresh | 0.03 | oz | 1 g | 0.2 | **FERMENTATION** |
| *Total weight:* | *1 lb 8* | *oz* | *721 g* | *160%* | 12–14 hours at 80°F (27°C) or 18 hours at 70°F (21°C) |

# RYE STARTER I

*For large-quantity measurements, see page 721.*

| Ingredients | U.S. | | Metric | % | Procedure |
|---|---|---|---|---|---|
| Rye flour | 1 lb | | 400 g | 100 | 1. Dissolve the yeast in the water. |
| Water | 12 | oz | 300 g | 75 | 2. Add the rye flour and mix until smooth. |
| Yeast, fresh | 0.16 oz (1 tsp) | | 4 g | 1 | 3. Bury the onion in the mix. |
| Onion, halved (optional) | 1 | | 1 | | 4. Let stand 24 hours. Desired temperature: 70°F (21°C) |
| *Total weight:* | *1 lb 12* | *oz* | *704 g* | *176%* | 5. Remove the onion. |

# RYE STARTER II

| Ingredients | U.S. | | Metric | % | Procedure |
|---|---|---|---|---|---|
| **Starter** | | | | | **MIXING** |
| Light rye flour | 1 lb | | 500 g | 100 | 1. Mix the starter ingredients. Let stand at shop temperature 24 hours. |
| Water | 12 | oz | 375 g | 75 | |
| Yeast, fresh | 0.16 oz (1 tsp) | | 4 g | 1 | 2. Add the first build ingredients. Ferment at 80°F (27°C) until the mixture falls back, about 3 hours. |
| **First build** | | | | | |
| Light rye flour | 4 lb | | 2000 g | 100 | |
| Water | 3 lb | | 1500 g | 75 | 3. Repeat with the remaining builds. The second build may be omitted if the schedule does not permit. Amounts added in the last build depend on production requirements. |
| **Second build** | | | | | |
| Light rye flour | 4 lb | | 2000 g | 100 | |
| Water | 3 lb | | 1500 g | 75 | |
| **Third build** | | | | | |
| Light rye flour | up to 24 lb | | up to 10,000 g | 100 | 4. Save about 2 lb (1 kg) sour as starter for the next day's production. |
| Water | up to 18 lb | | up to 7500 g | 75 | |
| *Total weight:* | *up to 57 lb* | | *up to 25,000 g* | | |

# RYE STARTER III

*For large-quantity measurements, see page 721.*

| Ingredients | U.S. | Metric | % | Procedure |
|---|---|---|---|---|
| Rye flour | 1 lb | 500 g | 100 | 1. Mix together all ingredients. |
| Water, warm (85–90°F/ 30–35°C) | 1 lb | 500 g | 100 | 2. Cover and let ferment at room temperature for about 15 hours. |
| Yeast, fresh | 0.25 oz | 7.5 g | 1.5 | |
| *Total weight:* | *2 lb* | *1007 g* | *201%* | |

# BASIC SOURDOUGH STARTER

*Yield: 1 lb 10 oz (815 g)*

| Ingredients | U.S. | Metric | % | Procedure |
|---|---|---|---|---|
| **Stage 1** | | | | 1. Combine the water and rye flour and mix together. Place in a nonreactive container (such as stainless steel or plastic) and cover. Let stand at room temperature until the mixture becomes bubbly and fermented and has a noticeable fermented aroma. This should take 2 or 3 days. |
| Water, warm | 8 oz | 250 g | 100 | |
| Whole rye flour | 8 oz | 250 g | 100 | |
| **Stage 2** | | | | 2. Mix together the ingredients in Stage 2 to make a stiff dough. Cover and let stand until well fermented. This may take 1 or 2 days. |
| Bread flour | 8 oz | 250 g | 100 | |
| Starter from Stage 1 | 1 lb | 500 g | 200 | |
| **Stage 3** | | | | 3. Combine the ingredients in Stage 3, discarding the leftover starter from the previous step. Mix into a stiff dough. Cover and let stand until the starter has fermented and the volume has increased by about half. This will probably take at least 1 day, possibly longer, depending on conditions and the strength of the wild yeast. |
| Bread flour | 12 oz | 375 g | 100 | |
| Water | 6 oz | 190 g | 50 | |
| Starter from Stage 2 | 8 oz | 250 g | 67 | |
| **To refresh starter as needed:** | | | | 4. Continue to refresh the starter as in step 3 until it is strong enough to double in volume in 8 to 12 hours. The procedure may take about 2 weeks in all. At this point, the starter is ready to use in bread. |
| Bread flour | 12 oz | 375 g | 100 | |
| Water | 6 oz | 190 g | 50 | |
| Starter | 8 oz | 250 g | 67 | 5. Refresh the starter at least once a day to keep it healthy and vigorous. If this is not possible, refresh the starter, let it ferment for a few hours, then refrigerate, tightly covered, for up to 1 week. To return the starter to active use, let it come back to room temperature and refresh it at least once before using in bread. |

# YOGURT SOUR

| Ingredients | U.S. | Metric | % | Procedure |
|---|---|---|---|---|
| Skim milk | 7 oz | 225 g | 180 | 1. Warm the milk to about 98°F (37°C), or body temperature. |
| Plain yogurt | 3 oz | 90 g | 72 | 2. Stir in the yogurt. |
| Bread flour | 4 oz | 125 g | 100 | 3. Mix in the flour until smooth. |
| *Total weight:* | *14 oz* | *440 g* | *352%* | 4. Pour into a sterile container, cover with a damp cloth, then cover tightly with plastic film. |
| | | | | 5. Allow to stand in a warm place for 2–5 days, until bubbles form. |

# POTATO SOUR

| Ingredients | U.S. | | Metric | % | Procedure |
|---|---|---|---|---|---|
| Bread flour | 8 | oz | 225 g | 100 | 1. Mix together the flour, water, salt, and sugar into a soft, smooth dough. Add the potato. |
| Water, warm | 6.5 | oz | 185 g | 82 | |
| Salt | 0.16 oz (1 tsp) | | 5 g | 2 | 2. Place in a sterilized bowl. Cover tightly with muslin or other clean fabric so the starter can breathe. Let rest in a warm place for up to 24 hours, until the mixture becomes frothy. |
| Sugar | 0.16 oz (1 tsp) | | 5 g | 2 | |
| Large potato, peeled | 1 | | 1 | | |
| *Total weight:* *(without potato)* | **14** | **oz** | **420 g** | **186%** | 3. Stir well and cover with plastic film. Leave to stand 2–3 days in a warm place, until the mixture becomes light and foamy. Stir thoroughly each day. |

4. Pour the fermented starter into a glass jar and store in the refrigerator for approximately 3 days, or until a clear liquid collects on top of the mixture. This indicates the mixture is ripened enough for use. Carefully pour all the liquid collected on the surface into a measuring jug, discarding the solid mixture that remains on the bottom. The weight of the liquid should be greater than the weight of the water used, because some of the flour will be poured off with the liquid.

# APPLE SOUR

*Yield: 2 lb (900 g)*

| Ingredients | U.S. | | Metric | Procedure |
|---|---|---|---|---|
| **Starter** | | | | 1. Leaving the skin on, grate the cored apple. |
| Whole apple, cored | 12 | oz | 360 g | 2. Combine the ingredients for the starter. Cover with a damp cloth and plastic film. Keep in a warm place 8–10 days. |
| Sugar | 2 | oz | 60 g | |
| Water | 1.33 oz | | 40 g | |
| **First build** | | | | 3. Each day, dampen the cloth, but do not mix the starter. Once the mixture starts to give off gases, it is ready. Remove any crust that may have formed on the surface. |
| Honey | 0.67 oz | | 20 g | |
| Water, warm | 4 | oz | 120 g | 4. For the first build, dissolve the honey in warm water. Mix in the apple starter and mash to a paste. Mix in the flour. Knead by hand 5–10 minutes to form a dough. |
| Apple starter (above) | 5 | oz | 160 g | |
| Bread flour (see *Note*) | 13 | oz | 390 g | 5. Place in a clean bowl and cover with a damp cloth and plastic film. Allow to ferment 8–10 hours. |
| **Second build** | | | | 6. Repeat step 3 with the ingredients for the second build. |
| Honey | 0.2 | oz | 6 g | |
| Water, warm | 3 | oz | 85 g | 7. Allow to ferment 5–8 hours. The dough should be well risen. |
| Starter from first build | 1 lb 6 | oz | 650 g | |
| Bread flour | 6 | oz | 195 g | |

*Note: For best results, use unbleached organic bread flour.*
*The total weight is less than the summed weights of the ingredients due to losses from evaporation and from skimming and other mixing losses.*

# OLD-FASHIONED RYE BREAD

*For large-quantity measurements, see page 721.*

| Ingredients | U.S. | Metric | % | Procedure |
|---|---|---|---|---|
| Water | 8 oz | 200 g | 50 | **MIXING** |
| Yeast, fresh | 0.16 oz | 4 g | 1 | 1. Dissolve the yeast in the water. |
| Fermented Rye Starter I or II | 9.5 oz | 240 g | 60 | 2. Add the starter and mix to break up the sour. |
| Clear flour | 1 lb | 400 g | 100 | 3. Add the flour, salt, and optional flavoring |
| Salt | 0.33 oz | 8 g | 2 | ingredients. Develop the dough 5 minutes at low speed. Do not overmix. |
| **Total weight:** | **2 lb 1 oz** | **852 g** | **213%** | |
| **Optional Ingredients** | | | | **FERMENTATION** |
| | | | | Rest 15 minutes, then scale. |
| Caraway seeds | up to 0.25 oz | up to 6 g | up to 1.5 | **MAKEUP** |
| Molasses or malt syrup | up to 0.5 oz | up to 12 g | up to 3 | See pages 172–175. Give only ¾ proof. |
| Caramel color | up to 0.25 oz | up to 6 g | up to 1.5 | **BAKING** |
| | | | | 425°F (218°C) with steam for first 10 minutes. |

# PUMPERNICKEL BREAD

*For large-quantity measurements, see page 722.*

| Ingredients | U.S. | Metric | % | Procedure |
|---|---|---|---|---|
| Water | 12 oz | 375 g | 50 | **MIXING** |
| Yeast, fresh | 0.25 oz | 8 g | 1 | 1. Dissolve the yeast in the water. |
| Fermented Rye Starter I or II | 10 oz | 315 g | 42 | 2. Add the starter and mix to break up the sour. |
| Rye meal (pumpernickel) | 5 oz | 150 g | 20 | 3. Add the rye meal, flour, salt, malt, molasses, and color. Develop the dough 5 minutes at |
| Clear flour | 1 lb 3 oz | 600 g | 80 | low speed. Do not overmix. |
| Salt | 0.5 oz | 15 g | 2 | |
| Malt syrup | 0.25 oz | 8 g | 1 | **FERMENTATION** |
| Molasses | 0.5 oz | 15 g | 2 | Rest 15 minutes, then scale. |
| Caramel color (optional) | 0.38 oz | 12 g | 1.5 | **MAKEUP** |
| **Total weight:** | **2 lb 15 oz** | **1498 g** | **199%** | See pages 172–175. Give only ¾ proof. |
| | | | | **BAKING** |
| | | | | 425°F (218°C) with steam for first 10 minutes. |

# RUSTIC SOURDOUGH BREAD

| Ingredients | U.S. | | Metric | % | Procedure |
|---|---|---|---|---|---|
| Bread flour | 2 lb 10 | oz | 1320 g | 88 | **MIXING** |
| Whole wheat flour | 3 | oz | 90 g | 6 | 1. Combine all the flours and the water and mix just until combined. |
| Dark rye flour | 3 | oz | 90 g | 6 | 2. Let stand 30 minutes (autolyse). |
| Water | 1 lb 15 | oz | 975 g | 65 | 3. Add the starter and salt. Mix at low speed 5–8 minutes to develop the dough. |
| Basic Sourdough Starter (p. 155), refreshed 8–12 hours earlier | 9.5 | oz | 300 g | 20 | **FERMENTATION** |
| | | | | | Ferment at 75°F (24°C) until almost double in bulk, about 8 hours. |
| Salt | 1 | oz | 30 g | 2 | **MAKEUP AND PROOFING** |
| *Total weight:* | *5 lb 9* | *oz* | *2805 g* | *187%* | Scale at 1 lb 12 oz (900 g). Make up into round loaves. Proof until almost double in bulk, about 3–4 hours. |

**BAKING**

425°F (218°C) with steam, 40–45 minutes.

**VARIATION**

Omit the rye flour and whole wheat flour and use 100% bread flour. If possible, use a high-extraction, high-ash European-style flour (see p. 60). You may need to use slightly less water, depending on the protein content of the flour.

# FIG HAZELNUT BREAD

| Ingredients | U.S. | | Metric | % | Procedure |
|---|---|---|---|---|---|
| Bread flour | 2 lb 9 | oz | 1290 g | 86 | **MIXING** |
| Whole wheat flour | 2 | oz | 60 g | 4 | 1. Combine all the flours and the water and mix just until combined. |
| Medium or light rye flour | 5 | oz | 150 g | 10 | 2. Let stand 30 minutes (autolyse). |
| Water | 1 lb 15 | oz | 975 g | 65 | 3. Add the starter and salt. Mix at low speed 5–8 minutes to develop the dough. |
| Basic Sourdough Starter (p. 155), refreshed 8–12 hours earlier | 12 | oz | 375 g | 25 | 4. Remove the dough from the mixer to a worktable. Add the figs and nuts and knead in by hand until evenly distributed in the dough. |
| Salt | | 1.2 oz | 38 g | 2.5 | **FERMENTATION** |
| Dried figs, diced (see note) | 1 lb | | 500 g | 33 | Ferment at 75°F (24°C) until almost double in bulk, about 8 hours. |
| Hazelnuts, lightly toasted (see note) | | 8 oz | 250 g | 17 | **MAKEUP** |
| **Total weight:** | **7 lb 4** | **oz** | **3638 g** | **242%** | Scale at 1 lb 8 oz (750 g). Make up into bâtard loaves (thick French-type loaves, p. 174). Proof until almost double in bulk, 3–4 hours. |

*Note: the quantities of fruit and nuts in this formula makes the dough somewhat difficult to handle. If desired, reduce the quantities of figs and nuts to taste.*

**BAKING**

425°F (218°C) with steam, 40–45 minutes

## VARIATION

### FIG ROLLS

Omit the hazelnuts. Make up into round rolls scaled at 4 oz (125 g) each. Bake at 450°F (232°C).

# FRENCH RYE

*For large-quantity measurements, see page 722.*

| Ingredients | U.S. | | Metric | % | Procedure |
|---|---|---|---|---|---|
| Rye Starter III (p. 154) | 1 lb 8 | oz | 750 g | 600 | **MIXING** |
| Bread flour | 4 | oz | 125 g | 100 | 1. Place the starter in a mixing bowl. Add the flour and salt. |
| Salt | 0.33 | oz | 10 g | 8 | 2. Mix at low speed for 10 minutes. The dough will be soft and somewhat sticky, and therefore a little difficult to handle. |
| **Total weight:** | **1 lb 12** | **oz** | **985 g** | **708%** | |

**FERMENTATION**

30 minutes at warm room temperature

**MAKEUP**

Scale at 1 lb (500 g). Shape into round or slightly oval loaves.

Brush or spray with water and dust heavily with flour. Proof 30–60 minutes at 85°F (27°C), or until about double in volume. Score the tops of the loaves.

**BAKING**

450°F (230°C) with steam, 40–45 minutes

# PAIN DE CAMPAGNE (COUNTRY-STYLE BREAD)

*For large-quantity measurements, see page 722.*

| Ingredients | U.S. | | Metric | % | Procedure |
|---|---|---|---|---|---|
| Rye Starter III (p. 154) | 6 | oz | 200 g | 20 | **MIXING** |
| Bread flour | 1 lb 8 | oz | 800 g | 80 | Straight dough method (mixed fermentation, p. 114) |
| Rye flour | 6 | oz | 200 g | 20 | 12 minutes at first speed |
| Salt | 0.6 | oz | 20 g | 2 | **FERMENTATION** |
| Yeast, fresh | 0.5 | oz | 15 g | 1.5 | 1 hour at warm room temperature (about 70°F/21°C) |
| Water | 1 lb 4 | oz | 650 g | 65 | |
| Lard or goose fat (optional) | 0.6 | oz | 20 g | 2 | |
| **Total weight:** | **3 lb 9** | **oz** | **1905 g** | **190%** | |

**MAKEUP**

Scale at 1 lb 12 oz (950 g). Round into tight, round loaves. Dust with flour before proofing. Before baking, score in a crosshatch or grid pattern.

**BAKING**

425°F (218°C) with steam, about 45 minutes

# APPLE SOURDOUGH

*Yield: 5 lb 10 oz (2400 g)*

| Ingredients | U.S. | | Metric | % |
|---|---|---|---|---|
| Granny Smith apples | 15 | oz | 450 g | 64 |
| Butter | 2.5 | oz | 80 g | 11 |
| Cinnamon | 0.25 | oz | 8 g | 1 |
| Yeast, dry | 0.25 | oz | 8 g | 1 |
| Water, warm | 12 | oz | 360 g | 51 |
| Honey | 0.2 | oz | 6 g | 0.85 |
| Salt | 0.5 | oz | 15 g | 2 |
| Apple Sour (p. 156) | 1 lb 14 | oz | 900 g | 129 |
| Bread flour (see *Note*) | 1 lb 2 | oz | 525 g | 75 |
| Rye flour | 6 | oz | 175 g | 25 |
| Raisins or dried cranberries | 7 | oz | 200 g | 29 |

*Note: For best results, use unbleached organic flour for this bread.*
*The dough yield is less than the summed weights of the ingredients due mostly to trimming and cooking loss of the apples.*

## Procedure

**MIXING**

1. Peel, core, and chop the apple into ¼-in. (5 mm) pieces. Sauté in the butter with the cinnamon until tender. Pour onto a tray and allow to cool.

2. Dissolve the yeast with half of the warm water. Mix to dissolve. Dissolve the honey and salt in the remaining water.

3. Cut the apple sour into pieces and place in the bowl of a mixer fitted with the dough hook.

4. Add the yeast liquid and then the honey, salt, and water, adding slowly to make a smooth paste.

5. Add in the flour slowly until a soft dough is formed.

6. Add the sautéed apples and raisins. Mix until combined.

7. Turn out the dough onto a light floured work surface and knead gently to form a smooth dough.

**FERMENTATION**

2½–3 hours at 80°F (27°C)

**MAKEUP**

Scale at 1 lb 6 oz (600 g).

Make up into long loaves like Italian or Vienna loaves (p. 174).

Allow 2–3 hours for proofing.

**BAKING**

425°F (220°C) for 20 minutes. Reduce the temperature to 375°F (190°C) for another 20 minutes.

# WHOLE WHEAT, RYE, AND NUT SOURDOUGH

| Ingredients | U.S. | | Metric | % | Procedure |
|---|---|---|---|---|---|
| **Sponge** | | | | | **MIXING** |
| Yogurt Sour (p. 155) | 10 | oz | 290 g | 27 | Sponge method (p. 115) |
| Water, warm | 13 | oz | 375 g | 35 | The sponge in this formula is an intermediate pre-ferment (see p. 137). It uses a sourdough starter rather than a commercial yeast. |
| Whole wheat flour | 12 | oz | 350 g | 32 | |
| **Dough** | | | | | **FERMENTATION** |
| Water | 8.5 | oz | 250 g | 23 | Sponge: 8 hours or overnight at room temperature |
| Yeast, dry | 0.5 | oz | 15 g | 1.4 | Dough: 1 hour at warm room temperature |
| Salt | 0.33 | oz | 10 g | 0.9 | |
| Whole wheat flour | 11 | oz | 325 g | 30 | **MAKEUP** |
| Rye flour | 8 | oz | 225 g | 21 | 1. Scale at 2 lb 4 oz (1050 g) for large loaves, 1 lb 8 oz (700 g) for medium loaves. |
| Bread flour | 6 | oz | 180 g | 17 | |
| Walnuts, chopped and lightly toasted | 2.5 | oz | 70 g | 6.5 | 2. Shape into round or elongated oval loaves. Spray tops with water and dust heavily with flour. Proof until double in volume. |
| Pecans, chopped and lightly toasted | 2.5 | oz | 70 g | 6.5 | 3. Score tops with desired pattern. |
| **Total weight:** | **4 lb 10** | **oz** | **2160 g** | **200%** | **BAKING** |
| | | | | | 425°F (220°C) for 30 minutes. Reduce to 350°F (180°C) until done. |

**VARIATIONS**

The nuts used may be varied—as, for example, all walnuts, all pecans, all hazelnuts, or all almonds. Raisins may be included in addition to the nuts.

# POTATO SOURDOUGH

| Ingredients | U.S. | | Metric | % | Procedure |
|---|---|---|---|---|---|
| **Sponge** | | | | | **MIXING** |
| Potato Sour (p. 156) | 8 | oz | 250 g | 29 | Sponge method |
| Bread flour | 6 | oz | 180 g | 21 | |
| Sugar | 1.75 | oz | 50 g | 6 | |
| Water | 4 | oz | 120 g | 14 | |
| Boiled potato, grated | 5 | oz | 150 g | 17 | |
| Sautéed onions | 5.25 | oz | 160 g | 18 | |
| Salt | 0.33 | oz | 10 g | 1 | |
| **Dough** | | | | | |
| Water, warm | 4 | oz | 120 g | 14 | |
| Milk powder | 3 | oz | 90 g | 10 | |
| Bread flour | 1 lb 7 | oz | 690 g | 79 | |
| Baking soda | 0.4 | oz (2½ tsp) | 12 g | 1.4 | |
| Cream of tartar | 0.4 | oz (5 tsp) | 12 g | 1.4 | |
| Butter | 2.67 | oz | 80 g | 9 | |
| Salt | 0.33 | oz | 10 g | 1 | |
| **Total weight:** | **4 lb 6** | **oz** | **1934 g** | **221%** | |

**MIXING**

Sponge method

1. The sponge in this formula is an intermediate pre-ferment (see p. 137). It uses a sourdough starter rather than a commercial yeast. For the sponge, mix together the sour and flour to make a very soft dough. Allow to rest for 2 hours.

2. Combine the sugar, water, potato, onions, and salt. Pour this mixture over the starter dough. Stir lightly. Cover tightly and allow to ferment overnight, or until the dough is risen and foamy.

3. For the dough, combine the sponge, water, milk powder, flour, baking soda, and cream of tartar. Add just enough of the flour to make a soft dough and mix about 2 minutes.

4. Beat in the butter, salt, and remaining flour. Knead by hand or with the machine at first speed for 10 minutes.

**FERMENTATION AND MAKEUP**

This dough is not fermented because the baking soda and cream of tartar begin to generate gas at once. Scale the dough at 1 lb (450 g). Shape into elongated oval loaves. Slash the tops of the loaves with diagonal slashes. Bake without proofing.

# FOUR-GRAIN BREAD

| Ingredients | U.S. | | Metric | % | Procedure |
|---|---|---|---|---|---|
| Water | 1 lb 10 | oz | 770 g | 63 | **MIXING** |
| Yeast, fresh | 0.5 | oz | 15 g | 1.25 | Straight dough method (p. 114) |
| Bread flour | 1 lb 4 | oz | 600 g | 49 | Sift together the four flours and mix well to |
| Rye flour | 14 | oz | 415 g | 34 | ensure even distribution. |
| Barley flour | 3 | oz | 85 g | 7 | Mix 10 minutes at first speed. Punch down |
| Oat flour | 4 | oz | 125 g | 10 | halfway through the fermentation. |
| Salt | 0.75 | oz | 24 g | 2 | **FERMENTATION** |
| Basic Yeast Starter (p. 153) or fermented dough | 1 lb | | 490 g | 40 | 1½ hours at 75°F (24°C) |
| *Total weight:* | *5 lb 4* | *oz* | *2524 g* | *206%* | **MAKEUP** |

See pages 175 and 179. Make up as desired for loaf pans or round loaves.

**BAKING**

425°F (220°C)

# ENGLISH MUFFINS

*For large-quantity measurements, see page 722.*

| Ingredients | U.S. | | Metric | % | Procedure |
|---|---|---|---|---|---|
| Water (see mixing instructions) | 12 | oz | 375 g | 75 | **MIXING** Straight dough method (p. 114) |
| Yeast, fresh | 0.25 | oz | 8 g | 1.5 | 20–25 minutes at second speed (see p. 116) |
| Bread flour | 1 lb | | 500 g | 100 | This dough is intentionally overmixed to develop |
| Salt | 0.25 | oz | 8 g | 1.5 | its characteristic coarse texture. Because of this |
| Sugar | 0.25 | oz | 8 g | 1.5 | long mixing time, use twice your normal machine |
| Nonfat milk solids | 0.4 | oz (2 tsp) | 12 g | 2.3 | friction factor (see p. 123) when calculating water |
| Shortening | 0.25 | oz | 8 g | 1.5 | temperature. For this reason, and because of the |
| *Total weight:* | *1 lb 13* | *oz* | *919 g* | *183%* | low fermentation temperature, it is usually nec- |

essary to use very cold water or part crushed ice.

**FERMENTATION**

Dough temperature: 70°F (21°C). Ferment 2½ to 3 hours.

**SCALING AND MAKEUP**

Because this dough is very soft and sticky, you must use plenty of dusting flour. Scale at 1.5 oz (45 g) per unit. Round and relax the units, then flatten with the palms of the hands. Place on cornmeal-covered trays to proof.

**BAKING**

Bake on both sides on a griddle at low heat.

# BAGELS

*For large-quantity measurements, see page 722.*

| Ingredients | U.S. | | Metric | % |
|---|---|---|---|---|
| Water | 9 | oz | 280 g | 56 |
| Yeast, fresh | 0.5 | oz | 15 g | 3 |
| High-gluten flour | 1 lb | | 500 g | 100 |
| Diastatic malt powder | 0.1 | oz (1 tsp) | 3 g | 0.6 |
| Salt | 0.33 | oz | 10 g | 2 |
| *Total weight:* | *1 lb 9* | *oz* | *808 g* | *161%* |

## Procedure

**MIXING**

Straight dough method (p. 114)

8–10 minutes at low speed

**FERMENTATION**

1 hour at 80°F (27°C)

**MAKEUP AND BAKING**

1. Scale at 2 oz (55 g) per unit.

2. One of two methods may be used for shaping bagels by hand:

   ◆ Roll with the palms of the hands into ropes (as for knotted or tied rolls). Loop around palms into doughnut shape (a). Seal the ends together well by rolling under the palms on the bench (b, c).

   ◆ Round the scaled unit and flatten into a thick disk. Press a hole in the center and tear open with the fingers. Pull the hole open and smooth the edges.

3. Give half proof.

4. Boil in a malt solution (⅓ qt malt syrup per 4 gal water, or 3 dL malt per 15 L water) about 1 minute.

5. Place on sheet pans about 1 in. (2.5 cm) apart. Bake at 450°F (230°C) until golden brown, turning them over when they are half baked.

Total baking time is about 20 minutes.

If desired, bagels may be sprinkled with sesame seeds, poppy seeds, diced onion, or coarse salt before baking.

## ❧ BAGELS ❧

As bagels have become more popular, bagel-like rolls that are really only ordinary bread shaped like bagels have proliferated. True bagels are dense, chewy rolls made with high-gluten flour and a low proportion of water. They are boiled in a malt solution before being baked to give them a glossy, distinctly flavored crust. Also, flavorings for true bagels are generally limited to toppings, such as poppy seeds, sesame seeds, coarse salt, and chopped onion or garlic. Two popular exceptions are pumpernickel bagels and cinnamon-raisin bagels.

The traditional baking method is to arrange them on wet canvas-covered boards and partially bake them in a hearth oven. When half done, they are tipped over directly onto the hearth to finish baking. They should be baked until well-browned. Proper bagels are not pale.

# OLIVE FOCACCIA

*For large-quantity measurements, see page 722.*

| Ingredients | U.S. | | Metric | % | Procedure |
|---|---|---|---|---|---|
| Water | 15 | oz | 470 g | 62.5 | **MIXING** |
| Yeast, fresh | 0.33 | oz | 10 g | 1.5 | Straight dough method (p. 114) |
| Bread flour | 1 lb 8 | oz | 750 g | 100 | Add the olives after the other ingredients have |
| Salt | 0.5 | oz | 15 g | 2 | formed a dough. |
| Olive oil | 1 | oz | 25 g | 3.5 | 12 minutes at first speed |
| Chopped, pitted oil-cured black olives | 8 | oz | 250 g | 33 | **FERMENTATION**<br>1½ hours at 80°F (27°C) |
| *Total weight:* | *3 lb* | | *1520 g* | *202%* | **MAKEUP AND BAKING** |
| | | | | | See Herb Focaccia (p. 167). |
| | | | | | This dough, without the olives, may also be used as a base for pizza (see p. 144). |

# HERB FOCACCIA (SPONGE METHOD)

*For large-quantity measurements, see page 723.*

| Ingredients | U.S. | | Metric | % |
|---|---|---|---|---|
| **Sponge** | | | | |
| Water | 6 | oz | 175 g | 21 |
| Yeast, fresh | 0.12 | oz | 4 g | 0.5 |
| Flour | 8 | oz | 225 g | 29 |
| Flour | 1 lb 4 | oz | 575 g | 71 |
| Water | 14 | oz | 400 g | 50 |
| Yeast, fresh | 0.12 | oz | 4 g | 0.5 |
| Salt | 0.5 | oz | 15 g | 1.75 |
| Olive oil | 1 | oz | 30 g | 3.5 |
| Rosemary and salt (see Makeup) | | | | |
| **Total weight:** | **3 lb 1** | **oz** | **1428 g** | **177%** |

| Procedure |
|---|

**MIXING**

Sponge method (p. 115)

**FERMENTATION**

Sponge: 8–16 hours at 70°F (21°C)

Dough: 30 minutes at 80°F (27°C)

**MAKEUP AND BAKING**

1. Scale at 3 lb (1400 g) for each half-size sheet pan.

2. Oil pans heavily with olive oil.

3. Roll and stretch the dough into a rectangle to fit the pans. Place in the pans (a).

4. Proof until doubled in thickness.

5. Top each unit with 2 oz (60 mL) olive oil (b). With your fingertips, poke holes heavily at regular intervals (c).

6. Top each unit with 2 tbsp (30 mL) fresh rosemary and with coarse salt to taste (d).

7. Bake at 400°F (200°C) for 30 minutes.

# CHESTNUT BREAD

*For large-quantity measurements, see page 723.*

| Ingredients | U.S. | | Metric | % | Procedure |
|---|---|---|---|---|---|
| Water | 12 | oz | 360 g | 60 | **MIXING** |
| Yeast, fresh | 1.2 | oz | 36 g | 6 | Straight dough method (p. 114) |
| High-gluten flour | 15 | oz | 450 g | 75 | 10 minutes at first speed |
| Chestnut flour | 5 | oz | 150 g | 25 | **FERMENTATION** |
| Salt | 0.5 | oz | 15 g | 2.5 | 40 minutes at 80°F (27°C) |
| Butter | 0.6 | oz | 18 g | 3 | **MAKEUP** |
| **Total weight:** | **2 lb** | **2 oz** | **1029 g** | **171%** | Scale at 10–11 oz (300–330 g). |
| | | | | | Oval-shaped loaves |
| | | | | | **BAKING** |
| | | | | | 450°F (230°C) |

**VARIATION**

For a more developed flavor, add 30% Basic Yeast Starter (p. 153)

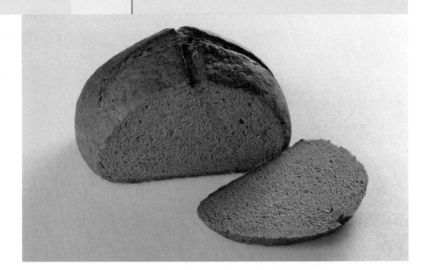

# PROSCIUTTO BREAD

*For large-quantity measurements, see page 723.*

| Ingredients | U.S. | | Metric | % | Procedure |
|---|---|---|---|---|---|
| Water | 9 | oz | 285 g | 57 | **MIXING** |
| Yeast, fresh | 0.33 | oz | 10 g | 2 | Straight dough method (mixed fermentation) |
| Bread flour | 1 lb | | 500 g | 100 | 1. Mix the water, yeast, flour, salt, and fat 6 minutes at first speed. |
| Salt | 0.33 | oz | 10 g | 2 | 2. Add the Basic Yeast Starter and mix another 4 minutes. |
| Rendered lard or prosciutto fat | 1 | oz | 30 g | 6 | 3. Add the prosciutto and mix another 1–2 minutes. |
| Basic Yeast Starter (p. 153) or fermented dough | 3.25 | oz | 100 g | 20 | **FERMENTATION** |
| | | | | | 1 hour at 80°F (27°C) |
| Prosciutto, chopped or diced into small pieces | 3.25 | oz | 100 g | 20 | **MAKEUP** |
| | | | | | Scale at 12–18 oz (360–540 g) or as desired. Shape like long Italian loaves. See page 174. |
| **Total weight:** | **2 lb 1** | **oz** | **1035 g** | **207%** | **BAKING** |
| | | | | | 425°F (220°C) with steam |

# OLIVE BREAD

*For large-quantity measurements, see page 723.*

| Ingredients | U.S. | | Metric | % | Procedure |
|---|---|---|---|---|---|
| Water | 12.5 oz | | 370 g | 62 | **MIXING** |
| Yeast, fresh | 0.3 oz | | 9 g | 1.5 | Straight dough method (mixed fermentation) |
| Bread flour | 15 oz | | 450 g | 75 | 1. Mix all the ingredients except the olives 10 minutes at first speed. |
| Whole wheat flour | 2 oz | | 60 g | 10 | |
| Rye flour | 3 oz | | 90 g | 15 | 2. Add the olives and mix another 4–5 minutes. |
| Salt | 0.4 oz | | 12 g | 2 | **FERMENTATION** |
| Olive oil | 1 oz | | 30 g | 5 | 90 minutes at 75°F (24°C) |
| Basic Yeast Starter (p. 153) or fermented dough | 2 oz | | 60 g | 10 | **MAKEUP** |
| | | | | | Same as Prosciutto Bread (p. 168) |
| Pitted black olives, whole or halved (see *Note*) | 6 oz | | 180 g | 30 | **BAKING** |
| | | | | | 425°F (220°C) with steam |
| **Total weight:** | **2 lb 10 oz** | | **1261 g** | **210%** | |

*Note: Use a flavorful brined olive such as Greek kalamata. Do not use canned, water-packed olives, as they have little flavor.*

# CRUMPETS

*For large-quantity measurements, see page 723.*

| Ingredients | U.S. | | | Metric | % | Procedure |
|---|---|---|---|---|---|---|
| Water, warm | 1 lb | 4 | oz | 550 g | 110 | 1. Mix the warm water, yeast, flour, salt, and sugar to form a soft dough or batter. Ferment 1½ hours at room temperature. |
| Yeast, fresh | | 1 | oz | 30 g | 5.5 | |
| Bread flour | 1 lb | 2 | oz | 500 g | 100 | |
| Salt | | 0.33 | oz | 10 g | 2 | 2. Dissolve the baking soda in the second quantity of water. Mix into the flour mixture until smooth. |
| Sugar | | 0.13 | oz (¾ tsp) | 3.5 g | 0.7 | |
| Baking soda | | 0.06 | oz (⅜ tsp) | 1.5 g | 0.3 | 3. Lightly grease crumpet rings or any round cutters. Place on a moderately hot griddle. Using a ladle or dropping funnel, fill the rings with the batter to a depth of about ½ in. (12 mm). The amount of batter for each crumpet varies from 1½ to 2 oz depending on the size of the rings. |
| Water, cold | | 5 | oz | 140 g | 28 | |
| **Total weight:** | **2 lb 12** | | **oz** | **1235 g** | **246%** | 4. As the crumpets bake, they will develop bubbles on the surface. When the bubbles become holes and the batter is set, remove the rings and turn the crumpets over with a spatula. Continue to bake until the second side just begins to color. |

# AMISH-STYLE SOFT PRETZELS

| Ingredients | U.S. | | Metric | % |
|---|---|---|---|---|
| Water | 10.5 | oz | 325 g | 65 |
| Yeast, fresh | 0.33 | oz | 11 g | 2.25 |
| Bread flour | 12 | oz | 375 g | 75 |
| Pastry flour | 4 | oz | 125 g | 25 |
| Salt | 0.1 | oz | 3 g | 0.6 |
| Sugar | 0.3 | oz | 10 g | 2 |
| **Soda wash** | | | | |
| Water, warm | 8 | oz | 250 g | |
| Baking soda | 1 | oz | 30 g | |
| Pretzel salt | | | | |
| or coarse salt | | | | |
| ***Total dough weight:*** | *1 lb 15* | *oz* | *849 g* | *170%* |

## Procedure

**MIXING**

Straight dough method

**FERMENTATION**

After mixing, allow a bench rest, covered, for 30–60 minutes before makeup.

**MAKEUP**

1. Scaling: With a bench scraper, cut off a long piece of dough 5 oz (150 g) in weight.

2. With the palms of the hands, roll on the bench to a uniform strip 30 in. (75 cm) long (a). Twist into a pretzel shape (b, c).

3. Dip in a solution of 2 oz (60 g) baking soda in 1 pt (500 mL) water. Arrange on baking sheets lined with parchment. Stretch and reform the pretzel shapes as necessary. (*Note:* After dipping in soda solution, the units are difficult to handle. If desired, pan the pretzels first, then brush thoroughly with the soda solution.)

4. Sprinkle with pretzel salt.

5. Bake immediately (without proofing) at 500°F (260°C) for 8–9 minutes, or until well browned.

6. *Optional:* Dip in melted butter immediately after baking and drain on racks (d).

# PITA

| Ingredients | U.S. | | | Metric | % | Procedure |
|---|---|---|---|---|---|---|
| Water | | 14 | oz | 435 g | 58 | **MIXING** |
| Yeast, fresh | | 1 | oz | 30 g | 4 | Straight dough method |
| Bread flour | 1 lb | 4 | oz | 625 g | 83 | **FERMENTATION** |
| Whole wheat flour | | 4 | oz | 125 g | 17 | Until doubled in bulk, about 1½ hours at 80°F (27°C) |
| Salt | | 0.5 | oz | 15 g | 2 | **MAKEUP AND BAKING** |
| Sugar | | 0.67 | oz | 22 g | 3 | 1. Scale at 3 oz (90 g). Round the units and bench-rest. |
| Yogurt, plain low-fat | | 3 | oz | 90 g | 12.5 | 2. With a rolling pin, roll out into circles about 4–5 in. (10–12 cm) in diameter. |
| Oil, preferably olive | | 1 | oz | 30 g | 4 | 3. Bake on oven hearth or on dry sheet pans at 500°F (260°C) until lightly golden around edges, about 5 minutes. Do not overbake, or the pitas will be dry and stiff. They should be soft when cool. |
| *Total weight:* | *2 lb 12* | | *oz* | *1372 g* | *183%* | |

# MAKEUP TECHNIQUES

The object of yeast dough makeup is to shape the dough into rolls or loaves that bake properly and have an attractive appearance. When you shape a roll or loaf correctly, you stretch the gluten strands on the surface into a smooth skin. This tight gluten surface holds the item in shape. This is especially important for loaves and rolls that are baked freestanding, not in pans. Units that are not made up correctly develop irregular shapes and splits and may flatten out.

## Use of Dusting Flour

In most cases, the bench and the dough must be dusted lightly with flour to prevent the dough from sticking to the bench and to the hands. Some bakers use light rye flour for dusting. Others prefer bread flour.

Whichever flour you use, one rule is very important: Use as little dusting flour as possible. Excessive flour makes seams difficult to seal and shows up as streaks in the baked product.

## Procedure for Scaling and Dividing Dough for Rolls

This procedure involves the use of a dough divider. A dough divider cuts a large unit of dough, called a *press*, into small units of equal weight. If this equipment is not available, you must scale individual roll units.

1. Scale the dough into presses of desired weight. One press makes 36 rolls.

2. Round the presses and allow them to relax.

3. Divide the press using a dough divider. Separate the pieces, using a little dusting flour to prevent sticking.

4. Make up the rolls as desired. In some cases, the pieces are rounded first. In other cases, the rolls are made up without rounding, just as they come from the divider.

# Crisp-Crusted Products and Rye Products

### Round Rolls

1. Scale the dough as required, such as 3½ lb (1600 g) per press or 1½ oz (45 g) per roll. Divide the presses into rolls.

2. Holding the palm of the hand fairly flat, roll the dough in a tight circle on the workbench (a). Do not use too much flour for dusting, as the dough must stick to the bench a little in order for the technique to work.

3. As the ball of dough takes on a round shape, gradually cup the hand (b, c).

4. The finished ball of dough should have a smooth surface, except for a slight pucker on the bottom.

5. Place rolls 2 in. (5 cm) apart on sheet pans sprinkled with cornmeal.

6. Proof, wash with water, and bake with steam.

A

B

C

### Oval Rolls

1. Scale and round the rolls as indicated above for round rolls.

2. Roll the rounded units back and forth under the palms of the hands so they become slightly elongated and tapered.

3. Proof and wash with water. Slash with one lengthwise cut or three diagonal cuts.

4. Bake with steam.

## Split Rolls

1. Round the rolls as for round rolls. Let them rest a few minutes.

2. Dust the tops lightly with rye flour. Using a lightly oiled ¾-in. (2 cm) thick wooden pin, press a crease in the center of each roll.

3. Proof upside down in boxes or on canvas dusted with flour. Turn right-side up and place on pans or peels dusted with cornmeal. Do not slash. Bake as for other hard rolls.

## Crescent Rolls

1. Scale the dough into 16–20-oz (450–575 g) units. Round and relax the units.

2. Flatten the dough and roll out into 12-in. (30 cm) circles.

3. With a pastry wheel, cut each dough circle into 12 equal wedges or tri-angles. (Alternative method: For large quantities of dough, roll out into a rectangle and cut like croissant dough; see p. 205.)

4. Roll the triangles into crescents using the same technique as for crois-sants (see p. 205). The rolls may be either left as straight sticks or bent into crescents.

5. Proof. Wash with water and, if desired, sprinkle with poppy seeds, car-away seeds, sesame seeds, or coarse salt. Bake with steam.

## Club Rolls

Rather than being rounded, these units are molded as they come from the divider.

1. Flatten the piece of dough roughly into a rectangle (a).

2. Begin to roll up the dough by folding over the back edge of the rectan-gle. Press the seam firmly with the fingertips (b).

3. Continue to roll the dough, always pressing the seam firmly after each turn. As you roll up the dough, the front edge will appear to shrink. Stretch the front corners, as shown by the arrows, to keep the width uni-form (c).

4. When the roll is finished, seal the seam well so the roll is tight (d).

5. Scoring the proofed roll with a single slash gives the baked roll this ap-pearance (e).

6. Place the units 2 in. (5 cm) apart on sheet pans sprinkled with cornmeal.

7. Proof, wash with water, and slash with one cut lengthwise. Bake with steam.

## Onion Rolls (for Rye or Hard Roll Dough)

1. Prepare the onion mixture:

   a. Cover 1 lb (500 g) dried onions with water and soak until soft. Drain.

   b. Mix with 2 oz (60 g) oil and ½ oz (15 g) salt.

   c. Place on a flat pan. Keep covered until ready to use.

2. Divide and round the dough for rolls. Let rest 10 minutes.

3. Place the rolls face down on top of the onions and flatten well with the hands. Place the flattened rolls onion-side up on paper-lined pans.

4. Proof. Press the center of each roll with two fingers to make an indenta-tion. Bake with steam.

a.

b.

c.

d.

e.

Kaiser Roll Tool

## Kaiser Rolls

1. Scale Vienna dough to produce rolls of desired size. For sandwich-size rolls, use 5-lb (2300 g) presses to yield 2-oz (60 g) baked rolls.

2. Press the dough in the divider and separate the pieces, dusting them with light rye flour.

3. Round the units and let them rest.

4. Flatten the pieces lightly with the hands.

5. Stamp each roll with a kaiser roll tool. The cuts should go about halfway through the rolls. Do not cut all the way through.

6. Place the rolls upside down on boxes or trays sprinkled generously with poppy seeds or lined with canvas cloth. Proof.

7. Place right-side up on cornmeal-dusted baking sheets or peels. Place in the oven and bake with steam.

## French, Italian, and Vienna Loaves

These loaves vary in shape from thick, elongated ovals and thick French-type loaves called *bâtards* to long, thin French baguettes.

1. Flatten the rounded, relaxed dough into an oval with the hands or with a rolling pin (a). Stretch the oval with the hands to lengthen it (b). Roll up tightly and seal the seam well (c, d). Roll the loaf on the bench under the palms of the hands to even out the shape. This will produce an elongated, oval-shaped loaf. The ends should be tapered and rounded, not pointed.

2. If a longer, thinner loaf is desired, relax these units again for a few minutes. Flatten them with the palms of the hands and stretch the dough lightly to increase its length. Once again, roll up tightly and seal the seam well. Roll on the bench under the palms of the hands to even it out and to stretch it to the desired shape and length.

3. Place seam-side down on pans dusted with cornmeal. Proofing the baguettes in these special pans (e) maintains their shape. Proof. Wash with water. Slash with diagonal cuts or one lengthwise cut; this can be done before or after proofing. Bake with steam for the first 10 minutes.

## Round Loaves and Oval Loaves

These techniques are used for many types of breads, including pain de campagne and French rye. A round loaf is called a *boule* or *miche*.

For round loaves, like pain de campagne:

1. Flatten the rounded, relaxed dough into a circle. Fold the sides over the center, then round again. Shape the dough into a seam-free ball (a).

2. Place on pans sprinkled with cornmeal or flour. Proof, wash the tops with water, and slash the tops in a crosshatch pattern (b, c). Bake with steam.

For oval loaves, like French rye:

1. As for round loaves, flatten the rounded, relaxed dough into a circle. Fold the sides over the center, then round again. Roll the dough under the palms of the hands into a smooth oval loaf (a).

2. Place on pans sprinkled with cornmeal or flour (b). Proof, wash the tops with water, and dredge with flour. Score as shown (c).

As an alternative to proofing on pans, proof upside down in special baskets called *bannetons*. Dust the inside of the banneton with flour and push the dough firmly into the basket (d). When the dough is proofed, turn out onto a sheet pan or a peel and slide into the oven.

Canvas-lined banneton

## Fougasse

1. Roll out the dough into a large, thin oval, letting it rest at intervals to allow the gluten to relax.

2. Oil a sheet pan with olive oil. Place the dough on the sheet pan and brush the dough well with olive oil (a).

3. Press the fingertips into the dough at regular intervals, as for focaccia (b) (see p. 167).

4. Cut slits in the dough (c). Stretch the dough to open the slits (d).

5. Proof for 30 minutes at room temperature.

# Soft Roll Doughs, Pan Loaves, and Braided Breads

## Tied or Knotted Rolls

1. Scale the dough into presses of desired size. Divide the presses.

2. With the palms of the hands, roll each unit on the workbench into a strip or rope of dough.

3. Tie the rolls as shown on page 177.

4. Place rolls 2 in. (5 cm) apart on greased or paper-lined baking sheets.

5. Proof, egg wash, and bake without steam.

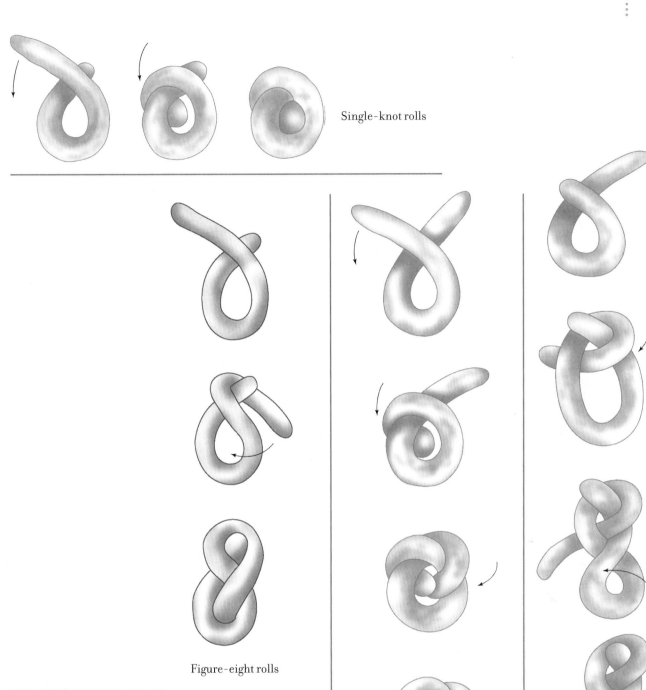

Single-knot rolls

Figure-eight rolls

Double-knot rolls

Braided rolls

## Sawtooth Rolls

1. Prepare elongated oval rolls.

2. With a scissors, cut a row of snips down the tops of the rolls.

### Crescent Rolls

1. Make up as for hard crescent rolls, except brush the triangles with melted butter before rolling up.

2. Proof, egg wash, and sprinkle with poppy seeds. Bake without steam.

### Pan Rolls

1. Scale the dough into presses of desired size. Divide.

2. Make up as for round hard rolls.

3. Place on greased pans ½ in. (1 cm) apart.

### Parker House Rolls

1. Scale the dough into presses of desired size. Divide.

2. Round the scaled piece of dough (a).

3. Flatten the center of the dough with a narrow rolling pin (b).

4. Fold the dough over and press down on the folded edge to make a crease (c).

5. Place on a greased baking sheet ½ in. (1 cm) apart. The baked rolls have a seam that splits open easily (d).

a.

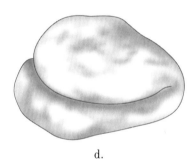

b.    c.    d.

### Cloverleaf Rolls

1. Scale the dough into presses of desired size. Divide each piece of dough into 3 equal parts and shape them into balls.

2. Place 3 balls in the bottom of each greased muffin tin (a). The balls merge as they bake to form a cloverleaf shape (b).

a.    b.

## Butterflake Rolls

1. Roll out the dough into a very thin rectangular shape. Brush it with melted butter. Cut it into strips 1 in. (2.5 cm) wide (a).

2. Stack 6 strips. Cut into 1½-in. (3.5 cm) pieces (b).

a.                                        b.

3. Place the pieces on end in greased muffin tins (c). Proof. The baked rolls have a flaky appearance (d).

c.                                        d.

## Pan Loaves

1. Start with the rounded, benched dough (a).

2. Stretch it into a long rectangle (b).

3. Fold into thirds (c, d).

4. Roll the dough into a tight roll that has the same length as the pan it is to be baked in (e). Seal the seam well and place the dough seam-side down in the greased pan.

For split-top loaves, make one cut from end to end in the top of the loaf after proofing.

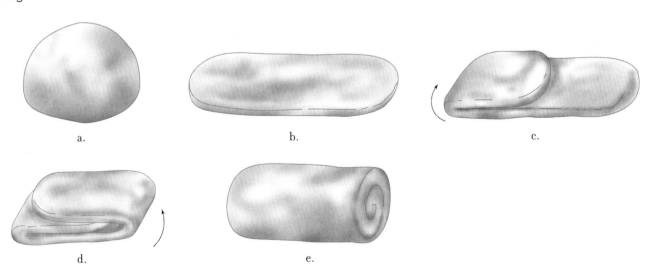

a.                          b.                          c.

d.                          e.

## Pullman Loaf

Pullman loaves are baked in loaf pans with sliding lids so slices from the baked loaf are square, ideal for sandwiches. Pans are usually of standard sizes to make 1-lb (450 g), 1½-lb (675 g), 2-lb (900 g), and 3-lb (1350 g) loaves.

1. Scale the dough to fit the loaf pans. Add an extra 2 oz (50 g) dough per pound (450 g) to allow for baking loss.

2. Make up loaves in one of two ways:

   ◆ Make up as standard pan loaves as in the preceding technique.

   ◆ Divide each scaled unit into 2 pieces. Roll out into strips and twist the 2 strips together. Seal the ends well. This method is preferred by many bakers because it gives extra strength to the loaf structure. The sides of the loaf are less likely to collapse.

3. Place the made-up loaves in lightly greased pans. Put on the lids (greased on the underside), but leave them open about 1 in. (2.5 cm).

4. Proof until the dough has risen almost to the lids.

5. Close the lids. Bake at 400°–425°F (200°–218°C) without steam.

6. Remove the lids after 30 minutes. The bread should be taking on color by this time. If the lid sticks, it may be because the bread requires a few more minutes of baking with the lid. Try again after a few minutes.

7. Complete baking with the lids off to allow moisture to escape.

## Braided Loaves

Egg-enriched soft roll dough and challah dough are the most appropriate for braided loaves. The dough should be relatively stiff so the braids hold their shape.

Braids of one to six strands are commonly made. More complicated braids of seven or more strands are not presented here because they are rarely made.

Braided breads are egg-washed after proofing. If desired, they may also be sprinkled with poppy seeds after washing.

## One-Strand Braid

1. Roll the dough into a smooth, straight strip with the palms of the hands. The strip should be of uniform thickness from end to end.

2. Tie or braid the strip as for a braided roll (see p. 177).

## Two-, Three-, Four-, Five-, and Six-Strand Braids

1. Divide the dough into equal pieces, depending on how many strips are required.

   For a double three-strand braid, divide the dough into 4 equal pieces, then divide one of these pieces into 3 smaller pieces to yield 3 large and 3 small pieces.

2. Roll the pieces with the palms of the hands into long, smooth strips. The pieces should be thickest in the middle and gradually tapered toward the ends.

3. Braid the strips as shown in the illustrations. Please note that the numbers used in these descriptions refer to the positions of the strands (numbered from left to right). At each stage in the braiding, number 1 always indicates the first strand on the left.

## Two-Strand Braids

1. Cross the 2 strands in the middle (a).

2. Fold the two ends of the bottom strand over the upper one (b).

3. Now fold the ends of the other strand over in the same way (c).

4. Repeat steps 2 and 3 until the braid is finished (d).

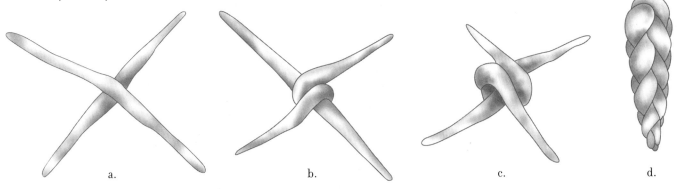

a.          b.          c.          d.

## Three-Strand Braids

1. Lay the 3 strands side by side. Starting in the center, fold the left strand over the center one (1 over 2) (a).

2. Now fold the right strand over the center (3 over 2) (b).

3. Repeat the sequence (1 over 2, 3 over 2) (c).

4. When you reach the end of the strands, turn the braid over (d).

5. Braid the other half (e).

6. If desired, a smaller three-strand braid can be placed on top (f).

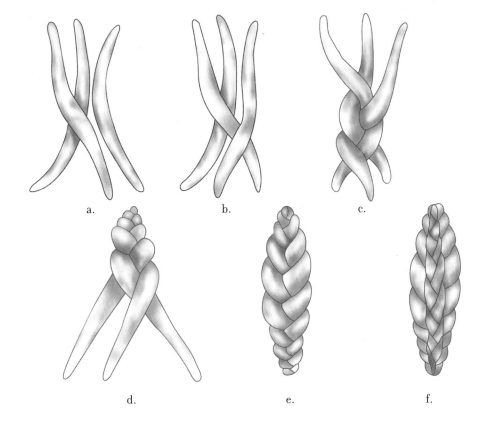

a.          b.          c.

d.          e.          f.

## Four-Strand Braids

**1.** Start with 4 strands, fastened at the end (a).

**2.** Move 4 over 2 (b).

**3.** Move 1 over 3 (c).

**4.** Move 2 over 3 (d).

**5.** Repeat steps 2, 3, 4 until the braid is finished (e, f).

a.

b.

c.

d.

e.

f.

## Five-Strand Braids

**1.** Start with 5 strands, fastened at the end (a).

**2.** Move 1 over 3 (b).

**3.** Move 2 over 3 (c).

**4.** Move 5 over 2 (d).

**5.** Repeat steps 2, 3, 4 until the braid is finished (e, f).

a.

b.

c.

d.

e.

f.

### Six-Strand Braids

1. Start with 6 strands, fastened at the end (a).
2. The first step, 6 over 1, is not part of the repeated sequence (b).
3. The repeated sequence begins with 2 over 6 (c).
4. Move 1 over 3 (d).
5. Move 5 over 1 (e).
6. Move 6 over 4 (f).
7. Repeat steps 3 to 6 until the braid is finished (g).

a.

b.

c.

d.

e.

f.

g.

## TERMS FOR REVIEW

| | | | |
|---|---|---|---|
| French bread | sour | press | pain de campagne |
| bagel | pumpernickel | ciabatta | fougasse |
| English muffin | Pullman loaf | focaccia | |

## QUESTIONS FOR DISCUSSION

1. How would the baked loaves be different if you increased the shortening in the French bread formula (p. 145) to 7%?

2. Why is the baking temperature for Italian bread (p. 144) higher than that for challah (p. 150)?

3. How could you modify the formula for Vienna bread (p. 143) if you didn't have any malt?

4. Why is it important not to use too much dusting flour when making up breads and rolls?

5. Describe the procedure for makeup of focaccia.

6. Describe the procedure for using a dough divider.

7. Describe the procedure for rounding rolls.

8. Describe the procedure for makeup of baguettes.

## Chapter 9

# Rich Yeast Doughs

**T**his chapter completes the study of yeast doughs with a survey of the most important rich yeast doughs. As explained in chapter 6, rich doughs are those with higher proportions of fat and, sometimes, sugar and eggs as well.

Simple sweet-roll doughs are the easiest of these products to handle. Even these, however, require care, as they are usually softer and stickier than bread doughs. Because their gluten structure is not as strong as that of lean doughs, more care must be taken in proofing and baking sweet dough products.

Rolled-in doughs, such as those for Danish pastries and croissants, are especially rich in fat because they consist of layers of butter between layers of dough. Like other sweet doughs, these yeast-leavened doughs are often considered the pastry chef's department rather than the bread baker's department. Considerable practice and skill are required for the makeup of fine Danish products.

As in chapter 8, the dough formulas and makeup techniques are given in separate sections of the chapter because each dough can be made up into a great many items. This chapter also includes a selection of fillings and toppings suitable for rich yeast-dough products. Review chapter 6 with respect to the basic mixing methods and other production procedures for yeast doughs.

**After reading this chapter, you should be able to:**

1. Produce simple sweet doughs.

2. Produce rolled-in yeast doughs.

3. Produce a variety of toppings and fillings for rich yeast doughs.

4. Make up a variety of products using sweet doughs and rolled-in doughs, including Danish pastry and croissants.

# SWEET DOUGH AND RICH DOUGH FORMULAS

It must be remembered that high percentages of fat and sugar in a yeast dough inhibit fermentation. For this reason, most of the doughs in this section are mixed by the sponge method so most of the fermentation can take place before the sugar and fat are added. The major exception is regular sweet dough or bun dough, which is low enough in fat and sugar to be mixed by the modified straight dough method. The quantity of yeast is also increased. Refer to pages 113–115 to review the basic mixing methods.

High levels of fat and eggs make rich doughs very soft. The amount of liquid is reduced to compensate for this.

Because they are so tender, rich doughs are generally underfermented and underproofed. About three-quarters proof is best for rich doughs. Overproofed units may collapse in baking.

Bun pans should be lined with silicone paper whenever there is danger of sticking. This is especially true for items with fruit fillings or other sugary fillings or toppings.

Note that the recipes exemplify two ways of mixing rich sponge doughs. Rich sweet dough and kugelhopf dough are high in sugar. To ensure even distribution in the dough, the sugar is creamed with the fat, just as in the modified straight dough method. **Brioche** and **baba** doughs contain little sugar, so this method is not used. The fat is mixed into the dough last.

## SWEET ROLL DOUGH

*For large-quantity measurements, see page 723.*

| Ingredients | U.S. | Metric | % | Procedure |
|---|---|---|---|---|
| Water | 8 oz | 200 g | 40 | **MIXING** |
| Yeast, fresh | 1.5 oz | 38 g | 7.50 | Modified straight dough method (p. 115) |
| Butter, margarine, or shortening (see *Note*) | 4 oz | 100 g | 20 | Develop the dough 4 minutes at second speed (see p. 116). |
| Sugar | 4 oz | 100 g | 20 | **FERMENTATION** |
| Salt | 0.4 oz | 10 g | 2 | 1½–2 hours at 75°F (24°C) |
| Nonfat milk solids | 1 oz | 25 g | 5 | **MAKEUP AND PROOFING** |
| Eggs | 3 oz | 75 g | 15 | See pages 206–215. |
| Bread flour | 1 lb | 400 g | 80 | **BAKING** |
| Cake flour | 4 oz | 100 g | 20 | 375°F (190°C) |
| **Total weight:** | 2 lb 9 oz | 1048 g | 209% | |

*Note: Any of the fats listed may be used alone or in combination.*

# RICH SWEET DOUGH

*For large-quantity measurements, see page 724.*

| Ingredients | U.S. | | Metric | % | Procedure |
|---|---|---|---|---|---|
| Milk, scalded and cooled | 8 | oz | 200 g | 40 | **MIXING** |
| Yeast, fresh | 1 | oz | 25 g | 5 | Sponge Method |
| Bread flour | 10 | oz | 250 g | 50 | 1. Make a sponge with the first 3 ingredients. Ferment until double. |
| Butter | 8 | oz | 200 g | 40 | 2. Cream butter, sugar, and salt until well blended. Blend in eggs. |
| Sugar | 4 | oz | 100 g | 20 | |
| Salt | 0.4 oz | | 10 g | 2 | 3. Add the sponge. Mix to break up the sponge. |
| Eggs | 5 | oz | 125 g | 25 | |
| Bread flour | 10 | oz | 250 g | 50 | 4. Add the flour and develop the dough. Mixing time: about 3 minutes. |
| *Total weight:* | *2 lb 14* | *oz* | *1160 g* | *232%* | |

**MIXING**

Sponge Method

1. Make a sponge with the first 3 ingredients. Ferment until double.

2. Cream butter, sugar, and salt until well blended. Blend in eggs.

3. Add the sponge. Mix to break up the sponge.

4. Add the flour and develop the dough. Mixing time: about 3 minutes.

**FERMENTATION**

30–40 minutes or retard immediately. Retarding makes it easier to handle the dough, which is very soft.

## VARIATIONS

### STOLLEN

*For large-quantity measurements, see page 724.*

| Ingredients | U.S. | | Metric | % |
|---|---|---|---|---|
| Almond extract | 0.12 oz (¾ tsp) | | 2 g | 0.5 |
| Lemon rind, grated | 0.12 oz (1½ tsp) | | 2 g | 0.5 |
| Vanilla extract | 0.12 oz (¾ tsp) | | 2 g | 0.5 |
| Raisins (light, dark, or a mixture) | 6 | oz | 150 g | 30 |
| Mixed glacéed fruit | 7 | oz | 175 g | 35 |

Add almond extract, lemon rind, and vanilla extract to the butter and sugar during the blending stage. Knead raisins and mixed glacéed fruit into the dough.

**MAKEUP**

1. Scale, round, and let rest. Scaling weights may range from 12 oz to 2 lb (350 g to 1 kg), depending on individual needs.

2. With hands or a rolling pin, flatten slightly into an oval shape.

3. Wash the top with butter.

4. Make a crease down the length of the oval about ½ in. (1 cm) off center. Fold one side (the smaller side) over the other, as though you are making a large, wide Parker House roll (see p. 178).

5. Give three-quarters proof. Wash the tops with melted butter.

6. Bake at 375°F (190°C).

7. Cool. Dredge heavily with 4X or 6X sugar.

### BABKA

*For large-quantity measurements, see page 724.*

| Ingredients | U.S. | | Metric | % |
|---|---|---|---|---|
| Vanilla extract | 0.12 oz (¾ tsp) | | 2 g | 0.5 |
| Cardamom | 0.06 oz (¾ tsp) | | 1 g | 0.25 |
| Raisins | 4 | oz | 100 g | 20 |

Add vanilla and cardamom to the butter during blending. Knead the raisins into the dough.

**MAKEUP**

Loaf-type coffee cake (p. 214). May be topped with streusel.

**BAKING**

350°F (175°C). Be sure to bake thoroughly; underbaked units will have sticky crumb and may collapse.

# KUGELHOPF

| Ingredients | U.S. | | Metric | % | Procedure |
|---|---|---|---|---|---|
| Milk, scalded and cooled | 6 | oz | 190 g | 30 | **MIXING** |
| Yeast, fresh | 1 | oz | 30 g | 5 | Sponge method |
| Bread flour | 6 | oz | 190 g | 30 | 1. Make a sponge with the first 3 ingredients. Ferment until double. |
| Butter | 8 | oz | 250 g | 40 | 2. Cream the butter, sugar, and salt until well |
| Sugar | 4 | oz | 125 g | 20 | blended. Blend in the eggs. |
| Salt | 0.4 | oz | 13 g | 2 | 3. Add the sponge. Mix to break up the sponge. |
| Eggs | 7 | oz | 220 g | 35 | 4. Add the flour and develop the dough. Mix- |
| Bread flour | 14 | oz | 440 g | 70 | ing time: about 3 minutes. Dough will be |
| Raisins | 2.5 | oz | 75 g | 12.5 | very soft and sticky. |
| **Total weight:** | **3 lb** | | **1527 g** | **244%** | 5. Carefully blend in the raisins. |

**FERMENTATION**

Needs only 15–20 minutes bench rest before scaling and panning. Or retard immediately.

**MAKEUP**

Heavily butter kugelhopf molds or tube pans. Line with sliced almonds (which will stick to the buttered sides). Fill molds halfway with dough (each quart of volume requires about 1 lb dough, or each liter requires about 500 g). Give three-quarters proof.

**BAKING**

375°F (190°C)

Unmold and cool completely. Dust with confectioners' sugar.

# HOT CROSS BUNS

*For large-quantity measurements, see page 724.*

| Ingredients | U.S. | | Metric | Procedure |
|---|---|---|---|---|
| Sweet Roll Dough (p. 188) | 2 lb 8 | oz | 1250 g | 1. Undermix the Sweet Roll Dough. Mix to- gether the fruits and spice until thoroughly mixed, then work into the dough until well incorporated. |
| Dried currants | 4 | oz | 125 g | |
| Golden raisins | 2 | oz | 60 g | |
| Mixed candied peel, diced | 1 | oz | 30 g | 2. See Sweet Roll Dough formula for fermenta- tion and baking. |
| Ground allspice | 0.07 oz (1 tsp) | | 2.5 g | |
| **Total weight:** | **2 lb 15** | **oz** | **1467 g** | |

**MAKEUP**

Scale into 2-oz (60 g) units and round. Place on greased or parchment-lined sheet pans, just touching. Egg wash. After baking, brush with Clear Glaze (p. 199). Pipe Flat Icing (p. 431) into a cross shape on each roll.

**VARIATION**

For a more traditional cross on top of the buns, mix together the in- gredients for Cross Paste (below) until smooth. Pipe crosses onto the buns after they are proofed but before they are baked.

## CROSS PASTE

| Ingredients | U.S. | | Metric | % |
|---|---|---|---|---|
| Water | 10 | oz | 300 g | 111 |
| Pastry flour or cake flour | 9 | oz | 270 g | 100 |
| Shortening | 2 | oz | 60 g | 22 |
| Milk powder | 1 | oz | 30 g | 11 |
| Baking powder | 0.06 oz (⅛ tsp) | | 2 g | 0.7 |
| Salt | 0.06 oz (⅛ tsp) | | 2 g | 0.7 |

# BABA/SAVARIN DOUGH

*For large-quantity measurements, see page 724.*

| Ingredients | U.S. | | Metric | % | Procedure |
|---|---|---|---|---|---|
| Milk | 4 | oz | 120 g | 40 | **MIXING** |
| Yeast, fresh | 0.5 | oz | 15 g | 5 | Sponge method |
| Bread flour | 2.5 | oz | 75 g | 25 | 1. Scald milk and cool to lukewarm. Dissolve |
| Eggs | 5 | oz | 150 g | 50 | yeast. Add flour and mix to make a sponge. |
| Bread flour | 7.5 | oz | 225 g | 75 | Let rise until double. |
| Sugar | 0.25 | oz | 8 g | 2.5 | 2. Gradually mix in eggs and then dry ingredi- |
| Salt | 0.2 | oz (1 tsp) | 4 g | 2 | ents (using the paddle attachment) to make |
| Butter, melted | 4 | oz | 120 g | 40 | a soft dough. |
| *Total weight:* | *1 lb 7* | *oz* | *719 g* | *239%* | |

**VARIATION**

Add 25% raisins (10 oz/300 g) to baba dough.

3. Beat in butter a little at a time until it is completely absorbed and the dough is smooth. Dough will be very soft and sticky.

**MAKEUP AND BAKING**

1. Fill greased molds half full. Average baba molds require about 2 oz (60 g). For savarin molds (ring molds), the following are averages:

| | |
|---|---|
| 5-in. ring: 5–6 oz | 13-cm ring: 140–170 g |
| 7-in. ring: 10–12 oz | 18-cm ring: 280–340 g |
| 8-in. ring: 14–16 oz | 20-cm ring: 400–450 g |
| 10-in. ring: 20–24 oz | 25-cm ring: 575–675 g |

2. Proof until dough is level with top of mold.

3. Bake at 400°F (200°C).

4. While still warm, soak in Dessert Syrup (p. 261) flavored with rum or kirsch. Drain.

5. Glaze with Apricot Glaze (p. 200). If desired, decorate with candied fruits.

# PANETTONE

| Ingredients | U.S. | | Metric | % | Procedure |
|---|---|---|---|---|---|
| Raisins | 2.5 | oz | 75 g | 11 | **MIXING AND FERMENTATION** |
| Golden raisins or sultanas | 2.5 | oz | 75 g | 11 | 1. *Prepare the marinated fruit mixture:* Combine the raisins, peel, almonds, zest, juice, rum, and nutmeg in a bowl. Cover and allow to marinate several hours or, refrigerated, overnight. |
| Mixed candied peel | 5 | oz | 150 g | 21 | |
| Blanched almonds, chopped | 2.5 | oz | 75 g | 11 | |
| Grated lemon zest | 0.12 | oz (1½ tsp) | 4 g | 0.6 | 2. Sift the flour into a bowl and make a well in the center. |
| Grated orange zest | 0.12 | oz (1½ tsp) | 4 g | 0.6 | 3. Warm the milk to 100°F (37°C) and mix with the yeast. Pour this mixture into the well in the flour. Sprinkle a little flour from the sides of the bowl on top of the yeast liquid. Cover the bowl and allow to stand at room temperature until the flour starts to appear cracked on top and the mixture bubbles, approximately 45 minutes. |
| Lemon juice | 2 | oz | 60 g | 9 | |
| Orange juice | 2 | oz | 60 g | 9 | |
| Rum | 4 | tsp | 20 g | 3 | |
| Nutmeg | ½ | tsp | 2 mL | 0.7 | |
| Bread flour | 1 lb 8 | oz | 700 g | 100 | |
| Milk | 10 | oz | 285 g | 41 | |
| Yeast, fresh | 1.5 | oz | 40 g | 6 | |
| Egg yolks | 4 | oz | 120 g | 17 | 4. Add the egg yolks, salt, and sugar to the flour mixture. Mix lightly to form a soft dough. Turn out onto a floured work surface and knead for 10 minutes, or until smooth. |
| Salt | 0.17 | oz (1 tsp) | 5 g | 0.7 | |
| Sugar | 4 | oz | 125 g | 17 | |
| Butter | 8 | oz | 225 g | 32 | 5. Place the dough in a lightly floured bowl, cover with a damp cloth, and let ferment at room temperature until doubled in size. |
| *Total weight:* | *3 lb 12* | *oz* | *2025 g* | *289%* | |

6. Drain the marinated fruit. Add the fruit and the butter, softened, into the dough until smooth and well incorporated. Put back into the bowl and let ferment a second time at room temperature until doubled in size.

**PAN PREPARATION AND BAKING**

*Note: This procedure makes 1 large loaf weighing about 3 lb (1500 g) after baking. For smaller loaves, divide the dough into 2, 3, or 4 equal parts and bake in smaller molds.*

1. Cut a double layer of parchment paper, long enough to line a 6-in. (15 cm) cake tin with an overlap of 1 in. (2 cm) and approximately 9 in. (23 cm) tall. Place into a buttered cake tin. Place on a baking sheet. Fold a sheet of foil several times to form a stiff collar on the outside of the tin. The foil should be the same height as the baking paper inside. Secure with string. Line the bottom of the tin with a double layer of paper cut into a 6-in. (15 cm) circle.

2. Punch down the dough and round it into a smooth ball.

3. Place the dough in the prepared cake tin and press down lightly with the knuckles.

4. Cover and proof at room temperature until doubled in volume.

5. Cut a cross in the top of the dough and brush with melted butter.

6. Bake in a preheated oven at 375°F (190°C) until lightly colored. Place a piece of butter (about 4 tsp/20 g) in the center of cross and continue to bake for 1 hour. Cover the top of the panettone with foil when golden in order to prevent excessive browning.

7. Reduce oven temperature to 325°F (160°C). Continue baking until a skewer inserted in the center comes out clean, approximately 1¾–2 hours in all.

8. Remove from the oven and brush with melted butter.

9. Once cold, dust the top with confectioners' sugar.

# BRIOCHE

*For large-quantity measurements, see page 724.*

| Ingredients | U.S. | | Metric | % | Procedure |
|---|---|---|---|---|---|
| Milk | 2 | oz | 60 g | 20 | **MIXING** |
| Yeast, fresh | 0.5 | oz | 15 g | 5 | Sponge method |
| Bread flour | 2 | oz | 60 g | 20 | 1. Scald the milk and cool to lukewarm. Dissolve the yeast. Add the flour and mix to make a sponge. Let rise until double. |
| Eggs | 5 | oz | 150 g | 50 | |
| Bread flour | 8 | oz | 240 g | 80 | 2. Gradually mix in the eggs and then the dry ingredients (using the paddle attachment) to make a soft dough. |
| Sugar | 0.5 | oz | 15 g | 5 | |
| Salt | 0.2 oz (1 tsp) | | 6 g | 2 | |
| Butter, softened (see Note) | 7 | oz | 210 g | 70 | 3. Beat in the butter a little at a time until it is completely absorbed and the dough is smooth. Dough will be very soft and sticky. |
| *Total weight:* | *1 lb 9* | *oz* | *760 g* | *252%* | |

*Note: To make the dough less sticky and easier to handle, the butter may be reduced to 50% (5 oz/150 g) or as low as 35% (3.5 oz/105 g). However, the product will not be as rich and delicate.*

**FERMENTATION**

1. If the dough will require much handling in makeup, as for small brioche rolls, it is easiest to retard the dough overnight. Making it up while chilled reduces stickiness.

2. If the dough is to be simply deposited in pans, its stickiness and softness is not a problem, so it need not be retarded. Ferment 20 minutes, then scale and pan.

**MAKEUP**

See page 206. Egg wash after proofing.

**BAKING**

400°F (200°C) for small rolls; 375°F (190°C) for large units

# ROLLED-IN DOUGH FORMULAS

R olled-in doughs contain many layers of fat sandwiched between layers of dough. These layers create the flakiness you are familiar with in Danish pastry.

In the classic pastry shop, there are two basic rolled-in yeast doughs:

1. *Croissant dough* (also called *Danish pastry dough, croissant-style*) resembles a puff pastry (see chapter 14) with the addition of yeast. It is based on a dough made of milk, flour, a little sugar, and, of course, yeast. The rolled-in butter gives the dough its flaky texture.

2. *Danish dough, brioche-style*, is a richer dough containing eggs, although it is not as rich in eggs as regular brioche. This dough is also called *brioche feuilletée*, or flaky brioche.

Both these doughs are used in making Danish pastries, although only the first one is generally used for croissants. In addition to the classic French recipes for these two pastry doughs, this section also includes two formulas similar to those widely used in North American bakeshops.

Take care not to overmix rolled-in doughs. The rolling-in procedure continues to develop the gluten. Overmixing the dough results in inferior baked products.

Butter is the preferred fat because of its flavor and melt-in-the-mouth qualities. The highest-quality products use butter for at least part of the rolled-in fat. However, butter is difficult to work because it is hard when cold and soft when a little too warm. Specially formulated shortenings and margarines (called *roll-in compounds*) can be used when lower cost and greater ease of handling are important considerations.

## ⁂ VIENNOISERIE ⁂

Viennoiserie (vee en wahz ree), or Viennese pastry, is the general term given to sweet yeast-raised dough goods, both laminated and non-laminated. Brioche, Danish, and croissants are classic examples of viennoiserie.

# Rolling-In Procedure for Danish and Croissant Dough

The rolling-in procedure has two major parts: enclosing the fat in the dough, and rolling out and folding the dough to increase the number of layers.

In these doughs, we use a **simple fold**, or three-fold, which means we fold the dough in thirds. Each complete rolling and folding step is called a *turn*. We give Danish dough three turns. Rest the dough in the refrigerator for 30 minutes after the first turn to allow the gluten to relax.

After each turn, use the fingertips to press indentations in the dough near the edge—one indentation after the first turn, two after the second, three after the third. This helps you keep track of your production if you have several batches in progress, and it is essential if you have several people working on the same dough.

1. Roll out the dough into a rectangle. Smear softened butter over two-thirds of the dough, leaving a margin around the edges.

2. Fold the unbuttered third of the dough over the center.

3. Fold the remaining third on top.

4. Rotate the dough 90 degrees on the countertop. This step is necessary before each rolling-out of the dough so the dough is stretched in all directions, not just lengthwise. In addition, always place the worse side up before rolling so it will be hidden after folding and the better side will be on the outside. Roll out the dough into a long rectangle.

5. Fold the dough into thirds by first folding the top third over the center.

6. Then fold over the remaining third. This is the first turn or first fold (enclosing the butter doesn't count as a turn). Let the dough rest in the refrigerator 30 minutes to relax the gluten. Repeat this rolling and folding two more times for a total of three turns.

# DANISH PASTRY DOUGH (CROISSANT-STYLE)

| Ingredients | U.S. | | Metric | % |
|---|---|---|---|---|
| Water | 7 | oz | 200 g | 18 |
| Yeast, fresh | 1.25 | oz | 40 g | 3.5 |
| Bread flour | 5 | oz | 150 g | 14 |
| Sugar | 2.5 | oz | 80 g | 7 |
| Salt | 0.75 | oz | 25 g | 2 |
| Milk | 12 | oz | 350 g | 32 |
| Water | 1.5 | oz | 50 g | 4.5 |
| Bread flour | 2 lb | | 950 g | 86 |
| Butter | 1 lb 4 | oz | 600 g | 55 |
| *Total weight:* | *5 lb 2* | *oz* | *2445 g* | *222%* |

## Procedure

### MIXING AND FERMENTATION

Modified straight dough method

1. In a bowl, mix the yeast and water (a). Sprinkle the first quantity of flour over the mixture (b). Let stand about 15 minutes.

2. In another bowl, mix the sugar, salt, milk, and water until the solids are dissolved

3. Sift the flour and add it to the yeast mixture. Add the liquid mixture. Begin mixing to form a dough (c).

4. Mix just until a uniform dough is formed. Continue mixing by hand; avoid overmixing (d).

5. Finish by kneading the dough on the countertop (e).

6. Cover and allow to ferment for 40 minutes at room temperature.

7. Punch down and place in refrigerator for 1 hour.

### ROLLING IN

Incorporate the butter and give 3 three-folds (see p. 195 for rolling-in procedure).

# DANISH PASTRY DOUGH (BRIOCHE-STYLE)

*For large-quantity measurements, see page 724.*

| Ingredients | U.S. | | Metric | % |
|---|---|---|---|---|
| Milk | 7 | oz | 225 g | 28 |
| Yeast, fresh | 1.33 | oz | 40 g | 5 |
| Bread flour | 1 lb 10 | oz | 800 g | 100 |
| Eggs | 3.25 | oz | 100 g | 12.5 |
| Butter, melted | 1.5 | oz | 50 g | 6 |
| Salt | 0.33 oz (2 tsp) | | 10 g | 1.25 |
| Sugar | 1.5 | oz | 50 g | 6 |
| Milk | 2.5 | oz | 75 g | 9 |
| Butter, softened | 1 lb | | 500 g | 62 |
| *Total weight:* | *3 lb 11* | *oz* | *1850 g* | *229%* |

## Procedure

### MIXING AND FERMENTATION

1. In a bowl, mix the first quantity of milk with the yeast (a).

2. Sift the flour on top of the yeast mixture. Add the eggs and melted butter (b).

3. Dissolve the salt and sugar in the second quantity of milk (c). Add to the bowl.

4. Mix for 1½ minutes with the dough hook to form a dough (d).

5. Place the dough in a mixing bowl, cover, and let ferment 30 minutes at room temperature or overnight in the refrigerator.

6. Punch down the dough and rest in the refrigerator for 45 minutes.

### ROLLING IN

Incorporate the last quantity of butter and give 3 three-folds (see p. 195 for rolling-in procedure).

# CROISSANTS

*For large-quantity measurements, see page 725.*

| Ingredients | U.S. | | Metric | % | Procedure |
|---|---|---|---|---|---|
| Milk | 8 | oz | 225 g | 57 | **MIXING** |
| Yeast, fresh | 0.5 | oz | 15 g | 4 | Straight dough method |
| Sugar | 0.5 | oz | 15 g | 4 | Scald the milk, cool to lukewarm, and dissolve |
| Salt | 0.25 | oz | 8 g | 2 | the yeast. Add the remaining ingredients ex- |
| Butter, softened | 1.5 | oz | 40 g | 10 | cept the last quantity of butter. Mix into a |
| Bread flour | 14 | oz | 400 g | 100 | smooth dough, but do not develop the gluten. |
| Butter | 8 | oz | 225 g | 57 | Gluten development will take place during |
| **Total weight:** | **2 lb** | | **928 g** | **234%** | rolling-in procedure. |

**FERMENTATION**

1–1½ hours at 75°F (24°C)

Punch down, spread out on a flat pan, and rest in refrigerator or retarder 30 minutes.

**ROLLING IN**

Incorporate the last amount of butter and give 3 three-folds (see p. 195). Rest in retarder overnight.

**MAKEUP**

See page 205.

Proof at 75°F (24°C) and 65% humidity. Egg wash before baking.

**BAKING**

400°F (200°C)

# DANISH PASTRY

*For large-quantity measurements, see page 725.*

| Ingredients | U.S. | | Metric | % | Procedure |
|---|---|---|---|---|---|
| Water | 8 | oz | 200 g | 40 | **MIXING** |
| Yeast, fresh | 1.25 | oz | 32 g | 6.25 | Modified straight dough method |
| Butter | 2.5 | oz | 62 g | 12.5 | Develop the dough 3–4 minutes at second |
| Sugar | 3 | oz | 75 g | 15 | speed (see p. 116). |
| Nonfat milk solids | 1 | oz | 25 g | 5 | Rest in retarder 30 minutes. |
| Salt | 0.4 | oz | 8 g | 2 | Roll in last quantity of butter. Give 4 three-folds |
| Cardamom or mace *(optional)* | 0.04 oz (½ tsp) | | 1 g | 0.2 | (see p. 195). |
| Whole eggs | 4 | oz | 100 g | 20 | **MAKEUP** |
| Egg yolks | 1 | oz | 25 g | 5 | See pages 206–215. |
| Bread flour | 1 lb | | 400 g | 80 | Proof at 90°F (32°C) with little steam. Egg wash |
| Cake flour | 4 | oz | 100 g | 20 | before baking. |
| Butter (for rolling in) | 10 | oz | 250 g | 50 | **BAKING** |
| **Total weight:** | **3 lb 3 oz** | | **1278 g** | **256%** | 375°F (190°C) |

# FILLINGS AND TOPPINGS

The formulas in this section include many of the most popular fillings and toppings for Danish pastry, coffee cakes, and other sweet yeast products. Several of these items, such as cinnamon sugar, streusel topping, almond filling, and clear glaze, are used for many other bakery products, including cakes, cookies, puff pastries, pies, and tarts. However, their primary use is in the production of yeast goods.

Many of these and similar fillings are available ready-made from bakery supply houses. For example, good-quality prune, poppy, apricot, and other fruit and nut fillings can be purchased in No. 10 cans.

## CINNAMON SUGAR

*For large-quantity measurements, see page 725.*

| Ingredients | U.S. | | Metric | % | Procedure |
|---|---|---|---|---|---|
| Sugar | 8 | oz | 250 g | 100 | Stir together thoroughly. |
| Cinnamon | 0.25 oz (4 tsp) | | 8 g | 3 | |
| *Total weight:* | *8* | *oz* | *258 g* | *103%* | |

## STREUSEL OR CRUMB TOPPING

*For large-quantity measurements, see page 725.*

| Ingredients | U.S. | | Metric | % | Procedure |
|---|---|---|---|---|---|
| Butter and/ or shortening | 4 | oz | 125 g | 50 | Rub all ingredients together until the fat is thoroughly blended in and the mixture appears crumbly. |
| Granulated sugar | 2.5 | oz | 75 g | 30 | |
| Brown sugar | 2 | oz | 60 g | 25 | |
| Salt | 0.04 | oz (¼ tsp) | 1 g | 0.5 | |
| Cinnamon or mace | 0.02–0.04 oz (¼–½ tsp) | | 0.6–1 g | 0.25–0.5 | |
| Pastry flour | 8 | oz | 250 g | 100 | |
| *Total weight:* | *1 lb* | | *514 g* | *206%* | |

**VARIATION**

### NUT STREUSEL
Add 25% chopped nuts (2 oz/60 g).

## CLEAR GLAZE

| Ingredients | U.S. | | Corn syrup at 100% | | Procedure |
|---|---|---|---|---|---|
| | | | Metric | % | |
| Water | 8 oz | | 250 g | 50 | 1. Mix the ingredients together and bring to a boil. Stir to ensure the sugar is completely dissolved. |
| Light corn syrup | 1 lb | | 500 g | 100 | |
| Granulated sugar | 8 oz | | 250 g | 50 | 2. Apply while hot, or reheat before use. |
| *Total weight:* | *2 lb* | | *1000 g* | *200%* | |

# APRICOT GLAZE I

*For large-quantity measurements, see page 725.*

Yield: 1 lb 10 oz (1880 g)

| Ingredients | U.S. | | Metric | % | Procedure |
|---|---|---|---|---|---|
| Apricots, canned | 1 lb | | 500 g | 50 | 1. Cut the fruit into small pieces, including the skins and seeds. Place in a heavy saucepan. |
| Apples | 1 lb | | 500 g | 50 | 2. Add the first quantity of sugar and water. Cook slowly, covered, over medium heat until the fruit is soft. |
| Sugar | 1 lb 14 | oz | 950 g | 95 | |
| Water | 1 | oz | 25 g | 2.5 | |
| Sugar | 2 | oz | 50 g | 5 | 3. Pass through a food mill. |
| Pectin | 0.67 | oz | 20 g | 2 | 4. Bring back to a boil. |
| | | | | | 5. Mix the second quantity of sugar and pectin together and add to the fruit. Cook another 3–4 minutes. |
| | | | | | 6. Strain, skim, and pour into a plastic container. Cool, then refrigerate. |

# APRICOT GLAZE II

*For large-quantity measurements, see page 725.*

Yield: 7 oz (220 g)

| | | | Preserves at 100% | | |
|---|---|---|---|---|---|
| Ingredients | U.S. | | Metric | % | Procedure |
| Apricot preserves | 8 oz | | 250 g | 100 | 1. Combine the preserves and water in a heavy saucepan. Bring to a simmer. Stir and cook until the preserves are melted and well mixed with the water. Simmer until reduced and thickened slightly. |
| Water | 2 oz | | 60 g | 25 | |
| | | | | | 2. Pass the mixture through a fine sieve. |
| | | | | | 3. Test the mixture by placing a small spoonful on a plate and refrigerating for a few minutes to see if it gels. If necessary, cook down for a few more minutes to make it thicker. |

# LEMON CHEESE FILLING

*For large-quantity measurements, see page 725.*

| | | | Cheese at 100% | | |
|---|---|---|---|---|---|
| Ingredients | U.S. | | Metric | % | Procedure |
| Cream cheese | 5 | oz | 150 g | 100 | Mix together the cheese, sugar, and zest until well blended. |
| Sugar | 1 | oz | 30 g | 20 | |
| Grated lemon zest | 0.1 | oz (1¼ tsp) | 3 g | 2 | |
| *Total weight:* | *6* | *oz* | *183 g* | *122%* | |

# DATE, PRUNE, OR APRICOT FILLING

*For large-quantity measurements, see page 725.*
*Yield: 1 lb 8 oz (750 g)*

| Ingredients | U.S. | | Metric | % | Procedure |
|---|---|---|---|---|---|
| | | | Fruit at 100% | | |
| Dates, prunes (pitted), or dried apricots | 1 lb | | 500 g | 100 | 1. Pass the fruit through a grinder. |
| Sugar | 3 | oz | 100 g | 20 | 2. Combine all ingredients in a saucepan. Bring to a boil. Simmer and stir until thick and smooth, about 10 minutes. |
| Water | 8 | oz | 250 g | 50 | 3. Cool before using. |

**VARIATIONS**

1. Date or prune filling may be flavored with lemon and/or cinnamon.
2. Add 12.5% (8 oz/250 g) chopped walnuts to date or prune filling.

# ALMOND FILLING I (FRANGIPANE)

*For large-quantity measurements, see page 726.*

| Ingredients | U.S. | Metric | % | Procedure |
|---|---|---|---|---|
| | | Almond paste at 100% | | |
| Almond paste | 8 oz | 250 g | 100 | 1. With the paddle attachment, mix the almond paste and sugar at low speed until evenly mixed. |
| Sugar | 8 oz | 250 g | 100 | |
| Butter and/or shortening | 4 oz | 125 g | 50 | 2. Mix in the fat and flour until smooth. |
| Pastry or cake flour | 2 oz | 62 g | 25 | 3. Beat in the eggs, a little at a time, until smooth. |
| Eggs | 2 oz | 62 g | 25 | |
| **Total weight:** | **1 lb 8 oz** | **750 g** | **300%** | |

# ALMOND FILLING II (FRANGIPANE)

| Ingredients | U.S. | Metric | % | Procedure |
|---|---|---|---|---|
| | | Almond paste at 100% | | |
| Almond paste | 8 oz | 200 g | 100 | 1. With the paddle attachment, mix the almond paste and sugar at low speed until evenly blended. |
| Sugar | 1 oz | 25 g | 12.5 | |
| Butter | 4 oz | 100 g | 50 | 2. Blend in the butter. |
| Cake flour | 1 oz | 25 g | 12.5 | 3. Blend in the flour. |
| Eggs | 4 oz | 100 g | 50 | 4. Blend in the eggs until smooth. |
| **Total weight:** | **1 lb 2 oz** | **450 g** | **225%** | |

# ALMOND CREAM (CRÈME D'AMANDE)

*For large-quantity measurements, see page 726.*

| Ingredients | U.S. | | Metric | Procedure |
|---|---|---|---|---|
| Butter | 3 | oz | 90 g | 1. Cream together the butter, sugar, and zest until pale and light. |
| Fine granulated sugar | 3 | oz | 90 g | |
| Grated lemon zest | 0.03 | oz (⅜ tsp) | 1 g | 2. Add the eggs, egg yolks, and vanilla a little at a time, beating well after each addition. |
| Whole egg | 1.67 | oz (1 egg) | 50 g | |
| Egg yolk | 0.67 | oz (1 yolk) | 20 g | 3. Stir in the powdered almonds and flour. |
| Vanilla extract | 2 | Drops | 2 drops | |
| Powdered almonds | 3 | oz | 90 g | |
| Cake flour | 1 | oz | 30 g | |
| *Total weight:* | *12* | *oz* | *370 g* | |

# LEMON FILLING

| Ingredients | U.S. | Pie filling at 100% | | Procedure |
|---|---|---|---|---|
| | | Metric | % | |
| Lemon Pie Filling (p. 307) | 1 lb | 500 g | 100 | Mix the ingredients together until smooth. |
| Cake crumbs | 8 oz | 250 g | 50 | |
| Lemon juice | 2 oz | 62 g | 12.5 | |
| *Total weight:* | *1 lb 10 oz* | *812 g* | *162%* | |

# APPLE COMPOTE FILLING

*For large-quantity measurements, see page 726.*
*Yield: about 1 lb (500 g), or 9 oz (275 g) drained*

| Ingredients | U.S. | | Apple at 100% | | Procedure |
|---|---|---|---|---|---|
| | | | Metric | % | |
| Apples, peeled and cored | 9 | oz | 275 g | 100 | 1. Cut the apple into ¼-in. (5–6 mm) dice. |
| Butter | 2.5 | oz | 75 g | 27 | 2. Combine all ingredients. Simmer, covered, over low heat about 15 minutes, until the apple dice are tender but still hold their shape. |
| Sugar | 4 | oz | 120 g | 44 | |
| Water | 2 | oz | 60 g | 22 | |

# CINNAMON RAISIN FILLING

*For large-quantity measurements, see page 726.*

| Ingredients | U.S. | | Almonds at 100% | | Procedure |
|---|---|---|---|---|---|
| | | | Metric | % | |
| Powdered almonds | 3.5 | oz | 100 g | 100 | 1. Using a wire whip (if mixing by hand) or the paddle attachment (if mixing by machine), mix together the almonds, sugar, syrup, egg whites, and cinnamon until smooth. |
| Sugar | 2 | oz | 60 g | 60 | |
| Maple syrup | 1 | oz | 30 g | 30 | |
| Egg whites | 2 | oz | 60 g | 60 | 2. The raisins may be mixed in at this point. For more even distribution, however, sprinkle them evenly over the filling after it has been spread. |
| Cinnamon | 0.33 | oz | 10 g | 10 | |
| Raisins, golden | 1.67 | oz | 50 g | 50 | |
| *Total weight:* | *10.5* | *oz* | *310 g* | *310%* | |

# PECAN MAPLE FILLING

*For large-quantity measurements, see page 726.*

| Ingredients | U.S. | | Metric | % | Procedure |
|---|---|---|---|---|---|
| | | | **Hazelnuts at 100%** | | |
| Powdered hazelnuts | 3.5 | oz | 100 g | 100 | Mix all ingredients together. |
| Sugar | 2 | oz | 60 g | 60 | |
| Egg whites | 2 | oz | 60 g | 60 | |
| Maple syrup | 1 | oz | 30 g | 30 | |
| Pecans, finely sliced or chopped | 2 | oz | 60 g | 60 | |
| **Total weight:** | **10** | **oz** | **310 g** | **310%** | |

# CHEESE FILLING

| Ingredients | U.S. | | Metric | % | Procedure |
|---|---|---|---|---|---|
| | | | **Cheese at 100%** | | |
| Baker's cheese | 1 lb | | 500 g | 100 | 1. Using the paddle attachment, cream the cheese, sugar, and salt until smooth. |
| Sugar | 5 | oz | 150 g | 30 | 2. Add the eggs, fat, vanilla, and zest. Blend in. |
| Salt | 0.12 | oz | 4 g | 0.7 | |
| Eggs | 3 | oz | 100 g | 20 | 3. Add the flour. Blend just until absorbed. Add the milk a little at a time, adding just enough to bring the mixture to a smooth, spreadable consistency. |
| Butter and/or shortening, softened | 3 | oz | 100 g | 20 | |
| Vanilla | 0.25 | oz | 8 g | 1.5 | 4. Stir in the raisins, if desired. |
| Grated lemon zest (*optional*) | 0.12 oz (1½ tsp) | | 4 g | 0.7 | |
| Cake flour | 1.5 | oz | 50 g | 10 | |
| Milk | 3–5 | oz | 100–150 g | 20–30 | |
| Raisins (*optional*) | 4 | oz | 125 g | 25 | |
| **Total weight:** | **2 lb** | | **1141 g** | **228%** | |
| | **to** | | **to** | **to** | |
| | **2 lb 6** | **oz** | **1191 g** | **238%** | |

# HAZELNUT FILLING

*For large-quantity measurements, see page 726.*

| Ingredients | U.S. | | Metric | % | Procedure |
|---|---|---|---|---|---|
| | | | **Nuts at 100%** | | |
| Hazelnuts, toasted and ground | 4 | oz | 125 g | 100 | 1. Blend together all ingredients except milk. |
| Sugar | 8 | oz | 250 g | 200 | 2. Mix in enough milk to bring the mixture to a spreadable consistency. |
| Cinnamon | 0.12 oz (2 tsp) | | 4 g | 3 | |
| Eggs | 1.5 | oz | 50 g | 37.5 | |
| Cake crumbs | 8 | oz | 250 g | 200 | |
| Milk | 4–8 | oz | 125–250 g | 100–200 | |
| **Total weight:** | **1 lb 9** | **oz** | **804 g** | **640%** | |
| | **to** | | **to** | **to** | |
| | **1 lb 13** | **oz** | **927 g** | **740%** | |

# POPPY SEED FILLING

| Ingredients | U.S. | | Metric | Poppy seeds at 100% % | Procedure |
|---|---|---|---|---|---|
| Poppy seeds | 8 | oz | 200 g | 100 | 1. Soak the seeds in the water overnight. Grind to a paste. |
| Water | 4 | oz | 100 g | 50 | |
| Butter, softened | 3 | oz | 75 g | 38 | 2. Add the remaining ingredients and blend until smooth. |
| Honey | 2 | oz | 50 g | 25 | |
| Sugar | 3 | oz | 75 g | 38 | 3. Add water as needed to bring to a spreadable consistency. |
| Cake crumbs | 8 | oz | 200 g | 100 | |
| Eggs | 1.5 | oz | 40 g | 19 | |
| Lemon zest, grated | 0.12 | oz (1½ tsp) | 3 g | 1.5 | |
| Cinnamon | 0.006 | oz (¾ tsp) | 1 g | 0.75 | |
| Water | (as needed) | | (as needed) | | |
| **Total weight:** | **1 lb 13** | **oz** | **744 g** | **372%** | |

*or more, depending on amount of water added*

# CHOCOLATE FILLING

*For large-quantity measurements, see page 726.*

| Ingredients | U.S. | | Metric | Cake crumbs at 100% % | Procedure |
|---|---|---|---|---|---|
| Sugar | 4 | oz | 100 g | 33 | 1. Sift together the sugar and cocoa. |
| Cocoa | 1.25 | oz | 40 g | 12 | 2. Mix in the cake crumbs. |
| Cake crumbs | 12 | oz | 300 g | 100 | 3. Add the eggs, butter, vanilla, and a little of the water. Blend in. Add enough additional water to bring to a smooth, spreadable consistency. |
| Eggs | 1 | oz | 25 g | 8 | |
| Butter, melted | 1.25 | oz | 40 g | 12 | |
| Vanilla | 0.25 | oz | 6 g | 2 | |
| Water (as needed) | 3 | oz | 75 g | 25 | |
| **Total weight:** | **1 lb 6** | **oz** | **582 g** | **192%** | |

**VARIATION**

Mix 50% (6 oz/150 g) miniature chocolate chips into the filling.

# HONEY PAN GLAZE (FOR CARAMEL ROLLS)

*For large-quantity measurements, see page 727.*

| Ingredients | U.S. | | Metric | Brown sugar at 100% % | Procedure |
|---|---|---|---|---|---|
| Brown sugar | 10 | oz | 25 g | 100 | 1. Cream together the sugar, fat, honey, and corn syrup. |
| Butter, margarine, or shortening | 4 | oz | 100 g | 40 | 2. Add enough water to bring the mixture to a spreadable consistency. |
| Honey | 2.5 | oz | 60 g | 25 | |
| Corn syrup (or malt syrup) | 2.5 | oz | 60 g | 25 | |
| Water (as needed) | 1 | oz | 25 g | 10 | |
| **Total weight:** | **1 lb 4** | **oz** | **274 g** | **200%** | |

# MAKEUP TECHNIQUES

J ust as for lean doughs, the object of rich dough makeup is to shape the dough into items that bake properly and have an attractive appearance. Most of the guidelines for making up lean yeast breads also hold true for rich doughs. In particular, review the use of dusting flour, discussed on page 171.

While lean doughs usually can be handled vigorously, rich doughs require more care. In particular, temperature control is important when handling rolled-in doughs so the butter is neither too hard nor too soft and so the dough does not become overproofed while you are making it up. Study the procedures for these doughs carefully.

Many sweet dough products, including most Danish pastries, are glazed with a clear glaze or apricot glaze after baking, preferably while they are still warm. After cooling, they may also be decorated with Flat Icing (p. 431). Flat icing is drizzled over the products; it doesn't cover them completely.

a.

b.

## Croissant Dough

### Plain Croissants

1. Roll out the dough into a rectangle 10 inches (25 cm) wide and about ⅛ inch (3 mm) thick. The length depends on the amount of dough used (a).

2. Cut the rectangle into triangles (b). Special roller cutters that do this quickly are available.

3. Place one of the triangles on the bench in front of you. Stretch the back corners outward slightly, as shown by the arrows (c).

4. Begin to roll the dough toward the point (d).

5. Stretch the point of the triangle slightly as you roll it up (e).

6. Finish rolling the dough (f).

7. Bend the roll into a crescent shape. The point of the triangle must face the inside of the crescent and be tucked under the roll so it won't pop up during baking (g).

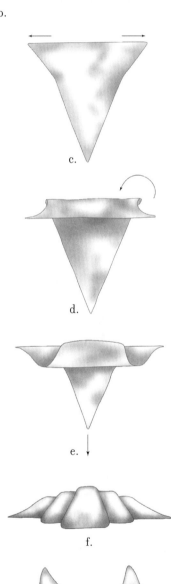

c.

d.

e.

f.

g.

### Filled Croissants

Make up as for plain croissants, except place a small amount of desired filling on the base of each triangle before rolling up.

The technique used for petits pains au chocolat (which follows) can also be used to create filled croissant-dough products with a variety of fillings. These rolls are often called *croissants*, but this use of the term is not accurate because the rolls are not crescent-shaped. (*Croissant* is the French word for "crescent").

### Petits Pains au Chocolat (Chocolate Rolls)

1. Roll out croissant dough into a sheet as for croissants.

2. Cut into rectangles 6 × 4 inches (15 × 10 cm).

3. Arrange a row of chocolate chips, or, preferably, special pain-au-chocolate bars, about 1½ inches (4 cm) from the narrow end of each rectangle. Use ⅓ ounce (10 g) chocolate per roll.

4. Egg wash the opposite end of each rectangle so the rolls will seal.

**5.** Roll the dough tightly around the chocolate.

**6.** Proof, egg wash, and bake as for croissants.

# Brioches

a.

b.

The traditional brioche shape, called *brioche à tête*, is shown here. Brioches may also be baked as pan loaves in many sizes and shapes.

**1.** For a small brioche, roll the dough into a round piece (a).

**2.** Using the edge of the hand, pinch off about one-fourth of the dough without detaching it. Roll the dough on the bench so both parts are round (b).

**3.** Place the dough in the tin, large end first. With the fingertips, press the small ball into the larger one (c).

**4.** For a large brioche, separate the two parts of the dough. Place the large ball in the tin and make a hole in the center. Form the smaller ball into a pear shape and fit it into the hole (d). The baked loaf has the traditional brioche shape (e).

c.

# Sweet Rolls and Danish Rolls

*Note:* Many sweet dough products, including most Danish products, are glazed with Clear Glaze (p. 199) after baking, while still hot. After cooling, they may also be decorated with Flat Icing (p. 431). Flat icing is drizzled over the products; it doesn't cover them completely.

## *Crumb Buns*

**1.** With a rolling pin, roll out sweet dough about ½-inch (12 mm) thick.

**2.** Cut into 2-inch (5 cm) squares.

**3.** Arrange the squares in rows on paper-lined sheet pans so they touch each other.

**4.** Wash with egg wash or milk.

**5.** Sprinkle the tops heavily with Streusel Topping (p. 199).

**6.** Proof. Bake at 400°F (200°C).

**7.** When the buns are cool, they may be dusted lightly with 6X sugar.

d.

## *Filled Buns*

**1.** Scale the sweet dough into presses of the desired size. Suggested size: 3 pounds (1400 g) for 36 rolls. Round the presses, relax, and divide.

**2.** Round the units and place them on paper-lined sheet pans in one of two ways:

　◆ Place them 2 inches (5 cm) apart so they bake without touching.

　◆ Place them in rows so they are just touching each other. Rolls baked in this way will rise higher and must be broken apart before being served.

**3.** Give the rolls a half-proof.

**4.** Using either the fingers or a small, round object, press a round 1-inch (2.5 cm) indentation in the center of each roll.

e.

5. Egg wash the tops of the rolls.

6. Fill the centers with desired filling, using about ½ ounce (15 g) per roll.

7. Continue proofing to about three-quarters proof. Bake at 400°F (200°C).

8. When cool, drizzle flat icing over the rolls.

## Cinnamon Raisin Rolls

1. Prepare Cinnamon Raisin Filling (p. 202), leaving the raisins separate for now; you will need 1 small batch, or about 10 ounces (300 g), for each unit of dough, as scaled in step 2.

2. Scale Danish Pastry Dough (Brioche-Style) (p. 197) into 22-ounce (615 g) units. Roll out each unit into a rectangle 20 × 10 in. (50 × 25 cm). For the neatest results, roll slightly larger and trim to size with a knife or pastry wheel.

3. Spread the filling evenly over the dough with a palette knife, sprinkling the raisins over the dough after the filling has been spread. Leave a narrow band of dough uncovered along the top edge (a).

4. Roll up tightly from the bottom edge into a cylinder 20 inches (50 cm) long (b).

5. Cut into 8 slices 2½ inches (6 cm) thick (c).

6. Place on a baking sheet lined with parchment and tuck the loose edge of the roll underneath. With the palm of the hand, flatten each roll to about 1 inch (2.5 cm) thick (d).

7. Proof for 25 minutes at 85°F (30°C).

8. Bake at 350°F (180°C) for 15 minutes.

9. Brush with clear glaze or apricot glaze when cool.

A

B

C

D

a.

b.

c.

A

B

C

## Cinnamon Rolls

1. Scale sweet dough into 20-ounce (570 g) units or as desired. On a floured bench, roll each piece of dough into a 9 × 12-inch rectangle about ¼-inch thick (23 × 30 × 0.5 cm). Brush off excess flour.

2. Brush with butter and sprinkle with 2 ounces (60 g) cinnamon sugar (a).

3. Roll up like a jelly roll 12 inches (30 cm) long (b).

4. Cut into 1-inch (2.5 cm) rolls (c).

5. Place cut side down in greased muffin tins or on greased sheet pans. One full-size 18 × 26-inch (46 × 66 cm) pan holds 48 rolls arranged in 6 rows of 8.

## Pecan Maple Rolls

1. Prepare Pecan Maple Filling (p. 203); you will need 1 small batch, or about 10 oz (300 g), for each unit of dough, as scaled in step 2.

2. Scale Danish Pastry Dough (Brioche-Style) (p. 197) into 22-ounce (615 g) units. Roll out each unit into a rectangle 20 × 10 in. (50 × 25 cm). For the neatest results, roll slightly larger and trim to size with a knife or pastry wheel.

3. Spread the filling evenly over the dough with a palette knife. Leave a narrow band of dough uncovered along the top edge (a).

4. Roll up from the bottom edge into a cylinder 20 inches (50 cm) long (b).

5. Cut into 20 slices 2 inches (5 cm) thick.

6. Butter and sugar 10 small brioche molds.

7. Place 1 slice of the dough roll cut side up in each mold, tucking the loose end of the roll underneath. Press lightly into molds (c).

8. Egg wash the tops.

9. Proof for 25 minutes at 85°F (30°C).

10. Egg wash a second time.

11. Bake at 350°F (180°C) for 20 minutes.

12. Brush with clear glaze when cool.

Clockwise from top left: Pecan Maple Rolls, Cinnamon Raisin Rolls, Lemon Cheese Pastries

## Caramel Rolls

1. Prepare like cinnamon rolls.

2. Before panning, spread the bottoms of the pans with Honey Pan Glaze (p. 204). Use about 1 ounce (30 g) per roll.

## Caramel Nut Rolls or Pecan Rolls

Prepare like caramel rolls, but sprinkle the pan glaze with chopped nuts or pecan halves before placing the rolls in the pans.

## Danish Spirals

1. Roll out Danish dough into a rectangle as for cinnamon rolls. The width of the roll may vary, depending on the desired size of the finished units. A wider rectangle will produce a thicker roll and, therefore, larger finished units.

2. Spread or sprinkle the rectangle with the desired filling. For example:

   Butter, cinnamon sugar, chopped nuts, and cake crumbs

   Butter, cinnamon sugar, and raisins

   Almond filling

   Prune filling

   Chocolate filling

   Loose fillings, such as chopped nuts, should be pressed on gently with a rolling pin.

3. Roll up like a jelly roll.

4. Slice to desired size.

5. Place the rolls on paper-lined pans and tuck the loose ends underneath.

6. Proof, egg wash, and bake at 400°F (200°C).

## Variations Made from Filled Dough Roll or Danish Spiral

The filled dough roll is the starting point for a variety of sweet dough and Danish products.

1. **Filled Spirals.** Make up like Danish Spirals, above. Give half-proof, then press an indentation in the center and fill with desired filling. Complete the proof and bake as above.

2. **Combs and Bear Claws.** Make the Danish Spiral roll thinner and cut it into longer pieces. Flatten the pieces slightly and cut partway through each in three to five places. Leave straight or bend into a curve to open the cuts (a).

3. **Figure-Eight Rolls.** Cut the Danish spiral rolls almost through. Open them up and lay them flat on the baking sheet (b).

4. **Three-Leaf Rolls.** Cut Danish spiral pieces in two places and spread the three segments apart (c).

5. **Butterfly Rolls.** Cut off slightly larger pieces from the Danish spiral roll. Crease them by pressing the center firmly with a wooden rod (d).

a.

b.

c.

d.

a.

b.

c.

d.

e.

f.

## *Filled Danish Crescents*

Make up like filled croissants (p. 205).

## *Danish Twists or Snails*

1. Roll out the dough into a rectangle 16 inches (40 cm) wide and less than ¼ inch (5 mm) thick. (The length of the rectangle depends on the quantity of dough.) Brush the dough with melted butter. Sprinkle half of it with cinnamon sugar (a).

2. Fold the unsugared half over the sugared half. You now have a rectangle 8 inches (20 cm) wide. Roll the dough very gently with a rolling pin to press the layers together (b).

3. Cut the dough into strips ½ inch (1 cm) wide (c).

4. Place one strip crosswise in front of you on the bench (d).

5. With the palms of your hands on the ends of the strip, roll one end toward you and the other end away from you, so the strip twists. Stretch the strip slightly as you twist it (e).

6. Curl the strip into a spiral shape on the baking sheet. Tuck the end underneath and pinch it against the roll to seal it in place (f). If desired, press a hollow in the center of the roll and place a spoonful of filling in it.

## *Danish Pockets*

1. Roll out the dough less than ¼ inch (5 mm) thick. Cut it into 5-inch (13 cm) squares. Place the desired filling in the center of each square (a). Brush the four corners lightly with water to help them seal when pressed together.

2. Fold two opposite corners over the center. Press down firmly to seal them together (b). (If desired, rolls may be left in this shape.)

3. Fold the other two corners over the center and, again, press them firmly together (c).

a.

b.

c.

## *Lemon Cheese Pastries*

1. Prepare Lemon Cheese Filling (p. 200); you will need 3 ounces (90 g) filling for each unit of dough, as scaled in step 2. Fill a pastry bag with a small plain tip with the filling.

2. Scale Danish Pastry Dough (Brioche-Style) (p. 197) into 22-ounce (615 g) units. Roll out each unit into a rectangle 16 × 12 inches (40 × 30 cm). For the neatest results, roll slightly larger and trim to size with a knife or pastry wheel.

3. Cut 4 by 3 into 12 squares, 4 inches (10 cm) on each side.

4. Egg wash the surface of each square.

5. Pipe the cheese mixture in a line down the center of each square (a).

6. Fold in half to make a rectangle. Press the edges well to seal (b).

7. Turn upside down and arrange on sheet pans lined with parchment. Egg wash the tops.

8. Proof for 15 minutes at 85°F (30°C).

9. Egg wash a second time. Sprinkle with sugar.

10. Bake at 350°F (180°C) for 12 minutes.

11. If desired, decorate the tops with slices of poached lemon.

## Cherry Vol-au-Vents

1. Scale Danish Pastry Dough (Croissant-Style) (p. 196) into 14-ounce (400 g) units.

2. Roll out into a rectangle 7 × 11 inches (18 × 27 cm) in size.

3. Cut into 2 strips 3½ × 11 inches (9 × 27 cm), then cut each strip into 3½-inch (9 cm) squares.

4. Fold each square in half diagonally to form a triangle (a).

5. With a chef's knife, cut a strip ½ inch (1 cm) wide along the two short sides of the triangle, starting at the folded edge and stopping about ¾ inch (2 cm) from the opposite corner (b).

6. Unfold the square. Brush with egg wash.

7. Fold each cut strip to the opposite side to make a diamond-shaped pastry with a raised border all around. Press corners to seal (c).

8. Proof for 20 minutes at 85°F (30°C).

9. Egg wash again.

10. With a pastry bag or spoon, deposit about 2 teaspoons (10 g) pastry cream in the center of each pastry. Fill with cherries. You will need about 1 ounce (25 g) cherries for each pastry (d).

11. Bake at 350°F (180°C) for 15 minutes.

12. Cool and brush with apricot glaze.

## *Apricot Pinwheels*

1. Scale Danish Pastry Dough (Croissant-Style) (p. 196) into 14-ounce (400 g) units.

2. Roll out into a rectangle about ½ inch (3 mm) thick and approximately 8 × 12 inches (20 × 30 cm). (For the neatest results, roll slightly larger and trim to size with a knife or pastry wheel.)

3. Cut into 6 squares 4 inches (10 cm) on a side (a).

4. Make a cut about 1½ inches (4 cm) long from the corner of each square toward the center (b).

5. Brush each square with egg wash. Fold alternating corner flaps toward the center to make a pinwheel (c).

6. Proof for 20 minutes at 85°F (30°C).

7. Egg wash again.

8. With a pastry bag or spoon, deposit about 2 teaspoons (10 g) pastry cream at the center of each pinwheel. Place an apricot half on top of the pastry cream, cut side down (d).

9. Bake at 350°F (180°C) for 15 minutes.

10. Cool and brush with clear glaze or apricot glaze.

Left to right:
Apple Rosettes,
Cherry Vol-au-Vents,
Apricot Pinwheels

## Apple Rosettes

1. Scale Danish Pastry Dough (Croissant-Style) (p. 196) into 14-ounce (400 g) units.

2. Roll out into a rectangle about ⅛ inch (3 mm) thick and approximately 8 × 12 inches (20 × 30 cm).

3. With a 4-inch (10 cm) round cutter, cut into 6 circles (a).

4. Make 4 equidistant cuts about 1½ inches (4 cm) long from the outside edge of each circle toward the center (b).

5. Brush each circle with egg wash. Fold alternating corner flaps toward the center to make a pinwheel. Press down corners to seal (c, d).

6. Proof for 20 minutes at 85°F (30°C).

7. Egg wash again.

8. With a pastry bag or spoon, deposit about 2 teaspoons (10 g) pastry cream at the center of each pinwheel (e). Top the pastry cream with about 1 ounce (25 g) Apple Compote Filling (p. 202) (f). Carefully press each mound of apple into place by hand.

9. Bake at 350°F (180°C) for 15 minutes.

10. Cool and brush with clear glaze or apricot glaze.

# Coffee Cakes

Coffee cakes can be made up into many sizes and shapes. The weight of the dough required and the size of the cake can be varied greatly according to the needs of the bakeshop. Except when a specific dough is indicated, the following can be made with either a sweet dough or Danish dough.

## Wreath Coffee Cake

1. Using a sweet dough or Danish dough, make a filled dough roll as for cinnamon rolls, but do not cut into separate pieces. Other fillings, such as prune or date, may be used instead of butter and cinnamon sugar.

2. Shape the roll into a circle (a). Place on a greased baking sheet. Cut partway through the dough at 1-inch (2.5 cm) intervals (b). Twist each segment outward to open the cuts (c).

3. Egg wash after proofing. Bake at 375°F (190°C).

a.

b.

c.

## Filled Coffee Cake

1. Scale sweet dough or Danish dough into 12-ounce (340 g) units.

2. Roll each unit into a rectangle 9 × 18 inches (23 × 46 cm).

3. Spread half of each rectangle with about 6 ounces (170 g) desired filling.

4. Fold the unspread half over the spread half to make a 9-inch (23 cm) square.

5. Place in a greased 9-inch (23 cm) square pan.

6. Sprinkle with streusel topping, about 4 ounces (110 g) per pan.

7. Proof. Bake at 375°F (190°C).

## Loaf Coffee Cake

1. Using babka dough, make a filled dough roll as for cinnamon rolls, using desired filling.

2. Fold the roll in half, then twist it up.

3. Place the twisted roll in a greased loaf pan, or coil the twist like a snail and place in a round pan.

4. Proof, wash with melted butter, and bake at 350°F (175°C).

## Danish Pretzel

1. Using almond filling, make up Danish dough into a long, thin dough roll as for cinnamon rolls.

2. Twist the roll into a pretzel shape. Place on a sheet pan.

3. Proof, egg wash, and bake at 375°F (190°C).

## Strip Coffee Cake or Danish Strip

1. Roll out the Danish dough about ¼ inch (6 mm) thick into a rectangle the length of the desired strip and about twice as wide.

2. Spread the desired filling lengthwise down the center of the dough, leaving a ½-inch (1 cm) margin at both ends.

3. Brush both ends and one edge of the rectangle with egg wash (in order to seal the seams).

4. Fold the side of the rectangle without the egg wash over the center of the filling. Fold the other side over the center, overlapping the first side by ½ inch (1 cm).

5. Turn the strip over and place it seam side down on a paper-lined pan. Make 5 or 6 diagonal slashes in the top of the dough; cut through to the filling but not to the bottom layer of dough.

6. Proof, egg wash, and bake at 375°F (190°C).

## Danish Ring

1. Using desired filling, make up Danish dough into a filled dough roll as for cinnamon rolls, but make it longer and thinner.

2. Flatten the roll slightly with a rolling pin. Make 2 parallel cuts lengthwise through the dough; cut through the bottom layer, but leave about 1 inch (2.5 cm) uncut at both ends.

3. Twist the strip as for Danish Twists (p. 210). Form the twist into a ring and seal the ends together.

4. Proof and egg wash. The ring may also be sprinkled with chopped or sliced nuts. Bake at 375°F (190°C).

# TERMS FOR REVIEW

| brioche | baba | croissant | panettone | simple fold |
| --- | --- | --- | --- | --- |

# QUESTIONS FOR DISCUSSION

1. What mixing method is used for brioche dough and kugelhopf dough? Why?

2. Butter is hard when cold and melts easily at room temperature. What precautions do you think are necessary when using butter as the rolling-in fat for Danish pastry dough?

3. Explain the difference between Danish dough, croissant-style, and Danish dough, brioche-style.

4. Describe the rolling-in procedure for Danish dough.

## Chapter 10

# Quick Breads

**Q**uick breads are the perfect solution for food service operations that want to offer their patrons fresh, homemade bread products but can't justify the labor cost of making yeast breads. Retail bakeries have discovered a great demand for such items as fresh muffins. Also, quick breads have the advantage of being easily made in almost unlimited varieties using such ingredients as whole wheat flour, rye flour, cornmeal, bran, oatmeal, and many kinds of fruits, nuts, and spices. Even breads made with vegetables have become popular.

As their name implies, quick breads are quick to make. Because they are leavened by chemical leaveners and steam, not by yeast, no fermentation time is necessary. And because they are usually tender products with little gluten development, mixing them takes just a few minutes.

Although prepared biscuit and muffin mixes are available, the only extra work that making these products from scratch requires is the time to scale a few ingredients. With a careful and imaginative selection of ingredients and an understanding of basic mixing methods, you can create superior products.

**After reading this chapter, you should be able to:**

1. Prepare baking powder biscuits and variations of them.

2. Prepare muffins, loaf breads or tea breads, coffee cakes, and corn breads.

3. Prepare popovers.

# MIXING AND PRODUCTION METHODS

D ough mixtures for quick breads are generally of two types:

+ *Soft doughs* are used for biscuits. They are, with a few exceptions, rolled out and cut into desired shapes.

+ Batters may be either **pour batters**, which are liquid enough to be poured, or **drop batters**, which are thick enough to be dropped from a spoon in lumps.

## Gluten Development in Quick Breads

Only slight gluten development is desirable in most quick breads. Tenderness is a desirable quality, rather than the chewy quality of many yeast breads.

In addition, chemical leavening agents do not create the same kind of texture yeast does, and they are not strong enough to create a light, tender product if the gluten is too strong.

Tunneling

Muffin, loaf bread, and pancake batters are mixed as little as possible, only until the dry ingredients are moistened. This, plus the presence of fat and sugar, keeps gluten development low. Overmixing muffin batter produces not only toughness but also irregular shapes and large, elongated holes inside the muffins. This condition is called **tunneling**.

Biscuit dough is often lightly kneaded, enough to help develop some flakiness but not enough to toughen the product.

Popovers are the exception among quick breads. They are made with a thin batter and leavened only by steam. Very large holes develop inside the product during baking, and the structure must be strong enough to hold up without collapsing. Thus, bread flour is used and the batter is mixed enough to develop the gluten. The high percentage of egg in popovers also helps build structure.

## Mixing Methods

Most quick-bread doughs and batters are mixed by using one of three mixing methods.

+ The **biscuit method** is used for biscuits, scones, and similar products. It is sometimes called the *pastry method* because it is like that used for mixing pie pastry.

+ The **muffin method** is used for muffins, pancakes, waffles, and many loaf-type or sheet-type quick breads. This method is fast and easy. However, the danger is the dough can quickly become overmixed, resulting in toughness. *Muffin batter should be mixed only until the dry ingredients are just moistened.* Do not attempt to achieve a smooth batter. Some loaf breads and coffee cakes are higher in fat and sugar than muffins, so they can withstand a little more mixing without becoming tough.

This mixing method is not as suitable for formulas high in fat, unlike the creaming method described next. Consequently, quick breads mixed by this method are not as rich and cakelike as muffins and other products mixed by the creaming method. They tend to be a little drier, more like breads than cake. High-fat muffins sell better in today's market (in spite of the public's concern about fat), so the muffin method is not as often used as it once was. Keep this in mind as you try the muffin-method formulas in this chapter.

♦ The **creaming method** is a cake-mixing method that is sometimes applied to muffins and loaf breads. Actually, there is no exact dividing line between muffin products and cakes, and, if they are rich enough, muffin products may be considered cakes rather than breads.

   The creaming method is a more time-consuming procedure than the muffin method. However, it produces fine-textured goods and carries less danger of overmixing. The creaming method is especially useful for products with high fat and sugar content because it helps mix the ingredients more uniformly.

   Some biscuits are also mixed by the creaming method. These have a texture that is more cakelike and less flaky than that produced by the biscuit method.

## Procedure—Biscuit Method

1. Scale all ingredients accurately.

2. Sift the dry ingredients together into a mixing bowl.

3. Cut in the shortening, using the paddle attachment or the pastry knife attachment; if you prefer, cut in the fat by hand, using a pastry blender or your fingers. Continue until the mixture resembles a coarse cornmeal (see variations below).

4. Combine the liquid ingredients.

5. Add the liquid to the dry ingredients. Mix just until the ingredients are combined and a soft dough is formed. Do not overmix.

6. Bring the dough to the bench and knead it lightly by pressing it out and folding it in half. Rotate the dough 90 degrees between folds.

7. Repeat this procedure 6 to 10 times, or for about 30 seconds. The dough should be soft and slightly elastic but not sticky. Overkneading toughens the biscuits.

   The dough is now ready for makeup.

### Variations

Changes in the basic procedure produce different characteristics in the finished product:

1. Using slightly more shortening and cutting it in less—only until the pieces are the size of peas—produces a flakier biscuit.

2. Omitting the kneading step produces very tender, crusty biscuits, but with less volume.

## Procedure—Muffin Method

1. Sift together the dry ingredients (a).

2. Combine all liquid ingredients, including melted fat or oil.

3. Add the liquids to the dry ingredients and mix just until all the flour is moistened. The batter will look lumpy. Be careful not to overmix (b).

4. Pan and bake immediately (c). The dry and liquid mixtures may be prepared in advance, but once the mixtures are combined, the batter should be baked without delay, or loss of volume may result.

## Procedure—Creaming Method for Biscuits

1. Combine the fat, sugar, salt, and milk powder (if used) in the bowl of a mixer fitted with the paddle attachment.

2. Blend to a smooth paste.

3. Add the eggs gradually and blend in thoroughly.

4. Add the water or milk (liquid) and mix in.

5. Sift together the flour and baking powder. Add to the bowl and mix to a smooth dough.

## Procedure—Creaming Method for Muffins, Loaves, and Coffee Cakes

1. Combine the fat, sugar, salt, spices, and milk powder (if used) in the bowl of a mixer fitted with the paddle attachment.

2. Cream the ingredients together until light.

3. Add the eggs in two or three stages. Cream well after each addition and before adding more eggs.

4. Sift together the flour, baking powder, and other dry ingredients.

5. Stir together the liquid ingredients until well combined.

6. Add the sifted dry ingredients alternately with the liquids. This is done as follows:

   ◆ Add one-fourth of the dry ingredients. Mix just until blended in.

   ◆ Add one-third of the liquid. Mix just until blended in.

   ◆ Repeat until all ingredients are used. Scrape down the sides of the bowl occasionally for even mixing.

# Makeup Methods

## *Makeup of Biscuits*

1. Roll out the biscuit dough into a sheet about ½ inch (1 cm) thick, being careful to roll it evenly and to a uniform thickness. Biscuits approximately double in height during baking.

2. Cut into desired shapes. When using round hand cutters, cut straight down. Do not twist the cutter. Space the cuts as closely as possible to minimize scraps. Reworked scrap dough produces tougher biscuits. Cutting into squares or triangles with a pastry cutter knife eliminates scraps that would have to be rerolled. Roller cutters also eliminate or reduce scraps. If cutting with a knife, cut straight down without dragging the knife.

3. Place the biscuits ½ inch (1 cm) apart on greased or paper-lined baking sheets. For straighter sides, place the biscuits upside down. For softer biscuits without crusty sides, arrange the units so they touch each other; these must be broken apart after baking.

4. If desired, brush the tops with egg wash or milk to aid browning.

5. Bake as soon as possible.

## *Makeup and Panning of Muffin Products*

Muffin tins and loaf pans should be greased with shortening or pan spray and dusted with flour or greased with a commercial pan grease preparation. Sheet pans for corn breads and other sheet products may be lined with silicone paper.

Paper liners may be used for muffin tins. However, because muffins do not stick to greased tins, they rise more freely and take a better shape and crust without paper liners.

When portioning batter into muffin tins, be careful not to stir the mix and toughen it. Scoop the batter from the outside edge of the bowl, using a portion scoop, for best results.

Batters for muffins and quick loaf breads are generally interchangeable. In other words, formulas for banana bread or date nut bread, for example, may be baked as muffins instead of as loaves. Similarly, standard muffin batters may also be baked as loaves or sheets.

Please note that some of the muffin and loaf bread formulas included here, especially those mixed by the muffin method, should be thought of as breads rather than as tea cakes. In particular, their fat and sugar contents are intentionally kept lower than those of the rather rich, oily muffins sometimes sold today. Formulas for richer, more cakelike muffins are included later in the chapter. If you wish to experiment with the two basic muffin recipes to make them richer in fat and sugar, first read the section on cake formula balance beginning on page 390.

# FORMULAS

## BISCUITS I

| Ingredients | U.S. | | | Metric | % | Procedure |
|---|---|---|---|---|---|---|
| Bread flour | 1 lb | 4 | oz | 600 g | 50 | **MIXING** |
| Pastry flour | 1 lb | 4 | oz | 600 g | 50 | Biscuit method (p. 219) |
| Salt | | 0.75 | oz | 24 g | 2 | **SCALING** |
| Sugar | | 2 | oz | 60 g | 5 | Approximately 1 lb (450 g) per dozen 2-in. |
| Baking powder | | 2.5 | oz | 72 g | 6 | (5 cm) biscuits |
| Shortening (regular) and/or butter | | 14 | oz | 420 g | 35 | **BAKING** |
| Milk | 1 lb | 10 | oz | 800 g | 65 | 400°F (200°C), about 15–20 minutes |
| *Total weight:* | *5 lb* | *5* | *oz* | *2576 g* | *213%* | |

### VARIATIONS

#### BUTTERMILK BISCUITS

Use buttermilk in place of regular milk. Reduce the baking powder to 4% (1.5 oz/50 g) and add 1% baking soda (0.4 oz/12 g).

#### CHEESE BISCUITS

| Ingredients | U.S. | Metric | % |
|---|---|---|---|
| Grated cheddar cheese | 12 oz | 360 g | 30 |

Add the cheese to the dry ingredients.

#### CURRANT BISCUITS

| Ingredients | U.S. | Metric | % |
|---|---|---|---|
| Sugar | 4 oz | 120 g | 10 |
| Dried currants | 6 oz | 180 g | 15 |

Increase the sugar to the above amount. Add the currants to the dry ingredients. Sprinkle the tops with cinnamon sugar before baking.

#### HERB BISCUITS

| Ingredients | U.S. | Metric | % |
|---|---|---|---|
| Fresh chopped parsley | 2 oz | 60 g | 5 |

Add the parsley to the dry ingredients.

## BISCUITS II

| Ingredients | U.S. | | | Metric | | % | Procedure |
|---|---|---|---|---|---|---|---|
| Shortening | | 6 | oz | 150 | g | 15 | **MIXING** |
| Sugar | | 4 | oz | 100 | g | 10 | Creaming method (p. 220) |
| Salt | | 0.5 | oz | 12.5 | g | 1.25 | **BAKING** |
| Nonfat milk solids | | 2 | oz | 0 | g | 5 | 400°F (200°C) |
| Eggs | | 3 | oz | 75 | g | 7.5 | |
| Water | 1 lb | 8 | oz | 600 | g | 60 | |
| Bread flour | 1 lb | 12 | oz | 700 | g | 70 | |
| Cake flour | | 12 | oz | 300 | g | 30 | |
| Baking powder | | 2 | oz | 50 | g | 5 | |
| *Total weight:* | *5 lb* | *1* | *oz* | *2037* | *g* | *203%* | |

### VARIATION

| Ingredients | U.S. | Metric | % |
|---|---|---|---|
| Butter | 7.5 oz | 190 g | 19 |

Substitute butter for the shortening.

# PLAIN MUFFINS

| Ingredients | U.S. | | | Metric | % | Procedure |
|---|---|---|---|---|---|---|
| Pastry flour | 2 lb | 8 | oz | 1200 g | 100 | **MIXING** |
| Sugar | 1 lb | 4 | oz | 600 g | 50 | Muffin method (p. 220) |
| Baking powder | | 2.5 | oz | 72 g | 6 | **PANNING** |
| Salt | | 0.5 | oz | 15 g | 1.25 | Grease and flour muffin tins. Fill them one-half |
| Eggs, beaten | | 12 | oz | 360 g | 30 | to two-thirds full. Exact weight depends on pan |
| Milk | 1 lb | 12 | oz | 840 g | 70 | size. Average sizes are 2 oz (60 g) for small |
| Vanilla extract | | 1 | oz | 30 g | 2.5 | muffins, 4 oz (110 g) for medium muffins, and |
| Butter or shortening, melted | 1 lb | | | 480 g | 40 | 5–6 oz (140–170 g) for large muffins. |
| | | | | | | **BAKING** |
| **Total weight:** | **7 lb** | **8** | **oz** | **3591 g** | **299%** | 400°F (200°C), about 20–30 minutes |

## VARIATIONS

### RAISIN SPICE MUFFINS

| Ingredients | U.S. | Metric | % |
|---|---|---|---|
| Raisins | 8 oz | 240 g | 20 |
| Cinnamon | 0.17 oz (2½ tsp) | 5 g | 0.4 |
| Nutmeg | 0.08 oz (1 tsp) | 2.5 g | 0.2 |

Add raisins, cinnamon, and nutmeg to dry ingredients.

### BLUEBERRY MUFFINS

| Ingredients | U.S. | Metric | % |
|---|---|---|---|
| Blueberries (well drained) | 1 lb | 480 g | 40 |

Fold blueberries into finished batter.

### WHOLE WHEAT MUFFINS

| Ingredients | U.S. | Metric | % |
|---|---|---|---|
| Pastry flour | 1 lb 12 oz | 840 g | 70 |
| Whole wheat flour | 12 oz | 360 g | 30 |
| Baking powder | 1.5 oz | 50 g | 4 |
| Baking soda | 0.3 oz (2 tsp) | 10 g | 0.75 |
| Molasses | 4 oz | 120 g | 10 |

Adjust the flour and leavening as listed above. Add the molasses to the liquid ingredients.

### CORN MUFFINS

| Ingredients | U.S. | Metric | % |
|---|---|---|---|
| Pastry flour | 1 lb 10 oz | 800 g | 65 |
| Cornmeal | 14 oz | 400 g | 35 |

Adjust the flour as listed above. (See also the Corn Bread formula on p. 225.)

### CORN CHEESE MUFFINS

| Ingredients | U.S. | Metric | % |
|---|---|---|---|
| Grated cheddar cheese | 1 lb 4 oz | 600 g | 50 |

Add the cheese to the dry ingredients in the above corn muffin formula. Use half the amount of sugar.

### BRAN MUFFINS

| Ingredients | U.S. | Metric | % |
|---|---|---|---|
| Pastry flour | 12 oz | 360 g | 30 |
| Bread flour | 1 lb | 480 g | 40 |
| Bran | 12 oz | 360 g | 30 |
| Raisins | 6 oz | 180 g | 15 |
| Butter, melted | 1 lb 4 oz | 600 g | 50 |
| Milk | 1 lb 14 oz | 900 g | 75 |
| Molasses | 6 oz | 180 g | 15 |

Adjust the flour, butter, and milk as listed above. Add the raisins to the dry ingredients and the molasses to the liquid ingredients.

### CRUMB COFFEE CAKE

| Ingredients | U.S. | Metric | % |
|---|---|---|---|
| Butter or shortening | 1 lb 4 oz | 600 g | 50 |
| Streusel (p. 199) | 2 lb | 1000 g | 80 |

Increase the fat as listed above. Pour the batter into a greased, paper-lined sheet pan and spread smooth. Top with streusel. Bake at 360°F (182°C) about 30 minutes.

Muffins, clockwise from top: blueberry, corn, bran

# MUFFINS (CREAMING METHOD)

| Ingredients | U.S. | | Metric | % | Procedure |
|---|---|---|---|---|---|
| Shortening and/or butter | 1 lb 4 | oz | 500 g | 50 | **MIXING** |
| Sugar | 1 lb 10 | oz | 650 g | 65 | Creaming method (p. 220) |
| Salt | 0.5 | oz | 12 g | 1.25 | **SCALING** |
| Nonfat milk solids | 3 | oz | 70 g | 7 | Fill tins one-half to two-thirds full. |
| Eggs | 12 | oz | 300 g | 30 | **BAKING** |
| Cake flour | 2 lb 8 | oz | 1000 g | 100 | 400°F (200°C), about 20–30 minutes |
| Baking powder | 2 | oz | 50 g | 5 | |
| Vanilla extract | 1 | oz | 25 g | 1.25 | |
| Water | 1 lb 14 | oz | 750 g | 75 | |
| **Total weight:** | **8 lb 6** | **oz** | **3357 g** | **334%** | |

## VARIATIONS

### CHOCOLATE CHIP MUFFINS

| Ingredients | U.S. | Metric | % |
|---|---|---|---|
| White granulated sugar | 1 lb 4 oz | 500 g | 50 |
| Brown sugar | 6 oz | 150 g | 15 |
| Chocolate chips | 12 oz | 300 g | 30 |

Adjust the sugar as listed above. Add the chocolate chips to the formula. Top with Cinnamon Sugar (p. 199) before baking.

### BLUEBERRY MUFFINS

| Ingredients | U.S. | Metric | % |
|---|---|---|---|
| Blueberries (well drained) | 1 lb 4 oz | 500 g | 50 |

Fold the blueberries into the finished batter.

### RAISIN SPICE MUFFINS

| Ingredients | U.S. | Metric | % |
|---|---|---|---|
| Raisins | 10 oz | 250 g | 25 |
| Cinnamon | 0.2 oz (3½ tsp) | 5 g | 0.5 |
| Nutmeg | 0.1 oz (1¼ tsp) | 2.5 g | 0.25 |

Add the raisins, cinnamon, and nutmeg to the dry ingredients.

# CORN BREAD, MUFFINS, OR STICKS

| Ingredients | U.S. | | | Metric | % | Procedure |
|---|---|---|---|---|---|---|
| Pastry flour | 1 lb | 4 | oz | 600 g | 50 | **MIXING** |
| Cornmeal | 1 lb | 4 | oz | 600 g | 50 | Muffin method (p. 220) |
| Sugar | | 6 | oz | 180 g | 15 | **SCALING** |
| Baking powder | | 2 | oz | 60 g | 5 | 60 oz (1700 g) per half-sheet pan (13 × 18 in./ |
| Nonfat milk solids | | 3 | oz | 90 g | 7.5 | 33 × 6 cm) |
| Salt | | 0.75 oz | | 24 g | 2 | |
| Eggs, beaten | | 8 | oz | 240 g | 20 | 24 oz (680 g) per 9-in. (23 cm) square pan or |
| Water | 2 lb | 2 | oz | 1000 g | 85 | per dozen muffins |
| Corn syrup | | 2 | oz | 60 g | 5 | 10 oz (280 g) per dozen corn sticks |
| Butter or shortening, melted | | 12 | oz | 360 g | 30 | **BAKING** |
| **Total weight:** | **6 lb 11** | | **oz** | **3214 g** | **269%** | 400°F (200°C) for corn bread, 25–30 minutes |

**BAKING**

425°F (218°C) for muffins or sticks, 15–20 minutes

**VARIATION**

Use buttermilk instead of water and omit nonfat milk solids. Reduce baking powder to 2.5% (1 oz/30 g) and add 1.25% (0.5 oz/15 g) baking soda.

# ZUCCHINI CARROT NUT MUFFINS

| Ingredients | U.S. | | Metric | | % | Procedure |
|---|---|---|---|---|---|---|
| Pastry flour | 2 lb | | 960 | g | 80 | **MIXING** |
| Bran | 8 | oz | 240 | g | 20 | Modified muffin method |
| Salt | 0.5 | oz | 15 | g | 1.25 | 1. Sift the flour, leavenings, and spices. Stir in |
| Baking powder | 0.6 oz (3½ tsp) | | 18 | g | 1.5 | the bran, nuts, and coconut. |
| Baking soda | 0.4 oz (2¼ tsp) | | 12 | g | 1 | 2. Beat the eggs and sugar until well mixed, |
| Cinnamon | 0.17 oz (2½ tsp) | | 5 | g | 0.4 | but do not whip into a foam. Stir in the |
| Nutmeg | 0.08 oz (1 tsp) | | 2.5 | g | 0.2 | grated vegetables and the oil. |
| Ginger | 0.04 oz (½ tsp) | | 1 | g | 0.1 | 3. Add the egg mixture to the dry ingredients |
| Pecans or walnuts, chopped | 10 | oz | 300 | g | 25 | and mix just until combined. |
| Shredded, unsweetened coconut | 4 | oz | 120 | g | 10 | **SCALING**<br>Fill the tins two-thirds full. |
| Eggs | 1 lb | | 480 | g | 40 | **BAKING** |
| Sugar | 1 lb 14 | oz | 900 | g | 75 | 400°F (200°C) about 30 minutes |
| Zucchini, grated | 12 | oz | 360 | g | 30 | |
| Carrot, grated | 12 | oz | 360 | g | 30 | |
| Vegetable oil | 1 lb | | 480 | g | 40 | |
| **Total weight:** | **8 lb 13** | **oz** | **4253** | **g** | **354%** | |

# SCONES

| Ingredients | U.S. | | Metric | % | Procedure |
|---|---|---|---|---|---|
| Bread flour | 1 lb 8 | oz | 600 g | 50 | **MIXING** |
| Pastry flour | 1 lb 8 | oz | 600 g | 50 | Biscuit method (p. 219). Chill dough after mixing if it is too soft to make up. |
| Sugar | 6 | oz | 150 g | 12.5 | |
| Salt | 0.5 | oz | 12 g | 1 | **MAKEUP VARIATIONS** |
| Baking powder | 3 | oz | 72 g | 6 | |
| Shortening and/or butter | 1 lb 3 | oz | 480 g | 40 | ◆ Scale at 1 lb (450 g), round up, and flatten to ½ in. (12 mm) thick. Cut into 8 wedges. |
| Eggs | 7 | oz | 180 g | 15 | ◆ Roll out into a rectangle ½ in. (12 mm) thick and cut into triangles as for croissants (see p. 205). |
| Milk | 1 lb 5 | oz | 540 g | 45 | |
| **Total weight:** | **6 lb 8** | **oz** | **2634 g** | **219%** | ◆ Roll out into a rectangle ½ in. (12 mm) thick and cut out with cutters like biscuits. |

*Note: Scones are traditionally cut into rounds in Britain but into triangles in the United States. British tea scones are usually moister and tenderer than American scones.*

Place on greased or paper-lined sheet pans. Egg wash tops.

**BAKING**

400°F (200°C) for 15–20 minutes

## VARIATIONS

| Ingredients | U.S. | Metric | % |
|---|---|---|---|
| Raisins or currants | 12 oz | 300 g | 25 |

Add the raisins or currants to the dry ingredients after cutting in the fat.

Left to right: Raisin Scones, Cranberry Drop Scones

# CRANBERRY DROP SCONES

*For large-quantity measurements, see page 727.*

| Ingredients | U.S. | | Metric | % | Procedure |
|---|---|---|---|---|---|
| Butter | 6 | oz | 185 g | 25 | **MIXING** |
| Sugar | 5 | oz | 150 g | 21 | Creaming method (p. 220) |
| Salt | 0.25 | oz | 8 g | 1 | **MAKEUP AND BAKING** |
| Egg yolks | 1.33 (2 yolks) | oz | 40 g (2 yolks) | 5.5 | Using a 2-oz (60-mL) scoop, drop mounds onto parchment-lined sheets pans. Bake as for regular scones, above. |
| Pastry flour | 1 lb 8 | oz | 750 g | 100 | |
| Baking Powder | 1.25 | oz | 38 g | 5 | |
| Milk | 14 | oz | 435 g | 58 | |
| Dried Cranberries | 4 | oz | 125 g | 17 | |
| **Total weight:** | **2 lb 9** | **oz** | **1296 g** | **171%** | |

# STEAMED BROWN BREAD

| Ingredients | U.S. | | Metric | % | Procedure |
|---|---|---|---|---|---|
| Bread flour | 8 | oz | 250 g | 28.5 | **MIXING** |
| Whole wheat flour | 4 | oz | 125 g | 14 | Muffin method (p. 220) |
| Light rye flour | 8 | oz | 250 g | 28.5 | **SCALING AND COOKING** |
| Cornmeal | 8 | oz | 250 g | 28.5 | |
| Salt | 0.25 | oz | 9 g | 1 | Fill well-greased molds one-half full, about |
| Baking soda | 0.5 | oz | 15 g | 1.8 | 16 oz for each quart of capacity (500 g per |
| Baking powder | 0.5 | oz | 15 g | 1.8 | liter). Cover molds and steam for 3 hours. |
| Raisins | 8 | oz | 250 g | 28.5 | |
| Buttermilk | 2 lb | | 1000 g | 114 | |
| Molasses | 15 | oz | 475 g | 54 | |
| Oil | 2 | oz | 60 g | 7 | |
| **Total weight:** | **5 lb 6** | **oz** | **2699 g** | **306%** | |

# ORANGE NUT BREAD

| Ingredients | U.S. | | Metric | % | Procedure |
|---|---|---|---|---|---|
| Sugar | 12 | oz | 350 g | 50 | **MIXING** |
| Orange zest, grated | 1 | oz | 30 g | 4 | Muffin method (p. 220). Blend the sugar and orange zest thoroughly before adding the remaining ingredients to ensure even distribution. |
| Pastry flour | 1 lb 8 | oz | 700 g | 100 | |
| Nonfat milk solids | 2 | oz | 60 g | 8 | |
| Baking powder | 1 | oz | 30 g | 4 | **SCALING** |
| Baking soda | 0.3 | oz (2 tsp) | 10 g | 1.4 | 1 lb 4 oz (575 g) per 7⅜ × 3⅝-in. (19 × 9 cm) loaf pan |
| Salt | 0.3 | oz (2 tsp) | 10 g | 1.4 | |
| Walnuts, chopped | 12 | oz | 350 g | 50 | |
| Eggs | 5 | oz | 140 g | 20 | 1 lb 10 oz (750 g) per 8½ × 4½-in. (22 × 11 cm) loaf pan |
| Orange juice | 6 | oz | 175 g | 25 | |
| Water | 1 lb | | 450 g | 65 | **BAKING** |
| Oil or melted butter or shortening | 6 | oz | 175 g | 25 | 375°F (190°C), about 50 minutes |
| **Total weight:** | **5 lb 6** | **oz** | **2480 g** | **344%** | |

**VARIATION**

## LEMON NUT BREAD

Substitute grated lemon zest for the orange zest. Omit the orange juice and add 8% (2 oz/60 g) lemon juice. Increase the water to 83% (1 lb 4 oz/580 g).

# BANANA BREAD

| Ingredients | U.S. | | | Metric | % | Procedure |
|---|---|---|---|---|---|---|
| Pastry flour | 1 lb | 8 | oz | 700 g | 100 | **MIXING** |
| Sugar | | 10 | oz | 280 g | 40 | Muffin method (p. 220) |
| Baking powder | | 1.25 | oz | 35 g | 5 | **SCALING** |
| Baking soda | | 0.14 oz (1 tsp) | | 4 g | 0.6 | 1 lb 4 oz (575 g) per 7⅜ × 3⅝-in. (19 × 9 cm) |
| Salt | | 0.33 oz (2 tsp) | | 9 g | 1.25 | loaf pan |
| Walnuts, chopped | | 6 | oz | 175 g | 25 | 1 lb 10 oz (750 g) per 8½ × 4½-in. (22 × 11 cm) |
| Eggs | | 10 | oz | 280 g | 40 | loaf pan |
| Ripe banana, pulp, puréed | 1 lb | 8 | oz | 700 g | 100 | **BAKING** |
| Oil or melted butter or shortening | | 8 | oz | 230 g | 33 | 375°F (190°C), about 50 minutes |
| **Total weight:** | **5 lb** | **4** | **oz** | **2413 g** | **344%** | |

**VARIATION**

For a more delicate, cakelike product, make the following adjustments:

1. Fat: Increase to 40% (10 oz/280 g). Use shortening and/or butter, not oil.
2. Sugar: Increase to 60% (15 oz/420 g).
3. Flour: Use cake flour.
4. Mixing: Mix by the creaming method.

# DATE NUT BREAD

| Ingredients | U.S. | | | Metric | % | Procedure |
|---|---|---|---|---|---|---|
| Shortening and/or butter | | 8 | oz | 200 g | 40 | **MIXING** |
| Brown sugar | | 8 | oz | 200 g | 40 | Creaming method (p. 220). Fold the dates and nuts into the finished batter. |
| Salt | | 0.25 | oz | 6 g | 1.25 | **SCALING** |
| Nonfat milk solids | | 1.5 | oz | 35 g | 7 | |
| Eggs | | 6 | oz | 150 g | 30 | 1 lb 4 oz (575 g) per 7⅜ × 3⅝-in. (19 × 9 cm) loaf pan |
| Cake flour | 1 lb | | | 400 g | 80 | 1 lb 10 oz (750 g) per 8½ × 4½-in. (22 × 11 cm) |
| Whole wheat flour | | 4 | oz | 100 g | 20 | loaf pan |
| Baking powder | | 0.75 | oz | 20 g | 3.75 | **BAKING** |
| Baking soda | | 0.25 | oz | 6 g | 1.25 | 375°F (190°C), about 50 minutes |
| Water | | 15 | oz | 375 g | 75 | |
| Dates (see *Note*) | | 10 | oz | 250 g | 50 | |
| Walnuts, chopped | | 6 | oz | 150 g | 30 | |
| **Total weight:** | **4 lb** | **11** | **oz** | **1891 g** | **378%** | |

*Note: After scaling the dates, soak them in hot water until very soft. Drain and chop.*

**VARIATIONS**

Substitute other nuts, or a mixture, for the walnuts. For example:

    pecans

    hazelnuts, toasted

    almonds, toasted

Substitute other dried fruits for the dates. For example:

    prunes      dried apples

    raisins      dried figs

    dried apricots

# PLUM CAKE

| Ingredients | U.S. | | | Metric | % | Procedure |
|---|---|---|---|---|---|---|
| Pastry flour | 1 lb | 4 | oz | 600 g | 100 | **MIXING** |
| Nonfat milk solids | | 0.5 | oz | 15 g | 3 | Biscuit method (p. 219). Because of the mois- |
| Salt | | 0.25 | oz | 8 g | 1.5 | ture in the brown sugar, the dry ingredients |
| Cinnamon | | 0.06 | oz (1 tsp) | 2 g | 0.3 | must be rubbed through a sieve when sifted. |
| Brown sugar | | 10 | oz | 300 g | 50 | |
| Butter | | 10 | oz | 300 g | 50 | **SCALING AND MAKEUP** |
| Eggs | | 9 | oz | 270 g | 45 | One recipe is enough for one half-sheet pan, |
| Milk | 1 lb | 2 | oz | 540 g | 90 | three 9-in. (23 cm) square pans, or four 8-in. |
| **Topping:** | | | | | | (20 cm) square pans. Spread the dough in |
| Italian-style | 3 lb | 12 | oz | 1800 g | 300 | greased and floured pans. Arrange plum |
| prune plums, | | | | | | halves, cut side up, on top of the dough. |
| halved and pitted | | | | | | Sprinkle with cinnamon sugar. |
| Cinnamon sugar | | 4 | oz | 120 g | 20 | **BAKING** |
| (p. 199) | | | | | | 400°F (200°C) for 35 minutes |
| **Total weight:** | **8 lb** | **3** | **oz** | **3955 g** | **659%** | |

**VARIATIONS**

For a more cakelike texture, mix the dough using the creaming method.

Top the cake with Streusel (p. 199) instead of cinnamon sugar before baking.

# ALMOND POPPY SEED MUFFINS

| Ingredients | U.S. | | | Metric | % | Procedure |
|---|---|---|---|---|---|---|
| Butter | | 14 | oz | 450 g | 60 | **MIXING** |
| Sugar | 1 lb | 2 | oz | 560 g | 75 | Creaming method (p. 220). Mix the poppy |
| Eggs | | 12 | oz | 375 g | 50 | seeds with the dry ingredients after sifting. |
| Pastry flour | 1 lb | 8 | oz | 750 g | 100 | **SCALING** |
| Baking powder | | 0.25 | oz (1½ tsp) | 8 g | 1 | Fill tins two-thirds full. |
| Baking soda | | 0.16 | oz (1 tsp) | 5 g | 0.7 | **BAKING** |
| Salt | | 0.2 | oz (1 tsp) | 6 g | 0.8 | 375°F (190°C) about 30 minutes |
| Poppy seeds | | 1 | oz | 30 g | 4 | |
| Almond extract | | 0.16 | oz (1 tsp) | 5 g | 0.7 | |
| Buttermilk | 1 pt | | | 500 g | 67 | |
| **Total weight:** | **5 lb** | **5** | **oz** | **2689 g** | **359%** | |

**VARIATION**

## LEMON POPPY SEED MUFFINS

Flavor the muffins with lemon extract instead of almond extract.

# APPLE SPICE MUFFINS

| Ingredients | U.S. | | Metric | | % | Procedure |
|---|---|---|---|---|---|---|
| Butter | 14 | oz | 435 | g | 60 | **MIXING** |
| Brown sugar | 1 lb 2 | oz | 540 | g | 75 | Creaming method (p. 220) |
| Salt | 0.25 oz (1½ tsp) | | 7 | g | 1 | |
| Cinnamon | 0.15 oz (2 tsp) | | 4 | g | 0.6 | **SCALING** |
| Nutmeg | 0.05 oz (¾ tsp) | | 1.5 | g | 0.2 | Fill tins two-thirds full. |
| Eggs | 8 | oz | 240 | g | 33 | **BAKING** |
| Pastry flour | 1 lb 4 | oz | 600 | g | 83 | 400°F (200°C), about 30 minutes |
| Whole wheat flour | 4 | oz | 120 | g | 17 | |
| Baking powder | 0.5 | oz | 15 | g | 2 | |
| Baking soda | 0.25 oz (1½ tsp) | | 7 | g | 1 | |
| Buttermilk | 12 | oz | 360 | g | 50 | |
| Applesauce | 1 lb 2 | oz | 540 | g | 75 | |
| **Total weight:** | **5 lb 14** | **oz** | **2869** | **g** | **397%** | |

# PUMPKIN MUFFINS

| Ingredients | U.S. | | Metric | | % | Procedure |
|---|---|---|---|---|---|---|
| Butter | 12 | oz | 375 | g | 50 | **MIXING** |
| Brown sugar | 1 lb | | 500 | g | 67 | Creaming method (p. 220) |
| Ginger | 0.05 oz (¾ tsp) | | 1.5 | g | 0.2 | |
| Cinnamon | 0.04 oz (½ tsp) | | 1.25 | g | 0.17 | **SCALING** |
| Nutmeg | 0.03 oz (⅓ tsp) | | 0.75 | g | 0.1 | Fill tins two-thirds full. |
| Allspice | 0.05 oz (¾ tsp) | | 1.5 | g | 0.2 | **BAKING** |
| Salt | 0.14 oz (¾ tsp) | | 4.5 | g | 0.6 | 400°F (200°C) about 30 minutes |
| Eggs | 6 | oz | 190 | g | 25 | |
| Pastry flour | 1 lb 8 | oz | 750 | g | 100 | |
| Baking powder | 0.33 oz (2 tsp) | | 10 | g | 1.4 | |
| Baking soda | 0.33 oz (2 tsp) | | 10 | g | 1.4 | |
| Buttermilk | 12 | oz | 375 | g | 50 | |
| Pumpkin purée, canned | 10 | oz | 300 | g | 40 | |
| **Total weight:** | **5 lb** | | **2519** | **g** | **336%** | |

# DOUBLE CHOCOLATE MUFFINS

| Ingredients | U.S. | | | Metric | | % | Procedure |
|---|---|---|---|---|---|---|---|
| Butter | | 10 | oz | 300 | g | 40 | **MIXING** |
| Sugar | | 11 | oz | 340 | g | 45 | Creaming method. Melt the chocolate, cool it |
| Semisweet chocolate | 1 lb | | | 500 | g | 67 | to room temperature, and cream it into the butter and sugar mixture. Fold the chocolate |
| Eggs | | 5 | oz | 150 | g | 20 | chips into the finished batter. (Note there is no baking powder in this formula, only baking |
| Flour | 1 lb | 8 | oz | 750 | g | 100 | soda.) |
| Baking soda | | 0.5 | oz | 15 | g | 2 | **SCALING** |
| Salt | | 0.14 | oz (¾ tsp) | 4.5 | g | 0.6 | Fill tins two-thirds full. |
| Buttermilk | 1 pt | 4 | oz | 625 | g | 83 | |
| Chocolate chips | | 12 | oz | 375 | g | 50 | **BAKING** |
| **Total weight:** | **6 lb** | **2** | **oz** | **3059** | **g** | **407%** | 400°F (200°C) about 30 minutes |

# POPOVERS

| Ingredients | U.S. | | | Metric | | % | Procedure |
|---|---|---|---|---|---|---|---|
| Eggs | 1 lb | 4 | oz | 625 | g | 125 | **MIXING** |
| Milk | 2 lb | | | 1000 | g | 200 | 1. Beat the eggs, milk, and salt together with the whip attachment until well blended. |
| Salt | | 0.25 | oz | 8 | g | 1.5 | Add the melted fat. |
| Butter or shortening, melted | | 2 | oz | 60 | g | 12.5 | 2. Replace the whip with the paddle. Mix in the flour until completely smooth. |
| Bread flour | 1 lb | | | 500 | g | 100 | 3. Strain the batter (optional but gives the popovers a better appearance). |
| **Total weight:** | **4 lb** | **6** | **oz** | **2193** | **g** | **439%** | |

**SCALING AND PANNING**

Grease popover tins or every other cup of muffin tins (to allow room for expansion). Fill the greased cups about one-half full, about 1½–3 oz (45 g) batter per unit, depending on the size of the tins.

**BAKING**

425°F (218°C) for 30–40 minutes. Before removing them from the oven, be sure the popovers are dry and firm enough to avoid collapsing. Remove from pans immediately.

## ❊〉 POPOVERS 〈❊

Popovers are similar to pâte à choux products such as cream puffs and éclairs in that both are strongly leavened by steam until they are hollow in the center, and both depend on egg and gluten proteins for their structure. The major difference between the two is that popovers are made from a thin batter, while choux products are made from a soft dough.

Proper mixing is important for both items. They must be mixed well enough to develop gluten but not so much that the gluten is too strong for the steam to expand. Mix popover batter until smooth, but do not overmix.

# GINGERBREAD

| Ingredients | Old-Fashioned Gingerbread | | | | Pain d'Épices (French Gingerbread) | | | |
|---|---|---|---|---|---|---|---|---|
| | U.S. | | Metric | % | U.S. | | Metric | % |
| Pastry flour | 2 lb 8 | oz | 1100 g | 100 | 1 lb 4 | oz | 550 g | 50 |
| Rye flour | — | | — | — | 1 lb 4 | oz | 550 g | 50 |
| Salt | 0.25 | oz | 7 g | 0.6 | 0.25 | oz | 7 g | 0.6 |
| Baking soda | 1.25 | oz | 33 g | 3 | 1.25 | oz | 33 g | 3 |
| Baking powder | 0.6 | oz | 16 g | 1.5 | 0.6 | oz | 16 g | 1.5 |
| Ginger | 0.5 | oz | 14 g | 1.25 | 0.5 | oz | 14 g | 1.25 |
| Cinnamon | — | | — | — | 0.25 | oz | 7 g | 0.6 |
| Cloves, ground | — | | — | — | 0.12 | oz | 3.5 g | 0.3 |
| Anise, ground | — | | — | — | 0.5 | oz | 14 g | 1.25 |
| Orange rind, grated | — | | — | — | 0.5 | oz | 14 g | 1.25 |
| Currants | — | | — | — | 8 | oz | 220 g | 20 |
| Molasses | 2 lb 8 | oz | 1100 g | 100 | — | | — | — |
| Honey | — | | — | — | 1 lb 14 | oz | 825 g | 75 |
| Hot water | 1 lb 4 | oz | 550 g | 50 | 1 lb 4 | oz | 550 g | 50 |
| Butter or shortening, melted | 10 | oz | 275 g | 25 | 10 | oz | 275 g | 25 |
| *Total weight:* | *7 lb 1* | *oz* | *3095 g* | *281%* | *6 lb 15* | *oz* | *3078 g* | *279%* |

## Procedure

**MIXING**

Muffin method (p. 220)

**PANNING**

Old-Fashioned Gingerbread: greased, paper-lined sheet pans, about 6.5 to 7 lb or 3 kg per sheet (one recipe per sheet).

Pain d'Épices (pronounced pan day peece): greased loaf pans. Fill about one-half full of batter.

**BAKING**

375°F (190°C)

---

### ✤{ GINGERBREAD }✤

The name *gingerbread* is given to a wide variety of cakes and shortbreads or cookies. Gingerbread in its various forms dates back to the Middle Ages, when highly spiced foods were common. Different regions of Europe developed their own varieties of gingerbread, using their own blends of spices.

Originally, gingerbreads were sweetened with honey, just as the French *pain d'épices* (pan day peece, meaning "spice bread") from the city of Dijon still is today. After sugarcane products became more widely available and economical, most regions switched to molasses to sweeten their gingerbread.

# SODA BREAD

| Ingredients | U.S. | | | Metric | % | Procedure |
|---|---|---|---|---|---|---|
| Pastry flour | 2 lb | 8 | oz | 1200 g | 100 | **MIXING** |
| Baking powder | | 2 | oz | 60 g | 5 | Biscuit method (p. 219). Stir in the currants af- |
| Baking soda | | 0.5 | oz | 15 g | 1.25 | ter cutting in the fat. Refrigerate after mixing if |
| Salt | | 0.5 | oz | 15 g | 1.25 | too soft to make up. |
| Sugar | | 2 | oz | 60 g | 5 | **SCALING** |
| Shortening or butter | | 4 | oz | 120 g | 10 | 1 lb (450 g) per unit |
| Currants or raisins | | 8 | oz | 240 g | 20 | **MAKEUP** |
| Buttermilk | 1 lb | 12 | oz | 840 g | 70 | Round into a ball-shaped loaf. Place on a sheet pan. Cut a deep cross into the top. |
| *Total weight:* | *5 lb* | *5* | *oz* | *2550 g* | *212%* | **BAKING** |

**VARIATION**

Add 1.25% (0.5 oz/15 g) caraway seeds. Omit currants or leave them in, as desired.

**BAKING**

375°F (140°C), 30–40 minutes

# TERMS FOR REVIEW

| | | |
|---|---|---|
| pour batter | tunneling | muffin method |
| drop batter | biscuit method | creaming method |

# QUESTIONS FOR DISCUSSION

1. If you made a batch of muffins that came out of the oven with strange, knobby shapes, what would you expect to be the reason?

2. What is the most important difference between the biscuit method and the muffin method?

3. Why do popovers require more mixing than other quick breads?

## Chapter : 11

# Doughnuts, Fritters, Pancakes, and Waffles

Unlike the products we have discussed so far, those included in this chapter are cooked not by baking in ovens but by deep-frying, by cooking in greased fry pans or on griddles, or, in the case of waffles, by cooking in specially designed griddles that heat the product from both sides at once.

Several types of doughs or batters are used for these products. To produce the two most popular types of doughnuts, you must understand the principles of yeast dough production (chapters 6–9) and the creaming method used for mixing some quick breads (chapter 10). French doughnuts are a fried version of the same pastry used to make cream puffs and éclairs (chapter 14). American pancakes are made from chemically leavened batters mixed by the muffin method, while French pancakes or crêpes are made from thin, unleavened batters made of milk, eggs, and flour.

**After reading this chapter, you should be able to:**

1. Prepare doughnuts and other deep-fried desserts and pastries.

2. Prepare pancakes and waffles.

3. Prepare crêpes and crêpe desserts.

# DOUGHNUTS

## Yeast-Raised Doughnuts

The mixing method used to prepare yeast-raised doughnuts is the *modified straight dough method* (p. 115). Review this procedure before beginning doughnut production. In addition, the following points will help you understand and produce high-quality doughnuts. Makeup and finishing procedures follow the formula.

1. The dough used for yeast doughnuts is similar to regular sweet dough or bun dough, except it is often not as rich—that is, doughnuts are made with less fat, sugar, and eggs (compare the formulas on pp. 188 and 238). Doughs that are too rich will brown too fast and absorb too much frying fat. The finished products will be greasy and either too dark on the outside or insufficiently cooked inside. Also, a leaner dough has stronger gluten, which can better withstand the handling involved in proofing and frying.

2. Punch the dough and bring it to the bench in sufficient time to allow for makeup. Remember that fermentation continues during makeup. If the dough gets too old (proofed too long), the doughnuts will require longer frying to become browned and thus will be greasier. When you are preparing a large quantity of doughnuts, it may be necessary to place some of the dough in the retarder so it doesn't become old.

3. Watch the dough temperature carefully, especially in warm weather. If the dough is much above 80°F (24°C), it will become old more quickly.

4. Proof the doughnuts at a lower temperature and humidity than you do breads. Some bakers proof them at room temperature, if there is a part of the bakeshop that isn't too hot (about 70°F/21°C). Doughnuts proofed this way are less likely to be deformed or dented when handled or brought to the fryer.

5. Handle fully proofed units carefully, as they are soft and easily dented. Many bakers give doughnuts only three-quarters proof. This makes a denser doughnut, but one that is more easily handled.

6. Heat the frying fat to the proper temperature. Fat temperature for raised doughnuts varies from 365° to 385°F (185° to 195°C), depending on the formula. Richer formulas require a lower temperature to avoid excessive browning. The formulas in this book require a frying temperature of 375° to 380°F (190° to 193°C).

7. Arrange the proofed units on screens on which they can be lowered into fat. (For small quantities, you can place them by hand in the fryer, but be careful not to burn yourself.) Frying time is about 2½ minutes. The doughnuts must be turned over when they are half done in order to brown evenly on both sides.

8. Lift from the frying fat with the screen, or, if you are frying in smaller quantities, with the frying basket or a spider, holding the doughnuts over the frying fat for a moment to let the fat drain from the doughnuts back into the kettle. Set the doughnuts on brown paper to absorb excess fat.

# Cake-Type Doughnuts

Operations that produce cake doughnuts in volume use equipment that drops batter directly into the hot fat. This equipment is usually automatic, although small hand-operated depositors are also available. Automatic depositors use a relatively slack dough that is generally made from prepared mixes. To use these mixes and depositors, follow two important guidelines:

- Follow manufacturers' directions closely when preparing the mix.

- Keep the depositor head 1½ inch (4 cm) above the fat. If the doughnut must drop much farther than this into the fat, poor shape may result.

Operations that make cake doughnuts by hand use a stiffer mix that is rolled out and cut with cutters. Two formulas for this type of mix are included in this chapter. Follow these guidelines when preparing cake doughnuts:

1. Scale ingredients carefully. Even small errors can result in products with unsatisfactory texture or appearance.

2. Mix the dough until smooth, but do not overmix. Undermixed doughs result in a rough appearance and excessive fat absorption. Overmixed doughs result in tough, dense doughnuts.

3. Dough temperature should be about 70° to 75°F (21° to 24°C) when the units are fried. Be especially careful of dough temperature during hot weather.

4. Let the cut-out units rest about 15 minutes before frying in order to relax the gluten. Failure to relax the dough results in toughness and poor expansion.

5. Fry at the proper temperature. Normal fat temperature for cake doughnuts is 375° to 385°F (190° to 195°C). Frying time is about 1½ to 2 minutes. Doughnuts must be turned over when half done.

# Preparation and Care of Frying Fat

Properly fried doughnuts absorb about 2 ounces fat per dozen. Therefore, frying fat should be of good quality and properly maintained; otherwise, the quality of the doughnuts will suffer. Observe the following guidelines for care of frying fat:

1. Use good-quality, flavorless fat. The best fat for frying has a high smoke point (the temperature at which the fat begins to smoke and to break down rapidly).

   Solid shortenings are popular for frying because they are stable and because they congeal when the doughnuts cool, making them appear less greasy. However, such doughnuts can have an unpleasant eating quality because the fat does not melt in the mouth.

2. Fry at the proper temperature. Using too low a temperature extends frying time, causing excessive greasiness.

   If you do not have automatic equipment with thermostatic temperature controls, keep a fat thermometer clipped to the side of the frying kettle.

3. Maintain the fat at the proper level in the fryer. When additional fat must be added, allow time for it to heat.

4. Do not fry too many doughnuts at a time. Overloading will lower the fat temperature, will not allow room for expansion of the doughnuts, and will make it difficult to turn them over.

5. Keep the fat clean. Skim out food particles as necessary. After each day's use, cool the fat until it is warm, strain it, and clean the equipment.

6. Discard spent fat. Old fat loses frying ability, browns excessively, and imparts a bad flavor.

7. Keep the fat covered when not in use. Try to aerate it as little as possible when filtering.

# FORMULAS

## YEAST-RAISED DOUGHNUTS

| Ingredients | U.S. | | Metric | % | Procedure |
|---|---|---|---|---|---|
| Water | 1 lb | | 410 g | 55 | **MIXING** |
| Yeast | 1.5 | oz | 38 g | 5 | Modified straight dough method (p. 115) |
| Shortening | 3 | oz | 75 g | 10 | Develop the dough completely, about 6–8 |
| Sugar | 4 | oz | 105 g | 14 | minutes at second speed. |
| Salt | 0.5 | oz | 13 g | 1.75 | **FERMENTATION** |
| Mace | 0.09 | oz (½ tsp) | 2 g | 0.3 | About 1½ hours at 80°F (24°C) |
| Nonfat milk solids | 1.5 | oz | 38 g | 5 | **SCALING** |
| Eggs | 4 | oz | 105 g | 14 | 1.5 oz (45 g) per unit |
| Bread flour | 1 lb 13 | oz | 750 g | 100 | See below for makeup. |
| **Total weight:** | **3 lb 11** | **oz** | **1536 g** | **205%** | Proof. |

**MIXING**

Modified straight dough method (p. 115)

Develop the dough completely, about 6–8 minutes at second speed.

**FERMENTATION**

About 1½ hours at 80°F (24°C)

**SCALING**

1.5 oz (45 g) per unit

See below for makeup.

Proof.

**FRYING**

375°F (190°C)

When the doughnuts are fried, lift them from the fat and let excess fat drip off. Place the doughnuts in one layer on absorbent paper. Cool.

### VARIATIONS

*Makeup of Yeast-Raised Doughnuts*

## RING DOUGHNUTS

1. Roll out the dough to ½ in. (12 mm) thick. Make sure the dough is of even thickness. Let the dough relax.

2. Cut out doughnuts with a doughnut cutter. Cut as close together as possible to minimize scrap.

3. Combine the scrap dough and let it relax. Roll it out and let it relax again. Continue cutting doughnuts.

## JELLY-FILLED DOUGHNUTS OR BISMARCKS

**METHOD 1**

1. Scale the dough into 3½ lb (1600 g) presses. Let them relax for 10 minutes.

2. Divide the dough. Round the small units.

3. Let them relax a few minutes, then flatten lightly.

**METHOD 2**

1. Roll out the dough to ½ in. (12 mm) thick, as for ring doughnuts.

2. Cut out with round cutters (biscuit cutters, or doughnut cutters with the "hole" removed).

After frying and cooling, use a doughnut pump or jelly pump to fill the doughnuts. Using a sharp, straight nozzle, pierce the side of the doughnut and inject the jelly into the center.

Other fillings besides jelly may be used, such as lemon, custard (see Pastry Cream, p. 271), and cream. If a filling containing egg, milk, or cream is used, the doughnuts must be kept refrigerated.

## LONG JOHNS

1. Roll out the dough to ½ in. (12 mm) thick, as for ring doughnuts.
2. With a pastry wheel, cut into strips 1½ in. (4 cm) wide and 3½ in. (9 cm) long.

## FRIED CINNAMON ROLLS

1. Make up like baked Cinnamon Rolls (p. 208), except omit the butter in the filling.
2. Make sure the edges are well sealed so the rolls don't unwind during frying.

## TWISTS

1. Scale into presses, divide the dough, and round the units, as for filled doughnuts.
2. Roll each unit on the bench with the palms of the hands to a strip about 8 in. (20 cm) long.
3. Place one hand over each end of the strip. Roll one end toward you and the other away from you to twist the strip.
4. Holding it by the ends, lift the strip off the bench and bring the two ends together. The strip will twist around itself.
5. Seal the ends together.

# CAKE DOUGHNUTS

| Ingredients | U.S. | | | Metric | % | Procedure |
|---|---|---|---|---|---|---|
| Shortening | | 3 | oz | 90 g | 9 | **MIXING** |
| Sugar | | 7 | oz | 220 g | 22 | Creaming method (p. 220) |
| Salt | | 0.25 | oz | 8 g | 0.8 | Mix the dough until it is smooth, but do not overmix. |
| Nonfat milk solids | | 1.5 | oz | 45 g | 4.7 | |
| Mace | | 0.12 oz (1¾ tsp) | | 4 g | 0.4 | **MAKEUP** |
| Vanilla extract | | 0.5 | oz | 15 g | 1.5 | 1. Place the dough on the bench and form into a smooth rectangular shape with the hands; rest 15 minutes. |
| Whole eggs | | 3 | oz | 90 g | 9 | |
| Egg yolks | | 1.5 | oz | 30 g | 3 | 2. Roll out to about ⅜ in. (1 cm) thick. Make sure the dough is of even thickness and not sticking to the bench. |
| Cake flour | 1 lb | 4 | oz | 750 g | 62.5 | |
| Bread flour | | 12 | oz | 250 g | 37.5 | 3. Cut out doughnuts with cutters. |
| Baking powder | | 1.25 | oz | 40 g | 4 | 4. Collect the scrap dough and let it relax. Roll it out again and continue cutting doughnuts. |
| Water | 1 lb | | | 500 g | 50 | 5. Place the doughnuts on lightly floured pans and let them relax 15 minutes. |
| *Total weight:* | *4 lb* | *4* | *oz* | *2042 g* | *204%* | |

**FRYING**

380°F (193°C)

Lift the doughnuts from fat, let the excess fat drip off, and place them in one layer on absorbent paper. Cool.

# CHOCOLATE CAKE DOUGHNUTS

*For large-quantity measurements, see page 727.*

| Ingredients | U.S. | | Metric | % | Procedure |
|---|---|---|---|---|---|
| Shortening | 1.5 | oz | 45 g | 9 | **MIXING** |
| Sugar | 4 | oz | 125 g | 25 | Creaming method (p. 220) |
| Salt | 0.13 oz (⅛ tsp) | | 4 g | 0.8 | Mix the dough until it is smooth, but do not |
| Nonfat milk solids | 0.75 oz | | 24 g | 4.7 | overmix. |
| Vanilla extract | 0.25 oz | | 8 g | 1.5 | **MAKEUP AND FRYING** |
| Whole eggs | 1.5 | oz | 45 g | 9 | Same as for Cake Doughnuts, above. *Caution:* |
| Egg yolks | 0.5 | oz | 15 g | 3 | Watch chocolate doughnuts carefully when fry- |
| Cake flour | 10 | oz | 315 g | 62.5 | ing because it is harder to tell doneness by |
| Bread flour | 6 | oz | 185 g | 37.5 | their color. |
| Cocoa powder | 1.25 oz | | 40 g | 7.8 | |
| Baking powder | 0.25 oz | | 15 g | 3 | |
| Baking soda | 0.1 oz (⅔ tsp) | | 3 g | 0.63 | |
| Water | 8.5 | oz | 265 g | 53 | |
| **Total weight:** | **2 lb 2** | **oz** | **1089 g** | **217%** | |

# RICH VANILLA SPICE DOUGHNUTS

*For large-quantity measurements, see page 727.*

| Ingredients | U.S. | | Metric | % | Procedure |
|---|---|---|---|---|---|
| Bread flour | 12 | oz | 375 g | 50 | **MIXING** |
| Cake flour | 12 | oz | 375 g | 50 | Muffin method (p. 220), modified as follows: |
| Baking powder | 0.75 oz | | 22 g | 3 | 1. Sift together the flour, baking powder, |
| Nutmeg | 0.2 oz (1 tbsp) | | 6 g | 0.8 | spices, and salt. |
| Cinnamon | 0.06 oz (1 tsp) | | 2 g | 0.25 | 2. Whip together the eggs, egg yolks, and |
| Salt | 0.3 oz (1 tsp) | | 9 g | 1.25 | sugar until light. Mix in the milk, vanilla, and |
| Whole eggs | 5 | oz | 155 g | 21 | melted butter. |
| Egg yolks | 1 | oz | 30 g | 4 | 3. Fold the liquid ingredients into the dry in- |
| Sugar | 10 | oz | 315 g | 42 | gredients to make a soft dough. |
| Milk | 9.5 | oz | 300 g | 40 | 4. Refrigerate at least 1 hour before rolling and |
| Vanilla extract | 0.75 oz | | 22 g | 3 | cutting. |
| Butter, melted | 3 | oz | 95 g | 12.5 | **MAKEUP** |
| **Total weight:** | **3 lb 6** | **oz** | **1712 g** | **227%** | Same as for Cake Doughnuts. |
| | | | | | **FRYING** |
| | | | | | 375°F (190°C) |

## Finishing Doughnuts

Doughnuts should be well drained and cooled before finishing with sugar or other coatings. If they are hot, steam from the doughnuts will soak the coating. The following are some popular coatings and finishes for doughnuts:

- ◆ Roll in cinnamon sugar.

- ◆ Roll in 4X sugar. (To keep the sugar from lumping and absorbing moisture, it may be sifted with cornstarch. Use 2 to 3 ounces starch per pound of sugar, or about 150 g per kg.)

- ◆ Ice the tops of the doughnuts with a fondant or fudge icing (see chapter 17).

- ◆ To **glaze**, dip in warm Doughnut Glaze (recipe follows) or in a warmed, thinned simple icing or fondant. Place on screens until glaze sets.

- ◆ After glazing, while glaze is still moist, doughnuts may be rolled in coconut or chopped nuts.

> ## ⁕{ FRENCH }⁕ DOUGHNUTS
>
> **French doughnuts** are made from Éclair Paste (p. 336) that is piped into ring shapes and deep-fried. They are included in the following section on fritters.

## DOUGHNUT GLAZE

| Ingredients | U.S. | | Metric | Sugar at 100% % | Procedure |
|---|---|---|---|---|---|
| Gelatin | 0.12 | oz | 3 g | 0.3 | 1. Soften the gelatin in the water. |
| Water | 8 | oz | 200 g | 20 | 2. Heat the water until the gelatin dissolves. |
| Corn syrup | 2 | oz | 50 g | 5 | 3. Add the remaining ingredients and mix until |
| Vanilla extract | 0.25 oz (1½ tsp) | | 6 g | 0.6 | smooth. |
| Confectioners' sugar | 2 lb 8 | oz | 1000 g | 100 | 4. Dip doughnuts into the warm glaze. Rewarm the glaze as necessary. |
| *Total weight:* | *3 lb 2* | *oz* | *1259 g* | *125%* | |

### VARIATION

#### HONEY GLAZE
Substitute honey for the corn syrup.

## FRITTERS

The term *fritter* is used for a great variety of fried items, both sweet and savory, including many made with vegetables, meats, or fish. Fried items of all types are often referred to by the French term for fritter, *beignet* (pronounced ben yay). In the pastry shop, we are concerned with two basic types of fritters:

1. Simple fritters, like doughnuts, are portions of dough that are deep-fried. They are usually dusted with sugar and often served with a sauce or a fruit preserve. This chapter includes recipes for four kinds of simple fritters, including the classic **beignet soufflé**, which is fried éclair paste.

2. Fruit fritters are made by dipping pieces of fresh, cooked, or canned fruit in batter and then deep-frying them, or by mixing chopped fruit into a

batter and dropping scoopfuls into frying fat. A basic procedure for making fruit fritters follows. Two recipes for fritter batters are included.

Also included in this chapter are **cannoli** shells. This type of fried pastry is not generally classified as a fritter. Nevertheless, cannoli shells are made in nearly the same way as two fritters in this chapter, fattigman and beignets de carnival—that is, they are made from a stiff dough that is rolled thin, cut out, and fried. Cannoli, however, are fried in a cylinder shape so they can take various fillings.

## Procedure for Preparing Fruit Fritters

1. Prepare batter (see formulas that follow).

2. Prepare the desired fruit. Popular fruits for fritters are:

   *Apples* Peel, core, and slice into rings ¼ in. (6 mm) thick.

   *Bananas* Peel, cut in half lengthwise, and then cut crosswise to make four quarters.

   *Pineapple* Use fresh or canned rings.

   *Apricots and plums* Split in half and remove the stones.

   For extra flavor, sprinkle fruits heavily with sugar and rum or kirsch and allow to marinate 1 to 2 hours.

3. Drain the fruit pieces well and dip them in batter to coat completely. Dip only as much as can be fried in one batch.

4. Drop into hot fat (375°F/190°C). Fry until golden brown on all sides.

5. Remove from fat and drain well.

6. Serve warm, sprinkled with cinnamon sugar. Crème Anglaise (p. 269) or Fruit Sauce (p. 277) may be served on the side.

# FRITTER BATTER I

*For large-quantity measurements, see page 727.*

| Ingredients | U.S. | | Metric | % | Procedure |
|---|---|---|---|---|---|
| Pastry flour | 9 | oz | 250 g | 100 | **MIXING** |
| Sugar | 0.5 | oz | 15 g | 6 | Muffin method (p. 220) |
| Salt | 0.12 oz (⅔ tsp) | | 4 g | 1.5 | 1. Sift together the dry ingredients. |
| Baking powder | 0.12 oz (¾ tsp) | | 4 g | 1.5 | |
| Eggs, beaten | 4.5 | oz | 125 g | 50 | 2. Combine the liquid ingredients. |
| Milk | 8 | oz | 225 g | 90 | 3. Gradually stir the liquid into the dry ingredi- |
| Oil | 0.5 | oz | 15 g | 6 | ents. Mix until nearly smooth, but do not |
| Vanilla extract | 0.08 oz (½ tsp) | | 2 g | 1 | overmix. |
| *Total weight:* | *1 lb 7* | *oz* | 640 g | 256% | 4. Let stand at least 30 minutes before using. |

# FRITTER BATTER II

*For large-quantity measurements, see page 728.*

| Ingredients | U.S. | | Metric | % | Procedure |
|---|---|---|---|---|---|
| Bread flour | 6 | oz | 190 g | 75 | 1. Sift together the dry ingredients. |
| Cake flour | 2 | oz | 60 g | 25 | 2. Combine the milk, egg yolks, and oil. |
| Salt | 0.12 oz (⅔ tsp) | | 4 g | 1.5 | 3. Stir the liquid into the dry ingredients. Mix |
| Sugar | 0.25 oz | | 8 g | 3 | until smooth. |
| Milk | 9 | oz | 312 g | 113 | 4. Let rest until ready to use, at least 30 minutes. |
| Egg yolks, beaten | 1 | oz | 30 g | 12.5 | 5. Whip the egg whites until stiff but not dry. |
| Oil | 1 | oz | 30 g | 12.5 | 6. Fold the egg whites into the batter. Use im- |
| Egg whites | 2 | oz | 60 g | 25 | mediately. |
| **Total weight:** | **1 lb 5** | **oz** | **694 g** | **267%** | |

# FRENCH DOUGHNUTS (BEIGNETS SOUFFLÉS)

*For large-quantity measurements, see page 727.*

| Ingredients | U.S. | | Metric | % | Procedure |
|---|---|---|---|---|---|
| Milk | 10 | oz | 250 g | 167 | **MIXING** |
| Butter | 4 | oz | 100 g | 67 | 1. In a saucepan, heat the milk, butter, salt, and sugar until the sugar dissolves and the butter is melted. |
| Salt | 0.18 oz (1 tsp) | | 5 g | 3 | 2. Bring to a rapid boil, then remove from the heat. Add the flour all at once and beat in vigorously with a wooden spoon. |
| Sugar | 0.18 oz (1 tsp) | | 5 g | 3 | |
| Bread flour | 6 | oz | 150 g | 100 | |
| Eggs | 8 | oz | 200 g | 133 | |
| **Total weight:** | **1 lb 12** | **oz** | **710 g** | **473%** | |

3. Set the pan over medium heat and beat the mixture for 2–3 minutes, until the mixture pulls away from the sides of the pan.

4. Turn the mixture into a stainless-steel bowl and cool slightly.

5. Add the eggs in 3 stages, beating well between additions.

6. Place the dough in a piping bag fitted with a large star tip.

**FRYING**

The doughnuts may be finished in either of two ways:

1. Pipe the mixture directly into a deep fryer heated to 340°F (170°C), cutting off the dough in 3-in. (7–8 cm) pieces using a knife dipped in the hot fat. Fry until puffed and golden. Drain on kitchen paper.

2. Pipe 2-in. (5 cm) circles onto parchment paper. (To make uniform shapes, mark 2-in./5 cm circles on the paper by tracing around a 2-in./5 cm cutter with a pencil. Turn the paper over and use the outlines as a guide.) Freeze. Fry the frozen units as in method 1.

See page 631 for presentation suggestions.

# BEIGNETS DE CARNIVAL

*For large-quantity measurements, see page 728.*

| Ingredients | U.S. | | Metric | % | Procedure |
|---|---|---|---|---|---|
| Bread flour | 7 | oz | 200 g | 100 | **MIXING** |
| Sugar | 0.5 | oz | 15 g | 8 | 1. Sift the flour, sugar, and salt into a bowl. |
| Salt | 0.18 | oz (1 tsp) | 5 g | 2.5 | 2. In a separate bowl, combine egg yolks, cream, kirsch, and rose water. |
| Egg yolks | 2 | oz | 60 g | 30 | |
| Light cream | 2 | oz | 60 g | 30 | 3. Make a well in the dry ingredients and pour in the liquids. Combine to a stiff dough. |
| Kirsch | 0.5 | oz | 15 g | 8 | |
| Rose water | 0.33 | oz (2 tsp) | 10 g | 5 | 4. Turn out onto a lightly floured surface and knead until a smooth ball forms. |
| **Total weight:** | **12** | **oz** | **365 g** | **183%** | |

5. Place the dough onto a lightly floured plate, cover tightly with plastic film, and chill overnight.

**FRYING**

1. Bring the dough back to room temperature.

2. Cut the rested dough into pieces ⅓ oz (10 g) each. Keep covered with a damp cloth or plastic film all the time you are working to prevent a crust forming.

3. Taking one piece of dough at a time, roll out very thinly until the dough starts to shrink back. Place under a damp cloth or plastic film and continue rolling all the pieces of dough.

4. Go back to the first piece and begin rolling again until the dough is nearly transparent. This process gives the dough time to rest and assists very thin rolling.

5. Once they are rolled for the second time, trim the circles to uniform size using a 4½-in. (11 cm) round cutter. Place the cut pieces on a sheet pan lined with parchment paper. Cover with plastic film.

6. Preheat the fryer to 355°F (180°C). Drop the beignets into the hot fat one at a time. Turn once when golden brown. The beignets can be either fried flat or shaped by holding them under the fat with a long-handled spoon, pressing firmly into the middle of each beignet; this causes them to cup slightly as they fry.

7. When golden, remove and drain on kitchen paper.

8. Serve with choice of poached fruit or fruit compote.

# FATTIGMAN

| Ingredients | U.S. | Metric | % | Procedure |
|---|---|---|---|---|
| Whole eggs | 3.33 oz (2 eggs) | 100 g (2 eggs) | 24 | 1. Whip the eggs and yolks until foamy. |
| Egg yolks | 1.33 oz (2 yolks) | 40 g (2 yolks) | 10 | 2. Beat in the salt, sugar, cardamom, and cream. |
| Salt | 0.13 oz (⅔ tsp) | 4 g | 1 | 3. Add the brandy and mix well. |
| Sugar | 2.5 oz | 70 g | 18 | 4. Add the flour and blend to make a dough. |
| Cardamom, ground | 0.07 oz (1 tsp) | 2 g | 0.5 | 5. Wrap or cover the dough and rest, refrigerated, for at least 1 hour. |
| Heavy cream | 3 oz | 85 g | 21 | 6. Roll out the dough ⅛ in. (3 mm) thick. |
| Brandy | 1.5 oz | 45 g | 11 | 7. Cut into small triangles about 2½ in. (6 cm) on a side. |
| Bread flour | 14 oz | 400 g | 100 | 8. Deep-fry at 375°F (190°C) until lightly browned and crisp. |
| Confectioners' sugar | as needed | as needed | | 9. Drain and cool. |
| **Total dough weight:** | **1 lb 9 oz** | **746 g** | **185%** | 10. Dust lightly with 10X sugar. |

See page 618 for presentation suggestion.

# VIENNOISE

*For large-quantity measurements, see page 728.*
*Yield: 10 pastries, 2 oz (60 g) each*

| Ingredients | U.S. | Metric | Procedure |
|---|---|---|---|
| Brioche Dough (p. 193) | 1 lb 4 oz | 600 g | 1. Scale the brioche dough into 2-oz (60 g) pieces. |
| Egg wash | as needed | as needed | 2. On a lightly floured work surface, roll each piece into a 4-in. (10 cm) circle. |
| Red currant jelly | 3.5 oz | 100 g | 3. Brush the tops with egg wash. |

4. Place ⅓ oz (10 g) jelly in the center of each circle. Enclose the jelly by gathering the edges of the circle together over the jelly to form a purse. Place upside down (seam on bottom) on a sheet pan lined with parchment. Proof in a warm place until double in size, about 40 minutes.

5. Deep-fry at 340°F (170°C) until golden brown, turning once. Frying time is about 8 minutes.

6. Drain.

# CANNOLI SHELLS

*For large-quantity measurements, see page 728.*

| Ingredients | U.S. | | Metric | % | Procedure |
|---|---|---|---|---|---|
| Bread flour | 6 | oz | 175 g | 50 | 1. Sift the flour, sugar, and salt together into a bowl. |
| Pastry flour | 6 | oz | 175 g | 50 | |
| Sugar | 1 | oz | 30 g | 8 | 2. Add the butter and work in with your hands until evenly blended. |
| Salt | 0.04 oz (⅛ tsp) | | 1 g | 0.3 | |
| Butter | 2 | oz | 60 g | 17 | 3. Add the egg and wine and work in to make a dough. Knead it a few times on a floured workbench until it is smooth. Cover and let rest for 30 minutes. |
| Egg, beaten | 1.67 oz (1 egg) | | 50 g (1 egg) | 14 | |
| Dry white wine or Marsala | 4 | oz | 125 g | 33 | |
| **Total weight:** | **1 lb 4** | **oz** | **616 g** | **172%** | 4. Roll out the pastry into a sheet about ⅛ in. (3 mm) thick. Dock it well. For small cannoli, cut into 3½-in. (9 cm) circles; for large cannoli, cut into 5-in. (12 cm) circles. Rework the scraps to cut additional circles. Twenty oz (600 g) dough is enough for 16–18 large cannoli or 32–36 small ones. |

### VARIATION

## SICILIAN CANNOLI

Using a pastry bag, fill cooled cannoli shells from both ends with Ricotta Cannoli Filling (below). Sprinkle lightly with confectioners' sugar. If desired, decorate the filling at the ends of the cannoli with halved candied cherries, colored sugar, or chopped pistachios.

5. Roll the circles around cannoli tubes. Where the edges of the circle overlap, press firmly to seal.

6. Deep-fry at 375°F (190°C) until golden brown. Cool for a few seconds, then carefully slip out the tube. Cool completely before filling. Shells may be filled with a variety of fillings, including vanilla and chocolate pastry creams and other thick creams and puddings.

# RICOTTA CANNOLI FILLING

*For large-quantity measurements, see page 728.*

| Ingredients | U.S. | | Metric | % | Procedure |
|---|---|---|---|---|---|
| Ricotta impasta- to (see p. 77) | 1 lb | | 500 g | 100 | 1. Process the ricotta in a blender until it is very smooth. |
| Confectioners' sugar | 8 | oz | 250 g | 50 | 2. Sift the sugar and fold in until well mixed. |
| Cinnamon extract | 0.25 oz (1½ tsp) | | 7 g | 1.5 | 3. Mix in the remaining ingredients. |
| Candied citron, candied citrus peel, or candied pumpkin, finely diced | 1.5 | oz | 45 g | 9 | |
| Sweet chocolate, finely chopped, or tiny chocolate bits | 1 | oz | 30 g | 6 | |
| **Total weight:** | **1 lb 10** | **oz** | **832 g** | **166%** | |

# JALEBIS

*Yield: approximately 100 pieces*

| Ingredient | U.S. | Metric | % | Procedure |
|---|---|---|---|---|
| Bread flour | 8 oz | 250 g | 50 | **MIXING** |
| Pastry flour | 8 oz | 250 g | 50 | 1. Sift together the bread flour and pastry flour into a bowl. |
| Plain yogurt | 4 oz | 125 g | 25 | |
| Water | 12 oz | 375 g | 75 | 2. Beat the yogurt until smooth. |
| Powdered saffron | ¼ tsp | 1 mL | | 3. Mix the first quantity of water into the yogurt. |
| Water | 6 oz | 185 g | 37.5 | 4. Stir the yogurt mixture and the saffron into the flour. Mix until smooth. |
| **Total weight of batter** | **2 lb  6 oz** | **800 g** | **237%** | 5. Stir in the second quantity of water to make a batter. |
| **Syrup** | | | | 6. Strain |
| Water | 1 lb 12 oz | 800 g | | 7. Let the batter stand several hours or overnight. |
| Sugar | 1 lb 12 oz | 800 g | | |
| Saffron | 1 tsp | 5 mL | | |
| Ground cardamom | ½ tsp | 2 mL | | |
| Rose water | 1 fl oz | 15 mL | | |

**PREPARING THE SYRUP**

1. Combine the water and sugar in a heavy saucepan. Bring to a boil.

2. Boil until the sugar is completely dissolved and the syrup reaches 230°F (110°C) when tested with a sugar thermometer.

3. Remove from the heat and stir in the saffron and cardamom.

4. When the syrup has cooled but is still warm, stir in the rose water.

**FRYING AND FINISHING**

1. Before frying, reheat the syrup until it is hot. Set aside.

2. Fill a squeeze bottle with batter. The opening of the squeeze bottle should be about ⅛ in. (3 mm) across, about the same as a ketchup squeeze bottle.

3. Heat frying fat to 350°F (175°C).

4. With the squeeze bottle, drop the batter into the fat in tight spirals 2½–3 in. (6-7 cm) across.

5. Fry on both sides until very lightly browned.

6. Remove from the fat and drain on absorbent paper for 1 minute.

7. Drop the jalebis into the warm syrup. Leave in the syrup for 2–4 minutes, then remove and drain.

**VARIATION**

For a less expensive version, omit both quantities of saffron. Instead, color the batter and syrup pale orange using red and yellow food colors, if desired.

## ❈⟩ INDIAN DESSERTS ⟨❈

Desserts from India are known for being aromatic and sweet. Many types of pastries are sweetened by soaking them in a flavored syrup. Jalebis are a deep-fried example of a pastry soaked in syrup. Freshly made, hot jalebis are often sold by street vendors in India.

# CHINESE SESAME BALLS

*Yield: 40 pieces, about 1 oz (25 g) each*

| Ingredient | U.S. | Metric | % | Procedure |
|---|---|---|---|---|
| Water | 10 oz | 250 g | 62.5 | **MIXING** |
| Brown sugar | 6 oz | 200 g | 37.5 | 1. Bring the water to a boil in a saucepan. Add the sugar and stir until dissolved. |
| Glutinous rice powder | 1 lb | 400 g | 100 | 2. Place the glutinous rice powder in a mixing bowl. |
| Red bean paste or lotus paste, canned | 8 oz | 150 g | 50 | 3. Mix the syrup into the rice powder to make a dough. Knead the dough until it is smooth. |
| Sesame seeds | as needed | as needed | | **MAKEUP** |
| **Total weight:** | **2 lb  8 oz** | **1000 g** | **262%** | 1. Divide the dough into 4 equal pieces. |

**MAKEUP**

1. Divide the dough into 4 equal pieces.

2. Using rice powder to dust the workbench and your hands, roll each piece of dough into a cylinder about 10 in. (25 cm) long.

3. Cut each cylinder into 10 equal pieces.

4. Roll each piece between the palms of your hands into a ball.

5. Roll the bean paste or lotus paste into small balls of about 1 tsp (5 g) each. If the paste is too soft to work with, refrigerate or partially freeze it.

6. For each rice dough ball, make a deep indentation in the ball with the thumb. Place a ball of bean paste inside and mold the dough to cover the hole completely. Make sure it is well sealed.

7. Place the sesame seeds in a pan or bowl.

8. Dip your hands in water, then roll a filled ball between the palms of the hands to moisten it slightly to help the seeds stick.

9. Roll the ball in the sesame seeds until well coated.

**FRYING**

1. Heat frying fat to 350°F (175°C).

2. Drop a few sesame balls into the hot fat. Fry about 2 minutes.

3. When the balls are lightly browned, they should be squeezed gently to help them expand in size slightly. This may be done in various ways. Use a pair of tongs to squeeze and turn the balls, or use a spatula to press them lightly against the side of the fryer. Release and repeat. (This technique takes a little practice.)

4. Continue frying until the balls are golden brown.

5. Drain. Serve warm.

## ❊{ CHINESE PASTRIES }❊

Chinese pastries are not usually very sweet, at least by European and North American standards, and desserts are not part of a typical Chinese dinner. Pastries are more often eaten as tea snacks or as part of a morning or midday meal of dumplings and other little dishes known as *dim sum*.

Pastes made from seeds, legumes, and nuts are often used as pastry fillings and are available already prepared. The red beans used for the paste in the recipe for sesame balls are small red dried beans known as *azuki beans*. They are also used to make a lightly sweetened soup sometimes served as dessert on banquet menus.

# PANCAKES AND WAFFLES

Although pancakes and waffles are rarely produced in the retail bake-shop, they are essential items on the breakfast, brunch, and dessert menus in food service operations. In addition, a French waffle formula that is especially well suited for dessert is included here. This batter is actually an éclair paste thinned with cream or milk. French pancakes, or *crêpes*, and desserts made from them are also presented.

## American-Style Pancakes and Waffles

American-style pancakes and waffles are made from pourable batters mixed by the muffin method, which is presented in chapter 10. As with muffins, it is important to avoid overmixing the batters for these products in order to prevent excessive gluten development.

Pancakes and waffles can be made in almost unlimited varieties by substituting other types of flour, such as buckwheat flour, whole wheat flour, and cornmeal, for part of the pastry flour. As some of these absorb more water than others, additional liquid may be needed to thin the batter.

Compare the formulas for pancakes and waffles. In particular, you should notice these differences:

- Waffle batter contains more fat. This makes the waffles richer and crisper and aids in their release from the waffle iron.

- Waffle batter contains less liquid, so it is slightly thicker. This, too, makes waffles crisp, as crispness depends on low moisture content.

- Whipping the egg whites separately and folding them into the batter gives waffles added lightness.

## Advance Preparation for Volume Service

1. Pancake and waffle batters leavened *only by baking powder* may be mixed the night before and stored in the cooler. Some rising power may be lost, so baking powder may have to be increased.

2. Batters leavened by *baking soda* should not be made too far ahead because the soda will lose its power. Mix dry ingredients and liquid ingredients ahead; combine just before service.

3. Batters using beaten *egg whites and baking powder* may be partially made ahead, but *incorporate the egg whites just before service.*

# PANCAKES AND WAFFLES

*Yield: about 1 qt (1 L)*

| Ingredients | Pancakes U.S. | | Metric | % | Waffles U.S. | | Metric | % |
|---|---|---|---|---|---|---|---|---|
| Pastry flour | 8 | oz | 225 g | 100 | 8 | oz | 225 g | 100 |
| Sugar | 1 | oz | 30 g | 12.5 | — | | — | — |
| Salt | 0.08 | oz (½ tsp) | 2.5 g | 1 | 0.08 | oz (½ tsp) | 2 g | 1 |
| Baking powder | 0.5 | oz (1 tbsp) | 15 g | 6 | 0.5 | oz (1 tbsp) | 15 g | 6 |
| Whole eggs, beaten | 3.5 | oz (2 large) | 100 g | 44 | — | | — | — |
| Egg yolks, beaten | — | | — | — | 2 | oz (3 large) | 55 g | 25 |
| Milk | 1 lb | | 450 g | 200 | 12 | oz | 340 g | 150 |
| Butter, melted, or oil | 2 | oz | 55 g | 25 | 4 | oz | 112 g | 50 |
| Egg whites | — | | — | — | 3 | oz (3 large) | 85 g | 38 |
| Sugar | — | | — | — | 1 | oz | 30 g | 12.5 |

## Procedure

### MIXING

Muffin method (p. 220)

1. Sift together the dry ingredients.

2. Combine the eggs or egg yolks, milk, and fat.

3. Add the liquid ingredients to the dry ingredients. Mix until just combined. Do not overmix.

4. For waffles: Just before they are to be cooked, whip the egg whites until they form soft peaks, then beat in the sugar until the meringue is stiff. Fold into the batter.

### COOKING PANCAKES

1. Using a 2-oz (60 mL) ladle, measure portions of batter onto a greased, preheated griddle (375°F/190°C), allowing space for spreading.

2. Fry the pancakes until the tops are full of bubbles and begin to look dry, and the bottoms are golden brown.

3. Turn and brown the other side.

4. Serve hot, accompanied by butter, maple syrup, fruit syrup, jams or preserves, applesauce, or fresh berries.

### COOKING WAFFLES

1. Pour enough batter onto a lightly greased, preheated waffle iron to almost cover the surface. Close the iron.

2. Cook the waffles until the signal light indicates they are done, or until steam is no longer emitted. The waffles should be brown and crisp.

3. Serve warm with confectioners' sugar, syrup, jam, or fresh fruit.

---

**VARIATION**

## BUTTERMILK PANCAKES AND WAFFLES

Use buttermilk instead of milk. Reduce baking powder to 3% (0.25 oz or 1½ tsp/7 g) and add ¾ tsp (3 g) baking soda. If the batter is too thick, thin it with milk or water as necessary (up to 50%).

# GAUFRES (FRENCH WAFFLES)

| Ingredients | U.S. | | Metric | % | Procedure |
|---|---|---|---|---|---|
| Milk | 1 lb | | 500 g | 200 | 1. Combine the milk, salt, and butter in a saucepan or kettle. Carefully bring to a boil. |
| Salt | | 0.25 oz | 8 g | 3 | |
| Butter | 3 | oz | 95 g | 37.5 | 2. Add the flour all at once and stir vigorously. Continue to stir until the mixture forms a ball and pulls away from the sides of the kettle. |
| Bread flour | 8 | oz | 250 g | 100 | |
| Eggs | 13 | oz | 400 g | 162.5 | |
| | (about 8 large eggs) | | | | 3. Remove from the heat and transfer to the bowl of a mixer. Let cool 5 minutes. |
| Cream | 8 | oz | 250 g | 100 | 4. With the mixer on low speed, add the eggs a little at a time. Wait until each addition is absorbed before adding more. |
| Milk | 4 | oz | 125 g | 50 | |
| *Total weight:* | *3 lb 4* | *oz* | *1628 g* | *653%* | 5. With the mixer continuing to run, slowly pour in the cream, then the milk. Don't worry if the batter is slightly lumpy even after all the milk is added; this is normal. The batter should be slightly thicker than regular waffle batter. If it is much thicker, add a little more milk. |

6. Bake as you would regular waffles.

# Crêpes

***Crêpes*** are thin, unleavened pancakes. They are rarely served plain but are instead used to construct a great variety of desserts by being rolled around fillings, layered with fillings, or served with sweet sauces. Unsweetened crêpes are used in similar ways but filled with meat, fish, or vegetable preparations.

Unlike leavened pancakes, crêpes may be made in advance, covered and refrigerated, and used as needed. When the crêpes are filled and rolled or folded, the side that was browned first, which is the more attractive side, should be on the outside.

# CRÊPES

*Yield: about 50 crêpes*

| Ingredients | U.S. | | Metric | % |
|---|---|---|---|---|
| Bread flour | 8 | oz | 250 g | 50 |
| Cake flour | 8 | oz | 250 g | 50 |
| Sugar | 2 | oz | 60 g | 12.5 |
| Salt | 0.5 | oz | 15 g | 3 |
| Eggs | 12 | oz | 375 g | 75 |
| | (7 large eggs) | | | |
| Milk | 2 lb | | 1000 g | 200 |
| Oil or clarified butter | 5 | oz | 150 g | 20 |
| *Total weight:* | **4 lb 3** | **oz** | **2100 g** | **421%** |

## Procedure

### MIXING

1. Sift the flour, sugar, and salt into a bowl.

2. Add the eggs and just enough of the milk to make a soft paste with the flour. Mix until smooth and lump-free.

3. Gradually mix in the rest of the milk and the oil. The batter should be about the consistency of heavy cream. If it is too thick, mix in a little water. If it has lumps, pour it through a strainer.

4. Let the batter rest 2 hours before frying.

### FRYING

1. Rub a 6- or 7-in. (15–18 cm) crêpe pan or skillet lightly with oil. Heat the pan over moderately high heat until it is very hot. Brush lightly with melted butter and pour off any excess (a).

2. Remove from heat and pour in about 3–4 tablespoons (45–60 mL) of the batter. Very quickly tilt the pan to cover the bottom with a thin layer. Immediately dump out any excess batter, as the crêpe must be very thin (b).

3. Return to the heat for about 1–1½ minutes, until the bottom is lightly browned. Flip the crêpe and brown the second side (c). The second side will brown only in a few spots and will not be as attractive as the first side. The first side should always be the visible side when the crêpe is served (d).

4. Slide the crêpe onto a plate. Continue making crêpes and stacking them as they are finished. Grease the pan lightly when necessary.

5. Cover the finished crêpes and refrigerate until needed.

## VARIATION

### CHOCOLATE CRÊPES

| Ingredients | U.S. | Metric | % |
|---|---|---|---|
| Bread flour | 6 oz | 190 g | 37.5 |
| Cake flour | 8 oz | 250 g | 50 |
| Cocoa powder | 2 oz | 60 g | 12.5 |

Reduce the quantity of flour in the crêpe formula and add cocoa powder in the proportion listed. Sift the cocoa with the flour in step 1 of the mixing procedure.

# Crêpe Desserts

The following are only a few of many possible suggestions. The variety of crêpe desserts you can prepare is limited only by your imagination.

**Crêpes Normande.** Sauté fresh sliced apples in butter and sprinkle with sugar and a dash of cinnamon. Roll the apples in crêpes and dust with confectioners' sugar.

**Banana Crêpes.** Sauté sliced bananas quickly in butter and sprinkle with brown sugar and a dash of rum. Roll the filling in the crêpes. Serve with apricot sauce (p. 277).

**Crêpes with Jam.** Spread apricot jam on crêpes and roll them up. Sprinkle with sugar and run under the broiler quickly to glaze the sugar.

**Glazed Crêpes.** Fill crêpes with vanilla pastry cream (p. 271) and roll them up. Sprinkle with sugar and run under the broiler to glaze the sugar.

**Crêpes Frangipane.** Spread the crêpes with Frangipane filling (p. 201) and roll them up or fold them in quarters. Brush with butter and sprinkle with sugar. Place in a buttered baking dish and bake in a hot oven about 10 minutes to heat through. Serve with chocolate sauce or vanilla sauce.

***Crêpes Suzette.*** This most famous of all crêpe desserts is generally prepared at tableside by the waiter according to the procedure in the following recipe. The crêpes, fruit, sugar, and butter are supplied by the kitchen. The dish can also be prepared in the kitchen or pastry department by coating crêpes with hot Sauce Suzette (p. 281).

# CRÊPES SUZETTE (DINING ROOM PREPARATION)

*Yield: 4 portions*

| Ingredients | U.S. | Metric | Procedure |
|---|---|---|---|
| Sugar | 3 oz | 85 g | 1. In a flambé pan, heat the sugar until it melts and begins to caramelize. |
| Orange | 1 | 1 | |
| Lemon | ½ | ½ | 2. Cut several strips of rind from the orange and one from the lemon; add them to the pan. |
| Butter | 2 oz | 60 g | |
| Orange-flavored liqueur | 1 oz | 30 mL | 3. Add the butter and squeeze the juice from the orange and lemon into the pan. Cook and stir until the sugar is dissolved and the mixture is a little syrupy. |
| Cognac | 2 oz | 60 mL | |
| Crêpes | 12 | 12 | 4. Add the orange liqueur. One by one, dip the crêpes in the sauce to coat them, then fold them into quarters in the pan. |

5. Add the cognac and allow it to heat for a few seconds. Flame by carefully tipping the pan toward the burner flame until the cognac ignites.

6. Shake the pan gently and spoon the sauce over the crêpes until the flame dies down.

7. Serve 3 crêpes per portion. Spoon a little of the remaining sauce over each serving.

# CRÊPES SOUFFLÉS SUZETTE

*Yield: 6 portions*

| Ingredients | U.S. | | Metric | Procedure |
|---|---|---|---|---|
| Orange juice | 8 | oz | 250 g | 1. Heat the orange juice. |
| Cornstarch | 1 | oz | 25 g | 2. Mix the cornstarch with enough cold water to make a smooth slurry. Stir into the orange juice and cook, stirring, until thickened. |
| Water | as needed | | as needed | |
| Sugar | 1 | oz | 30 g | |
| Orange liqueur, such as Grand Marnier | 1.67 oz | | 50 g | 3. Add the sugar, liqueur, and vanilla. Boil to dissolve the sugar. |
| Vanilla extract | ½ | tsp | 2 g | 4. Cool the mixture. |
| Egg whites | 4 | oz | 125 g | 5. Whip the egg whites to soft peaks. Add the sugar and whip to a firm meringue. |
| Sugar | 2.5 | oz | 75 g | |
| Crêpes | 18 | | 18 | 6. Whip one-third of the meringue into the orange base, then fold in the remaining meringue. |
| Confectioners' sugar | as needed | | as needed | 7. Fit a pastry bag with a medium plain tip. Fill with the orange meringue mixture. |
| Sauce Suzette (p. 281) | 8 | oz | 240 mL | 8. Fold the crêpes into quarters. Fill the folded pancakes with the orange meringue mixture using the pastry bag. The pancakes may now be frozen for later use if desired. |
| Candied orange zest | as desired | | as desired | 9. Arrange the filled pancakes on a greased baking sheet. Bake at 375°F (190°C) until well risen and firm to the touch. |
| Berries or other fruit garnish | as desired | | as desired | 10. Dust lightly with confectioners' sugar. |
| | | | | 11. Ladle a ring of sauce Suzette onto each plate. Arrange 3 crêpes on each plate. Garnish as desired with candied zest and berries. |

# CRÊPE GÂTEAU WITH PLUM COMPOTE

*Yield: 6 portions*

| Ingredients | U.S. | Metric | Procedure |
|---|---|---|---|
| Plum Compote (p. 600) | 1 lb | 450 g | 1. Place the plum compote in a fine strainer. Reserve the drained liquid for use as a sauce. |
| Crêpes (p. 252) | 9 | 9 | 2. Place a crêpe on the center of a lightly buttered oven-proof plate. Top with about one-eighth of the drained compote. |
| **Garnish** | | | 3. Repeat with the remaining crêpes and compote, ending with a crêpe. The stack should be about 4 in. (10 cm) high. |
| Confectioners' sugar | as needed | as needed | 4. Dust the top with confectioners' sugar. With a hot skewer, mark a lattice pattern in the top to resemble grill marks. |
| Quartered plum, fanned | as needed | as needed | 5. Dust again with confectioners' sugar. Brown lightly under a salamander or broiler. |
| Berries or other soft fruit | as needed | as needed | 6. Place in an oven at 325°F (160°C) until warm, about 10–to 15 minutes. |
| | | | 7. Remove from the oven. Decorate with the fruit. Ladle a little of the plum sauce (from step 1) around the gâteau. |
| | | | 8. To serve, cut into 6 wedges like a small cake. |

# CHOCOLATE SOUFFLÉ CRÊPES

*Yield: 6 portions*

| Ingredients | U.S. | | Metric | Procedure |
|---|---|---|---|---|
| Milk | 8 | oz | 250 g | 1. Heat the milk and chocolate together, stirring, until the chocolate is melted and well mixed with the milk. Bring to a simmer. |
| Bittersweet chocolate | 1.67 | oz | 50 g | |
| Cornstarch | 1 | oz | 25 g | 2. Combine the cornstarch and rum and mix to a smooth paste. Stir into the hot milk and simmer until thickened. |
| Rum | 1 | oz | 30 g | |
| Sugar | 1.67 | oz | 50 g | 3. Stir in the sugar and vanilla until the sugar is dissolved. |
| Vanilla extract | ½ | tsp | 2 g | |
| Egg whites | 4 | oz | 125 g | 4. Whip the egg whites to soft peaks. Add the sugar and whip to a firm meringue. |
| Sugar | 2.5 | oz | 75 g | |
| Chocolate Crêpes (p. 252) | 18 | | 18 | 5. Whip one-third of the meringue into the chocolate base, then fold in the remaining meringue. |
| Chocolate Sauce (pp. 278–279) | 8 | oz | 250 g | 6. Fit a pastry bag with a medium plain tip. Fill with the chocolate meringue mixture. |
| Plain yogurt | 4 | tsp | 20 g | 7. Fold the chocolate crêpes into quarters. Fill the folded pancakes with the chocolate meringue mixture using the pastry bag. The pancakes may now be frozen for later use if desired. |
| Candied orange zest | 0.5–1 | oz | 20 g | |

8. Arrange the filled pancakes on a greased baking sheet. Bake at 375°F (190°C) until well risen and firm to the touch.

9. Dust lightly with confectioners' sugar.

10. Ladle a pool of chocolate sauce onto each plate. Arrange 3 crêpes on each plate. Pipe a few dots of yogurt onto the sauce and feather. Garnish with candied orange zest.

# CRÊPES GEORGETTE

*Yield: 6 portions*

| Ingredients | U.S. | | Metric | Procedure |
|---|---|---|---|---|
| **Filling** | | | | 1. Heat the sugar to a golden caramel. Remove from the heat and add the butter, vanilla bean, and cloves. |
| Sugar | 3.5 | oz | 100 g | |
| Butter | 1 | oz | 30 g | 2. Add the diced pineapple and the kirsch. Flambé to burn off the alcohol. |
| Vanilla bean, split (see Note) | 1 | | 1 | |
| Cloves | 2 | | 2 | 3. Simmer until the pineapple is tender. Cool. |
| Pineapple, medium dice | 1 lb | | 500 g | 4. Place the crêpes on a tray or work surface upside down (that is, with the better side down). Place a spoonful of pineapple on each crêpe and roll up. |
| Kirsch | 1 | oz | 30 g | |
| Crêpes (p. 252) | 18 | | 18 | 5. Lightly butter 6 plates. Place 3 crêpes on each plate, seam side down. |
| **Passion fruit sabayon** | | | | 6. Cover with foil and keep warm in an oven at 325°F (160°C). |
| Whole eggs | 2 | | 2 | 7. Prepare the sabayon: Put the eggs, egg yolks, and sugar in a round-bottomed stainless-steel bowl. Whip over low heat until thick and pale, about 6 minutes. |
| Egg yolks | 2 | | 2 | |
| Fine granulated sugar | 2.75 oz | | 80 g | 8. Remove from the heat and continue whipping until cold. |
| Kirsch | 0.5 | oz | 15 g | 9. Stir in the kirsch and the passion fruit purée. |
| Passion fruit purée | 2 | oz | 60 g | 10. Spoon the sabayon over the crêpes, covering them completely. |

*Note: If vanilla beans are not available, add ½ tsp (2 mL) vanilla extract after step 2.*

11. Place the plates under a salamander or broiler until the sabayon is lightly browned.

12. If desired, dust lightly with confectioners' sugar and garnish with a sprig of mint, a few passion fruit seeds, and a few red berries.

# TERMS FOR REVIEW

| | | | |
|---|---|---|---|
| modified straight dough method | French doughnut | beignet soufflé | crêpe |
| | | cannoli | crêpes Suzette |
| glaze | fritter | gaufre | |

# QUESTIONS FOR DISCUSSION

1. Two yeast doughnut formulas have the same quantities of fat and milk, but one has more sugar than the other. Which one do you expect would require a higher frying temperature? Why?

2. Why is it important to carefully control the mixing time when making cake doughnuts?

3. List five rules for maintaining frying fat to produce good-quality fried foods.

4. What type of leavening is used in crêpes (French pancakes)? in French doughnuts?

5. Why does waffle batter often contain less liquid (water or milk) than pancake batter?

6. Which mixing method is used to make American-style pancakes? What are the steps in this method?

## Chapter 12

# Basic Syrups, Creams, and Sauces

**M**uch of the baker's craft consists of mixing and baking flour goods such as breads, cakes, and pastries. However, the baker also must be able to make a variety of other products, sometimes known as *adjuncts*, such as toppings, fillings, and sauces. These are not baked goods in themselves, but they are essential in the preparation of many baked goods and desserts.

Several of the procedures you learn in this chapter are used in many ways. For example, crème anglaise, or custard sauce, is used not only as a dessert sauce but is also the basis for such items as Bavarian creams and ice creams. Pastry cream, with a variety of flavorings, is also used for pie fillings, puddings, and soufflés.

**After reading this chapter, you should be able to:**

1. Cook sugar syrups to various stages of hardness.

2. Prepare whipped cream, meringues, custard sauces, and pastry cream variations.

3. Prepare dessert sauces.

# SUGAR COOKING

**U**nderstanding sugar cooking is important in the preparation of desserts and confections because sugar syrups of various strengths are often required (see, for example, Italian Meringue, p. 267).

## Syrup Strength

Syrup strength is an indication of the concentration of sugar in a solution. (When we talk of syrups in the bakeshop, we usually are referring to a solution of sugar in water, although of course sugar can be dissolved in other water-based liquids as well.) In small concentrations, sugar can be dissolved in water simply by stirring it in. With larger concentrations, however, we boil the syrup, because at higher temperatures, the sugar dissolves more quickly. Also, boiling water can hold more sugar in solution than cold water can.

Once the sugar has dissolved, we can increase the concentration of sugar by continuing to boil the syrup so water gradually evaporates. As the water is boiled off, the temperature of the syrup gradually rises. When all the water has evaporated, you are left with melted sugar. The sugar then begins to *caramelize*, or turn brown and change flavor. If heating continues, the sugar continues to darken and then burn.

A syrup cooked to a high temperature is harder when it is cooled than is a syrup cooked to a lower temperature. For example, a syrup cooked to 240°F (115°C) forms a soft ball when cooled. A syrup cooked to 300°F (150°C) is hard and brittle when cooled.

One pint (1 pound) water is enough to dissolve 3 or 4 pounds of sugar. There is no point in adding more water than you need for a particular purpose because you will just have to boil it off again.

Pure, clean granulated sugar is used to make syrups. Impurities cloud the syrup and form a scum or foam on the syrup as it is being boiled. Any scum should be carefully skimmed off.

## Crystallization and Inversion

Graininess is a common fault in many candies and desserts. Graininess results when cooked sugar *crystallizes*—that is, turns to tiny sugar crystals rather than staying dissolved in the syrup. If even one sugar crystal comes in contact with a cooked syrup, it can start a chain reaction that turns the whole thing into a mass of sugar crystals. This effect of sugar crystals on a syrup is called *seeding*.

To avoid crystallization during the first stages of boiling sugar syrups, use one of the following techniques. Do not stir the syrup in either method:

- As you boil the sugar, wash down the sides of the saucepan with a brush dipped in water. Do not let the brush touch the syrup, but let water from the brush run down the sides of the pan. This removes crystals that may seed the whole batch.

- When first bringing the syrup to a boil, cover the pan and boil for several minutes. This causes condensed steam to wash down the sides of the pan. Uncover and finish cooking without stirring.

---

## THE BRIX AND BAUMÉ SCALES

The Brix scale is a measure of the sugar concentration in a solution. It is named after Dr. Brix, who refined the earlier Balling scale to make it more accurate. Each degree (1°) of Brix is equal to a 1% concentration of sugar in solution when measured at 20°C (68°F). For example, a 15% sugar solution (15 grams of sugar in 100 grams of syrup; thus, a syrup consisting of 15 grams of sugar and 85 grams of water) would measure 15° Brix.

A simple way to measure sugar concentration is to use a *hydrometer*, a hollow glass tube with a weight at one end and a scale marked inside the length of the tube. (A hydrometer specifically intended to measure sugar concentration is also called a *saccharometer*.) The hydrometer is placed in the liquid at the correct temperature and the sugar concentration is read off the scale at the surface of the water. The higher the concentration of sugar, the higher the tube floats. This instrument is accurate enough for most purposes in the bakeshop.

A more scientific way to measure Brix is to use a *refractometer*, which measures the angle at which the solution bends a ray of light.

A second index used to indicate syrup density is the Baumé (boh may) scale, named after Antoine Baumé. Strictly speaking, the Baumé scale measures not the sugar concentration but the *specific gravity*, which is the ratio of the weight of the liquid compared to the weight of the same volume of water. Nevertheless, the measure is close enough to enable it to be used for sugar solutions. Each degree Baumé is equal to about 1.8% sugar concentration, although this varies slightly along the length of the scale. For example, 30° Brix equals 16.6° Baumé; 70° Brix equals 37.6° Baumé.

In this book, we make use of these sugar density scales in our discussion of frozen desserts. This is an important measurement because sugar concentration affects the freezing point of liquids.

Syrups cooked until they have a high concentration of sugar are liable to crystallize after they have been cooled. This can be controlled by a process called *inversion*. As explained in chapter 4 (p. 67), inversion is a chemical change of regular sugar (sucrose) into another form of sugar that resists crystallizing.

If an acid, such as cream of tartar or lemon juice, is added to a syrup before or during cooking, some of the sugar is inverted. The type and amount of acid used affect the amount of sugar that is inverted. Therefore, specific formulas should be followed carefully whenever acids are required in sugar boiling.

Glucose or corn syrup may also be added to control crystallization in boiling syrups. These are convenient to use and produce good results.

## Stages of Sugar Cooking

Testing the temperature with a candy thermometer is the most accurate way to determine the doneness of a syrup.

In the old days, a syrup was tested by dropping a little of it into a bowl of cold water and checking the hardness of the cooled sugar. The stages of doneness were given names that described their hardness.

The table below lists these stages of sugar cooking. Please note the names for the stages are not absolute; different sources may use slightly different names. In fact, all such tables are misleading because they suggest the syrup jumps from one stage to the next. Actually, of course, it changes gradually as the water is boiled off. For this reason, it is best to rely on the thermometer and not worry too much about the names.

### Stages of Doneness in Sugar Cooking

| Stage | Temperature | |
| --- | --- | --- |
| | °F | °C |
| Thread | 230 | 110 |
| Soft ball | 240 | 115 |
| Firm ball | 245 | 118 |
| Hard ball | 250–260 | 122–127 |
| Small crack | 265–270 | 130–132 |
| Crack | 275–280 | 135–138 |
| Hard crack | 290–310 | 143–155 |
| Caramel | 320–340 | 160–170 |

## Basic Syrups for the Bakeshop

Two basic syrups are kept in stock in the bakeshop and used in a variety of ways. **Simple syrup**, also known as *stock syrup*, is a solution of equal weights of sugar and water. It is used for such purposes as diluting Fondant (p. 422) and for preparing a variety of dessert syrups. **Dessert syrup** is simply a flavored simple syrup. It is used to moisten and flavor sponge cakes and various desserts, such as Babas au Rum (p. 191).

The concentration of both these syrups may be varied to taste. Some chefs prefer a sweeter syrup for some purposes, such as 1 part water to 1½ parts sugar. Others use a less sweet syrup, such as 2 parts water to 1 part sugar.

Following are procedures for preparing simple syrup and a basic dessert syrup. The recipes in this section also include a variety of flavored syrups. Other flavored syrups appear throughout the book as parts of formulas for cakes and pastries.

## Procedure for Preparing Simple Syrup

1. Combine the following ingredients in a saucepan:

   | | | |
   |---|---|---|
   | Water | 1 pt | 500 mL |
   | Sugar | 1 lb | 500 g |

2. Stir and bring to a boil over moderate heat. Cook and stir until the sugar is dissolved.

3. Remove any scum. Cool the syrup and store it in a covered container.

## Procedure for Preparing Dessert Syrup

### Method 1

Prepare and cool a simple syrup. Add any desired flavoring according to taste. Extracts such as vanilla or liquors such as rum or kirsch may serve as flavorings. Flavoring should be added after the syrup has cooled, as some of the flavor may evaporate if it is added to hot syrup.

### Method 2

Prepare a simple syrup, but add the rind of one orange and/or one lemon to the sugar and water before bringing it to a boil. Let the syrup simmer for 5 minutes before cooling. Remove the rind from the cooled syrup.

# VANILLA SYRUP

*For large-quantity measurements, see page 728.*

| Ingredients | U.S. | Metric | Procedure |
|---|---|---|---|
| Water | 7 oz | 200 g | 1. Place all the ingredients in a saucepan and heat gently until the sugar is dissolved. |
| Sugar | 6 oz | 180 g | |
| Vanilla bean, split (see variation) | 1 | 1 | 2. Remove from the heat and allow the vanilla to infuse for 30 minutes. |
| **Total weight:** | **13 oz** (about 12 fl oz) | **380 g** (about 325 mL) | |

### VARIATION

If vanilla beans are not available, flavor plain syrup to taste with vanilla extract.

# COFFEE RUM SYRUP

*For large-quantity measurements, see page 729.*

| Ingredients | U.S. | | Metric | Procedure |
|---|---|---|---|---|
| Sugar | 2.5 | oz | 65 g | 1. Boil the sugar and water until the sugar is dissolved. |
| Water | 2.5 | oz | 65 g | |
| Ground coffee | 0.16 | oz | 5 g | 2. Remove from the heat and add the coffee. Let stand 10 minutes. |
| Rum | 3.5 | oz | 90 g | |
| *Total weight:* | *8.5* | *oz* | *225 g* | 3. Add the rum. |
| | *(7–8 fl oz)* | | *(185–210 mL)* | 4. Strain. |

### VARIATION

## COFFEE SYRUP

*For large-quantity measurements, see page 729.*

| Ingredients | U.S. | Metric |
|---|---|---|
| Coffee liqueur | 1.67 oz | 40 g |

Omit the rum in the basic recipe and add the coffee-flavored liqueur.

## RUM SYRUP

*For large-quantity measurements, see page 729.*

| Ingredients | U.S. | Metric |
|---|---|---|
| Water | 3 oz | 75 g |
| Sugar | 2.5 oz | 65 g |
| Dark rum | 0.5 oz | 15 g |

Omit the coffee in the basic recipe and adjust the ingredient quantities as listed above.

# COCOA VANILLA SYRUP

*For large-quantity measurements, see page 728.*

| Ingredients | U.S. | Metric | Procedure |
|---|---|---|---|
| Water | 4 oz | 120 g | 1. Bring the water, sugar, and vanilla bean to a boil. Boil until the sugar is dissolved. |
| Sugar | 4 oz | 120 g | |
| Vanilla bean (see *Note*) | 1 | 1 | 2. Remove from the heat and add the cocoa powder a little at a time, whipping constantly. |
| Cocoa powder | 1 oz | 30 g | |
| *Total weight:* | *9 oz* | *270 g* | 3. Strain through a fine strainer or chinois. |
| | *(about 7½ fl oz)* | *(about 240 mL)* | |

*Note: If vanilla beans are not available, add ½ tsp vanilla extract just before straining.*

## BASIC CREAMS

**M**any of the preparations discussed in this section are among the most important and useful in the bakeshop or pastry shop. They find their way into a great variety of desserts—as fillings or components of cakes and pastries, as ingredients of such desserts as Bavarian creams and mousses, and as sauces or toppings. Learn these techniques well, because you will use them over and over again.

## Whipped Cream

Whipped cream is not only one of the most useful dessert toppings and fillings but also an ingredient in many desserts. Cream with a fat content of 30% or more, but preferably over 35%, can be whipped into a foam. One quart cream produces 2 to 2½ quarts whipped cream.

In the classical pastry shop, sweetened, vanilla-flavored whipped cream is known as **crème chantilly** (pronounced kremm shawn tee yee). A recipe is included on page 265. When making all whipped cream preparations, observe the following guidelines:

### Guidelines for Whipping Cream

1. Cream for whipping should be at least 1 day old. Very fresh cream doesn't whip well.

2. Chill the cream and all equipment thoroughly, especially in hot weather. Cream that is too warm is hard to whip and curdles easily.

3. Use a wire whip for beating by hand. For machine whipping, use the whip attachment and run the machine at medium speed.

4. If the cream is to be sweetened, use extra-fine granulated sugar or, for best stability, sifted confectioners' sugar.

5. Do not overwhip. Stop beating when the cream forms peaks that hold their shape. If the cream is whipped longer, it first becomes grainy in appearance and then separates into butter and whey.

## Procedure for Stabilizing Whipped Cream

During warm weather, it is sometimes helpful to add gelatin or a commercial stabilizer to whipped cream so it will hold up. This is especially true of whipped cream–topped items displayed on a buffet.

1. To use a commercial stabilizer, sift it with the sugar used to sweeten the cream. Use about ¼ ounce stabilizer per quart of cream (7 g/L). Add the sugar as in the basic procedure.

2. To use gelatin, use the following proportions:

| | | |
|---|---|---|
| Heavy cream | 1 qt | 1 L |
| Gelatin | 0.33 oz | 10 g |
| Cold water | 2 oz | 60 mL |

Soften the gelatin in the cold water, then warm it until the gelatin dissolves. Whip the cream until it just starts to thicken, then gradually but quickly and steadily whip the cream into the gelatin. Continue to whip the cream to the desired consistency.

6. Cream to be folded into other ingredients should be slightly under-beaten because the action of folding whips it more and may overbeat it.

7. Fold in flavoring ingredients last, after the cream is whipped.

8. If the cream is not to be used immediately, store it, covered, in the refrigerator.

## Procedure for Making Chocolate Whipped Cream

1. Use the following proportions:

| Heavy cream | 1 qt | 1 L |
| Sweet chocolate | 12 oz | 375 g |

2. Whip the cream as in the basic procedure, but underwhip it slightly.

3. Grate or chop the chocolate into small pieces and place it in a saucepan. Set over warm water and stir until the chocolate is melted. Let it cool to lukewarm. It must not cool too much or it will solidify before it can be mixed evenly with the cream.

4. Stir about one-fourth of the whipped cream into the chocolate until it is well mixed.

5. Fold the chocolate mixture into the rest of the cream carefully but thoroughly. Be careful not to overwhip the cream.

# CRÈME CHANTILLY

*For large-quantity measurements, see page 729.*

| Ingredients | U.S. | Metric | % | Procedure |
|---|---|---|---|---|
| Heavy cream or crème fraîche (see *Note*) | 8 oz | 250 g | 100 | 1. Make sure the cream and all equipment and utensils are chilled. |
| Confectioner's sugar | 1.25 oz | 40 g | 16 | 2. Whip the cream by hand or machine until it forms soft peaks. |
| Vanilla extract (see *Note*) | ½ tsp | 2 mL | 2 | 3. Add the sugar and vanilla. Continue to whip until the cream forms stiff peaks but is still smooth. Do not overwhip or the cream will become grainy and then separate to form particles of butter. |
| **Total weight:** | **9 oz** | **290 g** | **167%** | |

*Note: For best results, use crème fraîche or, if it is not available, heavy cream with a fat content of 40% or more. Crème chantilly can be made with cream having a fat content as low as 30%, but it is more likely to separate slightly or weep on standing.*

*For best-quality crème chantilly, flavor with seeds from a vanilla bean (p. 269) instead of vanilla extract.*

## Meringue

Meringues are whipped egg whites sweetened with sugar. They are frequently used for pie toppings and cake icings. They are also used to give volume and lightness to buttercream icings and to such preparations as mousses and dessert soufflés.

Another excellent use for meringues is to bake them in a slow oven until crisp. In this form, they can be used as cake layers or pastry shells to make light, elegant desserts. To add flavor, chopped nuts may be folded into meringues before forming and baking. Pastries and cakes incorporating crisp meringues are discussed in chapters 14 and 18.

## Basic Meringue Types

Meringues may be whipped to various degrees of stiffness as long as they are not overbeaten until they are too stiff and dry. For most purposes, they are beaten until they form stiff, or nearly stiff, moist peaks.

**Common meringue**, also called *French meringue*, is made from egg whites at room temperature, beaten with sugar. It is the easiest to make, and it is reasonably stable due to the high percentage of sugar.

**Swiss meringue** is made from egg whites and sugar that are warmed over a hot-water bath while they are beaten. This warming gives the meringue better volume and stability.

**Italian meringue** is made by beating a hot sugar syrup into the egg whites. This meringue is the most stable of the three because the egg whites are cooked by the heat of the syrup. When flavored with vanilla, it is also known as *boiled icing*. It is also used in meringue-type butter-cream icings.

The amount of sugar used in meringues may vary. **Soft meringues**, those used for pie toppings, may be made with as little as 1 pound of sugar per pound of egg whites. **Hard meringues**, those baked until crisp, are made with up to twice as much sugar as egg whites.

## Guidelines for Making Meringues

1. **Fats prevent whites from foaming properly.** This is very important. Make sure all equipment is free of every trace of fat or grease, and that the egg whites have no trace of yolks in them.

2. **Egg whites foam better if they are at room temperature than if they are cold.** Remove them from the cooler 1 hour before whipping.

3. **Do not overbeat.** Beaten egg whites should look moist and shiny. Over-beaten meringues look dry and curdled; they are difficult to fold into other ingredients and have lost much of their ability to leaven cakes and soufflés.

4. **Sugar makes egg white foams more stable.** Meringues are thicker and heavier than unsweetened egg white foams, and they are more stable. However, egg whites can hold only a limited amount of sugar without sacrificing volume. For this reason, when making common meringues, many cooks prefer to whip the egg whites with no more than an equal weight of sugar. Additional sugar can be folded in after the meringue is whipped.

5. **Mild acids help foaming.** A small amount of cream of tartar or lemon juice is sometimes added to egg whites for whipping in order to give them more volume and stability. This is especially helpful when the whipped whites are folded into other ingredients to provide lightness or leavening, as in the case of angel food cakes. Use about 2 teaspoons cream of tartar per pound of egg whites (15 g/kg).

# COMMON MERINGUE OR FRENCH MERINGUE

| Ingredients | U.S. | Metric | % | Procedure |
|---|---|---|---|---|
| Egg whites | 8 oz | 250 g | 100 | 1. With the whip attachment, beat the egg whites first at medium speed, then at high speed, until they form soft peaks. |
| Fine granulated sugar | 8 oz | 250 g | 100 | |
| Fine granulated sugar or sifted confectioners' sugar (see *Note*) | 8 oz | 250 g | 100 | 2. Add the first quantity of sugar, a little at a time, with the machine running. Whip until stiff. |
| **Total weight:** | **1 lb 8 oz** | **750 g** | **300%** | 3. Stop the machine. Fold in the remaining sugar with a spatula. |

*Note: For soft meringue pie toppings, the second quantity of sugar may be omitted.*

## VARIATION

### CHOCOLATE MERINGUE

| Ingredients | U.S. | Metric | % |
|---|---|---|---|
| Cocoa powder | 4 oz | 125 g | 25 |

Use the confectioners' sugar in step 3 of the basic formula. Sift the sugar twice with the cocoa powder.

# SWISS MERINGUE

| Ingredients | U.S. | Metric | % | Procedure |
|---|---|---|---|---|
| Egg whites | 8 oz | 250 g | 100 | 1. Place the egg whites and sugar in a stainless-steel bowl or in the top of a double boiler. Beat with a wire whip over hot water until the mixture is warm (about 120°F/50°C). |
| Fine granulated sugar or half granulated and half confectioners' | 1 lb | 500 g | 200 | |
| **Total weight:** | **1 lb 8 oz** | **750 g** | **300%** | 2. Transfer the mixture to the bowl of a mixing machine. Whip it at high speed until stiff peaks form and the meringue is completely cool. |

# ITALIAN MERINGUE

*Yield: about 2 qt (2 L)*

| Ingredients | U.S. | Metric | % | Procedure |
|---|---|---|---|---|
| Sugar | 1 lb | 500 g | 200 | 1. Heat the sugar and water in a saucepan until the sugar dissolves and the mixture boils. Boil until a candy thermometer placed in the syrup registers 243°F (117°C). |
| Water | 4 oz | 125 mL | 50 | |
| Egg whites | 8 oz | 250 g | 100 | 2. While the syrup is cooking, beat the egg whites in a mixing machine until they form soft peaks. |
| | | | | 3. With the machine running, very slowly beat in the hot syrup. |
| | | | | 4. Continue beating until the meringue is cool and forms firm peaks. |

# Crème Anglaise

***Crème anglaise*** (pronounced krem awng glezz), also known as *vanilla custard sauce*, is a stirred custard. It consists of milk, sugar, and egg yolks stirred over very low heat until slightly thickened, then flavored with vanilla.

The recipe that follows gives the method for preparing custard sauce. Special care is necessary in preparing this sauce because the eggs curdle easily if overcooked. The following guidelines will help you succeed:

1. Use clean, sanitized equipment and follow strict sanitation procedures. Egg mixtures are good breeding grounds for bacteria that cause food poisoning. Observe the sanitation guidelines discussed for pastry cream, page 270.

2. Before beginning the cooking process, set a stainless-steel bowl in a larger pan of ice water. Place a strainer over the bowl. This setup will enable you to cool the custard the instant it is cooked, to avoid any danger of overcooking the eggs.

3. When combining the egg yolks and sugar, whip the mixture as soon as the sugar is added. Letting sugar and egg yolks stand together without mixing creates lumps that cannot be beaten out. This is because the sugar absorbs water from the yolk, leaving lumps of dehydrated yolk. Using a stainless-steel bowl for this step makes the cooking and stirring easier in step 5.

4. Heat the milk to scalding (just below simmering) before combining with the egg yolks. This makes the final cooking much shorter. To avoid scorching the milk, you can set the pan of milk in a pan of boiling water. This takes longer than using direct heat, but the pan can be left unattended for a few minutes while you perform other tasks.

5. Slowly beat the hot milk into the beaten eggs and sugar. This raises the temperature of the eggs gradually and helps prevent curdling.

6. Set the bowl containing the egg mixture in a pan of simmering water and stir constantly to prevent curdling.

7. To test for doneness, two methods are available. Keep in mind that this is a very light sauce, so you can't expect a lot of thickening.

   ◆ Check the temperature with a thermometer. When it reaches 185°F (85°C), the sauce is cooked. Never let the temperature go above 190°F (87°C).

   ◆ When the mixture lightly coats the back of a spoon, instead of running off it like milk, the sauce is cooked.

8. Immediately pour the sauce through the strainer into the bowl set in ice water to cool the sauce quickly. Stir occasionally to cool it evenly.

9. If the sauce accidentally curdles, it is sometimes possible to save it. Immediately stir in 1 to 2 ounces (30–60 mL) cold milk, transfer the sauce to a blender, and blend at high speed.

Crème anglaise coating the back of a spoon

## Double Boiler or Direct Heat?

There are three possible ways to cook crème anglaise: in a double boiler above simmering water, in a bowl set directly into simmering water, or in a bowl over direct heat. Cooking in a double boiler above simmering water is the best way to avoid overcooking, but this method takes a long time. The guidelines above advocate cooking the crème anglaise in a bowl set in simmering water. This method is reasonably quick and still offers some protection against overcooking. Nevertheless, the mixture must be watched closely to avoid getting it too hot. Some experienced bakers prefer to cook the custard over direct heat rather than in a double boiler, feeling the stronger heat cooks the sauce faster, and their experience enables them to avoid overcooking. It is best to use one of the hot-water methods until you have some experience cooking this sauce.

# CRÈME ANGLAISE

*Yield: about 2½ pt (1.25 L)*

| Ingredients | U.S. | Metric | % | Procedure |
|---|---|---|---|---|
| Egg yolks | 8　oz (12 yolks) | 250 g (12 yolks) | 25 | 1. Review the guidelines for preparing crème anglaise preceding this recipe. |
| Sugar | 8　oz | 250 g | 25 | |
| Milk (see first variation below) | 2 lb (1 qt) | 1 L | 100 | 2. Combine the egg yolks and sugar in a stainless-steel bowl. Whip until thick and light. |
| Vanilla extract | 0.5 oz (1 tbsp) | 15 mL | 1.5 | 3. Scald the milk in a boiling-water bath or over direct heat. |

**Procedure**

1. Review the guidelines for preparing crème anglaise preceding this recipe.
2. Combine the egg yolks and sugar in a stainless-steel bowl. Whip until thick and light.
3. Scald the milk in a boiling-water bath or over direct heat.
4. Very gradually pour the hot milk into the egg yolk mixture while stirring constantly with the whip.
5. Set the bowl in a pan of simmering water. Heat it, stirring constantly, until it thickens enough to coat the back of a spoon or until it reaches 185°F (85°C).
6. Immediately remove the bowl from the heat and set it in a pan of cold water to stop the cooking. Stir in the vanilla. Stir the sauce occasionally as it cools.

## VARIATIONS

For a richer crème anglaise, substitute heavy cream for up to half the milk.

To flavor with a vanilla bean instead of vanilla extract, first split the bean in half lengthwise (a). Scrape the pulp from inside the bean with a paring knife, as shown in the illustration (b). Add the pulp and the split bean to the milk before heating it in step 3.

Vanilla bean technique

### CHOCOLATE CRÈME ANGLAISE

Melt 6 oz (180 g/18%) sweet chocolate. Stir it into the vanilla custard sauce while it is still warm (not hot).

### COFFEE CRÈME ANGLAISE

Add 2 tbsp (8 g) instant coffee to the warm custard sauce.

# Pastry Cream

Although it requires more ingredients and steps, pastry cream is easier to make than vanilla custard sauce because it is less likely to curdle. **Pastry cream**, also called *crème pâtissière*, contains a starch thickening agent that stabilizes the eggs. It can actually be boiled without curdling. In fact, it *must* be brought to a boil or the starch will not cook completely and the cream will have a raw, starchy taste.

*Strict observance of all sanitation rules is essential when preparing pastry cream* because of the danger of bacterial contamination. Use clean, sanitized equipment. Do not put your fingers in the cream; do not taste except with a clean spoon. Chill the finished cream rapidly in shallow pans. Keep the cream and all cream-filled products refrigerated at all times.

The procedure for preparing pastry cream is given in the formula that follows. Note the basic steps are similar to those for custard sauce. In this case, however, a starch is mixed with the eggs and half the sugar to make a smooth paste. (In some formulas with lower egg content, it is necessary to add a little cold milk to provide enough liquid to make a paste.) Meanwhile, the milk is scalded with the other half of the sugar. The egg mixture is then tempered with some of the hot milk and then returned to the kettle and brought to a boil. Some chefs prefer to add the cold paste gradually to the hot milk, but the tempering procedure described here seems to give better protection against lumping.

## Pastry Cream Variations

Pastry cream has many applications in the bakeshop, so it is important to master the basic technique. Pastry cream and its variations are used as fillings for cakes and pastries, as fillings for cream pies (p. 305), and as puddings (p. 520). With additional liquid, it can also be used as a custard sauce.

Cornstarch should be used as the thickening agent when the cream is to be used as a pie filling so the cut slices hold their shape. For other uses, either cornstarch or flour may be used. Remember that twice as much flour is needed to provide the same thickening power as cornstarch.

Other variations are possible, as you will see in the recipes. Sometimes whipped cream is folded into pastry cream to lighten it and to make a creamier product called *pastry cream mousseline*. Adding a meringue to pastry cream and stabilizing it with gelatin makes a cream called **Chiboust** (p. 272).

# PASTRY CREAM (CRÈME PÂTISSIÈRE)

*Yield: about 1⅛ qt (1.12 L)*

| Ingredients | U.S. | | Metric | Milk at 100% % |
|---|---|---|---|---|
| Milk | 2 lb (1 qt) | | 1 L | 100 |
| Sugar | 4 | oz | 125 g | 12.5 |
| Egg yolks | 3 | oz | 90 g | 9 |
| Whole eggs | 4 | oz | 125 g | 12.5 |
| Cornstarch | 2.5 | oz | 75 g | 8 |
| Sugar | 4 | oz | 125 g | 12.5 |
| Butter | 2 | oz | 60 g | 6 |
| Vanilla extract | 0.5 oz (1 tbsp) | | 15 mL | 1.5 |

## Procedure

1. In a heavy saucepan or kettle, dissolve the sugar in the milk and bring just to a boil.

2. With a whip, beat the egg yolks and whole eggs in a stainless-steel bowl.

3. Sift the cornstarch and sugar into the eggs. Beat with the whip until perfectly smooth.

4. Temper the egg mixture by slowly beating in the hot milk in a thin stream.

5. Return the mixture to the heat and bring to a boil, stirring constantly.

6. When the mixture comes to a boil and thickens, remove from the heat.

7. Stir in the butter and vanilla. Mix until the butter is melted and completely blended in.

8. Pour out into a clean, sanitized hotel pan or other shallow pan. Cover with plastic film placed directly in contact with the surface of the cream to prevent a crust from forming. Cool and chill as quickly as possible.

9. For filling pastries such as éclairs and napoleons, whip the chilled pastry cream until smooth before using.

## VARIATIONS

### DELUXE PASTRY CREAM

Omit the whole eggs in the basic recipe and use 30% egg yolks (10 oz/ 300 g).

### PASTRY CREAM MOUSSELINE

For a lighter pastry cream filling, fold whipped heavy cream into the chilled pastry cream. Quantities may be varied to taste. In general, for every 1 qt (1 L) pastry cream, use ½–1 cup (1.25–2.5 dL) heavy cream.

### CHOCOLATE PASTRY CREAM

For each 12 oz pastry cream, stir in 4 oz melted dark chocolate while the pastry cream is still warm (100 g chocolate for each 300 g pastry cream).

### PRALINE PASTRY CREAM

For each 12 oz pastry cream, stir in 4 oz softened praline paste while the pastry cream is still warm (100 g praline paste for each 300 g pastry cream).

### COFFEE PASTRY CREAM

Add 2 tbsp (8 g) instant coffee powder or coffee compound (flavoring) to the milk in step 1.

# CHIBOUST CREAM

*Yield: about 3 lb (1500 g)*

| Ingredients | U.S. | | Metric | Milk at 100%<br>% |
|---|---|---|---|---|
| Milk | 1 pt | | 500 g | 100 |
| Vanilla extract | ½ | tsp | 2 g | 0.4 |
| Sugar | 1 | oz | 30 g | 6 |
| Egg yolks | 5.33 oz | | 160 g | 33 |
| Sugar | 1 | oz | 30 g | 6 |
| Cornstarch | 1.33 oz | | 40 g | 8 |
| **Italian meringue** | | | | |
| Sugar | 13 | oz | 400 g | 80 |
| Water | 4 | oz | 120 g | 24 |
| Egg whites | 8 | oz | 240 g | 48 |
| Gelatin | 0.4 | oz | 12 g | 2.5 |

## Procedure

1. Combine the milk, vanilla, and sugar and bring to a boil, stirring to dissolve the sugar.

2. Whip the egg yolks with the second quantity of sugar. Stir in the cornstarch.

3. Temper the egg mixture with half of the hot milk. Pour this mixture back into the pan with the remaining milk. Return to a boil and boil for 1 minute, until thickened.

4. Turn out into a bowl and cover the surface with plastic film to prevent a skin from forming. Keep warm while making the Italian meringue.

5. Boil the sugar and water until the temperature of the syrup reaches 258°F (120°C). Whip the egg whites to firm peaks, then slowly pour the syrup into the whites, whipping constantly. Continue whipping until cool.

6. Soak the gelatin in cold water (see p. 88) and add to the hot pastry cream (a).

7. Mix until the gelatin is dissolved (b). (If the pastry cream is not warm enough, rewarm it slightly.)

8. Add one-third of the meringue to the cream and mix quickly to lighten the mixture (c).

9. Gently fold in the remaining meringue until evenly mixed (d, e).

### VARIATIONS

## CHOCOLATE CHIBOUST CREAM

| Ingredients | U.S. | | Metric | % |
|---|---|---|---|---|
| Rum | 1 | oz | 30 g | 6 |
| Bittersweet chocolate | 3.5 oz | | 100 g | 20 |

After step 3 in the basic recipe, stir in the rum and chopped bittersweet chocolate until the chocolate is melted and well blended.

## COFFEE CHIBOUST CREAM

| Ingredients | U.S. | | Metric | % |
|---|---|---|---|---|
| Coffee liqueur | 1 | oz | 30 g | 6 |
| Liquid coffee extract | 1.67 oz | | 50 g | 10 |

After step 3 in the basic recipe, stir in the coffee liqueur and liquid coffee extract.

## PRALINE CHIBOUST CREAM

| Ingredients | U.S. | | Metric | % |
|---|---|---|---|---|
| Rum | 1 | oz | 30 g | 6 |
| Praline paste | 2.5 oz | | 75 g | 15 |

After step 3 in the basic recipe, stir in the rum and praline paste.

# CHIBOUST CREAM WITH RASPBERRIES

*Yield: about 3 lb (1500 g)*

| Ingredients | U.S. | | Metric | Milk at 100% % | Procedure |
|---|---|---|---|---|---|
| Milk | 1 pt | | 500 g | 100 | 1. Combine the milk and sugar and bring to a boil, stirring to dissolve the sugar. |
| Sugar | 1.33 oz | | 40 g | 8 | |
| Egg yolks | 5.33 oz | | 160 g | 33 | 2. Whip the egg yolks with the second quantity of sugar. Stir in the cornstarch. |
| Sugar | 1.33 oz | | 40 g | 8 | |
| Cornstarch | 1.67 oz | | 50 g | 10 | |
| **Italian meringue** | | | | | 3. Temper the egg mixture with half of the hot milk. Pour this mixture back into the pan with the remaining milk. Return to a boil and boil for 1 minute, until thickened. |
| Sugar | 13 | oz | 400 g | 80 | |
| Water | 4 | oz | 120 g | 24 | 4. Turn out into a bowl and cover the surface with plastic film to prevent a skin from forming. Keep warm while making the Italian meringue. |
| Egg whites | 8 | oz | 240 g | 48 | |
| Raspberry purée (unsweetened) | 6 | oz | 180 g | 36 | |
| Gelatin | 0.5 | oz | 16 g | 3 | 5. Boil the sugar and water until the temperature of the syrup reaches 258°F (120°C). Whip the egg whites to firm peaks, then slowly pour the syrup into the whites, whipping constantly. Continue whipping until cool. |

*Note: The quantities of sugar, starch, and gelatin are greater in this recipe than in the basic Chiboust because the addition of raspberry purée requires additional sweetening and thickening.*

6. Fold the raspberry purée into the meringue.

7. Soak the gelatin in cold water (see p. 88). Stir the gelatin into the warm pastry cream until dissolved and evenly mixed. (If the pastry cream is not warm enough, rewarm it slightly.)

8. Add one-third of the meringue to the cream and mix quickly to lighten the mixture.

9. Gently fold this mixture into the remaining meringue until evenly mixed.

## CHIBOUST CREAM FLAVORED WITH ALCOHOL

| Ingredients | U.S. | | Metric | % |
|---|---|---|---|---|
| Lemon zest, grated | ½ | tsp | 2 g | 0.4 |
| Liqueur or other alcohol | 1.67 oz | | 50 g | 10 |

Omit the raspberry purée from the basic recipe. Add grated lemon zest to the egg yolk mixture in step 2, and stir rum, kirsch, brandy, or orange liqueur into the warm pastry cream when adding the gelatin in step 7.

# LIME OR LEMON CHIBOUST

Yield: about 1 lb 12 oz (750 g)

| Ingredients | U.S. | | Metric | % | Procedure |
|---|---|---|---|---|---|
| Lime or lemon juice | 10 | oz | 250 g | 100 | 1. Heat the juice, zest, and sugar to a simmer. |
| Lime or lemon zest, grated | 0.16 oz (2 tsp) | | 4 g | 1.5 | 2. Whip the egg yolks with the second quantity of sugar and the cornstarch. As when making pastry cream, gradually stir the juice into the egg yolk mixture, then return to the |
| Sugar | 1 | oz | 25 g | 10 | saucepan and bring to a boil. Remove from the heat. |
| Egg yolks | 3 | oz | 80 g | 32 | |
| Sugar | 1 | oz | 25 g | 10 | 3. Soak the gelatin in cold water (see p. 88). Add the gelatin to the egg yolk mixture and |
| Cornstarch | 1 | oz | 25 g | 10 | stir until dissolved. Cool. |
| Gelatin | 0.25 oz | | 6 g | 2.5 | |
| Italian Merigue (p. 267) | 1 lb | | 400 g | 160 | 4. Fold in the Italian meringue. |

# VANILLA CRÈME DIPLOMAT

For large-quantity measurements, see page 729.

| Ingredients | U.S. | | Metric | % | Procedure |
|---|---|---|---|---|---|
| Milk | 8 | oz | 250 g | 100 | 1. Heat the milk and vanilla bean to just below the boiling point. |
| Vanilla bean, split (see note) | ½ | | ½ | | 2. Whip the egg yolks and sugar until pale. Add the flour and cornstarch and mix well. |
| Egg yolks | 1.33 oz (2 yolks) | | 40 g (2 yolks) | 16 | |
| Fine granulated sugar | 1 | oz | 30 g | 12 | 3. Temper the egg mixture by gradually stirring in about half the hot milk. Pour this mixture back into the saucepan with the |
| Cake flour | 0.67 oz | | 20 g | 8 | remaining hot milk. Return to a boil, whipping constantly. |
| Cornstarch | 0.5 oz | | 15 g | 6 | |
| Orange liqueur, such as Grand Marnier | 1 | oz | 30 g | 12 | 4. Remove from the heat and stir in the liqueur. |
| | | | | | 5. Cover with plastic film and cool the pastry cream thoroughly, then chill. |
| Crème Chantilly (p. 211) | 6.5 | oz | 200 g | 80 | |
| **Total weight:** | **1 lb 3** | **oz** | **585 g** | **234%** | 6. Once the cream is cold, beat well until perfectly smooth. |

Note: If vanilla beans are not available, flavor the finished cream with vanilla extract to taste.

7. Fold in the crème chantilly.

## VARIATIONS

Crème diplomat is often stabilized with gelatin, using the same procedure as for Chiboust Cream (p. 272). For each 8 oz (250 g) milk, use ⅛ oz (4 g or 2 leaves) gelatin.

### CHOCOLATE CRÈME DIPLOMAT

For large-quantity measurements, see page 729.

| Ingredients | U.S. | Metric | % |
|---|---|---|---|
| Dark chocolate, finely chopped | 2.25 oz | 70 g | 28% |

Omit the orange liqueur from the basic recipe. Stir dark chocolate into the hot pastry cream in step 4. Stir until the chocolate is completely melted and well mixed.

Crème diplomat may also be flavored with coffee extract, praline paste, or chestnut purée.

# Chocolate Creams

*Ganache* (pronounced gah nahsh) is a rich chocolate cream filling with many uses. When freshly made and still warm, it can be used as a glaze or icing for cakes, much like fondant; pour it over the product to be iced and it will set into a soft icing. When cooled, ganache is used to make chocolate truffles or a filling for other candies. It can also be whipped to make a filling for cakes, tortes, and meringue pastries.

In its simplest form, ganache is a mixture of heavy cream and melted chocolate couverture. Butter can also be included, as illustrated in the second recipe in this section. The quality of a simple ganache depends primarily on the quality of the chocolate. More complex formulas for ganache include eggs and a variety of flavoring ingredients. You might like to experiment with the recipe for Passion Fruit Ganache (p. 276), substituting other fruit purées and flavoring ingredients for the passion fruit.

Chapter 17 includes a recipe for a ganache intended specifically for icing cakes, as well as other similar glazes.

The two chocolate mousse recipes included here are well suited for fillings and pastries. They can also be served by themselves as desserts. Additional chocolate mousses are included with the puddings in chapter 20.

# CHOCOLATE GANACHE I

| Ingredients | U.S. | Metric | Milk at 100% % |
|---|---|---|---|
| Dark chocolate | 1 lb | 500 g | 100 |
| Heavy cream | 12 oz | 375 g | 75 |
| *Total weight:* | *1 lb 12 oz* | *875 g* | *175%* |

**Procedure**

1. Chop the chocolate into small pieces.

2. Bring the cream just to a boil, stirring to prevent scorching. (Use very fresh cream; old cream is more likely to curdle when it is boiled.)

3. Add the chocolate. Remove from the heat, stir, and let stand for a few minutes. Stir again until the chocolate is completely melted and the mixture is smooth. If necessary, warm gently over low heat to completely melt the chocolate. At this point, the ganache is ready to be used as an icing or glaze. Apply it by pouring it over the item to be iced, like Fondant (see p. 422).

4. If the ganache is not to be used warm, let it cool at room temperature. Stir from time to time so it cools evenly. Cooled ganache may be stored in the refrigerator and rewarmed over a water bath when needed.

5. For whipped ganache, the mixture should first be cooled thoroughly, or it will not whip properly. Do not let it become too cold, however, or it will be too hard. With a wire whip or the whip attachment of a mixer, whip the ganache until it is light, thick, and creamy. Use at once. If stored, whipped ganache will become firm and hard to spread.

## VARIATIONS

The proportion of chocolate and cream may be varied. For a firmer product, or if the weather is warm, decrease the cream to as little as 50%. For a very soft ganache, increase the cream to 100%. This proportion makes a ganache that is too soft for truffles but may be whipped into a mousse.

The composition of the chocolate also affects the consistency of the ganache, and the formula may require slight adjustments depending on the chocolate used.

# CHOCOLATE GANACHE II

| Ingredients | U.S. | Metric | % | Procedure |
|---|---|---|---|---|
| Heavy cream | 1 lb 2 oz | 600 g | 100 | 1. Bring the cream and vanilla powder to a boil. |
| Vanilla powder | pinch | pinch | | 2. Chop the chocolate. |
| Bittersweet chocolate | 1 lb 2 oz | 600 g | 100 | 3. Pour the hot cream over the chocolate. Stir until the chocolate is melted. |
| Butter, softened | 3 oz | 100 g | 17 | |
| **Total weight:** | **2 lb 7 oz** | **1300 g** | **217%** | 4. When the mixture has cooled to 95°F (35°C), stir in the butter. Use the ganache at once. |

# PASSION FRUIT GANACHE

*For large-quantity measurements, see page 729.*

| Ingredients | U.S. | | Metric | % | Procedure |
|---|---|---|---|---|---|
| Heavy cream | 4 | oz | 120 g | 56 | 1. Combine the cream, juice, and butter in a saucepan and bring to a boil. |
| Passion fruit juice | 4 | oz | 120 g | 56 | |
| Butter | 2 | oz | 60 g | 28 | 2. Whip the egg yolks with the sugar until light. |
| Egg yolks | 1.67 | oz | 50 g | 23 | 3. Gradually beat the hot liquid into the egg mixture. |
| Sugar | 2 | oz | 60 g | 28 | |
| Dark chocolate, chopped | 7 | oz | 215 g | 100 | 4. Return this mixture to the heat and bring it quickly to a boil, then remove from heat. |
| **Total weight** | **1 lb 4** | **oz** | **625 g** | **291%** | 5. Strain the liquid over the chopped chocolate in a bowl. Stir until all the chocolate is melted and the mixture is evenly blended. |

# CHOCOLATE MOUSSE I

| Ingredients | U.S. | | Chocolate at 100% Metric | % | Procedure |
|---|---|---|---|---|---|
| Dark chocolate | 1 lb | | 500 g | 100 | 1. Melt the chocolate over hot water. |
| Butter | | 9 oz | 280 g | 56 | 2. Remove from the heat and add the butter. Stir until the butter is melted and completely mixed in. |
| Egg yolks | | 5 oz | 155 g | 31 | |
| Egg whites | | 12 oz | 375 g | 75 | 3. Add the egg yolks one at a time. Mix in each egg yolk completely before adding the next. |
| Sugar | | 2.5 oz | 80 g | 16 | |
| **Total weight** | **2 lb 12** | **oz** | **1390 g** | **278%** | 4. Beat the egg whites until they form soft peaks. Add the sugar and beat until the egg whites form stiff but moist peaks. Do not overbeat. |
| | | | | | 5. Fold the egg whites into the chocolate mixture. |

# CHOCOLATE MOUSSE II

*For large-quantity measurements, see page 729.*

| Ingredients | U.S. | | Metric | Chocolate at 100% % | Procedure |
|---|---|---|---|---|---|
| Egg yolks | 1.5 | oz | 40 g | 25 | |
| Fine granulated sugar | 1.33 | oz | 35 g | 22 | |
| Water | 1 | oz | 30 g | 19 | |
| Dark chocolate, melted | 6 | oz | 160 g | 100 | |
| Heavy cream | 11 | oz | 300 g | 190 | |
| **Total weight:** | **1 lb 4** | **oz** | **565 g** | **356%** | |

Procedure

1. In a round-bottomed stainless-steel bowl, whip the egg yolks until pale.

2. Make a syrup with the sugar and water and boil to 244°F (118°C). Whip the hot syrup into the yolks and continue whipping until cool.

3. Melt the chocolate and fold into the egg mixture.

4. Whip the cream until it forms soft peaks. Whip one-third of the cream into the chocolate mixture. Then fold in the remaining cream until well incorporated.

# DESSERT SAUCES

In addition to the recipes presented in this section, the following types of dessert sauces are discussed elsewhere in this book or can be made easily without recipes.

**Custard Sauces.** Vanilla custard sauce, or crème anglaise, is presented earlier in this chapter (p. 269). It is one of the most basic preparations in dessert cookery. Chocolate or other flavors may be added to create variations.

Pastry Cream (p. 271) can be thinned with heavy cream or milk to make another type of custard sauce.

**Chocolate Sauce.** In addition to the three recipes that follow, chocolate sauce may be made in several other ways. For example:

Flavor vanilla custard sauce with chocolate (see p. 269).

Prepare Chocolate Ganache I (p. 275) through step 3 in the procedure. Thin to desired consistency with cream, milk, or simple syrup.

**Lemon Sauce.** Prepare Lemon Filling (p. 307), but use only 1½ ounce (45 g) cornstarch, or use 1 ounce (30 g) waxy maize.

**Fruit Sauces.** Some of the best fruit sauces are also the simplest. These are of two types:

Purées of fresh or cooked fruits, sweetened with sugar. Such a purée is often called a **coulis** (pronounced koo-lee).

Heated, strained fruit jams and preserves, diluted with simple syrup, water, or liquor.

For greater economy, fruit sauces can be stretched by diluting them with water, adding more sugar, and thickening them with starch. Other sauces, such as those made of blueberries or pineapple, may have a more desirable texture when thickened slightly with starch. These may also be flavored with spices and/or lemon juice.

**Caramel Sauces.** The first section of this chapter explains the stages of sugar cooking, the last stage of which is caramel. In other words, caramel is simply sugar cooked until it is golden. The simplest caramel sauce is merely caramelized sugar diluted to sauce consistency with water. The addition of heavy cream makes a creamy caramel sauce, as shown by the recipe in this section.

Two methods are available for caramelizing sugar. In the *wet method*, the sugar is first combined with water and boiled to dissolve it, making a syrup. Glucose or an acid such as cream of tartar or lemon juice may be added to help prevent crystalization. The sugar caramelizes after the water has boiled off. The recipe for caramel sauce in this section is prepared using the wet method. Follow the guidelines for preparing syrups discussed at the beginning of this chapter.

The second method is called the *dry method*. In the dry method, the sugar is melted in a dry pan without first making it into a syrup. Often, an acid in the form of a small amount of lemon juice is added to the sugar and rubbed in so the crystals are slightly moist. Place the sugar in a heavy saucepan or sauté pan. Set it over moderately high heat. When the sugar begins to melt, stir constantly so it caramelizes evenly. Many chefs prefer to add the sugar to the pan a little at a time. More sugar is added only when the previous addition is fully melted. Butter caramel, included in this section, is prepared using the dry method.

Remember that sugar, when turning to caramel, is very hot, well over 300°F (150°C). Water or other liquids added to hot caramel can spatter dangerously. To minimize spattering, allow the caramel to cool slightly. To stop the cooking quickly and prevent the sugar from becoming too brown, dip the bottom of the pan in cold water for just an instant. Alternatively, heat the liquid first, then add it carefully to the caramelized sugar.

A more complex type of caramel is butter caramel. The recipe included in this section is rarely used by itself (except to make hard toffee candies). Rather, it is a component of other preparations, such as caramelized fruits. See, for example, the recipes for Caramelized Apricots, Figs in Port Wine, and Spiced Pineapple in chapter 22. Because butter caramel is somewhat difficult to make, it is included here to give you an opportunity to study it by itself and master it before trying one of the recipes mentioned. It is necessary to follow the instructions in the recipe procedure carefully in order to make the butter and caramelized sugar form a uniform, emulsified mixture.

---

## ⊱ COULIS ⊰

The word *coulis* has had many meanings in the past century or two. Originally the term referred to juices from cooked meats. By Escoffier's time, at the beginning of the twentieth century, a coulis was a type of thick soup made from puréed meat, game, or fish. More recently, as puréed meat soups were prepared more rarely, the term was used primarily for thick puréed shellfish soups.

The concept of a thick liquid made of puréed ingredients is preserved in the most common usage of the word *coulis* today. In modern cooking, a coulis is a thick sauce made of puréed fruits or vegetables, such as a raspberry coulis or a tomato coulis.

---

# CHOCOLATE SAUCE

*Yield: 1 qt (1 L)*

| Ingredients | U.S. | Metric | Procedure |
|---|---|---|---|
| Dark chocolate | 1 lb | 500 g | 1. Chop the chocolate into small pieces. |
| Water | 1 pt | 500 mL | 2. Place the chocolate and water in a saucepan. Heat over low heat or over hot water until the chocolate is melted. Bring to a simmer and simmer 2 minutes. Stir while cooking to make a smooth mixture. The mixture should thicken slightly as it simmers. |
| Butter | 6 oz | 190 g | |
| | | | 3. Remove from the heat and add the butter. Stir until the butter is melted and mixed in. |
| | | | 4. Set the pan in a bowl of ice water and stir the sauce until it is cool. |

# CHOCOLATE FUDGE SAUCE

*Yield: 1 qt (1 L)*

| Ingredients | U.S. | Metric | Procedure |
|---|---|---|---|
| Water | 1 pt | 0.5 mL | 1. Combine the water, sugar, and syrup and bring to a boil, stirring to dissolve the sugar. |
| Sugar | 2 lb | 1 kg | |
| Corn syrup | 6 oz | 375 g | 2. Boil 1 minute and remove from the heat. Let cool a few minutes. |
| Unsweetened chocolate | 8 oz | 250 g | 3. Melt the chocolate and butter together over low heat. Stir until smooth. |
| Butter | 2 oz | 62 g | 4. Very slowly stir the hot syrup into the chocolate. |
| | | | 5. Place over moderate heat and bring to a boil. Boil for 2 minutes. |
| | | | 6. Remove from the heat and cool. |

# CHOCOLATE SAUCE III

*Yield: 1 lb 8 oz (600 g)*

| Ingredients | U.S. | Metric | Procedure |
|---|---|---|---|
| Water | 12 oz | 300 g | 1. Combine the water, sugar, and chocolate. Bring to a boil, stirring to mix the chocolate with the syrup. |
| Sugar | 7 oz | 175 g | |
| Dark chocolate couverture | 3 oz | 75 g | 2. Mix the cornstarch and cocoa powder to a thin paste with a little water. |
| Cornstarch | 1 oz | 25 g | 3. Add this paste to the chocolate syrup mixture and return to a boil. Strain and cool. |
| Cocoa powder | 2 oz | 50 g | |
| Water, cold | as needed | as needed | |

# MELBA SAUCE

*Yield: about 1 pt (400 mL)*

| Ingredients | U.S. | Metric | Procedure |
|---|---|---|---|
| Frozen, sweetened raspberries | 1 lb 8 oz | 600 g | 1. Thaw the raspberries and force them through a sieve to purée them and remove the seeds. |
| Red currant jelly | 8 oz | 200 g | 2. Combine with the jelly in a saucepan. Bring to a boil, stirring until the jelly is melted and completely blended with the fruit purée. |

**VARIATIONS**

## RASPBERRY SAUCE

Purée and sieve frozen sweetened raspberries, or use fresh raspberries and sweeten to taste. Omit the red currant jelly. Use as is or simmer until thickened, as desired.

Other fruits can be puréed and sweetened to taste to make dessert sauces, using the same procedure. If purées from pulpy fruits (such as mangoes) are too thick, thin with water, simple syrup, or an appropriate fruit juice.

# CARAMEL SAUCE

*For large-quantity measurements, see page 729.*

*Yield: 12 oz (375 mL)*

| Ingredients | U.S. | Metric | Procedure |
|---|---|---|---|
| Sugar | 8 oz | 250 g | 1. Combine the sugar, water, and juice in a heavy saucepan. Bring to a boil, stirring to dissolve the sugar. Cook the syrup to the caramel stage (see p. 261). Toward the end of the cooking time, turn the heat to very low to avoid burning the sugar or letting it get too dark. It should be a golden color. |
| Water | 2 oz | 60 mL | |
| Lemon juice | ¾ tsp | 4 mL | |
| Heavy cream | 6 oz | 190 mL | |
| Milk or additional cream | 4 oz | 125 mL | |

2. Remove from the heat and cool 5 minutes. Alternatively, to stop the cooking completely and prevent the sugar from becoming any darker because of residual heat, dip the bottom of the pan in cold water for an instant.

3. Bring the heavy cream to a boil. Add a few ounces of it to the caramel.

4. Stir and continue to add the cream slowly. Return to the heat and stir until all the caramel is dissolved.

5. Let cool completely.

6. Stir the milk or additional cream into the cooled caramel to thin it.

**VARIATIONS**

### HOT CARAMEL SAUCE

Proceed as directed through step 4. Omit the milk or additional cream.

### CLEAR CARAMEL SAUCE

Substitute 2½–3 oz (75–90 mL) boiling water for the heavy cream and omit the milk. If the sauce is too thick when cool, add more water.

### BUTTERSCOTCH SAUCE

Use brown sugar instead of white granulated sugar in the basic recipe. Omit the lemon juice. In step 1, cook the syrup only to 240°F (115°C). Add 2 oz (60 g) butter before adding the heavy cream.

### CARAMEL CREAM

Prepare 2 oz Clear Caramel Sauce. Soften 0.06 oz (½ tsp/ 2 g) gelatin in 0.5 oz (1 tbsp/15 mL) water. Add to the warm caramel sauce and stir until dissolved (rewarm if necessary). Cool to room temperature but do not cool until set. Whip 4 oz (125 g) heavy cream to soft peaks. Mix about one-fourth of the cream into the caramel sauce, then fold in the remaining cream.

Clear caramel sauce and caramel sauce with cream

# BUTTER CARAMEL

*Yield: 11 oz (330 g)*

| Ingredients | U.S. | Metric | Procedure |
|---|---|---|---|
| Sugar | 8 oz | 250 g | 1. Heat the sugar over moderate heat until it melts and then turns to a golden brown caramel. |
| Butter | 4 oz | 125 g | |

2. Keep the pan over moderate heat. Add the butter. Stir constantly over heat until the butter has melted and is blended into the caramel. It is essential to stir vigorously in order to emulsify the butter and caramel. If you do not stir well enough, the butterfat will tend to separate.

3. The caramel will hold reasonably well for a short time over heat. It should be stirred from time to time. If the caramel is allowed to cool, it will become a hard, brittle toffee. If it is reheated, the butter will separate, but it can be reincorporated by adding a few drops of water and stirring vigorously.

# SABAYON I

*Yield: about 1½ pt (750 mL)*

| Ingredients | U.S. | Metric | Procedure |
|---|---|---|---|
| Egg yolks | 2.67 oz (4 yolks) | 80 g (4 yolks) | 1. Mix the egg yolks and syrup in a stainless-steel bowl. Place the bowl over a hot-water bath and whip until light, frothy, and pale in color. |
| Simple syrup (p. 261) | 3.5 oz | 100 g | 2. Remove the bowl from the hot-water bath and continue to whip until cool and doubled in volume. |
| Whipped cream | 2 oz | 60 g | 3. Gently fold in the whipped cream. |
| | | | 4. Use as a dessert sauce or topping that can be browned (gratinéed) under a salamander or broiler. |

# SABAYON II

*Yield: about 1 qt (900 mL)*

| Ingredients | U.S. | Metric | Procedure |
|---|---|---|---|
| Egg yolks | 4 oz (6 yolks) | 115 g (6 yolks) | 1. In a stainless-steel bowl, beat the yolks until foamy. |
| Sugar | 8 oz | 225 g | 2. Beat in the sugar and wine. Place over a hot-water bath and continue beating until thick and hot. |
| Dry white wine | 8 oz | 225 g | 3. Serve hot as a dessert or as a sauce for fruit or fritters. Serve without delay; it will lose some foaminess and begin to separate if allowed to stand. |

**VARIATIONS**

## COLD SABAYON

Dissolve 0.04 oz (½ tsp/1 g) gelatin in the wine. Proceed as in the basic recipe. When the sauce is done, place the bowl over ice and whip the sauce until it is cool.

## ZABAGLIONE

This is the Italian sauce and dessert that is the origin of sabayon. Use sweet Marsala wine instead of the dry white wine, and use only half the sugar. Other wines or spirits may be used, such as port or sherry. Adjust the sugar according to the sweetness of the wine.

# SAUCE SUZETTE

*Yield: about 1 pt (450 mL)*

| Ingredients | U.S. | Metric | Procedure |
|---|---|---|---|
| Orange juice | 7 oz | 200 g | 1. Warm the juice and zest in a saucepan. |
| Lemon juice | 2 oz | 60 g | 2. In a separate pan, cook the sugar to a golden caramel. |
| Orange zest, grated | 0.5 oz | 15 g | 3. Remove from the heat and add the butter. Stir to begin to dissolve the caramelized sugar. |
| Sugar | 7 oz | 200 g | |
| Butter | 2.5 oz | 80 g | 4. Add the warmed juices. Reduce by one-third, stirring continuously. |
| Orange liqueur such as Cointreau | 7 oz | 100 g | 5. Add the liqueur and brandy. Ignite to burn off the alcohol. |
| Brandy | 2 oz | 60 g | 6. Serve warm. |

# FRUIT COULIS

*Yield: 10–11 oz (300 g)*

| Ingredients | U.S. | | Metric | Procedure |
|---|---|---|---|---|
| Berries or other soft fruit | 7 | oz | 200 g | 1. Purée the fruit in a blender or food processor and pass through a fine sieve or chinois. |
| Fine granulated sugar | 3.5 | oz | 100 g | 2. Warm the fruit purée in a saucepan. |
| Water | 1.33 oz (8 tsp) | | 40 g | 3. Separately, make a syrup of the sugar and water and boil to 220°F (105°C). Mix into the fruit purée. |
| Lemon juice | 0.5 | oz (3 tsp) | 15 g | 4. Return to a boil, strain, and mix in the juice and alcohol. Cool. |
| Kirsch or other fruit brandy or liqueur *(optional)* | 0.67 oz (4 tsp) | | 20 g | |

# BLUEBERRY SAUCE

*Yield: about 10 oz (300 mL)*

| Ingredients | U.S. | | Metric | Procedure |
|---|---|---|---|---|
| Sugar | 1.5 | oz | 45 g | 1. Put the sugar in a heavy saucepan. Heat until the sugar melts and then caramelizes to a rich golden brown. |
| Water | 2 | oz | 60 mL | 2. Remove the pan from heat and add the water. Because the pan is very hot, the water will boil immediately, so be careful to avoid being scalded by steam. |
| Lemon juice | 1 | tsp | 30 mL | 3. Simmer until the caramelized sugar is dissolved. |
| Blueberries, fresh, washed and drained well | 12 | oz | 360 g | 4. Add the lemon juice and simmer 1 minute, until it is well blended. |
| | | | | 5. Add the blueberries and cook slowly for 5 to 10 minutes, until the berries pop and the sauce is slightly reduced and thickened. |
| | | | | 6. Taste for sweetness. If the berries are tart, add a little more sugar to taste. Cool. |

# DULCE DE LECHE

*Yield: about 1 pt (500 mL)*

| Ingredients | U.S. | Metric | Procedure |
|---|---|---|---|
| Milk | 2 pt | 1 L | 1. Combine the milk, sugar, and baking soda in a heavy saucepan. Set over medium heat. Bring to a slow boil without stirring. |
| Sugar | 12 oz | 375 mL | 2. As the mixture approaches the boil, it will foam up. Quickly remove it from the heat before it boils over; stir. |
| Baking soda | ¼ tsp | 1 mL | 3. Turn the heat to low, set the pan back on the heat, and cook slowly, stirring frequently with a wooden spoon, for about 45 to 60 minutes. The mixture will gradually caramelize. |
| Vanilla extract | ½ tsp | 2 mL | 4. When the mixture is a rich caramel brown and thickened but still pourable, remove from the heat and stir in the vanilla. |
| | | | 5. Cool thoroughly. |

# HARD SAUCE

*Yield: about 1 pt (500 mL)*

| Ingredients | U.S. | Metric | Procedure |
|---|---|---|---|
| Butter | 8 oz | 250 g | 1. Cream the butter and sugar until light and fluffy, as for simple buttercream. |
| Confectioners' sugar | 1 lb | 500 g | 2. Beat in the brandy or rum. |
| Brandy or rum | 1 oz | 30 mL | 3. Serve with steamed puddings, such as English Christmas pudding. |

# CREAM SAUCE FOR PIPING

*Yield: variable*

| Ingredients | U.S. | Metric | Procedure |
|---|---|---|---|
| Sour cream | as needed | as needed | 1. Stir the sour cream until it is smooth. |
| Heavy cream | as needed | as needed | 2. As this sauce is used for marbling or decorating other sauces, the quantity of cream needed depends on the texture of the other sauces. Gradually stir in heavy cream to thin the sour cream until it is the same consistency as the sauce to be decorated. |

# TERMS FOR REVIEW

| | | | |
|---|---|---|---|
| caramelize | common meringue | hard meringue | ganache |
| simple syrup | Swiss meringue | crème anglaise | crème Chantilly |
| dessert syrup | Italian meringue | pastry cream | coulis |
| crystallize | soft meringue | crème Chiboust | |

# QUESTIONS FOR DISCUSSION

1. How can you avoid unwanted crystallization when cooking sugar syrups?

2. Why is cream of tartar or lemon juice sometimes added to a sugar syrup before or during cooking?

3. Vanilla custard sauce and pastry cream both contain eggs. Why is it possible to boil pastry cream but not custard sauce?

4. Explain the importance of sanitation in the production of pastry cream. What specific steps should you take to ensure a safe product?

5. Explain the effects of fat, sugar, and temperature on the whipping of egg whites into foams.

6. Describe two simple ways of preparing fruit sauces.

## Chapter 13

# Pies

On the early American frontier, it was not uncommon for the pioneer housewife to bake twenty-one pies each week—one for every meal. Pies were so important to the settlers that in winter, when fruits were unavailable, cooks would bake dessert pies out of whatever materials were available, such as potatoes, vinegar, and soda crackers.

Few of us today eat pie at every meal. Nevertheless, pies are still a favorite American dessert. Most customers will order and pay a higher price for a piece of chocolate cream pie than for chocolate pudding, even if the pie filling is the same as the pudding and even if they leave the crust uneaten.

In this chapter, we study the preparation of pie doughs and fillings and the procedures for assembling and baking pies.

**After reading this chapter, you should be able to:**

1. Prepare pie doughs.
2. Roll pie doughs and line pie pans.
3. Fill, assemble, and bake single-crust pies, double-crust pies, and lattice-topped pies.
4. Form and bake pie shells for unbaked pies.
5. Prepare fruit fillings.
6. Prepare soft or custard-type pie fillings.
7. Prepare cream fillings.
8. Prepare chiffon fillings.

# PIE DOUGHS

**B**efore you begin studying this section, review the section on gluten development in chapter 5. Pie pastry is a simple product in terms of its ingredients: flour, shortening, water, and salt. Yet success or failure depends on how the shortening and flour are mixed and how the gluten is developed. The key to making pie dough is proper technique, and you will remember the techniques better if you understand why they work.

## Ingredients

**Flour.** Pastry flour is the best choice for pie doughs. It has enough gluten to produce the desired structure and flakiness, yet is low enough in gluten to yield a tender product, if handled properly. If stronger flours are used, the percentage of shortening should be increased slightly to provide more tenderness.

**Fat.** Regular hydrogenated shortening is the most popular fat for pie crusts because it has the right plastic consistency to produce a flaky crust. It is firm and moldable enough to make an easily workable dough. Emulsified shortening should not be used, as it blends too quickly with the flour and makes it difficult to achieve a flaky pastry.

Butter contributes excellent flavor to pie pastry, but it is frequently avoided in volume production for two reasons: It is expensive, and it melts easily, making the dough difficult to work.

It is desirable, if costs permit, to blend a quantity of butter into the shortening used for piecrusts in order to improve flavor. The large quantity of piecrust dumped into the garbage after customers have eaten the filling is evidence that many people are not satisfied with the taste of shortening piecrusts.

If butter is used to replace all the shortening for pie doughs, the percentage of fat in the formula should be increased by about one-fourth. (If 1 pound shortening is called for, use 1 pound 4 ounces butter.) The liquid can be reduced slightly, as butter contains moisture.

In the case of richer pastries and short doughs, butter is specified as the primary fat in the formulas here. These doughs are used primarily for European-style tarts and pastries, in which the flavor of the butter is an important part of the dessert.

Lard is an excellent shortening for pies because it is firm and plastic, properties that produce good flakiness. However, it is not widely used in food service.

**Liquid.** Water is necessary to develop some gluten in the flour and to give structure and flakiness to the dough. If too much water is used, the crust will become tough because of too much gluten development. If not enough water is used, the crust will fall apart because of inadequate gluten structure.

Milk makes a richer dough that browns more quickly. However, the crust is less crisp, and the production cost is higher. If dry milk is used, it should be dissolved in the water to ensure even distribution in the dough.

Whether water or milk is used, it must be added cold (40°F/4°C or colder) to maintain proper dough temperature.

---

### ✤ PIES IN HISTORY ✤

If we take the word *pie* to mean any of a variety of foods enclosed in pastry and baked, then there have been pies for nearly all of recorded history. In ancient Greece and Rome, doughs made with olive oil were used to cover or enclose various ingredients.

In English, the word *pie* used in this way dates back to at least 1300. It is probably a short form of *magpie*, a bird that collects a variety of things, just as bakers do when they are assembling ingredients to bake in a pie. In the Middle Ages, the word *pie* almost always referred to savory pies containing meats, poultry, or game. Today, in England, the word is still used largely for meat pies, both hot and cold (cold pies being similar to what we might call pâtés), while in North America, savory pies, such as chicken "pot pie," are still enjoyed.

North Americans, however, are responsible for turning the development of pies firmly away from savory and toward sweet. Fruit pies, especially apple pie, are perhaps still the most popular, but pastry cooks have devised dessert pie fillings from many other ingredients as well.

Pies are so popular that, across the continent, they are the feature of annual summer festivals. The little town of Braham, for example, which bills itself as the Pie Capital of Minnesota, hosts a popular festival called Pie Day, featuring pie sales, baking contests, art and craft shows, and daylong entertainment, all in celebration of pies.

**Salt.** Salt has some conditioning effect on the gluten (see page 94). However, it contributes mainly to flavor. Salt must be dissolved in the liquid before being added to the mix in order to ensure even distribution.

# Temperature

Pie dough should be kept cool, about 60°F (15°C), during mixing and makeup, for two reasons.

- Shortening has the best consistency when cool. If it is warm, it blends too quickly with the flour. If it is very cold, it is too firm to be easily worked.

- Gluten develops more slowly at cool temperatures than at warm temperatures.

# Pie Dough Types

There are two basic types of pie dough:

- Flaky pie dough.

- Mealy pie dough.

The difference between the two is in how the fat is blended with the flour. Complete mixing procedures are given in the formulas that follow. First, it is important to understand the basic distinction between the two types.

## Flaky Pie Dough

For *flaky pie dough*, the fat is cut or rubbed into the flour until the particles of shortening are about the size of peas or hazelnuts—that is, the flour is not completely blended with the fat, and the fat is left in pieces. (Many bakers distinguish between this crust, which they call *short-flake*, and *long-flake crusts*, in which the fat is left in pieces the size of walnuts and the flour is coated even less with shortening. Blitz puff paste, introduced in the next chapter, is actually a long-flake pie dough that is rolled and folded like puff paste.)

When water is added, the flour absorbs it and develops some gluten. When the dough is rolled out, the lumps of fat and moistened flour are flattened and become flakes of dough separated by layers of fat.

## Mealy Pie Dough

For *mealy pie dough*, the fat is blended into the flour more thoroughly, until the mixture looks like coarse cornmeal. The more complete coating of the flour with fat has several results:

- The crust is very short and tender because less gluten can develop.

- Less water is needed in the mix because the flour won't absorb as much as in flaky dough.

- The baked dough is less likely to absorb moisture from the filling and become soggy.

Mealy dough is used for bottom crusts, especially in baked fruit pies and soft or custard-type pies, because it resists sogginess. Flaky doughs are used for top crusts and sometimes for prebaked shells.

To produce mealy doughs with even more resistance to soaking, the flour and fat can be blended together completely to make a smooth paste. Such a dough is very short when baked. It is especially appropriate for custard pies.

The formula called Enriched Pie Pastry included in this section is essentially a mealy dough, except it contains more sugar, is enriched with egg yolks, and works especially well with butter as the only fat. Its delicate, rich flavor makes it suited for European-style tarts and single-crust pies.

### 3-2-1 Dough

A popular pie dough formula is called 3-2-1 dough. The numbers refer to the ratio of ingredients by weight: 3 parts flour, 2 parts shortening, and 1 part ice water. The ratios of ingredients in this chapter's basic pie dough formulas have been modified slightly from the 3-2-1 standard. In particular, they contain slightly less water to yield a somewhat more tender dough. However, the 3-2-1 ratio is easy to remember and is always reliable. It can be used for both mealy and flaky doughs. To mix the ingredients, use the same procedure as that given in the basic formulas below.

### Trimmings

Reworked scraps or trimmings are tougher than freshly made dough. They may be combined with mealy dough and used for bottom crusts only.

## Mixing

Hand mixing is best for small quantities of dough, especially flaky dough, because you have more control over the mixing. Quantities up to 10 pounds can be mixed almost as quickly by hand as by machine.

For machine mixing, use a pastry knife or paddle attachment. Blend at low speed.

## Crumb Crusts

Graham cracker crusts are popular because they have an appealing flavor and are much easier to make than pastry crusts. For variation, vanilla or chocolate wafer crumbs, gingersnap crumbs, or zwieback crumbs may be used instead of graham cracker crumbs. Ground nuts may be added for special desserts.

*Crumb crusts* are used primarily for unbaked pies, such as cream pies and chiffon pies. They can also be used for such desserts as cheesecake. Be sure the flavor of the crust is compatible with the filling. Lime chiffon pie with a chocolate crumb crust is not an appealing combination. Some cream fillings are so delicate in flavor they would be overwhelmed by a crust that is too flavorful.

Baking a crumb crust before filling it makes it firmer and less crumbly, and gives it a toasted flavor.

# PIE DOUGH

*For large-quantity measurements, see page 730.*

| | Flaky Pie Dough | | | Mealy Pie Dough | | |
|---|---|---|---|---|---|---|
| Ingredients | U.S. | Metric | % | U.S. | Metric | % |
| Pastry flour | 1 lb 4 oz | 500 g | 100 | 1 lb 4 oz | 500 g | 100 |
| Shortening, regular | 14 oz | 350 g | 70 | 13 oz | 325 g | 65 |
| Water, cold | 6 oz | 150 g | 30 | 5 oz | 125 g | 25 |
| Salt | 0.4 oz (2 tsp) | 10 g | 2 | 0.4 oz (2 tsp) | 10 g | 2 |
| Sugar (optional) | 1 oz | 25 g | 5 | 1 oz | 25 g | 5 |
| *Total weight:* | *2 lb 9 oz* | *1035 g* | *207%* | *2 lb 7 oz* | *985 g* | *197%* |

### Procedure

1. Sift the flour into a mixing bowl. Add the shortening.
2. Rub or cut the shortening into the flour to the proper degree:

   For flaky dough, until fat particles are the size of peas or hazelnuts.

   For mealy dough, until mixture resembles cornmeal.
3. Dissolve salt and sugar (if used) in water.
4. Add the water to the flour mixture. Mix very gently, just until the water is absorbed. Do not overwork the dough.
5. Place the dough in pans, cover with plastic film, and place in the refrigerator or retarder for at least 4 hours.
6. Scale portions of dough as needed.

# ENRICHED PIE PASTRY

*For large-quantity measurements, see page 730.*

| Ingredients | U.S. | Metric | % |
|---|---|---|---|
| Pastry flour | 12 oz | 375 g | 100 |
| Sugar | 2 oz | 62 g | 17 |
| Butter | 6 oz | 188 g | 50 |
| Egg yolks | 1 oz | 30 g | 8 |
| Water, cold | 3 oz | 94 g | 25 |
| Salt | 0.13 oz (⅞ tsp) | 4 g | 1 |
| *Total weight:* | *1 lb 8 oz* | *753 g* | *201%* |

### VARIATION

For quiches and other savory pies and tarts, omit the sugar.

### Procedure

This pastry is mixed somewhat like mealy pie dough, except the quantity of sugar is too large to dissolve easily in the water.

1. Sift the flour and sugar into a mixing bowl.
2. Add the butter and rub it in until it is well combined and no lumps remain.
3. Beat the egg yolks with the water and salt until the salt is dissolved.
4. Add the liquid to the flour mixture. Mix gently until it is completely absorbed.
5. Place the dough in pans, cover with plastic film, and place in refrigerator at least 4 hours. (Alternatively, if the sizes you need are known in advance, scale the dough, form into discs, wrap separately, and refrigerate.)
6. Scale portions as needed.

# GRAHAM CRACKER CRUST

*Yield: enough for four 9-in. (23 cm) pies or five 8-in. (20 cm) pies*

| Ingredients | U.S. | Metric | Crumbs at 100% % | Procedure |
|---|---|---|---|---|
| Graham cracker crumbs | 1 lb | 450 g | 100 | 1. Mix the crumbs and sugar in a mixing bowl. |
| Sugar | 8 oz | 225 g | 50 | 2. Add the melted butter and mix until evenly blended; crumbs should be completely moistened by the butter. |
| Butter, melted | 8 oz | 225 g | 50 | |
| **Total weight:** | **2 lb** | **900 g** | **200%** | |

**Procedure (continued)**

3. Scale the mixture into pie pans:

    8 oz (225 g) for 9-in. (23 cm) pans

    6 oz (180 g) for 8-in. (20 cm) pans

4. Spread the mixture evenly on the bottom and sides of the pan. Press another pan on top to pack the crumbs evenly.

5. Bake at 350°F (175°C) for 10 minutes.

6. Cool thoroughly before filling.

**VARIATIONS**

Substitute chocolate or vanilla wafer crumbs, gingersnap crumbs, or zwieback crumbs for the graham cracker crumbs.

# ASSEMBLY AND BAKING

**P**ies may be classified into two groups based on method of assembling and baking.

**Baked Pies.** Raw pie shells are filled and then baked. *Fruit pies* contain fruit fillings and usually have a top crust. *Soft pies* are those with custard-type fillings—that is, liquid fillings that become firm when their egg content coagulates. They are usually baked as single-crust pies.

**Unbaked Pies.** Prebaked pie shells are filled with a prepared filling, chilled, and served when the filling is firm enough to slice. *Cream pies* are made with pudding or boiled custard-type fillings. *Chiffon pies* are made with fillings that are lightened by the addition of beaten egg whites and/or whipped cream. Gelatin or starch gives them a firm consistency.

The two main components of pies are the dough or pastry and the filling. These two components are produced in quite separate and distinct operations. Once the pastry and fillings are made, rolling the dough and assembling and baking the pies can proceed rapidly.

Because these operations are separate and involve different kinds of problems and techniques, it is helpful to concentrate on them one at a time. The preparation of pie dough is discussed above. This section begins with procedures for making pie pastry into pie shells and for filling and baking pies, followed by a discussion of pie fillings.

Instead of being given a top crust, fruit pies are sometimes topped with Streusel (p. 199) or a lattice crust (see the following procedure). Streusel is especially good on apple pies. *Lattice crusts* are best for pies with attractive, colorful fruit, such as cherry or blueberry.

## Procedure for Rolling Pie Dough and Lining Pans

1. Select the best doughs for each purpose.

    Mealy pie doughs are used whenever soaking is a problem, so they are mainly used for bottom crusts, especially bottom crusts for soft pie fillings such as custard and pumpkin. This is because mealy doughs resist soaking better than flaky dough does.

    Flaky pie doughs are best for top crusts. They can also be used for prebaked pie shells if the shells are filled with cooled filling just before serving. However, if the prebaked shells are filled with hot filling, it is safer to use mealy dough.

2. Scale the dough.

    The following weights are only guidelines. The depth of pie tins, and hence their capacity, varies. For example, disposable tins are often shallower than standard tins.

    8 oz (225 g) for 9-in. (23 cm) bottom crusts

    6 oz (170 g) for 9-in. (23 cm) top crusts

    6 oz (170 g) for 8-in. (20 cm) bottom crusts

    5 oz (140 g) for 8-in. (20 cm) top crusts

    Experienced bakers are able to use less dough when rolling out crusts because they roll the dough to a perfect circle of the right size and need to trim away little excess dough.

    Be aware that pie pans are often mislabeled to suggest they are larger than they actually are. It is possible to find pans labeled as 9-inch that are actually smaller than 8-inch pans. *Pan size as used in this book refers to the inside top diameter of the pie pan.*

3. Dust the bench and rolling pin lightly with flour.

    Too much dusting flour toughens the dough, so use no more than needed to prevent sticking.

    Instead of rolling the dough directly on the bench, you may roll it out on flour-dusted canvas. Rolling on canvas does not require as much dusting flour.

4. Roll out the dough.

    Flatten the dough lightly and roll it out to a uniform ⅛-in. (3 mm) thickness. Use even strokes and roll from the center outward in all directions. Lift the dough frequently to make sure it is not sticking. The finished dough should be a nearly perfect circle.

5. Place the dough in the pan.

    To lift the dough without breaking it, roll it lightly around the rolling pin. A second method is to fold the dough in half, place the folded dough into the pan with the fold in the center, and unfold the dough.

    Allow the dough to drop into the pan; press it into the corners without stretching it. Stretched dough will shrink during baking.

    There should be no air bubbles between the dough and the pan.

6. For single-crust pies, flute or crimp the edges, if desired, and trim off excess dough. For double-crust pies, fill with cold filling, brush the edge of the crust with water, and top with the second crust, as explained in the procedure for preparing baked pies (p. 293). Seal the edges; crimp or flute, if desired. Trim off the excess dough.

    The simplest way to trim excess dough is to rotate the pie tin between the palms of the hands while pressing with the palms against the edge of the rim. This pinches off the excess dough flush with the rim.

7. Some bakers feel that fluted edges add to the appearance of the product. Others feel that fluting takes too much time and produces nothing more than a rim of heavy dough that most customers leave on their plates. Follow your instructor's directions on this procedure. Whether you flute the edges or not, be sure that double-crust pies are well sealed. Many bakers like to make a raised, fluted rim of dough on pie shells for soft-filled pies such as custard or pumpkin. This raised edge, as shown in the illustration, enables them to fill the shell quite full while reducing the chance of spillover.

8. Resting the made-up pies for 20–30 minutes, preferably refrigerated, helps prevent crust shrinkage.

# The Soggy Bottom

Underbaked bottom crusts or crusts that have soaked up moisture from the filling are a common fault in pies. Soggy bottoms can be avoided in several ways:

1. Use mealy dough for bottom crusts. Mealy dough absorbs less liquid than flaky dough does.

2. Use high bottom heat, at least at the beginning of baking, to set the crust quickly. Bake the pies at the bottom of the oven.

3. Do not add hot fillings to unbaked crusts.

4. For fruit pies, line the bottom of the pie shell with a thin layer of cake crumbs before pouring in the filling. This helps absorb some juice that might otherwise soak into the crust.

5. Use dark metal pie tins, which absorb heat. (Because so many bakers use disposable aluminum pans, other methods must be relied on. Disposable pans with black bottoms are sometimes available.)

6. If finished pies still have underbaked bottoms, they can be set on a flat-top range for a few minutes. However, exercise extreme care to avoid scorching.

## Procedure for Making a Lattice Top Crust

1. Roll out fresh pie dough (not scraps) ⅛ in. (3 mm) thick.

2. Cut long strips about ⅜ in. (1 cm) wide and long enough to cross the center of the pie.

3. Egg wash the strips and the rim of the filled pie.

4. Place the strips across the pie about 1 in. (2.5 cm) apart. Be sure they are parallel and evenly spaced. Seal them well onto the rim of the pie shell and trim off excess.

5. Place additional strips across the pie at an angle to the first. They may be at a 45-degree angle to make a diamond pattern or at a 90-degree angle to make a checkerboard pattern. Seal and trim excess.

*Note:* Instead of laying the strips across each other, you may interweave them (a, b, c), but this is usually too time-consuming for a bakeshop and generally done only in home kitchens. When you interweave the strips, some juices from the filling are likely to cling to the bottoms of the strips as in the illustration. It is best to remove most of these juices as you go, so that they do not mar the appearance of the crust when baked.

A

B

C

# Procedure for Preparing Baked Pies

*Note:* For pies without a top crust, omit steps 3 to 7.

1. Line pie pans with pie dough as in the basic procedure (a).

2. Fill with *cooled* fillings (b). See the table below for scaling instructions. Do not drop filling on the rims of the pie shells; this will make it harder to seal the rims to the top crusts, and leaking may result during baking.

   To avoid spilling custard fillings in single-crust pies, place the empty shells on the racks in the ovens before pouring in the filling.

3. Roll out dough for the top crusts.

4. Cut perforations in the top crusts to allow steam to escape during baking.

5. Moisten the rim of the bottom crusts with water or egg wash to help seal them to the top crusts.

6. Fit the top crusts in place (c). Seal the edges together firmly and trim excess dough. The rims may be fluted or crimped if desired. Pressing with the tines of a fork is a quick way to seal and crimp the edge (d). An efficient way to trim excess pastry is to rotate the pie tin while pressing on the edges with the palms of the hands.

7. Brush tops with desired wash: milk, cream, egg wash, or melted butter. Sprinkle lightly with granulated sugar, if desired.

   Egg-washed tops have a shiny appearance when baked. Tops brushed with fat, milk, or cream are not shiny but have a home-baked look.

8. Place pies on the lower level of an oven preheated to 425°–450°F (210°–220°C). The high initial heat helps set the bottom crust to avoid soaking. Fruit pies are baked at this high heat until done. For custard pies, reduce heat after 10 minutes to 325°–350°F (165°–175°C) to avoid overcooking and curdling the custard. Custard pies include all those containing large quantities of egg, such as pumpkin pie and pecan pie.

## Scaling Instructions for Baked Pies

| U.S. | | Metric | |
|---|---|---|---|
| Pie size | Weight of filling | Pie size | Weight of filling |
| 8 in. | 26–30 oz | 20 cm | 750–850 g |
| 9 in. | 32–40 oz | 23 cm | 900–1150 g |
| 10 in. | 40–50 oz | 25 cm | 1150–1400 g |

*Note:* Weights are guidelines only. Exact weights may vary, depending on the filling and the depth of the pans. Disposable tins are usually shallower than standard tins.

## Procedure for Preparing Unbaked Pies

1. Line the pie pans with pie dough as in the basic procedure.

2. Dock the crust well with a fork to prevent blistering.

3. Place another pan inside the first one so the dough is between two pans.

4. Place the pans upside down in a preheated oven at 450°F (230°C). Baking upside down helps keep the dough from shrinking down into the pan.

   Some bakers like to chill the crusts at least 20 or 30 minutes before baking to relax the gluten and help reduce shrinkage.

5. Bake at 450°F (230°C) for 10–15 minutes. One pan may be removed during the last part of baking so the crust can brown.

6. Cool the baked crust completely.

7. Fill with cream filling or chiffon filling. Fill as close as possible to service time to prevent soaking the crust.

8. Chill the pie until it is set enough to slice.

9. Most cream pies and chiffon pies are especially good topped with whipped cream. Some cream pies, especially lemon, are popular when topped with meringue and browned (procedure follows).

## Procedure for Making Meringue Pie Topping

1. Make common meringue or Swiss meringue, using 1 pound of sugar per pound of egg whites. Whip until just stiff. See page 267 for procedure.

2. Spread a generous amount of meringue on each pie. Mound it slightly, and be sure to attach it to the edge of the crust all around. If this is not done, the meringue may slide around on the finished pie. Leave the meringue in ripples or peaks.

3. Bake at 400°F (200°C) until the surface is attractively browned. Do not use higher temperatures, which will cause the surface of the meringue to shrink and toughen.

4. Remove from the oven and cool.

# FILLINGS

Most pie fillings require thickeners of some sort. The two most important thickeners for pies are starches and eggs.

## Starches for Fillings

Many kinds of pie filling, especially fruit fillings and cream fillings, depend on starch for their thickness. Some egg-thickened fillings, such as pumpkin, also sometimes contain starch. The starch acts as a stabilizer and may also reduce the cost by allowing for a lower egg content.

**Cornstarch** is used for cream pies because it sets up into a firm gel that holds its shape when sliced. It may also be used for fruit pies.

**Waxy maize** or **modified starches** are best for fruit pies because they are clear when set and make a soft paste rather than a firm gel. Waxy maize should be used for pies that are to be frozen, as this starch is not broken down by freezing.

**Flour, tapioca, potato starch, rice starch,** and other starches are used less frequently for fillings. Flour has less thickening power than other starches and makes fruit fillings cloudy.

**Instant or pregelatinized starch** needs no cooking because it has already been cooked. When used with certain fruit fillings, it eliminates the need to cook the filling before making up the pie. It loses this advantage, however, if the filling is made of raw fruit that must be cooked anyway. In the case of soft fillings such as pumpkin, *instant starch* can be used to eliminate a problem that often occurs with cornstarch: Cornstarch tends to settle out before gelatinizing. This creates a dense, starchy layer on the bottom and improperly thickened filling on top. Instant starches differ in thickening power, so follow the manufacturer's recommendations.

## Cooking Starches

To avoid lumping, starches must be mixed with a cold liquid or with sugar before being added to a hot liquid.

Sugar and strong acids, such as lemon juice, reduce the thickening power of starch. When possible, all or part of the sugar and strong acids should be added *after the starch has thickened.*

# Fruit Fillings

Fruit fillings consist of solid fruit pieces bound together by a gel. The gel consists of fruit juice, water, sugar, spices, and a starch thickener. As we have explained, modified starch such as waxy maize is the preferred thickener for fruit fillings because it makes a clear, not cloudy, gel.

Of course, other starches, such as cornstarch, tapioca, or potato starch, may also be used. Cornstarch is frequently used in food service operations in which baking is only part of the food preparation, making it inconvenient to have on hand all the specialty ingredients found in a bakery.

The functions of the gel are to bind the solid fruit pieces together, to help carry the flavors of the spices and the sweetness of the sugar, and to improve appearance by giving a shine or gloss to the fruit. However, the solid fruit is the most important part of the filling. To have a good-quality pie filling, you should have 2 to 3 pounds of drained fruit for each pound of liquid (juice plus water).

The two basic methods in food service for making pie fillings are the *cooked juice method* and the *cooked fruit method*. In the cooked juice method, the gel is made separately by cooking fruit juice, water, and sugar with a starch. The gel is then mixed with the fruit. In the cooked fruit method, the fruit, water, and juices (if any) are all cooked together and then thickened with a starch.

## Fruits for Pie Fillings

**Fresh fruits** are excellent in pies if they are at their seasonal peak. Fresh apples are used extensively for high-quality pies. The quality of fresh fruits can vary considerably, however, and many fruits require a lot of labor.

**Frozen fruits** are widely used for pies because they are consistent in quality and readily available. Frozen fruits for quantity use are commonly packed with sugar in 30-pound tins. They may be defrosted in the refrigerator for 2 to 3 days, or in a water bath. A third method of thawing is to thaw the fruit just enough to free it from its container, add the water to be used in making it into a pie filling, and heat it to 185° to 195°F (85° to 90°C). Then drain the juice well and make the filling. Whatever method you use, be sure the fruit is completely thawed before preparing the filling. If it is partially frozen, you will not be able to drain the juice properly to make the gel. The frozen, undrained juice will water down the filling later.

Some frozen fruits, especially berries, are packed without sugar. Naturally, the sugar content of any fruit must be taken into account when you are adding sugar to pie fillings.

**Canned fruits** are packed in four basic styles: solid pack, heavy pack, water pack, and syrup pack. *Solid pack* means no water is added, although you will be able to drain off a small quantity of juice. *Heavy pack* means only a small quantity of water or juice is added. *Water pack* fruits are canned with the water that was used to process them. Sour cherries are usually packed this way. *Syrup pack* fruits are packed in a sugar syrup, which may be light, medium, heavy, or extra-heavy. Heavy syrup means there is more sugar in the syrup. In general, fruits packed in heavy syrup are firmer and less broken than fruits in light syrup.

With water-pack and syrup-pack fruits, it is important to know the *drained weight* (the weight of the solid fruit without the juice). This information may be indicated on the label or available from the processor. The *net weight* is the weight of the total contents, including juice or syrup.

If the drained weight of a fruit is very low, you may need to add extra drained fruit to a batch of filling in order to get a good ratio of fruit to gel.

**Dried fruits** must be rehydrated by soaking and, usually, simmering before they are made into pie fillings.

Fruits must have sufficient acid (tartness) to make flavorful fillings. If they lack natural acid, you may need to add some lemon, orange, or pineapple juice to supply the acid.

### Cooked Juice Method

The advantage of this method is that only the juice is cooked. The fruit retains better shape and flavor because it is subjected to less heat and handling. This method is used when the fruit requires little or no cooking before filling the pie.

---

## Procedure—Cooked Juice Method

1. Drain the juice from the fruit.

2. Measure the juice and, if necessary, add water or other fruit juice to bring to the desired volume.

3. Bring the juice to a boil.

4. Dissolve the starch in cold water and stir it into the boiling juice. Return to a boil and cook until clear and thickened.

5. Add sugar, salt, and flavorings. Stir until dissolved.

6. Pour the thickened juice over the drained fruit and mix gently. Be careful not to break or mash the fruit.

7. Cool.

Most canned and frozen fruits are prepared this way. Fresh berries can also be prepared with this method: Part of the berries are cooked or puréed to provide juice, and the remaining berries are then mixed with the finished gel.

## Cooked Fruit Method

This method is used when the fruit requires cooking or when there is not enough liquid for the cooked juice method. Most fresh fruits (except berries) are prepared this way, as are dried fruits such as raisins and dried apricots. Canned fruits should not be prepared by this method because they have already been cooked and are likely to break up or turn to mush.

### Procedure—Cooked Fruit Method

1. Bring the fruit and juice or water to a boil. Some sugar may be added to the fruit to draw out juices.

2. Dissolve the starch in cold water and stir into the fruit. Return to a boil and cook until clear and thickened. Stir while cooking.

3. Add sugar, salt, flavorings, and other ingredients. Stir until dissolved.

4. Cool as quickly as possible.

**Variation**

Some fruits, such as fresh apples, may be cooked in butter, rather than boiled in water, for better flavor.

## Old-Fashioned Method

This method is commonly used for homemade apple pies and peach pies. However, it is not often used in food service operations because of its disadvantages. First, the thickening of the juices is difficult to control. Second, because raw fruit shrinks as it cooks, it is necessary to pile the fruit high in the shell. The fruit then shrinks, often leaving a large air space between the crust and fruit, and the top crust becomes misshapen. The juices given off are more likely to boil over than when the filling is cooked and the juice thickened before filling the pie.

For these reasons, the cooked fruit method usually gives better results than the old-fashioned method. See the Apple Pie formula and variations on page 300.

### Procedure—Old-Fashioned Method

1. Mix the starch and spices with the sugar until uniformly blended.

2. Mix the fruit with the sugar mixture.

3. Fill the unbaked pie shells with the fruit.

4. Place lumps of butter on top of the filling.

5. Cover with a top crust or Streusel (p. 199) and bake.

# APPLE PIE FILLING (CANNED FRUIT)

*Yield: about 9½ lb (4500 g)*

*Five 8-in. (20 cm) pies   Four 9-in. (23 cm) pies   Three 10-in. (25 cm) pies*

| Ingredients | U.S. | | Metric | Procedure |
|---|---|---|---|---|
| Canned apples, solid pack or heavy pack (one No. 10 can) | 6 lb 8 | oz | 3000 g | Use the cooked juice method. |
| Drained juice plus water | 1 pt 8 | fl oz | 750 mL | 1. Drain the apples and save the juice. Add enough water to the juice to measure 1½ pt (750 mL). |
| Water, cold | 8 | fl oz | 250 mL | 2. Mix the cold water and starch. |
| Cornstarch *or* | 3 | oz | 90 g | 3. Bring the juice mixture to a boil. Stir in the starch mixture and return to a boil. |
| Modified starch (waxy maize) | 2.5 | oz | 75 g | 4. Add the remaining ingredients, except the drained apples. Simmer until the sugar is dissolved. |
| Sugar | 1 lb 4 | oz | 570 g | 5. Pour the syrup over the apples and mix gently. Cool completely. |
| Salt | 0.25 | oz | 7 g | 6. Fill the pie shells. Bake at 425°F (220°C), 30–40 minutes. |
| Cinnamon | 0.25 | oz (4¼ tsp) | 7 g | |
| Nutmeg | 0.08 | oz (1 tsp) | 2 g | |
| Butter | 3 | oz | 90 g | |

## VARIATIONS

### DUTCH APPLE PIE FILLING

Simmer 8 oz (250 g) raisins in water. Drain and add to apple pie filling.

### CHERRY PIE FILLING

Use one No. 10 can sour cherries instead of apples and make the following ingredient adjustments:

Increase starch to 4 oz (125 g) cornstarch or 3 oz (90 g) waxy maize.

Increase sugar to 1 lb 12 oz (825 g).

Add 1½ oz (45 mL) lemon juice in step 4.

Omit cinnamon and nutmeg. Add almond extract to taste (optional).

If desired, color with 2 to 3 drops red coloring.

### PEACH PIE FILLING

Use one No. 10 can sliced peaches, preferably solid or heavy pack, instead of apples. Increase liquid in step 1 to 1 qt (1 L). Omit cinnamon and nutmeg.

### PINEAPPLE PIE FILLING

Use one No. 10 can crushed pineapple instead of apples. Gently press the fruit in a sieve to squeeze out the juice. Make the following ingredient adjustments:

Increase the liquid in step 1 to 1 qt (1 L).

Increase the starch to 4 oz (125 g) cornstarch or 3 oz (90 g) waxy maize.

Use 1 lb 8 oz (750 g) sugar and 8 oz (250 g) corn syrup.

Omit the cinnamon and nutmeg.

If desired, color with 2 to 3 drops yellow coloring.

# BLUEBERRY PIE FILLING (FROZEN FRUIT)

*Yield: about 7 lb 8 oz (3375 g)*
*Four 8-in. (20 cm) pies    Three 9-in. (23 cm) pies*

| Ingredients | U.S. | | Metric | Procedure |
|---|---|---|---|---|
| Blueberries, frozen, unsweetened | 5 lb | | 2250 g | Use the cooked juice method. |
| Drained juice plus water | 12 | oz | 375 mL | 1. Thaw the berries in their unopened original container. |
| Sugar | 6 | oz | 175 g | 2. Drain the berries. Add enough water to the juice to measure 12 oz (375 mL). Add the first quantity of sugar. |
| Water, cold | 6 | oz | 190 mL | 3. Mix the cold water and the starch. |
| Cornstarch *or* | 3 | oz | 90 g | 4. Bring the juice mixture to a boil. Stir in the starch mixture. Return to a boil to thicken. |
| Modified starch (waxy maize) | 2.25 | oz | 68 g | 5. Add the remaining ingredients, except the drained berries. Stir over heat until the sugar is dissolved. |
| Sugar | 14 | oz | 412 g | 6. Pour the syrup over the drained berries. Mix gently. Cool completely. |
| Salt | 0.25 | oz | 8 g | 7. Fill pie shells. Bake at 425°F (220°C) about 30 minutes. |
| Cinnamon | 0.12 | oz (2⅛ tsp) | 4 g | |
| Lemon juice | 1.5 | oz | 45 mL | |

## VARIATIONS

### APPLE PIE FILLING

Use 5 lb (2.25 kg) frozen apples instead of blueberries. Make the following ingredient adjustments:

 Reduce the starch to 1.5 oz (45 g) cornstarch or 1.25 oz (38 g) waxy maize.

 Reduce the second quantity of sugar to 8 oz (225 g).

 Add ½ tsp (1 g) nutmeg and 3 oz (87 g) butter in step 5.

### CHERRY PIE FILLING

Use 5 lb (2.25 kg) frozen cherries instead of blueberries. Make the following ingredient adjustments:

 Increase the liquid in step 2 to 1 pt (500 mL).

 Reduce the starch to 2.5 oz (75 g) cornstarch or 2 oz (60 g) waxy maize.

 Reduce the second quantity of sugar to 10 oz (285 g).

 Omit the cinnamon.

 Reduce the lemon juice to 0.75 oz (22 mL).

# RAISIN PIE FILLING

*For large-quantity measurements, see page 730.*
*Yield: about 2 lb/1 kg    One 9-in. (23 cm) pie*

| Ingredients | U.S. | | Metric | | Procedure |
|---|---|---|---|---|---|
| Raisins | 13 | oz | 360 | g | Use the cooked fruit method. |
| Water | 13 | oz | 400 | mL | 1. Combine the raisins and water in a saucepan. Simmer 5 minutes. |
| Water, cold | 2 | oz | 50 | mL | 2. Mix the water and starch. Stir into the raisins and simmer until thickened. |
| Cornstarch *or* | 0.5 | oz | 15 | g | 3. Add the remaining ingredients. Stir until the sugar is dissolved and the mixture is uniform. |
| Modified starch (waxy maize) | 0.4 | oz | 12 | g | 4. Cool thoroughly. |
| Sugar | 4 | oz | 114 | g | 5. Fill the pie shells. Bake at 425°F (220°C), 30–40 minutes. |
| Salt | 0.06 | oz (⅖ tsp) | 2 | g | |
| Lemon juice | 0.6 | oz | 18 | mL | |
| Grated lemon zest | 0.02 | oz (⅛ tsp) | 0.6 | g | |
| Cinnamon | 0.012 | oz (⅛ tsp) | 0.4 | g | |
| Butter | 0.6 | oz | 18 | g | |

# FRESH APPLE PIE FILLING I

*For large-quantity measurements, see page 731.*
Yield: about 2 lb 6 oz (1070 g)   One 9-in. (23 cm) pie

| Ingredients | U.S. | | Metric | | Procedure |
|---|---|---|---|---|---|
| Apples, peeled and sliced | 2 lb | | 900 | g | Use this variation of the cooked fruit method. |
| Butter | 1 | oz | 30 | g | |
| Sugar | 3 | oz | 90 | g | |
| Water, cold | 2 | oz | 60 | g | |
| Cornstarch | 0.75 | oz | 24 | g | |
| or | | | | | |
| Modified starch (waxy maize) | 0.5 | oz | 15 | g | |
| Sugar | 3.5 | oz | 100 | g | |
| Salt | 0.06 oz (⅛ tsp) | | 1 | g | |
| Cinnamon | 0.06 oz (1 tsp) | | 1 | g | |
| Nutmeg | 0.03 oz (¼ tsp) | | 0.5 | g | |
| Lemon juice | 0.33 oz (2 tsp) | | 10 | g | |
| Butter | 0.25 oz | | 7 | g | |

Procedure:

1. Sauté the apples lightly in the first quantity of butter until they are slightly softened. Add the first quantity of sugar as the apples cook. This will draw juices out of the apples, which will then simmer in these juices.
2. Mix the water and starch until smooth. Add the starch mixture to the apples and boil until the liquid is thick and clear.
3. Remove from the heat. Add the remaining ingredients. Stir gently until the sugar is dissolved and the butter is melted.
4. Cool completely.
5. Fill the pie shells. Bake at 425°F (220°C), 30–40 minutes.

## VARIATIONS

### FRESH APPLE PIE FILLING II

*For large-quantity measurements, see page 731.*

| Ingredients | U.S. | Metric |
|---|---|---|
| Water | 3.5 oz | 100 g |

Omit the first quantity of butter. Instead, simmer the apples in water and the first quantity of sugar as in the basic cooked fruit method, using the quantity of water listed above.

### APPLE GINGER PIE FILLING

*For large-quantity measurements, see page 731.*

| Ingredients | U.S. | Metric |
|---|---|---|
| Ground ginger (¼ tsp) | 0.03 oz | 0.5 g |
| Candied ginger, finely chopped | 0.67 oz | 20 g |

Prepare as for Fresh Apple Pie Filling I or II, but omit the cinnamon and instead add ground and candied ginger.

### APPLE PEAR PIE FILLING

Prepare as for Fresh Apple Pie Filling I or II, but substitute slightly firm pears for half the apples.

### APPLE WALNUT PIE FILLING

*For large-quantity measurements, see page 731.*

| Ingredients | U.S. | Metric |
|---|---|---|
| Chopped walnuts | 2.5 oz | 75 g |

Mix walnuts into Fresh Apple Pie Filling I or II.

### RHUBARB PIE FILLING

*For large-quantity measurements, see page 731.*

| Ingredients | U.S. | Metric |
|---|---|---|
| Fresh rhubarb | 1 lb 6 oz | 650 g |

Substitute rhubarb, cut into 1-in. (2.5 cm) pieces, for the apples. Omit the cinnamon, nutmeg, and lemon juice.

## ⁎{ APPLES FOR PIES }⁎

What varieties of apple are best for making pies? Two criteria are important: taste and texture. First, the apples should have a good flavor and a good level of acidity. Apples that are very mild make pies with little flavor. The sugar content, or sweetness, of the apple, is less important, as the sugar in the recipe can be adjusted.

Second, the apples should hold their shape when cooked. Apples that turn to mush, such as MacIntosh, are better for applesauce than for pies.

Popular apple varieties that have good taste and texture for use in pie fillings include Granny Smith, Jonathan, Jonagold, Newton Pippin, Rome, Macoun, Pink Lady, Stayman-Winesap, and Golden Delicious.

# PEACH SOUR CREAM PIE FILLING

*For large-quantity measurements, see page 730.*
*Yield: 2 lb 4 oz (1125 g)   One 9-in. (23 cm) pie*

| Ingredients | U.S. | | Metric | | Procedure |
|---|---|---|---|---|---|
| Sour cream | 8 | oz | 250 | g | 1. Mix the sour cream, sugar, and cornstarch until smooth. |
| Sugar | 4 | oz | 125 | g | 2. Add the eggs, vanilla, and nutmeg and mix in. |
| Cornstarch | 0.5 | oz | 15 | g | 3. Carefully fold the peaches into the sour cream mixture. |
| Eggs, beaten | 2 | | 2 | | 4. Fill unbaked pie shells. |
| Vanilla extract | ½ | tsp | 2 | mL | 5. Top with streusel. |
| Nutmeg | ⅛ | tsp | 0.5 | mL | 6. Bake at 425°F (220°C) about 30 minutes, until the filling |
| Fresh peaches, sliced (see Note) | 1 lb | | 500 | g | is set. |
| Streusel (p. 199) | 6 | oz | 180 | g | |

*Note: If fresh peaches are not available, substitute canned peaches packed in light syrup. Drain them well before weighing.*

**VARIATION**

## PEAR SOUR CREAM PIE

Substitute sliced pears for the sliced peaches.

# OLD-FASHIONED APPLE PIE FILLING

*Yield: about 11 lb (5 kg)*
*Six 8-in. (20 cm) pies   Five 9-in. (23 cm) pies   Four 10-in. (25 cm) pies*

| Ingredients | U.S. | | Metric | | Procedure |
|---|---|---|---|---|---|
| Apples, peeled and sliced | 9 lb | | 4100 g | | Use the old-fashioned method. |
| Lemon juice | 2 | oz | 60 mL | | 1. Select firm, tart apples. Scale after peeling and coring. |
| Sugar | 2 lb | | 900 g | | 2. Combine the apple slices and lemon juice in a large mixing bowl. Toss to coat apples with the juice. |
| Cornstarch | 3 | oz | 90 g | | |
| Salt | 0.25 | oz | 7 g | | 3. Mix together with sugar, cornstarch, salt, and spices. Add to the apples and toss gently until well mixed. |
| Cinnamon | 0.25 | oz | 7 g | | |
| Nutmeg | 0.08 | oz (1 tsp) | 2 g | | 4. Fill the pie shells, packing down the apples well. Dot the tops with pieces of butter before covering with top crusts. Bake at 400°F (200°C) about 45 minutes. |
| Butter | 3 | oz | 90 g | | |

# FRESH STRAWBERRY PIE FILLING

*Yield: about 12 lb (5.5 kg)*

*Six 8-in. (20 cm) pies    Five 9-in. (23 cm) pies    Four 10-in. (25 cm) pies*

| Ingredients | U.S. | | Metric | Procedure |
|---|---|---|---|---|
| Fresh whole strawberries | 9 lb | | 4100 g | Use the cooked juice method. |
| Water, cold | 1 pt | | 500 mL | 1. Hull, wash, and drain the berries. Set aside 7 lb (3.2 kg) berries. These may be left whole, if small, or cut in halves or quarters, if large. |
| Sugar | 1 lb 12 | oz | 800 g | 2. Mash or purée the remaining 2 lb (900 g) berries. Mix |
| Cornstarch *or* | 4 | oz | 120 g | with the water. (If a clear filling is desired, this mixture may be strained.) |
| Modified starch (waxy maize) | 3 | oz | 90 g | 3. Mix together the sugar, starch, and salt. Stir into the berry-and-water mixture until no lumps remain. |
| Salt | 0.17 oz (1 tsp) | | 5 g | 4. Bring to a boil, stirring constantly. Cook until thickened. |
| Lemon juice | 2 | oz | 60 mL | 5. Remove from the heat and stir in the lemon juice. |

6. Cool to room temperature but do not chill.

7. Stir to eliminate lumps. Fold in the reserved berries.

8. Fill baked pie shells and chill (do not bake).

---

## VARIATION

### FRESH BLUEBERRY TART FILLING

Substitute blueberries for the strawberries. This recipe works best with small berries and with cornstarch rather than modified starch. Adjust the sugar as desired, depending on the sweetness of the fruit. Force the cooked, thickened juices through a sieve (cooking the juices before straining gives more color to the gel). Fold the glaze into the berries while it is still hot.

This mixture is more suitable for tarts than for pies. Because pie shells are deeper, the filling may not hold its shape when sliced. One recipe makes enough filling for eight or nine 8-in. (20 cm) tarts, seven or eight 9-in. (23 cm) tarts, or six 10-in. (25 cm) tarts.

---

## Custard or Soft Fillings

Custard, pumpkin, pecan, and similar pies are made with an uncooked liquid filling containing eggs. The eggs coagulate during baking, which sets the filling. For more information on custards, see page 520.

The method for one pie in this section is unusual. Key Lime Pie is similar to other soft pies, except the pie is not baked. Instead, the acidity of the lime juice is sufficient to coagulate the proteins and thicken the pie filling.

Many soft fillings contain starch in addition to eggs. Flour, cornstarch, and instant starch are frequently used. Although starch is unnecessary if enough eggs are used, many bakers prefer to add a little starch because it allows them to reduce the egg content. Also, the use of starch helps bind the liquids and reduce the chance of separating, or weeping, in the baked pie. If starch is used, be sure the mix is well stirred before filling the pies in order to reduce the danger of the starch settling out.

The greatest difficulty in cooking soft pies is cooking the crust completely without overcooking the filling. Start the pie at the bottom of a hot oven (425° to 450°F/220° to 230°C) for the first 10 to 15 minutes in order to set the crust. Then reduce the heat to 325° to 350°F (165° to 175°C) in order to cook the filling slowly. An alternative approach is to *partially* bake the empty shells before filling. See page 294 for baking empty shells (called *baking blind*), but bake until about half cooked. Cool, fill, and bake the pie.

Use one of these methods to test for doneness:

1. Shake the pie very gently. If it is no longer liquid, it is done. The center will still be slightly soft, but its own heat will continue to cook the pie after it is removed from the oven.

2. Insert a thin knife blade an inch from the center. If it comes out clean, the pie is done.

# CUSTARD PIE FILLING

*For large-quantity measurements, see page 730.*
*Yield: 2 lb (0.9 kg)   One 9-in. (23 cm) pie*

| Ingredients | U.S. | | Metric | | Procedure |
|---|---|---|---|---|---|
| Eggs | 8 | oz | 225 | g | 1. Combine the eggs, sugar, salt, and vanilla and blend until smooth. Do not whip air into the mixture. |
| Sugar | 4 | oz | 112 | g | |
| Salt | ¼ | tsp | 1 | g | 2. Stir in the milk. Skim off any foam. |
| Vanilla extract | 0.25 | oz (1½ tsp) | 7.5 | mL | |
| Milk (see *Note*) | 1.25 | pt | 600 | mL | 3. Place the unbaked pie shells in preheated oven (450°F/230°C) and carefully ladle in the filling. Sprinkle tops with nutmeg. |
| Nutmeg | ¼–½ | tsp | 0.5–0.75 | g | |

*Note: For a richer custard, use part milk and part cream.*

4. Bake at 450°F (230°C) for 15 minutes. Reduce heat to 325°F (165°C) and bake until set, about 20–30 minutes more.

**VARIATION**

## COCONUT CUSTARD PIE FILLING

Use 2.5 oz (70 g) unsweetened, flaked coconut. Sprinkle the coconut into the pie shells before adding the custard mixture. The coconut may be lightly toasted in the oven before it is added to the pies. Omit the nutmeg.

# PECAN PIE FILLING

*For large-quantity measurements, see page 731.*
*Yield: 1 lb 12 oz (820 g) filling plus 5 oz (142 g) pecans   One 9-in. (23 cm) pie*

| Ingredients | U.S. | | Metric | | Procedure |
|---|---|---|---|---|---|
| Granulated sugar (see *Note*) | 7 | oz | 200 | g | 1. Using the paddle attachment at low speed, blend the sugar, butter, and salt until evenly blended. |
| Butter | 2 | oz | 60 | g | |
| Salt | ¼ | tsp | 1.5 | g | 2. With the machine running, add the eggs a little at a time until they are all absorbed. |
| Eggs | 7 | oz | 200 | g | |
| Dark corn syrup | 12 | oz | 350 | g | 3. Add the syrup and vanilla. Mix until well blended. |
| | | (about 8½ fl oz) | | | |
| Vanilla extract | 0.25 | oz (1½ tsp) | 8 | g | 4. To assemble pies, distribute the pecans evenly in the pie shells and then fill with the syrup mixture. |
| Pecans | 5 | oz | 142 | g | |

*Note: Brown sugar may be used if a darker color and stronger flavor are desired.*

5. Bake at 425°F (220°C) for 10 minutes. Reduce heat to 350°F (175°C). Bake 30–40 minutes more, until set.

**VARIATION**

## MAPLE WALNUT PIE FILLING

Substitute pure maple syrup for the corn syrup. Substitute coarsely chopped walnuts for the pecans.

# PUMPKIN PIE FILLING

*For large-quantity measurements, see page 731.*
*Yield: about 4.25 lb (2 kg)   Two 9-in. (23 cm) pies*

| Ingredients | U.S. | | Metric | | Procedure |
|---|---|---|---|---|---|
| Pumpkin purée (one No. 2½ can) | 1 lb 10.5 | oz | 750 | g | 1. Place the pumpkin in the bowl of a mixer fitted with the whip attachment. |
| Pastry flour | 1 | oz | 30 | g | 2. Sift together the flour, spices, and salt. |
| Cinnamon | 0.12 | oz | 4 | g | 3. Add the flour mixture and sugar to the pumpkin. Mix at second speed until smooth and well blended. |
| Nutmeg | ¼ | tsp | 1 | mL | |
| Ginger | ¼ | tsp | 1 | mL | 4. Add the eggs and mix in. Scrape down the sides of the bowl. |
| Cloves | ⅛ | tsp | 0.5 | mL | |
| Salt | 0.12 oz (⅝ tsp) | | 4 | g | 5. Turn the machine to low speed. Gradually pour in the syrup, then the milk. Mix until evenly blended. |
| Brown sugar | 10 | oz | 290 | g | |
| Eggs (see *Note*) | 10 | oz | 300 | g | 6. Let the filling stand for 30–60 minutes. |
| Corn syrup or half corn syrup and half molasses | 2 | oz | 60 | g | 7. Stir the filling to remix. Fill the pie shells. Bake at 450°F (230°C) for 15 minutes. Lower the heat to 350°F (175°C) and bake until set, about 30–40 minutes more. |
| Milk | 1 pt 4 | oz | 600 | mL | |

*Note: Pumpkin pie filling should be allowed to stand at least 30 minutes before being poured into the pie shells. This gives the pumpkin time to absorb the liquid and makes a smoother filling that is less likely to separate after baking. If the filling is to stand for much more than 1 hour, do not add the eggs until the pies are to be filled. If the eggs are added earlier, the acidity of the pumpkin and brown sugar may partially coagulate the eggs.*

**VARIATION**

## SWEET POTATO PIE FILLING

Substitute canned sweet potatoes, drained and puréed, for the pumpkin.

## SQUASH PIE FILLING

Substitute puréed squash for the pumpkin.

# KEY LIME PIE FILLING

*For large-quantity measurements, see page 731.*
*Yield: 1 lb 8 oz (750 g)   One 9-in. (23 cm) pie*

| Ingredients | U.S. | Metric | Procedure |
|---|---|---|---|
| Egg yolks, pasteurized | 4 | 4 | 1. Beat the egg yolks lightly, then stir in the sweetened condensed milk. |
| Sweetened condensed milk | 14 oz | 400 g | 2. Add the lime juice and beat until smooth. |
| Freshly squeezed Key lime juice (see *Note*) | 5 oz | 150 g | 3. Pour the filling into a baked pie shell or a graham cracker crumb pie shell. Refrigerate overnight. The acidity of the limes will partially coagulate the egg and milk proteins so the filling becomes firm. |
| | | | 4. Top with whipped cream. |

*Note: If Key limes are not available, substitute regular lime juice. Bottled or frozen Key lime juice is also available.*
*Classic Key lime pie filling is pale yellow in color, not green. However, if desired, tint the filling pale green with a few drops of food color.*

## Cream Pie Fillings

Cream pie fillings are the same as puddings, which in turn are the same as basic pastry cream with added flavorings such as vanilla, chocolate, or coconut. Lemon filling is made by the same method, using water and lemon juice instead of milk.

There is one difference between pastry cream and pie filling you should note: *Cream pie fillings are made with cornstarch, so slices hold their shape when cut.* Pastry cream may be made with flour, cornstarch, or other starches.

The basic principles and procedures for making pastry cream are included in chapter 12. See pages 270–271 to review this information. For your convenience, the formula for vanilla pastry cream is repeated here under the name Vanilla Cream Pie Filling. Popular flavor variations for cream pie fillings follow this basic recipe.

Opinion is divided as to whether pie shells should be filled with warm cream fillings, which are then cooled in the shell, or whether the filling should be cooled first and then added to the shell. For the best-looking slices, warm filling is best. The filling cools to a smooth, uniform mass and the slices hold sharp, clean cuts. However, you must be sure to use a good, mealy pie dough that resists soaking, or you risk having soggy bottom crusts. Enriched Pie Pastry (p. 289) is good for this purpose. Many food service operations prefer to fill each pie shell with cold filling shortly before the pie is to be cut and served. The slice does not cut as cleanly, but the crusts are crisp and you can use flaky dough for them. We use the warm filling method in this book, but you can, of course, modify the procedure to suit your needs.

# VANILLA CREAM PIE FILLING

*For large-quantity measurements, see page 732.*
Yield: about 1⅛ pt (0.5 L) or 13 oz (0.8 kg)    One 9-in. (23 cm) pie

| Ingredients | U.S. | | Metric | Procedure |
|---|---|---|---|---|
| Milk | 1 pt | | 500 g | Before beginning production, review the discussion of pastry cream on page 270. |
| Sugar | 2 | oz | 60 g | |
| Egg yolks | 1.5 | oz | 45 g | 1. In a heavy saucepan or kettle, dissolve the sugar in the milk and bring just to a boil. |
| Whole eggs | 2 | oz | 60 g | |
| Cornstarch | 1.25 | oz | 38 g | 2. With a whip, beat the egg yolks and whole eggs in a stainless-steel bowl. |
| Sugar | 2 | oz | 60 g | |
| Butter | 1 | oz | 30 g | 3. Sift the starch and sugar into the eggs. Beat with the whip until perfectly smooth. |
| Vanilla extract | 0.25 oz (1½ tsp) | | 8 g | |

4. Temper the egg mixture by slowly beating in the hot milk in a thin stream.

5. Return the mixture to the heat and bring it to a boil, stirring constantly.

6. When the mixture comes to a boil and thickens, remove it from the heat.

7. Stir in the butter and vanilla. Mix until the butter is melted and completely blended in.

8. Pour into baked, cooled pie shells. Cool, then keep chilled. Chilled pies may be decorated with whipped cream, using a pastry bag with a star tube.

## VARIATIONS

### COCONUT CREAM PIE FILLING

Add 2 oz (60 g) toasted, unsweetened coconut to the basic filling.

### BANANA CREAM PIE FILLING

Using vanilla cream filling, pour half the filling into pie shells, cover with sliced bananas, and fill with remaining filling. (Bananas may be dipped in lemon juice to prevent browning.)

### CHOCOLATE CREAM PIE FILLING I

*For large-quantity measurements, see page 732.*

| Ingredients | U.S. | Metric |
|---|---|---|
| Unsweetened chocolate | 1 oz | 30 g |
| Sweet chocolate | 1 oz | 30 g |

Melt together the unsweetened and sweet chocolate and mix into the hot vanilla cream filling.

## CHOCOLATE CREAM PIE FILLING II

*For large-quantity measurements, see page 732.*

| Ingredients | U.S. | | Metric |
|---|---|---|---|
| Milk | 14 | oz | 438 mL |
| Sugar | 2 | oz | 60 g |
| Egg yolks | 1.5 | oz | 45 g |
| Whole eggs | 2 | oz | 60 g |
| Cold milk | 2 | oz | 60 g |
| Cornstarch | 1.25 | oz | 38 g |
| Cocoa | 0.75 | oz | 22 g |
| Sugar | 2 | oz | 60 g |
| Butter | 1 | oz | 30 g |
| Vanilla extract | 0.25 | oz | 8 mL |

This variation uses cocoa instead of chocolate. The cocoa is sifted with the starch. Some of the milk must be included with the eggs in order to provide enough liquid to make a paste with the starch and cocoa. Follow the procedure in the basic recipe, but use the above ingredients.

## BUTTERSCOTCH CREAM PIE FILLING

*For large-quantity measurements, see page 732.*

| Ingredients | U.S. | | Metric |
|---|---|---|---|
| Brown sugar | 8 | oz | 250 g |
| Butter | 2.5 | oz | 75 g |

Combine brown sugar and butter in a saucepan. Heat over low heat, stirring, until the butter is melted and the ingredients are blended. Prepare the basic vanilla cream filling recipe, but omit all the sugar and increase the starch to 1½ oz (45 g). As the mixture comes to a boil in step 5, gradually stir in the brown sugar mixture. Finish as in the basic recipe.

## LEMON PIE FILLING

*For large-quantity measurements, see page 732.*

| Ingredients | U.S. | | Metric |
|---|---|---|---|
| Water | 14 | fl oz | 400 mL |
| Sugar | 7 | oz | 200 g |
| Egg yolks | 2.5 | oz | 75 g |
| Cornstarch | 1.5 | oz | 45 g |
| Sugar | 2 | oz | 60 g |
| Salt | 0.025 | oz (⅛ tsp) | 0.5 g |
| Lemon zest, grated | 0.16 | oz (2 tsp) | 5 g |
| Butter | 1 | oz | 30 g |
| Lemon juice | 3 | fl oz | 90 mL |

Follow the procedure for vanilla cream filling, but use the above ingredients. Note that the lemon juice is added after the filling is thickened.

# STRAWBERRY RHUBARB PIE FILLING

*For large-quantity measurements, see page 732.*
Yield: 3 lb 8 oz (1680 g)    Two 9-in. (20 cm) pies

| Ingredients | U.S. | | Metric | Procedure |
|---|---|---|---|---|
| Rhubarb, fresh or frozen, in 1-in. (2.5 cm) pieces | 1 lb 4 | oz | 600 g | 1. Place the rhubarb, sugar, and water in a heavy saucepan. Cover and set over low heat. Bring to a simmer. The sugar will help draw juices out of the rhubarb. Simmer until the rhubarb is soft and the sugar is dissolved. |
| Sugar | 12 | oz | 360 g | 2. Beat the egg yolks with the cream until well mixed. Add the cornstarch and stir until evenly blended. |
| Water | 4 | oz | 120 g | 3. Remove the rhubarb from the heat. Stir in the cream mixture. |
| Egg yolks | 4 | | 4 | 4. Return the rhubarb to the heat and bring to a simmer. Simmer about 1 minute, until thickened. |
| Heavy cream | 4 | oz | 120 g | 5. Pour the rhubarb out into a bowl and mix in the strawberries. Let stand until slightly warm. Mix again to blend the strawberry juices with the filling, then fill the baked pie shells. Chill until firm. |
| Cornstarch | 1.5 | oz | 45 g | |
| Fresh strawberries, hulled and quartered | 1 lb | | 480 g | |

# Chiffon Pie Fillings

Chiffon fillings have a light, fluffy texture created by the addition of beaten egg whites and, sometimes, whipped cream. The egg whites and cream are folded into a cream or fruit base that is stabilized with gelatin. The folding-in of the egg whites and the filling of the baked pie shells must be done before the gelatin sets. After the pie is chilled to set the gelatin, the filling should be firm enough to hold a clean slice.

When chiffon filling contains both egg whites and whipped cream, most chefs and bakers prefer to fold in the egg whites first, even though they may lose some volume. The reason is that if the cream is added first, there is more danger it will be overbeaten and turn to butter during the folding and mixing procedure.

For a review of the guidelines for beating egg whites, see page 266. For the guidelines for whipping cream, see page 264.

For safety, always use pasteurized egg whites.

Bases for chiffons include the following three main types:

1. **Thickened with starch.** The procedure is the same as for fruit pie fillings made by the cooked juice method or cooked fruit method, except the fruit is finely chopped or puréed. Most fruit chiffons are made this way.

2. **Thickened with egg.** The procedure is the same as for Crème Anglaise (p. 269). Chocolate chiffons and pumpkin chiffons are sometimes made this way.

3. **Thickened with egg and starch.** The procedure is the same as for pastry cream or cream pie fillings. Lemon chiffon is usually made this way.

## Procedure for Making Chiffon Fillings

1. Prepare the base (a).

2. Soften gelatin in cold liquid. Stir it into the hot base until dissolved (b). Chill until thickened, but not set.

3. Fold in beaten egg whites (c).

4. Fold in whipped cream, if used (d).

5. Immediately pour into pie shells and chill.

## Guidelines for Using Gelatin

Although some chiffons contain starch as their only stabilizer, most contain gelatin. Gelatin must be handled properly so it is completely dissolved and mixed evenly throughout the filling. All references to gelatin in this book mean unflavored gelatin, not flavored, sweetened gelatin mixes.

In addition to the guidelines below, please refer to chapter 4 for additional information on gelatin. There you will find guidelines for using leaf gelatin as well as powdered gelatin.

1. Measure gelatin accurately. Too much gelatin makes a stiff, rubbery product. Too little makes a soft product that does not hold its shape.

2. Do not mix raw pineapple or papaya with gelatin. These fruits contain enzymes that dissolve gelatin. These fruits may be used if they are cooked or canned.

3. To dissolve unflavored gelatin, stir it into *cold* liquid to avoid lumping. Let it stand for 5 minutes to absorb water. Then heat it until it is dissolved, or combine it with a hot liquid and stir until dissolved.

4. After the gelatin is dissolved in the base, cool or chill it until it is slightly thickened but not set. If the base starts to set, it will be difficult or impossible to fold in the egg whites uniformly.

5. Stir the base occasionally while it is cooling so it cools evenly. Otherwise, the outside edges may start to set before the inside is sufficiently cooled, which creates lumps.

6. If the gelatin sets before you can add the egg whites, warm the base slightly by stirring it over hot water just until the gelatin is melted and there are no lumps. Cool again.

7. When folding in egg whites and whipped cream, work rapidly and without pause, or the gelatin might set before you are finished. Fill the pie shells immediately, before the filling sets.

8. Keep the pies refrigerated, especially in hot weather.

In addition to the following chiffons, you may also use Bavarian creams (p. 532) as pie fillings. Although Bavarian creams contain gelatin and whipped cream, they are not, strictly speaking, chiffons, because they do not contain whipped egg whites. Nevertheless, their texture is similar to that of chiffons because of the lightening effect of the whipped cream.

# STRAWBERRY CHIFFON PIE FILLING

Yield: 6 lb 8 oz (3 kg)

Six 8-in. (20 cm) pies    Five 9-in. (23 cm) pies    Four 10-in. (25 cm) pies

| Ingredients | U.S. | | Metric |
|---|---|---|---|
| Frozen sweet-ened strawberries (see *Note*) | 4 lb | | 1800 g |
| Salt | 0.16 oz (1 tsp) | | 5 g |
| Cornstarch | 1 | oz | 30 g |
| Water, cold | 4 | oz | 120 mL |
| Gelatin | 1 | oz | 30 g |
| Cold water | 8 | oz | 240 mL |
| Lemon juice | 1 | oz | 30 mL |
| Egg whites, pasteurized | 1 lb | | 450 g |
| Sugar | 12 | oz | 350 g |

*Note: To use fresh strawberries, slice or chop 3 lb (1.4 kg) fresh, hulled strawberries and mix with 1 lb (450 g) sugar. Let stand in refrigerator for 2 hours. Drain and reserve juice and proceed as in basic recipe.*

## Procedure

1. Thaw and drain the strawberries. Chop them coarsely.
2. Place the drained juice and salt in a saucepan. Bring to a boil.
3. Dissolve the cornstarch in the water and stir into the juice. Cook until thick. Remove from the heat.
4. Soften the gelatin in the second quantity of water. Add it to the hot, thickened juice and stir until completely dissolved.
5. Stir in the lemon juice and the drained strawberries.
6. Chill the mixture until thickened, but not set.
7. Beat the egg whites until they form soft peaks. Gradually add the sugar and continue to beat until a thick, glossy meringue is formed.
8. Fold the meringue into the fruit mixture.
9. Pour the mixture into baked pie shells. Chill until set.

## VARIATIONS

### STRAWBERRY CREAM CHIFFON PIE FILLING

For a creamier filling, reduce the egg whites to 12 oz (350 g). Whip 1 pt (500 mL) heavy cream and fold it in after the meringue.

### RASPBERRY CHIFFON PIE FILLING

Substitute raspberries for strawberries in the basic recipe.

### PINEAPPLE CHIFFON PIE FILLING

Use 3 lb (1.4 kg) crushed pineapple. Mix the drained juice with an additional 1 pt (500 mL) pineapple juice and add 8 oz (240 g) sugar.

# CHOCOLATE CHIFFON PIE FILLING

Yield: 7 lb (3.2 kg)

Six 8-in. (20 cm) pies    Five 9-in. (23 cm) pies    Four 10-in. (25 cm) pies

| Ingredients | U.S. | | Metric | Procedure |
|---|---|---|---|---|
| Unsweetened chocolate | 10 oz | | 300 g | 1. Combine the chocolate and water in a heavy saucepan. Bring to a boil over moderate heat, stirring constantly until smooth. |
| Water | 1 pt | 8 oz | 750 mL | |
| Egg yolks | 1 lb | | 450 g | 2. With the whip attachment, beat the egg yolks and sugar together until thick and light. |
| Sugar | 1 lb | | 450 g | |
| Gelatin | | 1 oz | 30 g | 3. With the mixer running, gradually pour in the chocolate mixture. |
| Water, cold | | 8 oz | 240 mL | |
| Egg whites, pasteurized | 1 lb | 4 oz | 580 g | 4. Return the mixture to the saucepan and stir over very low heat until thickened. Remove from heat. |
| Sugar | 1 lb | 4 oz | 700 g | 5. Soften the gelatin in the second quantity of water. Add it to the hot chocolate mixture and stir until the gelatin is completely dissolved. |

6. Chill until thick, but not set.

7. Beat the egg whites until they form soft peaks. Gradually beat in the last quantity of sugar. Continue beating until a firm, glossy meringue is formed.

8. Fold the meringue into the chocolate mixture.

9. Pour the mixture into baked pie shells. Chill until set. Keep refrigerated.

**VARIATION**

## CHOCOLATE CREAM CHIFFON PIE FILLING

For a creamier filling, reduce the egg white to 1 lb (450 g). Whip 1 pt (500 mL) heavy cream and fold it in after the meringue.

# PUMPKIN CHIFFON PIE FILLING

*Yield: 7 lb 12 oz (3.4 kg)*

*Six 8-in. (20 cm) pies    Five 9-in. (23 cm) pies    Four 10-in. (25 cm) pies*

| Ingredients | U.S. | | Metric | Procedure |
|---|---|---|---|---|
| Pumpkin purée | 2 lb 8 | oz | 1200 g | 1. Combine the pumpkin, brown sugar, milk, egg yolks, salt, and spices. Mix until smooth and uniform. |
| Brown sugar | 1 lb 4 | oz | 600 g | |
| Milk | 12 | oz | 350 g | 2. Place mixture in a double boiler. Cook, stirring frequently, until thickened, or until the temperature of the mix is 185°F (85°C). Remove from heat. |
| Egg yolks | 12 | oz | 350 g | |
| Salt | 0.17 oz (1 tsp) | | 5 g | |
| Cinnamon | 0.25 oz (4 tsp) | | 7 g | 3. Soften the gelatin in the water. Add it to the hot pumpkin mixture and stir until dissolved. |
| Nutmeg | 0.16 oz (2 tsp) | | 4 g | |
| Ginger | 0.08 oz (1 tsp) | | 2 g | 4. Chill until very thick, but not set. |
| Gelatin | 1 | oz | 30 g | 5. Beat the egg whites until they form soft peaks. Gradually add the sugar and continue to beat until a thick, glossy meringue is formed. |
| Water, cold | 8 | oz | 240 mL | |
| Egg whites, pasteurized | 1 lb | | 450 g | 6. Fold the meringue into the pumpkin mixture. |
| Sugar | 1 lb | | 450 g | 7. Fill baked pie shells with mixture. Chill until set. |

**VARIATION**

### PUMPKIN CREAM CHIFFON PIE FILLING

For a creamier filling, reduce the egg whites to 12 oz (350 g). Whip 1 pt (500 mL) heavy cream and fold it in after the meringue.

# LEMON CHIFFON PIE FILLING

*Yield: 7 lb (3.2 kg)*

*Six 8-in. (20 cm) pies    Five 9-in. (23 cm) pies    Four 10-in. (25 cm) pies*

| Ingredients | U.S. | | Metric | Procedure |
|---|---|---|---|---|
| Water | 1 pt 8 | oz | 750 mL | 1. Dissolve the sugar in the water and bring to a boil. |
| Sugar | 8 | oz | 240 g | |
| Egg yolks | 12 | oz | 350 g | 2. Beat together the egg yolks, second quantity of water, cornstarch, sugar, and zest until smooth. |
| Water, cold | 4 | oz | 120 mL | 3. Gradually beat the boiling syrup into the egg yolk mixture in a thin stream. |
| Cornstarch | 3 | oz | 90 g | |
| Sugar | 8 | oz | 240 g | 4. Return the mixture to the heat and bring it to a boil, beating constantly with a whip. |
| Lemon zest, grated | 0.5 | oz | 15 g | |
| Gelatin | 1 | oz | 30 g | 5. As soon as the mixture thickens and boils, remove it from the heat. |
| Water, cold | 8 | oz | 250 mL | 6. Soften the gelatin in the third quantity of water. |
| Lemon juice | 12 | oz | 350 mL | 7. Add in the gelatin to the hot lemon mixture. Stir until it is dissolved. |
| Egg whites, pasteurized | 1 lb | | 450 g | 8. Stir in the lemon juice. |
| Sugar | 1 lb | | 450 g | 9. Chill it until thick, but not set. |

10. Beat the egg whites until they form soft peaks. Gradually add the sugar and continue to beat until a thick, glossy meringue is formed.

11. Fold the meringue into the lemon mixture.

12. Fill baked pie shells. Chill until set.

### VARIATIONS

## LIME CHIFFON PIE FILLING

Substitute lime juice and zest for the lemon juice and zest.

## ORANGE CHIFFON PIE FILLING

Make the following ingredient adjustments:

Use orange juice instead of water in step 1.

Omit the first 8 oz (240 g) sugar.

Substitute orange zest for the lemon zest.

Reduce the lemon juice to 4 oz (120 mL).

# PIE FAULTS AND THEIR CAUSES

**T**o remedy common pie faults, check the following troubleshooting guide for possible causes and correct your procedures.

| Fault | Causes |
|---|---|
| **CRUST** ||
| Dough too stiff | Not enough shortening |
| | Not enough liquid |
| | Flour too strong |
| Tough | Overmixing |
| | Not enough shortening |
| | Flour too strong |
| | Too much rolling or too much scrap dough used |
| | Too much water |
| Crumbly | Not enough water |
| | Too much shortening |
| | Improper mixing |
| | Flour too weak |
| Not flaky | Not enough shortening |
| | Shortening blended in too much |
| | Overmixing or too much rolling |
| | Dough or ingredients too warm |
| Soggy or raw bottom crust | Oven temperature too low; not enough bottom heat |
| | Filling hot when put in shell |
| | Not baked long enough |
| | Use of wrong dough (use mealy dough for bottom crusts) |
| | Not enough starch in fruit fillings |
| Shrinkage | Dough overworked |
| | Not enough shortening |
| | Flour too strong |
| | Too much water |
| | Dough stretched when put in pans |
| | Dough not rested |
| **FILLING** ||
| Filling boils out | No steam vents in top crust |
| | Top crust not sealed to bottom crust at edges |
| | Oven temperature too low |
| | Fruit too acidic |
| | Filling hot when put in shell |
| | Not enough starch in filling |
| | Too much sugar in filling |
| | Too much filling |
| Curdling of custard or soft fillings | Overbaked |

## TERMS FOR REVIEW

| | | | |
|---|---|---|---|
| flaky pie dough | soft pie | instant starch | heavy pack |
| mealy pie dough | cream pie | cooked juice method | water pack |
| crumb crust | chiffon pie | cooked fruit method | syrup pack |
| fruit pie | lattice crust | solid pack | drained weight |

## QUESTIONS FOR DISCUSSION

1. Discuss the factors that affect tenderness, toughness, and flakiness in pie dough. Why should emulsifier shortening not be used for pie dough?

2. What are some advantages and disadvantages of using butter in pie dough?

3. What would happen to a flaky pie dough if you mixed it too long before adding the water? after adding the water?

4. Describe the difference between mealy pie dough and flaky pie dough.

5. What kind of crust would you use for a pumpkin pie? an apple pie? a banana cream pie?

6. How can you prevent shrinkage when baking empty pie shells?

7. How can you prevent soggy or undercooked bottom piecrusts?

8. What starch would you use to thicken apple pie filling? chocolate cream pie filling? lemon pie filling? peach pie filling?

9. Why is lemon juice added to lemon pie filling after the starch has thickened the water? Wouldn't this thin the filling?

10. Why is the cooked juice method usually used when making pie fillings from canned fruits?

11. What problem might you have if you make blueberry pie filling out of blueberries that are still partially frozen?

12. How can you test a custard pie for doneness?

# 14

# Pastry Basics

The term *pastry* comes from the word *paste*, meaning, in this case, a mixture of flour, liquid, and fat. In the bakeshop, *pastry* refers both to various pastes and doughs and to the many products made from them.

We have already discussed two fundamental types of pastry: yeast-raised pastry, such as Danish dough, in chapters 6 and 9, and pie doughs in chapter 13. Besides these two, the most important types of pastry are short doughs of various types, puff pastry, also known as *pâte feuilletée*, and éclair paste, also known as *pâte à choux*. These three pastries are introduced in this chapter. We also take a look at strudel and phyllo doughs, which are important for some specialty items. Finally, we look at crisp meringues and other meringue-type sponges. These are not pastries in the original sense of the word, because they are not made from a flour paste. Nevertheless, they are used like flour pastries in combination with creams, fillings, fruits, and icings to create a wide range of desserts.

This chapter concentrates on production of the doughs themselves. It is important to master the production techniques for these preparations before applying them to more complicated pastry desserts. Some simple applications of puff paste and éclair paste are included to give you practice handling these doughs. In addition, the section on strudel and phyllo includes examples of pastries made with these doughs. Once you understand the fundamentals, continue to the next chapter, where these doughs are used in specialty pastry work.

**After reading this chapter, you should be able to:**

1. Prepare pâte brisée and short pastries.

2. Prepare puff pastry dough, blitz puff pastry dough, and reversed puff pastry dough, and prepare simple pastries from these doughs.

3. Prepare pâte à choux (éclair paste), and prepare simple pastries from it.

4. Prepare strudel dough, handle commercial phyllo (strudel) dough, and prepare pastries using either homemade or commercial dough.

5. Bake meringue and meringue-type sponges, and assemble simple desserts with these meringues.

# PÂTE BRISÉE AND SHORT PASTRIES

The quality of the pastry used to make tarts and tartlets is perhaps even more important than the quality of pie dough. Because tarts are generally thinner than pies, with less filling, the dough is a prominent part of the finished pastry and not just a holder for the filling, as often seems to be the case with American-style pies. The best of these doughs are made with pure butter, not shortening, and they generally are enriched with eggs and sugar.

This section includes two types of doughs, which differ in their mixing methods. *Pâte brisée* (pronounced pot bree zay; the term means "broken dough") is mixed the same way as mealy pie dough—that is, the fat is first combined with the flour. The amount of mixing determines how flaky the dough is. Review pie dough production (pp. 286–288) if necessary. If you compare the formula for pâte brisée in this chapter with the formula for Enriched Pie Pastry on page 289, you will see they are very similar. Pâte brisée is usually used for large tarts.

The remaining doughs in this section are mixed by the creaming method (see p. 220), in which the fat and sugar are mixed first. This method is also used for cookies and cakes. In fact, these doughs can be used to make plain cookies. Because they are fragile and more difficult to handle than pâte brisée, these doughs are used primarily for small items such as tartlets and petits fours.

## PÂTE BRISÉE

*For large-quantity measurements, see page 733.*

| Ingredients | U.S. | | Metric | % | Procedure |
|---|---|---|---|---|---|
| Pastry flour | 12 | oz | 400 g | 100 | 1. Sift the flour, salt, and sugar into a round-bottomed bowl. |
| Salt | 0.3 | oz (1½ tsp) | 10 g | 2.5 | |
| Sugar | 0.3 | oz (1½ tsp) | 10 g | 2.5 | 2. Cut the butter into small cubes. Rub it into the flour, using the fingertips, until the mixture looks like fine bread crumbs. Make a well in the center. |
| Butter, chilled | 6 | oz | 200 g | 50 | |
| Eggs | 4 | oz | 130 g | 33 | |
| Water | 0.6 | oz (4 tsp) | 20 g | 10 | 3. Mix the eggs, water, vanilla, and lemon zest. Pour the mixture into the well in the flour. Mix to form a soft dough. |
| Vanilla extract | 4 drops | | 4 drops | | |
| Lemon zest, grated | 0.12 | oz (1½ tsp) | 4 g | 1 | |
| *Total weight:* | *1 lb 7* | *oz* | *774 g* | *199%* | 4. Turn out the dough onto a lightly floured work surface. Knead gently just until it is smooth and well mixed. |
| | | | | | 5. Wrap in plastic film and chill for at least 30 minutes before use. |

# PÂTE SABLÉE

*For large-quantity measurements, see page 733.*

| Ingredients | U.S. | | Metric | % | Procedure |
|---|---|---|---|---|---|
| Butter, softened | 6 | oz | 150 g | 67 | 1. Cream together the butter, confectioners' sugar, lemon zest, and vanilla until the mixture is smooth and pale. |
| Confectioner's sugar | 3 | oz | 75 g | 33 | |
| Lemon zest, grated | 0.04 oz (½ tsp) | | 1 g | 0.5 | 2. Add the eggs a little at a time and beat well between each addition. |
| Vanilla extract | 2 drops | | 2 drops | | |
| Eggs, beaten | 1 | oz | 25 g | 11 | 3. Add the flour. With a plastic scraper, carefully blend into a soft dough. |
| Pastry flour | 9 | oz | 225 g | 100 | |
| **Total weight:** | **1 lb 3** | **oz** | **475 g** | **211%** | 4. Wrap in plastic film and flatten out. Chill until firm before use. |

**VARIATION**

## CHOCOLATE PÂTE SABLÉE

*For large-quantity measurements, see page 733.*

| Ingredients | U.S. | | Metric | % |
|---|---|---|---|---|
| Butter | 6 | oz | 150 g | 86 |
| Confectioners' sugar | 3 | oz | 75 g | 43 |
| Grated orange zest | 0.08 oz (1 tsp) | | 2 g | 0.2 |
| Eggs, beaten | 2 | oz | 50 g | 28 |
| Pastry flour | 7 | oz | 175 g | 100 |
| Cocoa powder | 1 | oz | 30 g | 17 |

Substitute the above ingredients and follow the basic procedure. Sift the flour with the cocoa.

# PÂTE SUCRÉE

*For large-quantity measurements, see page 733.*

| Ingredients | U.S. | | Metric | % | Procedure |
|---|---|---|---|---|---|
| Butter, softened | 7.5 | oz | 250 g | 62.5 | 1. Cream together the butter, confectioners' sugar, salt, lemon zest, and vanilla until the mixture is smooth and pale. |
| Confectioner's sugar | 3 | oz | 100 g | 25 | |
| Salt | 0.06 oz (⅓ tsp) | | 2 g | 0.5 | 2. Add the eggs a little at a time and beat well between each addition. |
| Lemon zest, grated | 0.06 oz (¾ tsp) | | 2 g | 0.5 | |
| Vanilla extract | 4 drops | | 4 drops | | 3. Add the flour. With a plastic scraper, carefully blend into a soft dough. |
| Eggs, beaten | 3 | oz | 100 g | 25 | |
| Pastry flour | 12 | oz | 400 g | 100 | 4. Wrap in plastic film and flatten out. Chill until firm before use. |
| **Total weight:** | **1 lb 9** | **oz** | **854 g** | **213%** | |

# SHORT DOUGH I

*For large-quantity measurements, see page 733.*

| Ingredients | U.S. | | Metric | % | Procedure |
|---|---|---|---|---|---|
| Butter or butter and shortening | 8 | oz | 250 g | 67 | 1. Using the paddle attachment, mix the butter, sugar, and salt at low speed until smooth and evenly blended. |
| Sugar | 3 | oz | 90 g | 25 | 2. Add the eggs and mix just until absorbed. |
| Salt | 0.06 oz (¼ tsp) | | 2 g | 0.5 | |
| Eggs | 2.25 oz | | 70 g | 19 | 3. Sift the flour and add it to the mixture. Mix just until evenly blended. |
| Pastry flour | 12 | oz | 375 g | 100 | 4. Chill several hours before using. |
| **Total weight:** | **1 lb  9** | **oz** | **787 g** | **211%** | |

# ALMOND SHORT DOUGH

*For large-quantity measurements, see page 733.*

| Ingredients | U.S. | | Metric | | % | Procedure |
|---|---|---|---|---|---|---|
| Butter | 8 | oz | 200 | g | 80 | 1. Using the paddle attachment, blend the butter, sugar, and salt at low speed until smooth and well mixed. Do not cream until light. |
| Sugar | 6 | oz | 150 | g | 60 | |
| Salt | 0.1 oz (½ tsp) | | 2.5 | g | 1 | 2. Add the almonds and blend in. |
| Powdered almonds | 5 | oz | 125 | g | 50 | 3. Add the eggs and vanilla. Mix just until absorbed. |
| Eggs | 1.6 oz | | 42 | g | 16.5 | 4. Sift the flour and add it to the mixture. Mix just until evenly blended. |
| Vanilla extract | ¼ | tsp | 1.25 | g | 0.5 | |
| Pastry flour | 10 | oz | 250 | g | 100 | 5. Chill several hours before using. |
| **Total weight:** | **1 lb 14** | **oz** | **770** | **g** | **308%** | |

### VARIATIONS

## LINZER DOUGH I

*For large-quantity measurements, see page 733.*

| Ingredients | U.S. | Metric | % |
|---|---|---|---|
| Cinnamon | 0.06 oz (1⅛ tsp) | 1.5 g | 0.6 |
| Nutmeg | 0.01 oz (⅛ tsp) | 0.25 g | 0.1 |

Use ground hazelnuts, ground almonds, or a mixture of the two. Mix in the cinnamon and nutmeg with the salt in the first step.

## LINZER DOUGH II

Prepare as for Linzer Dough I but, instead of the raw egg yolks, use finely sieved hard-cooked egg yolks.

# SHORT DOUGH II

*For large-quantity measurements, see page 734.*

| Ingredients | U.S. | | Metric | % | Procedure |
|---|---|---|---|---|---|
| Butter | 5 | oz | 150 g | 60 | 1. Using the paddle attachment, mix the butter, sugar, salt, vanilla powder, and almonds. |
| Sugar | 3.5 | oz | 100 g | 40 | |
| Salt | 0.07 oz (⅓ tsp) | | 2 g | 0.8 | 2. Add the eggs and flour. Mix until just combined. |
| Vanilla powder | 0.07 oz | | 2 g | 0.8 | |
| Powdered almonds | 1 | oz | 30 g | 12 | 3. Chill several hours before using. |
| Eggs | 1.75 oz | | 50 g | 22 | |
| Pastry flour | 8 | oz | 250 g | 100 | |
| **Total weight:** | **1 lb 3** | **oz** | **584 g** | **213%** | |

# PUFF PASTRY

**P**uff pastry is one of the most remarkable products of the bakeshop. Although it includes no added leavening agent, it can rise to 8 times its original thickness when baked.

*Puff pastry* is a laminated or rolled-in dough, like Danish and croissant doughs. This means it is made up of many layers of fat sandwiched between layers of dough. Unlike Danish dough, however, puff pastry contains no yeast. Steam, created when the moisture in the dough is heated, is responsible for the spectacular rising power of puff pastry. (See page 112 for a general discussion of laminated doughs.)

Because puff pastry or puff dough consists of over 1000 layers, many more than in Danish dough, the rolling-in procedure requires a great deal of time and care.

As with so many other products, there are nearly as many versions of puff pastry as there are bakers. Both formulas and rolling-in techniques vary. The formula provided here contains no eggs, for example, although some bakers add them.

Two methods for enclosing the butter and two rolling-in methods are illustrated.

Butter is the preferred fat for rolling in because of its flavor and melt-in-the-mouth quality. Special puff pastry shortening is also available. This shortening is easier to work because it is not as hard when refrigerated and because it doesn't soften and melt at warm temperatures as easily as butter does. It is also less expensive than butter. However, it can be unpleasant to eat because it tends to congeal and coat the inside of the mouth.

The quantity of rolled-in fat may vary from 50 to 100% of the weight of the flour, or 8 ounces to 1 pound of fat per pound of flour. If the lower quantity of fat is used, the dough should be left slightly thicker when rolled out. Puff pastry that is low in fat will not rise as high and may rise unevenly. This is because there is less fat between the dough layers, so the layers are more likely to stick together.

The illustrations in this section show in detail the procedures for mixing the dough, enclosing the butter, and rolling. The procedure below shows one complete method for making puff pastry using the *four-fold* method for rolling in. An alternative method for enclosing the butter in the dough is illustrated next. Finally, the *three-fold* method is shown as an alternative rolling-in procedure.

Formulas for *blitz puff pastry* and *reversed puff pastry* are also included. Blitz puff pastry is actually a very flaky pie dough that is rolled and folded like puff pastry. It is easier and quicker to make than classic puff dough (*blitz* is the German word for "lightning"). It does not rise as high as true puff pastry and its texture is not as fine, so it is not suitable for products in which a high, light pastry is desirable. However, it bakes up crisp and flaky and is perfectly suitable for *napoleons* and similar desserts that are layered with cream fillings.

Reversed puff pastry is somewhat unusual and rather difficult to work with. As the name suggests, the butter and dough are reversed—that is, the butter (which has flour mixed into it) encloses the dough rather than the dough enclosing the butter. Although it is more difficult to prepare, it can be made up and baked without a final rest, as it shrinks less than classic puff pastry.

# Procedure for Making Puff Pastry Dough

**1.** Make a well in the mound of flour and add the liquids.

**2.** Work the ingredients into a dough.

**3.** Knead the dough until it is smooth. Refrigerate for 30 minutes. Then roll it out into a large rectangle.

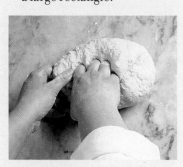

**4.** To prepare the butter, first soften it by beating it with a rolling pin.

**5.** Square off the butter. Roll it into a smooth rectangle two-thirds the size of the dough rectangle.

**6.** Place the butter on the dough so it covers the bottom two-thirds of the rectangle.

**7.** Fold down the top, unbuttered third of the dough so it covers half the butter.

**8.** Fold the bottom third over the center. The butter is now enclosed.

**9.** To give the dough its first four-fold, roll the dough into a long rectangle. Before rolling, beat the dough lightly as shown so that the butter is evenly distributed.

10. Before folding, always brush off excess dusting flour.

11. Fold down the top edge of the dough to the center.

12. Fold up the bottom edge to the center.

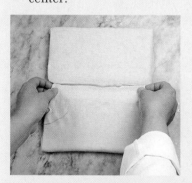

13. Fold in half to achieve the finished four-fold.

### Alternative Method: Rolling-in Procedure

1. Fold the dough rectangle in thirds, as for making Danish Pastry (p. 195).

2. Square off the finished three-fold with the rolling pin.

### Alternative Method: Enclosing the Butter in Puff Pastry

1. Roll the dough into a blunt cross shape as shown, leaving the center thicker than the arms of the cross.

2. Place the square of butter in the center. Fold one of the arms of dough over the butter to cover it.

3. Fold the remaining three arms of dough over the center.

# CLASSIC PUFF PASTRY
# (PÂTE FEUILLETÉE CLASSIQUE)

*For large-quantity measurements, see page 734.*

| Ingredients | U.S. | | Metric | % | Procedure |
|---|---|---|---|---|---|
| Bread flour | 1 lb | | 500 g | 100 | **MIXING** |
| Salt | 0.33 oz | | 10 g | 2 | 1. Mix the flour and the salt. Place the flour in a mound on a work surface and make a well in the center. |
| Butter, melted | 2.5 oz | | 75 g | 15 | |
| Water | 8 oz | | 250 g | 50 | |
| Butter, for rolling in | 9.5 oz | | 300 g | 60 | 2. Pour the melted butter and water into the center of the well. Gradually stir from the inside outward to incorporate the flour into the liquids, making a dough. |
| **Total weight:** | **2 lb 4 oz** | | **1135 g** | **227%** | |

3. Once the dough has formed, knead briefly, just until it is smooth. Do not overwork or the dough will become too elastic and difficult to work. Gather the dough into a smooth ball.

4. Decide which method for enclosing the butter (below) you will use. If method 1, wrap in plastic and refrigerate for 30 minutes. If method 2, cut a cross in the top of the dough and wrap in plastic film. Allow to rest for 30 minutes in the refrigerator.

**ENCLOSING THE BUTTER, METHOD 1**

1. Roll out the dough into a large rectangle.

2. Place the butter between 2 sheets of plastic film. Soften it and flatten it by beating it with a rolling pin. Set aside while the dough is rolled out.

3. Keeping the butter between the plastic sheets, roll it out and square the edges using the rolling pin to make a rectangle about two-thirds the size of the dough rectangle.

4. Remove the plastic from the rectangle of butter and place it on the bottom two-thirds of the dough rectangle. Fold the top third of the dough down over the center to cover half the butter. Fold the bottom one-third over the center. The butter is now enclosed in the dough, making 2 layers of butter between 3 layers of dough.

5. Give the dough 4 *four-folds*. This will give the dough 1028 layers of dough and butter. Rest the dough in a cool place between folds to allow the gluten to relax.

   Alternatively, give the dough 5 *three-folds*, making a total of 883 layers. (If you wish, you can double this number of layers by simply rolling and folding the dough in half after the last three-fold. This is preferable to giving the dough a sixth three-fold—for over 2400 layers—because the dough may not rise properly when the layers become this thin.)

**ENCLOSING THE BUTTER, METHOD 2**

1. With the rolling pin, spread open the four quarters of the dough made by cutting the cross and roll out the dough in the shape of a large, thick cross. Keep the dough thicker in the center than in the four arms of the cross.

2. Place the butter between 2 sheets of parchment or plastic film. Flatten it and soften it slightly by beating it lightly with a rolling pin. Then roll it out into a square about ¾ in. (2 cm) thick. The size of the square of butter should be smaller than the center section of dough so the butter will not overlap the edges of the dough in step 3.

3. Place the square of butter in the center of the dough cross. Fold the four arms of the dough over the butter to enclose it completely, as in an envelope.

4. Give the dough 6 *three-folds*. Rest the dough in a cool place between folds to allow the gluten to relax. This will give the dough 1459 layers of dough and butter.

# ORDINARY PUFF PASTRY

*For large-quantity measurements, see page 734.*

| Ingredients | U.S. | | Metric | % | Procedure |
|---|---|---|---|---|---|
| | | | | | **MIXING** |
| Bread flour | 12 | oz | 375 g | 75 | |
| Cake flour | 4 | oz | 125 g | 25 | 1. Place the first quantities of flour and butter in a mixing bowl. With the paddle attachment, mix at low speed until well blended. |
| Butter, softened | 2 | oz | 60 g | 12.5 | |
| Salt | 0.25 | oz | 8 g | 1.5 | 2. Dissolve the salt in the cold water. |
| Water, cold | 9 | | 282 g | 56 | 3. Add the salted water to the flour mixture and mix at low speed until a soft dough is formed. Do not overmix. |
| Butter | 1 lb | | 500 g | 100 | |
| Bread flour (see Note) | 2 | oz | 60 g | 12.5 | 4. Remove the dough from the mixer and let it rest in the refrigerator or retarder for 20 minutes. |
| **Total weight:** | **2 lb 13** | **oz** | **1410 g** | **282%** | |

*Note: The purpose of the second quantity of bread flour is to absorb some of the moisture of the butter and help make the dough more manageable. Omit this flour if shop temperature is cool or if puff paste shortening is used instead of butter.*

5. Blend the last quantities of butter and flour at low speed in the mixer until the mixture is the same consistency as the dough, neither too soft nor too hard.

6. Roll the butter into the dough following the procedure shown on pages 322–323. Give the dough 4 four-folds or 5 three-folds.

**VARIATION**

The butter for rolling in may be reduced to 75% or even to as little as 50%. If the butter is reduced, you should also reduce the last quantity of flour (for mixing with the butter) in the same proportion, so it is one-eighth the weight of the butter.

# BLITZ PUFF PASTRY

| Ingredients | U.S. | | Metric | % | Procedure |
|---|---|---|---|---|---|
| Bread flour | 8 | oz | 250 g | 50 | 1. Sift the two flours together into a mixing bowl. |
| Pastry flour | 8 | oz | 250 g | 50 | |
| Butter, slightly softened | 1 lb | | 500 g | 100 | 2. Cut the butter into the flour as for pie dough, but leave the fat in very large lumps, 1 in. (2.5 cm) across. |
| Salt | 0.25 | oz | 8 g | 1.5 | 3. Dissolve the salt in the water. |
| Water, cold | 8 | | 250 g | 50 | 4. Add the salted water to the flour/butter mixture. Mix until the water is absorbed. |
| **Total weight:** | **2 lb 8** | **oz** | **1258 g** | **251%** | |

5. Let the dough rest 15 minutes. Refrigerate it if the bakeshop is warm.

6. Dust the bench with flour and roll out the dough into a rectangle. Give the dough 3 four-folds.

**VARIATION**

Reduce the butter to 75% (12 oz/375 g).

# REVERSED PUFF PASTRY (PÂTE FEUILLETÉE INVERSÉE)

| Ingredients | U.S. | Metric | % | Procedure |
|---|---|---|---|---|
| Butter | 1 lb  4 oz | 500 g | 100 | 1. Combine the first quantities of butter and flour in a mixing bowl and mix together, either by hand or with the paddle attachment of a mixer, until completely blended. |
| Bread flour | 10 oz | 250 g | 50 | |
| Bread flour | 1 lb  4 oz | 500 g | 100 | 2. Roll the butter mixture between 2 sheets of parchment paper to make a large rectangle ¾ in. (2 cm) thick. Refrigerate for 30 minutes. |
| Salt | 1 oz | 25 g | 5 | |
| Water | 11 oz | 270 g | 54 | |
| Butter, melted | 7 oz | 175 g | 35 | |
| *Total weight:* | *4 lb  5 oz* | *1720 g* | *344%* | |

3. Mix the remaining ingredients into a dough using the procedure described in steps 1 and 2 of the formula for Classic Puff Pastry. Wrap and refrigerate for 30 minutes.

4. Roll out the dough to make a rectangle half the size of the butter rectangle.

5. Place the dough on the top half of the butter rectangle. Fold the butter over it to enclose completely, using the parchment to lift the butter.

6. Chill for 30 minutes.

7. Give the dough *5 three-folds*. Be sure to dust the work surface well with flour so the butter does not stick.

# Guidelines for Makeup and Baking of Puff Dough Products

1. The dough should be cool and firm when it is rolled and cut. If it is too soft, layers may stick together at the cuts, preventing proper rising.

2. Cut straight down with firm, even cuts. Use a sharp cutting tool.

3. Avoid touching the cut edges with your fingers, or the layers may stick together.

4. For best rising, place units upside down on baking sheets. Even sharp cutting tools may press the top layers of dough together. Baking upside down puts the stuck-together layers at the bottom.

5. Avoid letting egg wash run down the edges. Egg wash can cause the layers to stick together at the edges.

6. Rest made-up products for 30 minutes or more in a cool place or in the refrigerator before baking. This relaxes the gluten and reduces shrinkage.

7. Trimmings may be pressed together, keeping the layers in the same direction. After being rolled out and given a three-fold, they may be used again, although they will not rise as high.

8. Baking temperatures of 400° to 425°F (200° to 220°C) are best for most puff dough products. Cooler temperatures will not create enough steam

in the products to leaven them well. Higher temperatures will set the crust too quickly.

9. Larger products such as Pithiviers (p. 369) are harder to bake through than the small ones. To avoid underbaked, soggy interiors, start large items at a high temperature and bake until they are well risen. Then turn the temperature down to about 350°F (175°C) and finish baking until crisp.

## Puff Pastry Desserts

The following recipes include instructions for simple puff pastry products, including petits fours. If any of your products do not turn out well, consult the troubleshooting guide in the table below.

### Puff Pastry Faults and Their Causes

| Faults | Possible Causes |
|---|---|
| Shrinkage during baking | Dough not relaxed before baking |
| Poor lift or rising | Too little or too much fat used<br>Dough rolled out too thin or given too many turns<br>Oven too hot or too cold |
| Uneven lift or irregular shapes | Improper rolling-in procedure<br>Uneven distribution of fat before rolling<br>Dough not relaxed before baking<br>Uneven heat in oven |
| Fat running out during baking | Too much fat used<br>Not enough turns given<br>Oven too cool<br>(Note: Some fat running out is normal, but it should not be excessive.) |

## PINWHEELS

| Components | Procedure |
|---|---|
| Puff pastry dough<br>Egg wash<br>Fruit filling | 1. Roll out the puff pastry dough ⅛ in. (3 mm) thick.<br>2. Cut into squares 5 in. (12 cm) per side or to other size as desired.<br>3. Cut diagonally from the corners to about 2 in. (5 cm) from the center. Brush the pastry with egg wash.<br>4. Fold every other corner to the center and press into place, as for making Danish pinwheels (p. 212).<br>5. Brush with egg wash a second time.<br>6. Select a thick filling that will not run when baked (see step 9). Place a spoonful of the filling in the center of each pinwheel.<br>7. Bake at 400°F (200°C) until puffed and golden.<br>8. Cool. Dust with confectioners' sugar.<br>9. Pinwheels may also be filled after, instead of before, baking. This method is used for fillings that might run or burn when baked. |

# PATTY SHELLS

| Components | Procedure |
| --- | --- |
| Puff pastry dough<br>Egg wash | 1. Roll out puff pastry dough ⅛ in. (3 mm) thick.<br>2. Roll out a second piece of dough ¼ in. (6 mm) thick.<br>3. Cut the same number of circles from each piece of dough with a round 3-in. (7.5 cm) cutter.<br>4. With a 2-in. (5 cm) cutter, cut out the centers of the *thick* circles. |

5. Wash the thin circles with water or egg wash and place one of the rings on top of each. Wash the top carefully with egg wash (do not drip wash down the edges). Let them rest 30 minutes.
6. Place a sheet of greased parchment over the tops of the shells to prevent their toppling over while baking.
7. Bake at 400°F (200°C) until brown and crisp.

# TURNOVERS

| Components | Procedure |
| --- | --- |
| Puff pastry dough<br>Fruit filling<br>Egg wash<br>*or*<br>Milk or water and granulated sugar | 1. Roll puff pastry dough ⅛ in. (3 mm) thick.<br>2. Cut into 4-in. (10 cm) squares. Wash the edges of each with water.<br>3. Place a portion of the desired filling into the center of each square.<br>4. Fold the squares diagonally and press the edges together. With a knife, puncture the tops in 2 or 3 places to allow steam to escape. Let them rest 30 minutes.<br>5. Brush the tops with egg wash, if desired, or brush with milk or water and sprinkle with sugar.<br>6. Bake at 400°F (200°C) until crisp and brown. |

---

## ⁑{ NAPOLEONS }⁑

What does the layered puff pastry dessert have to do with the French emperor Napoleon? Actually, nothing. The name comes from the French adjective *napolitain*, meaning "pertaining to the Italian city of Napoli," or, as it is known in English, Naples. The pastry was thought to have originated there, and it has no connection with the emperor Napoleon. A better English name for it would be Neapolitan.

In fact, the dessert may have been the invention of Carême (p. 7) rather than of pastry cooks in Naples. Perhaps he was making a dessert in what he considered to be the style of Naples.

In French, the dessert is not called napoleon but *mille-feuille*, meaning "thousand leaves." Italians don't call it *napoleon*, either, but *mille foglie*, also meaning "thousand leaves."

# CREAM HORNS

| Components | Procedure |
|---|---|
| Puff pastry dough<br>Granulated sugar<br>Whipped cream<br>*or* Pastry Cream<br>(p. 271)<br>Confectioners'<br>sugar | 1. Roll out puff pastry dough ⅛ in. (3 mm) thick and about 15 in. (38 cm) wide.<br><br>2. Cut out strips 1¼ in. (3 cm) wide by 15 in. (38 cm) long.<br><br>3. Wash the strips with water.<br><br>4. Press one end of a strip, with the washed side facing outward, onto one end of a cream horn tube (a). If you are using conical tubes, start at the small end.<br><br>5. Roll the strip diagonally in a spiral by turning the tube (b). Overlap the edges by ⅜ in. (1 cm). Do not stretch the dough.<br><br>6. Roll up completely and press the end in place to seal (c).<br><br>7. Roll the horns in granulated sugar and lay them on baking sheets. The end of the dough strip should be on the bottom so it will not pop up during baking.<br><br>8. Bake at 400°F (200°C) until brown and crisp.<br><br>9. Slip out the tubes while still warm.<br><br>10. Just before service, fill the horns from both ends with whipped cream or pastry cream, using a pastry bag with a star tip. Dust with confectioners' sugar. |

# NAPOLEONS

| Components | Procedure |
|---|---|
| Puff pastry dough<br>Pastry Cream<br>(p. 271) or<br>mixture of pastry<br>cream and<br>whipped cream<br>Fondant (p. 422)<br>Chocolate Fondant<br>(p. 423) | 1. Roll puff pastry dough into a very thin sheet about the size of a sheet pan. Blitz puff paste or rerolled trimmings may be used.<br><br>2. Place on a sheet pan and let rest 30 minutes, preferably in the refrigerator.<br><br>3. Dock with a fork to prevent blistering.<br><br>4. Bake at 400°F (200°C) until brown and crisp.<br><br>5. Trim the edges of the pastry sheet and cut with a serrated knife into equal strips 3–4 in. (7.5–10 cm) wide. Set the best strip aside for the top layer. If one of the strips breaks, it can be used as the middle layer.<br><br>6. Spread one rectangle with pastry cream or with a mixture of pastry cream and whipped cream.<br><br>7. Top with a second sheet of pastry.<br><br>8. Spread with another layer of pastry cream.<br><br>9. Place third pastry rectangle on top, with the flattest side up.<br><br>10. Ice the top with the fondant (see p. 422).<br><br>11. To decorate, pipe 4 strips of chocolate fondant lengthwise on the white fondant. Draw a spatula or the back of a knife across the top in opposite directions to feather the design.<br><br>12. Cut into strips 1½–2 in. (4–5 cm) wide. |

# BAKED APPLE DUMPLINGS

| Components | Procedure |
|---|---|
| Small, tart baking apples<br>Puff pastry dough<br>Cake crumbs *(optional)*<br>Cinnamon Sugar (p. 199)<br>Raisins<br>Egg wash | 1. Peel and core as many apples as desired.<br><br>2. Roll out puff pastry dough to ⅛ in. (3 mm) thick. Cut out squares large enough to cover an apple completely when the points of the square are overlapped at the top of the apple. The dough must not be stretched over the apple or it will pull away during baking. *Caution:* Cut out one square and test it to be sure it is large enough to cover the apple. Then cut out the remaining squares.<br><br>3. If the dough becomes soft, refrigerate it for 15 to 30 minutes before continuing.<br><br>4. Place a teaspoonful of cake crumbs in the center of each pastry square. Then place an apple on top of the crumbs. (The crumbs are optional, but they help absorb the juice of the apple.)<br><br>5. Fill the center of the apples (where the cores used to be) with cinnamon sugar and raisins. Taste a small piece of apple for tartness to help you judge how much sugar to use.<br><br>6. Brush the edges of the dough with water or egg wash. Draw up the four corners of the dough and overlap them at the top of the apple. Press the corners together to seal. Pinch the edges of the dough together to seal the seams.<br><br>7. Cut out 1-in. (2.5 cm) circles of dough. Moisten the top of each apple with egg wash and cap with a circle of dough. This covers the overlapping corners and makes the product more attractive.<br><br>8. Arrange the apples on parchment-lined pans. Brush with egg wash.<br><br>9. Bake at 400°F (200°C) until the pastry is browned and the apples are cooked through but not too soft (or they will sag and flatten out). This will take 45 to 60 minutes, depending on the apples. Test for doneness by piercing one of the apples with a thin skewer. If the pastry browns too fast, cover lightly with a sheet of parchment or foil. |

## Fruit Tarts

Puff pastry may be used instead of short dough to make fruit tarts. Fruit strips are fruit tarts made in the shape of long strips about 4 to 5 inches (10 to 12 cm) wide.

The procedure for assembling these desserts is the same as that for unbaked fruit tarts described in chapter 15 (p. 358), except baked puff pastry should be assembled only at the last minute because the pastry quickly becomes soggy.

The shells can be made in any shape, but squares and rectangles are easiest, as in this procedure.

## ❊❴ PETITS FOURS ❵❊

The term *petit four*, French for "small oven," can be used for any small cake, pastry, or cookie that can be eaten in one or two bites. Petits fours are discussed in more detail on pages 479–480 and 491. The name may derive from the fact that, in the days of wood-fired brick ovens, petits fours were baked when the oven was cooling down, after the main baking of the day was finished.

For a long time, people in North America thought of petits fours only as small pieces of delicate layer cake individually iced in fondant. (Many of these cakes found in American bakeshops are not very "petit.") However, as many more restaurants have adopted the practice of serving a small tray or plate of tiny chocolates and petits fours of many types after dessert, Americans have become more familiar with the broader meaning of the term.

# FRUIT TARTS

| Components | Procedure |
|---|---|
| Puff pastry dough<br>Egg wash<br>Pastry Cream (p. 271)<br>Fruit, as desired<br>Apricot Glaze (p. 200)<br>  or other glaze | 1. Roll out the puff pastry dough ⅛ in. (3 mm) thick.<br><br>2. Cut out squares or rectangles of desired size.<br><br>3. With the remaining dough, cut strips about ¾ in. (2 cm) wide and long enough to make borders for the tarts.<br><br>4. Brush the rims of the dough squares with water or egg wash. Lay the strips in place on the moistened edges to make borders. Egg wash the tops of the borders.<br><br>5. With a fork, knife tip, or roller docker, dock the inside of the shell (not the borders) to prevent blistering.<br><br>6. Rest in the refrigerator 30 minutes before baking.<br><br>7. Bake at 400°F (200°C) until browned and crisp. Cool.<br><br>8. Fill with a thin layer of pastry cream, arrange fruit on top, and brush with apricot glaze. See page 358 for the detailed procedure for filling fruit tarts. |

**VARIATION**

### FRUIT STRIPS

Follow the above procedure, but make the rectangles 4–5 in. (10–12 cm) wide and as long as your sheet pans. Put borders on the two long sides, but leave the ends open.

## Puff Pastry Petits Fours

# CHAUSSONS

| Components | Procedure |
|---|---|
| Puff pastry dough<br>Egg wash<br>Apple Compote<br>  (p. 202) | 1. Roll out puff pastry dough to less than ⅛ in. (2 mm) thick. Place on a sheet pan lined with parchment paper. Chill for 30 minutes.<br><br>2. With a 2½-in. (6 cm) round cutter, cut out circles of dough.<br><br>3. Brush the edges with egg wash.<br><br>4. Spoon about ½ tsp (2–3 mL) apple compote onto the center of each circle.<br><br>5. Fold over to make a half-moon shape. Seal the edges by pressing with the reverse edge (the dull edge) of the round cutter.<br><br>6. Brush with egg wash. Score the tops lightly with the back of a fork to make a simple decoration.<br><br>7. Bake at 375°F (190°C) until puffed and golden brown. |

**VARIATION**

Use other fruit compotes (see chapter 22) or Frangipane (p. 201) instead of the apple filling.

# PALMIERS

| Components | Procedure |
|---|---|
| Puff pastry dough<br>Granulated sugar or sanding sugar | 1. Line a sheet pan with parchment. Alternatively, thickly butter a sheet pan and chill. |
| | 2. Dust the work surface heavily with granulated sugar. |
| | 3. Place puff pastry dough on top of the sugar and roll it out into a long strip about 12 in. (30 cm) wide and ⅛ in. (3 mm) thick. Turn it over once or twice as you roll it out so both sides become coated in sugar. |
| | 4. Trim the sides of the strip so they are straight. |
| | 5. Determine the center of the strip. Then fold each side halfway to the center (a). Then fold each side again so the two folds meet in the center (b). Each half of the strip should be 3 layers thick. |
| | 6. Fold one half over the other lengthwise to make a strip 6 layers thick and about 2 in. (5 cm) wide (c). |
| | 7. Refrigerate until firm. |
| | 8. Cut into slices ½ in. (6 mm) thick with a sharp knife (d) and lay on the prepared sheet pan in staggered rows, leaving plenty of space between them to give them room to expand. |
| | 9. Press down on the slices with the palm of the hand to flatten lightly. |
| | 10. Bake at 375°F (190°C) until golden brown. Turn the palmiers over and bake the second side until well colored. Transfer to a wire rack to cool. |

## VARIATIONS

Serve plain as a dry petit four.

Sandwich with buttercream and serve as a tea pastry.

Dip halfway into melted chocolate.

# ALLUMETTES

| Components | Procedure |
|---|---|
| Puff pastry dough<br>Royal Icing (p. 432) | 1. Roll out puff pastry dough to a rectangle ⅛ in. (3 mm) thick. Place on a sheet pan.<br><br>2. Spread a thin layer of royal icing thinly over the puff pastry. Freeze until icing sets.<br><br>3. Cut the pastry with a wet knife into batons or strips approximately ⅝ × 1½ in. (1.5 × 4 cm). Place on a sheet pan lined with parchment paper.<br><br>4. Bake at 375°F (190°C) until risen, then cover with a silicon mat and cook until golden and fully cooked, approximately 20 minutes.<br><br>5. Cool on a wire rack. |

# PAPILLONS (BUTTERFLIES OR BOW TIES)

| Components | Procedure |
|---|---|
| Puff pastry dough<br>Granulated sugar | 1. Line a sheet pan with parchment. Alternatively, thickly butter a baking tray and chill.<br><br>2. Scale 1 lb (500 g) puff pastry dough. On a work surface dusted with sugar, roll out to a rectangle 13 × 5 in. (33 × 13 cm). Trim the edges neatly.<br><br>3. Cut into 5 equal pieces, measuring about 2½ × 5 in. (6.5 × 13 cm). Brush 4 of them with a little water and stack them, placing the unbrushed one on top.<br><br>4. Using the back of a knife, mark a center line down the length of the pastry. Turn over and repeat in the same place on the underside. Chill.<br><br>5. Trim the edges of the stack to neaten if necessary. Using a sharp knife, cut crosswise into slices ¼ in. (5 mm) thick with an indention in the middle (a).<br><br>6. Twist the slices in the middle to splay the layers. Place on the tray and press down the edges lightly (b). Bake at 375°F (190°C) until golden brown. |

**VARIATION**

Add ground cinnamon or ginger to the sugar.

# CONVERSATIONS

| Components | Procedure |
|---|---|
| Puff pastry dough<br>Fruit jam, such as raspberry<br>Frangipane Filling (p. 201)<br>Royal Icing (p. 432) | 1. Roll out puff pastry dough as thin as possible. It should be nearly transparent. Chill for 30 minutes on a tray lined with parchment paper.<br><br>2. With a round cutter, cut out circles of dough large enough to line 2-in. (5 cm) tartlet cases. Cut out additional circles for the tops of each pastry and set aside. Keep the trimmings flat to use for the decoration.<br><br>3. Put about ½ tsp (3 g) jam in the bottom of each tartlet and top with 1 tsp (5 g) frangipane filling.<br><br>4. Brush the edges of the pastry with egg wash. Top with a circle of very thin puff pastry and chill.<br><br>5. Coat the top of the puff pastry with a thin layer of royal icing, using a small palette knife.<br><br>6. Cut strips of puff pastry very thinly and lay on top of the royal icing to form a lattice pattern. The small illustration at right shows one pastry without its top (right) and three ready to bake.<br><br>7. Bake at 375°F (190°C) until golden brown and cooked through. |

Puff pastry petits fours,
left to right: Palmiers,
Conversations, Papillons

# SACRISTAINS

| Components | Procedure |
|---|---|
| Puff pastry dough<br>Egg wash<br>Granulated sugar<br>Almonds, chopped<br>(optional) | 1. Roll out strips of puff pastry dough ⅛ in. (3 mm) thick. Cut into long strips 4 in. (10 cm) wide.<br>2. Brush the dough with egg wash and sprinkle with coarse granulated sugar or a mixture of sugar and chopped almonds. Lightly press the sugar and nuts into the dough with a rolling pin.<br>3. Turn the strips over and coat the other side with egg wash, sugar, and almonds in the same way.<br>4. Cut the strips crosswise into small strips ¾ in. (2 cm) wide and 4 in. (10 cm) long.<br>5. Twist each strip to make a shape like a corkscrew. Place on paper-lined baking sheets and press down the ends lightly so the twists do not unwind during baking.<br>6. Bake at 425°F (220°C) until brown and crisp. |

# ÉCLAIR PASTE

**É**clairs and cream puffs are made from a dough called *éclair paste*, or *choux paste*. The French name **pâte à choux** (pronounced pot a shoo) means "cabbage paste," referring to the resemblance of cream puffs to little cabbages.

Unlike puff pastry, éclair paste is extremely easy to make. The dough itself can be prepared in just a few minutes. This is fortunate, because for best baking results the dough should not be prepared more than 1 hour ahead of time.

The exact procedure for making éclair paste is detailed in the formula that follows. In general, the method consists of these steps:

1. Bring the liquid, fat, salt, and sugar (if used) to a boil. The liquid must be boiling rapidly so the fat is dispersed in the liquid, not just floating on top. If this is not done, the fat will not be as well incorporated into the paste, and some of it may run out during baking.

2. Add the flour all at once and stir until the paste forms a ball and pulls away from the sides of the pan. It should leave a thin film on the bottom of the pan.

3. Remove the paste from the heat and let it cool to 140°F (60°C). Beat or mix the paste so it cools evenly. If the paste is not cooled slightly, it will cook the eggs when they are added.

4. Beat in the eggs a little at a time. Completely mix in each addition of eggs before adding more. If the eggs are added too quickly, it will be difficult to get a smooth batter. The paste is now ready to use.

In principle, éclair paste is similar to popover batter (p. 231), even though the former is a thick dough and the latter a thin batter. Both products are leavened by steam, which expands the product rapidly and forms large holes in the center of the item. The heat of the oven then coagulates the gluten and egg proteins to set the structure and make a firm product. A strong flour is necessary in both for sufficient structure.

Éclair paste must be firm enough to hold its shape when piped from a pastry bag. You may occasionally find a formula that produces too slack a dough. Correct such a formula by reducing the water or milk slightly. On the other hand, éclair paste should not be too dry. It should look smooth and moist, not dry and rough. Paste that is too dry does not puff up well and is thick and heavy.

Éclair paste for cream puffs and éclairs is normally piped onto parchment-lined pans. It can also be piped onto greased pans, although this method is not used as often.

Proper baking temperatures are important. Start at a high temperature (425°F/220°C) for the first 15 minutes to develop steam. Then reduce the heat to 375°F (190°C) to finish baking and set the structure. The products must be firm and dry before being removed from the oven. If they are removed too soon or cooled too quickly, they may collapse. Some bakers like to leave them in a turned-off oven with the door ajar. However, if the oven must be heated again for other products, this may not be the best idea. It may be better to bake the products thoroughly, remove them carefully from the oven, and let them cool slowly in a warm place.

*Note:* French doughnuts or crullers, also made with éclair paste, are discussed in chapter 11 (p. 241).

# ÉCLAIR PASTE OR PÂTE À CHOUX

| Ingredients | U.S. | | Metric | % | Procedure |
|---|---|---|---|---|---|
| Water, milk, or half water, half milk | 1 lb | | 500 g | 133 | 1. Combine the liquid, butter, and salt in a heavy saucepan or kettle. Bring the mixture to a full, rolling boil. |
| Butter or regular shortening | 8 | oz | 250 g | 67 | 2. Remove the pan from the heat and add the flour all at once. Stir quickly. |
| Salt | 0.18 oz (1 tsp) | | 5 g | 1.5 | 3. Return the pan to moderate heat and stir vigorously until the dough forms a ball and pulls away from the sides of the pan. |
| Bread flour | 12 | oz | 375 g | 100 | |
| Eggs | 1 lb 4 | oz | 625 g | 167 | |
| *Total weight:* | *3 lb 8* | *oz* | *1755 g* | *468%* | 4. Transfer the dough to the bowl of a mixer. If you wish to mix it by hand, leave it in the saucepan. |

*Note: If a sweeter product is desired, add ½ oz (15 g) sugar in step 1.*

5. With the paddle attachment, mix at low speed until the dough has cooled slightly. It should be 110°–140°F (43°–60°C), which is still very warm but not too hot to touch.

6. At medium speed, beat in the eggs a little at a time. Add no more than one-quarter of the eggs at once, and wait until they are completely absorbed before adding more. When all the eggs are absorbed, the paste is ready to use.

## Éclair Paste Products

# CREAM PUFFS

| Components | Procedure |
|---|---|
| Éclair paste<br>Filling of choice<br>Confectioners' sugar | 1. Line sheet pans with parchment paper.<br><br>2. Fit a large pastry bag with a plain tube. Fill the bag with the éclair paste.<br><br>3. Pipe out round mounds of dough about 1½ in. (4 cm) in diameter onto the lined baking sheets. If you prefer, drop the dough from a spoon.<br><br>4. Bake at 425°F (215°C) for 10 minutes. Lower the heat to 375°F (190°C) and continue baking until the mounds are well browned and very crisp.<br><br>5. Remove them from the oven and let cool slowly in a warm place.<br><br>6. When cool, cut a slice from the top of each puff. Fill with whipped cream, Pastry Cream (p. 271), or other desired filling, using a pastry bag with a star tube.<br><br>7. Replace the tops and dust with confectioners' sugar.<br><br>8. Fill as close to service time as possible. If cream-filled puffs must be held, keep refrigerated.<br><br>9. Unfilled and uncut puffs, if thoroughly dry, may be held in plastic bags in the refrigerator for 1 week. Recrisp in the oven for a few minutes before use. |

# ÉCLAIRS

| Components | Procedure |
|---|---|
| Éclair paste<br>Pastry Cream<br>(p. 271)<br>Chocolate Fondant<br>(p. 422) | 1. Proceed as for cream puffs, except pipe the dough out into strips about ¾ in. (2 cm) wide and 3–4 in. (8–10 cm) long. Bake as for cream puffs.<br><br>2. Fill baked, cooled éclair shells with pastry cream. Two methods may be used:<br><br>a) Make a small hole in one end and fill with a pastry bag or a doughnut filling pump.<br><br>b) Cut a slice lengthwise from the top and fill with a pastry bag.<br><br>3. Dip the tops of the éclairs in chocolate fondant.<br><br>4. For service and holding, see Cream Puffs, above. |

**VARIATION**

### FROZEN ÉCLAIRS OR PROFITEROLES

1. Fill éclairs or small cream puffs (profiteroles) with softened ice cream. Keep frozen until service.

2. At service time, top with chocolate syrup.

# PARIS-BREST

| Components | Procedure |
|---|---|
| Éclair paste<br>Sliced or chopped almonds<br>Filling of choice | 1. Line a sheet pan with parchment paper. Using a round cake pan of the desired size as a guide, draw a circle on the parchment. An 8-in. (20 cm) circle is a popular size. |
| | 2. Fit a large pastry bag with a plain tube. Pipe a ring of éclair paste 1 in. (2.5 cm) thick just inside the drawn circle. Pipe a second ring inside the first one, just touching it. Then pipe a third ring on top of the other two. |
| | 3. Egg wash the paste circles and sprinkle with sliced or chopped almonds. |
| | 4. Bake as for cream puffs and éclairs. |
| | 5. When cool, cut a slice off the top of the pastry. Fill with whipped cream, vanilla pastry cream (p. 271), Pastry Cream Mousseline (p. 271), or Chiboust Cream (p. 272). Replace the top. |

## ❋{ PARIS-BREST-PARIS }❋

The bicycle race from Paris to Brest (in Britanny) and back to Paris again is the oldest regularly run bicycle race; it was begun in 1891. The race is a grueling 1200 kilometers (750 miles). The race is commemorated in the pastry known as Paris-Brest, made in the shape of a bicycle wheel.

# CHOUX PASTRY LATTICE

| Components | Procedure |
|---|---|
| Éclair paste<br>Poppy seeds | 1. Draw lattice designs on a sheet of parchment paper. Turn the paper over and place on a sheet pan. The drawings should show through. |
| | 2. Fill a paper cone with éclair paste and cut a small opening in the tip. Pipe the pastry over the outlines. If necessary, neaten the joints with the point of a small knife. |
| | 3. Sprinkle with poppy seeds. |
| | 4. Bake at 375°F (190°C) until evenly golden, 4–7 minutes. |
| | Use as a garnish for various cakes and plated desserts. |

## Choux Petits Fours

# PARIS-BREST

| Components | Procedure |
|---|---|
| Choux pastry<br>Flaked almonds<br>Praline Pastry Cream<br>  (p. 271)<br>Melted chocolate<br>Confectioners' sugar | 1. On a lightly buttered sheet pan, mark circles by dipping a 1-in. (2.5 cm) pastry cutter into flour and then tapping onto the tray.<br>2. Following this line, pipe a continuous ring of choux pastry using a small star tip.<br>3. Brush lightly with egg wash. Sprinkle with flaked almonds.<br>4. Bake at 375°F (190°C) until golden brown and hollow-sounding when tapped. Cool on a wire rack.<br>5. Slice the rings in half horizontally and pipe ⅓ oz (10 g) praline crème pâtissière in the lower half of each.<br>6. Flick the tops with melted chocolate, dust with confectioners' sugar, and replace the tops. |

Choux Petits Fours,
left to right:
Paris-Brest,
Mini Éclairs, Pralines,
Mini Cream Puffs,
Choux Florentines

# PRALINES

| Components | Procedure |
|---|---|
| Choux pastry<br>Praline Pastry Cream<br>(p. 271)<br>Nuts, lightly toasted<br>Caramelized sugar<br>(p. 278) | 1. Line a sheet pan with parchment paper, or butter it lightly. Pipe ¾-in. (2 cm) bulbs of choux pastry. Brush lightly with egg wash.<br>2. Bake at 375°F (190°C) until golden and well risen. Cool on a wire rack.<br>3. Once cold, pipe praline crème pâtissière into small holes in the bottom of each.<br>4. On a lightly oiled sheet pan, place lightly toasted nuts, slightly apart and one for each pastry.<br>5. Dip the top of each pastry in caramelized sugar and then place downward directly on top of each nut, allowing the caramel to cool around the nut and onto the flat tray.<br>6. Serve in paper petit four cases with the nut upward. |

# MINI CREAM PUFFS

| Components | Procedure |
|---|---|
| Choux pastry<br>Flaked almonds<br>Crème Chantilly<br>(p. 265)<br>Melted chocolate<br>Confectioners' sugar | 1. Line a sheet pan with parchment paper, or butter it lightly. Pipe ¾-in. (2 cm) bulbs of choux pastry. Brush lightly with egg wash and sprinkle with flaked almonds.<br>2. Bake at 375°F (190°C) until golden and hollow-sounding when tapped. Cool on a wire rack.<br>3. Slice in half horizontally. Pipe crème chantilly onto the bases.<br>4. Flick the tops with melted chocolate, dust with confectioners' sugar, and replace the tops.<br>5. Serve in paper petit four cases. |

# MINI ÉCLAIRS

| Components | Procedure |
|---|---|
| Choux pastry<br>Chocolate Pastry Cream<br>(p. 271)<br>Chocolate Fondant<br>(p. 422) or<br>caramelized sugar<br>(p. 278) | 1. Line a sheet pan with parchment paper, or butter it lightly. Pipe 2-in. (5 cm) fingers of choux pastry using a medium plain tip.<br>2. Brush with egg wash. Gently press down with the back of a fork.<br>3. Bake at 375°F (190°C) until hollow and golden. Cool on wire racks.<br>4. Make a hole at either end of the éclair. Pipe chocolate crème pâtissière inside, then dip the top in chocolate fondant icing or caramelized sugar.<br>5. Pipe designs in melted chocolate in the top of each and serve in paper petit four cases |

# CHOUX FLORENTINES

| Components | Procedure |
|---|---|
| Choux pastry<br>Flaked almonds<br>Caramelized sugar<br>(p. 278)<br>Crème Chantilly<br>(p. 265) | 1. On a lightly buttered sheet pan, mark circles by dipping a 1-in. (2.5 cm) pastry cutter in flour and then tapping onto the tray. Alternatively, using a round cutter as a guide, draw circles on a sheet of parchment. Turn the parchment over and place on a sheet pan. The circles should show through.<br>2. Following this line, pipe a ring of choux pastry using a small star tip.<br>3. Brush lightly with egg wash.<br>4. Bake at 375°F (190°C) until golden brown and hollow-sounding when tapped. Cool on a wire rack.<br>5. Dip the tops in caramelized sugar. Fill the center hole by piping a rosette of crème chantilly. |

# STRUDEL AND PHYLLO

Puff pastry dough, you will remember, consists of over 1000 layers of dough and fat. Starting with a single thick piece of dough, you fold in butter and then continue to roll out and fold until you have a very flaky pastry of extremely thin layers.

Pastries made from **strudel dough** or phyllo doughs are even flakier than puff pastries. Unlike puff pastries, these desserts start out with paper-thin layers of dough that are brushed with fat and then stacked or rolled up to make many-layered creations.

**Strudel** is an eastern European pastry that begins as a soft dough made of strong flour, eggs, and water. After the dough is mixed well to develop the gluten, it is stretched by hand into a very thin, transparent sheet. This is a skilled operation that takes practice to do well.

**Phyllo** (pronounced fee-lo and sometimes spelled filo or fillo) is a Greek version of this type of paper-thin dough. Although not exactly the same as strudel dough, it is interchangeable with strudel dough for most of our purposes. Because it is available commercially, phyllo dough is widely used today for strudel-making. In fact, commercial phyllo is often labeled "phyllo/strudel dough."

Commercially made phyllo is almost always available frozen, and in some locations it can also be purchased fresh (refrigerated). The sheets usually measure about 11 or 12 × 17 in. (28 to 30 × 43 cm). A 1-pound package contains about 25 sheets.

The following recipes are for homemade strudel dough and for two popular strudel fillings, apple and cheese. Included with these are procedures for assembling and baking a strudel using both homemade dough and commercial phyllo leaves. Finally, we include a procedure for assembling and baking baklava, the popular Greek phyllo pastry filled with nuts and soaked with a honey syrup.

## ❋ BAKLAVA ❋

There are countless varieties of baklava throughout the Mediterranean region, including Greece and southeastern Europe, Turkey, Lebanon and other countries in the Middle East, and parts of North Africa. The pastry seems to have originated with Turkish layered breads centuries ago. Today, connoisseurs of baklava can tell its origin by its filling (usually chopped nuts, including walnuts, pistachios, and almonds), its shape, and its flavorings (for example, honey and cinnamon in Greece, lemon and rose water in Lebanon.)

# STRUDEL DOUGH

*Yield: enough for 4 sheets, each about 3 × 4 ft (1 × 1.2 m)*

| Ingredients | U.S. | Metric | % | Procedure |
|---|---|---|---|---|
| Bread flour | 2 lb | 900 g | 100 | **MIXING** |
| Water | 1 lb 2 oz | 500 g | 56 | 1. Mix all ingredients into a smooth dough. To develop the gluten well, mix at moderate speed for about 10 minutes. The dough will be very soft. |
| Salt | 0.5 oz | 15 g | 1.5 | |
| Eggs | 5 oz | 140 g | 15 | |
| | (3 eggs) | (3 eggs) | | 2. Divide the dough into 4 equal parts. Flatten each piece into a rectangle. Place the 4 pieces of dough on an oiled sheet pan. Oil the top of the dough lightly and cover it with plastic film. |
| Vegetable oil | 2 oz | 55 g | 6 | |
| *Total weight:* | *3 lb 9 oz* | *1610 g* | *178%* | 3. Let the dough rest at least 1 hour at room temperature, or longer in the retarder. |

## Procedure for Stretching Strudel Dough

1. Strudel dough stretches best if it is slightly warm, so place the dough in a warm place. Allow at least 1 to 2 hours if the dough has been refrigerated.

2. Cover a large table (at least 3 × 4 ft/1 × 1.2 m) with a cloth. Dust the cloth well with flour and rub it in lightly.

3. Using plenty of dusting flour, place one piece of dough in the center of the table and, with a rolling pin, roll it out roughly into an oval or rectangle. This step is meant only to start the stretching, so don't try to roll the dough too thin.

4. Put your hands under the dough with the backs of the hands up. Carefully begin stretching the dough from the center outward, using the backs of your hands, not your fingers, to avoid poking holes in the dough. Work your way around the table, gently stretching the dough little by little in all directions. Concentrate on the thickest parts of the dough, so it is of even thickness all around.

5. Keep stretching the dough until it is paper-thin and nearly transparent. If small holes appear, you can ignore them; if large holes appear, patch them with pieces of dough from the edges after stretching is complete. Each piece of dough should make a sheet about 3 × 4 ft (1 × 1.2 m).

6. With scissors, cut off the heavy rim of dough around the edge and discard it.

7. Let the dough dry about 10 minutes, then fill it and roll it according to the following procedure.

## Procedure for Filling, Rolling, and Baking Strudel

### Method 1, Using Homemade Dough

1. Assemble the following ingredients:

| | | |
|---|---|---|
| 1 sheet freshly made strudel dough | 3 × 4 ft | 1 × 1.2 m |
| Melted butter | 8 oz | 250 g |
| Cake crumbs, bread crumbs, finely chopped nuts, or a mixture of these | 8 oz | 250 g |
| Cinnamon | 0.25 oz (1 tbsp) | 7 g |
| Cheese filling or | 5–5½ lb | 2300–2600 g |
| Apple filling | 4–4½ lb | 2000–2200 g |

2. Sprinkle or brush the dough all over with the melted butter. If you brush the fat on, draw the brush very lightly over the dough to avoid tearing it.

3. Mix the crumbs, nuts, and cinnamon and sprinkle them evenly over the dough (a).

4. Arrange the filling in a band 1½-in. (4 cm) thick along one long side of the dough. Leave a margin of about 2 in. (5 cm) between the row of filling and the edge of the dough.

5. Standing on the side where the filling is, grasp the edge of the cloth and lift it upward and forward to start the strudel rolling (b). Using the cloth as an aid, roll up the strudel like a jelly roll (c, d).

6. Cut the strudel in lengths to fit on a greased or paper-lined sheet, or bend the strudel to fit it on in one piece. Pinch the ends closed.

7. Brush the top with butter or egg wash. Bake at 375°F (190°C) until browned, about 45 minutes.

8. When cool, dust butter-washed strudel with confectioners' sugar, or brush egg-washed strudel with a clear syrup glaze (p. 199).

### Method 2, Using Phyllo Leaves

Each unit requires 4 phyllo leaves plus one-fourth of the filling ingredients needed in Method 1.

1. Assemble the following ingredients:

| Phyllo leaves | 4 sheets | 4 sheets |
|---|---|---|
| Melted butter | 2 oz | 60 g |
| Cake crumbs, bread crumbs, finely chopped nuts, or a mixture of these | 2 oz | 60 g |
| Cinnamon | ¾ tsp | 2 g |
| Cheese filling *or* | 20–22 oz | 575–625 g |
| Apple filling | 16–18 oz | 500–550 g |

2. Mix together the crumbs, nuts, and cinnamon.

3. Lay a cloth or a sheet of parchment on the bench. Lay a sheet of phyllo on the cloth or paper. Brush it with butter and sprinkle it with one-fourth of the crumb mixture.

4. Lay a second sheet on top of the first one. Brush with butter and sprinkle with crumbs.

5. Repeat with the remaining two sheets.

6. Arrange the filling in a band along the wide side of the sheet, leaving a margin of about 2 in. (5 cm) between the filling and the edge.

7. Roll up and bake as in Method 1 (steps 5 to 7). Each unit will fit crosswise on a standard baking sheet, four to six units per sheet.

8. In the retail shop, it is customary to cut each of these baked units in half and display the halves with the cut edges toward the customer.

## Handling Phyllo Dough

Commercially made phyllo is so thin and delicate it must be handled very carefully. Two guidelines are important. First, thaw frozen phyllo completely *before opening the plastic package*. Do not try to handle frozen dough; it will break.

Second, after opening the package and unfolding or unrolling the sheets of dough, keep the stack of leaves covered to prevent drying. Remove and work with one sheet at a time, keeping the rest covered. (*Note:* Instructions often say to cover the dough with a damp cloth, but this is risky because the sheets stick together if the dough becomes too damp.)

The modern trend to lighter pastries has inspired chefs to use baked layers of phyllo in place of puff pastry to make desserts such as napoleons.

## Procedure for Making Crisp Phyllo Layers for Napoleons

1. On a cutting board, lay out one sheet of phyllo dough. Brush very lightly with butter. It is not necessary to cover the surface thoroughly with butter; use a light hand. Top with a second and third layer, buttering each layer lightly.

2. Cut the pastry into squares or rectangles of desired size for individual pastries—for example, squares 3 in. (8 cm) on a side. Cut 2, 3, or 4 squares for each pastry, depending on the number of layers desired. A typical napoleon requires 3 layers.

3. Arrange the squares on baking sheets. Bake at 400°F (200°C) until brown, about 5 minutes.

4. The pastry squares to be used for top layers may be caramelized to enhance their appearance and flavor. To caramelize, coat with confectioners' sugar by sifting the sugar over them. Place under a hot broiler until the sugar is caramelized. Watch closely so neither the sugar nor the pastry burns or scorches.

### Phyllo Tartlet Shells

Prepare squares of pastry as in steps 1 and 2, making 4 layers. Press each square into a tartlet shell and bake. Use as shells for unbaked fruit tartlets, following the procedure on page 358.

# APPLE FILLING FOR STRUDEL

Yield: 4 lb (2000 g)

| Ingredients | U.S. | | Metric | % | Procedure |
|---|---|---|---|---|---|
| Apples, peeled and cored (see *Note*) | 3 lb | | 1500 g | 100 | 1. Cut the apples into thin slices or small dice. Mix with the lemon juice and the first quantity of sugar. Let stand for 30 minutes while preparing the pastry. |
| Lemon juice | 1 | oz | 30 g | 2 | |
| Sugar | 8 | oz | 250 g | 17 | |
| Sugar | 8 | oz | 250 g | 17 | 2. Drain the apples well. The sugar will have drawn out juice that would otherwise run out of the strudel and make the bottom soggy. |
| Raisins | 4 | oz | 125 g | 8 | |
| Walnuts, chopped | 4 | oz | 125 g | 8 | 3. Mix the apples with the remaining ingredients. |
| Cake crumbs | 2 | oz | 60 g | 4 | |
| Lemon zest, grated | 0.25 oz | | 8 g | 0.5 | |
| Cinnamon | 0.25 oz | | 8 g | 0.5 | |

*Note: Canned sliced apples may be used. Weigh after draining. Omit the lemon juice and the first quantity of sugar. Omit steps 1 and 2 in the procedure.*

# CHEESE FILLING FOR STRUDEL

Yield: enough for 4 strudels (each 16 in./41 cm long) or one 5-ft (1.6 m) strudel using homemade dough

| Ingredients | U.S. | | | Metric | % | Procedure |
|---|---|---|---|---|---|---|
| Baker's cheese | 2 lb | 8 | oz | 1200 g | 100 | 1. Combine the cheese and butter (at room temperature) and blend at low speed with the paddle attachment until smooth. |
| Butter | | 10 | oz | 300 g | 25 | |
| Sugar | | 12 | oz | 360 g | 30 | |
| Cake flour | | 3 | oz | 90 g | 7.5 | 2. Add the sugar, flour, salt, vanilla, and zest. Blend at low speed until just smooth and completely mixed. Do not cream too much air into the mixture or it will expand when baked and may burst the pastry. |
| Salt | | 0.5 | oz | 15 g | 1.25 | |
| Vanilla extract | | 0.5 | oz | 15 g | 1.25 | |
| Lemon zest, grated | | 0.25 oz (1 tbsp) | | 8 g | 0.6 | |
| Eggs | | 6 | oz | 180 g | 15 | 3. Add the eggs a little at a time, mixing in at low speed. Mix in the sour cream. |
| Sour cream | | 8 | oz | 240 g | 20 | |
| Raisins | | 8 | oz | 240 g | 20 | 4. Fold in the raisins. |
| **Total weight:** | **5 lb** | **8** | **oz** | **2648 g** | **220%** | |

## VARIATION

### CREAM CHEESE FILLING FOR STRUDEL

| Ingredients | U.S. | | Metric | % |
|---|---|---|---|---|
| Cream cheese | 3 lb | | 1440 g | 100 |
| Sugar | 12 | oz | 360 g | 25 |
| Cake flour | 3 | oz | 90 g | 6 |
| Salt | 0.5 | oz | 15 g | 1 |
| Vanilla extract | 0.5 | oz | 15 g | 1 |
| Lemon zest | 0.25 oz | | 8 g | 0.5 |
| Eggs | 6 | oz | 180 g | 12.5 |
| Sour cream | 8 | oz | 240 g | 17 |
| Raisins | 8 | oz | 240 g | 17 |

Substitute the above ingredients for those in the main recipe, using cream cheese instead of baker's cheese and omitting the butter. Mix as in basic recipe.

# BAKLAVA

*Yield: one 15 × 10-in. (38 × 25 cm) pan, about 48 pieces*

| Ingredients | U.S. | | Metric | |
|---|---|---|---|---|
| **Pastry** | | | | |
| Phyllo leaves | 1 | lb | 500 | g |
| Walnuts, chopped | 1 | lb | 500 | g |
| Sugar | 2 | oz | 60 | g |
| Cinnamon | 0.06 oz (1 tsp) | | 2 | g |
| Cloves, ground | 0.04 oz (½ tsp) | | 0.5 | g |
| Butter, melted, or mixture of butter and oil | 8 | oz | 250 | g |
| **Syrup** | | | | |
| Sugar | 12 | oz | 375 | g |
| Water | 9 | oz | 280 | g |
| Honey | 4.5 | oz | 140 | g |
| Lemon peel | 2 strips | | 2 strips | |
| Lemon juice | 1 | oz | 30 | g |
| Cinnamon stick | 1 | | 1 | |

## Procedure

1. Unfold the phyllo leaves and keep them covered.

2. Mix together the nuts, sugar, cinnamon, and cloves.

3. Butter the bottom and sides of a 15 × 10-in. (38 × 25 cm) baking pan.

4. Lay one of the phyllo sheets in the bottom of the pan, letting the ends of the dough fold upward at the sides of the pan. Brush the dough with butter (a).

5. Repeat until there are 10 buttered sheets in the pan.

6. Place one-third of the nut mixture in the pan in an even layer (b).

7. Put in 2 more phyllo leaves, buttering each as it is placed in the pan.

8. Put in another third of the nuts, another 2 buttered phyllo leaves, and the rest of the nuts.

9. Finally, lay each of the remaining leaves in the pan, buttering each, including the top one.

10. There will be excess dough sticking up around the edges of the pan. With a sharp knife, trim it level with the top of the pastry.

11. Chill the pastry to congeal the butter. This will make cutting easier.

12. Cut the pastry into 4 rows of 6 squares, each about 2½ in. (6 cm) on a side. Then cut the squares diagonally to make triangles (c). (A traditional method is to cut baklava into diamond shapes, but this always leaves small, odd-shaped pieces at the ends.)

13. Bake at 350°F (175°C) for 50–60 minutes, until golden brown.

14. While the baklava is baking, combine the syrup ingredients and bring to a boil. Simmer for 10 minutes, then cool to lukewarm. Remove the cinnamon stick and lemon peel. Skim off foam, if any.

15. When the pastry is baked, pour the warm syrup carefully over the hot baklava (d).

16. Let the baklava stand overnight so the syrup can be absorbed.

# BAKED MERINGUES

To refer to baked meringues as pastries may seem odd, as the term *pastry* usually refers to desserts made from flour goods such as puff pastry, short dough, or éclair paste. However, meringue that is bagged out into shapes and baked until crisp is used in many of the same ways as flour pastry. It can be filled or iced with many kinds of creams, icings, and fruits to make an interesting variety of attractive desserts.

Basic meringue mixtures are discussed in chapter 12, along with other creams and toppings. Common meringue and Swiss meringue are the types generally used to make crisp, baked shells. The basic procedure for baking meringue is presented in this section, followed by instructions for individual desserts. Also, a special meringue mixture containing nuts is introduced. This flavorful mixture is usually made into round, crisp layers that are used somewhat like cake layers. They may be filled and iced with buttercream, chocolate mousse, whipped cream, or similar light icings and creams.

The most common use for the preparations in this section is to pipe them out into disks and use the baked meringues as bases or layers for a variety of pastries. (To make meringue or sponge layers, mark a circle on a sheet of parchment and pipe the meringue or batter in a spiral to fill the circle.) Chopped or powdered nuts, especially almonds and hazelnuts, may be folded into a meringue before baking, making flavorful, crisp layers for a variety of pastries as well as specialty cakes. Two formulas of this type are included.

Four of the recipes in this section contain some cake flour and are mixed like sponge cakes. In fact, they are sometimes called *sponges*. The flour contributes structure. The quantity of flour is low, however, and the main ingredients are egg whites and sugar, as in regular meringues. Therefore, these recipes are grouped with meringues rather than with cakes.

You will find pastry recipes using these meringues in chapter 15. Chapter 18 includes cakes that incorporate one or more layers of meringue.

## CRISP BAKED MERINGUES

| Components | Procedure |
|---|---|
| Common Meringue (p. 267), Chocolate Meringue (p. 267) *or* Swiss Meringue (p. 267) | 1. Using a pastry bag, form the meringue into the desired shapes on baking sheets lined with parchment paper. Specific shapes are indicated in the procedures for specific desserts.<br><br>2. Bake at 200° to 225°F (100°C) until crisp but not browned. This will take 1 to 3 hours, depending on size.<br><br>3. Cool the meringues, then remove them from the parchment. Be careful, because they may be fragile. |

# ALMOND MERINGUES

*For large-quantity measurements, see page 734.*

| Ingredients | U.S. | Metric | Egg whites at 100%<br>% | Procedure |
|---|---|---|---|---|
| Egg whites | 4 oz | 120 g | 100 | |
| Fine granulated sugar | 4 oz | 120 g | 100 | |
| Powdered almonds | 4 oz | 120 g | 100 | |
| *Total weight* | *12 oz* | *360 g* | *300%* | |

Procedure

1. Prepare baking sheets by lining them with parchment paper. Draw circles of the desired size on the paper, using cake pans or other round objects as guides. Turn the sheets over so the circles are on the bottom but visible through the paper.

2. Add the sugar and continue whipping until firm and glossy.

3. Fold in the powdered almonds.

4. Whip the egg whites to soft peaks.

5. Using a pastry bag with a ½-in. (12 mm) plain tube, fill in the circles on the baking sheets by making spirals starting in the center of each circle, as on page 347. Each circle should be filled with a layer of meringue about ½ in. (12 mm) thick.

6. Bake at 325°F (160°C) until firm and dry, about 25 minutes.

# JAPONAISE MERINGUES

| Ingredients | U.S. | Metric | Egg whites at 100%<br>% | Procedure |
|---|---|---|---|---|
| Egg whites | 1 lb | 500 g | 100 | |
| Fine granulated sugar | 1 lb | 500 g | 100 | |
| Confectioners' sugar, sifted | 1 lb | 500 g | 100 | |
| Blanched hazelnuts or almonds, chopped very fine | 1 lb | 500 g | 100 | |
| *Total weight:* | *4 lb* | *2000 g* | *400%* | |

Procedure

1. Prepare baking sheets by lining them with parchment paper. Draw circles of the desired size on the paper, using cake pans or other round objects as guides. Turn the sheets over so the marks are on the bottom but visible through the paper.

2. With the whip attachment, beat the egg whites at medium speed until they form soft peaks.

3. Add the granulated sugar, a little at a time, with the machine running. Whip until the meringue forms stiff peaks.

4. Stop the machine. Mix together the confectioners' sugar and nuts. Fold this mixture into the meringue.

5. Using a pastry bag with a ½-in. (12 mm) plain tube, fill in the circles on the baking sheets by making spirals starting in the center of each circle, as on page 347. Each circle should be filled with a layer of meringue about ½ in. (12 mm) thick.

6. Bake at 250°F (120°C) until meringue is crisp and very lightly browned, about 1½ to 2 hours.

7. Use in place of or in addition to cake layers in assembling cakes and gâteaux (chapter 17).

# MARLY SPONGE

| Ingredients | U.S. | | Metric | Egg whites at 100% % | Procedure |
|---|---|---|---|---|---|
| Powdered almonds | 5 | oz | 150 g | 60 | 1. Line sheet pans with parchment paper. Draw circles of the desired size on the paper, using cake pans or other round objects as guides. Turn the sheets over so the marks are on the bottom but visible through the paper. |
| Cake flour | 2.25 | oz | 70 g | 28 | |
| Sugar | 8 | oz | 250 g | 100 | |
| Egg whites | 8 | oz | 250 g | 100 | 2. Sift the almonds, flour, and first quantity of sugar. |
| Sugar | 5 | oz | 150 g | 60 | |
| **Total weight:** | **1 lb 12** | **oz** | **870 g** | **248%** | 3. Whip the egg whites to soft peaks. Add the second quantity of sugar and whip to firm peaks. |

4. Fold in the almond powder mixture.

5. Using a pastry bag with a plain tip, pipe disks inside the circles marked on the paper, using the technique on page 347.

6. Bake at 350°F (180°C) for 12–15 minutes.

# COCONUT DACQUOISE

| Ingredients | U.S. | | Metric | Egg whites at 100% % | Procedure |
|---|---|---|---|---|---|
| Powdered almonds | 3 | oz | 90 g | 60 | 1. Draw circles of the desired size on the paper, using cake pans or other round objects as guides. Turn the sheets over so the marks are on the bottom but visible through the paper. |
| Sugar | 4 | oz | 120 g | 80 | |
| Cake flour | 1.5 | oz | 42 g | 28 | |
| Coconut, grated | 0.5 | oz | 15 g | 10 | |
| Egg whites | 5 | oz | 150 g | 100 | 2. Sift together the almond powder, first quantity of sugar, and flour. Stir in the coconut. |
| Sugar | 4 | oz | 120 g | 80 | |
| **Total weight:** | **1 lb 2** | **oz** | **537 g** | **358%** | 3. Whip the egg whites to soft peaks, add the second quantity of sugar, and continue whipping to firm peaks. |

4. Add the sifted dry ingredients and fold in.

5. Using a pastry bag with a medium plain tip, pipe disks inside the circles marked on the paper, using the technique shown on page 347.

6. Bake at 350°F (180°C) for 10 minutes or until golden.

# HAZELNUT COCONUT SPONGE

| Ingredients | U.S. | | Metric | % | Procedure |
|---|---|---|---|---|---|
| | | | **Egg whites at 100%** | | |
| Powdered hazelnuts | 5 | oz | 150 g | 83 | 1. Sift together the hazelnuts, confectioners' sugar, and cake flour. Stir in the coconut. |
| Confectioner's sugar | 4 | oz | 120 g | 67 | 2. Whip the egg whites and sugar to firm peaks. |
| Cake flour | 1 | oz | 30 g | 17 | 3. Fold in the dry ingredients. |
| Coconut, grated | 1.16 | oz | 35 g | 19 | 4. Using a medium plain tip, pipe the mixture onto parchment-lined pans into disks of desired size, as shown on page 347. |
| Egg whites | 6 | oz | 180 g | 100 | |
| Granulated sugar | 3 | oz | 90 g | 50 | 5. Bake at 350°F (180°C) for 10–12 minutes. |
| *Total weight:* | *1 lb 4* | *oz* | *605 g* | *336%* | |

# SUCCÈS

*For large-quantity measurements, see page 734.*

| Ingredients | U.S. | Metric | % | Procedure |
|---|---|---|---|---|
| | | **Egg whites at 100%** | | |
| Egg whites | 6 oz | 180 g | 100 | 1. Draw circles of the desired size on the paper, using cake pans or other round objects as guides. Turn the sheets over so the marks are on the bottom but visible through the paper. |
| Granulated sugar | 4 oz | 120 g | 67 | |
| Powdered almonds | 4 oz | 120 g | 67 | |
| Confectioner's sugar | 4 oz | 120 g | 67 | 2. Make a French meringue: Whip the egg whites until they form soft peaks. Add the granulated sugar and whip until the meringue is stiff and glossy. |
| Cake flour | 1 oz | 30 g | 17 | |
| *Total weight* | *1 lb 3 oz* | *570 g* | *318%* | 3. Sift together the remaining ingredients. Fold into the meringue. |

**VARIATION**

## PROGRÈS

This mixture can also be prepared with powdered hazelnuts, in which case it is more properly called Progrès. (The final *s* is not pronounced in either Succès or Progrès.)

Note that this preparation is similar to Marly Sponge (p. 349).

4. Using a pastry bag with a plain tip, pipe disks inside the circles marked on the paper using the technique shown on page 347.

5. Bake at 350°F (180°C) until dry to the touch but not completely hardened, 20–30 minutes.

# PISTACHIO MACAROON SPONGE

| Ingredients | U.S. | | Metric | Egg whites at 100%<br>% | Procedure |
|---|---|---|---|---|---|
| Almond paste | 9 | oz | 270 g | 90 | 1. Draw circles of the desired size on the paper, using cake pans or other round objects as guides. Turn the sheets over so the marks are on the bottom but visible through the paper. |
| Heavy cream | 2.5 | oz | 75 g | 25 | |
| Green pistachio paste | 2 | oz | 60 g | 20 | 2. Soften the almond paste with the heavy cream. Heat the mixture to 105°F (40°C). |
| Egg whites | 10 | oz | 300 g | 100 | 3. Mix in the pistachio paste. |
| Sugar | 4 | oz | 120 g | 40 | 4. Whip the egg whites to soft peaks. Add the sugar and whip to firm peaks. |
| *Total weight:* | *1 lb 11* | *oz* | *825 g* | *275%* | 5. Fold into the almond paste mixture. |

6. Using a pastry bag with a medium plain tip, pipe disks inside the circles marked on the paper, using the technique shown on page 347.

7. Bake at 350°F (180°C) for 8 minutes.

# CHOCOLATE HEADS

| Components | Procedure |
|---|---|
| Common Meringue (p. 267) *or* Chocolate Meringue (p. 267)<br>Chocolate Buttercream (p. 425)<br>Grated chocolate or chocolate sprinkles | 1. Prepare shells as for Meringue Chantilly (below).<br>2. Sandwich two shells together with chocolate buttercream.<br>3. Refrigerate shells until firm.<br>4. Spread each meringue sandwich with more chocolate buttercream so it is completely covered.<br>5. Roll in grated chocolate or chocolate sprinkles. |

# MERINGUE CHANTILLY

| Components | Procedure |
|---|---|
| Common Meringue (p. 267), Chocolate Meringue (p. 267), *or* Swiss Meringue (p. 267)<br>Crème Chantilly (p. 265) | 1. Shape the meringue into round mounds about 2 in. (5 cm) in diameter, using a ¾-in. (2 cm) plain tube in the pastry bag. Bake.<br>2. Optional step to allow more room for cream filling: When the shells are firm enough to handle but not completely crisp, remove them from the baking sheet. With your thumb, press a hollow in the base (the flat side). Return them to the oven to finish baking.<br>3. Cool the shells and store them in a dry place until needed.<br>4. Just before serving, sandwich two shells together with crème chantilly. Place the filled shells on their sides in paper cases.<br>5. Using a pastry bag with a star tube, decorate with additional whipped cream in the space between the shells.<br>6. If desired, the cream may be decorated with nuts or candied fruit. |

# MERINGUE GLACÉE

| Components | Procedure |
|---|---|
| Common Meringue (p. 267), Chocolate Meringue (p. 267), *or* Swiss Meringue (p. 267) <br> Ice cream <br> Whipped cream | 1. Prepare meringue shells as for Meringue Chantilly. <br> 2. Sandwich two shells together with ice cream instead of crème chantilly. <br> 3. Decorate with whipped cream. |

# MERINGUE MUSHROOMS

| Components | Procedure |
|---|---|
| Common Meringue (p. 267) | These are used primarily for decorating Bûche de Noël (Chocolate Christmas roll), page 477. <br> 1. Using a pastry bag with a small, plain tube, make small mounds of meringue in the shapes of mushroom caps. Make smaller, pointed mounds to use as stems. <br> 2. If desired, sprinkle very lightly with cocoa. <br> 3. Bake as for Crisp Baked Meringues (p. 347). <br> 4. When baked, make a small hole in the bottoms of the caps. Attach the stems with meringue or royal icing. |

# MERINGUE CREAM CAKES

| Components | Procedure |
|---|---|
| Japonaise Meringues (p. 348) <br> Buttercream (p. 425) | 1. For each cake, you will need two 2½-in. (6–7 cm) japonaise meringues and about 2 oz (60 g) buttercream in any flavor. <br> 2. Spread one japonaise circle with a thin layer of buttercream. Top with a second circle. <br> 3. Ice the top and sides smoothly. <br> 4. If desired, coat the iced cakes with chopped nuts, grated chocolate, toasted coconut, etc. |

# VACHERIN

| Components | Procedure |
|---|---|
| Common Meringue (p. 267), Chocolate Meringue (p. 267), *or* Swiss Meringue (p. 267)<br>Sweetened whipped cream<br>Fruit of choice<br>Sponge cake, cubed, moistened with flavored syrup *(optional)*<br>Fresh or candied fruit | 1. For a large vacherin, draw 8-in. (20 cm) or 9-in. (23 cm) circles on sheets of parchment, using a cake pan as a guide. For individual vacherins, draw 2½-in. (6–7 cm) circles.<br>2. Using a pastry bag with a plain tube, make one meringue base for each vacherin. Do this by making a spiral starting in the center of a circle and continuing until the circle is filled in with a layer of meringue about ½ in. (12 mm) thick.<br>3. For the sides of the vacherin, make rings of meringue the same size as the bases. For each large vacherin, you will need 4 or 5 rings. For each individual vacherin, make 2 rings.<br>4. Bake as for Crisp Baked Meringues (p. 347).<br>5. Carefully remove the baked meringues from the parchment. Be especially careful with the rings, as they are fragile.<br>6. Stack the rings on the bases, using additional unbaked meringue to stick the pieces together.<br>7. If the rings are neatly and uniformly made, you may leave the shell as is. If the sides are not attractive, you may spread the sides of the shell smoothly with fresh meringue, or you may later ice the sides of the finished shell with buttercream.<br>8. Bake the shells again to dry out the fresh meringue. Cool.<br>9. Fill the shells with sweetened whipped cream and fruit (such as strawberries or sliced peaches). Cubes of sponge cake moistened with a flavored syrup may be used in addition to fruit.<br>10. Using a pastry bag, decorate the top with more whipped cream. Also, arrange pieces of fresh or candied fruit in an attractive pattern on the top. |

# TERMS FOR REVIEW

| | | | |
|---|---|---|---|
| pâte brisée | blitz puff pastry | pâte à choux | phyllo dough |
| short dough | reversed puff pastry | éclair | baked meringue |
| puff pastry | napoleon | strudel dough | japonaise |
| three-fold | éclair paste | strudel | meringue glacée |
| four-fold | | | |

# QUESTIONS FOR DISCUSSION

1. Compare the mixing method for pâte brisée with the mixing method for short dough.

2. Describe two methods for enclosing the butter when making puff pastry.

3. Compare the mixing methods for puff pastry dough and blitz puff dough. Compare blitz puff dough and flaky pie dough.

4. What might happen to patty shells during baking if the puff dough is not relaxed before cutting and baking? What might happen to them if they are cut out of soft dough with a dull cutter?

5. Why is it important to bake cream puffs and éclairs thoroughly and to cool them slowly?

6. What precautions must you take when handling frozen commercial phyllo/strudel dough?

7. In order to bake meringue shells until crisp, should you use a hot, moderate, or cool oven? Why?

# Tarts and Special Pastries

To many bakers, pastry work is the most exciting and challenging part of their careers. It offers unlimited scope for developing artistic creativity, and it gives them opportunities for displaying their decorative skills. The basic doughs you learned in the preceding chapter combined with the creams and icings in other chapters are the components for a nearly infinite variety of delicious and eye-appealing desserts and sweets.

Chapter 14 presented the principal pastry doughs in detail. Procedures for preparing simple items were included for all these preparations, except short doughs, to help you become familiar with handling them. This chapter continues the study of pastries with more elaborate and advanced pastries.

The chapter is divided into two parts. The first explains the production of baked and unbaked tarts and presents a wide variety of recipes as examples. The remainder of the chapter is devoted to a selection of other special pastries, including modern creations as well as classic favorites.

**After reading this chapter, you should be able to:**

1. Prepare baked and unbaked tarts and tartlets.

2. Prepare a variety of special pastries based on puff pastry, choux pastry, and meringue-type sponges.

## TARTS AND TARTLETS

A *tart* is not just a pie without a top crust. Although they may resemble pies, tarts are actually more closely related to other European-style pastries. They are light, usually less than 1 inch (2.5 cm) thick, and often very colorful. Their appearance usually depends on a pattern of carefully arranged fruit. Tartlets are basically the same as tarts but prepared in small, individual-portion sizes.

Unlike pie pans, tart pans are shallow and straight-sided—that is, with sides that are perpendicular to the base. Often the sides are fluted. Because tarts are usually removed from the pans before serving, false-bottom pans are easiest to use. To remove a tart from a false-bottom pan, first remove the outside ring, then slide the tart from the flat base onto a cardboard circle or onto a serving dish. A flan ring, which is a simple metal hoop, is another form of tart pan. When a flan ring is placed on a baking sheet, it forms the side of the pan and the baking sheet serves as the bottom.

Small tartlet pans are not false-bottomed. Because the tartlets are quite small, it is easy to remove them from their tins. The tins may have straight or sloping sides, which may or may not be fluted.

Tarts need not be round. Square and rectangular tarts are also made, especially when puff pastry is used instead of short dough or pie pastry (see p. 330).

Because tarts contain less filling than pies do, the flavor of the dough is very important. Although regular pie dough can be used, the richer, buttery flavor of Pâte Brisée (p. 318) and Short Dough (p. 320) make them better choices. Short dough is a little harder to handle than enriched pie pastry, so it is used most often for individual tartlets. Almond short dough can also be used for tartlets.

The procedure on page 357 explains the method for making baked tart shells. Baked shells are most often filled with pastry cream, topped with fruit, and served without further baking. The procedure for making unbaked tarts from prebaked shells is illustrated in the recipe for Fresh Fruit Tart (p. 358). Small tartlets are made using the same procedure.

Baked tart shells may also be made of puff pastry dough, as explained on page 330.

## Baked Tarts

In its simplest form, a baked fruit tart is nothing more than an unbaked tart shell filled with a layer of fresh fruit and a little sugar and then baked. Many types of fruits may be used; the most popular are apples, pears, peaches, plums, apricots, and cherries.

A number of variations on this theme are possible, allowing you to create a wide range of tarts. The following are among the more popular varieties:

1. When using juicy fruits, sprinkle the bottom of the tart shell with a thin layer of cake crumbs, cookie crumbs, or even bread crumbs. These absorb some of the excess juices during baking and contribute to the texture and flavor of the filling.

2. Chopped nuts may be sprinkled in the bottom of the tart shell.

3. Frangipane (p. 201) may be spread on the bottom of the shell. This creates a rich, luxuriously almond-flavored fruit tart.

4. Pastry Cream (p. 271) may be used in place of frangipane cream, especially for small, individual tartlets. Arrange the fruit so it covers the cream completely.

# Procedure for Making Baked Tart Shells

This procedure is for making large tart shells. For individual tartlet shells, see the following variation.

1. Remove short dough or pâte brisée from refrigerator. Scale the dough as required.

   10–12 oz (300–340 g) for 10-in. (25 cm) tarts

   8–10 oz (225–300 g) for 9-in. (23 cm) tarts

   6–8 oz (175–225 g) for 8-in. (20 cm) tarts

   4–5 oz (115–140 g) for 6-in. (15 cm) tarts

2. Let the dough stand a few minutes or work it briefly with the hands to make it pliable. Dough should be cold, but if it is too cold and hard, it is difficult to roll out without cracking.

3. Roll out the dough on a floured surface or floured canvas. Pâte brisée should be rolled to about ⅛ in. (3 mm) thick. Short dough can be a little thicker, slightly less than ¼ in. (5 mm).

4. Place the dough in the tart pan. To lift the dough without breaking it, roll it loosely around the rolling pin. Allow the dough to drop into the pan and then press it into the corners without stretching it. Stretched dough shrinks during baking.

5. Flute the edges, if desired, and trim off excess dough. (The simplest way to trim the dough is to roll the rolling pin across the top of the pan (see photo).) At this point, the dough is ready to be filled with the fillings to be baked in the shell.

6. Refrigerate for at least 20–30 minutes before continuing. Resting the dough relaxes the gluten and helps prevent shrinkage. For tart shells to be baked empty, continue with step 7.

7. Prick the bottom of the dough all over with a fork (this is called *docking*). Line the shell with parchment and fill it with dried beans. These two steps keep the crust from puffing and blistering during baking.

8. Bake at 400°F (200°C) until the shells are fully baked and lightly browned, about 20 minutes. Remove the paper liners and beans. If the centers of the shells are still slightly underbaked, return them to the oven and bake for a few minutes more.

9. Cool the shells completely.

## Procedure Variation: Small Tartlet Shells

Individual tartlet molds come in many shapes, including plain round, fluted round, rectangular, and barquette (boat-shaped).

### Method 1

1. Arrange the tartlet shells close together on the work surface so there is as little space as possible between them. Different shapes may be used at the same time, as long as they are the same height.

2. Roll out the dough as in the basic procedure.

3. Lift the dough by rolling it loosely around the rolling pin. Drape it over the tartlet shells. Let the dough settle into the tins.

4. Run the rolling pin over the top of the dough to cut it off at the edges of the tins.

5. Using a small ball of scrap dough, press the pastry firmly into the shells.

6. Continue as in the basic procedure (step 5).

### Method 2: For Round Shells Only

1. Roll out the dough as in the basic procedure.

2. With a round cutter about ½ in. (1 cm) larger than the top diameter of the tartlet shells, cut the dough into circles.

3. For each shell, fit a circle of dough into a tin and press it well against the bottom and sides. If you are using fluted tins, make sure the dough is thick enough on the sides so it won't break apart at the ridges.

4. Continue as in the basic procedure.

5. If the raw fruit is hard (some apples, pears, and plums, for example), it may not cook to tenderness in the time it takes to bake the pastry. This is especially true if frangipane or pastry cream is used under the fruit. In such cases, precook the fruit by poaching it in a syrup (p. 587) or sautéing it in butter and sugar.

6. Before serving or displaying fruit tarts for sale, dress them up by brushing them with a glaze or by dusting them lightly with confectioners' sugar.

## Quantity Notice

Ingredient quantities in the following recipes may need to be adjusted. For example, especially sour fruit may need more sugar. Also, fruit may yield more or less than average quantities after trimming (peeling, pitting, etc.).

Most of the recipes on pages 359–365 are for 10-inch (25 cm) tarts. For smaller tarts, *multiply or divide each ingredient quantity by the factors indicated below* to get the approximate quantities needed.

| Tart size | Factor |
|---|---|
| 9-in. (23 cm) | multiply by 0.8 (or ⅘) |
| 8-in. (20 cm) | multiply by 0.66 (or ⅔) |
| 7-in. (18 cm) | divide by 2 |
| 6-in. (15 cm) | divide by 3 |
| 5-in. (13 cm) | divide by 4 |
| 4-in. (10 cm) | divide by 6 |
| 3-in. (7.5 cm) | divide by 10 |

# FRESH FRUIT TART

*Yield: one 10-in. (25 cm) tart*

| Ingredients | U.S. | Metric | Procedure |
|---|---|---|---|
| Fresh fruit (see Procedure) | 1.5–2 lb | 750–1000 g | 1. Select the fruit for the tart. Fresh fruit tarts may be made from all one fruit or a colorful combination of two or more fruits. Prepare fruit as necessary. Trim and wash. Cut large fruits such as peaches or pineapples into even slices or uniform bite-size pieces. Poach hard fruits such as apples or pears (see p. 587 for poaching methods). Drain all fruits well. |
| Pastry Cream (p. 271) | 14 oz | 400 g | 2. Spread a layer of pastry cream in the baked shell. Use enough pastry cream to fill it about half full. |
| 10-in. (25 cm) baked tart shell | 1 | 1 | 3. Carefully arrange the fruit on top of the pastry cream. |
| Apricot Glaze (p. 200) | 4 oz or as needed | 125 g or as needed | 4. Warm the apricot glaze and, if it is too thick, dilute it with a little water or simple syrup. Brush the glaze on the fruit to coat it completely. |

# APPLE TART

*Yield: one 10-in. (25 cm) tart*

| Ingredients | U.S. | Metric | Procedure |
|---|---|---|---|
| Firm, flavorful cooking apples | 1 lb 12 oz | 750 g | 1. Peel, core, and cut the apples into thin slices. You should have about 1 lb 6 oz (600 g) apple slices. |
| 10-in. (25 cm) unbaked tart shell | 1 | 1 | 2. Arrange the apple slices in the tart shell. Save the best, most uniform slices for the top; arrange them shingle-fashion in concentric rings. |
| Sugar | 3 oz | 90 g | 3. Sprinkle the sugar evenly over the apples. |
| Apricot Glaze (p. 200) | as needed | as needed | 4. Bake at 400°F (200°C) about 45 minutes, or until the pastry is browned and the apples are tender. |
| | | | 5. Cool. Brush with apricot glaze. |

## VARIATIONS

Saving enough of the best slices for a top layer, chop the rest of the apples and cook them with 2 oz (60 g) of the sugar and 0.5 oz (15 g) butter until they make a thick applesauce. Cool and spread in the bottom of the tart shell. Arrange apple slices on top. Sprinkle with remaining sugar and bake.

If the apple slices are very hard, sauté them lightly in 1–2 oz (30–60 g) butter and 1 oz (30 g) sugar until they begin to get soft and lightly browned. Turn them carefully to avoid breaking them. Proceed as in the basic recipe.

### PLUM, APRICOT, CHERRY, OR PEACH TART

Follow the basic recipe, but sprinkle a thin layer of cake crumbs, cookie crumbs, or bread crumbs in the unbaked shell before adding the fruit. Adjust the sugar according to the sweetness of the fruit.

Appropriate spices, such as cinnamon for plums or apples, may be added in small quantities.

### APPLE CUSTARD TART

Reduce the apples to 1 lb 4 oz/560 g (or 1 lb/450 g after peeling and coring). Reduce the sugar to 1.5 oz (45 g). Assemble and bake as in the basic recipe. When about half done, carefully pour in a custard mixture made by mixing the following ingredients.

| Ingredients | U.S. | Metric |
|---|---|---|
| Milk | 4 oz | 120 mL |
| Heavy cream | 4 oz | 120 mL |
| Sugar | 2 oz | 60 g |
| Whole egg | 1 | 1 |
| Egg yolk | 1 | 1 |
| Vanilla extract | 1 tsp | 5 mL |

Continue baking until set. Cool and dust with confectioners' sugar.

# PEAR ALMOND TART

*Yield: one 10-in. (25 cm) tart*

| Ingredients | U.S. | Metric | Procedure |
|---|---|---|---|
| 10-in. (25 cm) tart shell | 1 | 1 | 1. Spread the frangipane filling evenly in the tart shell. |
| Frangipane (p. 201) or Almond Cream (p. 202) | 12 oz | 350 g | 2. Drain the pears well. Cut them crosswise into thin slices, but keep the slices together in the shape of pear halves. |
| Pear halves, canned or poached | 8 | 8 | 3. Arrange the sliced pear halves on top of the frangipane like spokes of a wheel. Do not cover all the filling with the pears. Push them gently into the cream. |
| Apricot Glaze (p. 200) | as needed | as needed | 4. Bake at 375°F (190°C) about 40 minutes. |
| | | | 5. Cool. Brush the top with apricot glaze. |

## VARIATIONS

Cooked or canned peaches, apples, apricots, plums, or cherries may be used instead of pears. For small fruits such as apricots, plums, and cherries, reduce the quantity of frangipane and use enough fruit to cover the top completely.

### FRUIT TART WITH PASTRY CREAM

Omit the frangipane and, instead, cover the bottom of the tart shell with a ½-in. (1 cm) layer of pastry cream. Alternatively, use a mixture of 2 or 3 parts pastry cream blended smooth with 1 part almond paste. Cover the cream with a layer of fruit, arranged attractively.

### FRANGIPANE TART

Omit the fruit. Spread the bottom of the tart shell with a thin layer of apricot jam. Fill with frangipane filling. Bake and cool. Instead of glazing, dust lightly with confectioners' sugar. This recipe is especially appropriate for small, individual tartlets.

### FRUIT TARTLETS

The ingredients in the main recipe are the basis for all regular baked fruit tartlets. The following fresh or cooked fruits are the most commonly used: apples, pears, cherries, blueberries, pears, apricots, peaches, nectarines. Use only one type of fruit per tartlet. Approximately the following quantities will be needed for ten 3-in. (8 cm) tartlets.

| Ingredients | U.S. | Metric |
|---|---|---|
| Short Dough (p. 320) or Pâte Sucrée (p. 319) | 12 oz | 350 g |
| Frangipane (p. 201) or Almond Cream (p. 202) | 14 oz | 400 g |
| Fruit | 8–14 oz | 250–400 g |
| Apricot Glaze (p. 200) | 3–4 oz | 90–120 g |

# LEMON TART

*Yield: one 10-in. (25 cm) tart*

| Ingredients | U.S. | Metric | Procedure |
|---|---|---|---|
| 10-in. (25 cm) tart shell | 1 | 1 | 1. Bake the tart shell until it is golden but not too brown. Cool. |
| Sugar | 4 oz | 120 g | 2. In a mixer with the paddle attachment, blend the sugar and zest together thoroughly. |
| Lemon zest, grated | 1 tbsp | 15 mL | |
| Eggs | 4 | 4 | 3. Add the eggs. Mix until well combined, but do not whip. |
| Lemon juice | 6 oz | 175 mL | 4. Mix in first the lemon juice and then the cream. Pass the mixture through a strainer. |
| Heavy cream | 2 oz | 60 mL | 5. Pour the strained filling into the tart shell. Bake at 325°F (165°C) just until the filling is set, no longer, about 20 minutes. |

**VARIATION**

Arrange a few fresh raspberries on top of the tart. Dust lightly with confectioners' sugar.

# CHOCOLATE TART

*Yield: one 10-in. (25 cm) tart*

| Ingredients | U.S. | Metric | Procedure |
|---|---|---|---|
| 10-in. (25 cm) tart shell made with Short Dough (p. 320) | 1 | 1 | 1. Roll the short dough as thin as possible when making the tart shell. Bake until golden but not too brown. Cool. |
| Heavy cream | 6 oz | 175 mL | 2. Combine the cream and milk. Bring to a simmer and remove from the heat. |
| Milk | 6 oz | 175 mL | |
| Bittersweet chocolate | 8 oz | 240 g | 3. Add the chocolate. Stir in until completely melted and blended uniformly with the cream. |
| Egg | 1 | 1 | 4. Beat the egg lightly in a bowl. Gradually stir in the warm chocolate mixture. |
| | | | 5. Pour the chocolate into the tart shell. Bake at 375°F (190°C) until set, about 15 minutes. |

**VARIATIONS**

## CHOCOLATE BANANA TART

*In addition to the ingredients above, assemble the following:*

| Ingredients | U.S. | Metric |
|---|---|---|
| Ripe banana | 1 | 1 |
| Lemon juice | 0.5 oz | 15 g |
| Butter | 0.5 oz | 15 g |
| Sugar | 1.5 oz | 45 g |

Slice the banana and toss the pieces gently with the lemon juice. Heat the butter in a nonstick sauté pan over high heat. Add the banana pieces and then the sugar. Sauté over high heat so the bananas brown and become coated in the caramelized sugar. Do not cook until they are soft and mushy. Transfer to a sheet pan lined with parchment and let cool. Arrange the caramelized bananas in the bottom of the tart shell before pouring in the chocolate mixture. Proceed as in the basic recipe.

# TARTE TATIN

*Yield: one 9-in. (23 cm) tart*

| Ingredients | U.S. | Metric | Procedure |
|---|---|---|---|
| Apples | 3 lb | 1500 g | |
| Butter | 3 oz | 100 g | |
| Sugar | 8 oz | 250 g | |
| Puff Pastry (pp. 324–325), Blitz Puff Pastry (p. 325), Flaky Pie Dough (p. 289), or Pâte Brisée (p. 318) | 8 oz | 250 g | |

**Procedure**

1. Peel the apples, cut them in half vertically, and remove the cores. If the apples are large, cut the halves in half again to make quarters.

2. Select a heavy 10-in. (25 cm) skillet or sauté pan (a 10-in. skillet is needed to make a 9-in. tart). Melt the butter in the skillet. Cover the butter with the sugar in an even layer.

3. Arrange the apples in the pan on top of the sugar. Start by standing the apple halves on end in a circle around the sides of the pan. Fill in the center with the remaining apple halves. The pan should be completely full of apple halves standing on their edges and leaning against each other. They should protrude above the rim of the pan, but they will sink as they cook, making a tart about 1½ in. (4 cm) thick.

4. Set the pan over moderate heat and cook until the bottoms of the apples are soft and the juices are thick and syrupy, about 30 minutes. The tops of the apples will be barely cooked but will cook when the tart is baked. Remove from the heat and let cool slightly.

5. Roll out the pastry and cut a circle to fit over the top of the apples. Lay the pastry circle in place on top of the apples. Tuck the edges of the pastry inside the pan rather than letting it overlap the outside of the pan.

6. Bake at 425°F (220°C) for 30–40 minutes, until the pastry is brown and the apples are well caramelized.

7. Let the tart stand to cool slightly. The juices will gel or be partially reabsorbed so the tart can be turned out. Place a cake circle or a platter over the pan, then invert the pan and circle or platter to turn out the tart. The tops of the apples should have a rich caramel color. If more shine is desired, dust the top with sugar and caramelize it under a broiler or with a torch. Serve warm or at room temperature.

**VARIATIONS**

## PEAR TARTE TATIN AND PEACH TARTE TATIN

Although these are not traditional, they may be made following the basic procedure, substituting pears or peaches for the apples.

*Note on terminology:* These desserts are sometimes called *Tatins*, but strictly speaking, this is not correct. They are tarts. The term *Tatin* indicates what type of tart they are. **Tarte Tatin** is a shortened form of a French expression meaning, approximately, "tart made in the style of the Tatin sisters." These ladies owned a small hotel in the Loire Valley, where they became famous for this apple tart.

# ORANGE BRÛLÉE TART

*Yield: one 8-in. (20 cm) tart*

| Ingredients | U.S. | Metric | Procedure |
|---|---|---|---|
| Orange juice | 2.5 oz | 75 g | 1. Heat together the juice, first quantity of sugar, zest, and butter until the sugar is dissolved. |
| Sugar | 4 oz | 125 g | |
| Orange zest, grated | 0.14 oz (1¾ tsp) | 4 g | 2. Whip the eggs, egg yolks, and remaining sugar until the sugar is dissolved. |
| Butter | 3.5 oz | 100 g | 3. Stir the cornstarch into the egg mixture. |
| Whole eggs | 2 | 2 | 4. Bring the juice mixture to a boil. Temper the egg mixture by gradually beating in half the orange juice mixture, then return this mixture to the pan with the rest of the orange juice. |
| Egg yolks | 4 | 4 | |
| Sugar | 3.5 oz | 100 g | |
| Cornstarch | 0.5 oz | 15 g | |
| Prebaked 8-in. (20 cm) tart shell made with Short Dough II (p. 320) | 1 | 1 | 5. Heat, stirring constantly, and bring back to a boil. Boil for 1 minute. |
| | | | 6. Pour the mixture into a bowl and cool in an ice-water bath, stirring. |
| Fine granulated sugar | as needed | as needed | 7. Pour the mixture into the prebaked tart shell. |
| **Garnish (optional)** | | | 8. Sprinkle the surface with a thin, even layer of sugar. Heat under a salamander or with a blowtorch until the sugar is caramelized. (If using a salamander, mask the pastry rim with foil to prevent burning.) |
| Orange segments | as needed | as needed | 9. Chill the tart to set the custard before cutting. |
| Apricot Glaze (p. 200) | as needed | as needed | 10. If desired, decorate the top with orange segments just before serving. Brush the orange segments with apricot glaze. |

# CARAMELIZED APPLE TART WITH VANILLA

*Yield: one 10-in. (25 cm) tart*

| Ingredients | U.S. | Metric | Procedure |
|---|---|---|---|
| Firm, flavorful cooking apples | 2 lb 12 oz | 1300 g | 1. Peel the apples. Cut them into quarters and remove the cores. Cut each quarter in half to make 2 thick wedges. |
| Butter | 2 oz | 60 g | 2. Heat the butter in a large sauté pan over high heat. Add the apples and sauté for about 15 minutes, until the apples are lightly golden and soft but still holding their shapes. Adjust the heat as necessary; the heat should be high enough so the apples do not simmer in their own juices, but not so high they become too brown. |
| Vanilla extract | 0.33 oz (2 tsp) | 10 g | |
| 10-in. (25 cm) unbaked tart shell made with Pâte Brisée (p. 318) | 1 | 1 | |
| | | | 3. Add the vanilla and sauté another 5 seconds. Remove from the heat and cool completely. |
| Sugar | 3 oz | 90 g | 4. Arrange the apples in the tart shell. Sprinkle evenly with sugar. |
| | | | 5. Bake at 375°F (190°C) for 50–60 minutes, until the pastry has browned and the apples are lightly caramelized. |
| | | | 6. Serve warm (reheat if necessary). |

# WALNUT TART

*Yield: one 10-in. (25 cm) tart*

| Ingredients | U.S. | Metric | Procedure |
|---|---|---|---|
| Brown sugar | 8 oz | 225 g | 1. Cream the butter and sugar until well blended. |
| Butter | 2 oz | 55 g | 2. Beat in the eggs one at a time, waiting until one is absorbed before adding the next. |
| Eggs | 3 | 3 | |
| Flour | 1 oz | 30 g | 3. Add the flour and cinnamon. Blend in well. |
| Cinnamon | ½ tsp | 2 mL | 4. Mix in the nuts. |
| Walnuts, broken or coarsely chopped | 12 oz | 340 g | 5. Transfer the mixture to the tart shell. Bake at 350°F (175°C) for about 40 minutes, or until the pastry is golden and the filling is set. |
| Unbaked 10-in. (25 cm) tart shell | 1 | 1 | 6. Cool completely. |
| Chocolate Glaçage (p. 433) or tempered chocolate | as needed | as needed | 7. Using a paper cone (see pp. 440–442), drizzle the chocolate glaçage very lightly over the tart in a cross-hatch pattern. Let stand until the chocolate is set. |

# LINZERTORTE

*Yield: one 10-in. (25 cm) tart*

| Ingredients | U.S. | Metric | Procedure |
|---|---|---|---|
| Linzer Dough (p. 320) | 1 lb  8 oz | 700 g | 1. Roll out about two-thirds of the linzer dough to ¼–⅓ in. (6–8 mm) thick. |
| Raspberry jam | 14 oz (1¼ cups) | 400 g | 2. Line a greased 10-in. (25 cm) tart pan with the dough. |

*Note: This famous Austrian pastry is called a torte but it is actually a tart filled with raspberry jam.*

3. Spread the jam evenly in the shell.

4. Roll out the remaining dough and cut it into strips about ⅜ in. (1 cm) wide. Arrange the strips in a lattice pattern on top of the tarts. Set the strips at an angle so they form diamond shapes rather than squares.

5. Turn down the sides of the dough shell to make a border and to cover the ends of the lattice strips.

6. Bake at 375°F (190°C) for 35–40 minutes.

# PEASANT TART

*Yield: two 8-in. (20 cm) tarts*

| Ingredients | U.S. | | Metric | Procedure |
|---|---|---|---|---|
| **Marinated prunes** | | | | **MARINATED PRUNES** |
| Prunes, pitted and coarsely chopped | 10 | oz | 300 g | 1. Combine all the ingredients for the marinated prunes in a saucepan. Heat until the sugar dissolves. |
| Raisins | 1.75 | oz | 50 g | 2. Poach gently for 15 minutes, or until the prunes are tender. Drain. Discard the cinnamon stick. |
| Sugar | 3.5 | oz | 100 g | |
| Cinnamon stick | 1 | | 1 | **CUSTARD FILLING** |
| Tea bag | 1 | | 1 | 1. Heat the milk, cream, vanilla, cinnamon stick, and Armagnac to just below the simmer. Let stand for 30 minutes. Strain. |
| Armagnac | 1.33 oz (8 tsp) | | 40 g | |
| Water | 3.5 | oz | 100 g | |
| **Custard filling** | | | | 2. Whip together the sugar, honey, and eggs. Add the cornstarch and flour and mix until smooth. |
| Milk | 3.5 | oz | 100 g | |
| Heavy cream | 4 | oz | 125 g | 3. Pour the milk into the egg mixture and mix well. |
| Vanilla extract | ½ | tsp | 2 g | **TOPPING** |
| Cinnamon stick | 1 | | 1 | 1. Lightly toast the pine nuts, almonds, and hazelnuts. |
| Armagnac | 1.33 oz (8 tsp) | | 40 g | 2. Cook the sugar to a golden caramel and stir in the butter. |
| Sugar | 1.17 oz (6½ tsp) | | 35 g | |
| Honey | 2.5 | oz | 75 g | 3. Fold in the warm nuts and cook over low heat until the nuts separate. |
| Eggs | 7 | oz | 200 g | |
| Cornstarch | 1¼ | tsp | 3 g | 4. Pour onto an oiled marble slab, separating the nuts as they cool. |
| Flour | 1 | oz | 30 g | |
| **Topping** | | | | 5. Sift the flour and cinnamon. Rub in the butter until it resembles fine bread crumbs. |
| Pine nuts | 1.67 oz | | 40 g | |
| Blanched almonds, chopped | 1.67 oz | | 40 g | 6. Stir in the sugar and caramelized nuts. |
| Hazelnuts, whole | 1.67 oz | | 40 g | **ASSEMBLY AND BAKING** |
| Sugar | 1.67 oz | | 40 g | 1. Place the drained prunes and raisins in the bottom of the baked tart shells. |
| Butter | 2 | tsp | 10 g | |
| Flour | 5.5 | oz | 160 g | 2. Pour in the custard filling. |
| Cinnamon | 2 | tsp | 4 g | 3. Bake at 300°F (150°C) about 10 minutes, until the top is just set. |
| Butter | 3 | oz | 80 g | |
| Sugar | 3 | oz | 80 g | 4. Sprinkle the topping over the top. Dust with the remaining cinnamon. |
| 8-in. (20 cm) baked tart shells made with Pâte Brisée (p. 318) | 2 | | 2 | 5. Bake at 350°F (180°C) for 18–20 minutes, until the tart is golden brown and looks dry. |
| Cinnamon | 4 | tsp | 8 g | 6. Cool. Dust with confectioners' sugar. |
| Confectioners' sugar | 0.33 oz (4 tsp) | | 10 g | |

# SPECIAL PASTRIES

This section presents a collection of pastries of many types. The first three recipes are for famous classics based on puff pastry, pâte à choux, and short dough. These are items that all pastry chefs should know how to make well. The *Gâteau St-Honoré* is a spectacular assembly of choux pastry, short dough, caramel, and cream fillings. It is often decorated with a nest of spun sugar (p. 674) on top. The rich **Pithiviers** and the special napoleon or **millefeuille** test your ability to work with puff pastry.

The remaining recipes are mostly of the type sometimes known in North America as *French pastries*. They are individual portions made up of any of a number of creams, icings, Bavarian creams (from chapter 20), and layers of meringue, pastry, and even sponge cake. The first of these recipes, Passionata, is illustrated in detail to introduce you to the basic techniques for making this type of pastry. You can then apply the same techniques to other pastries in this section.

This chapter focuses primarily on pastries based on the doughs and meringue-type mixtures in chapter 14, but cake layers (chapter 16) are often used as well. Many of the cakes in chapter 18 could also be presented as French pastries, as discussed on page 438. Additional pastries based on cake batters are explained in that chapter. The most common way to make French pastries from cakes is to bake the cake layers as sheets rather than as rounds, cut the sheet cakes into long strips about 4 inches (10 cm) wide, and then slice the strips crosswise into portions, as explained on page 478. Note that several of the desserts in chapters 20 and 22 are made in large ring molds. These, too, can be made as individual pastries by assembling them in small ring molds instead.

Finally, the chapter includes a recipe for a popular pastry called **sfogliatelle** (pronounced sfo lee ah tell eh), a type of filled turnover from southern Italy. It is somewhat difficult to prepare. Follow the instructions carefully.

## ⋇❴ ST-HONORÉ ❵⋇

Two stories are told to explain the origin of the name of this elegant, classic pastry. One is that the confection was created in honor of the patron saint of pastry cooks, Saint Honoré (sant oh-no-ray). The other story is that it was developed in a pastry shop on the Paris street Rue Saint-Honoré. As a footnote to this second story, the pastry chef who developed the pastry was M. Chiboust, who supposedly invented a cream (see Chiboust Cream, p. 272) that is often used to fill a Gâteau St-Honoré.

# GÂTEAU ST-HONORÉ

*Yield: two 8-in. (20 cm) gâteaux*

| Ingredients | U.S. | | Metric | Procedure |
|---|---|---|---|---|
| Pâte Brisée (p. 318) | 10 | oz | 300 g | **PREPARING THE PASTRIES** |
| Pâte à Choux (p. 336) | 1 lb 4 | oz | 600 g | 1. Chill the pâte brisée for at least 30 minutes before use. |
| **Egg wash** | | | | 2. Fit a pastry bag with a medium plain tip and fill with the pâte à choux. |
| Egg yolks | 6 | | 6 | 3. Beat together the ingredients for the egg wash. (*Note:* You will not need the total quantity of egg wash. Reserve the remainder for another use.) |
| Whole egg | 1 | | 1 | |
| Sugar | ¼ | tsp | 1 g | |
| Salt | ¼ | tsp | 1 g | 4. Roll out the pâte brisée about ⅛ in. (3 mm) thick into a long oval shape (large enough to cut the circles in the next step). Place on a buttered sheet pan and dock well. Chill. |
| Water | 2 | tsp | 10 g | |
| Vanilla Crème Diplomat (p. 274) | 12–13 | oz | 385 g | 5. Cut two 8-in. (20 cm) circles from the pastry. Leave the circles on the pan and remove the excess dough. |
| Chocolate Crème Diplomat (p. 274) | 14 | oz | 425 g | 6. Brush around the edges of the circles with egg wash. |
| **Caramel** | | | | 7. Pipe a thick band of pâte à choux around the edge of the pastry circles about 1 in. (2.5 cm) from the outer edge. Brush lightly with egg wash. Press down the choux pastry lightly by running the back of a fork along the top. Pipe an additional small spiral of choux pastry in the center of each circle. |
| Fine granulated sugar | 7 | oz | 200 g | |
| Water | 2 | oz | 60 g | 8. Onto a parchment-lined or buttered sheet pan, pipe the remaining choux pastry into ¾-in. (2 cm) bulbs and brush with egg wash. (This will make more bulbs than necessary for the finished pastry, allowing you to select those of the best appearance.) |
| Glucose or corn syrup | 0.67 | oz | 20 g | |

9. Bake all the pastries at 375°F (190°F) until risen and golden and the bulbs sound hollow when tapped. Cool on wire racks.

**ASSEMBLING THE GÂTEAUX**

1. Select the best choux bulbs for the finished pastries. You will need 12–14 for each. Make a small hole in the bottom of each bulb and use a pastry bag to fill it with vanilla crème diplomat.

2. Spread a layer of chocolate crème diplomat in the bottom of each pastry circle.

3. Fit two pastry bags with St-Honoré tips. Fill with the remaining creams.

4. Holding the bag so the V-shaped point of the St-Honoré tip is up, pipe alternating lines of vanilla and chocolate creams to fill the pastry circles. See the photograph of the finished gâteau, as well as page 444, for piping with the St-Honoré tip. Chill the pastries.

5. Make a caramel by heating the sugar and water gently to dissolve the sugar. Bring to a boil, add the glucose, and cook until golden. Plunge the base of the pan into ice water briefly to stop the cooking.

6. Dip the filled choux bulbs into the caramel and then place caramel-side down onto an oiled marble slab until cold.

7. Reheat the remaining caramel and use to glue the bulbs around the edges of the pastry circles, keeping the flat caramel tops of the bulbs as level as possible.

# PRALINE MILLEFEUILLE

*Yield: one pastry, about 6 × 10 in. (15 × 25 cm) and weighing about 2½ lb (1200 g)*

| Ingredients | U.S. | Metric | Procedure |
|---|---|---|---|
| Classic Puff Pastry (p. 324) | 1 lb 4 oz | 630 g | 1. Roll out the puff pastry to a rectangle about 13 × 20 in. (33 × 52 cm). Place on a sheet pan lined with parchment paper. Dock the dough and refrigerate for 20 minutes. |
| Confectioners' sugar | as needed | as needed | 2. Bake at 400°F (200°C). When the pastry is about four-fifths baked, remove from the oven and dredge generously with confectioners' sugar. |
| Praline Cream (p. 542) | 1 lb | 500 g | 3. Increase the oven heat to 475°F (240°C). Return the pastry to the oven and bake until the sugar caramelizes, 2–3 minutes. |
| Praline Pailletine (recipe below) | 5 oz | 150 g | 4. Remove from the oven and let cool. |
| **Garnish** | | | 5. With a serrated knife, trim the edges of the pastry so they are straight and square. Then cut crosswise into 3 equal rectangles. (Exact size depends on how much the pastry shrank; approximate size is indicated above in the yield.) Select the best of the rectangles and reserve it for the top layer. |
| Caramelized nuts | as desired | as desired | 6. Spread one of the pastry rectangles with a layer of praline cream ⅝ in. (1.5 cm) thick. Cover with a second layer of pastry. |
| | | | 7. Top with the praline pailletine and then another layer of the praline cream. |
| | | | 8. Cover with the third layer of pastry. |
| | | | 9. Decorate the top as desired with caramelized nuts. |

# PRALINE PAILLETINE

| Ingredients | U.S. | Metric | Procedure |
|---|---|---|---|
| Milk chocolate couverture | 1 oz | 25 g | 1. Melt the chocolate and cocoa butter in a bowl over a hot-water bath. |
| Cocoa butter | 0.25 oz | 6 g | 2. Mix in the praline paste. |
| Almond-hazelnut praline paste | 4 oz | 100 g | 3. Add the crushed wafers and mix in. |
| Ice cream wafers (pailletine), crushed | 1 oz | 25 g | 4. To use in Praline Millefeuille (above), spread on a sheet pan to a thickness of about ¼ in. (5 mm), making a rectangle about 6 × 10 in. (15 × 25 cm), or the same size as the pastry rectangles. |
| *Total weight:* | *6 oz* | *156 g* | 5. Place in the refrigerator to harden. |

# MIRABELLE PITHIVIERS

*Yield: two 8-in. (20 cm) pastries, about 11 oz (325 g) each*

| Ingredients | U.S. | | Metric |
|---|---|---|---|
| Classic Puff Pastry (p. 324) | 1 lb | | 500 g |
| Almond Cream (p. 202) | 12 | oz | 370 g |
| Canned mirabelle plums, drained, syrup reserved (see variations) | 5 | oz | 150 g |
| **Egg wash** | | | |
| Egg yolks | 4 | oz | 120 g |
| Whole egg (1 egg) | 1.67 | oz | 50 g |
| Sugar | ¼ | tsp | 1 g |
| Salt | ¼ | tsp | 1 g |
| Water | 2 | tsp | 10 g |

*Note: This quantity of pastry allows for about 7 oz (200 g) trimmings. Each Pithiviers uses about 5 oz (150 g) pastry. Chefs who can roll pastry to accurate dimensions can get by with less pastry to start.*

## Procedure

1. Roll out the puff pastry to ⅛ in. (3 mm) thick. Place on a sheet pan lined with parchment. Cover with plastic film and chill.

2. Cut out two 8-in. (20 cm) and two 9-in. (23-cm) circles from the pastry. Chill again.

3. Beat together the ingredients for the egg wash.

4. For each pastry, brush egg wash around the outer edge of an 8-in. (20 cm) pastry disk. Dock the center.

5. Spread with a layer of almond cream, staying about 1–1½ in. (3–4 cm) from the edge.

6. Arrange the fruit on the top of the almond cream.

7. With a pastry bag, pipe the remaining almond cream over the plums to form a dome. Smooth with a palette knife.

8. Cover with the 9-in. (23 cm) pastry circle, pressing lightly to remove any trapped air. Select a bowl slightly larger than the dome of almond cream and invert it over the pastry. Press down to seal.

9. Using a bottle cap cut in half, cut a scalloped edge around the edge. (This can also be done with a knife, but an even finish is harder to achieve.) Remove the pastry trimmings (a).

10. Brush the top of the pastry with egg wash. Allow to dry in the refrigerator. Repeat with another layer of egg wash and again allow to dry.

11. With a paring knife, cut a pinwheel pattern in the top, stopping short of the scalloped edge (b).

12. If desired, score the scalloped edge lightly to decorate (c).

13. Bake at 375°F (190°C) until golden brown and well risen. Reduce the oven temperature to 325°F (160°C) and bake until a knife inserted in the center comes out clean. Total baking time is about 45 minutes.

14. Use the syrup from the canned fruit to brush the hot pastry and return to the oven at 425°F (220°C) until the syrup bubbles and the top is glazed.

15. Cool on a wire rack.

## VARIATIONS

Other canned fruits, such as pears or apricots, may be used.

For a classic plain Gâteau Pithiviers, omit the fruit and increase the quantity of almond cream.

## ❋⟨ PITHIVIERS ⟩❋

Gâteau Pithiviers (pee tee vyay) is a specialty of the town of Pithiviers in the Loire region of north central France. The dessert pastry is traditionally made with a filling of almond cream. The swirled design on top is also traditional. Some cooks also make savory pastries in the same shape, filled with meat or vegetable mixtures.

# PASSIONATA

*Yield: 12 pastries, about 5 oz (140 g) each*

| Ingredients | U.S. | | Metric | Procedure |
|---|---|---|---|---|
| Canned pineapple, drained | 10 | oz | 300 g | 1. Cut the pineapple into ¼ × ¾ in. pieces (5 mm × 2 cm). Add to the vanilla syrup. Simmer 10 minutes. Add the rum and flambé. Cool, then chill the mixture. |
| Vanilla Syrup (p. 262) | 6 | oz | 175 g | |
| Rum | 0.67 | oz (4 tsp) | 20 g | |
| Coconut Dacquoise disks (p. 349), 2¾ in. (7 cm) in diameter | 24 | | 24 | 2. Select 12 ring molds 2¾ in. (7 cm) in diameter and 1½ in. (4 cm) high. Place a disk of dacquoise on a cake card and set a ring mold over it so the disk is inside the mold. Trim the disks if necessary to fit snugly (a). |
| Passion Fruit Bavarian (p. 539) | 2 lb | | 1000 g | |
| Gelatin | 0.1 | oz | 3 g | |
| Fondant (p. 422) | 5 | oz | 150 g | |
| Passion fruit juice | 3.5 | oz | 100 g | |
| Passion fruit, fresh | 1 | | 1 | |
| Coconut, grated and toasted | as needed | | as needed | |

3. Drain the pineapple well and arrange half of it on top of the dacquoise (b).

4. Fill the molds halfway with passion fruit Bavarian (c).

5. Cover with a second dacquoise disk and add the remaining pineapple. Fill to the top with the remaining Bavarian and smooth with a palette knife.

6. Place in the freezer until set.

**Passionata Procedure continued**

7. Prepare the passion fruit mirror for the top. Soften the gelatin in water (see p. 88). Combine the fondant and passion fruit juice and bring to a boil. Add the gelatin. Stir to dissolve. Add the seeds and juice from a fresh passion fruit.

8. Spoon a thin layer of this mixture over the tops of the cold pastries to glaze (d); spread it to the edges with a palette knife (e). Allow to set.

9. Remove the ring molds by heating the sides gently with a blowtorch to release them (f). Lift off the mold (g).

10. Coat the sides of the pastries with coconut (h).

# CAPUCINE CHOCOLATE

*Yield: 12 pastries, about 3½ oz (100 g) each*

| Ingredients | U.S. | Metric | Procedure |
|---|---|---|---|
| Marly Sponge disks (p. 349), 2¾ in. (7 cm) in diameter | 24 | 24 | 1. For each pastry, place a disk of sponge inside a ring mold 2¾ in. (7 cm) in diameter and 1½ in. (4 cm) high. Trim the sponge disks as necessary to fit. |
| Chocolate Ganache II (p. 276) | 1 lb 12 oz | 775 g | 2. Cover the sponge disks with a layer of ganache about ¾ in. (2 cm) thick.<br>3. Top with a second sponge disk.<br>4. Place in the freezer until set. |
| Chocolate shavings | as needed | as needed | 5. Remove the ring molds, using a blowtorch to lightly warm the molds to release them. |
| Confectioners' sugar | as needed | as needed | 6. Press chocolate shavings onto the sides of the pastries.<br>7. Sprinkle the tops with confectioners' sugar. |
| Chocolate Ganache II (p. 276) *(optional)* | 2 oz | 60 g | 8. If desired, pipe about 1 tsp (5 g) ganache onto the centers of the tops of the pastries for additional decoration. |

# NOUGATINE PARISIENNE

*Yield: 8 pastries, about 5 oz (150 g) each*

| Ingredients | U.S. | | Metric | Procedure |
|---|---|---|---|---|
| Pistachio Macaroon Sponge disks (p. 351), 2¾ in. (7 cm) in diameter | 24 | | 24 | 1. For each pastry, place a sponge disk in the bottom of a ring mold 2¾ in. (7 cm) in diameter. |
| | | | | 2. Arrange half the caramelized apricots over the sponge disks. |
| Caramelized Apricots (p. 600) | 10 | oz | 300 g | 3. Cover with half of the nougatine cream. |
| Nougatine Cream (p. 542) | 1 lb 8 | oz | 750 g | 4. Place another sponge disk on top of the cream. |
| | | | | 5. Arrange the remaining apricots over the disks. |
| Dark chocolate | 7 | oz | 200 g | 6. Fill the molds with nougatine cream, smoothing the top with a palette knife. |
| Apricot Glaze (p. 200) | 3.5 oz | | 100 g | 7. Refrigerate or freeze until set. |
| | | | | 8. Carefully remove the ring molds by warming them briefly with a blowtorch. |
| **Garnish** | | | | 9. Select strips of acetate with the same width as the height of the molds. Temper the chocolate (see p. 641) and spread it over the strips as shown on page 645. |
| Apricots | as needed | | as needed | 10. While the chocolate is still soft, wrap around the pastries, chocolate side in, and allow to set. |
| Pistachios | as needed | | as needed | 11. Glaze the tops with apricot glaze and decorate as desired with pieces of apricot and pistachios. |
| | | | | 12. Peel the acetate off the chocolate just before serving. |

# CHOCOLATINES

*Yield: 10 pastries, about 2½ oz (75 g) each*

| Ingredients | U.S. | Metric | Procedure |
|---|---|---|---|
| Succès disks (p. 350), 2¾ in. (7 cm) in diameter | 20 | 20 | 1. For each pastry, place a succès disk in the bottom of a ring mold 2¾ in. (7 cm) in diameter. |
| | | | 2. Fill about two-thirds full with chocolate mousse. |
| Chocolate Mousse I (p. 276) | 14 oz | 400 g | 3. Top with a second succès disk and push down gently. |
| | | | 4. Fill the mold with additional chocolate mousse and smooth the top. |
| Confectioners' sugar | 2 oz | 60 g | 5. Chill several hours or overnight. |
| Cocoa powder | 1 oz | 30 g | 6. Remove the ring mold by warming it carefully and lifting off. |
| | | | 7. Sift together the confectioners' sugar and cocoa. Return the mixture to the sieve and sift the mixture over the tops of the pastries. |

# CREOLE DÉLICES

*Yield: 10 pastries, about 4 oz (120 g) each*

| Ingredients | U.S. | Metric | Procedure |
|---|---|---|---|
| Raisins | 5 oz | 150 g | 1. Combine the raisins and syrup in a small saucepan. Warm slightly, then remove from heat and let stand 1 hour to allow the raisins to soften. Drain well. |
| Dessert Syrup (p. 261) flavored with rum | 6 oz | 180 g | |
| Almond Meringue disks (p. 348), 2¾ in. (7 cm) in diameter | 20 | 20 | 2. Place half the meringue disks in the bottoms of 10 ring molds 2¾ in. (7 cm) in diameter.<br>3. Mix the raisins with the Bavarian cream. Fill the molds half full with the cream. Cover with the remaining cream and smooth the tops. Chill or freeze until set. |
| Liqueur Bavarian Cream (p. 534) flavored with dark rum | 1 lb 10 oz | 800 g | 4. Coat the tops with a thin layer of chocolate glaçage. Chill again until set. |
| Chocolate Glaçage (p. 433) | 5 oz | 150 g | 5. Warm the ring molds very gently with a blowtorch and lift off. |

**VARIATION**

## CHOCOLATE RUM DÉLICES

Prepare as in the main recipe except with the following changes: Use only half the quantity of Bavarian cream and omit the raisins and syrup. Use the cream in the bottom layer as in the main recipe. After placing the second meringue disk in the mold, fill the mold with Chocolate Mousse I (p. 276). Chill or freeze until set. Glaze the top as in the main recipe.

# FINANCIERS AU CAFÉ

*Yield: about 150 pastries, ½ oz (4 g) each*

| Ingredients | U.S. | Metric | Procedure |
|---|---|---|---|
| Raisins | 1.67 oz | 40 g | 1. Marinate the raisins and rum as long as possible (minimum 45 minutes). |
| Rum | 2 oz | 60 g | |
| Cake flour | 2.25 oz | 65 g | 2. Butter 1-in. (2.5 cm) round or boat-shaped molds.<br>3. Sift flour, sugar, and almonds into a bowl and make a well. |
| Confectioners' sugar | 6.5 oz | 185 g | |
| Powdered almonds | 2.25 oz | 65 g | 4. Lightly froth the egg whites with a fork. Pour into the well. |
| Egg whites | 4.5 oz | 125 g | 5. Cook the butter until it browns and takes on a nutty aroma and pour into the well with the coffee extract. |
| Butter, melted | 4.5 oz | 125 g | 6. Draw all the ingredients together to form a smooth paste. |
| Coffee extract | 1 drop | 1 drop | 7. Place the drained, marinated raisins into the prepared molds. |
| Dark rum | 3.5 oz | 100 g | 8. Pipe or spoon the mixture to fill the buttered molds three-quarters full. |
| Honey | 3.5 oz | 100 g | |
| Apricot Glaze (p. 200) or Clear Glaze (p. 199) | as needed | as needed | 9. Bake at 340°F (170°C) until firm. Remove from the molds and cool on a wire rack. Turn all the pastries bottom side up.<br>10. Heat the rum and honey to scalding point. Spoon the mixture over the baked financiers and brush with apricot glaze or clear glaze.<br>11. Place into paper petit four cases. |

# PRALINE CAKE (PRALINETTE)

*Yield: 12 individual-serving cakes, about 4 oz (110 g) each*

| Ingredients | U.S. | Metric | Procedure |
|---|---|---|---|
| Marjolaine Sponge Cake disks (p. 412), 2¾ in. (7 cm) in diameter | 24 | 24 | 1. For each cake, place one sponge disk in the bottom of a ring mold 2¾ in. (7 cm) in diameter and 1½ in. (4 cm) in height. |
| Light Praline Cream (p. 428) | 1 lb 8 oz | 680 g | 2. Using a pastry bag with a large plain tip, fill the mold with praline cream to within ½ in. (1 cm) of the top. |

1. For each cake, place one sponge disk in the bottom of a ring mold 2¾ in. (7 cm) in diameter and 1½ in. (4 cm) in height.

2. Using a pastry bag with a large plain tip, fill the mold with praline cream to within ½ in. (1 cm) of the top.

3. Place another sponge disk on top. Refrigerate to set.

4. Remove the ring mold.

| Milk chocolate couverture | 1 lb 4 oz–1 lb 12 oz | 600–800 g | |
| Cocoa powder | as needed | as needed | |

5. Following the procedure described for Feuille d'Automne (p. 466), coat the bottoms of sheet pans with melted milk chocolate (see p. 647) and, with a scraper, cut long strips of the chocolate to cover the cakes. (*Note:* For more information and further illustration of this procedure, refer to the recipe for Feuille d'Automne.)

6. Handling the chocolate as little and as lightly as possible, wrap it around the pastry.

7. Fold the top edge of the chocolate over the top of the pastry. Decorate the top with additional narrow strips of chocolate.

8. Sprinkle very lightly with cocoa powder.

# SFOGLIATELLE

*Yield: 10 large pastries, about 3½ oz (100 g) each, or 20 small pastries, about 1¾ oz (50 g) each*

| Ingredients | U.S. | Metric | | Procedure |
|---|---|---|---|---|
| **Dough** | | | | 1. To make the dough, sift the flour and salt into a bowl. Add the water and mix to make a dry dough. Turn out the mixture onto a work surface and knead until the dough holds together. |
| Bread flour | 12 oz | 375 | g | |
| Pastry flour | 4 oz | 125 | g | |
| Salt | 1 tsp | 5 | g | 2. Set the rollers of a pasta machine at their widest opening. Pass the dough through the rollers and fold in half. Repeat until the dough is smooth and elastic. Wrap the dough in plastic and rest for 1–2 hours in the refrigerator. |
| Water | 7 oz | 215 | g | |
| Butter | 4 oz | 125 | g | |
| Lard or shortening | 4 oz | 125 | g | |
| | | | | 3. Cut the dough into 4 equal pieces. Pass each piece through the rollers, set the rollers closer together, and repeat until you reach the narrowest setting of the rollers. You should have 4 long, paper-thin strips of dough. |
| **Filling** | | | | |
| Water, cold | 8 oz | 250 | g | |
| Sugar | 3 oz | 90 | g | 4. Melt together the butter and shortening or lard. Cool slightly. |
| Semolina | 3 oz | 90 | g | |
| Ricotta cheese | 12 oz | 375 | g | 5. Lay one strip of dough out on the workbench and brush heavily with the melted fat. Roll up tightly from one end until only about 1 in. (2.5 cm) of the strip remains. Move the roll back to the other end of the bench and lay the second strip out so the beginning of the first strip butts up against the end of the first strip to make a continuous roll. Again, brush heavily with the fat and continue to roll up. If you are making large pastries, repeat with the third and fourth strip. You should now have a roll of dough about 6 in. (15 cm) long and 2½ in. (6 cm) thick. If you are making small pastries, make a new roll with the third and fourth strips of dough, so you have two rolls about 6 in. (15 cm) long and 1¾ in. (4.5 cm) thick. Refrigerate for several hours. Save the remaining melted fat for step 10. |
| Egg yolks | 2 | 2 | | |
| Cinnamon extract | ⅛ tsp | 0.5 | mL | |
| Candied orange peel, finely diced | 3 oz | 90 | g | |

6. Prepare the filling. Combine the water, sugar, and semolina in a saucepan and mix until smooth. Bring to a boil over moderate heat, stirring constantly, and cook until the mixture is thick. Pass the ricotta through a fine sieve and add it to the pan. Cook for 2 or 3 minutes more. Remove from the heat and add the remaining filling ingredients, beating in well. Place in a bowl, cover tightly with plastic film, and chill. When the mixture is cold, beat until smooth and transfer to a pastry bag with a medium plain tip.

7. Remove the dough rolls from refrigeration and square off the ends with a sharp knife. Carefully slice each dough roll into 10 slices ½ in. (1.25 cm) thick.

8. For each pastry, place a slice of the dough on the workbench. With a small, light rolling pin, very gently roll the circle of dough from the center outward in all directions just until the layers of dough fan outward toward the edges of the circle. At this point, if it is warm in the bakeshop, chill the rolled-out slices briefly. Remove only a few at a time from refrigeration, because they are easier to work with if the fat between the layers is firm.

9. Pick up a circle of pastry with both hands, with the thumbs underneath and the fingers above the center of the circle. (The side that was up when the circle was rolled out should be on top.) Carefully shape the circle into a cone by working the thumbs into the center of the circle and working outward so the layers of dough slide away from each other. The side that was on top during rolling should be the outside of the cone. Hold the cone in one hand and, using the pastry bag, fill it with about 1 oz (30 g) filling for small pastries, 2 oz (60 g) for large pastries.

10. Lay the pastries on their sides on a sheet pan lined with parchment. Brush with the remaining fat.

11. Bake at 400°F (200°C) until golden, 25–30 minutes.

---

## ⊰ SFOGLIATELLE ⊱

This distinctive pastry, which somewhat resembles an oyster shell, is an ancient tradition from Naples. The pastry for sfogliatelle (sfo lee ah tell eh) is sort of an antique form of puff pastry. In Italian, *sfoglia* is a sheet of pasta dough, and *pasta sfoglia* is puff pastry.

# GÂTEAU SUCCÈS

*Yield: 1 gâteau, 7 in. (18 cm) in diameter*

| Ingredients | U.S. | | Metric | Procedure |
|---|---|---|---|---|
| Succès layers (p. 350), 7 in. (18 cm) in diameter | 2 | | 2 | 1. Place one succès layer on a cake card, anchoring it in place with a dab of buttercream. |
| Praline Buttercream (p. 427) | 8 | oz | 225 g | 2. Spread a layer of buttercream on the succès. |
| Nougatine (p. 668), crushed | 2 | oz | 60 g | 3. Sprinkle the crushed nougatine evenly over the buttercream. |
| Sliced almonds, toasted | 2.5 | oz | 75 g | 4. Top with the second layer of succès. |
| Confectioners' sugar | as needed | | as needed | 5. Spread the top and sides of the cake with buttercream. |
| | | | | 6. Coat the top and sides with the almonds. Sprinkle the top very lightly with confectioners' sugar. |

**VARIATION**

Individual succès pastries can be made using the same procedure. Use small succès disks 2¾ in. (7 cm) in diameter.

# TERMS FOR REVIEW

| | | | |
|---|---|---|---|
| tart | gâteau St-Honoré | tarte Tatin | millefeuille |
| Linzertorte | Pithiviers | peasant tart | sfogliatelle |
| French pastry | | | |

# QUESTIONS FOR DISCUSSION

1. What is the purpose of docking tart shells before they are baked?

2. List four or five ingredients besides fruit and sugar that are sometimes used for filling *baked* fruit tarts.

3. Describe the procedure for making baked tartlet shells.

4. Describe the procedure for making an unbaked fruit tart.

5. Describe, in as much detail as possible, the procedure for making a Gâteau St-Honoré.

6. Read the procedures for special cakes in chapter 18. Which do you think might be appropriate for making up as French pastries? Select one and describe how you would modify the procedure to make French pastries.

# Chapter 16

# Cake Mixing and Baking

C akes are the richest and sweetest of all the baked products we have studied so far. From the baker's point of view, producing cakes requires as much precision as producing breads, but for completely opposite reasons. Breads are lean products that require strong gluten development and careful control of yeast action during the long fermentation and proofing periods. Cakes, on the other hand, are high in both fat and sugar. The baker's job is to create a structure that supports these ingredients and yet to keep it as light and delicate as possible. Fortunately, producing cakes in quantity is relatively easy if the baker has good, well-balanced formulas, scales ingredients accurately, and understands basic mixing methods well.

Cakes owe their popularity not only to their richness and sweetness but also to their versatility. Cakes can be presented in many forms, from simple sheet cakes in cafeterias to elaborately decorated works of art for weddings and other important occasions. With only a few basic formulas and a variety of icings and fillings, the chef or baker can construct the perfect dessert for any occasion or purpose. In this chapter, we focus on the procedures for mixing and baking the basic types of cakes. In chapters 17 and 18, we discuss how to assemble and decorate many kinds of desserts, using baked cake layers and sheets in combination with icings, fillings, and other ingredients.

**After reading this chapter, you should be able to:**

1. Perform basic cake mixing methods.

2. Produce high-fat or shortened cakes, including high-ratio cakes and cakes mixed by creaming.

3. Produce foam-type cakes, including sponge, angel food, and chiffon cakes.

4. Scale and bake cakes correctly.

5. Correct cake failures or defects.

## MIXING

The selection of high-quality ingredients is, of course, necessary to produce a high-quality cake. However, good ingredients alone do not guarantee a fine cake. A thorough understanding of mixing procedures is essential. Slight errors in mixing can result in cakes with poor texture and volume.

The mixing methods presented in this chapter are the basic ones used for most types of cakes prepared in the modern bakeshop. Each of these methods is used for particular types of formulas.

- ◆ High-fat or shortened cakes

  Creaming method

  Two-stage method

  One-stage (liquid shortening) method

  Flour-batter method

- ◆ Low-fat or foam-type cakes

  Sponge method

  Angel food method

  Chiffon method

We discuss these methods and their variations in detail beginning on page 382.

The three main goals of mixing cake batters are:

- ◆ To combine all ingredients into a smooth, uniform batter.

- ◆ To form and incorporate air cells in the batter.

- ◆ To develop the proper texture in the finished product.

These three goals are closely related. They may seem fairly obvious, especially the first one. But understanding the goals in detail will help you avoid many errors in mixing. For example, inexperienced bakers often become impatient and turn the mixer to high speed when creaming fat and sugar, thinking high speed will do the same job faster. But air cells do not form as well at high speed, so the texture of the cake suffers.

Let's examine these three goals one at a time.

## Combining Ingredients into a Homogeneous Mixture

Two of the major ingredients in cakes—fat and water (including the water in milk and eggs)—are, by nature, unmixable. Therefore, careful attention to mixing procedures is important if this goal is to be reached.

As you recall from chapter 4 (p. 71), a uniform mixture of two unmixable substances is called an **emulsion**. Part of the purpose of mixing is to form such an emulsion. Properly mixed cake batters contain a water-in-fat emulsion—that is, the water is held in tiny droplets surrounded by fat and other ingredients. Curdling occurs when the fat can no longer hold the water in emulsion. The mixture then changes to a fat-in-water mixture, with small particles of fat surrounded by water and other ingredients.

The following factors can cause curdling:

1. **Using the wrong type of fat.** Different fats have different emulsifying abilities. High-ratio shortening contains emulsifiers that enable it to hold a large amount of water without curdling. You should not substitute regular shortening or butter in a formula that calls specifically for high-ratio, or emulsified, shortening.

   Butter has a desirable flavor but relatively poor emulsifying ability. Butter is, of course, used in many cake batters, but the formula should be specifically balanced so it contains no more liquid than the batter can hold. Also, remember that butter contains some water.

   Egg yolks, as you will recall, contain a natural emulsifier. When whole eggs or yolks are properly mixed into a batter, they help the batter hold the other liquids.

2. **Having the ingredients too cold.** Emulsions are best formed if the temperature of the ingredients is about 70°F (21°C).

3. **Mixing the first stage of the procedure too quickly.** If you do not cream the fat and sugar properly, for example, you will not form a good cell structure to hold the water (see "Forming Air Cells," below).

4. **Adding the liquids too quickly.** In most cases the liquids, including the eggs, must be added in stages—that is, a little at a time. If they are added too quickly, they cannot be absorbed properly.

   In batters made by the creaming method (p. 383), the liquid is often added alternately with the flour. The flour helps the batter absorb the liquid.

5. **Adding too much liquid.** This is not a problem if the formula is a good one. However, if you are using a formula that is not properly balanced, it might call for more liquid than the fat can hold in emulsion.

## Forming Air Cells

*Air cells* in cake batters are important for texture and for leavening. A fine, smooth texture is the result of small, uniform air cells. Large or irregular air cells result in a coarse texture. Also, you will recall from page 100 that air trapped in a mix helps leaven a cake when the heat of the oven causes the air to expand. When no chemical leavener is used, this trapped air, in addition to steam, provides nearly all the leavening. Even when baking powder or soda is used, the air cells provide places to hold the gases released by the chemical leavener.

Correct ingredient temperature and mixing speed are necessary for good air cell formation. Cold fat (below 60°F/16°C) is too hard to form good air cells, and fat that is too warm (above 75°F/24°C) is too soft. Mixing speed should be moderate (medium speed). If mixing is done on high speed, friction warms the ingredients too much. Not as many air cells are formed, and those that do form tend to be coarse and irregular.

Granulated sugar is the proper sugar for creaming-method cakes. Confectioners' sugar is too fine to produce good air cells.

In the case of egg-foam cakes (sponge, angel food, chiffon), the air cells are formed by whipping eggs and sugar. For the best foaming, the egg and sugar mixture should be slightly warm (about 100°F/38°C). Whipping may be done at high speed at first, but the final stages of whipping should be at medium speed in order to retain air cells.

## Developing Texture

Both the uniform mixing of ingredients and the formation of air cells are important to a cake's texture, as we discussed in the preceding sections. Another factor of mixing that affects texture is gluten development. For the most part, we want very little gluten development in cakes, so we use cake flour, which is low in gluten. Some sponge cake formulas call for cornstarch to replace part of the flour, so there is even less gluten (the high percentage of eggs in sponge cakes provides much of the structure). On the other hand, some pound cake and fruit cake formulas need more gluten than other cakes for extra structure and to support the weight of the fruit. Thus, you will sometimes see such cake formulas calling for part cake flour and part bread flour.

As you will recall from chapter 5, the amount of mixing affects gluten development. In the creaming method, the sponge method, and the angel food method, the flour is added at or near the end of the mixing procedure so there is very little gluten development in properly mixed batters. If the batter is mixed too long after the flour is added, or if it becomes too warm during mixing, the cakes are likely to be tough.

In the **two-stage method**, the flour is added in the first step. However, it is mixed with high-ratio shortening, which spreads well and coats the particles of flour with fat. This coating action limits gluten development. It is important to mix the flour and fat thoroughly for the best results. Observe all mixing times closely. Also, high-ratio cakes contain a high percentage of sugar, which is also a tenderizer.

# High-Fat Cakes

## Creaming Method

The **creaming method**, also called the *conventional method*, was for a long time the standard method for mixing **high-fat cakes**. The development of emulsified, or high-ratio, shortenings led to the development of simpler mixing methods for shortened cakes containing greater amounts of sugar and liquid. The creaming method is still used for many types of butter cakes, however.

The fat specified in creaming-method formulas in this book is butter. Butter cakes are highly prized for their flavor; shortening adds no flavor to cakes. Butter also influences texture because it melts in the mouth, while shortening does not.

However, many bakers may prefer to substitute shortening for all or part of the butter in these formulas. Shortening has the advantage of being less expensive and easier to mix. In creaming recipes, use regular shortening, not emulsified shortening. Regular shortening has better creaming abilities.

It is usually a good idea not to substitute an equal weight of shortening for butter. Remember that butter is only 80% fat, so you will need less shortening. Also, butter contains about 15% water, so you should adjust the quantity of milk or water. The procedures on page 384 explain how to adjust formulas for these substitutions.

## Two-Stage Method

This mixing method was developed for use with high-ratio plastic shortenings. High-ratio cakes contain a large percentage of sugar, more than 100% based on the weight of the flour. Also, they are made with more liquid than creaming-method cakes, and the batter pours more freely. The mixing method is a little simpler than the creaming method, and it produces a smooth batter that bakes up into a fine-grained, moist cake. It gets its name because the liquids are added in two stages.

The first step in making high-ratio cakes is blending the flour and other dry ingredients with shortening. When this mixture is smooth, the liquids (including eggs) are added in stages. Throughout this procedure, it is important to follow two rules:

- Mix at low speed and observe correct mixing times. This is important to develop proper texture.

- Stop the machine and scrape down the sides of the bowl frequently during mixing. This is important to develop a smooth, well-mixed batter.

## Procedure: Creaming Method

1. Scale ingredients accurately. Have all ingredients at room temperature (70°F/21°C).

2. Place the butter or shortening in the mixing bowl. With the paddle attachment, beat the fat slowly until it is smooth and creamy.

3. Add the sugar; cream the mixture at moderate speed until the mixture is light and fluffy (a). This will take about 8 to 10 minutes.

   Some bakers prefer to add the salt and flavorings with the sugar to ensure uniform distribution.

   If melted chocolate is used, it may be added during creaming.

4. Add the eggs a little at a time (b). After each addition, beat until the eggs are absorbed before adding more. After the eggs are beaten in, mix until light and fluffy. This step will take about 5 minutes.

5. Scrape down the sides of the bowl to ensure even mixing.

6. Add the sifted dry ingredients (including the spices, if they were not added in step 3), alternating with the liquids. This is done as follows:

   Add one-fourth of the dry ingredients (c). Mix just until blended in.

   Add one-third of the liquid (d). Mix just until blended in.

   Repeat until all ingredients are used. Scrape down the sides of the bowl occasionally for even mixing.

The reason for adding dry and liquid ingredients alternately is the batter may not absorb all the liquid unless some of the flour is present.

### Variation

A few creaming-method cakes require an extra step: Egg whites whipped to a foam with sugar are folded into the batter to provide additional leavening.

Note the variation following the basic procedure. Many bakers prefer this variation. It is somewhat simpler because it combines steps 2 and 3.

The two-stage method can sometimes be adapted to butter cakes, especially those high in fat. As an experiment, try making a butter cake formula with the creaming method and the two-stage method and comparing the texture of the finished cakes.

## Procedure for Substituting Butter and Shortening in Creaming-Method Batters

*To substitute regular shortening for all or part of the butter:*

1. Multiply the weight of the butter to be eliminated by 0.8. This gives the weight of regular shortening to use.

2. Multiply the weight of the eliminated butter by 0.15. This gives the weight of additional water or milk needed.

   Example: A formula calls for 3 lb butter and 3 lb milk. Adjust it so you use 1 lb (16 oz) butter. How much shortening and milk will you need?

$$\text{Weight of butter to be}$$
$$\text{eliminated} = 2\,\text{lb}$$
$$= 32\,\text{oz}$$
$$0.8 \times 32\,\text{oz} = 26\,\text{oz shortening}$$
$$\text{(rounded off)}$$
$$0.15 \times 32\,\text{oz} = 5\,\text{oz extra milk}$$
$$\text{(rounded off)}$$
$$\text{Total milk} = 3\,\text{lb}\,5\,\text{oz}$$

*To substitute butter for all or part of the regular shortening:*

1. Multiply the weight of the shortening to be eliminated by 1.25. This gives the weight of the butter to use.

2. Multiply the weight of the butter by 0.15. This gives the weight of water or milk to be subtracted from the formula.

   Example: A formula calls for 3 lb regular shortening and 3 lb milk. Adjust it so you use 1 lb (16 oz) shortening. How much butter and milk will you need?

$$\text{Weight of shortening}$$
$$\text{to be eliminated} = 2\,\text{lb}$$
$$= 32\,\text{oz}$$
$$1.25 \times 32\,\text{oz} = 40\,\text{oz butter}$$
$$0.15 \times 40\,\text{oz} = 6\,\text{oz milk to be subtracted}$$
$$\text{from the formula}$$
$$\text{Total milk} = 2\,\text{lb}\,10\,\text{oz}$$

## Procedure: Two-Stage Method

1. Scale the ingredients accurately. Have all ingredients at room temperature.

2. Sift the flour, baking powder, soda, and salt into the mixing bowl and add the shortening. With the paddle attachment, mix at low speed for 2 minutes. Stop the machine, scrape down the bowl and beater, and mix again for 2 minutes.

   If melted chocolate is used, blend it in during this step.

   If cocoa is used, sift it with the flour in this step or with the sugar in step 3.

3. Sift the remaining dry ingredients into the bowl and add part of the water or milk. Blend at low speed for 3 to 5 minutes. Stop the machine and scrape down the sides of the bowl and the beater several times to ensure even mixing.

4. Combine the remaining liquids and lightly beaten eggs. With the mixer running, add this mixture to the batter in 3 parts. After each part, turn off the machine and scrape down the bowl.

   Continue mixing for a total of 5 minutes in this stage.

   The finished batter is normally pourable.

### Variation

This variation combines steps 2 and 3 above into one step.

1. Scale the ingredients as in the basic method.

2. Sift all dry ingredients into the mixing bowl. Add the shortening and part of the liquid. Mix on low speed for 7 to 8 minutes. Scrape down the sides of the bowl and the beater several times.

3. Continue with step 4 in the basic procedure.

## One-Stage (Liquid Shortening) Method

High-ratio liquid shortening, described on p. 72, is so effective at emulsifying and at spreading through the batter to tenderize gluten that cake batters made from it can generally be mixed all in one step. Adding the liquid ingredients to the bowl first simplifies the procedure because there is less chance for moistened flour to coat the bottom and sides of the bowl, making scraping down difficult. Mix at low speed until the dry ingredients are moistened, so dry flour is not thrown from the bowl. Then mix for a period at high speed, followed by a period at medium speed, to properly develop air cells and create a smooth, fine-textured batter.

### Procedure: One-Stage Method

1. Scale all ingredients accurately. Have all ingredients at room temperature.

2. Combine all liquid ingredients, including high-ratio liquid shortening, in the mixing bowl (a).

3. Sift the dry ingredients together on top of the liquid ingredients in the bowl (b).

4. With the paddle attachment, mix at low speed for 30 seconds (c), until the dry ingredients are moistened. (The purpose of mixing slowly until the dry ingredients are moistened is to keep them from being thrown out of the bowl.)

5. Mix at high speed for 4 minutes. Stop the machine and scrape down the bowl and beater.

6. Mix at medium speed for 3 minutes (d).

## Flour-Batter Method

The **flour-batter method** is used for only a few specialty items. It produces a fine-textured cake, but there may be some toughening due to the development of gluten.

Flour-batter cakes include those made with either emulsified shortening or butter or both. There are no formulas in this book requiring this mixing method, although the batter for Old-Fashioned Pound Cake (p. 400) can be mixed this way instead of by the creaming method.

### Procedure: Flour-Batter Method

1. Scale all ingredients accurately. Have all ingredients at room temperature.

2. Sift the flour and other dry ingredients except the sugar into the mixing bowl. Add the fat. Blend together until smooth and light.

3. Whip the sugar and eggs together until thick and light. Add liquid flavoring ingredients, such as vanilla.

4. Combine the flour-fat mixture and the sugar-egg mixture and mix until smooth.

5. Gradually add water or milk (if any) and mix smooth.

# Low-Fat or Egg-Foam Cakes

Most *egg-foam cakes* contain little or no shortening and depend on the air trapped in beaten eggs for most or all of their leavening. Increasing interest in fine pastries and cakes has led to new appreciation of the versatility of sponge cakes. This chapter includes formulas for a great variety of egg-foam batters. These cakes are used in many of the special desserts assembled in chapter 18.

Egg-foam cakes have a springy texture and are tougher than shortened cakes. This makes them valuable for many kinds of desserts that require much handling to assemble. Most European cakes and tortes are made with sponge or egg-foam cakes. These cakes are baked either in thin sheets or disks or in thick layers that are then sliced horizontally into thinner layers. The thin sponge layers are then stacked with a variety of fillings, creams, mousses, fruits, and icings. In addition, sponge layers in this kind of cake are usually moistened with a flavored sugar syrup to compensate for their lack of moisture.

Sponge sheets for jelly rolls and other rolled cakes are often made without any shortening so they do not crack when rolled. Because fat weakens gluten, sponge cakes containing fat may split more easily.

Flour for egg-foam cakes must be weak in order to avoid making the cake tougher than necessary. Cornstarch is sometimes added to cake flour for these cakes to weaken the flour further.

## Sponge Methods

The many types of sponge cake have one characteristic in common: They are made with an egg foam that contains yolks. These are usually whole-egg foams but, in some cases, the base foam is a yolk foam and an egg white foam is folded in at the end of the procedure.

In its simplest form, sponge cake batter is made in two basic steps: (1) eggs and sugar are whipped to a thick foam, and (2) sifted flour is folded in. Additional ingredients, such as butter or liquid, complicate the procedure slightly. It would be too confusing to try to include all the variations in one procedure, so instead we describe four separate procedures.

Please note the difference between the main procedure and the first variation. There may be some confusion because in North American bakeshops, genoise nearly always contains butter. Nevertheless, in classical pâtisserie, genoise is often made without butter, and it is still commonly made with only eggs, sugar, and flour in European bakeshops. Furthermore, the main procedure as given here explains sponge cakes in their simplest and most basic form, and this procedure is the foundation for the variations that follow. If you work in a bakeshop in Canada or the United States, however, you can expect to use the first variation instead of the main procedure to mix basic *genoise*.

# Procedure: Plain Sponge or Genoise Method

1. Scale all ingredients accurately.

2. Combine the eggs, sugar, and salt in a stainless-steel bowl. Immediately set the bowl over a hot-water bath and stir or beat with a whip until the mixture warms to a temperature of about 110°F (43°C) (a). The reason for this step is that the foam attains greater volume if warm.

3. With a wire whip or the whip attachment of a mixer, beat the eggs at high speed until they are very light and thick (b). This may take as long as 10 to 15 minutes if the quantity is large.

4. If any liquid (water, milk, liquid flavoring) is included, add it now. Either whip it in in a steady stream or stir it in, as indicated in the recipe.

5. Fold in the sifted flour in 3 or 4 stages, being careful not to deflate the foam. Many bakers do this by hand, even for large batches. Fold gently until all the flour is blended in (c). If any other dry ingredients are used, such as cornstarch or baking powder, they should first be sifted with the flour.

6. Immediately pan and bake the batter. Delays will cause loss of volume.

### Variation: Butter Sponge or Butter Genoise

1. Follow the plain sponge procedure through step 5.

2. Carefully fold in the melted butter after the flour has been added. Fold in the butter completely, but be careful not to overmix or the cake will be tough (d).

3. Immediately pan and bake.

### Variation: Hot Milk and Butter Sponge

1. Scale all ingredients accurately. Heat the milk and butter together until the butter is melted.

2. Whip the eggs into a foam as in the plain sponge method, steps 2 and 3.

3. Fold in the sifted dry ingredients (flour, leavening, cocoa, etc.) as in the basic procedure.

4. Carefully fold in the hot butter and milk in 3 stages. Fold in completely, but do not overmix.

5. Immediately pan and bake.

### Variation: Separated Egg Sponge

1. Follow the basic plain sponge method, but use yolks for the basic foam (steps 2 and 3). Reserve the egg whites and part of the sugar for a separate step.

2. Whip the egg whites and sugar to firm, moist peaks. Fold into the batter alternately with the sifted dry ingredients. Fold in completely, but do not overmix.

3. Immediately pan and bake.

## Angel Food Method

Angel food cakes are based on egg-white foams and contain no fat. For success in beating egg whites, review the principles of egg white foams in chapter 12, p. 266. Egg whites for angel food cakes should be whipped until they form soft, not stiff, peaks. Overwhipped whites lose their ability to expand and to leaven the cake. This is because the protein network in stiffly beaten whites has already stretched as far as it can. If the whites are whipped to soft peaks instead, they can stretch more during baking, allowing the cake to rise.

### Procedure: Angel Food Method

1. Scale ingredients accurately. Have all ingredients at room temperature. The egg whites may be slightly warmed in order to achieve better volume.

2. Sift the flour with half the sugar. This step helps the flour mix more evenly with the foam.

3. Using the whip attachment, beat the egg whites until they form soft peaks. Add salt and cream of tartar near the beginning of the beating process.

4. Gradually beat in the portion of the sugar that was not mixed with the flour. Continue to whip until the egg whites form soft, moist peaks. Do not beat until stiff.

5. Fold in the flour-sugar mixture just until it is thoroughly absorbed, but no longer.

6. Deposit the mix in ungreased pans and bake immediately.

## Chiffon Method

Chiffon cakes and angel food cakes are both based on egg-white foams, but here the similarities in the mixing methods end. In angel food cakes, a dry flour-sugar mixture is folded into the egg whites. In chiffon cakes, a batter containing flour, egg yolks, vegetable oil, and water is folded into the whites.

Egg whites for chiffon cakes should be whipped until they are a little firmer than those for angel food cakes, but do not whip them until they are dry. Chiffon cakes contain baking powder, so they do not depend on the egg foam for all their leavening.

### Procedure: Chiffon Method

1. Scale all ingredients accurately. Have all ingredients at room temperature. Use a good-quality, flavorless vegetable oil.

2. Sift the dry ingredients, including part of the sugar, into the mixing bowl.

3. Mixing with the paddle attachment at second speed, gradually add the oil, then the egg yolks, water, and liquid flavorings, all in a slow, steady stream. While adding the liquids, stop the machine several times and scrape down the bowl and the beater. Mix until smooth, but do not overmix.

4. Whip the egg whites until they form soft peaks. Add the cream of tartar and sugar in a stream and whip to firm, moist peaks.

5. Fold the whipped egg whites into the flour-liquid mixture.

6. Immediately deposit the batter in ungreased center-tube pans (like angel food cakes) or in layer pans that have had the bottoms greased and dusted, but not the sides (like sponge layers).

# Combination Creaming/Sponge Method

Some European-style cakes are begun by using the creaming method. In other words, butter is creamed with sugar until the mixture is light. These cakes usually contain no chemical leavening, however. Instead, whipped egg whites are folded into the batter, as for some sponge cakes. Examples of this kind of cake are Hazelnut Sponge Cake (p. 413) and Baumkuchen (p. 414). Mixing hazelnut sponge is illustrated in the procedure below.

## Procedure: Combination Creaming/Sponge Method

**1.** Cream the butter and sugar.

**2.** Add the egg yolks a little at a time.

**3.** Mix well after each addition.

**4.** Whip the egg whites and sugar until they form soft peaks, as for angel food cake.

**5.** Fold the meringue into the butter mixture.

**6.** Sift the dry ingredients together.

**7.** Fold in the sifted dry ingredients.

**8.** Deposit the batter in prepared pans.

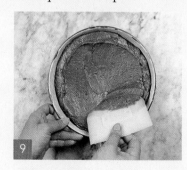

**9.** Level the top of the batter with a plastic scraper.

## Prepared Mixes

Many mixes are available that contain all ingredients except water and, sometimes, eggs. These products also contain emulsifiers to ensure even blending of ingredients. To use them, follow the package instructions exactly.

Most mixes produce cakes with excellent volume, texture, and tenderness. Whether or not they also taste good is a matter of opinion. On the other hand, cakes made from scratch are not necessarily better. They are better only if they are carefully mixed and baked; are prepared from good, tested formulas; and for parallelism incorporate high-quality ingredients.

# CAKE FORMULA BALANCE

**I**t is possible to change cake formulas, either to improve them or to reduce costs. However, ingredients and quantities can be changed only within certain limits. A cake formula whose ingredients fall within these limits is said to be in balance. Knowing the limits helps you not only modify recipes but also judge untested recipes and correct faults.

Keep in mind that new ingredients and procedures are frequently developed. Cake-balancing rules that have worked well until now may be changed as new developments come along that allow you to break the rules. A baker should be open to new ideas and willing to try them. For example, it was once a rule that the weight of sugar in a mix should not exceed the weight of flour. But the introduction of shortenings with emulsifiers led to formulas with higher proportions of sugar.

## Ingredient Functions

For the purpose of balancing cake formulas, we can classify cake ingredients according to four functions: tougheners (or stabilizers), tenderizers, dryers, and moisteners (or moisturizers). The idea of formula balancing is that tougheners should balance tenderizers and dryers should balance moisteners. In other words, if we increase the amount of tougheners in a formula, for example, we must compensate by also increasing the amount of tenderizers.

Many ingredients fill more than one function, sometimes even opposite functions. Egg yolks contain protein, which is a toughener, but they also contain fat, which is a tenderizer. The major cake ingredients are classified as follows:

**Tougheners** provide structure: flour, eggs (whites and yolks).

**Tenderizers** provide softness or shortening of protein fibers: sugar, fats (including butter, shortening, and cocoa butter), chemical leaveners.

**Moisteners** provide moisture or water: water, liquid milk, syrups and liquid sugars, eggs.

**Dryers** absorb moisture: flours and starches, cocoa, milk solids.

You can also use this table of ingredients as a troubleshooting guide for cake failures. A cake that fails even if mixed and baked correctly may require formula balancing. For example, if a cake is too dry, you might increase one or more of the moisteners or decrease the dryers.

This takes a certain amount of experience, however. Remember that most ingredients have more than one function. If you decide to increase the eggs in a dry cake, you may wind up with an even harder, tougher cake. Although whole eggs do provide some moisture, they provide even more toughening power because of their strong protein content.

As a further complication, many successful cake formulas apparently break the rules. For example, one rule for creaming-method cakes made with butter or regular shortening says the weight of the sugar should not exceed the weight of the flour. But, in fact, there are successful recipes calling for more than 100% sugar. Many baking manuals insist on these balancing rules rather strongly. But it may be better to think of them not as ironclad laws but as guidelines that give you a starting point for judging or correcting recipes.

In summary, it takes an experienced baker to be consistently successful at adjusting cake formulas. However, even beginning bakers should have some knowledge of formula balancing. It helps you understand the formulas you are using and practicing, and it helps you understand why you assemble and mix cakes in certain ways and what makes the mixtures work.

In the following discussion of balancing rules, it is helpful to think of ingredients in terms of baker's percentages (see p. 24) rather than as specific weights. This eliminates one variable: Flour is a constant 100%, so other ingredients are increased or decreased with respect to flour.

## Balancing Fat-Type or Shortened Cakes

A normal starting point in discussing cake balancing is old-fashioned *pound cake*. This cake is made of flour, sugar, butter, and eggs in equal parts. As bakers experimented with this basic recipe over the years, they reduced the quantities of sugar, fat, and eggs, and compensated by adding milk. This is the origin of the modern butter cake.

The general rules for balancing creaming-method cakes made with butter or regular shortening are as follows (all ingredient quantities are, of course, by weight):

- The sugar (a tenderizer) is balanced against the flour (a toughener). In most creaming-method cakes, the weight of sugar is less than or equal to the weight of flour.

- The fat (a tenderizer) is balanced against the eggs (tougheners).

- The eggs and liquids (moisteners) are balanced against the flour (a dryer).

Balancing one ingredient against another, as indicated in the above guidelines, means that if one ingredient is increased or decreased, then the balancing ingredients must also be changed. For example, if the fat is increased, then the eggs must be increased to keep the formula in balance.

With the development of emulsified shortening, it became possible to increase the quantities of sugar, eggs, and liquids. For example, the weight of sugar in high-ratio cakes is greater than the weight of flour, and the formula is still in balance. Similarly, the quantity of liquid can be greater because the emulsifiers in the shortening keep the batter stable. However, the general principles of balancing, as outlined above, still hold. If one ingredient is increased, other ingredients must be adjusted to compensate.

A common practice in balancing a formula is to decide on the sugar-flour ratio and then balance the rest of the ingredients against these. The following guidelines are helpful:

- If eggs are increased, increase the shortening.

- If extra milk solids are added as an enrichment, add an equal weight of water.

- If cocoa is added, add water equal in weight to 75 to 100% of the cocoa.

- If cocoa or bitter chocolate is added, increase the amount of sugar to as much as 180% of the weight of the flour in high-ratio cakes and to over 100% of the weight of the flour in creaming-method cakes. This is because of the starch content of the cocoa and chocolate.

- In cakes to be baked in very large units, use less liquid because less water will evaporate during baking.

- If a liquid sugar is added (honey, corn syrup, etc.), reduce other liquids slightly.

- If large quantities of moist ingredients, such as applesauce or mashed bananas, are added, reduce the liquid. Extra-large additions of moist ingredients may also require increasing the flour and eggs.

- Use less baking powder with creamed batters than two-stage batters because the creamed batters get more aeration in the creaming stage.

# SCALING, PANNING, AND BAKING

## Pan Preparation

Prepare pans before mixing cake batters so cakes can be baked without delay as soon as they are mixed.

- For high-fat cakes, layer pans must be greased, preferably with a commercial pan-greasing preparation. If this is not available, dust the greased pans with flour and tap out the excess.

- For sheet cakes, line the pans with greased parchment. For thin layers, such as Swiss rolls, it is necessary to use level pans without dents or warps. Silicone mats are especially good to use for lining pans for thin layers.

- For angel food cakes and chiffon cakes, do not grease the pan. The batter must be able to cling to the sides so it doesn't sink back into the pan after rising.

- For sponge cake layers with little or no fat, grease the bottoms but not the sides of the pans.

## Procedure for Scaling Creaming-Method Batters

These batters are thick and do not pour easily.

1. Place a prepared cake pan on the left side of the balance scale. Balance the scale by placing another pan on the right side.

2. Set the scale for the desired weight.

3. Add batter to the left pan until the scale balances.

4. Remove the pan from the scale and spread the batter smooth with a spatula.

5. Repeat with remaining pans.

6. Give the pans several sharp raps on the bench to free large trapped air bubbles. Bake immediately.

## Procedure for Scaling Two-Stage Batters

These batters are usually very liquid. They may be scaled like creamed batters or, for greater speed, as follows:

1. Place an empty volume measure on the left side of the balance scale. Balance the scale to zero.

2. Set the scale for the desired weight.

3. Pour batter into the measure until the scale balances.

4. Note the volume of batter in the measure.

5. Pour the batter into the prepared pan, quickly scraping out the measure to get all the batter.

6. Scale the remaining cakes with the volume measure, using the volume noted in step 4.

7. Give the pans several sharp raps on the bench to free large trapped air bubbles. Bake immediately.

## Procedure for Scaling Egg-Foam Cakes

Foam cake batters should be handled as little as possible and baked immediately to avoid deflating the beaten eggs. While these cakes may be scaled like creamed batters, many bakers prefer to eyeball them in order to minimize handling.

1. Have all prepared pans lined up on the bench.

2. Scale the first pan as for creamed batters.

3. Quickly fill the remaining pans to the same level as the first pan, judging the level by eye.

4. Spread the batter smooth and bake immediately.

See the table on page 394 for average scaling weights as well as baking temperatures and times.

## Average Cake Scaling Weights, Baking Temperatures, and Times

| Pan Type and Size | Scaling Weight[A] U.S. | Metric | Baking Temperature U.S. | Metric | Approximate Baking Time in Minutes |
|---|---|---|---|---|---|
| **HIGH-FAT CAKES AND CHIFFON CAKES** | | | | | |
| *Round layers* | | | | | |
| 6 in. (15 cm) | 8–10 oz | 230–285 g | 375°F | 190°C | 18 |
| 8 in. (20 cm) | 14–18 oz | 400–510 g | 375°F | 190°C | 25 |
| 10 in. (25 cm) | 24–28 oz | 680–800 g | 360°F | 180°C | 35 |
| 12 in. (30 cm) | 32–40 oz | 900–1100 g | 360°F | 180°C | 35 |
| *Sheets and square pans* | | | | | |
| 18 × 26 in. (46 × 66 cm) | 7–8 lb | 3.2–3.6 kg | 360°F | 180°C | 35 |
| 18 × 13 in. (46 × 33 cm) | 3.5–4 lb | 1.6–1.8 kg | 360°F | 180°C | 35 |
| 9 × 9 in. (23 × 23 cm) | 24 oz | 680 g | 360°F | 180°C | 30–35 |
| *Loaf (pound cake)* | | | | | |
| 2¼ × 3½ × 8 in. (6 × 9 × 20 cm) | 16–18 oz | 450–500 g | 350°F | 175°C | 50–60 |
| 2¾ × 4½ × 8½ in. (7 × 11 × 22 cm) | 24–27 oz | 680–765 g | 350°F | 175°C | 55–65 |
| *Cupcakes* | | | | | |
| per dozen | 18 oz | 510 g | 385°F | 195°C | 18–20 |
| **FOAM-TYPE CAKES** | | | | | |
| *Round layers* | | | | | |
| 6 in. (15 cm) | 5–6 oz | 140–170 g | 375°F | 190°C | 20 |
| 8 in. (20 cm) | 10 oz | 280 g | 375°F | 190°C | 20 |
| 10 in. (25 cm) | 16 oz | 450 g | 360°F | 180°C | 25–30 |
| 12 in. (30 cm) | 24 oz | 700 g | 360°F | 180°C | 25–30 |
| *Sheets (for jelly roll or sponge roll)* | | | | | |
| 18 × 26 in., ½ in. thick (46 × 66 cm, 12 mm thick) | 2.5 lb | 1.2 kg | 375°F | 190°C | 15–20 |
| 18 × 26 in., ¼ in. thick (46 × 66 cm, 6 mm thick) | 28 oz | 800 g | 400°F | 200°C | 7–10 |
| *Tube (angel food and chiffon)* | | | | | |
| 8 in. (20 cm) | 12–14 oz | 340–400 g | 360°F | 180°C | 30 |
| 10 in. (25 cm) | 24–32 oz | 700–900 g | 350°F | 175°C | 50 |
| *Cupcakes* | | | | | |
| per dozen | 10 oz | 280 g | 375°F | 190°C | 18–20 |

[A]The weights given are averages. Weights may be increased by 25% if thicker layers are desired. Baking times may need to be increased slightly.

## Baking and Cooling

Cake structure is fragile, so proper baking conditions are essential for high-quality products. The following guidelines will help you avoid cake failures.

◆ Preheat the ovens. To conserve expensive energy, don't preheat longer than necessary.

◆ Make sure ovens and shelves are level.

◆ Do not let pans touch each other. If pans touch, air circulation is inhibited and the cakes rise unevenly.

- Bake at the correct temperature.

- Too hot an oven causes the cake to set unevenly with a humped center, or to set before it has fully risen. Crusts will be too dark.

- Too slow an oven causes poor volume and texture because the cake doesn't set fast enough and may fall.

- If steam is available in the oven, use it for creamed and two-stage batters. These cakes bake with a flatter top if baked with steam because the steam delays the formation of the top crust.

- Do not open the oven or disturb cakes until they have finished rising and are partially browned. Disturbing the cakes before they are set may cause them to fall.

- Angel food and chiffon cakes should be cooled upside-down in their pans, so they won't collapse back into the pans. Because they are baked in ungreased pans, they won't fall out of their pans. When completely cool, they are sturdy enough to be pulled out of the pans without breaking.

## Tests for Doneness

- Shortened cakes shrink away slightly from sides of pan.

- Cake is springy. The center of the top of the cake springs back when pressed lightly.

- A cake tester or wooden pick inserted in center of cake comes out clean.

## Cooling and Removing from Pans

- Cool layer cakes and sheet cakes 15 minutes in pans and turn out while slightly warm. Because they are fragile, they may break if turned out when hot.

- Turn out layer cakes onto racks to finish cooling.

- To turn out sheet cakes:

  1. Sprinkle the top lightly with granulated sugar.

  2. Set a cake board on top of the cake, and then set an empty sheet pan on top, bottom-side down. (If a cake board is not available, just set the upside-down sheet pan on top.)

  3. Invert both pans.

  4. Remove the top pan.

  5. Peel the parchment off the cake.

- Cool angel food cakes and chiffon cakes upside down in pans so they do not fall back into the pans and lose volume. Support the edges of the pan so the top of the cake is off the bench. When cool, loosen the cake from sides of the pan with a knife or spatula and carefully pull out the cake.

Errors in mixing, scaling, baking, and cooling cakes cause many kinds of defects and failures. For easy reference, defects and their possible causes are summarized in the troubleshooting guide in the table on the next page.

## Common Cake Faults and Their Causes

| FAULT | CAUSES |
|---|---|
| **VOLUME AND SHAPE** | |
| Poor volume | Too little flour |
| | Too much liquid |
| | Too little leavening |
| | Oven too hot |
| Uneven shape | Improper mixing |
| | Batter spread unevenly |
| | Uneven oven heat |
| | Oven racks not level |
| | Cake pans warped |
| **CRUST** | |
| Too dark | Too much sugar |
| | Oven too hot |
| Too light | Too little sugar |
| | Oven not hot enough |
| Burst or cracked | Too much flour or flour too strong |
| | Too little liquid |
| | Improper mixing |
| | Oven too hot |
| Soggy | Underbaked |
| | Cooling in pans or with not enough ventilation |
| | Wrapping before cool |
| **TEXTURE** | |
| Dense or heavy | Too little leavening |
| | Too much liquid |
| | Too much sugar |
| | Too much shortening |
| | Oven not hot enough |
| Coarse or irregular | Too much leavening |
| | Too little egg |
| | Improper mixing |
| Crumbly | Too much leavening |
| | Too much shortening |
| | Too much sugar |
| | Wrong kind of flour |
| | Improper mixing |
| Tough | Flour too strong |
| | Too much flour |
| | Too little sugar or shortening |
| | Overmixing |
| **POOR FLAVOR** | |
| | Poor-quality ingredients |
| | Poor storage or sanitation |
| | Unbalanced formula |

# ALTITUDE ADJUSTMENTS

At high altitudes, atmospheric pressure is much lower than at sea level. This factor must be taken into account in cake baking. Formulas must be adjusted to suit baking conditions more than 2000 or 3000 feet above sea level.

Although general guidelines can be given, the exact adjustments required will vary for different kinds of cakes. Many manufacturers of flour, shortening, and other bakery ingredients supply detailed information and adjusted formulas for any given locality.

In general, the following adjustments must be made. See the table below for actual adjustments.

**Leavening.** Leavening gases expand more when air pressure is lower, so the amounts of baking powder and baking soda must be decreased.

Creaming and foaming procedures should also be reduced so less air is incorporated.

**Tougheners: Flour and Eggs.** Cakes require firmer structure at high altitudes. Both eggs and flour must be increased to supply adequate proteins for structure.

**Tenderizers: Shortening and Sugar.** For the same reasons, shortening and sugar must be decreased so that the structure will be firmer.

**Liquids.** At higher altitudes, water boils at a lower temperature and evaporates more easily. Liquids must be increased to prevent excess drying both during and after baking. This also helps compensate for the decrease in moisturizers (sugar and fat) and the increase in flour, which absorbs moisture.

**Baking Temperatures.** Increase baking temperatures by about 25°F (14°C) above 3500 feet.

**Pan Greasing.** High-fat cakes tend to stick at high altitudes. Grease pans more heavily. Remove baked cakes from pans as soon as possible.

**Storing.** To prevent drying, wrap or ice cakes as soon as they are cool.

## Approximate Formula Adjustment in Shortened Cakes at High Altitude

| Ingredient | Increase or Decrease | 2500 ft | 5000 ft | 7500 ft |
|---|---|---|---|---|
| Baking powder | decrease | 20% | 40% | 60% |
| Flour | increase | — | 4% | 9% |
| Eggs | increase | 2.5% | 9% | 15% |
| Sugar | decrease | 3% | 6% | 9% |
| Fat | decrease | — | — | 9% |
| Liquid | increase | 9% | 15% | 22% |

To make adjustments, multiply the percentage indicated by the amount of ingredient and add or subtract the result as indicated. *Example:* Adjust 1 lb (16 oz) eggs for 7500 ft.

$$.15 \times 16 \text{ oz} = 2.4 \text{ oz}$$
$$16 \text{ oz} + 2.4 \text{ oz} = 18.4 \text{ oz}$$

# FORMULAS

The following cake formulas will give you practice with all major cake-mixing methods. Many popular North American cake types are included, sometimes in the form of variations on the basic cake types. These variations show that by making small changes in flavoring ingredients, you can make many different cakes from the same basic recipe. Adding new flavorings sometimes requires other ingredient changes. For example, in the case of the Strawberry Cake (p. 403), the flavoring ingredient is high in sugar, so the amount of sugar in the formula is reduced.

Of course, many more variations are possible than there is room for here. As one example, we give a separate recipe for spice cake (made with brown sugar), but other spice cakes can be made by adding a similar spice mixture to a basic yellow cake.

The difference between chocolate cake and devil's food cake is in the amount of baking soda used. As was explained in chapter 4, an excess of soda causes a reddish color in chocolate. By reducing the amount of soda (and increasing the baking powder to make up the lost leavening power), a devil's food cake can be turned into a regular chocolate cake. Of course, both types of cake can be made with either cocoa powder or chocolate. See page 93 for instructions on substituting one type of cocoa product for another.

Because we have already discussed the mixing procedures in detail, the procedures are not repeated for each formula. If necessary, review pages 383–389 before beginning production.

## YELLOW BUTTER CAKE

*For large-quantity measurements, see page 734.*

| Ingredients | U.S. | | Metric | % | Procedure |
|---|---|---|---|---|---|
| Butter | 12 | oz | 360 g | 80 | **MIXING** |
| Sugar | 13 | oz | 390 g | 87 | Creaming method (p. 383) |
| Salt | 0.12 oz (⅔ tsp) | | 4 g | 0.75 | |
| Eggs | 7.5 | oz | 225 g | 50 | **SCALING AND BAKING** |
| Cake flour | 15 | oz | 450 g | 100 | See table on page 394. |
| Baking powder | 0.62 oz (3¾ tsp) | | 18 g | 4 | |
| Milk | 15 | oz | 450 g | 100 | |
| Vanilla extract | 0.25 oz | | 8 g | 1.5 | |
| *Total weight:* | *3 lb 15* | *oz* | *1905 g* | *423%* | |

*For large-quantity measurements, see page 734.*

### WALNUT CAKE

Add 50% (7.5 oz/225 g) chopped walnuts to the batter. Bake in small loaf pans. If desired, ice with chocolate buttercream.

### PAN SPREAD

*For large-quantity measurements, see page 734.*
*(for 9-in./23 cm square pan)*

| Ingredients | U.S. | | Metric |
|---|---|---|---|
| Brown sugar | 4 | oz | 112 g |
| Granulated sugar | 1.5 oz | | 42 g |
| Corn syrup or honey | 1 | oz | 30 g |
| Water (as needed) | | | |

Cream together the first three ingredients. Add enough water to thin to spreading consistency.

**VARIATIONS**

### UPSIDE-DOWN CAKE

Increase the eggs to 55% (8.25 oz/245 g). Decrease milk to 60% (9 oz/275 g). Add 0.75% (0.12 oz/4 g) lemon or orange flavor. Butter a sheet pan, spread with pan spread (at right), and arrange the desired fruit (pineapple rings, sliced peaches, etc.) on top of the pan spread. Scale the batter as indicated in the table on page 394. Bake at 360°F (180°C). Immediately after baking, turn out of the pan (see p. 395). Glaze with Clear Glaze (p. 199) or Apricot Glaze (p. 200).

# CHOCOLATE BUTTER CAKE

*For large-quantity measurements, see page 734.*

| Ingredients | U.S. | | Metric | % | Procedure |
|---|---|---|---|---|---|
| Butter | 9 | oz | 280 g | 75 | **MIXING** |
| Sugar | 15 | oz | 470 g | 125 | Creaming method (p. 383). Blend in the melted |
| Salt | 0.2 | oz (1 tsp) | 6 g | 1.5 | chocolate after the fat and sugar are well |
| Unsweetened chocolate, melted | 6 | oz | 188 g | 50 | creamed |
| Eggs | 8 | oz | 250 g | 67 | **SCALING AND BAKING** |
| Cake flour | 12 | oz | 250 g | 100 | See table on page 394. |
| Baking powder | 0.5 | oz | 15 g | 4 | |
| Milk | 14 | oz | 439 g | 115 | |
| Vanilla extract | 0.25 | oz | 8 g | 2 | |
| **Total weight:** | **4 lb** | | **2022 g** | **539%** | |

# BROWN SUGAR SPICE CAKE

| Ingredients | U.S. | | Metric | | % | Procedure |
|---|---|---|---|---|---|---|
| Butter | 12 | oz | 400 | g | 80 | **MIXING** |
| Brown sugar | 15 | oz | 500 | g | 100 | Creaming method (p. 383) |
| Salt | 0.25 | oz | 8 | g | 1.5 | **SCALING AND BAKING** |
| Eggs | 9 | oz | 300 | g | 60 | See table on page 394. |
| Cake flour | 15 | oz | 500 | g | 100 | |
| Baking powder | 0.5 | oz | 15 | g | 3 | |
| Baking soda | 0.05 | oz (⅜ tsp) | 1.5 | g | 0.3 | |
| Cinnamon | 0.08 | oz (1½ tsp) | 2.5 | g | 0.5 | |
| Cloves, ground | 0.05 | oz (¾ tsp) | 1.5 | g | 0.3 | |
| Nutmeg | 0.03 | oz (⅜ tsp) | 1 | g | 0.2 | |
| Milk | 15 | oz | 500 | g | 100 | |
| **Total weight:** | **4 lb** | **2 oz** | **2229** | **g** | **445%** | |

## VARIATIONS

### CARROT NUT CAKE

Reduce the milk to 90% (13.5 oz/450 g). Add 40% (6 oz/200 g) grated fresh carrots, 20% (3 oz/100 g) finely chopped walnuts, and 1 tsp (3 g) grated orange zest. Omit the cloves.

### BANANA CAKE

Omit the cinnamon and cloves. Reduce the milk to 30% (4.5 oz/150 g). Add 125% (1 lb 3 oz/625 g) ripe, puréed bananas. If desired, add 40% (6 oz/200 g) finely chopped pecans.

### APPLESAUCE CAKE

Reduce the milk to 50% (7.5 oz/250 g) and add 90% (13.5 oz/450 g) applesauce. Reduce the baking powder to 2% (0.3 oz or 2 tsp/10 g). Increase the baking soda to 1% (0.15 oz or 1 tsp/5 g).

# OLD-FASHIONED POUND CAKE

| Ingredients | U.S. | Metric | % | Procedure |
|---|---|---|---|---|
| Butter or part butter and part shortening | 1 lb | 500 g | 100 | **MIXING** |
| Sugar | 1 lb | 500 g | 100 | Creaming method (p. 383). After about half the eggs have been creamed in, add a little of the flour to avoid curdling. |
| Vanilla extract | 0.33 oz (2 tsp) | 10 g | 2 | |
| Eggs | 1 lb | 500 g | 100 | **SCALING AND BAKING** |
| Cake flour | 1 lb | 500 g | 100 | See table on page 394. Paper-lined loaf pans are often used for pound cakes. |
| *Total weight:* | *4 lb* | *2010 g* | *402%* | |

## VARIATIONS

Mace or grated lemon or orange zest may be used to flavor pound cake.

### RAISIN POUND CAKE

Add 25% (4 oz/125 g) raisins or currants that have been soaked in boiling water and drained well.

### CHOCOLATE POUND CAKE

Sift 25% (4 oz/125 g) cocoa and 0.8% (0.12 oz or ¾ tsp/4 g) baking soda with the flour. Add 25% (4 oz/125 g) water to the batter.

### MARBLE POUND CAKE

Fill loaf pans with alternating layers of regular and chocolate pound cake batters. Run a knife through the batter to marble the mixture.

### SHEET CAKE FOR PETITS FOURS AND FANCY PASTRIES

Increase eggs to 112% (1 lb 2 oz/560 g). Bake on sheet pans lined with greased paper. Scale 4 lb (1800 g) for ¼-in. (6 mm) layers to make three-layer petits fours. Increase the recipe and scale 6 lb (2700 g) for ⅜-in. (9 mm) layers to make two-layer petits fours.

### FRUIT CAKE

Use 50% cake flour and 50% bread flour in the basic recipe. Add 250–750% (2.5–7.5 lb/1.25–3.75 kg) mixed fruits and nuts to the batter. Procedure and suggested fruit mixtures follow.

1. *Prepare fruits and nuts:*

   Rinse and drain glazed fruits to remove excess syrup.

   Cut large fruits (such as whole dates) into smaller pieces.

   Mix all fruits and soak overnight in brandy, rum, or sherry.

   Drain well. (Reserve drained liquor for later batches or for other purposes.)

2. Mix batter as in basic procedure, using 80% of the flour. If spices are used, cream them with the butter and sugar.

3. Toss the fruits and nuts with the remaining flour. Fold them into the batter.

4. Baking: Use loaf, ring, or tube pans, preferably with paper liners. Bake at 350°F (175°C) for small cakes (1–1½ lb/450–700 g), and 300°F (150°C) for large cakes (4–5 lb/1.8–2.3 kg). Baking time ranges from about 1½ hours for small cakes to 3–4 hours or more for large cakes.

5. Cool. Glaze with Clear Glaze (p. 199), decorate with fruits and nuts, if desired, and glaze again.

Percentages in the following fruit mixes are based on the flour in the basic pound cake recipe.

## FRUIT MIX I (DARK)

| Ingredients | U.S. | | Metric | | % |
|---|---|---|---|---|---|
| Dark raisins | 1 lb | | 500 | g | 100 |
| Light raisins | 1 lb | | 500 | g | 100 |
| Currants | 8 | oz | 250 | g | 50 |
| Dates | 1 lb | | 500 | g | 100 |
| Figs | 8 | oz | 250 | g | 50 |
| Glacé cherries | 6.5 | oz | 200 | g | 40 |
| Nuts (pecans, walnuts, filberts, brazil nuts) | 9.5 | oz | 300 | g | 60 |
| *Spices* | | | | | |
|   Cinnamon | 0.08 oz (1½ tsp) | | 2 | g | 0.5 |
|   Cloves, ground | 0.04 oz (½ tsp) | | 1.25 | g | 0.25 |
|   Nutmeg | 0.04 oz (½ tsp) | | 1.25 | g | 0.25 |
| *Total weight:* | *5 lb* | | *2500* | *g* | *700%* |

## FRUIT MIX II (LIGHT)

| Ingredients | U.S. | | Metric | % |
|---|---|---|---|---|
| Golden raisins | 12 | oz | 375 g | 75 |
| Currants | 8 | oz | 250 g | 50 |
| Mixed glacé fruit | 8 | oz | 250 g | 50 |
| Glacé pineapple | 3 | oz | 100 g | 20 |
| Glacé orange peel | 2.5 | oz | 75 g | 15 |
| Glacé lemon peel | 2.5 | oz | 75 g | 15 |
| Glacé cherries | 5 | oz | 150 g | 30 |
| Blanched almonds | 4 | oz | 125 g | 25 |
| *Spices* | | | | |
|   Lemon zest, grated | 0.06 oz (¾ tsp) | | 2 g | 0.4 |
| *Total weight:* | *2 lb 13* | *oz* | *1400 g* | *280%* |

# ALMOND CAKE FOR PETITS FOURS

| Ingredients | U.S. | | Metric | % | Procedure |
|---|---|---|---|---|---|
| Almond paste | 3 lb 6 | oz | 1500 g | 300 | **MIXING** |
| Sugar | 2 lb 8 | oz | 1150 g | 225 | Creaming method (p. 383). To soften the al- |
| Butter | 2 lb 8 | oz | 1150 g | 225 | mond paste, blend it with a little of the egg un- |
| Eggs | 3 lb 2 | oz | 1400 g | 275 | til smooth before adding the sugar. Proceed as for mixing pound cake. |
| Cake flour | 12 | oz | 340 g | 67 | |
| Bread flour | 6 | oz | 170 g | 33 | **SCALING AND BAKING** |
| *Total weight:* | *12 lb 10* | *oz* | *5710 g* | *1125%* | 4 lb 3 oz (1900 g) per sheet pan. One recipe is enough for 3 pans. Pans must be level and without dents. Spread batter very smooth. |

**BAKING**

400°F (200°C)

See page 480 for makeup of petits fours.

# SACHER MIX I

| Ingredients | U.S. | | Metric | % | Procedure |
|---|---|---|---|---|---|
| Butter | 10 | oz | 250 g | 100 | **MIXING** |
| Sugar | 10 | oz | 250 g | 100 | Modified creaming method |
| Sweet chocolate, melted | 12.5 | oz | 312 g | 125 | 1. Cream the butter and sugar; add the chocolate; add the egg yolks and vanilla, as in the basic creaming method. |
| Egg yolks | 10 | oz | 250 g | 100 | 2. Whip the egg whites with the salt. Add the sugar and whip to soft peaks. |
| Vanilla extract | 0.33 | oz (2 tsp) | 8 g | 3.3 | |
| Egg whites | 15 | oz | 375 g | 150 | 3. Fold the egg whites into the batter alternately with the flour. |
| Salt | 0.08 | oz (½ tsp) | 2 g | 0.8 | **SCALING** |
| Sugar | 7.5 | oz | 188 g | 75 | 6-in. (15 cm) cake: 14 oz (400 g) |
| Cake flour, sifted | 10 | oz | 250 g | 100 | 7-in. (18 cm) cake: 19 oz (540 g) |
| **Total weight:** | **4 lb 11** | **oz** | **1885 g** | **750%** | 8-in. (20 cm) cake: 24 oz (680 g) |

Note: See page 461 for icing and decorating a Sachertorte. Layers may be iced and decorated like any other chocolate cake, but then the cake should not be called Sachertorte (see sidebar).

**SCALING**

6-in. (15 cm) cake: 14 oz (400 g)

7-in. (18 cm) cake: 19 oz (540 g)

8-in. (20 cm) cake: 24 oz (680 g)

9-in. (23 cm) cake: 30 oz (850 g)

10-in. (25 cm) cake: 36 oz (1020 g)

**BAKING**

325°F (165°C) for 45–60 minutes

# SACHER MIX II

*For large-quantity measurements, see page 735.*

| Ingredients | U.S. | | Metric | % | Procedure |
|---|---|---|---|---|---|
| Butter, softened | 4.5 | oz | 135 g | 337 | **MIXING** |
| Fine granulated sugar | 3.67 | oz | 110 g | 275 | Modified creaming method |
| Egg yolks | 4 | oz | 120 g | 300 | 1. Cream the butter and sugar. Add the egg yolks as in the basic creaming method. |
| Egg whites | 6 | oz | 180 g | 450 | 2. Whip the egg whites and sugar to a stiff meringue. |
| Fine granulated sugar | 2 | oz | 60 g | 150 | 3. Sift together the flour and cocoa powder. Mix in the almonds. |
| Cake flour | 1.33 | oz | 40 g | 100 | 4. Fold the meringue and dry ingredients alternately into the butter mixture, starting and ending with the meringue. |
| Cocoa powder | 1.33 | oz | 40 g | 100 | |
| Powdered almonds, toasted | 1.75 | oz | 55 g | 137 | |
| **Total weight:** | **1 lb 8** | **oz** | **740 g** | **1849%** | **SCALING** |

Note: See page 461 for icing and decorating Sachertorte. Layers may be iced and decorated like other kinds of chocolate cake, but then the cake should not be called Sachertorte.

**SCALING**

6-in. (15 cm) cake: 7 oz (200 g)

7-in. (18 cm) cake: 10 oz (280 g)

8-in. (20 cm) cake: 12 oz (370 g)

9-in. (23 cm) cake: 16 oz (470 g)

Butter the pans, line the bottoms with parchment, and dust with flour.

**BAKING**

325°F (160°C), 35–45 minutes, depending on size

## SACHERTORTE

The classic chocolate cake Sachertorte originated at the Hotel Sacher, an elegant hotel built in 1876, directly across the street from the Vienna Opera House. The cake became so popular that many bakers tried to imitate it, even though the hotel kept the original formula a secret. As a result, there are many recipes claiming to be authentic. Of course, the original is still available on the menu at the Hotel Sacher.

Austrians serve the cake with a generous portion of unsweetened whipped cream ("mit Schlag," in the Austrian dialect) because the texture of the cake is somewhat dry.

# WHITE CAKE

*For large-quantity measurements, see page 735.*

| Ingredients | U.S. | | Metric | % | Procedure |
|---|---|---|---|---|---|
| Cake flour | 12 | oz | 375 g | 100 | **MIXING** |
| Baking powder | 0.75 | oz | 22 g | 6.25 | Two-stage method (p. 384) |
| Salt | 0.25 | oz | 8 g | 2 | **SCALING AND BAKING** |
| Emulsified shortening | 6 | oz | 188 g | 50 | See table on page 394. |
| Sugar | 15 | oz | 470 g | 125 | |
| Skim milk | 6 | oz | 188 g | 50 | |
| Vanilla extract | 0.18 oz (1⅛ tsp) | | 5 g | 1.5 | |
| Almond extract | 0.09 oz (½ tsp) | | 2 g | 0.75 | |
| Skim milk | 6 | oz | 188 g | 50 | |
| Egg whites | 8 | oz | 250 g | 67 | |
| *Total weight:* | 3 lb 6 | oz | *1696 g* | *452%* | |

### VARIATIONS

Use water instead of milk and add 10% (0.62 oz/18 g) nonfat dry milk to the dry ingredients.

Flavor with lemon extract or emulsion instead of vanilla and almond.

## YELLOW CAKE

Make the following ingredient adjustments:

Reduce shortening to 45% (5.5 oz/168 g).

Substitute whole eggs for egg whites, using the same total weight (67%).

Use 2% (0.25 oz/8 g) vanilla and omit the almond extract.

## STRAWBERRY CAKE

Make the following ingredient adjustments:

Reduce the sugar to 100% (12 oz/375 g).

Reduce the milk in each stage to 33% (4 oz/ 125 g).

Thaw and purée 67% (8 oz/250 g) frozen, sweetened strawberries. Mix into the batter.

## CHERRY CAKE

Make the following ingredient adjustments:

Reduce the milk in each stage to 40% (4.75 oz/150 g).

Add 30% (3.5 oz/112 g) ground maraschino cherries, with juice, to the batter.

# DEVIL'S FOOD CAKE

*For large-quantity measurements, see page 735.*

| Ingredients | U.S. | | Metric | % | Procedure |
|---|---|---|---|---|---|
| Cake flour | 12 | oz | 375 g | 100 | **MIXING** |
| Cocoa | 2 | oz | 60 g | 17 | Two-stage method (p. 384) |
| Salt | 0.25 | oz | 8 g | 2 | **SCALING AND BAKING** |
| Baking powder | 0.375 | oz | 12 g | 3 | See table on page 394. |
| Baking soda | 0.25 | oz | 8 g | 2 | |
| Emulsified shortening | 7 | oz | 220 g | 58 | |
| Sugar | 1 lb | | 500 g | 133 | |
| Skim milk | 8 | oz | 250 g | 67 | |
| Vanilla extract | 0.18 | oz (1 tsp) | 5 g | 1.5 | |
| Skim milk | 6 | oz | 188 g | 50 | |
| Eggs | 8 | oz | 250 g | 67 | |
| **Total weight:** | **3 lb 12** | **oz** | **1876 g** | **500%** | |

# HIGH-RATIO POUND CAKE

| Ingredients | U.S. | | Metric | % | Procedure |
|---|---|---|---|---|---|
| Flour | 1 lb 2 | oz | 500 g | 100 | **MIXING** |
| Salt | 0.25 oz | | 8 g | 2 | Two-stage method (p. 384) |
| Baking powder | 0.25 oz | | 8 g | 2 | **SCALING AND BAKING** |
| Emulsified shortening | 12 | oz | 335 g | 67 | See table on page 394. |
| Sugar | 1 lb 5 | oz | 585 g | 117 | |
| Nonfat milk solids | 1 | oz | 30 g | 6 | |
| Water | 8 | oz | 225 g | 45 | |
| Eggs | 12 | oz | 335 g | 67 | |
| **Total weight:** | **4 lb 8** | **oz** | **2026 g** | **406%** | |

**VARIATIONS**

See variations following Old-Fashioned Pound Cake, page 400.

# YELLOW CAKE (LIQUID SHORTENING)

| Ingredient | U.S. | | | Metric | % | Procedure |
|---|---|---|---|---|---|---|
| Whole eggs | 1 lb | 8 | oz | 675 g | 150 | **MIXING** |
| Milk | | 8 | oz | 225 g | 50 | One-stage method (p. 385) |
| High-ratio liquid shortening | | 10 | oz | 280 g | 62.5 | **SCALING AND BAKING** |
| Vanilla extract | | 1 | oz | 30 g | 6.25 | See table on page 394. |
| Sugar | 1 lb | 4 | oz | 560 g | 125 | |
| Cake flour | 1 lb | | | 450 g | 100 | |
| Baking powder | | 1 | oz | 30 g | 6.25 | |
| Salt | | 0.5 | oz | 15 g | 3 | |
| *Total weight:* | *5 lb* | | | *2265 g* | *493%* | |

**VARIATIONS**

## WHITE CAKE (LIQUID SHORTENING)

Reduce the whole eggs to 12.5% (2 oz/60 g) and add 137.5% (1 lb 6 oz/615 g) egg whites. If desired, add 3% (½ oz /15 g) almond extract.

## CHOCOLATE CAKE (LIQUID SHORTENING)

In baker's percentages, substitute natural (not Dutched) cocoa powder for part of the flour, so the flour and cocoa together total 100%, as indicated in the following ingredient list. In addition, increase milk and sugar, decrease baking powder, and add baking soda as indicated. Mix and bake as in the basic formula.

| Ingredients | U.S. | | | Metric | % |
|---|---|---|---|---|---|
| Whole eggs | 1 lb | 8 | oz | 675 g | 150 |
| Milk | | 10 | oz | 280 g | 62.5 |
| High-ratio liquid shortening | | 10 | oz | 280 g | 62.5 |
| Vanilla extract | | 1 | oz | 30 g | 6.25 |
| Sugar | 1 lb | 6 | oz | 515 g | 137.5 |
| Cake flour | | 13 | oz | 365 g | 81.25 |
| Natural cocoa powder | | 3 | oz | 85 g | 18.75 |
| Baking powder | | 0.5 | oz | 15 g | 3 |
| Baking soda | | 0.25 | oz | 7 g | 1.5 |
| Salt | | 0.5 | oz | 15 g | 3 |

# YELLOW CHIFFON CAKE

| Ingredients | U.S. | | Metric | % | Procedure |
|---|---|---|---|---|---|
| Cake flour | 10 | oz | 250 g | 100 | **MIXING** |
| Sugar | 8 | oz | 200 g | 80 | Chiffon method (p. 388) |
| Salt | 0.25 | oz | 6 g | 2.5 | **SCALING AND BAKING** |
| Baking powder | 0.5 | oz | 12 g | 5 | See table on page 394. For layers, use the |
| Vegetable oil | 5 | oz | 125 g | 50 | weights for high-fat cakes. |
| Egg yolks | 5 | oz | 125 g | 50 | |
| Water | 7.5 | oz | 188 g | 75 | |
| Vanilla extract | 0.25 | oz | 6 g | 2.5 | |
| Egg whites | 10 | oz | 250 g | 100 | |
| Sugar | 5 | oz | 125 g | 50 | |
| Cream of tartar | 0.05 | oz (⅛ tsp) | 1 g | 0.5 | |
| **Total weight:** | **3 lb 3** | **oz** | **1288 g** | **515%** | |

## VARIATIONS

### CHOCOLATE CHIFFON CAKE

Make the following ingredient adjustments:

Add 20% (2 oz/50 g) cocoa. Sift it with the flour.

Increase egg yolks to 60% (6 oz/150 g).

Increase the water to 90% (9 oz/225 g).

### ORANGE CHIFFON CAKE

Make the following ingredient adjustments:

Increase the egg yolks to 60% (6 oz/150 g).

Use 50% (5 oz/125 g) orange juice and 25% (2.5 oz/62 g) water.

Add 0.5 oz (1 tbsp/6 g) grated orange zest when adding the oil.

# GENOISE

| Ingredients | U.S. | | | Metric | % | Procedure |
|---|---|---|---|---|---|---|
| Eggs | 1 lb | 2 | oz | 562 g | 150 | **MIXING** |
| Sugar | | 12 | oz | 375 g | 100 | Genoise or butter genoise method (p. 387) |
| Cake flour | | 12 | oz | 375 g | 100 | **SCALING AND BAKING** |
| Butter (optional; see p. 386) | | 4 | oz | 125 g | 33 | See table on page 394. |
| Vanilla extract or lemon flavor | | 0.25 | oz | 8 g | 2 | |
| *Total weight:* | *2 lb 14* | | *oz* | *1445 g* | *385%* | |

## VARIATIONS

### CHOCOLATE GENOISE

Substitute 2 oz (60 g) cocoa powder for 2 oz (60 g) of the flour.

### SPONGE FOR SEVEN-LAYER CAKE

Add 50% (6 oz/188 g) egg yolks and 10% (1.25 oz/38 g) glucose to the first stage of mixing. Scale at 1 lb 12 oz (800 g) per sheet pan or 14 oz (400 g) per half-pan.

### ALMOND SPONGE I

Make the following ingredient adjustments:

Add 50% (6 oz/188 g) yolks to the first mixing stage.

Increase the sugar to 150% (1 lb 2 oz/560 g).

Add 117% (14 oz/440 g) almond powder, mixed with the sifted flour.

(For more variations, substitute other nuts for the almonds.)

### ALMOND SPONGE II

Blend 125% (15 oz/470 g) almond paste with 50% (6 oz/188 g) egg yolks and blend until smooth. Blend in the sugar (from the basic recipe) until smooth. Add the eggs and proceed as in the basic recipe. (*Note:* This mix does not develop as much volume as regular genoise, and it makes a layer ⅞-in. (22 mm) thick if scaled like genoise. If desired, scale 25% heavier to make a thicker layer.)

### SPONGE ROLL I

Omit the butter from the basic recipe.

### CHOCOLATE SPONGE ROLL I

Omit the butter from the chocolate genoise mix.

# GENOISE MOUSSELINE

*For large-quantity measurements, see page 735.*

| Ingredients | U.S. | | | Metric | % | Procedure |
|---|---|---|---|---|---|---|
| Whole eggs | | 10 | oz | 300 g | 167 | **MIXING** |
| Egg yolks | | 1.33 | oz | 40 g | 22 | Plain sponge method (p. 387) |
| | | (2 yolks) | | (2 yolks) | | **SCALING AND BAKING** |
| Sugar | | 6 | oz | 180 g | 100 | See table on page 394. |
| Cake flour, sifted | | 6 | oz | 180 g | 100 | |
| *Total weight:* | *1 lb* | *7* | *oz* | *700 g* | *389%* | |

# SPONGE ROLL II (SWISS ROLL)

| Ingredients | U.S. | | Metric | % |
|---|---|---|---|---|
| Egg yolks | 12 | oz | 350 g | 100 |
| Sugar | 8 | oz | 235 g | 67 |
| Cake flour | 12 | oz | 350 g | 100 |
| Egg whites | 1 lb 2 | oz | 525 g | 150 |
| Salt | 0.25 | oz | 7 g | 2 |
| Sugar | 6 | oz | 175 g | 50 |
| Total weight: | 3 lb 8 | oz | 1642 g | 469% |

**Procedure**

**MIXING**

Separated-egg sponge method (p. 387)

**SCALING**

1 lb 12 oz (820 g) per sheet pan. Line the pans
with greased paper.

**BAKING**

425°F (220°C), about 7 minutes

## VARIATIONS

### DOBOS MIX

Blend 100% (12 oz/350 g) almond paste with the sugar. Add a little of
the yolks and blend until smooth. Add the rest of the yolks and proceed as in the basic formula.

#### SCALING AND PANNING

Seven layers are needed to make Dobos torte (see p. 460 for assembly instructions). For a round Dobos torte, spread a thin layer of mix
onto the greased, floured bottoms of upside-down cake pans or onto
circles traced on parchment. One recipe makes about seven 12-in.
(30 cm) circles or fourteen 8- or 9-in. (20–22 cm) circles. For rectangular torten, spread a thin layer of mix on greased, paper-lined pans.
Four times the basic recipe makes seven full-size sheets. To make only
one strip, scale 20 oz (550 g) onto one sheet pan. When baked, cut
into seven 3½-in. (9 cm) wide strips.

#### BAKING

400°F (200°C)

### CHOCOLATE SPONGE ROLL II (CHOCOLATE SWISS ROLL)

Sift 17% (2 oz/60 g) cocoa with the flour. Add
25% (3 oz/90 g) water to the whipped egg yolks.

# JELLY ROLL SPONGE

| Ingredients | U.S. | | Metric | % |
|---|---|---|---|---|
| Sugar | 11 | oz | 325 g | 100 |
| Whole eggs | 10 | oz | 292 g | 90 |
| Egg yolks | 2 | oz | 65 g | 20 |
| Salt | 0.25 | oz | 8 g | 2 |
| Honey or corn syrup | 1.5 | oz | 45 g | 14 |
| Water | 1 | oz | 30 g | 10 |
| Vanilla extract | 0.12 | oz (⅜ tsp) | 4 g | 1 |
| Water, hot | 4 | oz | 118 g | 36 |
| Cake flour | 11 | oz | 325 g | 100 |
| Baking powder | 0.16 | oz (1 tsp) | 5 g | 1.5 |
| Total weight: | 2 lb 7 | oz | 1217 g | 374% |

**Procedure**

**MIXING**

Plain sponge method (p. 387). Add the honey
or syrup, the first quantity of water, and the
vanilla to the sugar and eggs for the first mixing
stage.

**SCALING AND BAKING**

See the table on page 394. One recipe makes
2 sheet pans. Line the pans with *greased* paper.
Immediately after baking, turn out of the pans
onto a sheet of parchment and remove the
paper from the bottom of the cakes. Spread
with jelly and roll up tightly. When cool, dust
with confectioners' sugar.

# MILK AND BUTTER SPONGE

*For large-quantity measurements, see page 735.*

| Ingredients | U.S. | | Metric | % | Procedure |
|---|---|---|---|---|---|
| Sugar | 10 | oz | 312 g | 125 | **MIXING** |
| Whole eggs | 6 | oz | 188 g | 75 | Hot milk and butter sponge method (p. 387) |
| Egg yolks | 2 | oz | 60 g | 25 | |
| Salt | 0.12 oz (⅝ tsp) | | 4 g | 1.5 | **SCALING AND BAKING** |
| Cake flour | 8 | oz | 250 g | 100 | Cake layers; see table on page 394. |
| Baking powder | 0.25 oz | | 8 g | 3 | |
| Skim milk | 4 | oz | 125 g | 50 | |
| Butter | 2 | oz | 60 g | 25 | |
| Vanilla extract | 0.25 oz | | 8 g | 3 | |
| **Total weight:** | **2 lb 4** | **oz** | **1015 g** | **407%** | |

**VARIATION**

Instead of vanilla, add 1.5% (0.5 oz/15 g) lemon flavor.

# ANGEL FOOD CAKE

| Ingredients | U.S. | | Metric | % | Procedure |
|---|---|---|---|---|---|
| Egg whites | 2 lb | | 1000 g | 267 | **MIXING** |
| Cream of tartar | 0.25 oz | | 8 g | 2 | Angel food method (p. 388) |
| Salt | 0.17 oz (1 tsp) | | 5 g | 1.5 | |
| Sugar | 1 lb | | 500 g | 133 | **SCALING AND BAKING** |
| Vanilla extract | 0.33 oz (2 tsp) | | 10 g | 2.5 | See table on page 394. |
| Almond extract | 0.17 oz (1 tsp) | | 5 g | 1.25 | |
| Sugar | 1 lb | | 500 g | 133 | |
| Cake flour | 12 | oz | 375 g | 100 | |
| **Total weight:** | **4 lb 12** | **oz** | **2403 g** | **640%** | |

**VARIATIONS**

## CHOCOLATE ANGEL FOOD CAKE

Substitute 3 oz (90 g) cocoa for 3 oz (90 g) of the flour.

## COCONUT MACAROON CUPCAKES

Increase the first quantity of sugar to 167% (1 lb 4 oz/625 g). Mix 350% (2 lb 10 oz/1300 g) macaroon coconut with the flour/sugar mixture. Scale at 20 oz (575 g) per dozen cupcakes. Bake at 375°F (190°C) about 25 minutes.

# CHOCOLATE FUDGE CAKE

| Ingredients | U.S. | Metric | % | Procedure |
|---|---|---|---|---|
| Unsweetened chocolate | 1 lb | 500 g | 400 | **MIXING** |
| Butter | 1 lb | 500 g | 400 | Plain sponge method (p. 387). Melt the choco- |
| Eggs | 1 lb  4 oz | 625 g | 500 | late and butter together over a hot-water bath. |
| Sugar | 1 lb  4 oz | 625 g | 500 | Fold the chocolate mixture into the egg-sugar |
| Bread flour | 4 oz | 125 g | 100 | foam before folding in the flour. |
| **Total weight:** | **4 lb 12 oz** | **2375 g** | **1900%** | **SCALING** |

**VARIATIONS**

## CHOCOLATE SURPRISE CAKE

Fill large muffin tins or similar pans three-quarters full of batter. Insert a 1-oz (30 g) ball of cold ganache (p. 275) into the center of each. Bake at 350°F (175°C) about 15 minutes. Turn out and serve warm with whipped cream or ice cream. The melted ganache will run out when the cake is cut open.

**SCALING**

7-in. (18 cm) round pan: 19 oz (550 g)

8-in. (20 cm) round pan: 25 oz (750 g)

10-in. (25 cm) round pan: 38 oz (1100 g)

Butter the pans heavily before panning.

**BAKING**

350°F (175°C) until slightly underbaked, 20–30 minutes. Set the cake pans on sheet pans to avoid scorching the bottoms.

Cool and glaze with warm Ganache (p. 275).

# JOCONDE SPONGE CAKE (BISCUIT JOCONDE)

*For large-quantity measurements, see page 735.*

| Ingredients | U.S. | Metric | % | Procedure |
|---|---|---|---|---|
| Powdered almonds | 3.5  oz | 85 g | 340 | **MIXING** |
| Confectioners' sugar | 3  oz | 75 g | 300 | 1. Mix together the almonds, confectioners' sugar, and flour in a bowl. |
| Cake flour | 1  oz | 25 g | 100 | 2. Add the eggs a little at a time. Mix well after each addition. Mix until smooth and light. |
| Whole eggs | 4.75 oz | 120 g | 480 | |
| Egg whites | 3.25 oz | 80 g | 320 | 3. Whip the egg whites with the sugar until they form firm, glossy peaks. |
| Sugar | 0.4  oz (2½ tsp) | 10 g | 40 | 4. Gently fold the egg mixture into the whipped egg whites. |
| Butter, melted | 1.25 oz | 30 g | 120 | |
| **Total weight:** | **1 lb 1  oz** | **425 g** | **1700%** | 5. Fold in the melted butter. |

**VARIATION**

## HAZELNUT JOCONDE SPONGE CAKE

Substitute powdered hazelnuts for the powdered almonds. Omit the melted butter.

**SCALING AND BAKING**

Spread ¼ in. (5 mm) thick in half-sheet pans lined with parchment. Allow 1 lb (425 g) per half-sheet pan. Bake at 400°F (200°C) for 15 minutes, or until golden and firm to the touch. Remove from the pans and cool on a rack.

# RIBBON SPONGE

*Yield: 2 half-sheet pans*

| Ingredients | U.S. | | Metric |
|---|---|---|---|
| **Stencil paste** | | | |
| Butter | 7 | oz | 200 g |
| Confectioners' sugar | 7 | oz | 200 g |
| Egg whites | 7 | oz | 200 g |
| Cake flour | 7.75 | oz | 220 g |
| Powdered food coloring (see variation) | as needed | | as needed |
| Joconde Sponge batter (p. 410) | 2 lb | | 850 g |

*Note: This cake is used for decorative linings for cake molds and charlotte molds. Chapter 18 includes instructions for using the baked ribbon sponge. The stencil paste used to make the designs is another version of the batter used for Tuile cookies (pp. 508–509).*

*It is advisable to bake this sponge on a silicone mat so the bottom of the cake doesn't brown. If a mat is not available, double-pan (set one sheet pan on top of another) and bake on the top shelf of the oven.*

## Procedure

1. Beat the butter until soft. Add the sugar and mix well.

2. Add the egg whites, beating continuously.

3. Sift the flour into the mixture. Mix until smooth.

4. Color the paste with food coloring if desired.

5. Line the bottom of a sheet pan with a silicone mat.

6. Use one of the two following procedures to make the stencil design:

   (a) Cover the bottom of a sheet pan with a silicone mat. Place a stencil on top of the mat, spread with a thin layer of the paste, and remove the stencil.

   *or*

   (b) Spread a thin layer of the paste onto a silicone mat with a palette knife (a). Comb with a plastic pastry comb to make stripes, as shown here, or zigzags, wavy lines, or other patterns (b). Alternatively, an abstract finger-painted design can be applied by depositing dabs of colored stencil paste (c) and spreading them thin with a palette knife (d). If desired, make abstract finger-painted designs with the fingers (e)

7. Place the mat in the freezer until the paste is firm.

8. Cover the stencil paste with joconde sponge cake batter, spreading it to an even layer ¼ in. (5 mm) thick (f).

9. Bake in a 475°F (250°C) oven for about 15 minutes.

10. Transfer to a baking rack to cool.

11. Cut the strip to the desired length and use to line ring molds.

### VARIATIONS

For chocolate stencil paste to make brown and white ribbon sponge, substitute cocoa powder for *one-fifth* of the cake flour.

Plain genoise may be used instead of joconde sponge.

# LADYFINGER SPONGE

| Ingredients | U.S. | Metric | % | Procedure |
|---|---|---|---|---|
| Egg yolks | 6 oz | 180 g | 60 | |
| Sugar | 3 oz | 90 g | 30 | |
| Egg whites | 9 oz | 270 g | 90 | |
| Sugar | 5 oz | 150 g | 50 | |
| Lemon juice | ¼ tsp | 1 mL | 0.4 | |
| Pastry flour | 10 oz | 300 g | 100 | |
| **Total weight:** | **2 lb  1 oz** | **990 g** | **340%** | |

**MIXING**

Separated-egg sponge (p. 387)

**PANNING AND BAKING**

One recipe is enough for one full-size sheet pan. Use one of two methods for sponge sheets:

1. Using a pastry bag with a medium plain tip, pipe the sponge mix in diagonal lines on a sheet pan lined with parchment. Pipe the strips of batter so they touch each other and so the entire pan is filled with the sponge batter.

2. Alternatively, simply spread with a palette knife.

Bake at 375°F (190°F) for about 10 minutes.

### VARIATION

#### LADYFINGER COOKIES

Pipe batter as in method 1 above, but pipe strips of batter 3½ in. (9 cm) long and keep them separate, not touching. Dredge the pan generously with confectioners' sugar. Grasp the parchment by two adjacent corners and lift, letting excess sugar fall off. Bake as for method 1. One recipe makes about 100 ladyfingers.

# MARJOLAINE SPONGE CAKE

*For large-quantity measurements, see page 736.*

| Ingredients | U.S. | | Metric | % | Procedure |
|---|---|---|---|---|---|
| Confectioners' sugar | 4 | oz | 120 g | 133 | |
| Powdered almonds | 4 | oz | 120 g | 133 | |
| Egg yolks | 3.33 | oz | 100 g | 111 | |
| Egg whites | 2 | oz | 60 g | 67 | |
| Egg whites | 5 | oz | 150 g | 167 | |
| Sugar | 3 | oz | 90 g | 100 | |
| Pastry flour, sifted | 3 | oz | 90 g | 100 | |
| **Total weight:** | **1 lb 8** | **oz** | **730 g** | **811%** | |

**MIXING**

Sponge method variation

1. Combine the confectioners' sugar, almonds, and egg yolks. Beat well.

2. Add the first quantity of egg whites. Whip until thick and light.

3. Whip the second quantity of egg whites with the sugar to make a common meringue. Fold into the egg yolk mixture.

4. Fold in the flour.

**MAKEUP AND BAKING**

Line sheet pans with parchment paper. Fit a pastry bag with a medium plain tip. Pipe disks of the desired size using the technique shown on page 347. Bake for 10 minutes at 350°F (180°C).

# HAZELNUT SPONGE CAKE

*For large-quantity measurements, see page 736.*

| Ingredients | U.S. | | Metric | % | Procedure |
|---|---|---|---|---|---|
| Butter, softened | 4.5 | oz | 135 g | 337 | **MIXING** |
| Sugar | 3.67 | oz | 110 g | 275 | Combination creaming/sponge |
| Egg yolks | 4 | oz | 120 g | 300 | 1. Cream the butter and first quantity of sugar. |
| Egg whites | 6 | oz | 180 g | 450 | 2. Add the egg yolks in several stages, beating well after each addition. |
| Sugar | 2 | oz | 60 g | 160 | |
| Cake flour | 1.33 | oz | 40 g | 100 | 3. Whip the egg whites and second quantity of sugar to a stiff meringue. |
| Cocoa powder | 1.33 | oz | 40 g | 100 | 4. Sift together the flour and cocoa. Mix in the hazelnuts. |
| Ground hazelnuts, toasted | 1.75 | oz | 55 g | 138 | |
| **Total weight:** | **1 lb 8** | **oz** | **740 g** | **1860%** | 5. Fold the meringue and the dry ingredients alternately into the butter mixture, starting and finishing with the meringue. |

**SCALING**

12 oz (370 g) per 8-in. (20-cm) round pan. Grease the pans and line the bottoms with parchment. Flour the sides of the pans.

**BAKING**

325°F (160°C), about 40 minutes.

# ALMOND POUND CAKE (PAIN DE GÊNES)

| Ingredients | U.S. | | Metric | % | Procedure |
|---|---|---|---|---|---|
| Almond paste | 7.5 | oz | 225 g | 167 | **MIXING** |
| Confectioners' sugar | 5 | oz | 150 g | 111 | Separated-egg sponge |
| Egg yolks | 4 | oz | 120 g | 89 | 1. Mix the almond paste and confectioners' sugar to a sand-like consistency. |
| Whole eggs | 1.67 | oz | 50 g | 37 | |
| Vanilla extract | 0.07 | oz (½ tsp) | 2 g | 1.5 | 2. Mix in the egg yolks, a little at a time. Then add the whole egg and vanilla. Beat well until smooth and light. |
| Egg whites | 6 | oz | 180 g | 133 | |
| Sugar | 2.5 | oz | 75 g | 56 | 3. Whip the egg whites to soft peaks. Add the sugar and whip to stiff peaks. |
| Cake flour | 4.5 | oz | 135 g | 100 | |
| Butter, melted | 2.33 | oz | 70 g | 52 | 4. Fold the meringue into the almond paste mixture. |
| Sliced almonds | 2 | oz | 50 g | 37 | |
| **Total weight:** | **2 lb 1** | **oz** | **1057 g** | **783%** | 5. Fold in the flour and melted butter. |

**PAN PREPARATION, SCALING, AND BAKING**

1. Butter the bottom and sides of round or square cake pans. Line the insides of the pans with the sliced almonds.

2. For scaling, use the figures for high-fat cakes in the table on page 394 at the high end of the weight range.

3. Bake at 340°F (170°C) for 20–25 minutes.

# BAUMKUCHEN

| Ingredients | U.S. | | Metric | % |
|---|---|---|---|---|
| Butter | 7 | oz | 200 g | 114 |
| Sugar | 5 | oz | 150 g | 85 |
| Vanilla extract | 0.07 oz (½ tsp) | | 2 g | 1 |
| Lemon zest, grated | 0.03 oz (½ tsp) | | 1 g | 0.5 |
| Egg yolks | 2.5 | oz | 80 g | 43 |
| Egg whites | 7 | oz | 210 g | 120 |
| Sugar | 5 | oz | 150 g | 85 |
| Cornstarch | 6 | oz | 175 g | 100 |
| Powdered almonds | 2.25 oz | | 65 g | 37 |
| Salt | 0.07 oz (⅓ tsp) | | 2 g | 1 |
| *Total weight:* | *2 lb 2* | *oz* | *1035 g* | *586%* |

## Procedure

### MIXING

Combination creaming/sponge

1. Cream the butter, sugar, vanilla, and zest until light.

2. Beat in the egg yolks a little at a time.

3. Whip the egg whites until they form soft peaks. Add the sugar and whip until they form stiff, glossy peaks.

4. Fold the cornstarch into the egg whites.

5. Mix together the almonds and salt.

6. Fold the meringue and the almonds alternately into the butter mixture, starting and finishing with meringue.

### BAKING

1. Line the bottom of an 8-in. (20 cm) square cake pan with parchment.

2. Put about 1 oz (30 g) batter in the pan and spread it smooth with a small offset palette knife (a).

3. Place under a salamander or broiler until well and evenly browned (b).

4. Repeat steps 2 and 3 until the cake is about 1½ in. (4 cm) thick (c).

5. Chill.

6. The cut cake reveals a pattern of layers (d). It is used to line charlotte molds (see p. 455). It can also be cut into small pieces and served plain or iced with fondant (p. 422) as petits fours.

## ❧ BAUMKUCHEN ❧

*Baumkuchen* is an unusual cake that deserves extra explanation. The name means "tree cake" in German. Traditionally, it was made on a revolving wooden spit. The batter was ladled on in thin layers as the spit rotated in front of a heat source. As each layer cooked and browned on the surface, another layer was added. As a result, cutting into the cake revealed a series of concentric rings, resembling tree rings.

Today, baumkuchen is generally made in cake pans, as illustrated on this page. Its unusual striped interior makes it valuable for decorative lining of cake and charlotte molds.

# ALMOND CHOCOLATE SPONGE

*For large-quantity measurements, see page 736.*

| Ingredients | U.S. | Metric | % | Procedure |
|---|---|---|---|---|
| Marzipan | 4.33 oz | 130 g | 325 | **MIXING** |
| Egg yolks | 2.67 oz (4 yolks) | 80 g (4 yolks) | 200 | Separated-egg sponge |
| Egg whites | 4 oz (4 whites) | 120 g (4 whites) | 300 | |
| Sugar | 1.67 oz (4 tbsp) | 50 g | 125 | |
| Cake flour | 1.33 oz | 40 g | 100 | |
| Cocoa powder | 1.33 oz | 40 g | 100 | |
| Butter, melted | 1.33 oz | 40 g | 100 | |
| **Total weight:** | **1 lb** | **500 g** | **1250%** | |

**MIXING**

Separated-egg sponge

1. Beat the marzipan and egg yolks together until smooth and light.

2. Whip the egg whites and sugar to a stiff meringue.

3. Sift the flour and cocoa together. Fold the meringue and dry ingredients alternately into the egg yolk mixture, starting and ending with the meringue.

4. Fold in the butter.

**SCALING AND BAKING**

See table on page 394. For sponge circles (as for Monte Carlo Cake, p. 472), draw circles of the desired size on parchment. Turn the paper over and spread batter to fill the circles. Alternatively, pipe the batter using the technique shown on page 347. One 7-in. (18 cm) circle requires about 8 oz (250 g) batter. Bake at 425°F (220°C) for 10–12 minutes.

# CHOCOLATE SPONGE LAYERS

*For large-quantity measurements, see page 736.*

| Ingredients | U.S. | Metric | % | Procedure |
|---|---|---|---|---|
| Egg whites | 5 oz | 150 g | 150 | **MIXING** |
| Sugar | 4 oz | 120 g | 120 | |
| Egg yolks | 3.5 oz | 100 g | 100 | |
| Cake flour | 3.5 oz | 100 g | 100 | |
| Cocoa powder | 1 oz | 30 g | 30 | |
| **Total weight:** | **1 lb 1 oz** | **500 g** | **500%** | |

**MIXING**

1. Whip the egg whites until foamy, then add the sugar and whip to soft peaks.

2. Whip the egg yolks until they are light and pale.

3. Fold the yolks into the whites.

4. Sift the flour with the cocoa powder. Fold into the egg mixture.

**MAKEUP AND BAKING**

Using a pastry bag with a plain tip, pipe circles of batter on parchment as shown on page 347. Bake at 350°F (175°C) for 15 minutes.

# CHOCOLATE VELVET CAKE (MOELLEUX)

*For large-quantity measurements, see page 737.*

| Ingredients | U.S. | Metric | % | Procedure |
|---|---|---|---|---|
| Almond paste | 2.5 oz | 75 g | 188 | **MIXING** |
| Confectioners' sugar | 1.67 oz | 50 g | 125 | Modified separated-egg sponge |
| Egg yolks | 2 oz | 60 g | 150 | 1. Mix the almond paste and confectioners' sugar until the mixture has a sandy consistency. |
| Egg whites | 2 oz | 60 g | 150 | 2. Mix in the egg yolks a little at a time. Beat until the mixture is smooth and light. |
| Sugar | 0.83 oz (5 tsp) | 25 g | 63 | |
| Cake flour | 1.33 oz | 40 g | 100 | 3. Whip the egg whites and sugar to a stiff meringue. Fold into the almond paste mixture. |
| Cocoa powder | 0.33 oz | 10 g | 25 | 4. Sift together the flour and cocoa. Fold into the batter. |
| Butter, melted | 0.67 oz | 20 g | 50 | |
| **For baking** | | | | 5. Fold in the melted butter. |
| Almonds, chopped | 1 oz | 30 g | | **SCALING AND BAKING** |
| | | | | 7-in. (18 cm) square pan: 11 oz (340 g) |
| ***Total batter weight:*** | ***11 oz*** | ***340 g*** | ***851%*** | 8-in. (20 cm) square pan: 14 oz (425 g) |

9-in. (23 cm) square pan: 19 oz (600 g)

Butter the pans and line with the almonds before filling with batter.

340°F (170°C), 20–25 minutes

# LEMON MADELEINES

*For large-quantity measurements, see page 736.*

| Ingredients | U.S. | | Metric | % |
|---|---|---|---|---|
| Egg yolks | 2 | oz | 60 g | 67 |
| Demerara sugar (see Note) | 0.33 oz | | 10 g | 11 |
| Lemon zest, grated | 0.13 oz (1½ tsp) | | 4 g | 4.5 |
| Honey | 0.5 | oz | 15 g | 17 |
| Egg whites | 2 | oz | 60 g | 67 |
| Extra-fine granulated sugar | 2.5 | oz | 75 g | 83 |
| Salt | 0.03 oz (⅛ tsp) | | 1 g | 1 |
| Baking powder | 0.1 | oz (½ tsp) | 3 g | 3 |
| Cake flour | 3 | oz | 90 g | 100 |
| Butter, melted | 3 | oz | 90 g | 100 |
| **Total weight:** | **13** | **oz** | **408 g** | **453%** |

*Note: If Demerara sugar is not available, use regular white granulated sugar.*

## Procedure

### MIXING

Separated-egg sponge method. Fold the meringue and the sifted dry ingredients alternately into the whipped egg yolk mixture. Finish by folding in the melted butter. Chill the batter for 20 minutes.

### PANNING AND BAKING

1. Double-butter madeleine pans and dust with flour. Pipe batter into the pans using a pastry bag with a medium plain tip. Each small or petit four–size madeleine (1½ × 1 in. or 4 × 2.5 cm) requires about ⅙ oz (5 g) batter; a large madeleine (2½ × 1½ in. or 6.5 × 4 cm) requires about ⅔ oz (20 g) batter.

2. Bake at 350°F (180°C) until golden but still soft to the touch, about 6–7 minutes for small, at least twice as long for large madeleines.

3. Unmold onto wire racks to cool.

## VARIATION

### CHOCOLATE AND ORANGE MADELEINES

*For large-quantity measurements, see page 736.*

| Ingredients | U.S. | | Metric | % |
|---|---|---|---|---|
| Egg yolks | 2 | oz | 60 g | 100 |
| Demerara sugar (see *Note* above) | 0.33 oz | | 10 g | 17 |
| Orange zest, grated | 0.25 oz | | 8 g | 13 |
| Honey | 0.5 | oz | 15 g | 25 |
| Egg whites | 2 | oz | 60 g | 100 |
| Extra-fine granulated sugar | 2.5 | oz | 75 g | 125 |
| Salt | 0.03 oz (⅛ tsp) | | 1 g | 1.7 |
| Baking powder | 0.13 oz (¾ tsp) | | 4 g | 7 |
| Cocoa powder | 0.8 | oz (4 tbsp) | 25 g | 42 |
| Cake flour | 2 | oz | 60 g | 100 |
| Butter, melted | 3 | oz | 90 g | 150 |

Follow the basic procedure, but make changes to the ingredients as listed above.

# MARRONIER
## (CHESTNUT CAKE PETITS FOURS)

| Ingredients | U.S. | Metric | % | Procedure |
|---|---|---|---|---|
| Sweetened chestnut purée | 3.5 oz | 100 g | 133 | **MIXING** |
| Rum | 0.33 oz (2 tsp) | 10 g | 13 | 1. Soften the chestnut purée by mixing in the rum. |
| Egg whites | 8 oz | 240 g | 320 | 2. Whip the egg whites and granulated sugar to a stiff meringue. Fold into the chestnut purée. |
| Granulated sugar | 1.67 oz | 50 g | 67 | |
| Confectioners' sugar, sifted | 5 oz | 150 g | 200 | 3. Fold in the confectioners' sugar, almonds, and flour. |
| Powdered almonds | 2 oz | 60 g | 80 | 4. Fold in the melted butter. |
| Cake flour | 2.5 oz | 75 g | 100 | **SCALING AND BAKING** |
| Butter, melted | 3.5 oz | 100 g | 133 | 1. Butter and flour 2-in. (5 cm) tartlet molds. |
| **Garnish** | | | | 2. Fill each mold with ½ oz (15 g) batter. |
| Confectioners' sugar | as needed | as needed | | 3. Bake at 375°F (190°C) for 8 minutes. |
| Sugar-glazed chestnut halves | 48 | 48 | | 4. Remove from the molds immediately after baking. Cool on racks. |
| **Total batter weight:** | 1 lb 10 oz | 785 g | 1046% | 5. When completely cool, dust the tops with confectioners' sugar. Top each cake with a half chestnut. |

## TERMS FOR REVIEW

emulsion

air cell

creaming method

high-fat cake

two-stage method

one-stage method

flour-batter method

egg-foam cake

angel food method

chiffon method

sponge method

genoise

hot milk and butter
  sponge method

pound cake

fruit cake

sponge roll

ribbon sponge

baumkuchen

## QUESTIONS FOR DISCUSSION

1. What are the three main goals of mixing cake batter?

2. How are the following concepts related to the goals in question 1? (a) emulsion; (b) creaming of fat and sugar; (c) gluten development.

3. What are four precautions you should take to prevent a cake batter from curdling or separating?

4. List the steps in the creaming method of cake mixing.

5. List the steps in the two-stage, or high-ratio, mixing method.

6. List the steps in the sponge method. What extra steps are needed in the butter sponge method? in the hot milk and butter sponge method? in the separated-egg sponge method?

7. What are the advantages and disadvantages of using butter in high-fat cakes?

8. Why is there a lot of emphasis on scraping down the sides of the bowl and the beater in both the creaming method and the two-stage methods?

9. How is mixing a creaming-method cake different from mixing a combination creaming/sponge method cake?

10. Which of the following cake ingredients are considered tougheners, which are tenderizers, which are dryers, and which are moisteners?

| flour | egg whites | milk (liquid) |
| butter | egg yolks | cocoa |
| sugar | whole eggs | water |

11. Why should angel food cake pans not be greased?

## Chapter 17

# Assembling and Decorating Cakes

M uch of the appeal of cakes is due to their appearance. Cakes are a perfect medium in which a baker can express artistry and imagination.

A cake need not be elaborate or complex to be pleasing. Certainly, a simple but neatly finished cake is better than a gaudy, overdecorated cake that is done carelessly or without any plan for a harmonious overall design.

There are, of course, many styles of cake decorating, and within each style, hundreds or thousands of designs are possible. This chapter is, in part, an introduction to basic techniques for finishing cakes. The most important requirement for making effective desserts is hours and hours of practice with the pastry bag and paper cone—the decorator's chief tools. Even the simplest designs (such as straight lines) require a lot of practice. Only when you have mastered them should you proceed to the more advanced techniques presented in style manuals and cake decorating books.

A cake must be assembled and iced before it can be decorated. In this chapter, we begin with a study of icings, including recipes for many variations. Then we discuss the procedures for assembling basic layer cakes, sheet cakes, and other simple products. Examples of more elaborate cakes, including French and other European-style gâteaux and torten, are introduced in chapter 18.

**After reading this chapter, you should be able to:**

1. Prepare icings.
2. Assemble and ice simple layer cakes, sheet cakes, and cupcakes.
3. Make and use a paper decorating cone.
4. Use a pastry bag to make simple icing decorations.

# ICINGS

**cings, also called** *frostings,* are sweet coatings for cakes and other baked goods. Icings have three main functions:

- They contribute flavor and richness.
- They improve appearance.
- They improve keeping qualities by forming protective coatings around cakes.

There are eight basic types of icings and other cake coatings:

- Fondant.
- Buttercreams.
- Foam-type icings.
- Fudge-type icings.
- Flat-type icings.
- Royal or decorator's icing.
- Glazes.
- Rolled coatings.

Use top-quality flavorings for icings so they enhance the cake rather than detract from it. Use moderation when adding flavors and colors. Flavors should be light and delicate. Colors should be delicate pastel shades—except chocolate, of course.

## Fondant

**Fondant** is a sugar syrup that is crystallized to a smooth, creamy white mass. It is familiar as the icing for napoleons, éclairs, petits fours, and some cakes. When applied, it sets up into a shiny, nonsticky coating.

The word *crystallized* in the previous paragraph may cause some confusion. In chapter 12, the discussion of cooking sugar syrups stressed avoiding crystallization because crystallization causes graininess. So how can crystallization occur in a smooth icing? Reading the procedure for making fondant, you will see that this white icing starts out as a sugar solution as clear as water. It is crystallization that turns it white and opaque. The key is to control the temperature so when the crystals form, they are microscopically tiny. Keeping them so small keeps the fondant smooth and shiny. If the fondant is not made correctly, or if it is heated too much when used, the crystals become larger and the icing loses its shine and its smoothness.

Because it is difficult to make in the bakeshop, fondant is almost always purchased already prepared, either in the ready-to-use moist form or in the dry form, which requires only the addition of water. In an emergency (for instance, if you run out of fondant and there is no time to get more from your supplier), flat icing can be substituted, although it will not perform as well.

For those who wish to try making fondant in the bakeshop, a formula is included here. The purpose of the glucose or the cream of tartar in the formula is to invert some of the sugar in order to get the right amount of crystallization. If

---

### ❧ ICINGS AND FROSTINGS ❧

Most people use the terms *icing* and *frosting* interchangeably, and for the most part they mean the same thing. In general, however, products applied by pouring them over an item, such as fondant and flat icing, are rarely referred to as *frostings*. Royal icing, as well, is always called *icing*, not *frosting*. When the term *frosting* is used, it is likely to mean a thicker product applied with a palette knife or spatula, such as buttercream. But these are not absolute definitions. Many pastry chefs are in the habit of calling all these products *icings*.

none is used, the syrup will set up to be too unworkable, and it will not be smooth and white. When an excess of glucose or cream of tartar is added, not enough crystallization will take place and the fondant will be too soft and syrupy. Also, if the hot syrup is disturbed before it cools sufficiently (step 6 in the procedure), large crystals will form and the fondant will not be smooth and shiny.

Another type of fondant, **rolled fondant**, is handled and applied differently from poured fondant, as discussed on page 433.

## Procedure and Guidelines for Using Fondant

1. Heat the fondant over a warm-water bath, stirring constantly, to thin it and make it pourable. Do not heat it over 100°F (38°C) or it will lose its shine.

2. If it is still too thick, thin it with a little simple sugar syrup or water.

3. Flavorings and colorings may be added as desired.

4. To make *chocolate fondant*, stir melted bitter chocolate into the warm fondant until the desired color and flavor are reached (up to about 3 oz bitter chocolate per lb of fondant, or 190 g per kg). Chocolate will thicken the fondant, so the icing may require more thinning with sugar syrup.

5. Apply the warm fondant by pouring it over the item or by dipping items into it.

# FONDANT

*Yield: 6–7 lb (3–3.5 kg)*

| Ingredients | U.S. | | Metric | Sugar at 100% % | Procedure |
|---|---|---|---|---|---|
| Sugar | 6 lb | | 3000 g | 100 | 1. Clean a marble slab well and moisten it with water. Set 4 steel bars on the slab in the shape of a square to hold the hot syrup when it is poured onto the marble. |
| Water | 1 lb 8 | oz | 750 g | 25 | |
| Glucose | 1 lb 2 | oz | 570 g | 19 | |
| *or* | | | | | 2. Combine the sugar and water in a heavy kettle and heat to dissolve the sugar. Boil until the temperature reaches 225°F (105°C). |
| Cream of tartar | 0.5 oz | | 15 g | 0.5 | |

3. If glucose is used, warm it. If cream of tartar is used, disperse it in a little warm water. Add the glucose or the cream of tartar to the boiling syrup.

4. Continue to boil the syrup until it reaches 240°F (115°C).

5. Pour the boiling syrup onto the marble slab and sprinkle it with a little cold water to prevent crystallization.

6. Let the syrup cool undisturbed to about 110°F (43°C).

7. Remove the steel bars and work the sugar with a steel scraper, turning it from the outside to the center. It will turn white and begin to solidify.

8. Continue to work the fondant, either by hand or by putting it in a mixing bowl and working it slowly with the paddle attachment, until it is smooth and creamy.

9. Keep the fondant in a tightly covered container.

## Buttercreams

**Buttercream** icings are light, smooth mixtures of fat and sugar. They may also contain eggs to increase their smoothness or lightness. These popular icings for many kinds of cakes are easily flavored and colored to suit a variety of purposes.

There are many variations of buttercream formulas. We cover five basic kinds in this chapter:

1. **Simple buttercreams** are made by creaming together fat and confectioners' sugar to the desired consistency and lightness. A small quantity of egg whites, yolks, or whole eggs may be whipped in. Pasteurized eggs should be used for safety. Some formulas also include nonfat milk solids.

   **Decorator's buttercream** (sometimes called *rose paste*) is used for making flowers and other cake decorations. It is creamed only a little, at low speed, as too much air beaten into it would make it unable to hold delicate shapes. Because shortening has a higher melting point than butter, it is often used as the only fat in decorator's buttercream to give maximum stability to the finished décor. However, a little butter may be included to improve the flavor when possible.

2. **Meringue-type buttercreams** are a mixture of butter and meringue. These are very light icings. The most frequently made of these kinds of buttercreams is Italian buttercream, made with Italian meringue (p. 267). Swiss meringue can also be used as the base for buttercream.

3. **French buttercreams** are prepared by beating a boiling syrup into beaten egg yolks and whipping to a light foam. Soft butter is then whipped in. These are very rich, light icings.

4. **Pastry cream–type buttercream,** in its simplest form, is made by mixing together equal parts thick pastry cream and softened butter. If more sweetness is desired, mix in sifted confectioners' sugar. The recipe included in this chapter (Vanilla Cream, p. 427) contains a lower proportion of butter than usual. To give it the necessary body, a little gelatin is added.

5. **Fondant-type buttercream** is simple to make with only a few ingredients on hand. Simply cream together equal parts fondant and butter. Flavor as desired.

Butter, especially unsalted butter, is the preferred fat for buttercreams because of its flavor and melt-in-the-mouth quality. Icings made with shortening only can be unpleasant because the fat congeals and coats the inside of the mouth, where it does not melt. However, butter makes a less stable icing because it melts so easily. There are two ways around this problem:

◆ Use buttercreams only in cool weather.

◆ Blend a small quantity of emulsifier shortening with the butter to stabilize it.

Buttercreams may be stored, covered, in the refrigerator for several days. However, they should always be used at room temperature in order to have the right consistency. Before using, remove buttercream from the refrigerator at least 1 hour ahead of time and let it come to room temperature. If it must be warmed quickly, or if it curdles, warm it gently over warm water and beat it well until smooth.

## Flavoring Buttercreams

Because buttercreams may be combined with many flavorings, they are versatile and adaptable to many kinds of cakes and desserts.

The quantities given in the following variations are suggested amounts for each 1 pound (500 g) buttercream. In practice, flavorings may be increased or decreased to taste, but avoid flavoring icings too strongly.

Unless the instructions say otherwise, simply blend the flavoring into the buttercream.

1. **Chocolate.** Use 3 ounces (90 g) sweet dark chocolate.

    Melt chocolate and cool slightly (chocolate must not be too cool or it will solidify before completely blending with the buttercream). Blend with about one-quarter of the buttercream, then blend this mixture into the rest.

    If your buttercream base is very sweet, use 1½ ounces (45 g) unsweetened chocolate instead of the sweet chocolate.

2. **Coffee.** Use ⅔ fluid ounces (20 mL) coffee compound (coffee flavoring), or 1½ tablespoon (5 g) instant coffee dissolved in ½ ounce (15 mL) water.

3. **Marron (chestnut).** Use 8 ounces (250 g) chestnut purée.

    Blend with a little of the buttercream until soft and smooth, then blend this mixture into the remaining buttercream. Flavor with a little rum or brandy, if desired.

4. **Praline.** Use 2 to 3 ounces (60 to 90 g) praline paste.

    Blend with a little of the buttercream until soft and smooth, then blend this mixture into the remaining buttercream.

5. **Almond.** Use 6 ounces (180 g) almond paste.

    Soften almond paste with a few drops of water. Blend in a little of the buttercream until soft and smooth, then blend this mixture into the remaining buttercream.

6. **Extracts and emulsions** (orange, lemon, etc.). Add according to taste.

7. **Spirits and liqueurs.** Add according to taste. For example: kirsch, orange liqueur, rum, brandy.

# FRENCH BUTTERCREAM

*For large-quantity measurements, see page 737.*
*Yield: 1 lb 6 oz (688 g)*

| Ingredients | U.S. | | Metric | Sugar at 100% % | Procedure |
|---|---|---|---|---|---|
| Sugar | 8 | oz | 250 g | 100 | 1. Combine the sugar and water in a saucepan. Bring to a boil while stirring to dissolve the sugar. |
| Water | 2 | oz | 60 mL | 25 | |
| Egg yolks | 3 | oz | 90 g | 37.5 | 2. Continue to boil until the syrup reaches a temperature of 240°F (115°C). |
| Butter, softened | 10 | oz | 300 g | 125 | 3. While the syrup is boiling, beat the yolks with a wire whip or the whip attachment of a mixer until they are thick and light. |
| Vanilla extract | 0.12 oz (¾ tsp) | | 4 mL | 1.5 | |

**VARIATION**

For flavored buttercreams, see above.

4. As soon as the syrup reaches 240°F (115°C), pour it very slowly into the beaten yolks while whipping constantly.

5. Continue to beat until the mixture is completely cool and the yolks are very thick and light.

6. Whip in the butter a little at a time. Add it just as fast as it can be absorbed by the mixture.

7. Beat in the vanilla. If the icing is too soft, refrigerate it until it is firm enough to spread.

# SIMPLE BUTTERCREAM

*For large-quantity measurements, see page 737.*

| Ingredients | U.S. | | Metric | Sugar at 100%<br>% | Procedure |
|---|---|---|---|---|---|
| Butter | 8 | oz | 250 g | 40 | 1. Using the paddle attachment, cream together the butter, shortening, and sugar until well blended. |
| Shortening | 4 | oz | 125 g | 20 | |
| Confectioners' sugar | 1 lb 4 | oz | 625 g | 100 | |
| Egg whites, pasteurized | 1.25 oz | | 40 g | 7.5 | 2. Add the egg whites, lemon juice, and vanilla. Blend in at medium speed. Then mix at high speed until light and fluffy. |
| Lemon juice | 0.08 oz (½ tsp) | | 2 g | 0.4 | |
| Vanilla extract | 0.12 oz (¾ tsp) | | 4 g | 0.6 | 3. For a softer buttercream, blend in the water. |
| Water (optional) | 1 | oz | 30 g | 5 | |
| **Total weight:** | **2 lb 2** | **oz** | **1076 g** | **172%** | |

## VARIATIONS

*For flavored buttercreams, see pages 424–425.*

### SIMPLE BUTTERCREAM WITH EGG YOLKS OR WHOLE EGGS

Instead of the egg whites in the above recipe, substitute an equal weight of egg yolks or whole eggs. These substitutions make slightly richer icings. Also, the egg yolks help make a better emulsion.

### DECORATOR'S BUTTERCREAM OR ROSE PASTE

Use 7 oz (200 g) regular shortening and 3 oz (90 g) butter. Omit the lemon juice and vanilla. Add 0.75 oz (22 g) of either water or egg whites. Blend at low speed until smooth; do not whip.

### CREAM CHEESE ICING

Substitute cream cheese for the butter and shortening. Omit the egg whites. If necessary, thin the icing with cream or milk. If desired, flavor with grated lemon or orange zest instead of vanilla and use orange juice and/or lemon juice instead of milk for thinning the icing.

# ITALIAN BUTTERCREAM

*For large-quantity measurements, see page 737.*
*Yield: 1 lb 11 oz (850 g)*

| Ingredients | U.S. | | Metric | Sugar at 100%<br>% | Procedure |
|---|---|---|---|---|---|
| **Italian meringue** | | | | | 1. Make the meringue (Procedure on p. 267). Whip until completely cool. |
| Sugar | 8 | oz | 250 g | 100 | |
| Water | 2 | oz | 60 mL | 25 | 2. Little by little, add the soft butter and continue to whip. Add each piece after the previous one has been incorporated. In the same way, whip in the shortening, if using, or the additional butter. |
| Egg whites | 4 | oz | 125 g | 50 | |
| Butter, soft | 12 | oz | 375 g | 150 | |
| Emulsified shortening (or additional butter | 2 | oz | 60 mL | 25 | |
| Lemon juice | 0.08 oz (½ tsp) | | 2 mL | 1 | 3. When all the fat has been incorporated, whip in the lemon juice and vanilla. |
| Vanilla extract | 0.12 oz (¾ tsp) | | 4 mL | 1.5 | 4. Continue to whip until the buttercream is smooth. |

## VARIATION

*For flavored buttercreams, see pages 424–425.*

### SWISS BUTTERCREAM

Instead of making Italian buttercream, use the sugar and egg whites (omitting the water) in the formula to make a Swiss buttercream, as described on page 267. When the meringue has cooled to room temperature, continue with step 2 in the basic recipe.

# PRALINE BUTTERCREAM

*For large-quantity measurements, see page 737.*
*Yield: 1 lb 2 oz (550 g)*

| Ingredients | U.S. | | Metric | Sugar at 100% % | Procedure |
|---|---|---|---|---|---|
| Water | 1.5 | oz | 40 g | 33 | 1. Combine the water and sugar in a saucepan, bring to a boil to dissolve the sugar, and cook the syrup to 248°F (120°C). |
| Sugar | 4 | oz | 120 g | 100 | |
| Egg yolks | 3.33 | oz | 100 g | 83 | 2. Whip the egg yolks until light. Gradually add the hot syrup to the yolks, whipping constantly. Whip until cool. |
| | (5 yolks) | | (5 yolks) | | |
| Butter, softened | 6 | oz | 180 g | 150 | 3. Whip in the butter and the praline paste. |
| Praline paste | 5 | oz | 150 mL | 125 | |

# VANILLA CREAM

*For large-quantity measurements, see page 737.*

| Ingredients | U.S. | | Metric | Procedure |
|---|---|---|---|---|
| Pastry Cream (p. 271) | 1 lb | | 450 g | 1. Whip the pastry cream until smooth. |
| Gelatin | 0.25 | oz | 6 g | 2. Soften the gelatin in cold water (see p. 88). Heat the rum. Add the gelatin and stir until dissolved, warming as necessary. |
| Rum | 4 | tsp | 20 g | |
| Butter, softened | 7 | oz | 200 g | 3. Beat the gelatin mixture into the pastry cream. |
| *Total weight:* | **1 lb 7** | **oz** | **676 g** | 4. Beat in the butter a little at a time. |

# CARAMEL BUTTERCREAM

*For large-quantity measurements, see page 737.*
*Yield: 1 lb (500 g)*

| Ingredients | U.S. | | Metric | Sugar at 100% % | Procedure |
|---|---|---|---|---|---|
| Water | 1 | oz | 25 g | 14 | 1. Cook the first quantity of water and the sugar to the caramel stage. |
| Sugar | 6.5 | oz | 185 g | 100 | |
| Water | 1.75 | oz | 50 g | 27 | 2. Let the caramel cool to 250°F (120°C) and add the second quantity of water and the heavy cream. Cook until dissolved. |
| Heavy cream | 1.25 | oz | 35 g | 19 | |
| Coffee extract | 0.2 | oz (1 tsp) | 5 g | 2.7 | 3. Add the coffee extract. |
| Egg yolks | 2 | oz | 60 g | 32 | 4. Whip the egg yolks until light, then whip in the hot caramel. Whip until light and continue whipping until the mixture has cooled to about 85°F (30°C). |
| Butter, softened | 6.75 | oz | 190 g | 103 | |
| | | | | | 5. Whip in one-third of the butter. When this has been uniformly incorporated, whip in the remaining butter. |

# LIGHT PRALINE CREAM

*For large-quantity measurements, see page 738.*

| Ingredients | U.S. | | Metric | Sugar at 100% % | Procedure |
|---|---|---|---|---|---|
| Butter, softened | 8 | oz | 200 g | 100 | 1. Whip together the butter and praline paste until smooth and light. |
| Praline paste | 4 | oz | 100 g | 50 | 2. Whip in the cognac. |
| Cognac | 1.5 | oz | 40 g | 20 | 3. Mix in the Italian meringue. |
| Italian Meringue (p. 267) | 14 | oz | 340 g | 170 | |
| *Total weight:* | *1 lb 11* | *oz* | *680 g* | *340%* | |

## Foam-Type Icings

Foam icings, sometimes called **boiled icings**, are simply meringues made with a boiling syrup. Some also contain stabilizing ingredients like gelatin. Foam icings should be applied thickly to cakes and left in peaks and swirls.

These icings are not stable. Regular boiled icing should be used the day it is prepared. Marshmallow icing should be made just before using and applied while still warm, before it sets.

### Plain Boiled Icing

Follow the recipe for Italian Meringue (p. 267), but include 2 ounces (60 g) corn syrup with the sugar and water for the boiled syrup. Flavor the icing to taste with vanilla.

### Marshmallow Icing

Soak ¼ ounce (8 g) gelatin in 1½ ounces (45 mL) cold water. Warm the water to dissolve the gelatin. Prepare plain boiled icing. Add the dissolved gelatin to the icing after adding the hot syrup. Scrape down the sides of the bowl to make sure that the gelatin is evenly mixed in. Use while still warm.

### Chocolate Foam Icing and Filling

Prepare boiled icing. After the syrup has been added, blend in 5 ounces (150 g) melted, unsweetened chocolate.

## Fudge-Type Icings

Fudge-type icings are rich and heavy. Many of them are made somewhat like candy. Their predominant ingredient is sugar, and they contain less fat than buttercreams. Fudge icings may be flavored with a variety of ingredients and are used on cupcakes, layer cakes, loaf cakes, and sheet cakes.

Fudge icings are stable and hold up well on cakes and in storage. Stored icings must be covered tightly to prevent drying and crusting.

To use stored fudge icing, warm it in a double boiler until it is soft enough to spread.

# CARAMEL FUDGE ICING

*Yield: 2 lb (1 kg)*

| Ingredients | U.S. | | | Metric | Sugar at 100%<br>% | Procedure |
|---|---|---|---|---|---|---|
| Brown sugar | 1 lb | 8 | oz | 750 g | 100 | 1. Combine the sugar and milk in a saucepan. Bring to a boil, stirring to dissolve the sugar. Boil the mixture until it reaches 240°F (115°C). |
| Milk | | 12 | oz | 375 g | 50 | |
| Butter or part butter and part shortening | | 6 | oz | 188 g | 25 | 2. Pour the mixture into the bowl of a mixer. Let it cool to 110°F (43°C). |
| Salt | | 0.1 | oz (½ tsp) | 2 g | 0.4 | 3. Turn on the machine and mix at low speed with the paddle attachment. |
| Vanilla extract | | 0.25 | oz | 8 mL | 1 | 4. Add the butter, salt, and vanilla, and continue to mix at low speed until cool. Beat the icing until it is smooth and creamy in texture. If it is too thick, thin it with a little water. |

# QUICK WHITE FUDGE ICING I

*Yield: 2 lb (1 kg)*

| Ingredients | U.S. | | | Metric | Sugar at 100%<br>% | Procedure |
|---|---|---|---|---|---|---|
| Water | | 4 | oz | 125 mL | 12.5 | 1. Place the water, butter, shortening, syrup, and salt in a saucepan. Bring to a boil. |
| Butter | | 2 | oz | 60 g | 6 | |
| Emulsified shortening | | 2 | oz | 60 g | 6 | 2. Sift the sugar into the bowl of a mixer. |
| Corn syrup | | 1.5 | oz | 45 g | 4.5 | 3. Using the paddle attachment and with the machine running on low speed, add the boiling water mixture. Blend until smooth. The more the icing is mixed, the lighter it will become. |
| Salt | | 0.1 | oz (½ tsp) | 2 g | 0.25 | |
| Confectioners' sugar | 2 lb | | oz | 1000 g | 100 | |
| Vanilla extract | | 0.25 | oz | 8 mL | 0.75 | 4. Blend in the vanilla. |
| **Total weight:** | **2 lb 9** | | **oz** | **1300 g** | **129%** | 5. Use while still warm, or rewarm in a double boiler. If necessary, thin with hot water. |

**VARIATION**

### QUICK CHOCOLATE FUDGE ICING

Omit the butter in the basic recipe. After step 3, blend in 6 oz (188 g) melted unsweetened chocolate. Thin the icing with hot water as needed.

# QUICK WHITE FUDGE ICING II

*Yield: 2 lb (1 kg)*

| Ingredients | U.S. | | Metric | % | Procedure |
|---|---|---|---|---|---|
| **Fondant at 100%** | | | | | |
| Fondant | 1 lb 4 | oz | 500 g | 100 | 1. Warm the fondant to 95°F (35°C). |
| Corn syrup | 2 | oz | 50 mL | 10 | 2. Combine the fondant, corn syrup, butter, short-ening, and salt in the bowl of a mixer. Blend with the paddle attachment until smooth. |
| Butter, softened | 2 | oz | 50 g | 10 | |
| Emulsified shortening | 3 | oz | 75 g | 15 | 3. Blend in the desired flavoring (see below). |
| Salt | 0.12 oz | | 3 g | 0.6 | 4. Thin to spreading consistency with appropriate liquid (see below). |
| Flavoring (see procedure) | | | | | |
| Liquid, to thin (see procedure) | | | | | |
| **Total weight:** | 1 lb 11 **or more** | oz | 678 g **or more** | 135% **or more** | |

**FLAVORING VARIATIONS**

Add desired flavoring to taste, such as vanilla, almond, maple, lemon or orange (extract, emulsion, or grated zest), or instant coffee dissolved in water. Crushed fruit, such as pineapple, strawberries, or ground maraschino cherries, may be used.

For *chocolate icing,* add 6 oz (188 g) melted unsweetened chocolate.

**LIQUIDS FOR ADJUSTING CONSISTENCY**

With fruit flavorings such as orange or lemon, use lemon juice and/or orange juice. With other flavors, use simple syrup or evaporated milk.

# COCOA FUDGE ICING

*Yield: 2 lb 6 oz (594 g)*

| Ingredients | U.S. | | Metric | % | Procedure |
|---|---|---|---|---|---|
| **Granulated Sugar at 100%** | | | | | |
| Granulated sugar | 1 lb | | 500 g | 100 | 1. Combine the granulated sugar, syrup, water, and salt in a saucepan. Bring to a boil, stirring to dissolve the sugar. Boil the mixture until it reaches 240°F (115°C). |
| Corn syrup | 5 | oz | 150 g | 30 | |
| Water | 4 | oz | 125 mL | 25 | |
| Salt | 0.1 | oz (½ tsp) | 2 g | 0.5 | |
| Butter or part butter and part emulsified shortening | 4 | oz | 125 g | 25 | 2. While the sugar is cooking, mix the fat, confectioners' sugar, and cocoa until evenly combined, using the paddle attachment of the mixer. |
| Confectioners' sugar | 8 | oz | 250 g | 50 | 3. With the machine running at low speed, slowly pour in the hot syrup. |
| Cocoa | 3 | oz | 90 g | 18 | 4. Mix in the vanilla. Continue to beat until the icing is smooth, creamy, and spreadable. If necessary, thin with a little hot water. |
| Vanilla extract | 0.25 | oz | 8 mL | 1.5 | |
| Water, hot | as needed | | as needed | | 5. Use while still warm, or rewarm in a double boiler. |

**VARIATION**

## VANILLA FUDGE ICING

Use evaporated milk or light cream instead of water for the syrup. Omit the cocoa. Adjust consistency with additional confectioners' sugar (to thicken) or water (to thin). Other flavorings, such as almond, maple, peppermint, or coffee, may be used in place of vanilla.

# Flat Icings

Flat icings, also called *water icings*, are simply mixtures of confectioners' sugar and water, sometimes with corn syrup and flavoring added. They are used mostly for coffee cakes, Danish pastry, and sweet rolls.

Flat icings are warmed to 100°F (38°C) for application and are handled like fondant.

## FLAT ICING

*For large-quantity measurements, see page 738.*

| Ingredients | U.S. | | Metric | Sugar at 100% % | Procedure |
|---|---|---|---|---|---|
| Confectioners' sugar | 1 lb | | 500 g | 100 | 1. Mix all ingredients together until smooth. |
| Water, hot | 3 | oz | 90 mL | 19 | 2. To use, place the desired amount in a double boiler. Warm to 100°F (38°C) and then apply to the product to be iced. |
| Corn syrup | 1 | oz | 30 g | 6 | |
| Vanilla extract | 0.12 oz (¾ tsp) | | 4 g | 0.8 | |
| *Total weight:* | *1 lb* | *4 oz* | *630 g* | *125%* | |

# Royal Icing

*Royal icing*, also called *decorating* or *decorator's icing*, is similar to flat icings except it is much thicker and made with egg whites, which make it hard and brittle when dry. It is used almost exclusively for decorative work. Pure white royal icing is most often used, but it may also be colored as desired. Because it consists mostly of confectioners' sugar, it is sweet but has little taste.

Royal icing's trait of drying easily and quickly makes it useful for fine decorations, but it requires special handling and storage. It should be tightly covered whenever it is not in use. For even greater protection from drying, place a clean, damp towel on the surface of the icing, and then cover the container tightly with plastic film. If any icing dries or crusts on the sides of the container during storage, remove the dried icing carefully, without letting it fall back into the moist icing. Dried particles can clog the tips of paper cones and writing tubes.

Using a paper cone or, even better, a pastry bag fitted with a writing tip (a pastry tip with a small, round opening), royal icing can be piped into designs onto parchment or plastic and allowed to dry. They can then be lifted off carefully and stored in airtight containers for later use. See pages 440–442 for a discussion of using the paper cone.

A second use for royal icing is called *string work*, in which delicate strands or filaments of icing are suspended between two attachment points, as illustrated in the decoration of the pastillage showpiece on page 663. This technique is also used on some styles of wedding cakes. To produce string work, touch the tip of the paper cone to the first attachment point, then pull the bag away while squeezing the cone with constant pressure. Allow the loop to drop to the desired length, then touch the tip to the second attachment point.

A third use of royal icing is flooding outlined areas of a design with colored icing. This technique requires much thinner icing than that used for string work. Thin the icing with water until a teaspoonful dropped into the bowl of icing flattens to a smooth surface in about 10 seconds. The first step in flooding is to draw an outline using medium-stiff royal icing, either white or colored, as desired. Pipe the outline on the desired surface, such as a sheet of acetate. Allow the outline to dry at least until the surface of the icing is firm. Using a pastry bag with a small (No. 2) plain tip, pipe thinned icing, colored as desired, in a line next to but not touching the inside of the dried outline. The icing should be thin enough to flow up to the outline. Continue to pipe along the inside edge of the icing until the area is filled with a smooth layer of icing. When dry, the design can be lifted off and placed on the surface of a cake.

As you can see, the correct consistency or thickness of royal icing depends on its use. Piped designs and string work require fairly thick icing, while flood work requires a thinner product. For this reason, many pastry chefs do not use a recipe for royal icing but prepare small batches as needed, using the procedure given below. For those who prefer working with a recipe, one is provided.

## Procedure for Preparing Royal Icing

1. Place desired amount of confectioners' sugar in a mixing bowl. Add a small quantity of cream of tartar (for whiteness), about ⅛ tsp per pound of sugar (0.6 g per kilogram).

2. Beat in egg whites, a little at a time, until the sugar forms a smooth paste. You will need 2 to 3 oz egg whites per pound of sugar (125 g per kilogram).

3. Keep unused icing covered with a damp cloth or plastic film at all times to prevent hardening.

## ROYAL ICING

| Ingredients | U.S. | Metric | Procedure |
|---|---|---|---|
| Confectioners' sugar | 1 lb | 500　g | 1. Sift the sugar and cream of tartar into the bowl of a mixer fitted with the paddle attachment. |
| Cream of tartar | ⅛ tsp | 0.3 g (0.5 mL) | |
| Egg whites, pasteurized (see *Note*) | 3 oz | 95　g | 2. In a small bowl, beat the egg whites briefly to break them up. |
| ***Total weight:*** | ***1 lb　3 oz*** | ***595　g*** | 3. With the mixer running on low speed, gradually add the egg whites. |

*Note: Vary the quantity of egg whites depending on the consistency desired.*

4. Continue to mix until the ingredients are well blended and the icing stands in soft peaks.

## Glazes

*Glazes* are thin, glossy, transparent coatings that give a shine to baked products and help prevent drying.

The simplest glaze is a sugar syrup or diluted corn syrup brushed onto coffee cakes or Danish pastries while it is hot (see p. 199 for recipe). Syrup glazes may also contain gelatin or waxy maize starch.

Fruit glazes for pastries, the most popular of which are apricot and red currant, are available commercially prepared. They are melted, thinned with a little water, syrup, or liquor, and brushed on while hot. Fruit glazes may also be made by melting apricot or other preserves and forcing them through a strainer. It helps to add melted, strained preserves to commercial glazes because the commercial products usually have little flavor.

Glaze recipes included in this chapter are of two types: chocolate glazes and gelatin-based glazes. Chocolate glazes are usually melted chocolate containing additional fats or liquids, or both. They are applied warm and set up to form a thin, shiny coating. Gelatin-based glazes, which include many fruit glazes, are usually applied only to the tops of cakes and charlottes made in ring molds. There are several recipes in this chapter, and chapters 18 and 20 both contain examples of products finished with gelatin-based glazes.

## Rolled Coatings

The three commonly used rolled cake coatings are rolled fondant, marzipan, and modeling chocolate. Rather than being applied by spreading or pouring, like the other products discussed in this chapter, these are rolled into thin sheets, using a rolling pin, and draped over the cake to cover it. So the coating adheres to the cake, the cake is first brushed with apricot glaze (p. 200) or a similar product or iced with a thin layer of buttercream before the rolled coating is applied.

*Marzipan* is a paste made of ground almonds and sugar. Preparation and use of marzipan is discussed in chapter 25. Guidelines for applying rolled marzipan coatings are explained in chapter 18 (p. 456).

*Rolled fondant* is essentially a form of fondant (p. 422) that is firm and stiff enough to be kneaded. Like poured fondant, it is almost always purchased ready prepared.

*Modeling chocolate* is a stiff paste made of melted chocolate and corn syrup. It is discussed in chapter 24.

# CHOCOLATE GLAÇAGE OR SACHER GLAZE

| Ingredients | U.S. | Metric | Chocolate at 100% % | Procedure |
|---|---|---|---|---|
| Heavy cream | 6 oz | 150 g | 100 | 1. Prepare a ganache (pp. 275–276) with the cream and chocolate: Heat the cream to boiling and pour over the finely chopped chocolate. Stir until the chocolate is melted and the mixture is uniformly blended. |
| Dark chocolate, chopped | 6 oz | 150 g | 100 | |
| Butter | 2 oz | 50 g | 33 | |
| **Total weight:** | **14 oz** | **350 g** | **233%** | 2. Add the butter and stir to mix in. Use as soon as possible. |

# GANACHE ICING (GANACHE À GLACER)

| Ingredients | U.S. | Metric | Chocolate at 100% % | Procedure |
|---|---|---|---|---|
| Heavy cream | 10 oz | 250 g | 100 | 1. Heat the cream, sugar, and glucose to the boiling point. Remove from the heat. |
| Sugar | 2 oz | 50 g | 20 | |
| Glucose | 2 oz | 50 g | 20 | 2. Finely chop the chocolate and stir into the hot cream mixture until melted. |
| Dark chocolate couverture | 10 oz | 250 g | 100 | |
| **Total weight:** | **1 lb 8 oz** | **600 g** | **240%** | 3. Allow to cool slightly before use. This makes a thin, shiny coating when poured over cakes and charlottes. |

# OPERA GLAZE

*For large-quantity measurements, see page 738.*

| Ingredients | U.S. | | Metric | Procedure |
|---|---|---|---|---|
| Coating chocolate (see p. 92) | 8 | oz | 250 g | 1. Melt both chocolates in a hot-water bath. |
| Dark chocolate couverture | 3.5 | oz | 100 g | 2. Stir in the oil. |
| Peanut oil | 1.33 | oz | 40 g | 3. Allow to cool slightly before use. Makes a thin coat- |
| **Total weight:** | **12** | **oz** | **390 g** | ing that sets solid but can be cut with a hot knife. |

### VARIATIONS

If couverture is used alone instead of part coating chocolate and part couverture, the quantity of oil must be increased so the icing has the proper texture and can easily be cut with a cake knife.

*For large-quantity measurements, see page 738.*

| Ingredients | U.S. | Metric |
|---|---|---|
| Dark chocolate couverture | 11.5 oz | 350 g |
| Peanut oil | 2 oz | 60 g |

# COCOA JELLY

*For large-quantity measurements, see page 738.*

| Ingredients | U.S. | | Metric | Fondant at 100% % | Procedure |
|---|---|---|---|---|---|
| Water | 4 | oz | 100 g | 67 | 1. Combine the water, fondant, and glucose. Bring to a boil and skim if necessary. |
| Fondant | 6 | oz | 150 g | 100 | |
| Glucose | 1 | oz | 25 g | 17 | 2. Soften the gelatin in cold water (see p. 88). |
| Gelatin | 0.25 | oz | 7 g | 4.7 | 3. Add the gelatin and cocoa powder to the hot fondant mixture. Mix quickly and strain through a chinois or fine strainer. |
| Cocoa powder | 1.2 | oz (6 tbsp) | 30 g | 20 | |
| **Total weight:** | **12** | **oz** | **312 g** | **208%** | 4. This mixture is ready to use once the temperature has dropped to 95°F (35°C). |

# FRUIT GLAÇAGE

| Ingredients | U.S. | | Metric | Procedure |
|---|---|---|---|---|
| Gelatin | 0.5 | oz | 12 g | 1. Soften the gelatin in cold water (see p. 88). |
| Sugar | 3 | oz | 90 g | 2. Heat the sugar, water, and glucose until dissolved. Remove from the heat and stir in the gelatin until dissolved. |
| Water | 2 | oz | 60 g | |
| Glucose | 1 | oz | 30 g | |
| Fruit purée | 5 | oz | 150 g | 3. Add the fruit purée. |
| **Total weight:** | **11** | **oz** | **342 g** | 4. Strain through a chinois or fine strainer. |

### VARIATIONS

Two charlottes in this book, Passion Fruit Charlotte (p. 541) and Charlotte au Cassis (p. 540), use fruit glaçage. Passion fruit purée or juice and blackcurrant or cassis purée, respectively, are used to make the glaçage. For other uses, most fruit purées can be used.

5. To use, rewarm if necessary. Pour over the top of a cake or charlotte and quickly spread to the edges of the cake with a palette knife. One small batch makes enough glaze for a 7- or 8-in. (18–20 cm) cake.

# COFFEE MARBLE GLAZE

*For large-quantity measurements, see page 738.*

*Yield: about 11 oz (350 g)*

| Ingredients | U.S. | | Metric | Procedure |
|---|---|---|---|---|
| Gelatin | 0.33 | oz | 8 g | 1. Soften the gelatin in cold water (see p. 88). |
| Water | 8 | oz | 250 g | 2. Simmer the water, sugar, glucose, and vanilla bean until the sugar and glucose are completely dissolved. |
| Sugar | 1.33 | oz | 40 g | |
| Glucose | 1.33 | oz | 40 g | 3. Remove from the heat, cool slightly, and add the gelatin. Stir until dissolved. Scrape the seeds from the vanilla bean and add to the syrup. |
| Vanilla bean, split (see *Note*) | 1 | | 1 | |
| Coffee liqueur | 4 | tsp | 20 g | 4. When ready to use, rewarm the glaze if necessary. Add the coffee liqueur and extract and swirl them in slightly, but do not mix them in. Swirl the glaze over the surface of the cake so the coffee extract gives a marbled effect (see the photo of Julianna on p. 473). |
| Coffee extract | 2 | tsp | 10 g | |

*Note: If vanilla beans are not available, add ½ tsp vanilla extract.*

# ASSEMBLING AND ICING SIMPLE CAKES

This section deals with simple American-style cakes. Typical examples of this type are cupcakes, sheet cakes, and layer cakes made of two or three high-ratio or butter-cake layers. These are popular items in bakeshops and are standard desserts in many food service operations. They may be iced but otherwise undecorated, or they may be given some decorative touches.

## Selection of Icing

The flavor, texture, and color of the icing must be compatible with the cake.

In general, use heavy frostings with heavy cakes and light frostings with light cakes. For example, ice angel food cakes with a simple flat icing, fondant, or a light, fluffy, boiled icing. High-ratio cakes go well with buttercreams and fudge-type icings. Sponge layer cakes are often combined with fruits or fruit fillings, light French or meringue-type buttercreams, whipped cream, or flavored fondants.

Use the best-quality flavorings, and use them sparingly. The flavor of the frosting should not be stronger than that of the cake. Fudge-type icings may be flavored most strongly, as long as the flavor is of good quality.

Use color sparingly. Light, pastel shades are more appetizing than loud colors. Paste colors give the best results. To use either paste or liquid colors, mix a little color with a small portion of the icing, then use this icing to color the rest.

## Sheet Cakes

Sheet cakes are ideal for volume service because they require little labor to bake, ice, and decorate, and they keep well as long as they are uncut.

For special occasions, sheet cakes are sometimes decorated as a single unit with a design or picture in colored icing, and a "Happy Special Occasion" message. It is more common, however, to ice them for individual service, as in the procedure on page 437.

## Procedure for Assembling Layer Cakes

This is the basic procedure for assembling popular American-style layer cakes made with high-fat (that is, creaming method and two-stage method) batters. Layered sponge cakes are assembled slightly differently, as shown on page 451.

1. Cool cake layers completely before assembling and icing.

2. Trim layers if necessary. Remove any ragged edges. Slightly rounded tops are easily covered by icing, but excessively large bumps may have to be cut off.

   If desired, split layers in half horizontally. This makes the cake higher and increases the proportion of filling to cake (see p. 451).

3. Brush all crumbs from cakes. Loose crumbs make icing difficult.

4. Place the bottom layer upside down (to give a flat surface for the filling) on a cardboard cake circle of the same diameter. Place the cake in the center of a cake turntable. If a cake circle or turntable is not available, place the cake on a serving plate; slip sheets of wax paper or parchment under the edges of the cake to keep the plate clean.

5. Spread filling on the bottom layer out to the edges. If the filling is different from the outside frosting, be careful not to spread the filling over the edges. One way to avoid spilling the filling over the edge is to pipe a row of the icing used for the cake sides around the edge of the cake layer to form a dam to hold the filling inside.

   Use the proper amount of filling. If applied too heavily, filling will ooze out when top layer is put in place.

6. Place the top layer on the bottom layer, right-side up.

7. Ice the cake:

   If a thin or light icing is used, pour or spread the icing onto the center of the cake. Then spread it to the edges and down the sides with a spatula.

   If a heavy icing is used, it may be necessary to spread the sides first, then place a good quantity of icing in the center of the top and push it to the edges with the spatula.

   Pushing the icing rather than pulling or dragging it with the spatula prevents pulling up crumbs and getting them mixed with the icing.

   Use enough icing to cover the entire cake generously, but not excessively, with an even layer.

   Smooth the icing with the spatula, or leave it textured or swirled, as desired.

   An alternative way to apply icing is to pipe it on using an oversize basketweave tip, sometimes called a *speed icer*, in a pastry bag.

   The finished, iced cake should have a perfectly level top and perfectly straight, even sides.

# Cupcakes

There are three main methods for icing cupcakes. The first of these, dipping, is used for soft icings. The other methods are used when the icing is too stiff for dipping.

1. Dip the tops of the cupcakes in the icing. Do not dip them too deeply; only the tops should touch the icing.

   If the icing is reasonably stiff, not flowing, twist the cakes slightly and pull them out quickly in one smooth motion.

   If the icing is flowing (such as flat icing or fondant), pull the cakes straight out of the icing. Hold them sideways for a moment so the icing runs to one edge. Then turn them upright and wipe the icing from the edge of the cakes with your finger. Do not let icing run down the sides.

2. Spread the icing with a spatula. Take enough icing for one cake on the tip of a bowl knife and cover the top of the cake in a smooth, neat motion, twisting the cake in one hand. Practice is necessary to develop speed and efficiency.

**3.** With a pastry bag fitted with a star tube, apply a swirl of icing to each cake.

Before the icing dries, cupcakes may be decorated with glazed fruit, coconut, nuts, colored sugar, chocolate sprinkles, etc.

# Specialty Items

A number of popular cake items don't fit in the above categories (layer cake, sheet cake, or cupcake). Among them are the following:

## Boston Cream Pie

**Boston cream pie** is not a pie at all but a simple layer cake. Bake sponge cake in standard layer pans or pie tins. When cool, split each cake into two layers. Fill with Pastry Cream (p. 271) and ice the tops with chocolate fondant or sprinkle with confectioners' sugar.

## Cake Rolls

Besides the popular jelly rolls (p. 408), sponge rolls can be made with a variety of fillings, such as whipped cream, vanilla or chocolate boiled icing, marshmallow icing, or buttercream. Cake rolls are discussed in more detail in the section on European-style cakes (p. 476).

## Procedure for Icing Sheet Cakes

**1.** Turn out the cake onto a cake board or onto the bottom of another sheet pan or tray, as described on page 395. Cool the cake thoroughly.

**2.** Trim the edges evenly with a serrated knife.

**3.** Brush all crumbs from the cake.

**4.** Place a quantity of icing in the center of the cake and, with a spatula, push the icing to the edges. Smooth the top with the spatula, giving the entire cake an even layer of icing.

**5.** With a long knife or spatula, mark the entire cake into portions by pressing the back of the knife lightly into the icing. Do not cut the cake.

**6.** Using a paper cone or pastry bag fitted with a star tube, pipe a rosette or swirl onto the center of each marked-off portion. (If you prefer, select another kind of decoration.) Whatever decorations you use, keep them simple and make them the same for every portion.

**7.** Cut portions as close as possible to service time to keep the cake from drying.

Cake-cutting guides for sheet cakes and round layer cakes. For half-size sheets (13 × 18 in./33 × 46 cm), simply halve the diagrams for full-size sheet cakes below.

6 × 8 = 48 portions

8 × 8 = 64 portions

8 × 12 = 96 portions

8–10 in. (20–25 cm) layers
12 portions

10–12 in. (25–30 cm) layers
16 portions

## Ice Cream Cakes

Ice cream may be used in place of icing to fill layer cakes or cake rolls. If the bakeshop is cool, or if you have a walk-in refrigerator to work in, you can spread slightly softened ice cream on the layers or inside the rolls. Round cakes are best assembled inside cake rings lined with acetate (p. 52). If the temperature is warm, however, it is better to cut slices of hard-frozen ice cream to fill the cakes. Work quickly; do not allow the ice cream to melt and drip out of the cake.

As soon as the layers are stacked or the rolls tightly rolled, return them to the freezer until they are firm. Then quickly frost the tops and sides with whipped cream. Store in the freezer until needed.

## French Pastry

In parts of North America, the term **French pastry** is used for a wide range of decorated pastry and cake products usually made in single-portion pieces. The simplest of the cake-based varieties are tiny decorated layer cakes made in a variety of shapes. They are assembled as follows:

1. Using thin (½–¾-in./1–2 cm) sheet cakes, stack two or three sheets with filling or icing between them. The filled cake layers together should be about 1½–2 in. (4–5 cm) thick.

   Buttercream is the most popular filling. Fruit jams and fudge icings may also be used.

2. Press the layers together firmly and chill or freeze.

3. Using a sharp knife dipped in hot water before each cut, cut the sheet into desired shapes, such as squares, rectangles, or triangles. Circles may be cut out using large cutters. Pieces should be the size of a single portion.

4. Ice the sides and top of each piece with buttercream or fondant. After icing, sides may be coated with chopped nuts, coconut, chocolate sprinkles, etc.

5. Decorate the tops neatly.

French pastries are discussed further in the section on European-style cakes (p. 478).

# BASIC DECORATING TECHNIQUES

A number of simple decorating techniques are discussed in this section. Of these, perhaps the most difficult to learn are those using the pastry bag and paper cone. Some other techniques don't require as much practice but instead rely simply on your steady hand and your sense of neatness and symmetry.

## Tools

The following are needed for assembling and decorating cakes.

Palette knife

**Palette knife or steel spatula.** A spatula with a long, flexible blade for spreading and smoothing icings and fillings.

**Offset palette knife.** A palette knife with an angled blade that enables the chef to spread batters and creams inside pans.

Offset palette knife

**Serrated knife.** A scalloped-edge knife for cutting cakes and for splitting cake layers horizontally into thinner layers.

Serrated knife

*Icing screens* or *grates.* Open-mesh screens for holding cakes being iced with a flow-type icing such as fondant. Excess icing drips off the cake and is collected on a tray under the rack.

*Turntable.* A pedestal with a flat, rotating top, which simplifies the job of icing cakes.

*Icing comb.* A plastic triangle with toothed or serrated edges; used for applying a grooved or ridged pattern to the sides of iced cakes. The edge of the comb is held stationary in a vertical position against one side of the cake while the turntable is rotated.

Icing screen

**Plastic or steel scraper.** The flat edge is easily used to make the icing on the sides of cake perfectly smooth. The technique is the same as the technique for using the icing comb (see above).

**Brushes.** Used to remove crumbs from a cake, to apply dessert syrups to sponge cake layers, and to glaze the surfaces of cakes with apricot glaze and other coatings.

Pastry brushes

**Sugar dredger.** Looks like a large metal saltshaker. Used to dust cakes with confectioners' sugar.

**Cake rings or charlotte rings.** Stainless-steel rings of varying diameters and heights. Cakes are assembled inside these rings when they include soft fillings, such as Bavarian creams and other gelatin-based fillings, that must be held in place while the filling sets. Also used for charlottes (chapter 20).

**Cake cards and doilies.** Layer cakes are placed on cardboard circles (same diameter as the cake) when being assembled. Sheet cakes are placed on half- or full-size cardboard cake boards. This makes them easy to ice and to move after icing. For easy, attractive display, place a paper doily 4 inches (10 cm) larger than the cake on a cake card 2 inches (5 cm) larger than the cake. For example, to assemble, ice, and display a 10-inch cake, use a 10-inch circle, a 12-inch circle, and a 14-inch doily.

Sugar dredger

**Parchment paper.** For making paper cones.

**Pastry bag and tips.** For making borders, inscriptions, flowers, and other designs out of icing. The basic tips are described on page 440.

Many other specialized tips are used for unusual shapes. However, the plain and star tips are by far the most important. It is probably best for the beginner to concentrate on these. They make a wide variety of decorations. With the exception of roses and other flowers, the majority of cake decorations are made with the plain and star tips.

The usual way of using a pastry tip is simply to fit it inside the pastry bag. When you need to use more than one tip with the same icing, you must use a separate bag for each one or empty the bag to change the tip. Special *couplers* are available that allow you to attach the tip to the outside of the bag. It is then a simple matter to change tips even when the pastry bag is full of icing.

**Plain (round) tips**—for writing and for making lines, beads, dots, and so forth. Also used to pipe sponge batters, creams, and choux paste and to fill choux pastries and other items.

**Rose tip**—for making flower petals. These tips have a slit-shaped opening that is wider at one end than the other.

**Ribbon** or *basketweave tips*—for making smooth or ridged stripes or ribbons. These have a slit opening that is ridged on one side.

**Star tips**—for making rosettes, shells, stars, and borders.

**Leaf tips**—for making leaves.

**St-Honoré tip**—for filling Gâteaux St-Honoré (p. 367). This tip has a round opening with a V-shaped slit on one side.

# Using the Paper Cone

The **paper cone** is widely used in decorative work. It is inexpensive, easy to make, and can simply be discarded after use. It is especially valuable if you are working with different colors; simply make a separate cone for each color icing.

Although it is possible to fit metal decorating tubes inside paper cones, the cones are usually used without metal tubes for writing inscriptions and for making line drawings and patterns. In other words, they are used the same way you would use a pastry bag fitted with a small plain tube. Because paper cones can

## Procedure for Decorating with a Paper Cone

1. Make the paper cone as shown.

2. Fill the cone about half full of icing. If the cone is too full, it is hard to squeeze, and icing is likely to come out the top.

3. Fold down the top of the cone to close the open end.

4. With scissors, cut off a very small piece of the tip of the cone. (Be sure to discard the tiny paper tip, as it can easily become mixed with the icing.) It is better to make the opening too small than too large. Squeeze out a little of the icing to test the cone. If necessary, cut off a little more of the tip to enlarge the opening.

5. Hold the top end of the cone between the thumb and the first two fingers of your right hand (if you are right-handed). The fingers should be positioned so they hold the folded end closed and at the same time apply pressure to squeeze the icing from the cone.

6. The left hand does not squeeze the cone. Lightly hold the index finger of the left hand against the thumb of the right hand or against the cone in order to steady your right hand and help guide it.

7. Use either the contact method or the falling method (discussed on p. 442–443) to create different types of decorations and inscriptions.

Make a single cone out of a small triangle of parchment paper. Hold the cone with the fingertip in the center of the long side and curl one side

Curl the other side around to complete the cone.

Fold over the peak at the open end of the cone to secure it.

For a sturdier double cone, cut a longer triangle. Start as for a single cone.

Twist the long end around twice to complete the cone.

Complete single and double cones.

Note how the tip of the cone is held above the surface, allowing the icing to drop into place.

*(continues)*

An assortment of borders made with the paper cone

Paper-cone designs made by the contact method

be made rather small and are easy to control, pastry chefs generally prefer them to pastry bags when they are doing delicate work. For the most delicate work, a special type of plastic or cellophane is available that makes finer lines than paper because a smaller, cleaner opening can be cut on the tip.

Two factors are important if you are to be successful with both the paper cone and the pastry bag.

1. **Consistency of the icing.**  Icing must be neither too thick nor too thin. With the paper cone or the writing tube, the icing must be thin enough to flow freely from the opening but not too thin to form a solid thread. Stiff icing is difficult to force through the opening and tends to break off. For flowers and large decorations, the icing must be stiffer so it holds its shape.

2. **Pressure on the cone or bag.**  Pressure control is necessary for neat, exact decorations. As described below, sometimes you must keep the pressure steady and even. For other types of decorations, such as shell borders, you must vary the pressure from heavy to light and then stop the pressure at the right time. Learning to control the pressure with which you squeeze the decorator's cone or pastry bag takes a lot of practice.

Two methods are used to make decorations: the **contact method** and the **drop-string method**.

The drop-string method, also known as the *falling method,* is so called because the cone is held above the surface, and the icing is allowed to fall or drop from the tip of the cone onto the surface being decorated. This method is used to make lines of even thickness on horizontal surfaces. Much, if not most, paper-cone work is done this way, generally with royal icing, fondant, chocolate fondant, melted chocolate, or piping chocolate (p. 648).

Hold the cone vertically. Touch the tip of the cone to the surface to attach the icing to the point where you want the line to start. Then, as you begin to squeeze the cone, lift the tip of the cone from the surface and start your line. Hold the cone about 1 inch (2.5 cm) from the surface as you trace your pattern. The thread of icing is suspended in air between the tip of the cone and the surface being decorated. Keep the pressure light and constant. To finish a line, lower the tip of the cone and touch the surface at the point where you want the line to end. At the same time, stop squeezing the cone.

This method allows you to make fine, delicate lines and patterns while keeping the thickness of the line perfectly even. The opening in the tip of the cone should be cut quite small. At first, it may seem difficult to control the line while holding the cone an inch above the surface, but with practice, you will be able to make precise patterns.

The contact method is used in two situations: (1) when you want to vary the thickness of the line, and (2) when you want to decorate a vertical surface, such as the side of a cake.

Hold the cone as you would hold a pen, with the tip in contact with the surface and at an angle of about 30 to 45 degrees. Draw lines as though you were drawing on paper with a pen. Control the thickness of the line by adjusting the pressure of your thumb. Squeezing harder makes a thicker line.

It takes a fair amount of practice to control the thickness of the line. Normally, it is best to practice the drop-string method first, until you can make simple lines and patterns easily. Then, when you practice the contact method, you can concentrate on controlling pressure. In addition to royal icing, fondant, and chocolate, buttercream is also used for decorating with the contact method.

The following instructions for using the cone and pastry bag are written for right-handed people. If you are left-handed, simply reverse the hands in the instructions.

## Using the Pastry Bag

An advantage of the pastry bag is that it makes it easy to use different metal tips to create a wide variety of designs. Also, a pastry bag holds more icing than a paper cone. This is important when you are decorating with whipped cream or meringue. Buttercream flowers, shell borders, and many other decorations are made with the pastry bag.

### Procedure for Filling and Using a Pastry Bag

1. Fit the desired metal tip into the pastry bag.

2. If the filling or icing is thin, twist the bag just above the tip and force it into the tip. This prevents the filling from running out of the bag while the bag is being filled.

*(continues)*

3. Turn down the top of the bag into a sort of collar. Slip your hand under this collar and hold the top open with your thumb and forefinger.

4. Fill the bag half to three-quarters full. Remember that stiff icings are relatively hard to force from the bag, so the bag should be filled less. With meringue and whipped cream, the bag can be fuller.

5. Turn up the top of the bag again. Gather the loose top together and hold it shut with the thumb and forefinger of your right hand (if you are right-handed).

6. To force out the icing or cream, squeeze the top of the bag in the palm of your right hand.

7. Use the fingers of your left hand to lightly guide the tip of the bag, *not* to squeeze the bottom of the bag. The left hand is sometimes used to hold the item being filled or decorated.

Piping basic shells and shell borders

Simple bulbs, bead borders, and rosettes

Scrolls and borders made with a star tip

Additional scrolls and borders made with a star tip plus, at the bottom, an example of piping with a St-Honoré tip

Most pastry bags are made of one of the following four materials. *Disposable plastic* bags are designed to be thrown away after use. As a result, they are hygienic. *Reusable plastic* bags are made of a soft, reinforced plastic, making them durable and easy to use. They must be thoroughly cleaned after use, but they do not easily absorb odors and flavors. *Nylon* bags are soft and flexible. They must be cleaned thoroughly after use, but because they are made of a synthetic fabric, they are easier to clean than cotton. *Cotton* is the traditional material for pastry bags, but because it is so absorbent, bags made with it are harder to clean. It is important to wash them well and sterilize them after use.

Examples of marbled icing patterns

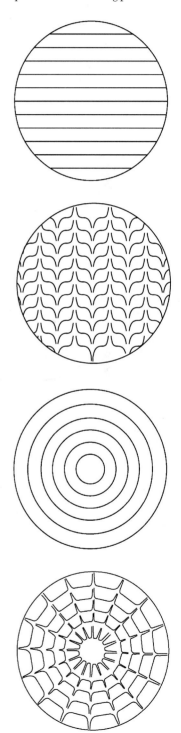

# Other Decorating Techniques

There are many dozens of techniques for decorating cakes. Below are some of the simpler, more commonly used techniques. In the next chapter and in the accompanying illustrations, you will see examples of these and other techniques.

A frequently used way of organizing the decoration of a cake is to divide the cake into portions by marking the icing on top with the back of a long knife. First mark the cake in quarters. Then divide each quarter in half, thirds, or fourths, depending on the size of the cake and the number of pieces desired.

Decorate the cake in a repetitive pattern so each slice has the same decorations. For example, you might decorate a Black Forest Torte (p. 458) with a rosette of cream at the wide end of each wedge, then place a cherry on each rosette.

The advantage of marking the cake into wedges is that it provides portion control. Thus, this approach is often used in restaurants and in retail shops that sell cakes by the slice. Each slice, when cut and served, retains an attractive decoration.

## Masking the Sides

Apply a coating of chopped or sliced nuts, coconut, chocolate sprinkles, chocolate shavings, cake crumbs, or another material to the sides of the cake. Hold the freshly iced cake (on a cardboard circle) in your left hand over the tray of nuts or other material. With your right hand, lightly press a handful of the material against the side of the cake, and let the excess fall back onto the tray. Turn the cake slightly and repeat until the coating is complete. You can coat the sides completely or just the bottom edge.

## Stenciling

Designs can be made on a cake by masking part of the top with paper cutouts or paper doilies and then sprinkling the top of the cake with confectioners' sugar, cocoa, ground nuts, shaved chocolate, cake crumbs, praline powder, or another fine material. Alternatively, spray the top of the cake with a chocolate sprayer, as shown on page 648. Carefully remove the paper pattern to reveal the design. A simple type of stenciling that is effective on chocolate icings is to place parallel strips of paper on the cake and dust with confectioners' sugar.

## Marbling

The **marbling** technique is most frequently used with fondant. Ice the top of the cake with fondant, then pipe lines or spirals in fondant of a contrasting color. Quickly, before the icing sets, draw the back of the knife through the icing to marble it. This is the same technique used to ice napoleons (p. 329). More elaborate marbled icing patterns are made by piping lines, circles, or spirals of a contrasting color fondant onto an iced cake top, then drawing the back of a knife or spatula across the lines before the icing sets.

## Palette Knife Patterns

Icing can be textured quickly and easily with a palette knife as soon as the cake is iced. To make a spiral pattern, leave the cake on the turntable and press the rounded end of the blade lightly into the icing at the center of the cake. Slowly turn the turntable and, at the same time, gradually draw the tip of the palette knife to the outer edge of the cake.

If you wish, this spiral can be marbled with the edge of the knife the same way you would marble fondant stripes. Other patterns, such as straight, parallel ridges, can be made with the palette knife and then marbled.

## Piping Jelly

**Piping jelly** is a transparent, sweet jelly used for decorating cakes. It is available in various colors and in a clear, colorless form you can color yourself. Piping jelly can be piped directly onto a cake with a paper cone. For example, you can add a touch of color to borders by first decorating them with one of the designs on page 442 and then filling in some of the small loops with colored piping jelly.

Another way to use piping jelly is to make jelly transfers. These are colored pictures that are made ahead of time and applied to cakes as needed. Their advantage is that they can be made during slack hours and stored until called for.

### Procedure for Making Piping Jelly Transfers

1. Trace the desired drawing onto a sheet of tracing paper, or, if you wish, draw a picture freehand.

2. Turn the drawing over so the tracing is underneath and can be seen through the paper. (The paper is turned over so the pen or pencil marks don't come off with the jelly.)

3. Outline the drawing with brown piping jelly.

4. Fill in the outlines with piping jelly of appropriate colors.

5. Let the jelly dry. This takes 1 day.

6. Turn the transfer over and place it, jelly-side down, on the iced cake.

7. Moisten the back of the paper lightly with a brush dipped in water.

8. Let the cake and paper stand a few minutes. Then carefully peel off the paper, leaving the jelly picture on the cake.

## Adding Fruits, Nuts, and Other Items

Arranging fruits, nuts, and other items in an attractive pattern is an easy and effective way to decorate a cake while adding to its flavor and its appeal to the customer. This technique is especially appropriate for cakes marked off into portions, as described at the beginning of this section. Each portion can be topped with an appropriate item, such as cherries on the Black Forest cake.

Many fresh or juicy fruits should be added as close to service or display time as possible, as they deteriorate quickly. Fruits in juice or syrup should be drained and dried well before applying.

Naturally, you should use items appropriate to the flavor of the cake. For example, you might place candy coffee beans on a mocha cake or mandarin orange segments on an orange-flavored cake.

Following are examples of items that can be arranged decoratively on cakes:

- Whole strawberries.
- Sweet cherries.
- Mandarin orange segments.
- Pineapple wedges.
- Glacéed fruits.
- Candied chestnuts.
- Pecan halves.
- Walnut halves.
- Small, crisp meringues.

- Chocolates, such as chocolate truffles.
- Chocolate curls or other chocolate decorations.
- Small candies (except hard candies, because a customer might break a tooth).
- Marzipan cutouts—cut from colored marzipan (p. 658) rolled out in sheets—and marzipan figures.

## Decorating Sequence

Although the order in which decorations are placed on the cake depends on the cake and the baker's preferences, many pastry chefs prefer the following sequence:

1. Mask the sides of the cake with nuts, crumbs, or other coatings, either before or after decorating. If the top decorations are delicate and might be damaged if the cake is handled, mask the sides first. However, if you are marbling the top of the cake or using some other technique that disturbs the icing on the sides of the cake, then mask the sides afterward.

2. If the cake is to have an inscription or message, such as a person's name or a holiday or birthday greeting, put this on first.

3. Add borders and paper-cone designs.

4. Add flowers, leaves, and similar decorations made with a pastry bag.

5. Add additional items such as fruits, nuts, or candies.

## TERMS FOR REVIEW

| | | | |
|---|---|---|---|
| fondant | royal icing | Boston cream pie | paper cone |
| buttercream | glaze | French pastry | contact method |
| boiled icing | marzipan | icing screen | drop-string method |
| marshmallow icing | rolled fondant | turntable | marbling (icing) |
| flat icing | modeling chocolate | icing comb | piping jelly |

## QUESTIONS FOR DISCUSSION

1. What is the most important rule to consider when using fondant? Why?

2. What are the advantages and disadvantages of using butter and using shortening in buttercream icings?

3. What are the steps for assembling and icing a two-layer cake?

4. What method would you use to ice cupcakes with fondant? With buttercream?

5. Why is the consistency of the icing important when you are decorating with a paper cone or pastry bag?

6. True or false: If you are right-handed, you should hold the top of the pastry bag shut with your right hand and squeeze the bag with your left hand. Explain your answer.

7. Name four techniques you can use for partially or completely decorating a cake without using a pastry bag or paper cone.

# Specialty Cakes, Gâteaux, and Torten

**A** typical American layer cake consists of two components: cake layers and icing. The cake has two or sometimes three fairly thick layers and is often a high-ratio or creaming-method cake. The iced cake may be 3 or 4 inches (7.5 or 10 cm) tall or more.

A typical European cake, on the other hand, can be described as follows: sponge cake, such as genoise, split into thin layers, moistened with a flavored syrup, filled and iced, and frequently set on a base of baked meringue, japonaise, or short dough. It is sometimes filled with fruit between the layers, and is almost always decorated on top. A European-style cake is usually less than 3 inches (7.5 cm) tall, and its broad, flat top provides an excellent medium for pastry chefs to display their decorating skills.

The above descriptions of American and European cakes are, of course, generalizations, so there are many exceptions to both. Nevertheless, they do give you some idea of the common differences and serve to introduce the subject of European-style cake assembly.

**After reading this chapter, you should be able to:**

1. Select from a variety of components to plan cakes that have well-balanced flavors and textures.

2. Line charlotte rings or cake rings for specialty cakes.

3. Coat a cake with marzipan.

4. Assemble a variety of European-style cakes, Swiss rolls, small cakes, and petits fours.

## PLANNING AND ASSEMBLING SPECIALTY CAKES

**A**s we have suggested several times in this book, much of a pastry cook's job is assembly work—that is, starting with basic elements such as creams, fillings, and baked doughs and batters, the pastry cook builds desserts by putting these elements together in different and attractive ways. This is especially true of the construction of European-style cakes.

Although the number of ingredients that can go into a cake is nearly limitless, the most commonly used components are listed below. Following this list is a general procedure for assembling a basic European-style cake. Following that are procedures for making specific desserts, most of which are popular classics. However, once you are familiar with the general procedure, you should be able to go beyond those included here and put together your own cakes. Just make sure the flavors of the cake layers, fillings, icings, and syrups you choose go well together.

A cake that comprises too many flavors is less pleasing than one with a few flavors that blend well or have a pleasing contrast. Texture, too, is an important consideration. A mixture of creamy, crisp, and cakelike textures is more interesting to the palate than a cake that consists mostly of mousse. Ingredients such as fruits, nuts, nougatine, caramel, chocolate, crisp meringue, and puff pastry add textural interest.

## Basic Cake Components

Following are some of the more important types of components pastry chefs use to construct specialty cakes.

| | |
|---|---|
| Optional bottom layer | Baked short dough circle (p. 320)<br>Baked meringue or japonaise (pp. 347–351) |
| Optional cake ring linings | (p. 453) |
| Cake layers | Genoise or other plain sponge (p. 407)<br>Almond sponge or other nut sponge (pp. 407, 413)<br>Chocolate sponge (pp. 407, 415) |
| Additional specialty layers | Puff paste disks (pp. 324–325)<br>Japonaise or meringue disks (pp. 347–351) |
| For moistening and flavoring cake layers | Dessert syrup (p. 261) |
| Fillings | Jam or jelly (especially apricot and raspberry)<br>Buttercream (pp. 424–428)<br>Crème chantilly (p. 265)<br>Ganache (pp. 275–276)<br>Chocolate mousse (p. 276–277)<br>Pastry cream and variations (pp. 271–274) |

## Procedure for Assembling a Basic Layered Sponge Cake

1. Trim the edges of the cake as necessary.

2. Cut a notch in the edge of the cake so the layers can be lined up again after cutting.

3. Split in half horizontally.

4. Place one half on a cake card and moisten it with a flavored syrup.

5. Applying the filling with a pastry bag is an easy way to get a layer of uniform thickness.

6. Top with the second layer and mask the top . . .

7. . . . and sides with the desired icing.

8. Smooth the sides with a plastic scraper.

9. With a palette knife, smooth the top. The cake is now ready for glazing, if desired, and decorating.

10. Most glazes are applied by pouring the warm glaze over the cake. If necessary, spread the glaze quickly with a palette knife before it sets.

Fillings *(continued)*

Bavarian cream (p. 534)
Fruits (fresh, poached, or canned)

Icings and coatings

Buttercream (pp. 424–428)
Fondant (pp. 423, 433)
Whipped cream (p. 264)
Marzipan (p. 659)
Glazes (pp. 433–435)

Because there are so many types of specialty cakes, some of which can be quite complex, we introduce the methods for making them in two stages. The first procedure, on page 451, is for assembling a basic layered sponge cake from baked cake layers and icing. Notice this procedure is somewhat different from the procedure used for high-fat cakes explained in chapter 17. The most important difference is the use of flavored syrups.

The second procedure introduces many of the techniques used for some of the more elaborate cakes later in this chapter. Please note this is only a general procedure. Some of the same steps appear in both procedures.

## General Procedure for Assembling European-Style Specialty Cakes

1. Assemble all ingredients and equipment.

2. Place a cake card on a turntable or on the work surface. The cake will be assembled on top of the card.

3. Split sponge cake horizontally into two or three layers, depending on the thickness of the cake. Alternatively, use a sponge baked in a thin layer, cutting it to the desired shape and size if necessary.

4. If using a charlotte ring (cake ring), line it as desired (see p. 453).

5. If using a japonaise, meringue, or short-dough base, place it on the cake card. Stick it down with a dab of icing or jam so it doesn't slide off the card. (If you are using a cake ring, place the base inside the ring.) Spread with a thin layer of filling or jam. Raspberry or apricot jam is often used on short-dough bases.

6. Place one sponge layer on top of the base or, if you are not using a base layer, place the sponge layer directly on the card.

7. Brush the cake layer with dessert syrup. Use enough to moisten the cake well, but not so much that it is soggy.

8. If fruit pieces are being used, arrange them either on top of the base or on top of the filling after the next step.

9. Apply a layer of the desired filling. Either spread it on with a palette knife or, to quickly apply an even layer, pipe it on as shown in step 5 of the procedure on assembling a basic layered sponge cake.

10. Top with another sponge layer and again brush with syrup.

11. If a third sponge layer is being used, repeat steps 9 and 10.

12. It is sometimes recommended that the top sponge layer be placed cut-side up, not crust-side up. This is especially helpful if a light, translucent icing such as fondant is being used. A dark crust will show through a thin fondant layer and detract from the appearance of the cake.

13. Ice the cake with the desired icing or glaze.

14. Decorate.

## Rectangular Cakes or Strips

Most popular cakes can also be made in a rectangular shape or strip about 2½ to 3½ inches (6 to 9 cm) wide and 16 to 18 inches (40 to 46 cm) long (the width of a sheet pan) or any fraction of that length. A cake baked in a standard sheet pan can be cut crosswise into seven pieces of this size.

To produce one cake, cut strips of desired size from sheet cakes and layer with fillings as in the basic procedure. Ice the top and sides. Ends may be iced, or they may be left uniced to show an attractive pattern of cake layers and fillings. Trim a thin slice off each end for a more attractive appearance. Use a sharp serrated knife, wiping it clean and dipping it in hot water before cutting each slice.

To produce rectangular or strip cakes in quantity, use full cake sheets and layer as in the basic procedure. Cut into strips of the desired width, then ice the top and sides of each strip.

Strip cakes are divided into portions by cutting off rectangular slices about 1½ inches (4 cm) wide. The tops may be marked into portions and decorated in a regular pattern, just as round cakes are often marked into wedges.

## Lining Charlotte Rings or Cake Rings

Sometimes a soft filling or mousse, such as Bavarian cream or other gelatin-based filling, is used in a layer cake. In these cases, it is necessary to use a ring mold to hold the filling in place until the cake is chilled enough to set the filling. These ring molds are often called **charlotte rings** because they are used to make charlottes, which are molded desserts made of Bavarian cream (see chapter 20). They may also be called *cake rings*.

Using a charlotte ring allows the pastry chef to create a decorative edge for the cake. The cake is finished by applying an icing or glaze only to the top. The decorated sides of the cake are revealed when the ring is removed.

For the neatest results, line the cake ring with a strip of acetate before assembling the cake. This makes it easier to remove the metal ring from the finished cake without marring the sides. Sponge cake, for example, sometimes sticks to the ring if acetate is not used.

Four popular linings for charlotte rings are sponge strips, sliced sponge, chocolate, and fruit.

### Sponge Strips

Sponge used to line a ring must be thin (about ¼ inch/0.5 cm) and flexible enough to bend without breaking. Sponges made with almond powder are good for this purpose because they stay moist and flexible. Joconde sponge (p. 410) is especially suitable. Ladyfinger Sponge (p. 412) is another good choice, even though it does not contain nut powder, because it is strong and flexible.

For a decorative edge, Ribbon Sponge (p. 411) is popular. Using colored stencil paste allows the chef to make many different designs for different cakes. In chapter 20, Passion Fruit Charlotte (p. 541) and L'Exotique (p. 544) are made with ribbon sponge. Caramelized sponge also makes an attractive lining and is suitable for cakes made with caramelized fruit or other caramel flavor, such as Bananier (p. 475). The procedure for making caramelized sponge follows.

## Procedure for Lining a Ring Mold with a Sponge Strip

1. Use the ring as a guide to measure the width and length of the strip of sponge to be cut (a). The strip may be cut slightly narrower than the ring so some of the filling can show above it. It should be slightly longer than the circumference of the ring so it will fit snugly.

2. Brush the sponge with dessert syrup before placing it in the mold to prevent discoloration by juices seeping through from the filling.

3. Place the ring on a cake card and fit the strip of sponge into the ring (b).

4. Trim the end of the strip with a small knife (c).

## Procedure for Caramelizing Sponge

1. Cut a strip of joconde sponge to the desired size for lining the mold.

2. Spread the sponge with a thin coating of Sabayon I (p. 281) and then sprinkle evenly with confectioners' sugar, using a fine sieve.

3. Brown the top of the sponge. For best results, use a hand-held electric salamander iron. If this is not available, brown under a salamander or broiler, but watch it closely to prevent it from scorching.

4. Repeat steps 2 and 3 for a second coat.

5. Turn the strip over and caramelize the other side in the same way.

### Sliced Sponge

Baumkuchen (p. 414) makes an attractive lining for molds because of the striped pattern of its cut surfaces. For a recipe using baumkuchen, see Caramelized Pear Charlotte (p. 598).

Another way to make a sliced sponge lining with attractive vertical stripes is to sandwich together thin layers of sponge with jam, ganache, or other filling. The procedure for cutting the slices and lining the mold is the same as for baumkuchen. Chocolate Indulgence (p. 548) and Charlotte au Cassis (p. 540) are made this way.

## Procedure for Lining a Mold with Slices of Baumkuchen

1. Cut a piece of baumkuchen into a strip just as wide as the desired height of the cake border (a).

Cut this strip crosswise into slices ¼ in. (0.5 cm) thick (b).

2. Fit these slices against the inside of the mold so the stripes are vertical (c).

### *Chocolate*

Chocolate is an especially popular lining for cake molds. Tempered chocolate is spread on a strip of acetate and placed inside the ring mold. The acetate can remain around the cake for display, but it is removed before the cake or charlotte is sliced and served. The procedure is illustrated on page 645. Plain chocolate can be used, but chocolate with a pattern—such as wood grain or marble—is even more attractive. These techniques are illustrated in chapter 24. See the procedure for Julianna (p. 473) for an example of a cake made in a ring lined with chocolate.

Ganache (pp. 275–276) may be used in the same way as tempered chocolate. Spread warm ganache on a strip of acetate and fit it inside the mold.

### *Fruit*

Fruits can be used to line a mold, as in the procedure for Strawberry Cake (p. 463). When using fresh fruits such as strawberries, remember the finished dessert cannot be frozen because the texture of the fruit will be ruined and the fruit will lose juices when thawed, marring the appearance of the cake.

Lining the mold with a strip of acetate gives the best results. (Use parchment if acetate is not available.) Take precautions so the filling does not run between the fruit and the mold, which would detract from the cake's appearance. In the case of halved strawberries or similar fruit, press the cut surface firmly against the side of the mold, but not so firmly as to crush the fruit. Thick fillings and gelatin-based fillings that are about to set are less likely to run between the fruit and mold.

## Fondant

Fondant provides a thin, smooth, shiny coating for cakes and serves as an excellent base for paper-cone decorations. Also, it is a good substitute for buttercream in hot weather, especially for cakes that, for one reason or another, may not be kept in a refrigerated case at all times.

When fondant is used to ice a cake, especially a sponge cake, it is a good idea to first brush the top and sides of the cake with hot apricot glaze. Let the glaze set before applying the fondant. This provides a moisture barrier between the fondant and the cake, and it reduces the chances of the fondant's drying out and losing its shine. Also, it reduces the problem of loose crumbs that might spoil the smoothness of the icing layer.

Guidelines for using fondant are on page 423. To ice a cake with fondant, set it on an icing screen, then pour the warm fondant over the cake, using a bowl knife to guide the fondant evenly over the sides.

This method can be used for coating products with melted chocolate.

# Applying Marzipan Coatings

A thin layer of marzipan, a confection or paste made of almonds and sugar, can be used to coat cakes. It can be colored and used in place of icing, or it can be used under fondant or other icing. When used under fondant, marzipan, like apricot coating, serves as a moisture barrier to protect the fondant. The production of marzipan is explained in chapter 25 (see p. 659).

The following are guidelines for using marzipan as a cake coating:

1. To make a sheet of marzipan, work the paste in your hands to make it pliable, if necessary. Using confectioners' sugar to dust the bench and rolling pin, roll out the marzipan into a thin sheet as though you are rolling out pastry.

2. If the marzipan is to be on the outside of the cake—that is, not covered with icing—the sheet can be textured with a ridged rolling pin. Roll the ridged pin over the sheet of marzipan once to make a ridged texture. To make a checked or dimpled texture, roll the pin across the sheet a second time at a right angle to the first.

3. For a round layer cake, it is easiest to coat only the top with marzipan. Before putting the top layer on the cake, brush it with apricot coating so the marzipan will stick. Place the layer upside down on a sheet of marzipan and press it on lightly. Trim off the excess marzipan. Set the layer right-side up on the cake.

   The sides of the cake can then be iced in a conventional manner.

4. To coat the sides of a round layer cake after coating the top, first ice the sides so the marzipan will stick. Roll out a strip of marzipan as wide as the cake is high and as long as 3 times the width of the cake. Roll up the strip loosely, then unroll it against the sides of the cake.

   The cake can now be coated with fondant or another light icing.

5. An alternative method for coating a cake is to roll out a sheet of marzipan large enough to cover the top and sides. Lift it with the rolling pin and drape it over the cake. With the hands, carefully mold the marzipan against the sides of the cake.

   This method produces a seamless coating for the cake, unlike the method above in step 3. However, it is more difficult to do. The sides must be molded carefully to avoid making ripples or folds in the marzipan.

6. To cover a strip cake or a sponge roll (Swiss roll) with marzipan, roll out a sheet of marzipan large enough to cover the strip or roll. Brush the marzipan with apricot glaze. Set the cake on the marzipan at one edge and roll it up in the sheet.

   As an alternative, you can first coat the cake with the apricot glaze rather than brushing the glaze onto the marzipan.

# PROCEDURES FOR POPULAR CAKES

The first half of this chapter concentrated on explaining general procedures and techniques for assembling specialty cakes. This second half is devoted to specific procedures for assembling a variety of cakes and cake-based desserts, including Swiss rolls and small cakes.

The instructions for specialty cakes in this chapter are assembly procedures rather than recipes, even though they may resemble recipes with their lists of ingredients or components. These procedures may be used for cakes of any size. In many cases, they can be used not only for round cakes but also for square cakes and rectangular strips. Consequently, the quantities of fillings and icings needed vary considerably. Presenting the procedures in this way reflects the normal working practices of a bakeshop. In a typical operation, cakes are baked ahead of time, and fillings, icings, and other components are prepared separately and in advance. Depending on demand or sales, individual desserts can be quickly assembled as needed using the materials on hand.

For a few of the more complex cakes, approximate quantities for the major components are given as guidelines. These quantities apply only to the size of cake indicated in the procedure. This does not prevent you, however, from using the procedures to make any size cake, changing the quantities as necessary.

## Large Cakes

Most of the procedures in this section are for round cakes. Many of these, except those made in ring molds, could also be made as rectangles or strips, as explained on page 453.

In addition, most of these cakes can be made in any size. Therefore, specific quantities of the individual components are not given in many cases; you have the freedom to make the cake in any size you wish. Also, bakeshops generally make cakes from the components they have on hand in larger quantities, so chefs simply use the quantities they feel they need without measuring specific amounts.

Later in this section are a number of cakes that are more complex, so quantities are included as guidelines to help you visualize the cakes. You should feel free to modify these quantities as necessary.

Finally, many molded desserts and pastries are made in the shape of cakes and decorated like cakes. For example, molded and decorated Bavarian creams, called **charlottes**, are often made in ring molds, as some cakes are. These are included with basic Bavarians in chapter 20 if they are made without cake layers. Other desserts made in the shape of cakes are found in chapters 15 and 22. Some of these are mentioned in the section above called "Lining Charlotte Rings or Cake Rings."

Each of the procedures in this section is accompanied by a diagram to help you visualize how the components are layered and built to make the completed cake. These drawings are intended to show the structure of the cake and the relationships of its components. They are not necessarily drawn to scale. For example, you may make layers of icings thicker or thinner than those shown. Also, decorations for the tops of the cakes are not shown.

# BLACK FOREST TORTE

| Components | Procedure |
|---|---|
| Chocolate Sponge (pp. 407, 415), split into 3 layers<br>Dessert syrup flavored with kirsch<br>Whipped cream flavored with kirsch<br>Sweet dark pitted cherries, drained<br>Chocolate shavings | 1. Moisten one chocolate sponge layer with syrup.<br>2. Spread with a thin layer of whipped cream.<br>3. With a pastry bag fitted with a large, plain tube, pipe a circle of cream in the center of the layer. Pipe a ring of cream around the edge. Then pipe another ring in the space between these two.<br>4. Fill the two spaces between these rings with well-drained cherries.<br>5. Top with a second sponge layer. Moisten with syrup.<br>6. Spread with a layer of whipped cream.<br>7. Top with a third sponge layer, moistened with syrup.<br>8. Ice the top and sides with whipped cream.<br>9. With the back of a knife, mark off the top of the cake into the desired number of wedges.<br>10. Mask the sides of the cake with chocolate shavings. Sprinkle chocolate shavings in the center of the cake.<br>11. With a star tube, pipe rosettes of whipped cream around the top edge of the cake so that there is one on each wedge. Place a cherry on each rosette. |

Chocolate shavings                                                    Whipped cream

Chocolate sponge moistened
with kirsch-flavored syrup                                    Cherries

---

### ❧ SCHWARZWALDER KIRSCHTORTE ☙

The Black Forest, or *Schwarzwald* (shvarts valt) in German, lies in southwestern Germany, just east of the Rhine River. One of the prominent agricultural products of this scenic region is the cherry, or *Kirsche* (keer sheh), which is used to make the clear white brandy (eau-de-vie) called *Kirschwasser*. The Schwarzwalder Kirschtorte, made of chocolate sponge flavored with kirschwasser (or *kirsch*, for short) and layered with cherries and whipped cream, is a popular dessert in this region and is sold in most pastry shops.

# MOCHA TORTE

| Components | Procedure |
|---|---|
| Genoise (p. 407), split into 3 or 4 layers<br><br>Buttercream flavored with coffee (p. 424)<br><br>Dessert syrup flavored with coffee or coffee liqueur | 1. Moisten the cake layers with syrup. Sandwich them together with buttercream.<br><br>2. Ice top and sides smoothly with buttercream.<br><br>3. Decorate as desired with a pastry bag filled with additional buttercream. Chocolate decorations are also appropriate. Sides may be masked with toasted, sliced almonds, if desired. |

**VARIATION**

Alternate 2 thin layers of vanilla genoise with 2 thin layers of chocolate genoise.

Coffee buttercream

Genoise moistened with coffee-flavored syrup

# FRUIT TORTE

| Components | Procedure |
|---|---|
| Short Dough (p. 320) or Almond Short Dough (p. 320) circle<br><br>Genoise (p. 407) or Almond Sponge (p. 407), split into 2 layers<br><br>Raspberry or apricot jam<br><br>Dessert syrup flavored with vanilla or kirsch<br><br>Buttercream flavored with vanilla or kirsch (p. 424)<br><br>Small fruits, preferably 3 or 4 kinds, in contrasting colors (such as mandarin orange slices, cherries, grapes, banana slices, strawberries, apricot halves, and pineapple wedges)<br><br>Apricot Glaze (p. 200)<br><br>Almonds, sliced or chopped | 1. Spread the short dough base with jam.<br><br>2. Top with a sponge layer. Moisten with syrup.<br><br>3. Spread with a thin layer of buttercream.<br><br>4. Top with second sponge layer.<br><br>5. Moisten with syrup.<br><br>6. Ice top and sides with buttercream.<br><br>7. Arrange the fruits on the top of the cake in neat, concentric circles, as though you were making an unbaked fruit tart (p. 358).<br><br>8. Glaze the fruits with apricot glaze.<br><br>9. Mask the sides of the cake with almonds. |

**VARIATION**

Instead of buttercream, use whipped cream or pastry cream.

Almonds    Fruit    Vanilla or kirsch buttercream

Genoise or almond sponge moistened with vanilla syrup or kirsch-flavored syrup    Short dough    Raspberry jam

# DOBOS TORTE

| Components | Procedure |
|---|---|
| 7 Dobos layers (p. 408)<br>Chocolate buttercream (p. 424)<br>Chopped almonds<br>Sugar, cooked to the light caramel stage (p. 261) | 1. Set aside the best Dobos layer for the top.<br>2. Sandwich the other 6 layers together with chocolate buttercream.<br>3. Ice the top and sides completely. Mask the sides with chopped almonds.<br>4. Cook the sugar to the light caramel stage. Pour the hot caramel over the reserved dobos layer to coat the top completely with a thin layer.<br>5. With a heavy, buttered knife, immediately cut the caramel layer into portion-size wedges. This must be done before the caramel hardens.<br>6. Top the cake with the layer of caramel-covered wedges. |

**VARIATION**

## SEVEN-LAYER CAKE

Seven-layer cake is a variation of the Dobos torte, except it is generally made as a strip or rectangle (see p. 453 for an explanation) rather than as a round cake. Use Dobos Mix (p. 408), seven-layer mix (p. 407), or any thin sponge layers. Sandwich together 7 layers of cake with chocolate buttercream. Coat the top and sides with chocolate buttercream, chocolate fondant, or melted chocolate.

Chocolate buttercream     Caramel     Dobos sponge

Almonds

# NAPOLEON GÂTEAU

| Components | Procedure |
|---|---|
| Blitz Puff Paste (p. 325) or scrap puff paste<br>Pastry Cream (p. 271)<br>White fondant<br>Chocolate fondant<br>Chopped almonds or puff paste crumbs<br><br>*Note: This is the same as a regular napoleon but made in the shape of a cake.* | 1. Roll out puff paste ⅛ in. (3 mm) thick. Cut out 3 circles 1 in. (2.5 cm) larger in diameter than the desired cake (this allows for shrinkage during baking). Dock the pastry well. Let rest 30 minutes.<br>2. Bake the puff paste at 400°F (200°C) until browned and crisp. Cool. With a serrated knife, carefully trim the circles, if necessary, so they are perfectly round and uniform.<br>3. Sandwich the 3 layers together with generous layers of pastry cream. Use the best pastry layer for the top and place it upside down so the top is flat and smooth.<br>4. Ice the top with white fondant and marble it with chocolate fondant (see p. 445).<br>5. Carefully smooth the sides, using additional pastry cream if necessary. Mask with almonds or pastry crumbs. |

Almonds or pastry crumbs     Marbled fondant     Puff pastry

Pastry cream

# SACHERTORTE

| Components | Procedure |
|---|---|
| 1 baked Sacher cake (p. 402)<br>Dessert syrup flavored with kirsch<br>Apricot jam<br>Ganache (p. 275)<br>Chocolate Glaçage (p. 433)<br>Grated dark chocolate | 1. Trim the cake, if necessary, and cut it into 2 layers. Moisten both layers with kirsch syrup.<br>2. Sandwich the layers together with a layer of apricot jam.<br>3. Mask the top and sides of the cake with ganache, spreading it perfectly smooth.<br>4. Chill the cake until the ganache is firm.<br>5. Place the cake on a wire rack on a tray. Ice the cake by pouring warm chocolate glaçage over it. Run a palette knife over the top and tap the tray to make the icing smooth. Chill until set.<br>6. Remove from the wire rack, neaten the bottom edge with a knife, and place on a cake board.<br>7. Using additional ganache, pipe the word *Sacher* across the middle of the cake. Coat the bottom of the sides with grated chocolate. (For background information on this classic Austrian cake, see page 403.) |

Grated chocolate

Chocolate glaçage

Ganache

Sacher cake layers moistened with kirsch syrup

Apricot jam

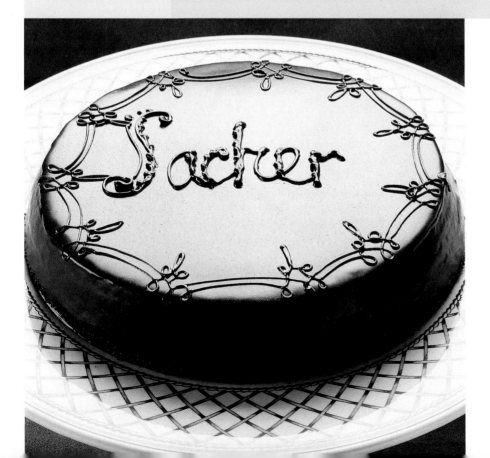

# KIRSCH TORTE

| Components | Procedure |
|---|---|
| 2 baked meringue or japonaise disks (pp. 347 and 348)<br>1 baked genoise layer (p. 407), about 1 in. (2.5 cm) thick<br>Dessert syrup flavored with kirsch<br>Buttercream flavored with kirsch (p. 424)<br>Confectioners' sugar<br>Chopped almonds or meringue crumbs | 1. Moisten the genoise with enough kirsch syrup to saturate it well.<br>2. Place a meringue or japonaise layer upside down (smooth side up) on a cake circle.<br>3. Spread it with a layer of buttercream.<br>4. Place the genoise on top and spread it with buttercream.<br>5. Top with the second meringue layer, smooth side up.<br>6. Spread the sides smoothly with buttercream and coat them with nuts or meringue crumbs.<br>7. Dust the top heavily with confectioners' sugar. With the back of a knife, mark the sugar in a diamond pattern. |

Almonds or meringue crumbs

Buttercream

Confectioners' sugar

Genoise moistened with kirsch-flavored syrup

Meringue disks

# ORANGE CREAM CAKE

| Components | Procedure |
|---|---|
| 1 meringue disk (p. 347)<br>Genoise (p. 407), split into 2 layers<br>Orange-flavored dessert syrup<br>Whipped cream lightly flavored with orange liqueur<br>Mandarin orange segments<br><br>*Note: This procedure can be used with any appropriate fruit, such as strawberries, pineapple, apricots, and cherries. The flavor of the syrup and the cream should be appropriate to the fruit.* | 1. Spread the meringue layer with whipped cream.<br>2. Top with a genoise layer and brush it with syrup.<br>3. Spread with whipped cream.<br>4. Arrange a layer of orange segments, well drained, on the cream.<br>5. Top with a second genoise layer. Moisten with syrup.<br>6. Ice the top and sides of the cake with whipped cream.<br>7. Mark the top of the cake into the desired number of wedges.<br>8. Decorate with rosettes of whipped cream around the top edge of the cake. Top each rosette with an orange segment. |

Whipped cream

Genoise moistened with orange-liqueur syrup

Mandarin orange segments

Meringue disk

# STRAWBERRY CAKE

| Components | Procedure |
|---|---|
| 2 genoise layers (p. 407), each ½ in. (1 cm) thick<br>Dessert syrup flavored with kirsch<br>Fresh strawberries<br>Vanilla Bavarian Cream (p. 534)<br>Buttercream flavored with vanilla (p. 424)<br>Piping chocolate (p. 648) | 1. Line a charlotte ring with a strip of acetate. Set the ring on a cake card.<br>2. Place a genoise layer in the ring and brush it with syrup.<br>3. Select the best-looking, most uniformly sized strawberries to line the ring and cut them in half vertically. Place them on the sponge evenly spaced around the edge, with the stem end down and the cut surface against the acetate. Distribute the remaining strawberries evenly on the sponge.<br>4. Cover the strawberries with the Bavarian cream, which has been cooled until it is thick and just about to set, filling the ring to within ½ in. (1 cm) of the top, making sure there are no air spaces around the berries.<br>5. Place the second genoise layer on top, pressing down gently. Brush the top with syrup.<br>6. Spread the top with a thin layer of buttercream.<br>7. Using a paper cone, decorate the top of the cake with piping chocolate, making desired patterns (see chapter 17).<br>8. Chill until set. Remove the ring, but leave the acetate around the cake until ready to serve. |

Vanilla buttercream

Vanilla Bavarian cream

Genoise moistened with kirsch-flavored syrup

Strawberries

# CHOCOLATE MOUSSE CAKE

| Components | Procedure |
|---|---|
| 3 chocolate meringue disks (p. 347)<br>Chocolate Mousse (p. 276)<br>Shaved chocolate | 1. Sandwich together the chocolate meringue disks with chocolate mousse.<br>2. Ice the top and sides completely with chocolate mousse.<br>3. Coat the top and sides of the cake with shaved chocolate. |

Chocolate shavings

Chocolate mousse

Chocolate meringue disks

# CHOCOLATE GANACHE TORTE

| Components | Procedure |
|---|---|
| 1 plain or chocolate meringue disk (p. 347) *(optional)*<br>Whipped ganache (p. 275)<br>Chocolate Genoise (p. 407), split into 3 layers<br>Dessert syrup flavored with rum or vanilla<br>Chocolate buttercream (p. 424) | 1. Spread the meringue disk with ganache.<br>2. Top with a genoise layer. Moisten with syrup and spread with a layer of ganache.<br>3. Repeat with a second genoise layer and more syrup and ganache.<br>4. Top with the remaining cake layer, moistened with syrup.<br>5. Ice the top and sides with buttercream.<br>6. Decorate as desired. |

Chocolate buttercream

Chocolate ganache

Chocolate genoise moistened with vanilla syrup or rum-flavored syrup

Meringue disk

# ABRICOTINE

| Components | Procedure |
|---|---|
| Genoise (p. 407), split into 2 layers<br>Dessert syrup flavored with kirsch<br>Apricot preserves<br>Italian Meringue (p. 267)<br>Sliced almonds<br>Confectioners' sugar | 1. Place a layer of genoise on a cake card and brush it with syrup.<br>2. Spread with a layer of apricot preserves.<br>3. Top with the second genoise layer and brush with syrup.<br>4. Coat the top and sides of the cake with Italian meringue.<br>5. Using a pastry bag with a star tip, pipe a decorative border of Italian meringue on top of the cake.<br>6. Fill the center of the top of the cake with a layer of sliced almonds and dust with confectioners' sugar.<br>7. Place in a hot oven (500°F/250°C) until lightly browned. |

Almonds, confectioners' sugar

Italian meringue

Genoise moistened with kirsch-flavored syrup

Apricot preserves

# ALMOND GÂTEAU

| Components | Procedure |
|---|---|
| Almond Sponge (p. 407), split into 2 layers<br>Dessert syrup flavored with rum<br>Apricot jam<br>Almond macaroon mixture (p. 504)<br>Apricot glaze (p. 200) | 1. Moisten the sponge layers with syrup and sandwich them together with apricot jam.<br>2. Coat the sides of the cake with the macaroon mixture. Using a star tube or basketweave tube, cover the top of the cake with macaroon mix in a basketweave pattern.<br>3. Let stand for at least 1 hour.<br>4. Brown quickly in a hot oven (450°F/230°C), about 10 minutes.<br>5. While still warm, glaze with apricot glaze. |

Apricot glaze   Almond macaroon mixture

Almond sponge moistened with rum-flavored syrup   Apricot jam

# BAVARIAN CREAM TORTE

| Components | Procedure |
|---|---|
| Genoise (p. 407) or other sponge cut into 3 very thin layers, about ¼ in. (6 mm) thick<br>Bavarian Cream in any flavor (pp. 534–535)<br>Whipped cream flavored to be compatible with the flavor of the Bavarian cream (use chocolate whipped cream with chocolate Bavarian torte)<br>Dessert syrup, flavored appropriately | 1. Line the bottom of a cake pan or springform pan with a thin sponge layer. Moisten with syrup.<br>2. Prepare the Bavarian cream. Pour enough of the mixture into the cake pan to make a layer about ¾ in. (2 cm) thick.<br>3. Place a second layer of sponge cake on top of the cream. Moisten with syrup.<br>4. Fill with another layer of Bavarian cream.<br>5. Top with the remaining sponge layer.<br>6. Chill until set.<br>7. Unmold.<br>8. Ice the top and sides with whipped cream.<br>9. Decorate as desired. |

Whipped cream   Genoise moistened with dessert syrup

Bavarian cream

# FEUILLE D'AUTOMNE

| Components | Procedure |
|---|---|
| Almond Meringues (p. 348), three 6½-in. (16 cm) disks<br>Chocolate Mousse IV (p. 546), 16–20 oz (450–550 g)<br>Dark chocolate couverture, about 14 oz (400 g)<br>Cocoa powder<br>Confectioners' sugar | 1. Place a 7-in. (18 cm) charlotte ring on a cake board. Place one of the meringue disks in the bottom. |

1. Place a 7-in. (18 cm) charlotte ring on a cake board. Place one of the meringue disks in the bottom.

2. Fill the ring slightly less than half full of mousse.

3. Place a second meringue on top and press down lightly. Fill nearly to the top with mousse, then place the third meringue on top. Press down lightly.

4. Spread the top with a thin layer of mousse.

5. Chill until firm.

6. Remove the charlotte ring, using a blowtorch to help release the sides. Chill again to firm the sides.

7. Melt the chocolate couverture.

8. Heat 3 clean half-sheet pans at 325°F (160°C) for 4 minutes. Spread the melted chocolate over the bottoms of the trays. Let cool at room temperature until the chocolate begins to get cloudy. (The purpose of warming the pans is to enable you to spread a thinner coat of chocolate; be careful, however, not to get the pans too hot. Some chefs prefer to use cold trays.)

   The procedure used here is illustrated and explained in more detail in chapter 24 (see p. 647). An experienced chef may need as little as 1 or 1½ pans of chocolate to coat the cake, but it is a good idea to prepare extra to allow for mistakes.

9. Refrigerate to set completely.

10. Bring back to room temperature. The chocolate must be pliable but not soft. Use a metal scraper to lift strips of chocolate off the trays, as shown on page 647. Wrap these around the sides of the cake. Use the same technique to make ruffles for the top of the cake. Chill.

11. Dust the top with a little cocoa powder. (The cake in the illustration is additionally decorated with chocolate leaves, made by brushing a leaf mold—real leaves could also be used—with tempered chocolate and letting the chocolate set before peeling off.)

Almond meringue disks     Chocolate strips

Chocolate mousse

# ALHAMBRA

| Components | Procedure |
|---|---|
| 1 8-in. (20 cm) round Hazelnut Sponge Cake (p. 413) | 1. Trim the top of the cake, if necessary, to make it level. Turn it upside down. Cut it in half horizontally to split into 2 layers. |

**Components**

1 8-in. (20 cm) round
  Hazelnut Sponge Cake
  (p. 413)
Coffee Rum Syrup
  (p. 263)
Ganache I (p. 275),
  made with equal parts
  cream and chocolate,
  about 8 oz (250 g)
Chocolate Glaçage
  (p. 433), 5–6 oz
  (150–175 g)
Decoration
  Chopped pistachios
  Marzipan rose

*Note: Assembly of this cake is illustrated on page 451.*

**Procedure**

1. Trim the top of the cake, if necessary, to make it level. Turn it upside down. Cut it in half horizontally to split into 2 layers.
2. Brush both halves with syrup to moisten.
3. Using a pastry bag with a medium plain tip, pipe the ganache onto the bottom layer, making a spiral that starts in the center and covers the layer completely.
4. Place the second layer on top and press down lightly.
5. Mask the top and sides of the cake with the remaining ganache. Chill.
6. Place the cake on a wire rack over a tray. Pour the glaçage over it. Carefully run a palette knife over the top and tap the tray to ensure the icing is perfectly smooth. Chill.
7. When the icing is chilled and set, remove the cake from the wire rack. Neaten the bottom edge with a knife.
8. Press chopped pistachios around the bottom ½ in. (1 cm) of the sides. Place on a cake card.
9. Using the remaining ganache, pipe the word *Alhambra* across the middle of the cake.
10. Make 2 marzipan roses and 2 leaves (see p. 661) and brush them with cocoa powder to highlight them. Place them next to the writing on top of the cake.

Chocolate glaçage

Hazelnut sponge cake moistened with coffee rum syrup

Ganache

Chopped pistachios

# GENOISE À LA CONFITURE FRAMBOISE (GENOISE WITH RASPBERRY FILLING)

| Components | Procedure |
|---|---|
| Genoise (p. 407), split into 2 layers<br>Dessert syrup flavored with framboise (raspberry alcohol)<br>Raspberry preserves or jam (p. 599)<br>Italian Meringue (p. 267)<br>Sliced almonds<br>Fresh raspberries<br>Confectioners' sugar | 1. Moisten one genoise layer with the syrup. Spread the top with an even layer of raspberry preserves.<br>2. Moisten the bottom of the second layer with syrup and place on top of the first layer. Brush the top with additional syrup.<br>3. Coat the top and sides with the Italian meringue and spread smooth with a palette knife. Using a pastry bag, decorate the top with additional meringue.<br>4. Press the almonds around the bottom edge of the sides of the cake.<br>5. Brown the meringue with a blowtorch.<br>6. Garnish the top of the cake with fresh raspberries and sprinkle with a little confectioners' sugar. |

Italian meringue

Sliced almonds

Genoise moistened with framboise-flavored syrup

Raspberry preserves

# BRASILIA

| Components | Procedure |
|---|---|
| 1 half-sheet pan Hazelnut Joconde Sponge Cake (p. 410)<br>Nougatine (p. 668), freshly prepared, 10 oz (300 g)<br>Dark chocolate, melted, about 2 oz (50 g)<br>Dessert syrup flavored with rum<br>Caramel Buttercream (p. 427), 1 lb (500 g)<br>Tempered white chocolate for decoration | 1. Cut the sponge into 3 equal rectangles, about 6 × 12 in. (15 × 30 cm).<br><br>2. Prepare the nougatine. Roll out into a thin rectangle slightly larger than the sponge rectangles. While it is still warm, trim the edges with a sharp knife so they are straight and the rectangle is about ½ in. (1 cm) smaller on a side than the sponge (to allow for later trimming of the sponge). (If you rolled the nougatine on a silicone mat, remove it from the mat before cutting.) Cut portions of the desired size, but leave them together. Let cool.<br><br>3. Spread one sponge layer with a thin layer of melted chocolate. Refrigerate to set.<br><br>4. Remove from the refrigerator, turn chocolate side down, and brush with the rum syrup.<br><br>5. Spread with a layer of buttercream about ¼ in. (5 mm) thick.<br><br>6. Place a second sponge layer on top, brush with syrup, and again spread with buttercream.<br><br>7. Repeat with the third layer and spread with buttercream.<br><br>8. Trim the edges and top with the nougatine.<br><br>9. Put the tempered white chocolate in a paper cone and decorate the top of the cake with a fancy border.<br><br>10. If desired, this large cake can be cut in half to make two 6-in. (15 cm) square cakes. |

Nougatine

Caramel buttercream    Hazelnut joconde sponge cake moistened with rum-flavored syrup    Chocolate

# RUSSIAN CAKE

| Components | Procedure |
|---|---|
| 1 half-sheet pan Joconde Sponge Cake (p. 410)<br>Dark chocolate, melted, about 2 oz (50 g)<br>Dessert syrup flavored with cognac<br>Praline Buttercream (p. 427), 1 lb (500 g)<br>Apricot Glaze (p. 200)<br>Toasted sliced almonds<br>Confectioners' sugar | 1. Cut the sponge into 3 equal rectangles, about 6 × 12 in. (15 × 30 cm).<br><br>2. Spread one sponge layer with a thin layer of melted chocolate. Refrigerate to set.<br><br>3. Remove from the refrigerator, turn chocolate side down, and brush with the cognac syrup.<br><br>4. Spread with a layer of buttercream about ½ in. (1 cm) thick.<br><br>5. Place a second sponge layer on top, brush with syrup, and again spread with buttercream.<br><br>6. Top with the third layer of sponge and brush with syrup. Trim the sides of the cake neatly.<br><br>7. Heat apricot glaze and thin with water to a consistency that can be poured and spread. Glaze the top of the cake.<br><br>8. With the remaining buttercream, decorate the top of the cake with a scroll border, using a pastry bag with a star tip.<br><br>9. Garnish the top of the cake with the almonds and dust them very lightly with confectioners' sugar. |

Apricot glaze

Joconde sponge cake moistened with cognac-flavored syrup

Praline buttercream

Chocolate

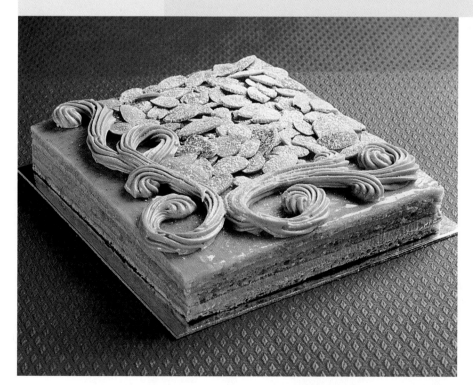

# OPERA CAKE

| Components | Procedure |
|---|---|
| 1 half-sheet pan Joconde Sponge Cake (p. 410)<br>Dark chocolate, melted, about 2 oz (50 g)<br>Dessert syrup flavored with coffee extract<br>French Buttercream flavored with coffee (p. 424), 12 oz (350 g)<br>Ganache, 5–6 oz (150 g)<br>Opera Glaze (p. 434) | 1. Cut the sponge into 3 equal rectangles, about 6 × 12 in. (15 × 30 cm).<br>2. Spread one sponge layer with a thin layer of melted chocolate. Refrigerate to set.<br>3. Remove from the refrigerator, turn chocolate-side down, and brush with the coffee syrup.<br>4. Spread with a layer of buttercream about ¼ in. (5 mm) thick.<br>5. Place a second sponge layer on top, brush with syrup, and spread with a thin layer of ganache.<br>6. Top with the third layer of sponge and brush with syrup. Spread with a layer of the buttercream. Smooth the top carefully with a palette knife. Refrigerate or freeze until firm. The cake must be quite cold so the warm glaze does not melt the buttercream.<br>7. Set the cake on a rack over a tray. Pour warm opera glaze over the cake. Pass a palette knife over the top of the cake and tap the tray to smooth the glaze.<br>8. Chill until set. Remove from the rack and trim the sides of the cake neatly and squarely with a hot knife.<br>9. With additional ganache in a paper cone, pipe the word Opera on top of the cake. |

Opera glaze     Ganache

Joconde sponge cake moistened with coffee-flavored syrup     Coffee-flavored buttercream     Chocolate

# MONTE CARLO

| Components | Procedure |
|---|---|
| Common Meringue (p. 267), 8 oz (225 g)<br>Almond Chocolate Sponge (p. 415), one circle 5, 6, or 7 in. (13–18 cm) in diameter<br>Jelled Spiced Apricot Compote (recipe opposite)<br>Almond Cream (p. 539), 14 oz (400 g)<br>Decoration<br>Crème Chantilly (p. 265)<br>Apricot halves<br>Cocoa powder<br>Red currants | 1. Pipe 7-in. (18 cm) circles of common meringue onto parchment paper (see p. 347 for technique). Use all the meringue—you will need two circles for the cake, plus crumbled meringue for decoration. Bake at 325°F (160°C) until firm. Using a 7-in. (18 cm) charlotte ring like a cookie cutter, trim two of the circles to fit inside the ring.<br>2. Trim the almond chocolate sponge, if necessary, to fit inside a 5-in. (13 cm) cake pan. Brush generously with the reserved syrup from the apricot compote. Pour warm apricot compote on top of the sponge in the tin. Chill until set.<br>3. Place one of the meringue layers on a cake card. Turn out the sponge and apricot compote from the tin upside down on top of the meringue so the almond sponge layer is on top. Be sure this 5-in. (13 cm) circle is centered on the meringue.<br>4. Place a 7-in. (18 cm) charlotte ring on the cake card enclosing the meringue layer.<br>5. Fill to just below the top of the ring with the almond cream. Top with the second meringue layer, pressing down gently. Chill until set.<br>6. Remove the charlotte ring, carefully using a blowtorch to release the ring from the sides.<br>7. Mask the top and sides of the cake by spreading on a thin layer of almond cream.<br>8. Crumble the remaining baked meringue and press the crumbs onto the sides and top of the cake.<br>9. Using a pastry bag with a star tip, pipe 8 rosettes of crème chantilly around the top edge of the cake. Top each with a fanned apricot half. Dust the center lightly with cocoa powder. If desired, add a few red currants for additional decoration. |

Broken meringue

Almond cream

Meringue disks

Chocolate sponge moistened with apricot-flavored syrup

Jelled spiced apricot compote

# JELLED SPICED APRICOT COMPOTE

| Ingredients | Procedure |
|---|---|
| Canned apricots with syrup, 12 oz (350 g)<br>Cinnamon stick, 1<br>Lemon peel, strips from 1 lemon<br>Gelatin, ⅛ oz (4 g or 2 leaves)<br>Amaretto liqueur, 2 oz (60 mL) | 1. Drain and reserve the syrup from the apricots. Add the cinnamon stick and lemon peel to the syrup and bring to a boil. Add the apricots and simmer until the fruit is beginning to fall apart (if necessary, remove the apricots and chop them). Remove the cinnamon stick and lemon peel. Drain and reserve the syrup to moisten the cake layer in step 2 above.<br>2. Soften the gelatin in cold water (see p. 88).<br>3. Add the gelatin to the hot apricots and stir until it is dissolved. Stir in the amaretto.<br>4. Rewarm, if necessary, to use in the Monte Carlo on the previous page. |

# JULIANNA

| Components | Procedure |
|---|---|
| Wood-grain chocolate strip<br>Plain genoise (p. 407), two 7-in. (18 cm) disks, ¼–⅜ in. (1 cm) thick<br>Coffee Syrup (p. 263)<br>Praline Cream II (p. 542), 10 oz (300 g)<br>Vanilla Cream (p. 427), 10 oz (300 g)<br>Coffee Marble Glaze (p. 435), 3–4 oz (100–110 g)<br>Decoration<br>  Chocolate fan<br>  Chocolate cigarettes<br>  Caramelized hazelnuts | 1. Line a 7-in. (18 cm) charlotte ring with a strip of acetate coated with wood-grain chocolate (see p. 645). Set the ring on a cake card.<br>2. Place a disk of genoise sponge in the base of the ring. (*Note:* The sponge circles may be cut from a thin sheet of sponge or cut horizontally from a thicker sponge layer.)<br>3. Brush the sponge with coffee syrup.<br>4. Fill the ring halfway with praline cream.<br>5. Top with a second sponge layer and press down gently and evenly. Brush the sponge with coffee syrup.<br>6. Fill the ring to the top with vanilla cream. Smooth with a palette knife. Chill until firm.<br>7. Add the coffee extract to the marble glaze (see p. 435) and swirl in lightly. Spread over the surface of the cake, swirling to give a marbled pattern. Chill well.<br>8. Remove the ring and peel away the acetate. Neaten the edge of the glaze with a small knife.<br>9. Decorate the top of the cake with a chocolate fan dusted with confectioners' sugar, a few chocolate cigarettes, and caramelized hazelnuts. |

Vanilla cream — Coffee marble glaze

Wood-grain chocolate strip — Genoise moistened with coffee-flavored syrup — Praline cream

# TIRAMISÙ

| Components | Procedure |
|---|---|
| 1 sheet Ladyfinger Sponge (p. 412)<br>Strong espresso coffee, 1 pt (500 mL)<br>Dessert syrup, 8 oz (250 mL)<br>Mascarpone Filling (recipe below)<br>Cocoa powder | 1. Cut the sponge sheet in half crosswise.<br>2. Combine the espresso and syrup. Brush the sponge sheets generously with this syrup, using it all.<br>3. Place one sponge sheet on a tray. Spread half the filling evenly over the sponge.<br>4. Top with the second layer of sponge, followed by the remaining filling. Smooth the top. Chill.<br>5. Dust the top with cocoa powder.<br>6. Cut 6 × 4 into 24 portions. |

*Note: This recipe is easily cut in half. Start with a half-size sponge sheet and use half the filling and coffee syrup. Alternatively, use ready-prepared ladyfinger cookies in place of the sponge sheet.*

Cocoa powder

Ladyfinger sponge moistened with espresso syrup

Mascarpone filling

# MASCARPONE FILLING

| Ingredients | U.S. | Metric | Procedure |
|---|---|---|---|
| Egg yolks | 2 yolks | 2 yolks | 1. Whip the egg yolks until light. |
| Sugar | 6 oz | 180 g | 2. Make a syrup of the sugar, water, and glucose and cook to 248°F (120°C). Gradually pour into the egg yolks while whipping constantly. Continue whipping until cool. |
| Water | 4 oz | 120 g | |
| Glucose or corn syrup | 2 oz | 60 g | 3. In a mixer with the paddle attachment, mix the mascarpone until soft. |
| Mascarpone | 1 lb | 500 g | 4. With the mixer running at low speed, add the egg yolk mixture a little at a time, waiting until each addition is blended in before adding more. |
| Heavy cream | 1 lb 8 oz | 740 g | |
| *Approximate weight:* | *3 lb* | *1600 g* | 5. Whip the cream to soft peaks. Fold into the mascarpone mixture. |

---

### ❊{ TIRAMISÙ }❊

Tiramisù has become so popular that many people consider it to be an old, classic Italian dessert. Some people have argued that it dates back hundreds of years to the Renaissance period. However, there are no printed recipes for tiramisù until the latter part of the twentieth century, so it is probable that the cake as we know it is a recent invention. The cake has become so widely copied that there are hundreds of different recipes for it, and almost the only thing they have in common is mascarpone cheese.

The word *tiramisù* means "pick-me-up," in reference to the two ingredients that contain caffeine, coffee and cocoa.

# BANANIER

| Components | Procedure |
|---|---|
| Joconde Sponge (p. 410)<br>Rum Syrup (p. 263)<br>Lime Chiboust (p. 274),<br>    7 oz (200 g)<br>Caramelized Banana Slices<br>    (below)<br>Banana Mousse (p. 543),<br>    7 oz (200 g)<br>Chocolate spray (p. 648)<br>Apricot glaze (p. 200)<br>Decoration<br>Chocolate fans<br>Slices of lime and banana | 1. Line a 6½-in. (16 cm) ring mold with a strip of acetate.<br><br>2. Cut two 6-in. (15 cm) circles from a sheet of joconde sponge. Cut one strip of joconde to line the side of the ring mold, making it slightly narrower than the height of the ring so the filling will show above it. Caramelize the sponge strip and circles according to the procedure on page 454.<br><br>3. Brush the caramelized sponge strip and circles with rum syrup. Line the mold with the strip of sponge and place it on a cake card. Place one sponge circle in the bottom.<br><br>4. Prepare the lime Chiboust. Before it sets, use it to fill the ring nearly half full, then place the second sponge circle on top and press down gently.<br><br>5. Arrange the banana slices on top of the sponge.<br><br>6. Prepare the banana mousse. Before it sets, fill the mold to the top and level it with a palette knife.<br><br>7. Place in the freezer for 45 minutes to set.<br><br>8. Place a decorative stencil on top of the cake and spray with a chocolate sprayer.<br><br>9. Coat the top with apricot glaze (p. 200).<br><br>10. Garnish as desired. The cake in the illustration is garnished with 2 chocolate fans and slices of lime and banana coated with apricot glaze. |

Apricot glaze — Caramelized banana slices — Banana mousse — Caramelized joconde sponge — Joconde sponge moistened with rum-flavored syrup — Lime chibouste

# CARAMELIZED BANANA SLICES FOR BANANIER

| Ingredients | Procedure |
|---|---|
| 1 banana<br>Brown sugar,<br>    1 oz (30 g)<br>Butter, 2 tsp (10 g) | 1. Cut the banana into slices ½ in. (1 cm) thick.<br><br>2. Heat the sugar in a small sauté pan and add the banana slices. Heat them quickly until caramelized on both sides but not soft.<br><br>3. Swirl in the butter.<br><br>4. Place the banana slices on a sheet of parchment paper to cool. |

# Swiss Rolls

*Swiss rolls* are made up in much the same way as American jelly rolls, except Swiss rolls are usually more delicate. They can be made with a great variety of fillings and are often iced and decorated.

## General Procedure for Making Swiss Rolls

1. Bake Swiss roll sponge as directed in the formula (p. 407 or 408). Turn out onto a sheet of parchment and carefully peel the paper off the back of the sponge. Cool it partially covered so the cake retains moisture and does not dry out. (The cake may also be moistened with dessert syrup.)

2. Trim the edges with a sharp knife. Crusty edges do not roll well.

3. Spread with desired filling, such as:

    Jam or jelly

    Buttercream (pp. 424–428)

    Ganache (pp. 275–276)

    Chocolate Mousse (pp. 276–277)

    Pastry cream variations (pp. 271–274)

    Whipped cream

    Lemon Filling (p. 202)

    Chopped fruits or nuts may be mixed with buttercream or pastry cream.

4. If any items—such as fruit pieces or a thin rope of marzipan—are to be rolled into the center of the roll, place these along one edge of the sheet on top of the filling. Begin rolling from this edge.

5. Roll up the cake tightly with the aid of the sheet of parchment under the sponge.

6. Ice or cover the outside of the roll as desired. For example:

    Brush with apricot glaze, then ice with fondant.

    Coat with melted chocolate.

    Coat with a sheet of marzipan (see p. 456), using apricot jam or glaze to make the marzipan stick.

    Spread with a thin layer of buttercream, then coat with marzipan.

    Spread with buttercream, then roll in coconut or chopped nuts.

7. Swiss rolls may be sold as whole cakes or cut into individual slices.

*Variation: Half Rolls*

1. Before icing the outside of the roll, chill the roll to make it firmer.

2. Cut a sheet of baked short pastry or sponge cake into 2 strips, each as long and as wide as the sponge roll. Spread the strips with a thin layer of icing or jam.

3. With a sharp knife, carefully cut the chilled sponge roll in half lengthwise.

4. Mount each half cut-side down on one of the prepared sponge or short dough bases.

5. Ice and decorate as in the basic procedure.

# ALMOND SWISS ROLLS

| Components | Procedure |
|---|---|
| Swiss Roll sponge (p. 408)<br>Apricot jam<br>Almond pastry cream<br>Apricot Glaze (p. 200)<br>White fondant<br>Toasted almonds | 1. Spread plain Swiss roll sponge with apricot jam, then with almond pastry cream.<br>2. Roll up.<br>3. Brush with apricot glaze and ice with white fondant.<br>4. While the fondant is soft, place a row of toasted almonds along the top of the roll. |

# BLACK FOREST ROLL

| Components | Procedure |
|---|---|
| Whipped cream fortified with gelatin (p. 264) and flavored with kirsch<br>Chocolate Swiss Roll sponge (p. 408)<br>Dark sweet cherries, well drained<br>Chocolate shavings | 1. Fit a pastry bag with a plain tube and fill it with the whipped cream.<br>2. Pipe strips of cream about ⅜ in. (1 cm) apart on a sheet of chocolate Swiss roll so the strips run the length of the roll.<br>3. Fill in the spaces between the strips with cherries.<br>4. Roll up.<br>5. Coat with additional cream and then with chocolate shavings. |

# BÛCHE DE NOËL
# (CHOCOLATE CHRISTMAS ROLL)

| Components | Procedure |
|---|---|
| Plain or chocolate Swiss Roll sponge (p. 408)<br>Chocolate buttercream (p. 424)<br>Vanilla buttercream (p. 424)<br>Meringue mushrooms (p. 352) | 1. Spread plain or chocolate Swiss roll sponge with chocolate buttercream.<br>2. Roll up.<br>3. Spread the ends with white buttercream and, with a paper cone, pipe on a spiral of chocolate buttercream or other chocolate icing to look like the end grain of wood.<br>4. Ice the rest of the roll with chocolate buttercream to resemble bark, either by using a pastry bag with a flattened star tube or by spreading on the cream and then texturing it with an icing comb.<br>5. Decorate with meringue mushrooms. |

# HARLEQUIN ROLL

| Components | Procedure |
|---|---|
| Plain Swiss Roll sponge (p. 408)<br>Vanilla buttercream (p. 424)<br>Chocolate buttercream (p. 424)<br>Melted chocolate, chocolate fondant, or marzipan colored with cocoa | 1. On a sheet of plain Swiss roll sponge, pipe alternating rows of vanilla and chocolate buttercream so the roll is completely covered with stripes of buttercream running the length of the roll.<br>2. Roll up.<br>3. Cover with melted chocolate, chocolate fondant, or marzipan colored with cocoa. |

# MOCHA ROLL

| Components | Procedure |
|---|---|
| Plain Swiss Roll sponge (p. 408)<br>Coffee buttercream (p. 424)<br>Chocolate shavings<br>Chocolate for drizzling | 1. Spread plain Swiss roll sponge with buttercream and sprinkle with chocolate shavings.<br>2. Roll up.<br>3. Ice with more buttercream. Decorate with chocolate drizzled over the icing. |

# PRALINE GANACHE ROLL

| Components | Procedure |
|---|---|
| Plain Swiss Roll sponge (p. 408)<br>Praline Buttercream (p. 425)<br>Ganache (p. 275)<br>Chopped or sliced hazelnuts | 1. Spread plain Swiss roll sponge with praline buttercream.<br>2. Using a large plain tube, pipe a strip of ganache along one edge.<br>3. Roll up so the ganache is in the center.<br>4. Cover with more buttercream. Roll in chopped or sliced hazelnuts. |

# STRAWBERRY CREAM ROLL

| Components | Procedure |
|---|---|
| Plain Swiss Roll sponge (p. 408)<br>Pastry cream (p. 271) flavored with orange flavor or orange liqueur<br>Fresh strawberries<br>Confectioners' sugar | 1. Spread plain Swiss roll sponge with flavored pastry cream.<br>2. Place a row of fresh strawberries along one edge.<br>3. Roll up so the strawberries are in the center. Dust with confectioners' sugar. |

## Small Cakes

Small fancy cakes in individual portion sizes can be made in many shapes and flavors. In some American bakeshops, these small cakes are known as *French pastries*. Using a variety of cakes, icings, fillings, and decorations, a baker can make an unlimited variety of small, attractive cakes. This section briefly discusses some of the more popular varieties.

### Slices

These are simply portion-size slices of rectangular strip cakes (p. 453), Swiss rolls (p. 476), and half-rolls (p. 476). An important part of the appearance of slices is the pattern of the icing and filling layers. Therefore, it is important to cut the slices carefully and neatly.

For best results, chill or freeze the rolls or strips before slicing so the fillings and icings are firm. Use a sharp knife. Wipe the knife clean and dip it into hot water before each cut.

Slices may be lined up on trays or placed in individual paper cases for display.

### Triangles

Sandwich together four or five layers of ¼-inch (6 mm) thick sponge (such as Swiss roll sponge or seven-layer sponge) with buttercream in a contrasting color. Press the layers together firmly. Chill to solidify the cream. Cut the cake into strips 2 to 2½ inches (5 to 6 cm) wide.

Place a strip at the edge of the bench and, using a sharp knife, cut diagonally into triangles (a). Turn the triangles so the layers are vertical (b). Attach them back to back with a layer of buttercream to form a larger triangle (c).

Coat with marzipan, chocolate glaçage, or icing. Cut into slices.

## Squares

Layer two or three sheets of cake and icing or filling so that the assembled layers are 1½ to 1¾ inches (4 cm) high. Press the layers together firmly. Chill to make the filling firm.

Cut the cake into small squares, 2 inches (5 cm) across or less. Ice the sides, then the top, with buttercream. Decorate as desired.

## Othellos

**Othellos** are small, round cakes made with a special sponge mixture. Prepare the mix for Sponge Roll I (p. 407), but reduce the first quantity of sugar to 25% (3 oz/90 g). Using a pastry bag with a plain tube, pipe 2-inch (5 cm) mounds onto silicone paper. Bake at 400°F (200°C). Cool. Scoop out a little of the cake from the flat side of each Othello base to make more room for the filling. Select half the cakes to be bottom halves and slice a little off the top of each to make a flat surface.

Sandwich two cakes together (one top and one bottom half) with appropriate filling (see below). Brush with apricot glaze. Set on screens and ice with fondant. To decorate, use a paper cone to pipe a spiral of fondant in the same color on the top of each Othello.

Although the term *Othello* is used for this whole category of pastries, it is traditional to use specific names for cakes of different flavors, as follows:

| | |
|---|---|
| Othellos | Filling: chocolate pastry cream<br>Icing: chocolate fondant |
| Iagos | Filling: coffee-flavored pastry cream<br>Icing: coffee fondant |
| Desdemonas | Filling: whipped cream flavored with vanilla<br>Icing: white fondant flavored with kirsch |
| Rosalinds | Filling: whipped cream flavored with rose water<br>Icing: pink fondant flavored with rose water |

> ## ❧ DRAMATIC PASTRIES
>
> The pastries known collectively as *Othellos* are named after characters in Shakespeare's drama *The Tragedy of Othello, the Moor of Venice*. The flawed hero Othello is misled by the evil Iago into believing that his wife, Desdemona, is unfaithful to him. He kills her in a fit of jealousy.
>
> Oddly, the character of Rosalind is from another of Shakespeare's plays, a comedy called *As You Like It*.

# Petits Fours

The term **petit four** can be used for almost any small cake or pastry item small enough to be eaten in one or two bites. *Petit* in French means "little" and *four* means "oven." Most petits fours are small baked items, although a few are not baked.

Petits fours are divided into two categories. *Petits fours secs* (sec means "dry") include a variety of small, dainty cookies, baked meringues, macaroons, and puff pastry products. These will be discussed further in the next chapter.

**Petits fours glacés** are iced petits fours (*glacé* means, in this case, "iced"). This category includes such items as tiny éclairs, tartlets, filled meringues, and cakes. In fact, nearly any iced or creamed pastry or cake item can be called a petit four as long as it is small enough to be eaten in one or two bites.

In North America, the usual type of petit four is a cake cutout iced with fondant. In fact, most people are probably not aware of any other kind. Because of its popularity, the fondant-glazed petit four should be in the repertoire of every pastry cook. See the general procedure given on page 480.

## Procedure for Making Fondant-Iced Petits Fours

1. Select a firm, close-grained cake. Cake that is too coarse, soft, or crumbly is difficult to cut evenly into small shapes. Of the formulas in this book, Almond Cake (p. 401) is recommended. Other suitable choices are Almond Sponge II (p. 407) and Pound Cake (see the variation for petits fours on p. 400). For one sheet of petits fours you will need 3 sheets of cake, ¼ in. (6 mm) thick each. The finished, iced petits fours should be no more than 1 in. (2.5 cm) high.

2. Lay one sheet of cake on a sheet pan and spread with a thin layer of hot apricot jam or of buttercream. Top with the second sheet.

3. Repeat with the third sheet. Spread the top with a thin layer of jam or whatever filling is used between the layers.

4. Roll out a thin sheet of marzipan the same size as the cake sheet. Roll it up loosely on the rolling pin and unroll it to cover the cake. Run the rolling pin over the top to make sure the layers are stuck together firmly.

5. Place a sheet of parchment on top of the marzipan, then place a sheet pan on the parchment. Invert the entire assembly so the marzipan layer is on the bottom. Remove the top sheet pan.

6. Wrap the cake in plastic film and freeze. This firms the cake so the neatest possible pieces can be cut from it.

7. Cut out small squares, rectangles, diamonds, ovals, circles, or other shapes with appropriate cutters. Remember to keep them small, no more than 1 in. (2.5 cm) across.

8. Prepare fondant for icing. Thin the fondant with simple syrup so it will coat the cakes with a very thin layer. You may also color it very lightly.

9. Place the petits fours 1 in. (2.5 cm) apart on an icing grate over a tray. Pour the fondant over each one, making sure the top and sides are completely covered.

   Alternatively, you may dip each cake in warm fondant. Push the cake upside down into the fondant until the bottom is level with the icing. With two chocolate forks (see p. 649), one on the bottom and one on the top, lift the cake out of the fondant, invert it, and set it on an icing grate to drain.

10. When the icing is set, use chocolate, piping gel, or colored fondant to decorate the tops of the petits fours.

11. As an interesting variation, before icing the petits fours, pipe a small bulb of buttercream on top of each cake. Refrigerate to harden the buttercream. Then coat the petits fours with fondant.

## TERMS FOR REVIEW

| | | | |
|---|---|---|---|
| gâteau | Black Forest torte | Sachertorte | petit four |
| torte | fruit torte | opera cake | petit four glacé |
| charlotte ring | Dobos torte | tiramisù | |
| Swiss roll | kirsch torte | Othello | |

## QUESTIONS FOR DISCUSSION

1. Briefly list the steps in assembling a typical basic European-style cake or gâteau.

2. Describe how to cut cake slices to achieve the neatest results.

3. Describe four ways to line a ring mold for a cake.

4. What precautions must be taken when using fruit to line a ring mold?

5. Describe the procedure for caramelizing a strip of sponge.

6. Describe the procedure for covering a cake with marzipan.

## Chapter 19

# Cookies

The word *cookie* means "small cake," and that's more or less what a cookie is. In fact, some cookies are made from cake batter. For some products, such as certain kinds of brownies, it's difficult to know whether to classify them as cakes or cookies.

Most cookie formulas, however, call for less liquid than cake formulas do. Cookie doughs range from soft to very stiff, unlike the thinner batters for cakes. This difference in moisture content means some differences in mixing methods, although the basic procedures are much like those for cakes.

The most obvious differences between cakes and cookies are in makeup. Because most cookies are individually formed or shaped, a great deal of hand labor is involved. Learning the correct methods and then practicing diligently are essential for efficiency.

**After reading this chapter, you should be able to:**

1. Understand the causes of crispness, moistness, chewiness, and spread in cookies.

2. Prepare cookie doughs by using the three basic mixing methods.

3. Prepare eight basic types of cookies: dropped, bagged, rolled, molded, icebox, bar, sheet, and stencil.

4. Bake and cool cookies properly.

# COOKIE CHARACTERISTICS AND THEIR CAUSES

*Cookies* come in an infinite variety of shapes, sizes, flavors, and textures. Characteristics that are desirable in some types are not desirable in others. For example, we want some cookies to be crisp, others to be soft. We want some to hold their shape, others to spread during baking. In order to produce the characteristics we want and to correct faults, it is useful to know what causes these basic traits.

## Crispness

Cookies are crisp if they are low in moisture. The following factors contribute to crispness:

1. Low proportion of liquid in the mix. Most crisp cookies are made from a stiff dough.

2. High sugar and fat content. A large proportion of these ingredients make it possible to mix a workable dough with low moisture content.

3. Baking long enough to evaporate most of the moisture. Baking in a convection oven also dries cookies more quickly, contributing to crispness.

4. Small size or thin shape, so the cookie dries faster during baking.

5. Proper storage. Crisp cookies can become soft if they absorb moisture.

## Softness

Softness is the opposite of crispness, so it has the opposite causes, as follows:

1. High proportion of liquid in the mix.

2. Low sugar and fat.

3. Honey, molasses, or corn syrup included in the formulas. These sugars are hygroscopic, which means they readily absorb moisture from the air or from their surroundings.

4. Underbaking.

5. Large size or thick shape, so they retain more moisture.

6. Proper storage. Soft cookies can become stale and dry if not tightly covered or wrapped.

## Chewiness

Moisture is necessary for chewiness, but other factors are also important. In other words, all chewy cookies are soft, but not all soft cookies are chewy. The following factors contribute to chewiness:

1. High sugar and liquid content, but low fat content.

2. High proportion of eggs.

3. Strong flour or gluten developed during mixing.

# Spread

Spread is desirable in some cookies, while others must hold their shape. Several factors contribute to spread or the lack of it.

1. High sugar content increases spread. Coarse granulated sugar increases spread, while fine sugar or confectioners' sugar reduces spread.

2. High baking soda or baking ammonia content encourages spread.

3. The creaming together of fat and sugar contributes to leavening by incorporating air. Creaming a mixture until light increases spread. Blending fat and sugar just to a paste (without creaming in a lot of air) reduces spread.

4. Low oven temperature increases spread. High temperature decreases spread because the cookie sets up before it has a chance to spread too much.

5. A slack batter—that is, one with a high liquid content—spreads more than a stiff dough.

6. Strong flour or activation of gluten decreases spread.

7. Cookies spread more if baked on heavily greased pans.

---

## ❊⟩ LITTLE CAKES ⟨❊

The word *cookie* comes from the Dutch word *koekje*, meaning "little cake." The word *cookie* is used only in North America. In Britain, these little cakes are known as *biscuits*, although English biscuits are usually smaller than North American cookies and almost always crisp rather than soft and chewy.

Immigrants from many countries brought their favorite little sweets with them to North America, and as a result there are cookies that originated in Scandinavia, Britain, Germany, France, Eastern Europe, and elsewhere.

Until recently, North American cookies were more likely to be small and crisp than they are today, staying closer to their European sources. In the latter part of the twentieth century, people began preferring soft or chewy cookies, and bakers started underbaking cookies so they wouldn't be crisp. As a result, it was not unusual to find doughy cookies with partly raw centers. Quickly, however, bakers modified cookie formulas so they could produce soft cookies that were fully baked. At the same time, the North American fondness for large portions led to cookies of increasing size. Today, it is common to find cookies 4 or 5 inches (10–12 cm) in diameter or even larger.

---

# MIXING METHODS

**C**ookie mixing methods are much like cake mixing methods. The major difference is that less liquid is usually incorporated, so mixing is somewhat easier. Less liquid means gluten is less developed by the mixing. Also, it is a little easier to get a smooth, uniform mix.

There are three basic cookie mixing methods:

- One-stage.

- Creaming.

- Sponge.

These methods are subject to many variations due to differences in formulas. The general procedures are as follows, but always be sure to follow the exact instructions with each formula.

## One-Stage Method

This method is the counterpart of the two-stage cake mixing method. There is more liquid in cake batters, so it must be added in two or more stages in order to blend uniformly. Low-moisture cookies, on the other hand, can be mixed all in one stage.

Because all the ingredients are mixed at once, the baker has less control over mixing with this method than with other methods. Therefore, the one-stage method is not frequently used. When overmixing is not a great problem, as with some chewy cookies, it can be used.

## Creaming Method

This is nearly identical to the creaming method for cakes. Because cookies require less liquid, it is not usually necessary to add the liquid alternately with the flour. It can be added all at once.

Note the importance of step 2, the creaming stage. The amount of creaming affects the texture of the cookie, the leavening, and the spread. Only a small amount of creaming is desired when the cookie must retain its shape and not spread too much. Also, if the cookie is very short (high in fat and low in gluten development), or if it is thin and delicate, too much creaming will make the cookie too crumbly.

---

### Procedure for One-Stage Method

1. Scale ingredients accurately. Have all ingredients at room temperature.

2. Place all ingredients in the mixer. With the paddle attachment, mix these ingredients at low speed until uniformly blended. Scrape down the sides of the bowl as necessary.

---

### Procedure for Creaming Method

1. Scale ingredients accurately. Have all ingredients at room temperature.

2. Place the fat, sugar, salt, and spices in the mixing bowl. With the paddle attachment, cream these ingredients at low speed.

3. For light cookies, cream until the mix is light and fluffy, in order to incorporate more air for leavening. For denser cookies, blend to a smooth paste, but do not cream until light.

4. Add the eggs and liquid, if any, and blend in at low speed.

5. Sift in the flour and leavening. Mix until just combined. Do not overmix, or gluten will develop.

---

## Sponge Method

This method is similar to the egg-foam methods for cakes. The procedure varies considerably, depending on the ingredients. Batches should be kept small because the batter is delicate.

---

### Procedure for Sponge Method

1. Scale all ingredients accurately. Have all ingredients at room temperature, or warm the eggs slightly for greater volume, as for sponge cakes.

2. Following the procedure given in the formula used, whip the eggs (whole, yolks, or whites) and the sugar to the proper stage: soft peaks for whites, thick and light for whole eggs or yolks.

3. Fold in the remaining ingredients as specified in the recipe. Be careful not to overmix or to deflate the eggs.

# TYPES AND MAKEUP METHODS

We can classify cookies by their makeup methods as well as by their mixing methods. Grouping them by makeup method is perhaps more useful, from the point of view of production, because their mixing methods are relatively simple, while their makeup procedures vary considerably. In this section, you will learn the basic procedures for producing eight cookie types:

- Bagged.
- Dropped.
- Rolled.
- Molded.
- Icebox.
- Bar.
- Sheet.
- Stencil.

No matter what makeup method you use, follow one important rule: *Make all cookies of uniform size and thickness.* This is essential for even baking. Because baking times are so short, small cookies may burn before large ones are done.

If the tops of the cookies are to be garnished with fruits, nuts, or other décor, place the garnishes on the cookies as soon as they are panned; press them on gently. If you wait until the surface of the dough begins to dry, the garnish may not stick and will fall off after baking.

## Bagged

Bagged or pressed cookies are made from soft doughs. The dough must be soft enough to be forced through a pastry bag but stiff enough to hold its shape. For stiffer doughs, you may want to double-bag the dough (for example, put a disposable bag inside a cloth bag) for extra strength.

1. Fit a pastry bag with a tip of the desired size and shape. Fill the bag with the cookie dough. Review page 444 for tips on the use of the pastry bag.

2. Press out cookies of the desired shape and size directly onto prepared cookie sheets.

## Dropped

Like bagged cookies, dropped cookies are made from a soft dough. Actually, this method can be considered the same as the bagged method, and many bakers use the term *drop* for both bagging out cookies and for depositing dough with a spoon or scoop. Usually, a pastry bag is faster, and it gives better control over the shape and size of the cookies. However, in the following situations, using a portion scoop to drop cookies may be preferred:

- When the dough contains pieces of fruit, nuts, or chocolate that would clog the pastry tube.

- When you want the cookies to have a rough, homemade look.

1. Select the proper size scoop for accurate portioning.

    A No. 30 scoop makes a large cookie, about 1 oz (30 g).

    A No. 40 scoop makes a medium cookie.

    A No. 50, 60, or smaller scoop makes a small cookie.

2. Drop the cookies onto the prepared baking sheets. Allow enough space between cookies for spreading.

3. Rich cookies spread by themselves, but if the formula requires it, flatten the mounds of batter slightly with a weight dipped in sugar.

## Rolled

Cookies rolled and cut from a stiff dough are not made as often in bakeshops and food service operations as they are made in homes because they require excessive labor. Also, there are always scraps left over after cutting. When rerolled, these scraps make inferior, tough cookies.

The advantage of this method is that it allows you to make cookies in a great variety of shapes for different occasions.

1. Chill dough thoroughly.

2. Roll out dough ⅛ in. (3 mm) thick on a floured canvas. Use as little flour as possible for dusting because this flour can toughen the cookies.

3. Cut out cookies with cookie cutters. Place cookies on prepared baking sheets. Cut as close together as possible to reduce the quantity of scraps. Roll scraps into fresh dough to minimize toughness.

4. Some décor may be applied before baking. For example, brush the tops with egg wash and sprinkle with colored sugars.

5. After baking, cutout cookies are often decorated with colored icing (royal icing, flat icing, or fondant) for holidays or special occasions. Cool cookies completely before applying icing.

## Molded

The first part of this procedure (steps 1 and 2) is simply a fast and fairly accurate way of dividing the dough into equal portions. Each piece is then molded into the desired shape. For some traditional cookies, special molds are used to flatten the dough and, at the same time, stamp a design onto the cookie. The use of such molds gives this procedure its name. However, today a more usual method is to flatten the pieces of dough with a weight rather than a special mold.

The pieces may also be shaped by hand into crescents, fingers, or other shapes.

1. Refrigerate the dough if it is too soft to handle. Roll it out into long cylinders about 1 inch (2.5 cm) thick, or whatever size is required.

2. With a knife or bench scraper, cut the roll into ½-oz (15 g) pieces, or whatever size is required.

3. Place the pieces on prepared baking sheets, leaving 2 inches (5 cm) space between each.

4. Flatten the cookies with a weight, such as a can, dipped in granulated sugar before pressing each cookie. A fork is sometimes used for flattening the dough, as for peanut butter cookies.

5. *Alternative method:* After step 2, shape the dough by hand into desired shapes.

## Icebox

The icebox or refrigerator method is ideal for operations that wish to have freshly baked cookies on hand at all times. The rolls of dough may be made up in advance and stored. Cookies can easily be cut and baked as needed.

This method is also used to make multicolored cookies in various designs, such as checkerboard and pinwheel cookies. The procedures for making these designs are included with the recipes in this chapter (p. 494).

1. Scale the dough into pieces of uniform size, from 1½ pounds (700 g), if you are making small cookies, to 3 pounds (1400 g) for large cookies.

2. Form the dough into cylinders 1–2 inches (2.5–5 cm) in diameter, depending on the cookie size desired. For accurate portioning, it is important to make all the cylinders of dough the same thickness and length.

3. Wrap the cylinders in parchment or wax paper, place them on sheet pans, and refrigerate overnight.

4. Unwrap the dough and cut into slices of *uniform thickness*. The exact thickness required depends on the size of the cookie and how much the dough spreads during baking. The usual range is ⅛–¼ inches (3–6 mm).
   A slicing machine is recommended for ensuring even thickness. Doughs containing nuts or fruits, however, should be sliced by hand with a knife.

5. Place the slices on prepared baking sheets, allowing 2 inches (5 cm) between cookies.

## Bar

This procedure is called the **bar method** because the dough is baked in long, narrow strips and later cut crosswise into bars. It should not be confused with **sheet cookies** (see next procedure), which are also called *bars* by many cooks.

1. Scale the dough into 1¾-pound (800 g) units. Units weighing 1 pound (450 g) may be used for smaller cookies.

2. Shape the pieces of dough into cylinders the length of the sheet pans. Place three strips on each greased pan, spacing them well apart.

3. Flatten the dough with the fingers into strips 3–4 inches (8–10 cm) wide and about ¼ inch (6 mm) thick.

4. If required, brush with egg wash.

5. Bake as directed in the formula.

6. After baking, while the cookies are still warm, cut each strip into bars about 1¾ inches (4.5 cm) wide.

7. In some cases, as with Italian-style *biscotti* (meaning "baked twice"), the strips are cut into thinner slices, placed on sheet pans, and baked a second time until dry and crisp. See page 514 for an example.

## Sheet

Sheet cookies vary so much that it is nearly impossible to give a single procedure for all of them. Some of them are almost like sheet cakes, only denser and richer; they may even be iced like sheet cakes. Others consist of two or three layers added and baked in separate stages. The following procedure is only a general guide.

1. Spread cookie mixture into prepared sheet pans. Make sure the thickness is even.

2. If required, add topping or brush with an egg wash.

3. Bake as directed. Cool.

4. Apply icing or topping, if desired.

5. Cut into individual squares or rectangles. Best practice is to turn the sheet out onto a board (see p. 395 for unmolding sheet cakes) before cutting to avoid damaging the sheet pans.

## Stencil

The stencil method is a special technique used with a particular type of soft dough or batter. This batter is often called **stencil paste**. It is used not only for making this type of cookie but also for making ribbon sponge cake (p. 411) for decorative work. The recipe for Almond Tuiles (p. 508) illustrates the stencil method using a simple round stencil, but it is possible to cut a stencil in nearly any shape for making decorative pieces or special desserts. For example, the recipe for Sesame Tuiles (p. 509) calls for a triangular stencil because the cookie is used in a special dessert plating (p. 633).

1. Line a sheet pan with a silicone mat. If a mat is not available, use a sheet of parchment paper.

2. Use a ready-made stencil. Stencils in many shapes are available from equipment purveyors. Alternatively, make a stencil by cutting a hole of the desired pattern in a sheet of thick plastic or thin cardboard (the cardboard used for cake boxes is suitable, but you may need to use a double thickness).

3. Place the stencil on the silicone mat or parchment. With an offset palette knife, spread the batter across the stencil to make a thin layer that completely fills in the hole.

4. Lift off the stencil and repeat to make additional cookies.

# PANNING, BAKING, AND COOLING

## Preparing the Pans

1. Use clean, unwarped pans.

2. Lining the sheets with parchment or silicone paper is fast, and it eliminates the necessity of greasing the pans.

3. A heavily greased pan increases the spread of the cookie. A greased and floured pan decreases spread.

4. Some high-fat cookies can be baked on ungreased pans.

## Baking

1. Most cookies are baked at a relatively high temperature for a short time.

2. Too low a temperature increases spreading and may produce hard, dry, pale cookies.

3. Too high a temperature decreases spreading and may burn the edges or bottoms.

4. Even a single minute of overbaking can burn cookies, so watch them closely. Also, the heat of the pan continues to bake the cookies if they are left on it after being removed from the oven.

5. Doneness is indicated by color. The edges and bottom should just be turning a light golden color.

6. Excessive browning is especially undesirable if the dough has been colored. The browning of the surface hides the color.

7. With some rich doughs, burned bottoms may be a problem. In these cases, double-pan the cookies by placing the sheet pan on a second pan of the same size.

# Cooling

1. Most cookies baked without silicone paper must be removed from the pans while they are still warm, or they may stick.

2. If the cookies are very soft, do not remove them from the pans until they are cool enough and firm enough to handle. Some cookies are soft when hot but become crisp when cool.

3. Do not cool cookies too rapidly or in cold drafts, or they may crack.

4. Cool completely before storing.

After the cookies have been baked, check them for defects. Use the troubleshooting guide in the table on page 492 to help correct problems.

# PETITS FOURS SECS

In the previous chapter, the subject of petits fours was introduced with a discussion of petits fours glacés, or iced petits fours (p. 479). Petits fours secs, or dry petits fours, are, by contrast, more properly discussed with cookies than with cakes.

As you may recall, nearly any pastry or cake item small enough to be eaten in one or two bites can be considered a petit four. The term *sec*, or "dry," means that these pastries have no icing or cream filling, although they may be dipped in chocolate. In practice, small quantities of creams or jellies are sometimes used—for example, in sandwich-type cookies.

Petits fours secs are usually served with after-dinner coffee or as an accompaniment for such cold desserts as ice cream, mousses, and Bavarian creams.

The following items from this chapter may be served as petits fours secs, provided they are quite small. In addition, petits fours secs made from puff pastry and pâte à choux are presented in chapter 14, and madeleines can be found in chapter 16.

- Butter Tea Cookies
- Almond Macaroons
- Coconut Macaroons (Meringue Type)
- Pistachio Macaroons
- Shortbread and Short Dough Cookies
- Fancy Icebox Cookies
- Nut Squares
- Spritz Cookies
- Langues de Chat
- Almond Tuiles
- Florentines
- Almond Slices
- Batons Marechaux and Eponges
- Diamonds

## Cookie Faults and Their Causes

| Fault | Causes |
|---|---|
| Too tough | Flour too strong<br>Too much flour<br>Not enough shortening<br>Incorrect amount of sugar<br>Mixed too long or improper mixing |
| Too crumbly | Improper mixing<br>Too much sugar<br>Too much shortening<br>Too much leavening<br>Not enough eggs |
| Too hard | Baked too long or baking temperature too low<br>Too much flour<br>Flour too strong<br>Not enough shortening<br>Not enough liquid |
| Too dry | Not enough liquid<br>Not enough shortening<br>Baked too long or baking temperature too low<br>Too much flour |
| Not browned enough | Baking temperature too low<br>Underbaked<br>Not enough sugar |
| Too brown | Baking temperature too high<br>Baked too long<br>Too much sugar |
| Poor flavor | Poor ingredients<br>Flavoring ingredients left out<br>Dirty baking pans<br>Ingredients improperly measured |
| Surface or crust sugary | Improper mixing<br>Too much sugar |
| Too much spread | Baking temperature too low<br>Not enough flour<br>Too much sugar<br>Too much leavening (chemical leaveners or creaming)<br>Too much liquid<br>Pans greased too much |
| Not enough spread | Baking temperature too high<br>Too much flour or flour too strong<br>Not enough sugar<br>Not enough leavening<br>Not enough liquid<br>Insufficient pan grease |
| Stick to pans | Pans improperly greased<br>Too much sugar<br>Improper mixing |

# FORMULAS

## OATMEAL RAISIN COOKIES

| Ingredients | U.S. | | Metric | % | Procedure |
|---|---|---|---|---|---|
| Butter or part butter and part shortening | 8 | oz | 250 g | 67 | **MIXING** |
| Brown sugar | 1 lb | | 500 g | 133 | Creaming method. Combine oats with other dry ingredients after they are sifted. Blend raisins in last. |
| Salt | 0.16 oz (1 tsp) | | 5 g | 1.5 | |
| Eggs | 4 | oz | 125 g | 33 | **MAKEUP** |
| Vanilla extract | 0.33 oz (2 tsp) | | 10 g | 3 | Drop method. Use greased or parchment-lined baking sheets. |
| Milk | 1 | oz | 30 g | 8 | |
| Pastry flour | 12 | oz | 375 g | 100 | **BAKING** |
| Baking powder | 0.5 | oz | 15 g | 4 | 375°F (190°C) for 10–12 minutes, depending on size |
| Baking soda | 0.25 | oz | 8 g | 2 | |
| Cinnamon (optional) | 0.12 oz (2 tsp) | | 4 g | 1 | |
| Rolled oats (quick cooking) | 10 | oz | 312 g | 83 | |
| Raisins (see note) | 8 | oz | 250 g | 67 | |
| *Total weight:* | *3 lb 12* | *oz* | *1880 g* | *501%* | |

Note: If raisins are hard and dry, soak them in hot water until soft, then drain them and dry them well before adding them to the cookie batter.

## CHOCOLATE CHIP COOKIES

| Ingredients | U.S. | | Metric | % | Procedure |
|---|---|---|---|---|---|
| Butter or half butter and half shortening | 5 | oz | 150 g | 50 | **MIXING** |
| Granulated sugar | 4 | oz | 120 g | 40 | Creaming method. Blend in chocolate chips and nuts last. |
| Brown sugar | 4 | oz | 120 g | 40 | |
| Salt | 0.12 oz (1⅛ tsp) | | 4 g | 1.25 | **MAKEUP** |
| Eggs | 3 | oz | 90 g | 30 | Drop method. Use greased or parchment-lined baking sheets. |
| Vanilla extract | 0.16 oz (1 tsp) | | 5 g | 1.5 | |
| Pastry flour | 10 | oz | 300 g | 100 | **BAKING** |
| Baking soda | 0.12 oz (¾ tsp) | | 4 g | 1.25 | 375°F (190°C) for 10–14 minutes, depending on size |
| Chocolate chips | 10 | oz | 300 g | 100 | |
| Chopped walnuts or pecans | 4 | oz | 120 g | 40 | |
| *Total weight:* | *2 lb 8* | *oz* | *1213 g* | *404%* | |

### VARIATION

#### BROWN SUGAR NUT COOKIES

Make the following ingredient adjustments:

Omit the granulated sugar and use 80% (8 oz/240 g) brown sugar.

Omit the chocolate chips and increase the nuts to 100% (10 oz/300 g).

### TOLL HOUSE COOKIES

Chocolate chip cookies, in their many varieties, are the most popular cookies in North America. They owe their origin to the Toll House cookie, said to have been developed in the 1920s or 1930s by Ruth Wakefield, owner of the Toll House Inn in Whitman, Massachusetts. The original Toll House cookies are simple butter cookies with semi-sweet chocolate morsels mixed into the dough. Today's chocolate chip or chocolate chunk cookies are likely to contain any kind of chocolate plus other ingredients, especially nuts, such as pecans, walnuts, or macadamia nuts.

# ICEBOX COOKIES

| Ingredients | U.S. | | Metric | % | Procedure |
|---|---|---|---|---|---|
| Butter, or half butter and half shortening | 1 lb | | 500 g | 67 | **MIXING** Creaming method |
| Granulated sugar | 8 | oz | 250 g | 33 | **MAKEUP** |
| Confectioners' sugar | 8 | oz | 250 g | 33 | Icebox method. Scale dough strips 1½ lb |
| Salt | 0.25 | oz | 8 g | 1 | (750 g) each. Slice cookies ¼ in. (6 mm) thick. |
| Eggs | 4 | oz | 125 g | 17 | Bake on ungreased pans. |
| Vanilla extract | 0.25 | oz | 8 g | 1 | **BAKING** |
| Pastry flour | 1 lb 8 | oz | 750 g | 100 | 375°F (190°C) for 10–12 minutes |
| *Total weight:* | *3 lb 12* | *oz* | *1891 g* | *252%* | |

## VARIATIONS

To reduce spread, use all confectioners' sugar.

### BUTTERSCOTCH ICEBOX COOKIES

Make the following ingredient adjustments:

In place of the sugars in the basic recipe, use 67% (1 lb/500 g) brown sugar.

Use only butter, no shortening.

Increase the eggs to 20% (5 oz/150 g).

Add ½ tsp (2 g) baking soda with the flour.

a.

### NUT ICEBOX COOKIES

Add 25% (6 oz/188 g) finely chopped nuts to the sifted flour in the basic recipe or the butterscotch cookie formula.

### CHOCOLATE ICEBOX COOKIES

Add 17% (4 oz/125 g) melted, unsweetened, chocolate to the creamed butter and sugar.

b.

### FANCY ICEBOX COOKIES

These are small cookies with designs in two colors. To make them, prepare white and chocolate icebox dough with only the 33% confectioners' sugar; omit the granulated sugar. This reduces the spread of the cookies and preserves the designs. Make the designs as follows:

### PINWHEEL COOKIES

Roll out a sheet of white dough about ⅛ in. (3 mm) thick. Roll out a sheet of chocolate dough the same size and thickness. Brush the white sheet lightly and evenly with egg wash, being careful not to leave any puddles. Lay the chocolate sheet on top and brush with egg wash. Roll up like a jelly roll until the roll is 1 in. (2.5 cm) thick (a). Cut off the dough evenly. Continue making rolls with the rest of the sheet. Refrigerate the rolls. Slice and bake as in the basic procedure.

c.

### CHECKERBOARD COOKIES

Roll out 1 sheet of white dough and 1 sheet of chocolate dough ¼ in. (6 mm) thick. Egg wash one sheet lightly and lay the second sheet on top. Cut the double sheet of dough in half. Egg wash one sheet and lay the second on top so you have four alternating colors. Chill until firm. Roll out another sheet of white dough very thin (less than ⅛ in.) and brush with egg wash. From the chilled four-layer sheet, cut off 4 slices ¼ in. (6 mm) thick (b). Lay one of these strips on the rolled-out sheet of

d.

**VARIATIONS CONTINUED**

dough along one edge. Egg wash the top. Lay a second strip on top with the colors reversed, so chocolate dough is on top of white dough and white is on top of chocolate. Egg wash the top. Repeat with the remaining two strips (c). Wrap in the thin sheet of dough (d). Chill, slice, and bake as in the basic procedure.

### BULL'S-EYE COOKIES

Roll out a cylinder of dough ½ in. (12 mm) thick. Roll out a sheet of contrasting-color dough ¼ in. (6 mm) thick. Egg wash the top. Wrap the cylinder in the sheet of dough (e). Chill, slice, and bake as in the basic procedure.

e.

# DOUBLE CHOCOLATE
# MACADAMIA CHUNK COOKIES

| Ingredients | U.S. | | | Metric | % | Procedure |
|---|---|---|---|---|---|---|
| Semisweet chocolate | 1 lb | 8 | oz | 750 g | 200 | **MIXING**<br>Modified sponge method |
| Butter | | 8 | oz | 250 g | 67 | 1. Melt the semisweet chocolate and the butter to-gether in a double boiler. Let the mixture cool to room temperature. |
| Sugar | | 4 | oz | 125 g | 33 | |
| Eggs | | 5 | oz | 150 g | 42 | |
| Salt | | 0.2 | oz (1 tsp) | 5 g | 1.5 | 2. Mix the sugar, eggs, and salt together until well blended, but do not whip. Whipping to a foam creates more leavening, resulting in a more crumbly cookie. If the eggs are not at room tem-perature, stir the mixture over a hot-water bath just until the mixture is at a slightly warm room temperature. |
| Bread flour | | 12 | oz | 375 g | 100 | |
| Cocoa powder | | 1 | oz | 30 g | 8 | |
| Baking powder | | 0.33 | oz (2 tsp) | 10 g | 3 | |
| White chocolate, cut into small bits | | 8 | oz | 250 g | 67 | 3. Blend in the chocolate mixture. |
| Macadamia nuts, coarsely chopped | | 4 | oz | 125 g | 33 | 4. Sift the flour, cocoa, and baking powder and fold in. |
| *Total weight:* | *4 lb* | *2* | *oz* | *2070 g* | *554%* | 5. Fold in the white chocolate pieces and nuts. |

**MAKEUP**

Dropped method. Use greased or parchment-lined baking sheets. Flatten to desired thickness; these cookies will not expand much.

Make up without delay, as the dough hardens as it sets. If it becomes too hard, let stand in a warm place for a few minutes to soften.

**BAKING**

350°F (175°C) for 10–15 minutes, depending on size

**VARIATION**

### CHOCOLATE CHOCOLATE CHUNK COOKIES

Substitute dark chocolate for the white chocolate. Omit the macadamia nuts or substitute pecans.

# SUGAR COOKIES

| Ingredients | U.S. | | Metric | % | Procedure |
|---|---|---|---|---|---|
| Butter and/or shortening | 8 | oz | 250 g | 40 | **MIXING** |
| Sugar | 10 | oz | 310 g | 50 | Creaming method |
| Salt | 0.16 | oz (1 tsp) | 5 g | 0.8 | **MAKEUP** |
| Eggs | 2 | oz | 60 g | 10 | Rolled method. Before cutting the rolled-out |
| Milk | 2 | oz | 60 g | 10 | dough, wash it with milk and sprinkle with |
| Vanilla extract | 0.25 | oz | 8 g | 1.25 | granulated sugar. Use greased or parchment-lined baking sheets. |
| Cake flour | 1 lb 4 | oz | 625 g | 100 | **BAKING** |
| Baking powder | 0.625 | oz | 18 g | 3 | 375°F (190°C) for 8–10 minutes |
| *Total weight:* | *2 lb 11* | *oz* | *1336 g* | *215%* | |

## VARIATIONS

Lemon zest, extract, or emulsion may be used in place of vanilla.

### BROWN SUGAR ROLLED COOKIES

Make the following ingredient adjustments:

Increase butter to 50% (10 oz/310 g).

Omit granulated sugar and use 60% (12 oz/375 g) brown sugar.

### CHOCOLATE ROLLED COOKIES

Substitute 2 oz (60 g) cocoa for 2 oz (60 g) of the flour.

# ALMOND SLICES

| Ingredients | U.S. | | Metric | % | Procedure |
|---|---|---|---|---|---|
| Butter | 6 | oz | 175 g | 40 | **MIXING** |
| Brown sugar | 12 | oz | 350 g | 80 | Creaming method. Blend each stage of mixing |
| Cinnamon | 0.07 | oz (1¼ tsp) | 2 g | 0.5 | until smooth, but do not cream until light. |
| Egg yolks | 3 | oz | 90 g | 20 | **MAKEUP** |
| Pastry flour | 15 | oz | 440 g | 100 | Icebox method. Scale the dough into 12-oz |
| Slivered almonds | 6 | oz | 175 g | 40 | (350 g) units. Roll into round strips about 1½ in. |
| *Total weight:* | *2 lb 10* | *oz* | *1232 g* | *280%* | (4 cm) in diameter, or into rectangular strips |

**MAKEUP** (continued)

Icebox method. Scale the dough into 12-oz (350 g) units. Roll into round strips about 1½ in. (4 cm) in diameter, or into rectangular strips about 1¼ × 1¾ in. (3.5 × 4.5 cm). Chill until very firm. Slice about ⅛ in. (3 mm) thick, using a sharp knife. Take care to slice through the almonds and not pull them out of the dough. Place slices on greased or paper-lined sheets.

**BAKING**

375°F (190°C) about 10 minutes, until just starting to brown at edges, no longer. Do not overbake, or the cookies will be hard.

# RICH SHORTBREAD

| Ingredients | U.S. | | Metric | % | Procedure |
|---|---|---|---|---|---|
| Butter | 12 | oz | 375 g | 75 | **MIXING** |
| Sugar | 8 | oz | 250 g | 50 | Creaming method |
| Salt | 0.12 oz (¾ tsp) | | 4 g | 0.75 | **MAKEUP** |
| Egg yolks | 4 | oz | 125 g | 25 | Rolled method. Roll the dough ¼ in. (6 mm) |
| Optional flavoring (see *Note*) | | | | | thick (this is thicker than most rolled cookies). Use greased or parchment-lined pans. |
| Pastry flour | 1 lb | | 500 g | 100 | **BAKING** |
| **Total weight:** | **2 lb 8** | **oz** | **1254 g** | **250%** | 350°F (175°C) for about 15 minutes |

*Note: Traditional Scottish shortbread is made with butter, flour, and sugar only—no eggs, flavoring, or liquid. Because this dough is very crumbly, it is usually not rolled out but rather pressed into pans or molds and baked. For the formula given here, you may make the cookies without added flavoring, or flavor to taste with vanilla, almond, or lemon extract.*

# BASIC SHORT DOUGH FOR COOKIES

| Ingredients | U.S. | | Metric | % | Procedure |
|---|---|---|---|---|---|
| Butter or half butter and half shortening | 1 lb | | 500 g | 63 | **MIXING** Creaming method |
| Sugar | 8 | oz | 250 g | 33 | **MAKEUP** |
| Salt | 0.25 oz | | 8 g | 1 | Rolled method. Roll out ⅛ in. (3 mm) thick and |
| Eggs | 3 | oz | 95 g | 12.5 | cut out with cutters of various shapes. See variations below. |
| Vanilla extract | 0.25 oz | | 8 g | 1 | |
| Pastry flour | 1 lb 8 | oz | 750 g | 100 | **BAKING** |
| **Total weight:** | **3 lb 3** | **oz** | **1611 g** | **214%** | 375°F (190°C) about 10 minutes |

## VARIATIONS

Short dough is a versatile mixture that can be made up in many ways to provide variety in the bakeshop. Some of the many possible variations are described here.

*Flavoring the dough:* During mixing, vary the dough by flavoring to taste with lemon, cinnamon, mace, maple, almond extract, or other flavoring. Fine coconut or chopped nuts may be mixed with the dough.

*Garnishing before baking:* Decorate the tops with chopped or whole nuts, colored sugar, chocolate sprinkles, coconut, glacéed fruits, or almond macaroon mixture. Tops may be egg washed first to help the toppings stick.

*Garnishing after baking:* Some examples of materials for garnishing cookies are fondant, royal icing, pecan halves on dabs of fudge or fondant icing, and melted chocolate (to coat completely or to drizzle on with a paper cone).

## JAM TARTS

Cut out dough with large, round cutters. With a ½-in. (12 mm) cutter, cut out the centers of half the rounds. These will be the tops of the sandwiched cookies. When baked, cool completely. Dust the tops (the ones with the cut-out centers) with confectioners' sugar. Sandwich tops and bottoms together with a small dab of jam, so the jam shows through the hole on top.

## ALMOND CRESCENTS

Cut crescent shapes from rolled-out dough. Spread tops with a layer of Almond Macaroon mixture (p. 504). Dip tops in chopped almonds. Bake at 350°F (175°C). When cooled, dip the tips of the crescents in melted chocolate.

# PEANUT BUTTER COOKIES

| Ingredients | U.S. | | Metric | % | Procedure |
|---|---|---|---|---|---|
| Butter or part butter and part shortening | 12 | oz | 375 g | 75 | **MIXING** |
| | | | | | Creaming method. Cream the peanut butter with the fat and sugar. |
| Brown sugar | 8 | oz | 250 g | 50 | **MAKEUP** |
| Granulated sugar | 8 | oz | 250 g | 50 | |
| Peanut butter (see Note) | 12 | oz | 375 g | 75 | Molded method. Use a fork instead of a weight to flatten the cookies. Use greased or parchment-lined pans. |
| Eggs | 4 | oz | 125 g | 25 | |
| Vanilla extract | 0.33 oz (2 tsp) | | 10 g | 2 | **BAKING** |
| Pastry flour | 1 lb | | 500 g | 100 | 375°F (190°C) for 11–14 minutes, depending on size |
| Baking soda | 0.16 oz (1 tsp) | | 5 g | 1 | |
| **Total weight:** | **3 lb 12** | **oz** | **1890 g** | **378%** | |

Note: This formula was developed with natural peanut butter, consisting of only ground peanuts and salt. You may need to add a little salt to the formula, depending on the salt content of the peanut butter you use. If you use unsalted peanut butter, add 1% (0.16 oz/ 5 g/1 tsp) salt to the creaming stage.

# CINNAMON COOKIES

| Ingredients | U.S. | | Metric | % | Procedure |
|---|---|---|---|---|---|
| Butter or part butter and part shortening | 1 lb | | 500 g | 80 | **MIXING** |
| | | | | | Creaming method. |
| Granulated sugar | 8 | oz | 250 g | 40 | **MAKEUP** |
| Brown sugar | 8 | oz | 250 g | 40 | |
| Salt | 0.17 oz (1 tsp) | | 5 g | 0.8 | Molded method. Roll pieces in cinnamon sugar before placing on greased baking sheets and pressing flat. |
| Cinnamon | 0.33 oz (2 tbsp) | | 10 g | 1.7 | |
| Eggs | 3 | oz | 90 g | 15 | **BAKING** |
| Milk | 1 | oz | 30 g | 5 | 375°F (190°C) for about 10 minutes. |
| Pastry flour | 1 lb 4 | | 625 g | 100 | |
| **Total weight:** | **3 lb 8** | **oz** | **1760 g** | **282%** | |

**VARIATION**

## CHOCOLATE CINNAMON COOKIES

Substitute 4 oz (125 g) cocoa for 4 oz (125 g) of the flour.

# NUT COOKIES

| Ingredients | U.S. | | Metric | % | Procedure |
|---|---|---|---|---|---|
| Butter | 14 | oz | 440 g | 87.5 | **MIXING** |
| Confectioners' sugar | 5 | oz | 155 g | 31 | Creaming method |
| Brown sugar | 2 | oz | 60 g | 12.5 | **MAKEUP** |
| Salt | 0.08 oz (⅜ tsp) | | 2 g | 0.5 | Molded method. Mold cookies by hand into desired shape, such as balls, fingers, or crescents. |
| Vanilla extract | 0.33 oz (2 tsp) | | 10 g | 2 | |
| Bread flour | 1 lb | | 500 g | 100 | **BAKING** |
| Ground nuts (hazelnuts, pecans, walnuts, almonds, etc.) | 12 | oz | 375 g | 75 | 350°F (175°C) for about 25 minutes. |
| *Total weight:* | *3 lb 1* | *oz* | *1542 g* | *308%* | **FINISH** |
| | | | | | Dust cooled cookies heavily with confectioners' sugar. |

# SPECULAAS

| Ingredients | U.S. | | Metric | % | Procedure |
|---|---|---|---|---|---|
| Butter or half butter and half shortening | 1 lb | | 500 g | 67 | **MIXING** |
| | | | | | Creaming method. Blend at each stage until smooth, but do not cream until light. |
| Confectioners' sugar | 13 | oz | 412 g | 55 | **MAKEUP** |
| Fine granulated sugar | 4 | oz | 125 g | 17 | The classic way to make these cookies is by the molded method. The dough is pressed into special wooden speculaas molds, then removed and placed on baking sheets. Alternatively, it is stamped with special tools to emboss a design in the dough. |
| Grated lemon zest | 0.16 oz (2 tsp) | | 5 g | 0.7 | |
| Cinnamon | 0.25 oz (4 tsp) | | 8 g | 1 | |
| Cloves | 0.05 oz (¾ tsp) | | 2 g | 0.2 | |
| Cardamom | 0.05 oz (¾ tsp) | | 2 g | 0.2 | If these molds are not available, make up the cookies either as icebox cookies or as rolled cookies cut with cookie cutters. They can be made small or large as desired. Large cookies should be about ¼ in. (6 mm) thick. |
| Eggs | 2.5 | oz | 75 g | 10 | |
| Pastry flour | 1 lb 8 | oz | 750 g | 100 | |
| *Total weight:* | *3 lb 12* | *oz* | *1879 g* | *251%* | *Optional:* Press sliced or whole blanched almonds onto the cookies after makeup. |
| | | | | | **BAKING** |
| | | | | | 375°F (190°C) for medium to large cookies; 400°F (200°C) for small, thin cookies |

# DIAMONDS

*For large-quantity measurements, see page 739.*

| Ingredients | U.S. | | Metric | % | Procedure |
|---|---|---|---|---|---|
| Butter cut in small pieces | 5 | oz | 140 g | 70 | **MIXING** |
| Cake flour | 7 | oz | 200 g | 100 | One-stage method |
| Confectioners' sugar | 2 | oz | 60 g | 30 | **MAKEUP AND BAKING** |
| Salt | 0.04 oz (⅛ tsp) | | 1 g | 0.5 | 1. Shape the dough into cylinders 1¼ in. (3 cm) in diameter, making sure the dough is very tight and there are no air pockets. |
| Grated orange zest | 0.08 oz (1 tsp) | | 2 g | 1 | |
| Vanilla extract | 0.08 oz (½ tsp) | | 2 g | 1 | |
| **For rolling** | | | | | 2. Refrigerate the dough for 30 minutes. |
| Crystal sugar | 2 | oz | 50 g | 25 | 3. Brush the cylinders with water. Roll in crystal sugar. |
| *Total dough weight:* | *14* | *oz* | *407 g* | *202%* | 4. Cut into rounds ½ in. (1 cm) thick. |

4. Cut into rounds ½ in. (1 cm) thick.

5. Bake on buttered sheet pans at 325°F (160°C) for 20 minutes.

# BUTTER TEA COOKIES

| Ingredients | U.S. | | Metric | % | Procedure |
|---|---|---|---|---|---|
| Butter or half butter and half shortening | 12 | oz | 335 g | 67 | **MIXING** |
| | | | | | Creaming method |
| Granulated sugar | 6 | oz | 165 g | 33 | **MAKEUP AND** |
| Confectioners' sugar | 3 | oz | 85 g | 17 | Bagged method. Make small cookies about the size of a quarter, using a plain tube or star tube. Bag out onto ungreased or parchment-lined baking sheets. |
| Eggs | 4.5 | oz | 125 g | 25 | |
| Vanilla extract | 0.16 oz (1 tsp) | | 4 g | 0.9 | |
| Cake flour | 1 lb 2 | oz | 500 g | 100 | |
| *Total weight:* | *2 lb 11* | *oz* | *1214 g* | *242%* | **BAKING** |

375°F (190°C), about 10 minutes

**VARIATION**

Flavor with almond extract instead of vanilla.

## FANCY TEA COOKIES

Add 17% (3 oz/85 g) almond paste to the first mixing stage.

## SANDWICH-TYPE COOKIES

Select cookies all of the same size and shape. Turn half of them over and dot the centers of the flat sides with a small amount of jam or fudge icing. Sandwich with the remaining cookies.

## CHOCOLATE TEA COOKIES

Substitute 3 oz (85 g) cocoa for 3 oz (85 g) of the flour.

# GINGERBREAD COOKIES

| Ingredients | U.S. | | Metric | % | Procedure |
|---|---|---|---|---|---|
| Butter or part butter and part shortening | 11 | oz | 340 g | 45 | **MIXING** Creaming method |
| Brown sugar | 8 | oz | 250 g | 33 | **MAKEUP** |
| Baking soda | 0.16 oz (1 tsp) | | 5 g | 0.7 | Rolled method |
| Salt | 0.12 oz (¾ tsp) | | 4 g | 0.5 | For small cookies, roll out ⅛ in. (3 mm) thick. |
| Ginger | 0.16 oz (2¼ tsp) | | 5 g | 0.7 | For large cookies, roll out ¼ in. (6 mm) thick. |
| Cinnamon | 0.12 oz (1 tsp) | | 2 g | 0.25 | Cut out cookies and place them on paper-lined |
| Cloves, ground | 0.03 oz (½ tsp) | | 1 g | 0.12 | or greased and floured baking sheets. |
| Eggs | 3.5 | oz | 110 g | 15 | **BAKING** |
| Molasses | 11 | oz | 340 g | 45 | 375°F (190°C) for small, thin cookies |
| Pastry flour | 1 lb 8 | oz | 750 g | 100 | 360°F (180°C) for larger, thicker cookies |
| **Total weight:** | **3 lb 10** | **oz** | **1807 g** | **240%** | |

# GINGERSNAPS

| Ingredients | U.S. | | Metric | % | Procedure |
|---|---|---|---|---|---|
| Shortening | 6 | oz | 190 g | 38 | **MIXING** |
| Sugar | 6 | oz | 190 g | 38 | Creaming method. Blend the molasses into the |
| Salt | 0.08 oz (1 tsp) | | 2 g | 0.5 | creamed fat-sugar mixture first. Then dissolve |
| Ginger | 0.25 oz (1 tbsp) | | 8 g | 1.5 | the soda in the water and blend in. Add the flour last. |
| Molasses | 10 | oz | 300 g | 63 | **MAKEUP** |
| Baking soda | 0.25 oz (1½ tbsp) | | 8 g | 1.5 | Bagged method. With a plain tube, bag out |
| Water | 2 | oz | 60 g | 13 | the size of a quarter. Flatten lightly. |
| Pastry flour | 1 lb | | 500 g | 100 | May also be chilled and made up by molded or |
| **Total weight:** | **2 lb 8** | **oz** | **1268 g** | **256%** | rolled methods. Use paper-lined or greased and floured pans. |
| | | | | | **BAKING** |
| | | | | | 375°F (190°C) for about 12 minutes |

# NUT SQUARES

*Yield: 150–300 cookies, depending on size*

| Ingredients | U.S. | Metric | Procedure |
|---|---|---|---|
| Old-Fashioned Pound Cake batter (p. 400) | 2 lb | 900 g | **MAKEUP** Sheet method |
| Chopped pecans, chopped walnuts, or sliced almonds | 8 oz | 225 g | 1. Spread the batter evenly onto a greased and floured full-size sheet pan (18 × 26 in./46 × 66 cm). |
| Cinnamon sugar | as needed | as needed | 2. Sprinkle with nuts, then with cinnamon sugar. |
| | | | **BAKING** 375°F (190°C) |
| | | | As soon as the sheet is baked, cut into small squares. |

# SPRITZ COOKIES

| Ingredients | U.S. | | Metric | % | Procedure |
|---|---|---|---|---|---|
| Almond paste | 12 | oz | 375 g | 100 | **MIXING** |
| Sugar | 6 | oz | 190 g | 50 | Creaming method. Blend the almond paste to a smooth, soft paste with a little of the egg. Add the butter and sugar, and cream as in basic Procedure. |
| Salt | 0.12 | oz (¾ tsp) | 4 g | 1 | |
| Butter | 12 | oz | 375 g | 100 | |
| Eggs | 4.5 | oz | 145 g | 38 | **MAKEUP** |
| Vanilla extract | 0.16 | oz (1 tsp) | 5 g | 1.5 | Bagged method. Bag out with star tube to desired shapes (small) on parchment-lined sheets. If desired, garnish tops with pieces of fruit or nuts. |
| Cake flour | 6 | oz | 190 g | 50 | |
| Bread flour | 6 | oz | 190 g | 50 | |
| *Total weight:* | *2 lb 14* | *oz* | *1474 g* | *390%* | **BAKING** |
| | | | | | 375°F (190°C) |

# LANGUES DE CHAT

| Ingredients | U.S. | | Metric | % | Procedure |
|---|---|---|---|---|---|
| Butter | 14 | oz | 350 g | 88 | **MIXING** |
| Extra-fine granulated sugar | 7 | oz | 175 g | 44 | Creaming method |
| Confectioners' sugar | 7 | oz | 175 g | 44 | **MAKEUP** |
| Egg whites | 10 | oz | 250 g | 63 | Bagged method. Using a ¼-in. (6 mm) plain tube, bag out onto silicone paper in the shape of small fingers 2 in. (5 cm) long. Allow at least 1 in. (2.5 cm) between cookies to allow for spreading. Double-pan for more even baking. |
| Vanilla extract | 0.25 | oz (1½ tsp) | 6 g | 1.6 | |
| Cake flour | 12 | oz | 300 g | 75 | |
| Bread flour | 4 | oz | 100 g | 25 | **BAKING** |
| *Total weight:* | *3 lb 6* | *oz* | *1356 g* | *340%* | 400°F (200°C) for about 10 minutes |
| | | | | | **FINISHING** |
| | | | | | Langues de chat may be served plain as petits fours sec. They may be used as decorations for ice cream, Bavarian cream, or other desserts. They may also be sandwiched together with ganache, buttercream, fudge, or jam. Sandwich cookies may be partially dipped in melted chocolate. |

# RAISIN SPICE BARS

| Ingredients | U.S. | | | Metric | % | Procedure |
|---|---|---|---|---|---|---|
| Granulated sugar | 1 lb | 4 | oz | 580 g | 83 | **MIXING** |
| Butter and/or shortening | | 8 | oz | 230 g | 33 | One-stage method |
| Eggs | | 8 | oz | 230 g | 33 | **MAKEUP** |
| Molasses | | 4 | oz | 115 g | 17 | Bar method. Egg wash strips with whole egg or egg whites. *Note:* This is a soft, sticky dough, difficult to handle. Do not worry if the units are not perfectly shaped. A homemade look is appropriate for this cookie. |
| Pastry flour | 1 lb | 8 | oz | 700 g | 100 | |
| Cinnamon | | 0.12 oz (2 tsp) | | 3 g | 0.5 | |
| Cloves, ground | | 0.04 oz (½ tsp) | | 1 g | 0.16 | |
| Ginger | | 0.07 oz (1 tsp) | | 2 g | 0.3 | **BAKING** |
| Baking soda | | 0.12 oz (¾ tsp) | | 3 g | 0.5 | 350°F (175°C) for about 15 minutes |
| Salt | | 0.17 oz | | 5 g | 0.75 | Cool partially and cut crosswise to make cookies of desired width. |
| Raisins (see *Note*) | 1 lb | | | 470 g | 67 | |
| **Total weight:** | **5 lb** | | | **2339 g** | **335%** | |

Note: If the raisins are hard and dry, soak them in hot water until soft, then drain them and dry them well before adding them to the cookie batter.

# LEMON WAFERS

| Ingredients | U.S. | | Metric | % | Procedure |
|---|---|---|---|---|---|
| Butter | 1 lb | | 500 g | 67 | **MIXING** |
| Sugar | | 12 oz | 375 g | 50 | Creaming method. Cream at each stage just until smooth; do not cream until light. |
| Lemon zest, grated | | 0.75 oz (3 tbsp) | 25 g | 3 | |
| Salt | | 0.25 oz (1½ tsp) | 8 g | 1 | **MAKEUP** |
| Baking soda | | 0.25 oz (1½ tsp) | 8 g | 1 | Bagged method. With a plain tube, bag out small mounds the size of a quarter on paper-lined pans, leaving 3 in. (8 cm) between them to allow for spread. Flatten slightly. |
| Eggs | | 4 oz | 125 g | 17 | |
| Milk | | 2 oz | 60 g | 8 | |
| Lemon juice | | 1 oz | 30 g | 4 | **BAKING** |
| Pastry flour | 1 lb | 8 | 750 g | 100 | 375°F (190°C) |
| **Total weight:** | **3 lb 12** | **oz** | **1881 g** | **251%** | |

**VARIATION**

## LIME WAFERS

Substitute lime zest and juice for the lemon. This is an unusual and tasty cookie.

# COCONUT MACAROONS (MERINGUE TYPE)

| Ingredients | U.S. | Metric | Sugar at 100% % | Procedure |
|---|---|---|---|---|
| Egg whites | 8 oz | 250 g | 40 | **MIXING** |
| Cream of tartar | 0.06 oz (1 tsp) | 2 g | 0.3 | Sponge method |
| Sugar | 1 lb 4 oz | 625 g | 100 | 1. Whip the egg whites with the cream of tartar |
| Vanilla extract | 0.5 oz | 15 g | 2.5 | until they form soft peaks. Gradually whip in |
| Macaroon coconut (see *Note*) | 1 lb | 500 g | 80 | the sugar. Continue to whip until stiff and glossy. |
| *Total weight:* | *2 lb 12 oz* | *1392 g* | *222%* | 2. Fold in the coconut. |

*Note: Macaroon coconut is finely ground or flaked, unsweetened, dried coconut.*

**MIXING**

Sponge method

1. Whip the egg whites with the cream of tartar until they form soft peaks. Gradually whip in the sugar. Continue to whip until stiff and glossy.
2. Fold in the coconut.

**MAKEUP**

Bagged method. Bag out with a star tube onto parchment-lined baking sheets.

**BAKING**

300°F (150°C) for about 30 minutes

# ALMOND MACAROONS I

*Yield: enough for about 150 1½-in. (4 cm) cookies*

| Ingredients | U.S. | Metric | Almond paste at 100% % | Procedure |
|---|---|---|---|---|
| Almond paste and/or macaroon paste | 1 lb | 500 g | 100 | **MIXING** |
| Egg whites | 6 oz | 190 g | 37.5 | |
| Granulated sugar | 1 lb | 500 g | 100 | |
| *Total weight:* | *2 lb 6 oz* | *1190 g* | *237%* | |

**MIXING**

One-stage method. Blend the almond paste with a little of the egg whites to soften it, then blend together all ingredients. If the mixture is too stiff for a pastry bag, add a little extra egg white.

**MAKEUP**

Bagged method. Using a plain tube, deposit the mix on silicone paper in mounds the size of a quarter. Double-pan.

**BAKING**

350°F (175°C). Let cool before removing from the paper. To make it easier to remove the macaroons from the paper, turn the sheets over and brush the bottoms of the sheets with water.

**VARIATION**

## AMARETTI

Make the following ingredient adjustments:

Use kernel paste instead of almond paste for a stronger flavor (optional).

Reduce the granulated sugar to 85% (13.5 oz/425 g).

Add 85% (13.5 oz/425 g) brown sugar.

# PISTACHIO MACAROONS

| Ingredients | U.S. | Metric | Procedure |
|---|---|---|---|
| Confectioners' sugar | 10.5 oz | 260 g | **MIXING** |
| Powdered almonds | 5 oz | 150 g | 1. Blend the confectioners' sugar and almonds in a food processor for 5 minutes. Sift into a bowl. |
| Egg whites | 2 oz | 50 g | |
| Green food coloring | 2 drops | 2 drops | 2. Mix in the first quantity of egg whites and the coloring until smooth and evenly blended. |
| Egg whites | 3 oz | 75 g | 3. Whip the remaining egg whites and cream of tartar to soft peaks. Add the sugar and whip until stiff. |
| Cream of tartar | ¼ tsp | 1 g | |
| Fine granulated sugar | 2 oz | 50 g | 4. Fold the egg whites one-third at a time into the sugar mixture until smooth. The mixture should look slightly wet. |
| Pistachio Filling (recipe follows) | 1 lb | 400 g | |
| **Batter weight (not including filling):** | **1 lb 6 oz** | **585 g** | |

**MAKEUP AND BAKING**

Bagged method. Using a medium plain tip, pipe 1-in. (2.5–3 cm) bulbs onto a parchment-lined sheet pan. Bake at 350°F (180°C) for 8–10 minutes. Remove from the oven and trickle water between the hot tray and parchment (the steam helps the macaroons release). Allow to cool completely before removing from the paper. Sandwich 2 macaroons together with pistachio filling.

# PISTACHIO FILLING FOR MACAROONS

| Ingredients | U.S. | Metric | Procedure |
|---|---|---|---|
| Heavy cream | 3 oz | 75 g | 1. Combine the cream, butter, and glucose. Bring to a boil. Remove from the heat and cool. |
| Butter | 1 oz | 25 g | |
| Glucose | 1 oz | 25 g | 2. Mix in the pistachio paste, vanilla, and kirsch. |
| Pistachio paste | 3 oz | 75 g | 3. Using a mixer with the paddle attachment, soften the marzipan, then add the cooked ingredients gradually to make a smooth paste. |
| Vanilla extract | ¼ tsp | 1 g | |
| Kirsch | 1 oz | 25 g | |
| Marzipan | 8 oz | 200 g | 4. For filling macaroons, place in a pastry bag with a small plain tip. |
| **Total weight:** | **1 lb 1 oz** | **426 g** | |

# ALMOND MACAROONS II

*For large-quantity measurements, see page 738.*

| Ingredients | U.S. | | Metric | % | Procedure |
|---|---|---|---|---|---|
| Confectioners' sugar at 100% | | | | | |
| Powdered almonds | 2 | oz | 60 g | 48 | |
| Confectioners' sugar | 4 | oz | 125 g | 100 | |
| Egg whites | 2 | oz | 60 g | 48 | |
| Fine granulated sugar | 0.83 oz (5½ tsp) | | 25 g | 20 | |
| Vanilla extract | 2 drops | | 2 drops | | |
| **Total weight:** | **8** | **oz** | **270 g** | **216** | |

**MIXING**

Sponge method

1. Process the almonds and confectioners' sugar in a food processor for 5 minutes. Sift into a bowl.

2. Whip the egg whites to soft peaks. Add the sugar and whip to stiff, glossy peaks.

3. Fold the dry ingredients and the vanilla into the egg whites, adding the dry ingredients a third at a time.

**MAKEUP**

Bagged method. Using a plain tip, deposit the mix on parchment paper in mounds the size of a quarter. Dust with confectioners' sugar and allow to stand 10–15 minutes.

**BAKING**

350°F (175°C), until golden and well risen. Remove from oven and drizzle a little water between the hot pan and the paper so the steam helps release the macaroons. Cool completely before removing the macaroons from the paper.

## VARIATION

### COCOA ALMOND MACAROONS

*For large-quantity measurements, see page 738.*

Prepare as in the basic recipe, using the following ingredients and quantities. Process the cocoa and cake flour with the almonds and sugar in step 1.

| Ingredients | U.S. | | Metric |
|---|---|---|---|
| Powdered almonds | 3 | oz | 75 g |
| Confectioners' sugar | 4 | oz | 100 g |
| Cocoa powder | 1 | oz | 25 g |
| Cake flour | 0.8 oz | | 20 g |
| Egg whites | 5 | oz | 120 g |
| Fine granulated sugar | 2 | oz | 50 g |

# CHOCOLATE MACAROONS I

| Ingredients | U.S. | Metric | Almond paste at 100%<br>% |
|---|---|---|---|
| Almond paste | 12 oz | 350 g | 100 |
| Sugar | 1 lb 5 oz | 600 g | 175 |
| Cocoa | 2 oz | 60 g | 17 |
| Macaroon coconut | 3 oz | 90 g | 25 |
| Egg whites | 8 oz | 225 g | 67 |
| *Total weight:* | *2 lb 14 oz* | *1325 g* | *384%* |

**Procedure**

**MIXING**

One-stage method. Blend the almond paste with a little of the egg whites until smooth. Mix in the remaining ingredients. If the mixture is still too stiff for a pastry bag, add a little extra egg white.

**MAKEUP**

Bagged method. Using a plain tube, deposit the mix on silicone paper in mounds the size of a quarter. Double-pan.

**BAKING**

350°F (175°C). Let cool before removing from the paper. To make it easier to remove the macaroons from the paper, turn the sheets over and brush the bottoms of the sheets with water.

**VARIATION**

Use ground nuts in place of the macaroon coconut.

# COCONUT MACAROONS (CHEWY TYPE)

| Ingredients | U.S. | Metric | Sugar at 100%<br>% |
|---|---|---|---|
| Sugar | 1 lb 8 oz | 700 g | 100 |
| Macaroon coconut | 1 lb 8 oz | 700 g | 100 |
| Corn syrup | 3 oz | 90 g | 13 |
| Vanilla extract | 0.33 oz (2 tsp) | 10 g | 1.5 |
| Pastry flour | 1.5 oz | 42 g | 6 |
| Salt | 0.12 oz (¾ tsp) | 4 g | 0.5 |
| Egg whites | 11 oz | 315 g | 45 |
| *Total weight:* | *3 lb 15 oz* | *1861 g* | *266%* |

**Procedure**

**MIXING**

One-stage method. Blend all ingredients together. Place in a kettle or stainless-steel bowl and set over a hot-water bath. Stir constantly until the mixture reaches 120°F (50°C).

**MAKEUP**

Using a star tube or plain tube, bag out onto paper-lined sheet pans. Make the cookies about 1 in. (2.5 cm) across.

**BAKING**

375°F (190°C)

**VARIATION**

## CHOCOLATE MACAROONS II

Add 1½ oz (45 g) cocoa to the basic recipe. Thin with an additional ½–1 oz (15–30 g) egg white, if necessary

# ALMOND TUILES I

*For large-quantity measurements, see page 739.*
*Yield: enough to make about 90 cookies, 2½ in. (6 cm) in diameter*

| Ingredients | U.S. | | Metric | % |
|---|---|---|---|---|
| Butter | 3 | oz | 90 g | 86 |
| Confectioners' sugar | 4 | oz | 120 g | 114 |
| Egg whites | 3 | oz | 90 g | 86 |
| Cake flour | 3.5 | oz | 105 g | 100 |
| **Garnish** | | | | |
| Sliced almonds | 2.5 | oz | 75 g | 70 |
| ***Batter weight:*** | **13** | **oz** | **405 g** | **386%** |

*Note: This batter is also known as stencil paste. Instead of the simple round stencils for tuiles, stencils of any shape or size can be cut and used for decorative effect. This stencil paste is interchangeable with the slightly different stencil paste included in the Ribbon Sponge recipe on page 411.*

*This recipe is not interchangeable with Almond Tuiles II, which is a very different batter, even though the makeup is similar.*

## Procedure

**MIXING**

Creaming method

1. Soften the butter to a creamy consistency, using the paddle attachment. Add the sugar and beat until thoroughly mixed.

2. Beat in the egg whites.

3. Sift the flour over the mixture and mix in well.

**MAKEUP**

Stencil method. Line a sheet pan with a silicone mat or, if a mat is not available, a sheet of parchment paper. Use a commercially made stencil, or make a stencil by cutting a round hole in a sheet of thick plastic or thin cardboard (the cardboard used for cake boxes is suitable). For petit-four-size tuiles, make the circle 2½ in. (6 cm) in diameter. Using an offset palette knife, spread the batter across the stencil, then lift off the stencil (a). Sprinkle with a few sliced almonds (b).

**BAKING**

350°F (175°C) 5–10 minutes depending on thickness, or until lightly browned. Remove the baked cookies from the baking sheet and immediately curve over a rolling pin or tuile rack (c) and allow to cool.

**VARIATION**

### TULIPES

Omit the almonds in the basic recipe. Immediately after baking, shape the cookies by molding them around the upturned bottom of a small glass or similar mold. Cup-shaped tulipes are used as edible containers for portions of ice cream and other desserts.

# ALMOND TUILES II

| Ingredient | U.S. | | Metric | % | Procedure |
|---|---|---|---|---|---|
| Sugar | 8 | oz | 240 g | 533 | **MIXING** |
| Sliced, blanched almonds | 9 | oz | 270 g | 600 | 1. Mix the sugar, almonds, and flour in a bowl. |
| Bread flour | 1.5 | oz | 45 g | 100 | 2. Add the egg whites and melted butter. Stir until well mixed. |
| Egg whites, lightly beaten | 4.5 | oz | 135 g | 300 | **MAKEUP** |
| Butter, melted | 1.5 | oz | 45 g | 100 | Dropped method. Drop by the tablespoonful 2 in. (5 cm) apart onto a greased and floured |
| **Total weight:** | **1 lb 8 oz** | | **735 g** | **1633%** | baking sheet. Use about ⅓–½ oz (10–15 g) per cookie. Flatten with a fork dipped in water, spreading the mixture so it is thin and flat. It will not spread during baking, and the cookies must be thin. |

**BAKING**

375°F (190°C) until browned. Immediately remove one by one from the baking sheet with a spatula and drape over a rolling pin to give a curved shape. The cookies will become crisp when cool. If they do not become crisp, they are underbaked; return them to the oven for 1 minute. If they become crisp before they can be curved, return them to the oven to soften them.

# SESAME TUILES

| Ingredient | U.S. | | Metric | % | Procedure |
|---|---|---|---|---|---|
| Confectioners' sugar | 7 | oz | 210 g | 100 | 1. Sift the sugar, flour, and nutmeg into a bowl. Make a well in the center. |
| Cake flour | 7 | oz | 210 g | 100 | 2. Lightly beat the egg whites and add to the well. Add the butter and lemon zest. |
| Nutmeg | large pinch | | large pinch | | |
| Egg whites | 5 | oz | 150 g | 71 | 3. Mix to make a soft batter. Add the first quantity of sesame seeds and mix in. Chill. |
| Butter, melted | 5 | oz | 150 g | 71 | |
| Lemon zest | 1 | tsp | 3 g | 1.5 | 4. Cut a triangle-shaped stencil and use it to spread the batter onto buttered, chilled sheet pans, using the procedure for making Almond Tuiles I (p. 508). Sprinkle with the remaining sesame seeds. |
| Sesame seeds | 1 | oz | 30 g | 15 | |
| **Garnish** | | | | | |
| Sesame seeds | 0.5 oz | | 15 g | 7 | 5. Bake at 375°F (190°C) until golden. |
| **Total weight:** | **1 lb 9 oz** | | **753 g** | **358%** | 6. Remove from the pan and immediately curve into an S-shape (see p. 633). |

# COCONUT TUILES

*For large-quantity measurements, see page 739.*

| Ingredients | U.S. | | Metric | Sugar at 100% % | Procedure |
|---|---|---|---|---|---|
| Confectioners' sugar | 4 | oz | 130 g | 100 | 1. Sift the sugar. |
| Egg, lightly beaten | 3 | oz | 100 g | 77 | 2. Mix in the egg, followed by the coconut and the butter. |
| Dessicated coconut | 4 | oz | 130 g | 100 | |
| Butter, melted | 0.75 | oz | 25 g | 19 | 3. Rest in refrigerator for 12 hours. |
| *Total weight:* | *11* | *oz* | *385 g* | *296%* | |

4. Divide the mixture into portions of the desired size and place on a silicone mat on a sheet pan. Cover with a sheet of dampened silicone paper and run a rolling pin over it to flatten the mixture.

5. Remove the paper. Bake at 350°F (180°C) until golden, about 8 minutes. Shape as required while still hot.

# CLASSIC BROWNIES

| Ingredients | U.S. | | Metric | % | Procedure |
|---|---|---|---|---|---|
| Unsweetened chocolate | 1 lb | | 450 g | 100 | **MIXING** |
| Butter | 1 lb 8 | oz | 675 g | 150 | Modified sponge method |
| Eggs | 1 lb 8 | oz | 675 g | 150 | 1. Melt the chocolate and butter together in a double boiler. Let the mixture cool to room temperature. |
| Sugar | 3 lb | oz | 1350 g | 300 | |
| Salt | 0.25 | oz | 7 g | 1.5 | 2. Mix the eggs, sugar, salt, and vanilla together until well blended, but do not whip. Whipping to a foam creates more leavening, resulting in a more crumbly, less fudgy brownie. |
| Vanilla | 1 | oz | 30 g | 6 | |
| Bread flour | 1 lb | | 450 g | 100 | 3. Blend in the chocolate mixture. |
| Chopped walnuts or pecans | 1 lb | | 450 g | 100 | 4. Sift the flour and fold in. |
| *Total weight:* | *9 lb 1* | *oz* | *4087 g* | *907%* | 5. Fold in the nuts. |

**MAKEUP**

Sheet method. Grease and flour the pans, or line them with parchment. One recipe fills 1 full sheet pan (18 × 26 in./46 × 66 cm), 2 half-sheet pans, four 9 × 13 in. (23 × 33 cm) pans, or six 9-in. (23 cm) square pans.

If desired, sprinkle the batter with an additional 50% (8 oz/225 g) chopped nuts after panning.

**BAKING**

325°F (165°C) for 45 to 60 minutes

For 2-in. (5 cm) square brownies, cut sheet pan into 8 rows of 12 to yield 96 pieces.

# RICH BROWNIES

*For large-quantity measurements, see page 739.*

| Ingredients | U.S. | | Metric | % |
|---|---|---|---|---|
| Unsweetened chocolate | 2 | oz | 60 g | 50 |
| Bittersweet chocolate | 5 | oz | 145 g | 125 |
| Butter | 10 | oz | 290 g | 250 |
| Eggs | 7 | oz | 200 g | 175 |
| Sugar | 9 | oz | 260 g | 225 |
| Salt | 0.06 | oz (¼ tsp) | 2 g | 1.5 |
| Vanilla extract | 0.25 | oz (1½ tsp) | 7 g | 6 |
| Bread flour | 4 | oz | 115 g | 100 |
| Walnuts or pecans, chopped | 4 | oz | 115 g | 100 |
| **Total weight:** | **2 lb 9** | **oz** | **1194 g** | **1032%** |

## Procedure

### MIXING

Modified sponge method

1. Melt the unsweetened chocolate, the bittersweet chocolate, and the butter together in a double boiler. Let the mixture cool to room temperature.

2. Mix the eggs, sugar, salt, and vanilla together until well blended, but do not whip (a). Whipping to a foam creates more leavening, resulting in a more crumbly, less fudgy brownie. If the eggs are not at room temperature, stir the mixture over a hot-water bath just until the mixture is at slightly warm room temperature.

3. Blend in the chocolate mixture (b).

4. Sift the flour and fold in (c).

5. Fold in the nuts.

### MAKEUP

Sheet method. For 2 lb 9 oz (1194 g) batter, use one 9 × 13 in. (23 × 33 cm) pan or two 8-in. (20 cm) square pans. Grease and flour the pans, or line them with parchment.

### BAKING

325°F (190°C) for about 45–50 minutes

For 2-in. (5 cm) square brownies, cut sheet pan into 4 rows of 6 to yield 24 pieces.

### VARIATION

*For large-quantity measurements, see page 739.*

| Ingredients | U.S. | Metric | % |
|---|---|---|---|
| Baking powder | 0.1 oz (½ tsp plus ⅛ tsp) | 3 g | 2.5% |

For a more cakelike brownie, sift the above quantity of baking powder with the flour in step 4.

# CREAM CHEESE BROWNIES

*For large-quantity measurements, see page 739.*

*Yield: 3 lb (1400 g) batter is enough for one 9 × 13 in. (23 × 33 cm) pan or two 8-in. (20 cm) square pans.*

| Ingredients | U.S. | Metric |
|---|---|---|
| Cream cheese | 8 oz | 225 g |
| Sugar | 2 oz | 55 g |
| Vanilla extract | ½ tsp | 2 mL |
| Egg yolks | 1 yolk | 20 g |
| Rich Brownie batter without walnuts (p. 511) (1 recipe) | 2 lb 9 oz | 1190 g |
| *Total weight:* | *3 lb 3 oz* | *1492 g* |

## Procedure

### MIXING

1. In a mixer with the paddle attachment, work the cream cheese at low speed until smooth and creamy.

2. Add the sugar and vanilla and mix in at low speed until smooth.

3. Add the egg yolks and blend in.

4. Prepare the brownie batter according to the recipe.

### MAKEUP

Sheet method. Grease and flour the pans, or line them with parchment.

Pour about half the brownie batter into the pans (a). Spread it evenly (b). Deposit half the cream cheese mixture in pools on top of the brownie batter (c). Pour in the remaining brownie batter (d). Spread evenly in the pan. Drop the remaining cream cheese mixture in pools on top (e). Swirl the two batters together slightly, using a palette knife or a spoon handle (f).

### BAKING

325°F (190°C) for about 45–50 minutes

Cut into 2-in. (5 cm) square brownies.

# FLORENTINES

| Ingredient | U.S. | Metric | % | Procedure |
|---|---|---|---|---|
| Butter | 7 oz | 210 g | 350 | **MIXING** |
| Sugar | 10 oz | 300 g | 500 | 1. Combine the butter, sugar, honey, and cream in a heavy saucepan. Bring to a strong boil, stirring constantly. Cook, stirring, until the mixture reaches 240°F (115°C). |
| Honey | 3 oz | 90 g | 150 | |
| Heavy cream | 3 oz | 90 g | 150 | |
| Sliced almonds | 12 oz | 360 g | 600 | 2. Mix together the remaining ingredients and add to the sugar mixture. Mix well. |
| Ground almonds or hazelnuts | 2 oz | 60 g | 100 | |
| Candied orange peel, chopped | 4 oz | 120 g | 200 | **MAKEUP**<br>Dropped method. Drop while the mixture is hot; it will get very stiff when cool. Drop ½ oz (15 g) mounds on baking sheets lined with silicone paper or greased and floured. Allow at least 2 in. (5 cm) between cookies for spreading. Flatten the cookies with a fork. |
| Bread flour | 2 oz | 60 g | 100 | |
| **For finishing**<br>Chocolate, melted | as needed | as needed | | |
| **Total weight:** | **2 lb 11 oz** | **1290 g** | **2150%** | **BAKING**<br>375°F (190°C) until browned. As soon as the pans are removed from the oven, use a round cookie cutter to pull the cookies back together into a round shape. Let cool. |

**FINISHING**
Spread the flat sides of the cookies with melted chocolate. Mark grooves in the chocolate with an icing comb.

# SWISS LECKERLI

| Ingredients | U.S. | | Metric | | % | Procedure |
|---|---|---|---|---|---|---|
| Honey | 10 | oz | 315 | g | 42 | **MIXING** |
| Sugar | 6 | oz | 185 | g | 25 | 1. Heat the honey and sugar together until the sugar is dissolved. Cool. |
| Baking soda | 0.25 | oz | 8 | g | 1 | 2. Dissolve the baking soda in the water. Add to the honey mixture. |
| Water | 4 | oz | 125 | g | 17 | |
| Salt | 0.17 | oz (1 tsp) | 5 | g | 0.7 | 3. Add the remaining ingredients. Mix to a smooth dough. |
| Cinnamon | 0.25 | oz (4½ tsp) | 8 | g | 1 | |
| Mace | 0.06 | oz (1 tsp) | 1.5 | g | 0.2 | **MAKEUP** |
| Cloves, ground | 0.06 | oz (1 tsp) | 1.5 | g | 0.2 | Sheet method. Roll out dough ¼ in. (6 mm) thick. Place on a well-greased baking sheet. Cut into small squares, but do not separate the squares until after they are baked. |
| Candied lemon peel, finely chopped | 2 | oz | 60 | g | 8 | |
| Candied orange peel, finely chopped | 2 | oz | 60 | g | 8 | Alternative method: Rolled method. Roll out ¼ in. (6 mm) thick and cut out with cutters, or cut into small squares. Place on greased, floured baking sheets. |
| Blanched almonds, chopped | 4 | oz | 125 | g | 17 | |
| Bread flour | 1 lb | | 500 | g | 67 | **BAKING** |
| Cake flour | 8 | oz | 250 | g | 33 | 375°F (190°C) for 15 minutes or more. Immediately after baking, while still hot, brush tops with flat icing. |
| **Total weight:** | **3 lb 5** | **oz** | **1644** | **g** | **220%** | |

# BISCOTTI

| Ingredients | U.S. | | Metric | % | Procedure |
|---|---|---|---|---|---|
| Eggs | 10 | oz | 300 g | 35 | **MIXING** |
| Sugar | 1 lb 2 | oz | 550 g | 65 | Sponge method |
| Salt | 0.5 | oz | 15 g | 2 | 1. Combine the eggs, sugar, and salt. Stir over hot water to warm the mixture, then whip until thick and light. |
| Vanilla extract | 0.3 | oz (2 tsp) | 8 g | 1 | |
| Orange zest, grated | 0.15 | oz (2 tsp) | 4 g | 0.5 | 2. Fold in the vanilla and orange zest. |
| Pastry flour | 1 lb 12 | oz | 850 g | 100 | 3. Sift together the flour and baking powder. Fold into the egg mixture. |
| Baking powder | 0.7 | oz | 20 g | 2.5 | |
| Blanched almonds | 10 | oz | 300 g | 35 | 4. Mix in the almonds. |
| **Total weight:** | **4 lb 3** | **oz** | **2047 g** | **241%** | |

*Note: These cookies are hard when cooled.*
*They are traditionally dipped in a sweet wine when eaten.*

### VARIATION

Omit the orange zest and flavor to taste with anise extract.

**MAKEUP**

Bar method. Scale at 1 lb (500 g). Shape into logs 2–2½ in. (6 cm) thick. Do not flatten the logs (the dough will be sticky and somewhat difficult to handle). Egg wash.

**BAKING**

325°F (160°C) for about 30–40 minutes, or until light golden

**FINISHING**

Let cool slightly. Slice diagonally ½ in. (12 mm) thick. Place cut side down on sheet pans. Bake at 275°F (135°C) until toasted and dry, about 30 minutes.

## ⊰ TWICE-BAKED ⊱

The Italian word *biscotto* (plural, *biscotti*) means "twice cooked." The British name for cookies, *biscuit*, comes from the same root and also means "twice cooked." In earlier times, when ovens were more primitive than they are today, double cooking was one method of producing dry, crisp flour goods. Dryness was desirable for these items because the low moisture content meant they kept longer.

Italian-style biscotti, made by the bar method—baked, sliced, and baked again until crisp—have become popular in the rest of Europe and in North America. Many flavor variations made today are recent innovations rather than classic Italian confections.

# ESPRESSO BISCOTTI

*For large-quantity measurements, see page 740.*

| Ingredients | U.S. | | Metric | % | Procedure |
|---|---|---|---|---|---|
| Butter | 4 | oz | 120 g | 40 | **MIXING** |
| Sugar | 6 | oz | 180 g | 60 | Creaming method. Dissolve the |
| Salt | 0.2 | oz (1 tsp) | 6 g | 2 | espresso powder in the hot water |
| Eggs | 3.33 | oz (2 eggs) | 100 g (2 eggs) | 33 | before adding to the creamed mix- |
| Water, hot | 0.5 | oz | 15 g | 5 | ture. Mix in the almonds after |
| Instant espresso powder | 0.2 | oz (2 tbsp) | 6 g | 2 | adding the sifted dry ingredients. |
| Pastry flour | 10 | oz | 300 g | 100 | **MAKEUP, BAKING,** |
| Baking powder | 0.25 | oz (1½ tsp) | 8 g | 2.5 | **AND FINISHING** |
| Blanched almonds | 3.5 | oz | 105 g | 35 | Same as Biscotti (p. 514) |
| **Total weight:** | **1 lb 11** | **oz** | **840 g** | **279%** | |

*Note: See discussion of biscotti, page 514.*

# CHOCOLATE PECAN BISCOTTI

*For large-quantity measurements, see page 740.*

| Ingredients | U.S. | | Metric | % | Procedure |
|---|---|---|---|---|---|
| Butter | 4 | oz | 120 g | 40 | **MIXING** |
| Sugar | 6 | oz | 180 g | 60 | Creaming method. Mix in the nuts |
| Salt | 0.1 | oz (½ tsp) | 3 g | 1 | and chocolate chips after adding |
| Orange zest, grated | 0.1 | oz (1½ tsp) | 3 g | 0.5 | the sifted dry ingredients. |
| Eggs | 3.33 | oz (2 eggs) | 100 g (2 eggs) | 33 | **MAKEUP, BAKING,** |
| Water | 2 | oz | 60 g | 20 | **AND FINISHING** |
| Vanilla extract | 0.16 | oz (1 tsp) | 5 g | 1.5 | Same as Biscotti (p. 514) |
| Pastry flour | 10 | oz | 300 g | 100 | |
| Cocoa powder | 1.5 | oz | 45 g | 15 | |
| Baking powder | 0.25 | oz (1½ tsp) | 8 g | 2.5 | |
| Baking soda | 0.08 | oz (½ tsp) | 2.5 g | 0.8 | |
| Pecan pieces | 2 | oz | 60 g | 20 | |
| Small chocolate chips | 2 | oz | 60 g | 20 | |
| **Total weight:** | **1 lb 15** | **oz** | **946 g** | **314%** | |

*Note: See discussion of biscotti, page 514.*

# BATONS MARECHAUX AND EPONGES

*For large-quantity measurements, see page 740.*

| Ingredients | U.S. | | Metric | % | Procedure |
|---|---|---|---|---|---|
| Confectioners' sugar | 3.33 | oz | 100 g | 333 | **MIXING** |
| Cake flour | 1 | oz | 30 g | 100 | Sponge method |
| Powdered almonds | 2.5 | oz | 75 g | 250 | 1. Sift together the confectioners' sugar, flour, and almonds. |
| Egg whites | 4 | oz | 120 g | 400 | 2. Whip the egg whites with the granulated sugar to make a common meringue. |
| Granulated sugar | 1.33 | oz | 40 g | 133 | |
| **For finishing Batons Marechaux** | | | | | 3. Fold the sifted ingredients into the meringue. |
| Chocolate, tempered | as needed | | as needed | 111 | **MAKEUP FOR BATONS MARECHAUX** |
| **For finishing Eponges** | | | | | Butter and flour sheet pans. Using a pastry bag with a plain tip (No. 8), pipe strips 2¼-in. (7 cm) long. Bake at 340°F (170°C) for 10 minutes. Remove from baking sheet and cool on rack. Dip the bottoms (flat sides) of the cookies in tempered chocolate and spread the chocolate thin with a palette knife. |
| Slivered almonds | as needed | | as needed | | |
| Raspberry jam | as needed | | as needed | | |
| *Total weight:* | *12* | *oz* | *365 g* | *1216%* | |

**MAKEUP FOR EPONGES**

Butter and flour sheet pans. Using a pastry bag with a plain tip, pipe small mounds ¾ in. (2 cm) in diameter. Sprinkle with slivered almonds. You will need about 1 oz (30 g) almonds for each 2 oz (60 g) dough. Bake at 340°F (170°C) for 10 minutes. Remove from the baking sheet and cool on rack. Sandwich together in pairs with a little raspberry jam spread on the bottoms.

## TERMS FOR REVIEW

| | | | |
|---|---|---|---|
| spread | dropped | molded | sheet |
| one-stage method | bagged | icebox | stencil |
| creaming method | rolled | bar | double-panning |
| sponge method | | | |

## QUESTIONS FOR DISCUSSION

1. What makes cookies crisp? How can you keep them crisp after they are baked?

2. If you baked cookies that were unintentionally chewy, how would you correct them in the next batch?

3. Describe briefly the difference between the creaming method and the one-stage method.

4. Besides cost control, why is accurate scaling and uniform sizing important when making up cookies?

## Chapter 20

# Custards, Puddings, Mousses, and Soufflés

This chapter discusses a variety of desserts not covered in earlier chapters. Although most of these items are not baked goods in the sense that breads, pastries, cakes, and cookies are, they are popular desserts that are important in food service. They include custards, puddings, creams, and frozen desserts.

Most of the items and techniques discussed are related to each other and to techniques discussed in earlier chapters. For example, many puddings, Bavarians and mousses, soufflés, and frozen desserts are based on two basic custards, crème anglaise and pastry cream, presented in chapter 12. Also, Bavarians, mousses, and soufflés depend on meringues (discussed in chapter 12), whipped cream, or both for their texture.

As you know, the art and science of baking and dessert preparation rely on a coherent set of principles and techniques applied over and over again to many kinds of product. The topics in this chapter are a further illustration of that fact.

**After reading this chapter, you should be able to:**

1. Prepare starch-thickened or boiled puddings.

2. Prepare baked custards and baked puddings.

3. Prepare steamed puddings.

4. Prepare Bavarian creams and mousses.

5. Use Bavarian creams to prepare cold charlottes.

6. Prepare hot dessert soufflés.

# CUSTARDS AND PUDDINGS

It is difficult to come up with a definition of *pudding* that includes everything called by that name. The term is used for such different dishes as chocolate pudding, blood sausages (blood puddings), and steak-and-kidney pudding. In this chapter, however, we are considering only popular North American dessert puddings.

Two kinds of puddings, starch-thickened and baked, are the most frequently prepared in food service kitchens. A third type, steamed pudding, is less often served, and then only in cold weather, because it is usually rather heavy and filling.

Because custards are the basis of so many puddings, we begin with a general discussion of this type of preparation. A **custard** is a liquid thickened or set by the coagulation of egg protein. There are two basic kinds of custards: **stirred custard**, which is stirred as it cooks and remains pourable when cooked (except for pastry cream—see below), and **baked custard**, which is not stirred and sets firm.

One basic rule governs the preparation of both types of custard: *Do not heat custards higher than an internal temperature of 185°F (85°C).* This temperature is the point at which egg-liquid mixtures coagulate. If they are heated beyond this, they tend to curdle. An overbaked custard becomes watery because the moisture separates from the toughened protein.

**Crème anglaise**, or vanilla custard sauce, discussed in detail in chapter 12 (p. 269), is a stirred custard. It consists of milk, sugar, and egg yolks stirred over very low heat until lightly thickened.

**Pastry cream**, also discussed in chapter 12 (p. 271), is stirred custard that contains starch thickeners as well as eggs, resulting in a much thicker and more stable product. Because of the stabilizing effect of the starch, pastry cream is an exception to the rule of not heating custards over 185°F (85°C). In addition to its use as a component of many pastries and cakes, pastry cream is also the basis for cream puddings.

Sweet baked custards, like custard sauce, consist of milk, sugar, and eggs—usually whole eggs for their thickening power. Unlike the sauce, this type of custard is baked rather than stirred over heat, so it sets and becomes firm. Baked custard is used as a pie filling, as a dessert by itself, and as a basis for many baked puddings.

## Rangetop Puddings

Most of the puddings in this category are thickened with starch, so they must be boiled in order to cook or gelatinize the starch. The first two types of pudding in the following list are of this type. The third type is bound with gelatin, so heating or cooking is necessary to dissolve the gelatin. This type of pudding may need only to be heated gently rather than simmered or boiled.

1. **Cornstarch pudding or blancmange.** *Cornstarch pudding* consists of milk, sugar, and flavorings and is thickened with cornstarch (or, sometimes, another starch). If enough cornstarch is used, the hot mixture may be poured into molds, chilled, and unmolded for service. (The term *blancmange*, pronounced, approximately, blaw mawnj, comes from the French words for "white" and "eat.")

2. **Cream puddings.** *Cream puddings*, as we have suggested, are the same as pastry cream. Puddings are usually made with less starch, however, and may contain any of several flavoring ingredients, such as coconut or

chocolate. The flavor of butterscotch pudding comes from using brown sugar instead of white sugar.

If you look again at the formula for pastry cream (p. 271), you will see that the only difference between cornstarch puddings and cream puddings is that the latter contain eggs. In fact, cream puddings may be made by stirring hot cornstarch pudding into beaten eggs and then heating the entire mixture to just below a simmer. Care must be taken to avoid curdling the eggs if this method is used.

Because these puddings are basically the same as pastry cream, which in turn is used for cream pie fillings, it is not necessary to give separate recipes here. *To prepare any of the following puddings, simply prepare the corresponding cream pie filling (pp. 305–307), but use only half the starch.* The following puddings can be made on this basis:

Vanilla pudding.

Coconut cream pudding.

Banana cream pudding (purée the bananas and mix with the pudding).

Chocolate pudding (two versions, using cocoa or melted chocolate).

Butterscotch pudding.

3. **Puddings bound with gelatin.** A pudding not thickened with starch or eggs must be bound or stabilized using another ingredient. Gelatin is often used for this purpose. One of the simplest and most popular desserts of this type is **panna cotta**, which is Italian for "cooked cream." In its most basic form, panna cotta is made by heating cream and milk with sugar, adding vanilla and gelatin, and chilling in molds until set. It is often served with fruits or caramel sauce.

Mousses and Bavarian creams, which owe their light texture to whipped cream or meringue, are often bound with gelatin. They are covered in detail later in this chapter.

# BLANCMANGE ENGLISH-STYLE
*Yield: about 2½ pt (1.25 L)*

| Ingredients | U.S. | | Metric | Milk at 100%<br>% | Procedure |
|---|---|---|---|---|---|
| Milk | 2 lb (1 qt) | | 1000 mL | 80 | 1. Combine the milk, sugar, and salt in a heavy saucepan and bring to a simmer. |
| Sugar | 6 | oz | 190 g | 15 | |
| Salt | 0.04 oz (¼ tsp) | | 1 g | 0.1 | 2. Mix the cornstarch and milk until perfectly smooth. |
| Cornstarch | 4 | oz | 125 g | 10 | 3. Pouring it in a thin stream, add about 1 cup (2.5 dL) of the hot milk to the cornstarch mixture. Stir this mixture back into the hot milk. |
| Milk, cold | 8 | oz (½ pt) | 250 mL | 20 | |
| Vanilla or<br>  almond extract | 0.25 oz | | 8 mL | 0.6 | |

*Note: French blancmange is very different from the English style. The French style is made from almonds or almond paste and gelatin.*

4. Stir over low heat until the mixture thickens and comes to a boil.

5. Remove from the heat and add desired flavoring.

6. Pour into ½-cup (125 mL) molds. Cool and then chill. Unmold for service.

**VARIATIONS**

Blancmange or cornstarch pudding may be flavored in any way cream puddings are. See the general discussion preceding this recipe.

For puddings to be served in dishes rather than unmolded, reduce the cornstarch to 2 oz (60 g).

# PANNA COTTA

| Ingredients | U.S. | | Metric | Procedure |
|---|---|---|---|---|
| Milk | 10 | oz | 300 g | 1. Heat the milk, cream, and sugar until the sugar is dissolved. |
| Heavy cream | 10 | oz | 300 g | |
| Sugar | 4 | oz | 125 g | 2. Soften the gelatin in cold water (see p. 88). Add the softened gelatin to the hot milk mixture and stir until dissolved. |
| Gelatin (see *Note*) | 1½ tsp–2¼ tsp | | 5–7 g (2½–3½ sheets) | |
| Vanilla extract | 1 | tsp | 5 g | 3. Stir in the vanilla. |
| **Total Weight:** | **1 lb 8** | **oz** | **740 g** | 4. Pour into 3- or 4-oz. (90 or 125 mL) molds. Chill until set. |
| | | | | 5. Unmold to serve. |

*Note: The lower quantity of gelatin makes a soft, delicate dessert. Use this quantity if the room temperature is cool. The larger quantity makes a firmer dessert that can withstand more handling when unmolded.*

# Baked Puddings

Many, if not most, baked puddings are custards that contain additional ingredients, usually in large quantities. Bread pudding, for example, is made by pouring a custard mixture over slices or cubes of bread arranged in a baking pan and placing it in the oven to bake. Rice pudding, made of cooked rice and custard, is another popular item.

Baked custard, a mixture of eggs, milk, sugar, and flavorings, is baked until the eggs coagulate and the custard sets. A good custard holds a clean, sharp edge when cut.

The amount of egg in a custard determines its firmness. A custard to be unmolded requires more egg than one to be served in its baking dish. Also, egg yolks make a richer custard with a softer texture than do whole eggs.

When baking custards, note in particular these points:

1. Scald the milk before beating it slowly into the eggs. This reduces cooking time and helps the product cook more evenly.

2. Remove any foam that would mar the appearance of the finished product.

3. Bake at 325°F (165°C) or lower. Higher temperatures increase the risk of overcooking and curdling.

4. Bake in a water bath so the outside edges do not overcook before the inside is set.

5. To test for doneness, insert a thin-bladed knife an inch or two from the center. If it comes out clean, the custard is done. The center may not be completely set, but it will continue to cook in its own heat after removal from the oven.

The procedure for making many baked puddings, such as bread pudding, is the same as that for making plain baked custard. A water bath may not be necessary if the starch content of the pudding is high.

Soft pie fillings, such as pumpkin, can also be considered baked puddings and can be served as such. These preparations are, strictly speaking, custards because they are liquids or semiliquids set by the coagulation of eggs. They may also contain small amounts of starch as a stabilizer.

This section also includes the popular baked custard called *crème brûlée*, which means "burnt cream." The *brûlée*, or "burnt," part of this name refers to the crunchy layer of sugar caramelized on the top of the dessert shortly before it is served. The custard portion of the dessert is especially rich because it is made with heavy cream. Some recipe books and food articles refer to the custard mixture as "the brûlée," which makes no sense when you consider the meaning of the term.

# BAKED CUSTARD

*Yield: 12 portions, 5 oz (150 g) each*

| Ingredients | U.S. | | Metric | | Milk at 100% % | Procedure |
|---|---|---|---|---|---|---|
| Eggs | 1 lb | | 500 | g | 40 | |
| Sugar | 8 | oz | 250 | g | 20 | |
| Salt | 0.08 | oz (½ tsp) | 2.5 | g | 0.2 | |
| Vanilla extract | 0.5 | oz | 15 | g | 1.25 | |
| Milk | 2 lb 8 | oz (2½ pt) | 1250 | mL | 100 | |

Procedure:

1. Combine the eggs, sugar, salt, and vanilla in a mixing bowl. Mix until thoroughly blended, but do not whip.

2. Scald the milk in a double boiler or in a saucepan over low heat.

3. Gradually pour the milk into the egg mixture, stirring constantly.

4. Skim all foam from the surface of the liquid.

5. Arrange custard cups in a shallow baking pan.

6. Carefully pour the custard mixture into the cups. If bubbles form during this step, skim them off.

7. Set the baking pan on the oven shelf. Pour enough hot water into the pan around the cups so the level of the water is about as high as the level of the custard mixture.

8. Bake at 325°F (165°C) until set, about 45 minutes.

9. Carefully remove the custard from the oven and cool. Store, covered, in the refrigerator.

## VARIATIONS

### CRÈME CARAMEL

Cook 12 oz (375 g) sugar with 2 oz (60 mL) water until it caramelizes (see the section on sugar cooking on page 261). Line the bottoms of the custard cups with this hot caramel. (Be sure the cups are clean and dry.) Fill with custard and bake as in a basic recipe. When cooled, refrigerate for 24 hours to allow some of the caramel to dissolve and form a sauce for the dessert when it is unmolded.

### VANILLA POTS DE CRÈME

*Pots de crème* (pronounced poh duh krem) are rich cup custards. Substitute 1 pt (500 mL) heavy cream for 1 pt (500 mL) of the milk in the basic recipe. Use 8 oz (250 g) whole eggs plus 4 oz (125 g) egg yolks.

### CHOCOLATE POTS DE CRÈME

Follow the procedure for vanilla pots de crème above, but stir 12 oz (375 g) chopped sweet chocolate into the hot milk until melted and evenly blended. Reduce the sugar to 4 oz (125 g).

# CRÈME BRÛLÉE

*Yield: 12 portions, about 5 oz (150 g) each*

| Ingredients | U.S. | | Metric | | Procedure |
|---|---|---|---|---|---|
| Brown sugar | 8 | oz | 250 | g | 1. Spread the brown sugar on a pan; dry out in a low oven. Cool, crush, and sift. |
| Egg yolks | 12 | | 12 | | 2. Mix together the egg yolks and granulated sugar until well combined. |
| Granulated sugar | 6 | oz | 180 | g | |
| Heavy cream, hot | 3 pt | | 1.5 | L | 3. Gradually stir in the hot cream. Add the vanilla and salt. Strain the mixture. |
| Vanilla extract | 0.25 oz (1½ tsp) | | 8 | mL | |
| Salt | ¾ | tsp | 3 | g | |

4. Set 12 shallow ramekins or gratin dishes, about 1 in. (2.5 cm) deep, on a towel in a sheet pan (the purpose of the towel is to insulate the bottoms of the ramekins from the strong heat). Divide the custard mixture equally among the dishes. Pour enough hot water into the sheet pan to come about halfway up the sides of the ramekins.

5. Bake at 325°F (165°C) until the custard is just set, about 25 minutes.

6. Cool, then refrigerate.

7. To finish, first dab any moisture from the tops of the custards. Sprinkle with an even layer of brown sugar. Caramelize the sugar under the broiler; place the custards very close to the heat so the sugar caramelizes quickly before the custard warms up too much (alternatively, use a blowtorch). When it cools, the caramelized sugar will form a thin, hard crust. Serve within an hour or two. If the custards are held too long, the caramel tops will soften.

## VARIATIONS

Granulated sugar may be used instead of brown sugar. White sugar need not be dried (as in step 1), but it is slightly harder to brown.

For a deluxe version, flavor with vanilla beans instead of extract. Split 2 vanilla beans in half lengthwise and scrape out the tiny seeds. Simmer the pods and seeds with the heavy cream. Remove the pods and continue with the basic recipe.

### COFFEE CRÈME BRÛLÉE

Flavor the hot cream to taste with coffee extract or instant coffee powder.

### CINNAMON CRÈME BRÛLÉE

Add 2 tsp (3.5 g) cinnamon to the hot cream.

### CHOCOLATE CRÈME BRÛLÉE

Use half milk and half cream. Mix 8 oz (250 g) melted bittersweet chocolate with the hot cream and milk mixture.

### RASPBERRY OR BLUEBERRY CRÈME BRÛLÉE

Place a few berries in the ramekins before adding the custard mixture.

### RASPBERRY PASSION FRUIT CRÈME BRÛLÉE

Reduce the quantity of cream to 2¾ pt (1375 mL). Omit the vanilla. Add 4 oz (125 mL) strained passion fruit juice and pulp to the mixture just before straining. Continue as for Raspberry Crème Brûlée.

## ❊{ BROILER OR }❊ BLOWTORCH?

Which tool is better for caramelizing the sugar on crème brûlée, a butane torch or a broiler/salamander? It's a matter of personal preference and equipment availability. When making individual desserts to order, chefs often find a torch is easiest and quickest. Besides, not every pastry department has a broiler, and the broiler in the hot kitchen may not be available. On the other hand, when you are preparing crèmes brûlées in quantity for a banquet, it may be easier to arrange the custards on sheet pans and pass them under a broiler.

# BREAD AND BUTTER PUDDING

*Yield: about 5 lb (2.5 kg)*

| Ingredients | U.S. | Metric | Procedure |
|---|---|---|---|
| White bread, in thin slices | 1 lb | 500 g | 1. Cut each slice of bread in half. Brush both sides of each piece with melted butter. |
| Butter, melted | 4 oz | 125 g | |
| Eggs | 1 lb | 500 g | 2. Arrange the bread slices so they overlap in a buttered 10 × 12 in. (25 × 30 cm) baking pan. (To use a full-size hotel pan, double the quantities.) |
| Sugar | 8 oz | 250 g | |
| Salt | 0.08 oz (½ tsp) | 2 g | 3. Mix together the eggs, sugar, salt, and vanilla until thoroughly combined. Add the milk. |
| Vanilla extract | 0.5 oz | 15 mL | |
| Milk | 2 lb 8 oz (1¼ qt) | 1250 mL | 4. Pour the egg mixture over the bread in the pan. |
| Cinnamon | as needed | as needed | |
| Nutmeg | as needed | as needed | |

1. Cut each slice of bread in half. Brush both sides of each piece with melted butter.

2. Arrange the bread slices so they overlap in a buttered 10 × 12 in. (25 × 30 cm) baking pan. (To use a full-size hotel pan, double the quantities.)

3. Mix together the eggs, sugar, salt, and vanilla until thoroughly combined. Add the milk.

4. Pour the egg mixture over the bread in the pan.

5. Let stand, refrigerated, for 1 hour or longer, so the bread absorbs the custard mixture. If necessary, push the bread down into the pan once or twice after the mixture has had time to stand.

6. Sprinkle the top lightly with cinnamon and nutmeg.

7. Set the pan in a larger pan containing about 1 in. (2.5 cm) hot water.

8. Place in an oven preheated to 350°F (175°C). Bake about 1 hour until set.

9. Serve warm or cold with whipped cream or crème anglaise (p. 269), a fruit purée, or confectioners' sugar.

## VARIATIONS

For a richer pudding, substitute cream for up to half of the milk.

Add 4 oz (125 g) raisins to the pudding, sprinkling them between the layers of bread.

### BRANDY OR WHISKEY BREAD PUDDING

Add 2 oz (60 mL) brandy or whiskey to the custard mixture.

### CABINET PUDDING

Prepare in individual custard cups instead of a baking pan. Substitute diced sponge cake for the bread and omit the melted butter. Add about 1½ tsp (4 g) raisins to each cup before pouring in the custard mix.

### DRIED CHERRY BREAD PUDDING

Add 4–6 oz (125–185 g) dried cherries to the bread pudding, sprinkling them between the layers of the bread. Substitute heavy cream for up to half of the milk.

# CHOCOLATE BREAD PUDDING

*Yield: about 5 lb (2500 g)*

| Ingredients | U.S. | | Metric | Procedure |
|---|---|---|---|---|
| Heavy cream | 1 lb | 4 oz | 625 g | 1. Combine the cream, milk, and sugar in a heavy saucepan. Heat, stirring, until the sugar is dissolved. |
| Milk | 1 lb | 4 oz | 625 g | |
| Sugar | | 6 oz | 180 g | 2. Remove the pan from the heat and let cool 1 minute. Then add the chocolate and stir until it is melted and completely blended in. |
| Bittersweet chocolate, chopped | | 12 oz | 350 g | |
| Dark rum | | 2 oz | 60 g | 3. Add the rum and vanilla. |
| Vanilla extract | | 2 tsp | 10 g | 4. Beat the eggs in a bowl, then gradually beat in the warm chocolate mixture. |
| Eggs | | 8 | 8 | |
| White bread, in thick slices, crusts trimmed (see *Note*) | 1 lb | | 500 g | 5. Cut the bread into large dice and place in a buttered half-size hotel pan or baking pan (10 × 12 in. or 25 × 30 cm), or use two 8-in. (20 cm) square pans. Pour the chocolate mixture over the bread. If any bread is not coated with the chocolate mixture, push it down into the chocolate to coat it. |

*Note: A good-quality, rich white bread, such as challah (p. 150), is recommended for this recipe.*

6. Let stand, refrigerated, for 1 hour or longer, so the bread absorbs the custard mixture. If necessary, push the bread down into the pan once or twice after the mixture has had time to stand.

7. Bake at 350°F (175°C) until set, about 30–45 minutes.

# RICE PUDDING

*Yield: about 4 lb 8 oz (2.25 kg)*

| Ingredients | U.S. | | Metric | Procedure |
|---|---|---|---|---|
| Rice, medium- or long-grain | 8 | oz | 250 g | 1. Wash the rice well. Drain. (See *Note*.) |
| Milk | 3 lb (3 pt) | | 1500 mL | 2. Combine the rice, milk, vanilla, and salt in a heavy saucepan. Cover and simmer over low heat until the rice is tender, about 30 minutes. Stir occasionally to be sure the mixture doesn't scorch on the bottom. Remove from the heat when cooked. |
| Vanilla extract | 0.16 oz (1 tsp) | | 5 mL | |
| Salt | 0.04 oz (¼ tsp) | | 2 g | |
| Egg yolks | 3 | oz | 95 g | 3. Combine the egg yolks, sugar, and cream in a mixing bowl. Mix until evenly combined. |
| Sugar | 8 | oz | 250 g | 4. Ladle some of the hot milk from the cooked rice into this mixture and mix well. Then slowly stir the egg mixture back into the hot rice. |
| Light cream | 8 | oz (½ pt) | 250 mL | |
| Cinnamon | as needed | | as needed | 5. Pour into a buttered 10 × 12 in. (25 × 30 cm) baking pan. Sprinkle the top with cinnamon. (To use a full-size hotel pan, double the quantities.) |

6. Bake in a water bath at 350°F (175°C) 30–40 minutes, or until set. Serve warm or chilled.

*Note: In order to remove even more loose starch, some cooks prefer to blanch the rice in boiling water for 2 minutes, then drain and rinse it.*

## VARIATIONS

### RAISIN RICE PUDDING

Add 4 oz (125 g) raisins to the cooked rice and milk mixture.

### RICE CONDÉ

Make the following adjustments:

Increase the rice to 10.5 oz (325 g).

Increase the egg yolks to 5 oz (150 g).

Omit the cinnamon.

As soon as the egg yolks have been incorporated, pour the rice mixture into shallow individual buttered molds. Bake as in the basic recipe, then chill until firm. Unmold onto serving dishes.

Rice Condé can be served plain or with whipped cream or fruit sauce, or used as a base for poached fruit. Arrange the fruit on top of the unmolded rice; brush with Apricot Glaze (p. 200). Dishes made in this way are named after their fruit, such as Apricot Condé or Pear Condé.

### TAPIOCA PUDDING

This pudding is prepared like rice pudding through step 4 in the procedure. However, it is not baked. Instead, whipped egg whites are folded in and the mixture is chilled. To prepare, make the following adjustments in the recipe:

Substitute 4 oz (125 g) tapioca for the 8 oz (250 g) rice. Do not wash the tapioca. Cook it in the milk until tender.

Reserve 2 oz (60 g) of the sugar (from step 3) for the meringue.

After the egg yolks are incorporated, return the pudding to low heat for a few minutes to cook the yolks. Stir constantly. Do not let the mixture boil.

Whip 4 oz (125 g) egg whites with the reserved 2 oz (60 g) sugar to a soft meringue. Fold into the hot pudding. Chill.

# CREAM CHEESECAKE

*Yield: enough for four 10-in. (25 cm) cakes, five 9-in. (23 cm) cakes, or six 8-in. (20 cm) cakes*

| Ingredients | U.S. | | Metric |
|---|---|---|---|
| Cream cheese | 10 lb | | 4500 g |
| Sugar | 3 lb 8 | oz | 1575 g |
| Cornstarch | 3 | oz | 90 g |
| Lemon zest, grated | 0.5 | oz | 15 g |
| Vanilla extract | 1 | oz | 30 g |
| Salt | 1.5 | oz | 45 g |
| Eggs | 2 lb | | 900 g |
| Egg yolks | 12 | oz | 340 g |
| Heavy cream | 1 lb | | 450 g |
| Milk | 8 | oz | 225 g |
| Lemon juice | 2 | oz | 60 g |
| Short Dough (p. 320) or sponge cake for lining pans | | | |
| **Total Weight:** | **18 lb 4** | **oz** | **8230 g** |

**Procedure**

1. Prepare the pans by lining the bottoms with either a very thin layer of sponge cake or a thin layer of short dough. Bake the short dough until it begins to turn golden.

2. Put the cream cheese in the mixing bowl and, with the paddle attachment, mix at low speed until it is smooth and lump free.

3. Add the sugar, cornstarch, lemon zest, vanilla, and salt. Blend in until smooth and uniform, but do not whip. Scrape down the sides of the bowl and the beater.

4. Add the eggs and egg yolks, a little at a time, blending in thoroughly after each addition. Scrape down the bowl again to make sure the mixture is well blended.

5. With the machine running at low speed, gradually add the cream, milk, and lemon juice.

6. Fill the prepared pans. Scale as follows:

   | | |
   |---|---|
   | 10-in. pans—4½ lb | 25-cm pans—2050 g |
   | 9-in. pans—3½ lb | 23-cm pans—1600 g |
   | 8-in. pans—3 lb | 20-cm pans—1350 g |

7. To bake without a water bath, place the filled pans on sheet pans and set them in an oven preheated to 400°F (200°C). After 10 minutes, turn down the oven to 225°F (105°C) and continue baking until the mixture is set, about 1–1½ hours, depending on the size of the cake.

8. To bake with a water bath, set the filled pans inside another, larger pan. Fill the outer pan with water and bake at 350°F (175°C) until set.

9. Cool the cakes completely before removing them from pans. To unmold a cake from a pan without removable sides, sprinkle the top of the cake with granulated sugar. Invert the cake onto a cardboard cake circle, then immediately place another circle over the bottom and turn it right-side up.

*Note: Cheesecake may be baked with or without a water bath. Baking in a water bath results in cakes with browned tops and unbrowned sides. Baking without a water bath results in browned sides and a lighter top. If you are not using a water bath, you may use either deep layer cake pans or springform pans (pans with removable sides). However, if you are using a water bath, you must use deep cake pans, not springform pans.*

**VARIATIONS**

## CHEESECAKE WITH BAKER'S CHEESE

In place of the 10 lb cream cheese, use 7½ lb (3400 g) baker's cheese plus either 3 lb (1350 g) butter or 2½ lb (1125 g) shortening. If desired, you may use all milk instead of part milk and part cream in step 5.

## FRENCH CHEESECAKE

This cheesecake has a lighter texture achieved by incorporating whipped egg whites into the batter of either the cream cheese version or the baker's cheese version. To make French cheesecake, make the following adjustments in either recipe above:

Increase the cornstarch to 5 oz (150 g).

Reserve 1 lb (450 g) of the sugar and whip it with 2 lb 4 oz (1040 g) egg whites to make a soft meringue.

Fold the meringue into the cheese batter before filling the pans.

## CHEESECAKE

One meaning of the word *cake* is a baked, leavened confection made of flour, eggs, sugar, and other ingredients, usually made in a round or rectangular shape. This type of cake is covered in chapter 16. Another meaning of *cake* is a shaped or molded mass of some substance, such as a cake of soap or a lump of snow caked on your boots. Many food preparations called *cakes* are closer to this second definition, and even some leavened flour goods, like pancakes, aren't normally discussed with the kind of cake discussed in chapter 16.

In some baking discussions, cheesecakes are discussed along with flour-based cakes. Technically, however, cheesecake is the same type of preparation as baked custard or pumpkin pie filling. It is a liquid mixture of milk, sugar, eggs, and cream cheese that becomes firm when the eggs coagulate. The fact that it happens to be called a cake has nothing to do with its composition. Cheesecake belongs in the cake chapter no more than do funnel cakes (a type of fritter), crab cakes, or black bean cakes.

Cheesecakes in many styles are made around the world, using local cheese. In North America, most cheesecake is made with cream cheese. New York–style cheesecake is perhaps the richest of these, being made with heavy cream in addition to cream cheese. Cakes made with lower-fat baker's cheese are also found, but less often. In Italy, the dessert is made with ricotta cheese, and in Germany it is made with a fresh cheese called *quark*. Unbaked cheesecakes, which rely on gelatin rather than coagulated eggs to enable them to set firm, are a type of Bavarian cream (see p. 532) rather than a baked custard.

## Steamed Puddings

Steamed puddings are primarily cold-weather fare. Their heavy, dense texture and richness make them warming, comforting desserts on winter nights. These same characteristics, however, make them inappropriate for year-round use.

The most famous steamed pudding is the English **Christmas pudding**, known in much of North America as *plum pudding*. A Christmas pudding, well made and with good ingredients, offers an unforgettable combination of flavors. The long list of ingredients makes the recipe look difficult, but once the ingredients are assembled and scaled, the pudding is simple to produce.

In addition to Christmas pudding, recipes for less complex steamed puddings are included to give you an idea of the range of possibilities. Many steamed puddings could be baked in a water bath, but steaming is more energy-efficient and helps keep the pudding moist during the long cooking time.

If a compartment steamer is available, simply set the filled, covered pudding molds in steamer pans and place them in the steamer. To steam on top of the stove, set the covered molds in large, deep pans and pour in enough hot water to come halfway up the sides of the molds. Bring the water to a boil, lower the heat to a gentle simmer, and cover the pan. Check the pan periodically and add more hot water as needed.

# CHRISTMAS PUDDING

*For large-quantity measurements, see page 740.*

| Ingredients | U.S. | | Metric | | Procedure |
|---|---|---|---|---|---|
| Dark raisins | 8 | oz | 250 | g | 1. Soak the fruits and almonds in the brandy for 24 hours. |
| Light raisins | 8 | oz | 250 | g | 2. Sift the flour with the spices. |
| Currants | 8 | oz | 250 | g | 3. Combine the flour mixture, suet, sugar, eggs, crumbs, and molasses. Add the fruit and brandy and mix well. |
| Dates, diced | 4 | oz | 125 | g | |
| Almonds, chopped | 3 | oz | 90 | g | |
| Candied orange peel, finely chopped | 2 | oz | 60 | g | 4. Fill greased pudding molds, allowing a little room for expansion. Cover the pudding mixture with rounds of greased parchment cut to fit inside the molds. Then cover the molds with foil and tie with string so steam does not get inside. |
| Candied lemon peel, finely chopped | 2 | oz | 60 | g | |
| Brandy | 6 | oz | 190 | mL | 5. Steam 4–6 hours, depending on size. |
| Bread flour | 4 | oz | 125 | g | 6. For storage, cool the puddings until just warm, then unmold. Wrap in cheesecloth and cool completely, then wrap again in plastic. The puddings will keep a year or more if sprinkled with brandy or rum every 7–10 days. |
| Cinnamon | ½ | tsp | 2 | mL | |
| Nutmeg | ⅛ | tsp | 0.5 | mL | |
| Mace | ⅛ | tsp | 0.5 | mL | |
| Ginger | ⅛ | tsp | 0.5 | mL | |
| Cloves, ground | ⅛ | tsp | 0.5 | mL | |
| Salt | 0.13 oz (⅝ tsp) | | 4 | g | 7. Christmas pudding must be served warm. To reheat it, place it in molds and steam 1–2 hours, or until heated through. Serve with Hard Sauce (p. 283). |
| Beef suet, finely chopped | 6 | oz | 190 | g | |
| Brown sugar | 4 | oz | 125 | g | |
| Eggs | 4 | oz | 125 | g | |
| Fresh bread crumbs | 2 | oz | 60 | g | |
| Molasses | 0.5 | oz | 15 | g | |
| *Total Weight:* | *3 lb 13* | *oz* | *1915* | *g* | |

# STEAMED BLUEBERRY PUDDING

*For large-quantity measurements, see page 741.*

| Ingredients | U.S. | | Metric | | Procedure |
|---|---|---|---|---|---|
| Brown sugar | 5 | oz | 150 | g | 1. Cream together the sugar, butter, salt, and cinnamon. |
| Butter | 2 | oz | 60 | g | 2. Blend in the eggs, a little at a time. Cream until light. |
| Salt | ⅛ | tsp | 0.5 | mL | 3. Sift the flour with the baking powder, then mix with the |
| Cinnamon | ¾ | tsp | 4 | mL | bread crumbs. |
| Eggs | 2 | oz | 60 | g | 4. Add the dry ingredients to the sugar mixture alternately |
| Bread flour | 1 | oz | 30 | g | with the milk. Blend to a smooth batter. |
| Baking powder | 0.18 oz (1 tsp) | | 6 | g | 5. Carefully fold in the blueberries. |
| Dry bread crumbs | 5 | oz | 150 | g | 6. Fill well-greased molds about two-thirds full. Cover |
| Milk | 4 | oz | 125 | g | tightly and steam for 1½–2 hours, depending on the |
| Blueberries, fresh or frozen, without sugar | 4 | oz | 125 | g | size of the molds. |
| **Total Weight:** | **1 lb 7** | **oz** | **706** | **g** | 7. Unmold and serve hot with Hard Sauce (p. 283) or Crème Anglaise (p. 269). |

### VARIATIONS

#### STEAMED RAISIN SPICE PUDDING

Add 1 oz (30 g) molasses, ¼ tsp (1 mL) ginger, and ⅛ tsp (0.5 mL) mace to the sugar mixture. In place of the blueberries, use 3 oz (90 g) raisins, soaked and drained, and 2 oz (60 g) chopped nuts. Serve hot with Hard Sauce (p. 283), Crème Anglaise (p. 269), or Lemon Sauce (p. 277).

# STEAMED CHOCOLATE ALMOND PUDDING

| Ingredients | U.S. | | Metric | Procedure |
|---|---|---|---|---|
| Butter | 4 | oz | 125 g | 1. Cream the butter, sugar, and salt until light. Blend in the |
| Sugar | 5 | oz | 150 g | chocolate. |
| Salt | 0.04 oz (¼ tsp) | | 1 g | 2. Add the egg yolks in 2 or 3 stages, then blend in the |
| Unsweetened chocolate, melted | 1.5 | oz | 45 g | milk or rum. Scrape down the bowl to eliminate lumps. |
| Egg yolks | 3 | oz | 90 g | 3. Blend in the almond powder and bread crumbs. |
| Milk or dark rum | 1 | oz | 30 g | 4. Whip the egg whites and sugar to a soft meringue. Fold |
| Powdered almonds | 6 | oz | 190 g | the meringue into the batter. |
| Dry bread crumbs | 1 | oz | 30 g | 5. Butter the insides of molds and sprinkle with sugar. Fill |
| Egg whites | 5 | oz | 150 g | three-fourths full with batter. Cover tightly and steam |
| Sugar | 1.5 | oz | 45 g | 1½ hours. |
| **Total Weight:** | **1 lb 12** | **oz** | **856 g** | 6. Unmold and serve hot with Chocolate Sauce (p. 278) or whipped cream. |

# BAVARIANS AND MOUSSES

Bavarians and mousses, along with soufflés, still-frozen desserts, and many other items discussed later in this chapter, have one thing in common: They all have a light, fluffy texture created by the addition of whipped cream, beaten egg whites, or both.

Bavarian creams are classic gelatin desserts containing custard and whipped cream. Chiffon pie fillings, discussed in chapter 13, are similar to Bavarians in that they are stabilized with gelatin and have a light, foamy texture. In the case of chiffons, however, this texture is due primarily to whipped egg whites; whipped cream may or may not be added. Chiffon pie fillings may also be served as puddings and chilled desserts.

Mousses may have a softer texture than Bavarians, although there is no precise dividing line between the two. Many desserts called *mousses* are made exactly like Bavarians. However, many mousses, especially chocolate mousses, are made without gelatin or with only a small amount. The light texture of mousses is created by adding whipped cream, meringue, or both.

## Bavarians

A Bavarian, also known as **Bavarian cream**, is made of three basic elements: custard sauce or crème anglaise (flavored as desired), gelatin, and whipped cream. That's all there is to it. Gelatin is softened in cold liquid, stirred into hot custard sauce until dissolved, and chilled until almost set. Whipped cream is then folded in, and the mixture is poured into a mold until set. It is unmolded for service.

Accurate measurement of the gelatin is important. If not enough gelatin is used, the dessert will be too soft to hold its shape. If too much is used, the cream will be too firm and rubbery. The use of gelatin is discussed in detail in chapter 4 (p. 86) and in the section of chapter 13 pertaining to chiffon pie fillings (p. 309).

Fruit Bavarians can be made like regular custard-based Bavarian creams by adding fruit purées and flavorings to the custard base. They can also be made without a custard base by adding gelatin to a sweetened fruit purée and then folding in whipped cream. A separate recipe is included for basic fruit Bavarian creams. In addition, recipes for several modern specialty Bavarian creams are found in this section.

Because they can be molded and decorated in many ways, Bavarian creams can be used to make elaborate, elegant desserts. They are the basis for a variety of desserts called **cold charlottes**, which are Bavarian creams molded in ring molds lined with various sponge cake products. Classic cold charlottes are usually decorated with whipped cream and fresh fruits, and are perhaps served with a fruit coulis. Procedures for assembling two famous charlottes from the classic pastry shop are included following the basic vanilla Bavarian recipe. (Although made in the same type of mold, hot charlottes are quite different from cold charlottes. See p. 592.)

Modern pastry chefs have created a new family of charlottes as a medium for displaying their decorative skills. This chapter includes several recipes of this type as examples of how flavorful and eye-appealing modern desserts can be created using classic techniques. These charlottes are made in large ring molds, but please note they can also be made in single-portion sizes by using small

---

### ✻{ CHARLOTTE }✻

The first printed use of the word *charlotte* for a dessert dates to 1796, and refers to the baked apple dessert still made today (p. 592). This dessert consists of apples baked in a mold lined with buttered slices of bread. It may have been named for Queen Charlotte, wife of the English King George III.

Only a few years later, the great pastry chef Carême (see p. 7) borrowed the name *charlotte* for one of his own creations, a cold, gelatin-based creamy dessert made in a mold lined with ladyfingers or sponge cake. He made the dessert while working in England and called it *Charlotte à la Parisienne*. Although no one knows for sure, the name *Charlotte Russe* may have been adopted at a banquet in honor of the Russian Tsar Alexander I.

ring molds 2¾ inches (7 cm) in diameter, just like several of the pastries in chapter 15. See page 370 for an illustration of the technique.

This section includes two other desserts made with the same techniques. *Rice Impératrice*, or empress rice, is an elegant molded rice pudding. The base is made somewhat like custard sauce (which is the base for Bavarian cream), except the rice is cooked in the milk before the egg yolks and gelatin are added. Whipped cream is then folded in. (Another way of arriving at the same result is to combine equal parts Rice Condé mixture, found on p. 527, and Vanilla Bavarian Cream mixture, plus the candied fruit mixture indicated in the recipe on p. 536.)

Cream cheese Bavarian is not made with a cooked custard base, but it contains gelatin and whipped cream. Thus it is similar in character and texture to other Bavarian creams. Similarly, three of the creams among the following recipes are based on pastry cream rather than crème anglaise like true Bavarian creams, although they belong in this section because of their gelatin and whipped cream content.

If a gelatin-based dessert is made in a bowl-shaped mold rather than a ring mold, unmold it by dipping the mold into hot water for 1 or 2 seconds. Quickly wipe the bottom of the mold and turn it over onto the serving plate (or invert the plate over the mold and flip the plate and mold over together). Alternatively, warm the mold carefully and briefly with a torch. If the dessert doesn't unmold after a gentle shake, repeat the warming procedure. Do not hold in the hot water for more than a few seconds or the gelatin will begin to melt.

## Procedure for Preparing Bavarian and Bavarian-Type Creams

1. Prepare the base—either Crème Anglaise (p. 269) or another base indicated in recipe.

2. Soften the gelatin in cold liquid and stir it into the hot base until dissolved. Or, if the base is not cooked, heat the gelatin and liquid until the gelatin is dissolved, then stir it into the base. Be careful the base isn't too cold, or the gelatin may congeal too quickly and form lumps.

3. Cool the mixture until thick but not set. This is done most quickly by setting the bowl in an ice-water bath and stirring constantly.

4. Fold in the whipped cream.

5. Pour the mixture into prepared molds and chill until set.

## Mousses

There are so many varieties of mousse it is impossible to give a rule for all of them. In general, we could define a *mousse* as any soft or creamy dessert made light and fluffy by the addition of whipped cream, beaten egg whites, or both. Note that Bavarians and chiffons fit this description. In fact, they are often served as mousses, but with the gelatin reduced or left out so the mousse is softer.

There are many kinds of bases for mousses. They may be nothing more than melted chocolate or puréed fresh fruit, or they may be more complex, like the bases for chiffons.

Some mousses contain both beaten egg whites and whipped cream. When this is the case, most chefs prefer to fold in the egg whites first, even though they may lose some volume. The reason is that if the cream is added first, there is more danger it will be overbeaten and turn to butter during the folding and mixing procedure.

If egg whites are folded into a *hot* base, they will cook or coagulate, making the mousse firmer and more stable. Whipped cream should never be folded into hot mixtures because it will melt and deflate.

In addition to the chocolate mousse recipes included in this section and the additional recipes in chapter 12 (pp. 276–277), you can also convert the chiffon pie filling recipes (p. 308) and the Bavarian cream recipes (pp. 534–536) to mousses. Just reduce the quantity of gelatin to one-third or one-half the amount indicated in the recipe. For creamier mousses made from the chiffon recipes, substitute whipped cream for part of the meringue. (Some of the variations following the main recipes indicate this substitution.) By making these recipe adjustments, you can make a number of popular mousses—including raspberry, strawberry, lemon, orange, and pumpkin—without needing separate recipes.

The chocolate terrine on page 547 could be said to be a chocolate mousse thick enough to be sliced. Compare this recipe to the recipe for Chocolate Mousse I on page 276. You will see that the procedures are almost the same, although the ingredient proportions are different.

# VANILLA BAVARIAN CREAM

*Yield: about 1½ qt (1.5 L)*

| Ingredients | U.S. | | Metric | Procedure |
|---|---|---|---|---|
| Gelatin | 0.75 oz | | 22 g | 1. Soak the gelatin in the cold water. |
| Water, cold | 5 | oz | 150 mL | |
| **Crème anglaise** | | | | 2. *Prepare the crème anglaise.* Whip the egg yolks and sugar until thick and light. Scald the milk and slowly stir it into the egg yolk mixture, beating constantly. Cook over a hot-water bath, stirring constantly, until it thickens slightly. (Review p. 268 for a detailed discussion of making crème anglaise.) |
| Egg yolks | 4 | oz | 125 g | |
| Sugar | 4 | oz | 125 g | |
| Milk | 1 pt | | 500 mL | |
| Vanilla | 0.25 oz | | 8 mL | |
| Heavy cream | 1 pt | | 500 mL | 3. Stir the gelatin mixture into the hot custard sauce until it is dissolved. |

4. Cool the custard sauce in the refrigerator or over crushed ice, stirring occasionally to keep the mixture smooth.

5. Whip the cream until it forms soft peaks. Do not overwhip.

6. When the custard is very thick but not yet set, fold in the whipped cream.

7. Pour the mixture into molds or serving dishes.

8. Chill until completely set. If prepared in molds, unmold for service.

## VARIATIONS

### CHOCOLATE BAVARIAN CREAM

Add 6 oz (190 g) dark chocolate, chopped or grated, to the hot custard sauce. Stir until completely melted and blended in.

### WHITE CHOCOLATE BAVARIAN CREAM

Add 8 oz (250 g) white chocolate, chopped or grated, to the hot custard sauce. Stir until completely melted and blended in.

### COFFEE BAVARIAN CREAM

Add 1½ tbsp (6 g) instant coffee powder to the hot custard sauce.

### STRAWBERRY BAVARIAN CREAM

Reduce the milk to 8 oz (250 mL) and the sugar to 3 oz (90 g). Mash 8 oz (250 g) strawberries with 3 oz sugar (90 g), or use 12 oz (375 g) frozen, sweetened strawberries. Stir this purée into the custard sauce before adding the whipped cream.

### RASPBERRY BAVARIAN CREAM

Prepare like Strawberry Bavarian Cream, using raspberries.

### LIQUEUR BAVARIAN CREAM

Flavor to taste with a liqueur or spirit, such as orange, kirsch, maraschino, amaretto, or rum.

### PRALINE BAVARIAN CREAM

Mix 3 oz (95 g) praline paste with the hot custard sauce.

## DIPLOMAT BAVARIAN CREAM

Moisten diced sponge cake (about 4 oz/125 g) and diced candied fruit (about 4 oz/125 g) with kirsch (about 1½ oz/45 ml). Mix gently with Vanilla Bavarian mixture.

## ORANGE BAVARIAN CREAM

Proceed as in the basic recipe, except omit the vanilla and reduce the milk to 8 oz (250 mL). Flavor the custard sauce with the grated zest of 1 orange or with orange flavor. Before adding the whipped cream, stir 8 oz (250 mL) orange juice into the cold custard mixture.

## CHARLOTTE RUSSE

Line the bottom and sides of a charlotte mold with ladyfingers (p. 412). For the bottom, cut the ladyfingers into triangles and fit them close together so the points meet in the center. The ladyfingers must fit tightly, with no space between them. Fill the mold with Bavarian cream mixture and chill until set. Before unmolding, trim the tops of the ladyfingers so they are level with the cream, if necessary.

Another method for making Charlotte Russe, although not authentic, yields an attractive dessert. Mold some Bavarian cream mixture in an unlined charlotte mold. After unmolding, cover the top and sides with ladyfingers or Langues de Chat (p. 502), using a little melted Bavarian mixture to make them stick. Decorate with whipped cream.

## CHARLOTTE ROYALE

Line a round mold with thin slices of a small jelly roll. Fit them close together so there is no space between them. Fill the mold with Bavarian mixture and chill until set. If desired, the charlotte may be glazed with Apricot Glaze (p. 200) after unmolding.

# FRUIT BAVARIAN

*Yield: about 2½ pt (1.25 L)*

| Ingredients | U.S. | | Metric | Procedure |
|---|---|---|---|---|
| Fruit purée (see Note) | 8 | oz | 250 g | 1. Force the fruit purée through a fine sieve. Mix it with the sugar and lemon juice. Stir the mixture or let it stand until the sugar is completely dissolved. |
| Extra-fine granulated sugar | 4 | oz | 125 g | |
| Lemon juice | 1 | oz | 30 mL | 2. Soften the gelatin in the cold water for 5 minutes. Heat the mixture gently until the gelatin is dissolved. |
| Gelatin | 0.5 | oz | 15 g | 3. Stir the gelatin mixture into the fruit purée. |
| Water, cold | 5 | oz | 150 mL | 4. Chill the mixture until thickened but not set. *Note:* If the fruit purée is cold when the gelatin is added, it will start to set very quickly, so further chilling may not be needed. |
| Heavy cream | 12 | oz | 375 mL | 5. Whip the cream until it forms soft peaks. Do not overwhip. |

*Note: Use 8 oz (250 g) unsweetened or lightly sweetened fresh, frozen, or canned fruit, such as strawberries, raspberries, apricots, pineapple, peaches, or bananas. For heavily sweetened fruit, such as frozen, sweetened strawberries, use 10 oz (300 g) fruit and reduce the sugar to 2 oz (60 g).*

6. Fold the cream into the fruit mixture. Pour it into molds and chill.

# RICE IMPÉRATRICE

*Yield: 1 qt (1 L)*

| Ingredients | U.S. | | Metric | | Procedure |
|---|---|---|---|---|---|
| Rice, long-grain | 3 | oz | 90 | g | 1. Rinse and drain the rice. Simmer it slowly in the milk, covered, until tender. Add the vanilla. |
| Milk | 1 pt | | 0.5 | L | |
| Vanilla | 0.25 | oz | 8 | mL | |
| Egg yolks | 2 | oz | 60 | g | 2. Whip the egg yolks and sugar together. Stir in a little of the hot milk from the rice mixture. Then stir the egg yolk mixture into the rice mixture. Cook very slowly for a few minutes, stirring constantly, until it is lightly thickened. |
| Sugar | 3 | oz | 90 | g | |
| Gelatin | 0.25 | oz | 8 | g | 3. Soften the gelatin in the water. Stir the gelatin mixture into the hot rice mixture until the gelatin is dissolved. (*Note:* For buffet service or in hot weather, increase the gelatin to 0.4 oz (11 g).) |
| Water, cold | 2 | oz | 60 | mL | |
| Candied fruits, diced | 3 | oz | 90 | g | 4. Stir in the candied fruits, which have been soaked in the kirsch. |
| Kirsch | 1 | oz | 30 | mL | 5. Chill the mixture until thick but not set. |
| Heavy cream | 6 | oz | 180 | mL | 6. Whip the heavy cream until it forms soft peaks. Fold it into the rice mixture. |

*Note: A traditional way of preparing this dish is to line the bottoms of the molds with about ¼ in. (6 mm) red fruit gelatin. For the quantity in this recipe, you will need about ¼ pt (125 mL) gelatin mixture. Use either 1 oz (30 g) flavored gelatin mix dissolved in 4 oz (125 mL) water or 1⁄16 oz (⅜ tsp/2 g) plain gelatin dissolved in 4 oz (125 mL) sweetened red fruit juice. Pour it into molds and chill until set.*

7. Pour into molds (see *Note*). Chill until set. Unmold onto serving plates. Decorate with candied fruits and whipped cream, if desired. Serve with Melba Sauce (p. 279).

# CREAM CHEESE BAVARIAN

*For large-quantity measurements, see page 741.*
*Yield: about 1½ qt (1.6 L)*

| Ingredients | U.S. | | Metric | | Procedure |
|---|---|---|---|---|---|
| Cream cheese | 12 | oz | 375 | g | 1. Place the cream cheese in the bowl of a mixer and mix at low speed to soften it. Add the sugar, salt, and flavorings and blend until smooth. Scrape down the sides of the bowl to eliminate lumps. |
| Sugar | 4 | oz | 125 | g | |
| Salt | 0.12 oz (⅝ tsp) | | 4 | g | |
| Lemon zest, grated | 0.03 oz (⅜ tsp) | | 1 | g | 2. Blend in the lemon juice. |
| Orange zest, grated | 0.02 oz (¼ tsp) | | 0.5 | g | 3. Soften the gelatin in the water, then heat the water gently until the gelatin is dissolved. |
| Vanilla extract | 0.06 oz (⅜ tsp) | | 2 | g | |
| Lemon juice | 1 | oz | 30 | g | 4. Whip the cream until it forms soft, not stiff peaks. Do not overwhip. |
| Gelatin | 0.25 | oz | 8 | g | 5. Blend the warm gelatin mixture into the cream cheese mixture. Scrape down the bowl to make sure the gelatin is mixed in well. |
| Water, cold | 2 | oz | 60 | g | |
| Heavy cream | 1 pt | | 500 | mL | 6. Immediately fold in the cream. Do not let the cheese mixture stand after adding the gelatin, as it will set very quickly. |
| **Total weight:** | **2 lb 3** | **oz** | **1105** | **g** | 7. Pour the mixture into prepared molds or serving dishes. Chill until set. |

VARIATIONS

## ICEBOX CHEESECAKE

Use one of the following methods:

1. Line the bottoms of cake pans or springform pans with thin sheets of sponge cake or with a crumb crust mixture. Pour in the cream cheese Bavarian mixture and chill until set. Unmold.

2. Follow the procedure for Bavarian Cream Torte (p. 465), using the cream cheese Bavarian mixture.

One full recipe is enough for one 9-in. (23 cm) cake.

# ORANGE CHEESE MOUSSE

| Ingredients | U.S. | | Metric | Procedure |
|---|---|---|---|---|
| **Italian meringue** | | | | 1. *Make the meringue:* Whip the egg whites to soft peaks. Make a syrup of the sugar and water and cook to 240°F (115°C). Gradually whip the hot syrup into the egg whites. Continue whipping until cold. Set aside. |
| Egg whites | 4 | oz | 125 g | |
| Sugar | 4 | oz | 125 g | |
| Water | 2.5 | oz | 70 g | |
| Gelatin | 0.33 | oz | 9 g | 2. Soften the gelatin in cold water (see p. 88). |
| Orange liqueur | 1.33 | oz | 40 g | 3. Heat the orange liqueur. Add the gelatin and stir to dissolve. |
| Cream cheese | 8 | oz | 250 g | 4. In a mixer with the paddle attachment, blend the cream cheese with the zest and a little of the orange juice until smooth. |
| Orange zest, grated | 1¾ | tsp | 4 g | |
| Orange juice, strained | 2 | oz | 60 g | 5. Mix in the gelatin and the remaining orange juice until smooth. |
| Heavy cream | 11 | oz | 350 g | 6. Whip the cream to soft peaks. Fold the meringue and the cream alternately into the cheese until smooth. |
| *Total Weight:* | *2 lb 1* | *oz* | *1033 g* | 7. Fill molds and chill. |

# UNBAKED ORANGE CHEESECAKE

*Yield: one 7-in. (18 cm) charlotte*

| Ingredients | U.S. | Metric | Procedure |
|---|---|---|---|
| Chocolate Pâte Sablée (p. 319) | 1 baked 7-in. circle, ⅛ in. thick | 1 baked 18-cm circle, 3 mm thick | 1. Spread the chocolate sablée circle with orange marmalade. Top with the sponge circle; brush the sponge with syrup. |
| Orange marmalade | 1–1.33 oz | 30–40 g | |
| Chocolate Genoise (p. 407) or other chocolate sponge | one 7-in. circle, ¼ in. thick | one 18-cm circle, 0.5 cm thick | 2. Place the sponge and sablée inside a 7-in. (18 cm) charlotte ring on a cake card. Fill to the top with the mousse and smooth the top with a palette knife. Chill until set. |
| Dessert syrup flavored with orange liqueur | as needed | as needed | 3. Remove the ring, using a blowtorch to gently warm the ring so it releases. |
| Orange Cheese Mousse (above) | 1 lb | 450–500 g | 4. Using a pastry bag with a star tip or a St-Honoré tip, decorate the border of the cake with crème chantilly as desired. Fill the center with kumquat compote. |
| **Decoration** | | | 5. Break the sheet of chocolate into random-size pieces and use to cover the sides of the cake. |
| Crème Chantilly (p. 265) | as needed | as needed | |
| Kumquat Compote (p. 601) | as needed | as needed | |
| Marbled or wood-grain chocolate slab (p. 644) | as needed | as needed | |

# THREE-CHOCOLATE BAVAROIS

*Yield: three 7-in. (18 cm) Bavarians*

| Ingredients | U.S. | | Metric | Procedure |
|---|---|---|---|---|
| Chocolate Sponge layers (p. 415), 6 in. (15 cm) in diameter | 3 | | 3 | 1. Line each of three 6½-in. (16 cm) charlotte rings with an acetate strip. |
| Cocoa Vanilla Syrup (p. 263) | 4 | oz | 125 g | 2. Place the rings on cake cards. Place a sponge layer in the base of each ring. (The sponge layers should be slightly smaller than the rings so there is a gap between the ring and sponge all the way around. If necessary, trim the sponge.) |
| **Crème anglaise** | | | | 3. Brush the sponge layers with the cocoa vanilla syrup. |
| Milk | 8 | oz | 250 g | |
| Heavy cream | 8 | oz | 250 g | 4. Prepare the crème anglaise according to the basic procedure on page 268. |
| Egg yolks | 5.5 | oz | 160 g | |
| Sugar | 3 | oz | 85 g | 5. Soften the gelatin in cold water (see p. 88). Add the gelatin to the hot crème anglaise and stir until dissolved. |
| Gelatin | 0.4 | oz | 12 g | |
| Dark chocolate, finely chopped | 2.75 oz | | 80 g | 6. Divide the crème anglaise into 3 equal portions. Add the dark chocolate to one bowl, the milk chocolate to the second, and the white chocolate to the third. Mix each thoroughly to melt the chocolate. |
| Milk chocolate, finely chopped | 2.75 oz | | 80 g | |
| White chocolate, finely chopped | 2.75 oz | | 80 g | |
| Heavy cream | 1 pt 5 | oz | 600 g | 7. Whip the cream into soft peaks. Divide the whipped cream into 3 equal portions. |
| Cocoa Jelly (p. 434) | 10 | oz | 300 g | |
| White chocolate for piping (p. 648) | as needed | | as needed | |

8. Cool the dark chocolate Bavarian over a cold-water bath until it is beginning to set. Fold in one-third of the whipped cream. Divide the chocolate Bavarian mixture among the 3 prepared charlotte rings, filling each about one-third full. Level the surfaces with an offset palette knife. Place in the refrigerator or freezer to set, approximately 20 minutes. The Bavarian should be firmly set before adding the next layer, or the layers will not be level.

9. Repeat step 8 with the milk chocolate, then with the white chocolate.

10. Place the finished layers in the freezer at least 1 hour.

11. Remove the charlottes from the freezer. Apply the cocoa jelly to the tops, running a palette knife across the top to smooth the glaze. Allow to set.

12. Decorate with piped white chocolate.

13. The ring molds may be removed at any time, but do not remove the acetate strips until ready to serve.

# ALMOND CREAM

| Ingredients | U.S. | | Metric | Procedure |
|---|---|---|---|---|
| **Crème anglaise** | | | | 1. *Make the crème anglaise:* Heat the milk, vanilla bean, and half the sugar until simmering. Meanwhile, whip the egg yolks with the remaining sugar. Gradually beat in the hot milk, then return to the heat and cook until just thickened enough to coat a spoon. |
| Milk | 10 | oz | 300 g | |
| Vanilla bean, split (see *Note*) | 1 | | 1 | |
| Sugar | 2.5 | oz | 75 g | 2. Stir in the marzipan in small pieces until smooth. |
| Egg yolks | 2 | oz | 60 g | 3. Soften the gelatin in cold water (see p. 88). |
| Marzipan | 1.67 | oz | 50 g | 4. Mix in the amaretto and the softened gelatin. Stir until the gelatin is dissolved. |
| Amaretto liqueur | 1 | oz | 30 g | |
| Gelatin | 0.4 | oz | 12 g | 5. Cool the mixture over ice, stirring to make sure it stays smooth as it thickens. |
| Heavy cream | 10 | oz | 300 g | 6. Before the mixture sets, whip the cream to soft peaks and fold in. Pour the mixture into molds and chill until set. |
| **Total Weight:** | **1 lb 11** | **oz** | **827 g** | |

*Note: If vanilla beans are not available, add ½ tsp (2 mL) vanilla extract in place of the vanilla bean.*

# PASSION FRUIT BAVARIAN

| Ingredients | U.S. | | Metric | Procedure |
|---|---|---|---|---|
| Milk | 7 | oz | 200 g | 1. Heat the milk and the first quantity of sugar in a pan. |
| Sugar | 3.5 | oz | 100 g | 2. Whip the yolks with the remaining second quantity of sugar. |
| Egg yolks | 6 | | 6 | |
| Sugar | 3.5 | oz | 100 g | 3. When the milk mixture comes to a boil, temper the yolks with one-fourth of this mix and return all to the pan. Cook to 185°F (85°C), being careful not to exceed this temperature. |
| Gelatin | 0.5 | oz | 14 g | |
| Passion fruit purée or juice | 7 | oz | 200 g | 4. Strain through a fine china cap. |
| | | | | 5. Soften the gelatin in cold water (see p. 88). |
| Heavy cream | 14 | oz | 400 g | 6. Bring the passion fruit pulp to a boil; add the gelatin and stir to dissolve. Stir over a cold-water bath until cooled to about 80°F (25°–28°C). Combine with the milk mixture. |
| **Total Weight:** | **2 lb 10** | **oz** | **920 g** | |
| | | | | 7. Whip the cream into soft peaks. Carefully fold in the whipped cream, working quickly before the gelatin sets. |
| | | | | 8. Pour into molds and chill. |

# CHARLOTTE AU CASSIS

*Yield: one 7-in. (18 cm) round charlotte*

| Ingredients | U.S. | Metric | Procedure |
|---|---|---|---|
| Plain Genoise sponge (p. 407) | Half-sheet pan, ¼ in. thick | Half-sheet pan, 0.5 cm thick | 1. Prepare the sponge for lining the mold. Cut one 6-in. (15 cm) circle from one end of the sponge sheet and reserve. Trim the remaining sponge to make a square about 12 in. (30 cm) on a side. Cut this square into 4 small squares of equal size. Spread 3 of the squares with raspberry jam and layer them. Top with the fourth sponge square. Press down lightly. Chill. (This makes enough for 2 charlottes; reserve the extra for later use.) |
| Raspberry jam | 3.5 oz | 100 g | |
| Sugar | 1.67 oz | 50 g | |
| Water | 1.67 oz | 50 g | |
| Crème de cassis liqueur | 1 oz | 30 g | |
| Mousse au Cassis (p. 541) | 1 lb 4 oz | 600 g | |
| Fruit Glaçage (p. 434) made with black-currant (cassis) purée | 2.5–3.5 oz | 75–100 g | |
| Berries and other soft fruits for decoration | as needed | as needed | |

2. Line a 7-in. (18 cm) charlotte ring. (This is the same procedure as for baumkuchen, illustrated on p. 455.) Cut the sponge square into strips whose width is two-thirds to three-fourths the height of the ring molds. The exact width is not important, as long as all the strips are the same width. Cut each of these strips crosswise into strips ¼ in. (5 mm) thick. Place the ring molds on cake cards. Arrange the strips of sponge around the inside of the ring molds, pressing them into place, so the stripes of raspberry jam are vertical. Continue until the ring is compactly lined with sponge.

3. Make a syrup by boiling the sugar and water until dissolved. Remove from the heat and add the liqueur. (This small amount of syrup is enough for at least 2 or 3 charlottes.)

4. Place the sponge circle inside the ring to make a base. Brush with the syrup.

5. Fill the ring to the top with the mousse aux cassis. Level with a palette knife. Chill until set.

6. Spread the warm glaçage over the tops and level with a palette knife. Chill until set.

7. Remove the rings by warming them slightly with a blowtorch to release them, then lifting off.

8. Decorate as desired.

### PASSION FRUIT CHARLOTTE

Make the following changes to the recipe:

Line the mold with yellow-striped Ribbon Sponge (p. 411), as illustrated on page 454.

In place of the cassis syrup for soaking the sponge, use a simple dessert syrup.

Substitute Passion Fruit Mousse (below) for the mousse aux cassis.

Use passion fruit purée for the glaçage. Add the seeds from one-half fresh passion fruit to the glaçage before applying to the charlotte.

The charlotte in the illustration is decorated with a bouquet of fruits and a free-form lattice made of piped choux pastry sprinkled with poppy seeds.

# MOUSSE AU CASSIS
# (BLACKCURRANT MOUSSE)

| Ingredients | U.S. | | Metric | Procedure |
|---|---|---|---|---|
| Gelatin | 0.33 oz | | 11 g | 1. Soften the gelatin in cold water (see p. 88). |
| Sugar | 1.67 oz | | 50 g | 2. Heat the sugar and water until the sugar is dissolved. Remove from the heat and add the softened gelatin. Stir until dissolved. |
| Water | 1 oz | | 30 g | |
| Blackcurrant (cassis) purée | 10 oz | | 300 g | 3. Add the fruit purée to the gelatin mixture. Stir over ice until it begins to set. |
| Heavy cream | 8 oz | | 250 g | 4. Whip the cream to soft peaks and immediately fold into the fruit purée. |
| *Total Weight:* | *1 lb 5 oz* | | *641 g* | 5. Fill molds and chill until set. |

### PASSION FRUIT MOUSSE

Substitute passion fruit purée for the blackcurrant purée in the main recipe. Omit the sugar and water syrup and instead use a syrup made of the following ingredients. Heat the water and sugar until dissolved. Remove from the heat and add the vodka.

| Ingredients | U.S. | Metric |
|---|---|---|
| Sugar | 1 oz | 27 g |
| Water | 1 oz | 27 g |
| Vodka | 0.5 oz | 16 g |

# NOUGATINE CREAM

| Ingredients | U.S. | | Metric | | Procedure |
|---|---|---|---|---|---|
| Gelatin | 0.25 | oz | 7.5 | g | 1. Soften the gelatin in cold water (see p. 88). |
| Pastry Cream (p. 271) | 11 | oz | 320 | g | 2. Heat the pastry cream just until hot. |
| Sugar | 3 | oz | 85 | g | 3. Add the softened gelatin and sugar. Stir until dissolved. |
| Crushed Nougatine (p. 668) | 8.5 | oz | 250 | g | 4. Add the nougatine. |
| | | | | | 5. When the temperature has dropped to about 85°F (30°C), stir in the kirsch. |
| Kirsch | 1.25 | oz | 35 | g | 6. Whip the cream into soft peaks and fold it into the mixture. |
| Heavy cream | 2 lb 6 | oz | 1100 | g | |
| **Total Weight:** | **3 lb 14** | **oz** | **1797** | **g** | 7. Pour into the desired molds and chill. |

# PRALINE CREAM I

| Ingredients | U.S. | | Metric | | Procedure |
|---|---|---|---|---|---|
| Gelatin | 0.12 | oz | 3 | g | 1. Soften the gelatin in cold water (see p. 88). |
| Pastry Cream (p. 271), freshly made and warm | 10 | oz | 250 | g | 2. Add the gelatin to the pastry cream and stir until dissolved. |
| Praline paste | 2 | oz | 50 | g | 3. Add the praline paste and mix in. |
| Heavy cream | 8 | oz | 200 | g | 4. Cool the mixture to about 75°–80°F (25°C). Whip the cream into soft peaks and mix about one-fourth of it into the mixture. |
| **Total Weight:** | **1 lb 4** | **oz** | **503 g** | | 5. Fold in the remaining whipped cream. |
| | | | | | 6. Pour into desired molds and chill. |

# PRALINE CREAM II

| Ingredients | U.S. | | Metric | | Procedure |
|---|---|---|---|---|---|
| Pastry Cream (p. 271) | 9 | oz | 225 | g | 1. Whip the pastry cream until it is smooth. Beat in the praline paste until well mixed in. |
| Praline paste | 3.5 | oz | 90 | g | 2. Soften the gelatin in cold water (see p. 88). |
| Gelatin | 0.25 | oz | 6 | g | 3. Heat the coffee liqueur. Add the gelatin and stir until dissolved, rewarming as necessary. |
| Coffee liqueur | 0.75 | oz | 20 | g | |
| Crushed Nougatine (p. 668) | 3 | oz | 75 | g | 4. Beat the gelatin mixture into the pastry cream. Chill. |
| | | | | | 5. Beat in the crushed nougatine. |
| Heavy cream | 8 | oz | 200 | g | 6. Whip the cream until it forms soft peaks. Fold in. |
| **Total Weight:** | **1 lb 8** | **oz** | **616** | **g** | |

# BANANA MOUSSE

| Ingredients | U.S. | | Metric | Procedure |
|---|---|---|---|---|
| Gelatin | 0.33 | oz | 8 g | 1. Soften the gelatin in cold water (see p. 88). |
| Banana pulp, fresh or frozen | 12 | oz | 310 g | 2. Heat one-third of the banana pulp to 140°F (60°C). Add the gelatin and stir until dissolved. |
| Lemon juice | 1 | oz | 25 g | 3. Mix in the lemon juice and sugar. Stir to dissolve the sugar. |
| Sugar | 1.33 | oz | 35 g | |
| White rum | 1 | oz | 25 g | 4. Add this mixture to the remaining banana pulp and mix in the rum. |
| Heavy cream | 1 lb | | 420 g | |
| *Total Weight:* | *1 lb 15* | *oz* | *823 g* | 5. Once this mixture has cooled to about 75°F (25°F), fold in the whipped cream. |
| | | | | 6. Fill molds and chill. |

# COCONUT MOUSSE WITH TROPICAL FRUIT

*Yield: about 1 lb 12 oz (800 g)*

| Ingredients | U.S. | | Metric | Procedure |
|---|---|---|---|---|
| Water | 4 | oz | 120 g | 1. For the fruit, heat together the water, coconut milk, and sugar to make a syrup. Add the diced mango and pineapple. Cover the surface with a round of parchment and poach the fruit for about 15 minutes, or until it is tender but still holding its shape. Do not overcook. Allow the fruit to cool in the syrup and then drain. |
| Coconut milk (unsweetened) | 4 | oz | 120 g | |
| Sugar | 7 | oz | 200 g | |
| Mango, diced | 5 | oz | 150 g | |
| Pineapple, diced | 5 | oz | 150 g | |
| Gelatin | 0.2 | oz | 6 g | 2. Soften the gelatin in cold water (see p. 88). |
| Milk | 1.67 | oz | 50 g | 3. Heat the milk, sugar, and coconut in a saucepan to about 175°F (80°C). Let stand a few minutes to allow the coconut to infuse. |
| Sugar | 1 | oz | 30 g | |
| Coconut, grated | 1 | oz | 30 g | |
| Coconut milk (unsweetened), chilled | 4.5 | oz | 140 g | 4. Remove from the heat and add the gelatin, stirring to dissolve. |
| Coconut-flavored liqueur | 4 | tsp | 20 g | 5. Add the second quantity of coconut milk. When the temperature has cooled to about 75°F (25°C), stir in the liqueur. |
| Heavy cream | 8 | oz | 250 g | 6. Whip the cream to soft peaks and fold in. |
| | | | | 7. Fold in the drained fruit. |
| | | | | 8. Pour into molds and chill. |

# L'EXOTIQUE

*Yield: one 6½-in. (16 cm) gâteau*

| Ingredients | U.S. | | Metric | Procedure |
|---|---|---|---|---|
| Ribbon Sponge (p. 411) | see step 1 | | see step 1 | 1. Line a 6½-in. (16 cm) charlotte ring with a strip of acetate. Prepare a multicolored sheet of ribbon sponge with an abstract pattern, as shown on p. 411. Cut a strip and line the charlotte ring as on p. 454, making the strip slightly narrower than the height of the ring so some of the filling shows above it. |
| Hazelnut Coconut Sponge layers (p. 350) 6 in. (15 cm) in diameter | 2 | | 2 | |
| Coconut Mousse with Tropical Fruit (p. 543) | 14 | oz | 400 g | 2. Place the ring on a cake card and put one of the sponge layers in the bottom.<br>3. Fill about one-third full with the coconut mousse. Smooth the top and chill until set. |
| Gelatin | 0.13 | oz | 4 g | 4. Soften the gelatin in cold water (see p. 88). |
| Mango pulp | 4 | oz | 125 g | 5. Heat about one-quarter of the mango pulp to 140°F (60°C), then stir in the gelatin and sugar until they are dissolved. Add the remaining mango pulp and stir. |
| Sugar | 0.4 | oz (2¾ tsp) | 12 g | |
| Passion Fruit Ganache (p. 276), warm | 6 | oz | 175 g | 6. Spread the jellied mango pulp on top of the coconut mousse once the mousse has set. Place in the freezer to set.<br>7. Spread a thin layer of the coconut mousse (about ½ in./1 cm thick) on top of the mango. |
| **Decoration** | | | | 8. Cover with the second layer of the sponge. |
| Chocolate for spraying | as needed | | as needed | 9. Finish with a third layer of the mousse, filling the mold to the top and leveling it. Place in the freezer to set. |
| Mango wedges | as needed | | as needed | 10. Spread a layer of warm ganache ½ in. (1 cm) thick over the frozen cake. (This depth is necessary because so much ganache is removed by the cake comb.) Before the ganache sets, quickly pass a cake comb over the top to make a design. |
| Passion fruit seeds and pulp | as needed | | as needed | |

11. Return to the freezer for 15 minutes to set.

12. Spray the top with a chocolate sprayer (see p. 648) to leave a velvety finish.

13. Remove the ring. Decorate the top with a few wedges of mango and a few passion fruit seeds.

L'Exotique cut to show the interior

# CHOCOLATE MOUSSE III

*Yield: about 2⅛ pt (1.12 L)*

| Ingredients | U.S. | Metric | Procedure |
|---|---|---|---|
| Bittersweet chocolate | 10 oz | 300 g | 1. In a saucepan, add the chocolate to the water and melt it over low heat, stirring constantly so the mixture is smooth. |
| Water | 2.5 oz | 75 g | |
| Egg yolks | 3 oz (9 yolks) | 90 g (9 yolks) | 2. Beat in the egg yolks. Whip the mixture over low heat for a few minutes until it thickens slightly. |
| Liqueur (see *Note*) | 1 oz | 30 g | 3. Remove the mixture from the heat and stir in the liqueur or other liquid. Cool it completely. |
| Egg whites | 4.5 oz (9 whites) | 135 g (9 whites) | 4. Whip the egg whites with the sugar to form a firm meringue. Fold it into the chocolate mixture. |
| Sugar | 2 oz | 60 g | 5. Whip the cream until it forms soft peaks. Fold it into the chocolate mixture. |
| Heavy cream | 8 oz | 250 mL | |
| **Total Weight:** | **1 lb 15 oz** | **950 g** | 6. Pour the mousse into serving bowls or individual dishes. Chill for several hours before serving. |

*Note: Any appropriate liqueur or spirit, such as orange liqueur, amaretto, rum, or brandy, may be used. If you don't wish to use a liqueur, use 1 oz (30 mL) strong coffee or 1½ tsp (8 mL) vanilla plus 1½ tbsp (22 mL) water.*

# CHOCOLATE MOUSSE IV

*Yield: about 1¾ qt (1.75 L)*

| Ingredients | U.S. | Metric | Procedure |
|---|---|---|---|
| Bittersweet chocolate | 1 lb | 500 g | 1. Melt the chocolate in a dry pan over a hot-water bath. |
| Butter | 4 oz | 125 g | 2. Remove from the heat. Add the butter and stir until melted. |
| Egg yolks | 6 oz | 180 g | 3. Add the egg yolks, mixing well. |
| Egg whites | 8 oz | 250 g | 4. Whip the egg whites with the sugar to form a soft meringue. Fold into the chocolate mixture. |
| Sugar | 2.5 oz | 75 g | 5. Whip the cream until it forms soft peaks. Fold it into the chocolate mixture. |
| Heavy cream | 8 oz | 250 mL | 6. Transfer the mousse to serving bowls or individual dishes. Chill for several hours before serving. |
| **Total Weight:** | **2 lb 12 oz** | **1378 g** | |

### VARIATIONS

The following variations are based on the above recipe. A few modifications are necessary due to the different composition and handling properties of milk chocolate and white chocolate.

## MILK CHOCOLATE MOUSSE

Substitute milk chocolate for the dark chocolate in the main recipe. Melt the chocolate with 4 oz (125 mL) water, stirring until smooth. Then remove from the heat and proceed with step 2 of the procedure. Reduce the quantity of yolks to 2 oz (60 g). Reduce the quantity of sugar to 2 oz (60 g).

## WHITE CHOCOLATE MOUSSE

Substitute white chocolate for milk chocolate in the preceding variation.

# CHOCOLATE MOUSSE V (WITH GELATIN)

| Ingredients | U.S. | Metric | Procedure |
|---|---|---|---|
| Gelatin | 0.2 oz | 6 g | 1. Soften the gelatin in cold water (see p. 88). |
| Sugar | 1.67 oz | 50 g | 2. Combine the sugar, water, and glucose and bring to a boil to make a syrup. Cook to 245°F (119°C). |
| Water | 1.67 oz | 50 g | |
| Glucose | 0.33 oz | 10 g | 3. Whip the egg yolks until thick and pale. Gradually beat in the hot syrup. Add the gelatin and beat until dissolved. Continue whipping until cold. |
| Egg yolks | 2.67 oz (4 yolks) | 80 g (4 yolks) | |
| Dark chocolate couverture, melted | 7.25 oz | 225 g | 4. Fold the melted chocolate into the egg-yolk mixture. |
| Heavy cream | 1 lb | 500 g | 5. Whip the cream into soft peaks. Fold in. |
| Italian Meringue (p. 267) | 6 oz | 180 g | 6. Fold in the Italian meringue. Pour into molds and chill until set. |
| **Total Weight:** | **2 lb 3 oz** | **1100 g** | |

# CHOCOLATE TERRINE

*Yield: 1 lb 8 oz (735 g)*

| Ingredients | U.S. | Metric | Procedure |
|---|---|---|---|
| Bittersweet chocolate | 12 oz | 375 g | |
| Eggs | 6 | 6 | |
| Orange liqueur | 2 oz | 60 mL | |
| Cocoa powder | as needed | as needed | |
| **Total Weight:** | **1 lb  8 oz** | **735 g** | |

**VARIATION**

Substitute 3 oz (90 g) strong espresso for the orange liqueur.

1. For each 12 oz chocolate, prepare a 1-pt (500 mL) loaf pan by lining it with parchment. [For broader slices of the finished terrine, double the recipe and use a 1-qt (1 L) loaf pan.]

2. Chop the chocolate into small pieces. Melt the chocolate over warm water. Do not allow any water to get into the chocolate.

3. Separate the eggs.

4. Whip the egg whites until they form soft peaks. Set aside. (It is necessary to whip the egg whites before beginning to mix the chocolate because once you add the first liquid to the chocolate, you must continue the procedure without interruption.)

5. Add the orange liqueur to the chocolate and beat in. The chocolate will become very thick.

6. Beat the yolks into the chocolate, 1 or 2 at a time, until well blended.

7. Beat the egg whites into the chocolate mixture. Use a stiff whip to beat them in. Do not try to fold them in gently, as the mixture is too stiff.

8. To create the necessary smooth texture, force the mixture through a sieve to remove lumps of unblended chocolate or egg.

9. Pour some of the chocolate into the prepared pan(s) to fill them about halfway. Rap the pans on the bench sharply to remove air bubbles. Fill with the remaining chocolate, and again remove air bubbles.

10. Cover and refrigerate overnight.

11. Unmold onto a platter. Dust the top and sides lightly with cocoa powder. Slice about ¼ in. (6 mm) thick using a sharp, thin-bladed knife dipped into hot water and wiped dry before each slice. Serve small portions, as this dessert is very rich.

# CHOCOLATE INDULGENCE

*Yield: 2 gâteaux, 7 in. (18 cm) in diameter*

| Ingredients | U.S. | Metric | Procedure |
|---|---|---|---|
| **To line mold** | | | 1. Prepare the joconde sponge cake for lining the mold. Cut two 6-in. (15 cm) circles from one end of the sponge sheet and reserve. Trim the remaining sponge to make a square about 12 in. (30 cm) on a side. Cut this square into 4 small squares of equal size. Spread one with a thin layer of Ganache I. Top with a second square and spread with a layer of Ganache II. Top with a third square and spread with a layer of Ganache I. Top with the fourth sponge square. Press down lightly. Chill. (If you wish to simplify production, you could omit the Ganache II and use Ganache I for all 3 layers.) |
| Joconde Sponge Cake (p. 410) | 1 half-sheet pan | 1 half-sheet pan | |
| Ganache I (p. 549) | as needed | as needed | |
| Ganache II (p. 549) | as needed | as needed | |
| **Syrup** | | | |
| Water | 2 oz | 60 g | |
| Sugar | 2 oz | 60 g | |
| Orange liqueur, such as Cointreau | 2 oz | 60 g | |
| Chocolate Mousse V (p. 546) | about 2 lb | 900–1000 g | |
| Ganache Icing (p. 433) | 7 oz | 200 g | |
| **Suggested decoration** | | | |
| Chocolate fans (p. 647) | as needed | as needed | |
| Cocoa powder | as needed | as needed | |
| Fresh berries | as needed | as needed | |
| Chocolate cigarettes (p. 646) | as needed | as needed | |

2. Line two 7-in. (18 cm) charlotte rings. (This is the same procedure as for baumkuchen, illustrated on p. 455.) Cut the sponge square into strips whose width is two-thirds to three-fourths the height of the ring molds. The exact width is not important, as long as all the strips are the same width. Cut each of these strips crosswise into strips ¼ in. (5 mm) thick. Place the ring molds on cake cards. Arrange the strips of sponge around the inside of the ring molds, pressing them into place, so the stripes of ganache are vertical. Continue until both rings are compactly lined with sponge.

3. Make a syrup by boiling the sugar and water until dissolved. Remove from the heat and add the liqueur.

4. Place one of the sponge circles inside each ring to make a base. Brush with the syrup.

5. Prepare the chocolate mousse and fill the rings to the top with the mousse. Level with a palette knife. Chill until set.

6. Spread the warm ganache icing over the tops and level with a palette knife. Chill until set.

7. Remove the rings by warming them slightly with a blowtorch to release them, then lifting off.

8. Decorate as desired.

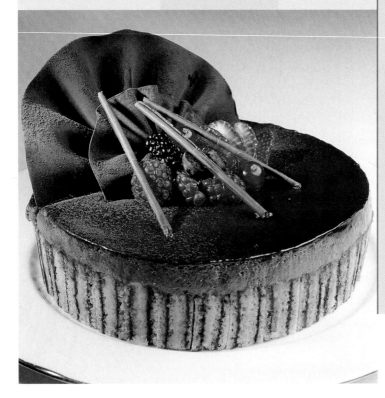

# GANACHE I

*Yield: 1 lb (450 g)*

| Ingredients | U.S. | Metric | Procedure |
|---|---|---|---|
| Dark chocolate, chopped | 7 oz | 200 g | Melt the chocolate in a water bath. Heat the cream and mix into the chocolate. Chill. |
| Heavy cream | 9 oz | 250 g | |

# GANACHE II

*Yield: 1 lb 4 oz (575 g)*

| Ingredients | U.S. | Metric | Procedure |
|---|---|---|---|
| White chocolate, chopped | 1 lb | 450 g | Melt the white chocolate in a water bath. Heat the cream and mix in. Add a little red color to give a pale pink color. Chill. |
| Heavy cream | 4.5 oz | 125 g | |
| Red coloring | few drops | few drops | |

# SOUFFLÉS

*Soufflés* are lightened with beaten egg whites and then baked. Baking causes the soufflé to rise like a cake because the air in the egg foam expands when heated. Toward the end of the baking time the egg whites coagulate, or become firm. However, soufflés are not as stable as cakes, and they fall shortly after they are removed from the oven. For this reason, they should be served immediately.

A standard soufflé consists of three elements:

1. **Base.** Many kinds of bases are used for dessert soufflés; most are heavy, starch-thickened preparations, such as pastry creams or sweetened white sauces. If egg yolks are used, they are added to the base.

2. **Flavoring ingredients.** These are added to the base and mixed in well. Popular flavorings include melted chocolate, lemon, and liqueurs. Small quantities of solid ingredients such as dried candied fruits or finely chopped nuts may also be added. The base and flavor mixture may be prepared ahead of time and kept refrigerated. Portions can then be scaled to order and mixed with egg whites.

3. **Egg whites.** Whenever possible, egg whites should be whipped with some of the sugar. This makes dessert soufflés more stable.

Butter soufflé dishes well and coat them with sugar. Fill dishes to about ½ in. (1 cm) below the rim. When baked, the soufflé should rise 1–1½ in. above the rim.

# VANILLA SOUFFLÉ

*Yield: 10–12 portions*

| Ingredients | U.S. | | Metric | Procedure |
|---|---|---|---|---|
| Bread flour | 3 | oz | 90 g | 1. Work the flour and butter together to form a paste. |
| Butter | 3 | oz | 90 g | |
| Milk | 1 pt | | 500 mL | 2. Dissolve the sugar in the milk and bring to a boil. Remove from the heat. |
| Sugar | 4 | oz | 120 g | |
| Egg yolks | 6 | oz | 180 g | 3. With a wire whip, beat in the flour paste. Beat vigorously to make sure there are no lumps. |
| | (8–9 yolks) | | (8–9 yolks) | |
| Vanilla extract | 0.33 oz (2 tsp) | | 10 mL | 4. Return the mixture to the heat and bring it to a boil, beating constantly. Simmer for several minutes until the mixture is very thick and no starchy taste remains. |
| Egg whites | 10 | oz | 300 g | |
| | (10 whites) | | (10 whites) | 5. Transfer the mixture to a mixing bowl. Cover and let cool 5–10 minutes. |
| Sugar | 2 | oz | 60 g | |

6. Beat in the egg yolks and vanilla.

7. Soufflés may be prepared ahead of time up to this point. Chill the mixture and scale portions of the base to order. Proceed with the following steps.

8. Prepare soufflé dishes by buttering the insides well and coating with granulated sugar. This recipe will fill 10–12 single-portion dishes or two 7-in. (18 cm) dishes.

9. Whip the egg whites until they form soft peaks. Add the sugar and whip until the mixture forms firm, moist peaks.

10. Fold the egg whites into the soufflé base.

11. Pour the mixture into the prepared baking dishes and smooth the tops.

12. Bake at 375°F (190°C). Approximate baking times are 30 minutes for large dishes, 15 minutes for single-portion dishes.

13. *Optional step:* 3–4 minutes before soufflés are done, dust the tops generously with confectioners' sugar.

14. Serve as soon as removed from the oven.

## VARIATIONS

### CHOCOLATE SOUFFLÉ

Melt together 3 oz (90 g) unsweetened chocolate and 1 oz (30 g) sweet chocolate. Add to the base after step 5.

### LEMON SOUFFLÉ

Instead of vanilla, use the grated zest of 2 lemons for flavoring.

### LIQUEUR SOUFFLÉ

Flavor with 2–3 oz (60–90 mL) desired liqueur, such as kirsch or orange liqueur, added after step 5.

### COFFEE SOUFFLÉ

Flavor with 2 tbsp (15 g) instant coffee powder, or to taste, added to the milk in step 2.

### PRALINE SOUFFLÉ

Blend 4–5 oz (125–150 g) praline paste with the base after step 5.

## TERMS FOR REVIEW

| | | | |
|---|---|---|---|
| custard | pastry cream | pot de crème | rice impératrice |
| stirred custard | cornstarch pudding | Christmas pudding | mousse |
| baked custard | cream pudding | Bavarian cream | soufflé |
| crème anglaise | panna cotta | cold charlotte | |

## QUESTIONS FOR DISCUSSION

1. What is the internal temperature at which the eggs in custard mixtures become cooked or coagulated? What happens to stirred custards and baked custards if they are cooked beyond this point?

2. The basic techniques used to make crème anglaise and baked custard are also used for some of the following preparations. Identify which of the following desserts are made using a stirred custard (custard sauce) technique, which are made using a baked custard technique, and which are made without any custard.

   | | |
   |---|---|
   | Bread pudding | Apple cobbler |
   | Christmas pudding | Charlotte russe |
   | Chocolate Bavarian | Chocolate pots de crème |
   | Baked cheesecake | Apple charlotte |

3. What is the main difference between cornstarch pudding and cream pudding?

4. In the production of Bavarian creams and other desserts stabilized with gelatin, why is it important to measure the gelatin carefully?

5. When making a Bavarian or chiffon pie filling, what difficulty would you encounter if you chilled the gelatin mixture too long before folding in the whipped cream or egg whites?

6. When making dessert soufflés, what is the advantage of adding part of the sugar to the whipped egg whites?

## Chapter 21

# Frozen Desserts

The popularity of ice cream needs no explanation. Whether it is a plain scoop of vanilla ice cream in a dish or an elaborate assemblage of fruits, syrups, toppings, and numerous flavors of ice cream and sherbet, a frozen dessert appeals to everyone.

Until recently, few establishments made their own ice cream because of the labor involved, the equipment required, and the sanitation regulations and health codes that had to be followed. In addition, the convenience and high quality of commercially made ice creams make it unnecessary for many operations to make their own. But today, many restaurants find that serving their own homemade sorbets and ice creams is appealing to customers. In fact, in the finest restaurants, customers may expect the pastry chef to produce frozen desserts as well as pastries. Learning to make ice cream has become an important skill.

You will find that much of this chapter seems familiar. The base for ice cream, for example, is the same crème anglaise you have used in many other preparations. Other techniques in this chapter, such as preparing syrups and whipping meringues, are used in many areas of the bakeshop.

**After reading this chapter, you should be able to:**

1. Judge the quality of commercial ice creams.

2. Prepare ice creams and sorbets.

3. Prepare ice cream and sorbet desserts using commercial or homemade ice creams and sorbets.

4. Prepare still-frozen desserts, including bombes, frozen mousses, and frozen soufflés.

# CHURN-FROZEN DESSERTS

Ice cream and sherbet are churn-frozen, meaning they are mixed constantly while being frozen. If they were not churned, they would freeze into solid blocks of ice. The churning keeps the ice crystals small and incorporates air into the dessert.

*Ice cream* is a smooth, frozen mixture of milk, cream, sugar, flavorings, and, sometimes, eggs. *Philadelphia-style* ice cream contains no eggs, and *French-style* ice cream contains egg yolks. The eggs add richness and help make a smoother product because of the emulsifying properties of the yolks.

*Ice milk* is like ice cream, but with a lower butterfat content. *Frozen yogurt* contains yogurt in addition to the normal ingredients for ice cream or ice milk.

*Sherbets* and *ices* are usually made from fruit juices, water, and sugar. American sherbets usually contain milk or cream and, sometimes, egg whites. The egg whites increase smoothness and volume. Ices, also called *water ices*, contain only fruit juice, water, sugar, and, sometimes, egg whites; they do not contain milk products. The French word *sorbet* (pronounced sor-bay) is sometimes used for these products. *Granité* (pronounced grah-nee-tay) is coarse, crystalline ice, made without egg whites.

Italian versions of ice cream, sorbet, and granité are called *gelato* (plural, *gelati*), *sorbetto* (plural, *sorbetti*), and *granita* (plural, *granite*). Traditional Italian gelato is usually lower in fat than other ice creams. Gelato flavors such as vanilla and chocolate are often made with milk only, and no cream. Fruit gelati often contain cream, but because they are mostly fruit purée, they are still low in fat. In addition, many gelati are made without egg yolks, and most are made without other emulsifiers and stabilizers. Thus, they melt quickly and have a light texture and flavor in the mouth. On the other hand, they are mixed less than ice creams and have low overrun (see below), contributing to a rich mouth feel. (The basic meaning of *gelato* in Italian is "frozen.")

## Production and Quality

A basic French- or custard-style ice cream mix is simply a crème anglaise or custard sauce mixed with 1 or 2 parts heavy cream for every 4 parts milk used in the sauce. This base is flavored, as desired, with vanilla, melted chocolate, instant coffee, sweetened crushed strawberries, and so on, chilled thoroughly, and then frozen according to the instructions for the particular equipment in use.

When the mix has frozen, it is transferred to containers and placed in a deep freeze at below 0°F (−18°C) to harden. (Soft-frozen or soft-serve ice creams and gelati are served directly as they come from the churn freezer, without being hardened.)

Whether you make ice cream or buy it, you should be aware of several quality factors:

1. **Smoothness** is related to the size of the ice crystals in the product. Ice cream should be frozen rapidly and churned well during freezing so large crystals don't have a chance to form.

    Rapid hardening helps keep crystals small, as do eggs and emulsifiers or stabilizers added to the mix.

    Large crystals may form if ice cream is not stored at a low enough temperature (below 0°F/−18°C).

2. **Overrun** is the increase in volume due to incorporation of air when freezing ice cream. It is expressed as a percentage of the original volume of the mix. (For example, if the mixture doubles in volume, then the amount of increase is equal to the original volume and the overrun is 100%.)

   Some overrun is necessary to give a smooth, light texture. If ice cream has too much overrun, it is airy and foamy and lacks flavor. It was once thought that ice cream should have from 80% to 100% overrun and that less would make it heavy and pasty. This may be true for ice creams containing gums and other stabilizers. However, some high-quality manufacturers produce rich (and expensive) ice cream with as little as 20% overrun.

   Overrun is affected by many factors, including the type of freezing equipment, the length of churning time, the fat content of the mix, the percentage of solids in the mix, and how full the freezer is.

3. **Mouth feel** or body depends, in part, on smoothness and overrun as well as on other qualities. Good ice cream melts in the mouth to a smooth, not too heavy liquid. Some ice creams have so many stabilizers they never melt to a liquid. Unfortunately, many people are so accustomed to these products that an ice cream that actually does melt in the mouth strikes them as "not rich enough."

   Butterfat from cream contributes to a rich mouth feel. However, too high a fat content can detract from the texture. This is because, when fat content is especially high, some of the fat may congeal into tiny lumps of butter during churn-freezing, producing a grainy texture.

   A good gelato has a light, smooth mouth feel from low fat content and lack of emulsifiers combined with low overrun.

## Storage and Service

1. Store ice creams and sherbets below 0°F (–18°C). This low temperature helps prevent the formation of large ice crystals.

2. To prepare for serving, temper frozen desserts at 8° to 15°F (–13° to –9°C) for 24 hours so they will be soft enough to serve.

3. When serving, avoid packing the ice cream. The best method is to draw the scoop across the surface of the product so the product rolls into a ball in the scoop.

4. Use standard scoops for portioning ice cream. Normal portions for popular desserts are as follows:

   | | |
   |---|---|
   | Parfait | 3 No. 30 scoops |
   | Banana split | 3 No. 30 scoops |
   | "À la mode" topping for pie or cake | 1 No. 20 scoop |
   | Sundae | 2 No. 20 scoops |
   | Plain dish of ice cream | 1 No. 10, No. 10, 12, or 16 scoop |

5. Measure syrups, toppings, and garnishes for portion control. For syrups, use pumps that dispense measured quantities, or use standard ladles.

# Popular Ice Cream Desserts

*Parfaits* are made by alternating layers of ice cream and fruit or syrup in tall, narrow glasses. They are usually named after the syrup or topping. For example, a chocolate parfait has three scoops of vanilla or chocolate ice cream alternating with layers of chocolate syrup and topped with whipped cream and shaved chocolate. (This is the most common meaning of the term *parfait* in North America. See page 566 for the original parfait.)

*Sundaes* or **coupes** consist of one or two scoops of ice cream or sherbet placed in a dish or glass and topped with any of a number of syrups, fruits, toppings, and garnishes. They are quick to prepare, unlimited in variety, and as simple or as elegant as you wish—served in an ordinary soda fountain glass or in a silver cup or crystal champagne glass.

Coupes are often elegant, attractively decorated desserts. Many types have been handed down from the classic cuisine of years ago. The following are classic coupes and similar desserts that are still made today, but often with different names (the classical names are given as a point of interest, but, with the exception of Peach Melba, Pear Belle Hélène, and Coupe au Marrons, these names aren't often used today).

**Coupe Arlesienne.** In the bottom of the cup, place a spoonful of diced candied fruits that have been soaked in kirsch. Add a scoop of vanilla ice cream, top with a poached pear half, and coat with apricot sauce.

**Coupe Black Forest.** Place a scoop of chocolate ice cream in the cup and add sweet, dark cherries flavored with a little cherry brandy. Decorate with rosettes of whipped cream and shaved chocolate.

**Coupe Edna May.** Top vanilla ice cream with sweet cherries. Decorate with whipped cream mixed with enough raspberry purée to color it pink.

**Coupe Gressac.** Top vanilla ice cream with three small almond macaroons moistened with kirsch. Top with a small poached peach half, cut side up, and fill the center of the peach with red currant jelly. Decorate with a border of whipped cream.

**Coupe Jacques.** Place a scoop each of lemon sherbet and strawberry ice cream in a cup. Top with a mixture of diced, fresh fruit flavored with kirsch.

**Coupe aux Marrons.** Top vanilla ice cream with candied chestnuts (marrons glacés) and whipped cream.

**Coupe Orientale.** Place diced pineapple in the bottom of the cup and add pineapple sherbet. Top with apricot sauce and toasted almonds.

**Peach Melba.** Top vanilla ice cream with a poached peach half covered with Melba sauce (p. 279) and topped with slivered almonds.

**Pear Belle Hélène.** Top vanilla ice cream with a poached pear half covered with chocolate sauce and garnished with toasted, sliced almonds.

Among other popular ice cream desserts mentioned earlier in this book are Meringues Glacées (p. 352) and Frozen Éclairs and Profiteroles (p. 337). The popular festive dessert called **Baked Alaska** is discussed in the following procedure. Although no one is surprised by it any more, one of the classic names for this dessert is Soufflé Surprise, so called because it looks like baked whipped eggs on the outside but is frozen inside.

## Procedure for Making Baked Alaska

1. Pack softened ice cream into a dome-shaped mold of the desired size. Freeze solid.

2. Prepare a layer of sponge cake the same size as the flat side of the mold and about ½ in. (12 mm) thick.

3. Unmold the frozen ice cream onto the cake layer so the cake forms the base for the ice cream.

4. With a spatula, cover the entire dessert with a thick layer of meringue. If desired, decorate with more meringue forced from a pastry bag.

5. Bake at 450°F (230°C) until the raised edges of the meringue decorations turn golden brown.

6. Serve immediately.

# Homemade Ice Creams and Sorbets

The same quality factors that apply to commercially made frozen desserts, as discussed above, apply to those you make yourself.

The first two recipes that follow illustrate the basic procedures for making ice cream and sorbet. Using the procedures in these two recipes, you can make an unlimited variety of frozen desserts, as exemplified by the many variations that follow each main recipe. Following these basic recipes are additional recipes for specialty ice creams and sorbets.

## Ice Cream Production

As in other areas in the bakeshop, accurate measurement of ingredients is important. In the case of frozen desserts, proper measurement is important to ensure the mix freezes properly. This is because the ratio of sugar weight to total weight has a strong effect on freezing. If an ice cream or sorbet mix contains too much sugar, it will not freeze enough to become firm. On the other hand, an ice cream with too little sugar will not be as smooth as one with the correct amount.

For a basic vanilla ice cream, the weight of the sugar is usually 16–20% of the total weight. Adding other ingredients makes the calculation more complicated because many ingredients, such as fruits, contain sugar. When you are developing new recipes, test a small batch of the mixture to see how hard it freezes, and increase or decrease the quantity of sugar as necessary.

Ice creams have a better texture if the finished mix is refrigerated for about 12 hours before freezing. This maturing time enables the proteins of the eggs and milk to bond with more of the water molecules in the mixture. This bonding leaves fewer water molecules available to form ice crystals that can give ice cream a grainy texture.

Careful sanitation procedures are critical because ice cream mix is a good breeding ground for bacteria. Equipment should be made of stainless steel or other nonporous and noncorrosive material, and it should be properly cleaned and sanitized after every use.

## Sorbet Production

A basic sorbet mixture is simply a sugar syrup mixed with flavoring ingredients. For sorbets, the proportion of sugar in the mix is even more critical to the texture of the final product than it is for ice cream, because sorbets do not contain the cream or egg yolks that contribute to the smooth texture of ice cream. The size of the ice crystals is the most important factor in texture.

The sugar content of fruit varies with its ripeness and other factors. Therefore, testing the sugar concentration of sorbet mix is the surest way to ensure proper texture. Sugar concentration can be measured with a hydrometer, also called a *saccharometer*. Basic measurement of sugar concentration, using the Brix and Baumé scales, is discussed on page 260. For best freezing, sorbet mixtures should be at a concentration of 30°–32.5° Brix or 16°–18° Baumé. If the sugar density is too high, dilute with a little water. If it is too low, add a little sugar syrup to increase the sugar content.

Rapid freezing produces smaller ice crystals, and thus smoother texture, than slow freezing. For sorbets as well as for ice creams, chill the mixture well before freezing so it freezes in the shortest possible time.

Using a little corn syrup in place of some of the sugar for the syrup may also contribute slightly to smoothness in some sorbets. Classic sorbets, however, are based on a syrup made only with regular granulated sugar. Using corn syrup in a syrup for sorbets darkens the syrup somewhat, because of increased browning of the sugars and starches in the corn syrup. This may be a disadvantage for some white or light-colored sorbets.

For granitas, unlike for sorbets, large crystals are characteristic of the product and are desirable. Classic granitas are made with sorbet-like mixes, but with two differences. First, the sugar content is slightly lower, so the ice crystals are larger. Second, rather than being churn-frozen, the mixture is still-frozen in a pan and stirred periodically as it freezes. This freezing method gives granitas their typical icy texture.

# VANILLA ICE CREAM

*Yield: about 2 qt (2 L), depending on overrun*

| Ingredients | U.S. | | Metric | Procedure |
|---|---|---|---|---|
| Egg yolks (12 yolks) | 8 | oz | 250 g | 1. Vanilla ice cream mix is basically a custard sauce or crème anglaise with the addition of heavy cream. Review the guidelines for preparing crème anglaise on page 268. |
| Sugar | 12 | oz | 375 g | |
| Milk | 2 | pt | 1 L | 2. Combine the egg yolks and sugar in a bowl. Whip until thick and light. |
| Heavy cream | 1 | pt | 500 mL | 3. Scald the milk and gradually beat it into the egg mixture. |
| Vanilla extract | 2 | tsp | 10 mL | |
| Salt | pinch | | pinch | 4. Heat over a hot-water bath or in a double boiler, stirring constantly, until the mixture thickens enough to coat the back of a spoon. Immediately remove from the heat. |

4. Heat over a hot-water bath or in a double boiler, stirring constantly, until the mixture thickens enough to coat the back of a spoon. Immediately remove from the heat.

5. Stir in the cold cream to stop the cooking. Add the vanilla and salt. (*Note:* If you are not using freshly opened, pasteurized cream, it is best to scald and cool the cream or else to heat it with the milk in step 3. In this case, set the cooked custard in an ice-water bath as soon as it is cooked to stop the cooking.)

6. Chill the mixture thoroughly. Refrigerate overnight to mature the mix (see p. 557).

7. Freeze in an ice cream freezer according to the manufacturer's directions.

## VARIATIONS

For a less rich ice cream, substitute milk for part of the cream. In addition, the quantity of egg yolks may be decreased to 6 (4 oz/125 g).

### VANILLA BEAN ICE CREAM

Split 1 or 2 vanilla beans, scrape out the seeds, and simmer the seeds and pods with the cream. Cool. Remove and discard the pods. Omit the vanilla extract from the basic recipe.

### CHOCOLATE ICE CREAM

Reduce the sugar to 9 oz (280 g). Melt together 4 oz (125 g) unsweetened chocolate and 4 oz (125 g) bittersweet chocolate. When the custard has cooled to tepid, carefully stir it into the melted chocolate. Reduce the cream to 12 oz (375 mL).

**MORE VARIATIONS**

## CINNAMON ICE CREAM

Add 1 tbsp (5 g) cinnamon to the egg mixture before cooking.

## COFFEE ICE CREAM

Flavor the hot custard mix to taste with instant coffee powder or instant espresso powder.

## CAROB ICE CREAM

After the scalded milk is added to the egg mixture, beat in 3 oz (90 g) roasted carob powder. Proceed as in basic recipe.

## COCONUT ICE CREAM

Reduce the number of egg yolks to 6 (4 oz/125 g). Reduce the sugar to 4 oz (125 g). Add 12 fl oz (375 mL) canned sweetened coconut cream to the yolks and sugar. Omit the heavy cream and vanilla. Stir the cooked mix over ice until cold to prevent the coconut fat from separating.

## CARAMEL ICE CREAM

Omit the vanilla. Caramelize the sugar, following the procedure in the recipe for Caramel Sauce (p. 280) but omitting the lemon. Add the 1 pt (500 mL) heavy cream from the basic recipe and simmer until the caramel is dissolved, again following the procedure in the caramel sauce recipe, steps 2–4. Beat the eggs, add the hot milk and caramel cream, make the custard, and finish the ice cream as in the basic recipe.

## ALMOND, HAZELNUT, OR MACADAMIA PRALINE ICE CREAM

Make a praline with any of the above nuts, following the recipe for Nougatine (p. 668). Crush 6 oz (185 g) praline and add it to chilled vanilla or caramel ice cream mix before freezing.

## CHEESECAKE ICE CREAM

Prepare the basic vanilla ice cream mix, but use only 4 oz (125 g) egg yolks and substitute milk for half of the cream. In a mixer with the paddle attachment, blend 2 lb (1 kg) cream cheese, 7 oz (200 g) sugar, 1 tsp (3 g) each grated lemon zest and orange zest, and 1½ oz (50 mL) lemon juice until light and free of lumps. Gradually add the chilled custard and mix until smooth. Chill well. Freeze.

## STRAWBERRY ICE CREAM

Reduce the number of yolks to 6 (4 oz/125 g). Mash 1½ lb (750 g) strawberries with 6 oz (185 g) sugar and refrigerate at least 2 hours. Mix the strawberries with the cold ice cream mix before freezing.

## RASPBERRY SWIRL ICE CREAM

Reduce the number of yolks to 6 (4 oz/125 g). Mash 1 lb (500 g) raspberries with 4 oz (125 g) sugar. Refrigerate at least 2 hours. Make vanilla ice cream and freeze in an ice cream freezer. After the churn-freezing is finished but before hardening the ice cream, fold in the raspberries, but do not mix in completely; leave it in swirls.

## MANGO ICE CREAM

Reduce the number of yolks to 6 (4 oz/125 g). Combine 1½ lb (750 g) sieved mango purée, 3 oz (90 mL) lime juice, and 3 oz (90 g) sugar. Refrigerate at least 2 hours. Combine with cold custard mix and freeze.

## PEACH ICE CREAM

Mash 2 lb (1 kg) sliced fresh peaches, 4 oz (125 g) sugar, and 1 oz (30 mL) lemon juice. Reduce the number of egg yolks to 6 (4 oz/125 g). Omit the milk, increase the cream to 2 pt (1 L), and make the custard with the cream. Mix the peaches with the cold custard and freeze.

## GINGERBREAD-SPICE ICE CREAM

| Ingredients | U.S. | Metric |
|---|---|---|
| Ginger | 1½ tsp | 2.8 g (7 mL) |
| Cinnamon | 1 tsp | 1.7 g (5 mL) |
| Cloves, ground | ½ tsp | 1 g (2 mL) |
| Nutmeg | ¼ tsp | 0.5 g (1 mL) |
| Molasses | 2 oz | 60 g |

Add the spices to the egg mixture before cooking. Add the molasses to the mixture after cooking.

## LEMON ICE CREAM

Reduce the quantity of milk to 1 pt (500 mL) and the sugar to 8 oz (250 g). Scald the milk and cream together. Omit the vanilla. With these exceptions, make the ice cream mix as in the basic recipe.

Separately, combine 2 tbsp (15 g) grated lemon zest and 1 oz (30 g) sugar. Work the zest and sugar together with the back of a spoon or with a mortar and pestle to make a coarse paste. Beat this lemon sugar with 3 egg yolks (2 oz/60 g). Add 12 oz (375 mL) lemon juice and beat over hot water until thick and creamy, as for making crème anglaise. Cool over ice. Refrigerate the lemon mixture and the custard mixture separately until ready to freeze. Combine the mixtures and freeze.

## LIME ICE CREAM

Substitute lime zest and juice for the lemon in the preceding recipe.

## ❧ ICE CREAM FREEZERS ❧

Modern commercial ice cream freezers operate on the same principal as old-fashioned hand-cranked freezers. In those home devices, refrigeration is provided by a mixture of ice, water, and salt. The salt lowers the temperature of the melting ice below the freezing point of water to enable it to freeze the ice cream mix. The ice cream mix is placed in a cylinder surrounded by the ice and salt. A paddle or dasher continuously scrapes the freezing ice cream mixture off the walls of the cylinder and at the same time incorporates air into the mix.

Modern batch freezers work the same way, except an electric refrigeration unit does the freezing instead of salt and ice. In vertical batch freezers, the cylinder is vertical, just as in the old-style hand-cranked machines. This type of freezer incorporates the least amount of air into the mix, resulting in low overrun. Horizontal batch freezers, with a horizontal cylinder, incorporate more air and produce ice cream with overrun up to 100%. Depending on the model, horizontal machines freeze ice cream quickly, finishing a batch of 6 quarts (6 L) or more in about five minutes.

Continuous ice cream freezers are used by high-volume operations. Instead of producing one batch at a time, the mix flows continuously into one end of the cylinder and the frozen product is extruded at the other end. Such machines can produce 150 to as much as 3000 quarts (liters) or more of ice cream in an hour. Continuous ice cream freezers also incorporate the most air, resulting in ice cream with overrun from 60 to 140%.

# SORBET

*Yield: variable*

| Ingredients | U.S. | Metric | Procedure |
|---|---|---|---|
| Sugar (see *Note*) | 12 oz | 375 g | 1. Make a syrup by heating the sugar and first quantity of water to dissolve the sugar. Cool. |
| Water | 8 fl oz | 250 mL | |
| Fruit juice or pulp or other flavor ingredients | (see variations) | (see variations) | 2. Prepare the desired flavor ingredients as indicated in the variations that follow. If additional water is required, mix it with the flavor ingredient. |
| Water | (see variations) | (see variations) | 3. Mix the syrup with the remaining ingredients. |

*Note: Including corn syrup as part of the sugar may slightly increase smoothness in some sorbets, although traditional sorbets are made with only granulated sugar. To include corn syrup, decrease the sugar to 11.5 oz (360 g) and add 2 oz (60 g) corn syrup to the syrup ingredients.*

4. If possible, test the sugar concentration with a hydrometer (saccharometer). The mixture should be between 16° and 18° Baumé, or between 30° and 32.5° Brix. If the concentration is too low, add a little more syrup. If it is high, dilute with a little water.

5. Chill the mixture well, then freeze in an ice cream freezer according to the manufacturer's instructions.

### VARIATIONS

The following sorbet variations indicate the quantities of flavor ingredients and additional water to be used in the above recipe. If the ingredients require special preparation instructions, they are indicated. If no special directions are given, simply follow the basic procedure above. Note that most fruit sorbets require strained fruit purée. for the smoothest texture. This means fruit pulp that has been puréed and then forced through a sieve.

## LEMON OR LIME SORBET

| Ingredients | U.S. | Metric |
|---|---|---|
| Lemon or lime zest, grated | 1 tbsp | 8 g |
| Lemon juice or lime juice | 8 fl oz | 250 mL |
| Water | 12 fl oz | 375 mL |

Boil the zest with the syrup. Cool and strain.

## ORANGE OR TANGERINE SORBET

| Ingredients | U.S. | Metric |
|---|---|---|
| Orange or tangerine juice | 20 fl oz | 625 mL |
| Water | 4 fl oz | 125 mL |

## RASPBERRY, STRAWBERRY, MELON, OR KIWI SORBET

| Ingredients | U.S. | Metric |
|---|---|---|
| Strained fruit purée | 1 lb 12 oz | 875 g |
| Water | none | none |

Taste the mix before freezing. Some fruit is low in acidity, so a little lemon juice may improve the flavor of the mix.

## MANGO SORBET

| Ingredients | U.S. | Metric |
|---|---|---|
| Strained mango purée | 1 lb 12 oz | 875 g |
| Lemon juice | 1.5 fl oz | 60 mL |
| Water | 8 fl oz | 250 mL |

## PINEAPPLE SORBET

| Ingredients | U.S. | Metric |
|---|---|---|
| Fresh pineapple chunks | 1 lb 8 oz | 750 g |
| Water | 12 fl oz | 375 mL |

Poach the pineapple in the syrup. Cool. Purée and force through a sieve. Add the water. Freeze.

## BLUEBERRY SORBET

| Ingredients | U.S. | Metric |
|---|---|---|
| Blueberries | 2 lb 4 oz | 1125 g |
| Lemon juice | 2 fl oz | 60 mL |
| Cinnamon | ¼ tsp | 0.4 g (1 mL) |
| Water | none | none |

Simmer the blueberries, lemon juice, and cinnamon in the syrup until the berries are tender. Strain through a fine sieve.

## BANANA PASSION FRUIT SORBET

| Ingredients | U.S. | Metric |
|---|---|---|
| Banana pulp, strained | 12 oz | 375 g |
| Passion fruit pulp or juice, strained | 1 lb | 500 g |
| Water | none | none |

## RHUBARB SORBET

| Ingredients | U.S. | Metric |
|---|---|---|
| Rhubarb | 2 lb | 1000 g |
| Water | 1 pt | 500 mL |

Cut the rhubarb into 1-in. (2.5 cm) slices. Combine the syrup, rhubarb, and water in a stainless-steel saucepan. Bring to a simmer and cook until the rhubarb is tender, about 10 minutes. Let the mixture cool, then strain through a fine strainer. Do not press down on the rhubarb solids, but let the rhubarb stand in the strainer about 30 minutes to let all the flavored syrup drain off. This will keep the syrup clear. Measure the syrup and add enough cold water to bring the volume to 20 oz (625 mL). Freeze the syrup. Reserve the rhubarb for another use (for example, add sugar to taste to make a simple rhubarb compote).

## WHITE WINE OR CHAMPAGNE SORBET

| Ingredients | U.S. | Metric |
|---|---|---|
| White wine or champagne | 2.5 pt | 1.25 L |
| Water | 4 fl oz | 125 mL |

## CHOCOLATE SORBET

| Ingredients | U.S. | Metric |
|---|---|---|
| Cocoa powder | 1 oz | 30 g |
| Bittersweet or semisweet chocolate | 6 oz | 185 g |

Reduce the quantity of sugar in the syrup to 6 oz (185 g). Increase the water in the syrup to 1 pt (500 mL). Add the cocoa powder to the syrup ingredients. When the sugar has dissolved, remove the syrup from the heat and let it cool slightly. Melt the chocolate. Carefully stir the syrup into the melted chocolate. Bring to a simmer, stirring constantly, and simmer 1–2 minutes, until slightly thickened. Chill and freeze.

## MASCARPONE SORBET

| Ingredients | U.S. | Metric |
|---|---|---|
| Mascarpone (soft Italian cream cheese) | 1 lb 8 oz | 750 g |
| Lemon juice | 1.5 fl oz | 45 mL |
| Water | 10 fl oz | 300 mL |

Be sure to chill the mixture thoroughly, and do not leave in the ice cream freezer too long. Overmixing in the churn-freezer may cause some milkfat to separate and form chunks of butter.

# HONEY ICE CREAM

*Yield: about 1 qt (1 L), depending on overrun*

| Ingredients | U.S. | | Metric | Procedure |
|---|---|---|---|---|
| Milk | 8 | oz | 250 g | 1. Heat the milk and the vanilla bean to the scalding point. |
| Vanilla bean, split | 1 | | 1 | |
| Honey | 4.33 | oz | 130 g | 2. Whip the honey and egg yolks until light. Slowly beat in the hot milk. |
| Egg yolks | 4 | oz | 120 g | |
| | (6 yolks) | | (6 yolks) | 3. Return the mixture to the pan. Cook over low heat, stirring constantly, until thick enough to coat the back of a spoon. Remove from the heat and cool. Scrape the seeds from the vanilla bean and return them to the mixture. Chill. |
| Heavy cream | 8 | oz | 250 g | |
| | | | | 4. Add the heavy cream. Freeze in an ice cream freezer. |

# DULCE DE LECHE ICE CREAM

*Yield: about 3½ pt (1750 mL), depending on overrun*

| Ingredients | U.S. | Metric | Procedure |
|---|---|---|---|
| Milk | 1 pt 8 oz | 750 g | 1. Heat the milk and the dulce de leche together until the dulce de leche is completely dissolved. |
| Dulce de Leche | 1 lb 2 oz | 560 g | |
| (p. 282) | (about 14 fl oz) | (about 425 mL) | 2. Remove from the heat and add the remaining ingredients. |
| Heavy cream | 6 oz | 185 g | |
| Vanilla extract | ¼ tsp | 1 g | 3. Chill well. Refrigerate 12 hours to mature the mix (see p. 557). |
| Salt | pinch | pinch | |
| | | | 4. Freeze in an ice cream freezer. |

# BITTER CHOCOLATE ICE CREAM

*Yield: about 3 qt (3 L), depending on overrun*

| Ingredients | U.S. | Metric | Procedure |
|---|---|---|---|
| Egg yolks | 8 oz | 250 g | 1. Combine the egg yolks and the first quantity of sugar in a bowl. Whip until thick and light. |
| | (12 yolks) | (12 yolks) | |
| Sugar | 6 oz | 190 g | 2. Combine the milk and the second quantity of sugar in a heavy saucepan. Bring to a simmer, stirring to dissolve the sugar. |
| Milk | 2 pt 8 oz | 1250 mL | |
| Sugar | 12 oz | 375 g | 3. Gradually beat the milk into the egg yolk mixture. Set over a hot-water bath and heat, stirring constantly, until the mixture thickens enough to coat the back of a spoon. Immediately remove from the heat. Let cool until lukewarm. |
| Bittersweet chocolate | 8 oz | 250 g | |
| Cocoa powder, sifted | 8 oz | 250 g | |
| Heavy cream | 1 pt | 500 mL | |
| | | | 4. Melt the chocolate and let cool slightly. |
| | | | 5. Gradually stir in the custard mixture. |
| | | | 6. Add the cocoa and beat with a whip until it is thoroughly mixed in. |
| | | | 7. Stir in the heavy cream. |
| | | | 8. Chill the mixture. Refrigerate 12 hours to mature the mix (p. 557). |
| | | | 9. Freeze in an ice cream freezer. |

# RASPBERRY FROZEN YOGURT

*Yield: about 3 pt (1.5 L), depending on overrun*

| Ingredients | U.S. | Metric | Procedure |
|---|---|---|---|
| Raspberries, fresh or frozen, unsweetened | 1 lb | 500 g | 1. Combine the raspberries, sugar, and water in a food processor. Process until the raspberries are puréed and the sugar is dissolved. |
| Granulated sugar | 8 oz | 250 g | 2. Force the mixture through a fine sieve to remove the seeds. |
| Water | 4 oz | 125 g | 3. Combine with the yogurt and mix until evenly blended. |
| Plain low-fat or whole milk yogurt | 12 oz | 375 g | 4. Chill the mixture well. |
| | | | 5. Freeze in an ice cream freezer. |

# PISTACHIO GELATO

*Yield: about 2½ pt (1250 mL), depending on overrun.*

| Ingredients | U.S. | Metric |
|---|---|---|
| Shelled, unsalted pistachios | 8 oz | 250 g |
| Whole milk | 2 pt | 1 L |
| Sugar | 7 oz | 220 g |

### Procedure

1. Grind the pistachios in a food processor until fine. Transfer to a bowl.

2. Combine the milk and sugar in a saucepan. Bring to a boil. Stir to dissolve the sugar.

3. Pour the milk over the ground pistachios and stir.

4. Cover and refrigerate overnight.

5. Strain the pistachio mixture in a chinois or other fine strainer lined with several layers of cheesecloth (a). Gather up the corners of the cheesecloth to make a bag and squeeze gently to force the remaining liquid from the ground nuts (b).

6. Chill the liquid again, if necessary, and then freeze in an ice cream freezer (c).

# COCONUT SORBET

*Yield: about 1¾ pt (850 mL), depending on overrun*

| Ingredients | U.S. | | Metric | Procedure |
|---|---|---|---|---|
| Frozen coconut purée, thawed (see variation) | 1 | lb | 480 g | 1. Mix together all ingredients. |
| Confectioners' sugar | 3.5 | oz | 100 g | 2. Freeze in an ice cream freezer. |
| Lime juice, fresh | 1.75 | oz | 50 g | |
| Coconut-flavored rum | 2 | oz | 60 g | |

### VARIATION

The coconut purée used in this recipe contains 20% sugar. If this product is not available, use canned, unsweetened coconut milk and adjust the quantities as follows:

| Ingredients | U.S. | | Metric |
|---|---|---|---|
| Canned, unsweetened coconut milk | 14 | oz | 400 g |
| Confectioners' sugar | 6 | oz | 180 g |
| Lime juice | 1.75 | oz | 50 g |
| Coconut-flavored rum | 2 | oz | 60 g |

# CIDER APPLE SORBET

*Yield: about 1½ pt (700 mL)*

| Ingredients | U.S. | Metric | Procedure |
|---|---|---|---|
| Sugar | 4.5 oz | 135 g | 1. Heat the sugar and water until the sugar is dissolved. |
| Water | 4 oz | 120 g | 2. Peel, core, and chop the apples. Add to the syrup and cook until tender. |
| Cooking apples | 7 oz | 200 g | 3. Add the cider. Place in a blender and blend until smooth. Pass through a fine strainer. |
| Fermented cider | 5.5 oz | 165 g | 4. Cool, then freeze in an ice cream freezer. |

# COFFEE OR ESPRESSO GRANITA

*Yield: about 2 pt 4 fl oz (1125 mL)*

| Ingredients | U.S. | Metric | Procedure |
|---|---|---|---|
| Sugar | 4 oz | 125 g | 1. Dissolve the sugar in the coffee. |
| Very strong coffee or espresso, freshly brewed | 2 pt | 1 L | 2. Pour the coffee into a hotel pan or similar pan and place in the freezer. |
| | | | 3. When the coffee begins to freeze around the edges, stir with a spoon, fork, or whip. Return to the freezer. |
| | | | 4. Repeat every 15 or 20 minutes, until the mixture resembles crushed ice. When finished, it should be completely frozen but loose, or else it will freeze into a block when stored. |
| | | | 5. Cover and store in the freezer. |

# CASSATA ITALIENNE

| Ingredients | U.S. | Metric | Procedure |
|---|---|---|---|
| Common Meringue (p. 267) | 3 oz | 90 g | 1. Using a pastry bag with a plain tip, pipe the meringue onto a parchment-lined sheet pan in a rectangle the same size as the top of the mold. Bake at 250°F (120°C) for 1 hour. Cool. |
| Vanilla Ice Cream (p. 558), softened | 7 oz | 200 g | 2. Line the mold with plastic film. |
| Raspberry jam | 1.5–2 oz | 50 g | 3. Using a pastry bag with a plain tip, pipe the ice cream into the bottom of the mold and smooth the surface (using a pastry bag makes it easier to avoid air bubbles). Freeze until firm. |
| Raspberry Sorbet (p. 561), softened | 7 oz | 200 g | |
| **Total weight:** | **1 lb 2 oz** | **540 g** | 4. Spread the raspberry jam onto the ice cream in an even layer. Freeze until firm. |

*Note: This procedure is for rectangular (loaf) molds approximately 6½ × 3½ in. (17 × 9 cm). It can be modified for any size or shape mold.*

5. Pipe the raspberry sorbet into the mold and smooth the surface.

6. Place the baked, cooled meringue on top of the sorbet and press down gently. Freeze until firm.

7. Unmold, remove the plastic film, and slice to serve.

# STILL-FROZEN DESSERTS

**T**he air mixed into ice cream by churn-freezing is important to its texture. Without this air, the ice cream would be hard and heavy rather than smooth and creamy. Desserts that are still-frozen—that is, frozen in a container without mixing—also must have air mixed into them in order to be soft enough to eat. In this case, the air is incorporated before freezing by mixing in whipped cream, whipped egg whites, or both.

Thus, still-frozen desserts are closely related to products such as Bavarians, mousses, and hot soufflés. These products are all given lightness and volume by adding whipped cream or an egg foam. In fact, many of the same mixtures used for these products are also used for frozen desserts. However, because freezing serves to stabilize or solidify frozen desserts, they don't depend as much on gelatin or other stabilizers.

Still-frozen desserts include bombes, frozen soufflés, and frozen mousses. In classical theory, each type is made with a different mix, but in actual practice today, many of these mixes are interchangeable.

A note on the use of alcohol in frozen desserts: Liqueurs and spirits are often used to flavor these items. However, even a small amount of alcohol lowers the freezing point considerably. If you find that liqueur-flavored parfaits, bombes, and mousses aren't freezing hard enough, you can add more whipped cream. This will raise the freezing point. In future batches, you might try using less alcohol.

A high sugar concentration also inhibits freezing. It is important to avoid using too much sugar in these items so they freeze properly.

## Parfaits and Bombes

In North America, the term **parfait** usually means an ice cream dessert consisting of layers of ice cream and topping in a tall, thin glass. The original parfait, however, is a still-frozen dessert frozen in a tall, thin mold and unmolded for service. (No doubt the ice cream parfait is so named because the glass it is served in is similar in shape to a parfait mold.) The mixture for parfaits consists of three elements: a thick, sweet egg-yolk foam, an equal volume of whipped cream, and flavorings.

The parfait mixture is also called a *bombe mixture* because it is used in the production of a dessert called a **bombe**. The bombe is one of the most elegant frozen desserts, and it is often elaborately decorated with fruits, whipped cream, petits fours secs, and other items after unmolding. It is made by lining a chilled mold (usually spherical or dome-shaped) with a layer of ice cream or sherbet and freezing it hard. The center is then filled with a bombe mixture of compatible flavor and then frozen again.

Mixtures for frozen mousses can also be used to fill bombes, as can regular ice cream or sherbet, but a special bombe mixture is most often used.

Two recipes are given below for bombe mixtures. The ingredients and final results are nearly the same, but the techniques differ. Note that the technique for the first mixture is the same as that used to make French buttercream (p. 425). The second recipe requires a sugar syrup of a specific strength; the recipe for this syrup is also provided.

A procedure for assembling bombes is given, followed by descriptions of a number of classic bombes that have been popular for many decades.

# BASIC BOMBE MIXTURE I

*Yield: 1½ qt (1.5 L)*

| Ingredients | U.S. | Metric | Procedure |
|---|---|---|---|
| Sugar | 8 oz | 250 g | 1. Dissolve the sugar in the water over high heat and boil the mixture until it reaches 240°F (115°C). (See p. 260 for information on boiling sugar.) |
| Water | 2 oz | 60 g | |
| Egg yolks | 4 oz<br>(6 yolks) | 125 g<br>(6 yolks) | 2. While the syrup is boiling, whip the egg yolks (using the whip attachment of the mixing machine) until light and foamy. |
| Flavoring (see variations following recipe for Basic Bombe Mixture II) | | | 3. With the machine running, slowly pour the hot syrup into the egg yolks. Continue whipping until the mixture is cool. It should be very thick and foamy. |
| Heavy cream | 1 pt | 500 mL | 4. This mixture will keep, covered and refrigerated, up to 1 week. When you are ready to assemble a dessert, proceed with the next steps. |

5. Stir the desired flavorings into the egg yolk mixture.
6. Whip the cream until it forms soft, not stiff, peaks. Do not overwhip.
7. Fold the cream into the base mixture. Pour the result into prepared molds or other containers and freeze it until firm.

# SYRUP FOR BOMBES

*Yield: about 1½ qt (1.5 L)*

| Ingredients | U.S. | Metric | Procedure |
|---|---|---|---|
| Sugar | 3 lb | 1.5 kg | 1. Combine the water and sugar in a saucepan. Bring the mixture to a boil, stirring until the sugar is completely dissolved. |
| Water | 2 lb | 1 kg | 2. Remove the syrup from the heat and let it cool. Store it in a covered container in the refrigerator. |

*Note: Simple syrup of this concentration is used in the Basic Bombe Mixture II (p. 568) and Frozen Mousse II (p. 571).*

# BASIC BOMBE MIXTURE II

*Yield: 1½ qt (1.5 L)*

| Ingredients | U.S. | Metric | Procedure |
|---|---|---|---|
| Egg yolks | 6 oz (9 yolks) | 180 g (9 yolks) | 1. Whip the egg yolks lightly in a stainless-steel bowl, then gradually beat in the syrup. |
| Syrup for bombes (see p. 567) | 8 oz | 250 mL | 2. Set the bowl over hot water and whip the mixture with a wire whip until it is thick and creamy, about the consistency of a thick hollandaise sauce. |
| Flavoring (see variations below) | | | 3. Remove the mixture from the heat, set it over ice, and continue whipping until it is cold. |
| Heavy cream | 12 oz | 375 mL | 4. Add the desired flavoring. |

5. Whip the cream until it forms soft peaks. Do not over-whip. Fold it into the egg yolk mixture.

6. Pour the mixture into molds or other containers. Freeze until firm.

## VARIATIONS

To create bombes of different flavors, add the suggested flavorings to either of the egg-yolk mixtures in the above two recipes before folding in the whipped cream.

### VANILLA

Add ½–¾ oz (15–22 mL) vanilla extract.

### CHOCOLATE

Melt 2 oz (60 g) unsweetened chocolate. Stir in a little stock syrup to make a thick sauce. Then fold this into the yolk mixture. (For a stronger chocolate flavor, melt 1–1½ oz (30–45 g) sweet chocolate with the 2 oz (60 g) unsweetened chocolate.)

### LIQUEUR

Add 1–1½ oz (30–45 mL), or to taste, desired liqueur or spirit, such as orange liqueur, kirsch, or rum.

### COFFEE

Add ¼ oz (8 g) instant coffee dissolved in ½ oz (15 mL) water.

### PRALINE

Add 2½ oz (75 g) praline paste, softened with a little water, to the yolk mixture.

### FRUIT (RASPBERRY, STRAWBERRY, APRICOT, PEACH, ETC.)

Add up to 8 oz (250 g) fruit purée.

### BOMBE OR PARFAIT WITH FRUIT

Instead of flavoring the bombe mixture with a fruit purée, add solid fruits cut in small dice to plain or liqueur-flavored bombe mixture.

### BOMBE OR PARFAIT WITH NUTS, SPONGE CAKE, OR OTHER INGREDIENTS

Solid ingredients besides fruit may be mixed with plain or flavored bombe mixture, including chopped nuts, crumbled almond macaroons, marrons glacés (candied chestnuts), and diced sponge cake or ladyfingers moistened with liqueur.

## Procedure for Making Bombes

1. Place the bombe mold in the freezer until very cold.

2. Line the mold with a layer of slightly softened ice cream, using your hand to press it against the sides and smooth it. The ice cream layer should be about ¾ in. (2 cm) thick for small molds, up to 1½ in. (4 cm) for large molds.

    If the ice cream becomes too soft to stick to the sides, place it in the freezer to harden it, then try again.

3. Freeze the mold until the ice cream layer is hard.

4. Fill the mold with bombe mixture, cover, and freeze until firm.

5. To unmold, dip the mold in warm water for a second, wipe the water from the outside of the mold, and turn out the bombe onto a cold serving plate. (*Note:* To keep the bombe from sliding around on the plate, turn it out onto a thin sheet of genoise, which acts as a base.)

6. Decorate with whipped cream and appropriate fruits or other items.

7. Serve immediately. Cut into wedges or slices so all portions are uniform.

## *A Selection of Classic Bombes*

### BOMBE AFRICAINE

Coating: chocolate ice cream

Filling: apricot bombe mixture

### BOMBE AIDA

Coating: strawberry ice cream

Filling: kirsch-flavored bombe mixture

### BOMBE BRESILIENNE

Coating: pineapple sherbet

Filling: bombe mixture flavored with vanilla and rum and mixed with diced pineapple

### BOMBE CARDINALE

Coating: raspberry sherbet

Filling: praline vanilla bombe mixture

### BOMBE CEYLON

Coating: coffee ice cream

Filling: rum-flavored bombe mixture

### BOMBE COPPELIA

Coating: coffee ice cream

Filling: praline bombe mixture

### BOMBE DIPLOMAT

Coating: vanilla ice cream

Filling: bombe mixture flavored with maraschino liqueur and mixed with candied fruit

### BOMBE FLORENTINE

Coating: raspberry sherbet

Filling: praline bombe mixture

### BOMBE FORMOSA

Coating: vanilla ice cream

Filling: bombe mixture flavored with strawberry purée and mixed with whole strawberries

### BOMBE MOLDAVE

Coating: pineapple sherbet

Filling: bombe mixture flavored with orange liqueur

### BOMBE SULTANE

Coating: chocolate ice cream

Filling: praline bombe mixture

### BOMBE TUTTI-FRUTTI

Coating: strawberry ice cream or sherbet

Filling: lemon bombe mixture mixed with candied fruits

### CASSATA NAPOLETANA

Cassatas are Italian-style bombes lined with three layers of different ice creams and filled with Italian meringue mixed with various ingredients. The most popular, Cassata Napoletana, is made as follows. Line the mold first with vanilla, then with chocolate, and finally with strawberry ice cream. Fill with Italian Meringue (p. 267) flavored with vanilla, kirsch, or maraschino and mixed with an equal weight of diced candied fruits. A little whipped cream may be added to the meringue, if desired.

# Frozen Mousses and Frozen Soufflés

*Frozen mousses* are light frozen desserts containing whipped cream. Although they are all similar in character because of their whipped cream content, the bases for them are made in several ways. Three types of preparation are included here:

◆ Mousse with Italian meringue base.

◆ Mousse with syrup and fruit base.

◆ Mousse with custard base.

The mixture for bombes and parfaits can also be used for mousses.

The simplest method for serving mousse is to pour the mixture into individual serving dishes and freeze them. The mixture can also be poured into molds of various shapes. After unmolding, cut the mousse into portions and decorate it with whipped cream and appropriate fruits, cookies, or other items.

*Frozen soufflés* are simply mousse or bombe mixtures frozen in soufflé dishes or other straight-sided dishes. A band of heavy paper or foil, called a *collar*, is tied around the mold so it extends 2 inches (5 cm) or more above the rim of the dish. The mousse or bombe mixture is poured in so it comes within ½ inch (12 mm) of the top of this band. After the dessert is frozen, the band is removed. The dessert thus looks like a hot soufflé that has risen above its baking dish.

Other items may be incorporated in the frozen soufflé, such as sponge cake, ladyfingers, baked meringue, fruits, and so forth. For example, you might pour one-third of the mousse mixture into the prepared dish, place a japonaise disk (p. 348) on top, pour in another layer of mousse, add a second japonaise, then fill with the mousse mixture. This technique can also be used with thin sponge cake layers. For further variety, arrange a layer of fruit on top of each genoise layer before adding more mousse.

# FROZEN MOUSSE I (MERINGUE BASE)

*Yield: 1½ qt (1.5 L)*

| Ingredients | U.S. | Metric | Procedure |
|---|---|---|---|
| **Italian meringue** | | | 1. *For the Italian meringue:* Dissolve the sugar in the water in a saucepan and boil the syrup until it reaches 250°F (120°C). Meanwhile, whip the egg whites until they form soft peaks. Whipping constantly, slowly pour the hot syrup into the egg whites. Continue to whip the meringue until it is completely cool (unless you are flavoring it with liqueur—see next step). |
| Sugar | 8 oz | 250 g | |
| Water | 2 oz | 60 mL | |
| Egg whites | 4 oz | 125 g L | |
| Flavoring (see *Note*) | | | 2. Stir or fold in flavoring ingredients. If you are using melted chocolate or a thick fruit purée, stir a little of the meringue into the flavoring, then fold this into the rest of the meringue. If you are using a liqueur or spirit, add it while the meringue is still warm so most of the alcohol evaporates. |
| Heavy cream | 12 oz | 375 mL | |

*Note: Possible flavorings include fruit purées, liqueurs, and chocolate. Use up to 3 oz (90 mL) strong spirits (brandy or dark rum, for example) or 4 oz (125 mL) sweet liqueur. Use 4 oz (125 g) melted unsweetened chocolate or up to 8 oz (250 g) thick fruit purée. Specific flavors are suggested in the variations following the basic procedure.*

3. Whip the cream until it forms soft peaks. Fold it into the meringue mixture. Freeze.

## VARIATIONS

*The following are a few of many possible flavors for frozen mousse.*

### LIQUEUR MOUSSE

Flavor with 3 oz (90 mL) brandy, dark rum, or Calvados, or with 4 oz (125 mL) sweet liqueur.

MORE VARIATIONS

## CHOCOLATE MOUSSE

Melt 4 oz (125 g) unsweetened chocolate. Stir in a little Syrup for Bombes (p. 567) to make a thick sauce. Stir some of the meringue into this mixture, then fold the chocolate mixture into the rest of the meringue.

## APRICOT MOUSSE

Soak 6 oz (188 g) dried apricots in water overnight, then simmer until tender. Drain and purée in a food mill. Fold into the meringue. If desired, add ½ oz (15 mL) rum or kirsch.

## BANANA MOUSSE

Purée 8 oz (250 g) very ripe bananas with ½ oz (15 mL) lemon juice. Add to meringue.

## LEMON MOUSSE

Add 3 oz (90 mL) lemon juice and the grated zest of 1 lemon to the meringue.

## CHESTNUT MOUSSE

Soften 7 oz (220 g) chestnut purée by blending it with 1 oz (30 mL) dark rum until smooth. Add it to the meringue.

## RASPBERRY OR STRAWBERRY MOUSSE

Force 8 oz (250 g) fresh or frozen (unsweetened) raspberries or strawberries through a sieve. Add to the meringue.

# FROZEN MOUSSE II (SYRUP AND FRUIT BASE)

*Yield: about 2½ pt (1.25 L)*

| Ingredients | U.S. | Metric | Procedure |
|---|---|---|---|
| Syrup for Bombes (p. 567) | 8 oz | 250 mL | 1. Mix the syrup and fruit purée until uniformly blended. |
| Fruit purée | 8 oz | 250 mL | 2. Whip the cream until it forms soft peaks. |
| Heavy cream | 1 pt | 500 mL | 3. Fold the cream into the syrup mixture. |
| | | | 4. Pour the mixture into molds or dishes and freeze. |

# FROZEN MOUSSE III (CUSTARD BASE)

*Yield: about 1½ qt (1.5 L)*

| Ingredients | U.S. | Metric | Procedure |
|---|---|---|---|
| Egg yolks | 5 oz (7–8 yolks) | 150 g (7–8 yolks) | 1. Whip the egg yolks with half the sugar until they are light and foamy. |
| Sugar | 8 oz | 250 g | 2. Meanwhile, bring the milk to a boil with the rest of the sugar. |
| Milk | 8 oz | 250 mL | 3. Pour the milk over the yolks, whipping constantly. |
| Flavoring (see step 6) | | | 4. Set the milk and egg mixture over a hot-water bath and cook, stirring constantly, until the mixture thickens like crème anglaise (p. 268). Do not overcook, or the custard will curdle. |
| Heavy cream | 1 pt | 500 mL | 5. Cool the mixture, then chill it in the refrigerator or over ice. |
| | | | 6. Add the desired flavoring. The same flavorings and quantities may be used as in Frozen Mousse I (p. 570). |
| | | | 7. Whip the cream and fold it into the custard mixture. |
| | | | 8. Pour the mousse into molds or dishes and freeze. |

# WHITE CHOCOLATE PARFAIT WITH FLAMBÉED CHERRIES

*Yield: 10 parfaits, 3 oz (95 g) each*

| Ingredients | U.S. | | Metric | Procedure |
|---|---|---|---|---|
| **Flambéed cherries** | | | | 1. *Prepare the cherries:* Pit the cherries and place them and the sugar in a saucepan. Heat gently until liquid begins to cook out of the cherries. Continue to heat until the liquid is almost evaporated. Add the vanilla and the port. Place over high heat and flambé to burn off the alcohol. Continue to cook, lightly covered, over low heat until the juices are thick and syrupy. Drain the cherries for use in step 7. Reserve the syrup. |
| Fresh cherries (see *Note*) | 10 | oz | 300 g | |
| Sugar | 2 | oz | 60 g | |
| Vanilla extract | ½ | tsp | 2 g | |
| Port wine | 5 | oz | 150 g | |
| Baked disks of Chocolate Meringue (p. 347), 2½ in. (6 cm) in diameter | 10 | | 10 | 2. Set 2¾-in. (7 cm) ring molds on a tray. Place a disk of baked chocolate meringue in the base of each. |
| Sugar | 3.67 | oz | 110 g | 3. For the parfait, dissolve the sugar in the water and bring to a boil. |
| Water | 2.5 | oz | 75 g | |
| Egg yolks | 4 | oz | 120 g | 4. Whip the egg yolks until light and gradually whip in the hot syrup. Continue whipping until cool. |
| White chocolate, chopped | 5 | oz | 150 g | 5. Melt the white chocolate over a hot-water bath. |
| Heavy cream | 12 | oz | 375 g | 6. Quickly mix the chocolate into the egg-yolk sabayon. Do not overmix, or the sabayon may fall. |
| **Decoration** | | | | 7. Whip the cream and quickly fold it in. |
| Chocolate curls | as needed | | as needed | |
| Pistachios | as needed | | as needed | 8. Without delay, fill the molds about two-thirds full. Place 6–8 cherries in each one, pushing some of them down into the mix. (Reserve the remaining cherries and syrup to serve with the parfaits.) Fill to the top with parfait mix and level the tops. Freeze for at least 1 hour or until firm. |
| ***Total weight of parfait mix:*** | **1 lb 9** | **oz** | **775 g** | |

*Note: Cherries packed in syrup may also be used.*
*Morello cherries (griottes) are especially good in this preparation.*
*Drain the cherries and proceed as in the basic recipe.*

9. To serve, unmold by lightly warming the mold and lifting it off. Top with chocolate curls and pistachios and a few cherries. Spoon some of the cherry syrup and a few more cherries onto the plate.

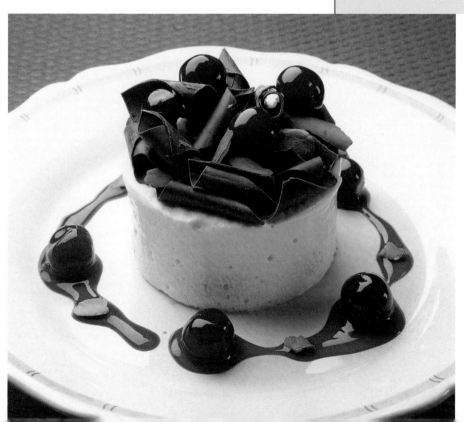

# COINTREAU ICED SOUFFLÉ

| Ingredients | U.S. | Metric | Procedure |
|---|---|---|---|
| Milk | 7 oz | 200 g | 1. *Make a crème anglaise:* Combine the milk and vanilla bean and bring to a simmer. Whip the egg yolks with sugar until light, then temper by beating in half the hot milk. Return this mixture to the pan with the rest of the milk and cook gently until slightly thickened. Cool over an ice bath. |
| Vanilla bean, split (see *Note*) | ½ | ½ | |
| Egg yolks | 4 oz | 120 g | |
| Sugar | 7 oz | 200 g | |
| Cointreau liqueur (see *Note*) | 2 oz | 60 g | 2. Add the liqueur. Chill. |
| Heavy cream | 14 oz | 400 g | 3. Whip the cream to soft peaks. Fold into the chilled custard mixture. Pour into prepared mold (see below) and level the top with a palette knife. Freeze. |
| **Mold Preparation** | | | **MOLD PREPARATION** |
| Almond Macaroons II (p. 506) | 12 | 12 | 1. Use a doubled sheet of parchment paper to tie a collar around a 5-in. (12.5 cm) soufflé dish, so the collar extends 1½ in. (4 cm) above the rim. Secure with string. |
| Cointreau liqueur | 1.5–2 oz | 50 g | 2. Dip the almond macaroons in liqueur and arrange them in the bottom of the dish. |
| **For Service** | | | 3. Fill with the soufflé mix. |
| Crème Chantilly (p. 265) | as needed | as needed | **SERVICE** |
| Candied Orange Zest (p. 602) | as needed | as needed | Remove the paper collar. Decorate the top with rosettes of crème chantilly around the edge. Arrange candied orange zest in the center. Top each cream rosette with a macaroon. |
| Additional Almond Macaroons | as needed | as needed | |
| **Total weight of soufflé mix:** | **2 lb 2 oz** | **980 g** | |

Note: If vanilla beans are not available, add ¼ tsp (1 g) vanilla extract to the cooked egg mixture.
Other orange liqueurs can be used, but the name of the recipe should be changed to reflect that.

# POPPY SEED PARFAIT

| Ingredients | U.S. | | Metric | Procedure |
|---|---|---|---|---|
| Milk | 8 | oz | 250 g | 1. Heat the first quantity of milk with the poppy seeds. Simmer for 10 minutes. Skim and cool. |
| Poppy seeds | 3.25 | oz | 100 g | |
| Milk | 4 | oz | 125 g | 2. *Make a crème anglaise:* Heat the remaining milk. Whip the egg yolks and sugar until pale. Temper the egg mixture with half the hot milk, then pour this mixture back into the pan with the remaining milk and cook gently until just thickened enough to coat the back of a spoon. Add the vanilla, the amaretto, and the poppy seeds and milk from step 1. Chill over ice. |
| Egg yolks | 2.67 oz (4 yolks) | | 80 g (4 yolks) | |
| Sugar | 3.75 | oz | 120 g | |
| Vanilla extract | ¼ | tsp | 1 g | |
| Amaretto liqueur | 1.25 | oz | 40 g | |
| Heavy cream | 13 | oz | 400 g | 3. Whip the cream to stiff peaks. (It is important to whip the cream until stiff to prevent the poppy seeds from sinking to the bottom of the parfait, but take care not to over-whip.) Fold the whipped cream into the chilled poppy seed mixture. |
| *Total weight:* | **2 lb 3** | **oz** | **1116 g** | |
| | | | | 4. Pour into molds and freeze. |

# ICED LOW-FAT RASPBERRY PARFAIT

*Yield: about 3 pt (1.5 L)*

| Ingredients | U.S. | | Metric | Procedure |
|---|---|---|---|---|
| **Italian Meringue** | | | | 1. *Make an Italian meringue:* Dissolve the sugar in the water and boil to 250°F (120°C). Whip the egg whites to soft peaks. While whipping constantly, slowly pour in the hot syrup. Continue whipping until the meringue is cool. |
| Sugar | 3.5 | oz | 100 g | |
| Water | 2.25 | oz | 65 g | |
| Egg whites | 3 | oz | 90 g | |
| Raspberries, fresh or frozen | 7 | oz | 200 g | 2. Purée the raspberries and force the purée through a sieve to remove the seeds. |
| Plain low-fat yogurt | 7 | oz | 200 g | 3. Whip the yogurt until smooth and mix in the raspberry purée. |
| | | | | 4. Fold the cold meringue, one-third at a time, into the yogurt mixture. |
| | | | | 5. Pour into molds and freeze. |

**VARIATION**

Other fruit purées can be substituted for the raspberries.

See page 620 for a serving suggestion.

## TERMS FOR REVIEW

| | | | |
|---|---|---|---|
| ice cream | frozen yogurt | granita | Baked Alaska |
| Philadelphia-style ice cream | ice | overrun | bombe |
| French-style ice cream | granité | sundae | frozen mousse |
| ice milk | gelato | coupe | frozen soufflé |
| sherbet | sorbetto | parfait | |

## QUESTIONS FOR DISCUSSION

1. Why do ice cream and sherbet have to be frozen in a special freezer that mixes the product while it is being frozen? Why is it possible to freeze frozen mousses and similar desserts without this kind of freezer?

2. How does sugar affect the freezing properties of frozen desserts?

3. How does alcohol affect the freezing properties of frozen desserts?

4. How are still-frozen desserts similar to Bavarians?

5. Describe the procedure for making a Baked Alaska or Soufflé Surprise.

6. Describe the basic procedure for making bombes.

## Chapter 22

# Fruit Desserts

**I**nterest in desserts with less fat and fewer calories has stimulated interest in fruit desserts as alternatives to richer pastries and cakes. Fruits are, of course, important components of many pastries, cakes, and sauces, and many fruit desserts contain significant amounts of fat and sugar, including some in this chapter. Nevertheless, customers often perceive such desserts as more healthful, and this may account, in part, for their popularity. Another factor is the fresh, stimulating flavors of many fruit desserts.

In earlier chapters, we discussed fruit pies, fritters, pastries, tarts, cakes, and sauces. Many other types of fruit-based dessert, however, do not fit neatly into these categories. A representative sampling of recipes is included here, although, of course, they are only a small fraction of the many hundreds of recipes to be found elsewhere.

**After reading this chapter, you should be able to:**

1. Select good-quality fresh fruits and prepare them for use in desserts.

2. Calculate fresh fruit yields based on trimming losses.

3. Prepare various fruit desserts, including poached fruits and fruit compotes.

# HANDLING FRESH FRUITS

Advances in transportation and refrigeration have made fresh fruits widely available year-round. Even exotic tropical fruits are increasingly common in the market. Not long ago, most fresh fruits were available during limited seasons only. For example, strawberries were usually available for a short time in the spring, when they were in season. Now, however, almost everything is in season somewhere in the world, and it is easy to ship that crop to any market.

Unlimited availability is a mixed blessing, however. Shipped-in, out-of-season fruits may not be at the peak of quality. Many fruit varieties, in addition, are bred for shipping rather than for flavor. Thus it is important to be able to evaluate the quality of fresh fruit.

---

### ☙ FRUIT VERSUS VEGETABLE ❧

In culinary terms, a vegetable is a plant part that is used primarily in savory dishes. Plant parts include roots, tubers, stems, leaves, and fruits. Yes, fruits. A fruit is, in botanical terms, the part of the plant that bears the seeds. Cucumbers, squash, green beans, eggplant, okra, pea pods, tree nuts such as walnuts, avocado, and chiles are all fruits. And they are all vegetables. There is no contradiction in this statement any more than in saying that carrots, parsnips, and turnips are all roots and all vegetables.

In culinary terms, a fruit is the part of a plant that bears the seeds and that is used primarily in sweet dishes. In most cases, the fruits used are those that are high in natural sugar content. In nature, however, most fruits are not sweet—think of milkweed pods and prickly burdock, for example. Similarly, many fruits used in the kitchen are not sweet—that is, they are vegetables.

---

## Ripening

Part of evaluating the quality of fruits is judging their ripeness. As explained in the sidebar, some fruits continue to ripen after they are harvested, and the chef must be able to judge their degree of ripeness. Other fruits are harvested ripe and must be used quickly, before they deteriorate.

Ripening is a complex phenomenon. Some fruits change more than others. The main kinds of changes are the following:

- **Aroma.** Bitter or unpleasant aromas fade, and attractive aromas develop. With few exceptions, this happens only before harvest.

- **Sweetness.** Sugar content increases. Some sugar comes from the plant before harvest, and some results as stored starches in the fruit break down.

- **Juiciness and texture.** Cell walls break down. This releases juices and makes the fruit softer.

- **Color.** Many fruits are green when immature and turn red, orange, purple, or other color when they ripen.

The following table indicates which of our common fruits undergo which of these changes. Except for pears, which can be refrigerated before they ripen completely to avoid mushiness, do not refrigerate fruits until they have ripened. After they have ripened, refrigerate to slow deterioration. Fruits that are picked fully ripe should be refrigerated upon receipt.

| | |
|---|---|
| These fruits undergo changes in aroma, sweetness, juiciness and texture, and color when they ripen after picking. | Avocado (usually used as a vegetable, not in the bakeshop)<br>Banana |
| These fruits become sweeter, juicier, and softer, and their color changes when they ripen after picking. | Apple (still crisp, unless overripe, but not as hard as unripe apples)<br>Kiwi<br>Mango<br>Papaya<br>Pear |
| These fruits do not become sweeter, but they do become juicier and softer, and their color changes when they ripen after picking. | Apricot<br>Blueberry<br>Fig<br>Melon (hollow types)<br>Nectarine<br>Passion fruit<br>Peach<br>Persimmon<br>Plum |
| These fruits are harvested fully ripe and do not ripen further after picking. | Berries (except blueberries)<br>Citrus fruits (grapefruit, orange, tangerine, lemon, lime, kumquat)<br>Cherries<br>Grapes<br>Pineapple<br>Watermelon |

## Trimming Loss: Calculating Yields and Amounts Needed

All fresh fruits must be washed before being used. Following washing, nearly all fruits require further preparation and trimming. Sometimes prep is simple—pulling grapes from their stems or picking over blueberries to remove bits of stem and leaf. In other cases, further trimming, peeling, and cutting may be required. The next section describes basic preparation for individual fruits.

Because parts of a fruit may be removed and discarded, the amount purchased is not the same as the amount served. The percentage yield of a fruit indicates, on the average, how much of the *AP weight* (as purchased weight) is left after pre-prep to produce the ready-to-cook item, or *EP weight* (edible portion weight). You can use this figure to do two basic calculations.

1. **Calculating yield.**
   Example: You have 10 lb AP kiwi fruit. Yield after trimming is 80 percent. What will your EP weight be?

   First, change the percentage to a decimal number by moving the decimal point two places to the left.

   $$80\% = 0.80$$

   Multiply the decimal by your AP weight to get EP yield.

   $$10 \text{ lb} \times 0.80 = 8 \text{ lb}$$

2. **Calculating amount needed.**
   Example: You need 10 lb EP kiwi fruit. What amount of untrimmed fruit do you need?

> ### ❈{ MATURITY }❈ AND RIPENESS
>
> A *mature* fruit is one that has completed its development and is physiologically capable of continuing the ripening process. A *ripe* fruit is one that is at its peak for texture and flavor and is ready to be consumed. In other words, maturity refers to biological development and ripeness refers to eating quality. Fruit that is harvested before it is mature will not soften and develop good eating quality. On the other hand, the riper a fruit is at harvest, the shorter its potential storage life, so growers, when possible, harvest fruit that is mature but not yet ripe. As indicated in the table, however, not all fruits are capable of ripening after they have been picked.

Change the percentage to a decimal number.

80% = 0.80

Divide the EP weight needed by this number to get the AP weight.

$$\frac{10 \text{ lb}}{0.80} = 12\frac{1}{2} \text{ lb}$$

# Evaluating and Preparing

The following is a summary of the most commonly available fresh fruits. Emphasis is on what qualities to look for when purchasing them and on how to trim and prepare them for use. In addition, identification information is included for certain exotic items. Nearly everyone knows what apples, bananas, and strawberries are, but not everyone can identify a persimmon or a passion fruit. Trimming yields are also given.

**Apples.** Mature apples have a fruity aroma, brown seeds, and a slightly softer texture than unripe fruit. Overripe or old apples are soft and sometimes shriveled. Avoid apples with bruises, blemishes, decay, or mealy texture. Summer varieties (sold until fall) do not keep well. Fall and winter varieties keep well and are available for a longer period. Apples with a good acid content are usually better for cooking than bland eating varieties like Red Delicious. Granny Smith and Golden Delicious are widely used for cooking.

To prepare, wash; pare if desired. Quarter and remove core, or leave whole and core with a special coring tool. Use a stainless-steel knife for cutting to avoid discoloring the fruit. After paring, dip in solution of lemon juice (or other tart fruit juice) or ascorbic acid to prevent browning.

Percentage yield: 75%

**Apricots.** Only tree-ripened apricots have sufficient flavor, and they keep for only a week or less under refrigeration. They should be golden yellow, firm, and plump, not mushy. Avoid fruit that is too soft, blemished, or decayed.

Wash, split in half, and remove pit. Peeling is not necessary for most purposes.

Percentage yield: 94%

**Bananas.** Look for plump, smooth bananas without bruises or spoilage. All bananas are picked green, so you don't need to avoid unripe fruit. Avoid overripe fruit, however.

Ripen at room temperature for three to five days; fully ripe fruit is all yellow with small brown flecks and no green. Refrigerating the ripe fruit will darken the skin but not the flesh. Peel and dip in fruit juice to prevent browning.

Percentage yield: 70%

**Berries.** This category includes blackberries, blueberries, cranberries, blackcurrants (cassis), red currants, white currants, lingonberries, raspberries, and strawberries. Berries should be full, plump, and clean, with bright, fully ripe color. Watch for moldy or spoiled fruits. Wet spots on the carton indicate damaged fruit.

Granny Smith apple

Golden Delicious apple

Rome apple

Gala apple

Bananas

Blackberries

Blueberries

Cranberries

White currants

Raspberries

Strawberries

Refrigerate in the original container until ready to use in order to reduce handling. Except for cranberries, berries do not keep well. Sort out spoiled berries and foreign materials. Wash with gentle spray and drain well. Remove the stems and hulls from strawberries. Red currants for garnishing are often left on the stem. Handle berries carefully to avoid bruising.

Percentage yield: 92–95%

**Cherries.** Look for plump, firm, sweet, juicy cherries. Bing or black cherries should be uniform dark red to almost black.

Refrigerate in the original container until ready to use. Just before use, remove stems and sort out damaged fruit. Rinse and drain well. Pit with a special pitting tool.

Percentage yield: 82% (pitted)

Cherries

**Coconuts.** Shake to hear liquid inside; fruits with no liquid are dried out. Avoid cracked fruits and fruits with wet eyes.

Pierce an eye with an ice pick or nail and drain the liquid. Crack the coconut with a hammer and remove the meat from the shell (this job is easier if the shell is placed in a 350°F/175°C oven 10–15 minutes). Peel the brown skin with a paring knife or vegetable peeler.

Percentage yield: 50%

Coconut

**Figs.** Calimyrna figs, also called Smyrna figs, are light green; Black Mission figs and Black Spanish figs (also called Brown Turkey) are purple. All figs are sweet when ripe and soft and delicate in texture. They should be plump and soft, without spoilage or sour odor.

Keep refrigerated (although firm, unripe figs can be left at room temperature, spread in one layer, for a few days to ripen slightly). Rinse and drain, handling carefully. Trim off hard stem ends.

Percentage yield: 95% (80–85% if peeled)

Figs

**Grapefruit.** Select fruit that is heavy for its size and has a firm, smooth skin. Avoid puffy, soft fruits and those with pointed ends, which have low yield and a lot of rind. Cut and taste for sweetness.

For sections and slices, peel with a chef's knife, removing all white pith. Free sections from membrane with a small knife.

Percentage yield: 45–50% (flesh without membrane); 40–45% (juiced)

Grapefruit

Peeling a grapefruit

a. Cut off the ends of the grapefruit and turn it on a flat end so it is stable. Slice off a section of the peel, following the contour of the grapefruit.

b. Make sure the cut is deep enough to remove the peel but not so deep as to waste the product.

c. Continue making slices around the grapefruit until all the peel is removed.

d. Slice or section the fruit. (Squeeze the remaining pulp for juice.)

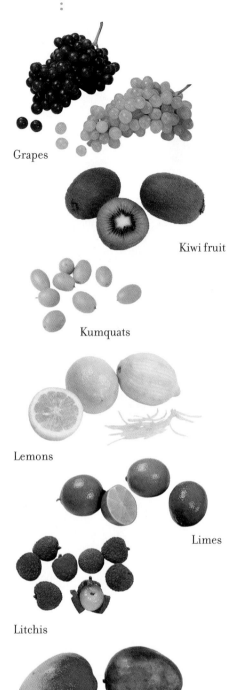

Grapes

Kiwi fruit

Kumquats

Lemons

Limes

Litchis

Mangoes

Cantaloupe

**Grapes.** Look for firm, ripe, good-colored fruits in full bunches. Grapes should be firmly attached to stems and should not fall off when shaken. Watch for rotting or shriveling at stem ends.

Refrigerate in the original container. Wash and drain. Except for seedless varieties, cut in half and remove seeds with the point of a paring knife.

Percentage yield: 90%

**Kiwi fruit.** Kiwis are firm when unripe; they become slightly softer when ripe but do not change color significantly. Allow them to ripen at room temperature. Avoid fruits with bruises or soft spots.

Pare the thin outer skin. Cut crosswise into slices. Alternative method for slices with smooth, round edges: Cut off ends. Insert spoon into end, sliding it just beneath the skin; twist the spoon to completely free the flesh from the skin.

Percentage yield: 80%

**Kumquats.** These look like tiny, elongated oranges, about the size of a medium olive. The skin and even the seeds can be eaten. In fact, the skin is sweet, while the flesh and juice are tart. Avoid soft or shriveled fruit. Kumquats keep well and are usually in good condition in the market.

Wash, drain well, and cut as desired.

Percentage yield: 95–100%

**Lemons and limes.** Look for firm, smooth skins. Colors may vary: Limes may be yellow and lemons may have some green on skin. The most commonly used limes are called Persian limes, usually with a deep green rind. Key limes are much smaller and may be green or yellow. A special variety of lemon called Meyer lemon has a higher sugar concentration than regular lemons and thus has a sweeter taste. Once rare, Meyer lemons have become more widely available.

Cut in wedges, slices, or other shapes for garnish, or cut in half crosswise for juicing.

Percentage yield: 40–45% (juiced)

**Litchis** (or lychees). This Chinese fruit is about the size of a walnut or Ping-Pong ball. Its rough, leathery outer skin, which ranges from reddish to brown, is easily peeled away to reveal aromatic, juicy white flesh that surrounds an inedible pit. Look for heavy, plump fruit with good color.

Peel, cut in half, and remove the seed.

Percentage yield: 50%

**Mangoes.** The two main types of this tropical fruit are oval ones with a skin that ranges from green to orange to red, and kidney-shaped fruit with skin that is a more uniform yellow when ripe. Mangoes have a thin but tough skin and yellow to yellow-orange flesh that is juicy and aromatic. Fruit should be plump and firm, with clear color and no blemishes. Avoid rock-hard fruit, which may not ripen properly.

Let ripen at room temperature until slightly soft. Peel and cut the flesh away from the center stone, or cut in half before peeling, working a thin-bladed knife around both sides of the flat stone.

Percentage yield: 75%

**Melons.** Look for the following characteristics when selecting melons. *Cantaloupes:* Smooth scar on stem end, with no trace of stem (called *full slip,* meaning the melon was picked ripe). Yellow rind, with little or no green. Heavy, with good aroma. *Honeydew:* Good aroma, slightly soft, heavy, creamy white to yellowish rind, not too green. Large sizes have best quality. *Crenshaw, Casaba, Persian, Canary, Santa Claus:* Heavy, with a rich aroma and slightly soft blossom end. *Watermelon:* Yellow underside, not white. Firm and symmetrical. Large sizes have best yield. Velvety surface, not too shiny. When cut, look for hard dark brown seeds and no white heart (hard white streak running through center).

Honeydew                    Canary melon                    Watermelon

To prepare hollow melons, wash, cut in half, and remove seeds and fibers. Cut into wedges and cut flesh from rind, or cut balls with ball cutter. Alternatively, cut the rind from the whole melon with a heavy knife, using same technique as illustrated for grapefruit, above. Then cut in half, remove the seeds, and cut the flesh as desired. For watermelon, wash, cut in half or into pieces, and cut balls with ball cutter, or cut flesh from rind and remove seeds.

Percentage yield: Watermelons, 45%; others, 50–55%

**Nectarines.**  See peaches and nectarines.

**Oranges and mandarins (including tangerines).**  To buy high-quality oranges, use the same guidelines as for grapefruit. Mandarins may feel puffy, but they should be heavy for their size. Unusual varieties include blood oranges, with dark red flesh and juice and intense flavor, and Seville oranges, with tart rather than sweet flesh. Seville oranges are prized for making marmalade.

Peel mandarins by hand and separate the sections. For juicing, cut oranges in half crosswise; for sections, see grapefruit.

Percentage yield: 60–65% (sections with no membranes); 50% (juiced)

**Papayas.**  Papayas are pear-shaped tropical fruits with a mild, sweet flavor and slightly floral aroma. The flesh is yellow or pinkish, depending on the variety, and the center cavity holds a mass of round, black seeds. Papayas may weigh from less than 1 pound to several pounds (less than 500 g to more than 1 kg) each. Their skin is green when unripe, becoming yellow as they ripen. For best quality, select fruits that are firm and symmetrical, without bruises or rotten spots. Avoid dark green papayas, which may not ripen properly.

Let ripen at room temperature until slightly soft and nearly all yellow, with only a little green. Wash. Cut in half lengthwise and scrape out the seeds. Peel, if desired, or serve the seeded halves as they are, like small melon halves.

Percentage yield: 65%

**Passion fruit.**  These are tropical fruits about the size of eggs, with a brownish purple skin that becomes wrinkled when ripe. (There is also a yellow-skinned variety.) They are mostly hollow when ripe, with juice, seeds, and a little flesh inside. The tart juice has an intense, exotic flavor and aroma that is greatly prized by pastry chefs. Select fruits that are large and heavy for their size. If they are smooth, let ripen at room temperature until the skin is wrinkled.

To use, cut in half, taking care not to lose any juice. Scrape out the seeds, juice, and pulp. The seeds can be eaten, so do not discard them. If you need only the juice, it is much more economical to buy the frozen juice, as fresh fruits are expensive.

Percentage yield: 40–45%

**Peaches and nectarines.**  Peaches should be plump and firm, without bruises or blemishes. Avoid dark green fruits, which are immature and will not ripen well. Avoid fruits that have been refrigerated before ripening, as they may be mealy. Select freestone varieties of peaches. Clingstone varieties require too much labor (they are used primarily for canning).

Nectarines

Oranges

Tangerines

Papaya

Passion fruit

Peaches

Pears

Persimmons

Prune plums

Red plums

Black freestone plums

Santa Rosa plums

Pomegranate

Let ripen at room temperature, then refrigerate. Peel peaches by blanching in boiling water 10 to 20 seconds, until the skin slips off easily, and cool in ice water. (Nectarines do not need to be peeled unless you wish.) Cut in half, remove the pit, and drop into fruit juice, sugar syrup, or ascorbic acid solution to prevent darkening.

Percentage yield: 75%

**Pears.** Pears should be clean, firm, and bright, with no blemishes or bruises.

Pears for eating raw should be fully ripe and aromatic. However, once they have ripened, pears are likely to become mushy within a day, so refrigerate immediately upon ripening. For cooking, they are better if slightly underripe, as fully ripe pears are too soft when cooked. Wash, pare, cut in halves or quarters, and remove core. To prevent browning, dip in fruit juice.

Percentage yield: 75% (peeled and cored)

**Persimmons.** Persimmons are orange-red fruits available in two varieties. The most common is Hachiya, which is shaped somewhat like a large acorn (about 8 oz/250 g each). It is extremely tannic when unripe, nearly inedible, but it ripens to a soft, jellylike mass. Ripe persimmons are sweet, juicy, and mild but rich in flavor. The other variety, Fuyu, is smaller and more squat in shape. It lacks the tannin content of Hachiya persimmons and can be eaten even when not fully ripe. Select plump persimmons with a good red color and stem cap attached.

Ripen at room temperature until very soft, then refrigerate. Remove stem cap, cut as desired, and remove seeds, if there are any.

Percentage yield: 80%

**Pineapple.** Pineapples should be plump and fresh-looking, with an orange-yellow color and abundant fragrance. Avoid soft spots, bruises, and dark, watery spots.

Store at room temperature for a day or two to allow some tartness to disappear, then refrigerate. Pineapples may be cut in many ways. For slices, chunks, and dice, cut off top and bottom and pare the rough skin from the sides, using a stainless-steel knife. Remove all eyes. Cut into quarters lengthwise and cut out the hard center core. Slice or cut as desired.

Percentage yield: 50%

Pineapple

**Plums.** Look for plump, firm, but not hard plums, with no bruises or blemishes.

Wash, cut in half, and remove pits.

Percentage yield: 95% (pitted only)

**Pomegranates.** The pomegranate is a subtropical fruit about the size of a large apple. It has a dry red skin or shell enclosing a mass of seeds. Each seed is surrounded by a small sphere of juicy, bright red pulp. Pomegranates are used mostly for their red, tart-sweet juice. The seeds with their surrounding pulp can also be used as an attractive garnish for desserts and even meat dishes. Look for heavy fruits without bruises. When squeezed, they should yield to gentle pressure; if they are too hard, they may be dried out.

To prepare, lightly score the skin without cutting into the seeds and carefully break the fruit into sections. Separate the seeds from the membranes. Juicing is difficult. Some methods crush the seeds and make the juice bitter. This method makes a better juice: Roll the whole pomegranate on the countertop under the palm of the hand to break the juice sacs. Then pierce a hole in the side of the fruit and squeeze out the juice.

Percentage yield: 55%

**Prickly pears or cactus pears.** This is a barrel-shaped fruit about the size of a large egg. Its skin color ranges from magenta to greenish red and it has a bright pinkish red, spongy interior with black seeds. The pulp is sweet and aromatic, but with a mild flavor. Good-quality fruits are tender but not mushy, with a good skin color, not faded. Avoid fruits with rotten spots.

If the fruit is firm, allow to ripen at room temperature, then refrigerate. As it is the fruit of a cactus, thorns grow on the skin. These are removed before shipping, but small, hard-to-see thorns may remain. To avoid getting stung, hold the fruit with a fork while you slice off the top and bottom. Still holding it with a fork, pare the sides with a knife and discard the peels without touching them. Cut or slice the pulp as desired, or force it through a sieve to purée it and remove the seeds.

Percentage yield: 70%

Prickly pears

**Quince.** Quinces grow in temperate climates and were once very popular in Europe and North America. Many old, neglected quince trees remain in New England and elsewhere. The fruit resembles a large, yellow, lumpy pear with either a smooth or slightly downy skin. The raw fruit is never eaten, as it is dry and hard. When cooked (usually stewed or poached in a sugar syrup), it becomes aromatic, flavorful, and sweet, and the color of the flesh turns slightly pink. The fruit keeps well. Select fruit with good color and free of bruises or blemishes.

Cut, pare, and core like apples or pears, then cook.
Percentage yield: 75%

Quince

**Rhubarb.** Rhubarb is a stem, not a fruit, but it is used like a fruit. Buy firm, crisp, tender rhubarb with thick stalks, not thin and shriveled.

Cut off all traces of leaf, which is poisonous. Trim the root end, if necessary. Peel with a vegetable peeler, if desired, or omit this step if the skin is tender. Cut into desired lengths.

Percentage yield: 85–90% (if purchased without leaves)

Rhubarb

**Star fruit or carambola.** The star fruit is a shiny, yellow, oblong fruit with five ridges running its length, so it forms stars when sliced crosswise. It is fragrant, ranging from tart to sweet, with a crisp texture. Look for full, firm fruits. Avoid fruits with ribs that have browned and shrunk.

Wash and slice crosswise.
Percentage yield: 99%

---

### ❧ FRUIT LIQUEURS AND ALCOHOLS ❧

A variety of alcoholic beverages are distilled from or flavored with fruits. Many of these are useful as flavoring ingredients in the bakeshop.

Most of the alcohols we use in the bakeshop fall into two categories: white alcohols and liqueurs. White alcohols, also known as *eaux-de-vie* (oh duh vee; singular form: *eau-de-vie*, French for "water of life") are true brandies, meaning they are distilled from fruit, and they are not aged in wood barrels, so they are clear and colorless. White alcohols have no sweetness and have a fresh, fruity aroma. The most common in the bakeshop is kirsch (made from cherries). Other white alcohols include poire (pear), mirabelle (yellow plum), and framboise (raspberry).

Liqueurs, also called *cordials*, are sweet alcoholic beverages flavored with fruit, herbs, or other ingredients. Orange-flavored liqueurs, such as curaçao, Cointreau, and Grand Marnier, are the most commonly used in the bakeshop.

# FRUIT DESSERTS

## Simple Fruit Salads and Cooked Fruits

After a rich meal, a piece of fresh fruit can be a light and refreshing dessert. Most diners, however, are happier with something that requires a little more effort from the kitchen. Serving fresh fruit, such as berries, with cream or a sauce such as sabayon, crème anglaise, or coulis often satisfies these desires. (See chapter 12 for a selection of dessert sauces.) A simple fruit salad can be an attractive alternative. Marinating fresh fruit in a flavored syrup adds a new dimension to the fruit and also allows the pastry chef to make an attractive mixture of colorful, carefully cut seasonal items.

A simple and versatile category of fruit dessert is the **compote**, which can be defined as cooked fruit, usually small fruits or cut fruit, served in its cooking liquid. Mixed fruit compotes are versatile because they can be seasoned and sweetened as desired, and the combination of fruits is infinitely variable. Cooking media range from light syrups to concentrated spiced caramel, honey, or liqueur mixtures.

There is no clear dividing line between fresh fruit salads and lightly cooked fruit compotes. If a boiling syrup is poured over a mixture of fruit and the fruit is marinated without additional cooking, it could be called either a compote or a fresh fruit salad.

Hard fruits and mixtures of dried fruits are usually cooked longer, until they are tender. Larger, whole fruits cooked in syrup are not usually called compotes, but the cooking procedure is the same. Pears poached in wine is a classic dessert that remains popular and can be found on the menus of many restaurants.

This chapter contains two types of compotes. The first part of the recipe section includes light mixtures of fresh fruit in syrup that are served as desserts. Later in the chapter you will find sweeter, more intensely flavored compotes that are not served by themselves but are used as sauces, condiments, and ingredients in pastries and other preparations.

Many fruits can also be sautéed for serving as desserts. This procedure is similar to sautéing vegetables, except that sugar is added to the fruit and butter in the pan. The sugar caramelizes and forms a rich sauce as it combines with the juices that are drawn out of the fruit. Apples, apricots, bananas, pears, peaches, pineapples, plums, and cherries are especially suited to this style of preparation. For examples of this type of preparation, see the recipe for Caramelized Pears (p. 590) and the variations that follow.

## Traditional and Specialty Fruit Desserts

This chapter also includes a selection of recipes ranging from the old-fashioned and rustic to the stylishly modern. Traditional North American favorites include **cobblers**, which are like fruit pies made in large baking pans, but without bottom crusts; **crisps**, which are like cobblers but with brown sugar streusel topping instead of a pastry crust; and **betties**, which have alternating layers of rich cake crumbs and fruit. These homey desserts are, for the most part, easy to prepare.

At the other end of the range of difficulty is the Caramelized Pear Charlotte (p. 598), perhaps the most complex recipe in this chapter. Before preparing this dessert, you may need to review the information on Bavarians, mousses, and charlottes in chapter 20.

# Fruit Preserves, Condiments, and Garnishes

Finally, you will find at the end of the chapter a variety of preparations that are not served as desserts but rather used as elements or ingredients in other dishes. These include jams and marmalades, sweet compotes used as sauces or garnishes, and specialty items such as fruit crisps and candied citrus zests that add appeal to plated desserts and petit four trays.

## POACHED FRUIT (FRUIT COMPOTE)

*Yield: about 3 lb (1.5 kg), plus syrup*

| Ingredients | U.S. | Metric | Procedure |
|---|---|---|---|
| Water | 1 qt | 1 L | 1. Combine the water and sugar in a saucepan. Bring to a boil, stirring until the sugar is dissolved. |
| Sugar (see Note) | 1–2 lb | 0.5–0.75 kg | |
| Vanilla extract (see Note) | 2 tsp | 10 mL | 2. Add the vanilla. |
| Prepared fruit (see individual variations) | 3 lb | 1.5 kg | 3. Add the prepared fruit to the syrup or, if using tender fruit, place the fruit in a shallow pan and pour the syrup over it. |

*Note: The amount of sugar used depends on the desired sweetness of the dessert and the natural sweetness of the fruit. Other flavoring may be used in place of the vanilla. A popular alternative is to add 2 or 3 strips lemon peel and 1 oz (30 mL) lemon juice to the syrup.*

4. Cook very slowly, just below a simmer, until the fruit is just tender.

5. Let the fruit cool in the syrup. When cool, refrigerate in the syrup until needed.

### VARIATIONS

#### POACHED APPLES, PEARS, OR PINEAPPLE

Peel, quarter, and core the fruit. For pineapple, cut into small wedges. Poach as in basic recipe.

#### PEARS IN WINE

Substitute red or white table wine for the water. Omit the vanilla. Add ½ sliced lemon to the syrup. Peel the pears, but leave them whole.

#### POACHED PEACHES

Peel the peaches by blanching them in boiling water for a few seconds and slipping off the skins. Cut in half and remove the stones. Poach as in the basic recipe.

#### PEACHES IN WINE

Prepare the peaches as above. Poach as for pears in wine, flavoring the syrup with lemon.

#### POACHED APRICOTS, PLUMS, OR NECTARINES

Cut the fruits in half and remove the stones. (Nectarines may be peeled like peaches, if desired.) Poach as in the basic recipe.

#### POACHED CHERRIES

Pit the cherries with a cherry pitter. Poach as in the basic recipe.

#### POACHED DRIED FRUIT

Soak dried fruit in water overnight. Use the soaking liquid for making the syrup. Poach as in the basic recipe, adding 1 oz (30 mL) lemon juice to the syrup.

#### TROPICAL FRUIT COMPOTE

Prepare the syrup as in the basic recipe, flavoring it with lemon and orange zest in addition to the vanilla and substituting white wine for half the water. Prepare a mixture of kiwi fruit, peeled and sliced crosswise; papayas, peeled, seeded, and cut into thin wedges or slices; mangoes, peeled, pitted, and sliced; orange wedges; and strawberries, trimmed and halved. While the syrup is still hot, pour it over the fruit. Cool, cover, and refrigerate overnight. If desired, top each portion with toasted or untoasted shredded coconut.

#### FRESH FRUIT SALAD

This is an uncooked version of fruit compote. Prepare the syrup as in the basic recipe. Cool it completely. Prepare a mixture of fresh fruits; dice large fruits or cut them into bite-size pieces. Combine the fruits and cold syrup and let them stand several hours or overnight in the refrigerator.

# FRUIT SALAD

*Yield: about 2 lb 8 oz (1100 g), including syrup*

| Ingredients | U.S. | Metric | Procedure |
|---|---|---|---|
| Apple | 1 | 1 | 1. Prepare all the fruit as necessary (wash, peel, pit, core, and so on, depending on the fruit). Cut all the fruit, except the passion fruit, into large bite-size pieces and place in a bowl. Add the pulp, juice, and seeds from the passion fruit to the bowl. |
| Pear | 1 | 1 | |
| Orange | 1 | 1 | |
| Peach | 1 | 1 | |
| Strawberries | 10 | 10 | |
| Raspberries | 10 | 10 | 2. Heat the sugar, water, cinnamon sticks, vanilla bean, and bay leaves gently until the sugar has dissolved. Bring to a boil. Remove from the heat and pour over the prepared fruit. |
| Red plum | 1 | 1 | |
| Passion fruit | 1 | 1 | |
| Sugar | 11 oz | 300 g | |
| Water | 14 oz | 400 g | 3. Let the mixture steep and infuse 2–3 hours. |
| Cinnamon sticks | 2 | 2 | 4. Drain or serve with a slotted spoon. Reserve the syrup for other uses, if desired. |
| Vanilla bean | 1 | 1 | |
| Bay leaves | 2 | 2 | |

# MARINATED TROPICAL FRUITS

*Yield: about 4 lb (2 kg), including syrup*

| Ingredients | U.S. | Metric | Procedure |
|---|---|---|---|
| Mangoes | 3 | 3 | 1. Peel the fruit. Core the pineapple and remove the pit from the mangoes. Cut into large cubes (about 1 in./2.5 cm). Place the fruit in a saucepan. |
| Large pineapple | 1 | 1 | |
| Kiwi fruits | 5 | 5 | |
| Water | 7 oz | 200 g | 2. Combine the remaining ingredients, stirring to dissolve the sugar. (If desired, the spices may be tied in a cheesecloth bag so they can be removed easily before serving.) |
| Sugar | 7 oz | 200 g | |
| Cinnamon stick | 1 | 1 | |
| Orange rind, in strips | 0.3 oz | 8 g | |
| Lemon | ½ | ½ | 3. Pour the boiling syrup over the fruit, cover with a round of parchment, and simmer 5 minutes. Cool and then chill the fruit in the syrup. |
| Cloves, whole | 4 | 4 | |
| Mint sprig | 1 | 1 | |
| Vanilla bean | 1 | 1 | |

# CHILLED SUMMER FRUIT SOUP

*Yield: approximately 3 pt (1.5 L)*

| Ingredients | U.S. | | | Metric | Procedure |
|---|---|---|---|---|---|
| Water | 2 pt | 8 | oz | 1250 mL | 1. Combine the sugar and water in a saucepan. Bring to a boil and stir to dissolve the sugar. |
| Sugar | 1 lb | 8 | oz | 750 g | |
| Lime juice | | 5 | oz | 150 mL | 2. Add the lime juice and zest, the strawberries, and the bananas. Remove from the heat, cover, and let stand until cooled to room temperature. |
| Grated lime zest | | 0.25 | oz | 8 g | |
| Strawberries, sliced | | 8 | oz | 250 g | |
| Bananas, sliced | | 12 | oz | 375 g | 3. Pass the soup through a fine sieve. Let the liquid drain, but do not press down on the solids, which would make the soup cloudy. |
| Gelatin | | 0.25 | oz | 8 g | 4. Soften the gelatin in the cold water. Reheat the soup until just below the simmering point and add the gelatin. Stir until dissolved. |
| Cold water | | 4 | oz | 125 g | |
| Garnish: assorted fresh fruit, such as strawberries, raspberries, blackberries, plums, red currants, blueberries, kiwi fruit | | as desired | | as desired | 5. Cool and then chill the soup. The quantity of gelatin is just enough to give the soup a little body without gelling it. |
| | | | | | 6. Prepare the desired fruit for garnish. Leave small berries whole, and cut larger fruit as desired. |
| | | | | | 7. To serve, ladle the soup into soup plates and add the desired garnish. |

# CARAMELIZED PEARS

*Yield: 8 portions*

| Ingredients | U.S. | Metric | Procedure |
|---|---|---|---|
| Pears, ripe | 8 | 8 | |
| Butter | 2 oz | 60 g | |
| Granulated sugar | 4 oz | 125 g | |

1. Peel, core, and quarter the pears.

2. Heat the butter in a sauté pan. Add the pears and sugar. Cook over moderately high heat. The pears will give off juice, which will combine with the sugar to form a syrup. Continue to cook, turning and basting the pears, until the syrup reduces and thickens and the pears are lightly caramelized. The syrup will become light brown; do not try for a dark brown color or the fruit will overcook.

3. Serve warm. A small scoop of vanilla ice cream is a good accompaniment. Caramelized fruits are most often used as components of other desserts, and are also used as garnish for savory items such as pork and duck.

## VARIATIONS

Cut the pears into halves instead of quarters. To serve, place them cut side down on a plate, slice crosswise, and fan the slices. For a more caramelized surface, sprinkle the top of the fruit with sugar and caramelize under a salamander or broiler, being careful not to let the sugar scorch.

The following fruits can be prepared using the same basic method. Adjust the quantities of butter and sugar according to taste and the sweetness of the fruit.

### CARAMELIZED APPLES

Peel, core, and slice the apples. Use white or brown sugar, depending on the desired flavor. If desired, season with cinnamon and nutmeg, vanilla, or lemon zest.

### CARAMELIZED PEACHES

Blanch and skin the peaches. Cut in half and remove the pits. Slice or cut into wedges.

### CARAMELIZED PINEAPPLE

Peel, slice crosswise, and remove the core from each slice using a small, round cutter. Use white or brown sugar, as desired.

### CARAMELIZED BANANAS

Peel; quarter by cutting in half crosswise and then lengthwise. Use brown sugar. Because bananas release little juice, you may add a little orange juice or pineapple juice. Flavor with cinnamon and nutmeg or mace.

# APPLE CRISP

*Yield: 1 pan, 12 × 20 in. (30 × 50 cm)*
*48 portions, 4 oz (120 g) each*

| Ingredients | U.S. | | Metric | Procedure |
|---|---|---|---|---|
| Peeled, sliced apples | 8 lb | | 4000 g | 1. Toss the apples gently with the sugar and lemon juice. Spread evenly in a 12 × 20-in. (30 × 50 cm) baking pan. |
| Sugar | 4 | oz | 125 g | 2. Rub the butter, sugar, cinnamon, and flour together until well blended and crumbly. |
| Lemon juice | 2 | oz | 60 mL | |
| Butter | 1 lb | | 500 g | 3. Sprinkle evenly over the apples. |
| Brown sugar | 1 lb 8 | oz | 750 g | 4. Bake at 350°F (175°C) for about 45 minutes, until the top is browned and the apples are tender. |
| Cinnamon | 0.12 oz (2 tsp) | | 4 g | |
| Pastry flour | 1 lb 8 | oz | 750 g | |

**VARIATIONS**

### PEACH, CHERRY, OR RHUBARB CRISP

Substitute peaches, cherries, or rhubarb for the apples. If rhubarb is used, increase the sugar in step 1 to 12 oz (375 g).

# FRUIT COBBLER

*Yield: 1 pan, 12 × 20 in. (30 × 50 cm)*
*48 portions, 5 oz (150 g) each*

| Ingredients | U.S. | Metric | Procedure |
|---|---|---|---|
| Fruit pie filling | 12–15 lb | 5.5–7 kg | 1. Place the fruit filling in a 12 × 20-in. (30 × 50 cm) baking pan. |
| Flaky Pie Dough (p. 289) | 2 lb | 1 kg | 2. Roll out the pastry to fit the top of the pan. Place on top of the filling and seal the edges to the pan. Pierce small holes in the pastry to allow steam to escape. |

**VARIATION**

In place of the pie pastry, use biscuit dough. Roll out the dough ¼ in. (6 mm) thick and cut it into 1½-in. (4 cm) rounds. Place the rounds on top of the fruit filling.

3. Bake at 425°F (220°C) for about 30 minutes, until the top is browned.

4. Cut the dessert in 6 rows of 8, or 48 portions. Serve warm or cold.

# APPLE BETTY

*Yield: 1 pan, 12 × 20 in. (30 × 50 cm)*
*48 portions, 4 oz (120 g) each*

| Ingredients | U.S. | Metric | Procedure |
|---|---|---|---|
| Peeled, sliced apples | 8 lb | 4000 g | 1. Combine the apples, sugar, salt, nutmeg, zest, and lemon juice in a bowl. Toss gently until well mixed. |
| Sugar | 1 lb 8 oz | 750 g | 2. Place one-third of the apple mixture in an even layer in a well-buttered 12 × 20-in. (30 × 50 cm) baking pan. |
| Salt | 0.25 oz (1½ tsp) | 7 g | |
| Nutmeg | 0.08 oz (1 tsp) | 2 g | 3. Top with one-third of the cake crumbs. |
| Lemon zest, grated | 0.12 oz (1½ tsp) | 3 g | 4. Continue until all the apples and crumbs have been used. You will have 3 layers of fruit and 3 layers of crumbs. |
| Lemon juice | 2 oz | 60 mL | |
| Yellow or white cake crumbs | 2 lb | 1000 g | 5. Pour the butter evenly over the top. |
| Butter, melted | 8 oz | 250 g | 6. Bake at 350°F (175°C) for about 1 hour, until the fruit is tender. |

# APPLE CHARLOTTE

*Yield: one 1-qt (1 L) mold*

| Ingredients | U.S. | Metric | Procedure |
|---|---|---|---|
| Tart cooking apples | 2 lb | 900 g | 1. Peel, core, and slice the apples. Combine them with the butter, zest, and cinnamon in a broad, shallow pan. Cook over moderate heat until soft. Mash the apples lightly with a spoon and continue to cook until they form a thick purée (a few remaining lumps of apple are acceptable). |
| Butter | 1 oz | 30 g | |
| Lemon zest, grated | 0.08 oz (1 tsp) | 2 g | |
| Cinnamon | 0.01 oz (¼ tsp) | 0.4 g | |
| Puréed apricot jam | 2 oz | 60 g | 2. Stir in the apricot jam. Add sugar to taste, depending on the sweetness of the apples. |
| Sugar | 1–2 oz | 30–60 g | 3. Line a 1-qt (1 L) charlotte mold, two 1-pt (500 mL) charlotte molds, or other straight-sided molds in the following manner: Dip the bread slices in the melted butter and line the mold with the buttered side against the inside of the mold. The bottom may be lined with one round slice or with wedges of bread cut to fit. Line the sides with half-slices of bread overlapping shingle-fashion. |
| Firm white bread, trimmed of crusts | 12 slices | 12 slices | |
| Butter, melted | 4 oz | 110 g | |

*Note: Apple charlottes should normally not be made in sizes larger than 1 qt (1 L), or they are likely to collapse after unmolding. Also, to avoid collapse, the apple mixture must be cooked until it is quite thick. The bread should be firm, and the charlotte should be baked long enough to brown the bread well.*

4. Fill with the apple purée and top with the remaining bread.

5. Bake at 400°F (200°C) 30–40 minutes.

6. Cool for 20 minutes, then carefully unmold. Serve warm or cold.

# STRAWBERRIES ROMANOFF

*Yield: 8–12 portions*

| Ingredients | U.S. | | Metric | Procedure |
|---|---|---|---|---|
| Strawberries, fresh | 2 | qt | 2 L | 1. Trim the stems and hulls from the strawberries. Cut the berries in half if they are large. |
| Confectioners' sugar | 2 | oz | 60 g | |
| Orange juice | 4 | oz | 125 mL | 2. Combine the berries with the first quantities of sugar, orange juice, and liqueur. Let stand for 1 hour, refrigerated. |
| Orange liqueur, such as curaçao | 2 | oz | 60 mL | |
| Heavy cream | 12 | oz | 400 mL | 3. Prepare whipped cream flavored with orange liqueur, following the procedure on page 264. |
| Confectioners' sugar | 0.75 oz (3 tbsp) | | 20 g | |
| Orange liqueur, such as curaçao | 0.75 oz (1½ tbsp) | | 20 mL | 4. To serve, put the berries and juices in a serving bowl or individual dessert dishes. Put the whipped cream in a pastry bag fitted with a star tube. Pipe the cream decoratively over the berries to cover them completely. |

**VARIATION**

Place a small scoop of orange sorbet in each dessert dish and cover it with the marinated berries. Cover with whipped cream as in the basic recipe.

# RASPBERRY OR CHERRY GRATIN

| Ingredients per portion | U.S. | | Metric | Procedure |
|---|---|---|---|---|
| Genoise layer (p. 407; see step 2) | | | | 1. Select a shallow gratin dish or other heatproof dish large enough to hold the fruit in a shallow layer. |
| Raspberries or sweet, pitted cherries | 3 | oz | 90 g | 2. Cut a thin slice of genoise (about ⅜ in./1 cm thick) to cover the bottom of the dish. |
| Pastry Cream (p. 271) | 2 | oz | 60 g | 3. Arrange the fruit on top of the genoise. (If desired, marinate the fruit ahead of time in fruit brandy or liqueur and a little sugar. Drain and use the liquid in step 4.) |
| Whipped cream | 1 | oz | 30 g | |
| Kirsch, orange liqueur, or raspberry or cherry brandy | to taste | | to taste | |
| Sliced almonds | 0.25 oz | | 7 g | 4. Combine the pastry cream, whipped cream, and flavoring. Spread the mixture over the fruit to cover completely. |
| Butter, melted | 0.25 oz | | 7 g | |
| Confectioners' sugar (optional) | | | | 5. Mix the almonds and butter and sprinkle over the pastry cream. Dredge the top heavily with confectioners' sugar. |

6. Place under a broiler or in the top of a hot oven for a few minutes to brown the top. Serve hot or warm.

# GRATIN DE FRUITS ROUGES
# (BERRY GRATIN)

*Yield: 5 portions, 5 oz (150 g) each*

| Ingredients | U.S. | Metric | Procedure |
|---|---|---|---|
| Sponge layers (see step 1) | 5 | 5 | 1. Cut 5-in. (12 cm) circles of sponge ¼ in. (6 mm) thick. (Sponge Roll II, p. 408, is recommended, but Genoise, p. 407, or other sponges can be used.) |
| Dessert syrup flavored with kirsch (p. 262) | as needed | as needed | 2. Place the circles of sponge on serving plates. Brush with the syrup. |
| Strawberries | 7 oz | 200 g | 3. Clean the fruit as necessary, and cut the strawberries into halves or quarters, depending on size. Arrange the fruit on top of the sponge. |
| Blackberries | 3.5 oz | 100 g | |
| Raspberries | 3.5 oz | 100 g | |
| Red currants | 2.5 oz | 75 g | |
| Sabayon I (p. 281) | 5 oz (about 15 fl oz) | 150 g (about 450 mL) | 4. With a spoon, cover the fruit with a layer of sabayon at least ⅛ in. (3 mm) thick. |
| | | | 5. Place under a hot salamander or broiler until lightly browned. |
| Raspberry Sauce (p. 279) | 3.5 oz | 100 g | 6. Pour a ribbon of raspberry sauce around each gratin and serve immediately. |
| Additional fruit for garnish | as needed | as needed | |

# BAKED APPLES TATIN-STYLE

*Yield: 6 apples, about 4½ oz (130 g) each*

| Ingredients | U.S. | | Metric | Procedure |
|---|---|---|---|---|
| Puff pastry | 6 | oz | 150 g | 1. Roll out the pastry until it is very thin. Dock and chill. Cut 6 circles 4½ in. (11 cm) in diameter. Return to the refrigerator until needed. |
| **Stuffing** | | | | |
| Brown sugar | 2 | oz | 50 g | 2. Butter 6 pudding molds about 3 in. (7–8 cm) in diameter on top, or large enough to hold an apple. Set aside. |
| Butter | 2 | oz | 50 g | |
| Almonds, chopped | 2 | oz | 50 g | 3. *Prepare the stuffing:* Cream the butter and sugar. Mix in the remaining stuffing ingredients. |
| Pecans, chopped | 1 | oz | 25 g | 4. *Prepare the topping:* Cook the sugar to the caramel stage. Keeping the pan over moderate heat, add the vanilla and butter and stir constantly until the butter is incorporated into the caramel (see p. 280 for information on butter caramel). Pour a little of the caramel into the bottoms of the pudding molds, using about one-fourth of the caramel in all. Add the remaining topping ingredients to the caramel and keep warm. |
| Raisins | 2 | oz | 50 g | |
| Prunes, chopped | 2 | oz | 50 g | |
| Armagnac or brandy | 0.5 | oz | 15 g | |
| Cinnamon | 1 | tsp | 2 g | |
| **Topping** | | | | 5. Peel and core the apples. Brush with melted butter. |
| Sugar | 5 | oz | 150 g | 6. Place the apples in the pudding molds and fill the cores with the stuffing mixture. Press down well. |
| Vanilla bean (see *Note*) | ½ | | ½ | |
| Butter | 3 | oz | 70 g | 7. Cover with foil and bake at 350°F (180°C) until the apples start to soften, about 15 minutes. Remove from the oven and allow to cool slightly. |
| Sliced almonds, toasted | 0.75 | oz | 20 g | |
| Pecans, chopped | 0.75 | oz | 20 g | 8. Place a disk of puff pastry on top of each apple and tuck in the sides. |
| Pine nuts | 0.75 | oz | 20 g | |
| Raisins | 0.75 | oz | 20 g | 9. Bake at 400°F (200°C) until the pastry is browned. |
| Pistachios | 0.75 | oz | 20 g | 10. Mix the crème anglaise with the Calvados. Ladle pools of this sauce onto serving plates. Turn out the apples onto the pools with the puff pastry on the bottom. Spoon a little of the topping over the apples. |
| Granny Smith apples | 6 | | 6 | |
| Butter, melted | 2 | oz | 50 g | |
| Crème Anglaise (p. 269) | 12 | oz | 300 g | |
| Calavados | 2 | oz | 50 g | |

*Note: If vanilla beans are not available, add ¼ tsp (1 g) vanilla extract to the caramel in step 4.*

# PEAR AND APPLE GRATIN

*Yield: 6 portions*

| Ingredients | U.S. | | Metric | Procedure |
|---|---|---|---|---|
| Apples | 4 | | 4 | 1. Peel and core the apples and pears. Chop into bite-size pieces. |
| Pears | 4 | | 4 | |
| Sugar | 10 | oz | 300 g | 2. Heat the sugar to a golden caramel. Add the butter, then the apples, pears, and vanilla. Cook gently until the fruit is tender. Add the Calvados. Remove the fruit with a slotted spoon and reserve. |
| Butter | 5 | oz | 150 g | |
| Vanilla extract | ½ | tsp | 2 g | |
| Calvados brandy | 1 | oz | 30 g | |
| Flour | 1.33 oz | | 40 g | 3. Sift the flour with the ground almonds into a bowl. Add the sugar and mix. Make a well in the center. |
| Ground almonds | 1.33 oz | | 40 g | |
| Extra-fine granulated sugar | 3.5 oz | | 100 g | 4. Froth the egg whites lightly with a fork and pour into the well. Heat the butter until it is browned and pour into the well. Draw the ingredients to form a paste. Place this mixture in a pastry bag with a small plain tip. |
| Egg whites | 3.5 oz | | 100 g | |
| Butter | 3.5 oz | | 100 g | |
| Confectioners' sugar for dusting | as needed | | as needed | 5. Lightly butter 6 ovenproof serving plates. Arrange the fruit on the plates, leaving the centers empty. |
| Apple Crisps (p. 602) | 12 | | 12 | 6. Pipe the almond mixture over the fruit in a random pattern. Dust with confectioners' sugar. |
| Cider Apple Sorbet (p. 564) | 6 small scoops or quenelles | | 6 small scoops or quenelles | 7. Clean the edges of the plates. Bake at 350°F (180°C) until golden brown. |

8. Place an apple crisp in the center of each plate. Top with a small quenelle of sorbet, then another apple crisp. If desired, decorate with a sprig of mint. Serve immediately.

**VARIATION**

In place of the cooked pears and apples, use uncooked berries.

# CRÈME BRÛLÉE SOPHIA

*Yield: 6 portions*

| Ingredients | U.S. | | Metric | Procedure |
|---|---|---|---|---|
| Grapefruits | 2 | | 2 | 1. Segment the grapefruits. If any segments are thick, cut them in half horizontally to make thinner segments. Drain on absorbent paper until thoroughly dry to the touch. |
| Peaches, fresh or canned, drained and chopped | 8 | oz | 250 g | |
| Sugar | 1.75 | oz | 50 g | 2. Cook the peach flesh with the sugar over low heat until soft, then purée. Divide the purée among 6 shallow 5-oz (150 mL) ramekins, spreading it evenly on the bottom. |
| Milk | 9 | oz | 280 g | 3. Bring the milk and cream to scalding point. |
| Heavy cream | 3 | oz | 90 g | |
| Whole eggs | 5 | oz | 150 g | 4. Whip the eggs, yolks, and sugar until light. Temper with half of the hot milk, then stir this back into the remaining milk mixture. Add the vanilla. |
| Egg yolks | 1.33 | oz | 40 g | |
| Sugar | 3.5 | oz | 100 g | |
| Vanilla extract | ½ | tsp | 2 g | 5. Strain through a fine china cap. |
| Peach schnapps | 2 | oz | 60 g | 6. Add the peach schnapps. Pour carefully into the ramekins so as not to stir the peach purée. |
| Extra-fine granulated sugar | 3.5 | oz | 100 g | 7. Place in a hot-water bath and bake at 215°F (100°C) until just set. |
| | | | | 8. Cool completely. |
| | | | | 9. Arrange the grapefruit wedges on top in a pinwheel pattern. Just before serving, dust with sugar and caramelize the tops with a blowtorch. |

# FIGS IN PORT WINE

*Yield: about 1 lb 4 oz (600 g) figs in sauce, depending on size of figs*

| Ingredients | U.S. | | Metric | Procedure |
|---|---|---|---|---|
| Sugar | 3.75 | oz | 100 g | 1. Cook the sugar to a golden caramel. |
| Butter | 1.5 | oz | 40 g | 2. Keeping the pan over moderate heat, add the butter and stir constantly until the butter is incorporated into the caramel (see p. 280 for information on butter caramel). |
| Red wine | 3 | oz | 80 g | |
| Port wine | 3 | oz | 80 g | |
| Vanilla extract | ½ | tsp | 2 g | 3. Add the red wine, port, and vanilla extract. Simmer until the caramelized sugar is dissolved. |
| Blackcurrant purée | 2 | oz | 50 g | 4. Add the blackcurrant purée and reduce by one-third. |
| Fresh, whole figs | 8 | | 8 | 5. Trim the hard stem ends of the figs and cut the figs in half lengthwise. |
| | | | | 6. Place the figs in a baking dish and pour the caramel-wine syrup over them. |
| | | | | 7. Bake at 350°F (180°C) until the figs are slightly puffed, 10–20 minutes, longer if the figs are not ripe. |
| | | | | 8. Serve the figs with the sauce. See page 633 for a serving idea. |

# CARAMELIZED PEAR CHARLOTTE

*Yield: 3 cakes, 7 in. (18 cm) each*

| Ingredients | U.S. | | Metric | Procedure |
|---|---|---|---|---|
| **Caramelized pears** | | | | 1. *For the pears:* Make a syrup with the sugar and water and cook to a golden caramel. Carefully add the cream and vanilla bean. Stir and simmer until the caramel is dissolved. Add the pears. Cover with a round of parchment and simmer until tender. Drain and reserve both the caramel and the pears. Scrape the seeds from the vanilla bean and add them to the caramel. There should be about 7 oz (200 g) caramel. |
| Sugar | 10 | oz | 270 g | |
| Water | 4 | oz | 110 g | |
| Heavy cream | 11 | oz | 310 g | |
| Vanilla bean, split (see *Note*) | 1 | | 1 | |
| Pears, peeled, cored, and quartered | 6 | | 6 | |
| **Syrup** | | | | 2. *For the syrup:* Heat the water and sugar until the sugar is dissolved. Remove from the heat and add the Poire Williams. |
| Sugar | 2 | oz | 60 g | |
| Water | 2 | oz | 60 g | |
| Poire Williams | 3.33 oz | | 100 g | |
| **Assembly** | | | | 3. Line three 7-in. (18 cm) charlotte rings with baumkuchen, as shown on page 455. Place the rings on cake cards. Cut 6 thin layers from the genoise and place one in the bottom of each ring. (Reserve the other 3 layers for step 8.) Brush the genoise with the syrup. |
| Baumkuchen (p. 414) | see step 3 | | see step 3 | |
| Genoise layer (p. 407) | see step 3 | | see step 3 | |
| **Mousse** | | | | 4. Reserve 3 pear quarters for decorating the charlottes and chop the remaining pears into bite-size pieces, retaining any juices they release when cut. Add these juices to the caramel. Place the chopped pears on top of the genoise layers. |
| Milk | 7.5 | oz | 220 g | |
| Egg yolks | 3 | oz | 90 g | |
| Sugar | 4 | tsp | 20 g | |
| Gelatin, softened in water | 0.5 | oz | 14 g | 5. *For the mousse:* Heat the milk to scalding point. Whip the egg yolks and sugar until light, then whip in half the milk. Return this mixture to the pan with the remaining milk and heat until thick enough to coat the back of a spoon. |
| Caramel from the pears | 8 | oz | 240 g | |
| Heavy cream | 1 lb 7 | oz | 650 g | |
| **Glaçage** | | | | 6. Add the gelatin and two-thirds of the reserved caramel from the pears. Stir until the gelatin is dissolved. |
| Gelatin | 0.25 oz | | 6 g | |
| Caramel from the pears | 4 | oz | 120 g | 7. Cool the mixture by stirring over ice. Before it sets, whip the cream to soft peaks and fold in. |
| Glucose | 1 | oz | 30 g | |
| Poire Williams | 1 | oz | 30 g | 8. Fill the rings three-fourths full with the mousse mixture and level the tops. Place a layer of genoise on top and press down gently. Brush with syrup. |
| **Decoration** | | | | |
| Italian Meringue (p. 267) | as needed | | as needed | 9. Fill the rings to the top with the remaining mousse and level the tops with a palette knife. Chill until set. |
| Chocolate cigarettes (p. 646) | as needed | | as needed | |
| Red currants or other berries | as needed | | as needed | 10. *For the glaçage:* Soften the gelatin in cold water (see p. 88). Heat the remaining caramel with the glucose. Stir in the gelatin until dissolved. Add the Poire Williams. Cool slightly. |
| Mint leaves | as needed | | as needed | |

*Note: If vanilla beans are not available, add ½ tsp (2 g) vanilla extract to the caramel in step 1.*

11. Spoon the glaçage over the mousse. Smooth with a palette knife and chill.

12. Remove the charlotte rings by warming them slightly with a blowtorch and lifting them off.

13. Decorate the tops with a few scrolls of Italian meringue, piped with a star or plain tip, a fanned quartered pear, some chocolate cigarettes, berries, and mint leaves.

# SPICED PINEAPPLE

*Yield: about 2 lb (950 g) pineapple and sauce*

| Ingredients | U.S. | Metric | Procedure |
|---|---|---|---|
| Baby pineapples (see Note) | 4 | 4 | 1. Peel, core, and eye the pineapples. |
| Sugar | 7 oz | 200 g | 2. Cook the sugar to a golden caramel. Keeping the pan over moderate heat, add the butter and spices. Stir constantly until the butter is incorporated into the caramel (see p. 280 for information on butter caramel). |
| Butter | 3.5 oz | 100 g | |
| Star anise, whole | 2 | 2 | |
| Cloves, whole | 2 | 2 | 3. Roll the pineapple in the caramel and transfer the fruit to a baking dish. |
| Cinnamon sticks | 2 | 2 | |
| Rum | 1.5 oz | 40 g | 4. Add the rum and vanilla to the caramel and flambé. Pour this mixture over the pineapple. |
| Vanilla extract | ½ tsp | 2 g | |
| Heavy cream | 3.5 oz | 100 g | 5. Bake at 350°F (180°C), basting regularly, until the pineapple is tender, about 35 minutes. |

6. Slice the pineapples and serve warm. Heat the caramel sauce, add the cream, and strain. Pour the sauce over the pineapple. See page 632 for a serving suggestion.

*Note: Baby pineapples weigh about 8 oz (250 g) each and yield about 5 oz (150 g) flesh. If they are not available, substitute 20 oz (600 g) peeled, cored fresh pineapple, in large pieces.*

# RASPBERRY JAM

*For large-quantity measurements, see page 741.*
*Yield: 7½ oz (240 g)*

| Ingredients | U.S. | Metric | Fruit at 100% % | Procedure |
|---|---|---|---|---|
| Sugar | 3 oz | 94 g | 75 | 1. Place the first quantity of sugar and water in a saucepan and bring to a boil, dissolving the sugar. |
| Water | 1 oz | 30 g | 25 | |
| Raspberries, fresh | 4 oz | 125 g | 100 | |
| Glucose | 0.4 oz | 12 g | 10 | 2. Add the raspberries and glucose. Boil until the fruit has broken down and the consistency is thick. |
| Sugar | 0.6 oz | 18 g | 15 | 3. Mix together the pectin and the remaining sugar. Add to the cooked fruit. Mix well and simmer another 3 minutes. |
| Pectin | 0.33 oz | 10 g | 8 | |

4. Pour into a clean glass jar and seal. Keep refrigerated.

**VARIATIONS**

Other soft fruits may be prepared in the same way.

# APPLE MARMALADE

*For large-quantity measurements, see page 741.*
*Yield: 2 lb 2 oz (1060 g)*

| Ingredients | U.S. | Metric | Fruit at 100% % | Procedure |
|---|---|---|---|---|
| Apples, peeled and cored | 2 lb | 1000 g | 100 | 1. Chop the apples. |
| Water | 4 oz | 125 g | 12.5 | 2. Place all ingredients in a saucepan and cook over low heat until very soft and of a purée consistency. |
| Sugar | 10 oz | 300 g | 30 | |

3. Force through a sieve or food mill.

4. Pour into clean glass jars. Refrigerate.

# STRAWBERRY MARMALADE

*For large-quantity measurements, see page 741.*
*Yield: 13 oz (400 g)*

| Ingredients | U.S. | | Metric | % | Procedure |
|---|---|---|---|---|---|
| | | | | **Fruit at 100%** | |
| | | | | | |
| Strawberries | 8 | oz | 250 g | 100 | 1. If the strawberries are large, cut them into halves or quarters. Otherwise, leave them whole. |
| Sugar | 8 | oz | 250 g | 100 | |
| Pectin | 0.17 | oz | 5 g | 2 | |
| Lemon juice | 0.5 | oz | 15 g | 3 | 2. Mix the berries with the sugar. Refrigerate overnight. |
| | | | | | 3. Bring the sugared fruit to a simmer and cook until a purée consistency is obtained. |
| | | | | | 4. Remove from the heat. Sprinkle the pectin over the fruit and stir in. Return to the heat and cook 3–4 minutes. |
| | | | | | 5. Add the lemon juice and mix in. |
| | | | | | 6. Pour into clean glass jars and seal. Refrigerate. |

# CARAMELIZED APRICOTS

*For large-quantity measurements, see page 741.*
*Yield: 12 oz (300 g)*

| Ingredients | U.S. | Metric | Procedure |
|---|---|---|---|
| Sugar | 4 oz | 100 g | 1. Combine the sugar, water, and honey, and cook to the caramel stage. |
| Water | 1 oz | 25 g | |
| Honey | 2 oz | 50 g | 2. Keeping the pan over moderate heat, add the butter and stir constantly until the butter is incorporated into the caramel (see p. 280 for information on butter caramel). |
| Butter | 1 oz | 25 g | |
| Canned apricots, drained | 12 oz | 300 g | 3. Add the apricots to the caramel mixture. Heat until the apricots are well coated with the caramel. |
| | | | 4. Remove the apricots from the caramel mixture and place on a tray or sheet pan. Cover with plastic film and cool. |

# PLUM COMPOTE

*Yield: 2 lb 4 oz (1000 g)*

| Ingredients | U.S. | Metric | Procedure |
|---|---|---|---|
| Sugar | 7 oz | 200 g | 1. Melt the sugar in a heavy saucepan. Cook to a pale caramel. |
| Butter | 2 oz | 50 g | |
| Star anise, whole | 2 | 2 | 2. Remove from heat; cool slightly. |
| Vanilla bean (see *Note*) | 1 | 1 | 3. Add the butter, star anise, plums, lemon juice, zest, wine, and vanilla. |
| Red or black plums, stoned and quartered | 2 lb 4 oz | 1000 g | |
| Lemon juice | 1 oz | 30 g | 4. Bring to a boil, then reduce to a simmer. Cook until the fruit is tender but the pieces remain intact. Cool. |
| Lemon zest, grated | 1 tsp | 2 g | |
| Port wine, warmed | 2 oz | 50 g | |

*Note: If desired, omit the vanilla bean and add ½ tsp (2 mL) vanilla extract to the simmering fruit in step 4.*

# APRICOT COMPOTE

*For large-quantity measurements, see page 741.*
*Yield: 9.5 oz (240 g)*

| Ingredients | U.S. | Metric | Procedure |
|---|---|---|---|
| Sugar | 4.5 oz | 112 g | 1. Combine the sugar and water in a saucepan and bring to a boil to dissolve the sugar and make a syrup. Cook to 221°F (105°C). |
| Water | 0.6 oz | 15 g | |
| Apricots, fresh or canned, halved and pitted | 5 oz | 125 g | 2. Cut the apricot halves into halves or thirds, depending on size. Add to the syrup. Cook an additional 15–17 minutes if the apricots are fresh, about 3 minutes if canned. |
| Pectin | 0.4 oz | 10 g | 3. Add the pectin and glucose and mix in well. Cook an additional 3 minutes. |
| Glucose | 0.5 oz | 12 g | |

### VARIATION

## APRICOT AND ALMOND COMPOTE

*For large-quantity measurements, see page 741.*

| Ingredients | U.S. | Metric |
|---|---|---|
| Whole blanched almonds | 2 oz | 50 g |

Add the almonds to the apricots at the same time as the pectin and glucose.

# PINEAPPLE KUMQUAT COMPOTE

*For large-quantity measurements, see page 742.*
*Yield: 11 oz (270 g)*

| Ingredients | U.S. | Metric | Procedure |
|---|---|---|---|
| Sugar | 4.5 oz | 112 g | 1. Place the sugar, water, and vanilla bean in a saucepan. Bring to a boil. Cook to 238°F (120°C). |
| Water | 0.6 oz | 15 g | |
| Vanilla bean (see *Note*) | ½ | ½ | 2. Add the fruit and nuts to the syrup. |
| Glucose | 0.5 oz | 12 g | 3. Cook over high heat 2–3 minutes. Remove the vanilla bean. |
| Canned pineapple, drained and diced | 5 oz | 125 g | 4. Pour into clean glass jars and seal. Refrigerate. |
| Kumquats, sliced and blanched | 2 oz | 50 g | |
| Pistachios | 0.4 oz | 10 g | |

### VARIATION

## KUMQUAT COMPOTE

*For large-quantity measurements, see page 742.*

| Ingredients | U.S. | Metric |
|---|---|---|
| Sugar | 4.5 oz | 112 g |
| Water | 0.6 oz | 15 g |
| Glucose | 0.5 oz | 12 g |
| Kumquats, halved or sliced, blanched | 5 oz | 125 g |
| Pistachios | 0.75 oz | 20 g |

Follow the procedure in the basic recipe, but omit the pineapple and vanilla and adjust the quantities as listed above.

*Note: If vanilla beans are not available, flavor the finished compote with vanilla extract to taste.*

# CANDIED ORANGE OR LEMON ZEST

*Yield: variable*

| Ingredients | U.S. | Metric | Procedure |
|---|---|---|---|
| Oranges or lemons | 4 | 4 | 1. Peel the zest from the oranges in strips, using a vegetable peeler. Using a small, sharp knife, remove the white pith. Square off the strips and then cut them into julienne. |
| Water | as needed | as needed | |
| Sugar | 7 oz | 200 g | 2. Boil the zest in a generous quantity of water until tender. Drain and discard the water. |
| Water | 7 oz | 200 g | 3. Boil the sugar and water to make a syrup. |
| | | | 4. Poach the zest in the syrup until tender and translucent. Cool. |
| | | | 5. The zest can be stored in the syrup and drained as needed. Alternatively, drain and pat off excess syrup with absorbent paper. Then roll in extra-fine granulated sugar and shake in a sieve to remove excess sugar. |

# APPLE CRISPS

*Yield: variable, depending on size of apple and thickness of cuts*

| Ingredients | U.S. | Metric | Procedure |
|---|---|---|---|
| Sugar | 7 oz | 200 g | 1. Heat the sugar and water until the sugar is dissolved. |
| Water | 7 oz | 200 g | 2. Cut the apple crosswise into paper-thin slices, preferably using a slicing machine or a mandoline. Immediately drop the slices into the syrup and heat gently for 2 minutes. |
| Green apple, peeled | 2 | 2 | 3. Allow the fruit to cool in the syrup. |

**VARIATIONS**

Other fruits, such as oranges, pineapple, pears, and large strawberries, may be prepared in the same way.

4. Carefully remove the slices from the syrup and arrange on a silicone mat on a sheet pan. Dry in an oven at 175°F (80°C) until dry and crisp.

5. Use as a garnish for fruit desserts (see, for example, p. 596).

# APPLESAUCE

*Yield: about 1 qt (1 L)*

| Ingredients | U.S. | Metric | Procedure |
|---|---|---|---|
| Apples | 4 lb | 2 kg | 1. Cut the apples into quarters and remove the cores. Skins may be left on because they will be strained out later. (Red peels will color the applesauce pink.) Coarsely dice the apples. |
| Sugar | as needed | as needed | |
| Flavoring (see step 5) | | | |
| Lemon juice | to taste | to taste | |

1. Cut the apples into quarters and remove the cores. Skins may be left on because they will be strained out later. (Red peels will color the applesauce pink.) Coarsely dice the apples.

2. Place the apples in a heavy saucepan with about 2 oz (60 ml) water. Cover.

3. Set the pan over a low heat and cook the apples until very soft. Stir occasionally.

4. Remove the cover. Add sugar to taste. The amount depends on the desired sweetness of the sauce and the sweetness of the apples.

5. Add desired flavoring to taste, such as grated lemon zest, vanilla, or cinnamon. Add lemon juice to taste, especially if the apples lack tartness. Simmer for a few minutes to blend in flavors.

6. Pass the sauce through a food mill.

7. If the sauce is too thin or watery, let it simmer uncovered until thickened.

# TERMS FOR REVIEW

| | | |
|---|---|---|
| compote | fruit crisp | apple charlotte |
| fruit cobbler | fruit betty | fruit gratin |

# QUESTIONS FOR DISCUSSION

1. Briefly describe each of the following fruits.

   | | |
   |---|---|
   | kumquat | persimmon |
   | litchi | pomegranate |
   | mango | prickly pear |
   | papaya | quince |
   | passion fruit | |

2. True or false: Berries should be removed from their containers and washed as soon as possible after delivery or purchase. Explain.

3. For the following fruits, describe how to select produce of good quality.

   | | |
   |---|---|
   | apples | grapefruit |
   | apricots | grapes |
   | bananas | peaches |
   | coconuts | pineapples |

4. Describe in general terms how to sauté a fruit for a dessert.

5. Describe the procedure for preparing pears poached in red wine.

## Chapter 23

# Dessert Presentation

I n recent years, chefs have devoted more of their creativity to the arrangement of food on the plate. This is something of a change from earlier decades, when much of the plating of foods in elegant restaurants was done by the dining room staff at tableside. This trend has extended to the service of desserts as well. A piece of pastry or a wedge of cake that was at one time served by itself on a small dessert plate is now likely to be served on a large plate with a sauce and one or more items of garnish.

A pastry chef may devote as much attention to the appearance of a plated dessert as he or she gives to the decoration of a cake or the assembly of a large pastry for the display case or retail counter. The purpose of this chapter is to present guidelines and general suggestions for the presentation of individual desserts. The discussion concludes with a list of specific suggestions that employ recipes from throughout this book.

**After reading this chapter, you should be able to:**

1. Plate and serve attractive presentations of desserts with appropriate sauces and garnishes.

# BACKGROUND AND GUIDELINES

## A Brief Overview

The art of the plated dessert is a fairly new aspect of the pastry chef's craft. Until recently, desserts in fine restaurants were presented on a pastry cart and plated by the dining room staff, or else they were plated very simply in the kitchen, again by the dining room staff or, sometimes, a pantry cook. Hot desserts such as soufflés may have been prepared by a line cook. The head chef or one of the cooks, perhaps a pantry cook, often prepared the desserts, or they were purchased from an outside vendor. If the restaurant employed a pastry chef, she or he was simply an anonymous cook.

Today the situation is very different. Many restaurants—not just the finest white-tablecloth restaurants but even casual neighborhood spots—proudly display the names of their pastry chefs on their menus. Dessert menus are likely to be printed separately and not just added to the bottom of the dining menus. Desserts, prepared by a high-profile pastry chef, are seen as products that not only will increase the check average but also draw public attention to the restaurant and to the creativity of the kitchen, thus bringing in more customers.

Plating styles have changed noticeably in a few short years. Many of the pastry chefs who were pioneers in this area created complex architectural assemblies that were impressive and beautiful to look at but difficult to eat. Diners were fascinated but found they had to take the construction apart in order to begin to eat it. Often, chefs added to the complexity by decorating the rims of the plates with squirts of sauce or sprinklings of cocoa powder or 10X sugar, which was likely to end up on the sleeves of the diners. Gradually, pastry chefs began to return their focus to flavor, discovering they could make great-looking and great-tasting desserts without building towering constructions.

An important factor in the development of plating styles is the way pastry chefs and kitchen chefs work together as a team to shape the culinary identity of the restaurant. Dessert menus are treated as continuations of the dining experience, not simply as an unrelated sweet course tacked on at the end. The pastry chef's work complements and harmonizes with the hot food in plating styles as well as in ingredients and flavors.

## Plated Desserts Today

Dessert plating styles are constantly changing and evolving, thanks to today's creative pastry chefs. There are many opinions on what makes a successful presentation, and chefs have thought and discussed and written a great deal about this subject. There is much disagreement, of course. When chefs try to develop an individual style to showcase their talents, the result is more variety to attract and satisfy customers.

Because pastry chefs do not always agree on how best to present a dessert, it is impossible to set down a list of rules that must be followed. But we can discuss some of the ideas that influence chefs in their decisions and some of the factors pastry chefs consider when planning a dessert menu.

### Three Essentials of Dessert Presentation

Making desserts look good requires that the pastry chef pay careful attention to all of his or her tasks. In order to create attractive plated desserts, the chef should observe the following three basic principles. Note that only the third one concerns the actual design of the plating.

1. **Good basic baking and pastry skills.**

   A pastry chef cannot make superior plated desserts without having mastered basic skills and techniques. Individual components must be properly prepared. If puff pastry doesn't rise evenly and well because the chef hasn't mastered correct rolling-in techniques, if cake layers have poor texture because of incorrect mixing methods, if a slice of cake is poorly cut, if sauces have poor texture, or if whipped cream is over-whipped and curdled, then no amount of fancy plate design will correct those faults.

2. **Professional work habits.**

   Plating attractive and appealing desserts is partly a matter of being neat and careful and using common sense. This is an aspect of the professional pride we discussed at the end of chapter 1. Professionals take pride in their work and in the food they serve. Pride in workmanship means that chefs care about the quality of their work and do not serve a dessert they aren't proud of.

3. **Visual sense.**

   Beyond being neat, effective dessert presentation depends on developing an understanding of techniques involving balance of colors, shapes, textures, and flavors and of arranging dessert, garnish, and sauce on a plate to achieve this balance. This is the subject of our next sections.

## Flavor First

"Too much presentation and not enough flavor." That is an often-expressed opinion of some of the complicated towering constructions that were common on dessert plates not long ago. It is true that you can be more structural with dessert presentations than with hot food. It is also true, as the old saying goes, that "the eye eats first." But it is important to remember that food is still food. After the customers have demolished the structure on the plate and finished eating, it is the flavor—or lack of it—they will remember. The presentation should enhance the flavor experience, not cover up a lack of flavor.

Flavor begins with ingredients. In baking as well as in cooking, there is no substitute for the best ingredients available. To get maximum flavor from fruits and other perishable ingredients, look for the freshest locally grown products in season. This means the dessert menu changes as certain good-quality items become unavailable. Chefs get their inspiration from the best in the market. A new crop of fresh summer berries, for example, gets chefs thinking about how best to feature them on the menu. In the fall, local apples and pears show up on menus in many forms.

## Simplicity and Complexity

Getting the best and freshest flavors on the plate frequently means knowing when to stop. It is often harder to leave a presentation alone than to keep adding to it. One pastry expert has written that a good chef can take a great peach and make something original and inventive out of it, but a great chef will know when to let the peach speak for itself. Sometimes, with the best ingredients, a simple presentation is the best, and the more complexity you add, the more it distracts from the flavors.

This doesn't mean there is no place for complex presentations on dessert menus. It is good to offer customers variety. Furthermore, elaborate presentations often draw attention in the dining room and stimulate additional sales and raise check averages. But you should consider the function and importance of each additional element you place on a plate. Does it harmonize with the rest of the presentation? Does it serve a purpose, or did you add it just because you could? Even a simple garnish, such as the mint sprigs that appear on every dessert plate in some restaurants, should not be added without thought. What is the mint for? If only to add color, is the color necessary? Some chefs argue that nothing should be put on the plate that isn't intended to be eaten. You may or may not agree, but at least have a reason for what you do to the dessert presentation.

One argument for elaborate dessert presentations is that customers should be offered desserts they can't prepare at home. For some people this is true, but many others are attracted most of all to familiar comfort foods. The creative pastry chef can find ways to satisfy both types of customers with a varied dessert menu. Even when presenting homestyle desserts, chefs can add a distinctive touch in the form of garnish or sauces while keeping the base of the dessert recognizable. Even more important, they can make the base dessert extremely well, so even the familiar is lifted to a new level of excellence.

Which dessert do you think is more successful: one the customer thinks is too beautiful to eat or one the customer can't wait to start eating?

Another factor to consider when designing your presentations concerns kitchen capabilities. A pastry chef's hours vary from establishment to establishment, but in many cases the pastry chef starts early, finishes all the baking, and goes home before dinner service begins. Desserts are then plated by the kitchen staff or even the dining room staff. If the pastry chef's artful designs are too complex for anyone else to construct, simpler presentations are probably advisable.

## Plating for the Customer

Customers love desserts. However, not all customers order them. What should the pastry chef do to create and present desserts that more customers will order? Variety is the key—something for everyone.

Some people would love a little sweet after a satisfying restaurant meal but are simply too full for a large, rich dessert. In the average restaurant, perhaps two-thirds, at most, of the diners order dessert. Of the remaining third, some undoubtedly would order dessert if something light and refreshing were on the menu, or if an item was so attractive they couldn't resist. When planning for variety, don't neglect to include lighter, simpler presentations to appeal to reluctant diners.

If most of your dessert presentations are elaborate or complex, try to include at least one or two simple comfort foods.

Think of the convenience of the diner. Don't make the dessert into a presentation that is difficult or awkward to eat.

For each presentation, select plates large enough to hold the arrangement without overcrowding (but not so large that the dessert looks sparse). Besides looking sloppy and unprofessional, desserts spilling over the rims of plates risk spilling on the customer.

Be honest on the menu so people know what to expect. Don't take such liberties with menu terminology in an effort to be creative that you confuse your customers. If people order apple pie, for example, they are likely to be disappointed if what they get is a disk of puff pastry with artfully arranged slices of sautéed apple placed on top, no matter how attractive the presentation is or how flavorful the apples are.

## Plating Guidelines

The baker's art consists of two stages: first, cooking and baking doughs, batters, fillings, creams, and sauces; and second, assembling these components into finished desserts and pastries. In chapter 18, for example, you learned how to take an assortment of baked cake and pastry layers, icings, mousses, fruits, and fillings and build them into attractive and sometimes complex cakes and tortes.

The same principle is used in plating dessert presentations. A plated dessert is an arrangement of one or more components. For most desserts, all the components are prepared well in advance. The plated dessert itself, however, is assembled at the last minute. All the components discussed throughout this book, including meringues, mousses, ice creams and sorbets, cookies, puff pastry, sponge and other cake layers, pastry cream, and dessert sauces, are used to make a presentation that is more than the sum of its parts. Of course, this means that in order to make successful plated desserts, you first have to learn how to prepare the components.

The basic elements of a plated dessert are the following:

- Main item.

- Garnish.

- Sauce.

In its simplest form, a dessert can be a portion of a single main item, such as a slice of cake or a wedge of pie, served unadorned on a plate. More often, other items are added to enhance flavor, texture, and eye appeal. In some cases, a presentation may have two or more main items, as in the case of dessert samplers. Usually, however, the secondary items on the plate are considered garnishes. They serve to enhance and add contrast to the main item.

When deciding what to put on the plate, you should consider five characteristics of the components of the dessert. Three of these characteristics are related to tastes and mouth feel and are the most important:

- Flavor.

- Texture.

- Temperature.

The other two are visual elements:

- Color.

- Shape.

Flavors should enhance or complement each other, such as a caramel sauce with a caramelized fruit gratin, or offer a pleasing contrast, such as a soothing crème anglaise with a slightly tart fruit. If the main item is soft, such as a mousse or ice cream, add a crisp or crunchy garnish, such as small cookies or caramelized nuts, for texture contrast. Temperature contrasts are also pleasing, such as a spoonful of ice cream with a warm fruit tart.

Visually, a variety of colors and shapes can be attractive, but be careful not to make too much of a jumble. And don't feel compelled to add color to every plate. Brown is a good color, too, and a well-prepared dessert in a few shades of brown can be very appetizing.

## Garnish

Many if not most dessert presentations are improved with one or more items of garnish. But first take a moment to consider whether serving the dessert alone, without garnish, wouldn't be effective. A simple, ungarnished plating is usually used for homestyle desserts or, at the opposite extreme, for elegant pastries or gâteaux that are beautiful on their own and need no added elements.

Although the term *garnish* may refer to a purely decorative item, such as a sprig of mint, it is usually best to plate only components that are intended to be eaten. Thus, we use the term to mean an edible item that complements the main item on the plate. Following are examples. The first two of these are the most versatile because they include the greatest variety of items and possible presentations.

*Fruit* is a good garnish for many pastries, cakes, and other desserts. Nearly any fresh or cooked fruit can be used. Depending on size and shape, they can be used whole, such as berries, or cut into slices, wedges, or other shapes (such as apples, pears, pineapple, mango, kiwi, and peaches).

*Ice creams* and *sorbets* can provide both temperature and texture contrasts in a dessert presentation. For homestyle desserts such as pies, the ice cream is usually served with a standard scoop. For more elegant presentations, the ice cream is often shaped into a small, oval *quenelle*. To shape a quenelle, first make sure the ice cream or sorbet is tempered to a soft consistency and not too hard. Scoop a portion of the frozen dessert with a tablespoon dipped in water. With a second spoon, scoop the ice cream out of the first spoon. This shapes the ice cream into a neat, oval shape about the size of the bowl of the spoon. Repeat the scooping action with the first spoon if necessary to make the oval neater.

*Whipped cream,* applied with a pastry bag or spoon, is a classic garnish for many desserts. (Whipped cream could also be considered a sauce rather than a garnish.)

A small *cookie (petit four sec)* or two gives textural contrast to soft desserts such as mousses, Bavarians, and ice creams.

*Fruit crisps* or *chips* (p. 602) are used to decorate fruit desserts of a corresponding flavor. Not only do they give a textural contrast but also they add flavor interest by providing a variation on the flavor of the main item. For example, one or more apple crisps can garnish a plating of baked apple with apple sorbet.

*Chocolate decorations* of many types, including curls, cigarettes, cutouts, and piped lacework, go well with many kinds of dessert, not only chocolate desserts. Decorative chocolate work is discussed in chapter 24.

A *choux lattice* is used in the photo of a decorated slice of Passion Fruit Charlotte (p. 634). This decoration is made as follows: Draw lattice designs on a sheet of parchment, then turn the parchment over (the drawing should show through). Using a paper cone (p. 440), pipe pâte à choux over the outlines. Use the point of a small knife to make the joints neat, as necessary. Sprinkle with poppy seeds, if you like, and bake at 375°F (190°C) until golden. Choux paste can be used to make décor not just in lattice shapes but in many others as well.

*Stencil paste* or *tuile batter* (pp. 411 and 508) can be piped in designs the same way choux paste is, then baked until crisp. Alternatively, use the stencil method of cookie makeup (p. 490) to make wafers in decorative shapes for dressing up dessert presentations.

Sugar spirals, spun sugar, and other forms of decorative *sugar work,* as well as caramelized or toasted nuts, are other items used to garnish appropriate desserts. Sugar work is discussed in chapter 26.

These are only some of the simplest and most commonly used garnishes. For more ambitious plating styles, you can also garnish with small portions of pastries and confections that, in a larger portion size, could stand on their own as a main item—for example, a frozen pineapple mousse cake garnished with pineapple fritters, or a chocolate tart accompanied by a small raspberry crème brûlée. Sometimes it is difficult to determine which is the main item and which are the garnishes. Usually, however, one of the items dominates and the others play supporting roles. The possible combinations are limitless.

In summary, always keep in mind these general concepts when planning dessert presentations:

- Every component should have a purpose. Don't add elements merely to make the plate fuller.

- Components or elements can work together by complementing or by contrasting.

- When elements contrast, be sure they balance. For example, when you balance a rich mousse with a tart fruit sauce, be sure the sauce isn't so tart or strong-flavored that it overwhelms the mousse.

One final point: It is possible to get carried away with the concept of balance. It is not necessary to garnish every soft dessert with something crisp or every hot dessert with something cold. Sometimes customers prefer just a plain, unadorned dish of ice cream or a simple slice of warm apple pie.

## Sauce

Dessert sauces enhance desserts both by their flavor and by their appearance, just as savory sauces enhance meats, fish, and vegetables. The most popular and useful dessert sauces are discussed in chapter 12. Crème anglaise variations, chocolate sauce, caramel sauce, and the many fruit sauces or sweetened fruit purées are the most versatile. One or another of these complements nearly every dessert.

Except in the case of some homestyle desserts and frozen desserts, sauces are usually not ladled over a dessert because this would mar its appearance by covering it up. Sauces are usually plated as a small pool, either around the dessert portion or to its side. Another way to serve a sauce is to drizzle it in a ribbon or in a random pattern onto the plate.

Sauces served in a pool are often marbled or feathered, as shown in the accompanying photographs. This is done by piping lines or dots of a sauce of a contrasting color and then drawing a pick or skewer through the piped sauce to make the pattern. For this technique to work properly, the piped sauce must be of about the same weight and consistency as the sauce in the pool. If you pipe a heavier sauce onto a pool of another sauce, the heavy piping will sink out of sight. On the other hand, if the piped sauce is much lighter, it may float and spread across the top of the sauce pool. The easiest way to pipe a sauce is to use a small squeeze bottle.

For dark-colored sauces, such as chocolate sauce or raspberry purée, a white sauce such as that on page 283 is a good choice for piping. Crème anglaise or other light-colored sauces can be decorated with chocolate crème anglaise or other dark sauces. Contrasting fruit sauces can also be used to decorate each other.

# EXAMPLES OF DESSERT PRESENTATIONS

The techniques and recipes presented in other chapters of this book and in the first part of this chapter give you the tools to prepare an unlimited variety of modern, stylish desserts.

This section follows a format similar to the one used to explain the procedures for preparing gâteaux and torten that begins on page 457. In other words, no new recipes are required; individual components—as prepared from recipes elsewhere in this book—are assembled and arranged as indicated.

The following presentations are merely a few suggestions, selected to provide a sampling of ideas using different types of desserts and a variety of styles of arrangement. In order to give you realistic and practical information, the plating and garnish styles selected for this chapter are a reflection of currently popular styles and are similar to desserts actually served in a variety of North American and European restaurants. Chefs derive inspiration from one another's work and often create presentations by combining their own ideas with existing styles and plating concepts.

Distributed among the more elaborate or complex presentations are a number of the simplest arrangements—for example, ideas for plating a slice of cake. By contrast, toward the end of the chapter are several medleys of three or more desserts on a plate. The list includes both homey, rustic desserts and elegant desserts.

Each procedure begins with a list of the components required for the presentation. Page numbers refer to recipes or procedures elsewhere in this book. Where no page number is given, there may be two or more recipes, any of which is suitable; refer to the index for page numbers.

## Decorating with Sauces

# MOCHA TORTE

| Components | Procedure |
|---|---|
| Mocha Torte (p. 459)<br>Chocolate Sauce (p. 278)<br>Crème Anglaise (p. 269) | 1. Place a wedge of mocha torte in the center of a plate.<br>2. Spoon a small pool of chocolate sauce on one side of the cake. Spoon a small pool of crème anglaise on the other side of the cake.<br>3. If desired, marble the chocolate sauce with a little crème anglaise, and marble the crème anglaise with a little chocolate sauce (see p. 612). |

# PANNA COTTA WITH CARAMEL AND FRESH BERRIES

| Components | Procedure |
|---|---|
| Caramel for Cages (p. 676)<br>Panna Cotta (p. 522)<br>Clear Caramel Sauce (p. 280)<br>Assorted fresh berries | 1. *Prepare the caramel decorations:* Drizzle the caramel onto a silicone mat or an oiled sheet pan into desired shapes or patterns. Allow to cool and harden.<br>2. Unmold a portion of panna cotta onto a broad soup plate or other suitable plate.<br>3. Ladle a little caramel sauce around the panna cotta.<br>4. Distribute the mixed berries around the panna cotta on top of the caramel sauce.<br>5. Top with the caramel decoration immediately before serving. Do not let it stand, or the caramel decoration may begin to dissolve in the moisture from the dessert. |

# APPLE WALNUT TURNOVER

| Components | Procedure |
|---|---|
| Apple Walnut Pie Filling (p. 300)<br>Puff Pastry (pp. 324–325)<br>Sabayon (p. 281)<br>Walnuts | 1. Prepare the pie filling as directed, but chop the apples into fairly small pieces.<br>2. Prepare and bake the turnovers (p. 328), filling each one generously.<br>3. Cut a warm turnover in half and spread it open on a plate to display the filling.<br>4. In the space between the two cut surfaces, spoon a pool of sabayon. Sprinkle the sauce with walnut pieces. |

**VARIATIONS**

Instead of sabayon, use Crème Anglaise (p. 269) flavored with cinnamon.

# PEACH NAPOLEON

| Components | Procedure |
|---|---|
| 3 phyllo layers for napoleons, one of which is caramelized (p. 344)<br>Pastry Cream (p. 271) flavored with amaretto<br>Caramelized peach slices (p. 590)<br>Clear Caramel Sauce (p. 280)<br>Peach Ice Cream (p. 559) | 1. Place a plain phyllo layer just to one side of the center of a plate. Cover with caramelized peach slices.<br>2. With a pastry bag filled with a star tube, pipe pastry cream over the peaches. Alternatively, place a small spoonful of pastry cream on the peaches and spread gently over the center with the back of a spoon.<br>3. Top with another phyllo layer and additional peaches and pastry cream.<br>4. Top with the caramelized phyllo layer.<br>5. Drizzle caramel sauce onto the plate around the napoleon.<br>6. Place a quenelle (see p. 610) of ice cream next to the napoleon. Serve at once. |

**VARIATIONS**

Instead of the peach ice cream, use Caramel Ice Cream (p. 559), Cinnamon Ice Cream (p. 559), or whipped cream flavored with amaretto.

# STRAWBERRY CREAM CAKE

| Components | Procedure |
|---|---|
| Strawberry Cream Cake (p. 462; see the recipe note)<br>Strawberry sauce (p. 277)<br>Cream Sauce for Piping (p. 283) | 1. Prepare the cake following the procedure for Orange Cream Cake but using strawberries instead of oranges and kirsch to flavor the syrup and cream.<br>2. Place a wedge of cake on one side of a plate.<br>3. On the other half of the plate, spoon a pool of strawberry sauce.<br>4. Pipe 2 or 3 lines of cream sauce onto the strawberry sauce and draw a pick through the lines to marble them. |

# ANGEL FOOD CAKE WITH PLUM COMPOTE AND MASCARPONE SORBET

| Components | Procedure |
|---|---|
| Angel Food Cake batter (p. 409)<br>Plum Compote (p. 600)<br>Florentines (p. 513) without chocolate, or Coconut Tuiles (p. 510), made in 2½-in. (6 cm) rounds and left flat<br>Mascarpone Sorbet (p. 561) | 1. Bake the cake batter in 2½-in. (6 cm) ring molds. Cool and remove from the molds.<br>2. Spoon the plum compote onto a dessert plate.<br>3. Place a cake round on top of the plums in the center of the plate.<br>4. Top with a florentine or coconut tuile.<br>5. Place a small scoop of sorbet on top of the cookie. |

# OLD-FASHIONED POUND CAKE WITH HONEY ICE CREAM AND BLUEBERRIES

| Components | Procedure |
|---|---|
| Blueberry Sauce (p. 282)<br>Honey Ice Cream (p. 562)<br>Old-Fashioned Pound Cake (p. 400)<br>Crème fraîche<br>Toasted sliced almonds | 1. Spoon a pool of blueberry sauce onto a dessert plate.<br>2. Place a scoop of ice cream on the center of the plate.<br>3. Slice a slice of pound cake about ¾ in. (2 cm) thick. Cut this slice into thirds vertically. Lean the slices against the ice cream.<br>4. Drizzle crème fraîche over the cake and blueberries.<br>5. Sprinkle with toasted almonds. |

# SPICE CAKE WITH CARAMELIZED APPLES

| Components | Procedure |
|---|---|
| Brown Sugar Spice Cake (p. 399), baked as a sheet cake<br>Caramelized Apples (p. 590), apples cut into medium dice before caramelizing<br>Crème Anglaise (p. 269), made with half milk and half heavy cream<br>Apple Crisps (p. 602) | 1. Place a square of spice cake in the center of a dessert plate.<br>2. Top with caramelized apples.<br>3. Ladle a generous pool of crème anglaise around the cake. If desired, drizzle a little over the cake as well.<br>4. Dot the pool of sauce with a few additional dice of caramelized apple.<br>5. Stick an apple crisp into the mound of apples on top of the cake so it stands upright. |

# LEMON TART

| Components | Procedure |
|---|---|
| Lemon Tart (p. 361)<br>Whipped cream<br>Fruit, as desired<br>Sprig of mint | 1. Place a wedge of tart slightly to the left of the center of the plate with the point toward you.<br>2. To the right of the tart wedge, pipe a rosette or shell of whipped cream using a pastry bag with a large star tube.<br>3. As garnish, place a colorful piece of fruit and a mint sprig next to the cream. |

# PECAN PIE WITH ORANGE

| Components | Procedure |
|---|---|
| Pecan Pie (p. 303)<br>Soft whipped cream<br>Grated orange zest<br>Candied Orange Zest (p. 602)<br>Kumquat Compote (p. 601) or<br>   Clear Caramel Sauce (p. 280) | 1. Place a wedge of pie on the center of a dessert plate.<br>2. Flavor the whipped cream by folding in a little grated orange zest. Top the pie with a spoonful of the cream.<br>3. Garnish the top of the whipped cream with a few short strips of candied orange zest.<br>4. Drizzle a little kumquat compote or caramel sauce on the plate around the pie. (Alternatively, use just the syrup from the compote.)<br>5. Sprinkle the whole dessert with a little chopped candied orange zest. |

# APPLE CRISP WITH CARAMEL SAUCE OR BUTTERSCOTCH SAUCE

| Components | Procedure |
|---|---|
| Caramel Sauce or Butterscotch Sauce (p. 280)<br>Apple Crisp (p. 591)<br>Vanilla ice cream | 1. Spoon a pool of sauce into the center of a plate.<br>2. With a large serving spoon, place a generous spoonful of apple crisp on the pool of sauce slightly to one side of the center of the plate.<br>3. Garnish with a small scoop of vanilla ice cream. |

**VARIATION**

Substitute a generous spoonful of whipped cream for the ice cream.

# FATTIGMAN WITH LINGONBERRIES

| Components | Procedure |
|---|---|
| Fattigman (p. 245)<br>Lingonberry preserves<br>Vanilla ice cream<br>Mint | 1. Arrange 3 to 5 fattigman on one side of a dessert plate.<br>2. Place a spoonful of lingonberries next to the fattigman.<br>3. In the space remaining on the plate, place a scoop of vanilla ice cream.<br>4. Decorate with a sprig of mint. |

# CHARLOTTE AU CASSIS

| Components | Procedure |
|---|---|
| Charlotte au Cassis (p. 540)<br>Chocolate fan (p. 647)<br>Fresh berries<br>Candied Orange Zest (p. 602)<br>Mint<br>Crème Chantilly (p. 265)<br>Sauces (see step 4) | 1. Place a wedge of charlotte toward the back of a plate.<br><br>2. In front of the charlotte, place a chocolate fan and fill it with berries. Garnish with a few pieces of candied orange zest and a sprig of mint.<br><br>3. Make a quenelle of crème chantilly and place it next to the chocolate fan. Alternatively, pipe a rosette of the cream with a star tip.<br><br>4. Spoon a band of sauce around the plate and marble it with a sauce of a contrasting color. (The sauces in the photograph are syrup from kumquat compote and raspberry coulis.) |

# BROWNIE CHERRY CHEESECAKE ICE CREAM SANDWICH

| Components | Procedure |
|---|---|
| Two 2-in. Cream Cheese Brownies (p. 512)<br>1½–2 oz Cheesecake Ice Cream (p. 559)<br>1 oz Cherry Pie Filling (p. 299)<br>Whipped cream<br>Chocolate shavings or other chocolate decorations | 1. Place one brownie slightly off center on a plate. Top with the ice cream, which has been flattened slightly.<br><br>2. Place the second brownie on top.<br><br>3. Spoon the cherry pie filling onto the plate next to the brownie sandwich.<br><br>4. Decorate with whipped cream and chocolate decorations. |

# ICED LOW-FAT RASPBERRY PARFAIT WITH ALMOND MACAROONS

| Components | Procedure |
|---|---|
| Iced Low-Fat Raspberry Parfait (p. 574)<br>Italian Meringue (p. 267)<br>Raspberry Sauce (p. 279)<br>Fresh raspberries and other berries<br>Almond Macaroons II (p. 506) | 1. Freeze the parfait in a gutter mold lined with plastic film.<br>2. Unmold the parfait onto a tray and remove the plastic film. Using a pastry bag with a star tip, coat the top and sides of the parfait with Italian meringue. Brown lightly with a blowtorch.<br>3. For each portion, cut a slice of the parfait 1¼–1½ in. (3–4 cm) thick and stand on one side of a plate. Spoon a crescent of raspberry sauce on the other side of the plate. Top the pool of sauce with a bouquet of fruit and 2 or 3 macaroons. |

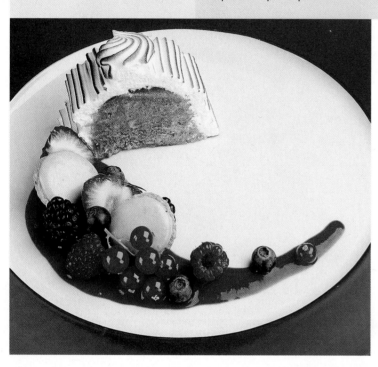

# TRICOLOR FRUIT MOUSSE

| Components | Procedure |
|---|---|
| Ingredients for strawberry, pineapple, and raspberry Bavarians (p. 535)<br>Peach sauce, made by puréeing fresh or canned peaches (p. 277)<br>Pistachio Macaroons (p. 505) or Almond Macaroons II (p. 506) | 1. Prepare the strawberry Bavarian, *using half the quantity of gelatin indicated in the recipe*. Pour the mixture into a flat-bottomed, straight-sided mold so the mousse is about ¾ in. (2 cm) thick. Chill until set.<br>2. Prepare the pineapple Bavarian, using canned or poached pineapple (raw pineapple does not work with gelatin) and *only half the indicated quantity of gelatin*. Pour a layer of pineapple Bavarian on top of the strawberry layer. Chill until set.<br>3. Repeat with the raspberry Bavarian, *again using half the gelatin*.<br>4. Pour a pool of peach purée sauce onto a plate.<br>5. Remove a spoonful of the tricolor mousse by holding a tablespoon vertically and inserting it into the mousse so each spoonful contains all three layers. Place several spoonfuls of the mousse onto the sauce.<br>6. Arrange 2 or 3 macaroons next to the mousse. |

# POACHED PEAR WITH BAKLAVA AND MASCARPONE CREAM

| Components | Procedure |
| --- | --- |
| Whole pear poached in white wine (p. 587), with some of the poaching syrup<br>Mascarpone<br>Crème fraîche<br>Confectioners' sugar<br>Baklava (p. 346)<br>Pistachios or walnuts, coarsely chopped<br>Cinnamon | 1. With a melon baller, remove the core of the pear through the blossom end, leaving the pear whole. Cut a thin slice off the bottom of the pear so it stands upright.<br>2. Reduce the poaching syrup until it is thickened and syrupy.<br>3. Mix together equal parts mascarpone and crème fraîche. Sweeten lightly with confectioners' sugar. Whip until stiff.<br>4. Using a pastry bag, fill the pear with the whipped mascarpone cream.<br>5. Stand the pear on a dessert plate.<br>6. Lean a triangle of baklava against the pear, taking care so the pastry layers don't fall apart. Alternatively, simply place the baklava on the plate next to the pear.<br>7. Drizzle a little crème fraîche and a little of the pear syrup around the pear.<br>8. Sprinkle with chopped nuts and just a dash of cinnamon. |

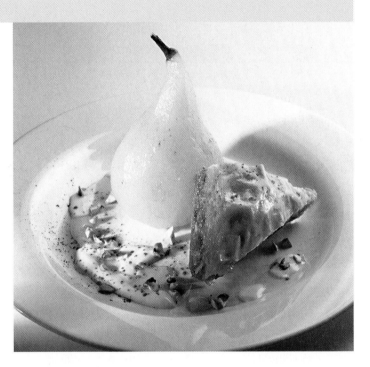

# CREAM CHEESE BAVARIAN WITH FRUIT COMPOTE

| Components | Procedure |
| --- | --- |
| Genoise (p. 407)<br>Cream Cheese Bavarian (p. 536)<br>Toasted sliced almonds<br>Fruit Compote (p. 587) made with a mixture of colorful fresh fruit | 1. Select a round, straight-sided, flat-bottomed mold 3–4 in. (8–10 cm) in diameter. Cut a layer of genoise as thin as possible and line the bottom of the mold.<br>2. Prepare the Bavarian and pour a layer into the mold about 1½ in. (4 cm) thick. Sprinkle the top with a few almonds. Chill until set.<br>3. Unmold the Bavarian and place in the center of a plate.<br>4. Spoon the fruit compote around the Bavarian. |

# PUMPKIN PROFITEROLES

| Components | Procedure |
|---|---|
| 4 unfilled profiteroles (cream puffs), about 1½–2 in. (4–5 cm) in diameter<br>Pumpkin Cream Chiffon (p. 312) made with half the gelatin<br>Crème Anglaise (p. 269)<br>Whipped cream | 1. Cut the tops off the profiteroles. Fill with the pumpkin chiffon, using a pastry bag with a star tube, and replace the tops. Dust with confectioners' sugar.<br>2. Ladle a pool of crème anglaise onto a plate.<br>3. Arrange 3 profiteroles in a triangle in the center of the plate.<br>4. Pipe a rosette of whipped cream in the center of the triangle.<br>5. Place the fourth profiterole on the center of the whipped cream. |

# STEAMED CHOCOLATE ALMOND PUDDING WITH CARAMEL SAUCE

| Components | Procedure |
|---|---|
| Steamed Chocolate Almond Pudding (p. 531)<br>Caramel Sauce (p. 280)<br>Praline Ice Cream (p. 559) | 1. Prepare the pudding in single-serving molds, or make it in large molds and then slice or break it coarsely into portions, depending on whether an elegant appearance or a homestyle, rustic appearance is desired.<br>2. Ladle a pool of caramel sauce onto a plate.<br>3. Place a portion of pudding on the sauce.<br>4. Garnish with a small scoop or spoonful of ice cream placed next to the pudding. |

# BOMBE BRESILIENNE

| Components | Procedure |
|---|---|
| Bombe Bresilienne (p. 569)<br>Whipped cream<br>Caramelized Pineapple (p. 590) | 1. Cut a wedge of bombe and place it on its side on a plate so the thick part of the wedge is against the rim of the plate and the point of the wedge lies across the center of the plate.<br>2. Using a pastry bag with a small star tube, pipe a row of whipped cream rosettes along the thin edge of the bombe.<br>3. In the remaining space on the plate, arrange a few pieces of caramelized pineapple and their juices.<br>4. If desired, decorate the pineapple with a few fresh berries, a little toasted coconut, or candied orange zest. |

# CHOCOLATE BREAD PUDDING
# WITH CARAMELIZED BANANAS
# AND CINNAMON ICE CREAM

| Components | Procedure |
|---|---|
| Tuile batter (p. 508)<br>Caramelized Bananas (p. 590)<br>Chocolate Bread Pudding<br>  (p. 526), warm<br>Chocolate Sauce (p. 278)<br>Crème Anglaise (p. 269),<br>  flavored with a little cinnamon<br>Cinnamon Ice Cream (p. 559) | 1. With the tuile batter, prepare 2-in. (5 cm) tuiles, using the procedure on page 508 but omitting the almonds.<br>2. Place 3 or 4 pieces of caramelized banana side by side in the center of a dessert plate.<br>3. Place a square of warm pudding on top of the bananas.<br>4. Drizzle a few spoonfuls each of the cinnamon crème anglaise and the chocolate sauce around the dessert.<br>5. Place a tuile on top of the pudding.<br>6. Place a small ball of ice cream inside the tuile. |

**Alternative Procedure**

Instead of cutting squares of pudding, use a round cutter or ring mold to cut portions, or bake individual portions of the pudding in round molds.

# CHILLED SUMMER FRUIT SOUP
# WITH STRAWBERRY SORBET

| Components | Procedure |
|---|---|
| Tuile batter (p. 508)<br>Chilled Summer Fruit Soup<br>(p. 589)<br>Grated lime zest<br>Strawberry Sorbet (p. 561) | 1. With the tuile batter, make wafers about 1 in. (2.5 cm) wide and long enough to place across the rim of the soup plates in which you intend to serve the soup.<br>2. Plate the soup in shallow soup plates.<br>3. Sprinkle the soup lightly with grated lime zest.<br>4. Place a wafer across the top of the plate with the ends resting on opposite rims.<br>5. Place a small scoop or quenelle of sorbet on the center of the wafer, above the soup.<br>6. Serve immediately. |

**VARIATION**

In place of the strawberry sorbet, use another sorbet appropriate to the fruit used in the soup garnish, such as raspberry, mango, or pineapple.

# TRIO OF FRUIT SORBETS

| Components | Procedure |
|---|---|
| Fruit purée sauces (p. 277):<br>raspberry, kiwi, mango,<br>strawberry<br>Three fruit sorbets (p. 561)<br>of contrasting colors, such as<br>lemon, melon, and raspberry | 1. Spoon pools of the sauces onto a dinner plate, using about 1 oz (30 mL) each. Tap the plate gently so the pools run together and cover the entire center of the plate. With a fork or other utensil, swirl the sauces together to make an attractive pattern.<br>2. Place a spoonful of each of 3 sorbets in the center of the plate. |

# CHOCOLATE MOUSSE TRIO

| Components | Procedure |
|---|---|
| Crème Anglaise (p. 269)<br>White Chocolate Mousse (p. 546)<br>Milk Chocolate Mousse (p. 546)<br>Dark Chocolate Mousse (p. 546)<br>Toasted sliced almonds<br>Chocolate and Orange Madeleines (p. 417) | 1. Ladle a pool of crème anglaise onto a plate.<br>2. Place a spoonful of each mousse on the sauce.<br>3. Garnish the tops of the mousses with a few toasted sliced almonds.<br>4. Arrange 1 or 2 madeleines on the side of the plate. |

**VARIATION**

Garnish each mousse with a different kind of nut.

# RASPBERRY MILLEFEUILLE

| Components | Procedure |
|---|---|
| Almond Tuile batter (p. 508)<br>Fresh raspberries<br>Whipped cream flavored with orange liqueur<br>Confectioners' sugar (optional)<br>Raspberry Sauce (p. 279)<br>Cream Sauce for Piping (p. 283) (optional) | 1. Bake tuile wafers about 3 in. (7 cm) in diameter, but leave them flat; do not bend or mold them.<br>2. Place 1 wafer in the center of a plate. Arrange a ring of berries on the wafer lining the outside edge. Using a pastry bag, fill the space in the center of the berry ring with the flavored whipped cream.<br>3. Top with a second wafer and repeat with the berries and cream.<br>4. Dredge a third wafer generously with confectioners' sugar, if desired. Carefully place it on top of the dessert.<br>5. Spoon a ring of raspberry sauce onto the plate around the pastry. If desired, marble the raspberry sauce with the cream sauce for piping. Serve at once, while the wafers are crisp. |

**VARIATION**

Garnish with a spoonful of Raspberry or Orange Sorbet (p. 561)

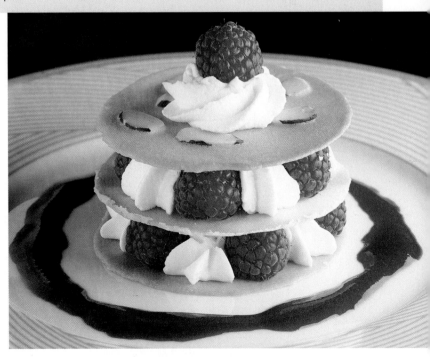

# APPLE-FILLED BRIOCHE WITH BERRIES

| Components | Procedure |
|---|---|
| Brioche (p. 193)<br>Applesauce (p. 603;<br>  see procedure)<br>Pastry Cream Mousseline<br>  (p. 271)<br>Crème Anglaise (p. 269)<br>Assorted fresh berries | 1. Slice off the top of the brioche. Hollow out the brioche and toast the resulting case lightly in the oven.<br>2. Prepare an applesauce that is sweet, not too tart, and well flavored with vanilla. Leave it slightly chunky; do not force it through a food mill.<br>3. Spoon a little pastry cream mousseline into the bottom of the brioche case. Fill almost to the top with the applesauce. Place a little more pastry cream on top and replace the top of the brioche.<br>4. Ladle a pool of crème anglaise onto a plate. Place the filled brioche in the center of the plate. Scatter fresh berries around the brioche. |

# FRENCH-TOASTED CHALLAH WITH CHEESECAKE ICE CREAM

| Components | Procedure |
|---|---|
| Challah (p. 150)<br>Batter for French toast<br>  (mixture of beaten eggs,<br>  milk, a little sugar, cinnamon)<br>Confectioners' sugar<br>Cheesecake Ice Cream<br>  (p. 559)<br>Melba Sauce (p. 279)<br>Whipped cream *(optional)* | 1. Slice the bread. Soak it in the egg batter and pan-fry it in butter to make French toast.<br>2. Overlap 2 or 3 slices of French toast on one side of a plate. Dust heavily with confectioners' sugar.<br>3. Place a scoop of ice cream in the center of the plate.<br>4. Spoon a pool of Melba sauce on the other side of the plate.<br>5. Garnish with a few rosettes of whipped cream, if desired. |

# LINZER "SHORTCAKE" WITH BERRIES

| Components | Procedure |
|---|---|
| Linzer Dough (p. 320)<br>Fresh raspberries or a mixture<br>  of raspberries, blackberries,<br>  and strawberries<br>Simple syrup<br>Confectioners' sugar<br>Crème Chantilly (p. 265)<br>Grated lime zest<br>Crushed nougatine (p. 668) | 1. Make small shortbread cookies with the Linzer dough. Roll out thin, cut into squares 1½–2 in. (4–5 cm) across, and bake until crisp. (*Note:* The dough is very soft and difficult to roll thin; be sure it is not too warm, and use plenty of flour for dusting, or else roll out between two sheets of parchment.) Cool completely.<br>2. If you are using strawberries, cut them into quarters or wedges. Place the berries in a bowl and add enough simple syrup to cover. Refrigerate several hours or overnight.<br>3. Dust the cookies very lightly with confectioners' sugar.<br>4. On a dessert plate or in shallow soup bowl, ladle some berries and a little of the syrup.<br>5. Place 1 shortbread cookie in the center of the berries. Place a dollop of crème chantilly on top of the cookie, using either a pastry bag or a spoon. Repeat with 2 more cookies and additional cream. Either stack the cookies vertically, like a napoleon, or lean them against the first one, like a stack that has tipped on its side. Top with a fourth cookie, but do not top this one with cream.<br>6. If desired, dust the dessert very lightly with confectioners' sugar by holding a sieve over the plate and giving it one or two light taps, taking care not to get the sugar on the rim of the plate.<br>7. Sprinkle the berries lightly with lime zest.<br>8. Finish with a light sprinkle of crushed nougatine. |

# SAVARIN WITH BERRIES

| Components | Procedure |
|---|---|
| Sabayon (p. 281)<br>Small (single-portion size)<br>  Savarin (p. 191)<br>Fresh berries | 1. Ladle a pool of sabayon onto a plate.<br>2. Place a savarin in the center of the plate.<br>3. Fill the savarin with berries. |

# WARM TROPICAL FRUIT COMPOTE WITH COCONUT ICE CREAM

| Components | Procedure |
|---|---|
| Tropical Fruit Compote (p. 588)<br>Coconut Ice Cream (p. 559)<br>Toasted coconut | 1. If the compote is not warm, heat it.<br>2. Spoon the compote in a soup plate or shallow bowl.<br>3. Place a scoop of the ice cream in the center.<br>4. Sprinkle lightly with toasted coconut.<br>5. If the compote is not colorful, sprinkle with a few pomegranate seeds or fresh berries. |

# APPLE FRITTERS WITH MASCARPONE SORBET

| Components | Procedure |
|---|---|
| Apple fritters (p. 242)<br>Confectioners' sugar<br>Raspberry Sauce (p. 279)<br>Mascarpone Sorbet (p. 561)<br>A strawberry or a few raspberries for garnish | 1. Place 2 fritters on one side of a plate. Dust with confectioners' sugar.<br>2. On the other side of the plate, spoon a pool of raspberry sauce.<br>3. Place a spoonful of the sorbet on the pool of sauce.<br>4. Garnish the plate with a fresh strawberry or a few raspberries. |

# POACHED PEAR WITH WINE SORBET

| Components | Procedure |
|---|---|
| Small pear, such as Seckel<br>Ingredients for Pears in Wine<br>(p. 587)<br>White Wine Sorbet (p. 561)<br>Sabayon (p. 281) | 1. Peel the pear and core it from the blossom end, but leave the stem in. Poach it in red wine, as directed in the recipe. Cool the pear.<br>2. Slice the cooled poached pear vertically, but leave the slices attached at the stem end; do not slice all the way through. Carefully fan the pear and place slightly off center on a plate.<br>3. Place a spoonful of wine sorbet next to the pear.<br>4. Place a spoonful of sabayon in front of the pear and sorbet. |

# POPPY SEED PARFAIT

| Components | Procedure |
|---|---|
| Poppy Seed Parfait (p. 574)<br>Genoise or Chocolate Genoise<br>(p. 407)<br>Crème Chantilly (p. 265)<br>Kumquat Compote (p. 601)<br>Chocolate cigarettes (p. 646) | 1. Fill a loaf-shaped mold nearly to the top with the parfait mixture. Top with a thin slice of genoise. Freeze until solid.<br>2. Unmold the parfait so the genoise forms the base.<br>3. Cut 3 slices, about 1½ oz (45 g) each. Overlap the slices off center on a cold plate.<br>4. Decorate with rosettes of crème chantilly.<br>5. On the empty side of the plate, spoon 2–3 oz (60–90 g) kumquat compote.<br>6. Lay 2 or 3 chocolate cigarettes across the plate. |

# HOT AND COLD BANANA SPLIT

| Components | Procedure |
|---|---|
| Strawberries, lightly sugared<br>Caramelized Bananas,<br>hot (p. 590)<br>Crème Anglaise (p. 269)<br>Raspberry Sauce (p. 279)<br>Strawberry Sauce (p. 277)<br>Chocolate Sauce (p. 278)<br>Chocolate Ice Cream (p. 558)<br>Strawberry Ice Cream (p. 559)<br>Peach Ice Cream (p. 559)<br>Vanilla Ice Cream (p. 558)<br>Whipped cream (optional) | 1. Place a small mound of strawberries in the center of a plate.<br>2. Arrange 4 caramelized banana quarters, cut side up, on the plate like spokes of a wheel, with the strawberries as the hub, so they divide the plate into quadrants. The round ends of the banana should be toward the outside and the cut or square ends against the strawberries.<br>3. In each quadrant, between the banana pieces, spoon a small pool of one of the four sauces.<br>4. Place a small scoop of the chocolate ice cream on the crème anglaise, vanilla ice cream on the chocolate sauce, strawberry ice cream on the raspberry sauce, and peach ice cream on the strawberry sauce. Use no more than about 1 oz (30 g) of each ice cream, or the dessert will be too big.<br>5. If desired, decorate the dessert with a few rosettes of whipped cream. |

# MERINGUE GLACÉ WITH MACÉDOINE OF FRESH FRUIT

| Components | Procedure |
|---|---|
| Vanilla ice cream<br>Whipped cream<br>Crisp baked meringues (p. 347) made in the shape of whipped cream rosettes<br>Mixture of diced fresh fruit (such as kiwi, strawberries, mango, papaya, melon, apple, pear)<br>Chocolate Sauce (p. 278) | 1. Place a scoop of ice cream in the center of a dish.<br>2. Surround the ice cream with crisp meringues alternating with rosettes of whipped cream, piped so the whipped cream rosettes look just like the meringues.<br>3. Spoon the fruit mixture over the dessert.<br>4. Serve the chocolate sauce in a small pitcher on the side. |

# CORNUCOPIA OF FRESH FRUIT WITH LEMON ICE CREAM

| Components | Procedure |
|---|---|
| Florentine batter (p. 513)<br>Whipped cream flavored with orange liqueur<br>Raspberry Sauce (p. 279)<br>Assorted fresh fruit<br>Lemon Ice Cream (p. 559) | 1. Prepare florentines as directed in the recipe, but while the baked cookies are still hot and pliable, bend them into cones.<br>2. Fill a florentine cone two-thirds full of the flavored whipped cream. Place it on a plate so the point of the cone is at the back rim of the plate and the open end is near the center. (To keep it from rolling, stick it in place with a dab of whipped cream.)<br>3. Spoon the raspberry sauce onto the plate so it appears to have spilled out of the cone and spread across the front of the plate.<br>4. Arrange a colorful assortment of fresh fruit on top of the sauce, so it appears to have spilled out of the cone.<br>5. Place an oval spoonful of lemon ice cream on each side of the cone. |

**VARIATION**

In place of the florentine horn, use tulipe or almond tuile cookies bent into cones, or puff pastry horns.

# FRENCH DOUGHNUTS, PRESENTATION 1

| Components | Procedure |
|---|---|
| 3 French Doughnuts, fried by method 1 (p. 243)<br>2–2½ oz (70 g) Praline Cream II (p. 542)<br>3 oz (90 g) Apricot and Almond Compote (p. 601)<br>Crushed Nougatine (p. 668)<br>Red currants<br>Sugar spirals (p. 675)<br>Mint sprig | 1. On one side of a plate, arrange 3 doughnuts alternating with 2 quenelles of praline cream.<br>2. Place the apricot and almond compote on the other side of the plate.<br>3. Garnish with a few pieces of nougatine and the currants, sugar spirals, and a mint sprig. |

# FRENCH DOUGHNUTS, PRESENTATION 2

| Components | Procedure |
|---|---|
| 2 French Doughnuts, fried by method 2 (p. 243)<br>Confectioners' sugar<br>2 oz (60 g) Coconut Sorbet (p. 564)<br>Toasted coconut<br>Blanched pineapple leaves (optional)<br>2½–3 oz (80 g) Pineapple Kumquat Compote (p. 601)<br>Pistachios<br>Red currants | 1. Dust the doughnuts lightly with confectioners' sugar.<br>2. Place 1 doughnut on one side of a plate. Top with a scoop of sorbet and then with the second doughnut.<br>3. Sprinkle a little toasted coconut around the doughnuts and, if desired, decorate with 3 blanched pineapple leaves.<br>4. Place the pineapple kumquat compote on the other side of the plate and decorate with a few pistachios and red currants. |

# PEAR PECAN TART, CHOCOLATE GANACHE TORTE, AND RASPBERRY SORBET

| Components | Procedure |
|---|---|
| Pastry for pear tart (see step 1)<br>Caramel Sauce (p. 280)<br>Chopped pecans<br>Caramelized pear half (p. 590)<br>Apricot glaze (p. 200)<br>Chocolate genoise, dessert syrup, and ganache for Chocolate Ganache Torte (p. 464; see procedure for assembly)<br>Tulipe (p. 508)<br>Raspberry sorbet | 1. *Prepare the pastry for the tart:* Bake a thin, round disk of pastry 2½– 3 in. (7 cm) in diameter, using puff pastry, phyllo pastry, short dough, or enriched pie pastry, as desired.<br>2. Brush or spread the baked pastry with a thin layer of caramel sauce. Sprinkle with chopped pecans. Slice a caramelized pear half and fan it out on the pastry base. Brush the top with apricot glaze.<br>3. Prepare a chocolate ganache torte as a sheet cake, but without the meringue layer and buttercream; you will have an uniced cake consisting of 3 thin layers of chocolate genoise, flavored with rum or vanilla syrup, and 2 layers of ganache. Cut the cake into 2-in. (5 cm) squares, then cut each square in half diagonally to make 2 triangles. If desired, dust the top of the cake with confectioners' sugar.<br>4. Place a spoonful of raspberry sorbet in a tulipe.<br>5. Arrange a tart, a cake triangle, and a sorbet-filled tulipe on a plate. |

# SPICED PINEAPPLE WITH COCONUT SORBET AND COCONUT TUILE

| Components | Procedure |
|---|---|
| Spiced Pineapple (p. 599)<br>Coconut Tuile (p. 510) shaped as a cup or tulipe<br>Coconut Sorbet (p. 564)<br>Pistachios<br>Pine nuts<br>Red currants, dusted with confectioners' sugar<br>Toasted coconut | 1. Rewarm the pineapple if it was prepared in advance, and finish the sauce with the cream as in the basic recipe. Strain it, reserving the spices. Slice the pineapple and arrange the slices on one side of a plate. Pour the sauce over the pineapple.<br>2. Place a coconut tuile cup on the other side of the plate. Place one or more scoops of coconut sorbet in the tuile.<br>3. Garnish the plate with some of the spices from the sauce. Garnish the pineapple with a few pistachios and pine nuts.<br>4. Decorate the sorbet with a small cluster of red currants.<br>5. Finish the plate by sprinkling with a little toasted coconut. |

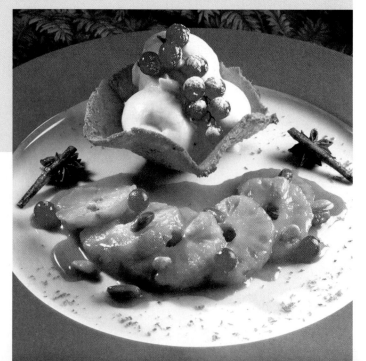

# FIGS IN PORT WINE WITH HONEY ICE CREAM AND SESAME TUILE

| Components | Procedure |
|---|---|
| Figs in Port Wine (p. 597)<br>Sesame Tuile (p. 509)<br>Honey Ice Cream (p. 562)<br>Caramelized almonds<br>Mint sprig | 1. If the figs were prepared ahead of time, reheat them in the oven with the syrup.<br>2. Spoon the syrup onto a plate.<br>3. Stand a sesame tuile on its side on the plate.<br>4. In the broad curve of the tuile, arrange 3 or 4 fig halves.<br>5. On the other side of the tuile, place a scoop of honey ice cream. (Optionally, pipe the ice cream using a star tip, as in the illustration.)<br>6. Place a few caramelized almonds in front of the figs.<br>7. Garnish the ice cream with a sprig of mint. |

# WINTER DESSERT MEDLEY WITH FROZEN BANANA AND CHOCOLATE MOUSSE CAKE

| Components | Procedure |
|---|---|
| Crisp meringue, chocolate meringue, or japonaise disks to fit inside a 7-in. (18 cm) cake pan, springform pan, or charlotte ring<br>Frozen Banana Mousse mixture (p. 571)<br>Bananas<br>Frozen Chocolate Mousse mixture (p. 571)<br>Orange Bavarian (p. 535) prepared in 2-oz (60 mL) molds<br>Whipped cream<br>Raspberry Sauce (p. 279)<br>Segments (free of membranes) from a small sweet orange, blood orange, or tangerine | 1. *Prepare the frozen mousse cake:* Place 1 meringue disk in the bottom of a 7-in. (18 cm) cake pan. Add a layer ½ in. (12 mm) thick of the banana mousse mixture. Cut the bananas in half lengthwise and again crosswise. Arrange them at intervals (that is, not touching each other) in the pan and push them down into the mousse. Add a layer about ¾ in. (2 cm) thick of chocolate mousse mixture. Top with another meringue disk and press down gently. Freeze.<br>2. Unmold the mousse cake and cut it into wedges. Place a wedge on one side of a plate.<br>3. Unmold an orange Bavarian and place on the plate, leaving at least one-third of the plate empty. Decorate the Bavarian with whipped cream.<br>4. Ladle a pool of raspberry sauce onto the remaining space on the plate. Arrange orange segments in a star pattern on top of the sauce. |

# PASSION FRUIT CHARLOTTE

| Components | Procedure |
|---|---|
| Passion Fruit Charlotte (p. 541)<br>Kumquat Compote (p. 601)<br>Red currants<br>Choux pastry lattice (p. 338)<br>Crème anglaise<br>Confectioners' sugar | 1. Place a wedge of the charlotte toward the back of a plate.<br>2. Place a spoonful of kumquat compote in front of the charlotte wedge and garnish with a few red currants or other small red berries to add color.<br>3. Prop a piece of choux pastry lattice in front of the compote so it leans against the wedge of charlotte.<br>4. Spoon a little crème anglaise on the plate in a decorative fashion.<br>5. Dust the pastry lattice lightly with confectioners' sugar. |

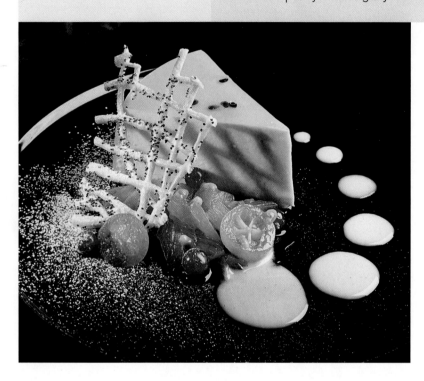

# CARAMEL MEDLEY

| Components | Procedure |
|---|---|
| Crème Brûlée (p. 524) in a<br>  small dish<br>Tarte Tatin (p. 362)<br>Clear Caramel Sauce (p. 280)<br>Tulipe (p. 508)<br>Caramel Ice Cream (p. 559) | 1. Place the crème brûlée on a dinner plate large enough so only a third of the plate is covered.<br>2. Place a thin wedge of tarte Tatin next to the crème brûlée.<br>3. In the remaining space on the plate, drizzle caramel sauce in a lattice pattern. Place a tulipe on the sauce. Place a scoop of caramel ice cream in the tulipe. |

# CHOCOLATE MEDLEY

| Components | Procedure |
|---|---|
| Chocolate Mousse (p. 276)<br>Crisp chocolate meringue disk, 2 in. (5 cm) in diameter<br>Chocolate shavings<br>Chocolate Ice Cream (pp. 558, 562) or Chocolate Sorbet (p. 561)<br>Tulipe (p. 508) or Almond Tuile (p. 508)<br>Raspberries<br>White Chocolate Bavarian (p. 534), prepared in 2-oz (60 mL) mold<br>Tempered chocolate<br>Chocolate Sauce (p. 278)<br>Chocolate Ganache (pp. 275, 276), soft but not whipped<br>Crème anglaise | This dessert consists of five separate elements—in small quantities—arranged on a large plate:<br><br>1. Chocolate mousse, piped in a mound onto a chocolate meringue disk and coated with chocolate shavings.<br><br>2. Chocolate ice cream or sorbet in a tulipe or tuile, garnished with a few raspberries placed next to the ice cream.<br><br>3. White chocolate Bavarian on a pool of chocolate sauce. Decorate the top of the Bavarian with a piped chocolate decoration (see p. 648).<br><br>4. A quenelle of chocolate ganache.<br><br>5. A pool of crème anglaise marbled with chocolate sauce. (This is a separate element on the plate, with nothing placed on it.) |

# QUESTIONS FOR DISCUSSION

1. Discuss how the quality of ingredients affects dessert plating presentations.

2. Discuss the advantages and disadvantages of simple presentations and of elaborate or complex presentations.

3. What are the three basic elements of a plated dessert? Is it necessary to have all three of these elements in each presentation?

4. Each component of a dessert can be said to have five characteristics. What are they? Which are visual characteristics, and which are flavor or mouth-feel characteristics? Suggest examples of how to balance each of these characteristics when designing a plated dessert.

5. What is a quenelle of ice cream? Describe how to make it.

6. Name four types of items that can be used as garnish for a dessert.

7. Describe how to marble or feather a sauce.

# Chocolate

Chocolate is not only one of the world's most popular confections but also a wonderful medium for decorative work, ranging from simple garnishes for desserts to elaborate showpieces. Many pastry chefs make a specialty of chocolate work and become well known for their imaginative and skillful pieces.

Because of its composition, chocolate is difficult to work with. It is sensitive to temperature and moisture. Proper melting and cooling require accurate temperature control. Unless a liquid is to be added, chocolate must be protected from moisture. A single drop of water will ruin its texture and make it unusable for dipping or molding.

This chapter provides an introduction to fine chocolate work. The fundamentals of handling chocolate are discussed, followed by procedures for simple decorative work and molding. A brief look at chocolate confections closes the chapter.

**After reading this chapter, you should be able to:**

1. Temper chocolate couverture.

2. Use tempered chocolate for dipping and molding.

3. Produce a variety of chocolate decorations.

4. Make chocolate truffles.

# PRODUCTION OF CHOCOLATE

*Chocolate* is produced from the seeds of a tropical tree called the *cocoa* or, more properly, *cacao* tree. As with coffee, the quality of cocoa is sensitive to growing conditions, so cocoa from the best growing regions commands the highest prices. Cocoa trees produce large pods full of seeds called **cocoa beans**.

---

## ❊❴ CHOCOLATE HISTORY ❴❊

The cacao tree originated in the western hemisphere, where it grows in tropical climates from northern South America to southern Mexico. Long before the European discovery of the Americas, native peoples, including the Mayas and Aztecs, brewed a bitter, unsweetened beverage from the beans, which they had learned to ferment and dry. The beverages, probably enjoyed hot, were often flavored with chiles, vanilla, and other ingredients.

Because the cacao tree grew in limited areas, the pods were prized and became objects of trade. They were even used for currency. In addition, they were important in religious ceremonies.

Spanish conquerors at first disliked the bitter, black beverage the natives brewed from cacao, but they soon learned to appreciate it and began carrying cocoa beans back to Europe in the 1500s. Availability was limited at first, but by 1700 cocoa had spread through much of Europe. Its use was still mostly as a beverage, although Europeans found they enjoyed the drink more when it was sweetened. Cocoa was also used as a medicine and as a cooking spice.

In the early 1800s, a Dutchman named van Houten developed a process for removing much of the cocoa butter from raw cocoa, using a powerful press. He also discovered that processing the cocoa with an alkali yielded a milder product with a darker color. This "dutching" process is still used today for some cocoa.

Van Houten's inventions enabled the development of modern chocolate manufacturing and the use of chocolate for confections and not just as a beverage. Manufacturers discovered that by adding cocoa butter back to ground cocoa, they could make a smooth paste that hardened into blocks. In 1842, the Cadbury brothers began selling block chocolate in England. In the 1880s, the Swiss Rudolphe Lindt invented the conching process (described in the text) to make a smoother product. Around the same time, another Swiss, Daniel Peter, created milk chocolate by adding dried milk to the paste. (Dried milk had been invented by Henri Nestlé.)

---

After the pods are harvested, the beans are quickly removed and allowed to ferment until they lose most of their moisture. There are several ways of doing this, but the traditional method is to spread them between layers of banana leaves and leave them for several days, turning them often so they ferment evenly.

The chemical changes that take place during fermentation turn the beans from yellowish to brown and begin to develop the flavor. The fermented beans are next dried in the open air, because they still contain a great deal of moisture. The dried beans are now ready to be shipped to processors. A single tree yields only 1 to 2 pounds (500 g to 1 kg) dried beans.

Cocoa processors clean the dried beans thoroughly and then roast them. The true flavor of the cocoa develops during roasting, and the temperature and degree of roasting are important factors in the quality of the finished chocolate. After roasting, the beans are cracked and the shells are removed. The broken particles of cocoa that result are called *nibs*. Nibs contain more than 50 percent fat, in the form of cocoa butter, and very little moisture.

Grinding the nibs produces a paste and releases the cocoa butter from inside the cell walls. This paste is called **chocolate liquor** or **cocoa mass** and is the basis of chocolate production. When chocolate liquor cools, it sets into a hard block. (Chocolate liquor contains no alcohol, in spite of its slightly misleading name.)

The next stage of manufacturing is to separate the cocoa powder from the cocoa butter. This is done with powerful hydraulic presses that squeeze out the melted fat, leaving hard cakes that are then ground into cocoa powder. Meanwhile, the cocoa butter is purified to remove odor and color.

To manufacture chocolate, the cocoa powder is blended with sugar and, in the case of milk chocolate, milk solids. These ingredients are ground and blended together. At this point comes the critical procedure called **conching**. This is a two-stage process that first removes additional moisture and refines the flavor. During the second stage of conching, cocoa butter is added back and the liquid mass is ground and mixed for hours or even days to develop a fine, smooth texture. In general, higher-quality, more expensive chocolates derive their superior texture from longer conching. Finally, the liquid chocolate is tempered, as explained below, and molded into blocks for sale as couverture.

## Couverture

The basic types of chocolate are introduced in chapter 4. Please review pages 91–94 and, in particular, note the difference between *couverture* and *coating chocolate* or *baking chocolate*. Genuine couverture contains cocoa butter and no other fat. Coating chocolate is chocolate that had part or most of the cocoa butter replaced with other fats in order to make it easier to handle and in order to reduce the cost. In this chapter, we are concerned entirely with couverture, also known as *confectioners' chocolate*.

There are three main ingredients of dark couverture:

♦ Cocoa solids.

♦ Sugar.

♦ Cocoa butter.

In addition, it may also contain small quantities of vanilla (a flavoring) and lecithin (an emulsifier). On the packaging of a block of professional couverture, you may see a series of numbers such as the following: 65/35/38. The first two numbers refer to the ratio of cocoa solids to sugar—in this case, 65% cocoa solids to 35% sugar. The last number is the total fat content (38% in the example) and indicates the viscosity or thickness of the chocolate. The higher the fat content, the thinner the chocolate will be when melted. Couverture must contain at least 31% cocoa butter.

The quantities of cocoa solids and sugar determine whether **dark couverture** is referred to as *semisweet*, *bitter*, or *extra-bitter*. The higher the percentage of cocoa solids, the lower the sugar content will be. Semisweet chocolate couverture contains 50 to 60% cocoa solids. Chocolates with more cocoa solids (and, therefore, less sugar) are called *bitter* and *extra-bitter*. The highest practical percentage of cocoa is 75 to 76%.

**Milk chocolate couverture** contains milk solids in addition to cocoa solids and sugar. It usually contains about 36% cocoa solids and no more than 55% sugar. **White couverture** cannot be called chocolate because it contains no cocoa solids, only cocoa butter, sugar, milk solids, and flavoring.

In this chapter, the term *couverture*, when used by itself, always refers to dark chocolate. Milk chocolate couverture or white couverture is specified if those types are intended.

Tools for chocolate. Clockwise from top left: grooved scraper, wood-grain tool, molds for truffles and small chocolates, dipping forks, plastic mat for textured cutouts, cotton wool for polishing molds and acetate, and inexpensive molds for larger pieces.

## Tempering

For most chocolate work, couverture will not handle properly if simply melted. It will take too long to set, and when it does set, it will not have the desired shine or the proper texture. The process of preparing couverture for dipping, coating, molding, and other purposes is called *tempering*.

The reason for tempering can be explained as follows: Cocoa butter consists of several fats. Some of these melt at low temperatures, and others melt at high temperatures. The fats that melt at high temperatures are, of course, the first ones to solidify as the melted chocolate is cooled. These high-melt-point fats give high-quality chocolate its shine and its snap (high-quality chocolate that has been properly tempered and cooled breaks with a clean, sharp snap). The objective of tempering is to create a very fine fat-crystal structure in the chocolate. In a melted, tempered chocolate, the high-melt-point fats have begun to solidify into fine crystals that are distributed throughout the melted chocolate. When the chocolate is left to cool, the chocolate sets or solidifies quickly because the fine crystals act as seeds around which the rest of the chocolate crystallizes.

To summarize, tempered chocolate sets quickly and has a good texture and shine. Melted, untempered chocolate takes a long time to set. Its texture will not be as good. Its surface will be cloudy because some of the cocoa butter floats to the surface and makes a whitish coating called **bloom**.

The actual process of melting and tempering chocolate consists of three steps. The proper temperatures for each of these three stages depend on the type of chocolate and its exact composition. The table below indicates the range of temperatures appropriate to the basic chocolate types. The manufacturer or the supplier should be able to indicate the exact temperatures that are best for each of its products.

1. **Melting.** The chocolate is placed in a pan or bowl and set over hot water to melt. It should not be set over direct heat because the chocolate is easily damaged by heat, which destroys both the texture and the flavor. Stir constantly while the chocolate is melting. The chocolate must be brought to a temperature high enough to completely melt all the fats, including the high-melt-point fats. Refer to the table below.

2. **Cooling or precrystallizing.** When the chocolate is melted, it is removed from the heat. All or part of the chocolate is then cooled until it is thick and pasty. At this point, fine fat crystals have formed.

3. **Rewarming.** The chocolate is too thick at this point for dipping, molding, or most other uses and must be warmed slightly before it is ready to be used. Set it over warm water and stir it until it is the proper temperature and thickness to be used. This step must be done carefully. Do not let the chocolate get warmer than the recommended temperature. If this happens, too many of the fat crystals melt and the chocolate is no longer tempered, making it necessary to repeat the whole procedure. If the chocolate is too thick at the proper temperature, thin it with a little melted cocoa butter. Do not thin it by heating it.

---

### ❧ BETA 6 ❧ CRYSTALS

Technology has brought simplification to the tricky process of tempering chocolate. Now available commercially, beta 6 crystals are crystals of cocoa butter in their most stable form. By simply adding the crystals to melted couverture, the pastry chef can quickly and easily temper the chocolate. The basic procedure for tempering with beta 6 crystals consists of three steps:

1. Bring melted couverture to 95°F (35°C).

2. Add beta 6 crystals equal to 1 percent of the weight of the chocolate. (For example, for 6 lb chocolate, you need only 1 ounce of crystals; for 3 kg chocolate, 30 g crystals.) Stir well to make sure they are blended in thoroughly.

3. Wait 10 minutes. The couverture is now tempered.

---

## Critical Temperatures for Tempering Chocolate

| Process | Dark Chocolate Couverture | Milk Chocolate and White Couverture |
|---|---|---|
| Melting | 122°–131°F (50°–55°C) | 113°–122°F (45°–50°C) |
| Precrystallizing (cooling) | 80°–84°F (27°–29°C) | 78°–82°F (26°–28°C) |
| Rewarming | 86°–89°F (30°–32°C) | 84°–86°F (29°–30°C) |

Manufacturers and large processors use precise thermostatically controlled equipment to automatically heat, cool, and rewarm the chocolate to the exact temperatures required. In the pastry shop, however, two other methods are used for tempering small quantities of couverture. The first method, **tablage**, below is quick to do and is, perhaps, the most popular. The second method is **seeding**.

Once the chocolate is tempered, it is ready for molding, dipping, and other uses. The following sections describe procedures for a variety of chocolate work.

For all work with tempered chocolate, the work area should be at a temperature between 65° and 77°F (18° and 25°C). If it is colder, the chocolate will set up too quickly and be difficult to handle. If warmer, the chocolate will take

# Procedures for Tempering Chocolate

## Method 1: Tablage

*Caution:* In all stages of this procedure, do not let even a trace of moisture come in contact with the chocolate.

1. With a heavy knife, chop the chocolate into small pieces. Place the pieces in a dry stainless-steel bowl.

2. Set the bowl in a pan of warm water. Stir the chocolate constantly so it melts uniformly.

3. Continue stirring until the chocolate is completely melted and reaches the proper temperature, as indicated in the table on page 640.

4. Remove the bowl from the water bath. Wipe all traces of moisture from the bottom of the bowl to avoid contaminating the chocolate.

5. Pour about two-thirds of the chocolate onto a marble slab (a). With a metal scraper and a spatula, spread the chocolate and quickly scrape it back together, continuing to mix the chocolate so it cools uniformly (b).

6. When the chocolate cools to the proper temperature (78°–84°F or 26°–29°C, as indicated in the table on page 640), it will become thick and pasty. Quickly scrape it back into the bowl with the remaining melted chocolate (c).

7. Mix and reheat the chocolate over hot water to the proper rewarming temperature (84°–89°F or 29°–32°C, depending on the chocolate). Do not warm it above the recommended temperature. The chocolate is now ready for use.

### Procedure Variation

Instead of working the chocolate on a marble slab in step 5, some chefs prefer to set the entire bowl over cold water and stir until the chocolate cools to the proper temperature. Then they rewarm the chocolate as in step 7. This method may not produce chocolate with as good a temper, and it raises the risk of getting water in the chocolate. However, it has the advantage of speed.

## Method 2: Seeding or Injection

1. Chop the chocolate to be melted into small pieces, as in method 1.

2. Cut fine shreds or shavings from a block of tempered chocolate and set them aside.

3. Melt the chopped chocolate as in method 1.

4. Remove the melted chocolate from the water bath. Stir in some of the shaved chocolate.

5. When these shavings are nearly all melted, add a few more shavings. Continue adding and stirring until the melted chocolate is cooled to the proper tempering point and all the added shavings are melted. Do not add the shavings too fast, or they may not all melt.

6. Rewarm the chocolate as in method 1.

too long to set; in addition, the marble slab will be too warm for some techniques to work.

## MOLDING CHOCOLATE

Molding is possible because chocolate contracts when it sets. Thus, it pulls away from the mold and can be easily removed. Molds are made of metal or plastic. They must be kept clean and dry, and the insides must be kept shiny and free of scratches. If they are scratched, chocolate will stick to them.

To be sure the molds are completely clean and smooth, hold them briefly over steam, then polish the inside surfaces with cotton wool. Be sure they are completely dry before proceeding to mold the chocolate.

Procedures for molding chocolate truffles and other candies are covered in the last part of this chapter. The following discussion deals with molding decorative chocolates as well as display pieces.

Molding chocolate eggs is one of the simpler molding procedures; it also illustrates the techniques used in other types of molds. The following procedures explain in detail how to mold eggs. Next is a more general discussion of other types of molds and how to use them.

These procedures explain molding single-color chocolates. You can also use contrasting colors of chocolate for decorative effects. This is done by decorating the inside of the mold with one color and then coating it with another color. Use the same techniques as described in the discussion of chocolate cutouts, below.

Two-part molds are used to make hollow chocolate items. There are two kinds: completely enclosed molds and molds with open bottoms. The first step for using either kind of mold is to paint the inside surfaces with a thin layer of tempered chocolate, using a soft brush. This step is frequently omitted, but it is recommended because it eliminates small air bubbles that might otherwise mar the surface of the chocolate. When the chocolate is set but not hard, continue with one of the following procedures.

To use two-part molds with open bottoms, clip the two parts together. Pour tempered chocolate into the opening until the mold is nearly full. Tap the mold with a wooden stick to release air bubbles. After a few moments, invert the mold over the chocolate pot and pour out the chocolate, leaving a layer of chocolate coating the mold. Set the mold, open end down, on a sheet of parchment. Additional melted chocolate will run down the inside and seal the open end. Leave the filled mold in a cool place until set, then open it and remove the chocolate.

If you are using plastic molds, you can easily see when the chocolate has set and pulled away from the mold. With metal molds, however, you just have to let the molds stand long enough until you are certain the chocolate is set.

To use enclosed molds, pour enough tempered chocolate into one half of the mold to completely coat the insides of both halves. Place the second half of the mold on top and clip it in place. Turn the mold over and over so the inside is completely coated with chocolate. Tap the mold several times while rotating it in order to release air bubbles. Let the chocolate stand until set, then unmold.

## Procedures for Molding Chocolate Eggs

### Method 1

1. Polish the insides of the mold with cotton wool.

2. Using a clean, dry brush, brush the inside of the mold with tempered chocolate. Be sure to cover the inside of the mold completely with an even layer.

3. Let the mold stand until the chocolate is partially set. It should be firm but not hard.

4. Using a metal scraper, scrape the excess chocolate from the top of the mold so the half-egg has a smooth, sharp edge.

5. Let stand in a cool place until the chocolate is completely set and hard.

6. Turn the mold over and tap it gently to unmold the egg. To avoid getting fingerprints on the shiny surface of the unmolded chocolate, handle it with disposable plastic gloves.

7. To glue two halves together to make a whole hollow egg, use one of two methods:

   ◆ Using a paper cone filled with tempered chocolate, pipe a fine line of chocolate onto the edge of one of the halves, then press the two halves together.

   ◆ Place one of the halves open side down on a warm baking sheet for just an instant to melt the edge slightly, then fasten the two halves together.

8. Use the point of a small knife to trim excess chocolate from the seam.

### Method 2

1. Polish the inside of the mold with cotton wool.

2. Fill the mold with tempered chocolate until it runs over the top.

3. Invert the chocolate over the container of tempered chocolate to dump out the chocolate, leaving a coating on the insides of the molds.

4. Prop the molds upside down over two sticks set on a sheet of parchment or clean sheet pan to allow the excess to drip out.

5. Continue with step 3 of method 1.

# CHOCOLATE DECORATIONS

Tempered chocolate can be used to make a variety of decorations for cakes, pastries, and other items. The most popular of these are described here.

## Chocolate Cutouts

Polish a sheet of acetate with cotton wool. Pour tempered chocolate onto the acetate and spread into a thin layer with a palette knife. Let the chocolate stand until it clouds over and becomes firm but not hard. Cut with a small, sharp knife, cutting straight through to the acetate, or use a metal cutter, slightly warmed, to cut out desired shapes. Do not attempt to remove the cutouts at this point. Let stand until the chocolate is hard and the acetate peels away easily from the chocolate.

For decorative effects, the acetate can be coated with two colors of chocolate, making attractive patterns. The following are some of the easiest and most popular techniques:

1. Flick or spatter streaks of one color of chocolate—for example, white couverture. Let the chocolate set, and then coat the acetate with a contrasting color of chocolate.

2. With a paper cone, pipe a latticework design of fine stripes with one color of chocolate. Let the chocolate set, and then coat the acetate with a contrasting color.

3. With a paper cone, pipe large dots of chocolate at regular intervals. Let the chocolate set, and then coat the acetate with a contrasting color.

4. Spread with one color of chocolate, then scrape with a comb scraper, using the same technique as for ribbon sponge (p. 411). Then cover with another color.

5. Use *chocolate transfer sheets*, which are commercially made acetate sheets with designs on them. Use as you would a plain acetate sheet, making sure the raised or textured side—that is, the side that has the design on it—is up. After the chocolate has set, the design remains on the chocolate when the acetate is peeled off. Custom-made transfer sheets, embossed with a company's name or logo, for example, are available.

6. To marble chocolate, add a little tempered white couverture to tempered dark couverture and mix just until the white shows streaks against the dark (top left). Then coat the acetate.

Mix dark and white couverture very lightly to marble.

Pour some of the chocolate onto a sheet of acetate.

Lift the acetate and tilt it from side to side so the chocolate coats the entire sheet.

When the chocolate clouds over and is set but not hard, cut out desired shapes with a sharp knife or cutter.

Broken pieces of dark chocolate streaked with white and cutouts of marbled white and milk chocolate.

# Chocolate Strips

Strips of acetate can be coated with decorative chocolate in the same way as sheets. Strips have many uses, such as ribbons and bows for showpieces (p. 646) and liners for charlotte molds. The procedure for coating a strip of acetate with tempered chocolate is similar to coating a large sheet, as described above. Use a palette knife to spread the chocolate in an even layer to cover the strip. Then carefully lift the strip and run your fingers along the edges of the strip to remove excess chocolate and make a neat, straight edge.

Chocolate strips may be decorated with patterns of chocolate in two colors, using the same techniques as above. An additional technique, which creates a pattern with the appearance of wood grain, requires a special tool shown on page 639.

1. Drizzle a little tempered dark chocolate onto an acetate strip (a) and, with a palette knife, spread it into a thin layer covering the strip (b).

2. Scrape the wood-grain tool down the length of the strip, rocking it back and forth to make the grain pattern (c). Let stand a few minutes to allow the chocolate to set.

3. Spread the strip with a layer of tempered white couverture (d).

4. Lift the acetate strip and run your fingers along both edges to remove excess chocolate (e). The acetate side of the strip shows the pattern (f).

5. Fit the strip into a ring mold and allow it to set (g). This mold is to be used to make a Julianna cake (p. 473). For a freestanding chocolate ring, such as the one used for the candy box on page 643, spread the chocolate more thickly so the ring will be sturdier.

## *Chocolate Bows*

For chocolate bows, cut strips of acetate to the desired size. Spread with tempered chocolate, either in a single color or in a pattern of two colors. Allow the chocolate to cloud and partially set, then bend into a teardrop shape and fasten the ends together with a paper clip. If necessary, pipe a little tempered chocolate with a paper cone into the joint between the ends of the chocolate in order to strengthen the seam. Let set until hardened.

Peel the acetate from the bows after they are completely set (a). Cut the ends to points so they will fit together on the box (b). To hold the bows in place, pipe a little tempered chocolate with a paper cone (c). Fit the bow in place. Hold steady until the chocolate sets (d).

Chocolate strips made into teardrops (like bows, but larger) are used for plating presentations of desserts such as chocolate mousse. Place the teardrop on the plate and use a pastry bag to fill it with mousse.

## Chocolate Cigarettes and Curls

Melted chocolate can be used for these decorations. Tempered chocolate may also be used but is not necessary. For cigarettes, spread the chocolate in a long strip on a slab of marble. Allow the chocolate to set. It should be completely set but not hard and brittle. If it becomes too hard, warm it slightly by rubbing it with the palm of your hand. Hold a metal scraper and push it forward so the chocolate curls up ahead of the metal edge (a).

For curls and shavings, score the strip of chocolate with the point of a knife (b) and then scrape up the curls with the knife (c).

# Chocolate Strips and Fans

Chocolate strips are used for coating cakes and pastries (see Pralinette, p. 374, and Feuille d'Automne, p. 466). Chocolate fans are used as decorations for various cakes and pastries. As in the case of chocolate strips, chocolate does not have to be tempered for this procedure. Melted, untempered chocolate may be used.

Heat a clean half-sheet pan at 325°F (160°C) for 4 minutes. Use a clean, unwarped pan, preferably one reserved for chocolate work only. The tray should be warm but not too hot to handle. (The purpose of warming the pan is to enable you to spread a thinner coat of chocolate; be careful, however, not to get the pan too hot. Some chefs prefer to use cold trays.) Turn the sheet upside down and spread melted chocolate in a thin, even layer on the bottom of the pan. Let stand until the chocolate looks cloudy, then refrigerate until set. Remove from the refrigerator and let warm to room temperature.

To make chocolate strips, push the scraper against the tray and, with the other hand, lift off the strip of chocolate as it is released by the scraper (a). Handle the strip of chocolate very lightly (b). After coating the sides of the cake (c), make more strips for the top (d). Arrange the strips on the top (e). Finish the cake with coiled strips (f), touching them as little as possible to prevent melting (g). (The cake pictured here is a Feuille d'Automne.)

To make chocolate fans, scrape the chocolate as for strips, except hold your thumb against one corner of the scraper so the strip bunches or gathers on one side (a). Carefully neaten the ruffles or folds of the fan as necessary (b).

## Piping Chocolate

With the use of a paper cone, as described in chapter 17, tempered chocolate can be made into decorations for cakes, pastries, and other desserts. It can be piped directly onto the dessert or piped onto parchment paper in small designs and left to harden. After they are set, the decorations can be removed from the paper and placed on the desserts. In this way, decorations can be made during slack hours and stored until needed.

Ordinary tempered chocolate is adequate for small, fine decorations, such as those for petits fours (see p. 479), but it is too thin for most other piped decorations. To make piping chocolate, add a very little warm simple syrup to the tempered chocolate. This will thicken the chocolate immediately. Stirring constantly, add more syrup very slowly until the chocolate is thinned to piping consistency.

## Modeling Chocolate

Modeling chocolate is a thick paste that can be molded by hand to make a variety of shapes, just as you might use marzipan. Simply combine melted chocolate with half its weight of glucose (corn syrup) that has been warmed to the temperature of the chocolate. Mix them together well. Place them in an airtight container and let stand for an hour or more. Knead the mixture until it forms a workable paste.

## Spraying Chocolate

A standard paint sprayer can be used to spray liquid chocolate. The sprayed chocolate creates a velvety coating on cakes, pastries, and showpieces.

To enable the chocolate to pass through the sprayer, thin it with melted cocoa butter. It is not possible to give exact quantities, as the cocoa butter content of couverture varies considerably.

A chocolate sprayer
being used to stencil a
pattern on a dessert

# CHOCOLATE TRUFFLES AND CONFECTIONS

Chocolate truffles get their name because of their resemblance to black truffles, the aromatic underground fungus prized by gourmets.

In their simplest form, *chocolate truffles* are simply balls of chocolate ganache, the thick mixture of chocolate and cream that was introduced in chapter 12. Ganache can be made not only with dark chocolate but also milk chocolate and white couverture. Many flavorings and other ingredients can be added to create a variety of confections. Review the discussion of ganache on page 275.

The simplest way of finishing truffles, and one of the most popular, is simply to coat the balls of ganache with cocoa powder. This technique is used in the first recipe in this section, Dark Chocolate Truffles.

For more elaborate presentations, the truffles may be coated with chocolate by dipping or molding.

## Dipping Chocolates

For candy makers, the techniques for dipping and molding candies are basic. There are two basic procedures for dipping small items such as truffles, other candy centers, and nuts.

For the first method, place the items one at a time on the surface of the tempered chocolate. With a dipping fork, turn them over to cover them completely, then lift them out. Tap the fork holding the chocolate on the edge of the bowl to even the coating. Draw the fork holding the coated chocolate over the edge of the bowl to wipe off excess chocolate from the bottom of the fork, then set the item on a sheet of parchment. To mark the chocolate, touch the top of the item lightly with the dipping fork. Each kind of fork will leave its own distinctive pattern, so you can mark different flavors with different patterns. Let stand until hardened.

The second dipping method is hand-dipping. To hand-dip plain truffles, pipe bulbs of ganache onto a parchment sheet (a). Using plastic gloves, hand-roll the truffles with a little cornstarch to round them (b). Still wearing plastic gloves, coat the truffles with a thin layer of tempered chocolate by hand-rolling them in tempered chocolate (c). Drop into a bowl of cocoa powder (d). Remove from the cocoa with a dipping fork and drop into a sieve to remove excess cocoa (e).

# Molding Chocolates

Small molds for individual candies are lined with chocolate using the same techniques as for larger molds, as discussed on page 642. Either of the two methods above may be used. The procedure described here is an example of the first method. It shows how to make white couverture molds decorated with dark chocolate brushstrokes. Other decorative techniques, as described on page 644, can be applied to this molding method as well.

First prepare the molds by holding them over steam, then brushing with cotton wool to make sure they are clean, smooth, and dry (a). Brush the insides lightly with tempered dark couverture to create a marbled or stippled effect (b). Coat with tempered white couverture (c). Let set. Repeat this step to make a thicker coating, if desired. After each layer, it is essential to remove excess chocolate by scraping the flat top of the mold with a metal scraper. This should be done before the chocolate becomes too hard. Failure to do this will mar the appearance of the finished chocolates and may make it impossible to seal them properly.

Pipe in the ganache filling (d). Do not fill the molds too full, and do not get any filling on the top edge of the chocolate. Doing so will make it impossible to seal the candies with the final layer of chocolate.

With a paper cone, cover with tempered couverture (e). Scrape off excess chocolate (f). If the filling is soft, it is necessary to use the paper cone for this step. For firmer fillings, scrape a layer of tempered couverture back and forth over the top of the mold until the chocolates are sealed.

To unmold the candies, turn over the mold onto a sheet of parchment. Most of them should fall out easily. If necessary, tap the mold lightly on the work surface to release the remaining chocolates.

# DARK CHOCOLATE TRUFFLES

*Yield: about 75 truffles, ⅓ oz (10 g) each*

| Ingredients | U.S. | Metric | Procedure |
|---|---|---|---|
| **Ganache** | | | 1. Heat the cream and vanilla to a simmer. |
| Heavy cream | 7 oz | 225 g | 2. Pour over the chopped chocolate in a bowl. Stir until the chocolate is completely melted and blended in. Cool the mixture until it is just slightly warm to the touch. |
| Vanilla extract | ½ tsp | 2.5 g | |
| Dark chocolate couverture, chopped | 1 lb | 500 g | |
| Butter | 2 oz | 60 g | 3. Stir in the butter until it is melted and completely blended in. |
| **Coating** | | | 4. Let the mixture stand until it starts to thicken, then put it in a pastry bag fitted with a medium plain tip. |
| Cocoa powder | as needed | as needed | 5. Pipe the mixture into small mounds, about 2 tsp (10 mL) each, on sheets of parchment paper. Chill until firm. |
| | | | 6. One by one, roll between the palms of the hands to round the pieces of ganache; drop them into a bowl of cocoa powder. |
| | | | 7. Remove the truffles from the cocoa and shake in a sieve to remove excess cocoa. |

# BANANA TRUFFLES

*Yield: about 120 truffles, ⅓ oz (9 g) each*

| Ingredients | U.S. | | Metric | Procedure |
|---|---|---|---|---|
| **Ganache centers** | | | | 1. Mash the bananas with the rum until smooth. |
| Banana pulp | 5 | oz | 150 g | 2. Heat the cream, butter, and honey to the boiling point. Remove from heat. |
| Rum | 4 | tsp | 20 g | |
| Heavy cream | 3.33 | oz | 100 g | 3. Melt the milk and dark chocolates and stir into the cream mixture. |
| Butter | 4 | tsp | 20 g | |
| Honey | 3.33 | oz | 100 g | 4. Mix in the bananas. Let stand until completely cold. |
| Milk chocolate couverture | 4 | oz | 125 g | 5. Prepare polycarbonate molds by holding them over steam and then polishing them with cotton wool. |
| Dark chocolate couverture | 3.33 | oz | 100 g | 6. Brush the inside of the molds very lightly with tempered dark chocolate, allow to set, and then brush with white couverture to give a marbled effect. Scrape the top surface level. (If desired, brush a second time with white couverture for a thicker coating.) |
| **Coating** | | | | |
| Dark chocolate couverture, tempered | 7 | oz | 200 g | |
| White couverture, tempered | 1 lb 5 | oz | 600 g | 7. Put the ganache mixture into a piping bag with a small plain tip and fill the molds three-quarters full. |
| | | | | 8. Seal the molds by piping additional white chocolate over the filling, using a paper cone. Scrape off excess chocolate and chill before unmolding. |

*Note: The quantity of chocolate needed for the coating is approximate. Because you need enough for the molding procedure, you must temper more chocolate than will actually be used.*

# ORANGE TRUFFLES

*Yield: about 125 truffles, ⅓ oz (9 g) each*

| Ingredients | U.S. | | Metric | Procedure |
|---|---|---|---|---|
| Heavy cream | 4 | oz | 120 g | 1. Combine the cream, juice, liqueur, and butter in a saucepan and bring to a boil. |
| Orange juice, strained | 1 | oz | 30 g | 2. Whip the egg yolks with the sugar until light. |
| Orange liqueur | 3 | oz | 90 g | 3. Gradually beat the hot liquid into the egg mixture. |
| Butter | 2 | oz | 60 g | 4. Return this mixture to the heat and bring quickly to a boil, then remove from heat. |
| Egg yolks | 1.67 | oz | 50 g | 5. Strain the liquid over the chopped chocolate in a bowl. Stir until all the chocolate is melted and the mixture is evenly blended. |
| Sugar | 1.67 | oz | 50 g | |
| Dark chocolate, chopped | 7 | oz | 215 g | 6. Let the mixture stand until it starts to thicken. This may take an hour or longer, depending on the room temperature. If necessary, the mixture can be chilled briefly, but do not let it become too hard. Then put it in a pastry bag fitted with a medium plain tip. |
| **Coating** | | | | |
| Dark chocolate couverture, tempered | 1 lb 4 | oz | 600 g | 7. Pipe the mixture into small mounds, about 2 tsp (10 mL) each, on sheets of parchment paper. Chill until firm. |

*Note: The quantity of chocolate needed for the coating is approximate. Because you need enough for the molding procedure, you must temper more chocolate than will actually be used.*

8. One by one, roll between the palms of the hands to round the pieces of ganache. Place them back onto the parchment.

9. Coat the truffles in one of two ways:

   ◆ Drop them a few at a time in a bowl of tempered chocolate, then remove with a dipping fork and place on a parchment-lined tray.

   ◆ Roll in tempered chocolate in the palms of the hands while wearing disposable plastic gloves, as shown on page 649, then place on a parchment-lined tray.

Let stand until the chocolate is completely set.

# ROCHER WITH ALMONDS

*For large-quantity measurements, see page 742.*

| Ingredients | U.S. | Metric | Procedure |
|---|---|---|---|
| Dark chocolate | 4 oz | 100 g | 1. Melt the first quantity of dark chocolate over a hot-water bath. |
| Praline paste | 6 oz | 150 g | 2. Add the praline paste and mix quickly. |
| Ice cream wafers (pailletine), finely crushed | 2 oz | 50 g | 3. Add the crushed wafers and mix. |
| Dark chocolate | 6 oz | 150 g | 4. As soon as the mixture starts to thicken but before it starts to solidify, use a spoon to drop 1-tbsp (12 g) pieces onto a parchment-lined sheet pan. If desired, roll between palms to shape into balls. |
| Almonds, toasted and chopped | 1 oz | 25 g | 5. Allow to set at room temperature 2–3 hours. |
| *Total weight:* | *1 lb 3 oz* | *475 g* | 6. Temper the remaining dark chocolate and add the chopped almonds. |

7. Dip each ball into the tempered chocolate and retrieve using a chocolate fork.

8. Place onto a parchment-lined baking sheet and allow to harden.

# LEMON TRUFFLES

*Yield: about 110 truffles, ½ oz (14 g) each*

| Ingredients | U.S. | | Metric |
|---|---|---|---|
| **Ganache centers** | | | |
| Milk | 4 | oz | 125 g |
| Heavy cream | 4 | oz | 125 g |
| Glucose | 1.67 | oz | 50 g |
| White couverture, chopped | 1 lb | | 500 g |
| Lemon juice | 3.25 | oz | 100 g |
| **Coating** | | | |
| White couverture, tempered | 1 lb 10 | oz | 800 g |

*Note: The quantity of chocolate needed for the coating is approximate. Because you need enough for the molding and dipping procedure, you must temper more chocolate than will actually be used.*

### Procedure

1. Heat the milk, cream, and glucose until the mixture is warm and the glucose is dissolved.

2. Add the white couverture and stir until it is melted and uniformly blended with the cream mixture.

3. Stir in the lemon juice.

4. Let the mixture cool completely. Place the ganache in a pastry bag fitted with a small, plain tip.

5. Prepare hemispherical polycarbonate truffle molds by holding them over steam and then polishing them with cotton wool.

6. Brush the insides of the molds with tempered white chocolate. Scrape off the top surface. Repeat if a thicker coating is desired. Let stand until the chocolate has hardened.

7. Fill to the top with the ganache filling. Unmold. For each truffle, stick 2 half-spheres together to make a round ball.

8. Dip in tempered white chocolate, remove with a dipping fork, and place on a wire rack. To create a textured surface, allow to set a few moments, then roll along the rack to give a spiked coating to the truffle. Allow to harden completely before removing from the rack.

### Alternative Procedure

Use ready-made chocolate shells. Fill them using a pastry bag with a small plain tip and seal the opening by covering it with tempered couverture using a paper cone. Dip as in the basic procedure above.

# MUSCADINES

*Yield: about 45 truffles, ⅓ oz (10 g) each*

| Ingredients | U.S. | | Metric | Procedure |
|---|---|---|---|---|
| **Ganache** | | | | 1. Melt the first quantity of chocolate and stir in the praline paste. |
| Milk chocolate couverture | 6.75 | oz | 200 g | |
| Praline paste | 1 | oz | 30 g | 2. Add the water and stir until evenly mixed. |
| Water, boiling | 1 | oz | 30 g | |
| Butter, softened | 4 | tsp | 20 g | 3. Mix in the butter and liqueur. Chill over an ice-water bath until the mixture is thick enough to hold its shape. |
| Orange liqueur, such as Cointreau | 1 | oz | 30 g | |
| **Coating** | | | | 4. Place in a piping bag with a large star tip (approximately ½ in./1 cm wide at the opening). Pipe long logs of the mixture onto a baking sheet lined with parchment paper. Cut the logs into 1½-in. (4 cm) lengths. Chill. |
| Confectioners' sugar | as needed | | as needed | |
| Milk chocolate couverture | 8 | oz | 250 g | |
| Cocoa butter, melted | 3.25 oz | | 100 g | 5. Sift confectioners' sugar onto a tray or sheet pan until it is about ½ in. (1 cm) deep. |

6. Temper the milk chocolate and stir in the cocoa butter.

7. Dip each piece of chilled ganache into the chocolate, remove with a dipping fork, and tap off the excess chocolate. Place in the confectioners' sugar. Shake the tray to cover the chocolates in sugar. Allow to set before removing.

# TERMS FOR REVIEW

| | | | |
|---|---|---|---|
| chocolate | couverture | dark chocolate | tablage |
| cocoa beans | coating chocolate | milk chocolate | seeding |
| chocolate liquor | baking chocolate | white couverture | chocolate truffle |
| cocoa mass | confectioners' chocolate | tempering | |
| conching | cocoa butter | bloom | |

# QUESTIONS FOR DISCUSSION

1. Why is it necessary to temper chocolate for making chocolate molds?

2. Briefly explain two methods for tempering chocolate.

3. If tempered chocolate is at the correct temperature for molding but is too thick, how should you thin it?

4. Why is *white chocolate* an inaccurate term?

5. Why are chocolate molds polished with cotton wool before use?

6. Describe one procedure for molding chocolate eggs.

7. Describe five techniques for making decorative patterns using two colors of chocolate for cutouts.

8. Describe the procedure for making chocolate fans, starting with melted chocolate.

9. What are chocolate truffles? Give as complete an answer as you can, describing various types and forms.

## Chapter 25

# Marzipan, Nougatine, and Pastillage

T his chapter and the next are an introduction to the pastry chef's art of making decorative items out of sugar and other materials. Although all the ingredients used for these pieces are edible, and many of these items are used to decorate cakes and other desserts, they are, in many cases, made as showpieces, such as centerpieces for dessert buffet tables, and are not intended to be eaten.

In hotels and other food service and retail operations, such showpieces can be useful and even profitable. They serve to draw the customers' attention to the skill and artistry of the pastry chef and, thus, indirectly lead to greater sales of desserts. Perhaps even more important, from a pastry chef's point of view, they are an enjoyable outlet for creative skills.

Some of the items in these two chapters are comparatively easy to make, while others, such as pulled sugar, require a great deal of practice before you can expect to achieve good results. The text and the many photographs that illustrate the techniques provide an introduction but, for the most part, the only effective way to learn these skills is with the guidance of an instructor.

**After reading this chapter, you should be able to:**

1. Make and handle marzipan and mold decorative items from it.

2. Make pastillage and use it to create decorative items.

3. Make nougatine and shape it into simple decorative items.

# MARZIPAN

*Marzipan* is a paste made of almonds and sugar that is worked to a plastic consistency. Its texture allows it to be rolled out with a rolling pin like dough or to be modeled into the shapes of fruits, animals, flowers, and so forth.

Pastry chefs and confectioners once had to grind almonds in order to make marzipan, but today the ready availability of almond paste makes the job much easier. As you can see in the accompanying formula, making marzipan involves moistening the almond paste and blending it with confectioners' sugar. Formulas may vary slightly, but the principle behind them is the same. Some formulas call for more or less sugar or use different moistening agents, such as fondant or egg whites.

In order to preserve the color of the marzipan, be sure that all equipment, including bowls, mixer attachments, and work surfaces, is very clean. Use stainless steel rather than aluminum mixing bowls because aluminum discolors marzipan.

Marzipan dries quickly when exposed to air and forms a crust on the surface. To avoid this when you are working with marzipan, keep unused portions in a bowl covered with a damp cloth. To store marzipan, keep it wrapped or covered in an airtight container. It keeps indefinitely if protected from air. If left uncovered, it eventually becomes hard as a rock.

When marzipan is kneaded and worked, the oil content (from the almonds) comes to the surface and makes the marzipan sticky. To avoid this, dust the work surface lightly with confectioners' sugar. Keep a pan of confectioners' sugar handy for dusting as needed.

## Marzipan Sheets and Cutouts

Marzipan can be rolled out into sheets with a rolling pin in the same way that you roll out short dough. Confectioners' sugar is used for dusting the workbench and rolling pin. Make sure the bench and the pin are completely clean.

Marzipan sheets are useful for covering cakes and petits fours, as explained in chapter 17. They may be left smooth or textured with a ribbed roller or basketweave roller (see p. 456).

Colored patterns, such as stripes or polka dots, can be made on marzipan sheets as follows. Roll out a sheet of marzipan partway, so it is about twice as thick as desired. Roll out another small piece of marzipan in a contrasting color until it is ⅛ inch (3 mm) thick. Cut out small circles or strips and arrange them carefully on top of the thick sheet. Now continue to roll out this sheet to the desired thickness. Be careful to roll it evenly in all directions to keep the design uniform.

Using round or fancy cutters, cut out small shapes from the marzipan sheets and use them to decorate cakes and desserts. For additional effect, spread the sheet of marzipan with tempered chocolate and texture it with an icing comb. Make cutouts before the chocolate hardens completely. Make another variation by texturing the marzipan with ribbed rollers and then spinning fine lines of chocolate over the sheet, using a paper cone with a very small opening.

Note that the Easter plaque on the chocolate egg pictured on page 643 is made of a textured marzipan sheet.

Marzipan petits fours can be made to look like fancy icebox cookies. Using two colors of marzipan instead of icebox cookie dough, make checkerboard or pinwheel slices using the procedures for the icebox cookies (p. 494). (Do not bake the slices.)

# MARZIPAN

| Ingredients | U.S. | Metric | Procedure |
|---|---|---|---|
| Almond paste | 1 lb | 500 g | 1. In a clean stainless-steel bowl, blend the almond paste and glucose, using the paddle attachment, until smooth. |
| Glucose or corn syrup | 3 oz | 90 g | |
| Confectioners' sugar, sifted | 1 lb | 500 g | 2. Add the sifted sugar, a little at a time, just as fast as it is absorbed. Stop adding sugar when the desired consistency is reached. The marzipan should be stiff but workable and not too dry. |
| *Total weight:* | *2 lb 3 oz* | *1090 g* | 3. If colored marzipan is desired, add a small amount of color and work it in. |

## Modeling with Marzipan

Fruits, vegetables, animals, flowers, and many other shapes can be molded with marzipan. Small marzipan fruits, served as petits fours or candies, are perhaps the most popular items.

### Fruits and Flowers

To make small fruits, first divide the paste into equal portions. For example, to make ¾-ounce (22 g) pieces, flatten 1½ pound (700 g) marzipan into a fairly thick rectangle of uniform thickness. With a knife, carefully cut the rectangle into four rows of eight to make 32 equal pieces.

Begin by rolling each piece between the palms of your hands into a round ball that is perfectly smooth and free of seams and cracks (bananas are an exception—begin by rolling the pieces into smooth sausage shapes). Then start modeling the balls with the fingers into the shapes of pears, apples, and other fruits. The best way to make realistic-looking fruits is to use real fruits as models. Imitate the shapes of the real fruits as closely as possible.

Special effects can be made with ordinary tools or with special modeling tools. For example, make the crease on the sides of peaches, apricots, plums, and cherries with the back of a knife. Texture the surfaces of strawberries by poking them lightly with a toothpick. Imitate the rough surface of lemons and oranges by rolling them lightly on a cheese grater.

Let the fruits dry overnight before coloring. Coloring can be done in two ways:

Marzipan tools. Top: basketweave roller. Middle row: metal rolling pin, small cutters with release plungers, strawberry leaf cutter, nippers, modeling tools, smoother for covering cakes with sheets of marzipan. Bottom: color sprayer

1. Start with tinted marzipan—green for apples and pears, yellow for bananas, peaches, and lemons, and so on. Apply food color with a brush to color in highlights and markings, such as the brown streaks and dots on bananas, the red blush on apples and peaches, and so on.

2. Start with untinted marzipan. Color the finished fruits with background colors, using either a brush or a sprayer. Let the color dry, then color in the highlights.

Flowers such as carnations and roses are useful items to make because they can be used to decorate cakes as well as display pieces.

Marzipan rose, carnation, strawberry, and oranges

## Procedure for Making a Marzipan Strawberry

1. Roll the ball of marzipan into a strawberry shape with the palms of your hands.

2. Indent the stem end of the strawberry with an appropriate modeling tool.

3. Roll the strawberry in sugar to simulate the textured surface of the real berry.

4. Cut out a leaf shape for the stem end and fasten it in place using an appropriate modeling tool.

## Procedure for Making a Marzipan Orange

1. Roll a piece of marzipan into a round ball.

2. Using a marzipan molding tool, make an indentation in the ball to resemble the stem end of the orange.

## Procedure for Making a Marzipan Carnation

1. Flatten a strip of marzipan on the workbench so the edges are paper thin. Feather the edge with the point of a knife.

2. Release the strip of marzipan by sliding a knife under it. Gather it together into a carnation shape.

## Procedure for Making a Marzipan Rose

1. Taper a ball of marzipan to serve as the base of the rose.

2. Mold the ball with the tapered end pointing up to serve as the center of the flower.

3. For the petals, roll a log of marzipan and cut pieces of equal size. Flatten these pieces into small disks.

4. With the back of a spoon, flatten the disks, using a circular motion to taper the edges to paper thinness.

5. Wrap the petal around the base, leaving one edge free so the second petal can be inserted under it.

6. Attach the second petal.

7. Continue adding petals in the same fashion until the rose is the desired size. With a sharp knife, cut the rose from the base.

## Other Items

The variety of objects that can be modeled from marzipan is limited only by the imagination and talent of the pastry cook. Vegetables such as carrots, asparagus, potatoes, and peas in the pod can be made in the same way as fruits. Marzipan snowmen and holly leaves are often used to decorate the Bûche de

Noël (p. 477). Animals such as dogs, pigs, and frogs are popular subjects. Features such as eyes, nose, and tongue can be applied with royal icing, chocolate, or fondant.

Frames for chocolate paintings on pastillage (p. 663) are generally made of marzipan. Roll marzipan into long, round strips of perfectly uniform thickness and fasten them around the pastillage plaque. With assorted marzipan nippers and modeling tools, texture the marzipan to look like a carved frame. Highlight the raised details by very carefully browning them with a blowtorch.

# PASTILLAGE

*Pastillage* (pronounced pahss tee yahzh) is a sugar paste used for modeling decorative items. Unlike marzipan and other modeling pastes, it is rarely, if ever, intended to be eaten. Although it is made entirely of edible items, pastillage is as hard and brittle as plaster of Paris when it dries, and nearly as tasteless. It is used primarily for making display pieces, such as centerpieces for dessert buffet tables, or small baskets or boxes to hold petits fours and candies. Pastillage is normally left pure white, although it may be colored in pastel shades.

The formula given here is a simple and popular one using readily available ingredients: confectioners' sugar, cornstarch (as a drying agent), water, cream of tartar (to help preserve whiteness), and gelatin (as a stiffening and stabilizing agent). Pastillage is sometimes called **gum paste**, although that term is more correctly used when a vegetable gum (usually gum tragacanth) is used instead of gelatin (see sidebar).

## Making and Handling Pastillage

Many of the same precautions must be taken in the production of pastillage as in the production of marzipan. Great care is essential to preserve the pure white color. Make sure all equipment is scrupulously clean, and use a stainless-steel bowl, not aluminum, for mixing (aluminum imparts a grayish color to the paste). Likewise, the work surface, rolling pin, and molds must be clean and dry.

Pastillage dries and crusts over even faster than marzipan, so it must be kept covered at all times. While working with pastillage, keep unused portions in a bowl covered with a damp cloth. Work quickly and without pause until your products are formed and ready for drying.

Most pastillage pieces are made of thin sheets of the paste cut to shape with the aid of paper patterns. The pieces are left flat or curved around molds and allowed to dry, then assembled by gluing them together with royal icing. A marble slab is ideal for rolling out pastillage because it gives the paste a smooth surface. Use cornstarch to dust the work surface. Be careful not to use more starch than is necessary to keep the paste from sticking. Excessive starch dries the surface of the paste quickly and causes it to crust over and crack.

For the most attractive, delicate pieces, the pastillage sheets should be rolled thin (about ⅛ in./3 mm thick). Thick sheets make heavy, clumsy-looking pieces. Have paper patterns ready, and as soon as the pastillage is rolled out, place the patterns on it and cut cleanly and accurately with a sharp knife or cutter.

For pieces to be molded, have the molds clean, dry, and dusted with cornstarch. For example, to make a pastillage bowl, you can use the outside of an-

Pastillage tools: Ribbed roller, molds, and cutters

other bowl, placed upside down on the workbench, as your mold. Carefully fit the sheet of paste outside or inside the mold, gently fitting it to the shape of the mold with your hands.

When the pastillage is partially dry and firm, turn it over to allow the bottom to dry. Continue turning it over from time to time so it dries evenly. Pastillage that does not dry evenly tends to curl or distort out of shape. Drying time depends on the size and thickness of the pieces and may take from 12 hours to several days.

Dried pastillage may be lightly sanded with extra-fine sandpaper until it is very smooth. This also helps smooth the cut edges, which may be rough or sharp. Finally, assemble the pieces using royal icing as cement. Use very little icing; any excess is likely to squeeze out at the seams, which spoils the appearance of the piece.

The procedure below illustrates most of the steps discussed above. In the photos, the pastry chef is making and assembling the display piece pictured on this page. The flowers are tinted with food colors using the sprayer depicted on page 659.

Because of its pure white, smooth surface, pastillage makes an ideal canvas for chocolate painting. Make a round, oval, or rectangular plaque of pastillage, let it dry, and sand it smooth. Using an artist's brush, draw a picture using melted unsweetened chocolate. Create light and dark shades by diluting the chocolate with varying proportions of melted cocoa butter. For fine detail, etch lines in the chocolate with a sharp wooden pick. After the chocolate has set, the painting can be finished off with a marzipan frame (p. 662).

## ❧ GUM PASTE ❧

Although the terms *gum paste* and *pastillage* are sometimes used interchangeably, they are slightly different products in spite of their similar appearance. Gum paste is made with a vegetable gum called *gum tragacanth* (see p. 88). Because this gum is somewhat expensive, gum paste is less practical than pastillage for large pieces or high-volume work. Also, because gum paste dries more slowly than pastillage, it is inconvenient when time is an important factor in finishing a display piece.

The slow-drying property of gum paste is sometimes an important advantage as well. Because it doesn't dry or crust as quickly as pastillage, it is a good choice when you are doing a detailed, intricate piece that takes a long time to shape. And because it is more pliable, it can be rolled thinner and used to make more delicate items. For those interested in comparing gum paste and pastillage, a formula is included on page 742.

# PASTILLAGE

| Ingredients | U.S. | | Metric | Sugar at 100%<br>% | Procedure |
|---|---|---|---|---|---|
| Gelatin | 0.5 | oz | 12 g | 1.25 | 1. Stir the gelatin into the water. Let stand 5 minutes, then heat until the gelatin is dissolved. |
| Water, cold | 5.5 | oz | 140 g | 14 | |
| Confectioners' sugar (10X) | 2 lb 8 | oz | 1000 g | 100 | 2. Sift together the sugar, starch, and cream of tartar. |
| Cornstarch | 5 | oz | 125 g | 12.5 | 3. Place the gelatin mixture in a stainless-steel mixer bowl. Fit the mixing machine with the dough hook. |
| Cream of tartar | 0.04 oz (½ tsp) | | 1 g | 0.1 | |
| *Total weight:* | *3 lb 3* | *oz* | *1278 g* | *127%* | 4. With the machine running at low speed, add most of the sugar mixture just as fast as it is absorbed, keeping back a little of the sugar in case the texture must be adjusted. Mix to a smooth, pliable paste. It should have the consistency of a firm dough. If it is too moist, add some or all of the remaining sugar. |

5. Keep the paste covered at all times.

Techniques for creating this pastillage showpiece are illustrated on pages 664–665.

# Techniques for Creating a Showpiece from Pastillage

The techniques shown here are used to create the showpiece pictured on page 663.

1. Roll out the pastillage on a work surface, preferably marble, dusted lightly with cornstarch.

2. Check the thickness.

3. Lift the rolled-out pastillage by draping it over a rolling pin. Always dust off excess cornstarch.

4. Create a textured surface with a ribbed roller.

5. Cut out desired shapes. Working on a tray allows you to remove the pieces from the workbench for drying without disturbing them. The tray should be dusted with cornstarch.

6. Some shapes can be cut freehand with a knife.

7. Use small cutters to cut additional pieces.

8. Use a ring mold to measure the width of a strip to form the sides of the box.

9. Cut a strip of pastillage and fit it inside the ring mold. Trim the ends so the joint fits smoothly.

10. Trim excess from the top.

11. For leaves and petals, cut appropriate shapes.

12. Press the cut-out shapes in a leaf mold.

13. Fit the petals into a mold lined with a little square of parchment to prevent sticking.

14. To make the center of the flower, press a ball of pastillage into a sieve.

15. Set the center of the flower in place.

16. To use this type of cutter/molder, stamp out a piece of pastillage, press it in to mold it, and push it out with the spring-loaded plunger.

17. For the feet of the box, press balls of pastillage into a chocolate mold. Pass a scraper over the top of the mold to remove excess and flatten the tops.

18. Once the pastillage has dried, sand it with fine sandpaper to achieve a smooth surface.

19. Fasten pieces together with royal icing.

20. Fasten the dried top of the box, textured with a ribbed roller, in place.

21. Fasten the side pieces in place.

22. Make the decorative lacework by coloring royal icing and piping it using a paper cone.

# NOUGATINE

*Nougatine* is a candy made of caramelized sugar and almonds. (Almonds are traditional, but other sliced nuts are sometimes used as well.) It looks somewhat like peanut brittle but is more attractive because of the sliced almonds. The caramelized sugar should be a clear amber, not cloudy. Because the sugar is soft and pliable when it is hot, it can be cut and molded into shapes to make decorative pieces.

## Production and Shaping

As can be seen in the following formula, cooking nougatine involves two fairly simple steps: caramelizing the sugar and adding the almonds. The glucose inverts some of the sugar (see p. 67), thus preventing unwanted crystallization. Cream of tartar or lemon juice is sometimes used instead of glucose.

Nougatine can be cut into many shapes and is often cut freehand. If your display piece requires precise shapes, however, it is best to cut patterns out of sheets of parchment. Lay the patterns on top of the sheet of nougatine to guide your cutting. Have all your patterns ready before starting to make the nougatine.

When the nougatine is ready, pour it onto a silicone mat or an oiled tray or marble slab. It will cool quickly, so you must work fast. When the sheet has begun to set, flip it over with a spatula so it cools evenly. Have your paper pattern ready. Flatten the sheet with an oiled rolling pin to even the thickness. Place the patterns on the sheet and quickly cut out shapes with a heavy oiled knife. Because of the oiled surface, the patterns shouldn't stick, but don't press them down or leave them on the nougatine too long.

Prepare the molds ahead of time by oiling them lightly. For example, to make a nougatine bowl, you can use the bottom of a stainless-steel bowl placed upside-down on the bench and rubbed with oil. Place the soft, cut nougatine over the bowl and carefully press it into shape.

If the nougatine cools and hardens before you can shape it, place it on an oiled baking sheet and place it in a hot oven for a moment to soften it. You can even stick two sheets together by placing them next to each other and heating them. However, every time you reheat nougatine it darkens a little more. Several shades of nougatine in a display piece detract from its appearance.

When the molded nougatine pieces have cooled and hardened, cement them together as necessary, using either royal icing or a hot sugar syrup boiled to 310°F (190°C). Nougatine pieces can also be decorated with royal icing.

## Other Uses of Nougatine

Unlike some decorative materials, such as pastillage, nougatine is a tasty confection. Thin nougatine sheets can be cut into fancy shapes and used to decorate cakes and other desserts.

Hard nougatine can be crushed and used like chopped nuts for masking the sides of cakes. Finely ground and sifted, or ground to a paste, it makes an excellent flavoring for creams and icings. This product is similar to praline paste, except that praline generally contains hazelnuts.

## Techniques for Working with Nougatine

1. Pour out the hot nougatine mixture onto a silicone mat.

2. With a spatula or your hands (using rubber gloves), fold the mass over on itself as it cools so it cools evenly.

3. While it is still hot and soft, roll out the nougatine with a rolling pin to the desired thickness.

4. This nougatine is to be used as the base of a centerpiece. It is molded to shape in a lightly oiled cake tin.

5. Trim off excess with a chef's knife.

6. Thinly rolled nougatine can be cut into shapes for decorating cakes (such as the top layer of Brasilia, p. 469) and pastries.

7. Bend the cutout to the desired shape while still hot, or rewarm until pliable.

# NOUGATINE

*Yield: about 2 lb 8 oz (1220 g)*

| Ingredients | U.S. | Metric | Sugar at 100% % | Procedure |
|---|---|---|---|---|
| Sliced almonds | 12 oz | 375 g | 50 | 1. Place the almonds on a heated baking sheet in a 320°F (160°C) oven, mixing occasionally until light golden in color. |
| Sugar | 1 lb 8 oz | 750 g | 100 | 2. Cook the water, sugar, and glucose to a blond caramel. |
| Glucose | 9.5 oz | 300 g | 40 | 3. Add the almonds to the caramel all at once and mix in carefully. Do not overmix, or the almonds will break into small pieces. |
| Water | 6.5 oz | 200 g | 27 | 4. Pour the mixture onto an oiled baking sheet or silicone mat. |

5. Spread the nougatine in small quantities and use a metal rolling pin to make an even layer.

6. Work the nougatine near the opening of the oven, as this will keep it pliable much longer. The nougatine should not stick to the rolling pin or table. If it does, allow the nougatine to cool a little before continuing, returning it to the oven to achieve the correct consistency.

7. Trimmings may be used again after gentle reheating, but be careful not to use nougatine once it has become dark in color and the almonds are broken to a fine powder.

# TERMS FOR REVIEW

marzipan            pastillage            gum paste            nougatine

# QUESTIONS FOR DISCUSSION

1. What precaution must be taken when mixing marzipan in order to preserve its color?

2. Suppose you wanted to cover a strawberry-filled Swiss roll with white marzipan decorated with pink polka dots. How would you make the marzipan sheet?

3. Describe the procedure for making a marzipan carnation.

4. What procedure is used to make sure pastillage dries properly?

5. How are dried pieces of pastillage fastened together?

6. Describe the procedure for making, cutting, and molding nougatine.

7. What are some uses for leftover nougatine trimmings?

## Chapter 26

# Sugar Techniques

**M**any pastry chefs consider sugar work the pinnacle of their decorative art. One reason is surely the sheer beauty of skillfully made pulled- and blown-sugar pieces, which can be elaborate constructions of multicolored sugar flowers in blown-sugar vases, large sprays of sugar flowers cascading down the side of a wedding cake, or sugar baskets filled with sugar fruit and set on sugar pedestals wrapped with sugar ribbons and bows.

Another reason is, no doubt, the difficulty of decorative work. Becoming proficient at this art requires dedication and hours, even years, of practice and study, so chefs who have mastered it have earned the respect this accomplishment brings them. Students are often irresistibly drawn to the challenge of learning these techniques when they see what results are possible.

This chapter is an introduction to sugar work, beginning with the simpler techniques of spun sugar and sugar cages and proceeding to the more difficult pulled and blown sugar. The chapter concludes with an introduction to confections based on boiled sugar.

**After reading this chapter, you should be able to:**

1. Boil sugar syrups correctly for decorative sugar work.

2. Make spun sugar, sugar cages, and poured sugar.

3. Pull sugar and use it to make simple pulled- and blown-sugar decorative items.

4. Prepare basic boiled-sugar confections.

# BOILING SYRUPS FOR SUGAR WORK

In chapter 12, we discussed the boiling of sugar syrups for use in various desserts. When syrups are boiled until nearly all the water is evaporated, the sugar becomes solid when it cools. This process enables us to make decorative pieces out of sugar that is boiled to 300°F (149°C) or more and shaped while still hot.

As you learned in chapter 4 (p. 67), sugar that is boiled in a syrup containing an acid undergoes a chemical change called *inversion*, in which a molecule of double sugar (sucrose) combines with a molecule of water and changes into two molecules of simple sugar (dextrose and levulose). Invert sugar, you remember, resists crystallization, and plain sucrose (granulated sugar) crystallizes easily. The amount of sugar that is inverted depends on the amount of acid present. This principle is used in the production of fondant icing (p. 422): Just enough cream of tartar or glucose is added to the syrup to create a mass of extremely fine sugar crystals that give fondant its pure white color.

This technique is also used for the sugar work discussed in this section, especially in pulled sugar. If too much cream of tartar or glucose is used, too much sugar is inverted, so the sugar is too soft and sticky to work and doesn't harden enough when cool. If not enough cream of tartar or glucose is used, too little sugar is inverted and the sugar is hard, so it is difficult to work and easily broken.

As long as it is kept within limits, the exact amount of tartar or glucose to be used depends largely on the preferences of the pastry chef or confectioner. Some artists prefer to work with a harder sugar, while some prefer a softer one. Consequently, you will see many formulas. Your instructor may have his or her own favorite to substitute for those in this book.

The temperature to which syrup is boiled is also important. The higher the temperature, the harder the sugar will be. The temperature range recommended in this book is 311°–320°F (155°–160°C), and the actual temperature used for the pulled and blown sugar items shown in the illustrations was 320°F (160°C). Nevertheless, you may see slightly different temperatures used in other books, because all chefs have their own preferred procedures.

Cooking the sugar to a higher temperature makes it harder and more brittle and thus more difficult to work. Cooking to a lower temperature makes a softer sugar that is easier to work, but the pieces may not hold up as well, especially in a humid climate. Inexperienced cooks may want to start with temperatures at the lower end of the range, not worrying about the keeping qualities of their pieces, until they develop some familiarity with sugar work.

Two more precautions are necessary regarding temperature and the addition of tartaric acid (cream of tartar). First, boiled invert sugar discolors more rapidly than pure sucrose. Therefore, the acid should not be added until near the end of the boiling process. In the recipes in this book, the tartaric acid is not added to the syrup until it has reached 275°F (135°C). Second, the syrup should be boiled rapidly over moderately high heat. Boiling slowly gives the syrup more time to discolor, and it will not be clear white.

If color is added to the syrup during boiling (for poured or pulled sugar), it should be added partway through the cooking, at about 260°F (125°C). If it is added earlier, it has more time to discolor, but it must be added early enough for the alcohol or water to cook off.

Slightly different syrups are used for each of the techniques in this chapter. Follow the specific recipes in each section, keeping these guidelines in mind:

1. Use pure white granulated cane sugar. Sift the sugar to remove any impurities that may have fallen into it during storage.

2. Place the sugar and water in a clean, heavy pan. Place the mixture over low heat and stir gently until the sugar is dissolved.

3. When the sugar is dissolved, raise the heat to moderately high and do not stir any more. To prevent crystallization, use a clean pastry brush dipped in hot water to wash any sugar crystals down the side of the pan. Do not let the brush touch the syrup.

4. Always use a sugar thermometer.

5. Add coloring and tartaric acid solution at the temperatures specified in the recipes.

6. Liquid colors in an acid solution should not be used. For best results, use powdered colors and dissolve them in a little water or alcohol. Good-quality paste colors can also be used.

# SPUN SUGAR AND CARAMEL DECORATIONS

## Spun Sugar

*Spun sugar* is a mass of threadlike or hairlike strands of sugar used to decorate cakes and showpieces. Gâteau St-Honoré (p. 367) is often decorated with spun sugar.

Spun sugar should be made just before it is needed because it does not keep well. It gradually absorbs moisture from the atmosphere and becomes sticky. Eventually, this absorbed moisture causes the sugar to dissolve.

Prepare a workstation by propping a lightly oiled wooden rod or rolling pin on the edge of a table so it projects horizontally beyond the edge of the table by 1 to 2 feet (30–60 cm). Place plenty of paper on the floor below to catch drippings. To spin the sugar, you will need a wire whip with the ends cut off.

Tools for sugar work. Top: sugar lamp. Bottom, left to right: sugar thermometer, rubber gloves, leaf molds, blowpipe, cut-off wire whip for spun sugar.

## Procedure for Making Spun Sugar

1. Prepare the syrup as in the formula on page 676. When the correct temperature is reached, remove the pan from the heat and allow the syrup to stand for a few minutes until it is slightly cooled and thickened.

2. Dip the cut-off wire whip in the syrup and tap lightly to remove excess. Wave or flick the whip vigorously over the wooden rod so the sugar is thrown off in fine, long threads.

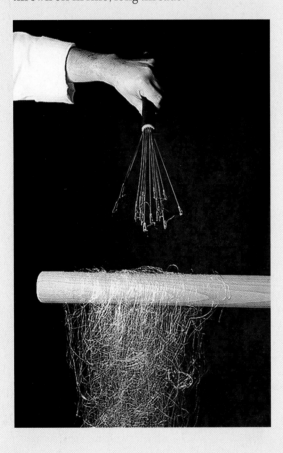

3. Repeat until the desired amount of spun sugar is hanging from the rod. Carefully lift the mass from the rod.

4. Coil the sugar, or shape as desired for decoration.

5. If the syrup cools too much to spin, simply rewarm it over low heat.

## Caramel Cages and Other Shapes

*Sugar cages* are delicate, lacy sugar domes made of caramelized sugar. Their decorative effect can be impressive and elegant. Sugar cages can be made large enough to cover whole cakes, bombes, Bavarian creams, and other desserts, or small enough to decorate individual portions.

Bowls of the desired size can be used as molds for large cages. Ladles are usually used for small, single-portion cages. Lightly oil the bottom of the ladle or other mold so the sugar can be removed when it is hard.

## Procedure for Making Caramel Cages

1. Prepare a syrup as in the formula on page 676. Testing with a sugar thermometer is the most accurate way to determine the stage of the boiled syrup.

2. Cool the syrup slightly. Holding the mold in one hand, dip a spoon in the sugar and drizzle it in a random, lacy pattern over the mold, turning the mold so all sides receive some of the syrup.

3. Trim off excess, let the sugar cool until hard, and carefully lift off.

Other shapes can be made by piping or drizzling the sugar onto a silicone mat or oiled work surface. To create fine, even lines of sugar, use a paper cone, as described in the formula procedure. Wear rubber gloves to protect your hands from the heat. For a rougher or more casual look, dip a spoon in the sugar and drizzle it onto the mat. The caramel shape decorating the panna cotta dessert pictured on page 613 was made this way.

Sugar spirals make elegant garnishes for some plated desserts (see, for example, the photo on p. 631). These are made using the following procedure.

## Procedure for Making a Sugar Spiral

1. Prepare a syrup as for making caramel cages (p. 676).

2. Wind a strand of hot syrup around a lightly oiled pencil or thin wooden rod.

3. Slip the spiral off the pencil when the sugar has hardened.

# SPUN SUGAR

*Yield: about 12 oz (360 g)*

| Ingredients | U.S. | Metric | Sugar at 100% % | Procedure |
|---|---|---|---|---|
| Sugar | 10 oz | 300 g | 100 | 1. Make a syrup of the sugar, water, and glucose. See page 260 for guidelines on cooking sugar syrups. |
| Water | 5 oz | 150 g | 50 | 2. Boil to 255°F (125°C) and add coloring, if desired. |
| Glucose | 2 oz | 60 g | 20 | 3. Continue to boil to 320°F (160°C), and then stop the cooking immediately by plunging the base of the pan into cold water. Remove from the cold water and allow to stand 2–3 minutes to thicken slightly. |
| Coloring, if desired | | | | 4. Lightly oil a rolling pin or metal pole and suspend it horizontally. Place sheets of paper on the floor under the pole to catch drips. |
| | | | | 5. Dip a cut-off wire whip in the syrup and flick it over the pole, as in the illustrations. Continue until the desired quantity is made. |
| | | | | 6. Lift the spun sugar from the pole and shape as desired. |

---

### ❧ CARNIVAL TREAT ❧

Cotton candy, the popular circus and carnival treat, is nothing more than spun sugar made from a flavored, colored syrup. The syrup is forced through tiny holes in a spinning head that flings the fine threads of sugar against the sides of a bowl, where it is wound around a paper cone. The amount of sugar in an entire portion of cotton candy is usually less than 1 ounce (30 g).

---

# CARAMEL FOR CAGES AND OTHER SHAPES

*Yield: about 10 oz (300 g)*

| Ingredients | U.S. | | Metric | Sugar at 100% % | Procedure |
|---|---|---|---|---|---|
| Sugar | 10 | oz | 300 g | 100 | 1. Make a syrup of the sugar, water, and glucose. See page 260 for guidelines on cooking sugar syrups. |
| Water | 10 | oz | 300 g | 100 | 2. Boil to 320°F (160°C), then stop the cooking immediately by plunging the base of the pan into cold water. Remove from the cold water and allow to stand 2–3 minutes to thicken slightly. |
| Glucose | 1.33 | oz | 40 g | 13 | 3. Wear rubber gloves to protect your hands from the hot syrup. Pour the syrup into a paper cone. Snip off the tip and pipe desired shapes onto a silicone mat or oiled work surface. Allow to cool. Remove and store in an airtight container until use. |
| | | | | | 4. For cages, lightly oil the bottom of a ladle. Dip a spoon in the syrup (or, for more delicate sugar, dip the point of a knife in the syrup) and drizzle it in a lace pattern over the bottom of the ladle. Trim off excess with scissors. Let stand 2 minutes, then carefully lift off. |

# POURED SUGAR

**Poured sugar**, also called *cast sugar*, is boiled sugar that is allowed to harden in various shapes. Usually it is cast in flat sheets like glass, although, like nougatine, it can be bent and shaped while it is hot and pliable. The syrup can also be colored before it finishes cooking.

There are several ways of preparing molds for casting the sugar. For round shapes, simply use a flan ring or charlotte ring. Metal molds in other shapes (like large cookie cutters) can also be used. For other shapes, bend a strip of metal into the desired shape. An easy way to make a mold of any shape is to roll heat-resistant plasticine (a type of modeling clay) into a rope and work it to the desired shape on an oiled marble slab or silicone mat. Whatever mold you use, it should be lightly oiled to prevent the sugar from sticking.

Once the edges of the sugar shape have hardened enough, remove the mold. When the entire shape has hardened enough, slide a palette knife under it to detach it from the work surface. (This is not necessary if you are using a silicone mat, which will peel away easily.)

To bend cast sugar, remove it from the work surface while it is still soft enough to be pliable. If it gets too hard, simply place it on an oiled baking sheet and heat it in an oven just until it is pliable. Then bend as desired, or use an oiled mold to shape it as you would nougatine (p. 666).

Another item that can be made by simply pouring sugar onto a surface is sugar lace. Sugar lace can be seen in the display piece pictured on page 682. The base of this piece is made with poured sugar.

## Procedure for Pouring Sugar

1. Prepare the syrup as in the formula on page 678. Color the syrup as desired, as indicated in the formula.

2. When the syrup reaches the proper temperature, briefly plunge the base of the saucepan into cold water to stop the cooking. Let stand for a moment.

3. Place a lightly oiled mold on a sheet of parchment. Pour the hot syrup—in this case, colored black—into the mold to the desired thickness.

4. Before the sugar cools, it can be marbled with another color—here, a little white coloring.

## Procedure for Making Sugar Lace

1. Pour a small pool of boiled sugar onto a square of silicone paper.

2. Quickly spread it to a thin layer with a palette knife.

3. Before the sugar hardens, crinkle the paper to shape the sugar.

# POURED SUGAR

*Yield: about 2 lb 6 oz (1200 g)*

| Ingredients | U.S. | Metric | Sugar at 100% %  | Procedure |
|---|---|---|---|---|
| Sugar | 2 lb | 1000 g | 100 | 1. Prepare molds for the desired shape: Brush metal rings with oil, or roll heat-resistant plasticine to the desired shape, then brush it with oil. Place the molds on a silicone mat or an oiled or parchment-covered marble slab. |
| Water | 1 lb | 500 g | 50 | |
| Glucose | 6.5 oz | 200 g | 0 | |
| Coloring, as desired | | | | |

2. Make a syrup of the sugar, water, and glucose. See page 260 for guidelines on cooking sugar syrups.

3. Boil to 255°F (125°C) and add coloring, if desired.

4. Continue to boil to 330°F (165°C). If desired, add a few drops of another color at this point without mixing to create a marbled effect.

5. Stop the cooking immediately by plunging the base of the pan into cold water. Remove from the cold water and allow to stand 2–3 minutes to thicken slightly.

6. Pour into desired mold until approximately ¼ in. (5 mm) thick.

7. Once the edges have set enough, remove the rings. Score lightly with an oiled knife, if desired.

8. Use a little reheated sugar as glue to attach pieces together.

# PULLED SUGAR AND BLOWN SUGAR

**Pulled sugar** and **blown sugar** are, perhaps, the most difficult of the pastry chef's decorative art forms. This section explains the basic procedure for making pulled sugar. Several techniques for making ribbons, flowers, leaves, and blown fruits are illustrated in detail, and a number of other techniques are explained in the text.

Before beginning work, assemble your equipment. The following tools are the most important items you will need, depending on what pieces you are making:

- Sugar thermometer, for accurate control of the temperature of the boiling syrup.
- Sugar lamp or other warmer, to keep the stock of sugar warm and soft.
- Scissors and knife, lightly oiled, for cutting the sugar.
- Alcohol lamp, for melting sugar in order to fasten pieces together.
- Blowpipe, for blowing sugar; a pipe with a bulb for inflating is easier to use than one that is blown with the mouth.
- Silicone mat or oiled marble slab, for pouring out the cooked syrup.
- Fan or hair dryer, for cooling sugar items.
- Rubber gloves, to protect from burns when handling hot sugar (some experienced chefs prefer to work without gloves).

Prepare the syrup according to the formula below. Note the need for liquid tartaric acid, which is a solution of equal weights of cream of tartar and water, prepared as indicated in the recipe.

Once the pulled sugar is prepared, it can be used at once, or it can be cooled and stored in an airtight container for later use. To use stored sugar for pulled or blown items, first reheat it under a sugar lamp (warming lamp) or in an oven preheated to 170°F (75°C). Turn the lumps of sugar over from time to time so they warm evenly. This is particularly important when working with a sugar lamp and should be done regularly the entire time you are working with the sugar, because the heat comes only from above.

After it has been heated to the proper temperature, the sugar must again be pulled and folded as in step 7 of the formula below until it is cooled to a workable temperature and even in texture. Test the sugar by pulling a bit from the edge of the ball with the thumb and forefinger and attempting to break it off. If it breaks off cleanly, the sugar is ready. This pulling and folding procedure is sometimes called *pearling* because of the pearl-like appearance it gives the sugar. This appearance is caused by the incorporation of air in the sugar structure during the pulling. For this reason, another common name for pearling is *aerating*. If this process is not done, it will not be possible to work the sugar properly.

## GOING TO THE NEXT LEVEL

Success at advanced decorative work requires not only good instruction but also a great deal of practice and repetition. Many of the most commonly used sugar techniques are explained and illustrated in this chapter. Doing these procedures only once or twice, however, will not make you an accomplished *décorateur* (a pastry chef specializing in or skilled at decorative work). To develop your sugar skills, it is suggested that you practice the techniques in this chapter repeatedly until you are comfortable with them.

Once you have some mastery of the basic techniques, you will have skills that will help you produce a great variety of décor. You might want to consult any of a number of advanced books on decorative work, some of which are listed in the bibliography on page 757. The variety of shapes that can be made with sugar is limited only by the imagination and skill of the chef.

# PULLED SUGAR AND BLOWN SUGAR

*Yield: about 2 lb 6 oz (1200 g)*

| Ingredients | U.S. | Metric | Sugar at 100% % | Procedure |
|---|---|---|---|---|
| Sugar | 2 lb | 1000 g | 100 | |
| Water | 9.5 oz | 300 g | 30 | |
| Glucose | 6.5 oz | 200 g | 20 | |
| Color | as desired | as desired | | |
| Tartaric acid solution (see *Note*) | 8 drops | 8 drops | | |

*Note: To prepare tartaric acid solution, use equal weights of cream of tartar and water. Bring the water to a boil, remove from the heat, and add the cream of tartar. Let cool.*

**Procedure**

1. Make a syrup of the sugar, water, and glucose. See page 260 for guidelines on cooking sugar syrups.

2. Boil to 255°F (125°C) and add coloring, if desired. (Color can also be added when the sugar is poured out in step 5.)

3. Continue to boil to 275°F (135°C) and add the tartaric acid.

4. Continue boiling. When the temperature reaches 320°F (160°C), or whatever final temperature is desired (see p. 672), stop the cooking immediately by plunging the base of the pan into cold water. Remove from the cold water and allow to stand 2–3 minutes to thicken slightly.

5. Pour out onto an oiled marble slab or, preferably, onto a silicone mat. If color was not added in step 2, it can be added now, as on page 681.

6. Let cool slightly, but before the sugar begins to harden around the outside edges, fold the edges into the center. Repeat until the sugar mass can be picked up off the table.

7. Begin stretching the sugar and folding it back onto itself. Repeat until the mixture is cooler and makes a faint crackling or clicking sound when pulled. Do not attempt to pull when the sugar becomes too cool, as it could start to crystallize. Cut the sugar into smaller pieces with a scissors and place under a sugar lamp to keep them at workable temperature. Pull and fold the pieces one at a time so they will have a uniform texture and temperature. The sugar will take on a silky or pearled appearance after about 12 to 20 folds. Do not pull too much, or the sugar will lose this pearled appearance and become less shiny.

8. The sugar is now ready to be made into blown or pulled sugar decorations.

## Ribbons

A ribbon of a single color is made by simply pulling a piece of sugar out into a thin ribbon shape. This sounds easy, but making a thin, delicate ribbon of perfectly even thickness and width takes a great deal of practice and skill. Be sure the piece of sugar is uniformly warm and that all parts of the strip stretch the same amount.

To make a two-colored ribbon, start with two pieces of sugar in contrasting colors. Shape them into strips of the same size and shape. Press them together side by side, then stretch them into a ribbon. For multiple stripes, cut the two-colored strip in half when it is partly stretched. Place the two pieces together side by side so you have four alternating stripes. Finish stretching them into a ribbon shape.

A ribbon of three or more colors can be made with the same technique.

To make a bow, cut off a length of ribbon with scissors and bend it into a loop. Cool the loop in front of a fan so it holds its shape. Make as many loops as desired. Fasten them together into a bow by heating one end of each loop over a gas flame to soften the sugar and then pressing the heated ends together.

## Procedure for Making Pulled Sugar

1. Pour the cooked sugar onto a silicone mat.

2. If a color is desired and was not added during cooking, add the color now with an eyedropper.

3. As the sugar cools, fold the edges toward the center so it cools evenly.

4. When the color is blended in, pick up the mass of sugar and begin to stretch and fold it.

5. Pull and fold the sugar until it has a silky or pearly appearance and makes a faint clicking sound when stretched.

6. Store the lumps of sugar under the sugar lamp as you work them in order to keep them at the proper temperature.

---

### ❧ THE SUGAR LAMP ❧

A sugar lamp is simply a fixture for an infrared heat bulb, usually a 250-watt bulb. The bulb housing is on a long, flexible neck that enables the pastry chef to adjust the distance between the heat source and the sugar, which is placed on a silicone mat.

To be workable, sugar for pulling or blowing must be warm enough to be pliable, generally around 100°–130°F (38°–55°C) for pulling and as high as 175°F (80°C) for blowing, depending, in part, on the preference of the chef. Because the heat lamp warms the sugar mostly from the top, the sugar must be turned and folded so it warms uniformly. Let the lump of sugar rest under the lamp until the surface is shiny and almost liquid in appearance. Then pull the sugar gently into an oblong shape and fold the ends over so they meet in the middle. (Alternatively, simply fold it in half.) Be careful not to trap air bubbles between the layers of sugar. Repeat several times until the sugar is uniformly warmed and soft.

As you work with one piece of sugar creating decorative items, repeatedly turn over the remaining lumps of sugar under the lamp so they stay uniformly heated and soft.

## Procedure for Making Pulled Sugar Ribbons

**1.** Make equal-size ropes of the selected colors and place them side by side under the sugar lamp.

**2.** Pull or stretch to begin to form the ribbon.

**3.** Fold the ribbon so the two ends are side by side; snip in half with an oiled scissors.

**4.** Repeat this pulling and doubling procedure until you have a ribbon of the desired pattern and width.

**5.** Before the sugar hardens, bend it into folds to resemble a slightly crinkled ribbon.

**6.** Snip the ribbon into desired lengths with a lightly oiled scissors.

## Flowers and Leaves

The basic techniques for making simple flowers are detailed in the procedure on page 683. The illustrations show the production of a lily and a leaf. Note the mold used to mark the veins in the leaf. If a mold is not available, you can mark the pattern of veins using the back of a knife.

Another popular flower to make with pulled sugar is, of course, the rose. Rose petals are made using the same basic technique as for lily petals, except the petal is pulled into a round shape rather than being stretched into a long shape. Roll the first petal into a tight cone shape. Then curl additional petals around the center cone just as you would for a marzipan rose (p. 661). Make the outer petals a little larger than the inner ones, and curl back the edges to resemble real rose petals.

An alternative method is to make all the petals first without assembling them. Heat the bottom edges of the petals over the flame of an alcohol lamp so they stick together, and assemble them to make the flower.

To make a stem that will support the weight of a flower, pull a strong piece of wire through warm pulled sugar so it is completely coated. While the sugar is still soft, bend the covered wire to the desired shape.

## Procedure for Making a Pulled Sugar Lily

1. Stretch one side of a ball of pulled sugar to make a thin edge.

2. Grasp this thin edge and pull outward to make a pointed petal.

3. Snip off the petal with an oiled scissors. Repeat to make additional petals.

4. Attach the petals together into the shape of a lily.

5. For the inside of the flower, stretch pulled sugar into thin strands.

6. Fold two pieces of this sugar strand as shown and insert in the flower.

7. To make leaves, pull sugar as for the petals, but make the piece wider to resemble a leaf.

8. Lay the leaf pieces on one half of a leaf mold.

9. Press the piece of sugar with the other half of the mold to give it the texture of a leaf. The finished flowers are shown on page 684.

# Simple Baskets

Roll out a piece of pulled sugar with a rolling pin into a thin sheet. Mold it over an oiled bowl or large tin can, just as you would mold nougatine. You can also attach a handle.

# Woven Baskets

A woven pulled-sugar basket filled with pulled-sugar flowers or fruit is one of the most impressive of all display pieces. To make the basket, you need a base board into which an uneven number of holes has been drilled. The holes should be evenly spaced and should form a circle, oval, or square. In addition, you need wooden pegs that fit loosely into these holes. The holes should be drilled at an angle so the pegs tilt outward. This makes the basket wider at the top than at the bottom. Oil the pegs and board lightly before weaving the basket.

Take a ball of soft pulled sugar and start to pull a rope or cord of sugar from the ball. Starting at the inside edge of one of the pegs, weave the sugar cords in and out around the pegs, pulling out more of the sugar as you go. Be careful to keep the thickness of the cord uniform. Continue weaving the sugar around the pegs until the basket is as high as desired.

Make pulled sugar rods the same size and number as the wooden pegs. One by one, pull out the pegs and replace them with the pulled sugar rods. If necessary, trim the tops of the rods with a hot knife or scissors.

Make a base for the basket with poured sugar (p. 677) or with pulled sugar rolled out with a rolling pin. Attach it to the basket with hot boiled syrup.

To finish off the top and bottom edges, twist two cords of pulled sugar together to make a rope. Coil the rope around the top and bottom edges of the basket and seal the ends together. Make a handle for the basket by shaping heavy wire and then weaving a rope of sugar around it.

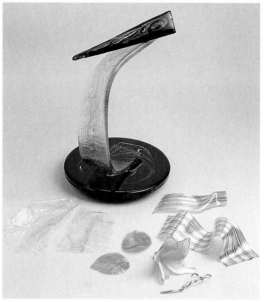

Parts of the sugar display piece before assembly

Finished sugar display piece

# Blown Sugar

Hollow sugar fruits and other items are blown from pulled sugar in much the same way glass is blown. Traditionally, sugar was blown with the mouth, using a length of tube, and many chefs still prefer this method. Today, however, the use of a blowpipe inflated with a squeeze bulb (see p. 673) has become common and makes the work a little easier. Especially for the beginner, this type of blowpipe is easier to control than a tube blown with the mouth.

The shape of the sugar piece depends on how it is manipulated and supported with the hands and on how it is cooled or warmed. To make round objects, such as apples, hold the blowpipe and sugar upward at an angle, so the weight of the sugar does not cause it to elongate. For long, thin objects such as bananas, stretch the sugar gently as you blow.

If the sugar on one side becomes too thin, cool that side slightly with a fan so it hardens. By watching demonstrations and practicing, you can learn to control the temperature of the piece on all sides in order to shape it as you want. The best sugar pieces have a thin, delicate wall of sugar that is of even thickness all around.

More complex pieces, such as animals, birds, and fish, can be made with practice. For example, make a long-necked bird by blowing the sugar into the shape of a vase and stretching out the neck to form the long neck of the bird. An animal's head and body may be blown separately and attached. Parts such as wings and fins are made separately from pulled sugar.

When the blown sugar has hardened, add more coloring to make the fruit more realistic. If the pieces were blown from colored pulled sugar, you may need to add only a few highlights and markings with an artist's brush. An alternative method is to use uncolored sugar for blowing and then a sprayer for adding layers of color to give a more blended effect. If done skillfully, this can give the fruit a more natural look. For spraying, dissolve powdered color in alcohol. If a dull rather than a shiny surface is appropriate for the item, dust the finished piece with cornstarch.

The procedure below illustrates the major steps in making blown-sugar fruits.

## Procedure for Blowing Sugar

1. Make a depression in a lump of hot pulled sugar and insert the end of the blowpipe.

2. Press the sugar firmly around the pipe to seal.

3. For a pear, inflate the bulb of sugar slowly, shaping the fruit as it is blown up.

4. Continue to inflate the sugar, shaping it with the fingers. When the desired shape and size are achieved, harden the sugar by cooling it with a fan.

5. Heat the neck of the pipe over a flame and detach the pear from the pipe. Mold the stem end with the fingers.

6. Mold other fruit in a similar fashion, such as bananas . . .

7. . . . and apples.

8. These finished fruits have been colored with a sprayer (see p. 648) and highlighted with a small paintbrush.

# BOILED SUGAR CONFECTIONS

Except for chocolates, a large proportion of old-fashioned candies are based on a boiled sugar solution. The background material in chapter 12 and in this chapter prepare you to make the recipes that follow. In particular, review the material on boiling sugar syrups, including steps to avoid crystallization, explained in chapter 12.

Hard candies are simply a flavored syrup boiled to the hard crack stage. Note that the recipe below is the same as for pulled sugar, with the addition of flavoring. Fancy candies, such as multicolored ribbon, can be made using the procedures for pulled sugar. Alternatively, simple candies can be made by preparing the candy through step 6 in the recipe procedure. Then roll the sugar to a uniform thickness with an oiled rolling pin and cut it into small squares with an oiled knife.

## HARD CANDIES

*Yield: about 2 lb 6 oz (1200 g)*

| Ingredients | U.S. | Metric | Sugar at 100% % | Procedure |
|---|---|---|---|---|
| Sugar | 2 lb | 1000 g | 100 | 1. Make a syrup of the sugar, water, and glucose. See page 260 for guidelines on cooking sugar syrups. |
| Water | 9.5 oz | 300 g | 30 | |
| Glucose or corn syrup | 6.5 oz | 200 g | 20 | 2. Boil to 255°F (125°C) and add coloring, if desired. (Color can also be added when the sugar is poured out in step 5.) |
| Tartaric acid solution (see p. 680) | 8 drops | 8 drops | | 3. Continue to boil to 275°F (135°C) and add the tartaric acid. |
| Coloring | as desired | as desired | | 4. Continue boiling. When the temperature reaches 320°F (160°C), or whatever final temperature is desired (see p. 672), stop the cooking immediately by plunging the base of the pan into cold water. Remove from the cold water and allow to stand 2–3 minutes to thicken slightly. |
| Flavoring, such as peppermint, lemon or other citrus, cinnamon | few drops | few drops | | |

5. Pour out onto an oiled marble slab or, preferably, onto a silicone mat. If color was not added in step 2, it can be added now, as on page 681.

6. Let cool slightly and add the flavoring to the top of the sugar. Before the sugar begins to harden around the outside edges, fold the edges into the center. Repeat until the sugar mass can be picked up off the table.

7. Begin stretching the sugar and folding it back onto itself. Repeat until the mixture is cooler and makes a faint crackling or clicking sound when pulled. Do not attempt to pull when the sugar becomes too cool, as it could start to crystallize. Cut the sugar into smaller pieces with a scissors and place under a sugar lamp to keep them at workable temperature. Pull and fold the pieces one at a time so they will have a uniform texture and temperature. The sugar will take on a silky or pearled appearance after about 12 to 20 folds. Do not pull too much, or the sugar will lose this pearled appearance and become less shiny.

8. Pull each lump of sugar into a rope about ½ in. (12 mm) thick. With a scissors, snip off pieces ½ in. (12 mm) long.

9. Let cool. Store in an airtight container.

Toffee is essentially the same as the butter caramel introduced in chapter 12 (p. 280), with the addition of flavorings and other ingredients that transform it into a delectable candy. Note that the core of the toffee recipe, the sugar and butter, are the same as in the butter caramel recipe. Peanut brittle is a similar confection, but with less butter and with the addition of a large quantity of peanuts. Soft caramels, too, are made in a similar fashion, except the syrup is made with cream or milk instead of water and the candy is cooked to a lower temperature so less moisture is cooked away, resulting in confections that are soft rather than hard.

Finally, classic, old-fashioned fudge should also be understood as a boiled sugar confection rather than as a chocolate candy. Although chocolate is often used as a flavoring, other flavorings may be used as well. The basic procedure is similar to the procedure for making fondant icing—that is, the boiled syrup is cooled to the proper temperature and then agitated to create extremely fine crystals. Review the fondant recipe and compare with the fudge recipe given here. A critical point in both procedures is the temperature to which the syrup is cooled. If it is stirred or agitated while it is still too warm, the crystals will be too large and the texture will be grainy.

# TOFFEE

*Yield: about 3 lb 6 oz (1650 g)*

| Ingredients | U.S. | | Metric | Sugar at 100% % | Procedure |
|---|---|---|---|---|---|
| Granulated sugar | 2 lb | | 1000 g | 100 | 1. Lightly oil a marble slab and arrange oiled caramel rulers (see p. 688) on the slab to make a rectangle about 15 × 16 inches (38 × 40 cm). |
| Water | | 8 oz | 250 g | 25 | |
| Glucose or corn syrup | | 5 oz | 160 g | 16 | 2. Make a syrup of the sugar, water, and glucose. See page 260 for guidelines on cooking sugar syrups. |
| Butter | 1 lb | | 500 g | 50 | 3. Boil to 280°F (138°C). |
| Salt | | 0.2 oz (1 tsp) | 6 g | 0.6 | 4. Add the butter and salt and stir in. Continue to boil to 315°F (157°C). |
| Almonds, chopped fine | | 3 oz | 90 g | 9 | 5. Stir in the almonds and vanilla. Continue to boil to 320°F (160°C). |
| Vanilla extract | | 0.2 oz (1 tsp) | 6 g | 0.6 | 6. Pour the syrup onto the prepared marble slab. |

7. When the syrup has begun to firm up but is still soft and hot, score or mark the toffee into 1-in. (2.5 cm) squares using a knife, a wheel knife, or a caramel cutter.

8. When the toffee has cooled and hardened, break apart into squares.

### VARIATION

After scoring the toffee, allow it to cool until just warm, and spread it with a thin layer of melted chocolate. Sprinkle with finely chopped almonds. Cool and break into pieces.

---

### { CARAMEL RULERS AND }
### CARAMEL CUTTERS

Caramel rulers are heavy steel bars used to contain hot syrups when poured out onto a marble slab or other flat surface. They are useful in many boiled sugar preparations, especially in the production of soft caramels, toffee, and similar confections.

A caramel cutter, also called a *toffee cutter*, consists of a row of wheel cutters spaced along a steel rod, with handles on both ends like a rolling pin. Spacers of various lengths enable the worker to adjust the cutter to cut multiple rows of the desired width. Using a caramel cutter, you can cut or score a sheet of caramel into uniform squares with one pass of the cutter lengthwise and one pass crosswise.

---

# PEANUT BRITTLE
*Yield: 4 lb 4 oz (2125 g)*

| Ingredients | U.S. | | Metric | Sugar at 100% %| Procedure |
|---|---|---|---|---|---|
| Granulate sugar | 2 lb | | 1000 g | 100 | 1. Lightly oil a marble slab. |
| Glucose or corn syrup | 1 lb 7 | oz | 720 g | 72 | 2. Combine the sugar, corn syrup, and water in a heavy saucepan. Bring to a boil to dissolve the sugar and make a syrup. See page 260 for guidelines on cooking sugar syrups. |
| Water | 12 | oz | 380 g | 38 | |
| Raw peanuts (see *Note*) | 1 lb 8 | oz | 750 g | 75 | 3. Boil the syrup until the temperature reaches 250°F (121°C). |
| Butter | 1.75 | oz | 55 g | 5.5 | 4. Add the peanuts and butter. |
| Vanilla extract | 0.33 oz (2 tsp) | | 10 g | 1 | 5. Continue to boil until the mixture reaches 312°F (155°C). Stir constantly and gently to prevent burning on the bottom. |
| Salt | 0.2 oz (1 tsp) | | 6 g | 0.6 | |
| Baking soda | 0.33 oz (2 tsp) | | 10 g | 1 | 6. Remove the pan from the heat. Stir in the vanilla, salt, and baking soda. Use caution, as the hot syrup will foam up for a moment. |

*Note: If raw peanuts are not available, use unsalted, roasted peanuts and add them just before pouring out onto marble.*

7. Pour the mixture onto the marble slab.

8. The syrup will flow outward more than the peanuts. To ensure an even distribution of nuts, use an oiled palette knife to carefully spread some of the peanuts toward the edges of the slab of syrup.

9. Put on a pair of latex gloves to protect your hands during this next step. As soon as the syrup has cooled enough so the edges can be lifted with the palette knife, carefully raise the edges with gloved hands and pull outward to stretch the candy so it becomes thinner between the nuts. This is easiest to do with two or more workers on opposite sides of the slab, as it cools and hardens quickly. Be careful not to touch any part of the sugar that is still molten. As the candy hardens, break off pieces from the edge, and continue stretching the rest of the brittle. (This step is optional, but it makes a thinner, finer-textured candy.)

10. Cool completely and store in airtight containers.

# SOFT CARAMELS

*Yield: 3 lb (1.5 kg)*

| Ingredients | U.S. | | Metric | | Sugar at 100% % |
|---|---|---|---|---|---|
| Heavy cream | 3 pt | | 1.5 | L | 200 |
| Granulated sugar | 1 lb 8 | oz | 750 | g | 100 |
| Glucose or corn syrup | 6.5 | oz | 200 | g | 27 |
| Salt | 0.15 | oz (¾ tsp) | 4 | g | 0.6 |
| Butter | 6.5 | oz | 200 | g | 27 |
| Vanilla extract | 0.5 | oz (1 tbsp) | 15 | mL | 2 |

## Procedure

1. Place a sheet of parchment on a marble slab or other work surface. Arrange oiled caramel rulers on the parchment in a rectangle about 12 × 16 inches (30 × 40 cm).

2. Combine the cream, sugar, and glucose in a heavy saucepan. Bring to a boil, stirring to dissolve the sugar.

3. Turn the heat to low and cook, stirring, until the mixture reaches 230°F (110°C).

4. Add the butter and vanilla. Continue to cook slowly, stirring constantly, until the mixture reaches 245°F (118°C).

5. Pour the mixture onto the prepared parchment. Allow to cool completely.

6. When completely cool, cut into 1-in. (2.5 cm) squares or other desired shape.

7. If desired, cooled caramels may be dipped in tempered chocolate (p. 647).

## VARIATION

### CHOCOLATE CARAMELS

Add 3.5 oz (100 g) melted, unsweetened chocolate after the butter has been stirred in.

### NUT CARAMELS

Before pouring out the cooked mixture onto the parchment, stir in 10 oz (300 g) finely chopped walnuts or pecans.

## ❧ CARAMEL TEXTURE ❧

Within a narrow range, the texture of soft caramels may vary from soft to fairly firm but still chewy. To test the texture as you are cooking, drop a small amount into a bowl of cold water and examine the texture of the cooled caramel. It should form a ball that is soft but firm enough to hold its shape. If it is too soft, cook the mixture a little longer. If it is too firm, stir a little water into the mixture and test again.

# CHOCOLATE FUDGE

*Yield: 2 lb 12 oz (1375 g) without walnuts*

| Ingredients | U.S. | | Metric | Sugar at 100% % | Procedure |
|---|---|---|---|---|---|
| Granulated sugar | 2 lb | | 1000 g | 100 | |
| Milk | 12 | oz | 375 g | 37.5 | |
| Glucose or corn syrup | 4 | oz | 125 g | 12.5 | |
| Butter | 4 | oz | 125 g | 12.5 | |
| Unsweetened chocolate, chopped fine | 5 | oz | 155 g | 15.5 | |
| Salt | 0.1 | oz (½ tsp) | 3 g | 0.3 | |
| Vanilla extract | 0.5 | oz (1 tbsp) | 15 g | 1.5 | |
| Walnuts, chopped (optional) | 6 | oz | 200 g | 20 | |

**Procedure**

1. Prepare a 9-inch (23-cm) square pan by lining it with aluminum foil.

2. Combine the sugar, milk, and glucose in a heavy saucepan. Bring to a boil, stirring constantly, until the sugar is dissolved. See page 260 for guidelines on cooking sugar syrups.

3. Continue to cook the mixture over moderate heat until the temperature reaches 230°F (110°C). Stir gently and slowly as the mixture cooks to prevent scorching on the bottom of the pan.

4. Add the butter and stir gently until it is blended in.

5. Add the chocolate, salt, and vanilla. Stir until the chocolate is melted and blended in.

6. Continue to boil, stirring very gently, until the mixture reaches 236°F (113°C).

7. Pour onto a marble slab. Let cool, *undisturbed*, until the temperature reaches 110°F (43°C).

8. When the fudge has reached the proper temperature, mix and stir it with a bench scraper or metal spatula until it thickens and becomes less shiny. If using nuts, add them at this time.

9. Quickly, while the mixure is still quite soft, transfer the fudge to the prepared sheet pan to cool completely.

10. When cool, cover tightly and let stand at room temperature overnight. This ripening period improves the texture.

11. Cut into squares of desired size.

## VARIATION

### VANILLA FUDGE

Omit the chocolate.

### BROWN SUGAR FUDGE

Use brown sugar instead of white sugar. The acidity of the sugar will curdle the milk during the first stages of cooking, but this will not harm the finished product.

### PEANUT BUTTER FUDGE

Omit the chocolate and instead add 25% (8 oz/250 g) peanut butter in step 5.

## TERMS FOR REVIEW

| | | |
|---|---|---|
| inversion | sugar cage | pulled sugar |
| spun sugar | poured sugar | blown sugar |

## QUESTIONS FOR DISCUSSION

1. When boiling sugar for pulled sugar, why is it important to boil it rapidly?

2. Describe the procedure for making spun sugar (assuming you have already boiled the syrup).

3. Explain the importance of the final cooking temperature when cooking a syrup for pulled sugar.

4. Discuss the effect of tartaric acid in the production of pulled sugar. Include in your discussion the time it is added and the total quantity used.

5. Describe the procedure for making a pulled-sugar ribbon using two alternating colors of sugar.

6. If pulled sugar is made in advance and stored, what must be done to make it workable?

## Chapter 27

# Baking for Special Diets

hat is "healthful" food? First, of course, the food must not do harm. In light of our increasing awareness of food allergies, some foods that are perfectly safe for some people are anything but healthful for those who are allergic to one or more of their ingredients. Second, to be healthful, a food must contribute to our well-being. It might be argued that even a rich dessert with no nutritional value but high in fat and sugar can contribute to our emotional well-being by being delicious and satisfying. Most pastry chefs would probably agree with that statement. However, what we usually mean when we say a food is healthful is that it is high in nutrients and low in calories from fat and sugar.

It is sometimes said that bakers are in the "fat business" because the products they make are high in fat. This is not completely true, or at best it is misleading. Many of the most important products of the bakeshop are low in fat or fat-free, from French breads to fruit compotes and meringues. Nevertheless, other products, such as pastries and cookies, are high in fat and low in nutrients other than calories. Pastry chefs are responding by trying to develop more healthful versions of popular items.

More importantly—because allergic reactions can be fatal—cooks, bakers, and pastry chefs must become aware of the problem of food allergies so they can produce foods that are both delicious and safe for their customers.

**After reading this chapter, you should be able to:**

1. Identify and describe nutritional concerns associated with baked goods and desserts.

2. Identify and describe allergy and food intolerance concerns associated with baked goods and desserts.

3. Identify the three ways to modify an ingredient in a baking formula to make the formula suitable for a specialized diet.

4. Using a knowledge of ingredient functions, describe how to reduce or eliminate fat, sugar, gluten, and dairy products in baking formulas.

693

# DIETARY CONCERNS

Diet and health are increasingly in the news. Rising obesity rates regularly are in the headlines. Increasing numbers of people suffer from food allergies. Health problems caused by diet are increasing the costs of medical care. Often, it seems, people are too afraid of food to enjoy it. At the same time, our love affair with restaurants and bakeries continues to grow. People want food they can enjoy and that is also healthful.

Dietary concerns can be divided into two broad areas: concerns about nutrition, and concerns about food allergies and intolerances.

Good nutrition means consuming a varied diet that includes all essential vitamins, minerals, protein, and other nutrients. At the same time, it means limiting our intake of foods that can be harmful in large quantities. Managing weight gain requires limiting calories, especially calories from fats and sugar. The term *empty calories* refers to foods that provide few nutrients per calorie. Foods of high *nutrient density* are those that have lots of nutrients per calorie. Fruits, vegetables, and whole grains are examples of foods with high nutrient density, while refined sugar and flour have low nutrient density.

For the customer, choosing nutritious foods is optional. Even people who usually choose nutritious foods can enjoy a rich pastry or choose a piece of white bread over whole grain. Enjoying limited sweets as part of a balanced diet provides enjoyment without necessarily having ill effects. For those with food allergies, however, choosing the right foods can be a matter of life or death. Allergic reactions can range from discomfort to severe illness and even death, so addressing these concerns is of great importance to all food service workers.

In this chapter, we approach nutrition concerns and allergies in separate discussions because they require somewhat different approaches to finding alternatives in the bakeshop. After the main dietary issues are explored, we examine ways to modify formulas for special needs. The chapter concludes with a selection of formulas that give examples of ways to satisfy special dietary needs.

Dietary baking is a large subject that encompasses many subtopics, such as gluten-free baking and baking with sugar substitutes. Many books have been written about each of these subtopics, so this chapter can only serve as an introduction that familiarizes you with the main issues and the general procedures for devising formulas suitable for restricted diets. Consult the bibliography on page 757 for a sample of books on the subtopics considered here.

# NUTRITION IN THE BAKESHOP

The role of the baker or pastry chef in preparing nutritious foods varies greatly, depending on the part of the industry in which he or she works. School, hospital, and nursing home food services must, of course, plan menus to meet basic nutritional needs. A qualified dietitian is usually required in such establishments. On the other hand, retail bakers and restaurant pastry chefs have a primary responsibility to prepare a variety of attractive and flavorful items that will sell. It is often good business to include more healthful preparations among the items for sale, but many customers will still choose white bread over whole grain or chocolate mousse over fruit compote.

Satisfying nutritional concerns has two aspects: providing desirable nutrients and avoiding undesirable nutrients. A **nutrient** is a substance that is essential for the functioning or growth of an organism. For this discussion, we divide nutrients into two categories:

1. Nutrients that provide energy: fats, carbohydrates, and proteins. (Note that proteins can be used by the body for energy, but their more important function is to provide the building blocks of all cells. See sidebar.)

2. Nutrients that are needed for metabolism, or basic body functioning, including all the chemical processes that take place within cells: vitamins, minerals, and water.

A healthful, balanced diet is one that includes all the nutrients in just the right amounts, not too much or too little of any of them. For many people, balancing the diet means consuming foods with more vitamins and minerals—the metabolism nutrients—and less fat and carbohydrates—the energy nutrients.

## Increasing Desirable Nutrients

In our culture, foods from the bakeshop form a relatively small part of the normal diet. Thus, we don't normally look to these foods—desserts, pastries, and breads—to give us more than a small part of our essential nutrients each day.

Nevertheless, bakers can take some steps to give customers the option of choosing items with more vitamins, minerals, and fiber (see sidebar). The most significant sources of valuable vitamins and minerals among bakeshop ingredients are whole grains, fruits, and nuts. Bakers have ways of incorporating these ingredients to give customers the option of choosing more nutritious breads and desserts. For example:

◆ Replace part of the white flour in doughs and batters with whole wheat flour. Replacing up to 2 ounces per pound (125 g per kg) usually has only

---

### ✵{ FIBER }✵

The term **fiber** refers to a group of complex carbohydrates that can't be absorbed and used by the body. Thus, fiber supplies no calories. However, fiber is important for the proper functioning of the intestinal tract and the elimination of body waste. In addition, there is evidence that sufficient dietary fiber helps prevent some kinds of cancers and helps decrease cholesterol in the blood. Fruits and vegetables, especially raw, and whole grains supply dietary fiber.

---

### ✵{ BASIC NUTRIENTS REVIEWED }✵

**Carbohydrates** are the body's most important sources of food energy. These compounds consist of long chains of carbon atoms with oxygen and hydrogen atoms attached to the sides. Starches and sugars are the most important dietary carbohydrates.

**Fats** supply energy to the body in highly concentrated form. Also, some fatty acids are necessary for regulating certain body functions. Third, fats act as carriers of fat-soluble vitamins.

**Proteins** are essential for growth, for building body tissue, and for basic body functions. They can also be used for energy if the diet doesn't contain enough carbohydrates and fats.

**Vitamins** are present in foods in extremely small quantities, but they are essential for regulating body functions. Unlike proteins, fats, and carbohydrates, they supply no energy, but some of them must be present in order for energy to be utilized in the body. Water-soluble vitamins (the B vitamins and vitamin C) are not stored in the body, so they must be eaten every day. Fat-soluble vitamins (A, D, E, and K) can be stored in the body, but the total amount eaten over time must be sufficient.

**Minerals**, like vitamins, are also consumed in small quantities and are essential for regulating certain body functions. Major minerals include calcium, chloride, magnesium, phosphorus, sulfur, sodium, and potassium. Trace minerals, eaten in even smaller amounts, include chromium, copper, iron, zinc, and iodine. Of all these, sodium, the major mineral in table salt, can contribute to high blood pressure if eaten in large quantities, as it often is.

**Water** supplies no energy, but the body can't function without it. The adult human body is 50 to 60 percent water by weight.

a small effect on dough formation. Replacing more than this can be done, but the bread or other product is likely to be heavier.

♦ Replace part of the white flour with whole-grain flour from another grain, such as oats, barley, amaranth, buckwheat, soy, or millet, or grain product such as wheat germ, wheat bran, or oat bran. For yeast breads, you may need to use a wheat flour with higher gluten to compensate for the lack of gluten in these other grains.

♦ Add a small amount of flaxseed meal to doughs to provide beneficial fiber and fatty acids.

♦ Use flaxseeds, rolled oats, sunflower seeds, and other grains and seeds as toppings for breads, rolls, and quick breads.

♦ Seek out more whole-grain and mixed-grain bread formulas. There are several in this book and many more available in bookstores, libraries, and online.

♦ Add ground nuts in small quantities to dough formulas, and add chopped nuts to muffins and pastries.

♦ Add raisins and other dried fruits to breads and other baked goods. (See, for example, the Fig Hazelnut Bread on p. 159.)

♦ Offer more desserts made with fruits, such as fruit compotes and fruit coulis.

# Reducing Undesirable Nutrients

The idea of reducing nutrients to be more nutritious may seem odd, but the fact is that many people consume far too many energy-producing nutrients in the form of fats, sugars, and starches. As a result, many people suffer from obesity, heart disease, diabetes, and other ailments related to diet. For the baker, this is a difficult problem to address because these components, especially starches, are the baker's stock in trade. For the consumer, one of the best ways to cut down on consumption of fats, starches, and sugars is simply to avoid breads and desserts, or at least reduce consumption of them. Nevertheless, the baker can take some measures to make choices easier for health-conscious consumers. To understand how to approach the problem, a short review of these energy nutrients and issues concerning them is needed.

## Calories and Weight Gain

The **calorie** (or, more correctly, the kilocalorie; see sidebar) is a unit of measurement of energy. It is defined as the amount of heat needed to raise the temperature of 1 kilogram of water by 1°C.

The calorie is used to measure how much certain foods supply for the energy the body needs to function. Carbohydrates, proteins, and fats can be used by the body to supply energy.

1 gram of carbohydrate supplies 4 calories

1 gram of protein supplies 4 calories

1 gram of fat supplies 9 calories

There is a direct connection between calorie intake, physical activity, and weight gain or loss. Simply put, if you consume more calories than you burn, you gain weight. If you consume fewer calories than you burn, you lose weight. All the diet schemes and fashions in the world—at least the ones that are medically sound—can be

---

### ⁂ CALORIES AND KILOCALORIES

In scientific terminology, the amount of heat needed to raise the temperature of 1 kilogram of water by 1°C is called a *kilocalorie*, sometimes written *Calorie* (with a capital *C*) and abbreviated *kcal*. When written with a small *c*, the term *calorie* refers to a unit of energy measurement that is only 1,000th as large—the amount of heat needed to raise the temperature of 1 *gram* of water by 1°C.

Nevertheless, in discussions of nutrition, the word *calorie* is commonly substituted for *kilocalorie*. Just remember that when you see *calorie* in connection with food, the real meaning is *Calorie* (or *kilocalorie*).

reduced to this. In other words, losing weight is possible only by eating fewer calories, burning more calories through exercise, or both.

## Fat

As the above list shows, fats are a concentrated form of energy, supplying more than twice as many calories per gram as do carbohydrates and proteins. This suggests that reducing fats in the diet is an effective dietary method of weight loss. Always keep in mind, however, that some fat is necessary in the diet, both for regulating certain body functions and for carrying fat-soluble vitamins.

Fats may be classified as saturated, monounsaturated, or polyunsaturated. **Saturated fats** are solid at room temperature. Animal products—eggs and dairy products as well as meats, poultry, and fish—and solid shortenings are the major source of saturated fats. Tropical oils such as coconut oil and palm kernel oil are also rich in saturated fats. Health experts believe these fats contribute significantly to heart disease and other health problems.

Polyunsaturated fats and monounsaturated fats are liquid at room temperature. Although consuming too much of any kind of fat is unhealthy, these fats are considered more healthful than saturated fats. **Polyunsaturated fats** are found in vegetable oils such as corn oil, safflower oil, sunflower oil, and cottonseed oil. High levels of **monounsaturated fats** are found in olive oil and canola oil. Recent research has suggested that monounsaturated fat may actually lower the levels of the most harmful kinds of cholesterol in the body. Both kinds of unsaturated fats are also found in other plant products as well, including whole grains, nuts, and some fruits and vegetables.

One group of saturated fats of special concern is **trans fats**. These fats occur only in small amounts in nature. Most of the trans fats in our diets are from manufactured fats subjected to a process called *hydrogenation*. Hydrogenated fats are fats that are changed from liquid to solid by adding hydrogen atoms to the fat molecules. This is the process used to make products such as solid shortening and margarine. Trans fats are of concern because they limit the body's ability to rid itself of cholesterol that builds up on the walls of arteries.

Fats are members of a group of compounds called **lipids**. Another lipid found in the body is **cholesterol**, a fatty substance that has been closely linked with heart disease because it collects on the walls of arteries and blocks the flow of blood to the heart and other vital organs. It is found only in animal products and is especially high in egg yolks, butterfat, and organ meats such as liver and brains. The human body can manufacture its own cholesterol, so not all the cholesterol in the blood is necessarily from foods. Although some cholesterol is necessary for body functions, it is not considered a nutrient because the body is able to manufacture all the cholesterol it needs. Experts generally agree it is best to keep the cholesterol in the diet as low as possible.

## Sugars and Starches

Sugars are simple carbohydrates. Simple sugars, such as glucose, are small compounds containing 6 carbon atoms. Table sugar, or sucrose, is a larger sugar molecule with 12 carbon atoms. Sugars are found in sweets and, to a lesser extent, in fruits and vegetables.

Starches are complex carbohydrates consisting of long chains of simple sugars bound together. They are found in such foods as grains, bread, peas and beans, and many vegetables and fruits.

Most authorities believe that complex carbohydrates, especially those from whole grains and unrefined foods, are better for you than simple carbohydrates. This is partly because starchy foods also have many other nutrients, while sweets have few other nutrients. Also, there is some evidence that a lot of sugar in the diet may contribute to heart and circulatory diseases. Simple sugars and refined starches are primary sources of empty calories.

Many consumers believe that honey, raw sugar, and some other sweeteners are more nutritious than refined white sugar. It is true that these products have some beneficial minerals and other nutrients, but only in tiny amounts. They are still mostly sugar. Substituting one of these for white sugar does not reduce the amount of carbohydrate in a formula.

### Sodium

As explained above, excess sodium in the diet has been linked to high blood pressure, so people with this ailment are generally advised to reduce their sodium intake. Salt is the primary source of sodium in the diet. Most of a person's salt intake, however, does not come from baked goods and desserts but rather from main courses, side dishes, and salty snacks. Some people are on salt-free diets, so reducing or eliminating salt in desserts and pastries may be advised for them and can be done with only a small effect on flavor. For most people, however, this change will have only a small effect on total sodium intake. Be careful, also, when reducing the salt content of yeast breads, as one of the functions of salt is to regulate yeast activity (see p. 94).

### Vegetarian Diets

A vegetarian diet is one consisting entirely or mostly of foods derived from plants. Reasons that people follow vegetarian diets may be based on concerns for nutrition and health or on ethical, moral, religious, or cultural beliefs.

There are several types of vegetarian diets. The **vegan** diet is the most restrictive. It includes plant products only. All animal products, including dairy and eggs, are off limits. **Lacto-vegetarians** eat dairy products in addition to plant products but will not eat other animal products. **Ovo-vegetarians** eat eggs in addition to plant products. **Lacto-ovo-vegetarians** eat dairy and egg products as well as plant products.

For the baker or pastry chef, the main ingredients of concern to vegetarians are the following:

Dairy products, including milk, cream, butter, and cheese must not be included in products intended for vegans. Lacto-vegetarians and lacto-ovo-vegetarians, on the other hand, will eat them.

Eggs must not be included in products intended for vegans, although they are permitted for ovo-vegetarians and lacto-ovo-vegetarians.

Honey should not be used in baked goods and desserts for vegans, because it is an animal product.

Refined sugar poses problems for vegans. Because some cane sugar is refined with the use of animal bone char, many vegans avoid all refined sugar to be on the safe side. If you can assure the customer that the sugar is made from sugar beets and not refined with bone char, some vegans may be willing to eat it. A safer approach is to substitute a product like date sugar or maple sugar. These products impart a distinctive flavor, however, and are also more expensive than refined white sugar. In addition, avoid using any prepared ingredient that contains sugar, because you can't be sure of the source of that sugar.

Gelatin is an animal product, so it must be avoided in vegetarian products. Agar-agar, a gelatin-like product made from seaweed, can be substituted (see p. 88).

## Allergens in the Bakeshop

An **allergen** is any substance that triggers an allergic reaction. Many foods, including many ingredients used in the bakeshop, are potential allergens. Health agencies report that more and more people are being diagnosed with food allergies each year, so this is a growing problem worldwide.

A food allergy is an abnormal response to a food triggered by the immune system. In other words, the body's immune system mistakenly believes a food item is harmful and reacts to protect the body. This reaction may include the production of chemicals that are actually harmful to the body, sometimes even fatal. A sudden, severe, allergic reaction of the immune system is called **anaphylaxis**.

The foods that most commonly spur allergic reactions are peanuts, tree nuts, eggs, fish, shellfish, milk, soybeans, and wheat. Note that, with the exception of fish and shellfish, all of these products may be found in the bakeshop. Wheat, milk, and eggs are among the baker's main ingredients.

A food allergy is not the same as a **food intolerance**. For example, a person may develop gas and bloating after eating a particular food, but this reaction does not involve the immune system. For example, people with lactose intolerance lack an enzyme that enables them to digest milk sugar, or lactose. These persons may develop gas and abdominal pain when they consume dairy products. For the purpose of this discussion, we treat allergies and intolerances together because they both involve foods that must be avoided by the affected customer.

In food service operations and retail bakeries, precautions must be taken both in the preparation of food and in service to customers. The following are just a few of the steps you should take.

> **Food Preparation.** Train staff to be aware of ingredients that can cause allergic reactions. Read the ingredient labels on all prepared food items used in the kitchen. Don't make casual or unannounced ingredient substitutions. Avoid cross-contamination; for example, a "safe" food could become dangerously allergenic if it is prepared on an inadequately cleaned prep table containing dust from peanuts used in prepping an earlier item. Ideally, keep a separate prep area for preparing foods for allergy sufferers.

> **Food Service.** Service and sales personnel should be aware of the ingredients in all menu items and should be prepared to answer questions about ingredients or to consult someone on staff who knows the answer. Be sensitive to customers' questions; if someone asks whether an ingredient is used, find out if that customer has an allergy. If a customer's questions cannot be answered with confidence, admit it and be prepared to suggest alternative choices.

Among bakeshop ingredients, nuts, gluten, dairy products, soy products, and eggs are the primary culprits for sufferers of food allergies and intolerances. To this list we add alcohol, which is not an allergen but which must be completely avoided by some people.

## Nuts

Peanuts and tree nuts—such as walnuts, almonds, brazil nuts, and pecans—are some of the most potent allergens and are responsible for many of the 150 to 200 deaths from food allergies each year in the United States. (*Note:* Peanuts are not true nuts but legumes, like peas and beans, so the allergies are somewhat different.) Even trace amounts, such as dust from peanuts left on a work surface, can trigger an allergic reaction. The only safe measure that can be taken is complete avoidance. It is not enough to leave the nuts out of a baked item or dessert. The surest way to guarantee a product is nut-free is to make it in a separate prep area with separate equipment that never is used for goods containing nuts.

Fortunately, nuts are not a critical ingredient for most baked goods. Most formulas do not call for nuts, and it is not difficult to eliminate them from those that do or to substitute similar preparations—for example, substitute a plain meringue disk for japonaise (p. 348), or use plain short dough instead of linzer dough (p. 320).

### Gluten

*Celiac disease* is a genetic (inherited) disorder in which the intestine is unable to process gluten proteins (see sidebar). Symptoms may be severe, and there is no cure. The only remedy is to avoid gluten completely.

The difficulty for the baker is that gluten is the backbone of breads and many other baked goods and is a component of wheat flour, the baker's main ingredient. In addition, gluten proteins are found in rye, barley, spelt, and oats.

Nevertheless, it is possible to bake a variety of products using gluten-free flours, such as rice, millet, buckwheat, amaranth, and quinoa flours, potato starch, cornstarch and cornmeal, and flours from chickpeas and other legumes. The structure-building properties of gluten proteins must be supplied by other ingredients, such as egg proteins and vegetable gums. These ingredients don't work the same way as gluten, however, so the texture of the products will differ. Doughs are less elastic, and baked items are likely to be more crumbly than similar items baked with wheat flour.

> ### ❋❳ CELIAC DISEASE ❲❋
>
> Celiac (pronounced see lee ak) is a disease of the immune system, like other food allergies. When gluten is ingested by someone with this disease, the gluten proteins damage the lining of the small intestine. As a result, the body is less able to absorb other nutrients. The disease has many symptoms, including anemia, fatigue, intestinal pain, and malnutrition. Because the symptoms are many and varied, it is difficult for doctors to diagnose. Only recently has the scope of the problem become recognized. There are still probably many people who suffer from the disease without knowing what it is.

## Lactose Intolerance and Milk Allergies

*Lactose*, also called *milk sugar*, is a form of simple sugar found in dairy products. Some people are unable to digest lactose, and drinking milk or eating products containing lactose results in intestinal discomfort, gas, bloating, and other symptoms. Because lactose is not an important component of baked goods, lactose-free milk and other lactose-free dairy products can easily be substituted in most formulas. Other milk replacers, such as soy milk, can also be used.

Milk allergies are immune reactions to milk proteins rather than to lactose. This allergy is fairly common in infants, but most children grow out of it. The allergy is uncommon in adults. Those who suffer from it must usually avoid all dairy products.

## Soy

Soy products contain at least fifteen proteins, and it is not clear if allergic reactions are caused by one or more of these proteins or by yet other components of soybeans. A great many prepared foods contain soy products, so it is necessary to read ingredient labels carefully. The emulsifier **lecithin** is used in many products, including chocolate, and may not be identified as derived from soybeans. However, soy products are not essential ingredients in most formulas, so avoiding them does not pose great problems, as long as bakers are attentive to ingredient labels.

## Eggs

Like milk allergy, egg allergy affects primarily infants and children, and most people outgrow it by the time they are about five years old. Nevertheless, it does affect some adults, who may react with stomach cramps, skin rashes, coughing and wheezing, or, in some cases, severe anaphylaxis (see above). The allergic reactions are triggered by one or more of the proteins in the egg. Some people are allergic to egg white proteins, while others have a reaction to the yolks.

Because many common egg substitutes are made with egg whites, these products can't be used as baking ingredients for allergy sufferers. *Eggless egg substitutes*, on the other hand, contain no egg products. They are made of flour or other starches, plus vegetable gums and stabilizers, and, sometimes, soy protein. They are intended for use in baked goods only—that is, in doughs and batters—and are not suitable for use in custards or breakfast egg preparations.

## Alcohol

Unlike the other food items discussed so far, alcohol is not an allergen, but it must be avoided by people suffering from the disease alcoholism. Trace quantities of alcohol are present in a number of products of the bakeshop or pastry department. Alcohol is a byproduct of yeast fermentation and so is present in freshly baked bread, but the amount is so small it doesn't generally pose a problem. After the bread cools and is stored, nearly all the alcohol evaporates. Similarly, small quantities of liqueurs may flavor dessert syrups used to moisten cakes, but the amount per portion is usually minute. Be prepared to advise customers, however, if a dessert contains significant amounts of alcohol. In some cases, merely the flavor of the alcoholic beverage, even if the alcohol has been burned away, can trigger an undesirable reaction.

# MODIFYING FORMULAS FOR SPECIAL NEEDS

The first part of this chapter focused on what ingredients or components of baking formulas and desserts may have to be modified for special diets, and why some customers may need or desire to avoid those ingredients. From this discussion, it can be seen that there is no single solution to dietary baking. For example, the discussion of increasing vitamins and minerals suggests adding nuts to baked goods to increase nutrients. However, the discussion of allergens indicates that nuts must be completely avoided by some customers. People with lactose intolerance may substitute soy milk for dairy milk as an ingredient, but that substitution makes the product unsuitable for people with soy allergy.

In other words, there are many approaches to baking for special needs, but each is directed at a specific problem. No one of them is suitable for every problem or every customer.

## Ingredient Functions

Whether you want to want modify an ingredient of a baking formula to reduce fat or calories or to eliminate an allergen, you must first understand the functions of that ingredient in the formula.

Three ways to modify an ingredient are to *eliminate* it, *reduce* it, or *substitute* another ingredient for it.

Eliminating an ingredient may be the best method if that ingredient does not have a major structural or flavor function in a formula. For example, eliminating the chopped nuts in a brownie or cookie formula does not affect the dough or batter, so this step can be done easily.

Reducing the amount of an ingredient may be successful, even if the reduction makes a slight change in the finished product. For example, some quick bread formulas are high in fat. Perhaps the fat can be reduced to make a more healthful product, one that is still appealing even if the texture is slightly drier.

Substituting other ingredients is the only option if the ingredient has a critical structural function in the baked item. Wheat flour is the main example. The gluten in wheat flour is important for the structure of many baked goods. Eliminating it would make the formula unworkable. The only option is to substitute other ingredients that can take on those structure-building functions.

The explanations of basic ingredients in chapter 4 include lists of the primary functions of the principal ingredients. Review these sections so the functions are fresh in your mind for the following discussion. In addition, reread the discussion on cake formula balance on pages 390–392. The basic principles explained there apply to all doughs and batters. Recall that:

- Tougheners or structure builders include flour and eggs.

- Tenderizers have the opposite function of structure builders. They include fats, sugars, and leaveners.

- Moisteners include water, liquid milk, syrups, and eggs.

- Dryers include flours, other starches, milk solids, and cocoa powder.

Apply the principle of formula balance when you are modifying a formula for dietary purposes. When an ingredient is eliminated or reduced, you must balance the formula by doing one or both of the following:

**1.** Replace the ingredient with another that performs the same functions. For example, when reducing fat, which is a tenderizer, add or increase other tenderizers, such as sugars.

**2.** Reduce the amount of ingredients that have the opposite effect. For example, if you are eliminating gluten, a toughener or structure builder, also reduce the tenderizers to maintain structure.

The following section applies these principles to ingredients bakers may want to eliminate or reduce for health or dietary reasons.

# Ingredient Substitutions

The following ingredients or components are those that may have to be reduced or omitted for dietary reasons. However, these components perform important functions in baking formulas. When one of them is reduced or eliminated, its functions must be performed by other ingredients.

## Fat

Modifying the fat content of a formula usually involves one of the following goals:

### Replacing Saturated Fats and Trans-Fats with More Healthful Unsaturated Fats.

Recall that saturated fats are solid at room temperature. Saturated fats include the most important fats in the bakeshop: butter, shortening, and margarine. Unsaturated fats are liquid oils.

Fats in doughs and batters function as tenderizers, and they improve the mouth feel of cakes and quick breads by giving the feel of moistness. When an oil is used in place of a solid fat, the oil still performs these tenderizing and moisturizing functions. In fact, because the oil doesn't solidify at room temperature, a muffin made with oil may seem even moister than one made with solid fat.

Another important function of solid fats is to form and retain air cells when creamed with sugar. Some creaming-method batters depend entirely on these air cells for leavening. Oils can not be creamed with sugar to form air cells. Therefore, oil can not be substituted for solid fats when creaming is essential to leavening. However, sometimes it is possible to substitute oil for *part* of the fat. When trying this substitution, make a test batch and compare the quality of the resulting product with the regular formula. In most cases, the best procedure is to cream the solid fat with the sugar and add the oil to the batter with other liquids.

To make up for lost leavening power, increase the baking powder, or fold in whipped egg whites.

Liquid fats work better when incorporated using the muffin method rather than the creaming method. Try reworking creaming-method formulas to convert them to the muffin method.

When the fat is butter, flavor is also an important contribution of fats. If butter is a primary flavor in the product, substituting other fats for butter is likely to decrease quality. The substitution works better for products with other dominant flavors, such as chocolate cake, spice cake, and many quick breads.

There is no substitute for solid fat in laminated doughs. The rolled-in fat in some formulas may be reduced slightly, but the resulting product may not rise as well or be as flaky.

Finally, remember that oil has as much fat and calories per gram as solid fat—even more, in the case of butter—so substituting oil for solid fat does not reduce total fat or calories. It reduces unhealthful saturated fats only.

## Reducing the Total Amount of Fat

Reducing the fat in a formula means reducing the total amount of tenderizers. To maintain the desired texture of the baked item, one must either substitute other tenderizers, reduce the tougheners, or both. The following techniques can be used when reducing total fat:

- Reducing tougheners:

    Use a softer flour. For example, substitute cake flour for pastry flour, or substitute pastry flour for part of the bread flour.

    Substitute whole-grain flours, especially of a gluten-free grain, for part of the wheat flour.

    Reduce the quantity of egg. You will probably have to increase other liquids to make up for the lost moisture of the egg.

    Avoid overmixing, which develops gluten.

    Avoid overbaking, which dries the product and also toughens protein.

- Increasing tenderizers in the formula or adding other tenderizers or moisteners in place of the fat:

    Increase sugars. Liquid sweeteners such as honey, molasses, corn syrup, and maple syrup are useful for this purpose.

    Add a fruit or vegetable purée. Many purées can substitute for fats to increase the tenderness and moistness of a baked item, such as applesauce, prune purée, date purée, squash or pumpkin purée, fruit jelly or jam, banana purée, and fruit juice concentrates. Select a flavor that blends well with the flavors of the baked item.

    Add a dairy fat substitute. Fat-free buttermilk, sour cream, and yogurt can be substituted for part of the fat. They increase moistness, and their acidity tenderizes the gluten. Unlike fruit or vegetable purées, they don't change the flavor significantly.

    Use reduced-fat margarine or butter. These products contain less fat and more water and milk protein than regular margarine and butter. They can be substituted in many quick breads and cakes.

Finally, remember that there are many low-fat desserts already in the baker's standard repertory. For example:

- Use a low-fat icing, such as fondant or boiled icing, instead of buttercreams on cakes.

- Use angel food or sponge cakes instead of high-fat creaming-method and high-ratio cakes.

- Use baked meringues instead of short doughs in pastries and tarts.

- Use fruit fillings instead of high-fat fillings such as frangipane and cream cheese.

## Sugar

In addition to adding sweetness and flavor, sugars perform the following functions in baked goods:

- They create tenderness and fineness of texture.

- They retain moisture, thus improving texture and keeping qualities.

- They act as creaming agents with fats to provide leavening.

- They give crust color because of their browning properties.

When sugar in a formula is reduced, these functions must be performed by other ingredients.

Some customers want to reduce or eliminate refined white sugar in their diets but have no objection to natural sugars like honey, even though they may have the same number of calories. Another granular sugar, such as date sugar or maple sugar, can be substituted for white sugar in equal weights without other changes to the formula. If a liquid sugar, such as honey, brown rice syrup, molasses, or maple syrup, the following adjustments to the formula may be necessary:

- Liquid sugars have no creaming ability, so other forms of leavening must be substituted. You may be able to mix the batter by the muffin method rather than the creaming method, providing the quantity of baking powder is increased.

- If a large quantity of liquid sugar is used, reduce the other liquids in the formula.

- Not all liquid sugars have the same sweetening power, so you may have to adjust quantities. Brown rice syrup, for example, is only 30 to 60 percent as sweet as white sugar, while honey is sweeter than white sugar.

*Sugar substitutes* are used when it is necessary to reduce the total quantity of sugar in a formula. Sugar substitutes are chemicals that have a sweet taste, usually much sweeter than sugar, but no or little nutritional value. Aspartame and saccharin are intensely sweet chemicals often used as beverage sweeteners, but they have little use in baking because they don't perform any of the functions of sugar listed above, other than providing sweetness. Also, aspartame is destroyed by heat, so it is of no use in baked goods. These sweeteners have aftertastes that are unpleasant to many people, and there are also questions about their safety.

**Sucralose** is the most useful sugar substitute in baked goods. It is sold under the brand name Splenda. Pure sucralose is 600 times sweeter than sugar. For baking, it is mixed with a bulking agent called *maltodextrin* so it has the same sweetening power and texture as an equal volume of sugar. This product is called *granular sucralose*. In pies, cookies, quick breads, dessert sauces, and custards, substitute an equal volume of granular sucralose for the sugar in the formula. (Granular sucralose has 96 calories per cup/240 mL, primarily from the bulking agents, while granulated sugar has 770 calories for the same volume.)

Granular sucralose, however, does not have good creaming abilities, it does not contribute to browning, it doesn't contribute to texture, and it does not improve keeping quality as sugar does. When these functions are important, the usual technique is to substitute granular sucralose for *half* of the sugar in the formula, thus reducing the number of calories from sugar by half. A so-called baker's blend, consisting of half granular sucralose mixed with half sugar, is available, but buying it is not as cost-effective as making the blend yourself.

Please note that, when you are substituting granular sucralose for sugar, you must substitute an equal *volume*, not an equal *weight*, because the granular sucralose is much lighter than sugar. One cup (240 mL) granular sucralose weighs about 25 grams, slightly less than 1 ounce.

When baking with sucralose, monitor the products carefully for doneness. You can't rely on the usual amount of crust browning as a doneness indicator because the product won't brown as well.

Sucralose

## Gluten

Perhaps the biggest challenge for a baker is making baked goods without gluten. Gluten is a component of wheat flour and is a major structural component of most baked goods.

Wheat flour supplies the bulk of most baked goods. This bulk-forming function can be duplicated by simply substituting other flours and starches for wheat flour. The structure-building functions of gluten proteins, however, are more difficult to duplicate (see pages 101–104 to review gluten formation and functions). Gluten-free baked goods must contain other ingredients that help build structure, or the item will be excessively crumbly, will not hold together, or will not rise. For some items, such as certain quick breads, egg protein can provide the necessary structure.

Vegetable gums, including pectin, are also used to provide necessary structure. Pectin is a component of fruit jellies, preserves, and purées. Adding these to gluten-free quick breads and other batters may improve the structure and texture. Powdered vegetable gums (see p. 88) can be used for the same purpose without adding the sweetness and flavor of fruit products. Xanthan gum is perhaps the most useful gum in gluten-free baking.

Some starches, such as cornstarch, can also partly compensate for an absence of gluten. Gelatinized cornstarch, for example, forms a firm gel that can improve the structure of some baked goods.

The following flours and starches can be used to make gluten-free baked goods. Usually a mixture of several performs better than any single one. Keep in mind that each of these absorbs a different quantity of water, so you will have to do some experimenting and adjusting of liquids when making substitutions in formulas.

Xanthan gum

Amaranth flour[*]

Arrowroot

Buckwheat flour

Chickpea (garbanzo) flour

Fava bean flour

Garfava flour (blend of garbanzo and fava flours)

Cornmeal

Corn flour (like cornmeal but finer in texture)

Cornstarch

Millet flour*

Nut flours (not suitable, obviously, for nut allergies)

Potato starch

Quinoa flour*

Rice flour

Sorghum flour

Soy flour

Tapioca flour and starch

*These items are sometimes contaminated with wheat during processing and shipping, so caution is necessary.*

Of the above ingredients, rice flour, potato starch, tapioca starch, and cornstarch are especially useful because they have relatively little flavor of their own and thus most closely approximate white wheat flour.

Commercial gluten-free mixes are available for various purposes. For example, one commercial pizza dough mix contains rice flour, potato starch, cornstarch, crystallized honey, guar gum, and salt.

The following grains and other ingredients contain gluten proteins and are *not* suitable for gluten-free diets:

Barley

Kamut

Malt (made from barley)

Oats

Puffed rice cereal (may be processed in a facility that also processes wheat)

Rye

Semolina

Spelt (farro)

Triticale

Wheat

Gluten-free items, even with structure-building ingredients added, always have a markedly different texture from similar items made with wheat flour. The strength and elasticity of gluten can't be duplicated by other ingredients. In general, gluten-free baked goods have a more crumbly or grainy texture.

## Dairy

Dairy ingredients in baking formulas are modified for either of two goals: to reduce the fat and calories from full-fat dairy products and to make the product lactose- and allergen-free.

In many formulas, full-fat milk can be replaced with low-fat or nonfat milk without significantly changing the characteristics of the finished product. If the fat from the milk is an important structural component of the baked item, you may have to compensate by making some of the adjustments discussed above in the section on fat. Low-fat and fat-free sour cream can be substituted for regular sour cream in some formulas, and fat-free yogurt often works in place of sour cream, as does whole-milk yogurt.

Lactose intolerance and milk allergies require a different approach, usually the complete elimination of all dairy ingredients. Recall that lactose, which some people can't digest, is a form of sugar present in milk. Milk allergies, on the other hand, involve the proteins in milk products. Many lactose-free dairy products, including fluid milk, are available and can be consumed by people who are lactose intolerant. Lactose-free, however, is not the same as dairy-free. People with milk allergies can not consume lactose-free milk.

Many types of milk substitutes are available. These can replace milk in most formulas to make the product suitable for anyone with a milk allergy or lactose intolerance. Soy milk is perhaps the most familiar, although this is of course not suitable for people with soy allergies. Other commercially available milk substitutes are made from rice, almonds, quinoa, potatoes, sesame seeds, and coconut. (Coconut milk, unlike the other products, is high in fat—17% or more.) Some of these are available in powdered as well as liquid form.

Dairy-free margarines can be substituted for butter in almost any formula. Read the label carefully, however, as many margarines contain milk protein. Margarines labeled *parve* or *pareve* are dairy-free.

## Eggs

Egg yolks contain fat and cholesterol, while egg whites are fat-free. If the goal is to reduce fat and cholesterol, use egg whites in place of an equal weight of whole eggs in doughs and batters when the egg is used as a binder.

When egg foams are used for leavening, egg-white foams can often be substituted for whole-egg foams. Of course when the eggs are also a main structural component of a baked item, using egg-white foams in place of whole eggs makes too great a change in the product. For example, if you substitute egg whites in a genoise sponge cake formula, the product will no longer be a genoise but something like an angel food cake.

For egg allergies, substituting egg whites is not acceptable. All egg product must be eliminated. Commercial baking egg substitutes (described on p. 700) containing starches and gums are designed to be used in place of eggs in doughs and batter.

Other starches, gums, and proteins can substitute for eggs to replace their binding power. Flaxseed meal is rich in gums and soluble fiber and is a useful egg replacement. To use, mix 1 tablespoon (15 mL) flaxseed meal with each 4 ounces (120 g) flour in the formula. Tapioca flour and arrowroot can be used in the same way. Alternatively, try substituting an equal weight of puréed tofu or puréed banana for the eggs in batter formulas. (Tofu, a soy product, can't be used for people with soy allergies.)

# FORMULAS

As writers, publishers, dieticians, and chefs have become aware of dietary issues related to baking and desserts, many specialized books have become available containing collections of recipes for all sorts of diets, from low-fat and sugar-free diets to gluten-free, lactose-free, and other allergen-free diets. A few of these books are listed in the bibliography on page 757. More recipes can be found online and at any bookstore.

The following recipes are examples of various techniques for solving dietary problems in the bakeshop. Included are gluten-free formulas, low-fat versions of high-fat baked goods, sugar-free formulas, and lactose-free formulas.

# LOW-FAT APPLE HONEY MUFFINS

| Ingredient | U.S. | | | Metric | % | Procedure |
|---|---|---|---|---|---|---|
| Whole wheat flour | | 12 | oz | 340 g | 75 | **MIXING** |
| Oat flour | | 4 | oz | 110 g | 25 | Muffin method (p. 220) |
| Baking powder | | 1 | oz | 30 g | 6 | 1. Sift together the flours, baking powder, and cardamom. |
| Cinnamon | | 0.1 | oz (1½ tsp) | 3 g | 0.6 | |
| Cardamom | | 0.03 | oz (½ tsp) | 1 g (2 mL) | 0.2 | 2. Mix together the applesauce, honey, and egg whites. |
| Applesauce, unsweetened | 1 lb | 4 | oz | 560 g | 125 | 3. Add the liquid ingredients to the dry ingredients and mix just until combined. |
| Honey | | 10 | oz | 280 g | 62.5 | |
| Egg whites, beaten | | 4 | oz | 110 g | 25 | 4. Mix in the raisins. |
| Raisins | | 6 | oz | 170 g | 38 | |
| **Total weight:** | **3 lb 9** | | **oz** | **1617 g** | **356%** | |

**PANNING**

Use paper muffin cups to line muffin pans, or spray the pan with a nonstick spray. Fill tins one-half to two-thirds full. Exact weight depends on pan size. Average sizes are 2 oz (60 g) for small muffins, 4 oz (110 g) for medium muffins, and 5–6 oz (140–170 g) for large muffins.

**BAKING**

375°F (190°C) for approximately 20 minutes, depending on size.

# LOW-FAT MULTIGRAIN BROWN BREAD

| Ingredient | U.S. | | Metric | | % | Procedure |
|---|---|---|---|---|---|---|
| Whole wheat flour | 7 | oz | 200 | g | 44 | **MIXING** |
| Cornmeal | 4 | oz | 110 | g | 25 | Muffin method (p. 220): |
| Rye flour | 3 | oz | 85 | g | 19 | 1. Sift together the flours, baking soda, and spices. |
| Oat flour | 2 | oz | 55 | g | 12 | |
| Baking soda | 0.7 | oz (4 tsp) | 18 | g | 4 | 2. Mix together the buttermilk, molasses, prune purée, and egg whites. |
| Ginger | 0.14 | oz (2 tsp) | 4 | g (10 mL) | 0.9 | |
| Nutmeg | 0.07 | oz (1 tsp) | 2 | g (5 mL) | 0.45 | 3. Stir the liquids into the dry ingredients just until combined. |
| Cinnamon | 0.06 | oz (1 tsp) | 1.8 | g (5 mL) | 0.4 | |
| Low-fat buttermilk | 1 | lb | 450 | g | 100 | **PANNING** |
| Molasses | 6 | oz | 170 | g | 38 | Spray the insides of 8½ × 4½ in. (22 × 11 cm) loaf pans with nonstick spray. Scale 1 lb 8 oz (700 g) batter per pan. |
| Prune purée (see *Note*) | 8 | oz | 225 | g | 50 | |
| Egg whites, lightly beaten | 3 | oz | 85 | g | 19 | **BAKING** |
| **Total weight:** | **3 lb 1** | **oz** | **1405** | **g** | **313%** | 375°F (190°C) about 50 minutes. |

Note: If prune purée is not available, soak pitted prunes in just enough warm water to cover, then purée the prunes and water in a food processor.

# LOW-FAT CHOCOLATE PIE

*Yield: one 9-inch (23 cm) pie*

| Ingredient | U.S. | | Metric | Procedure |
|---|---|---|---|---|
| Skim milk | 1 | pt | 500 mL | 1. Combine the first quantities of milk and sugar in a heavy saucepan. Heat to dissolve the sugar, and bring the liquid just to a boil. |
| Sugar | 2 | oz | 60 g | |
| Cornstarch | 2 | oz | 60 g | 2. Sift the cornstarch, sugar, and cocoa powder into a bowl. Gradually stir in the second quantity of (cold) milk, making a smooth, lump-free mixture. |
| Sugar | 2.5 | oz | 75 g | |
| Cocoa powder | 1 | oz | 30 g | 3. Gradually stir in the hot milk from step 1. |
| Skim milk | 8 | fl oz | 250 mL | |
| Vanilla extract | 0.25 fl oz (1½ tsp) | | 7 mL | 4. Return the mixture to the saucepan and set over moderate heat. Bring to a boil, stirring constantly. |
| 9-inch (23 cm) low-fat graham cracker pie shell (below) | 1 | | 1 | 5. When the mixture comes to a boil, remove it from the heat and set the pan in an ice-water bath. Stir constantly to cool the mixture to lukewarm. |

6. Stir in the vanilla.

7. Pour the mixture into the prepared pie shell.

8. Chill until cold and set.

## VARIATION

### LOW-FAT CHOCOLATE PUDDING

Reduce the cornstarch to 1.5 oz (45 g). Prepare as in basic recipe, omitting pie shell.

# LOW-FAT GRAHAM CRACKER PIE SHELL

*Yield: one 9-inch (23 cm) pie shell*

| Ingredient | U.S. | | Metric | Procedure |
|---|---|---|---|---|
| Graham cracker crumbs | 4.5 oz | | 125 g | 1. In a food processor or a mixer with the paddle attachment, mix together the crumbs and jam until evenly blended and crumbly. |
| Raspberry jam | 2 | oz | 55 g | 2. Spray the inside of a 9-in. (23 cm) pie tin with nonstick spray. |

3. Put the crumbs in the pie tin. Pack them evenly against the bottom and sides of the tin. The mixture is sticky, so you may want to use a disposable glove. Alternatively, use the back of a kitchen spoon and dip it in sugar as needed to keep the crumbs from sticking to it.)

4. Bake at 350°F (175°C) for 10 minutes.

5. Cool thoroughly before filling.

# NO-SUGAR-ADDED LEMON COOKIES

| Ingredient | U.S. | | Metric | | % | Procedure |
|---|---|---|---|---|---|---|
| Butter, soft | 8 | oz | 225 | g | 50 | |
| Sucralose, granular | 1.3 | oz (12 fl oz) | 36 | g | 8 | |
| Salt | 0.12 | oz (¾ tsp) | 3.5 | g | 0.8 | |
| Grated lemon zest | 0.5 | oz | 14 | g | 3 | |
| Eggs | 3 | oz | 85 | g | 19 | |
| Vanilla | 0.33 | oz (2 tsp) | 10 | g | 2.4 | |
| Pastry flour | 1 lb | | 450 | g | 100 | |
| Baking powder | 0.4 | oz (2½ tsp) | 11 | g | 2.5 | |
| *Total weight:* | *1 lb 13* | *oz* | *834* | *g* | *185%* | |

### MIXING

Creaming method:

1. Combine the butter, sucralose, salt, and zest in the bowl of a mixer fitted with the paddle attachment. Cream until light, scraping down the bowl as necessary to make sure all ingredients are evenly blended. (Note that the mixture will not cream as well as butter and sugar.)
2. Add the eggs a little at a time, and mix until each addition is completely absorbed before adding more.
3. Blend in the vanilla.
4. Sift together the flour and baking powder. Add to the mixing bowl and mix at low speed until evenly blended and smooth.

### MAKEUP

Icebox method: Divide the dough into approximately 8-oz (230 g) parts. Roll each into a cylinder 1 in (2.5 cm) thick. Wrap each tightly in plastic film and refrigerate for several hours or overnight. Slice ¼ in. (6 mm) thick. Bake on parchment-lined sheet pans.

### BAKING

350°F (160°C), about 10 minutes.

## VARIATION

### NO-SUGAR-ADDED CINNAMON COOKIES

Omit the lemon zest. Add 1% (0.16 oz or 4.5 g; about 1 tsp or 5 mL).

# REDUCED-SUGAR APPLE SPICE CAKE

| Ingredient | U.S. | | Metric | | % | Procedure |
|---|---|---|---|---|---|---|
| Pastry flour | 1 lb | | 500 | g | 100 | **MIXING** |
| Sucralose, granular | | 1.25 oz | 40 | g | 8 | Muffin method: |
| Baking soda | | 0.5 oz | 15 | g | 3 | 1. Sift together the dry ingredients. |
| Baking powder | | 0.16 oz (1 tsp) | 5 | g | 1 | 2. Mix together the applesauce, molasses, oil, and eggs until well blended. |
| Salt | | 0.16 oz (¾ tsp) | 5 | g | 1 | |
| Cinnamon | | 0.08 oz (1½ tsp) | 2.5 | g | 0.5 | 3. Add the dry ingredients to the liquids and mix just until smooth. |
| Ginger | | 0.05 oz (¾ tsp) | 1.5 | g | 0.3 | |
| Ground cloves | | 0.05 oz (¾ tsp) | 1.5 | g | 0.3 | **SCALING AND BAKING** |
| Nutmeg | | 0.03 oz (⅜ tsp) | 1 | g | 0.2 | Refer to the weights for high-fat cakes in the table on p. 394. When a weight range is given, use the lower end of the range. Use the temperatures indicated in the table. |
| Applesauce, unsweetened | 1 lb | 4 oz | 625 | g | 125 | |
| Molasses | | 11.5 oz | 360 | g | 72 | |
| Vegetable oil | | 3 oz | 95 | g | 19 | |
| Eggs, beaten (or liquid egg substitute) | | 6 oz | 190 | g | 38 | |
| **Total weight:** | **3 lb 10** | **oz** | **1841** | **g** | **368%** | |

*Note: This formula is called "reduced-sugar" rather than "no-sugar-added" because of the sugar content of the molasses. No other sugar is added.*

# GLUTEN-FREE YELLOW CHIFFON CAKE

| Ingredient | U.S. | | Metric | | % | Procedure |
|---|---|---|---|---|---|---|
| Rice flour | 5 | oz | 125 | g | 50 | **MIXING** |
| Potato starch | 3 | oz | 75 | g | 30 | Chiffon method: |
| Tapioca flour | 2 | oz | 50 | g | 20 | 1. Sift together the flours, sugar, salt, xanthan gum, and baking powder into the bowl of a mixer fitted with the paddle attachment. |
| Sugar | 8 | oz | 200 | g | 80 | |
| Salt | 0.25 | oz | 6 | g | 2.5 | |
| Xanthan gum | 0.05 | oz (½ tsp) | 1.25 | g | 0.5 | 2. With the mixer running at second speed, gradually add the oil and then the egg yolks, water, and vanilla. Stop the machine several times during these additions to scrape down the bowl and mixer. |
| Baking powder | 0.5 | oz | 12 | g | 5 | |
| Vegetable oil | 5 | oz | 125 | g | 50 | |
| Egg yolks | 5 | oz | 125 | g | 50 | |
| Water | 7.5 | oz | 188 | g | 75 | |
| Vanilla extract | 0.25 | oz | 6 | g | 2.5 | 3. Whip the egg whites until they form soft peaks. Add the sugar and cream of tartar in a stream and whip to firm, moist peaks. |
| Egg whites | 10 | oz | 250 | g | 100 | |
| Sugar | 5 | oz | 125 | g | 50 | 4. Fold the egg whites into the flour-liquid mixture. |
| Cream of tartar | 0.05 | oz (⅝ tsp) | 1 | g | 0.5 | |
| **Total weight:** | **3 lb 3** | **oz** | **1288** | **g** | **515%** | |

**SCALING AND BAKING**

See the table on p. 394.

*Note: This formula is adapted from the formula on p. 406.*

# GLUTEN-FREE YEAST BREAD

| Ingredient | U.S. | | Metric | % |
|---|---|---|---|---|
| Rice flour | 1 lb | | 500 g | 67 |
| Potato starch | 3 | oz | 95 g | 12.5 |
| Cornstarch | 2 | oz | 60 g | 8 |
| Tapioca flour | 3 | oz | 95 g | 12.5 |
| Sugar | 1 | oz | 30 g | 4 |
| Nonfat milk solids (or powdered milk replacer) | 2.5 | oz | 75 g | 10 |
| Xanthan gum | 0.5 | oz (5 tsp) | 15 g | 2 |
| Salt | 0.5 | oz | 15 g | 2 |
| Instant yeast | 0.5 | oz | 15 g | 2 |
| Butter or margarine, melted | 2 | oz | 60 g | 8 |
| Water, warm | 1 lb 12 | oz | 875 g | 117 |
| Distilled (white) vinegar | 0.33 | oz (2 tsp) | 10 g | 1.4 |
| Egg whites, lightly beaten | 6 | oz | 190 g | 25 |
| *Total weight:* | *4 lb 1* | *oz* | *2035 g* | *271%* |

### Procedure

**MIXING**

1. Sift all the dry ingredients (a) into the bowl of a mixer fitted with the paddle attachment. Mix on low speed until the ingredients are uniformly blended.

2. With the machine running on low speed, slowly add the melted butter (b), water (c), and vinegar. Blend the ingredients together.

3. Add the egg whites. Turn the machine to high speed and mix for 3 minutes. Note that the mixture forms a batter, not a dough (d).

**PANNING, PROOFING, AND BAKING**

Note that this batter does not have a fermentation period like regular yeast doughs.

1. Grease loaf pans and dust with rice flour.

2. Fill pans half full of the batter.

3. Proof until double in bulk.

4. Bake at 400°F (200°C) for about 50 minutes, depending on the size of the loaves.

# GLUTEN-FREE CHOCOLATE CHIP COOKIES

| Ingredient | U.S. | | Metric | | % | Procedure |
|---|---|---|---|---|---|---|
| Butter or margarine | 5 | oz | 150 | g | 50 | **MIXING** |
| Granulated sugar | 4 | oz | 120 | g | 40 | Creaming method: |
| Brown sugar | 4 | oz | 120 | g | 40 | 1. Cream together the butter, sugars, and salt until light. |
| Salt | 0.12 | oz | 4 | g | 1.25 | |
| Eggs | 3 | oz | 90 | g | 30 | 2. Add the eggs a little at a time, waiting before each addition is absorbed before adding the next. |
| Vanilla extract | 0.16 oz (1 tsp) | | 5 | g | 1.6 | |
| Cornstarch | 3.5 | oz | 105 | g | 35 | 3. Add the vanilla. |
| Tapioca flour | 3.5 | oz | 105 | g | 35 | 4. Sift or mix together the dry ingredients and blend them into the creamed mixture. |
| Chickpea (garbanzo) flour | 2 | oz | 60 | g | 20 | |
| Rice flour | 1 | oz | 30 | g | 10 | 5. Stir in the chocolate chips. |
| Baking soda | 0.12 oz (¾ tsp) | | 4 | g | 1.25 | **MAKEUP** |
| Xanthan gum | 0.05 oz (½ tsp) | | 1.5 | g | 0.5 | Drop method: Drop ¾ oz (22 g) portions onto parchment-lined sheet pans. |
| Chocolate chips | 7 | oz | 210 | g | 70 | |
| **Total weight:** | **2 lb 1** | **oz** | **1004** | **g** | **334%** | **BAKING** |
| | | | | | | Bake at 350°F (175°C) about 12 minutes. |

*Note: This formula is adapted from the formula on p. 493.*

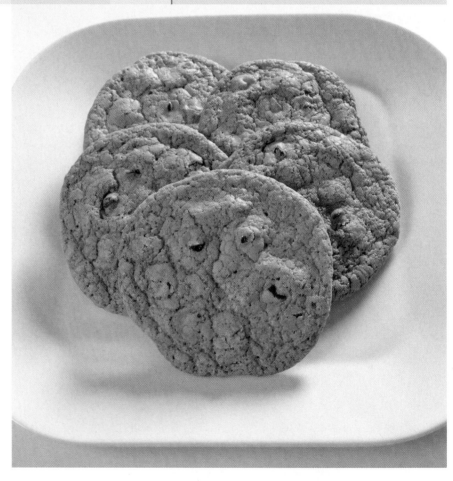

# GLUTEN-FREE BROWNIES

| Ingredient | U.S. | | Metric | % | Procedure |
|---|---|---|---|---|---|
| Unsweetened chocolate | 12 | oz | 338 g | 75 | **MIXING** |
| Butter | 1 lb 8 | oz | 675 g | 150 | 1. Melt the chocolate and butter together in a double boiler. Let the mixture cool to room temperature. |
| Eggs | 1 lb 3 | oz | 525 g | 117 | 2. Mix the eggs, sugar, salt, and vanilla together until well blended, but do not whip to a foam. |
| Sugar | 2 lb 5 | oz | 1050 g | 233 | |
| Salt | 0.25 | oz | 7 g | 1.5 | |
| Vanilla extract | 1 | oz | 30 g | 6 | 3. Blend in the chocolate mixture. |
| Rice flour | 10 | oz | 284 g | 63 | 4. Sift together the dry ingredients. Fold them into the chocolate mixture. |
| Potato starch | 4 | oz | 112 g | 25 | |
| Tapioca flour | 2 | oz | 54 g | 12 | 5. Fold in the nuts, if desired. Leave them out, of course, if nut allergies are a concern. |
| Xanthan gum | 0.25 | oz | 7 g | 1.5 | |
| Chopped walnuts or pecans (*optional*) | 12 | oz | 338 g | 75 | |
| **Total weight** | **7 lb 9** | **oz** | **3420 g** | **759%** | |

**PANNING**

Grease sheet pans or other baking pans and dust them with rice flour. Pour the batter into the pans. One recipe is enough for one full-size sheet pan, two half-sheet pans, four 9 × 13-in. (23 × 33 cm) pans, or six 9-in. (23 cm) or 8-in. (20 cm) square pans.

**BAKING**

325°F (165°C) for 45–50 minutes.

# LACTOSE-FREE CRÈME CARAMEL

*Yield: 12 portions, 5 oz (150 g) each*

| Ingredient | U.S. | | Metric | | Procedure |
|---|---|---|---|---|---|
| Sugar | 12 | oz | 375 | g | 1. Cook the first quantity of sugar with the water until it caramelizes. (See the section on sugar cooking on p. 260.) |
| Water | 2 | fl oz | 60 | mL | |
| Eggs | 1 lb | | 500 | g | 2. Line the bottoms of twelve 6-oz (180 mL) custard ramekins with the hot caramel. (Be sure the cups are clean and dry before adding the caramel.) Let cool. |
| Sugar | 8 | oz | 250 | g | |
| Salt | ½ | tsp | 2.5 | g | 3. Combine the eggs, sugar, salt, and vanilla in a mixing bowl. Mix thoroughly but do not whip. |
| Vanilla extract | 1 | tbsp | 15 | mL | |
| Soy milk (see *Note*) | 2½ pt | | 1250 | mL | 4. Scald the soy milk in a double boiler or in a saucepan over low heat. |

*Note: For soy allergies, use another of the milk substitutes listed on p. 707 in place of the soy milk.*

5. Gradually pour the milk into the egg mixture, stirring constantly.

6. Skim off all foam from the surface of the liquid.

7. Arrange the caramel-lined custard ramekins in a shallow baking pan.

8. Carefully pour the custard mixture into the ramekins.

9. Set the baking pan on the oven shelf. Pour enough hot water into the pan around the cups so the level of the water is about as high as the level of the custard mixture.

10. Bake at 325°F (165°C) until set, about 45 minutes.

11. Carefully remove the custard from the oven and cool. Cover and refrigerate at least 12 hours to allow the caramel time to partly dissolve and form a sauce.

12. Before serving, carefully unmold onto a serving dish.

# LACTOSE-FREE MANGO COCONUT ICE CREAM

*Yield: about 3 qt (3 L), depending on overrun*

| Ingredient | U.S. | | Metric | | Procedure |
|---|---|---|---|---|---|
| Egg yolks | 4 oz (6 yolks) | | 125 g (6 yolks) | | 1. Combine the egg yolk, sugar, and first quantity of coconut milk in a bowl. Whip until smooth and evenly mixed. |
| Sugar | 12 | oz | 375 | g | 2. Scald the remaining coconut milk and gradually beat it into the egg mixture. |
| Coconut milk | 8 | fl oz | 250 | mL | |
| Coconut milk | 2 pt 8 | fl oz | 1250 | mL | 3. Heat in a hot-water bath or a double boiler, stirring constantly, until the mixture thickens enough to coat the back of a spoon. Immediately remove from the heat and set in an ice-water bath to stop the cooking. (See p. 268 for guidelines on preparing crème anglaise.) |
| Mango purée | 1 lb 8 | oz | 750 | g | |
| Lime juice | 3 | fl oz | 90 | mL | |
| Sugar | 3 | oz | 90 | g | |

4. Chill the mixture thoroughly. Refrigerate overnight.

5. Mix the mango purée, lime juice, and sugar until evenly blended. Chill for several hours or overnight.

6. Combine the custard mixture and the mango purée. Freeze in an ice cream freezer.

# TERMS FOR REVIEW

| | | | |
|---|---|---|---|
| empty calorie | mineral | lipid | anaphylaxis |
| nutrient density | fiber | cholesterol | food intolerance |
| nutrient | calorie | vegan | celiac disease |
| carbohydrate | saturated fat | lacto-vegetarian | lactose |
| fat | polyunsaturated fat | ovo-vegetarian | lecithin |
| protein | monounsaturated fat | lacto-ovo-vegetarian | sucralose |
| vitamin | trans fat | allergen | |

# QUESTIONS FOR DISCUSSION

1. Describe five ways to increase the vitamin, mineral, and fiber content of yeast breads.

2. True or false: Replacing the sugar in a muffin formula with honey makes the muffins more nutritious. Explain your answer.

3. A guest at a catered banquet tells the waiter she is allergic to nuts and can't eat the cake that is being served for dessert, a white cake with chocolate icing decorated with walnut halves. The waiter removes the nuts from the cake and serves it to the customer. Is this the proper response? Explain your answer.

4. Which of the following ingredients can be used to make cookies for people with celiac disease: barley flour, rye flour, whole wheat flour, spelt flour, oat flour?

5. Name and describe the three basic ways to modify an ingredient or ingredient quantity in a formula in order to make the formula suitable for special dietary needs.

6. Explain why it is important to understand the function of an ingredient in a baking formula when you want to eliminate that ingredient for customers who are allergic to it.

7. Why is it especially important to avoid overmixing if you reduce the butter content of a muffin formula?

# Large-Quantity Measurements

## HARD ROLLS (P. 143)

| Ingredients | U.S. | Metric |
|---|---|---|
| Water | 3 lb 4 oz | 1480 g |
| Yeast, fresh | 3 oz | 90 g |
| Bread flour | 5 lb 8 oz | 2500 g |
| Salt | 2 oz | 55 g |
| Sugar | 2 oz | 55 g |
| Shortening | 2 oz | 55 g |
| Egg whites | 2 oz | 55 g |
| **Total weight:** | **9 lb 7 oz** | **4290 g** |

## VIENNA BREAD (P. 143)

| Ingredients | U.S. | Metric |
|---|---|---|
| Water | 3 lb 4 oz | 1480 g |
| Yeast, fresh | 3 oz | 90 g |
| Bread flour | 5 lb 8 oz | 2500 g |
| Salt | 2 oz | 55 g |
| Sugar | 2.5 oz | 75 g |
| Malt syrup | 1 oz | 25 g |
| Oil | 2.5 oz | 75 g |
| Eggs | 3.5 oz | 100 g |
| **Total weight:** | **9 lb 10 oz** | **4400 g** |

## ITALIAN BREAD (P. 144)

| Ingredients | U.S. | Metric |
|---|---|---|
| Water | 4 lb 4 oz | 1840 g |
| Yeast, fresh | 3 oz | 80 g |
| Bread flour | 7 lb | 3000 g |
| Salt | 2 oz | 60 g |
| Malt syrup | 0.5 oz | 15 g |
| **Total weight:** | **11 lb 9 oz** | **4995 g** |

### VARIATION

#### WHOLE WHEAT ITALIAN BREAD

*Use the following proportions of flour in the above formula.*

| Ingredients | U.S. | Metric |
|---|---|---|
| Whole wheat flour | 3 lb | 1300 g |
| Bread flour | 4 lb | 1700 g |

Increase the water to 63–65% to allow for the extra absorption by the bran. Mix 8 minutes.

## BAGUETTE (P. 146)

| Ingredients | U.S. | Metric |
|---|---|---|
| Bread flour | 6 lb 6 oz | 3000 g |
| Salt | 2 oz | 60 g |
| Yeast, fresh | 2.25 oz | 75 g |
| Water | 3 lb 12 oz | 1800 g |
| **Total weight:** | **10 lb 6 oz** | **4935 g** |

## FRENCH BREAD (STRAIGHT DOUGH) (P. 145)

| Ingredients | U.S. | | Metric |
|---|---|---|---|
| Water | 4 lb 4 | oz | 1840 g |
| Yeast, fresh | 3 | oz | 80 g |
| Bread flour | 7 lb | | 3000 g |
| Salt | 2 | oz | 60 g |
| Malt syrup | 0.5 | oz | 15 g |
| Sugar | 2 | oz | 50 g |
| Shortening | 2 | oz | 50 g |
| **Total weight:** | **11 lb 13** | **oz** | **5095 g** |

### VARIATION

#### WHOLE WHEAT FRENCH BREAD
*Use the following proportions of flour in the above formula.*

| Ingredients | U.S. | Metric |
|---|---|---|
| Whole wheat flour | 3 lb | 1300 g |
| Bread flour | 4 lb | 1700 g |

Increase the water to 63–64% to allow for the extra absorption by the bran. Mix 8 minutes.

## FRENCH BREAD (SPONGE) (P. 145)

| Ingredients | U.S. | | Metric |
|---|---|---|---|
| **Sponge** | | | |
| Bread flour | 2 lb | | 1000 g |
| Water | 2 lb | | 1000 g |
| Yeast, fresh | 2 | oz | 60 g |
| Malt syrup | 1 | oz | 30 g |
| **Dough** | | | |
| Bread flour | 4 lb | | 2000 g |
| Water | 1 lb 10 | oz | 810 g |
| Salt | 1.75 oz | | 52 g |
| **Total weight:** | **9 lb 14** | **oz** | **4952 g** |

### VARIATION

#### COUNTRY-STYLE FRENCH BREAD
*Use the following proportions of flour and water in the dough stage of the above formula.*

| Ingredients | U.S. | Metric |
|---|---|---|
| Clear or bread flour | 1 lb 8 oz | 740 g |
| Whole wheat flour | 2 lb 8 oz | 1260 g |
| Water | 1 lb 13 oz | 900 g |

Make up the dough into round loaves.

## CUBAN BREAD (P. 146)

| Ingredients | U.S. | Metric |
|---|---|---|
| Water | 3 lb 12 oz | 1860 g |
| Yeast, fresh | 4 oz | 120 g |
| Bread flour | 6 lb | 3000 g |
| Salt | 2 oz | 60 g |
| Sugar | 4 oz | 120 g |
| **Total weight:** | **10 lb 6 oz** | **5160 g** |

## CIABATTA (P. 147)

| Ingredients | U.S. | Metric |
|---|---|---|
| **Sponge** | | |
| Water | 4 lb 4 oz | 1920 g |
| Yeast, fresh | 4 oz | 120 g |
| Bread flour | 4 lb | 1800 g |
| Virgin olive oil | 1 lb 8 oz | 720 g |
| **Dough** | | |
| Salt | 2 oz | 60 g |
| Bread flour | 2 lb | 880 g |
| **Total weight:** | **12 lb 2 oz** | **5550 g** |

## WHITE PAN BREAD (P. 148)

| Ingredients | U.S. | Metric |
|---|---|---|
| Water | 3 lb | 1200 g |
| Yeast, fresh | 3 oz | 75 g |
| Bread flour | 5 lb | 2000 g |
| Salt | 2 oz | 50 g |
| Sugar | 3 oz | 75 g |
| Nonfat milk solids | 4 oz | 100 g |
| Shortening | 3 oz | 75 g |
| **Total weight:** | **8 lb 15 oz** | **3575 g** |

### VARIATION

#### WHOLE WHEAT BREAD
*Use the following proportions of flour in the above formula.*

| Ingredients | U.S. | Metric |
|---|---|---|
| Bread flour | 2 lb | 800 g |
| Whole wheat flour | 3 lb | 1200 g |

## WHITE PAN BREAD (SPONGE) (P. 148)

| Ingredients | U.S. | Metric |
|---|---|---|
| **Sponge** | | |
| Flour | 4 lb | 2000 g |
| Water | 2 lb 12 oz | 1350 g |
| Yeast, fresh | 2.5 oz | 75 g |
| Malt syrup | 0.5 oz | 15 g |
| **Dough** | | |
| Flour | 2 lb | 1000 g |
| Water | 14 oz | 450 g |
| Salt | 2 oz | 60 g |
| Nonfat milk solids | 3 oz | 90 g |
| Sugar | 5 oz | 150 g |
| Shortening | 3 oz | 90 g |
| **Total weight:** | **10 lb 10 oz** | **5280 g** |

## 100% WHOLE WHEAT BREAD (P. 149)

| Ingredients | U.S. | Metric |
|---|---|---|
| Water | 4 lb 8 oz | 2070 g |
| Yeast, fresh | 3 oz | 90 g |
| Whole wheat flour | 6 lb 8 oz | 3000 g |
| Sugar | 2 oz | 60 g |
| Malt syrup | 2 oz | 60 g |
| Nonfat milk solids | 3 oz | 90 g |
| Shortening | 4 oz | 120 g |
| Salt | 2 oz | 60 g |
| **Total weight:** | **12 lb** | **5550 g** |

## SOFT ROLLS (P. 149)

| Ingredients | U.S. | Metric |
|---|---|---|
| Water | 3 lb 2 oz | 1500 g |
| Yeast, fresh | 3 oz | 90 g |
| Bread flour | 5 lb 4 oz | 2500 g |
| Salt | 1.5 oz | 50 g |
| Sugar | 8 oz | 240 g |
| Nonfat milk solids | 4 oz | 120 g |
| Shortening | 4 oz | 120 g |
| Butter | 4 oz | 120 g |
| **Total weight:** | **9 lb 14 oz** | **4740 g** |

## CHALLAH (P. 150)

| Ingredients | U.S. | Metric |
|---|---|---|
| Water | 2 lb | 800 g |
| Yeast, fresh | 3 oz | 80 g |
| Bread flour | 5 lb | 2000 g |
| Egg yolks | 1 lb | 400 g |
| Sugar | 6 oz | 150 g |
| Malt syrup | 0.5 oz | 10 g |
| Salt | 1.5 oz | 38 g |
| Vegetable oil | 8 oz | 250 g |
| **Total weight:** | **9 lb 3 oz** | **3728 g** |

## EGG BREAD AND ROLLS (P. 149)

| Ingredients | U.S. | Metric |
|---|---|---|
| Water | 2 lb 10 oz | 1250 g |
| Yeast, fresh | 3 oz | 90 g |
| Bread flour | 5 lb 4 oz | 2500 g |
| Salt | 1.5 oz | 50 g |
| Sugar | 8 oz | 240 g |
| Nonfat milk solids | 4 oz | 120 g |
| Shortening | 4 oz | 120 g |
| Butter | 4 oz | 120 g |
| Eggs | 8 oz | 240 g |
| **Total weight:** | **9 lb 14 oz** | **4730 g** |

## MILK BREAD (PAIN AU LAIT) (P. 150)

| Ingredients | U.S. | Metric |
|---|---|---|
| Bread flour | 6 lb 12 oz | 3000 g |
| Sugar | 10 oz | 300 g |
| Salt | 2.25 oz | 60 g |
| Yeast, fresh | 3 oz | 90 g |
| Eggs | 10 oz | 300 g |
| Milk | 3 lb 6 oz | 1500 g |
| Butter or margarine | 15 oz | 450 g |
| Malt syrup | 1 oz | 30 g |
| **Total weight:** | **12 lb 11 oz** | **5730 g** |

## LIGHT AMERICAN RYE BREAD AND ROLLS (P. 151)

| Ingredients | U.S. | | Metric |
|---|---|---|---|
| Water | 3 lb | | 1400 g |
| Yeast, fresh | | 3 oz | 90 g |
| Light rye flour | 2 lb | | 1000 g |
| Bread flour or clear flour | 3 lb | | 1400 g |
| Salt | | 1.5 oz | 45 g |
| Shortening | | 2 oz | 60 g |
| Molasses or malt syrup | | 2 oz | 60 g |
| Caraway seeds (optional) | | 1 oz | 30 g |
| Rye flavor | | 1 oz | 30 g |
| **Total weight:** | **8 lb 10 oz** | | **4115 g** |

## ONION RYE (P. 151)

| Ingredients | U.S. | | Metric |
|---|---|---|---|
| Water | 3 lb | | 1200 g |
| Yeast, fresh | | 3 oz | 75 g |
| Light rye flour | 1 lb 12 oz | | 700 g |
| Clear flour | 3 lb 4 oz | | 1300 g |
| Dried onions, scaled, soaked in water, and well drained | | 4 oz | 100 g |
| Salt | | 1.5 oz | 40 g |
| Caraway seeds | | 1 oz | 25 g |
| Rye flavor | | 1 oz | 25 g |
| Malt syrup | | 2 oz | 50 g |
| **Total weight:** | **8 lb 12 oz** | | **3515 g** |

### VARIATION

#### ONION PUMPERNICKEL (NONSOUR)
*Use the following proportions of flour in the above formula.*

| Ingredients | U.S. | Metric |
|---|---|---|
| Rye meal (pumpernickel flour) | 1 lb | 400 g |
| Medium rye flour | 12 oz | 300 g |
| Clear flour | 3 lb 4 oz | 1300 g |

Dough may be colored with caramel color or cocoa powder.

## BASIC YEAST STARTER (BIGA) (P. 153)

| Ingredients | U.S. | | Metric |
|---|---|---|---|
| Bread flour | 3 lb 12 oz | | 1800 g |
| Water | 2 lb 4 oz | | 1080 g |
| Yeast, fresh | | 0.12 oz | 4 g |
| Salt | | 1.2 oz | 36 g |
| **Total weight:** | **6 lb 1 oz** | | **2920 g** |

## RYE STARTER I (P. 154)

| Ingredients | U.S. | | Metric |
|---|---|---|---|
| Rye flour | 5 lb | | 2000 g |
| Water | 3 lb 12 oz | | 1500 g |
| Yeast, fresh | | 0.8 oz | 20 g |
| Onion, halved (optional) | 1 | | 1 |
| **Total weight:** | **8 lb 12 oz** | | **3500 g** |

## RYE STARTER III (P. 154)

| Ingredients | U.S. | | Metric |
|---|---|---|---|
| Rye flour | 4 lb | | 2000 g |
| Water, warm (85°–90°F or 30°–35°C) | 4 lb | | 2000 g |
| Yeast, fresh | | 1 oz | 30 g |
| **Total weight:** | **8 lb** | | **4030 g** |

## OLD-FASHIONED RYE BREAD (P. 157)

| Ingredients | U.S. | | Metric |
|---|---|---|---|
| Water | 3 lb | | 1200 g |
| Yeast, fresh | | 1 oz | 25 g |
| Fermented rye starter I or II | 3 lb 8 oz | | 1440 g |
| Clear flour | 6 lb | | 2400 g |
| Salt | | 2 oz | 50 g |
| **Total weight:** | **12 lb 11 oz** | | **5115 g** |
| **Optional** | | | |
| Caraway seeds | up to 1.5 oz | | up to 35 g |
| Molasses or malt syrup | up to 3 oz | | up to 70 g |
| Caramel color | up to 1.5 oz | | up to 35 g |

## PUMPERNICKEL BREAD (P. 157)

| Ingredients | U.S. | | Metric |
|---|---|---|---|
| Water | 3 lb | | 1500 g |
| Yeast, fresh | 1 | oz | 30 g |
| Fermented rye starter I or II | 2 lb 8 | oz | 1260 g |
| Rye meal (pumpernickel) | 1 lb 4 | oz | 600 g |
| Clear flour | 4 lb 12 | oz | 2400 g |
| Salt | 2 | oz | 60 g |
| Malt syrup | 1 | oz | 30 g |
| Molasses | 2 | oz | 60 g |
| Caramel color (optional) | 1.5 | oz | 45 g |
| *Total weight:* | *11 lb 15* | *oz* | *5985 g* |

## ENGLISH MUFFINS (P. 164)

| Ingredients | U.S. | | Metric |
|---|---|---|---|
| Water (see mixing instructions) | 3 lb | | 1500 g |
| Yeast, fresh | 1 | oz | 30 g |
| Bread flour | 4 lb | | 2000 g |
| Salt | 1 | oz | 30 g |
| Sugar | 1 | oz | 30 g |
| Nonfat milk solids | 1.5 | oz | 45 g |
| Shortening | 1 | oz | 30 g |
| *Total weight:* | *7 lb 5* | *oz* | *3665 g* |

## FRENCH RYE (P. 160)

| Ingredients | U.S. | | Metric |
|---|---|---|---|
| Rye Starter III (p. 154) | 6 lb | | 3000 g |
| Bread flour | 1 lb | | 500 g |
| Salt | 1.25 | oz | 40 g |
| *Total weight:* | *7 lb 1* | *oz* | *3540 g* |

## BAGELS (P. 165)

| Ingredients | U.S. | | Metric |
|---|---|---|---|
| Water | 2 lb 4 | oz | 1120 g |
| Yeast, fresh | 2 | oz | 60 g |
| High-gluten flour | 4 lb | | 2000 g |
| Diastatic malt powder | 0.4 | oz | 12 g |
| Salt | 1 | oz | 30 g |
| Oil | 0.5 | oz | 16 g |
| *Total weight:* | *6 lb 7* | *oz* | *3238 g* |

## PAIN DE CAMPAGNE (COUNTRY-STYLE BREAD) (P. 160)

| Ingredients | U.S. | | Metric |
|---|---|---|---|
| Rye Starter III (p. 154) | 1 lb 2 | oz | 600 g |
| Bread flour | 4 lb 8 | oz | 2400 g |
| Rye flour | 1 lb 2 | oz | 600 g |
| Salt | 1.75 | oz | 60 g |
| Yeast, fresh | 1.5 | oz | 45 g |
| Water | 3 lb 12 | oz | 1950 g |
| Lard or goose fat (optional) | 1.75 | oz | 60 g |
| *Total weight:* | *10 lb 13* | *oz* | *5675 g* |

## OLIVE FOCACCIA (P. 166)

| Ingredients | U.S. | | Metric |
|---|---|---|---|
| Water | 3 lb 12 | oz | 1875 g |
| Yeast, fresh | 1.5 | oz | 45 g |
| Bread flour | 6 lb | | 3000 g |
| Salt | 2 | oz | 60 g |
| Olive oil | 3.5 | oz | 100 g |
| Chopped, pitted oil-cured black olives | 2 lb 3 | oz | 1105 g |
| *Total weight:* | *12 lb 6* | *oz* | *6185 g* |

## HERB FOCACCIA (SPONGE METHOD) (P. 167)

| Ingredients | U.S. | | Metric |
|---|---|---|---|
| **Sponge** | | | |
| Flour | 2 lb | | 925 g |
| Water | 1 lb 8 | oz | 675 g |
| Yeast, fresh | 0.5 | oz | 15 g |
| Flour | 5 lb | | 2275 g |
| Water | 3 lb 8 | oz | 1600 g |
| Yeast, fresh | 0.5 | oz | 15 g |
| Salt | 2 | oz | 60 g |
| Olive oil | 4 | oz | 125 g |
| Rosemary and salt (see Makeup) | | | |
| **Total weight** | **12 lb 7** | **oz** | **5690 g** |

## CHESTNUT BREAD (P. 168)

| Ingredients | U.S. | | Metric |
|---|---|---|---|
| Water | 2 lb 4 | oz | 1080 g |
| Yeast, fresh | 3.5 | oz | 100 g |
| High-gluten flour | 2 lb 13 | oz | 1350 g |
| Chestnut flour | 15 | oz | 450 g |
| Salt | 1.5 | oz | 45 g |
| Butter | 1.75 | oz | 54 g |
| **Total weight:** | **6 lb 6** | **oz** | **3079 g** |

## PROSCIUTTO BREAD (P. 168)

| Ingredients | U.S. | | Metric |
|---|---|---|---|
| Water | 1 lb 11 | oz | 855 g |
| Yeast, fresh | 1 | oz | 30 g |
| Bread flour | 3 lb | | 1500 g |
| Salt | 1 | oz | 30 g |
| Rendered lard or prosciutto fat | 3 | oz | 90 g |
| Basic Yeast Starter (p. 153) or fermented dough | 10 | oz | 300 g |
| Prosciutto, chopped or diced into small pieces | 10 | oz | 300 g |
| **Total weight:** | **6 lb 4** | **oz** | **3105 g** |

## OLIVE BREAD (P. 169)

| Ingredients | U.S. | | Metric |
|---|---|---|---|
| Water | 3 lb 2 | oz | 1480 g |
| Yeast, fresh | 1.2 | oz | 36 g |
| Bread flour | 3 lb 12 | oz | 1800 g |
| Whole wheat flour | 8 | oz | 240 g |
| Rye flour | 12 | oz | 360 g |
| Salt | 1.5 | oz | 50 g |
| Olive oil | 4 | oz | 120 g |
| Basic Yeast Starter (p. 153) or fermented dough | 8 | oz | 240 g |
| Pitted black olives, whole or halved | 1 lb 8 | oz | 720 g |
| **Total weight:** | **10 lb 8** | **oz** | **5046 g** |

## CRUMPETS (P. 169)

| Ingredients | U.S. | | Metric | |
|---|---|---|---|---|
| Water, warm | 3 lb 12 | oz | 1650 | g |
| Yeast, fresh | 3 | oz | 90 | g |
| Bread flour | 3 lb 6 | oz | 1500 | g |
| Salt | 1 | oz | 30 | g |
| Sugar | 0.4 | oz | 10 | g |
| Baking soda | 0.16 | oz | 4.5 | g |
| Water, cold | 15 | oz | 420 | g |
| **Total weight:** | **8 lb 5** | **oz** | **3704** | **g** |

## SWEET ROLL DOUGH (P. 188)

| Ingredients | U.S. | | Metric |
|---|---|---|---|
| Water | 2 lb | | 800 g |
| Yeast, fresh | 6 | oz | 150 g |
| Butter, margarine, or shortening | 1 lb | | 400 g |
| Sugar | 1 lb | | 400 g |
| Salt | 1.5 | oz | 40 g |
| Nonfat milk solids | 4 | oz | 100 g |
| Eggs | 12 | oz | 300 g |
| Bread flour | 4 lb | | 1600 g |
| Cake flour | 1 lb | | 400 g |
| **Total weight:** | **10 lb 7** | **oz** | **4190 g** |

## RICH SWEET DOUGH (P. 189)

| Ingredients | U.S. | Metric |
|---|---|---|
| Milk, scalded and cooled | 2 lb | 800 g |
| Yeast, fresh | 4 oz | 100 g |
| Bread flour | 2 lb 8 oz | 1000 g |
| Butter | 2 lb | 800 g |
| Sugar | 1 lb | 400 g |
| Salt | 1.5 oz | 40 g |
| Eggs | 1 lb 4 oz | 500 g |
| Bread flour | 2 lb 8 oz | 1000 g |
| **Total weight:** | **11 lb 9 oz** | **4640 g** |

### VARIATIONS

#### STOLLEN

| Ingredients | U.S. | Metric |
|---|---|---|
| Almond extract | 0.5 oz | 10 g |
| Lemon rind, grated | 0.5 oz | 10 g |
| Vanilla extract | 0.5 oz | 10 g |
| Raisins (light, dark, or a mixture) | 1 lb | 600 g |
| Mixed glacéed fruit | 1 lb 12 oz | 700 g |

Add almond extract, lemon rind, and vanilla extract to the butter and sugar during the blending stage. Knead the raisins and mixed glacéed fruit into the dough.

#### BABKA

| Ingredients | U.S. | Metric |
|---|---|---|
| Vanilla extract | 0.5 oz | 10 g |
| Cardamom | 0.25 oz | 5 g |
| Raisins | 1 lb | 400 g |

Add the vanilla and cardamom to the butter during blending. Knead the raisins into the dough.

## BABA/SAVARIN DOUGH (P. 191)

| Ingredients | U.S. | Metric |
|---|---|---|
| Milk | 1 lb | 480 g |
| Yeast, fresh | 2 oz | 60 g |
| Bread flour | 10 oz | 300 g |
| Eggs | 1 lb 4 oz | 600 g |
| Bread flour | 1 lb 14 oz | 900 g |
| Sugar | 1 oz | 30 g |
| Salt | 0.8 oz | 24 g |
| Butter, melted | 1 lb | 500 g |
| **Total weight:** | **5 lb 15 oz** | **2894 g** |

## HOT CROSS BUNS (P. 190)

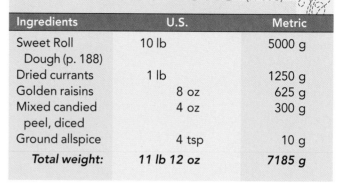

| Ingredients | U.S. | Metric |
|---|---|---|
| Sweet Roll Dough (p. 188) | 10 lb | 5000 g |
| Dried currants | 1 lb | 1250 g |
| Golden raisins | 8 oz | 625 g |
| Mixed candied peel, diced | 4 oz | 300 g |
| Ground allspice | 4 tsp | 10 g |
| **Total weight:** | **11 lb 12 oz** | **7185 g** |

## BRIOCHE (P. 193)

| Ingredients | U.S. | Metric |
|---|---|---|
| Milk | 8 oz | 250 g |
| Yeast, fresh | 2 oz | 60 g |
| Bread flour | 8 oz | 250 g |
| Eggs | 1 lb 4 oz | 600 g |
| Bread flour | 2 lb | 950 g |
| Sugar | 2 oz | 60 g |
| Salt | 0.8 oz | 24 g |
| Butter, softened | 1 lb 12 oz | 850 g |
| **Total weight:** | **6 lb 4 oz** | **3044 g** |

## DANISH PASTRY DOUGH (BRIOCHE-STYLE) (P. 197)

| Ingredients | U.S. | Metric |
|---|---|---|
| Milk | 1 lb 6 oz | 675 g |
| Yeast, fresh | 4 oz | 120 g |
| Bread flour | 4 lb 14 oz | 2400 g |
| Eggs | 10 oz | 300 g |
| Butter, melted | 4.5 oz | 150 g |
| Salt | 1 oz | 30 g |
| Sugar | 4.5 oz | 150 g |
| Milk | 7.5 oz | 225 g |
| Butter, softened | 3 lb | 1500 g |
| **Total weight:** | **11 lb 3 oz** | **5550 g** |

## CROISSANTS (P. 198)

| Ingredients | U.S. | Metric |
|---|---|---|
| Milk | 2 lb | 900 g |
| Yeast, fresh | 2 oz | 60 g |
| Sugar | 2 oz | 60 g |
| Salt | 1 oz | 30 g |
| Butter, softened | 6 oz | 160 g |
| Bread flour | 3 lb 8 oz | 1600 g |
| Butter | 2 lb | 900 g |
| *Total weight:* | *8 lb 3 oz* | *3710 g* |

## CINNAMON SUGAR (P. 199)

| Ingredients | U.S. | Metric |
|---|---|---|
| Sugar | 2 lb | 1000 g |
| Cinnamon | 1 oz | 30 g |
| *Total weight:* | *2 lb 1 oz* | *1030 g* |

## DANISH PASTRY (P. 198)

| Ingredients | U.S. | Metric |
|---|---|---|
| Water | 2 lb | 800 g |
| Yeast, fresh | 5 oz | 125 g |
| Butter | 10 oz | 250 g |
| Sugar | 12 oz | 300 g |
| Nonfat milk solids | 4 oz | 100 g |
| Salt | 1.5 oz | 40 g |
| Cardamom or mace (optional) | 0.16 oz (2 tsp) | 4 g |
| Whole eggs | 1 lb | 400 g |
| Egg yolks | 4 oz | 100 g |
| Bread flour | 4 lb | 1600 g |
| Cake flour | 1 lb | 400 g |
| Butter (for rolling in) | 2 lb 8 oz | 1000 g |
| *Total weight:* | *12 lb 12 oz* | *5119 g* |

## APRICOT GLAZE I (P. 200)

*Yield: 3 lb 4 oz (3760 g)*

| Ingredients | U.S. | Metric |
|---|---|---|
| Apricots, canned | 2 lb | 1000 g |
| Apples | 2 lb | 1000 g |
| Sugar | 3 lb 12 oz | 1900 g |
| Water | 2 oz | 50 g |
| Sugar | 4 oz | 100 g |
| Pectin | 1.33 oz | 40 g |

## STREUSEL OR CRUMB TOPPING (P. 199)

| Ingredients | U.S. | Metric |
|---|---|---|
| Butter and/or shortening | 1 lb | 500 g |
| Granulated sugar | 10 oz | 300 g |
| Brown sugar | 8 oz | 250 g |
| Salt | 0.16 oz (1 tsp) | 5 g |
| Cinnamon or mace | 0.08–0.16 oz (1–2 tsp) | 2.5–5 g |
| Pastry flour | 2 lb | 1000 g |
| *Total weight:* | *4 lb 2 oz* | *2060 g* |

## APRICOT GLAZE II (P. 200)

*Yield: 1 lb 12 oz (880 g)*

| Ingredients | U.S. | Metric |
|---|---|---|
| Apricot preserves | 2 lb | 1000 g |
| Water | 8 oz | 250 g |

## LEMON CHEESE FILLING (P. 200)

| Ingredients | U.S. | Metric |
|---|---|---|
| Cream cheese | 1 lb 4 oz | 600 g |
| Sugar | 4 oz | 120 g |
| Grated lemon zest | 0.4 oz (5 tsp) | 12 g |
| *Total weight:* | *1 lb 8 oz* | *732 g* |

## DATE, PRUNE, OR APRICOT FILLING (P. 201)

*Yield: about 6 lb (3000 g)*

| Ingredients | U.S. | Metric |
|---|---|---|
| Dates, prunes (pitted), or dried apricots | 4 lb | 2000 g |
| Sugar | 12 oz | 400 g |
| Water | 2 lb | 1000 g |

## ALMOND FILLING I (FRANGIPANE) (P. 201)

| Ingredients | U.S. | Metric |
|---|---|---|
| Almond paste | 2 lb | 1000 g |
| Sugar | 2 lb | 1000 g |
| Butter and/or shortening | 1 lb | 500 g |
| Pastry or cake flour | 8 oz | 250 g |
| Eggs | 8 oz | 250 g |
| **Total weight:** | **6 lb** | **3000 g** |

## APPLE COMPOTE FILLING (P. 202)

*Yield: about 4 lb (2 kg) or 2 lb 4 oz (1100 g) drained*

| Ingredients | U.S. | Metric |
|---|---|---|
| Apples, peeled and cored | 2 lb 4 oz | 1100 g |
| Butter | 10 oz | 300 g |
| Sugar | 1 lb | 480 g |
| Water | 8 oz | 240 g |

## CINNAMON RAISIN FILLING (P. 202)

| Ingredients | U.S. | Metric |
|---|---|---|
| Powdered almonds | 14 oz | 400 g |
| Sugar | 8 oz | 240 g |
| Maple syrup | 4 oz | 120 g |
| Egg whites | 8 oz | 240 g |
| Cinnamon | 1.33 oz | 40 g |
| Raisins, golden | 7 oz | 200 g |
| **Total weight:** | **2 lb 10 oz** | **1240 g** |

## PECAN MAPLE FILLING (P. 203)

| Ingredients | U.S. | Metric |
|---|---|---|
| Powdered hazelnuts | 14 oz | 400 g |
| Sugar | 8 oz | 240 g |
| Egg whites | 8 oz | 240 g |
| Maple syrup | 4 oz | 120 g |
| Pecans, finely sliced or chopped | 8 oz | 240 g |
| **Total weight:** | **2 lb 10 oz** | **1240 g** |

## ALMOND CREAM (CRÈME D'AMANDE) (P. 202)

| Ingredients | U.S. | Metric |
|---|---|---|
| Butter | 12 oz | 360 g |
| Fine granulated sugar | 12 oz | 360 g |
| Grated lemon zest | 0.12 oz (1½ tsp) | 4 g |
| Whole eggs | 6.67 oz (4 eggs) | 200 g |
| Egg yolks | 2.67 oz (4 yolks) | 80 g |
| Vanilla extract | 8 drops | 8 drops |
| Powdered almonds | 12 oz | 360 g |
| Cake flour | 4 oz | 120 g |
| **Total weight:** | **3 lb** | **1480 g** |

## HAZELNUT FILLING (P. 203)

| Ingredients | U.S. | Metric |
|---|---|---|
| Hazelnuts, toasted and ground | 1 lb | 500 g |
| Sugar | 2 lb | 1000 g |
| Cinnamon | 0.5 oz | 15 g |
| Eggs | 6 oz | 190 g |
| Cake crumbs | 2 lb | 1000 g |
| Milk | 1–2 lb | 500–1000 g |
| **Total weight:** | **6 lb 6 to 7 lb 6 oz** | **3205 g to 3705 g** |

## CHOCOLATE FILLING (P. 204)

| Ingredients | U.S. | Metric |
|---|---|---|
| Sugar | 1 lb | 400 g |
| Cocoa | 6 oz | 150 g |
| Cake crumbs | 3 lb | 1200 g |
| Eggs | 4 oz | 100 g |
| Butter, melted | 6 oz | 150 g |
| Vanilla | 1 oz | 25 g |
| Water (as needed) | 12 oz | 300 g |
| **Total weight:** | **5 lb 13 oz** | **2425 g** |

# HONEY PAN GLAZE (FOR CARAMEL ROLLS) (P. 204)

| Ingredients | U.S. | | Metric |
|---|---|---|---|
| Brown sugar | 2 lb | 8 oz | 100 g |
| Butter, margarine, or shortening | 1 lb | | 400 g |
| Honey | | 10 oz | 250 g |
| Corn syrup or malt syrup | | 10 oz | 250 g |
| Water (as needed) | | 4 oz | 100 g |
| *Total weight:* | *5 lb* | | *2000 g* |

# CRANBERRY DROP SCONES (P. 226)

| Ingredients | U.S. | | Metric |
|---|---|---|---|
| Butter | 1 lb | 2 oz | 550 g |
| Sugar | | 15 oz | 450 g |
| Salt | | 1.25 oz | 25 g |
| Egg yolks | | 4 oz (6 yolks) | 120 g |
| Pastry flour | 4 lb | 8 oz | 2250 g |
| Baking powder | | 4.5 oz | 135 g |
| Milk | 2 lb | 10 oz | 1300 g |
| Dried cranberries | | 12 oz | 375 g |
| *Total weight:* | *7 lb* | *14 oz* | *3905 g* |

# CHOCOLATE CAKE DOUGHNUTS (P. 240)

| Ingredients | U.S. | | Metric |
|---|---|---|---|
| Shortening | | 6 oz | 180 g |
| Sugar | 1 lb | | 500 g |
| Salt | | 0.5 oz | 15 g |
| Nonfat milk solids | | 3 oz | 90 g |
| Vanilla extract | | 1 oz | 30 g |
| Whole eggs | | 6 oz | 180 g |
| Egg yolks | | 2 oz | 60 g |
| Cake flour | 2 lb | 8 oz | 1500 g |
| Bread flour | 1 lb | 8 oz | 500 g |
| Cocoa powder | | 5 oz | 155 g |
| Baking powder | | 2 oz | 60 g |
| Baking soda | | 0.4 oz (2⅔ tsp) | 13 g |
| Water | 2 lb | 2 oz | 1060 g |
| *Total weight:* | *8 lb* | *11 oz* | *4343 g* |

# RICH VANILLA SPICE DOUGHNUTS (P. 240)

| Ingredients | U.S. | | Metric |
|---|---|---|---|
| Bread flour | 1 lb 8 | oz | 750 g |
| Cake flour | 1 lb 8 | oz | 750 g |
| Baking powder | 1.5 | oz | 45 g |
| Nutmeg | 0.4 | oz (2 tbsp) | 12 g |
| Cinnamon | 0.12 | oz (2 tsp) | 4 g |
| Salt | 0.6 | oz (1 tbsp) | 18 g |
| Whole eggs | 10 | oz | 310 g |
| Egg yolks | 2 | oz | 60 g |
| Sugar | 1 lb 4 | oz | 630 g |
| Milk | 1 lb 3 | oz | 600 g |
| Vanilla extract | 1.5 | | 45 g |
| Butter, melted | 6 | oz | 190 g |
| *Total weight:* | *6 lb 13* | *oz* | *3414 g* |

# FRITTER BATTER I (P. 242)

| Ingredients | U.S. | | Metric |
|---|---|---|---|
| Pastry flour | 2 lb 4 | oz | 1000 g |
| Sugar | 2 | oz | 60 g |
| Salt | 0.5 | oz | 15 g |
| Baking powder | 0.5 | oz | 15 g |
| Eggs, beaten | 1 lb 2 | oz | 500 g |
| Milk | 2 lb | | 900 g |
| Oil | 2 | oz | 60 g |
| Vanilla extract | 0.33 | oz (2 tsp) | 10 g |
| *Total weight:* | *5 lb 11* | *oz* | *2560 g* |

# FRITTER BATTER II (P. 243)

| Ingredients | U.S. | | Metric |
|---|---|---|---|
| Bread flour | 1 lb 8 | oz | 750 g |
| Cake flour | 8 | oz | 250 g |
| Salt | 0.5 oz | | 15 g |
| Sugar | 1 | oz | 30 g |
| Milk | 2 lb 4 | oz | 1125 g |
| Egg yolks, beaten | 4 | oz | 125 g |
| Oil | 4 | oz | 125 g |
| Egg whites | 8 | oz | 250 g |
| *Total weight:* | *5 lb 5* | *oz* | *2670 g* |

# FRENCH DOUGHNUTS (BEIGNETS SOUFFLÉS) (P. 243)

| Ingredients | U.S. | | Metric |
|---|---|---|---|
| Milk | 1 lb 14 | oz | 750 g |
| Butter | 12 | oz | 300 g |
| Salt | 0.5 | oz | 15 g |
| Sugar | 0.5 | oz | 15 g |
| Bread flour | 1 lb 2 | oz | 450 g |
| Eggs | 1 lb 8 | oz | 600 g |
| *Total weight:* | *5 lb 5* | *oz* | *2130 g* |

# BEIGNETS DE CARNIVAL (P. 244)

| Ingredients | U.S. | | Metric |
|---|---|---|---|
| Bread flour | 1 lb 5 | oz | 600 g |
| Sugar | 1.5 | oz | 45 g |
| Salt | 0.5 | oz | 15 g |
| Egg yolks | 6 | oz | 180 g |
| Light cream | 6 | oz | 180 g |
| Kirsch | 1.5 | oz | 45 g |
| Rose water | 1 | oz | 30 g |
| *Total weight:* | *2 lb 5* | *oz* | *1095 g* |

# VIENNOISE (P. 245)

| Ingredients | U.S. | Metric |
|---|---|---|
| Brioche dough (p. 193) | 5 lb | 2400 g |
| Egg wash | as needed | as needed |
| Red currant jelly | 14 oz | 400 g |

# CANNOLI SHELLS (P. 246)

| Ingredients | U.S. | | Metric |
|---|---|---|---|
| Bread flour | 1 lb 8 | oz | 700 g |
| Pastry flour | 1 lb 8 | oz | 700 g |
| Sugar | 4 | oz | 120 g |
| Salt | 0.15 oz (⅔ tsp) | | 4 g |
| Butter | 8 | oz | 240 g |
| Egg, beaten | 6.5 | oz | 200 g |
| Dry white wine or Marsala | 1 lb | | 500 g |
| *Total weight:* | *5 lb 2* | *oz* | *2464 g* |

# RICOTTA CANNOLI FILLING (P. 246)

| Ingredients | U.S. | Metric |
|---|---|---|
| Ricotta impastato (see p. 77) | 4 lb | 2000 g |
| Confectioners' sugar | 2 lb | 1000 g |
| Cinnamon extract | 1 oz | 30 g |
| Candied citron, candied citrus peel, or candied pumpkin, finely diced | 6 oz | 180 g |
| Sweet chocolate, finely chopped, or tiny chocolate bits | 4 oz | 120 g |
| *Total weight:* | *6 lb 11 oz* | *3530 g* |

# VANILLA SYRUP (P. 262)

| Ingredients | U.S. | Metric |
|---|---|---|
| Water | 1 lb 12 oz | 800 g |
| Sugar | 1 lb 8 oz | 720 g |
| Vanilla bean, split | 2 | 2 |
| *Total weight:* | *3 lb 4 oz* *(about 2¼ pt)* | *1520 g* *(about 1300 mL)* |

# COCOA VANILLA SYRUP (P. 263)

| Ingredients | U.S. | Metric |
|---|---|---|
| Water | 1 lb | 500 g |
| Sugar | 1 lb | 500 g |
| Vanilla bean | 2 | 2 g |
| Cocoa powder | 4 oz | 125 g |
| *Total weight:* | *2 lb 4 oz* *(about 30 fl oz)* | *1125 g* *(about 1 L)* |

# COFFEE RUM SYRUP (P. 263)

| Ingredients | U.S. | | Metric |
|---|---|---|---|
| Sugar | 10 | oz | 260 g |
| Water | 10 | oz | 260 g |
| Ground coffee | 0.67 | oz | 20 g |
| Rum | 14 | oz | 360 g |
| **Total weight:** | **2 lb 2** | **oz** | **900 g** |
| | **(29–31 fl oz)** | | **(770–800 mL)** |

## VARIATIONS

### COFFEE SYRUP

| Ingredients | U.S. | Metric |
|---|---|---|
| Coffee liqueur | 6.5 oz | 160 g |

Omit the rum in the basic formula and add the coffee-flavored liqueur.

### RUM SYRUP

| Ingredients | U.S. | Metric |
|---|---|---|
| Water | 12 oz | 300 g |
| Sugar | 10.5 oz | 260 g |
| Dark rum | 2 oz | 60 g |

Omit the coffee in the basic formula and adjust the ingredient quantities as listed above.

# CRÈME CHANTILLY (P. 265)

| Ingredients | U.S. | Metric |
|---|---|---|
| Heavy cream or crème fraîche | 2 pt | 1000 g |
| Confectioners' sugar | 5 oz | 155 g |
| Vanilla extract | 2 tsp | 10 mL |
| **Total weight:** | **2 lb 5 oz** | **1165 g** |

# PASSION FRUIT GANACHE (P. 276)

| Ingredients | U.S. | Metric |
|---|---|---|
| Heavy cream | 12 oz | 360 g |
| Passion fruit juice | 12 oz | 360 g |
| Butter | 6 oz | 180 g |
| Egg yolks | 5 oz | 150 g |
| Sugar | 6 oz | 180 g |
| Dark chocolate, chopped | 1 lb 5 oz | 645 g |
| **Total weight:** | **3 lb 14 oz** | **1875 g** |

# VANILLA CRÈME DIPLOMAT (P. 274)

| Ingredients | U.S. | | Metric |
|---|---|---|---|
| Milk | 1 pt 8 | oz | 750 g |
| Vanilla bean, split | 1 | | 1 |
| Egg yolks | 4 | oz | 120 g |
| Fine granulated sugar | 3 | oz | 90 g |
| Cake flour | 2 | oz | 60 g |
| Cornstarch | 1.5 | oz | 45 g |
| Orange liqueur, such as Grand Marnier | 3 | oz | 90 g |
| Crème Chantilly (p. 265) | 1 lb 4 | oz | 600 g |
| **Total weight:** | **3 lb 9** | **oz** | **1755 g** |

## VARIATION

### CHOCOLATE CRÈME DIPLOMAT

| Ingredients | U.S. | Metric |
|---|---|---|
| Dark chocolate, finely chopped | 7 oz | 210 g |

Omit the orange liqueur from the basic formula. Stir the dark chocolate into the hot pastry cream in step 4. Stir until the chocolate is completely melted and well mixed.

# CHOCOLATE MOUSSE II (P. 277)

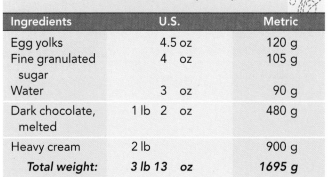

| Ingredients | U.S. | | Metric |
|---|---|---|---|
| Egg yolks | 4.5 | oz | 120 g |
| Fine granulated sugar | 4 | oz | 105 g |
| Water | 3 | oz | 90 g |
| Dark chocolate, melted | 1 lb 2 | oz | 480 g |
| Heavy cream | 2 lb | | 900 g |
| **Total weight:** | **3 lb 13** | **oz** | **1695 g** |

# CARAMEL SAUCE (P. 280)

*Yield: 1½ qt (1.5 L)*

| Ingredients | U.S. | | Metric |
|---|---|---|---|
| Sugar | 2 | lb | 1 kg |
| Water | | 8 oz | 250 mL |
| Lemon juice | | 1 tbsp | 15 mL |
| Heavy cream | 1.5 | pt | 750 mL |
| Milk | 1 | pt | 500 mL |

## PIE DOUGH (P. 289)

| Ingredients | Flaky Pie Dough U.S. | Metric | Mealy Pie Dough U.S. | Metric |
|---|---|---|---|---|
| Pastry flour | 5 lb | 2000 g | 5 lb | 2000 g |
| Shortening, regular | 3 lb 8 oz | 1400 g | 3 lb 4 oz | 1300 g |
| Water, cold | 1 lb 8 oz | 600 g | 1 lb 4 oz | 500 g |
| Salt | 1.5 oz | 40 g | 1.5 oz | 40 g |
| Sugar *(optional)* | 4 oz | 100 g | 4 oz | 100 g |
| *Total weight:* | *10 lb 5 oz* | *4140 g* | *9 lb 13 oz* | *3940 g* |

## ENRICHED PIE PASTRY (P. 289)

| Ingredients | U.S. | Metric |
|---|---|---|
| Pastry flour | 3 lb | 1500 g |
| Sugar | 8 oz | 250 g |
| Butter | 1 lb 8 oz | 750 g |
| Egg yolks | 4 oz | 120 g |
| Water, cold | 12 oz | 375 g |
| Salt | 0.5 oz | 15 g |
| *Total weight:* | *6 lb* | *3010 g* |

## PEACH SOUR CREAM PIE FILLING (P. 301)

Yield: 5 lb (4500 g)

*Five 8-in. (20 cm) pies    Four 9-in. (23 cm) pies*

*Three 10-in. (25 cm) pies*

| Ingredients | U.S. | Metric |
|---|---|---|
| Sour cream | 2 lb | 1000 g |
| Sugar | 1 lb | 500 g |
| Cornstarch | 2 oz | 60 g |
| Eggs, beaten | 8 | 8 |
| Vanilla extract | 2 tsp | 8 mL |
| Nutmeg | ½ tsp | 2 mL |
| Fresh peaches, sliced | 4 lb | 2000 g |
| Streusel (p. 199) | 1 lb 8 oz | 720 g |

## RAISIN PIE FILLING (P. 299)

Yield: about 10½ lb (4.8 kg)

*Six 8-in. (20 cm) pies    Five 9-in. (23 cm) pies*

*Four 10-in. (25 cm) pies*

| Ingredients | U.S. | Metric |
|---|---|---|
| Raisins | 4 lb | 1800 g |
| Water | 4 pt | 2000 mL |
| Water, cold | 8 oz | 250 mL |
| Cornstarch | 2.5 oz | 75 g |
| or | | |
| Modified starch (waxy maize) | 2 oz | 60 g |
| Sugar | 1 lb 4 oz | 570 g |
| Salt | 0.33 oz (2 tsp) | 10 g |
| Lemon juice | 3 oz | 90 mL |
| Grated lemon zest | 0.1 oz (1 tbsp) | 3 g |
| Cinnamon | 0.06 oz (1 tsp) | 2 g |
| Butter | 3 oz | 90 g |

## CUSTARD PIE FILLING (P. 303)

Yield: 8 lb (3.7 kg)

*Five 8-in. (20 cm) pies    Four 9-in. (23 cm) pies*

*Three 10-in. (25 cm) pies*

| Ingredients | U.S. | Metric |
|---|---|---|
| Eggs | 2 lb | 900 g |
| Sugar | 1 lb | 450 g |
| Salt | 0.17 oz (1 tsp) | 5 g |
| Vanilla extract | 1 oz | 30 mL |
| Milk | 5 pt | 2400 mL |
| Nutmeg | 1–2 tsp | 2–3 g |

# FRESH APPLE PIE FILLING I (P. 300)

*Yield: about 12 lb (5300 g)*
*Six 8-in. (20 cm) pies    Five 9-in. (23 cm) pies*
*Four 10-in. (25 cm) pies*

| Ingredients | U.S. | | Metric | |
|---|---|---|---|---|
| Apples, peeled and sliced | 10 lb | | 4500 | g |
| Butter | 5 | oz | 150 | g |
| Sugar | 15 | oz | 450 | g |
| Water, cold | 10 | oz | 300 | g |
| Cornstarch or | 3.75 | oz | 120 | g |
| Modified starch (waxy maize) | 2.5 | oz | 75 | g |
| Sugar | 1 lb | | 500 | g |
| Salt | 0.3 | oz (1 tsp) | 5 | g |
| Cinnamon | 0.3 | oz (5 tsp) | 5 | g |
| Nutmeg | 0.15 | oz (1¼ tsp) | 2.5 | g |
| Lemon juice | 1.67 | oz | 50 | g |
| Butter | 1.25 | oz | 35 | g |

### VARIATIONS

#### FRESH APPLE PIE FILLING II

| Ingredients | U.S. | Metric |
|---|---|---|
| Water | 1 lb | 500 g |

Omit the first quantity of butter. Instead, simmer the apples in water and the first quantity of sugar as in the basic cooked fruit method, using the quantity of water listed above.

#### APPLE GINGER PIE FILLING

| Ingredients | U.S. | | Metric | |
|---|---|---|---|---|
| Ground ginger | 0.15 oz (1¼ tsp) | | 2.5 | g |
| Candied ginger, finely chopped | 3.5 | oz | 100 | g |

Prepare as for Fresh Apple Pie Filling I or II, but omit the cinnamon and instead add ground and candied ginger.

#### APPLE WALNUT PIE FILLING

| Ingredients | U.S. | Metric |
|---|---|---|
| Chopped walnuts | 12 oz | 375 g |

Mix the walnuts into Fresh Apple Pie Filling I or II.

#### RHUBARB PIE FILLING

| Ingredients | U.S. | Metric |
|---|---|---|
| Fresh rhubarb | 7 lb | 3200 g |

Substitute the rhubarb, cut into 1-in. (2.5 cm) pieces, for the apples. Omit the cinnamon, nutmeg, and lemon juice.

# PECAN PIE FILLING (P. 303)

*Yield: 7 lb (3.3 kg) filling plus 1 lb 4 oz (570 g) pecans*
*Five 8-in. (20 cm) pies    Four 9-in. (23 cm) pies*
*Three 10-in. (25 cm) pies*

| Ingredients | U.S. | | Metric | |
|---|---|---|---|---|
| Granulated sugar | 1 lb 12 | oz | 800 | g |
| Butter | 8 | oz | 230 | g |
| Salt | 0.25 oz | | 7 | g |
| Eggs | 1 lb 12 | oz | 800 | g |
| Dark corn syrup | 3 lb | | 1400 | g |
| | (about 34 fl oz ) | | | |
| Vanilla extract | 1 | oz | 30 | g |
| Pecans | 1 lb 4 | oz | 570 | g |

# PUMPKIN PIE FILLING (P. 304)

*Yield: about 17 lb (8 kg)*
*Ten 8-in. (20 cm) pies    Eight 9-in. (23 cm) pies*
*Six 10-in. (25 cm) pies*

| Ingredients | U.S. | | Metric | |
|---|---|---|---|---|
| Pumpkin purée | 6 lb 10 | oz | 3000 | g |
| | (1 No. 10 can or 4 No. 2 ½ cans) | | | |
| Pastry flour | 4 | oz | 120 | g |
| Cinnamon | 0.5 | oz | 15 | g |
| Nutmeg | 0.08 | oz (1 tsp) | 2 | g |
| Ginger | 0.08 | oz (1 tsp) | 2 | g |
| Cloves | 0.04 | oz (½ tsp) | 1 | g |
| Salt | 0.5 | oz | 15 | g |
| Brown sugar | 2 lb 8 | oz | 1150 | g |
| Eggs | 2 lb 8 | oz | 1200 | g |
| Corn syrup or half corn syrup and half molasses | 8 | oz | 240 | g |
| Milk | 5 pt | | 2400 | mL |

# KEY LIME PIE FILLING (P. 305)

*Yield: 6 lb (3000 g)*
*Five 8-in. (20 cm) pies    Four 9-in. (23 cm) pies*
*Three 10-in. (25 cm) pies*

| Ingredients | U.S. | Metric |
|---|---|---|
| Egg yolks | 16 | 16 |
| Sweetened condensed milk | 3 lb 8 oz | 1600 g |
| Freshly squeezed Key lime juice | 1 lb 4 oz | 600 g |

# VANILLA CREAM PIE FILLING (P. 306)

*Yield: about 2¼ qt (2.25 L) or 6 lb 4 oz (3.1 kg)*
*Five 8-in. (20 cm) pies    Four 9-in. (23 cm) pies*
*Three 10-in. (25 cm) pies*

| Ingredients | U.S. | Metric |
| --- | --- | --- |
| Milk | 4 pt | 2000 mL |
| Sugar | 8 oz | 250 g |
| Egg yolks | 6 oz | 180 g |
| Whole eggs | 8 oz | 240 g |
| Cornstarch | 5 oz | 150 g |
| Sugar | 8 oz | 250 g |
| Butter | 4 oz | 125 g |
| Vanilla extract | 1 oz | 30 mL |

## VARIATIONS

### CHOCOLATE CREAM PIE FILLING I

| Ingredients | U.S. | Metric |
| --- | --- | --- |
| Unsweetened chocolate | 4 oz | 125 g |
| Sweet chocolate | 4 oz | 125 g |

Melt together the unsweetened and sweet chocolate and mix into the hot vanilla cream filling.

### CHOCOLATE CREAM PIE FILLING II

| Ingredients | U.S. | Metric |
| --- | --- | --- |
| Milk | 3 lb 8 oz (3½ pt) | 1750 mL |
| Sugar | 8 oz | 250 g |
| Egg yolks | 6 oz | 180 g |
| Whole eggs | 8 oz | 240 g |
| Cold milk | 8 oz | 250 g |
| Cornstarch | 5 oz | 150 g |
| Cocoa | 3 oz | 90 g |
| Sugar | 8 oz | 250 g |
| Butter | 4 oz | 125 g |
| Vanilla extract | 1 oz | 30 mL |

This variation uses cocoa instead of chocolate. The cocoa is sifted with the starch. Some of the milk must be included with the eggs to provide enough liquid to make a paste with the starch and cocoa. Follow the procedure in the basic formula, but use the above ingredients.

## VARIATIONS (CONT.)

### BUTTERSCOTCH CREAM PIE FILLING

| Ingredients | U.S. | Metric |
| --- | --- | --- |
| Brown sugar | 2 lb | 1000 g |
| Butter | 10 oz | 300 g |

Combine the brown sugar and butter in a saucepan. Heat over low heat, stirring, until the butter is melted and the ingredients are blended. Prepare the basic vanilla cream filling formula, but omit all the sugar and increase the starch to 6 oz (180 g). As the mixture comes to a boil in step 5, gradually stir in the brown sugar mixture. Finish as in the basic formula.

### LEMON PIE FILLING

| Ingredients | U.S. | | Metric |
| --- | --- | --- | --- |
| Water | 4 | pt | 2000 mL |
| Sugar | 1 | lb | 500 g |
| Egg yolks | 10 | oz | 300 g |
| Cornstarch | 6 | oz | 180 g |
| Sugar | 8 | oz | 250 g |
| Lemon zest, grated | 0.5 | oz | 15 g |
| Butter | 4 | oz | 125 g |
| Lemon juice | 8 | oz | 250 mL |

Follow the procedure for vanilla cream filling, but use the above ingredients. Note the lemon juice is added after the filling is thickened.

# STRAWBERRY RHUBARB PIE FILLING (P. 307)

*Yield: 10 lb 8 oz (5000 g)*
*Five 8 inch (20-cm) pies    Four 9 inch (23-cm) pies*
*Three 10 inch (25-cm) pies*

| Ingredients | U.S. | Metric |
| --- | --- | --- |
| Rhubarb, fresh or frozen, in 1-in. (2.5 cm) pieces | 2 lb 8 oz | 1200 g |
| Sugar | 1 lb 8 oz | 720 g |
| Water | 8 oz | 240 g |
| Egg yolks | 8 | 8 |
| Heavy cream | 8 oz | 240 g |
| Cornstarch | 3 oz | 90 g |
| Fresh strawberries, hulled and quartered | 2 lb | 1000 g |

## PÂTE BRISÉE (P. 318)

| Ingredients | U.S. | | | Metric |
|---|---|---|---|---|
| Pastry flour | 1 lb | 8 | oz | 800 g |
| Salt | | 0.6 | oz | 20 g |
| Sugar | | 0.6 | oz | 20 g |
| Butter, chilled | | 12 | oz | 400 g |
| Eggs | | 8 | oz | 260 g |
| Water | | 1.2 | oz | 40 g |
| Vanilla extract | | 8 drops | | 8 drops |
| Lemon zest, grated | | 0.25 oz | | 8 g |
| *Total weight:* | *2 lb* | *14* | *oz* | *1548 g* |

## PÂTE SUCRÉE (P. 319)

| Ingredients | U.S. | | | Metric |
|---|---|---|---|---|
| Butter, softened | | 15 | oz | 500 g |
| Sugar | | 6 | oz | 200 g |
| Salt | | 0.12 oz (¾ tsp) | | 4 g |
| Lemon zest, grated | | 0.12 oz (1½ tsp) | | 4 g |
| Vanilla extract | | 8 drops | | 8 drops |
| Eggs, beaten | | 6 | oz | 200 g |
| Pastry flour | 1 lb | 8 | oz | 800 g |
| *Total weight:* | *3 lb* | *3* | *oz* | *1708 g* |

## PÂTE SABLÉE (P. 319)

| Ingredients | U.S. | | | Metric |
|---|---|---|---|---|
| Butter, softened | 1 lb | 8 | oz | 600 g |
| Confectioners' sugar | | 12 | oz | 300 g |
| Lemon zest, grated | | 0.12 oz | | 4 g |
| Vanilla extract | | 8 drops | | 8 drops |
| Egg, beaten | | 4 | oz | 100 g |
| Pastry flour | 2 lb | 4 | oz | 900 g |
| *Total weight:* | *4 lb* | *12* | *oz* | *1904 g* |

**VARIATION**

### CHOCOLATE PÂTE SABLÉE

| Ingredients | U.S. | | | Metric |
|---|---|---|---|---|
| Butter | 1 lb | 8 | oz | 600 g |
| Confectioners' sugar | | 12 | oz | 300 g |
| Grated orange zest | | 0.33 oz | | 8 g |
| Eggs, beaten | | 8 | oz | 200 g |
| Pastry flour | 1 lb | 12 | oz | 700 g |
| Cocoa powder | | 4 | oz | 120 g |

Substitute the above ingredients and follow the basic procedure. Sift the flour with the cocoa.

## SHORT DOUGH I (P. 320)

| Ingredients | U.S. | | | Metric |
|---|---|---|---|---|
| Butter *or* butter and shortening | 2 lb | | | 1000 g |
| Sugar | | 12 | oz | 375 g |
| Salt | | 0.25 oz | | 8 g |
| Eggs | | 9 | oz | 280 g |
| Pastry flour | 3 lb | | | 1500 g |
| *Total weight:* | *6 lb* | *5* | *oz* | *3163 g* |

## ALMOND SHORT DOUGH (P. 320)

| Ingredients | U.S. | | | Metric |
|---|---|---|---|---|
| Butter | 2 lb | | | 800 g |
| Sugar | 1 lb | 8 | oz | 600 g |
| Salt | | 0.4 oz (2½ tsp) | | 10 g |
| Powdered almonds | 1 lb | 4 | oz | 500 g |
| Eggs | | 6.5 | oz | 165 g |
| Vanilla extract | | 0.2 oz (1¼ tsp) | | 5 g |
| Pastry flour | 2 lb | 8 | oz | 1000 g |
| *Total weight:* | *7 lb* | *11* | *oz* | *3080 g* |

**VARIATION**

### LINZER DOUGH I

| Ingredients | U.S. | Metric |
|---|---|---|
| Cinnamon | 0.25 oz (4½ tsp) | 6 g |
| Nutmeg | 0.04 oz (½ tsp) | 1 g |

Use ground hazelnuts, ground almonds, or a mixture of the two. Mix in the cinnamon and nutmeg with the salt in the first step.

## SHORT DOUGH II (P. 320)

| Ingredients | U.S. | | | Metric |
|---|---|---|---|---|
| Butter | 1 lb 4 | | oz | 600 g |
| Sugar | 14 | | oz | 400 g |
| Salt | 0.25 | oz | | 8 g |
| Vanilla powder | 0.25 | oz | | 8 g |
| Powdered almonds | 4 | | oz | 120 g |
| Eggs | 7 | | oz | 200 g |
| Pastry flour | 2 lb 2 | | oz | 1000 g |
| *Total weight:* | *4 lb 15* | | *oz* | *2336 g* |

## CLASSIC PUFF PASTRY (PÂTE FEUILLETÉE CLASSIQUE) (P. 324)

| Ingredients | U.S. | | Metric |
|---|---|---|---|
| Bread flour | 3 lb | | 1500 g |
| Salt | 1 | oz | 30 g |
| Butter, melted | 8 | oz | 225 g |
| Water | 1 lb 8 | oz | 750 g |
| Butter, for rolling in | 1 lb 12 | oz | 900 g |
| *Total weight:* | *6 lb 13* | *oz* | *3405 g* |

## ORDINARY PUFF PASTRY (P. 325)

| Ingredients | U.S. | | Metric |
|---|---|---|---|
| Bread flour | 3 lb | | 1500 g |
| Cake flour | 1 lb | | 500 g |
| Butter, softened | 8 | oz | 250 g |
| Salt | 1 | oz | 30 g |
| Water, cold | 2 lb 4 | oz | 1125 g |
| Butter | 4 lb | | 2000 g |
| Bread flour | 8 | oz | 250 g |
| *Total weight:* | *11 lb 5* | *oz* | *5655 g* |

## ALMOND MERINGUES (P. 348)

| Ingredients | U.S. | Metric |
|---|---|---|
| Egg whites | 1 lb | 500 g |
| Fine granulated sugar | 1 lb | 500 g |
| Powdered almonds | 1 lb | 500 g |
| *Total weight:* | *3 lb* | *1500 g* |

## SUCCÈS (P. 350)

| Ingredients | U.S. | | Metric |
|---|---|---|---|
| Egg whites | 1 lb 2 | oz | 540 g |
| Granulated sugar | 12 | oz | 360 g |
| Powdered almonds | 12 | oz | 360 g |
| Confectioners' sugar | 12 | oz | 360 g |
| Cake flour | 3 | oz | 90 g |
| *Total weight:* | *3 lb 9* | *oz* | *1710 g* |

## YELLOW BUTTER CAKE (P. 398)

| Ingredients | U.S. | | | Metric |
|---|---|---|---|---|
| Butter | 2 lb 4 | | oz | 1100 g |
| Sugar | 3 lb | | | 1450 g |
| Salt | 0.5 | oz | | 15 g |
| Eggs | 1 lb 11 | | oz | 810 g |
| Cake flour | 3 lb 12 | | oz | 1800 g |
| Baking powder | 2.5 | oz | | 72 g |
| Milk | 2 lb 8 | | oz | 1200 g |
| Vanilla extract | 1 | | oz | 30 g |
| *Total weight:* | *13 lb 7* | | *oz* | *6477 g* |

**VARIATION**

### PAN SPREAD

*For one sheet pan:*

| Ingredients | U.S. | | Metric |
|---|---|---|---|
| Brown sugar | 1 lb | | 450 g |
| Granulated sugar | 6 | oz | 170 g |
| Corn syrup or honey | 4 | oz | 120 g |
| Water (as needed) | | | |

Cream together the first three ingredients. Thin with water to spreading consistency.

## CHOCOLATE BUTTER CAKE (P. 399)

| Ingredients | U.S. | | | Metric |
|---|---|---|---|---|
| Butter | 2 lb | | | 1000 g |
| Sugar | 3 lb 8 | | oz | 1725 g |
| Salt | 0.75 | oz | | 22 g |
| Unsweetened chocolate, melted | 1 lb | | | 500 g |
| Eggs | 1 lb 8 | | oz | 750 g |
| Cake flour | 3 lb | | | 1500 g |
| Baking powder | 2 | | oz | 60 g |
| Milk | 1 lb 8 | | oz | 750 g |
| Vanilla extract | 1 | | oz | 30 g |
| *Total weight:* | *12 lb 11* | | *oz* | *6337 g* |

## SACHER MIX II (P. 402)

| Ingredients | U.S. | | Metric |
|---|---|---|---|
| Butter, softened | 13.5 oz | | 400 g |
| Fine granulated sugar | 11 oz | | 330 g |
| Egg yolks | 12 oz | | 360 g |
| Egg whites | 1 lb 2 oz | | 540 g |
| Fine granulated sugar | 6 oz | | 180 g |
| Cake flour | 4 oz | | 120 g |
| Cocoa powder | 4 oz | | 120 g |
| Powdered almonds, toasted | 5.5 oz | | 165 g |
| **Total weight:** | **4 lb 10 oz** | | **2215 g** |

## WHITE CAKE (P. 403)

| Ingredients | U.S. | | Metric |
|---|---|---|---|
| Cake flour | 3 lb | | 1500 g |
| Baking powder | 3 oz | | 90 g |
| Salt | 1 oz | | 30 g |
| Emulsified shortening | 1 lb 8 oz | | 750 g |
| Sugar | 3 lb 12 oz | | 1875 g |
| Skim milk | 1 lb 8 oz | | 750 g |
| Vanilla extract | 0.75 oz (4½ tsp) | | 20 g |
| Almond extract | 0.36 oz (2¼ tsp) | | 10 g |
| Skim milk | 1 lb 8 oz | | 750 g |
| Egg whites | 2 lb | | 1000 g |
| **Total weight:** | **13 lb 9 oz** | | **6775 g** |

## JOCONDE SPONGE CAKE (BISCUIT JOCONDE) (P. 410)

| Ingredients | U.S. | | Metric |
|---|---|---|---|
| Powdered almonds | 14 oz | | 340 g |
| Confectioners' sugar | 12 oz | | 300 g |
| Cake flour | 4 oz | | 100 g |
| Whole eggs | 1 lb 3 oz | | 480 g |
| Egg whites | 13 oz | | 320 g |
| Sugar | 1.6 oz | | 40 g |
| Butter, melted | 5 oz | | 120 g |
| **Total weight:** | **4 lb 5 oz** | | **1700 g** |

## DEVIL'S FOOD CAKE (P. 404)

| Ingredients | U.S. | | Metric |
|---|---|---|---|
| Cake flour | 3 lb | | 1500 g |
| Cocoa | 8 oz | | 250 g |
| Salt | 1 oz | | 30 g |
| Baking powder | 1.5 oz | | 45 g |
| Baking soda | 1 oz | | 30 g |
| Emulsified shortening | 1 lb 12 oz | | 870 g |
| Sugar | 4 lb | | 2000 g |
| Skim milk | 2 lb | | 1000 g |
| Vanilla extract | 0.75 oz (4½ tsp) | | 20 g |
| Skim milk | 1 lb 8 oz | | 750 g |
| Eggs | 2 lb | | 1000 g |
| **Total weight:** | **15 lb** | | **7495 g** |

## GENOISE MOUSSELINE (P. 407)

| Ingredients | U.S. | | Metric |
|---|---|---|---|
| Whole eggs | 1 lb 14 oz | | 900 g |
| Egg yolks | 4 oz (6 yolks) | | 120 g (6 yolks) |
| Sugar | 1 lb 2 oz | | 540 g |
| Cake flour, sifted | 1 lb 2 oz | | 540 g |
| **Total weight:** | **4 lb 6 oz** | | **2100 g** |

## MILK AND BUTTER SPONGE (P. 409)

| Ingredients | U.S. | | Metric |
|---|---|---|---|
| Sugar | 2 lb 8 oz | | 1250 g |
| Whole eggs | 1 lb 8 oz | | 750 g |
| Egg yolks | 8 oz | | 250 g |
| Salt | 0.5 oz | | 15 g |
| Cake flour | 2 lb | | 1000 g |
| Baking powder | 1 oz | | 30 g |
| Skim milk | 1 lb | | 500 g |
| Butter | 8 oz | | 250 g |
| Vanilla extract | 1 oz | | 30 g |
| **Total weight:** | **8 lb 2 oz** | | **4075 g** |

## MARJOLAINE SPONGE CAKE (P. 412)

| Ingredients | U.S. | Metric |
|---|---|---|
| Confectioners' sugar | 12 oz | 360 g |
| Powdered almonds | 12 oz | 360 g |
| Egg yolks | 10 oz | 300 g |
| Egg whites | 6 oz | 180 g |
| Egg whites | 15 oz | 450 g |
| Sugar | 9 oz | 270 g |
| Pastry flour, sifted | 9 oz | 270 g |
| **Total weight:** | **4 lb 9 oz** | **2190 g** |

## HAZELNUT SPONGE CAKE (P. 413)

| Ingredients | U.S. | Metric |
|---|---|---|
| Butter, softened | 14 oz | 400 g |
| Sugar | 11 oz | 330 g |
| Egg yolks | 12 oz | 360 g |
| Egg whites | 1 lb 2 oz | 540 g |
| Sugar | 6 oz | 180 g |
| Cake flour | 4 oz | 120 g |
| Cocoa powder | 4 oz | 120 g |
| Ground hazelnuts, toasted | 5.5 oz | 165 g |
| **Total weight:** | **4 lb 10 oz** | **2215 g** |

## ALMOND CHOCOLATE SPONGE (P. 415)

| Ingredients | U.S. | Metric |
|---|---|---|
| Marzipan | 13 oz | 390 g |
| Egg yolks | 8 oz | 240 g |
| Egg whites | 12 oz | 360 g |
| Sugar | 5 oz | 150 g |
| Cake flour | 4 oz | 120 g |
| Cocoa powder | 4 oz | 120 g |
| Butter, melted | 4 oz | 120 g |
| **Total weight:** | **3 lb 2 oz** | **1500 g** |

## CHOCOLATE SPONGE LAYERS (P. 415)

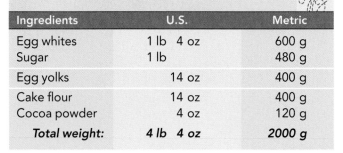

| Ingredients | U.S. | Metric |
|---|---|---|
| Egg whites | 1 lb 4 oz | 600 g |
| Sugar | 1 lb | 480 g |
| Egg yolks | 14 oz | 400 g |
| Cake flour | 14 oz | 400 g |
| Cocoa powder | 4 oz | 120 g |
| **Total weight:** | **4 lb 4 oz** | **2000 g** |

## LEMON MADELEINES (P. 417)

| Ingredients | U.S. | Metric |
|---|---|---|
| Egg yolks | 6 oz | 180 g |
| Demerara sugar | 1 oz | 30 g |
| Lemon zest, grated | 0.4 oz (4½ tsp) | 12 g |
| Honey | 1.5 oz | 45 g |
| Egg whites | 6 oz | 180 g |
| Extra-fine granulated sugar | 7.5 oz | 225 g |
| Salt | 0.1 oz (½ tsp) | 3 g |
| Baking powder | 0.3 oz (1½ tsp) | 9 g |
| Cake flour | 9 oz | 270 g |
| Butter, melted | 9 oz | 270 g |
| **Total weight:** | **2 lb 8 oz** | **1224 g** |

**VARIATION**

### CHOCOLATE AND ORANGE MADELEINES

| Ingredients | U.S. | Metric |
|---|---|---|
| Egg yolks | 6 oz | 180 g |
| Demerara sugar | 1 oz | 30 g |
| Orange zest, grated | 0.75 oz | 24 g |
| Honey | 1.5 oz | 45 g |
| Egg whites | 6 oz | 180 g |
| Extra-fine granulated sugar | 7.5 oz | 225 g |
| Salt | 0.1 oz (½ tsp) | 3 g |
| Baking powder | 0.4 oz (2¼ tsp) | 12 g |
| Cocoa powder | 2.5 oz | 75 g |
| Cake flour | 6 oz | 180 g |
| Butter, melted | 9 oz | 270 g |

Follow the basic procedure, but change the ingredients as listed above.

# CHOCOLATE VELVET CAKE (MOELLEUX) (P. 416)

| Ingredients | U.S. | Metric |
|---|---|---|
| Almond paste | 7.5 oz | 225 g |
| Confectioners' sugar | 5 oz | 150 g |
| Egg yolks | 6 oz | 180 g |
| Egg whites | 6 oz | 180 g |
| Sugar | 2.5 oz | 75 g |
| Cake flour | 4 oz | 120 g |
| Cocoa powder | 1 oz | 30 g |
| Butter, melted | 2 oz | 60 g |
| **For baking** | | |
| Almonds, chopped | 3 oz | 90 g |
| ***Total batter weight:*** | ***2 lb 2 oz*** | ***1020 g*** |

# FRENCH BUTTERCREAM (P. 425)

Yield: 5 lb 8 oz (2750 g)

| Ingredients | U.S. | Metric |
|---|---|---|
| Sugar | 2 lb | 1000 g |
| Water | 8 oz | 250 mL |
| Egg yolks | 12 oz | 375 g |
| Butter, softened | 2 lb 8 oz | 1250 g |
| Vanilla extract | 0.5 oz | 15 mL |

# SIMPLE BUTTERCREAM (P. 426)

| Ingredients | U.S. | Metric |
|---|---|---|
| Butter | 2 lb | 1000 g |
| Shortening | 1 lb | 500 g |
| Confectioners' sugar | 5 lb | 2500 g |
| Egg whites, pasteurized | 5 oz | 160 g |
| Lemon juice | 0.33 oz (2 tsp) | 10 g |
| Vanilla extract | 0.5 oz | 15 g |
| Water *(optional)* | 4 oz | 125 g |
| ***Total weight:*** | ***8 lb 9 oz*** | ***4310 g*** |

# ITALIAN BUTTERCREAM (P. 426)

Yield: 6 lb 12 oz (3400 g)

| Ingredients | U.S. | Metric |
|---|---|---|
| **Italian meringue** | | |
| Sugar | 2 lb | 1000 g |
| Water | 8 oz | 250 mL |
| Egg whites | 1 lb | 500 g |
| Butter | 3 lb | 1500 g |
| Emulsified shortening | 8 oz | 250 g |
| Lemon juice | 0.33 oz (2 tsp) | 10 mL |
| Vanilla extract | 0.5 oz | 15 mL |

# PRALINE BUTTERCREAM (P. 427)

Yield: 3 lb 6 oz (1650 g)

| Ingredients | U.S. | Metric |
|---|---|---|
| Water | 4 oz | 120 g |
| Sugar | 12 oz | 360 g |
| Egg yolks | 10 oz | 300 g |
| Butter, softened | 1 lb 2 oz | 540 g |
| Praline paste | 15 oz | 450 g |

# VANILLA CREAM (P. 427)

| Ingredients | U.S. | Metric |
|---|---|---|
| Pastry Cream (p. 271) | 2 lb 8 oz | 1125 g |
| Gelatin | 0.5 oz | 16 g |
| Rum | 1.75 oz | 50 g |
| Butter, softened | 1 lb 2 oz | 500 g |
| ***Total weight:*** | ***3 lb 12 oz*** | ***1690 g*** |

# CARAMEL BUTTERCREAM (P. 427)

Yield: 4 lb (2000 g)

| Ingredients | U.S. | Metric |
|---|---|---|
| Water | 4 oz | 100 g |
| Sugar | 1 lb 10 oz | 740 g |
| Water | 7 oz | 200 g |
| Heavy cream | 5 oz | 140 g |
| Coffee extract | 0.75 oz | 20 g |
| Egg yolks | 8 oz | 240 g |
| Butter, softened | 1 lb 11 oz | 760 g |

## LIGHT PRALINE CREAM (P. 428)

| Ingredients | U.S. | Metric |
|---|---|---|
| Butter, softened | 2 lb | 1000 g |
| Praline paste | 1 lb | 500 g |
| Cognac | 6 oz | 200 g |
| Italian Meringue (p. 267) | 3 lb 6 oz | 1700 g |
| **Total weight:** | **6 lb 12 oz** | **3400 g** |

## FLAT ICING (P. 431)

| Ingredients | U.S. | Metric |
|---|---|---|
| Confectioners' sugar | 4 lb | 2000 g |
| Water, hot | 12 oz | 375 mL |
| Corn syrup | 4 oz | 125 g |
| Vanilla extract | 0.5 oz | 15 g |
| **Total weight:** | **5 lb** | **2500 g** |

## OPERA GLAZE (P. 434)

| Ingredients | U.S. | Metric |
|---|---|---|
| Coating chocolate (p. 92) | 1 lb 8 oz | 750 g |
| Dark chocolate couverture | 10.5 oz | 300 g |
| Peanut oil | 4 oz | 120 g |
| **Total weight:** | **2 lb 6 oz** | **1170 g** |

**VARIATION**

If couverture is used alone instead of part coating chocolate and part couverture, the quantity of oil must be increased so the icing has the proper texture and can easily be cut with a cake knife.

| Ingredients | U.S. | Metric |
|---|---|---|
| Dark chocolate couverture | 2 lb 2.5 oz | 1050 g |
| Peanut oil | 6 oz | 180 g |

## COCOA JELLY (P. 434)

| Ingredients | U.S. | Metric |
|---|---|---|
| Water | 1 lb | 450 g |
| Fondant | 1 lb 8 oz | 675 g |
| Glucose | 8 oz | 225 g |
| Gelatin | 1 oz | 30 g |
| Cocoa powder | 4.75 oz | 135 g |
| **Total weight:** | **3 lb 5 oz** | **1515 g** |

## COFFEE MARBLE GLAZE (P. 435)

*Yield: 2 lb (1000 g)*

| Ingredients | U.S. | Metric |
|---|---|---|
| Gelatin | 1 oz | 24 g |
| Water | 1 lb 8 oz | 750 g |
| Sugar | 4 oz | 120 g |
| Glucose | 4 oz | 120 g |
| Vanilla bean, split | 2 | 2 |
| Coffee liqueur | 2 oz | 60 g |
| Coffee extract | 1 oz | 30 g |

## ALMOND MACAROONS II (P. 506)

| Ingredients | U.S. | Metric |
|---|---|---|
| Powdered almonds | 8 oz | 240 g |
| Confectioners' sugar | 1 lb | 500 g |
| Egg whites | 8 oz | 240 g |
| Fine granulated sugar | 3.5 oz | 100 g |
| Vanilla extract | 8 drops | 8 drops |
| **Total weight:** | **2 lb 3 oz** | **1080 g** |

**VARIATION**

### COCOA ALMOND MACAROONS

Prepare as in the basic formula, using the following ingredients and quantities. Process the cocoa and cake flour with the almonds and sugar in step 1.

| Ingredients | U.S. | Metric |
|---|---|---|
| Powdered almonds | 12 oz | 300 g |
| Confectioners' sugar | 1 lb | 400 g |
| Cocoa powder | 4 oz | 100 g |
| Cake flour | 3.5 oz | 80 g |
| Egg whites | 1 lb 3 oz | 480 g |
| Fine granulated sugar | 8 oz | 200 g |

## DIAMONDS (P. 500)

| Ingredients | U.S. | | Metric |
|---|---|---|---|
| Butter, cut in small pieces | 1 lb 4 | oz | 560 g |
| Cake flour | 1 lb 12 | oz | 800 g |
| Confectioners' sugar | 8 | oz | 240 g |
| Salt | 0.16 oz (¾ tsp) | | 4 g |
| Grated orange zest | 0.3 oz (4 tsp) | | 8 g |
| Vanilla extract | 0.3 oz (2 tsp) | | 8 g |
| **For rolling** | | | |
| Crystal sugar | 7 | oz | 200 g |
| **Total dough weight:** | **3 lb 15** | **oz** | **1620 g** |

## ALMOND TUILES I (P. 508)

| Ingredients | U.S. | | Metric |
|---|---|---|---|
| Butter | 12 oz | | 360 g |
| Confectioners' sugar | 1 lb | | 480 g |
| Egg whites | 12 oz | | 360 g |
| Cake flour | 14 oz | | 420 g |
| **Garnish** | | | |
| Sliced almonds | 10 oz | | 300 g |
| **Batter weight:** | **3 lb 6 oz** | | **1620 g** |

## COCONUT TUILES (P. 510)

| Ingredients | U.S. | | Metric |
|---|---|---|---|
| Confectioners' sugar | 1 lb | | 520 g |
| Egg, lightly beaten | 12 oz | | 400 g |
| Desiccated coconut | 1 lb | | 520 g |
| Butter, melted | 3 oz | | 100 g |
| **Total weight:** | **2 lb 15 oz** | | **1540 g** |

## RICH BROWNIES (P. 511)

*Yield: one large formula (about 10 lb 5 oz or 4652 g)*
*fills one full-size sheet pan (18 × 26 in./46 × 66 cm),*
*two half-size sheet pans, four 9 × 13 in. (23 × 33 cm) pans,*
*or six 9-in. (23 cm) square pans.*

| Ingredients | U.S. | | Metric |
|---|---|---|---|
| Unsweetened chocolate | 8 | oz | 225 g |
| Bittersweet chocolate | 1 lb 4 | oz | 560 g |
| Butter | 2 lb 8 | oz | 1125 g |
| Eggs | 1 lb 12 | oz | 790 gm |
| Sugar | 2 lb 4 | oz | 1015 g |
| Salt | 0.25 oz | | 7 g |
| Vanilla extract | 1 | oz | 30 mL |
| Bread flour | 1 lb | | 450 g |
| Walnuts or pecans, chopped | 1 lb | | 450 g |
| **Total weight:** | **10 lb 5** | **oz** | **4652 g** |

### VARIATION

| Ingredients | U.S. | Metric |
|---|---|---|
| Baking powder | 0.4 oz | 11 g |

For a more cakelike brownie, sift the above quantity of baking powder with the flour in step 4.

## CREAM CHEESE BROWNIES (P. 512)

*Yield: one large formula (about 12 lb or 5600 g)*
*fills one full-size sheet pan (18 × 26 in./46 × 66 cm),*
*two half-size sheet pans, four 9 × 13 in. (23 × 33 cm) pans,*
*or six 9-in. (23 cm) square pans.*

| Ingredients | U.S. | | Metric |
|---|---|---|---|
| Cream cheese | 2 lb | | 900 g |
| Sugar | 8 | oz | 225 g |
| Vanilla extract | 2 | tsp | 7 mL |
| Egg yolks | 2.7 oz (4 yolks) | | 80 g |
| Rich Brownie batter without walnuts (p. 511) (1 recipe) | 10 lb 5 | oz | 4650 g |
| **Total weight:** | **12 lb 15** | **oz** | **5862 g** |

# ESPRESSO BISCOTTI (P. 515)

| Ingredients | U.S. | | Metric |
|---|---|---|---|
| Butter | 12 | oz | 360 g |
| Sugar | 1 lb 2 | oz | 540 g |
| Salt | 0.6 | oz | 18 g |
| Eggs | 10 | oz | 300 g |
| Water, hot | 1.5 | oz | 45 g |
| Instant espresso powder | 0.6 | oz | 18 g |
| Pastry flour | 1 lb 14 | oz | 900 g |
| Baking powder | 0.75 | oz | 24 g |
| Blanched almonds | 11 | oz | 315 g |
| **Total weight:** | **5 lb 2** | **oz** | **2520 g** |

# CHOCOLATE PECAN BISCOTTI (P. 515)

| Ingredients | U.S. | | Metric |
|---|---|---|---|
| Butter | 12 | oz | 360 g |
| Sugar | 1 lb | | 540 g |
| Salt | 0.3 | oz | 9 g |
| Orange zest, grated | 0.3 | oz | 9 g |
| Eggs | 10 | oz | 300 g |
| Water | 6 | oz | 180 g |
| Vanilla extract | 0.5 | oz | 15 g |
| Pastry flour | 1 lb 14 | oz | 900 g |
| Cocoa powder | 4.5 | oz | 135 g |
| Baking powder | 0.75 | oz | 24 g |
| Baking soda | 0.25 | oz | 8 g |
| Pecan pieces | 6 | oz | 180 g |
| Small chocolate chips | 6 | oz | 180 g |
| **Total weight:** | **5 lb 12** | **oz** | **2840 g** |

# BATONS MARECHAUX AND EPONGES (P. 516)

| Ingredients | U.S. | | Metric |
|---|---|---|---|
| Confectioners' sugar | 10 | oz | 300 g |
| Cake flour | 3 | oz | 90 g |
| Powdered almonds | 7.5 | oz | 225 g |
| Egg whites | 12 | oz | 360 g |
| Granulated sugar | 4 | oz | 120 g |
| **For finishing Batons Marechaux** | | | |
| Chocolate, tempered | as needed | | as needed |
| **For finishing Eponges** | | | |
| Slivered almonds | as needed | | as needed |
| Raspberry jam | as needed | | as needed |
| **Total weight:** | **2 lb 4** | **oz** | **1095 g** |

# CHRISTMAS PUDDING (P. 530)

| Ingredients | U.S. | | Metric |
|---|---|---|---|
| Dark raisins | 2 lb | | 1000 g |
| Light raisins | 2 lb | | 1000 g |
| Currants | 2 lb | | 1000 g |
| Dates, diced | 1 lb | | 500 g |
| Almonds, chopped | 12 | oz | 375 g |
| Candied orange peel, finely chopped | 8 | oz | 250 g |
| Candied lemon peel, finely chopped | 8 | oz | 250 g |
| Brandy | 1 pt 8 | oz | 750 mL |
| Bread flour | 1 lb | | 500 g |
| Cinnamon | 0.12 oz (2 tsp) | | 4 g |
| Nutmeg | 0.03 oz (½ tsp) | | 1 g |
| Mace | 0.03 oz (½ tsp) | | 1 g |
| Ginger | 0.03 oz (½ tsp) | | 1 g |
| Cloves, ground | 0.03 oz (½ tsp) | | 1 g |
| Salt | 0.5 | oz | 15 g |
| Beef suet, finely chopped | 1 lb 8 | oz | 750 g |
| Brown sugar | 1 lb | | 500 g |
| Eggs | 1 lb | | 500 g |
| Fresh bread crumbs | 8 | oz | 250 g |
| Molasses | 2 | oz | 60 g |
| **Total weight:** | **15 lb 7** | **oz** | **7700 g** |

## STEAMED BLUEBERRY PUDDING (P. 531)

| Ingredients | U.S. | | Metric |
|---|---|---|---|
| Brown sugar | 1 lb 4 | oz | 625 g |
| Butter | 8 | oz | 250 g |
| Salt | 0.08 oz (½ tsp) | | 3 g |
| Cinnamon | 0.17 oz (1 tbsp) | | 5 g |
| Eggs | 8 | oz | 250 g |
| Bread flour | 4 | oz | 125 g |
| Baking powder | 0.75 oz | | 22 g |
| Dry bread crumbs | 1 lb 4 | oz | 625 g |
| Milk | 1 lb | | 500 g |
| Blueberries, fresh or frozen, without sugar | 1 lb | | 500 g |
| **Total weight:** | **5 lb 13** | **oz** | **2905 g** |

## CREAM CHEESE BAVARIAN (P. 536)
*Yield: about 6 qt (6.5 L)*

| Ingredients | U.S. | | Metric |
|---|---|---|---|
| Cream cheese | 3 lb | | 1500 g |
| Sugar | 1 lb | | 500 g |
| Salt | 0.5 oz | | 15 g |
| Lemon zest, grated | 0.12 oz (1½ tsp) | | 4 g |
| Orange zest, grated | 0.08 oz (1 tsp) | | 2.5 g |
| Vanilla extract | 0.25 oz (1½ tsp) | | 8 g |
| Lemon juice | 4 | oz | 125 g |
| Gelatin | 1 | oz | 30 g |
| Water, cold | 8 | oz | 250 g |
| Heavy cream | 4 pt | | 2000 mL |
| **Total weight:** | **8 lb 13** | **oz** | **4434 g** |

## RASPBERRY JAM (P. 599)
*Yield: 1 lb 14 oz (950 g)*

| Ingredients | U.S. | | Metric |
|---|---|---|---|
| Sugar | 12 | oz | 375 g |
| Water | 1 | oz | 125 g |
| Raspberries, fresh | 1 lb | | 500 g |
| Glucose | 1.6 | oz | 50 g |
| Sugar | 2.5 | oz | 75 g |
| Pectin | 1.33 oz | | 40 g |

## APPLE MARMALADE (P. 599)
*Yield: 8 lb 8 oz (4240 g)*

| Ingredients | U.S. | Metric |
|---|---|---|
| Apples, peeled and cored | 8 lb | 4000 g |
| Water | 1 lb | 500 g |
| Sugar | 2 lb 8 oz | 1200 g |

## STRAWBERRY MARMALADE (P. 600)
*Yield: 3 lb 4 oz (1600 g)*

| Ingredients | U.S. | | Metric |
|---|---|---|---|
| Strawberries | 2 lb | | 1000 g |
| Sugar | 2 lb | | 1000 g |
| Pectin | 0.67 oz | | 20 g |
| Lemon juice | 2 | oz | 30 g |

## CARAMELIZED APRICOTS (P. 600)
*Yield: 2 lb 8 oz (1200 g)*

| Ingredients | U.S. | | Metric |
|---|---|---|---|
| Sugar | 1 lb | | 400 g |
| Water | 4 | oz | 100 g |
| Honey | 8 | oz | 200 g |
| Butter | 4 | oz | 100 g |
| Canned apricots, drained | 2 lb 8 oz | | 1200 g |

## APRICOT COMPOTE (P. 601)
*Yield: 2 lb 6 oz (960 g)*

| Ingredients | U.S. | | Metric |
|---|---|---|---|
| Sugar | 1 lb 2 | oz | 450 g |
| Water | 2.5 oz | | 60 g |
| Apricots, fresh or canned, halved and pitted | 1 lb 4 | oz | 500 g |
| Pectin | 1.5 oz | | 40 g |
| Glucose | 2 | oz | 50 g |

### VARIATION

#### APRICOT AND ALMOND COMPOTE

| Ingredients | U.S. | Metric |
|---|---|---|
| Whole blanched almonds | 8 oz | 200 g |

Add the almonds to the apricots at the same time as the pectin and glucose.

# PINEAPPLE KUMQUAT COMPOTE (P. 601)

*Yield: 2 lb 12 oz (1080 g)*

| Ingredients | U.S. | Metric |
|---|---|---|
| Sugar | 1 lb 2 oz | 450 g |
| Water | 2.5 oz | 60 g |
| Vanilla bean | 1 | 1 |
| Glucose | 2 oz | 48 g |
| Canned pineapple, drained and diced | 1 lb 4 oz | 500 g |
| Kumquats, sliced and blanched | 8 oz | 200 g |
| Pistachios | 1.5 oz | 40 g |

**VARIATION**

### KUMQUAT COMPOTE

| Ingredients | U.S. | Metric |
|---|---|---|
| Sugar | 1 lb 2 oz | 450 g |
| Water | 2.5 oz | 60 g |
| Glucose | 2 oz | 48 g |
| Kumquats, halved or sliced, blanched | 1 lb 4 oz | 500 g |
| Pistachios | 3 oz | 80 g |

Follow the procedure in the basic recipe, but omit the pineapple and vanilla and adjust the quantities as listed above.

# ROCHER WITH ALMONDS (P. 652)

| Ingredients | U.S. | Metric |
|---|---|---|
| Dark chocolate | 1 lb | 450 g |
| Praline paste | 1 lb 8 oz | 675 g |
| Ice cream wafers (pailletine), finely crushed | 8 oz | 225 g |
| Dark chocolate | 1 lb 8 oz | 675 g |
| Almonds, toasted and chopped | 4 oz | 112 g |
| **Total weight:** | **4 lb 12 oz** | **2137 g** |

# GUM PASTE (P. 663)

| Ingredient | U.S. | Metric |
|---|---|---|
| Confectioners' sugar | 2 lb 8 oz | 1250 g |
| Gum tragacanth | 1 oz (3 tbsp) | 30 g |
| Water | 6 fl oz | 190 mL |
| Glucose syrup | 2 oz | 60 g |
| Confectioners sugar | 8 oz or as needed | 250 g |
| **Total weight:** | **3 lb 9 oz** | **1780 g** |

## Procedure

1. Sift the confectioner's sugar into a bowl.
2. Add the gum tragacanth and mix in.
3. Add the water and glucose. Mix until smooth.
4. Transfer the mixture to a work surface. Knead in the remaining sugar, or enough to make a smooth, firm dough.
5. Roll the gum paste into a cylinder. Coat it with a light film of shortening (to prevent drying) and wrap tightly in plastic film. Let stand overnight.

# Metric Conversion Factors

## Weight

1 ounce equals 28.35 grams

1 gram equals 0.035 ounce

1 pound equals 454 grams

1 kilogram equals 2.2 pounds

## Volume

1 fluid ounce equals 29.57 milliliters

1 milliliter equals 0.034 fluid ounce

1 cup equals 237 milliliters

1 quart equals 946 milliliters

1 liter equals 33.8 fluid ounces

## Length

1 inch equals 25.4 millimeters

1 centimeter equals 0.39 inch

1 meter equals 39.4 inches

## Temperature

To convert Fahrenheit to Celsius: Subtract 32, then multiply by $5/9$.

*Example:* Convert 140°F to Celsius.

$$140 - 32 = 108$$

$$108 \times 5/9 = 60°C$$

To convert Celsius to Fahrenheit: Multiply by $9/5$, then add 32.

*Example:* Convert 150°C to Fahrenheit.

$$150 \times 9/5 = 270$$

$$270 + 32 = 302°F$$

*Note:* The metric measurements in the recipes in this book are not equivalent to the corresponding U.S. measurements. See page 22 for a complete explanation.

# Decimal Equivalents of Common Fractions

| Fraction | Rounded to 3 places | Rounded to 2 places |
|---|---|---|
| ⅚ | 0.833 | 0.83 |
| ⅘ | 0.8 | 0.8 |
| **¾** | **0.75** | **0.75** |
| **⅔** | **0.667** | **0.67** |
| ⅝ | 0.625 | 0.63 |
| ⅗ | 0.6 | 0.6 |
| **½** | **0.5** | **0.5** |
| **⅓** | **0.333** | **0.33** |
| **¼** | **0.25** | **0.25** |
| ⅕ | 0.2 | 0.2 |
| ⅙ | 0.167 | 0.17 |
| **⅛** | **0.125** | **0.13** |
| 1/10 | 0.1 | 0.1 |
| 1/12 | 0.083 | 0.08 |
| 1/16 | 0.063 | 0.06 |
| 1/25 | 0.04 | 0.04 |

# Approximate Volume Equivalents of Dry Foods

The following equivalents are rough averages only. Actual weight varies considerably. For accurate measurement, all ingredients should be weighed.

Following common practice, volume measures in this chart are represented as common fractions rather than as decimals.

**Bread flour, sifted**
- 1 lb = 4 cups
- 1 cup = 4 oz

**Bread flour, unsifted**
- 1 lb = 3⅓ cups
- 1 cup = 4.75 oz

**Cake flour, sifted**
- 1 lb = 4¼ cups
- 1 cup = 3.75 oz

**Cake flour, unsifted**
- 1 lb = 3½ cups
- 1 cup = 4.5 oz

**Granulated sugar**
- 1 lb = 2¼ cups
- 1 cup = 7 oz

**Confectioners' sugar, sifted**
- 1 lb = 4 cups
- 1 cup = 4 oz

**Confectioners' sugar, unsifted**
- 1 lb = 3½ cups
- 1 cup = 4.5 oz

**Cornstarch, sifted**
- 1 lb = 4 cups
- 1 cup = 4 oz
- 1 oz = 4 tbsp = ¼ cup
- 1 tbsp = 0.25 oz

**Cornstarch, unsifted**
- 1 lb = 3½ cups
- 1 cup = 4.5 oz
- 1 oz = 3½ tbsp
- 1 tbsp = 0.29 oz

**Cocoa, unsifted**
- 1 lb = 5 cups
- 1 cup = 3.2 oz
- 1 oz = 5 tbsp
- 1 tbsp = 0.2 oz

**Gelatin, unflavored**
- 1 oz = 3 tbsp
- ¼ oz = 2¼ tsp
- 1 tbsp = 0.33 oz
- 1 tsp = 0.11 oz

**Baking powder (phosphate type and sodium aluminum sulfate type)**
- 1 oz = 2 tbsp
- ¼ oz = 1½ tsp
- 1 tbsp = 0.5 oz
- 1 tsp = 0.17 oz

**Baking soda**
- (same as for Baking Powder)

**Cream of tartar**
- 1 oz = 4 tbsp
- ¼ oz = 1 tbsp
- 1 tsp = 0.08 oz

**Salt**
- 1 oz = 5 tsp
- ¼ oz = 1¼ tsp
- 1 tsp = 0.2 oz

**Cinnamon**
- 1 oz = 17 tsp
- ¼ oz = 4¼ tsp
- 1 tsp = 0.06 oz

**Ground spices (except cinnamon)**
- 1 oz = 14 tsp
- ¼ oz = 3½ tsp
- 1 tsp = 0.07 oz

**Grated lemon zest**
- 1 oz = 4 tbsp
- 1 tsp = 0.08 oz

# Temperature Calculations for Yeast Doughs

In chapter 6 (p. 123), a simple formula is presented to enable you to calculate what the water temperature should be in order to get a mixed dough of a specified temperature. This formula is sufficient for most straight doughs made in small batches. However, other calculations may sometimes be required. These are detailed here.

## Machine Friction

Machine friction depends on many factors, including the type of mixer, amount of dough, stiffness of dough, and mixing time. This friction may be determined for each dough prepared, assuming a constant batch size.

## Ice Calculation

If your tap water is warmer than the water temperature you need for a batch of dough, you can cool the water with crushed ice. A simple formula can be used to calculate how much crushed ice to use.

This formula is based on the fact that it requires 144 BTUs of heat energy to melt 1 pound ice. A BTU (British thermal unit) is the amount of heat needed to raise the temperature of 1 pound water 1°F. Therefore, it takes 144 BTUs to melt 1 pound ice, but only 1 more BTU to heat that pound of melted ice from 32° to 33°F.

You can use the following formula without having to understand how it is derived. However, if you wish to know where the formula comes from, an explanation follows the formula and sample calculation. Please note this formula is more accurate than many of the formulas you will see elsewhere. Many other formulas allow for the heat energy needed to melt the ice, but they don't allow for the fact that the melted ice is also warmed up to the final water temperature.

Also, please remember that the ice counts as part of the water for the dough.

---

## Procedure for Determining Machine Friction

1. Prepare a batch of dough, first measuring the room temperature, flour temperature, and water temperature. Add these three figures.

2. Measure the temperature of the dough as it comes from the mixer. Multiply this figure by 3.

3. Subtract the result of step 1 from the result of step 2. This is the machine friction.

4. Use this factor when calculating the water temperature required for subsequent batches of this particular dough, as explained on page 123.

Example:

Room temperature = 72°F
Flour temperature = 65°F
Water temperature = 75°F
Dough temperature = 77°F

1. $72 + 65 + 75 = 212$

2. $77 \times 3 = 231$

3. $231 - 212 = 19$

Machine friction = 19°F

## Procedure for Determining Ice Requirement

1. Measure the temperature of the tap water. Subtract the water temperature needed for your dough from the tap water temperature. This number is the temperature decrease needed.

$$\text{Tap water temperature} - \text{desired water temperature} = \text{temperature decrease}$$

2. Calculate the weight of ice needed by using the following formula.

$$\text{Ice weight} = \frac{\text{Total water} \times \text{temperature decrease}}{\text{Tap water temperature} + 112}$$

Total water is the weight of water needed for the dough recipe.

3. Subtract the ice weight from the total water needed to get the weight of the tap water needed.

$$\text{Total water} - \text{ice} = \text{tap water}$$

Example: For a batch of bread, you need 16 lb water at 58°F. Your tap water is 65°F. How much tap water and how much ice should you use?

$$\text{Ice} = \frac{16\,\text{lb} \times (65 - 58)}{65 + 112} = \frac{16\,\text{lb} \times 7}{177}$$

$$= \frac{112\,\text{lb}}{177} = 0.63\,\text{lb} = 10\,\text{oz}$$

$$\text{Tap water} = 16\,\text{lb} - 10\,\text{oz} = 15\,\text{lb}\ 6\,\text{oz}$$

You need 10 oz ice plus 15 lb 6 oz tap water.

---

The above formula is based on the fact that the number of BTUs needed to raise the ice to the desired water temperature equals the number of BTUs lost by the tap water when it is cooled to the desired temperature. This can be expressed as follows:

$$\left.\begin{array}{l}\text{BTUs to melt ice } plus \\ \text{BTUs to heat melted ice to} \\ \text{desired temperature}\end{array}\right\} = \text{BTUs lost by tap water}$$

Remember, as explained earlier, that 144 BTUs are needed to melt 1 pound ice and that 1 BTU is needed to heat 1 pound water 1°F.

Therefore, the three BTU values in the above equation can each be expressed mathematically:

BTUs to melt ice = Ice weight (in pounds) *times* 144

$$\begin{array}{l}\text{BTUs to heat melted} \\ \text{ice to temperature}\end{array} = \begin{array}{l}\text{Ice weight } times \\ \text{degrees of temperature rise}\end{array}$$

*or*

Ice weight *times* (desired temperature minus 32°F)

BTUs lost by tap water = weight of tap water *times* degrees of temperature drop

*or*

(total water *minus* ice) *times* (tap water temperature *minus* desired temperature)

To make the calculations easier to read, we adopt the following abbreviations. Then we substitute them in our basic equation and proceed to simplify it mathematically.

$$I = \text{ice weight}$$
$$W = \text{tap water weight}$$
$$W + I = \text{total water required in recipe}$$
$$T = \text{tap water temperature}$$
$$D = \text{desired temperature}$$

$$\left.\begin{array}{l}\text{BTUs to melt ice } plus \\ \text{BTUs to heat melted ice to 6} \\ \text{desired temperature}\end{array}\right\} = \text{BTUs lost by tap water}$$

$$(I \times 144) + (I \times (D - 32)) = ((W + I) - I) \times (T - D)$$

$$I \times (144 + D - 32) = ((W + I) \times (T - D)) - (I \times (T - D))$$

$$(I \times (144 + D - 32)) + (I \times (T - D)) = (W + I) \times (T - D)$$

$$I \times (144 + D - 32 + T - D) = (W + I) \times (T - D)$$

$$I \times (112 + T) = (W + I) \times (T - D)$$

$$I = \frac{(W + I) \times (T - D)}{112 + T}$$

$$\text{Ice} = \frac{\text{Total water} \times \text{temperature decrease}}{\text{Tap water temperature} + 112}$$

# Eggs and Safety

The following guidelines are reprinted from Joan K. Loken, *The HACCP Food Safety Manual.* New York: John Wiley & Sons, 1995, pp. 122–123.

## Eggs and Egg-Based Products

Outbreaks of salmonellosis have been traced to clean, whole, uncracked-shell eggs contaminated with *Salmonella enteritidis.* Whole-shell eggs are now classified as potentially hazardous foods by the [U.S. Food and Drug Administration].

The following guidelines, which treat eggs as potentially hazardous foods during storage, handling, preparation, and service, must be followed to prevent the possibility of food-borne illness:

* Store eggs at refrigerated temperatures of 40°F [4°C] or lower.

* When using eggs for menu service, it is best to keep them refrigerated and pull as needed. If this is not feasible, pull one layer at a time if used quickly, or ice eggs in a pan.

* Cooked eggs must be held at 140°F [60°C] or higher.

* Cook eggs thoroughly until both the yolk and white are firm, not runny.

    *Scrambled*—1 minute on cooking surface of 250°F [121°C]

    *Poached*—5 minutes in boiling water

    *Soft-boiled*—7 minutes in boiling water

    *Sunnyside*—7 minutes on cooking surface of 250°F [121°C], or covered 4 minutes at 250°F [121°C]

    *Fried, over easy*—3 minutes at 250°F [121°C], then turn and fry another 2 minutes on the other side.

* Avoid pooling raw eggs for holding. Eggs may be pooled in small quantities for immediate cooking and serving.

* For lightly cooked egg items, such as custards, French toast, mousse, and meringues, pasteurized eggs should be used.

* Avoid raw egg menu items. Review menus, recipes, and preparation procedures using raw eggs. Pasteurized eggs may be substituted for Caesar salad, hollandaise and béarnaise sauces, eggnog, ice cream, and egg-fortified beverages.

* Pasteurized eggs require the same time and temperature handling as other potentially hazardous foods.

* Wash hands with hot, soapy water before and after handling eggs and egg products.

* Wash and sanitize utensils, equipment, and the work area after handling eggs and egg products.

* Do not reuse a container that has held a raw egg mixture. Use a clean, sanitized container for each batch.

# Glossary

Many culinary terms in common use are taken from French. Phonetic guides for difficult words are included here, using English sounds. However, exact renderings are impossible in many cases because French has a number of sounds that do not exist in English.

**Absorption:** The amount of water a flour can take up and hold while being made into a simple dough, based on a predetermined standard dough consistency or stiffness; expressed as a percentage of the weight of flour.

**Aerobic:** Requiring oxygen to live and grow; said of bacteria.

**Air cell:** A tiny bubble of air, created by creaming or foaming, that assists in leavening a dough or batter.

**Allergen:** A substance that triggers an allergic reaction.

**Allumette:** Any puff pastry item made in thin sticks or strips (French word for "matchstick").

**Almond paste:** A mixture of finely ground almonds and sugar.

**Amylase:** An enzyme in flour that breaks down starches into simple sugars.

**Anaerobic:** Requiring an absence of oxygen to live and grow; said of bacteria.

**Anaphylaxis:** A sudden, severe, allergic reaction of the immune system.

**Angel food cake:** A type of cake made of meringue (egg whites and sugar) and flour.

**Angel food method:** A cake-mixing method involving folding a mixture of flour and sugar into a meringue.

**AP weight:** As purchased; the weight of an item before trimming.

**Apple charlotte:** A dessert of apples cut up and baked in a mold lined with bread slices.

**Artisan bread:** Bread made by a skilled manual worker; usually referring to handmade breads made using traditional methods and with natural ingredients only.

**Ash:** The mineral content of flour; expressed as a percentage of the total weight.

**Autolyse:** A resting period early in the mixing procedure of yeast doughs during which the flour fully absorbs the water.

**Baba:** A type of yeast bread or cake that is soaked in syrup.

**Babka:** A type of sweet yeast bread or coffee cake.

**Bagel:** A ring-shaped lean yeast dough product made from a very stiff dough.

**Bagged:** A cookie makeup method in which the dough is shaped and deposited with a pastry bag.

**Baked Alaska:** A dessert consisting of ice cream on a sponge cake base, covered with meringue and browned in the oven.

**Baked custard:** A custard that is baked without being disturbed so it sets into a solid.

**Baked meringue:** Any meringue mixture that is baked until dry.

**Baker's percentage:** A method of expressing ratios of ingredients in a baking formula, in which the weight of each ingredient is expressed as a percentage of the weight of the flour.

**Baking ammonia:** A leavening ingredient that releases ammonia gas and carbon dioxide.

**Baklava:** A Greek or Middle Eastern dessert made of nuts and phyllo dough and soaked with syrup.

**Bar:** A cookie makeup method in which the dough is shaped into flattened cylinders, baked, and sliced crosswise into individual cookies; a cookie made by this method.

**Batter:** A semiliquid mixture containing flour or other starch, used for the production of such products as cakes and breads and for coating products to be deep fried.

**Baumé:** A unit of measure indicating the specific gravity of a solution, often used to indicate sugar concentration.

**Baumkuchen** (bowm koo khen): A cake made by adding one thin layer of batter at a time to a pan and browning lightly under a broiler after each addition, repeating until the cake is the desired thickness.

**Bavarian cream:** A light, cold dessert made of gelatin, whipped cream, and custard sauce or fruit.

**Beignet soufflé** (ben yay soo flay): A type of fritter made with éclair paste, which puffs up greatly when fried.

**Biga:** A yeast pre-ferment made as a stiff dough.

**Biscuit method:** A mixing method in which the fat is mixed with the dry ingredients before the liquid ingredients are added.

**Black Forest torte:** A chocolate sponge layer cake filled with whipped cream and cherries.

**Blancmange** (bla mahnge): (1) An English pudding made of milk, sugar, and cornstarch; (2) A French dessert made of milk, cream, almonds, and gelatin.

**Blitz puff pastry:** A type of pastry mixed like a very flaky pie dough, then rolled and folded like puff pastry.

**Bloom:** A whitish coating on chocolate caused by separated cocoa butter.

**Blown sugar:** Pulled sugar made into thin-walled, hollow shapes by being blown up like a balloon.

**Boiled icing:** Italian meringue used as a cake icing.

**Bolting:** The process of sifting flour, primarily to separate the bran.

**Bombe:** A type of frozen dessert made in a dome-shaped mold.

**Boston cream pie:** A sponge cake or other yellow cake filled with pastry cream and topped with chocolate fondant or confectioners' sugar.

**Boulanger** (boo lawn zhay): Bread baker.

**Boulanger:** An eighteenth-century Parisian credited with starting the first restaurant.

**Bran flour:** Flour to which bran flakes have been added.

**Bran:** The hard outer covering of kernels of wheat and other grains.

**Bread flour:** Strong flour, such as patent flour, used for breads.

**Break system:** A milling system to produce various grades of flour by repeatedly breaking the grains between rollers and sifting.

**Brioche:** Rich yeast dough containing large amounts of eggs and butter; a product made from this dough.

**Brix:** A unit of measure indicating the sugar concentration of a solution.

**Brown sugar:** Regular granulated sucrose containing impurities that give it a distinctive flavor.

**Buttercream:** An icing made of butter and/or shortening blended with confectioners' sugar or sugar syrup and, sometimes, other ingredients.

**Cabinet pudding:** A baked custard containing sponge cake and fruit.

**Cake flour:** A fine, white flour made from soft wheat.

**Calorie:** The amount of heat needed to raise the temperature of 1 kilogram of water 1 degree Celsius.

**Cannoli:** Fried Italian pastries made in tube shapes, generally with a sweet cream or cheese filling (singular form is *cannolo*).

**Caramelization:** The browning of sugars caused by heat.

**Carbohydrate:** Any of a group of compounds, including starches and sugars, that supply energy to the body.

**Carême, Marie-Antoine:** Important nineteenth-century cook and pastry chef.

**Cassata:** An Italian-style bombe, usually with three layers of different ice creams, plus a filling of Italian meringue.

**Cast sugar:** Sugar boiled to the hard crack stage and then poured into molds to harden. Also called *poured sugar*.

**Celiac disease:** A reaction to gluten in which the lining of the intestine is damaged.

**Celsius scale:** The metric system of temperature measurement, with 0°C at the freezing point of water and 100°C at the boiling point of water.

**Centi-:** Prefix in the metric system meaning "one-hundredth."

**Challah:** A rich egg bread, often made as a braided loaf.

**Charlotte ring:** A metal ring used as a mold for charlottes and other desserts.

**Charlotte:** (1) A cold dessert made of Bavarian cream or other cream in a special mold, usually lined with ladyfingers or other sponge products; (2) A hot dessert made of cooked fruit and baked in a special mold lined with strips of bread.

**Chemical leavener:** A leavener such as baking soda, baking powder, or baking ammonia, which releases gases produced by chemical reactions.

**Chiffon cake:** A light cake made by the chiffon method.

**Chiffon method:** A cake-mixing method involving the folding of whipped egg whites into a batter made of flour, egg yolks, and oil.

**Chiffon pie:** A pie with a light, fluffy filling containing egg whites and, usually, gelatin.

**Chocolate liquor:** Unsweetened chocolate, consisting of cocoa solids and cocoa butter.

**Chocolate truffle:** A small ball of chocolate ganache, served as a confection.

**Cholesterol:** A fatty substance found in foods derived from animal products and in the human body; it has been linked to heart disease.

**Christmas pudding:** A dark, heavy steamed pudding made of dried and candied fruits, spices, beef suet, and crumbs.

**Ciabatta:** A type of Italian bread made from a very slack dough deposited on pans with minimal shaping.

**Clear flour:** A tan-colored wheat flour made from the outer portion of the endosperm.

**Coagulation:** The process by which proteins become firm, usually when heated.

**Cobbler:** A fruit dessert similar to a pie, but without a bottom crust.

**Cocoa butter:** A white or yellowish fat found in natural chocolate.

**Cocoa:** The dry powder that remains after cocoa butter is pressed out of chocolate liquor.

**Common meringue:** Egg whites and sugar whipped to a foam; also called *French meringue*.

**Complex presentation:** A style of plating a dessert consisting of an arrangement of two or more desserts plus sauces and garnishes.

**Compote:** Cooked fruit served in its cooking liquid, usually a sugar syrup.

**Conching:** A step in the manufacturing of chocolate, the purpose of which is to create a fine, smooth texture.

**Confectioners' sugar:** Sucrose ground to a fine powder and mixed with a little cornstarch to prevent caking.

**Confisseur** (cone fee sur): A candy maker.

**Contaminated:** Containing a harmful substance not originally present in the food.

**Cooked fruit method:** A method for making pie fillings in which the fruit is cooked and thickened before being placed in the pie crust.

**Cooked juice method:** A method for making pie fillings in which the fruit juices are cooked, thickened, and mixed with the fruit.

**Cornstarch pudding:** A sweetened liquid, usually milk and flavorings, that is boiled with cornstarch to thicken it.

**Coulis:** A sweetened fruit purée, used as a sauce.

**Coupe:** A dessert consisting of one or two scoops of ice cream or sherbet placed in a dish or glass and topped with any of a number of syrups, fruits, toppings, and garnishes; a sundae.

**Couverture:** Natural, sweet chocolate containing no added fats other than natural cocoa butter; used for dipping, molding, coating, and similar purposes.

**Cream pie:** An unbaked pie containing a pastry cream–type filling.

**Cream pudding:** A boiled pudding made of milk, sugar, eggs, and starch.

**Creaming method:** A mixing method that begins with the blending of fat and sugar; used for cakes, cookies, and similar items.

**Creaming:** The process of beating fat and sugar together to blend them uniformly and to incorporate air.

**Crème anglaise** (krem awng glezz): A light vanilla-flavored custard sauce made of milk, sugar, and egg yolks.

**Crème brûlée:** A rich custard with a brittle top crust of caramelized sugar (French name means "burnt cream").

**Crème caramel:** A custard baked in a mold lined with caramelized sugar, then unmolded.

**Crème chantilly** (krem shawn tee yee): Sweetened whipped cream flavored with vanilla.

**Crème Chiboust:** A cream filling made of pastry cream, gelatin, meringue, and flavorings.

**Crème fraîche** (krem fresh): A slightly aged, cultured heavy cream with a slightly tangy flavor.

**Crêpe** (krep): A very thin French pancake, often served rolled around a filling.

**Crêpes Suzette:** French pancakes served in a sweet sauce flavored with orange.

**Croissant** (krwah sawn): A flaky, buttery yeast roll shaped like a crescent and made from a rolled-in dough.

**Cross-contamination:** The transfer of pathogens to food from another food or from work surfaces or equipment.

**Crumb crust:** A piecrust made of cookie crumbs, butter, and sugar.

**Crumb:** The interior of a baked item, distinct from the crust.

**Crystallize:** To form crystals, as in the case of dissolved sugar.

**Cuisinier** (kwee zee nyay): A cook; the head of a kitchen.

**Custard:** A liquid thickened or set by the coagulation of egg protein.

**Dark chocolate:** Sweetened chocolate that consists of chocolate liquor and sugar.

**Deci-:** Prefix in the metric system meaning "one-tenth."

**Décorateur:** A pastry chef who specializes in or is skilled at decorative work, such as showpieces, sugar work, and fancy cakes.

**Demerara sugar:** A type of crystalline brown sucrose.

**Dessert syrup:** A flavored sugar syrup used to flavor and moisten cakes and other desserts.

**Devil's food cake:** A chocolate cake made with a high percentage of baking soda, which gives the cake a reddish color.

**Diastase:** Various enzymes, found in flour and in diastatic malt, that convert starch into sugar.

**Disaccharide:** A complex or double sugar, such as sucrose.

**Dobos torte:** A Hungarian cake made of seven thin layers filled with chocolate buttercream and topped with caramelized sugar.

**Docking:** Piercing or perforating pastry dough before baking in order to allow steam to escape and to avoid blistering.

**Double-acting baking powder:** Baking powder that releases some of its gases when it is mixed with water and the remaining gases when it is heated.

**Double-panning:** Placing a baking sheet or pan on or in a second pan to prevent scorching the bottom of the product being baked.

**Dough relaxation:** A period of rest in the production of yeast dough during which gluten strands become adjusted to their new length and become less tight.

**Drained weight:** The weight of solid canned fruit after draining off the juice.

**Dredge:** To sprinkle thoroughly with sugar or another dry powder.

**Drop batter:** A batter that is too thick to pour but will drop from a spoon in lumps.

**Dropped:** A cookie makeup method in which portions of dough are measured with a scoop or spoon and dropped onto a baking pan.

**Dutch process cocoa:** Cocoa processed with an alkali to reduce its acidity.

**Éclair paste:** A paste or dough made of boiling water or milk, butter, flour, and eggs; used to make éclairs, cream puffs, and similar products.

**Egg-foam cake:** A cake leavened primarily by whipped eggs; it usually has a low percentage of fat.

**Empty calorie:** A food that provide few nutrients per calorie.

**Emulsified shortening:** Shortening containing emulsifiers so it can be used for high-ratio cakes.

**Emulsion:** A uniform mixture of two or more unmixable substances.

**Endosperm:** The starchy inner portion of grain kernels.

**English muffin:** A yeast dough product made in the shape of a disk and cooked on a griddle.

**EP weight:** Edible portion; the weight of an item after trimming.

**Escoffier, Georges-August:** Most important chef of late nineteenth and early twentieth century; organized cooking principles and kitchen hierarchy.

**Extract:** A flavoring ingredient consisting of flavorful oils or other substances dissolved in alcohol.

**Extraction:** The portion of the grain kernel that is separated into a particular grade of flour. Usually expressed as a percentage.

**Facultative:** Able to live and grow with or without the presence of oxygen; said of bacteria.

**Fat:** Any of a group of compounds, consisting of chains of fatty acids, that supply energy to the body in a concentrated form.

**Fermentation:** The process by which yeast changes carbohydrates into carbon dioxide gas and alcohol.

**Fiber:** A type of complex carbohydrate that is not absorbed by the body but is necessary for the proper functioning of the digestive system.

**Flaky piecrust:** A piecrust that has a flaky texture due to layers of fat sandwiched between layers of dough.

**Flat icing:** A simple icing made of confectioners' sugar and water, usually used for Danish pastries and sweet rolls.

**Flour-batter method:** A cake-mixing method in which the flour is first mixed with the fat.

**Flow of food:** The path food travels in a food service operation from receiving to serving.

**Foaming:** The process of whipping eggs, with or without sugar, to incorporate air.

**Focaccia:** A flat Italian bread similar to a thick pizza dough.

**Fondant:** A type of icing made of boiled sugar syrup that is agitated so it crystallizes into a mass of extremely small white crystals.

**Food Danger Zone:** The temperature range of 41° to 135°F (5° to 57°C), in which bacteria grow rapidly.

**Food intolerance:** A nonallergic reaction to a food that may be characterized by any of a variety of undesirable symptoms.

**Formula:** A set of instructions for preparing a bakery product; a baker's recipe.

**Fougasse:** A regional French bread made in the shape of a trellis or ladder.

**Four-fold:** A technique used to increase the number of layers in puff pastry or Danish pastry by folding the dough in fourths.

**Frangipane:** A type of almond-flavored cream.

**French doughnut:** A fried pastry made of choux paste.

**French meringue:** Egg whites and sugar whipped to a foam; also called *common meringue*.

**French pastry:** Any of a variety of small fancy cakes and other pastries, usually in single-portion sizes.

**French-style ice cream:** Ice cream containing egg yolks.

**Fritter:** A deep-fried item made of or coated with a batter or dough.

**Frozen mousse:** A still-frozen dessert containing whipped cream.

**Fruit betty:** A baked dessert consisting of layers of fruit and cake crumbs.

**Fruit cake:** A loaf cake containing a high percentage of dried and candied fruits and, usually, nuts.

**Fruit cobbler:** A baked fruit dessert with a pastry topping or top crust.

**Fruit crisp:** A baked fruit dessert with a streusel topping.

**Fruit gratin:** A dessert consisting of fruit plus a topping, browned under a broiler.

**Fruit pie:** A baked single- or double-crust pie with a fruit filling.

**Fruit torte:** A layer cake topped with a decorative arrangement of fruit.

**Fusion cuisine:** The use of techniques and ingredients from more than one regional cuisine in a single dish.

**Ganache** (gah nahsh): A rich cream made of sweet chocolate and heavy cream.

**Garnish:** An edible item added to another food as a decoration or accompaniment.

**Gâteau St-Honoré:** A pastry consisting of a base made of short pastry and pâte à choux and a cream filling, usually crème Chiboust or crème diplomat.

**Gâteau** (gah toe): French word for "cake."

**Gaufre** (go fr): French for "waffle."

**Gelatin:** A water-soluble protein extracted from animal tissue; used as a jelling agent.

**Gelatinization:** The process by which starch granules absorb water and swell in size.

**Gelato:** Italian ice cream.

**Genoise:** A sponge cake made by whipping whole eggs with sugar and folding in flour and, sometimes, melted butter.

**Germ:** The plant embryo portion of a grain kernel.

**Glacé** (glah say): (1) Glazed; coated with icing; (2) Frozen.

**Glacier** (glah see yay): A chef who makes ice cream.

**Glaze:** (1) A shiny coating, such as a syrup, applied to a food; (2) To make a food shiny or glossy by coating it with a glaze or by browning it under a broiler or in a hot oven.

**Gliadin:** A protein in wheat flour that combines with another protein, glutenin, to form gluten.

**Glucose:** A simple sugar available in the form of a clear, colorless, tasteless syrup.

**Gluten:** An elastic substance, formed from proteins present in wheat flours, that gives structure and strength to baked goods.

**Glutenin:** See Gliadin.

**Gram:** The basic unit of weight in the metric system; equal to about one-thirtieth of an ounce.

**Granité** (grah nee tay): A coarse, crystalline frozen dessert made of water, sugar, and fruit juice or another flavoring.

**Granulated sugar:** Sucrose in a fine crystalline form.

**Gum paste:** A type of sugar paste or pastillage made with vegetable gum.

**HACCP:** Hazard Analysis Critical Control Points; a food safety system of self-inspection designed to highlight hazardous foods and to control food handling to avoid hazards.

**Hard sauce:** A flavored mixture of confectioners' sugar and butter; often served with steamed puddings.

**Hard wheat:** Wheat high in protein.

**Hazard:** A potentially dangerous food condition due to contamination, growth of pathogens, survival of pathogens, or presence of toxins.

**Hearth bread:** A bread baked directly on the bottom of the oven, not in a pan.

**Heavy pack:** A type of canned fruit or vegetable with very little added water or juice.

**High-fat cake:** A cake with a high percentage of fat; distinguished from a sponge or egg-foam cake.

**High-ratio method:** See Two-stage method.

**High-ratio:** (1) Term referring to cakes and cake formulas mixed by a special method and containing more sugar than flour; (2) The mixing method used for these cakes; (3) Term referring to certain specially formulated ingredients used in these cakes, such as shortening.

**Homogenized milk:** Milk processed so the cream does not separate out.

**Hot milk and butter sponge:** A sponge cake batter in which a mixture of warm milk and melted butter is mixed into the batter.

**Hydration:** The process of absorbing water.

**Hydrogenation:** A process that converts liquid oils to solid fats (shortenings) by chemically bonding hydrogen to the fat molecules.

**Ice cream:** A churn-frozen mixture of milk, cream, sugar, flavorings, and, sometimes, eggs.

**Ice milk:** A frozen dessert similar to ice cream, but with a lower fat content.

**Ice:** A frozen dessert made of water, sugar, and fruit juice.

**Icebox:** A cookie makeup method in which the dough is shaped into cylinders, refrigerated, and sliced.

**Icing comb:** A plastic triangle with toothed or serrated edges; used for texturing icings.

**Instant starch:** A starch that thickens a liquid without cooking because it has been precooked.

**Inversion:** A chemical process in which a double sugar splits into two simple sugars.

**Invert sugar:** A mixture of two simple sugars, dextrose and levulose, resulting from the breakdown of sucrose.

**Italian meringue:** A meringue made by whipping a boiling syrup into egg whites.

**Jalebi:** A type of Indian dessert made of deep-fried batter soaked in syrup.

**Japonaise** (zhah po nez): A baked meringue flavored with nuts.

**Kernel paste:** A nut paste, similar to almond paste, made of apricot kernels and sugar.

**Kilo-:** Prefix in the metric system meaning "one thousand."

**Kirsch:** A clear alcoholic beverage distilled from cherries.

**Kirschtorte:** A torte made of genoise, meringue disks, and buttercream and flavored with kirsch.

**Kugelhopf:** A type of rich, sweet bread or coffee cake, usually made in a tube-type pan.

**Lactobacillus:** A group of bacteria primarily responsible for creating the acidity in sourdough starters.

**Lacto-ovo-vegetarian:** Referring to a vegetarian diet that includes dairy products and eggs.

**Lacto-vegetarian:** Referring to a vegetarian diet that includes milk and other dairy products.

**Ladyfinger:** A small, dry, finger-shaped sponge cake or cookie.

**Lag phase:** A period after bacteria are introduced to a new environment and before they begin to grow and reproduce.

**Langue de chat** (lahng duh shah): A thin, crisp cookie. The French name means "cat's tongue," referring to the shape of the cookie.

**Lattice crust:** A top crust for a pie made of strips of pastry in a criss-cross pattern.

**Lean dough:** A dough low in fat and sugar.

**Leavening:** The production or incorporation of gases in a baked product to increase volume and to produce shape and texture.

**Levain:** Sourdough starter.

**Levain-levure:** French for "yeast pre-ferment."

**Levure:** Commercial yeast.

**Linzertorte:** A tart made of raspberry jam and a short dough containing nuts and spices.

**Lipid:** Any of a group of compounds containing fats and cholesterol.

**Liter:** The basic unit of volume in the metric system; equal to slightly more than 1 quart.

**Macaroon:** A cookie made of eggs (usually whites) and almond paste or coconut.

**Maillard reaction:** A chemical reaction that causes the browning of proteins and sugars together when subjected to heat.

**Malt syrup:** A type of syrup containing maltose sugar, extracted from sprouted barley.

**Marble:** To partly mix two colors of cake batter or icing so the colors are in decorative swirls.

**Margarine:** An artificial butter product made of hydrogenated fats and flavorings.

**Marron:** French for "chestnut."

**Marshmallow icing:** Boiled icing with the addition of gelatin.

**Marshmallow:** A light confection, icing, or filling made of meringue and gelatin (or other stabilizers).

**Marzipan:** A paste or confection made of almonds and sugar and often used for decorative work.

**Mature (dough):** At the ideal stage of development for a yeast dough.

**Mature (fruit):** Having completed its development and physiologically capable of continuing the ripening process, even when the fruit has been removed from the tree.

**Maza:** An early type of bread; cakes of grain paste baked by the ancient Greeks.

**Meal:** Coarsely ground grain.

**Mealy piecrust:** A piecrust in which the fat has been mixed in thoroughly enough so the dough does not have a flaky texture.

**Melba sauce:** A sweet sauce made of puréed raspberries and, sometimes, red currants.

**Meringue chantilly** (shawn tee yee): Baked meringue filled with whipped cream.

**Meringue glacée:** Baked meringue filled with ice cream.

**Meringue:** A thick, white foam made of whipped egg whites and sugar.

**Meter:** The basic unit of length in the metric system; slightly longer than 1 yard.

**Metric system:** A measurement system based entirely on decimals.

**Microorganism:** A life form, such as bacteria, too small to be seen without a microscope.

**Milk chocolate:** Sweetened chocolate containing milk solids.

**Millefeuille** (mee foy): French term for napoleon; literally, "thousand leaves." Also used for various layered desserts.

**Milli-:** Prefix in the metric system meaning "one-thousandth."

**Modeling chocolate:** A thick paste made of chocolate and glucose that can be molded by hand into decorative shapes.

**Modified straight dough method:** A mixing method similar to the straight dough method, except the fat and sugar are mixed together first to ensure uniform distribution; used for rich doughs.

**Molasses:** A heavy brown syrup made from sugarcane.

**Molded:** A cookie makeup method in which the dough is shaped into cylinders, cut into equal portions, and shaped as desired.

**Monosaccharide:** A simple or single sugar such as glucose and fructose.

**Monounsaturated fat:** A type of fat, normally liquid at room temperature, that contains one double bond in its carbon chain.

**Mousse:** A soft or creamy dessert made light by the addition of whipped cream, egg whites, or both.

**Muffin method:** A mixing method in which the mixed dry ingredients are combined with the mixed liquid ingredients.

**Napoleon:** A dessert made of layers of puff pastry filled with pastry cream.

**Natural sour:** See Sourdough starter.

**Natural starter:** See Sourdough starter.

**Net weight:** The weight of the total contents of a can or package.

**No-time dough:** A bread dough made with a large quantity of yeast and given no fermentation time, except for a short rest after mixing.

**Nougatine:** A mixture of caramelized sugar and almonds or other nuts, used in decorative work and as a confection and flavoring.

**Nouvelle cuisine:** Important cooking style of 1960s and 1970s, known for lighter flavors and elaborate plating styles.

**Nutrient density:** The quantity of nutrients per calorie.

**Nutrient:** A substance essential for the functioning or growth of an organism.

**Old dough:** A dough that is overfermented.

**One-stage method:** (1) A cookie-mixing method in which all ingredients are added to the bowl at once; (2) A cake-mixing method in which all the ingredients, including high-ratio liquid shortening, are mixed together at once.)

**Opera cake:** A layer cake made of thin sponge layers, coffee-flavored buttercream, and chocolate ganache.

**Opson:** In ancient Greece, any food eaten with bread.

**Othello:** A small (single-portion size), spherical sponge cake filled with cream and iced with fondant.

**Oven spring:** The rapid rise of yeast goods in the oven due to the production and expansion of trapped gases caused by the oven heat.

**Overrun:** The increase in volume of ice cream or frozen desserts due to the incorporation of air while freezing.

**Ovo-vegetarian:** Referring to a vegetarian diet that includes eggs.

**Pain d'épice** (pan day peece): A type of gingerbread (French name means "spice bread").

**Pain de campagne:** French country-style bread.

**Palmier** (palm yay): A small pastry or petit four sec made of rolled, sugared puff pastry cut into slices and baked.

**Panna cotta:** An Italian pudding made of cream, gelatin, and flavorings; literally, "cooked cream."

**Pannetone:** An Italian sweet bread made in a large loaf, generally containing dried and candied fruits.

**Parfait:** (1) A type of sundae served in a tall, thin glass; (2) A still-frozen dessert made of egg yolks, syrup, and heavy cream.

**Paris-Brest:** A dessert consisting of a ring of baked éclair paste filled with cream.

**Pasteurized:** Heat-treated to kill bacteria that might cause disease or spoilage.

**Pastillage:** A sugar paste, used for decorative work, that becomes very hard when dry.

**Pastry cream:** A thick custard sauce containing eggs and starch.

**Pastry flour:** A weak flour used for pastries and cookies.

**Pâte à choux** (pot ah shoo): Éclair paste.

**Pâte brisée:** A type of rich pastry dough used primarily for tarts.

**Pâte fermentée:** Fermented dough, used as a starter.

**Pâte feuilleté** (pot foo ya tay): French name for puff pastry.

**Patent flour:** A fine grade of wheat flour milled from the inner portions of the kernel.

**Pathogen:** A disease-causing microorganism.

**Peasant tart:** A baked tart with a custard filling containing prunes.

**Pectin:** A soluble plant fiber, used primarily as a jelling agent for fruit preserves and jams.

**Peel:** A flat wooden shovel used to place hearth breads in an oven and to remove them.

**Pentosan:** A category of carbohydrate gums present in wheat flour and having strong water absorption ability.

**Petit four glacé:** An iced or cream-filled petit four.

**Petit four sec:** An un-iced or unfilled petit four (*sec* means "dry"), such as a small butter cookie or palmier.

**Petit four:** A delicate cake or pastry small enough to be eaten in one or two bites.

**pH:** A measure of the acidity or alkalinity of a substance.

**Philadelphia-style ice cream:** Ice cream containing no eggs.

**Phyllo** (fee lo): A paper-thin dough or pastry used to make strudels and various Middle Eastern and Greek desserts.

**Piping jelly:** A transparent, sweet jelly used for decorating cakes.

**Pithiviers** (pee tee vyay): A cake made of puff pastry filled with almond cream.

**Polyunsaturated fat:** A type of fat, normally liquid at room temperature, that contains more than one double bond in its carbon chain.

**Poolish:** A thin yeast starter made with equal parts flour and water, plus commercial yeast.

**Pot de crème** (poh duh krem): A rich baked custard.

**Pound cake:** (1) A cake made of equal weights of flour, butter, sugar, and eggs; (2) Any cake resembling this.

**Pour batter:** A batter liquid enough to pour.

**Poured sugar:** Sugar boiled to the hard crack stage and then poured into molds to harden. Also called *cast sugar*.

**Praline:** A confection or flavoring made of nuts and caramelized sugar.

**Pre-ferment:** A fermented dough or batter used to provide leavening for a larger batch of dough.

**Press:** A scaled piece of dough divided into small, equal units in a dough divider.

**Profiterole:** A small puff made of éclair paste. Often filled with ice cream and served with chocolate sauce.

**Protein:** Any of a group of nutrients essential for growth, building body tissue, and basic body functions, and that can also be used for energy if the diet doesn't contain enough carbohydrates and fats.

**Puff pastry:** A very light, flaky pastry made from a rolled-in dough and leavened by steam.

**Pulled sugar:** Sugar boiled to the hard crack stage, allowed to harden slightly, then pulled or stretched until it develops a pearly sheen.

**Pullman loaf:** A long, rectangular loaf of bread.

**Pumpernickel flour:** A coarse, flaky meal made from whole rye grains.

**Punching:** A method of expelling gases from fermented dough.

**Purée:** A food made into a smooth pulp, usually by being ground or forced through a sieve.

**Quenelle** (kuh nell): A small oval portion of food.

**Recipe:** A set of instructions for preparing a certain dish.

**Regular shortening:** Any basic shortening without emulsifiers, used for creaming methods and for icings.

**Retarder-proofer:** An automated, timer-controlled combination of retarder/freezer and proofer, used for holding and proofing yeast products.

**Retarding:** Refrigerating a yeast dough to slow its fermentation.

**Reversed puff pastry:** A type of puff pastry made with the dough enclosed between layers of butter.

**Ribbon sponge:** A thin sponge cake layer with a decorative design made of stencil paste.

**Rice condé:** A thick, molded rice pudding, usually topped with fruit.

**Rice impératrice:** A rich rice pudding containing whipped cream, candied fruits, and gelatin.

**Rich dough:** A dough high in fat, sugar, and/or eggs.

**Ripe (fruit):** At its peak of texture, flavor, and sweetness, and ready to be consumed.

**Rolled:** A cookie makeup method in which the dough is rolled out into a sheet and cut into shapes with cutters.

**Rolled-in dough:** Dough in which a fat has been incorporated in many layers by using a rolling and folding procedure.

**Rôtisseur** (ro tee sur): Roast cook or meat cook.

**Rounding:** A method of molding a piece of dough into a round ball with a smooth surface or skin.

**Royal icing:** A form of icing made of confectioners' sugar and egg whites; used for decorating.

**Rye blend:** A mixture of rye flour and hard wheat flour.

**Rye meal:** Coarse rye flour.

**Sabayon:** A foamy dessert or sauce made of egg yolks whipped with wine or liqueur.

**Sachertorte:** A rich chocolate cake from Vienna.

**Sacristain** (sak ree stan): A small pastry made of a twisted strip of puff paste coated with nuts and sugar.

**Saturated fat:** A fat that is normally solid at room temperature.

**Savarin:** A type of yeast bread or cake soaked in syrup.

**Scaling:** Weighing, usually of ingredients or of doughs or batters.

**Scone flour:** A mixture of flour and baking powder used when very small quantities of baking powder are needed.

**Scone:** A type of biscuit or biscuitlike bread.

**Seeding:** A technique for tempering chocolate by adding grated tempered chocolate to melted chocolate to cool it.

**Sfogliatelle** (sfo lee ah tell eh): A Southern Italian flaky turnover pastry with a sweet cheese filling.

**Sheet:** A cookie makeup method in which the dough is baked in sheets and cut into portions.

**Sherbet:** A frozen dessert made of water, sugar, fruit juice, and, sometimes, milk or cream.

**Short dough:** A pastry dough, similar to a basic cookie dough, made of flour, sugar, and fat. See also Short.

**Short:** Having a high fat content, which makes the product (such as a cookie or pastry) very crumbly and tender.

**Shortbread:** A crisp cookie made of butter, sugar, and flour.

**Shortening:** (1) Any fat used in baking to tenderize the product by shortening gluten strands; (2) A white, tasteless, solid fat formulated for baking or deep frying.

**Simple presentation:** A style of plating a dessert consisting of a portion of one dessert plus optional sauces and garnishes.

**Simple syrup:** A syrup consisting of sucrose and water in varying proportions.

**Single-acting baking powder:** Baking powder that releases gases as soon as it is mixed with water.

**Soft pie:** A single-crust pie with a custard-type filling—that is, a filling that sets or coagulates due to its egg content.

**Soft wheat:** Wheat low in protein.

**Solid pack:** A type of canned fruit or vegetable with no water added.

**Sorbet** (sor bay): French for "sherbet."

**Sorbetto:** Italian for "sherbet."

**Soufflé:** (1) A baked dish containing whipped egg whites, which cause the dish to rise during baking; (2) A still-frozen dessert made in a soufflé dish so it resembles a baked soufflé.

**Sour:** Sourdough starter.

**Sourdough starter:** A dough or batter that contains wild yeasts and bacteria, has a noticeable acidity as a result of fermentation by these organisms, and is used to leaven other doughs.

**Sourdough:** A dough leavened by a sourdough starter.

**Sponge cake:** A type of cake made by whipping eggs and sugar to a foam, then folding in flour.

**Sponge method:** A cake-mixing method based on whipped eggs and sugar.

**Sponge roll:** See Swiss roll.

**Sponge:** A batter or dough of yeast, flour, and water that is allowed to ferment and is then mixed with more flour and other ingredients to make a bread dough.

**Spread:** The tendency of a cookie to spread out and flatten when baked.

**Spun sugar:** Boiled sugar made into long, thin threads by dipping wires into the sugar syrup and waving them so the sugar falls off in fine streams.

**Staling:** The change in texture and aroma of baked goods due to the loss of moisture by the starch granules.

**Standardized formula:** A set of instructions describing the way a particular establishment prepares a certain baked item.

**Starch retrogradation:** A chemical change of starch molecules that is responsible for staling.

**Stencil:** A pattern cut from plastic or cardboard, used for depositing batter for thin cookies made in decorative shapes.

**Stencil paste:** A type of thin cookie or wafer dough used to make cookies in decorative shapes and for making decorative patterns in ribbon sponge.

**St-Honoré:** (1) A dessert made of a ring of cream puffs set on a short dough base and filled with a type of pastry cream; (2) The cream used to fill this dessert, made of pastry cream and whipped egg whites.

**Stirred custard:** A custard stirred while it is cooked so it thickens but does not set.

**Stollen:** A type of sweet yeast bread with fruit.

**Straight dough method:** A mixing method for yeast goods in which all ingredients are mixed together at once.

**Straight flour:** Flour made from the entire wheat kernel minus the bran and germ.

**Streusel** (stroy sel): A crumbly topping for baked goods, consisting of fat, sugar, and flour rubbed together.

**Strong flour:** Flour with a high protein content.

**Strudel:** (1) A type of dough that is stretched until paper thin; (2) A baked item consisting of a filling rolled up in a sheet of strudel dough or phyllo dough.

**Sucralose:** A type of synthetic sweetener derived from sucrose.

**Sucrose:** The chemical name for regular granulated sugar and confectioners' sugar.

**Sugar cage:** A lacy dome of hard or caramelized sugar.

**Swiss meringue:** Egg whites and sugar warmed, usually over hot water, and then whipped to a foam.

**Swiss roll:** A thin sponge cake layer spread with a filling and rolled up.

**Syrup:** One or more types of sugar dissolved in water, often with small amounts of other compounds or impurities that give the syrup flavor.

**Syrup pack:** A type of canned fruit containing sugar syrup.

**Tablage:** A technique for tempering chocolate by cooling it on a marble slab.

**Tart:** A flat, baked item consisting of a pastry and a sweet or savory topping or filling; similar to a pie but usually thinner.

**Tarte Tatin:** An upside-down apple tart.

**Tempering:** The process of melting and cooling chocolate to a specific temperature in order to prepare it for dipping, coating, or molding.

**Three-fold:** A technique used to increase the number of layers in puff pastry or Danish pastry by folding the dough in thirds.

**Tiramisù:** An Italian dessert made of ladyfinger sponge flavored with espresso coffee and a creamy cheese filling.

**Torte:** German for various types of cakes, usually layer cakes.

**Trans fat:** A solid fat, usually manufactured by hydrogenation, that limits the body's ability to rid itself of cholesterol.

**Tulipe:** A thin, crisp cookie molded into a cup shape.

**Tunneling:** A condition of muffin products characterized by large, elongated holes; caused by overmixing.

**Turntable:** A pedestal with a flat, rotating top, used for holding cakes while they are being decorated.

**Two-stage method:** A cake-mixing method beginning with the blending of flour and high-ratio shortening and followed by the addition of liquids. Also called the *high-ratio method*.

**Vacherin** (vah sher ran): A crisp meringue shell filled with cream, fruits, or other items.

**Vegan:** Referring to a vegetarian diet that excludes all animal products, including dairy products and eggs.

**Vitamin:** any of a group of compounds that are present in foods in very small quantities and that are necessary for regulating body functions.

**Wash:** (1) A liquid brushed onto the surface of a product, usually before baking. (2) To apply such a liquid.

**Water hardness:** The mineral content of water.

**Water pack:** A type of canned fruit or vegetable containing the water used to process the item.

**Weak flour:** Flour with a low protein content.

**White couverture:** A confection consisting of cocoa butter, milk solids, and sugar. Sometimes erroneously called *white chocolate*.

**Whole wheat flour:** Flour made by grinding the entire wheat kernel, including the bran and germ.

**Yeast starter:** A type of sourdough starter made with a cultivated yeast.

**Young dough:** A dough that is underfermented.

**Zabaglione:** An Italian dessert or sauce made of whipped egg yolks and Marsala wine.

**Zest:** The colored outer portion of the peel of citrus fruits.

# Bibliography

Amendola, Joseph, and Nicole Rees. *The Baker's Manual*, 5th ed. Hoboken, N.J.: John Wiley & Sons, 2003.

———. *Understanding Baking*, 3rd ed. Hoboken, N.J.: John Wiley & Sons, 2003.

Bilheux, Roland, et al. *Special and Decorative Breads*. 2 vols. New York: John Wiley & Sons, 1989.

Bilheux, Roland, and Alain Escoffier. *Professional French Pastry Series*. 4 vols. New York: John Wiley & Sons, 1988.

Boyle, Peter T. *Sugar Work*. New York: John Wiley & Sons, 1988.

Boyle, Tish, and Timothy Moriarty. *Grand Finales: The Art of the Plated Dessert*. New York: John Wiley & Sons, 1997.

———. *Grand Finales: A Neoclassic View of Plated Desserts*. New York: John Wiley & Sons, 2000.

Bundy, Ariana. *Sweet Alternative*. North Vancouver, B.C.: Whitecap Books, 2005.

Clayton, Bernard. *The Breads of France*. Indianapolis: Bobbs-Merrill, 1978.

———. *Bernard Clayton's New Complete Book of Breads*. New York: Fireside, 1995.

Culinary Institute of America. *Baking and Pastry*. Hoboken, N.J.: John Wiley & Sons, 2004.

Daley, Regan. *In the Sweet Kitchen*. New York: Artisan, 2001.

D'Ermo, Dominique. *The Modern Pastry Chef's Guide to Professional Baking*. New York: Harper & Row, 1962.

Drummond, Karen Eich, Joseph F. Vastano, and Josephine C. Vastano. *Cook's Healthy Handbook*. New York: John Wiley & Sons, 1993

Duchene, Laurent, and Bridget Jones. *Le Cordon Bleu Dessert Techniques*. New York: William Morrow, 1999.

Eagan, Maureen, and Susan Davis Allen. *Healthful Quantity Baking*. New York: John Wiley & Sons, 1992.

Escoffier, A. *The Escoffier Cook Book*. New York: Crown, 1969.

Fance, Wilfred. J., ed. *The New International Confectioner*, 5th ed. London: Virtue & Co., 1981.

Figoni, Paula. *How Baking Works*. Hoboken, N.J.: John Wiley & Sons, 2004.

Fleming, Claudia. *The Last Course*. New York: Random House, 2001.

Friberg, Bo. *The Professional Pastry Chef*, 4th ed. New York: John Wiley & Sons, 2002.

———. *The Advanced Professional Pastry Chef*. Hoboken, N.J.: John Wiley & Sons, 2003.

Garrett, Toba M. *Professional Cake Decorating*. Hoboken, N.J.: John Wiley & Sons, 2006.

Gioannini, Marilyn. *The Complete Food Allergy Cookbook*. Roseville, CA: Prima, 1997.

Glezer, Maggie. *Artisan Baking Across America*. New York: Artisan, 2000.

Hagman, Bette. *The Gluten-Free Gourmet*. New York: Henry Holt, 2000.

Hamelman, Jeffrey. *Bread: A Baker's Book of Techniques and Recipes*. Hoboken, N.J.: John Wiley & Sons, 2004.

Hanneman, L. J. *Patisserie*. London: Heinemann, 1977.

———. *Baker: Bread and Fermented Goods*. London: Heinemann, 1980.

Hermé, Pierre, and Dorie Greenspan. *Desserts by Pierre Hermé*. Boston: Little, Brown, 1998.

Labensky, Sarah R., Eddy van Damme, Priscilla Martel, and Klaus Tenbergen. *On Baking*. Upper Saddle River, N.J.: Prentice Hall.

Leach, Richard. *Sweet Seasons*. New York: John Wiley & Sons, 2001.

Lenôtre, Gaston. *Lenôtre's Desserts and Pastries*. Woodbury, N.Y.: Barron's, 1977.

———. *Lenôtre's Ice Creams and Candies*. Woodbury, N.Y.: Barron's, 1979.

Matz, S. A. *Bakery Technology and Engineering*, 3rd ed. Pan-Tech International, 1999.

MacLauchlan, Andrew. *New Classic Desserts*. New York: John Wiley & Sons, 1995.

———. *The Making of a Pastry Chef*. New York: John Wiley & Sons, 1999.

National Restaurant Association Educational Foundation. *ServSafe Coursebook, 3rd ed.* Chicago, 2004.

Payard, François. *Simply Sensational Desserts*. New York: Broadway Books, 1999.

Pyler, E. J. *Baking Science and Technology*, 2nd ed. 2 vols. Chicago: Siebel, 1973.

Reinhart, Peter. *The Bread Baker's Apprentice*. Berkeley, CA: Ten Speed Press, 2001.

Roux, Michel. *Michel Roux's Finest Desserts*. New York: Rizzoli, 1995.

Schünemann, Claus, and Günter Treu. *Baking: The Art and Science*. Calgary, Alberta: Baker Tech, 1986.

Sultan, William J. *The Pastry Chef*. New York: Van Nostrand Reinhold, 1983.

———. *Practical Baking*, 5th ed. New York: John Wiley & Sons, 1989.

Teubner, Christian. *The Chocolate Bible*. New York: Penguin, 1997.

Trotter, Charlie. *Charlie Trotter's Desserts*. Berkeley, CA: Ten Speed Press, 1998.

Woodruff, Sandra. *Secrets of Fat-Free Baking*. Garden City Park, N.Y.: Avery, 1995.

# Recipe Index

# Subject Index